CORRY Robinson
744 Dexter
Denver Co 80220
303 388 2513 H
270 5209 O

# *THE*
# *STATE OF THE STATES*
# *IN*
# *DEVELOPMENTAL DISABILITIES*

## FOURTH EDITION

*by*

**David Braddock  Richard Hemp**
**Lynn Bachelder  Glenn Fujiura**

**INSTITUTE ON DISABILITY AND HUMAN DEVELOPMENT**
**THE UNIVERSITY OF ILLINOIS AT CHICAGO**

**Published by the**
**American Association on Mental Retardation**

**1995**

# THE
# STATE OF THE STATES
# IN
# DEVELOPMENTAL DISABILITIES
## Fourth Edition

*by*

**David Braddock, Ph.D.    Richard Hemp, M.A.**
**Lynn Bachelder, Ph.D.    Glenn Fujiura, Ph.D.**

**INSTITUTE ON DISABILITY AND HUMAN DEVELOPMENT**
**THE UNIVERSITY OF ILLINOIS AT CHICAGO**

*Gary N. Siperstein*
*Editor, AAMR Special Publications*

**American Association on Mental Retardation**
**Washington, DC**

Published by

American Association on Mental Retardation
444  N. Capitol Street, NW, Suite 846
Washington, DC 20001-1512

Printed in the United States of America

**Library of Congress Cataloging-in-Publication Data**

The state of the states in developmental disabilities / by David Braddock
. . . [et al.]. -- 4th ed.
    p.      cm.
Includes bibliographical references.
ISBN 0-940898-37-3
    1. Developmentally disabled—Services for—United States—States.
2. Developmentally disabled—Government policy—United States—States.
I. Braddock, David L.   II. American Association on Mental Retardation.
HV1570.5.U65S74        1995
362.1'968--dc20
                                                              95-4283
                                                                 CIP

# Contents

**PART II: STATE PROFILES**

## PART III: TECHNICAL NOTES

# Listing of Figures and Tables

**PART I: THE STATE OF THE STATES IN DEVELOPMENTAL DISABILITIES: AN OVERVIEW**

FIGURES

TABLES

## PART II: .STATE PROFILES

## PART III:  TECHNICAL NOTES FOR THE STATE PROFILES

# *Acknowledgments*

The assistance of the state directors of developmental disabilities services and their counterparts in state Medicaid and human services agencies was central to the successful completion of this study. Nearly 200 persons in state government agencies throughout the United States participated in the study. These individuals are identified by name beginning on page 383. We are extremely grateful for their cooperation. The support and assistance of Robert M. Gettings and Gary Smith of the National Association of State Directors of Developmental Disabilities Services are also sincerely appreciated.

At the University of Illinois at Chicago, research assistants Raymond E. Belstner, Jr., Tom McGovern, Sudheera Kanuri, and Carol Davis provided technical support in the production of graphics and development of the data base. We extend appreciation to Susan Yoder for her careful editing of the manuscript in preparation for AAMR's publication of the book.

The authors express their gratitude to Commissioner Bob Williams and the Administration on Developmental Disabilities for ADD's financial support to help carry out the project (Project # HHS 90 DD 0347). The University of Illinois at Chicago, through the Institute on Disability and Human Development, has also helped underwrite the costs of this research. We wish to gratefully acknowledge the continuing support of the University over the past 14 years.

# PART I

# *The State of the States in Developmental Disabilities: An Overview*

# PART I
# THE STATE OF THE STATES
# IN DEVELOPMENTAL DISABILITIES: AN OVERVIEW

This is the fourth edition of a study conceived in 1982 to monitor the growth and development of mental retardation and developmental disabilities (MR/DD) services on a state by state basis. Relying primarily on a financial perspective, three previous study editions were published, in 1984 (Braddock, Hemp, & Howes, 1984), 1986 (Braddock, Hemp, & Fujiura, 1986; 1987), and 1990 (Braddock, Hemp, Fujiura, Bachelder, & Mitchell, 1990). The previous studies examined the structure and financing of MR/DD services in the states for the periods 1977-84, 1985-86, and 1987-88, respectively. This fourth update of the study extends the longitudinal analysis of financial and programmatic data in the states through fiscal year 1992. Thus, a 16-year time frame, 1977-92, is encompassed in the data base analyzed in this fourth iteration of the study.

The book has three parts. Part I is an analysis of trends in developmental disabilities in the states. Part II consists of detailed profiles for each of the states in terms of resource allocation and service delivery. Technical notes for each state's profile are presented in Part III of the book. The notes describe data sources utilized and special characteristics of each state's profile.

The present study identifies emerging trends in the provision of MR/DD services across the country with an emphasis on the 1988-92 period. The current study updates all data collected in the 1990 edition (Braddock et al., 1990), and it expands the data collected to include information on assistive technology,

**TABLE 1**
***Classification Categories Used in the Collection and Analysis of MR/DD Expenditures: FYs 1977-92***

| |
|---|
| **TOTAL FUNDS** |
| **CONGREGATE (16+ BEDS) SERVICES FUNDS** |
| *INSTITUTIONAL SERVICES FUNDS* |
|   **STATE FUNDS** |
|     **General Funds** |
|     **Other State Funds** |
|     **Local/County Overmatch** |
|   **FEDERAL FUNDS** |
|     **Federal ICF/MR** |
|     **Title XX/SSBG** |
|     **Other Federal Funds** |
| *LARGE PRIVATE RESIDENTIAL FUNDS* |
|   **STATE FUNDS** |
|     **General Funds** |
|     **Other State Funds** |
|     **Local/County Overmatch** |
|   **FEDERAL FUNDS** |
|     **Large Private ICF/MR** |
| **COMMUNITY SERVICES FUNDS** |
|   **STATE FUNDS** |
|     **General Funds** |
|     **Other State Funds** |
|     **Local/County Overmatch** |
|     **SSI State Supplement** |
|   **FEDERAL FUNDS** |
|     **ICF/MR Funds** |
|       **Small Public** |
|       **Small Private** |
|     **HCBS Waiver** |
|     **Model 50/200 Waiver** |
|     **Waiver Participants' SSI/ADC** |
|     **Other Title XIX Programs** |
|     **Title XX/SSBG** |
|     **Other Federal Funds** |

supported living, and personal assistance. There are also important refinements in the comparative analysis of resource allocation patterns in the states. "Community residential services" in previous editions of the study were operationally defined to include facilities with 15 or fewer residents. The current study presents supplementary analyses of state financial patterns using a six-bed or less construct to define community services. This has a profound impact on the assessment of patterns of service delivery in any given state.

# METHOD

The initial procedure employed, as in the 1984, 1986, and 1990 studies, was to obtain copies of published executive budget documents from each of the states and the District of Columbia. Next, an interview guide for analysts was prepared describing important study definitions (outlined in Table 1 and discussed below) and interview procedures. Activities of the *principal mental retardation and developmental disabilities state agency* were the primary focus of the study; however, it was often necessary to consult by telephone and in writing with representatives of the state Medicaid and social services agencies because these organizations typically administered the Intermediate Care Facility/Mental Retardation and Social Services Block Grant (SSBG) Programs, respectively.

Two broad classification categories were employed in the analysis of trends in spending: large (16+ beds) congregate care services and community services. The large congregate care category was subdivided into state institutional funding and large private 16+ beds residential funding. These general subcategories were further broken down in terms of state or federal revenue sources. State revenues for community services were subclassified into four components: general funds, other state funds, local/county overmatch (over and above the required Medicaid and SSBG match), and state supplement payments for Supplemental Security Income (SSI).

Federal funds for community services were subclassified into eight different categories, as shown in Table 1. As noted above, special analyses were also completed using the six-bed or less construct to define community services.

Income maintenance payments associated with individuals receiving services under Home and Community Based Services (HCBS) Waivers were included within the community services category of the analysis. All other federal income maintenance funds were excluded from the states' data sets. It was appropriate to exclude non-Waiver associated federal income maintenance data from the analytic model because the primary purpose of the study was to gauge *state government* effort in developmental disabilities. SSI state supplement payments, which were included within the community services spending construct, *require* state legislative action before funds can be budgeted for this purpose, and several states, most notably California, have large supplement programs. To strengthen the integrity of the econometric model in terms of measuring state fiscal effort, state supplement funding was included within the operational definition of community services expenditures.

## Definitions

The following definitions were employed in data collection and analysis. An *institutional expenditure* was defined in the study to include all operating funds, including related fringe-benefit costs, for all 16+ bed state-operated institutions, developmental centers, training centers, state schools, and for designated MR/DD units in state psychiatric hospitals. In many states, fringe benefits were budgeted for state employees in institutions or in the community by

state agencies other than the principal state MR/DD agency. These funds were included in computing expenditures for these state-operated programs. Funds budgeted in institutional accounts supporting group homes and related services in community settings were excluded from institutional expenditures and included within community services funds in the study. Institutional funds supporting group homes on institutional grounds were considered institutional expenditures due to the location of these homes. Institutional construction expenditures, except those funds allocated for routine maintenance, equipment purchases, and debt service, were excluded from the computation of institutional operating costs.

*State general funds* for institutional services included all funds, exclusive of federal moneys, budgeted under general appropriations acts of the state legislatures. *Other state funds* included the state and local/county ICF/MR match, which ranged between 22 and 50% of federal ICF/MR reimbursement payments, when that match was budgeted outside the general funds accounts of the principal MR/DD state agency. If the state match was carried in the principal MR/DD state agency's budget, it was included in the state general funds category. *Other state funds* in the institutional category also included dedicated revenues such as special funds, lottery receipts, and client fees. Client fees constituted approximately 1% of the total state funds for institutional operations. *Other federal funds* financing institutional services included moneys expended for Title I/Chapter I Educational Aid, Medicare, CHAMPUS, and various other small research, training, and demonstration projects.

*Institutional staffing ratio* (or staff-to-resident ratio) referred to total full time equivalent (FTE) staff employed by all state-operated institutions in a given state divided by the number of institutional residents in those facilities. This is consistent with the definition employed by Epple, Jacobson, and Janicki (1985) in their 1983 national survey. An *institutional closure* was defined as a completed or in-progress termination of a state-operated mental retardation institution. An in-progress closure implied that the MR/DD state agency was implementing a legislatively sanctioned phase-out of the facility. Typically, this was verifiable by examining published state budget documentation (Braddock & Heller, 1985).

*Large private residential* expenditures referred to funding associated with 24-hour residential facilities serving 16 or more persons with developmental disabilities in the same location. This included state-funded facilities (not state-operated facilities) whether or not the facilities were certified as ICFs/MR. The large private residential category included spending for county-operated facilities in a few states, notably Iowa and Ohio. Programmatic data were also collected on privately provided nursing home services (ICFs/SNFs) to persons with mental retardation.

*Community services expenditures* consisted of federal and state spending for publicly or privately operated community-based programs providing 15-bed or less (or 6-bed or less) residential services. Also reflected in this category was federal and state funding for the purchase of nonresidential services such as habilitation, day training, sheltered work, supported and competitive employment, family support, early intervention, and other state assisted residential living arrangements and supports including services and income maintenance associated with the Title XIX Waiver program. Regional office costs associated with the oversight and development of community services were included within these expenditures. Local and county funding of community services were included in this category to the extent that such funds were used to match the state-federal Medicaid and Social Services Block Grant (SSBG) programs. In those states known to employ extensive local or county *overmatch* funding in the provision of MR/DD services (i.e., local or county funding in addition to the required match for the Social Services and Medicaid programs), a special effort was mounted to gather these data. Significant local and county overmatch funds are reported in the state profiles for Colorado, Illinois, Iowa, Kansas, Michigan, Minnesota, Missouri, Nebraska, Ohio, Pennsylvania, Texas, Virginia, and Wisconsin.

*Special community initiatives* of the principal MR/DD state agencies were gauged in terms of individuals served and funding levels in family support, early intervention, supported employment, aging services, assistive technology, supported living, and personal assistance services. Funding associated with these initiatives represented a subset of total community services spending within the state. An activity was described as a special initiative if it attained either line item status in an MR/DD agency's published executive budget or was identified in the agency's internal planning or accounting systems.

*Family support* consisted of any community-based service administered by the state MR/DD agency providing for vouchers, direct cash payments to families, reimbursement, or direct payments to service providers which the state agency itself identified as family support. Examples of family support programs, other than cash subsidy, include respite care (a distinct category of data collection employed in the study), family counseling, equipment, architectural adaptation of the home, in-home training, education, and behavior management services. In many states, even though a formal family support program initiative was not in place, the state agency reported a variety of relevant discretionary family support activities being carried out by local providers with state assistance.

*Supported employment* referred to state MR/DD agency programs and projects for the long-term support of individuals in integrated work settings, work stations in industry, enclaves, or work crews where the goal was development of independent work skills and the ability to earn wages commensurate with those earned by individuals without disabilities doing similar work.

*Early intervention services* referred to developmental programs for infants and children ages birth to five years administered by the state MR/DD agency. Activities sponsored by the state special education agency were not reflected in data collected for this study. Specialized *aging/DD services* referred to any community-based residential or supportive service funded by the state MR/DD agency providing assistance to older individuals with developmental disabilities. The age requirement, usually 55 years or older, was defined by each state agency. Aging/DD services funded by state units and local area agencies on aging were not included in the present survey.

*Assistive technology* consisted of state MR/DD agency support in the purchase of assistive devices or services. This included funding directly to individuals with disabilities, to universities, private agencies, technology centers, or other providers of assistive technology devices or services.

*Supported living* met the criteria of choice by the individual of where and with whom she or he lived; ownership of the housing arrangement by someone other than the support provider (e.g. individual, family, landlords who might have support agencies serve as "guarantors," or housing cooperatives); and individualized support plans which recognized that individuals' needs for support change over time. *Personal assistance services* consisted of the state MR/DD agencies' use of Medicaid Personal Care Assistance funds, HCBS Waiver federal funds, or other state or federal funds to support individuals in their own homes. These criteria were based on the documentation of expanding state and local efforts to supplant traditional services with individualized support (e.g., Consortium for Citizens with Disabilities [CCD], 1991; Karan, Granfield, & Furey, 1992; Lakin & Stehly, 1990; Racino & Taylor, 1993; Smith, 1990; Smull, 1989).

## Reliability of the Data

Published state executive budgets for 1988-92 were collected directly from the states during 1992-93. The content analysis of budget documents began in January, 1992, and communication with state officials continued for 24 months through January, 1994. Extensive interviews and written communication with financial management and program staff in the medical assistance, social services, and developmental disabilities state agencies were conducted because amplification of published budget detail was invariably required. State data sets were reviewed by state mental retardation program directors.

Reliability of the classification of the data into the various funding categories has, in previous editions of the study, been demonstrated to be quite high (Braddock & Fujiura, 1991). Winer's (1971) unbiased intraclass correlation coefficients were between .88 and 1.00 in each of the state data sets. Less than perfect reliabilities are usually due to identifying additional expenditures overlooked in a previous edition of the study (e.g., fringe benefits) or, occasionally, reclassifying expenditures from institutional to the community services categories and vice versa.

## Analysis

The national data set was analyzed for the presence or absence of trends across the 1977-92 study period in three major service domains: institutional services, large private residential services, and community services. In selected analyses, the first two listed service domains were consolidated for purposes of creating an analytical category termed *large congregate care services*. Trends in the states were analyzed with respect to facility size, public or private sponsorship, and revenue source by level of government and statutory authorization. Recent institutional closures in the state were identified. Community services program initiatives were summarized.

In addition to a statistical summary of trends, fiscal effort was calculated for each of the states and the District of Columbia. Fiscal effort was computed for four time periods: 1977, 1988, 1992, and cumulatively across 1977-92. The fiscal effort computations were computed separately for large congregate care services, community services, and total (consolidated) spending. The calculation involved dividing the level of MR/DD expenditure in each state by aggregate statewide personal income, for each year and with respect to each of the three service domains. States were ranked in terms of fiscal effort during the four identified time periods, and these rankings were inspected to ascertain rates of change across the 1977-92 period.

Inflation during the 1977-92 period totaled 122%. In some analyses, financial data were adjusted for the impact of inflation. The state and local subindex of the Gross National Product implicit price deflator was used to express the data in terms of constant dollars. (Bureau of Economic Analysis, 1987a, 1987b, 1988a, 1988b, 1988c, 1989, 1993).

# RESULTS

## Total Spending Advances

Total public (federal, state, local) spending for MR/DD services in the U.S. has grown from $3.457 billion in 1977 to $17.228 billion in 1992. Adjusted for inflation, this was a total growth rate of 124%. During the four year period from 1988 to 1992, MR/DD spending continued its rapid upward momentum and advanced from $11.733 billion to $17.228 billion. Adjusted for inflation, the 1988-92 growth rate of 28% slightly exceeded the 25% adjusted growth rate for

MR/DD spending during 1984-88, and adjusted spending growth in both recent quadrennial periods exceeded the 18% growth rate during 1980-84.

The increase in total spending is almost entirely attributable to the expansion of funds allocated to community services activities. In the 1988-92 study update period, spending for "large congregate care services," which consisted of institutional and large privately operated residential care services, increased only 5%. Spending for community services advanced 52%.

The following analysis of the national data set is organized in four sections: 1) out-of-home placement trends; 2) institutional services; 3) large private residential services; and 4) community services.

## Out-of-Home Residential Placements

The changing structure of the residential care system is reflected in the growing percentage of individuals being served in smaller community settings.

Figure 1 illustrates out-of-home residential placements in 1977 compared to 1992. In 1977, only 14% of the 291,551 persons with developmental disabilities residing in out-of-home residential settings lived in settings with 15 or fewer residents. (Just 20,409 persons, 7%, resided in settings of 6 or fewer persons.) In contrast, by 1992, 52% of the 346,874 persons in out-of-home placements were residing in 15 or fewer settings. (Thirty-four percent of the total, or 117,920 individuals, resided in 6-person or fewer settings.)

There is diversity among the states in the utilization of the smaller settings. Table 2 presents state by state data with respect to the proportion of residents living in 16+ bed, 15-bed or less, or 6-bed or less settings. These statistics underscore the large congregate care orientation of the residential service system nationally in 1992. However, since 1977, smaller, more individualized services and supports have expanded rapidly in the states. New Hampshire, for example, in 1992 supported 97% of all residents in 15-bed or less settings and 71% in 6-bed or less settings. At the other end of the spectrum, 90% of Mississippi's residents are in large congregate 16+ bed settings.

States with the greatest proportion of their out-of-home placements in 6 bed or less settings in 1992, in addition to New Hampshire, were Hawaii, Arizona, Vermont, Michigan, Montana, Rhode Island, Maryland, Oregon, California, and North Dakota.

## Institutional Services

The plateau in institutional spending noted in previous national studies continued. Real growth across the 1988-92 period in institutional spending totaled just 2%. In fact, since 1977 the total resources allocated to operate the nation's institutions grew just 10%. During this 16-year period, however, the number of residents living in state-operated institutions was reduced by one-half--falling from 149,681 residents to 77,618. Per diem rates skyrocketed. Improved staffing ratios accounted for most of the cost-per-resident increase. Ratios grew from 1.6:1 in 1983 to 2.08:1 in 1992.

**FIGURE 1**

*Individuals Served by Size of Residential Setting: FYs 1977 and 1992*

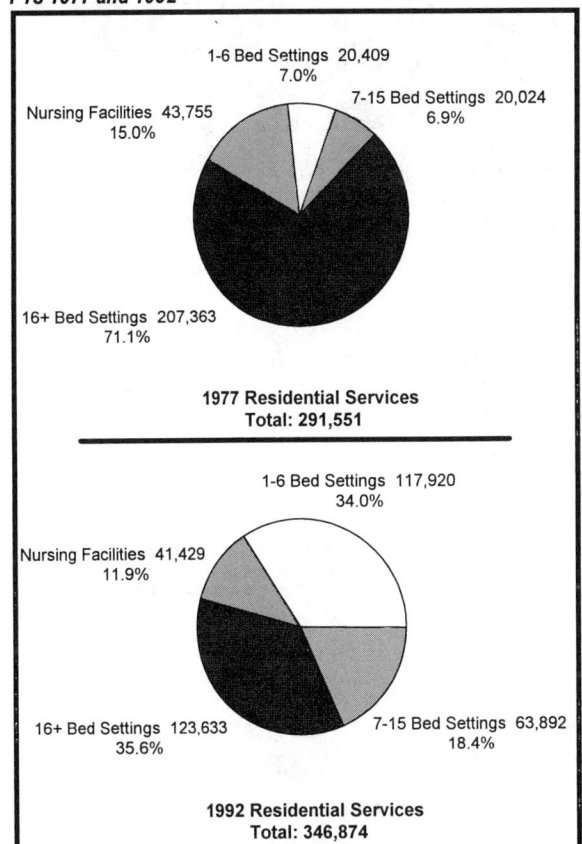

1-6 Bed Settings  20,409
7.0%

7-15 Bed Settings  20,024
6.9%

Nursing Facilities  43,755
15.0%

16+ Bed Settings  207,363
71.1%

**1977 Residential Services**
**Total: 291,551**

1-6 Bed Settings  117,920
34.0%

Nursing Facilities  41,429
11.9%

16+ Bed Settings  123,633
35.6%

7-15 Bed Settings  63,892
18.4%

**1992 Residential Services**
**Total: 346,874**

## TABLE 2

*Number and Percentage of Individuals Served by Size of Residential Setting: FY 1992* [1]

| Rank | State | 1-6 Bed Settings | | 7-15 Bed Settings | | 16 + Bed Settings | | Total Served |
|---|---|---|---|---|---|---|---|---|
| | | n | % of Total | n | % of Total | n | % of Total | |
| 1 | HAWAII | 949 | 87.0 | 6 | 0.5 | 136 | 12.5 | 1,091 |
| 2 | ARIZONA | 2,055 | 85.4 | 0 | 0.0 | 350 | 14.6 | 2,405 |
| 3 | VERMONT | 552 | 71.5 | 0 | 0.0 | 220 | 28.5 | 772 |
| 4 | NEW HAMPSHIRE | 907 | 71.2 | 322 | 25.3 | 45 | 3.5 | 1,274 |
| 5 | MICHIGAN | 7,271 | 70.8 | 404 | 3.9 | 2,594 | 25.3 | 10,269 |
| 6 | MONTANA | 982 | 70.4 | 8 | 0.6 | 404 | 29.0 | 1,394 |
| 7 | RHODE ISLAND | 1,241 | 63.6 | 444 | 22.8 | 265 | 13.6 | 1,950 |
| 8 | MARYLAND | 3,093 | 63.4 | 0 | 0.0 | 1,783 | 36.6 | 4,876 |
| 9 | OREGON | 2,473 | 57.1 | 611 | 14.1 | 1,248 | 28.8 | 4,332 |
| 10 | CALIFORNIA | 23,101 | 56.8 | 3,055 | 7.5 | 14,537 | 35.7 | 40,693 |
| 11 | NORTH DAKOTA | 1,147 | 56.2 | 469 | 23.0 | 424 | 20.8 | 2,040 |
| 12 | COLORADO | 2,163 | 54.7 | 842 | 21.3 | 949 | 24.0 | 3,954 |
| 13 | CONNECTICUT | 3,335 | 54.0 | 573 | 9.3 | 2,265 | 36.7 | 6,173 |
| 14 | MAINE | 1,078 | 53.5 | 354 | 17.6 | 582 | 28.9 | 2,014 |
| 15 | MINNESOTA | 5,589 | 51.6 | 1,884 | 17.4 | 3,367 | 31.1 | 10,840 |
| 16 | WISCONSIN | 5,466 | 48.1 | 984 | 8.7 | 4,921 | 43.3 | 11,371 |
| 17 | NEVADA | 263 | 47.4 | 0 | 0.0 | 292 | 52.6 | 555 |
| 18 | PENNSYLVANIA | 7,255 | 46.2 | 1,423 | 9.1 | 7,023 | 44.7 | 15,701 |
| 19 | WASHINGTON | 2,412 | 45.9 | 440 | 8.4 | 2,398 | 45.7 | 5,250 |
| 20 | NORTH CAROLINA | 2,899 | 44.5 | 276 | 4.2 | 3,342 | 51.3 | 6,517 |
| 21 | DELAWARE | 368 | 42.9 | 66 | 7.7 | 423 | 49.4 | 857 |
| 22 | ALASKA | 291 | 41.3 | 328 | 46.6 | 85 | 12.1 | 704 |
| 23 | KANSAS | 1,669 | 40.6 | 824 | 20.1 | 1,614 | 39.3 | 4,107 |
| 24 | NEW JERSEY | 3,954 | 37.8 | 0 | 0.0 | 6,504 | 62.2 | 10,458 |
| 25 | IDAHO | 478 | 37.3 | 485 | 37.8 | 320 | 24.9 | 1,283 |
| 26 | MASSACHUSETTS | 3,775 | 37.0 | 2,206 | 21.6 | 4,214 | 41.3 | 10,195 |
| 27 | NEW MEXICO | 533 | 33.6 | 380 | 24.0 | 671 | 42.4 | 1,584 |
| 28 | SOUTH DAKOTA | 618 | 33.3 | 715 | 38.5 | 522 | 28.1 | 1,855 |
| 29 | WEST VIRGINIA | 445 | 32.1 | 532 | 38.4 | 410 | 29.6 | 1,387 |
| 30 | DIST OF COLUMBIA | 324 | 30.7 | 649 | 61.5 | 82 | 7.8 | 1,055 |
| 31 | WYOMING | 207 | 30.0 | 180 | 26.1 | 302 | 43.8 | 689 |
| 32 | LOUISIANA | 2,146 | 29.1 | 333 | 4.5 | 4,907 | 66.4 | 7,386 |
| 33 | KENTUCKY | 930 | 27.9 | 148 | 4.4 | 2,258 | 67.7 | 3,336 |
| 34 | GEORGIA | 1,489 | 27.2 | 7 | 0.1 | 3,976 | 72.7 | 5,472 |
| 35 | UTAH | 563 | 26.8 | 350 | 16.7 | 1,187 | 56.5 | 2,100 |
| 36 | INDIANA | 2,310 | 23.5 | 2,716 | 27.7 | 4,788 | 48.8 | 9,814 |
| 37 | OHIO | 3,765 | 22.5 | 3,112 | 18.6 | 9,890 | 59.0 | 16,767 |
| 38 | NEBRASKA | 716 | 22.2 | 1,151 | 35.6 | 1,363 | 42.2 | 3,230 |
| 39 | SOUTH CAROLINA | 919 | 21.5 | 1,109 | 25.9 | 2,252 | 52.6 | 4,280 |
| 40 | FLORIDA | 2,203 | 21.4 | 3,782 | 36.7 | 4,319 | 41.9 | 10,304 |
| 41 | IOWA | 1,627 | 20.0 | 1,875 | 23.1 | 4,621 | 56.9 | 8,123 |
| 42 | MISSOURI | 1,825 | 19.4 | 2,085 | 22.2 | 5,497 | 58.4 | 9,407 |
| 43 | NEW YORK | 5,856 | 17.4 | 15,137 | 45.0 | 12,670 | 37.6 | 33,663 |
| 44 | OKLAHOMA | 857 | 14.7 | 395 | 6.8 | 4,575 | 78.5 | 5,827 |
| 45 | TEXAS | 2,469 | 13.3 | 3,195 | 17.2 | 12,941 | 69.6 | 18,605 |
| 46 | ILLINOIS | 1,780 | 9.1 | 4,870 | 24.8 | 13,002 | 66.2 | 19,652 |
| 47 | TENNESSEE | 454 | 9.0 | 1,593 | 31.7 | 2,984 | 59.3 | 5,031 |
| 48 | ARKANSAS | 341 | 8.1 | 1,496 | 35.6 | 2,370 | 56.3 | 4,207 |
| 49 | VIRGINIA | 379 | 7.6 | 906 | 18.2 | 3,701 | 74.2 | 4,986 |
| 50 | MISSISSIPPI | 220 | 7.1 | 82 | 2.6 | 2,806 | 90.3 | 3,108 |
| 51 | ALABAMA | 178 | 4.5 | 1,090 | 27.7 | 2,663 | 67.7 | 3,931 |
| | **UNITED STATES** | **117,920** | **34.0** | **63,892** | **18.4** | **165,062** | **47.6** | **346,874** |

[1] *States are ranked by percentage of individuals served in settings of 6 beds or less; columns entitled "16+ Bed Settings" and "Total Served" include persons in nursing facilities; see Table 7 for state-by-state nursing facility detail.*

## The ICF/MR Program

The percentage of federal ICF/MR funding being allocated to reimburse placements in state institutions and other large 16+ bed residential settings is slowly declining. In 1992, 74% of the $4.889 billion in federal ICF/MR funds was being deployed to institutions and large 16+ bed privately operated residential settings. Twenty-six percent of federal ICF/MR funds were being spent to reimburse placements in settings of 15 beds or less (see Figure 2). For comparison, in 1986, 87% of all ICF/MR reimbursements supported placements in large congregate care settings. In 1977, 99% of all federal ICF/MR funds supported placements in large congregate settings.

The proportionately large federal commitment to institutional settings is disturbing to community services advocates because of the tremendous volume of federal funding associated with the ICF/MR program. The program remained by far the largest federal services program in the field. When matched with the state and local funding required under Medicaid provisions, it accounted for 52% of all financial resources for MR/DD services and supports allocated nationally in 1992.

Thirty-six states used more than two-thirds of their federal ICF/MR resources to support placements in large congregate care settings greater than 15 beds in size. In 1988, the state of Rhode Island was the *only* state which used a majority of its ICF/MR resources in 15-bed or less settings. In 1992, six states were doing so: Washington, DC, Michigan, New Hampshire, New York, Rhode Island, and West Virginia. It should be noted, however, that only Michigan and Rhode Island deployed 75% or more of 15 or less ICF/MR funds to settings with six or fewer residents. Nationally, the ICF/MR program supported only 34% of all 15 or less ICF/MR residents in settings as small as 6 beds or less.

## FIGURE 2
*ICF/MR Spending by Facility Setting in the United States: FY 1992*

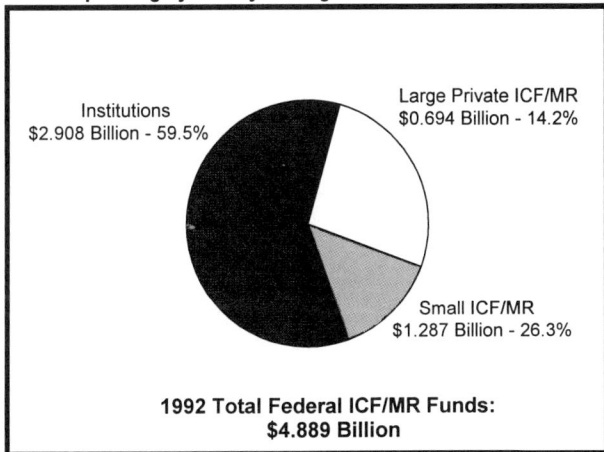

Institutions
$2.908 Billion - 59.5%

Large Private ICF/MR
$0.694 Billion - 14.2%

Small ICF/MR
$1.287 Billion - 26.3%

**1992 Total Federal ICF/MR Funds:
$4.889 Billion**

## Census Trends

The number of institutional residents continued to decline steadily. The population residing in these facilities dropped from 91,432 in 1988 to 77,618 in 1992. This 15% drop over a 4-year period is similar to the rate of decline experienced for the past 25 years. The institutional census peaked at 194,650 in 1967 (Lakin, 1979) and has diminished by between 3% and 4% percent per year since then. The census decline between 1984 and 1988 was 16.6%. The average daily number of residents in institutions in the U.S. is depicted in Figure 3.

All states with the exception of Mississippi, Kentucky, and Georgia reduced institutional populations during 1988-92. The most notable development nationally during 1988-92 was the complete termination of institutional operations in New Hampshire and the District of Columbia. An additional 11 states had fewer than 250 individuals residing in institutional settings in 1992. These states were West Virginia, North Dakota, Hawaii, Rhode Island, Vermont, Idaho, Wyoming, Maine, Alaska, Montana, and Nevada. The 10 states, besides Washington, DC, and New Hampshire, that reduced their institutional census at the most rapid rate on a percentage basis during 1988-92 were West Virginia (75% decline), Michigan (57%), Hawaii (49%), Oregon (47%) Rhode Island (42%), North Dakota (42%), Colorado (40%), Wyoming (36%), Minnesota (34%), and Oklahoma (31%). Most of these states were involved in class action litigation requiring community placement of institutional residents.

The 10 states with the greatest absolute reduction in resident populations included New York (2,277), Michigan (821), Massachusetts (706), Texas (621), Pennsylvania (619), Connecticut (612), Ohio (556), Oregon (527), Minnesota (523), and New Jersey (499). These 10 states accounted for nearly 60% of the nationwide reduction in institutional residents during the 1988-92 period. Table 3 presents detailed institutional census data on a state-by-state basis.

## FIGURE 3
*Institutional Census: FYs 1977 - 92*

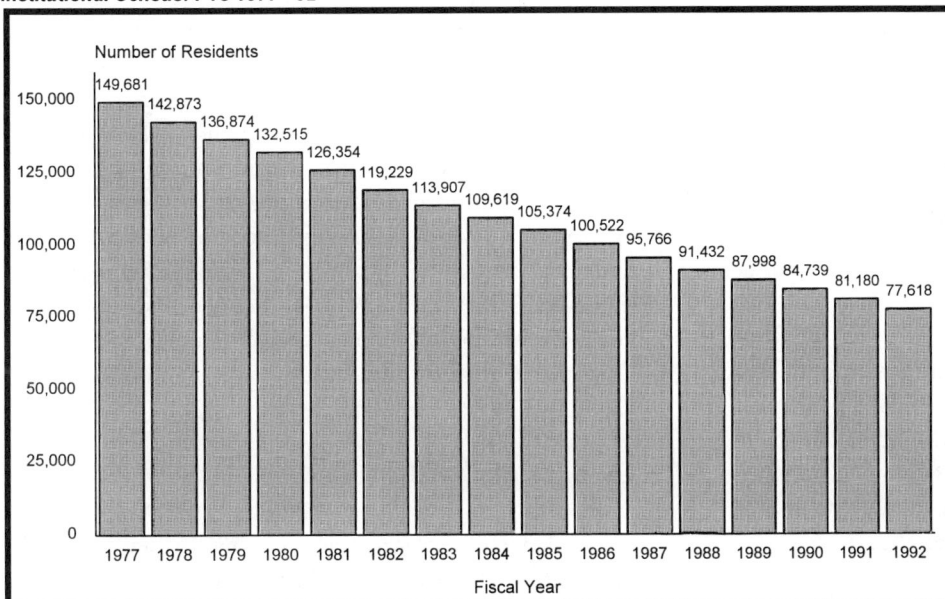

Number of Residents

| Fiscal Year | Number |
| --- | --- |
| 1977 | 149,681 |
| 1978 | 142,873 |
| 1979 | 136,874 |
| 1980 | 132,515 |
| 1981 | 126,354 |
| 1982 | 119,229 |
| 1983 | 113,907 |
| 1984 | 109,619 |
| 1985 | 105,374 |
| 1986 | 100,522 |
| 1987 | 95,766 |
| 1988 | 91,432 |
| 1989 | 87,998 |
| 1990 | 84,739 |
| 1991 | 81,180 |
| 1992 | 77,618 |

## Per Diem Costs of Care

As noted above, a declining census coupled with a plateau in total institutional spending has resulted in escalating per diems across the 1977-92 period. During the 1988-92 period, per diems advanced from $154 to $212. Adjusted for the impact of inflation, this is a 20%, 4-year increase. The per diem increase during the 1984-88 comparison period was 23%. Figure 4 displays the rapid growth of per diems across

## TABLE 3
*Institutional Census by State: 1977, 1988, and 1992[1]*

| Rank | State | 1977 | 1988 | 1992 | % Decline 1988-92 | % Decline 1977-92 |
|---|---|---|---|---|---|---|
| 1 | D.C. | 1,100 | 257 | 0 | 100.0 | 100.0 |
| 2 | NEW HAMPSHIRE | 684 | 167 | 0 | 100.0 | 100.0 |
| 3 | WEST VIRGINIA | 1,165 | 508 | 125 | 75.4 | 89.3 |
| 4 | MICHIGAN | 6,047 | 1,477 | 656 | 55.6 | 89.2 |
| 5 | NORTH DAKOTA | 1,139 | 347 | 203 | 41.5 | 82.2 |
| 6 | HAWAII | 562 | 227 | 116 | 48.9 | 79.4 |
| 7 | COLORADO | 1,580 | 554 | 334 | 39.7 | 78.9 |
| 8 | RHODE ISLAND | 736 | 283 | 165 | 41.7 | 77.6 |
| 9 | ARIZONA | 959 | 388 | 264 | 32.0 | 72.5 |
| 10 | VERMONT | 443 | 191 | 135 | 29.3 | 69.5 |
| 11 | OREGON | 1,873 | 1,130 | 603 | 46.6 | 67.8 |
| 12 | MINNESOTA | 3,085 | 1,556 | 1,033 | 33.6 | 66.5 |
| 13 | OHIO | 6,838 | 2,990 | 2,434 | 18.6 | 64.4 |
| 14 | MARYLAND | 2,725 | 1,441 | 1,014 | 29.6 | 62.8 |
| 15 | IDAHO | 454 | 250 | 172 | 31.2 | 62.1 |
| 16 | NEW YORK | 18,799 | 9,534 | 7,257 | 23.9 | 61.4 |
| 17 | OKLAHOMA | 2,158 | 1,213 | 839 | 30.8 | 61.1 |
| 18 | PENNSYLVANIA | 9,189 | 4,426 | 3,807 | 14.0 | 58.6 |
| 19 | FLORIDA | 4,414 | 1,993 | 1,949 | 2.2 | 55.8 |
| 20 | WYOMING | 533 | 374 | 238 | 36.4 | 55.3 |
| 21 | NEBRASKA | 1,008 | 470 | 458 | 2.6 | 54.6 |
| 22 | SOUTH DAKOTA | 843 | 440 | 385 | 12.5 | 54.3 |
| 23 | MAINE | 522 | 307 | 245 | 20.2 | 53.1 |
| 24 | ALASKA | 100 | 61 | 47 | 23.0 | 53.0 |
| 25 | UTAH | 841 | 527 | 410 | 22.2 | 51.2 |
| 26 | MASSACHUSETTS | 5,229 | 3,320 | 2,614 | 21.3 | 50.0 |
| 27 | CONNECTICUT | 3,058 | 2,157 | 1,545 | 28.4 | 49.5 |
| 28 | MONTANA | 299 | 253 | 174 | 31.2 | 41.8 |
| 29 | WASHINGTON | 2,504 | 1,794 | 1,498 | 16.5 | 40.2 |
| 30 | DELAWARE | 534 | 378 | 325 | 14.0 | 39.1 |
| 31 | SOUTH CAROLINA | 3,440 | 2,354 | 2,135 | 9.3 | 37.9 |
| 32 | NEW JERSEY | 7,603 | 5,236 | 4,737 | 9.5 | 37.7 |
| 33 | IOWA | 1,397 | 1,062 | 895 | 15.7 | 35.9 |
| 34 | KANSAS | 1,456 | 1,149 | 943 | 17.9 | 35.2 |
| 35 | TEXAS | 10,843 | 7,662 | 7,041 | 8.1 | 35.1 |
| 36 | NORTH CAROLINA | 3,848 | 2,805 | 2,502 | 10.8 | 35.0 |
| 37 | WISCONSIN | 2,405 | 1,790 | 1,581 | 11.7 | 34.3 |
| 38 | VIRGINIA | 3,836 | 2,821 | 2,554 | 9.5 | 33.4 |
| 39 | ILLINOIS | 6,580 | 4,518 | 4,398 | 2.7 | 33.2 |
| 40 | CALIFORNIA | 9,764 | 6,772 | 6,683 | 1.3 | 31.6 |
| 41 | INDIANA | 2,477 | 1,945 | 1,767 | 9.2 | 28.7 |
| 42 | GEORGIA | 2,909 | 2,080 | 2,089 | -0.4 | 28.2 |
| 43 | LOUISIANA | 3,245 | 2,841 | 2,372 | 16.5 | 26.9 |
| 44 | MISSOURI | 2,102 | 1,888 | 1,538 | 18.5 | 26.8 |
| 45 | ALABAMA | 1,643 | 1,285 | 1,262 | 1.8 | 23.2 |
| 46 | NEW MEXICO | 584 | 493 | 483 | 2.0 | 17.3 |
| 47 | MISSISSIPPI | 1,720 | 1,458 | 1,493 | -2.4 | 13.2 |
| 48 | KENTUCKY | 839 | 742 | 753 | -1.5 | 10.3 |
| 49 | ARKANSAS | 1,380 | 1,316 | 1,259 | 4.3 | 8.8 |
| 50 | TENNESSEE | 2,071 | 2,024 | 1,914 | 5.4 | 7.6 |
| 51 | NEVADA | 118 | 178 | 174 | 2.2 | -47.5 |
| | UNITED STATES | 149,681 | 91,432 | 77,618 | 15.1 | 48.1 |

[1] States are ranked by percentage decline, 1977-92.

## FIGURE 4
*Daily Costs Per Resident: FYs 1977 - 92*

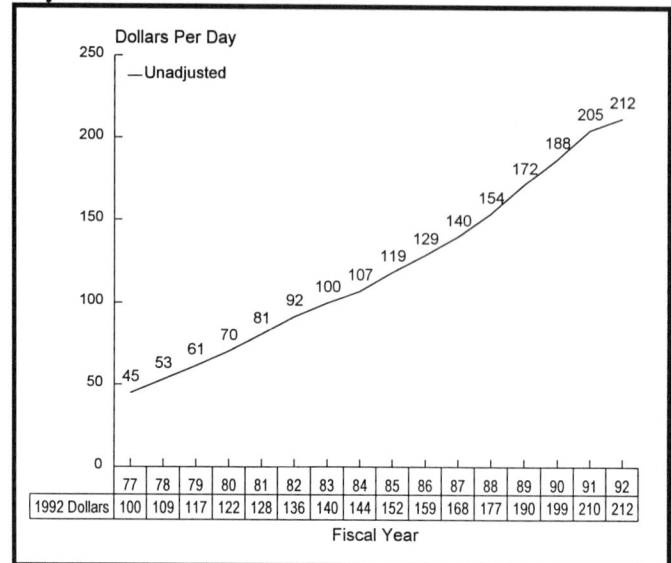

the entire 16-year study period. In real economic terms, the increase is 112%.

The states exhibited great variations in per diem rates in 1992. Rates ranged from over $435 per day in Alaska, Maine, Massachusetts, and Rhode Island, to $124-$160 per day in Arkansas, Illinois, Kentucky, Louisiana, Mississippi, Nebraska, South Carolina, Tennessee, and Texas. In 1992, per diems exceeded $300 in 11 states. Maine had the highest per diem at $505. The most rapid rates of growth in per diems during 1988-92 occurred in the following five states: Maine, West Virginia, Hawaii, Oregon, and Oklahoma. Per diems in the states during the 1988-92 period are presented in Table 4.

## Staff-to-Resident Ratios

As reported in the previous national study (Braddock et al., 1990) staff-to-resident ratios increased 18% between 1983 and 1988. The increase for the 1988-92 period was 11%--from 1.88:1 in 1988 to 2.08:1 in 1992. There were, however, 10,611 fewer full-time equivalent staff working in institutional facilities in 1992 versus 1988. This is due to the continuing reduction in the institutional census and the closure of numerous institutions. Thirty-three states reduced the number of institutional personnel between 1988-92; in all but seven of these states, staff-to-resident ratios increased. There were absolute increases in institutional personnel in 18 states. Staff-to-resident ratios varied from a low of between 1.5:1 and 1.6:1 in California, Illinois, and Michigan to in excess of 3.00:1 in Idaho, Massachusetts, North Dakota, Oklahoma, Oregon, Rhode Island, and West Virginia. Data from the states are presented in Table 5.

## Closure of Institutions

The trend toward closing institutions gained momentum during the recession of the early 1980s and has continued. In a 1984 national survey, Braddock & Heller (1985) identified 24 closures in 12 states. The 1988 national study of public spending (Braddock et al., 1990) identified a total of 44 closures in 20 states. The current study has identified a total of 94 scheduled or completed institutional closures in 29 states.

In 1992, New Hampshire closed the Laconia State School and became an institution-free state. About a year later, the District of Columbia closed Forest Haven, an institution that since 1925 had served persons with mental retardation who were residents of the District. Vermont and Rhode Island closed their re-

## TABLE 4
### Institutional Per Diem Costs: 1992, 1988, and Percentage Change 1988-92 [1]

| State | Per Diem Costs ($) 1992 | Per Diem Costs ($) 1988 | % Change 1988-92 |
|---|---|---|---|
| ALABAMA | 174.57 | 145.11 | 20.3 |
| ALASKA | 461.92 | 302.82 | 52.5 |
| ARIZONA | 181.27 | 222.24 | -18.4 |
| ARKANSAS | 136.83 | 99.50 | 37.5 |
| CALIFORNIA | 228.61 | 176.82 | 29.3 |
| COLORADO | 202.03 | 128.16 | 57.6 |
| CONNECTICUT | 308.69 | 185.11 | 66.8 |
| DELAWARE | 204.62 | 137.19 | 49.2 |
| DIST OF COLUMBIA | 0.00 | 235.77 | -100.0 |
| FLORIDA | 172.05 | 140.83 | 22.2 |
| GEORGIA | 203.52 | 164.12 | 24.0 |
| HAWAII | 292.97 | 124.89 | 134.6 |
| IDAHO | 320.31 | 167.85 | 90.8 |
| ILLINOIS | 157.03 | 129.78 | 21.0 |
| INDIANA | 212.55 | 115.57 | 83.9 |
| IOWA | 207.47 | 154.57 | 34.2 |
| KANSAS | 212.90 | 144.54 | 47.3 |
| KENTUCKY | 161.00 | 107.10 | 50.3 |
| LOUISIANA | 124.05 | 85.99 | 44.3 |
| MAINE | 504.95 | 175.10 | 188.4 |
| MARYLAND | 223.87 | 172.05 | 30.1 |
| MASSACHUSETTS | 435.75 | 274.22 | 58.9 |
| MICHIGAN | 329.58 | 217.72 | 51.4 |
| MINNESOTA | 291.88 | 179.58 | 62.5 |
| MISSISSIPPI | 119.45 | 89.91 | 32.9 |
| MISSOURI | 234.95 | 133.53 | 76.0 |
| MONTANA | 234.17 | 150.04 | 56.1 |
| NEBRASKA | 151.26 | 111.20 | 36.0 |
| NEVADA | 247.50 | 145.02 | 70.7 |
| NEW HAMPSHIRE | 0.00 | 277.68 | -100.0 |
| NEW JERSEY | 182.72 | 132.52 | 37.9 |
| NEW MEXICO | 192.21 | 118.37 | 62.4 |
| NEW YORK | 253.13 | 216.88 | 16.7 |
| NORTH CAROLINA | 210.72 | 151.59 | 39.0 |
| NORTH DAKOTA | 335.54 | 227.59 | 47.4 |
| OHIO | 230.66 | 157.83 | 46.1 |
| OKLAHOMA | 290.64 | 133.94 | 117.0 |
| OREGON | 361.76 | 160.54 | 125.3 |
| PENNSYLVANIA | 206.80 | 150.09 | 37.8 |
| RHODE ISLAND | 438.73 | 244.61 | 79.4 |
| SOUTH CAROLINA | 150.67 | 107.20 | 40.6 |
| SOUTH DAKOTA | 161.61 | 105.24 | 53.6 |
| TENNESSEE | 134.81 | 106.07 | 27.1 |
| TEXAS | 158.88 | 116.25 | 36.7 |
| UTAH | 185.52 | 122.59 | 51.3 |
| VERMONT | 267.61 | 163.50 | 63.7 |
| VIRGINIA | 167.67 | 128.40 | 30.6 |
| WASHINGTON | 296.77 | 153.17 | 93.8 |
| WEST VIRGINIA | 319.05 | 113.62 | 180.8 |
| WISCONSIN | 197.26 | 142.51 | 38.4 |
| WYOMING | 232.16 | 109.71 | 111.6 |
| **UNITED STATES** | **211.77** | **154.07** | **37.5** |
| *INDIVIDUALS SERVED* | 77,618 | 91,432 | |

[1] Per diem costs are in nominal dollars (not adjusted for inflation).

## TABLE 5
### Staffing Ratios in Public Mental Retardation Institutions, 1992, 1988, and Percentage Change 1988-92

| State | # FTE Staff 1992 | Staff Ratio 1992 | Staff Ratio 1988 | % Change 1988-92 |
|---|---|---|---|---|
| ALABAMA | 2,430 | 1.93 | 1.86 | 3.5 |
| ALASKA | 136 | 2.89 | 2.26 | 28.0 |
| ARIZONA * | 550 | 2.08 | 1.98 | 5.1 |
| ARKANSAS | 2,344 | 1.86 | 1.87 | -0.4 |
| CALIFORNIA | 10,807 | 1.62 | 1.42 | 13.9 |
| COLORADO | 772 | 2.31 | 1.59 | 45.3 |
| CONNECTICUT | 3,748 | 2.43 | 2.16 | 12.3 |
| DELAWARE | 696 | 2.14 | 1.96 | 9.3 |
| DIST OF COLUMBIA | 0 | 0.00 | 2.06 | -100.0 |
| FLORIDA | 4,015 | 2.06 | 2.10 | -1.9 |
| GEORGIA | 5,004 | 2.40 | 2.30 | 4.1 |
| HAWAII | 334 | 2.88 | 1.94 | 48.4 |
| IDAHO | 560 | 3.26 | 2.15 | 51.4 |
| ILLINOIS | 6,948 | 1.58 | 1.54 | 2.6 |
| INDIANA | 3,423 | 1.94 | 1.78 | 8.8 |
| IOWA | 1,967 | 2.20 | 2.11 | 4.2 |
| KANSAS | 2,418 | 2.56 | 2.01 | 27.6 |
| KENTUCKY * | 1,400 | 1.82 | 1.72 | 5.7 |
| LOUISIANA | 4,399 | 1.85 | 1.45 | 27.9 |
| MAINE | 703 | 2.87 | 2.44 | 17.6 |
| MARYLAND | 2,423 | 2.39 | 1.95 | 22.5 |
| MASSACHUSETTS | 8,000 | 3.06 | 3.01 | 1.7 |
| MICHIGAN | 962 | 1.51 | 2.14 | -29.2 |
| MINNESOTA | 1,835 | 1.78 | 1.64 | 8.3 |
| MISSISSIPPI | 2,704 | 1.77 | 1.88 | -5.6 |
| MISSOURI | 4,000 | 2.60 | 2.18 | 19.3 |
| MONTANA | 487 | 2.80 | 2.10 | 33.3 |
| NEBRASKA | 860 | 1.88 | 1.81 | 3.7 |
| NEVADA | 380 | 2.18 | 1.38 | 58.3 |
| NEW HAMPSHIRE | 0 | 0.00 | 3.04 | -100.0 |
| NEW JERSEY | 9,720 | 1.98 | 1.87 | 6.1 |
| NEW MEXICO | 1,137 | 2.35 | 1.71 | 37.7 |
| NEW YORK | 14,672 | 2.02 | 2.05 | -1.4 |
| NORTH CAROLINA | 5,628 | 2.25 | 1.99 | 13.0 |
| NORTH DAKOTA | 743 | 3.66 | 3.18 | 15.1 |
| OHIO | 4,993 | 2.05 | 1.83 | 12.1 |
| OKLAHOMA | 2,534 | 3.02 | 1.97 | 53.3 |
| OREGON | 2,047 | 3.39 | 2.10 | 61.7 |
| PENNSYLVANIA | 6,404 | 1.68 | 1.55 | 8.5 |
| RHODE ISLAND | 703 | 4.26 | 1.62 | 163.0 |
| SOUTH CAROLINA | 4,526 | 2.12 | 1.79 | 18.4 |
| SOUTH DAKOTA | 832 | 2.16 | 1.78 | 21.4 |
| TENNESSEE | 3,289 | 1.72 | 1.64 | 4.8 |
| TEXAS | 15,768 | 2.24 | 1.93 | 16.0 |
| UTAH | 835 | 2.04 | 1.93 | 5.4 |
| VERMONT | 400 | 2.96 | 2.20 | 34.7 |
| VIRGINIA | 4,926 | 1.93 | 1.66 | 16.2 |
| WASHINGTON | 3,631 | 2.42 | 1.75 | 38.5 |
| WEST VIRGINIA | 605 | 4.84 | 2.25 | 115.1 |
| WISCONSIN | 2,734 | 1.73 | 1.63 | 6.1 |
| WYOMING | 705 | 2.96 | 1.35 | 119.4 |
| **UNITED STATES** | **161,137** | **2.08** | **1.88** | **10.5** |

* 1992 staffing ratios estimated for Arizona and Kentucky

maining institutions in 1993 and 1994, respectively. In other important developments, Governor Mario Cuomo announced the intention of the state of New York to phase out and close all of the state's developmental centers. Minnesota also put forward a similar plan, but stopped short of announcing closures of all institutional facilities. During 1988-92, several states without previous closure experience announced plans to close facilities. These included Indiana, Maine, New Jersey, Oklahoma, Texas, Washington, and West Virginia.

As noted in the 1990 study, in most states the number of persons with mental retardation residing in institutions continues to decline at a consistent rate and the cost of supporting these individuals in such settings is climbing rapidly. Aggregate staffing of institutions has remained fairly constant while the census has declined, resulting in a substantial rise in per diems.

As the institutional census continues to fall and per diems increase in corresponding, inverse fashion, pressures on states to close additional institutions will grow. It seems quite likely that by the year 2000, only 50,000 to 60,000 persons will be residing in state-operated institutions. If the federal government adopts significant new incentives for community placement, the numbers of persons residing in institutions and the numbers of institutions could decline even more rapidly over the next several years. Closures are summarized in Table 6. The table is current as of August, 1994.

## Large Private Residential Services

The powerful national trend of reducing the populations of state institutions did not carry over during the 1988-92 period into large privately operated residential care facilities. The total population in these 16+ bed facilities remained essentially the same (47,154 in 1988 versus 46,015 in 1992). There was a significant increase in the number of persons residing in large ICF/MR certified private facilities (increase of 1,649 individuals) and a counter-balancing decline of 2,788 persons residing in large private settings not certified as ICFs/MR. It appears likely that some of the non-certified facilities sought and achieved ICF/MR certification during the 1988-92 period.

With this certification came additional public funding. Financial support for large private settings grew very rapidly during the 1988-92 period from $.941 billion to $1.372 billion. This was an increase of 27% expressed in real economic terms. Most of the increase was attributable to ICF/MR spending growth. The rate of growth of overall nationwide adjusted spending in the large private residential sector during 1988-92 was slightly over one-half the adjusted growth rate for community services funding during that period (27% vs. 53%). The expansion of funding in the MR/DD field was therefore not restricted to smaller scale 15-bed or less community services. Expansion occurred in the large private residential sector as well (see Figure 5).

## Nursing Home Utilization

An additional objective of the study included the collection of data from the states on the number of persons with mental retardation residing in nursing homes. Data, collected by telephone interviews in many instances, were based on figures the states reported to the Health Care Financing Administration in accord with their reporting requirements under P.L. 100-203. Table 7 summarizes the estimated 1992 utilization of nursing home placements for persons with mental retardation and related conditions.

The number of persons with mental retardation reported to be residing in nursing homes declined from 50,606 in 1988 to 41,429 in 1992. Nearly three-fourths of this decline was associated with five states: Ohio (1,756 decline), New Jersey (1,733), Wisconsin (1,643), Illinois (1,196), and Pennsylvania (889). The number of persons with mental retardation reported in nursing homes increased by 3,013 in 14 states: New Mexico, Mississippi, Nevada, Oregon, Nebraska, District of Columbia, Kentucky, Missouri, Oklahoma, Massachusetts, Arkansas, Nevada, Louisiana, and Indiana. This increase apparently reflected improved assessment procedures mandated by P.L. 100-203.

## Trends in Community Services

The growing proportion of residential placements in smaller, more individualized community settings is dramatically reflected in the financing of these services over time. Total spending for community services, defined in terms of 15-bed or less

## TABLE 6
### Completed and In-Progress Closures of State-Operated Mental Retardation Institutions in the United States

| State | Institution | Year Built/ Became MR | Original Use | # Served, Closure Announcement | Year of Closure | Alternate Use |
|-------|-------------|----------------------|--------------|-------------------------------|-----------------|---------------|
| ARIZONA | Phoenix | 1974 | MR Facility | 46 | 1988 | Pending Sale: Commercial |
| CALIFORNIA | DeWitt | 1942/1947 | Army Hospital | 819 | 1972 | Placer County Recreation |
| | Modesto Unit | 1943/1948 | Army Hospital | 1,394 | 1969 | Modesto County Community College |
| | Napa | 1875/1967 | Asylum for MR/MI | 30 | 1988 | MI Use Only |
| COLORADO | Pueblo | 1935 | MI/MR Facility | 163 | 1989 | Pueblo Regional Center |
| | Wheatridge | 1912 | MR Facility | 80 | 1995 | Colorado Land Board |
| CONNECTICUT | Mansfield | 1906/1917 | Epileptic Colony | 146 | 1993 | Corrections/U. of Connecticut |
| | New Haven | 1964 | MR Facility | 56 | 1994 | Job Corps |
| | Waterbury | 1963/1972 | Convent | 40 | 1989 | Administrative Offices |
| DIST. OF COLUMBIA | Forest Haven | 1925 | MR Facility | 1,000 | 1991 | Private Rehab/PH Infirmary |
| FLORIDA | Orlando | 1929/1959 | TB Hospital | 1,000 | 1984 | Unoccupied: asbestos |
| | Tallahassee | 1928/1967 | TB Hospital | 350 | 1983 | Unoccupied: asbestos |
| ILLINOIS | Adler | 1967 | MI/MR Facility | 16 | 1982 | Water Survey Offices |
| | Alton | 1914/1974 | MI Facility | 108 | 1994 | MI Forensic Services |
| | Bowen | 1965 | MR Facility | 105 | 1982 | Corrections |
| | Choate (Anna) | 1873/1993 | MI | 17 | 1993 | Closed child/adolescent section |
| | Dixon | 1918 | MR Facility | 820 | 1987 | Corrections/Opened New MR Facility |
| | Galesburg | 1950/1969 | Army Hospital | 350 | 1985 | Head Start/Community Programs |
| | Meyer | 1966/1970 | MI Facility | 53 | 1993 | MI Facility |
| INDIANA | Central State | 1848 | MI/MR Facility | 83 | 1994 | Undetermined |
| KANSAS | Norton | 1926/1963 | TB Hospital | 60 | 1988 | Corrections |
| KENTUCKY | Frankfort | 1860 | MR Facility | 650 | 1972 | Demolition |
| | Outwood | 1922/1962 | TB Hospital | 80 | 1983 | Demolition/New Campus |
| MAINE | Pineland | 1908 | MR Facility | 265 | 1995 | Undetermined |
| MARYLAND | Walter P. Carter | 1978/1979 | MI/MR Facility | 10 | 1990 | MH |
| | Victor Cullen | 1908/1974 | TB Hospital | 79 | 1991 | Private Juvenile Facility |
| | Henryton | 1928/1962 | TB Hospital | 312 | 1985 | State Juvenile Facility |
| | Highland Health | 1870/1972 | General Hospital | 88 | 1989 | Department of Mental Health |
| MASSACHUSETTS | Belchertown | 1922 | MR Facility | 297 | 1992 | Vacant |
| | Paul A. Dever | 1940/1946 | P.O.W. Camp | 294 | 1995 | No Plans |
| MICHIGAN | Alpine | 1937/1959 | TB Hospital | 200 | 1981 | Notsego County Offices |
| | Coldwater | 1874/1939 | Orphanage | 113 | 1987 | Corrections |
| | Fort Custer | 1942/1956 | Army Hospital | 1,000 | 1972 | Back to U.S. Dept. of Defense |
| | Hillcrest | 1905/1961 | TB Hospital | 350 | 1982 | Demolition |
| | Macomb-Oakland | 1967/1970 | CDA | 100 | 1989 | Reverted to Community Development |
| | Muskegon | 1969 | MR Facility | 157 | 1992 | Vacant |
| | Newberry | 1896/1941 | MI Facility | 39 | 1992 | Vacant |
| | Northville | 1952/1972 | MI/MR Facility | 180 | 1983 | Revert to MI Use |
| | Oakdale | 1895 | MR Facility | 100 | 1991 | Vacant/County Negotiating |
| | Plymouth | 1960 | MR Facility | 837 | 1984 | County/State Offices |
| MINNESOTA | Faribault | 1879 | MR Facility | 501 | Pending | Portion used by Corrections |
| | Moose Lake | 1938/1970 | Psychiatric Hosp | 34 | 1995 | Corrections |
| | Owatonna | 1895/1947 | Orphanage | 250 | 1970 | County/City/Substance Abuse |
| | Rochester | 1879/1972 | MI Facility | 150 | 1982 | Federal Corrections |
| NEW HAMPSHIRE | Laconia | 1903 | MR Facility | 4 | 1991 | Corrections |
| NEW JERSEY | Johnstone | 1955 | MR Facility | 239 | 1992 | Corrections |
| NEW MEXICO | Fort Stanton | 1964 | Army Apache | 145 | 1995 | Skilled Nursing/Respite |
| | Villa Solano | 1964/1967 | Missile Base | 82 | 1982 | Demolition/Community Housing |
| NEW YORK | J.N. Adams | 1912/1967 | TB Hospital | 180 | 1993 | Potential City of Buffalo Use |
| | Bronx | 1977 | MR Facility | 217 | 1992 | Plans Not Final |
| | Brooklyn | 1972 | MR Facility | 378 | 2000 | Proposed Substance Abuse |
| | Broome | 1970 | MR Facility | 446 | 2000 | No Plans |
| | Craig | 1896/1935 | Epilepsy Hospital | 120 | 1988 | Corrections |
| | B.M. Fineson | 1971 | Hospital/Hotel for | 478 | 2000 | No Plans |
| | Oswald D. Heck | 1972 | MR Facility | 274 | 2000 | No Plans |
| | Letchworth | 1911 | MR Facility | 704 | 2000 | No Plans |
| | Long Island | 1965 | MR Facility | 682 | 1993 | No Plans |
| | Manhattan | 1919/1972 | Warehouse | 197 | 1992 | OMR/DD Office |
| | Newark | 1878 | Custodial Asylum | 325 | 1993 | Community College/Substance Abuse |
| | Rome | 1825/1894 | County Poorhouse | 638 | 1989 | Corrections |
| | Staten Island | 1942/1952 | Army Hospital | 692 | 1987 | OMR/DD & Community College |
| | Sunmount | 1965 | TB Facility | 322 | 2000 | No Plans |
| | Syracuse | 1851/1972 | MR Facility | 409 | 2000 | No Plans |
| | Wassaic | 1930 | MR Facility | 979 | 2000 | No Plans |
| | Westchester | 1932/1979 | MI Facility | 195 | 2000 | Office of MH |
| | West Seneca | 1962 | MR Facility | 683 | 1988 | No Plans |
| | Wilton | 1960 | MR Facility | 370 | 1995 | No Plans |
| NORTH DAKOTA | San Haven | 1922/1973 | TB Hospital | 86 | 1987 | Vacant |
| OHIO | Broadview | 1930/1967 | TB Hospital | 178 | 1992 | City Administration Building/Retirement |
| | Cleveland | 1855/1963 | MI Facility | 149 | 1988 | Vacant/Negotiating with City of Cleveland |
| | Dayton | 1855/1979 | MI/MR Facility | 52 | 1983 | DMH |
| | Orient | 1898 | MR Facility | 800 | 1984 | Corrections |
| OKLAHOMA | Hissom | 1967 | MR Facility | 451 | 1994 | Possible Corrections/Educational |
| OREGON | Columbia Park | 1929/1963 | TB Hospital | 304 | 1977 | Columbia Gorge Community College |
| | Eastern Oregon | 1929/1963 | TB Hospital | 240 | 1984 | Corrections/Opened New MR Facility |
| PENNSYLVANIA | Allentown | 1974 | MI/MR Facility | 40 | 1988 | Revert to MI Use |
| | Clarks Summit | 1974 | MR Facility | 40 | 1991 | Revert to MI Use |
| | Cresson | 1912/1964 | TB Hospital | 155 | 1982 | Corrections |
| | Harrisburg | 1972 | MI/MR Facility | 60 | 1982 | Revert to MI Use |
| | Hollidaysburg | 1974 | MR Facility | 60 | 1976 | Revert to MI Use |
| | Marcy Center | 1915/1974 | TB Hospital | 152 | 1982 | Vacant |
| | Pennhurst Center | 1908 | MR Facility | 179 | 1988 | Veterans' Medical Center |
| | Philadelphia | 1983 | MI/MR Facility | 60 | 1989 | Vacant |
| | Warren | 1975 | MI/MR Facility | 50 | 1976 | Revert to MI Use |
| | Wernersville | 1974 | MI/MR Facility | 40 | 1988 | Revert to MI Use |
| RHODE ISLAND | Dix Building | 1945/1982 | WPA | 80 | 1989 | Corrections |
| | Ladd Center | 1907 | MR Facility | 292 | 1994 | No Plans |
| TEXAS | Forth Worth | 1976 | MR Facility | 339 | 1995 | No Plans |
| | Travis | 1934 | MR Facility | 585 | 1999 | No Plans |
| VERMONT | Brandon | 1915 | MR Facility | 26 | 1993 | For Sale, Local Realty |
| WASHINGTON | Interlake School | 1946/1967 | Geriatric MI | 123 | 1995 | Other State Agency |
| WEST VIRGINIA | Greenbrier | 1801/1974 | Women's College | 56 | 1994 | Community College |
| | Spencer | 1893 | MI/MR Facility | 150 | 1989 | Vacant/Possible Corrections |
| | Weston | 1864/1985 | MI/MR Facility | 99 | 1988 | Revert to MI Use |

## FIGURE 5
*Growth of Public Funds for Large Privately Operated Facilities*

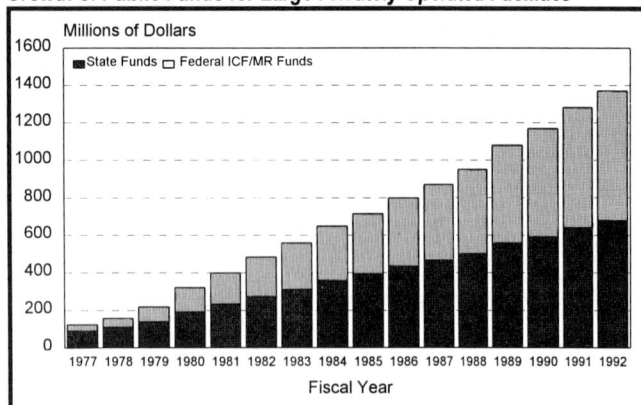

residential placements and related day programs and other services and supports, advanced from $.872 billion in 1977 to $9.840 billion in 1992. This is an average annual percentage growth rate of 11.5% in real economic terms and a total real growth rate of 408% across the 16-year period. During the 1988-92 period, real growth totaled 52% (11.1% per year). Four-year growth during 1984-88 totaled 57%; during 1980-84 overall adjusted community spending growth was 56%. For three consecutive four-year periods, the rate of expansion of resources for financing community services in the United States has been remarkably stable and strong.

Figure 6 illustrates the steady 16-year growth of community spending set against the modest increases in resources for large congregate care services. In 1989 for the first time in the nation's history, the volume of public funds deployed for supporting persons with developmental disabilities in community settings *exceeded* the amount of funds allocated for institutions and other large congregate 16+ bed services. In 1992, 57% of funding was being used to support individuals in 15-bed or less community settings.

A contrasting graphic is presented in Figure 7, which redefines the 15-bed or less community services construct employed in Figure 6 to refer to 6-bed or less settings. As previously noted, this has a profound effect on the analysis of patterns of financial support across the 16 year period. By classifying facilities with 7-15 beds in the large congregate category, it becomes clear that the nation has a great distance to travel before the allocation of our financial resources will reflect the programmatic values of small, family-scale services and supports that are so widely espoused today.

## TABLE 7
*Persons with Mental Retardation and Related Conditions in Nursing Homes, Estimated Costs, and Placement Rate per 100,000 of the General Population [1]*

| Rank | State | 1992 State Population | Persons with MR in NHs | Estimated Costs ($) | Rate per 100,000 |
|---|---|---|---|---|---|
| 1 | OKLAHOMA | 3,157,000 | 1,763 | 26,953,202 | 55.84 |
| 2 | IOWA | 2,787,000 | 1,278 | 24,343,766 | 45.86 |
| 3 | MISSOURI | 5,254,000 | 2,230 | 37,262,631 | 42.44 |
| 4 | NEBRASKA | 1,600,500 | 649 | 11,857,749 | 40.55 |
| 5 | INDIANA | 5,648,000 | 2,241 | 48,409,380 | 39.68 |
| 6 | ARKANSAS | 2,438,500 | 928 | 1,349,612 | 38.06 |
| 7 | ALABAMA | 4,211,625 | 1,401 | 28,843,088 | 33.27 |
| 8 | LOUISIANA | 4,343,000 | 1,331 | 16,872,691 | 30.65 |
| 9 | MONTANA | 791,000 | 230 | 5,178,482 | 29.08 |
| 10 | KENTUCKY | 3,749,500 | 1,067 | 24,442,967 | 28.46 |
| 11 | OHIO | 10,934,000 | 3,000 | 54,092,386 | 27.44 |
| 12 | NORTH DAKOTA | 650,500 | 175 | 4,527,460 | 26.90 |
| 13 | MASSACHUSETTS | 5,952,000 | 1,600 | 56,217,600 | 26.88 |
| 14 | MISSISSIPPI | 2,671,000 | 718 | 14,059,158 | 26.88 |
| 15 | GEORGIA | 6,801,500 | 1,777 | 36,922,186 | 26.13 |
| 16 | MICHIGAN | 9,327,000 | 1,938 | 61,389,167 | 20.78 |
| 17 | TEXAS | 17,247,250 | 3,355 | 58,424,909 | 19.45 |
| 18 | MINNESOTA | 4,422,000 | 845 | 25,309,355 | 19.11 |
| 19 | SOUTH DAKOTA | 717,500 | 137 | 2,786,391 | 19.09 |
| 20 | ILLINOIS | 11,720,500 | 2,159 | 63,215,520 | 18.42 |
| 21 | WISCONSIN | 4,907,500 | 857 | 23,562,289 | 17.46 |
| 22 | TENNESSEE | 5,084,500 | 870 | 24,336,841 | 17.11 |
| 23 | MAINE | 1,255,000 | 207 | 15,639,399 | 16.49 |
| 24 | NEW YORK | 17,872,375 | 2,882 | 113,320,217 | 16.13 |
| 25 | VIRGINIA | 6,390,000 | 1,020 | 22,821,052 | 15.96 |
| 26 | UTAH | 1,756,500 | 279 | 6,089,058 | 15.88 |
| 27 | CONNECTICUT | 3,293,000 | 510 | 21,420,483 | 15.49 |
| 28 | OREGON | 2,849,500 | 420 | 11,546,118 | 14.74 |
| 29 | VERMONT | 579,500 | 85 | 2,015,886 | 14.67 |
| 30 | WYOMING | 459,000 | 64 | 2,237,315 | 13.94 |
| 31 | DIST OF COLUMBIA | 596,875 | 82 | 3,369,747 | 13.74 |
| 32 | NEW MEXICO | 1,569,000 | 188 | 4,996,223 | 11.98 |
| 33 | COLORADO | 3,358,000 | 390 | 10,319,861 | 11.61 |
| 34 | WASHINGTON | 4,889,000 | 493 | 23,680,762 | 10.08 |
| 35 | NEVADA | 1,180,000 | 118 | 3,135,065 | 10.00 |
| 36 | RHODE ISLAND | 1,005,000 | 100 | 3,394,500 | 9.95 |
| 37 | NEW JERSEY | 7,892,000 | 746 | 17,550,754 | 9.45 |
| 38 | WEST VIRGINIA | 1,815,000 | 164 | 5,115,812 | 9.04 |
| 39 | IDAHO | 1,017,000 | 90 | 2,500,000 | 8.85 |
| 40 | MARYLAND | 4,894,000 | 428 | 8,690,831 | 8.75 |
| 41 | DELAWARE | 699,000 | 52 | 1,455,766 | 7.44 |
| 42 | ALASKA | 533,500 | 38 | 3,268,380 | 7.12 |
| 43 | NORTH CAROLINA | 6,841,000 | 316 | 6,893,098 | 4.62 |
| 44 | CALIFORNIA | 30,052,500 | 1,226 | 26,670,896 | 4.08 |
| 45 | PENNSYLVANIA | 12,062,500 | 435 | 11,509,291 | 3.61 |
| 46 | FLORIDA | 13,423,500 | 377 | 10,020,253 | 2.81 |
| 47 | SOUTH CAROLINA | 3,626,000 | 72 | 1,373,918 | 1.99 |
| 48 | HAWAII | 1,170,000 | 20 | 2,694,789 | 1.71 |
| 49 | NEW HAMPSHIRE | 1,180,500 | 20 | 488,005 | 1.69 |
| 50 | ARIZONA | 3,810,000 | 58 | 1,407,416 | 1.52 |
| 51 | KANSAS | 2,534,500 | 0 | 0 | 0.00 |
| | TOTAL | 253,019,125 | 41,429 | 993,981,724 | 16.37 |

[1] *States ranked by 1992 placement rate per 100,000 of the general population.*

National data inevitably obscure great variations in the states as revealed by inspecting the state-specific data in Figure 8. Each individual state's chart presents 16 years of resource allocation data, across

**FIGURE 6**
*Adjusted MR/DD Spending for Congregate (16+ Beds) and Community Services*

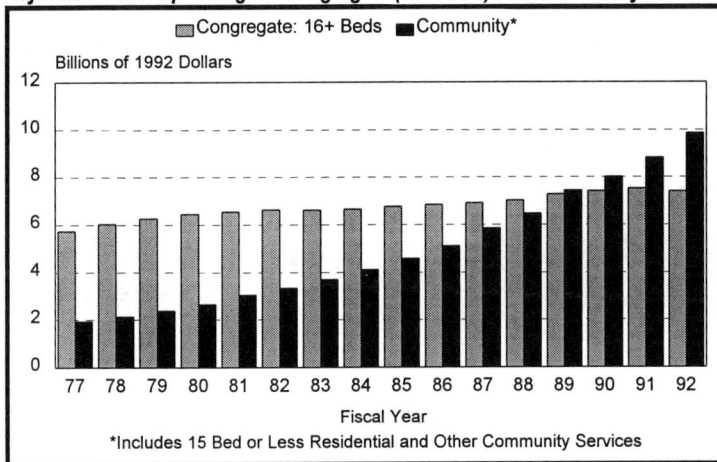

*Includes 15 Bed or Less Residential and Other Community Services*

**FIGURE 7**
*Adjusted MR/DD Spending for Congregate (7+ Beds) and Community Services*

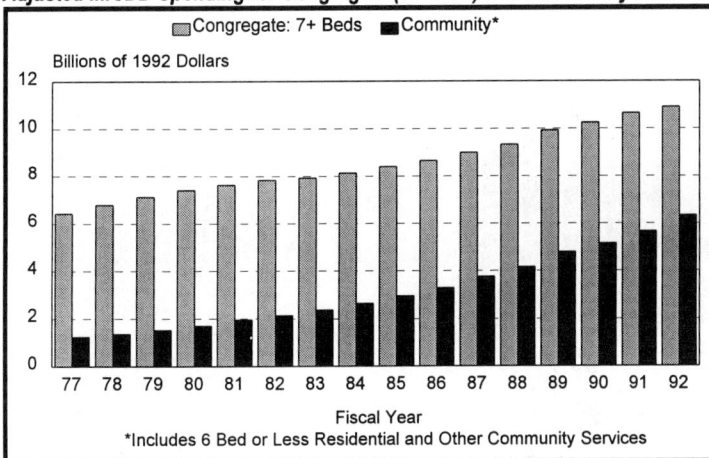

*Includes 6 Bed or Less Residential and Other Community Services*

the 1977-92 period, for all 50 states and the District of Columbia. Community services spending is denoted by the solid black bars; large congregate spending, defined in terms of 16+ bed settings, is represented by the hash-marked bars.

Inspection of Figure 8 also reveals that community services funding has grown rapidly in virtually all the states. However, the initiation of a substantial commitment to fund community services began at different times across the 16-year period in individual states, and the states exhibited significant variations in the intensity and duration of this growth. In addition, while some states rapidly phased down support for large congregate care settings as they were at-

tempting to expand community services (e.g., Michigan and New Hampshire), the majority of states funded growth in both the large congregate and community services sectors simultaneously. Two states following this dual priority approach, Massachusetts and Texas, recently began implementing institutional closures, however.

## Sources of Revenue

State government general revenues continue to be the major source of funds in the states to finance community services. These funds, including state SSI supplementation, comprised 62% of total community services revenues of $9.840 billion in 1992. The state fund percentage decline from 70% of total community funding in 1988 was due primarily to the rapid expansion of federal funding available under the Medicaid Home and Community Based Services (HCBS) Waiver program and the ICF/MR program. As shown in Figure 9, federal HCBS Waiver funds and associated federal income maintenance represented one-eighth of all community services funding available in the United States in 1992 and over one-third of federal funding for community services.

ICF/MR funds supporting 15-bed or less community residential services also grew rapidly from 1988-92. In 1988, 28,066 persons were supported in ICF/MR settings of 15 or fewer beds at a federal reimbursement cost of $.552 billion. The comparable figures for 1992 were 42,398 persons and $1.287 billion in federal reimbursements. Federal ICF/MR reimbursements grew 100% in real economic terms during the total four-year period. Federal ICF/MR funding for community services in New York State in 1992 ($.411 billion) represented 32% of all federal ICF/MR funding for community services in the nation. New York State operates an extensive network of ICF/MR financed group homes. As noted previously, the state is committed to closing all institutions and relocating residents to community settings. In contrast to New York's use of ICF/MR funds, the state of Maryland has chosen not to employ ICF/MR resources for financing community services options, relying instead on the HCBS waiver.

## FIGURE 8

*Adjusted MR/DD Spending for Congregate 16+ Beds Residential and Community Services in the States: FYs 1977-1992*[1]

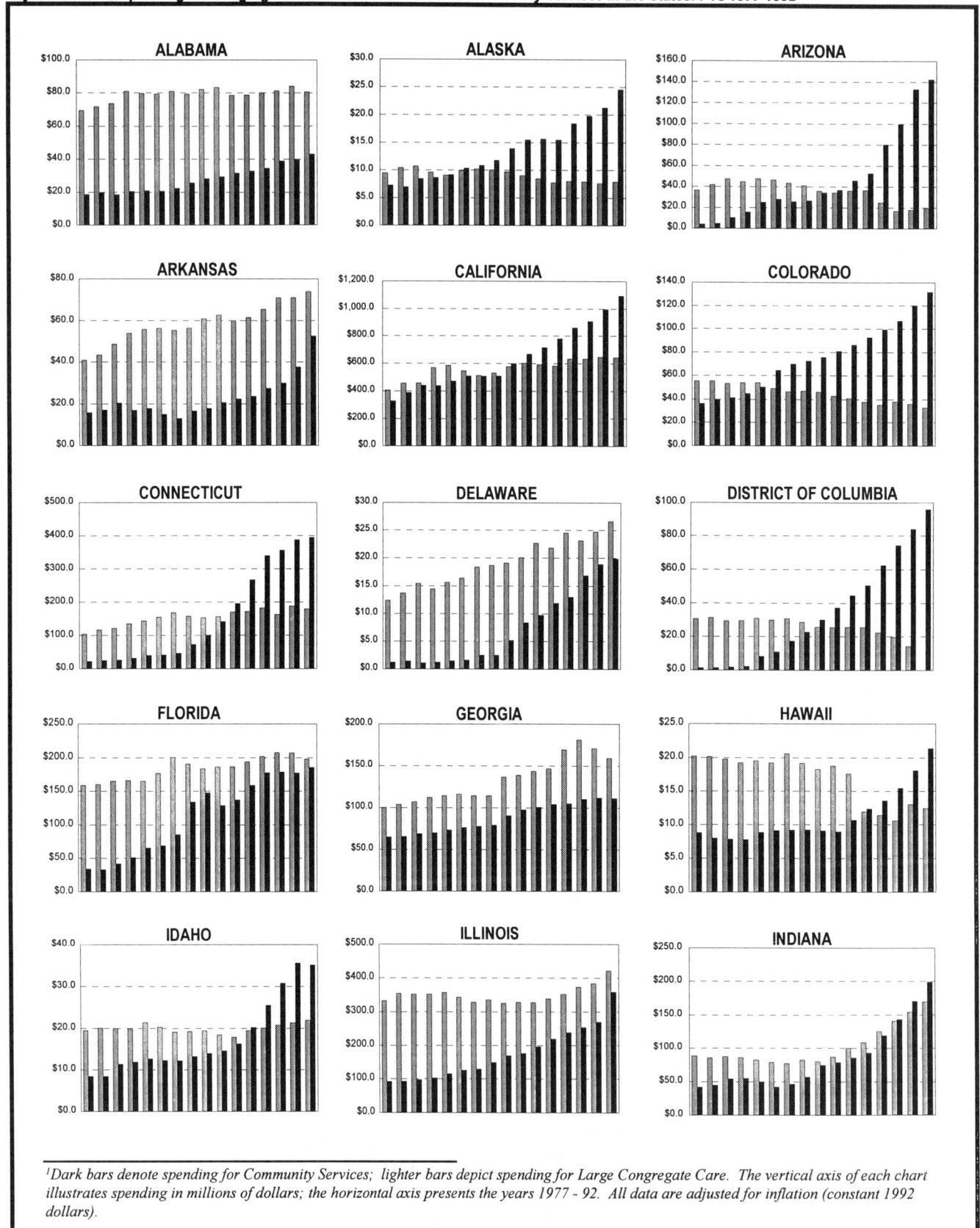

[1]*Dark bars denote spending for Community Services; lighter bars depict spending for Large Congregate Care. The vertical axis of each chart illustrates spending in millions of dollars; the horizontal axis presents the years 1977 - 92. All data are adjusted for inflation (constant 1992 dollars).*

## FIGURE 8 (continued)
*Adjusted MR/DD Spending for Congregate 16+ Beds Residential and Community Services in the States: FYs 1977-1992[1]*

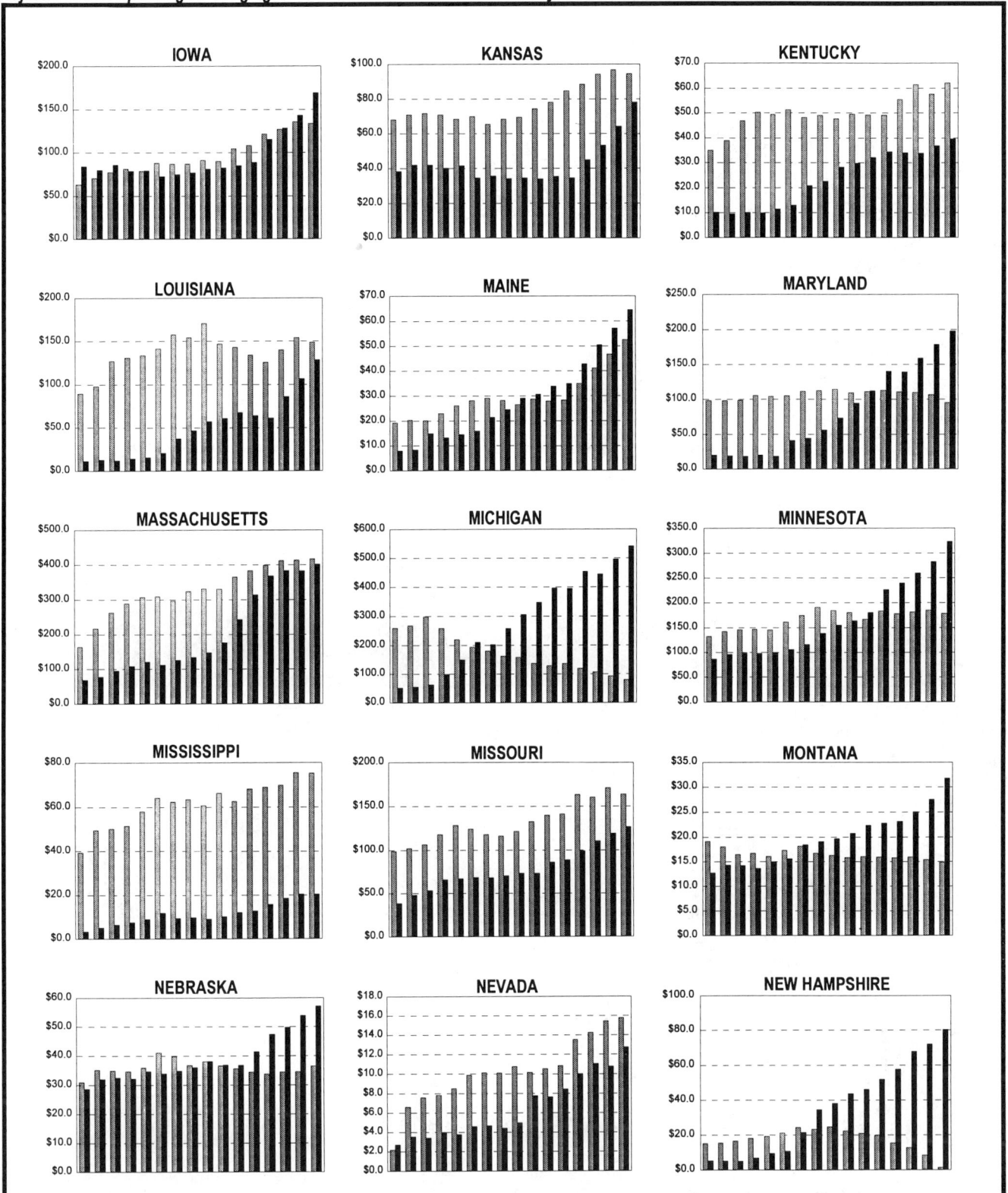

IOWA, KANSAS, KENTUCKY, LOUISIANA, MAINE, MARYLAND, MASSACHUSETTS, MICHIGAN, MINNESOTA, MISSISSIPPI, MISSOURI, MONTANA, NEBRASKA, NEVADA, NEW HAMPSHIRE

[1]*Dark bars denote spending for Community Services; lighter bars depict spending for Large Congregate Care. The vertical axis of each chart illustrates spending in millions of dollars; the horizontal axis presents the years 1977 - 92. All data are adjusted for inflation (constant 1992 dollars).*

# FIGURE 8 (continued)

*Adjusted MR/DD Spending for Congregate 16+ Beds Residential and Community Services in the States: FYs 1977-1992[1]*

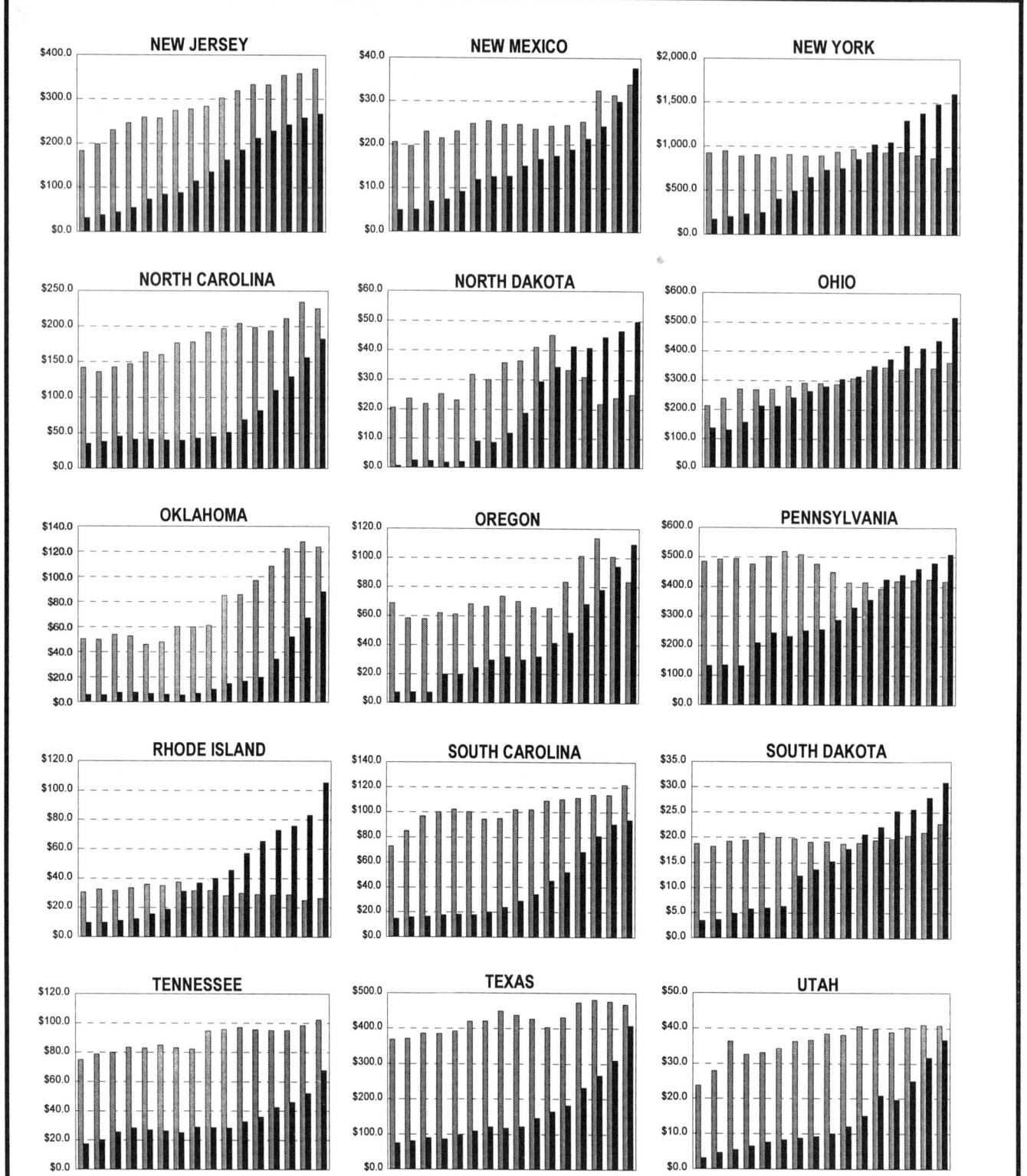

[1]*Dark bars denote spending for Community Services; lighter bars depict spending for Large Congregate Care. The vertical axis of each chart illustrates spending in millions of dollars; the horizontal axis presents the years 1977 - 92. All data are adjusted for inflation (constant 1992 dollars).*

**FIGURE 8 (continued)**
*Adjusted MR/DD Spending for Congregate 16+ Beds Residential and Community Services in the States: FYs 1977-1992[1]*

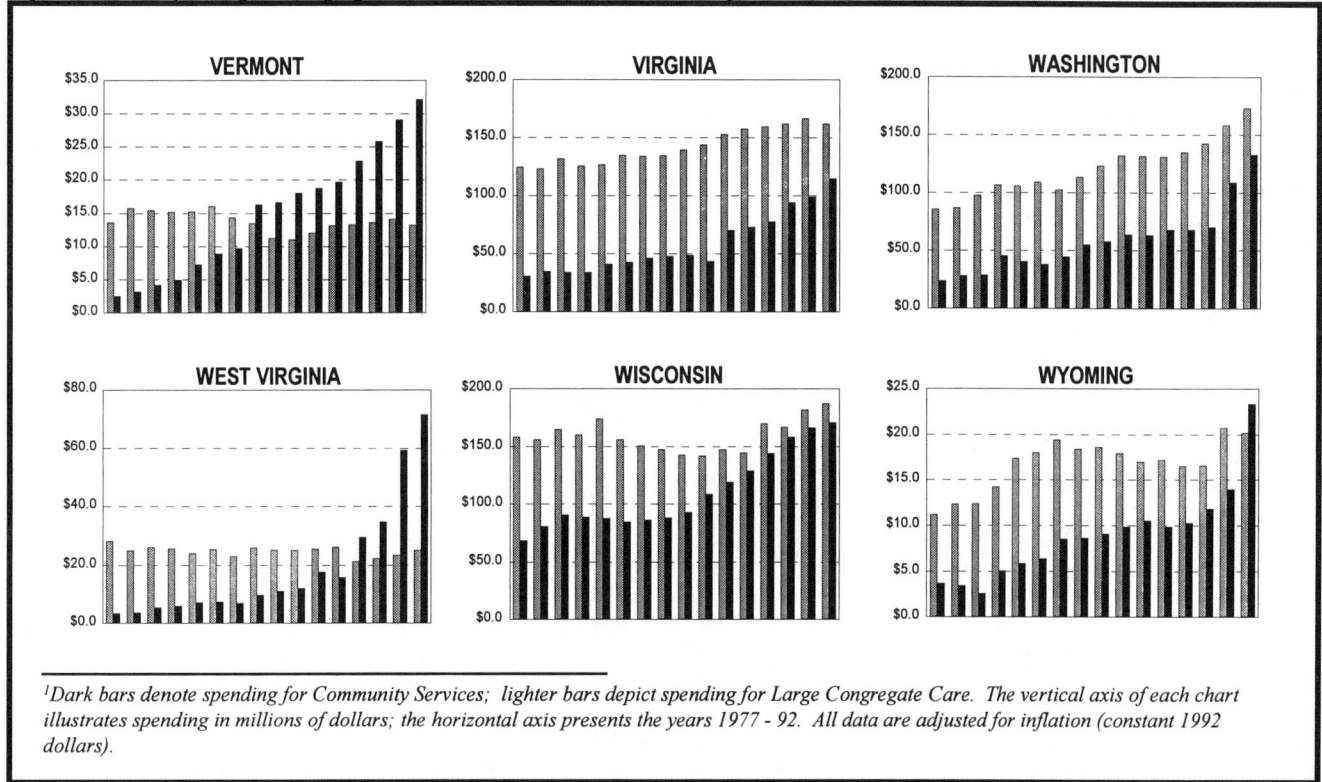

VERMONT · VIRGINIA · WASHINGTON · WEST VIRGINIA · WISCONSIN · WYOMING

[1]*Dark bars denote spending for Community Services; lighter bars depict spending for Large Congregate Care. The vertical axis of each chart illustrates spending in millions of dollars; the horizontal axis presents the years 1977 - 92. All data are adjusted for inflation (constant 1992 dollars).*

**The Home and Community-Based Services Waiver**

In the 1990 edition of this study, which reported on data through 1988, it was noted that the Waiver program grew from $1.2 million in federal reimbursements in 1982 to $.248 billion in 1988. This rapid rate of growth has continued. In 1992, federal HCBS Waiver reimbursements totaled $.877 billion and supported 63,206 participants. The types of services financed by the Waiver included case management, homemakers, home health aides, personal care, residential habilitation, day habilitation, respite care, transportation,

supported employment, adapted equipment and home modification, and occupational, speech, physical, and behavioral therapists.

On a per capita basis, North Dakota, New Hamp-

**FIGURE 9**
**Community Services Funding Sources: FY 1992**

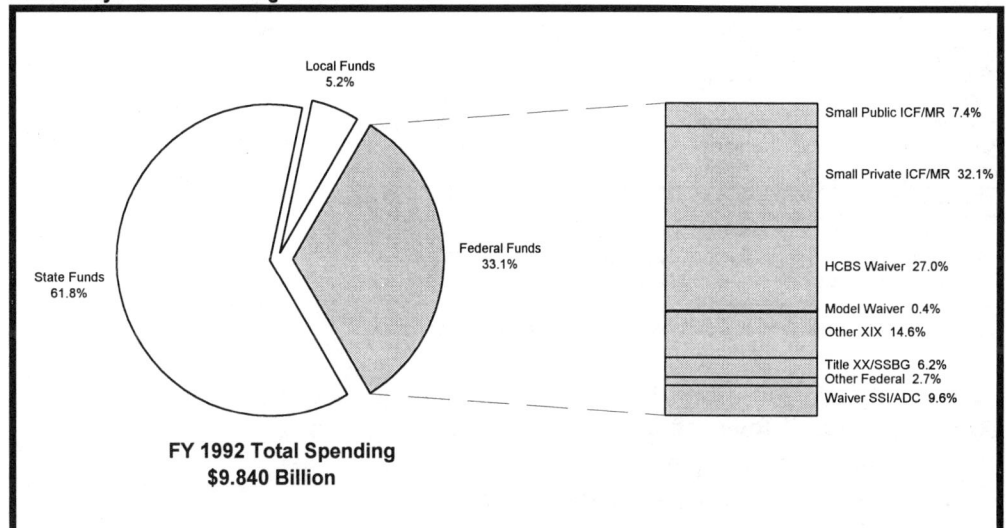

Local Funds 5.2%
State Funds 61.8%
Federal Funds 33.1%

FY 1992 Total Spending $9.840 Billion

Small Public ICF/MR 7.4%
Small Private ICF/MR 32.1%
HCBS Waiver 27.0%
Model Waiver 0.4%
Other XIX 14.6%
Title XX/SSBG 6.2%
Other Federal 2.7%
Waiver SSI/ADC 9.6%

**TABLE 8**
*HCBS Waiver Expenditures in the United States, 1992 [1]*

| State | Federal Expenditures ($) | Partici- pants | Years in Effect | Waiver Expendi- tures Per Capita ($) | Per Capita Rank |
|---|---|---|---|---|---|
| ALABAMA | 12,244,044 | 2,176 | 10 | 2.91 | 30 |
| ALASKA | 0 | 0 | 0 | 0.00 | 48 |
| ARIZONA | 44,339,788 | 4,494 | 4 | 11.64 | 9 |
| ARKANSAS | 3,303,992 | 411 | 3 | 1.35 | 36 |
| CALIFORNIA | 52,200,000 | 3,360 | 8 | 1.74 | 33 |
| COLORADO | 29,705,426 | 2,135 | 9 | 8.85 | 15 |
| CONNECTICUT | 43,696,015 | 1,920 | 5 | 13.27 | 7 |
| DELAWARE | 3,846,778 | 272 | 8 | 5.50 | 22 |
| DIST OF COLUMBIA | 0 | 0 | 0 | 0.00 | 49 |
| FLORIDA | 9,594,343 | 2,631 | 9 | 0.71 | 40 |
| GEORGIA | 4,137,720 | 353 | 3 | 0.61 | 42 |
| HAWAII | 3,719,910 | 401 | 9 | 3.18 | 29 |
| IDAHO | 1,841,200 | 385 | 9 | 1.81 | 32 |
| ILLINOIS | 30,038,700 | 3,110 | 9 | 2.56 | 31 |
| INDIANA | 36,357 | 28 | 3 | 0.01 | 46 |
| IOWA | 0 | 0 | 0 | 0.00 | 50 |
| KANSAS | 12,961,993 | 948 | 9 | 5.11 | 23 |
| KENTUCKY | 13,848,568 | 797 | 9 | 3.69 | 27 |
| LOUISIANA | 683,257 | 494 | 6 | 0.16 | 44 |
| MAINE | 13,203,703 | 584 | 9 | 10.52 | 10 |
| MARYLAND | 39,045,928 | 1,896 | 9 | 7.98 | 16 |
| MASSACHUSETTS | 43,706,099 | 2,811 | 8 | 7.34 | 18 |
| MICHIGAN | 37,299,151 | 2,228 | 5 | 4.00 | 26 |
| MINNESOTA | 43,562,408 | 2,942 | 8 | 9.85 | 12 |
| MISSISSIPPI | 0 | 0 | 0 | 0.00 | 51 |
| MISSOURI | 18,438,892 | 2,280 | 4 | 3.51 | 28 |
| MONTANA | 7,064,410 | 459 | 11 | 8.93 | 13 |
| NEBRASKA | 14,232,466 | 931 | 5 | 8.89 | 14 |
| NEVADA | 1,116,522 | 179 | 10 | 0.95 | 38 |
| NEW HAMPSHIRE | 21,700,000 | 1,055 | 9 | 18.38 | 2 |
| NEW JERSEY | 52,462,000 | 3,800 | 9 | 6.65 | 19 |
| NEW MEXICO | 2,688,857 | 282 | 8 | 1.71 | 34 |
| NEW YORK | 69,259 | 168 | 1 | 0.00 | 47 |
| NORTH CAROLINA | 6,425,645 | 1,075 | 9 | 0.94 | 39 |
| NORTH DAKOTA | 13,145,248 | 1,339 | 9 | 20.21 | 1 |
| OHIO | 1,695,743 | 482 | 2 | 0.16 | 45 |
| OKLAHOMA | 15,847,994 | 1,050 | 7 | 5.02 | 24 |
| OREGON | 33,408,612 | 1,471 | 11 | 11.72 | 8 |
| PENNSYLVANIA | 75,113,844 | 2,657 | 9 | 6.23 | 21 |
| RHODE ISLAND | 13,648,644 | 1,200 | 9 | 13.58 | 6 |
| SOUTH CAROLINA | 1,798,354 | 253 | 1 | 0.50 | 43 |
| SOUTH DAKOTA | 11,584,315 | 945 | 10 | 16.15 | 4 |
| TENNESSEE | 6,776,723 | 630 | 6 | 1.33 | 37 |
| TEXAS | 25,502,913 | 1,335 | 7 | 1.48 | 35 |
| UTAH | 18,331,475 | 1,500 | 5 | 10.44 | 11 |
| VERMONT | 9,429,167 | 545 | 10 | 16.27 | 3 |
| VIRGINIA | 4,010,000 | 250 | 2 | 0.63 | 41 |
| WASHINGTON | 36,818,360 | 2,078 | 9 | 7.53 | 17 |
| WEST VIRGINIA | 11,628,000 | 513 | 9 | 6.41 | 20 |
| WISCONSIN | 24,139,631 | 1,890 | 9 | 4.92 | 25 |
| WYOMING | 6,719,626 | 463 | 2 | 14.64 | 5 |
| **UNITED STATES** | **876,812,080** | **63,206** | -- | **3.47** | -- |

[1] *Zero ("0") indicates the state did not provide HCBS Waiver services for persons with MR/DD. Years in Effect indicates the number of fiscal years the state has reported expenditures for the HCBS Waiver. Expenditures consist of federal Title XIX funds only; state/local match funds of $667.9 million supported HCBS Waiver services.*

shire, Vermont, and South Dakota had the largest Waiver programs, followed by Wyoming, Rhode Island, Connecticut, Oregon, Arizona, Maine, and Utah. In absolute terms, the largest HCBS Waiver

programs in 1992 were in Arizona, California, Connecticut, Minnesota, Pennsylvania, and New Jersey. Table 8 shows data on individuals served under the HCBS Waiver along with reimbursement levels, years in effect, and per capita spending rank (based on general population). The Model 50/200 Waiver program, in 1992, provided Medicaid coverage in seven states for 1,003 children living at home at a cost of $12.12 million nationally. Although still modest in size, the Model Waiver program more than tripled in number of participants between 1988 and 1992.

Over the past decade, the HCBS Waiver has more than replaced Title XX/SSBG as a major source of federal funding for community services. In 1982, the year the Waiver program was initiated, adjusted federal Title XX/SSBG funds declined by over $100 million and federal support for community services declined that year by 10% in real terms. Throughout the remainder of the 1980s, federal community funding increased by more than 10% annually in real terms. The Waiver played an important part in this increase. The HCBS Waiver was established in 29 states by 1984 (see "years in effect" column in Table 8). In the decade since, real federal Waiver revenues increased 38% per year. The other major federal source of community services funding, small (15 bed or less) ICFs/MR, increased by 21% annually in real economic terms.

### Local Funding

Total local/county resources allocated for community services grew from $419.8 million in 1988 to $627.1 million in 1992. This was an absolute growth rate of 49% over the total four-year period. About one-third of these resources were used as state matching funds for the Medicaid HCBS Waiver or ICF/MR programs. The remaining funds supported local or county government operated group homes, day programs, or other community supports.

Local government or county funding of community services represents only about 5% of community services resources nationally. However, these funds are major revenue components in several states—most notably in Ohio where county funding comprises nearly 50% of total community spending in the state. In Iowa, Kansas, Missouri, Virginia, Minnesota, Texas, Wisconsin, and Nebraska, local or county government resources contributed between

35% and 10% of total community services resources in 1992. It should be stressed that one-half of all local or county funding supporting community services in the United States was attributable to a single state-- Ohio.

## Community Services Special Initiatives

One of the major objectives of the current study was to assess the emergence and growth of community services special priorities in the states. The intent was to identify initiatives in the states that had achieved *status* as a line item in the state's budget or in the agency's planning, accounting, or reporting systems. The current study built upon the 1990 effort which had collected data on initiatives in four emergent priority areas: family support, supported employment, early intervention, and special programs serving older individuals with developmental disabilities. Updating the previous study's 1988 data set permitted comparisons to be made with 1992 funding and numbers of individuals supported. In addition, baseline 1992 data sets were collected for new priority initiatives in assistive technology, supported living, and personal assistance services. The initiatives summarized below were undertaken by state mental retardation and developmental disabilities agencies.

### Family Support

The *family support* data were collected in three specific categories: cash subsidy payments, respite care, and other family support. In 1992, 17 states reported cash subsidy payments, up from 11 states in 1988 (see Table 9). The states reporting the implementation of new programs since 1988 were Arkansas, Connecticut, Illinois, Iowa, Kansas, and New York. Total cash payments to families doubled to a level of $26.74 million between 1988-92, and the number of families supported increased from 5,275 to 12,304. The average monthly subsidy payment to a family in the U.S. was $181 ($2,173 per year).

Texas and Michigan, however, accounted for two-thirds of all subsidy payments in the U.S. during 1992. Other than these two states, only Minnesota, Illinois, and Louisiana budgeted in excess of $1 million annually for subsidy payments. There is a growing interest in the states to experiment with cash subsidy programs. Apparently that interest is tem-

pered with a reluctance to expand the size of the programs beyond the pilot stage.

*Respite care* program activity was identified in 38 states, up from 33 states in 1988. Total nationwide expenditures doubled from 1988--to $107 million in 1992. In total, 58,359 families received respite services, more than 133% above the 1988 level. Large programs were identified in New York, California, Illinois, Massachusetts, South Carolina, Texas, and Wisconsin. New Hampshire, a state with a modest population, also had an unusually strong program that reached 2,609 families.

*Other family support* included activities ranging from family counseling to in-home behavior therapy support. General support activities were identified in 37 states with services provided to a total of 105,503 families. Reported funding increased nearly 50% in this area to $146 million in 1992. The increase in spending closely paralleled the overall rate of increase in community services spending across the U.S. The states, however, reported serving about twice the number of families in 1992, compared to 1988.

Taken in the aggregate, total expenditures for the three categories of family support advanced from $171 million in 1988 to $279 million in 1992. The number of families supported also grew rapidly from an imputed total of 168,314 to an imputed total of 193,753. While it is important not to attribute infallibility to the data being collected from individual states--comparisons in family support are problematic among state reporting and accounting systems-- the emerging strength of this priority is evident across the nation in Figure 10. Forty-seven states and the District of Columbia reported a special family support initiative in either cash subsidies, respite care, or other family support activity. The next several years should bring continuing growth and maturity to family support as a priority in the states.

### Supported Employment, Early Intervention, and Aging Services

There was very rapid growth in *supported employment* services financed by state developmental disabilities agencies. The growth in spending more than tripled during 1988-92 from $62 million to $220 million. Individuals supported increased from 13,981 to 57,989. This expansion of supported employment was evident throughout the country although data were unavailable from a few states. Large programs were identified in California, Connecticut, Georgia, Illinois, Maryland, Massachusetts, Minnesota, New Hampshire, Louisiana, North Carolina, New York, Ohio, Oregon, Virginia, Washington State, and Wisconsin. These 16 states accounted for about three-fourths of the supported employment activity across the U.S. in terms of funds budgeted. Data presented in Table 10 were from 42 states.

## TABLE 9
### Family Support Programs Administered by State MR/DD Agencies in 1992 [1]

| State | Cash Subsidy Expenditure ($) | Families | Respite Care Expenditure ($) | Families | Other Family Support Expenditure ($) | Families | Total Family Support Expenditure ($) | Families |
|---|---|---|---|---|---|---|---|---|
| ALABAMA | 0 | 0 | 350,000 | 650 | 100,000 | 3,150 | 645,000 | 3,800 |
| ALASKA | 0 | 0 | 2,051,542 | 785 | 0 | 0 | 2,051,542 | 785 |
| ARIZONA | 0 | 0 | 1,040,102 | 1,245 | 0 | 0 | 1,040,102 | 1,245 |
| ARKANSAS | 218,451 | 116 | 272,912 | 731 | 0 | 0 | 491,363 | 847 |
| CALIFORNIA | 0 | 0 | 26,146,125 | 10,273 | 30,414,502 | 15,588 | 56,560,627 | 21,585 |
| COLORADO | 0 | 0 | 292,559 | 465 | 1,400,316 | 268 | 1,692,875 | 733 |
| CONNECTICUT | 589,820 | 243 | 1,273,244 | 1,483 | 2,356,802 | * | 4,219,866 | * |
| DELAWARE | 0 | 0 | 63,444 | 824 | 0 | 0 | 63,444 | 824 |
| DIST OF COLUMBIA | * | 746 | 782,996 | 655 | 616,016 | 91 | 1,399,012 | 1,492 |
| FLORIDA | 373,777 | 232 | 699,840 | 1,255 | 101,285 | 385 | 699,840 | 1,255 |
| GEORGIA | 0 | 0 | 0 | 0 | 644,083 | 607 | 644,083 | 607 |
| HAWAII | 0 | 0 | 0 | 0 | 359,500 | 265 | 359,500 | 265 |
| IDAHO | 0 | 0 | 77,000 | 334 | 70,000 | 134 | 147,000 | 468 |
| ILLINOIS | 1,202,800 | 250 | 6,072,500 | 3,900 | 13,691,600 | 17,102 | 20,966,900 | 21,252 |
| INDIANA | 0 | 0 | 502,350 | 1,500 | 0 | 0 | 502,350 | 1,500 |
| IOWA | 653,000 | 193 | 0 | 0 | 55,000 | 42 | 708,000 | 235 |
| KANSAS | 600,000 | 250 | 1,948,200 | 191 | 0 | 0 | 2,548,200 | 441 |
| KENTUCKY | 0 | 0 | 1,175,832 | * | 348,349 | * | 1,524,181 | * |
| LOUISIANA | 1,043,845 | 609 | 1,395,337 | 715 | 1,296,742 | 156 | 3,735,924 | 1,480 |
| MAINE | 0 | 0 | 200,000 | 100 | 0 | 0 | 200,000 | 100 |
| MARYLAND | 0 | 0 | 0 | 0 | 11,116,817 | 3,880 | 11,116,817 | 3,880 |
| MASSACHUSETTS | 0 | 0 | 14,600,000 | * | 3,400,000 | * | 18,000,000 | * |
| MICHIGAN | 10,414,137 | 3,922 | 0 | 0 | 8,822,781 | 9,762 | 19,236,918 | 13,684 |
| MINNESOTA | 1,410,000 | 641 | 2,400,000 | 1,343 | 5,586,280 | 997 | 9,396,280 | 2,981 |
| MISSISSIPPI | 0 | 0 | 0 | 0 | 0 | 0 | 0 | 0 |
| MISSOURI | 0 | 0 | 1,007,407 | 682 | 2,434,723 | 1,747 | 3,442,130 | 2,429 |
| MONTANA | 0 | 0 | 352,775 | 599 | 4,762,667 | 1,753 | 5,115,442 | 2,352 |
| NEBRASKA | 0 | 0 | 0 | 0 | 0 | 0 | 0 | 0 |
| NEVADA | 266,740 | 108 | 51,077 | 228 | 0 | 0 | 317,817 | 336 |
| NEW HAMPSHIRE | 0 | 0 | 2,193,049 | 2,609 | 500,000 | * | 2,693,049 | * |
| NEW JERSEY | 0 | 0 | 6,973,249 | * | 165,000 | * | 7,138,249 | * |
| NEW MEXICO | 0 | 0 | 617,175 | 522 | 0 | 0 | 617,175 | 522 |
| NEW YORK | 700,000 | 500 | 16,778,000 | 18,000 | 9,153,800 | 16,500 | 26,631,800 | 35,000 |
| NORTH CAROLINA | 0 | 0 | 416,936 | 1,922 | 62,390 | 117 | 479,326 | 2,039 |
| NORTH DAKOTA | 378,563 | 226 | 108,161 | 161 | 902,230 | 345 | 1,388,954 | 564 |
| OHIO | 0 | 0 | 0 | 0 | 4,777,305 | 7,258 | 4,777,305 | 7,258 |
| OKLAHOMA | 0 | 0 | 408,580 | 260 | 95,427 | 125 | 504,007 | 385 |
| OREGON | 466,542 | 183 | 0 | 0 | 474,564 | 252 | 941,106 | 435 |
| PENNSYLVANIA | 0 | 0 | 0 | 0 | 16,073,702 | 16,288 | 16,073,702 | 16,288 |
| RHODE ISLAND | 273,244 | * | 261,932 | * | 2,200,000 | * | 2,735,176 | * |
| SOUTH CAROLINA | 509,293 | 512 | 6,794,966 | 984 | 0 | 0 | 7,304,259 | 1,496 |
| SOUTH DAKOTA | 0 | 0 | 33,686 | * | 0 | 0 | 33,686 | * |
| TENNESSEE | 0 | 0 | 165,810 | 456 | 477,660 | 419 | 643,470 | 875 |
| TEXAS | 7,600,000 | 3,450 | 3,330,607 | 1,513 | 15,646,175 | 4,661 | 26,576,782 | 9,624 |
| UTAH | 39,970 | 123 | 545,178 | 808 | 656,684 | * | 1,241,832 | * |
| VERMONT | 0 | 0 | 548,591 | 450 | 20,000 | 60 | 568,591 | 510 |
| VIRGINIA | 0 | 0 | 0 | 0 | 600,000 | 600 | 600,000 | 600 |
| WASHINGTON | 0 | 0 | 3,166,094 | * | 2,368,292 | * | 5,534,386 | 1,846 |
| WEST VIRGINIA | 0 | 0 | * | * | 546,250 | 600 | 546,250 | 600 |
| WISCONSIN | 0 | 0 | 1,932,306 | 2,716 | 3,572,514 | 2,351 | 5,504,820 | 5,067 |
| WYOMING | 0 | 0 | 0 | 0 | 0 | 0 | 0 | 0 |
| **Reporting States** | **26,740,182** | **12,304** | **107,029,562** | **58,359** | **145,869,456** | **105,503** | **279,359,138** | **167,685** |
| **U.S. TOTAL (Imputed)** | -- | | -- | 77,286 | -- | 114,956 | -- | 193,753 |

[1] An asterisk indicates that data were not available and "0" indicates that special family support activity was not identified.

Data on numbers of families supported may include duplicate counts. Several states were able to report expenditures, but not numbers supported.

The imputed U.S. totals include estimates for these states based on the average cost/family of reporting states.

*Early intervention* activities were reported in 35 states. Total spending increased from $115 million in 1988 to $176 million in 1992 even though four fewer states provided data. The number of infants and children served increased from 57,314 in 1988 to 70,708 in 1992. The largest programs were in California, Connecticut, Illinois, Indiana, Massachusetts, North Carolina, Oregon, Pennsylvania, Texas, Virginia, Wisconsin, and Wyoming. Early intervention services financed by state/local special education or health agencies were not included in Table 10.

Ten states reported identifiable funding in 1992 for *aging services* for older individuals with mental retardation, down from 11 states reporting this initiative in 1988. The largest special programs were funded in Connecticut, New York, North Dakota, and Washington State. These four states accounted for nearly 80% of the $16 million in identifiable funding in 1992. A total of 3,123 older individuals were reported to be supported under special aging initiatives, up from 1,551 in 1988. Funding in 1988 was $11 million.

The effort to identify state MR/DD agency initiatives in family support, supported employment, early intervention, and aging services should be considered exploratory. However, the growth of program initiatives in two of these areas--family support and supported employment--seems quite strong. Growth at a lesser rate was also evident in early intervention and aging services. The accounting of state-by-state data presented in Tables 9 and 10 for the four initiatives obviously does not represent a comprehensive assessment of all of the special services actually being provided in community settings throughout the country. The data presented in Tables 9 and 10 are a starting point for further study and they provide some insight into the degree to which the four activity areas are emerging as state-level policy priorities. For additional information on special community initiatives, please consult each state's data profile in Part II.

## Assistive Technology, Supported Living, and Personal Assistance

As discussed in the introduction to this section, data were collected from the states on a preliminary basis for three new community program initiatives. The objective was to obtain 1992 baseline data for

**FIGURE 10**
*The Growth of Family Support 1988, 1990, & 1992*

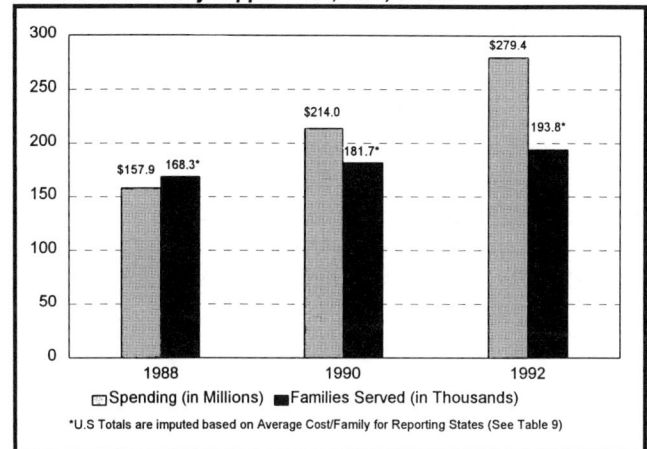

□Spending (in Millions) ■Families Served (in Thousands)
*U.S Totals are imputed based on Average Cost/Family for Reporting States (See Table 9)

three community initiatives that seemed likely to emerge as future priorities in the states. The activity areas were assistive technology, supported living, and personal assistance services.

*Assistive technology* was defined for purposes of the study to include funding by the principal state MR/DD agency for off-the-shelf, adapted, or fabricated assistive technology devices, and any services contributing to individuals' use of technology, including assessments, counseling, training, and technical assistance. The current study identified discretely budgeted assistive technology funding by state MR/DD agencies in 11 states (Table 11). Funding totaled $6.78 million on a national basis and the largest programs were in California, Florida, Nevada, New Hampshire, and New York. It seems likely that two recent legislative events at the federal level will stimulate the future growth of assistive technology services in state MR/DD agencies. The events are enactment and implementation of the Technology Related Assistance for Individuals with Disabilities Act of 1988 (P.L. 100-407) and the P.L. 100-203 nursing home legislation. The nursing home reform legislation will require technology evaluations of residents; the Technology Act legislation will broaden the field's understanding of how technology can be applied to promote community integration, productivity, and personal empowerment.

*Supported living* was defined to refer to housing in which individuals with developmental disabilities choose where and with whom they live, housing which is owned by someone other than the support provider (i.e., by the individual, the family, a landlord, or a housing cooperative), and housing in which the individual has a personalized support plan which changes as her or his needs and abilities change. According to this definition, 21 states indicated that they were providing supported living services to 14,779 individuals in 1992. Total spending was $102 million and the largest state funded programs were in California, Oklahoma, Ohio, North Dakota, and Connecticut.

*Personal assistance services (PAS)* were defined as principal state agencies' use of state funds, or federal/state Medicaid or HCBS Waiver funds to pro-

## TABLE 10
### *State-by-State Data on Supported Employment, Early Intervention, and Aging Services [1]*

| State | Supported Employment | | Early Intervention | | Aging/DD | |
|---|---|---|---|---|---|---|
| | Expenditure ($) | Individuals | Expenditure ($) | Individuals | Expenditure ($) | Individuals |
| ALABAMA | 225,000 | 171 | 1,750,000 | 152 | 0 | 0 |
| ALASKA | 936,151 | 127 | 0 | 0 | 0 | 0 |
| ARIZONA | 6,000,000 | 1,600 | 1,939,255 | 1,135 | 0 | 0 |
| ARKANSAS | 196,659 | 182 | 690,676 | 456 | 0 | 0 |
| CALIFORNIA | 26,700,000 | 5,023 | 10,457,159 | * | 0 | 0 |
| COLORADO | 8,904,026 | 1,880 | 3,325,583 | 1,581 | 783,720 | 178 |
| CONNECTICUT | 21,241,799 | 2,320 | 6,645,468 | 1,125 | 5,491,013 | 679 |
| DELAWARE | 810,402 | 144 | 150,384 | 461 | 0 | 0 |
| DIST OF COLUMBIA | * | 49 | 0 | 0 | 0 | 0 |
| FLORIDA | 2,956,407 | 2,328 | 3,183,952 | 3,030 | 0 | 0 |
| GEORGIA | 6,117,144 | 986 | 2,786,474 | 1,423 | 0 | 0 |
| HAWAII | * | 126 | 0 | 0 | 0 | 0 |
| IDAHO | 502,000 | 450 | * | 638 | * | 217 |
| ILLINOIS | 4,725,400 | 1,370 | 8,558,200 | 6,223 | 0 | 0 |
| INDIANA | 2,100,000 | 881 | 6,000,000 | 2,489 | 0 | 0 |
| IOWA | 2,860,191 | 1,052 | 0 | 0 | 0 | 0 |
| KANSAS | 3,500,000 | 592 | * | 325 | 0 | 0 |
| KENTUCKY | 759,365 | * | 2,185,749 | * | 85,554 | * |
| LOUISIANA | 3,829,465 | 578 | 3,072,562 | 1,287 | 0 | 0 |
| MAINE | 2,384,275 | 389 | 0 | 0 | 0 | 0 |
| MARYLAND | 14,031,566 | 1,767 | 0 | 0 | 0 | 0 |
| MASSACHUSETTS | 10,100,000 | 1,325 | 19,000,000 | 8,500 | 0 | 0 |
| MICHIGAN | * | 3,000 | 133,500 | 64 | 558,700 | * |
| MINNESOTA | 13,584,625 | 4,453 | 0 | 0 | 0 | 0 |
| MISSISSIPPI | * | 451 | 800,006 | 430 | 0 | 0 |
| MISSOURI | 393,936 | 131 | 929,220 | 1,101 | 0 | 0 |
| MONTANA | 973,367 | 233 | 1,195,191 | 153 | 756,636 | 122 |
| NEBRASKA | * | 397 | 0 | 0 | 0 | 0 |
| NEVADA | 76,292 | 35 | 978,531 | 253 | 0 | 0 |
| NEW HAMPSHIRE | 5,692,775 | 550 | 2,964,845 | 1,305 | 0 | 0 |
| NEW JERSEY | 6,300,000 | 823 | 0 | 0 | 0 | 0 |
| NEW MEXICO | 2,413,636 | 436 | 2,674,636 | 862 | 0 | 0 |
| NEW YORK | 9,725,000 | 4,917 | 665,800 | 5,500 | 2,562,000 | 538 |
| NORTH CAROLINA | 3,089,400 | 950 | 10,116,087 | 3,862 | * | * |
| NORTH DAKOTA | 908,963 | 449 | 1,041,431 | 455 | 1,638,026 | 166 |
| OHIO | 7,473,600 | 6,228 | 2,373,750 | 3,165 | 1,041,600 | 868 |
| OKLAHOMA | 2,968,297 | 392 | 0 | 0 | 0 | 0 |
| OREGON | 10,354,739 | 1,617 | 8,681,082 | 2,358 | 0 | 0 |
| PENNSYLVANIA | 312,469 | * | 30,923,000 | 10,597 | 0 | 0 |
| RHODE ISLAND | 0 | 0 | 0 | 0 | 0 | 0 |
| SOUTH CAROLINA | 1,867,761 | 1,092 | 4,040,500 | 1,144 | 0 | 0 |
| SOUTH DAKOTA | * | 339 | 0 | 0 | 0 | 0 |
| TENNESSEE | 1,283,800 | 425 | 4,511,658 | 1,117 | 0 | 0 |
| TEXAS | * | 650 | 5,500,000 | * | 0 | 0 |
| UTAH | 2,357,185 | 376 | 2,627,310 | 1,322 | 119,710 | 96 |
| VERMONT | 1,031,809 | 487 | 0 | 0 | 0 | 0 |
| VIRGINIA | 9,453,032 | * | 7,539,631 | * | 0 | 0 |
| WASHINGTON | 8,822,954 | 2,506 | 2,492,516 | 1,583 | 2,762,497 | 259 |
| WEST VIRGINIA | * | 385 | 0 | 0 | 0 | 0 |
| WISCONSIN | 10,485,943 | 3,091 | 9,029,805 | 5,190 | 0 | 0 |
| WYOMING | 1,995,616 | 236 | 6,650,000 | 1,422 | 0 | 0 |
| **Reporting States** | **220,445,049** | **57,989** | **175,613,961** | **70,708** | **15,799,456** | **3,123** |
| **U.S. TOTAL (Imputed)** | -- | -- | -- | **81,692** | -- | -- |

[1] An asterisk indicates that data were not available and "0" indicates that special initiative activity was not identified. Some states were able to report expenditures, but not numbers supported. The imputed U.S. totals include estimates for these states based on the average cost/individual of reporting states.

vide assistance for individuals in their own homes. Substantial special initiatives in personal assistance were identified in California, New York, North Carolina, and West Virginia. Not presented in Table 11 are personal assistance data for individuals participating in nonprincipal MR/DD agency programs; e.g., to those managed by states' Medicaid or social service agencies.

## Structuring Systems of Support

Clearly, state-wide systems of support for individuals and families are being established in a growing number of states. *Family supports* were ini-

### TABLE 11
*State-by-State Data on Assistive Technology, Supported Living, and Personal Assistance* [1]

| State | Assistive Technology | | Supported Living | | Personal Assistance | |
|---|---|---|---|---|---|---|
| | Expenditure ($) | Individuals | Expenditure ($) | Individuals | Expenditure ($) | Individuals |
| ALABAMA | 0 | 0 | 0 | 0 | 0 | 0 |
| ALASKA | 0 | 0 | 0 | 0 | 0 | 0 |
| ARIZONA | 0 | 0 | 466,459 | 62 | 0 | 0 |
| ARKANSAS | 0 | 0 | 250,053 | 44 | 0 | 0 |
| CALIFORNIA | 1,239,497 | 1,324 | 24,913,657 | 6,815 | 6,979,677 | 2,195 |
| COLORADO | 0 | 0 | 0 | 0 | 0 | 0 |
| CONNECTICUT | 0 | 0 | 8,687,261 | 638 | 0 | 0 |
| DELAWARE | 71,785 | * | 161,332 | 28 | 0 | 0 |
| DIST OF COLUMBIA | 0 | 0 | 0 | 0 | 0 | 0 |
| FLORIDA | 2,291,799 | 2,848 | 1,633,537 | 496 | 0 | 0 |
| GEORGIA | 0 | 0 | 0 | 0 | 0 | 0 |
| HAWAII | 23,277 | 138 | 0 | 0 | 0 | 0 |
| IDAHO | 0 | 0 | 0 | 29 | * | 624 |
| ILLINOIS | 172,500 | 170 | 99,000 | 200 | 0 | 0 |
| INDIANA | 0 | 0 | 0 | 0 | 0 | 0 |
| IOWA | 0 | 0 | 1,171,284 | 1,380 | 0 | 0 |
| KANSAS | 0 | 0 | 0 | 0 | 0 | 0 |
| KENTUCKY | 0 | 0 | 0 | 0 | 0 | 0 |
| LOUISIANA | 0 | 0 | 30,824 | 23 | 0 | 0 |
| MAINE | * | 436 | 2,500,000 | 125 | 0 | 0 |
| MARYLAND | 0 | 0 | 0 | 0 | 0 | 0 |
| MASSACHUSETTS | 0 | 0 | 0 | 0 | 0 | 0 |
| MICHIGAN | 0 | 0 | * | 301 | 0 | 0 |
| MINNESOTA | 0 | 0 | 0 | 0 | 0 | 0 |
| MISSISSIPPI | 0 | 0 | 0 | 0 | 0 | 0 |
| MISSOURI | 0 | 0 | * | 661 | * | 0 |
| MONTANA | 0 | 0 | 0 | 0 | 0 | 0 |
| NEBRASKA | 0 | 0 | 3,967,394 | 714 | 0 | 0 |
| NEVADA | 680,081 | 5,600 | 967,019 | 128 | 0 | 0 |
| NEW HAMPSHIRE | 703,000 | 220 | 0 | 0 | 240,000 | 30 |
| NEW JERSEY | 200,000 | * | 0 | 0 | 0 | 0 |
| NEW MEXICO | 0 | 0 | 2,856,730 | 370 | 0 | 0 |
| NEW YORK | 772,325 | 1,100 | 1,231,000 | 140 | 1,639,000 | 1,922 |
| NORTH CAROLINA | * | * | * | * | 1,462,800 | 318 |
| NORTH DAKOTA | 0 | 0 | 10,124,278 | 800 | 0 | 0 |
| OHIO | 0 | 0 | 12,712,360 | 1,099 | 0 | 0 |
| OKLAHOMA | 0 | 0 | 24,573,133 | 349 | 127,500 | 50 |
| OREGON | 0 | 0 | 0 | 0 | 349,355 | 477 |
| PENNSYLVANIA | 0 | 0 | 0 | 0 | 0 | 0 |
| RHODE ISLAND | 0 | 0 | 0 | 0 | 0 | 0 |
| SOUTH CAROLINA | 0 | 0 | 0 | 0 | 0 | 0 |
| SOUTH DAKOTA | 0 | 0 | 0 | 0 | 0 | 0 |
| TENNESSEE | 608,300 | 1,827 | 0 | 0 | 0 | 0 |
| TEXAS | 0 | 0 | 0 | 0 | 0 | 0 |
| UTAH | 0 | 0 | 336,150 | 156 | 323,685 | 50 |
| VERMONT | 20,000 | 39 | 0 | 0 | 0 | 0 |
| VIRGINIA | 0 | 0 | 3,173,563 | * | 0 | 0 |
| WASHINGTON | 0 | 0 | 0 | 0 | 0 | 0 |
| WEST VIRGINIA | 0 | 0 | 0 | 0 | 2,090,243 | 1,872 |
| WISCONSIN | 0 | 0 | 1,637,818 | 159 | 0 | 0 |
| WYOMING | 0 | 0 | 881,000 | 62 | 0 | 0 |
| **Reporting States** | 6,782,564 | 13,702 | 102,373,852 | 14,779 | 13,212,260 | 7,538 |
| **U.S. TOTAL (Imputed)** | -- | 13,820 | -- | -- | -- | -- |

[1] *An asterisk indicates that data were not available and "0" indicates that special initiative activity was not identified. Some states were able to report expenditures, but not numbers supported.*
*The imputed U.S. totals include estimates for these states based on the average cost/individual of reporting states.*

tiated by the majority of state MR/DD agencies in the early 1980s (Fujiura, Garza, & Braddock, 1990). *Supported living* was incorporated into community residential systems in the mid-1980s in Colorado, Florida, Missouri, North Dakota, Ohio, Oregon, and Wisconsin (Bauer & Smith, 1993; Pittsley, 1990; Smith, 1990). Nearly all the states are expanding *supported employment*. The increased availability of supported living, personal assistance, and supported employment reflects in part the priorities of self-advocacy organizations across the country (Longhurst, 1994). Individuals with disabilities are articulating what services and supports are needed, and they are sharing insights about how best to assure quality (Kennedy, 1990).

Responding to a survey about creative community financing efforts, state MR/DD agency directors and community provider organizations emphasized replacing previously acceptable service models such as sheltered workshops and group homes (Hemp, 1994). One state director expressed, "the best programs are those support systems that are the most invisible" (p. 286). To structure such systems of support, state MR/DD agencies must address three broad priority areas: 1) new administrative and financial policies and procedures, 2) new and reallocated funding, and 3) effective management of staff resources. Each priority area is briefly discussed below.

Statewide systems of support require substantial revision of state administrative and financial policies and procedures. As exemplified in Florida's supported living initiative: 1) supported persons' choices take precedence over providers' convenience; 2) "own home" means that the name of the person with a disability is on the lease or mortgage; 3) there are flexible and natural supports which are responsive to individuals' changing needs; and 4) support planning incorporates person-centered methodologies (Lepore, 1992). California, North Dakota, and Ohio, states with large supported living initiatives, designed policies and procedures to clarify staff responsibilities, to specify methods of funding, and to address administrative issues including quality assurance. Massachusetts was beginning to implement statewide initiatives by developing new and revised policies for supported living. Vermont was focusing on a quality assurance system for individuals in supported living.

The second priority for state agencies is a commitment to the reallocation of existing resources coupled with the identification of new funds. Forty-seven states now use the federal HCBS Waiver to reallocate funds consistent with the federal requirement for "budget neutrality" (reducing or avoiding the expansion of ICF/MR capacity) (Smith, 1993, p. 880). Supplanting ICF/MR funding with Waiver resources expands participants' options for supported living and employment. By 1992, 15 states offered supported living as a specific Waiver service; and 31 states offered supported employment (Smith & Gettings, 1992). For example, Colorado's Waiver-reimbursed "personal care alternatives" (PCA) served over one thousand persons in 1992. This was more than one-third of the total 15-bed or less community residential placements in that state. Waiver PCA participants lived with one or two other people, and costs per person ranged from $12-$50 thousand annually. Although Colorado's PCA option usually involved ownership of housing by the support provider (inconsistent with one of the criteria for supported living and personal assistance), it nevertheless represented a substantial redirection of federal and state funding. Many of the PCA Waiver participants were formerly residents of private ICFs/MR, facilities which Colorado converted to the Waiver program in 1984.

Some states without substantial federal Waiver programs have also redirected state funding to supported living. In 1991, Ohio increased supported living spending from $2 to $10 million with a combination of new Department of Mental Retardation/Developmental Disabilities appropriations and the transfer of $6 million from DMR/DD's group homes budget line. Florida officials earmarked new state appropriations for supported living and specified that funding levels in group residences be maintained as persons transition to supported living.

The 1990 Medicaid amendment authorizing Community Supported Living Arrangements (CSLA) offers the clearest federal statement to date about structuring state-wide systems of support. CSLA (P.L. 101-508) stresses individualized supports rather than standardized packages of services more common to the ICF/MR program. Total state-federal spending for CSLA in the eight pilot states is projected to grow from $14 million in 1993 to $36 million in 1994 (*Community Services Reporter*, 1994a). (There was $2.1 million in state-federal spending in 1992.) The eight CSLA states (California, Colorado, Florida, Illinois, Maryland, Michigan, Rhode Island, and Wisconsin) built their successful applications on their experiences with the HCBS Waiver, such as Wisconsin's Community Integration Program-CIP, and on local initiatives such as Illinois' Supporting People in Integrated Community Environments-SPICE program. California's substantial state-wide supported living initiative began in 1988 financed by state purchase of service funding. Colorado, as noted above, completely redirected private ICF/MR funding to the HCBS Waiver, while Maryland has never utilized the private ICF/MR model. Both states substantially expanded their Waiver programs in recent years. Michigan and Rhode Island's Waiver programs contributed to their successful CSLA applications.

States implementing structured systems of supported living are creatively redirecting staff resources for direct individual support and for regional oversight and case management. Direct support staff must exercise considerable discretion each day, as the people they support learn to manage their daily activities, their homes, and a range of new experiences with others in the community around them. Unfortunately, a pattern of lower compensation and benefit levels compared to those of institutional employees negatively impacts support staff in most states (Mitchell & Braddock, 1993). It also complicates effective community staff recruitment, training, and retention (Larson, Hewitt, & Lakin, 1994).

Dispersed support staff usually interact on a very limited basis with co-workers who have similar responsibilities. Managers must make special arrangements to support these staff through training and technical assistance (Bachelder & Braddock, 1994; Karan, Furey, & Granfield, 1991). Support staff should also be given the opportunity to work together in teams and to assume responsibility for the basic organizational decisions affecting their support relationships (Leavitt, 1975; Smull, 1993). Ultimately, structuring systems of support means re-directing the activities of managers, professionals, and direct care staff in profound ways.

## ASSESSING FISCAL EFFORT IN THE STATES

Fiscal effort is a ratio which can be utilized to rank states according to the proportion of their total state-wide personal income devoted to developmental disabilities services. Bahl (1982) defined the measurement of fiscal performance, or "fiscal effort," in state and local governments as an index predicated on relative, rather than absolute, values. Braddock and Fujiura (1987a), utilizing the effort index to examine the determinants of states' support for community alternatives, further defined fiscal effort as

...tied theoretically to the competitive resource allocation struggle described by Key (1949) and Wildavsky (1974) as the essence of politics. Some states are addressing a given political objective such as mental retardation more vigorously than others. Comparative state financial performance analysis enables distinctions to be made between those states making a strong effort and those that are not. This knowledge, according to Caiden (1978), is useful in providing objective standards of comparison among the states and relevant information for policy making and is an important component in the enforcement of accountability. (pp. 450-451)

Figure 11 illustrates changes in fiscal effort across the U.S. during the 1977-92 period. In 1977, $2.27 per thousand dollars of aggregate U.S. personal income was expended for MR/DD services across the U.S. By 1988, fiscal effort had increased to $3.01, and in 1992 the figure was $3.33 per thousand. The composition of this robust 16-year trend consists of two major subcomponents: the dynamic and continuing growth of community services resources and a steady decline in fiscal effort in the states allocated for the large congregate care sector. Community services fiscal effort has tripled from $.57/$1,000 in 1977 to $1.90/$1,000 of personal income in 1992; in marked contrast, fiscal effort for congregate care peaked in 1980 at $1.75/$1,000 and declined annually to $1.43/$1,000 in 1992. In summary, the proportion of the nation's wealth being spent on MR/DD services increased 11% overall between 1988 and 1992; it declined by 8% in the congregate care sector and advanced by 32% in community services programs.

## State Spending Patterns

There were wide variations in fiscal effort among the states in 1992 and several important developments in the performance of individual states over the preceding four years. North Dakota led the nation in total fiscal effort, as it also did in 1988, expending $7.68/$1,000 of state wealth on MR/DD services. Other states with the most substantial financial commitments to MR/DD services in 1992 included Rhode Island, Connecticut, the District of Columbia, Iowa, Wyoming, Minnesota, New York, and Massachusetts. The most remarkable changes in nationwide fiscal effort rankings in the states occurred in West Virginia, Oklahoma, Indiana, and New Mexico. These four states climbed between 27 and 12 positions in the rankings. West Virginia advanced from 46th in 1988 to 19th in 1992. (A special analysis of the transformation of the West Virginia MR/DD service system is available from the West Virginia Developmental Disabilities Planning Council (Braddock & Bachelder, 1992)). Oklahoma also moved dramatically forward in the rankings--from

34th in 1988 to 14th in 1992. Underlying this movement in West Virginia and Oklahoma, as well as in New Mexico, was the rapid expansion of community services programs and related spending. All three states were also involved in class action litigation promoting institutional downsizing and community placements. Other states moving up at least five positions in the rankings included Maine, Washington, Arizona, Kansas, Wyoming, Arkansas, and Connecticut.

A declining pattern of overall MR/DD fiscal effort was particularly evident during 1988-92 in New Hampshire, which fell 14 positions to 33rd nationally. New Hampshire closed its state institution at Laconia during 1992, and the state has been able to significantly reduce its total MR/DD spending effort while developing an extensive alternative array of community services. Michigan, with only 656 residents remaining in its developmental institutions in 1992, declined 7 positions in overall spending during 1988-92. Severe, unprecedented budget cuts associated with a major state revenue crisis led to a decline of 14

## FIGURE 11
### *MR/DD Spending Per $1,000 of Personal Income: FYs 1977-92*

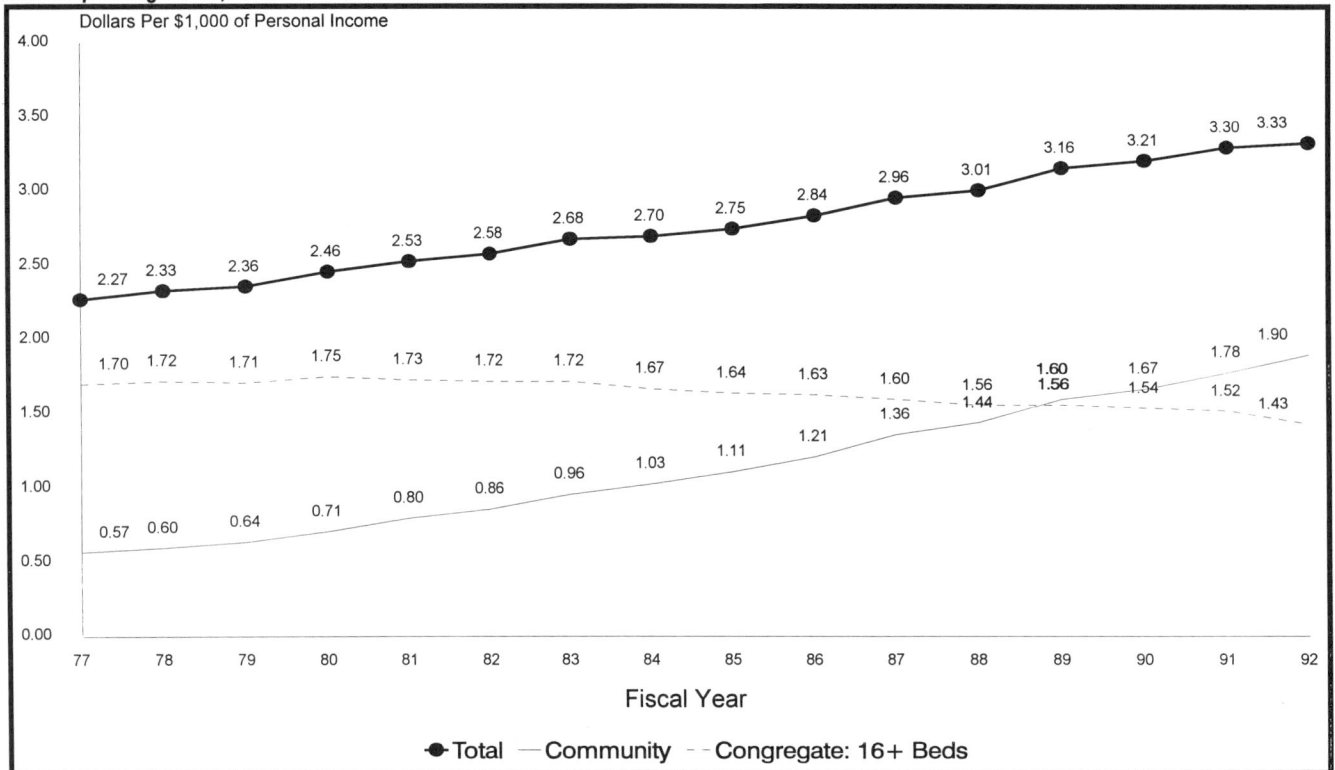

positions in the national ranking for New Jersey. Maryland, Georgia, Utah, Montana, Mississippi, Pennsylvania, Nebraska, and New York dropped between 11 and 5 positions in total fiscal effort.

Fiscal effort for community services in the states during 1988-92 showed unusually strong advances in West Virginia (+31 positions), Oklahoma (+22 positions), Arizona (+16 positions), and Wyoming (+15 positions). Significant but less rapid increases of from 6 to 9 positions were noted in Louisiana, Iowa, and Kansas. Arkansas, Oregon, New Mexico, and Texas increased positions in the ranking. There were major declines (10 - 17 positions) in community services fiscal effort in New Jersey, Georgia, and Missouri. Declines between 6 and 9 positions occurred in California, Wisconsin, Maryland, Massachusetts, Nebraska, Pennsylvania, Delaware, and Florida.

In the congregate care sector, the most dramatic shift in fiscal effort was in the District of Columbia. The District closed its only MR/DD institution, Forest Haven, in 1992. Fiscal effort correspondingly plunged 28 positions between 1988-92. There was also a substantial decline in congregate effort in New York, which began the process of closing all its institutions. New York declined in the congregate rankings from first in 1977 to 3rd in 1988 and to 17th in 1992. A decline of 7 positions from 6th to 13th was evident in Minnesota, which also embarked on a series of facility closures during the past few years. Colorado and Rhode Island both reduced their institutional censuses significantly, and Rhode Island dropped 8 positions in the rankings to 34th; Colorado had congregate fiscal effort rankings of 48th in 1988 and 47th in 1992.

There were major enhancements of congregate fiscal effort in Maine, which advanced 21 positions to 7th in the rankings between 1988-92. There was a doubling of federal ICF/MR reimbursements in Maine during 1988-92 and an even more rapid increase in state general funds allocated for institutional operations. This infusion of resources occurred while the resident population at the institutions (Pineland and Levinson) dropped from 307 to 245. Per diems as a result skyrocketed to $505/day--the highest in the nation. Rapid growth in congregate fiscal effort between 1988 and 1992 was also observed in Indiana, which moved upward 14 positions to 24th, and in New Mexico which advanced 10 posi-

tions to 29th. Other states with significant congregate fiscal effort growth were Wisconsin, Nevada, Oklahoma, and Washington State.

Table 12 (following page) summarizes the fiscal effort data for the states. The state rankings are presented for three individual years--1977, 1988, and 1992--and also cumulatively. The cumulative measure reflects aggregate spending for MR/DD services across the states for the entire 1977-92 period divided by aggregate statewide personal income during that entire 16-year period. The cumulative measure is the best representation of state financial performance over a substantial period of time. States that have supported MR/DD services at consistently high levels over many years were rated higher on the cumulative ranking than states that only recently began exhibiting major commitments to MR/DD services.

## Determinants of Community Spending

The state rankings presented in Table 12 raise intriguing questions. How can the goal of community integration be universally accepted among state service systems if state governments vary so dramatically in the implementation of its principles? Why does North Dakota spend over 1,000% more dollars per $1,000 of state wealth for community MR/DD services than Mississippi and Nevada? How is it that the Great Lakes state of Michigan, so similar in geography, demographics, and economy to Illinois, exhibits twice the fiscal effort of Illinois in supporting community services?

Definitive answers to these types of questions will require a sustained research effort in individual states, focused on policy development, and with greater emphasis given to the process of governmental action. The National Study of Public Spending data base, national in scope, longitudinal in design, and program specific, provides a unique empirical opportunity to develop and evaluate a model of state spending with specific and theoretically relevant variables (Braddock & Fujiura, 1991).

Despite the size of the federal fiscal commitment to MR/DD services generally, state government has been central to the development of community-based services. As noted earlier, state-source revenues formed the fiscal foundation of community services programs in 1992. The fundamental importance of this role has been essentially unchanged throughout the 16 years of our analysis. It is government at the state level that raises most of the revenue and allocates the funds that drive the community services agenda. Thus, it is with the state as the basic unit of

analysis that an inquiry into the determinants of community services spending must begin.

## Models of State Spending

Economists (Fabricant, 1952; Hofferbert, 1972; Horowitz, 1968) and political scientists (Dye, 1966;

**TABLE 12**
*Ranking of States by Fiscal Effort for MR/DD Services in 1992, 1988, 1977, and Cumulatively* [1]

| State | COMMUNITY | | | | CONGREGATE | | | | TOTAL MR/DD | | | |
|---|---|---|---|---|---|---|---|---|---|---|---|---|
| | 1992 | 1988 | 1977 | Cumulative | 1992 | 1988 | 1977 | Cumulative | 1992 | 1988 | 1977 | Cumulative |
| DISTRICT OF COLUMBIA | 1 | 3 | 50 | 2 | 51 | 23 | 9 | 25 | 4 | 6 | 21 | 7 |
| NORTH DAKOTA | 2 | 1 | 51 | 3 | 4 | 1 | 3 | 1 | 1 | 1 | 14 | 1 |
| RHODE ISLAND | 3 | 2 | 15 | 1 | 33 | 25 | 5 | 17 | 2 | 7 | 8 | 5 |
| CONNECTICUT | 4 | 4 | 30 | 5 | 15 | 10 | 14 | 10 | 3 | 2 | 19 | 6 |
| NEW YORK | 5 | 6 | 17 | 4 | 17 | 3 | 1 | 3 | 8 | 3 | 1 | 2 |
| MINNESOTA | 6 | 5 | 2 | 6 | 13 | 6 | 7 | 6 | 7 | 4 | 2 | 3 |
| IOWA | 7 | 15 | 1 | 7 | 3 | 5 | 28 | 9 | 5 | 8 | 3 | 8 |
| WYOMING | 8 | 23 | 18 | 23 | 1 | 4 | 19 | 7 | 6 | 12 | 18 | 14 |
| NEW HAMPSHIRE | 9 | 9 | 25 | 8 | 50 | 45 | 44 | 46 | 32 | 19 | 40 | 21 |
| VERMONT | 10 | 11 | 32 | 9 | 36 | 30 | 8 | 29 | 15 | 13 | 11 | 11 |
| MICHIGAN | 11 | 8 | 34 | 10 | 48 | 46 | 20 | 44 | 27 | 20 | 28 | 22 |
| WEST VIRGINIA | 12 | 43 | 46 | 34 | 40 | 41 | 45 | 42 | 19 | 46 | 48 | 45 |
| SOUTH DAKOTA | 13 | 10 | 27 | 15 | 14 | 15 | 6 | 14 | 11 | 9 | 10 | 10 |
| MAINE | 14 | 16 | 20 | 13 | 7 | 29 | 37 | 20 | 10 | 18 | 31 | 12 |
| MASSACHUSETTS | 15 | 7 | 11 | 11 | 2 | 2 | 17 | 2 | 9 | 5 | 13 | 4 |
| OHIO | 16 | 12 | 10 | 12 | 18 | 16 | 41 | 24 | 13 | 10 | 25 | 13 |
| MONTANA | 17 | 14 | 4 | 14 | 38 | 32 | 15 | 34 | 21 | 14 | 6 | 18 |
| IDAHO | 18 | 20 | 13 | 20 | 30 | 31 | 23 | 32 | 25 | 24 | 17 | 24 |
| ARIZONA | 19 | 35 | 49 | 24 | 49 | 48 | 46 | 50 | 43 | 49 | 49 | 47 |
| PENNSYLVANIA | 20 | 13 | 12 | 16 | 20 | 18 | 2 | 8 | 17 | 11 | 4 | 9 |
| LOUISIANA | 21 | 27 | 42 | 32 | 6 | 7 | 18 | 4 | 12 | 15 | 29 | 17 |
| OREGON | 22 | 26 | 43 | 28 | 26 | 17 | 16 | 19 | 23 | 21 | 27 | 25 |
| COLORADO | 23 | 19 | 8 | 19 | 46 | 49 | 38 | 49 | 41 | 40 | 23 | 41 |
| NEBRASKA | 24 | 17 | 3 | 17 | 32 | 36 | 35 | 35 | 28 | 23 | 9 | 19 |
| INDIANA | 25 | 29 | 22 | 25 | 24 | 38 | 47 | 39 | 22 | 39 | 42 | 38 |
| ALASKA | 26 | 22 | 14 | 21 | 44 | 47 | 49 | 48 | 39 | 41 | 44 | 42 |
| WISCONSIN | 27 | 18 | 6 | 18 | 11 | 20 | 4 | 13 | 16 | 17 | 5 | 15 |
| OKLAHOMA | 28 | 50 | 45 | 46 | 5 | 11 | 40 | 21 | 14 | 34 | 46 | 37 |
| MARYLAND | 29 | 21 | 37 | 26 | 42 | 40 | 33 | 40 | 42 | 31 | 36 | 39 |
| KANSAS | 30 | 39 | 5 | 27 | 12 | 13 | 12 | 16 | 20 | 26 | 7 | 20 |
| SOUTH CAROLINA | 31 | 28 | 26 | 29 | 8 | 8 | 10 | 5 | 18 | 16 | 12 | 16 |
| NEW MEXICO | 32 | 36 | 35 | 35 | 29 | 39 | 36 | 37 | 29 | 42 | 38 | 40 |
| CALIFORNIA | 33 | 24 | 9 | 22 | 41 | 42 | 48 | 41 | 40 | 37 | 34 | 35 |
| NORTH CAROLINA | 34 | 38 | 23 | 37 | 16 | 12 | 11 | 12 | 26 | 25 | 15 | 23 |
| ARKANSAS | 35 | 40 | 16 | 39 | 10 | 14 | 24 | 15 | 24 | 29 | 22 | 26 |
| ILLINOIS | 36 | 32 | 24 | 36 | 25 | 28 | 21 | 28 | 30 | 33 | 24 | 29 |
| UTAH | 37 | 34 | 44 | 40 | 27 | 21 | 29 | 22 | 35 | 27 | 41 | 31 |
| TEXAS | 38 | 42 | 33 | 42 | 28 | 26 | 13 | 27 | 37 | 38 | 20 | 36 |
| DELAWARE | 39 | 33 | 47 | 41 | 19 | 22 | 42 | 23 | 31 | 28 | 47 | 32 |
| MISSOURI | 40 | 30 | 21 | 30 | 23 | 24 | 32 | 26 | 34 | 30 | 30 | 28 |
| WASHINGTON | 41 | 37 | 31 | 38 | 21 | 27 | 31 | 30 | 33 | 35 | 35 | 34 |
| NEW JERSEY | 42 | 25 | 39 | 33 | 22 | 19 | 30 | 18 | 36 | 22 | 39 | 27 |
| GEORGIA | 43 | 31 | 7 | 31 | 31 | 33 | 25 | 31 | 44 | 36 | 16 | 33 |
| HAWAII | 44 | 46 | 19 | 44 | 47 | 50 | 39 | 47 | 50 | 50 | 32 | 50 |
| VIRGINIA | 45 | 45 | 29 | 45 | 37 | 34 | 22 | 36 | 45 | 43 | 26 | 43 |
| TENNESSEE | 46 | 48 | 36 | 48 | 35 | 37 | 34 | 38 | 46 | 45 | 37 | 46 |
| FLORIDA | 47 | 41 | 38 | 43 | 43 | 44 | 43 | 45 | 49 | 48 | 45 | 48 |
| KENTUCKY | 48 | 44 | 41 | 49 | 39 | 43 | 50 | 43 | 48 | 47 | 50 | 49 |
| ALABAMA | 49 | 47 | 28 | 47 | 34 | 35 | 26 | 33 | 47 | 44 | 33 | 44 |
| MISSISSIPPI | 50 | 51 | 48 | 50 | 9 | 9 | 27 | 11 | 38 | 32 | 43 | 30 |
| NEVADA | 51 | 49 | 40 | 51 | 45 | 51 | 51 | 51 | 51 | 51 | 51 | 51 |

[1] *States are ranked by 1992 Community MR/DD Spending as a percentage of personal income. Ranks for community, congregate, and total MR/DD spending are indicated for 1992, 1988, 1977, and cumulative. "Cumulative" consists of annual spending across 1977-92 divided by annual personal income across 1977-92.*

Dye & Robey, 1980) have noted a strong association between the magnitude of state expenditure in any given program area and the general economic wealth or per capita income of the state and its population base. The theory underlying this relationship has been postulated by Cyert and March (1963) and others in terms of states having greater slack resources available to them for adopting new programs or innovations. In a seminal study, Walker (1969) derived state innovation scores based on the rapidity with which state legislatures adopted 88 specific programs in a variety of issue areas. He obtained Pearson product-moment correlations with total state population and state per capita income of .59 and .55 respectively. Populous and wealthy states such as New York, California, Massachusetts, and New Jersey scored much higher on the composite innovation index than did smaller, less wealthy states. Savage's (1978) work on the measurement of a state innovation trait generally supports Walker's earlier findings.

However, it does not appear that state MR/DD spending is a simple function of state size and wealth. In a direct test of these traditional hypotheses, Braddock and Fujiura (1987a) conducted a hierarchical regression analysis on the 1977-84 MR/DD spending data set. The dependent variable was the cumulative state funding, per $1,000 of personal income devoted to community-based services. State population, wealth, and degree of federal assistance to MR/DD services (proportion of the MR/DD budget composed of federal revenue) were the independent variables. All three variables were poor predictors; total predicted variance was .13 and failed to achieve statistical significance. It appeared that deterministic models of state spending based on economics and demographics did not apply to the MR/DD field.

To further test the hypothesis that MR/DD funding is somehow distinctive, a broader expenditure data base was established, including 1977-91 state spending on corrections, natural resources, education, and highways. This was a replication of the analysis of the 1977-84 data set (Braddock & Fujiura, 1987b). Data for the current analysis were obtained from the U.S. Bureau of the Census (1993) and in annual publications for the prior fourteen years--1977-90. In a manner parallel to the foregoing analysis, a hierarchical regression was

employed to regress per-capita spending in each of these areas on three commonly employed predictors: state wealth, state population, and tax rate. The two former variables were the same predictors employed in the other analysis; the latter predictor (tax revenue of state governments divided by state-wide aggregate personal income) was another proxy for a state's fiscal capacity. The distinctiveness of MR/DD fiscal effort appeared to be a robust finding. The three predictors, as a group, were consistent in their predictive strength across all areas of state spending *with the exception of MR/DD services* (Table 13).

**TABLE 13**
*Regression of State Spending in the Areas of Corrections, Natural Resources, Education, and Community MR/DD Services on State Size, State Wealth, and Tax Rate for 1977-91*

| | TYPE OF STATE SPENDING | | | |
| --- | --- | --- | --- | --- |
| | Corrections | Natural Resources | Education | Community MR/DD Services |
| Order of Entry | Predicted Variance ($R^2$) | | | |
| 1. State Size | .178 | .109 | .104 | .000 |
| 2. State Wealth | .000 | .003 | .047 | .066 |
| 3. Tax Rate | .160 | .764 | .245 | .067 |
| TOTAL $R^2$ | .338** | .876** | .396** | .133 |

*$p < .01$. **$p < .001$.

## A Politics and Advocacy Model

The divergence of MR/DD community services spending from the typical pattern illustrated in the foregoing analysis suggests other determinants, perhaps of a complex and idiosyncratic character. There are, however, logical bases upon which preliminary models of MR/DD spending can be built and, therefore, tested. A more detailed discussion of policy analysis theory and model building is described by Braddock and Fujiura (1991).

Two potentially important covariates of contemporary community services spending are a state's historical innovativeness on civil rights issues generally and the effect of special interest groups. The importance of this history is suggested by the extent of MR/DD class action litigation in the nation after 1971. Braddock (1981) for example, identified 38 pending and completed class action right-to-habilitation suits in 27 states between 1971 and 1981. Significantly, most of the cases filed or reformulated after 1974 resulted in court orders or consent agreements requiring the states to develop community-based alternatives to institutions (Herr, 1983). This stimulated many defendant state governments to request substantial additional funds from their legislatures to implement new community services. The linkage between interest group activity and spending is often direct; for example, mental retardation advocacy organizations were frequently the moving parties or plaintiff intervenors in key litigation (Table 14), and most state Associations for Retarded Citizens (The Arc) operated active governmental affairs programs. Theoretically, the state governments most responsive from a fiscal standpoint to community services development were influenced in significant degree by the efforts of these highly motivated special interest groups.

**TABLE 14**
*Top 10 States in Community Services Fiscal Effort for Persons with DD, Right to Habilitation Class Action Litigation, and The Arc Activity*

| Rank | State | Class Action Litigation Filed | Arc Involvement |
|---|---|---|---|
| 1 | DIST OF COLUMBIA | Evans v Washington (1976) | Court Monitor |
| 2 | NORTH DAKOTA | ARC of North Dakota v Olson (1980) | Plaintiff |
| 3 | RHODE ISLAND | Iasimone v Garrahy (1977) | Court Monitor |
| 4 | CONNECTICUT | Connecticut ARC v Thorne (1978) | Plaintiff |
| 5 | NEW YORK | New York State ARC v Rockefeller (1972) | Plaintiff |
| 6 | MINNESOTA | Welsch v Likins (1972) | No Official Role |
| 7 | IOWA | Conner v Branstad (1986) | No Official Role |
| 8 | WYOMING | Weston v Wyoming (1990) | No Official Role |
| 9 | NEW HAMPSHIRE | Garrity v Gallen (1978) | Plaintiff Intervenor |
| 10 | VERMONT | *In re* Brace (1978) (Judicial Review) | No Official Role |

There was extremely rapid growth of community services fiscal effort during the recent 1988-92 four year period in the states of West Virginia, Oklahoma, Wyoming, Arizona, Kansas, Texas, Arkansas, Louisiana, Indiana, North Carolina, Oregon, New Mexico, Washington, DC, and Iowa. Community services fiscal effort in 1992 increased between 328% and 74% over 1988 levels in these states. This compared to an average nationwide rate of increase in fiscal effort across 1988-92 of 32%. Thus, spending for MR/DD community services grew from 2-10 times faster in these 15 states than in the average state. One factor many of these 15 community services expansion states had in common was class action litigation. The following cases stimulated substantial expansion of community placements and resources: West Virginia (*Hartley*), Oklahoma (*Hissom*), Wyoming (*Weston*), Texas (*Lelsz*), North Carolina (*Thomas*), Oregon (*U.S. Department of*

*Justice*), New Mexico (*Jackson*), Washington, DC (*Evans*), and Iowa (*Conner*).

It should be noted that state protection and advocacy agencies (P&As) played key roles in many of these cases, including Wyoming (as counsel), Iowa (plaintiff), Texas (plaintiff intervenor), Oregon (counsel), and New Mexico (counsel). The P&A also served as counsel in an extremely important community services development case in California (*Coffelt*).

To quantitatively assess the relationship of spending to civil rights history, a variable from the political science field, civil rights innovativeness (Gray, 1973), was employed to serve as a proxy for the dynamics undergirding the histories of civil rights activities in the states. The variable was defined in terms of the rapidity of states' adoption of three civil rights laws over a period of 30 years between 1937-66. An *innovative* state was an early adopter of civil rights statutes in public accommodations, fair housing, and fair employment. Adoption of these statutes at the state level preceded their adoption federally and thus very likely reflects a purer measure of general state orientation toward civil rights historically. Per capita membership in 1992 in the Arc state organizations was employed as a proxy for interest group activity.

A hierarchical regression was conducted on the 1977-92 data set in a manner paralleling the Braddock and Fujiura (1991) analysis. The three demographic and economic variables from the original analysis were employed in an effort to replicate those findings with the updated 1977-92 data set: state size, defined as the average total state population over the 16-year period; state wealth, defined as a state's 16-year total aggregate per capita income; and degree of federal assistance, defined as the 16-year average of the percentage of the community services' MR/DD spending that represented federal revenues. The fourth predictor was Gray's (1973) civil rights innovativeness index. The Arc per capita membership was entered into the equation last.

The choice of predictors reflects the direct comparison of the deterministic model of state spending to a model that presumes distinctive dynamics for MR/DD services, dynamics that reflect political concerns rather than economic and demographic forces. The analysis asks first, is MR/DD fiscal effort a simple function of states' size and wealth? Second, has the growing role of federal revenue transfers impacted on state spending? Finally, to what extent might states' civil rights histories account for variance in community spending above and beyond traditional predictors of state spending? The order of entry into the regression equation was predicated on this latter point; the civil rights and The Arc membership variables were entered last.

The dependent variable was also historical in character, represented by the cumulative, 16-year, 1977-92 fiscal effort devoted to community services. Fiscal effort was defined as before--total dollars expended on community services per $1,000 of personal income, aggregated over the 16-year period.

Fifty-three percent of the variance was accounted for in the overall regression, and the equation, with all variables entered, was statistically significant at the $p < .001$ level, $F (5,42) = 9.549$ (Table 15). None of the three variables representing the deterministic model of state spending was a statistically significant

## TABLE 15

*Regression of State Fiscal Effort FYs 1977-92 on State Size, Wealth, Degree of Federal Assistance, Civil Rights Innovativeness, and Consumer Advocacy*

| Entry | Multiple R | $R^2$ Change | Beta | F Equation |
|---|---|---|---|---|
| 1. Population | .0137 | .0002 | -.0137 | .009 |
| 2. Wealth | .2969 | .0879 | .3223 | 2.175 |
| 3. Federal Assistance | .3239 | .0168 | .1662 | 1.719 |
| 4. Civil Rights | .5527 | .2005 | .5649 | 4.728* |
| 5. Consumer Advocacy | .7294 | .2266 | .4912 | 9.547** |
| | TOTAL $R^2$ | .5320 | | |

*$p < .01$. **$p < .001$.*

predictor. The state size and degree of federal assistance variables accounted for virtually none of the total variance. *It was the entry of the civil rights and consumer advocacy variables that made the overall regression equation statistically significant.* They accounted for the bulk of the total predicted variance, even after the demographic and economic variables were entered. The simple correlation of civil rights innovativeness and The Arc membership was .168.

An additional regression was completed to determine if the variance accounted for during the recent 1988-92 period contrasted significantly with the variance accounted for across the entire 1977-92 time span. *It did not. Forty-six percent* of the variance was accounted for in the 1988-92 regression. The equation was statistically significant at the $p < .001$ level, $F (5,42) = 7.225$.

Thus, regression analyses of the 1977-92 and 1988-92 data sets both indicated the absense of a relationship between indices of state size, wealth, and federal assistance to community services fiscal effort in the states. This finding essentially replicates the outcome of the Braddock and Fujiura (1991) analysis on the 1977-88 data set.

These results quantify what many individuals involved in the field intuitively understand--that the development of services for persons with developmental disabilities is inextricably intertwined in the cultural and political contexts of the states. The policies that foster these services are affected by complex determinants and even more complicated political processes. Many are idiosyncratic to individual states, and a comprehensive portrait requires extensive and detailed analyses on a state-by-state basis.

# PART II

## State Profiles

# PART II
## STATE RESOURCE ALLOCATION AND SERVICE DELIVERY PROFILES

Each state's resource allocation profile consists of five pages of figures, tables, and a financial spreadsheet, in the following sequence:

- Comparative 1977-92 spending for congregate, 16+ beds, residential and for community residential (15 bed or less) and nonresidential services;
- Numbers of individuals served in out-of-home residential settings and in other services;
- Community revenue detail and state spending for special community initiatives;
- Revenue, expenditure, and program detail for congregate residential services;
- Total MR/DD fiscal effort across 1977-92, and comparative congregate and community services fiscal effort; and
- The financial spreadsheet with resource detail for institutional, large private residential, and community services across the 16-year period, FYs 1977-92.

Each page of the state profile is briefly described below.

**Comparative Spending.** The first page of figures summarizes 1977-92 constant dollar spending for congregate, 16+ beds, residential services, compared to 15 beds or less residential and non-residential community services. A pie chart indicates the proportions of community and congregate 16+ beds spending in 1992. A single bar chart extending from the congregate services section of the pie chart depicts the proportions of congregate spending dedicated to state institutions, to 16+ bed private ICFs/MR, and to 16+ bed private facilities not certified as ICFs/MR.

**Individuals Served.** On the second page of a state's profile a pie chart summarizes the proportions of individuals served in out-of-home settings in 1992. Settings are categorized according to size and ICF/MR certification status:

Facilities of 16+ beds:
- state institutions

- nursing facilities[1]
- private ICFs/MR
- other private residential settings
Facilities of 7-15 beds:
- public and private ICFs/MR
- other residential settings
Facilities of 1-6 beds:
- public and private ICFs/MR
- other small community residences

The first table on this page presents data on individuals served across 1986-92. The table includes detail on publicly and privately operated community-based ICFs/MR of 7-15 beds or 6 beds or less. The second table summarizes the numbers of individuals served in day/work programs, in case management, in the Home and Community Based Services (HCBS) Waiver, and in the Model 50/200 Waiver.

**Community Revenues and Special Community Initiatives.** The proportions of community revenues which are contributed by state and local government or federal sources are depicted in a pie chart. (Local government funding consists of "local/county overmatch"; the local matches for Medicaid or other federal programs are included with state funds). A single bar chart extends from the federal funding section of the community revenue pie chart to indicate the proportion of all 1992 federal revenue deriving from one or more of the following sources:

- Small private ICF/MR (facilities with 15 beds or less),
- Small public ICF/MR (facilities with 15 beds or less),
- HCBS Waiver (including the OBRA 87 Waiver, if applicable),
- Model 50/200 Waiver,
- Title XX/Social Services Block Grant (SSBG),
- Other Title XIX program funds (including day training, day habilitation, targeted case management, or CSLA), and
- Other federal funds.

---

[1] Nursing home data (individuals with mental retardation and related conditions served, expenditures) are not included in figures or tables on other pages of the state profile.

Principal state MR/DD agencies funded one or more of the *special community initiatives* summarized in the tables on the third page of the state profile. The seven initiatives, defined in Part I, Overview, are:

- Family support, including financial subsidy/payment, family assistance (respite care), and other family supports,
- Aging/DD services,
- Assistive technology
- Early intervention services,
- Personal assistance,
- Supported employment, and
- Supported living.

**Congregate Residential Services.** The fourth page of the state profile summarizes revenue sources for private, 16+ bed settings and for institutional services. Also displayed are average daily residents in institutions during 1977-92; and institutional per diem rates across those 16 years.

**Fiscal Effort.** The final page of figures in the state profile summarizes the state's fiscal effort on behalf of individuals with developmental disabilities and their families. Line charts encompassing 1977-92 depict annual spending per thousand dollars of statewide aggregate personal income for total MR/DD services; congregate 16+ beds services; and community services. Additional 1977-92 line charts present a) total MR/DD spending in the state, and b) statewide aggregate personal income.

**The Financial Spreadsheet.** The spreadsheet encompasses the 16 years of the extended data set, 1977-92. Revenues and expenditures are presented according to the outlined budget categories in Table 1, Overview. The United States financial spreadsheet aggregates data for each of the 50 states and the District of Columbia.

**Technical Notes to the State Profiles.** Technical notes in Part III following the state and U.S. profiles include a brief summary of the study's data collection process, information on each principal state agency, and a summary of data sources employed in the analysis. Also presented in the technical notes are descriptions of calculations or estimations integral to constructing the states' resource allocation profiles.

# ALABAMA

## MR/DD Spending for Congregate Residential & Community Services

▨Congregate: 16+ Beds*  ■Community**

Millions of 1992 Dollars

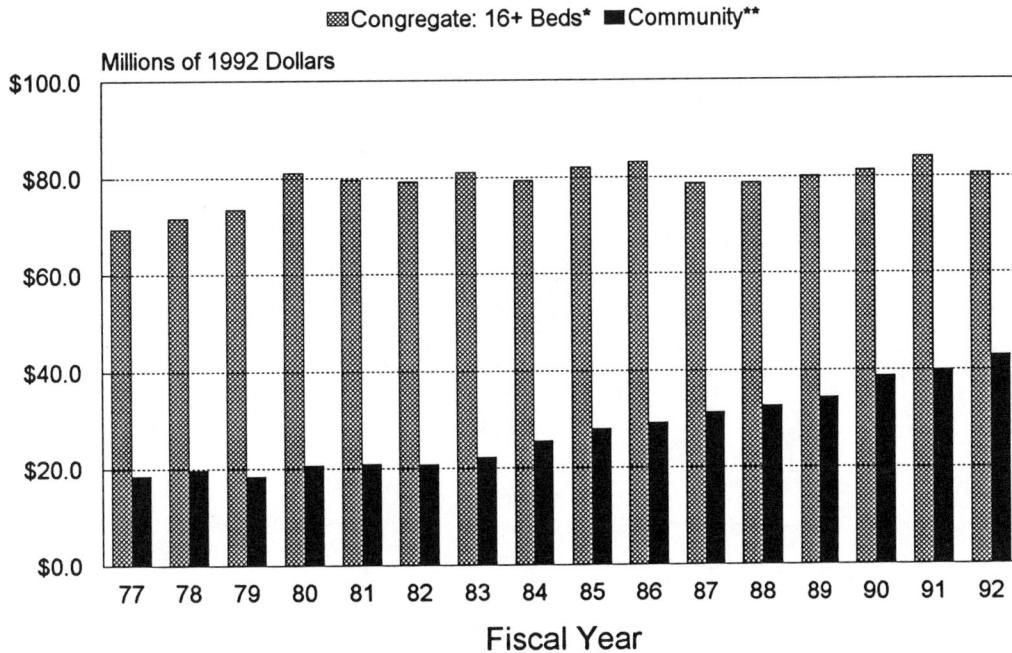

Fiscal Year

*Excludes nursing homes; ** Includes resources for
15 bed or less residential settings & non-residential community services

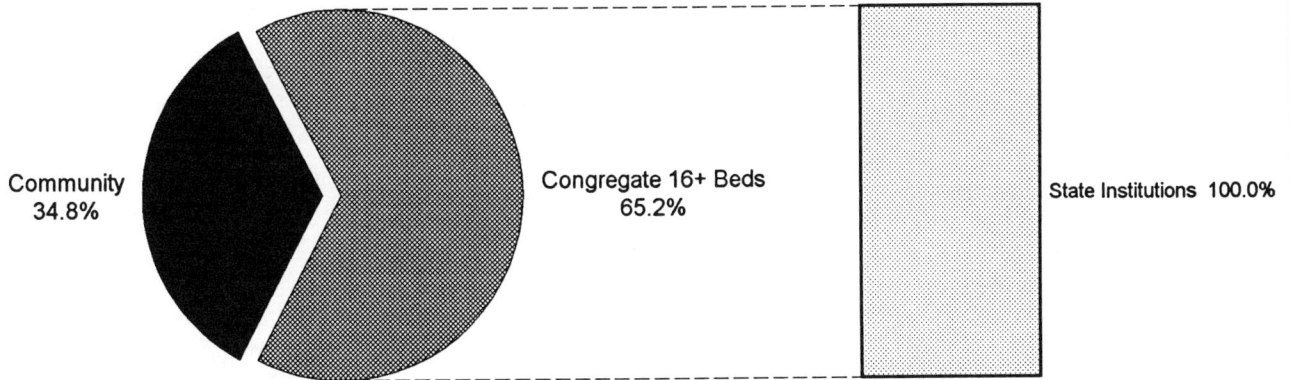

Community
34.8%

Congregate 16+ Beds
65.2%

State Institutions  100.0%

FY 1992 Total Spending:
$123.7 Million

*Source:*
Institute on Disability and Human Development (UAP),
University of Illinois at Chicago, 1994

# ALABAMA

## Number of Persons Served by Residential Setting: FY 1992

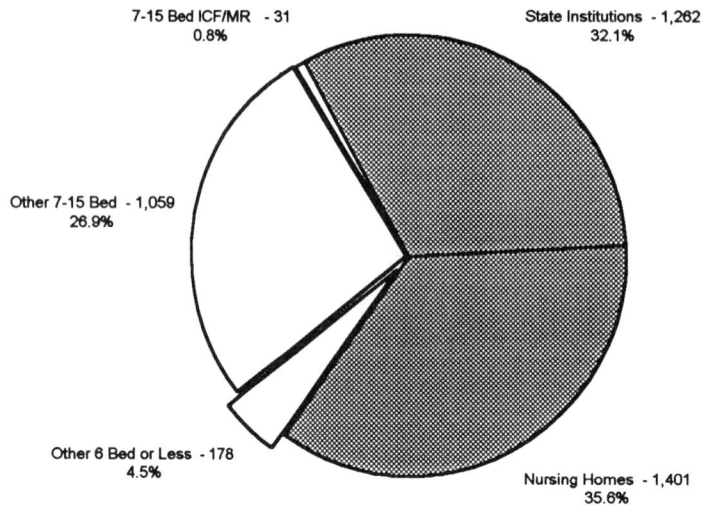

7-15 Bed ICF/MR  - 31
0.8%

State Institutions  - 1,262
32.1%

Other 7-15 Bed  - 1,059
26.9%

Other 6 Bed or Less  - 178
4.5%

Nursing Homes  - 1,401
35.6%

Total Served: 3,931

## Persons Served by Residential Setting:1986-92

|  | 1986 | 1987 | 1988 | 1989 | 1990 | 1991 | 1992 |
|---|---|---|---|---|---|---|---|
| CONGREGATE 16 + BED SETTINGS | NA | NA | 2,930 | NA | NA | 2,539 | 2,663 |
| Nursing Homes* | NA | NA | 1,645 | NA | NA | 1,321 | 1,401 |
| State Institutions | 1,307 | 1,303 | 1,285 | 1,318 | 1,308 | 1,218 | 1,262 |
| Private 16+Bed ICF/MR | 0 | 0 | 0 | 0 | 0 | 0 | 0 |
| Other 16+Bed Residential | 30 | 30 | 0 | 0 | 0 | 0 | 0 |
| 15 BED OR LESS RESIDENTIAL SETTINGS | 690 | 736 | 762 | 897 | 957 | 1,083 | 1,268 |
| Public 7-15 Bed ICF/MR | 0 | 0 | 0 | 0 | 0 | 0 | 0 |
| Private 7-15 Bed ICF/MR | 31 | 31 | 31 | 31 | 31 | 31 | 31 |
| Other 7-15 Bed Residential | 659 | 705 | 731 | 866 | 926 | 874 | 1,059 |
| Public 6 Bed or Less ICF/MR |  |  |  |  |  | 0 | 0 |
| Private 6 Bed or Less ICF/MR |  |  |  |  |  | 0 | 0 |
| Other 6 Bed or Less Residential |  |  |  |  |  | 178 | 178 |
| TOTAL PERSONS SERVED | NA | NA | 3,692 | NA | NA | 3,622 | 3,931 |

## Persons Served in Non-Residential Community Services:1986-92

|  | 1986 | 1987 | 1988 | 1989 | 1990 | 1991 | 1992 |
|---|---|---|---|---|---|---|---|
| DAY/WORK PROGRAMS | 2,569 | 2,656 | 2,571 | 3,234 | 3,213 | 3,379 | 3,297 |
| Sheltered Employment/Work Activity |  |  |  |  |  |  | 525 |
| Day Habilitation ("Day Training") |  |  |  |  |  |  | 2,544 |
| Supported/Competitive Employment | 0 | 16 | 26 | 217 | 156 | 183 | 228 |
| CASE MANAGEMENT | 2,000 | 2,000 | 2,000 | 3,311 | 3,343 | 3,432 | 3,732 |
| HCBS WAIVER | 1,491 | 1,526 | 1,593 | 1,734 | 1,934 | 2,101 | 2,176 |
| MODEL 50/200 WAIVER | 0 | 0 | 0 | 0 | 0 | 0 | 0 |

*Source:*
Institute on Disability and Human Development (UAP),
University of Illinois at Chicago, 1994

# ALABAMA

## Community Services: FY 1992 Revenue Sources

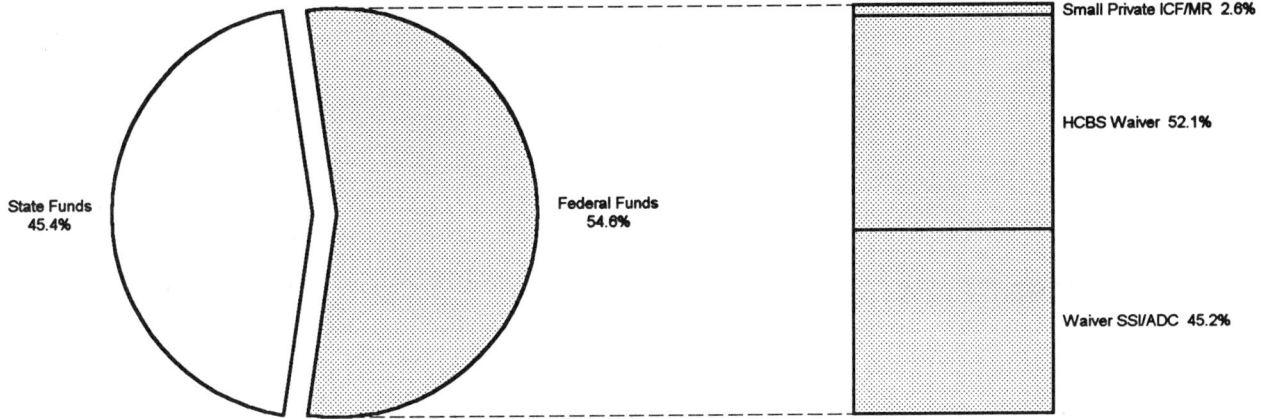

State Funds 45.4%

Federal Funds 54.6%

Small Private ICF/MR 2.6%

HCBS Waiver 52.1%

Waiver SSI/ADC 45.2%

Total Funds: $43.0 Million

## Family Support Initiatives*

|  | 1986 | 1987 | 1988 | 1989 | 1990 | 1991 | 1992 |
|---|---|---|---|---|---|---|---|
| **FAMILY SUPPORT: TOTAL SPENDING** | $0 | $240,000 | $325,000 | $365,000 | $400,000 | $430,000 | $645,000 |
| **Total # of Families Supported** | 211 | 3,210 | 3,378 | 3,786 | 3,677 | 3,722 | 3,800 |
| A. Financial Subsidy/Payment | $0 | $0 | $0 | $0 | $0 | $0 | $0 |
| # of Families | 0 | 0 | 0 | 0 | 0 | 0 | 0 |
| B. Family Assistance Payments |  | $240,000 | $250,000 | $265,000 | $300,000 | $330,000 | $350,000 |
| # of Families | 211 | 315 | 341 | 475 | 334 | 609 | 650 |
| C. Other Family Support Payments |  |  | $75,000 | $100,000 | $100,000 | $100,000 | $100,000 |
| # of Families |  | 2,895 | 3,037 | 3,311 | 3,343 | 3,113 | 3,150 |

## Other Community Services Initiatives*

|  | 1986 | 1987 | 1988 | 1989 | 1990 | 1991 | 1992 |
|---|---|---|---|---|---|---|---|
| **AGING/DD SPENDING** | $138,000 | $138,000 | $138,000 | $0 | $0 | $0 | $0 |
| # of Persons Served | 20 | 20 | 20 | 0 | 0 | 0 | 0 |
| **ASSISTIVE TECHNOLOGY SPENDING** |  |  |  |  |  |  | $0 |
| # of Persons Served |  |  |  |  |  |  | 0 |
| **EARLY INTERVENTION SPENDING** | NA | $1,198,000 | $1,870,000 | $1,500,000 | $2,000,000 | $2,250,000 | $1,750,000 |
| # of Persons Served | 195 | 202 | 198 | 148 | 237 | 267 | 152 |
| **PERSONAL ASSISTANCE SPENDING** |  |  |  |  |  |  | $0 |
| # of Persons Served |  |  |  |  |  |  | 0 |
| **SUPPORTED EMPLOYMENT SPENDING** | $0 | $82,600 | $80,000 | $150,000 | $150,000 | $225,000 | $225,000 |
| # of Persons Served | 0 | 16 | 26 | 100 | 100 | 183 | 171 |
| **SUPPORTED LIVING SPENDING** |  |  |  |  |  |  | $0 |
| # of Persons Served |  |  |  |  |  |  | 0 |

*Expenditures associated with Special Community Initiatives are a subset of funding within the community services component of the state's chart series and spreadsheet; Family Support Client figures may include duplicate client counts; HCBS Waiver counts include Waiver case management numbers.
0= Services not provided in the state; NA= Data not available from state; blank= Services not applicable (eg. CSLA prior to authorization, Special Community Initiatives prior to request for data by this study)

*Source:*
Institute on Disability and Human Development (UAP),
University of Illinois at Chicago, 1994

# ALABAMA

## Large Congregate Care Facilities: FY 1992 Revenue Sources*

### Private 16+Bed Settings

### Public Institutions

**Does Not Apply**

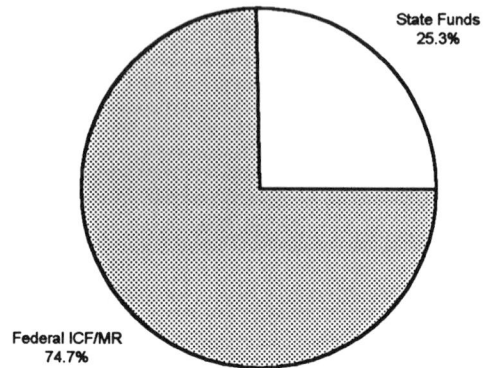

State Funds
25.3%

Federal ICF/MR
74.7%

Total Funds: $80.6 Million

**\*Excludes nursing homes**

## Average Daily Residents in Institutions

Number of Residents

2,000

1,643 1,663 1,659 1,630 1,602 1,491 1,458 1,437 1,390 1,307 1,303 1,285 1,318 1,308 1,218 1,262

1,500

1,000

500

0

77 78 79 80 81 82 83 84 85 86 87 88 89 90 91 92

Fiscal Year

## Institutional Daily Costs Per Resident

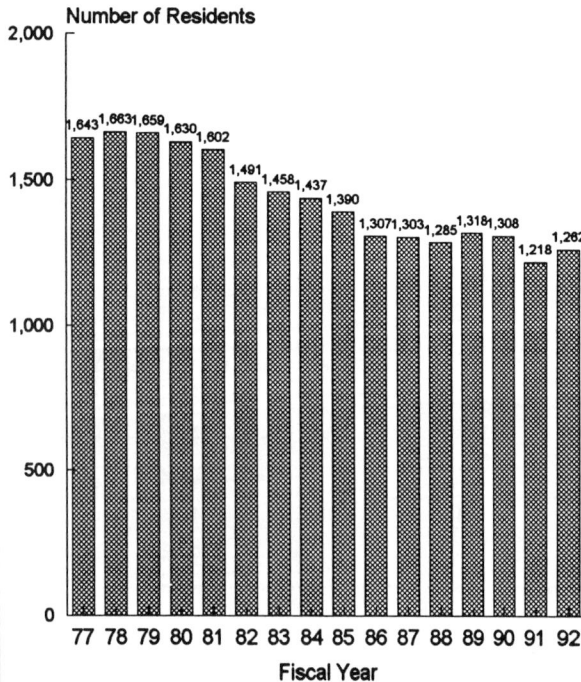

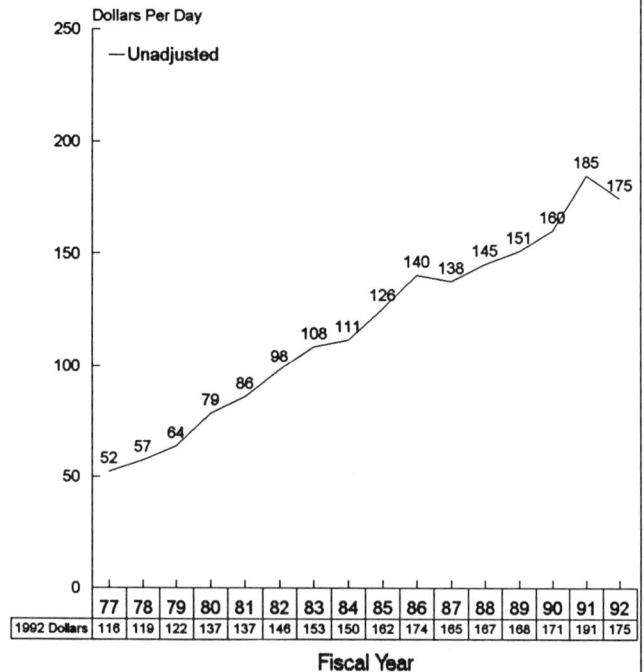

Dollars Per Day

250

— Unadjusted

200

185
175

160
151
145
140 138
126
111
108
98
86
79
64
57
52

150

100

50

0

| 1992 Dollars | 77 | 78 | 79 | 80 | 81 | 82 | 83 | 84 | 85 | 86 | 87 | 88 | 89 | 90 | 91 | 92 |
|---|---|---|---|---|---|---|---|---|---|---|---|---|---|---|---|---|
| | 116 | 119 | 122 | 137 | 137 | 146 | 153 | 150 | 162 | 174 | 165 | 167 | 168 | 171 | 191 | 175 |

Fiscal Year

*Source:*
Institute on Disability and Human Development (UAP),
University of Illinois at Chicago, 1994

# ALABAMA FISCAL EFFORT

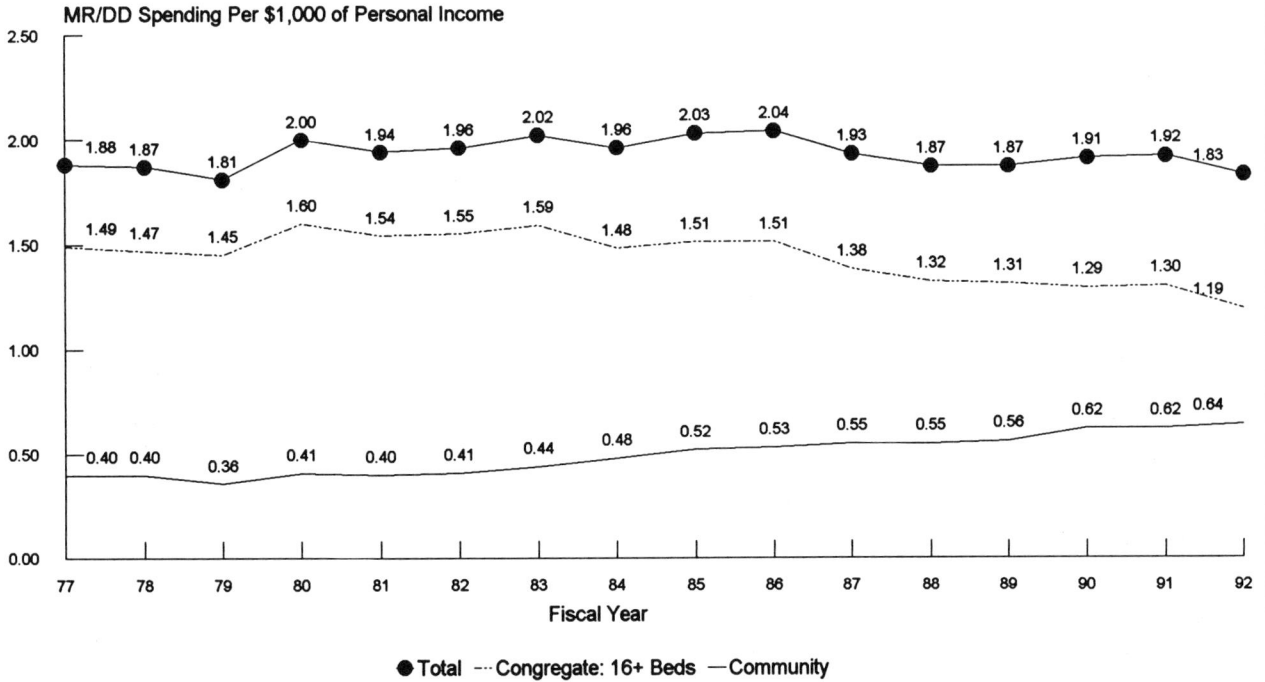

MR/DD Spending Per $1,000 of Personal Income

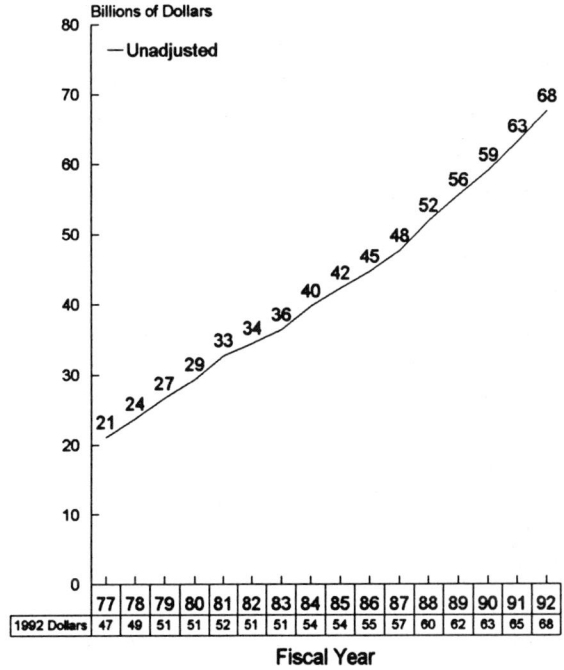

| | |
|---|---|
| 2.50 | |
| 2.00 | 1.88 1.87 1.81 2.00 1.94 1.96 2.02 1.96 2.03 2.04 1.93 1.87 1.87 1.91 1.92 1.83 |
| 1.50 | 1.49 1.47 1.45 1.60 1.54 1.55 1.59 1.48 1.51 1.51 1.38 1.32 1.31 1.29 1.30 1.19 |
| 1.00 | |
| 0.50 | 0.40 0.40 0.36 0.41 0.40 0.41 0.44 0.48 0.52 0.53 0.55 0.55 0.56 0.62 0.62 0.64 |
| 0.00 | |

77   78   79   80   81   82   83   84   85   86   87   88   89   90   91   92

Fiscal Year

● Total  --- Congregate: 16+ Beds  — Community

## Total MR/DD Spending

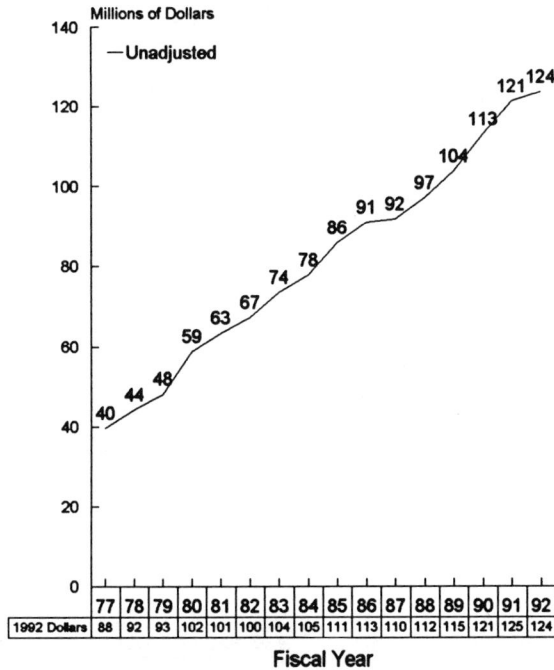

Millions of Dollars
— Unadjusted

| | |
|---|---|
| 140 | |
| 120 | 121 124 |
| 100 | 113 104 97 |
| 80 | 91 92 86 78 74 |
| 60 | 67 63 59 |
| 40 | 40 44 48 |
| 20 | |
| 0 | |

| | 77 | 78 | 79 | 80 | 81 | 82 | 83 | 84 | 85 | 86 | 87 | 88 | 89 | 90 | 91 | 92 |
|---|---|---|---|---|---|---|---|---|---|---|---|---|---|---|---|
| 1992 Dollars | 88 | 92 | 93 | 102 | 101 | 100 | 104 | 105 | 111 | 113 | 110 | 112 | 115 | 121 | 125 | 124 |

Fiscal Year

## Personal Income

Billions of Dollars
— Unadjusted

| | |
|---|---|
| 80 | |
| 70 | 68 |
| 60 | 63 59 56 |
| 50 | 52 48 45 42 |
| 40 | 40 36 |
| 30 | 33 34 29 27 |
| 20 | 21 24 |
| 10 | |
| 0 | |

| | 77 | 78 | 79 | 80 | 81 | 82 | 83 | 84 | 85 | 86 | 87 | 88 | 89 | 90 | 91 | 92 |
|---|---|---|---|---|---|---|---|---|---|---|---|---|---|---|---|
| 1992 Dollars | 47 | 49 | 51 | 51 | 52 | 51 | 51 | 54 | 54 | 55 | 57 | 60 | 62 | 63 | 65 | 68 |

Fiscal Year

*Source:*
Institute on Disability and Human Development (UAP),
University of Illinois at Chicago, 1994

# ALABAMA
## Financial Support for MR/DD Services: FY 1977-92

| | 1977 | 1978 | 1979 | 1980 | 1981 | 1982 | 1983 | 1984 |
|---|---|---|---|---|---|---|---|---|
| **TOTAL FUNDS** | $39,617,500 | $44,323,700 | $48,194,200 | $58,733,000 | $63,342,000 | $67,321,500 | $73,530,851 | $77,809,477 |
| **CONGREGATE 16+ BEDS** | 31,261,000 | 34,773,000 | 38,542,000 | 46,838,000 | 50,205,000 | 53,381,000 | 57,693,600 | 58,856,425 |
| INSTITUTIONAL SERVICES FUNDS | 31,261,000 | 34,773,000 | 38,542,000 | 46,838,000 | 50,205,000 | 53,381,000 | 57,693,600 | 58,611,500 |
| STATE FUNDS | 30,828,000 | 34,381,000 | 36,905,000 | 36,015,000 | 37,342,000 | 33,978,000 | 17,730,500 | 34,372,200 |
| General Funds | 10,970,000 | 8,874,000 | 8,473,000 | 8,388,000 | 15,895,000 | 9,563,000 | 5,380,900 | 9,899,100 |
| Local | 0 | 0 | 0 | 0 | 0 | 0 | 0 | 0 |
| Other State Funds | 19,858,000 | 25,507,000 | 28,432,000 | 27,627,000 | 21,447,000 | 24,415,000 | 12,349,600 | 24,473,100 |
| FEDERAL FUNDS | 433,000 | 392,000 | 1,637,000 | 10,823,000 | 12,863,000 | 19,403,000 | 39,963,100 | 24,239,300 |
| Federal ICF/MR | 433,000 | 392,000 | 1,637,000 | 10,823,000 | 12,863,000 | 19,403,000 | 39,772,900 | 24,081,900 |
| Title XX / SSBG Funds | 0 | 0 | 0 | 0 | 0 | 0 | 0 | 0 |
| Other Federal Funds | 0 | 0 | 0 | 0 | 0 | 0 | 190,200 | 157,400 |
| LARGE PRIVATE RESIDENTIAL | 0 | 0 | 0 | 0 | 0 | 0 | 0 | 244,925 |
| STATE FUNDS | 0 | 0 | 0 | 0 | 0 | 0 | 0 | 244,925 |
| General Funds | 0 | 0 | 0 | 0 | 0 | 0 | 0 | 244,925 |
| Other State Funds | 0 | 0 | 0 | 0 | 0 | 0 | 0 | 0 |
| Local/County Overmatch | 0 | 0 | 0 | 0 | 0 | 0 | 0 | 0 |
| FEDERAL FUNDS | 0 | 0 | 0 | 0 | 0 | 0 | 0 | 0 |
| Large Private ICF/MR | 0 | 0 | 0 | 0 | 0 | 0 | 0 | 0 |
| **COMMUNITY SERVICES FUNDS** | 8,356,500 | 9,550,700 | 9,652,200 | 11,895,000 | 13,137,000 | 13,940,500 | 15,837,251 | 18,953,052 |
| STATE FUNDS | 4,466,500 | 5,534,700 | 5,397,200 | 7,329,000 | 8,913,000 | 9,419,500 | 7,680,700 | 8,364,600 |
| General Funds | 1,143,000 | 1,076,000 | 917,000 | 1,380,000 | 3,226,000 | 2,254,000 | 2,039,000 | 2,101,400 |
| Other State Funds | 2,622,500 | 3,664,700 | 3,644,200 | 5,166,000 | 4,921,000 | 6,363,500 | 4,679,700 | 5,195,200 |
| Local/County Overmatch | 0 | 0 | 0 | 0 | 0 | 0 | 0 | 0 |
| SSI State Supplement | 701,000 | 794,000 | 836,000 | 783,000 | 766,000 | 802,000 | 962,000 | 1,068,000 |
| FEDERAL FUNDS | 3,890,000 | 4,016,000 | 4,255,000 | 4,566,000 | 4,224,000 | 4,521,000 | 8,156,551 | 10,588,452 |
| ICF/MR Funds | 0 | 0 | 0 | 0 | 0 | 0 | 0 | 0 |
| Small Public | 0 | 0 | 0 | 0 | 0 | 0 | 0 | 0 |
| Small Private | 0 | 0 | 0 | 0 | 0 | 0 | 0 | 0 |
| HCBS Waiver | 0 | 0 | 0 | 0 | 0 | 0 | 1,757,200 | 3,329,800 |
| Model 50/200 Waiver | 0 | 0 | 0 | 0 | 0 | 0 | 0 | 0 |
| Other Title XIX Programs | 0 | 0 | 0 | 0 | 0 | 0 | 0 | 0 |
| Title XX / SSBG Funds | 3,315,000 | 3,436,000 | 3,403,000 | 3,714,000 | 3,372,000 | 3,645,000 | 2,838,100 | 923,400 |
| Other Federal Funds | 575,000 | 580,000 | 852,000 | 852,000 | 852,000 | 876,000 | 1,043,200 | 911,300 |
| Waiver Clients' SSI/ADC | 0 | 0 | 0 | 0 | 0 | 0 | 2,518,051 | 5,423,952 |

| | 1985 | 1986 | 1987 | 1988 | 1989 | 1990 | 1991 | 1992 |
|---|---|---|---|---|---|---|---|---|
| **TOTAL FUNDS** | $85,882,516 | $90,915,481 | $91,849,629 | $97,028,045 | $103,753,002 | $112,940,623 | $121,211,357 | $123,671,974 |
| **CONGREGATE 16+ BEDS** | 63,976,816 | 67,234,598 | 65,663,561 | 68,556,295 | 72,637,079 | 76,440,557 | 82,155,285 | 80,633,339 |
| INSTITUTIONAL SERVICES FUNDS | 63,719,000 | 66,965,198 | 65,418,261 | 68,245,095 | 72,637,079 | 76,440,557 | 82,155,285 | 80,633,339 |
| STATE FUNDS | 22,280,000 | 31,828,003 | 29,449,832 | 32,381,740 | 30,330,580 | 22,298,797 | 16,408,357 | 20,406,985 |
| General Funds | 6,821,600 | 15,982,484 | 13,551,344 | 0 | 0 | 0 | 0 | 0 |
| Local | 0 | 0 | 0 | 0 | 0 | 0 | 0 | 0 |
| Other State Funds | 15,458,400 | 15,845,519 | 15,898,488 | 32,381,740 | 30,330,580 | 22,298,797 | 16,408,357 | 20,406,985 |
| FEDERAL FUNDS | 41,439,000 | 35,137,195 | 35,968,429 | 35,863,355 | 42,306,499 | 54,141,760 | 65,746,928 | 60,226,354 |
| Federal ICF/MR | 41,297,000 | 35,040,555 | 35,871,009 | 35,824,355 | 42,306,499 | 54,141,760 | 65,746,928 | 60,226,354 |
| Title XX / SSBG Funds | 0 | 0 | 0 | 0 | 0 | 0 | 0 | 0 |
| Other Federal Funds | 142,000 | 96,640 | 97,420 | 39,000 | 0 | 0 | 0 | 0 |
| LARGE PRIVATE RESIDENTIAL | 257,816 | 269,400 | 245,300 | 311,200 | 0 | 0 | 0 | 0 |
| STATE FUNDS | 257,816 | 269,400 | 245,300 | 311,200 | 0 | 0 | 0 | 0 |
| General Funds | 257,816 | 269,400 | 245,300 | 311,200 | 0 | 0 | 0 | 0 |
| Other State Funds | 0 | 0 | 0 | 0 | 0 | 0 | 0 | 0 |
| Local/County Overmatch | 0 | 0 | 0 | 0 | 0 | 0 | 0 | 0 |
| FEDERAL FUNDS | 0 | 0 | 0 | 0 | 0 | 0 | 0 | 0 |
| Large Private ICF/MR | 0 | 0 | 0 | 0 | 0 | 0 | 0 | 0 |
| **COMMUNITY SERVICES FUNDS** | 21,905,700 | 23,680,883 | 26,186,068 | 28,471,750 | 31,115,923 | 36,500,066 | 39,056,072 | 43,038,635 |
| STATE FUNDS | 9,193,100 | 10,642,906 | 12,853,440 | 14,687,871 | 16,238,319 | 17,011,582 | 18,460,662 | 19,547,293 |
| General Funds | 2,468,700 | 7,116,047 | 9,190,265 | 11,177,204 | 12,481,496 | 12,260,371 | 13,324,124 | 13,430,632 |
| Other State Funds | 5,594,400 | 2,346,859 | 2,513,175 | 2,406,667 | 2,597,623 | 3,534,051 | 3,858,520 | 4,774,742 |
| Local/County Overmatch | 0 | 0 | 0 | 0 | 0 | 0 | 0 | 0 |
| SSI State Supplement | 1,130,000 | 1,180,000 | 1,150,000 | 1,104,000 | 1,159,200 | 1,217,160 | 1,278,018 | 1,341,919 |
| FEDERAL FUNDS | 12,712,600 | 13,037,977 | 13,332,628 | 13,783,879 | 14,877,604 | 19,488,484 | 20,595,410 | 23,491,342 |
| ICF/MR Funds | 330,900 | 528,168 | 563,664 | 603,666 | 662,689 | 783,996 | 603,094 | 619,714 |
| Small Public | 0 | 0 | 0 | 0 | 0 | 0 | 0 | 0 |
| Small Private | 330,900 | 528,168 | 563,664 | 603,666 | 662,689 | 783,996 | 603,094 | 619,714 |
| HCBS Waiver | 5,247,700 | 5,596,814 | 6,028,635 | 6,000,032 | 6,402,666 | 9,033,197 | 9,682,375 | 12,244,044 |
| Model 50/200 Waiver | 0 | 0 | 0 | 0 | 0 | 0 | 0 | 0 |
| Other Title XIX Programs | 0 | 0 | 0 | 0 | 0 | 0 | 0 | 0 |
| Title XX / SSBG Funds | 714,500 | 900,000 | 0 | 0 | 0 | 0 | 0 | 0 |
| Other Federal Funds | 933,100 | 448,583 | 972,049 | 986,597 | 695,913 | 1,130,747 | 678,957 | 0 |
| Waiver Clients' SSI/ADC | 5,486,400 | 5,564,412 | 5,768,280 | 6,193,584 | 7,116,336 | 8,540,544 | 9,630,984 | 10,627,584 |

*Source:*
Institute on Disability and Human Development (UAP),
University of Illinois at Chicago, 1994

# ALASKA

## MR/DD Spending for Congregate Residential & Community Services

▦ Congregate: 16+ Beds*  ■ Community**

Millions of 1992 Dollars

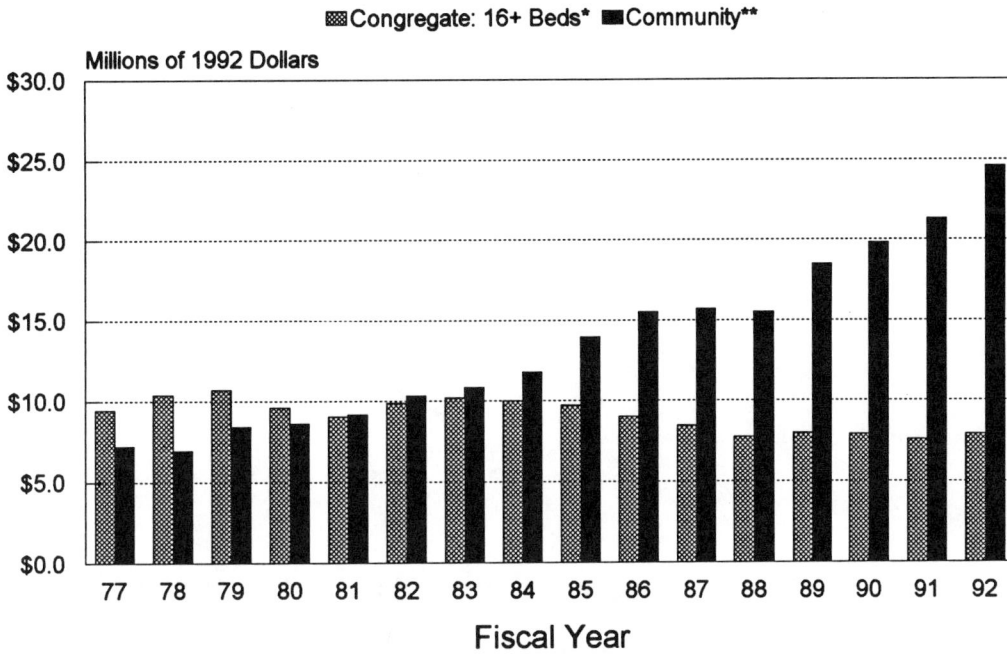

Fiscal Year

*Excludes nursing homes; ** Includes resources for
15 bed or less residential settings & non-residential community services

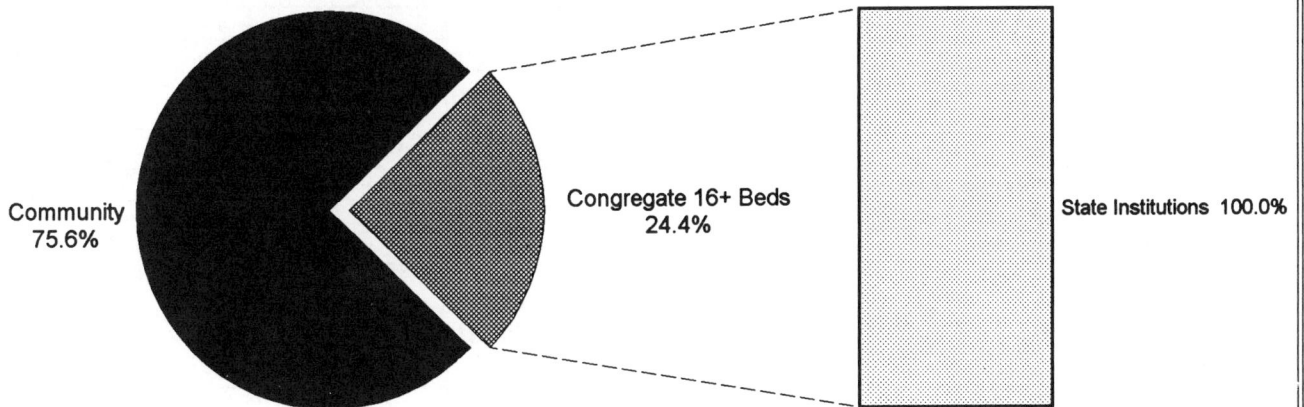

Community
75.6%

Congregate 16+ Beds
24.4%

State Institutions  100.0%

FY 1992 Total Spending:
$32.6 Million

*Source:*
Institute on Disability and Human Development (UAP),
University of Illinois at Chicago, 1994

# ALASKA

## Number of Persons Served by Residential Setting: FY 1992

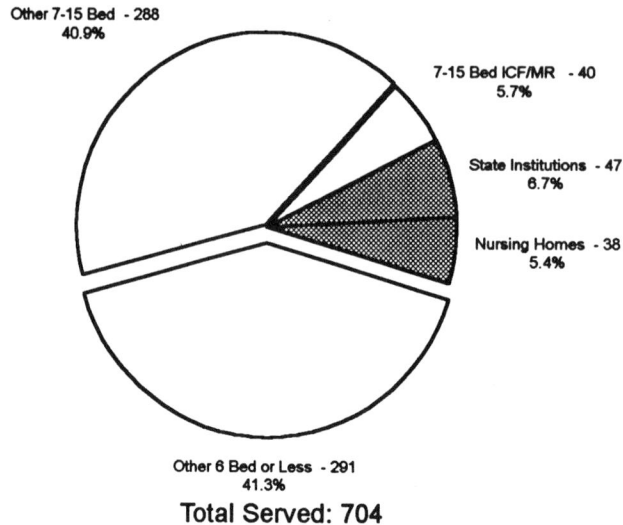

Other 7-15 Bed  - 288
40.9%

7-15 Bed ICF/MR  - 40
5.7%

State Institutions  - 47
6.7%

Nursing Homes - 38
5.4%

Other 6 Bed or Less  - 291
41.3%

Total Served: 704

## Persons Served by Residential Setting:1986-92

|  | 1986 | 1987 | 1988 | 1989 | 1990 | 1991 | 1992 |
|---|---|---|---|---|---|---|---|
| CONGREGATE 16 + BED SETTINGS | 60 | 61 | 102 | 105 | 105 | 95 | 85 |
| Nursing Homes | NA | NA | 41 | 48 | 48 | 42 | 38 |
| State Institutions | 60 | 61 | 61 | 57 | 57 | 53 | 47 |
| Private 16+Bed ICF/MR | 0 | 0 | 0 | 0 | 0 | 0 | 0 |
| Other 16+Bed Residential | 0 | 0 | 0 | 0 | 0 | 0 | 0 |
| 15 BED OR LESS RESIDENTIAL SETTINGS | 247 | 264 | 308 | 315 | 321 | 619 | 619 |
| Public 7-15 Bed ICF/MR | 0 | 0 | 0 | 0 | 0 | 0 | 0 |
| Private 7-15 Bed ICF/MR | 40 | 40 | 40 | 40 | 40 | 40 | 40 |
| Other 7-15 Bed Residential | 207 | 224 | 268 | 275 | 281 | 288 | 288 |
| Public 6 Bed or Less ICF/MR | 0 | 0 | 0 | 0 | 0 | 0 | 0 |
| Private 6 Bed or Less ICF/MR | 0 | 0 | 0 | 0 | 0 | 0 | 0 |
| Other 6 Bed or Less Residential | NA | NA | NA | NA | NA | 291 | 291 |
| TOTAL PERSONS SERVED | 307 | 325 | 410 | 420 | 426 | 714 | 704 |

## Persons Served in Non-Residential Community Services:1986-92

|  | 1986 | 1987 | 1988 | 1989 | 1990 | 1991 | 1992 |
|---|---|---|---|---|---|---|---|
| DAY/WORK PROGRAMS | 190 | 239 | NA | NA | NA | NA | NA |
| Sheltered Employment/Work Activity | 190 | 197 | NA | NA | NA | NA | NA |
| Day Habilitation ("Day Training") | 0 | 0 | NA | NA | NA | NA | NA |
| Supported/Competitive Employment | 0 | 42 | 127 | NA | NA | NA | NA |
| CASE MANAGEMENT | NA | NA | NA | NA | NA | NA | NA |
| HCBS WAIVER | 0 | 0 | 0 | 0 | 0 | 0 | 0 |
| MODEL 50/200 WAIVER | 0 | 0 | 0 | 0 | 0 | 0 | 0 |

Source:
Institute on Disability and Human Development (UAP),
University of Illinois at Chicago, 1994

# ALASKA

## Community Services: FY 1992 Revenue Sources

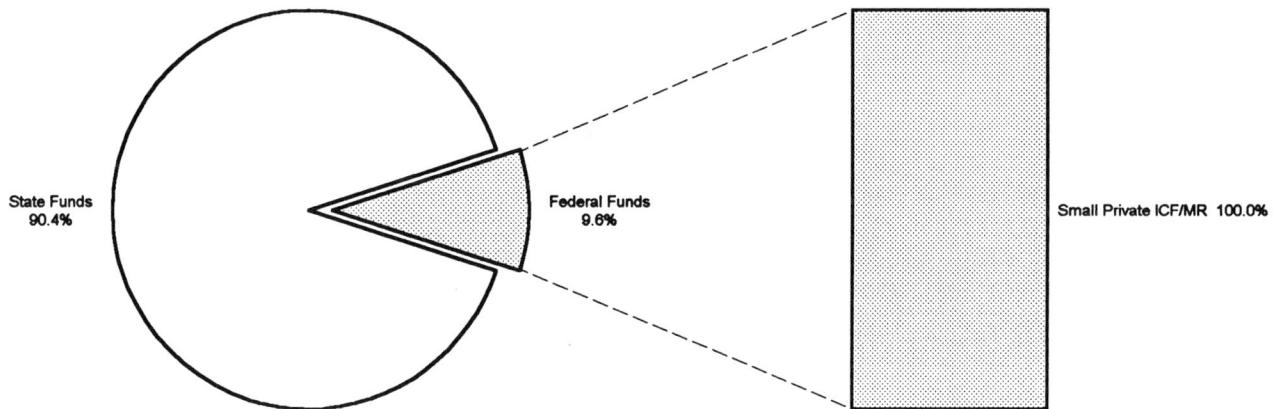

State Funds
90.4%

Federal Funds
9.6%

Small Private ICF/MR  100.0%

Total Funds: $24.6 Million

## Family Support Initiatives*

|  | 1986 | 1987 | 1988 | 1989 | 1990 | 1991 | 1992 |
|---|---|---|---|---|---|---|---|
| **FAMILY SUPPORT: TOTAL SPENDING** | $0 | $0 | $718,900 | $1,094,813 | $1,330,944 | $1,403,638 | $2,051,542 |
| **Total # of Families Supported** | 0 | 0 | 436 | 469 | 513 | 681 | 785 |
| A. Financial Subsidy/Payment | $0 | $0 | $0 | $0 | $0 | $0 | $0 |
| # of Families | 0 | 0 | 0 | 0 | 0 | 0 | 0 |
| B. Family Assistance Payments | NA | NA | $718,900 | $1,094,813 | $1,330,944 | $1,403,638 | $2,051,542 |
| # of Families | NA | NA | 436 | 469 | 513 | 681 | 785 |
| C. Other Family Support Payments | $0 | $0 | $0 | $0 | $0 | $0 | $0 |
| # of Families | 0 | 0 | 0 | 0 | 0 | 0 | 0 |

## Other Community Services Initiatives*

|  | 1986 | 1987 | 1988 | 1989 | 1990 | 1991 | 1992 |
|---|---|---|---|---|---|---|---|
| **AGING/DD SPENDING** | $0 | $0 | $0 | $0 | $0 | $0 | $0 |
| # of Persons Served | 0 | 0 | 0 | 0 | 0 | 0 | 0 |
| **ASSISTIVE TECHNOLOGY SPENDING** |  |  |  |  |  |  | $0 |
| # of Persons Served |  |  |  |  |  |  | 0 |
| **EARLY INTERVENTION SPENDING** | $0 | $0 | $0 | $0 | $0 | $0 | $0 |
| # of Persons Served | 0 | 0 | 0 | 0 | 0 | 0 | 0 |
| **PERSONAL ASSISTANCE SPENDING** |  |  |  |  |  |  | $0 |
| # of Persons Served |  |  |  |  |  |  | 0 |
| **SUPPORTED EMPLOYMENT SPENDING** | $0 | $250,000 | $762,300 | NA | NA | NA | NA |
| # of Persons Served | 0 | 42 | 127 | NA | NA | NA | NA |
| **SUPPORTED LIVING SPENDING** |  |  |  |  |  |  | $0 |
| # of Persons Served |  |  |  |  |  |  | 0 |

*Expenditures associated with Special Community Initiatives are a subset of funding within the community services component of the state's chart series and spreadsheet; Family Support Client figures may include duplicate client counts; HCBS Waiver counts include Waiver case management numbers.
0= Services not provided in the state; NA= Data not available from state; blank= Services not applicable (eg. CSLA prior to authorization, Special Community Initiatives prior to request for data by this study)

*Source:*
Institute on Disability and Human Development (UAP),
University of Illinois at Chicago, 1994

# ALASKA

## Large Congregate Care Facilities: FY 1992 Revenue Sources*

### Private 16+Bed Settings

### Does Not Apply

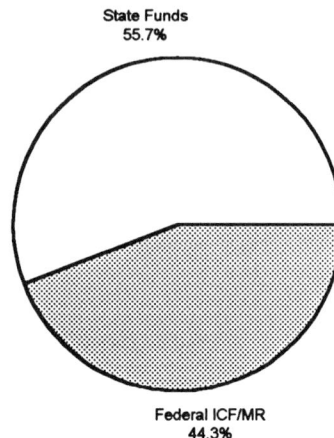

### Public Institutions

State Funds
55.7%

Federal ICF/MR
44.3%

Total Funds: $7.9 Million

*Excludes nursing homes

## Average Daily Residents in Institutions

Number of Residents

| Fiscal Year | Residents |
|---|---|
| 77 | 100 |
| 78 | 104 |
| 79 | 91 |
| 80 | 92 |
| 81 | 89 |
| 82 | 88 |
| 83 | 85 |
| 84 | 75 |
| 85 | 72 |
| 86 | 60 |
| 87 | 61 |
| 88 | 61 |
| 89 | 57 |
| 90 | 57 |
| 91 | 53 |
| 92 | 47 |

Fiscal Year

## Institutional Daily Costs Per Resident

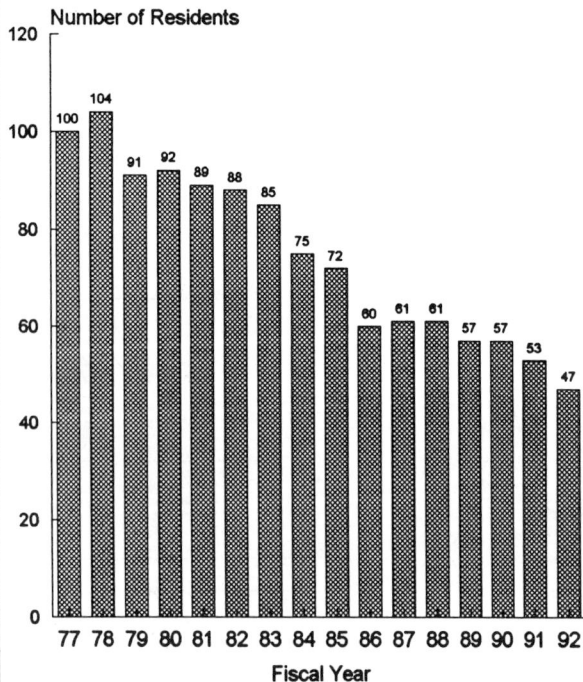

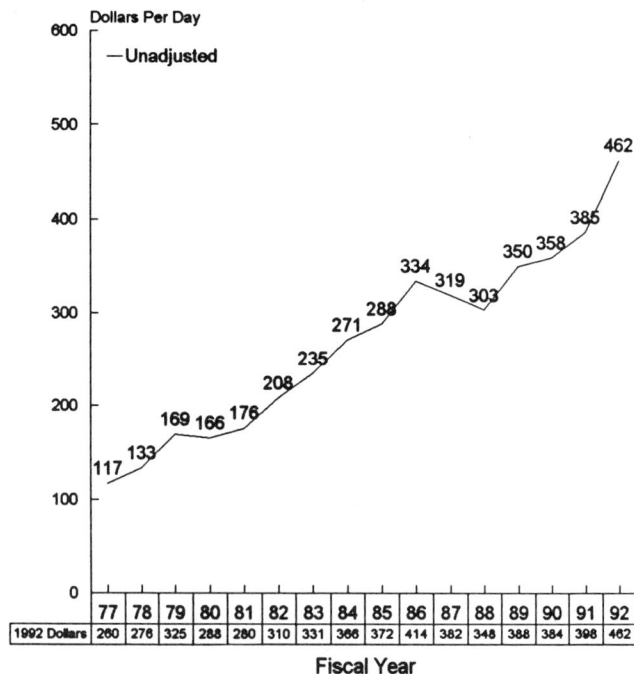

Dollars Per Day

— Unadjusted

117  133  169  166  176  208  235  271  288  334  319  303  350  358  385  462

| | 77 | 78 | 79 | 80 | 81 | 82 | 83 | 84 | 85 | 86 | 87 | 88 | 89 | 90 | 91 | 92 |
|---|---|---|---|---|---|---|---|---|---|---|---|---|---|---|---|---|
| 1992 Dollars | 260 | 276 | 325 | 288 | 280 | 310 | 331 | 366 | 372 | 414 | 382 | 348 | 388 | 384 | 398 | 462 |

Fiscal Year

*Source:*
Institute on Disability and Human Development (UAP),
University of Illinois at Chicago, 1994

# ALASKA FISCAL EFFORT

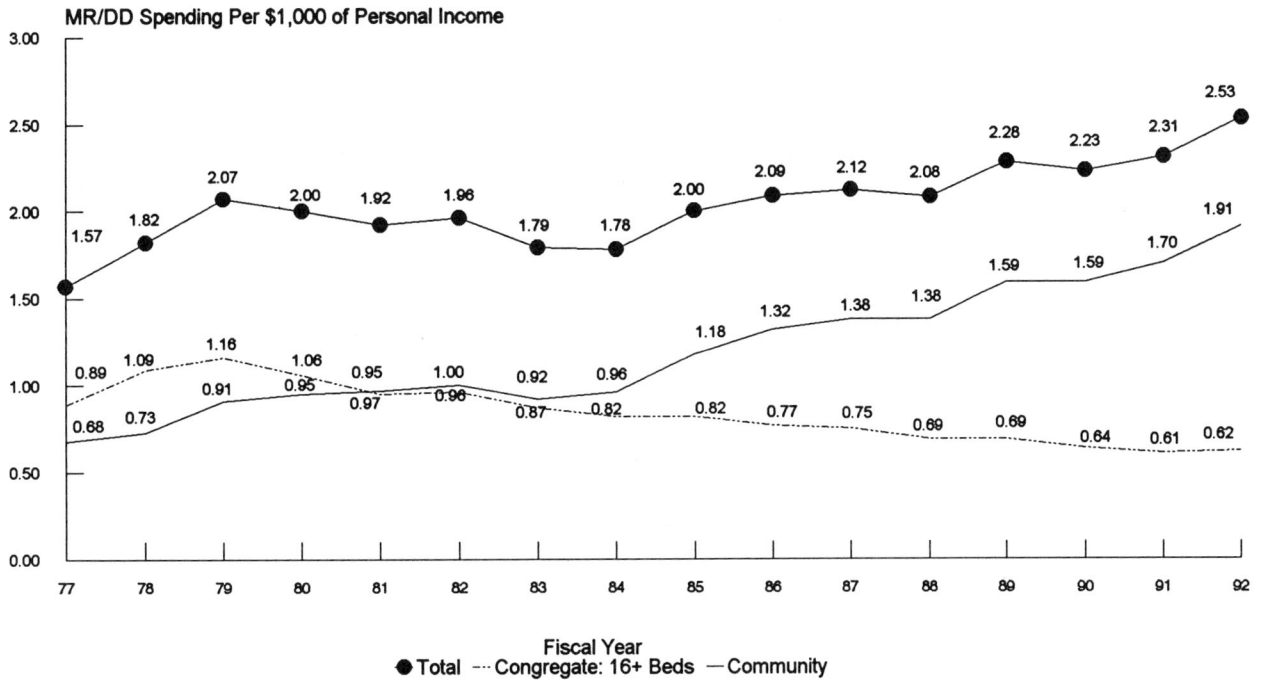

MR/DD Spending Per $1,000 of Personal Income

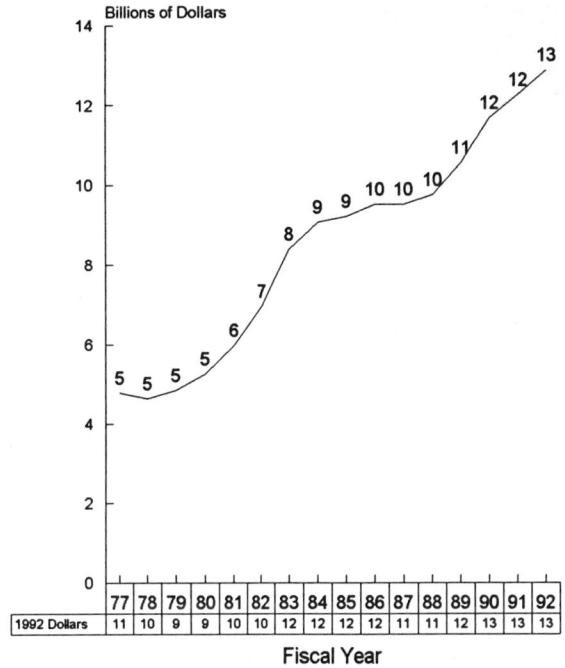

| | |
|---|---|
| 3.00 | |

Fiscal Year

● Total   --- Congregate: 16+ Beds   — Community

Total values (Total line): 1.57, 1.82, 2.07, 2.00, 1.92, 1.96, 1.79, 1.78, 2.00, 2.09, 2.12, 2.08, 2.28, 2.23, 2.31, 2.53

Congregate: 16+ Beds: 0.89, 1.09, 1.16, 1.06, 0.95, 1.00, 0.92, 0.96, 0.82, 0.77, 0.75, 0.69, 0.69, 0.64, 0.61, 0.62

Community: 0.68, 0.73, 0.91, 0.95, 0.97, 0.96, 0.87, 0.82, 1.18, 1.32, 1.38, 1.38, 1.59, 1.59, 1.70, 1.91

## Total MR/DD Spending

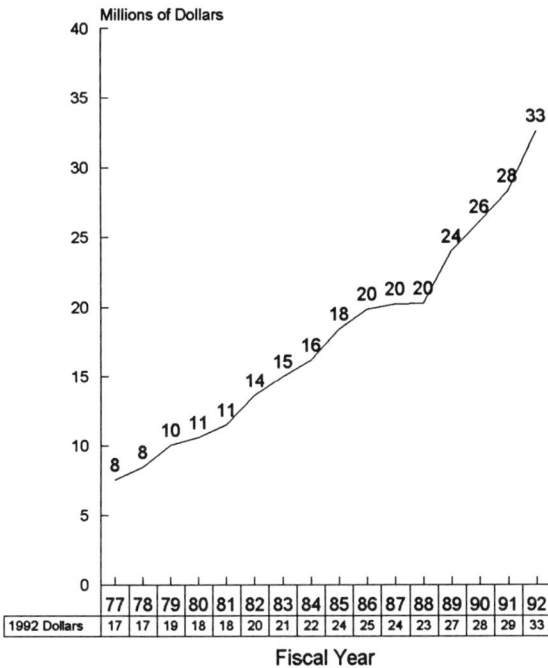

Millions of Dollars

Values: 8, 8, 10, 11, 11, 14, 15, 16, 18, 20, 20, 20, 24, 26, 28, 33

| | 77 | 78 | 79 | 80 | 81 | 82 | 83 | 84 | 85 | 86 | 87 | 88 | 89 | 90 | 91 | 92 |
|---|---|---|---|---|---|---|---|---|---|---|---|---|---|---|---|---|
| 1992 Dollars | 17 | 17 | 19 | 18 | 18 | 20 | 21 | 22 | 24 | 25 | 24 | 23 | 27 | 28 | 29 | 33 |

Fiscal Year

## Personal Income

Billions of Dollars

Values: 5, 5, 5, 5, 6, 7, 8, 9, 9, 10, 10, 10, 11, 12, 12, 13

| | 77 | 78 | 79 | 80 | 81 | 82 | 83 | 84 | 85 | 86 | 87 | 88 | 89 | 90 | 91 | 92 |
|---|---|---|---|---|---|---|---|---|---|---|---|---|---|---|---|---|
| 1992 Dollars | 11 | 10 | 9 | 9 | 10 | 10 | 12 | 12 | 12 | 12 | 11 | 11 | 12 | 13 | 13 | 13 |

Fiscal Year

*Source:*
Institute on Disability and Human Development (UAP),
University of Illinois at Chicago, 1994

# ALASKA
## Financial Support for MR/DD Services: FY 1977-92

| | 1977 | 1978 | 1979 | 1980 | 1981 | 1982 | 1983 | 1984 |
|---|---|---|---|---|---|---|---|---|
| **TOTAL FUNDS** | $7,539,000 | $8,432,000 | $10,048,000 | $10,572,000 | $11,498,000 | $13,642,000 | $15,012,000 | $16,187,100 |
| **CONGREGATE 16+ BEDS** | 4,263,000 | 5,054,000 | 5,618,000 | 5,573,000 | 5,711,000 | 6,681,000 | 7,285,000 | 7,442,600 |
| INSTITUTIONAL SERVICES FUNDS | 4,263,000 | 5,054,000 | 5,618,000 | 5,573,000 | 5,711,000 | 6,681,000 | 7,285,000 | 7,442,600 |
| STATE FUNDS | 2,216,700 | 2,628,100 | 2,921,300 | 2,897,900 | 2,969,700 | 3,474,100 | 3,788,200 | 5,222,200 |
| General Funds | 2,216,700 | 2,628,100 | 2,921,300 | 2,897,900 | 2,969,700 | 3,474,100 | 3,788,200 | 2,712,700 |
| Local | 0 | 0 | 0 | 0 | 0 | 0 | 0 | 0 |
| Other State Funds | 0 | 0 | 0 | 0 | 0 | 0 | 0 | 2,509,500 |
| FEDERAL FUNDS | 2,046,300 | 2,425,900 | 2,696,700 | 2,675,100 | 2,741,300 | 3,206,900 | 3,496,800 | 2,220,400 |
| Federal ICF/MR | 2,046,300 | 2,425,900 | 2,696,700 | 2,675,100 | 2,741,300 | 3,206,900 | 3,496,800 | 2,220,400 |
| Title XX / SSBG Funds | 0 | 0 | 0 | 0 | 0 | 0 | 0 | 0 |
| Other Federal Funds | 0 | 0 | 0 | 0 | 0 | 0 | 0 | 0 |
| LARGE PRIVATE RESIDENTIAL | 0 | 0 | 0 | 0 | 0 | 0 | 0 | 0 |
| STATE FUNDS | 0 | 0 | 0 | 0 | 0 | 0 | 0 | 0 |
| General Funds | 0 | 0 | 0 | 0 | 0 | 0 | 0 | 0 |
| Other State Funds | 0 | 0 | 0 | 0 | 0 | 0 | 0 | 0 |
| Local/County Overmatch | 0 | 0 | 0 | 0 | 0 | 0 | 0 | 0 |
| FEDERAL FUNDS | 0 | 0 | 0 | 0 | 0 | 0 | 0 | 0 |
| Large Private ICF/MR | 0 | 0 | 0 | 0 | 0 | 0 | 0 | 0 |
| **COMMUNITY SERVICES FUNDS** | 3,276,000 | 3,378,000 | 4,430,000 | 4,999,000 | 5,787,000 | 6,961,000 | 7,727,000 | 8,744,500 |
| STATE FUNDS | 2,770,000 | 2,783,000 | 3,747,000 | 4,163,000 | 4,916,000 | 5,938,000 | 6,706,000 | 7,399,900 |
| General Funds | 2,374,000 | 2,340,000 | 3,329,000 | 3,959,000 | 4,754,000 | 5,661,000 | 5,712,000 | 6,057,900 |
| Other State Funds | 0 | 0 | 0 | 0 | 0 | 0 | 0 | 0 |
| Local/County Overmatch | 0 | 0 | 0 | 0 | 0 | 0 | 0 | 0 |
| SSI State Supplement | 396,000 | 443,000 | 418,000 | 204,000 | 162,000 | 277,000 | 994,000 | 1,342,000 |
| FEDERAL FUNDS | 506,000 | 595,000 | 683,000 | 836,000 | 871,000 | 1,023,000 | 1,021,000 | 1,344,600 |
| ICF/MR Funds | 506,000 | 595,000 | 683,000 | 836,000 | 871,000 | 1,023,000 | 1,021,000 | 1,344,600 |
| Small Public | 0 | 0 | 0 | 0 | 0 | 0 | 0 | 0 |
| Small Private | 506,000 | 595,000 | 683,000 | 836,000 | 871,000 | 1,023,000 | 1,021,000 | 1,344,600 |
| HCBS Waiver | 0 | 0 | 0 | 0 | 0 | 0 | 0 | 0 |
| Model 50/200 Waiver | 0 | 0 | 0 | 0 | 0 | 0 | 0 | 0 |
| Other Title XIX Programs | 0 | 0 | 0 | 0 | 0 | 0 | 0 | 0 |
| Title XX / SSBG Funds | 0 | 0 | 0 | 0 | 0 | 0 | 0 | 0 |
| Other Federal Funds | 0 | 0 | 0 | 0 | 0 | 0 | 0 | 0 |
| Waiver Clients' SSI/ADC | 0 | 0 | 0 | 0 | 0 | 0 | 0 | 0 |

| | 1985 | 1986 | 1987 | 1988 | 1989 | 1990 | 1991 | 1992 |
|---|---|---|---|---|---|---|---|---|
| **TOTAL FUNDS** | $18,430,400 | $19,868,880 | $20,211,000 | $20,266,200 | $24,025,824 | $26,091,548 | $28,301,516 | $32,567,323 |
| **CONGREGATE 16+ BEDS** | 7,572,000 | 7,311,480 | 7,095,000 | 6,760,700 | 7,277,200 | 7,455,800 | 7,455,800 | 7,946,000 |
| INSTITUTIONAL SERVICES FUNDS | 7,572,000 | 7,311,480 | 7,095,000 | 6,760,700 | 7,277,200 | 7,455,800 | 7,455,800 | 7,946,000 |
| STATE FUNDS | 5,351,600 | 5,081,080 | 4,148,500 | 3,814,200 | 4,151,400 | 4,151,400 | 4,151,400 | 4,425,500 |
| General Funds | 2,832,100 | 2,561,500 | 862,300 | 689,400 | 661,200 | 573,100 | 0 | 0 |
| Local | 0 | 0 | 0 | 0 | 0 | 0 | 0 | 0 |
| Other State Funds | 2,519,500 | 2,519,580 | 3,286,200 | 3,124,800 | 3,490,200 | 3,578,300 | 4,151,400 | 4,425,500 |
| FEDERAL FUNDS | 2,220,400 | 2,230,400 | 2,946,500 | 2,946,500 | 3,125,800 | 3,304,400 | 3,304,400 | 3,520,500 |
| Federal ICF/MR | 2,220,400 | 2,230,400 | 2,946,500 | 2,946,500 | 3,125,800 | 3,304,400 | 3,304,400 | 3,520,500 |
| Title XX / SSBG Funds | 0 | 0 | 0 | 0 | 0 | 0 | 0 | 0 |
| Other Federal Funds | 0 | 0 | 0 | 0 | 0 | 0 | 0 | 0 |
| LARGE PRIVATE RESIDENTIAL | 0 | 0 | 0 | 0 | 0 | 0 | 0 | 0 |
| STATE FUNDS | 0 | 0 | 0 | 0 | 0 | 0 | 0 | 0 |
| General Funds | 0 | 0 | 0 | 0 | 0 | 0 | 0 | 0 |
| Other State Funds | 0 | 0 | 0 | 0 | 0 | 0 | 0 | 0 |
| Local/County Overmatch | 0 | 0 | 0 | 0 | 0 | 0 | 0 | 0 |
| FEDERAL FUNDS | 0 | 0 | 0 | 0 | 0 | 0 | 0 | 0 |
| Large Private ICF/MR | 0 | 0 | 0 | 0 | 0 | 0 | 0 | 0 |
| **COMMUNITY SERVICES FUNDS** | 10,858,400 | 12,557,400 | 13,116,000 | 13,505,500 | 16,748,624 | 18,635,748 | 20,845,716 | 24,621,323 |
| STATE FUNDS | 9,776,100 | 11,226,200 | 11,219,900 | 11,596,500 | 14,620,743 | 16,459,086 | 18,625,222 | 22,246,854 |
| General Funds | 8,357,100 | 9,814,200 | 9,263,900 | 9,407,900 | 12,322,713 | 14,046,154 | 16,091,644 | 19,586,597 |
| Other State Funds | 0 | 0 | 0 | 0 | 0 | 0 | 0 | 0 |
| Local/County Overmatch | 0 | 0 | 0 | 0 | 0 | 0 | 0 | 0 |
| SSI State Supplement | 1,419,000 | 1,412,000 | 1,956,000 | 2,188,600 | 2,298,030 | 2,412,932 | 2,533,578 | 2,660,257 |
| FEDERAL FUNDS | 1,082,300 | 1,331,200 | 1,896,100 | 1,909,000 | 2,127,881 | 2,176,662 | 2,220,494 | 2,374,469 |
| ICF/MR Funds | 1,082,300 | 1,331,200 | 1,896,100 | 1,909,000 | 2,127,881 | 2,176,662 | 2,220,494 | 2,374,469 |
| Small Public | 0 | 0 | 0 | 0 | 0 | 0 | 0 | 0 |
| Small Private | 1,082,300 | 1,331,200 | 1,896,100 | 1,909,000 | 2,127,881 | 2,176,662 | 2,220,494 | 2,374,469 |
| HCBS Waiver | 0 | 0 | 0 | 0 | 0 | 0 | 0 | 0 |
| Model 50/200 Waiver | 0 | 0 | 0 | 0 | 0 | 0 | 0 | 0 |
| Other Title XIX Programs | 0 | 0 | 0 | 0 | 0 | 0 | 0 | 0 |
| Title XX / SSBG Funds | 0 | 0 | 0 | 0 | 0 | 0 | 0 | 0 |
| Other Federal Funds | 0 | 0 | 0 | 0 | 0 | 0 | 0 | 0 |
| Waiver Clients' SSI/ADC | 0 | 0 | 0 | 0 | 0 | 0 | 0 | 0 |

Source:
Institute on Disability and Human Development (UAP),
University of Illinois at Chicago, 1994

# ARIZONA

## MR/DD Spending for Congregate Residential & Community Services

▨Congregate: 16+ Beds*  ■Community**

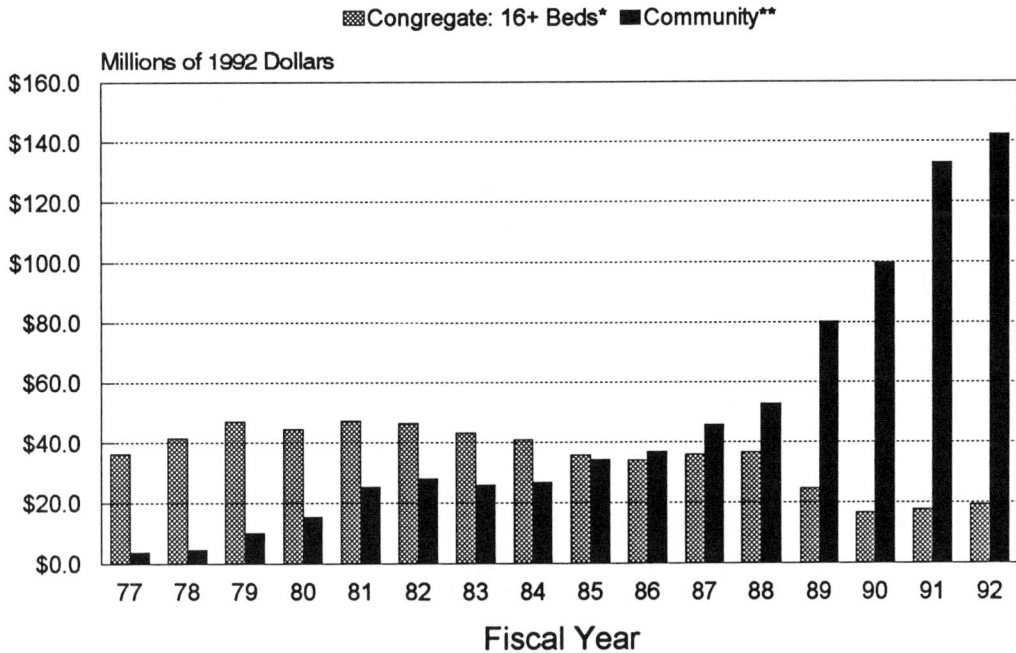

Millions of 1992 Dollars

Fiscal Year

*Excludes nursing homes; ** Includes resources for
15 bed or less residential settings & non-residential community services

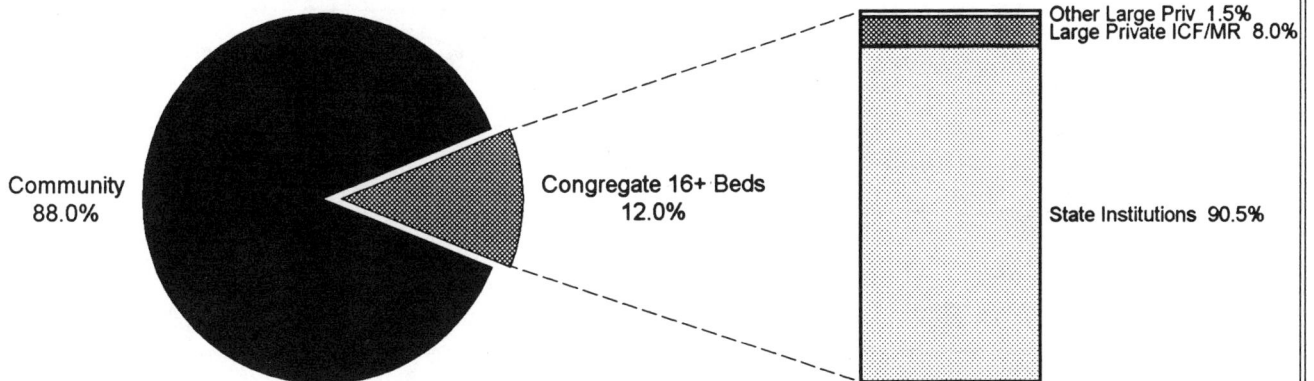

Other Large Priv  1.5%
Large Private ICF/MR  8.0%

Community
88.0%

Congregate 16+ Beds
12.0%

State Institutions  90.5%

FY 1992 Total Spending:
$161.9 Million

*Source:*
Institute on Disability and Human Development (UAP),
University of Illinois at Chicago, 1994

# ARIZONA

## Number of Persons Served by Residential Setting: FY 1992

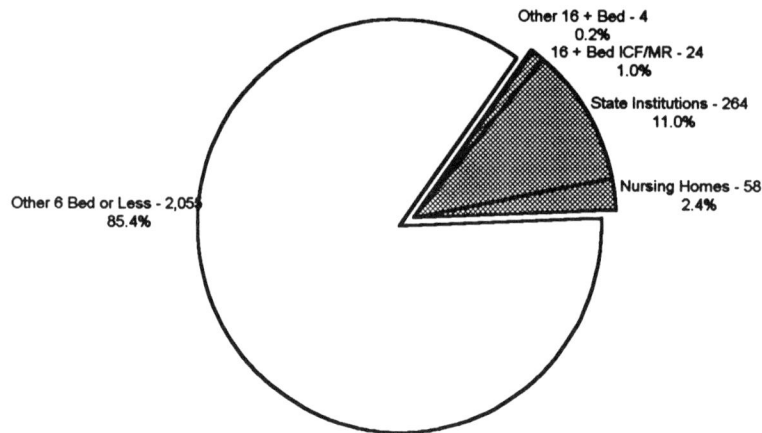

Other 16 + Bed - 4
0.2%
16 + Bed ICF/MR - 24
1.0%
State Institutions - 264
11.0%

Nursing Homes - 58
2.4%

Other 6 Bed or Less - 2,055
85.4%

Total Served: 2,405

## Persons Served by Residential Setting:1986-92

|  | 1986 | 1987 | 1988 | 1989 | 1990 | 1991 | 1992 |
|---|---|---|---|---|---|---|---|
| CONGREGATE 16 + BED SETTINGS | NA | NA | 688 | NA | 412 | 353 | 350 |
| Nursing Homes* | NA | NA | 300 | NA | 48 | 47 | 58 |
| State Institutions | 423 | 400 | 388 | 361 | 333 | 277 | 264 |
| Private 16+Bed ICF/MR | 0 | 0 | 0 | 0 | 16 | 20 | 24 |
| Other 16+Bed Residential | 0 | 0 | 0 | 0 | 15 | 9 | 4 |
| 15 BED OR LESS RESIDENTIAL SETTINGS | 1,334 | 1,495 | 1,548 | 1,464 | 1,379 | 1,878 | 2,055 |
| Public 7-15 Bed ICF/MR | 0 | 0 | 0 | 0 | 0 | 0 | 0 |
| Private 7-15 Bed ICF/MR | 0 | 0 | 0 | 0 | 0 | 0 | 0 |
| Other 7-15 Bed Residential | 1,334 | 1,495 | 0 |  | 0 | 0 | 0 |
| Public 6 Bed or Less ICF/MR | 0 | 0 | 0 | 0 | 0 | 0 | 0 |
| Private 6 Bed or Less ICF/MR | 0 | 0 | 0 | 0 | 0 | 0 | 0 |
| Other 6 Bed or Less Residential |  |  | 1,548 | 1,464 | 1,379 | 1,878 | 2,055 |
| TOTAL PERSONS SERVED | NA | NA | 2,236 | NA | 1,791 | 2,231 | 2,405 |

## Persons Served in Non-Residential Community Services:1986-92

|  | 1986 | 1987 | 1988 | 1989 | 1990 | 1991 | 1992 |
|---|---|---|---|---|---|---|---|
| DAY/WORK PROGRAMS | 1,729 | 1,252 | 1,280 | NA | NA | NA | NA |
| Sheltered Employment/Work Activity | 995 | 792 | 820 | NA | NA | NA | NA |
| Day Habilitation ("Day Training") | 608 | 334 | 334 | NA | 1,300 | 1,179 | 1,353 |
| Supported/Competitive Employment | 126 | 126 | 126 | NA | 1,399 | 1,600 | 1,600 |
| CASE MANAGEMENT | 42 | 42 | 42 | NA | 10,610 | 11,917 | 12,835 |
| HCBS WAIVER | 0 | 0 | 0 | 464 | 2,220 | 3,706 | 4,494 |
| MODEL 50/200 WAIVER | 0 | 0 | 0 | 0 | 0 | 0 | 0 |

*Source:*
Institute on Disability and Human Development (UAP),
University of Illinois at Chicago, 1994

# ARIZONA

## Community Services: FY 1992 Revenue Sources

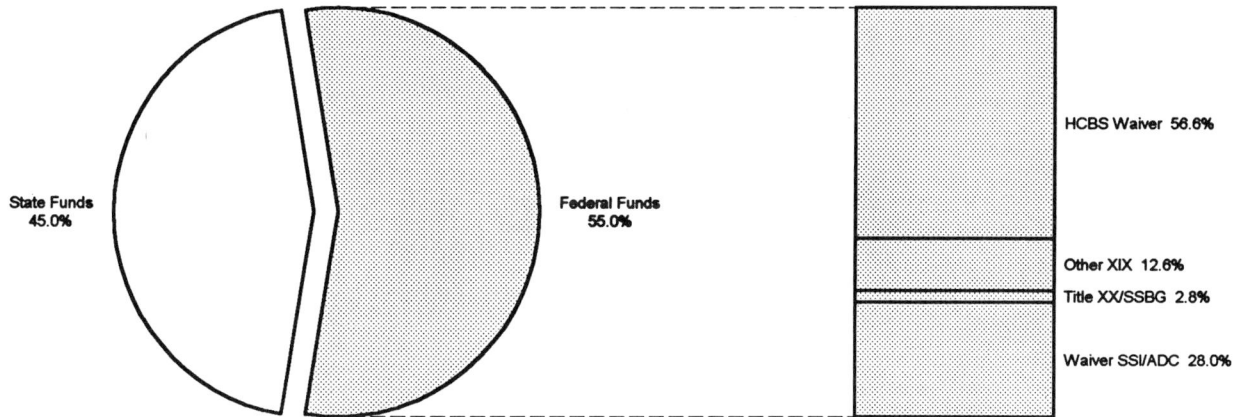

State Funds
45.0%

Federal Funds
55.0%

HCBS Waiver 56.6%

Other XIX 12.6%

Title XX/SSBG 2.8%

Waiver SSI/ADC 28.0%

Total Funds: $142.5 Million

## Family Support Initiatives*

| | 1986 | 1987 | 1988 | 1989 | 1990 | 1991 | 1992 |
|---|---|---|---|---|---|---|---|
| FAMILY SUPPORT: TOTAL SPENDING | $237,100 | $2,634,500 | $3,975,900 | $0 | $2,014,177 | $1,974,013 | $1,040,102 |
| Total # of Families Supported | 674 | 1,409 | 1,781 | 0 | 2,311 | 2,686 | 1,245 |
| A. Financial Subsidy/Payment | $0 | $0 | $0 | $0 | $0 | $0 | $0 |
| # of Families | 0 | 0 | 0 | 0 | 0 | 0 | 0 |
| B. Family Assistance Payments | $237,100 | $210,000 | $227,600 | NA | $2,014,177 | $1,974,013 | $1,040,102 |
| # of Families | 674 | 744 | 754 | NA | 2,311 | 2,686 | 1,245 |
| C. Other Family Support Payments | NA | $2,424,500 | $3,748,300 | NA | $0 | $0 | $0 |
| # of Families | NA | 665 | 1,027 | NA | 0 | 0 | 0 |

## Other Community Services Initiatives*

| | 1986 | 1987 | 1988 | 1989 | 1990 | 1991 | 1992 |
|---|---|---|---|---|---|---|---|
| AGING/DD SPENDING | $0 | $0 | $0 | $0 | $0 | $0 | $0 |
| # of Persons Served | 0 | 0 | 0 | 0 | 0 | 0 | 0 |
| ASSISTIVE TECHNOLOGY SPENDING | | | | | | | $0 |
| # of Persons Served | | | | | | | 0 |
| EARLY INTERVENTION SPENDING | $0 | $0 | $0 | NA | $1,151,300 | $2,011,957 | $1,939,255 |
| # of Persons Served | 0 | 0 | 0 | NA | 881 | 1,210 | 1,135 |
| PERSONAL ASSISTANCE SPENDING | | | | | | | $0 |
| # of Persons Served | | | | | | | 0 |
| SUPPORTED EMPLOYMENT SPENDING | $0 | $0 | $194,400 | NA | $5,820,271 | $6,000,000 | $6,000,000 |
| # of Persons Served | 0 | 0 | 56 | NA | 1,399 | 1,600 | 1,600 |
| SUPPORTED LIVING SPENDING | | | | | | | $466,459 |
| # of Persons Served | | | | | | | 62 |

*Expenditures associated with Special Community Initiatives are a subset of funding within the community services component of the state's chart series and spreadsheet; Family Support Client figures may include duplicate client counts; HCBS Waiver counts include Waiver case management numbers.
0= Services not provided in the state; NA= Data not available from state; blank= Services not applicable (eg. CSLA prior to authorization, Special Community Initiatives prior to request for data by this study)

Source:
Institute on Disability and Human Development (UAP),
University of Illinois at Chicago, 1994

# ARIZONA

## Large Congregate Care Facilities: FY 1992 Revenue Sources*

### Private 16+Bed Settings

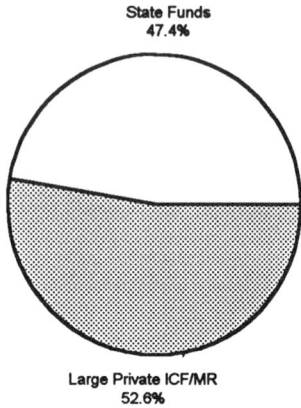

State Funds
47.4%

Large Private ICF/MR
52.6%

Total Funds: $1.8 Million

### Public Institutions

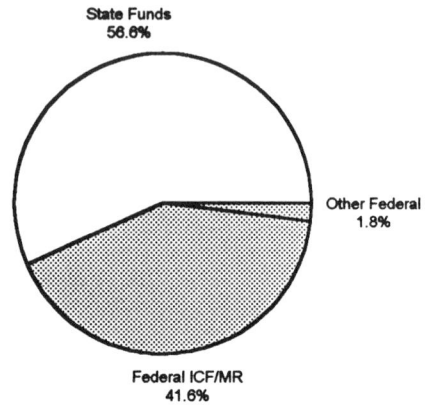

State Funds
56.6%

Other Federal
1.8%

Federal ICF/MR
41.6%

Total Funds: $17.5 Million

*Excludes nursing homes

## Average Daily Residents in Institutions

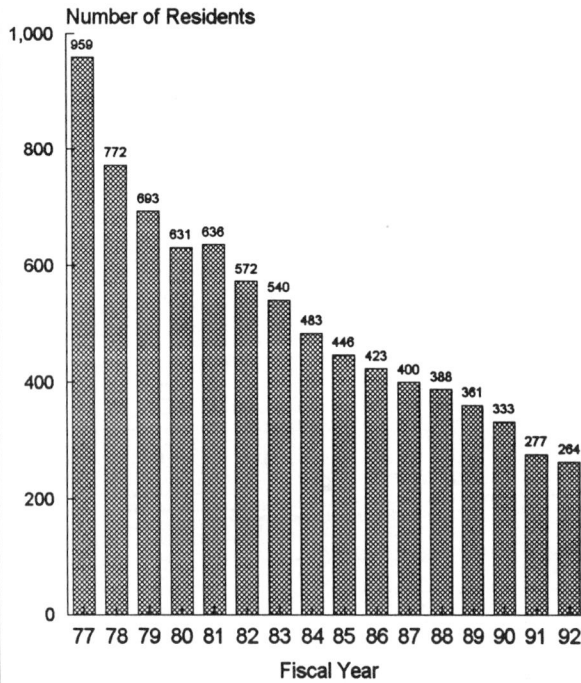

Number of Residents

| Fiscal Year | Residents |
|---|---|
| 77 | 959 |
| 78 | 772 |
| 79 | 693 |
| 80 | 631 |
| 81 | 636 |
| 82 | 572 |
| 83 | 540 |
| 84 | 483 |
| 85 | 446 |
| 86 | 423 |
| 87 | 400 |
| 88 | 388 |
| 89 | 361 |
| 90 | 333 |
| 91 | 277 |
| 92 | 264 |

## Institutional Daily Costs Per Resident

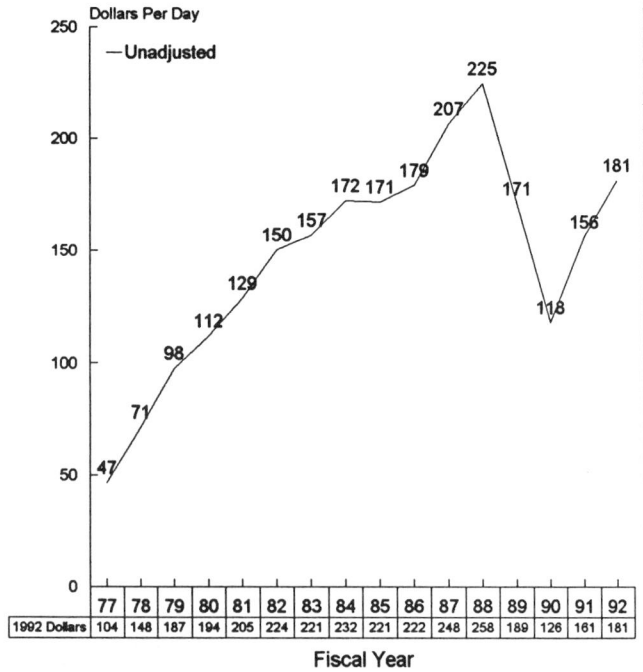

Dollars Per Day

—Unadjusted

Values: 47, 71, 98, 112, 129, 150, 157, 172, 171, 179, 207, 225, 171, 118, 156, 181

| | 77 | 78 | 79 | 80 | 81 | 82 | 83 | 84 | 85 | 86 | 87 | 88 | 89 | 90 | 91 | 92 |
|---|---|---|---|---|---|---|---|---|---|---|---|---|---|---|---|---|
| 1992 Dollars | 104 | 148 | 187 | 194 | 205 | 224 | 221 | 232 | 221 | 222 | 248 | 258 | 189 | 126 | 161 | 181 |

Fiscal Year

*Source:*
Institute on Disability and Human Development (UAP),
University of Illinois at Chicago, 1994

# ARIZONA FISCAL EFFORT

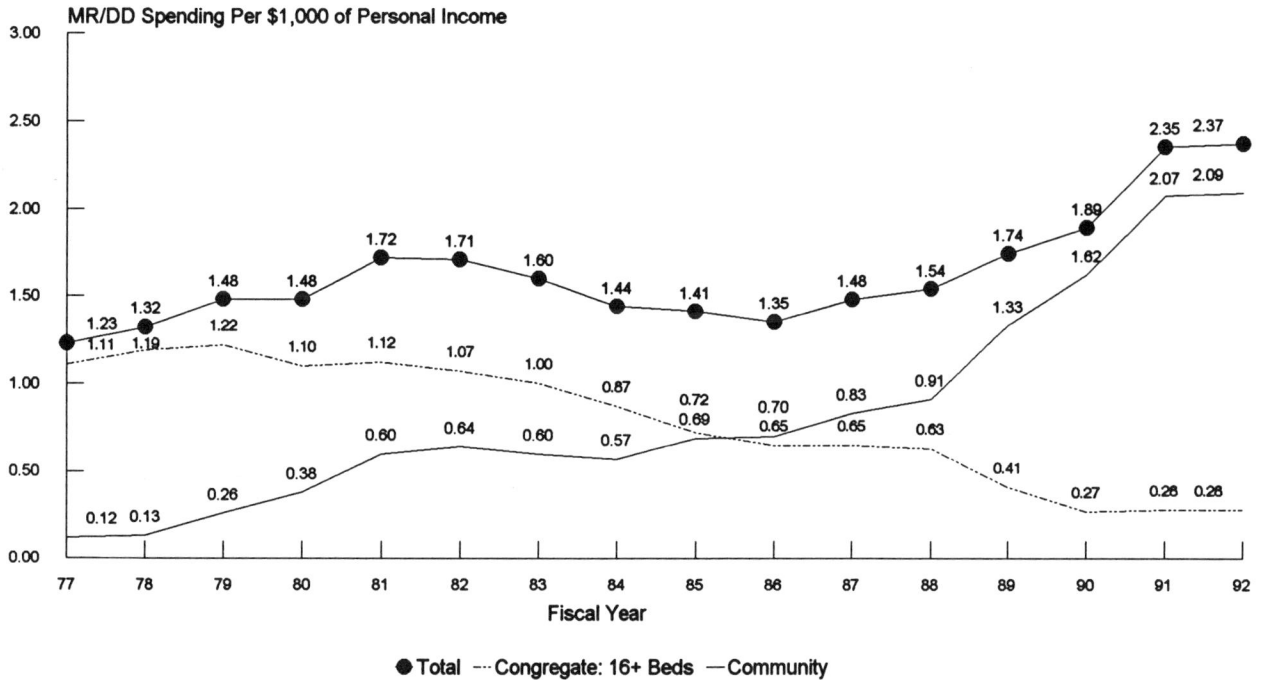

MR/DD Spending Per $1,000 of Personal Income

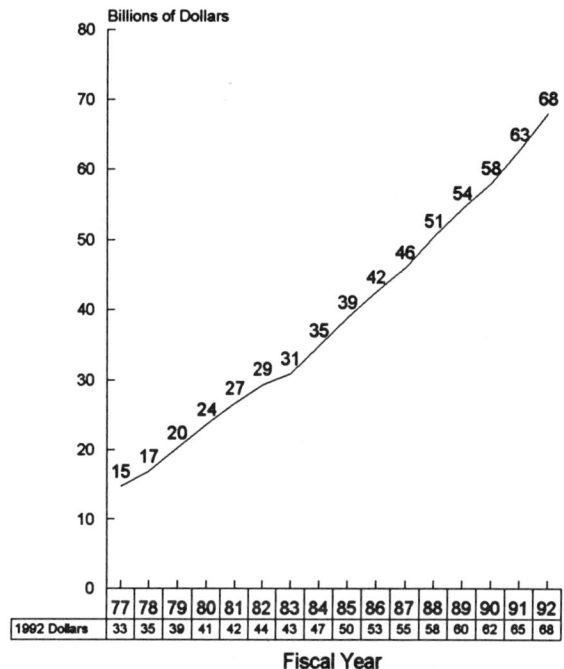

| Year | Total | Congregate: 16+ Beds | Community |
|------|-------|----------------------|-----------|
| 77 | 1.23 | 1.11 | 0.12 |
| 78 | 1.32 | 1.19 | 0.13 |
| 79 | 1.48 | 1.22 | 0.26 |
| 80 | 1.48 | 1.10 | 0.38 |
| 81 | 1.72 | 1.12 | 0.60 |
| 82 | 1.71 | 1.07 | 0.64 |
| 83 | 1.60 | 1.00 | 0.60 |
| 84 | 1.44 | 0.87 | 0.57 |
| 85 | 1.41 | 0.72 / 0.69 | |
| 86 | 1.35 | 0.70 / 0.65 | |
| 87 | 1.48 | 0.83 | 0.65 |
| 88 | 1.54 | 0.91 | 0.63 |
| 89 | 1.74 | 1.33 | 0.41 |
| 90 | 1.89 | 1.62 | 0.27 |
| 91 | 2.35 | 2.07 | 0.26 |
| 92 | 2.37 | 2.09 | 0.26 |

Fiscal Year

● Total　---Congregate: 16+ Beds　—Community

## Total MR/DD Spending

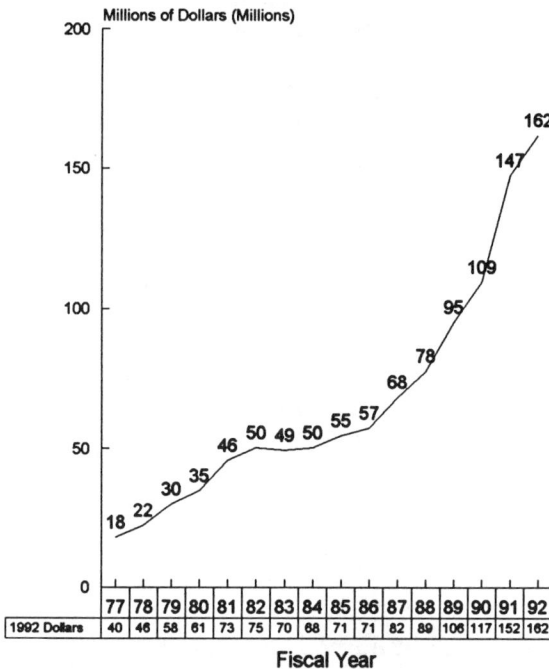

Millions of Dollars (Millions)

| Fiscal Year | 77 | 78 | 79 | 80 | 81 | 82 | 83 | 84 | 85 | 86 | 87 | 88 | 89 | 90 | 91 | 92 |
|-------------|----|----|----|----|----|----|----|----|----|----|----|----|----|----|----|----|
| | 18 | 22 | 30 | 35 | 46 | 50 | 49 | 50 | 55 | 57 | 68 | 78 | 95 | 109 | 147 | 162 |
| 1992 Dollars | 40 | 46 | 58 | 61 | 73 | 75 | 70 | 68 | 71 | 71 | 82 | 89 | 106 | 117 | 152 | 162 |

## Personal Income

Billions of Dollars

| Fiscal Year | 77 | 78 | 79 | 80 | 81 | 82 | 83 | 84 | 85 | 86 | 87 | 88 | 89 | 90 | 91 | 92 |
|-------------|----|----|----|----|----|----|----|----|----|----|----|----|----|----|----|----|
| | 15 | 17 | 20 | 24 | 27 | 29 | 31 | 35 | 39 | 42 | 46 | 51 | 54 | 58 | 63 | 68 |
| 1992 Dollars | 33 | 35 | 39 | 41 | 42 | 44 | 43 | 47 | 50 | 53 | 55 | 58 | 60 | 62 | 65 | 68 |

*Source:*
Institute on Disability and Human Development (UAP),
University of Illinois at Chicago, 1994

# ARIZONA
## Financial Support for MR/DD Services: FY 1977-92

| | 1977 | 1978 | 1979 | 1980 | 1981 | 1982 | 1983 | 1984 |
|---|---|---|---|---|---|---|---|---|
| **TOTAL FUNDS** | $18,057,000 | $22,384,000 | $29,974,000 | $34,773,000 | $45,812,000 | $50,254,000 | $49,376,000 | $50,350,000 |
| **CONGREGATE 16+ BEDS** | 16,312,000 | 20,123,000 | 24,690,000 | 25,806,000 | 29,870,000 | 31,357,000 | 30,889,000 | 30,413,000 |
| INSTITUTIONAL SERVICES FUNDS | 16,312,000 | 20,123,000 | 24,690,000 | 25,806,000 | 29,870,000 | 31,357,000 | 30,889,000 | 30,413,000 |
| STATE FUNDS | 15,848,000 | 19,501,000 | 23,348,000 | 25,018,000 | 29,071,000 | 30,707,000 | 30,061,000 | 29,288,000 |
| General Funds | 15,848,000 | 19,501,000 | 23,348,000 | 25,018,000 | 29,071,000 | 30,619,000 | 29,756,000 | 28,973,000 |
| Local | 0 | 0 | 0 | 0 | 0 | 0 | 0 | 0 |
| Other State Funds | 0 | 0 | 0 | 0 | 0 | 88,000 | 305,000 | 315,000 |
| FEDERAL FUNDS | 464,000 | 622,000 | 1,342,000 | 788,000 | 799,000 | 650,000 | 828,000 | 1,125,000 |
| Federal ICF/MR | 0 | 0 | 0 | 0 | 0 | 0 | 0 | 0 |
| Title XX / SSBG Funds | 0 | 0 | 743,000 | 788,000 | 799,000 | 650,000 | 828,000 | 1,125,000 |
| Other Federal Funds | 464,000 | 622,000 | 599,000 | 0 | 0 | 0 | 0 | 0 |
| LARGE PRIVATE RESIDENTIAL | 0 | 0 | 0 | 0 | 0 | 0 | 0 | 0 |
| STATE FUNDS | 0 | 0 | 0 | 0 | 0 | 0 | 0 | 0 |
| General Funds | 0 | 0 | 0 | 0 | 0 | 0 | 0 | 0 |
| Other State Funds | 0 | 0 | 0 | 0 | 0 | 0 | 0 | 0 |
| Local/County Overmatch | 0 | 0 | 0 | 0 | 0 | 0 | 0 | 0 |
| FEDERAL FUNDS | 0 | 0 | 0 | 0 | 0 | 0 | 0 | 0 |
| Large Private ICF/MR | 0 | 0 | 0 | 0 | 0 | 0 | 0 | 0 |
| **COMMUNITY SERVICES FUNDS** | 1,745,000 | 2,261,000 | 5,284,000 | 8,967,000 | 15,942,000 | 18,897,000 | 18,487,000 | 19,937,000 |
| STATE FUNDS | 1,745,000 | 2,261,000 | 4,438,000 | 8,070,000 | 13,398,000 | 16,877,000 | 16,640,000 | 18,385,000 |
| General Funds | 1,739,000 | 2,247,000 | 4,398,000 | 8,013,000 | 12,293,000 | 15,472,000 | 15,680,000 | 16,944,000 |
| Other State Funds | 0 | 0 | 0 | 0 | 1,042,000 | 1,328,000 | 816,000 | 1,247,000 |
| Local/County Overmatch | 0 | 0 | 0 | 0 | 0 | 0 | 0 | 0 |
| SSI State Supplement | 6,000 | 14,000 | 40,000 | 57,000 | 63,000 | 77,000 | 144,000 | 194,000 |
| FEDERAL FUNDS | 0 | 0 | 846,000 | 897,000 | 2,544,000 | 2,020,000 | 1,847,000 | 1,552,000 |
| ICF/MR Funds | 0 | 0 | 0 | 0 | 0 | 0 | 0 | 0 |
| Small Public | 0 | 0 | 0 | 0 | 0 | 0 | 0 | 0 |
| Small Private | 0 | 0 | 0 | 0 | 0 | 0 | 0 | 0 |
| HCBS Waiver | 0 | 0 | 0 | 0 | 0 | 0 | 0 | 0 |
| Model 50/200 Waiver | 0 | 0 | 0 | 0 | 0 | 0 | 0 | 0 |
| Other Title XIX Programs | 0 | 0 | 0 | 0 | 0 | 0 | 0 | 0 |
| Title XX / SSBG Funds | 0 | 0 | 846,000 | 897,000 | 2,544,000 | 2,020,000 | 1,847,000 | 1,552,000 |
| Other Federal Funds | 0 | 0 | 0 | 0 | 0 | 0 | 0 | 0 |
| Waiver Clients' SSI/ADC | 0 | 0 | 0 | 0 | 0 | 0 | 0 | 0 |

| | 1985 | 1986 | 1987 | 1988 | 1989 | 1990 | 1991 | 1992 |
|---|---|---|---|---|---|---|---|---|
| **TOTAL FUNDS** | $54,653,200 | $57,457,100 | $68,401,900 | $77,738,400 | $95,153,121 | $109,466,771 | $147,448,249 | $161,863,260 |
| **CONGREGATE 16+ BEDS** | 27,909,300 | 27,615,400 | 30,151,600 | 31,884,600 | 22,442,920 | 15,645,717 | 17,400,196 | 19,360,933 |
| INSTITUTIONAL SERVICES FUNDS | 27,909,300 | 27,615,400 | 30,151,600 | 31,884,600 | 22,442,920 | 14,316,389 | 15,770,418 | 17,514,656 |
| STATE FUNDS | 26,783,900 | 26,534,200 | 29,026,200 | 30,760,300 | 20,871,654 | 10,983,008 | 9,406,506 | 9,906,646 |
| General Funds | 26,322,000 | 25,561,000 | 28,059,000 | 29,823,700 | 19,289,799 | 8,755,898 | 5,080,537 | 5,041,799 |
| Local | 0 | 0 | 0 | 0 | 0 | 0 | 0 | 0 |
| Other State Funds | 461,900 | 973,200 | 967,200 | 936,600 | 1,581,855 | 2,227,110 | 4,325,969 | 4,864,847 |
| FEDERAL FUNDS | 1,125,400 | 1,081,200 | 1,125,400 | 1,124,300 | 1,571,266 | 3,333,381 | 6,363,912 | 7,608,010 |
| Federal ICF/MR | 0 | 0 | 0 | 0 | 1,571,266 | 3,142,531 | 6,079,748 | 7,285,878 |
| Title XX / SSBG Funds | 1,125,400 | 1,081,200 | 1,125,400 | 1,124,300 | 0 | 0 | 0 | 0 |
| Other Federal Funds | 0 | 0 | 0 | 0 | 0 | 190,850 | 284,164 | 322,132 |
| LARGE PRIVATE RESIDENTIAL | 0 | 0 | 0 | 0 | 0 | 1,329,328 | 1,629,778 | 1,846,277 |
| STATE FUNDS | 0 | 0 | 0 | 0 | 0 | 906,163 | 947,776 | 875,493 |
| General Funds | 0 | 0 | 0 | 0 | 0 | 623,740 | 486,473 | 253,999 |
| Other State Funds | 0 | 0 | 0 | 0 | 0 | 282,423 | 461,303 | 621,494 |
| Local/County Overmatch | 0 | 0 | 0 | 0 | 0 | 0 | 0 | 0 |
| FEDERAL FUNDS | 0 | 0 | 0 | 0 | 0 | 423,165 | 682,002 | 970,784 |
| Large Private ICF/MR | 0 | 0 | 0 | 0 | 0 | 423,165 | 682,002 | 970,784 |
| **COMMUNITY SERVICES FUNDS** | 26,743,900 | 29,841,700 | 38,250,300 | 45,853,800 | 72,710,202 | 93,821,054 | 130,048,053 | 142,502,327 |
| STATE FUNDS | 25,144,700 | 27,044,200 | 35,424,500 | 42,806,400 | 47,583,846 | 52,362,427 | 64,382,190 | 64,100,514 |
| General Funds | 22,304,800 | 24,486,400 | 32,183,700 | 39,967,200 | 36,330,013 | 32,692,825 | 31,771,392 | 30,294,173 |
| Other State Funds | 2,633,900 | 2,268,800 | 2,813,800 | 2,385,200 | 10,777,134 | 19,169,067 | 32,085,236 | 33,254,501 |
| Local/County Overmatch | 0 | 0 | 0 | 0 | 0 | 0 | 0 | 0 |
| SSI State Supplement | 206,000 | 289,000 | 427,000 | 454,000 | 476,700 | 500,535 | 525,562 | 551,840 |
| FEDERAL FUNDS | 1,599,200 | 2,797,500 | 2,825,800 | 3,047,400 | 25,126,356 | 41,458,627 | 65,665,863 | 78,401,813 |
| ICF/MR Funds | 0 | 0 | 0 | 0 | 0 | 0 | 0 | 0 |
| Small Public | 0 | 0 | 0 | 0 | 0 | 0 | 0 | 0 |
| Small Private | 0 | 0 | 0 | 0 | 0 | 0 | 0 | 0 |
| HCBS Waiver | 0 | 0 | 0 | 0 | 21,028,203 | 23,398,278 | 38,321,600 | 44,339,788 |
| Model 50/200 Waiver | 0 | 0 | 0 | 0 | 0 | 0 | 0 | 0 |
| Other Title XIX Programs | 0 | 0 | 0 | 0 | 0 | 6,600,982 | 7,760,554 | 9,881,585 |
| Title XX / SSBG Funds | 1,599,200 | 2,693,000 | 2,713,900 | 2,734,900 | 2,195,374 | 1,655,847 | 2,595,405 | 2,231,744 |
| Other Federal Funds | 0 | 104,500 | 111,900 | 312,500 | 0 | 0 | 0 | 0 |
| Waiver Clients' SSI/ADC | 0 | 0 | 0 | 0 | 1,902,779 | 9,803,520 | 16,988,304 | 21,948,696 |

*Source:*
Institute on Disability and Human Development (UAP),
University of Illinois at Chicago, 1994

# ARKANSAS

## MR/DD Spending for Congregate Residential & Community Services

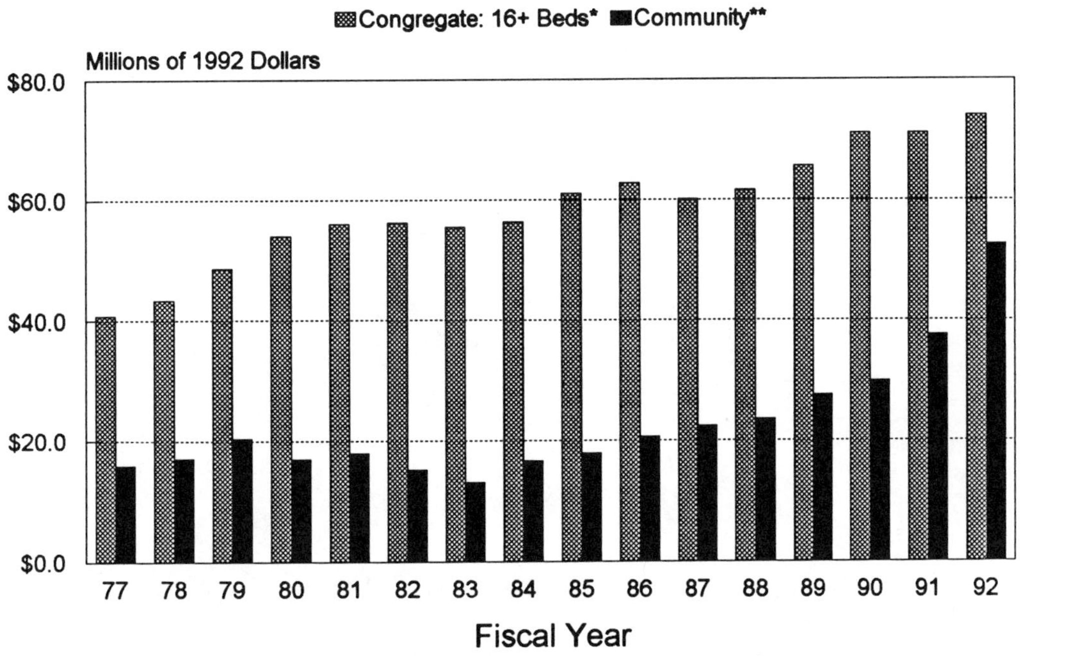
Congregate: 16+ Beds* Community**
Millions of 1992 Dollars
$80.0
$60.0
$40.0
$20.0
$0.0
77 78 79 80 81 82 83 84 85 86 87 88 89 90 91 92
Fiscal Year

*Excludes nursing homes; ** Includes resources for 15 bed or less residential settings & non-residential community services

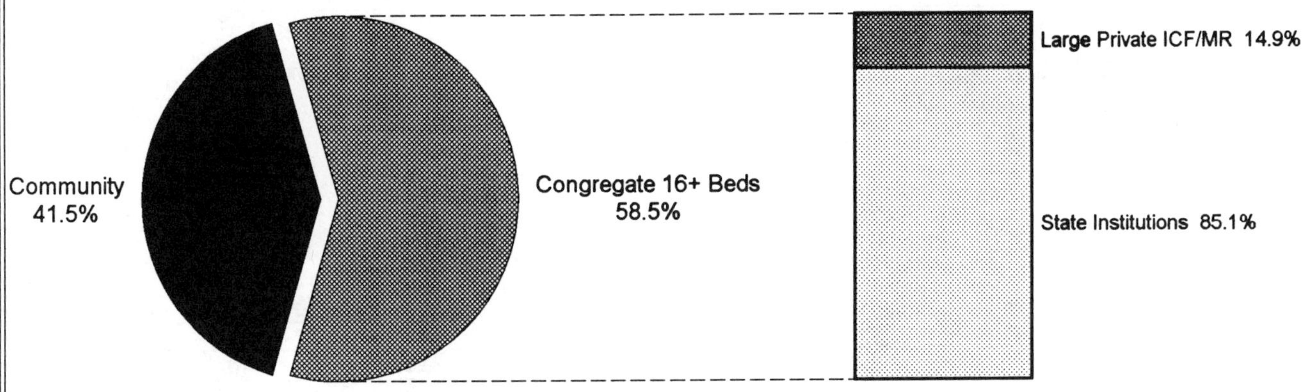
Community 41.5%
Congregate 16+ Beds 58.5%
Large Private ICF/MR 14.9%
State Institutions 85.1%

FY 1992 Total Spending:
$126.7 Million

*Source:*
Institute on Disability and Human Development (UAP), University of Illinois at Chicago, 1994

# ARKANSAS

## Number of Persons Served by Residential Setting: FY 1992

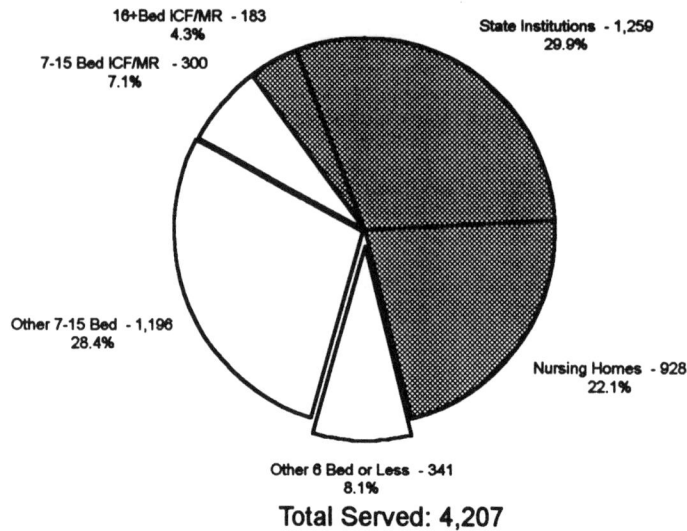

16+Bed ICF/MR - 183
4.3%

7-15 Bed ICF/MR - 300
7.1%

State Institutions - 1,259
29.9%

Other 7-15 Bed - 1,196
28.4%

Nursing Homes - 928
22.1%

Other 6 Bed or Less - 341
8.1%

Total Served: 4,207

## Persons Served by Residential Setting:1986-92

| | 1986 | 1987 | 1988 | 1989 | 1990 | 1991 | 1992 |
|---|---|---|---|---|---|---|---|
| CONGREGATE 16 + BED SETTINGS | NA | NA | 2,244 | NA | NA | NA | 2,370 |
| Nursing Homes* | NA | NA | 800 | NA | NA | NA | 928 |
| State Institutions | 1,341 | 1,329 | 1,316 | 1,294 | 1,260 | 1,250 | 1,259 |
| Private 16+Bed ICF/MR | 102 | 128 | 128 | 177 | 179 | 182 | 183 |
| Other 16+Bed Residential | 0 | 0 | 0 | 0 | 0 | 0 | 0 |
| 15 BED OR LESS RESIDENTIAL SETTINGS | 494 | 593 | 604 | 1,123 | 1,132 | 1,496 | 1,837 |
| Public 7-15 Bed ICF/MR | 0 | 0 | 0 | 0 | 0 | 0 | 0 |
| Private 7-15 Bed ICF/MR | 0 | 0 | 0 | 0 | 25 | 262 | 300 |
| Other 7-15 Bed Residential | 494 | 593 | 604 | 1,123 | 1,107 | 1,234 | 1,196 |
| Public 6 Bed or Less ICF/MR | 0 | 0 | 0 | 0 | 0 | 0 | 0 |
| Private 6 Bed or Less ICF/MR | 0 | 0 | 0 | 0 | 0 | 0 | 0 |
| Other 6 Bed or Less Residential | 0 | 0 | 0 | 0 | 0 | 0 | 341 |
| TOTAL PERSONS SERVED | NA | NA | 2,848 | NA | NA | NA | 4,207 |

## Persons Served in Non-Residential Community Services:1986-92

| | 1986 | 1987 | 1988 | 1989 | 1990 | 1991 | 1992 |
|---|---|---|---|---|---|---|---|
| DAY/WORK PROGRAMS | 1,732 | 2,446 | 2,454 | 5,013 | 5,004 | 5,125 | 5,694 |
| Sheltered Employment/Work Activity | 1,037 | 1,037 | 1,024 | 1,398 | 1,356 | 1,304 | 1,468 |
| Day Habilitation ("Day Training") | 695 | 1,409 | 1,418 | 3,604 | 3,591 | 3,688 | 4,044 |
| Supported/Competitive Employment | NA | NA | 12 | 11 | 57 | 133 | 182 |
| CASE MANAGEMENT | 3,489 | 3,520 | 3,588 | 882 | 1,528 | 1,747 | 3,598 |
| HCBS WAIVER | 0 | 0 | 0 | 0 | 132 | 182 | 411 |
| MODEL 50/200 WAIVER | 0 | 0 | 0 | 0 | 0 | 0 | 0 |

*Source:*
Institute on Disability and Human Development (UAP),
University of Illinois at Chicago, 1994

# ARKANSAS

## Community Services: FY 1992 Revenue Sources

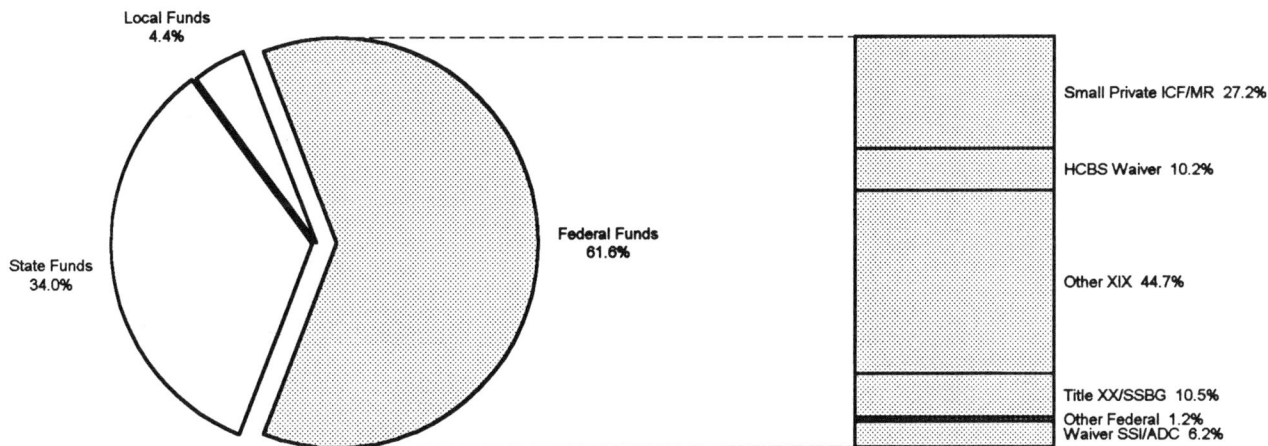

Local Funds
4.4%

State Funds
34.0%

Federal Funds
61.6%

Small Private ICF/MR 27.2%

HCBS Waiver 10.2%

Other XIX 44.7%

Title XX/SSBG 10.5%
Other Federal 1.2%
Waiver SSI/ADC 6.2%

Total Funds: $52.5 Million

## Family Support Initiatives*

|  | 1986 | 1987 | 1988 | 1989 | 1990 | 1991 | 1992 |
|---|---|---|---|---|---|---|---|
| FAMILY SUPPORT: TOTAL SPENDING | $188,700 | $178,500 | $206,000 | $291,130 | $513,465 | $499,447 | $491,363 |
| Total # of Families Supported | 40 | 40 | 40 | 444 | 544 | 591 | 847 |
| A. Financial Subsidy/Payment | $0 | $0 | $0 | $0 | $138,337 | $218,451 | $218,451 |
| # of Families | 0 | 0 | 0 | 0 | 65 | 76 | 116 |
| B. Family Assistance Payments | $188,700 | $178,500 | $206,000 | $291,130 | $375,128 | $280,996 | $272,912 |
| # of Families | 40 | 40 | 40 | 444 | 479 | 515 | 731 |
| C. Other Family Support Payments | $0 | $0 | $0 | $0 | $0 | $0 | $0 |
| # of Families | 0 | 0 | 0 | 0 | 0 | 0 | 0 |

## Other Community Services Initiatives*

|  | 1986 | 1987 | 1988 | 1989 | 1990 | 1991 | 1992 |
|---|---|---|---|---|---|---|---|
| AGING/DD SPENDING | $0 | $0 | $0 | $0 | $0 | $0 | $0 |
| # of Persons Served | 0 | 0 | 0 | 0 | 0 | 0 | 0 |
| ASSISTIVE TECHNOLOGY SPENDING |  |  |  |  |  |  | $0 |
| # of Persons Served |  |  |  |  |  |  | 0 |
| EARLY INTERVENTION SPENDING | $397,500 | $386,500 | $444,200 | $178,696 | $350,448 | $323,736 | $690,676 |
| # of Persons Served | 394 | 304 | 269 | 255 | 454 | 310 | 456 |
| PERSONAL ASSISTANCE SPENDING |  |  |  |  |  |  | $0 |
| # of Persons Served |  |  |  |  |  |  | 0 |
| SUPPORTED EMPLOYMENT SPENDING | $64,300 | $62,100 | $71,600 | $6,258 | $90,272 | $271,705 | $196,659 |
| # of Persons Served | NA | NA | 12 | 11 | 57 | 133 | 182 |
| SUPPORTED LIVING SPENDING |  |  |  | $69,318 | $606,980 | $358,639 | $250,053 |
| # of Persons Served |  |  |  | 42 | 55 | 55 | 44 |

*Expenditures associated with Special Community Initiatives are a subset of funding within the community services component of the state's chart series and spreadsheet; Family Support Client figures may include duplicate client counts; HCBS Waiver counts include Waiver case management numbers.
0= Services not provided in the state; NA= Data not available from state; blank= Services not applicable (eg. CSLA prior to authorization, Special Community Initiatives prior to request for data by this study)

*Source:*
Institute on Disability and Human Development (UAP),
University of Illinois at Chicago, 1994

# ARKANSAS

## Large Congregate Care Facilities: FY 1992 Revenue Sources*

### Private 16+Bed Settings

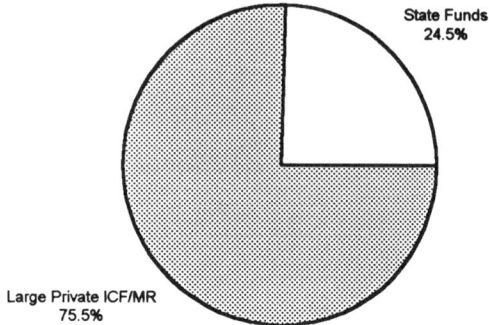

State Funds
24.5%

Large Private ICF/MR
75.5%

Total Funds: $11.0 Million

### Public Institutions

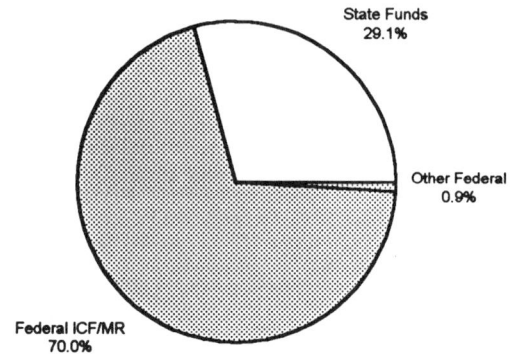

State Funds
29.1%

Other Federal
0.9%

Federal ICF/MR
70.0%

Total Funds: $63.0 Million

*Excludes nursing homes

## Average Daily Residents in Institutions

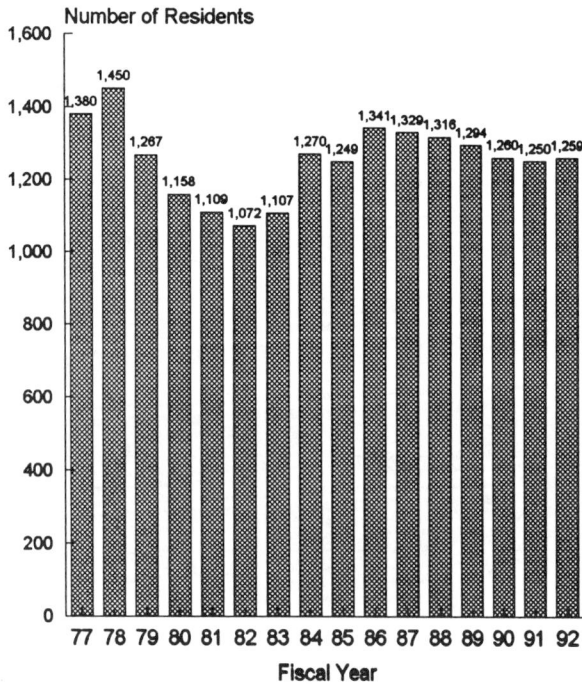

Number of Residents

| Fiscal Year | Residents |
|---|---|
| 77 | 1,380 |
| 78 | 1,450 |
| 79 | 1,267 |
| 80 | 1,158 |
| 81 | 1,109 |
| 82 | 1,072 |
| 83 | 1,107 |
| 84 | 1,270 |
| 85 | 1,249 |
| 86 | 1,341 |
| 87 | 1,329 |
| 88 | 1,316 |
| 89 | 1,294 |
| 90 | 1,260 |
| 91 | 1,250 |
| 92 | 1,259 |

Fiscal Year

## Institutional Daily Costs Per Resident

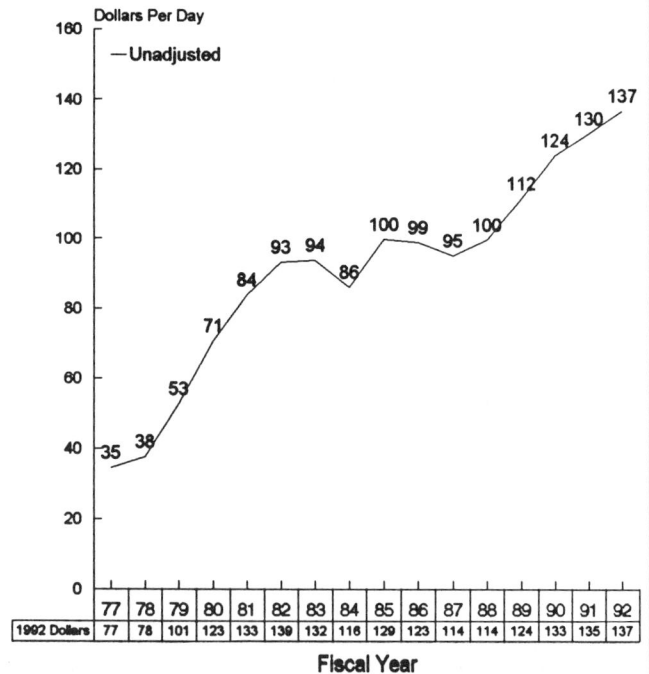

Dollars Per Day

—Unadjusted

| Fiscal Year | 77 | 78 | 79 | 80 | 81 | 82 | 83 | 84 | 85 | 86 | 87 | 88 | 89 | 90 | 91 | 92 |
|---|---|---|---|---|---|---|---|---|---|---|---|---|---|---|---|---|
| Unadjusted | 35 | 38 | 53 | 71 | 84 | 93 | 94 | 86 | 100 | 99 | 95 | 100 | 112 | 124 | 130 | 137 |
| 1992 Dollars | 77 | 78 | 101 | 123 | 133 | 139 | 132 | 116 | 129 | 123 | 114 | 114 | 124 | 133 | 135 | 137 |

Fiscal Year

*Source:*
Institute on Disability and Human Development (UAP),
University of Illinois at Chicago, 1994

# ARKANSAS FISCAL EFFORT

MR/DD Spending Per $1,000 of Personal Income

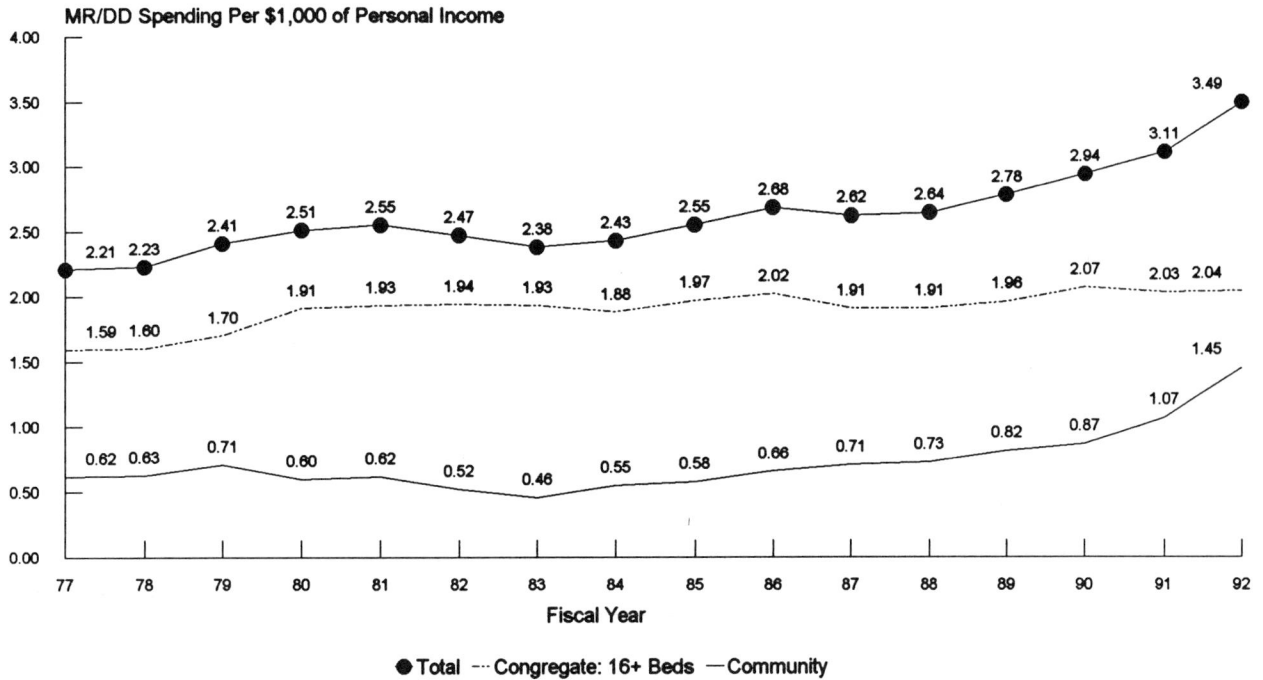

● Total  --- Congregate: 16+ Beds  — Community

## Total MR/DD Spending

Millions of Dollars (Millions)

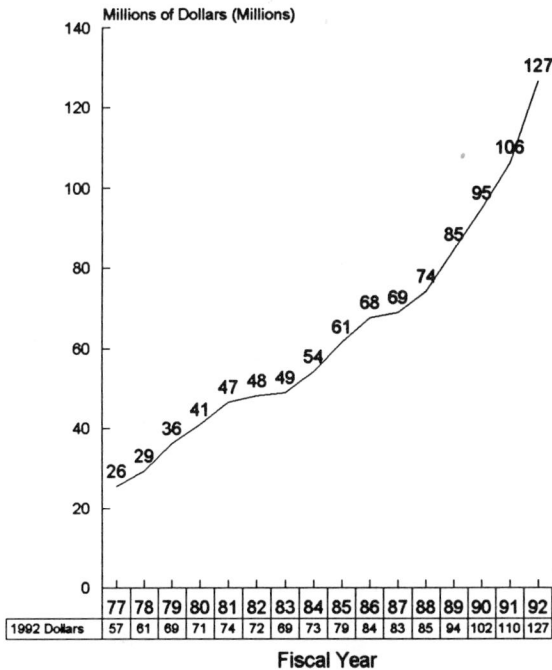

| | 77 | 78 | 79 | 80 | 81 | 82 | 83 | 84 | 85 | 86 | 87 | 88 | 89 | 90 | 91 | 92 |
|---|---|---|---|---|---|---|---|---|---|---|---|---|---|---|---|---|
| 1992 Dollars | 57 | 61 | 69 | 71 | 74 | 72 | 69 | 73 | 79 | 84 | 83 | 85 | 94 | 102 | 110 | 127 |

Fiscal Year

## Personal Income

Billions of Dollars

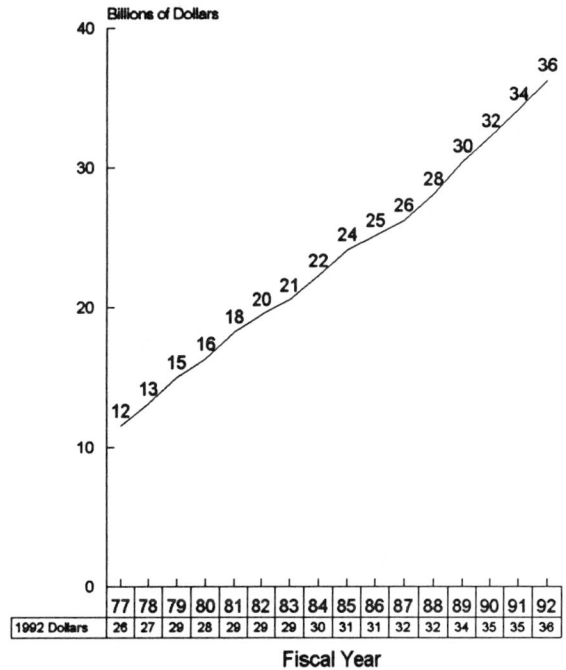

| | 77 | 78 | 79 | 80 | 81 | 82 | 83 | 84 | 85 | 86 | 87 | 88 | 89 | 90 | 91 | 92 |
|---|---|---|---|---|---|---|---|---|---|---|---|---|---|---|---|---|
| 1992 Dollars | 26 | 27 | 29 | 28 | 29 | 29 | 29 | 30 | 31 | 31 | 32 | 32 | 34 | 35 | 35 | 36 |

Fiscal Year

*Source:*
Institute on Disability and Human Development (UAP),
University of Illinois at Chicago, 1994

# ARKANSAS
## Financial Support for MR/DD Services: FY 1977-92

| | 1977 | 1978 | 1979 | 1980 | 1981 | 1982 | 1983 | 1984 |
|---|---|---|---|---|---|---|---|---|
| **TOTAL FUNDS** | $25,531,689 | $29,304,620 | $36,185,103 | $41,006,645 | $46,581,723 | $48,122,789 | $48,893,516 | $54,183,892 |
| **CONGREGATE 16+ BEDS** | 18,378,689 | 21,020,820 | 25,478,903 | 31,214,294 | 35,295,825 | 37,925,366 | 39,553,447 | 41,862,772 |
| INSTITUTIONAL SERVICES FUNDS | 17,418,000 | 19,990,000 | 24,345,000 | 29,965,866 | 33,923,802 | 36,471,021 | 37,869,178 | 39,976,882 |
| STATE FUNDS | 3,967,000 | 5,082,000 | 6,299,000 | 7,897,000 | 8,936,000 | 9,870,000 | 11,840,800 | 10,995,900 |
| General Funds | 3,967,000 | 5,082,000 | 6,299,000 | 7,897,000 | 8,936,000 | 9,870,000 | 11,840,800 | 10,995,900 |
| Local | 0 | 0 | 0 | 0 | 0 | 0 | 0 | 0 |
| Other State Funds | 0 | 0 | 0 | 0 | 0 | 0 | 0 | 0 |
| FEDERAL FUNDS | 13,451,000 | 14,908,000 | 18,046,000 | 22,068,866 | 24,987,802 | 26,601,021 | 26,028,378 | 28,980,982 |
| Federal ICF/MR | 11,651,000 | 13,108,000 | 16,246,000 | 21,124,000 | 24,002,000 | 25,582,000 | 25,284,700 | 28,151,600 |
| Title XX / SSBG Funds | 0 | 0 | 0 | 0 | 0 | 0 | 0 | 0 |
| Other Federal Funds | 1,800,000 | 1,800,000 | 1,800,000 | 944,866 | 985,802 | 1,019,021 | 743,678 | 829,382 |
| LARGE PRIVATE RESIDENTIAL | 960,689 | 1,030,820 | 1,133,903 | 1,248,428 | 1,372,023 | 1,454,345 | 1,684,269 | 1,885,890 |
| STATE FUNDS | 244,015 | 281,414 | 316,812 | 341,195 | 372,230 | 402,272 | 468,900 | 503,910 |
| General Funds | 244,015 | 281,414 | 316,812 | 341,195 | 372,230 | 402,272 | 468,900 | 503,910 |
| Other State Funds | 0 | 0 | 0 | 0 | 0 | 0 | 0 | 0 |
| Local/County Overmatch | 0 | 0 | 0 | 0 | 0 | 0 | 0 | 0 |
| FEDERAL FUNDS | 716,674 | 749,406 | 817,091 | 907,233 | 999,793 | 1,052,073 | 1,215,369 | 1,381,980 |
| Large Private ICF/MR | 716,674 | 749,406 | 817,091 | 907,233 | 999,793 | 1,052,073 | 1,215,369 | 1,381,980 |
| **COMMUNITY SERVICES FUNDS** | 7,153,000 | 8,283,800 | 10,706,200 | 9,792,351 | 11,285,898 | 10,197,423 | 9,340,069 | 12,321,120 |
| STATE FUNDS | 3,403,000 | 4,489,800 | 6,677,200 | 5,541,700 | 6,933,700 | 6,018,200 | 5,168,524 | 6,618,241 |
| General Funds | 2,903,000 | 3,984,000 | 6,140,000 | 5,080,000 | 6,462,000 | 5,579,000 | 4,199,524 | 5,576,541 |
| Other State Funds | 500,000 | 505,800 | 537,200 | 461,700 | 471,700 | 439,200 | 969,000 | 1,041,700 |
| Local/County Overmatch | 0 | 0 | 0 | 0 | 0 | 0 | 0 | 0 |
| SSI State Supplement | 0 | 0 | 0 | 0 | 0 | 0 | 0 | 0 |
| FEDERAL FUNDS | 3,750,000 | 3,794,000 | 4,029,000 | 4,250,651 | 4,352,198 | 4,179,223 | 4,171,545 | 5,702,879 |
| ICF/MR Funds | 0 | 0 | 0 | 0 | 0 | 0 | 0 | 0 |
| Small Public | 0 | 0 | 0 | 0 | 0 | 0 | 0 | 0 |
| Small Private | 0 | 0 | 0 | 0 | 0 | 0 | 0 | 0 |
| HCBS Waiver | 0 | 0 | 0 | 0 | 0 | 0 | 0 | 0 |
| Model 50/200 Waiver | 0 | 0 | 0 | 0 | 0 | 0 | 0 | 0 |
| Other Title XIX Programs | 0 | 0 | 0 | 0 | 0 | 0 | 0 | 1,830,800 |
| Title XX / SSBG Funds | 3,750,000 | 3,794,000 | 4,029,000 | 3,463,000 | 3,538,000 | 3,294,000 | 3,343,000 | 3,159,100 |
| Other Federal Funds | 0 | 0 | 0 | 787,651 | 814,198 | 885,223 | 828,545 | 712,979 |
| Waiver Clients' SSI/ADC | 0 | 0 | 0 | 0 | 0 | 0 | 0 | 0 |

| | 1985 | 1986 | 1987 | 1988 | 1989 | 1990 | 1991 | 1992 |
|---|---|---|---|---|---|---|---|---|
| **TOTAL FUNDS** | $61,494,733 | $67,529,539 | $68,905,897 | $74,172,285 | $84,543,304 | $95,007,958 | $106,336,116 | $126,658,116 |
| **CONGREGATE 16+ BEDS** | 47,531,014 | 50,837,507 | 50,186,926 | 53,635,711 | 59,585,332 | 66,907,459 | 69,587,257 | 74,090,365 |
| INSTITUTIONAL SERVICES FUNDS | 45,427,200 | 48,394,400 | 46,045,800 | 47,926,600 | 52,662,434 | 57,013,468 | 59,416,051 | 63,051,420 |
| STATE FUNDS | 11,990,000 | 12,582,400 | 13,885,200 | 13,910,900 | 17,729,715 | 19,943,391 | 17,735,837 | 18,338,109 |
| General Funds | 11,990,000 | 12,582,400 | 13,885,200 | 13,910,900 | 15,498,046 | 17,588,813 | 15,235,837 | 15,433,215 |
| Local | 0 | 0 | 0 | 0 | 0 | 0 | 0 | 0 |
| Other State Funds | 0 | 0 | 0 | 0 | 2,231,669 | 2,354,578 | 2,500,000 | 2,904,894 |
| FEDERAL FUNDS | 33,437,200 | 35,812,000 | 32,160,600 | 34,015,700 | 34,932,719 | 37,070,077 | 41,680,214 | 44,713,311 |
| Federal ICF/MR | 32,612,500 | 35,024,800 | 31,147,000 | 32,911,600 | 34,241,855 | 36,388,794 | 41,100,744 | 44,129,627 |
| Title XX / SSBG Funds | 0 | 0 | 0 | 0 | 0 | 0 | 0 | 0 |
| Other Federal Funds | 824,700 | 787,200 | 1,013,600 | 1,104,100 | 690,864 | 681,283 | 579,470 | 583,684 |
| LARGE PRIVATE RESIDENTIAL | 2,103,814 | 2,443,107 | 4,141,126 | 5,709,111 | 6,922,898 | 9,893,991 | 10,171,206 | 11,038,945 |
| STATE FUNDS | 554,355 | 640,338 | 1,077,935 | 1,475,234 | 1,788,877 | 2,525,936 | 2,543,819 | 2,701,230 |
| General Funds | 554,355 | 640,338 | 1,077,935 | 1,475,234 | 1,788,877 | 2,525,936 | 2,543,819 | 2,701,230 |
| Other State Funds | 0 | 0 | 0 | 0 | 0 | 0 | 0 | 0 |
| Local/County Overmatch | 0 | 0 | 0 | 0 | 0 | 0 | 0 | 0 |
| FEDERAL FUNDS | 1,549,459 | 1,802,769 | 3,063,191 | 4,233,877 | 5,134,021 | 7,368,055 | 7,627,387 | 8,337,715 |
| Large Private ICF/MR | 1,549,459 | 1,802,769 | 3,063,191 | 4,233,877 | 5,134,021 | 7,368,055 | 7,627,387 | 8,337,715 |
| **COMMUNITY SERVICES FUNDS** | 13,963,719 | 16,692,032 | 18,718,971 | 20,536,574 | 24,957,972 | 28,100,499 | 36,748,859 | 52,567,751 |
| STATE FUNDS | 6,971,959 | 8,686,632 | 10,020,771 | 10,764,274 | 13,882,617 | 14,555,997 | 16,142,832 | 20,195,852 |
| General Funds | 5,610,559 | 6,517,332 | 6,540,871 | 9,900,274 | 11,990,981 | 12,361,554 | 13,943,533 | 17,117,389 |
| Other State Funds | 1,361,400 | 2,169,300 | 3,479,900 | 863,900 | 668,226 | 877,031 | 790,675 | 771,869 |
| Local/County Overmatch | 0 | 0 | 0 | 100 | 1,223,410 | 1,317,412 | 1,408,624 | 2,306,594 |
| SSI State Supplement | 0 | 0 | 0 | 0 | 0 | 0 | 0 | 0 |
| FEDERAL FUNDS | 6,991,760 | 8,005,400 | 8,698,200 | 9,772,300 | 11,075,355 | 13,544,502 | 20,606,027 | 32,371,899 |
| ICF/MR Funds | 0 | 0 | 0 | 0 | 0 | 763,674 | 6,044,735 | 8,801,126 |
| Small Public | 0 | 0 | 0 | 0 | 0 | 0 | 0 | 0 |
| Small Private | 0 | 0 | 0 | 0 | 0 | 763,674 | 6,044,735 | 8,801,126 |
| HCBS Waiver | 0 | 0 | 0 | 0 | 0 | 195,583 | 1,307,779 | 3,303,992 |
| Model 50/200 Waiver | 0 | 0 | 0 | 0 | 0 | 0 | 0 | 0 |
| Other Title XIX Programs | 3,758,200 | 4,707,700 | 5,476,400 | 6,360,100 | 7,322,099 | 7,680,071 | 8,516,639 | 14,473,174 |
| Title XX / SSBG Funds | 2,767,800 | 3,086,600 | 3,015,200 | 3,220,900 | 3,341,134 | 3,885,154 | 3,453,380 | 3,408,410 |
| Other Federal Funds | 465,760 | 211,100 | 206,600 | 191,300 | 412,122 | 437,108 | 449,206 | 377,873 |
| Waiver Clients' SSI/ADC | 0 | 0 | 0 | 0 | 0 | 582,912 | 834,288 | 2,007,324 |

*Source:*
Institute on Disability and Human Development (UAP),
University of Illinois at Chicago, 1994

# CALIFORNIA

## MR/DD Spending for Congregate Residential & Community Services

▨Congregate: 16+ Beds*  ■Community**

Millions of 1992 Dollars

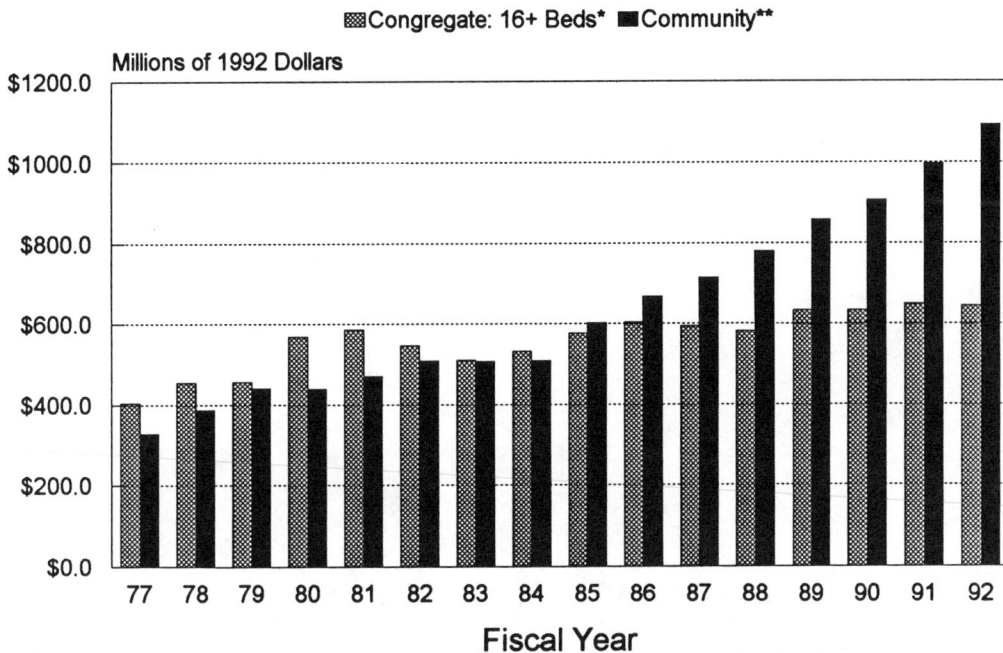

**Fiscal Year**

*Excludes nursing homes; ** Includes resources for
15 bed or less residential settings & non-residential community services

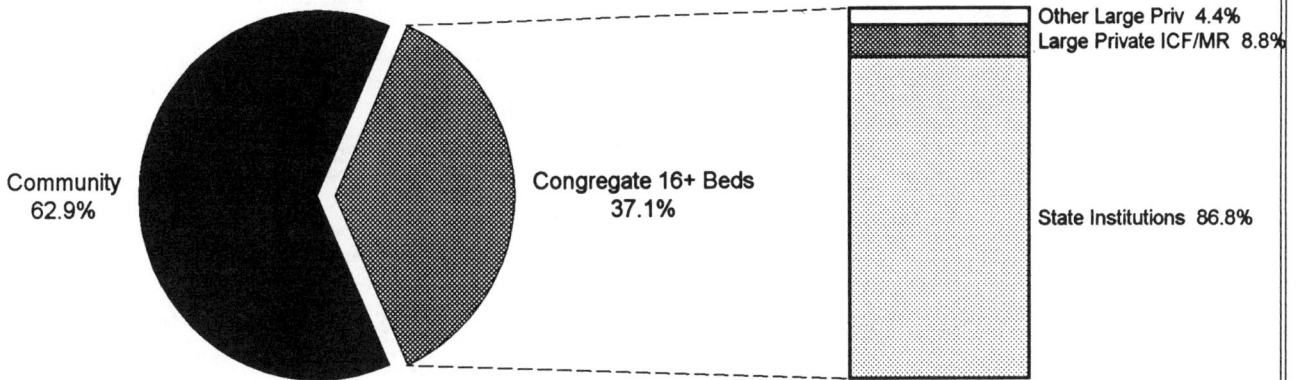

Community
62.9%

Congregate 16+ Beds
37.1%

Other Large Priv  4.4%
Large Private ICF/MR  8.8%

State Institutions  86.8%

FY 1992 Total Spending:
$1.74 Billion

*Source:*
Institute on Disability and Human Development (UAP),
University of Illinois at Chicago, 1994

# CALIFORNIA

## Number of Persons Served by Residential Setting: FY 1992

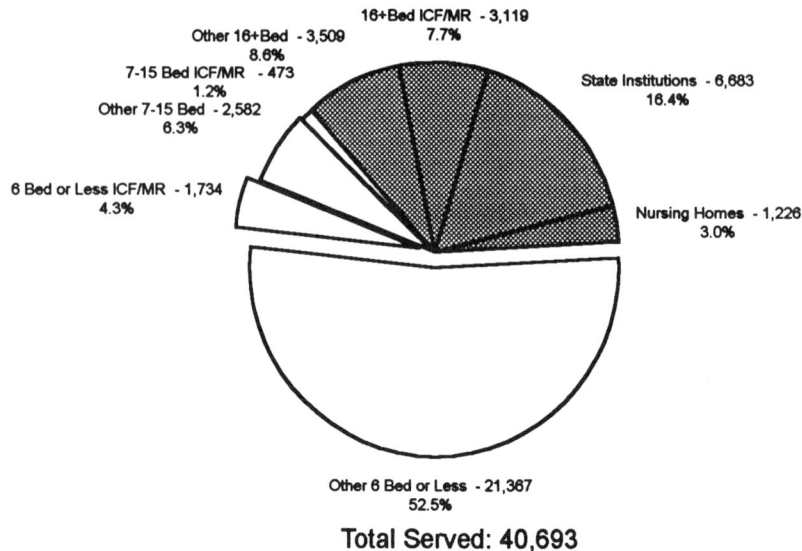

16+Bed ICF/MR - 3,119
7.7%

Other 16+Bed - 3,509
8.6%

7-15 Bed ICF/MR - 473
1.2%

Other 7-15 Bed - 2,582
6.3%

State Institutions - 6,683
16.4%

6 Bed or Less ICF/MR - 1,734
4.3%

Nursing Homes - 1,226
3.0%

Other 6 Bed or Less - 21,367
52.5%

Total Served: 40,693

## Persons Served by Residential Setting:1986-92

|  | 1986 | 1987 | 1988 | 1989 | 1990 | 1991 | 1992 |
|---|---|---|---|---|---|---|---|
| CONGREGATE 16 + BED SETTINGS | 13,135 | 13,237 | 15,345 | 15,030 | 14,817 | 14,770 | 14,537 |
| Nursing Homes | NA | NA | 1,860 | 870 | 976 | 1,128 | 1,226 |
| State Institutions | 6,956 | 6,804 | 6,772 | 6,738 | 6,722 | 6,720 | 6,683 |
| Private 16+Bed ICF/MR | 2,829 | 2,757 | 2,685 | 3,358 | 3,228 | 3,191 | 3,119 |
| Other 16+Bed Residential | 3,350 | 3,676 | 4,028 | 4,064 | 3,891 | 3,731 | 3,509 |
| 15 BED OR LESS RESIDENTIAL SETTINGS | 14,371 | 14,759 | 20,487 | 20,928 | 22,347 | 25,296 | 26,156 |
| Public 7-15 Bed ICF/MR | 0 | 0 | 0 | 0 | 0 | 0 | 0 |
| Private 7-15 Bed ICF/MR | 859 | 1,199 | 466 | 412 | 428 | 442 | 473 |
| Other 7-15 Bed Residential | 13,512 | 13,560 | 2,575 | 2,592 | 2,618 | 2,616 | 2,582 |
| Public 6 Bed or Less ICF/MR | 0 | 0 | 0 | 0 | 0 | 0 | 0 |
| Private 6 Bed or Less ICF/MR | NA | NA | 1,089 | 1,212 | 1,446 | 1,598 | 1,734 |
| Other 6 Bed or Less Residential | NA | NA | 16,357 | 16,712 | 17,855 | 20,640 | 21,367 |
| TOTAL PERSONS SERVED | 27,506 | 27,996 | 35,832 | 35,958 | 37,164 | 40,066 | 40,693 |

## Persons Served in Non-Residential Community Services:1986-92

|  | 1986 | 1987 | 1988 | 1989 | 1990 | 1991 | 1992 |
|---|---|---|---|---|---|---|---|
| DAY/WORK PROGRAMS | 10,123 | 10,965 | 11,945 | 16,516 | 17,272 | 19,567 | 37,753 |
| Sheltered Employment/Work Activity | NA | NA | NA | NA | NA | NA | 12,341 |
| Day Habilitation ("Day Training") | NA | NA | NA | 16,516 | 17,272 | 19,567 | 20,389 |
| Supported/Competitive Employment | NA | NA | NA | NA | NA | NA | 5,023 |
| CASE MANAGEMENT | 67,427 | 72,430 | 79,196 | 84,658 | 88,946 | 93,639 | 99,716 |
| HCBS WAIVER | 2,500 | 2,500 | 2,500 | 3,360 | 3,360 | 3,360 | 3,360 |
| MODEL 50/200 WAIVER | 0 | 0 | 0 | 0 | 0 | 0 | 0 |

*Source:*
Institute on Disability and Human Development (UAP),
University of Illinois at Chicago, 1994

# CALIFORNIA

## Community Services: FY 1992 Revenue Sources

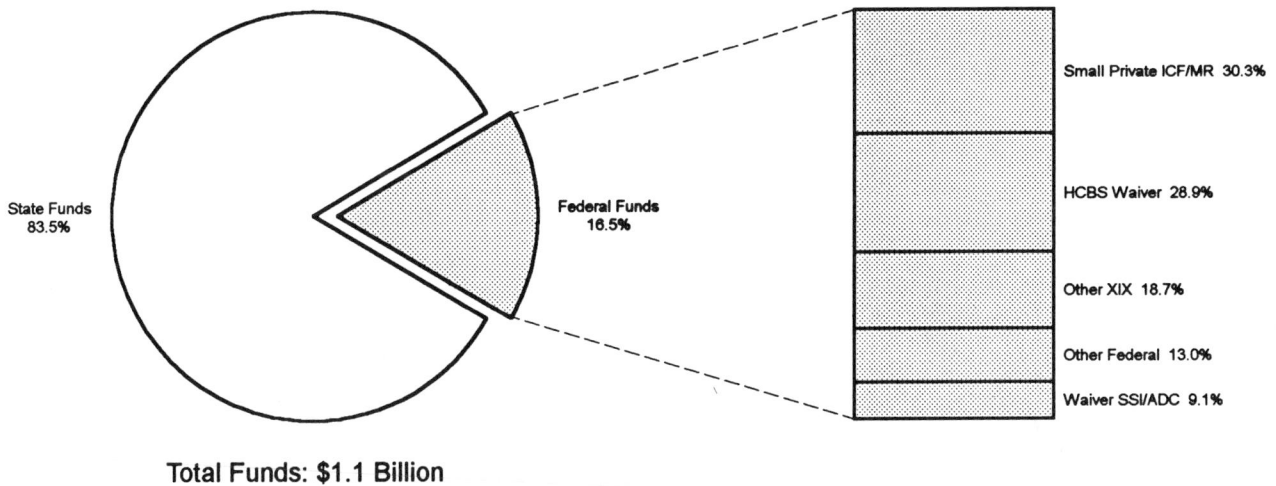

State Funds 83.5%

Federal Funds 16.5%

Small Private ICF/MR 30.3%

HCBS Waiver 28.9%

Other XIX 18.7%

Other Federal 13.0%

Waiver SSI/ADC 9.1%

Total Funds: $1.1 Billion

## Family Support Initiatives*

|  | 1986 | 1987 | 1988 | 1989 | 1990 | 1991 | 1992 |
|---|---|---|---|---|---|---|---|
| FAMILY SUPPORT: TOTAL SPENDING | $24,513,483 | $26,887,321 | $30,511,839 | $31,849,044 | $40,436,663 | $49,529,612 | $56,560,627 |
| Total # of Families Supported | NA | NA | NA | 17,188 | 19,279 | 20,064 | 21,585 |
| A. Financial Subsidy/Payment | $0 | $0 | $0 | $0 | $0 | $0 | $0 |
| # of Families | 0 | 0 | 0 | 0 | 0 | 0 | 0 |
| B. Family Assistance Payments | $7,172,632 | $8,770,612 | $10,791,546 | $12,931,181 | $16,963,828 | $24,539,069 | $26,146,125 |
| # of Families | 8,498 | 9,321 | 10,754 | 7,795 | 8,418 | 9,121 | 10,273 |
| C. Other Family Support Payments | $17,340,851 | $18,116,709 | $19,720,293 | $18,917,863 | $23,472,835 | $24,990,543 | $30,414,502 |
| # of Families | 19,501 | 19,570 | 22,159 | 12,546 | 14,408 | 15,060 | 15,588 |

## Other Community Services Initiatives*

|  | 1986 | 1987 | 1988 | 1989 | 1990 | 1991 | 1992 |
|---|---|---|---|---|---|---|---|
| AGING/DD SPENDING | $0 | $0 | $0 | $0 | $0 | $0 | $0 |
| # of Persons Served | 0 | 0 | 0 | 0 | 0 | 0 | 0 |
| ASSISTIVE TECHNOLOGY SPENDING |  |  | $737,810 | $829,907 | $1,204,629 | $1,532,614 | $1,239,497 |
| # of Persons Served |  |  | 905 | 1,078 | 1,389 | 1,739 | 1,324 |
| EARLY INTERVENTION SPENDING | $0 | $0 | $914,000 | $2,107,196 | $6,137,414 | $9,809,332 | $10,457,159 |
| # of Persons Served | 0 | 0 | NA | NA | NA | NA | NA |
| PERSONAL ASSISTANCE SPENDING |  |  | $2,423,036 | $3,169,830 | $3,878,659 | $6,614,064 | $6,979,677 |
| # of Persons Served |  |  | 1,484 | 1,498 | 1,406 | 2,122 | 2,195 |
| SUPPORTED EMPLOYMENT SPENDING | NA | NA | NA | NA | NA | NA | $26,700,000 |
| # of Persons Served | NA | NA | NA | NA | NA | NA | 5,023 |
| SUPPORTED LIVING SPENDING |  |  | $10,250,427 | $11,702,902 | $14,280,050 | $22,502,120 | $24,913,657 |
| # of Persons Served |  |  | 4,075 | 4,075 | 4,633 | 6,781 | 6,815 |

*Expenditures associated with Special Community Initiatives are a subset of funding within the community services component of the state's chart series and spreadsheet; Family Support Client figures may include duplicate client counts; HCBS Waiver counts include Waiver case management numbers.
0= Services not provided in the state; NA= Data not available from state; blank= Services not applicable (eg. CSLA prior to authorization, Special Community Initiatives prior to request for data by this study)

*Source:*
Institute on Disability and Human Development (UAP),
University of Illinois at Chicago, 1994

# CALIFORNIA

## Large Congregate Care Facilities: FY 1992 Revenue Sources*

### Private 16+Bed Settings

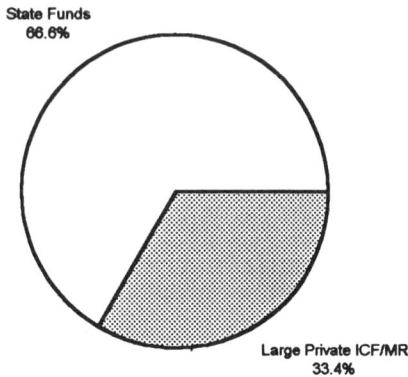

State Funds
66.6%

Large Private ICF/MR
33.4%

Total Funds: $85.1 Million

### Public Institutions

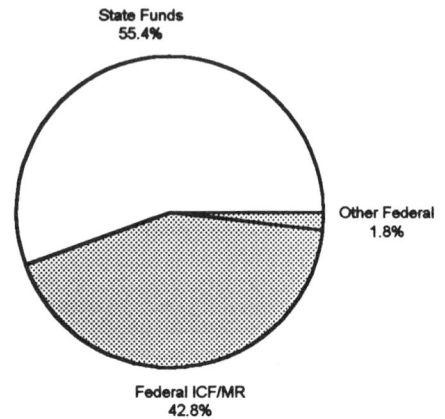

State Funds
55.4%

Other Federal
1.8%

Federal ICF/MR
42.8%

Total Funds: $559.2 Million

*Excludes nursing homes

## Average Daily Residents in Institutions

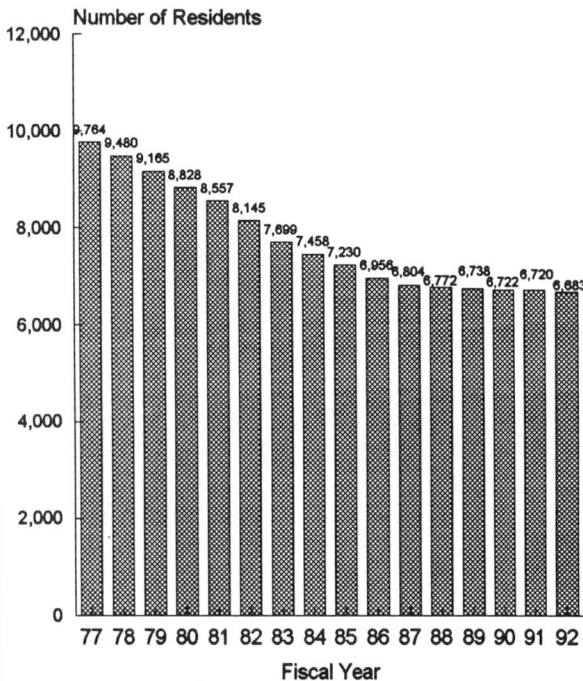

Number of Residents

| Fiscal Year | Residents |
|---|---|
| 77 | 9,764 |
| 78 | 9,480 |
| 79 | 9,165 |
| 80 | 8,828 |
| 81 | 8,557 |
| 82 | 8,145 |
| 83 | 7,699 |
| 84 | 7,458 |
| 85 | 7,230 |
| 86 | 6,956 |
| 87 | 6,804 |
| 88 | 6,772 |
| 89 | 6,738 |
| 90 | 6,722 |
| 91 | 6,720 |
| 92 | 6,683 |

Fiscal Year

## Institutional Daily Costs Per Resident

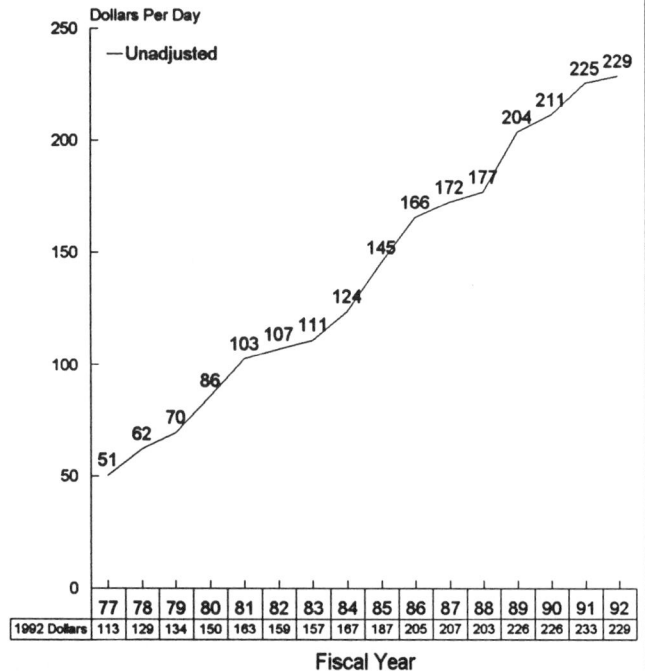

Dollars Per Day

—Unadjusted

Values (unadjusted): 51, 62, 70, 86, 103, 107, 111, 124, 145, 166, 172, 177, 204, 211, 225, 229

| Fiscal Year | 77 | 78 | 79 | 80 | 81 | 82 | 83 | 84 | 85 | 86 | 87 | 88 | 89 | 90 | 91 | 92 |
|---|---|---|---|---|---|---|---|---|---|---|---|---|---|---|---|---|
| 1992 Dollars | 113 | 129 | 134 | 150 | 163 | 159 | 157 | 167 | 187 | 205 | 207 | 203 | 226 | 226 | 233 | 229 |

Fiscal Year

*Source:*
Institute on Disability and Human Development (UAP),
University of Illinois at Chicago, 1994

# CALIFORNIA FISCAL EFFORT

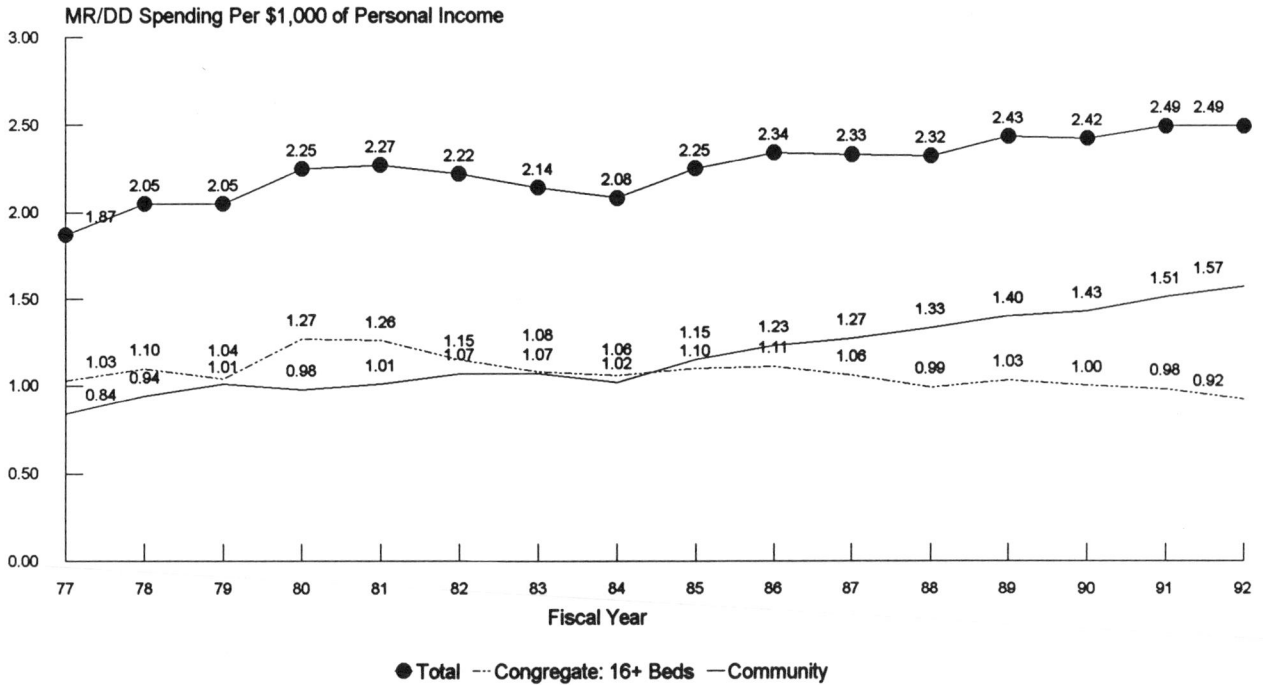

MR/DD Spending Per $1,000 of Personal Income

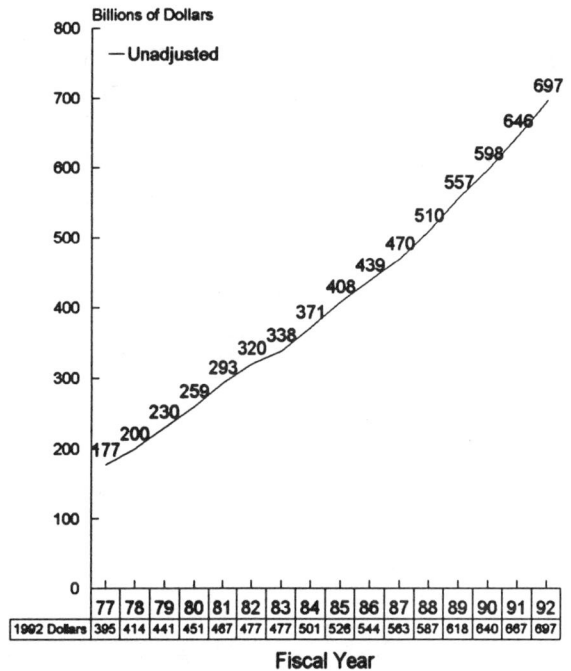

| | |
|---|---|
| 3.00 | |

Total values: 1.87, 2.05, 2.05, 2.25, 2.27, 2.22, 2.14, 2.08, 2.25, 2.34, 2.33, 2.32, 2.43, 2.42, 2.49, 2.49

Congregate: 16+ Beds values: 1.03, 1.10, 1.04, 1.27, 1.26, 1.15, 1.08, 1.06, 1.15, 1.23, 1.27, 1.33, 1.40, 1.43, 1.51, 1.57

Community values: 0.84, 0.94, 1.01, 0.98, 1.01, 1.07, 1.07, 1.02, 1.10, 1.11, 1.06, 0.99, 1.03, 1.00, 0.98, 0.92

Fiscal Year: 77 78 79 80 81 82 83 84 85 86 87 88 89 90 91 92

● Total  --- Congregate: 16+ Beds  — Community

## Total MR/DD Spending

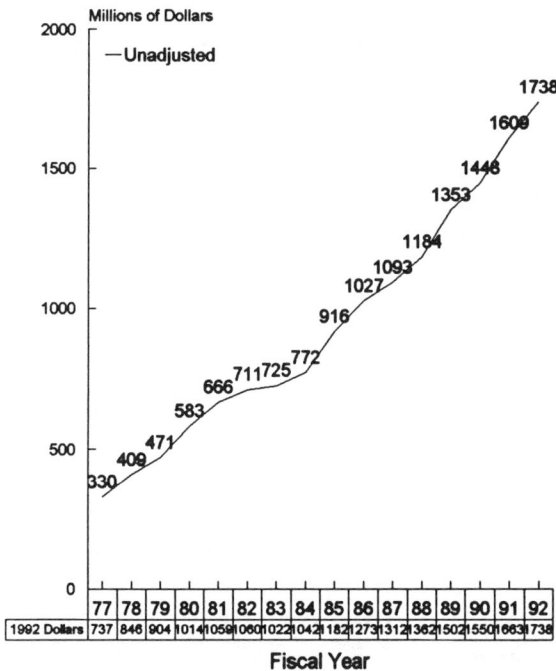

Millions of Dollars

— Unadjusted

Values: 330, 409, 471, 583, 666, 711, 725, 772, 916, 1027, 1093, 1184, 1353, 1448, 1609, 1738

| | 77 | 78 | 79 | 80 | 81 | 82 | 83 | 84 | 85 | 86 | 87 | 88 | 89 | 90 | 91 | 92 |
|---|---|---|---|---|---|---|---|---|---|---|---|---|---|---|---|---|
| 1992 Dollars | 737 | 846 | 904 | 1014 | 1059 | 1060 | 1022 | 1042 | 1182 | 1273 | 1312 | 1362 | 1502 | 1550 | 1663 | 1738 |

Fiscal Year

## Personal Income

Billions of Dollars

— Unadjusted

Values: 177, 200, 230, 259, 293, 320, 338, 371, 408, 439, 470, 510, 557, 598, 646, 697

| | 77 | 78 | 79 | 80 | 81 | 82 | 83 | 84 | 85 | 86 | 87 | 88 | 89 | 90 | 91 | 92 |
|---|---|---|---|---|---|---|---|---|---|---|---|---|---|---|---|---|
| 1992 Dollars | 395 | 414 | 441 | 451 | 467 | 477 | 477 | 501 | 526 | 544 | 563 | 587 | 618 | 640 | 667 | 697 |

Fiscal Year

*Source:*
Institute on Disability and Human Development (UAP),
University of Illinois at Chicago, 1994

# CALIFORNIA
## Financial Support for MR/DD Services: FY 1977-92

| | 1977 | 1978 | 1979 | 1980 | 1981 | 1982 | 1983 | 1984 |
|---|---|---|---|---|---|---|---|---|
| **TOTAL FUNDS** | $330,301,000 | $408,851,000 | $471,036,000 | $582,668,000 | $666,075,000 | $711,255,000 | $724,803,000 | $772,122,000 |
| **CONGREGATE 16+ BEDS** | 182,517,000 | 220,774,820 | 239,591,820 | 328,373,820 | 369,075,000 | 368,477,155 | 363,786,105 | 394,670,420 |
| INSTITUTIONAL SERVICES FUNDS | 180,112,000 | 215,822,000 | 232,678,000 | 278,109,000 | 320,504,000 | 317,811,000 | 312,108,000 | 338,092,000 |
| STATE FUNDS | 129,463,000 | 176,714,000 | 173,146,000 | 218,811,000 | 199,929,000 | 190,819,000 | 163,835,000 | 187,209,000 |
| General Funds | 125,906,000 | 170,112,000 | 167,812,000 | 210,584,000 | 188,206,000 | 181,858,000 | 153,351,000 | 175,610,000 |
| Local | 0 | 0 | 0 | 0 | 0 | 0 | 0 | 0 |
| Other State Funds | 3,557,000 | 6,602,000 | 5,334,000 | 8,227,000 | 11,723,000 | 8,961,000 | 10,484,000 | 11,599,000 |
| FEDERAL FUNDS | 50,649,000 | 39,108,000 | 59,532,000 | 59,298,000 | 120,575,000 | 126,992,000 | 148,273,000 | 150,883,000 |
| Federal ICF/MR | 48,246,000 | 36,250,000 | 57,364,000 | 56,534,000 | 116,539,000 | 123,751,000 | 143,379,000 | 145,743,000 |
| Title XX / SSBG Funds | 0 | 0 | 0 | 0 | 0 | 0 | 0 | 0 |
| Other Federal Funds | 2,403,000 | 2,858,000 | 2,168,000 | 2,764,000 | 4,036,000 | 3,241,000 | 4,894,000 | 5,140,000 |
| LARGE PRIVATE RESIDENTIAL | 2,405,000 | 4,952,820 | 6,913,820 | 50,264,820 | 48,571,000 | 50,666,155 | 51,678,105 | 56,578,420 |
| STATE FUNDS | 2,405,000 | 4,952,820 | 6,913,820 | 29,569,820 | 28,781,000 | 30,454,155 | 31,540,105 | 34,628,420 |
| General Funds | 2,405,000 | 4,952,820 | 6,913,820 | 29,569,820 | 28,781,000 | 30,454,155 | 31,540,105 | 34,628,420 |
| Other State Funds | 0 | 0 | 0 | 0 | 0 | 0 | 0 | 0 |
| Local/County Overmatch | 0 | 0 | 0 | 0 | 0 | 0 | 0 | 0 |
| FEDERAL FUNDS | 0 | 0 | 0 | 20,695,000 | 19,790,000 | 20,212,000 | 20,138,000 | 21,950,000 |
| Large Private ICF/MR | 0 | 0 | 0 | 20,695,000 | 19,790,000 | 20,212,000 | 20,138,000 | 21,950,000 |
| **COMMUNITY SERVICES FUNDS** | 147,784,000 | 188,076,180 | 231,444,180 | 254,294,180 | 297,000,000 | 342,777,845 | 361,016,895 | 377,451,580 |
| STATE FUNDS | 140,111,000 | 181,063,180 | 231,444,180 | 254,294,180 | 297,000,000 | 342,777,845 | 359,841,895 | 374,251,580 |
| General Funds | 62,956,000 | 98,683,180 | 116,817,180 | 137,109,180 | 176,851,000 | 219,361,845 | 241,967,895 | 252,956,580 |
| Other State Funds | 0 | 0 | 0 | 0 | 0 | 0 | 0 | 0 |
| Local/County Overmatch | 0 | 0 | 0 | 0 | 0 | 0 | 0 | 0 |
| SSI State Supplement | 77,155,000 | 82,380,000 | 114,627,000 | 117,185,000 | 120,149,000 | 123,416,000 | 117,874,000 | 121,295,000 |
| FEDERAL FUNDS | 7,673,000 | 7,013,000 | 0 | 0 | 0 | 0 | 1,175,000 | 3,200,000 |
| ICF/MR Funds | 0 | 0 | 0 | 0 | 0 | 0 | 1,175,000 | 3,200,000 |
| Small Public | 0 | 0 | 0 | 0 | 0 | 0 | 0 | 0 |
| Small Private | 0 | 0 | 0 | 0 | 0 | 0 | 1,175,000 | 3,200,000 |
| HCBS Waiver | 0 | 0 | 0 | 0 | 0 | 0 | 0 | 0 |
| Model 50/200 Waiver | 0 | 0 | 0 | 0 | 0 | 0 | 0 | 0 |
| Other Title XIX Programs | 0 | 0 | 0 | 0 | 0 | 0 | 0 | 0 |
| Title XX / SSBG Funds | 7,673,000 | 7,013,000 | 0 | 0 | 0 | 0 | 0 | 0 |
| Other Federal Funds | 0 | 0 | 0 | 0 | 0 | 0 | 0 | 0 |
| Waiver Clients' SSI/ADC | 0 | 0 | 0 | 0 | 0 | 0 | 0 | 0 |

| | 1985 | 1986 | 1987 | 1988 | 1989 | 1990 | 1991 | 1992 |
|---|---|---|---|---|---|---|---|---|
| **TOTAL FUNDS** | $916,467,925 | $1,026,590,850 | $1,093,059,175 | $1,184,092,302 | $1,352,975,291 | $1,447,785,354 | $1,608,657,885 | $1,738,095,966 |
| **CONGREGATE 16+ BEDS** | 448,629,015 | 487,233,420 | 495,769,085 | 506,205,400 | 574,609,673 | 595,413,238 | 633,609,946 | 644,265,925 |
| INSTITUTIONAL SERVICES FUNDS | 383,505,000 | 420,479,000 | 428,251,000 | 438,266,000 | 500,847,272 | 518,591,564 | 552,714,774 | 559,180,000 |
| STATE FUNDS | 227,520,000 | 236,617,300 | 240,583,300 | 240,577,600 | 276,741,272 | 282,777,261 | 303,775,822 | 309,821,000 |
| General Funds | 213,051,000 | 223,783,800 | 227,749,800 | 38,355,500 | 34,767,000 | 30,745,000 | 42,647,000 | 45,369,000 |
| Local | 0 | 0 | 0 | 0 | 0 | 0 | 0 | 0 |
| Other State Funds | 14,469,000 | 12,833,500 | 12,833,500 | 202,222,100 | 241,974,272 | 252,032,261 | 261,128,822 | 264,452,000 |
| FEDERAL FUNDS | 155,985,000 | 183,861,700 | 187,667,700 | 197,688,400 | 224,106,000 | 235,814,303 | 248,938,952 | 249,359,000 |
| Federal ICF/MR | 151,907,000 | 175,351,000 | 179,157,000 | 189,427,000 | 217,775,000 | 228,002,000 | 236,682,000 | 239,317,000 |
| Title XX / SSBG Funds | 0 | 0 | 0 | 0 | 0 | 0 | 0 | 0 |
| Other Federal Funds | 4,078,000 | 8,510,700 | 8,510,700 | 8,261,400 | 6,331,000 | 7,812,303 | 12,256,952 | 10,042,000 |
| LARGE PRIVATE RESIDENTIAL | 65,124,015 | 66,754,420 | 67,518,085 | 67,939,400 | 73,762,401 | 76,821,674 | 80,895,172 | 85,085,925 |
| STATE FUNDS | 40,346,715 | 41,977,120 | 42,703,885 | 42,647,700 | 47,609,742 | 49,808,056 | 53,750,679 | 56,696,415 |
| General Funds | 40,346,715 | 41,977,120 | 42,703,885 | 17,356,000 | 21,457,083 | 22,794,428 | 26,606,186 | 28,306,905 |
| Other State Funds | 0 | 0 | 0 | 25,291,700 | 26,152,659 | 27,013,628 | 27,144,493 | 28,389,510 |
| Local/County Overmatch | 0 | 0 | 0 | 0 | 0 | 0 | 0 | 0 |
| FEDERAL FUNDS | 24,777,300 | 24,777,300 | 24,814,200 | 25,291,700 | 26,152,659 | 27,013,618 | 27,144,493 | 28,389,510 |
| Large Private ICF/MR | 24,777,300 | 24,777,300 | 24,814,200 | 25,291,700 | 26,152,659 | 27,013,618 | 27,144,493 | 28,389,510 |
| **COMMUNITY SERVICES FUNDS** | 467,838,910 | 539,357,430 | 597,290,090 | 677,886,902 | 778,365,618 | 852,372,116 | 975,047,939 | 1,093,830,041 |
| STATE FUNDS | 435,280,310 | 504,085,430 | 555,710,990 | 624,005,001 | 702,827,963 | 764,413,596 | 861,398,046 | 913,063,706 |
| General Funds | 305,982,310 | 362,246,430 | 405,329,990 | 428,637,100 | 489,062,542 | 526,043,322 | 610,056,689 | 616,497,095 |
| Other State Funds | 996,000 | 1,122,000 | 1,291,000 | 38,753,901 | 91,075,421 | 106,016,274 | 113,728,357 | 144,631,611 |
| Local/County Overmatch | 0 | 0 | 0 | 0 | 0 | 0 | 0 | 0 |
| SSI State Supplement | 128,302,000 | 140,717,000 | 149,090,000 | 156,614,000 | 122,690,000 | 132,354,000 | 137,613,000 | 151,935,000 |
| FEDERAL FUNDS | 32,558,600 | 35,272,000 | 41,579,100 | 53,881,901 | 75,537,655 | 87,958,520 | 113,649,893 | 180,766,335 |
| ICF/MR Funds | 7,807,600 | 10,003,000 | 14,731,200 | 22,612,701 | 29,820,421 | 37,028,142 | 46,290,357 | 54,841,845 |
| Small Public | 0 | 0 | 0 | 0 | 0 | 0 | 0 | 0 |
| Small Private | 7,807,600 | 10,003,000 | 14,731,200 | 22,612,701 | 29,820,421 | 37,028,142 | 46,290,357 | 54,841,845 |
| HCBS Waiver | 12,611,000 | 13,100,000 | 13,650,900 | 13,681,200 | 27,454,000 | 28,734,000 | 27,200,000 | 52,200,000 |
| Model 50/200 Waiver | 0 | 0 | 0 | 0 | 0 | 0 | 0 | 0 |
| Other Title XIX Programs | 0 | 0 | 0 | 0 | 437,794 | 249,618 | 13,182,296 | 33,778,250 |
| Title XX / SSBG Funds | 0 | 0 | 0 | 0 | 0 | 0 | 0 | 0 |
| Other Federal Funds | 3,260,000 | 2,959,000 | 3,867,000 | 7,958,000 | 4,036,000 | 7,109,000 | 11,575,000 | 23,536,000 |
| Waiver Clients' SSI/ADC | 8,880,000 | 9,210,000 | 9,330,000 | 9,630,000 | 13,789,440 | 14,837,760 | 15,402,240 | 16,410,240 |

*Source:*
Institute on Disability and Human Development (UAP),
University of Illinois at Chicago, 1994

# COLORADO

## MR/DD Spending for Congregate Residential & Community Services

▨Congregate: 16+ Beds*   ■Community**

Millions of 1992 Dollars

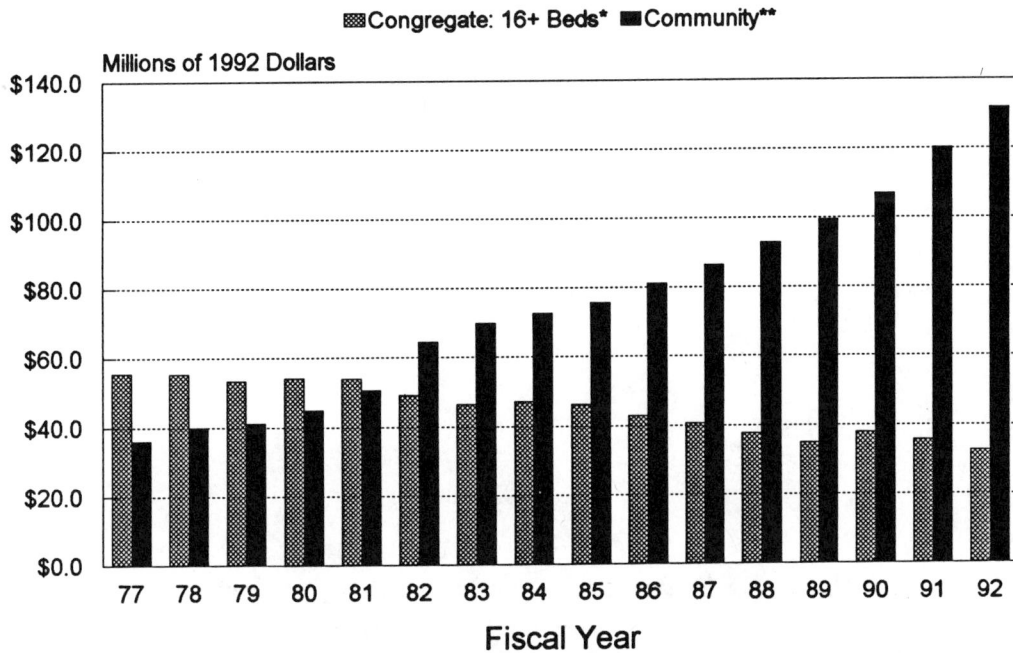

Fiscal Year

*Excludes nursing homes; ** Includes resources for
15 bed or less residential settings & non-residential community services

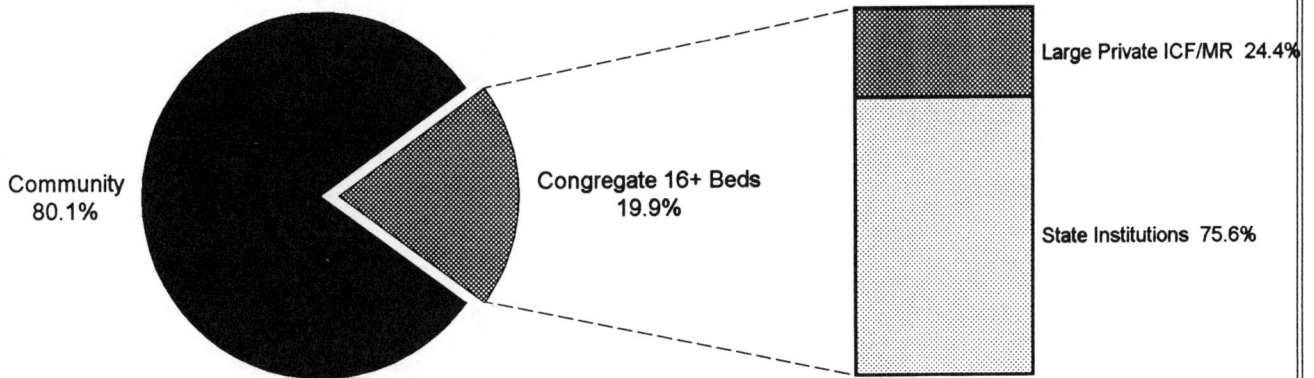

Community
80.1%

Congregate 16+ Beds
19.9%

Large Private ICF/MR  24.4%

State Institutions  75.6%

FY 1992 Total Spending:
$164.4 Million

*Source:*
Institute on Disability and Human Development (UAP),
University of Illinois at Chicago, 1994

# COLORADO

## Number of Persons Served by Residential Setting: FY 1992

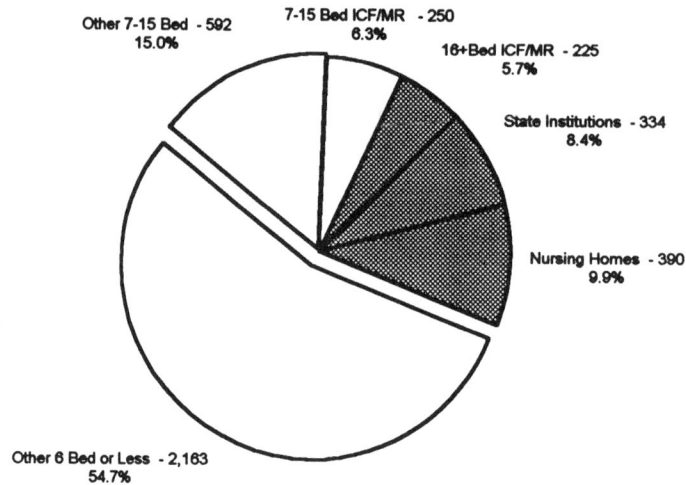

Other 7-15 Bed - 592
15.0%

7-15 Bed ICF/MR - 250
6.3%

16+Bed ICF/MR - 225
5.7%

State Institutions - 334
8.4%

Nursing Homes - 390
9.9%

Other 6 Bed or Less - 2,163
54.7%

Total Served: 3,954

## Persons Served by Residential Setting:1986-92

| | 1986 | 1987 | 1988 | 1989 | 1990 | 1991 | 1992 |
|---|---|---|---|---|---|---|---|
| CONGREGATE 16 + BED SETTINGS | NA | NA | 1,371 | 1,251 | 1,166 | 1,076 | 949 |
| Nursing Homes | NA | NA | 484 | 460 | 440 | 420 | 390 |
| State Institutions | 745 | 670 | 554 | 511 | 466 | 406 | 334 |
| Private 16+Bed ICF/MR | 336 | 336 | 333 | 280 | 260 | 250 | 225 |
| Other 16+Bed Residential | 0 | 0 | 0 | 0 | 0 | 0 | 0 |
| 15 BED OR LESS RESIDENTIAL SETTINGS | 1,970 | 2,114 | 2,313 | 2,522 | 2,628 | 2,785 | 3,005 |
| Public 7-15 Bed ICF/MR | 280 | 280 | 280 | 274 | 277 | 275 | 250 |
| Private 7-15 Bed ICF/MR | 0 | 0 | 0 | 0 | 0 | 0 | 0 |
| Other 7-15 Bed Residential | 1,690 | 1,834 | 2,033 | 1,305 | 693 | 448 | 592 |
| Public 6 Bed or Less ICF/MR | 0 | 0 | 0 | 0 | 0 | 0 | 0 |
| Private 6 Bed or Less ICF/MR | 0 | 0 | 0 | 0 | 0 | 0 | 0 |
| Other 6 Bed or Less Residential | | | | 943 | 1,658 | 2,062 | 2,163 |
| TOTAL PERSONS SERVED | NA | NA | 3,684 | 3,773 | 3,794 | 3,861 | 3,954 |

## Persons Served in Non-Residential Community Services:1986-92

| | 1986 | 1987 | 1988 | 1989 | 1990 | 1991 | 1992 |
|---|---|---|---|---|---|---|---|
| DAY/WORK PROGRAMS | 3,157 | 3,362 | 3,438 | 3,837 | 3,654 | 3,875 | 4,277 |
| Sheltered Employment/Work Activity | NA | NA | NA | NA | NA | NA | NA |
| Day Habilitation ("Day Training") | NA | NA | NA | NA | NA | NA | NA |
| Supported/Competitive Employment | 219 | 708 | 809 | 1,009 | 1,426 | 1,673 | 1,880 |
| CASE MANAGEMENT | 5,345 | 5,648 | 5,771 | 5,942 | 5,919 | 6,176 | 6,463 |
| HCBS WAIVER | 1,074 | 1,223 | 1,432 | 1,639 | 1,735 | 1,900 | 2,135 |
| MODEL 50/200 WAIVER | 0 | 0 | 0 | 0 | 0 | 0 | 0 |

*Source:*
Institute on Disability and Human Development (UAP),
University of Illinois at Chicago, 1994

# COLORADO

## Community Services: FY 1992 Revenue Sources

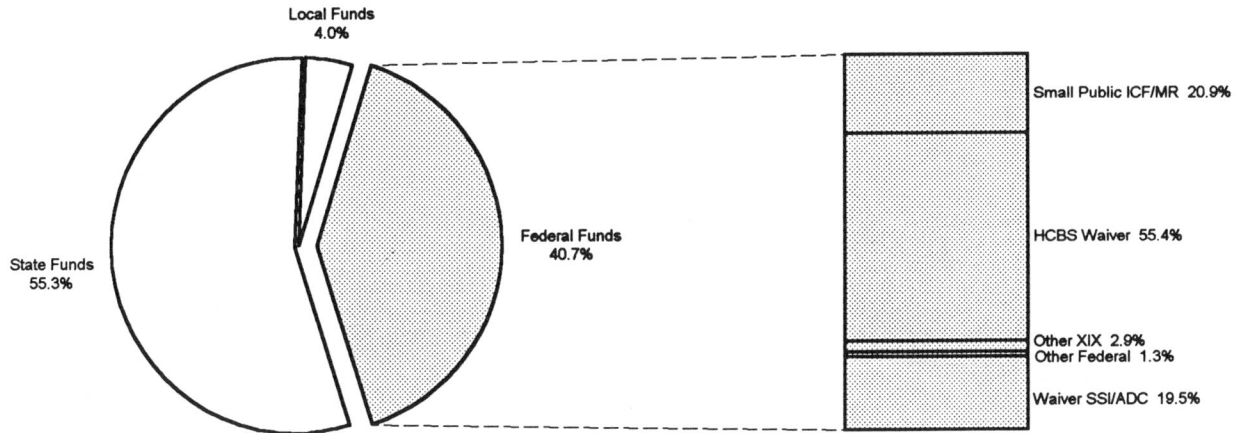

Local Funds
4.0%

State Funds
55.3%

Federal Funds
40.7%

Small Public ICF/MR 20.9%

HCBS Waiver 55.4%

Other XIX 2.9%
Other Federal 1.3%

Waiver SSI/ADC 19.5%

Total Funds: $131.8 Million

## Family Support Initiatives*

|  | 1986 | 1987 | 1988 | 1989 | 1990 | 1991 | 1992 |
|---|---|---|---|---|---|---|---|
| **FAMILY SUPPORT: TOTAL SPENDING** | $177,131 | $264,422 | $289,894 | $417,400 | $466,520 | $729,165 | $1,692,875 |
| **Total # of Families Supported** | 256 | 50 | 65 | 115 | 115 | 200 | 733 |
| A. Financial Subsidy/Payment | $0 | $0 | $0 | $0 | $0 | $0 | $0 |
| # of Families | 0 | 0 | 0 | 0 | 0 | 0 | 0 |
| B. Family Assistance Payments | $92,131 | $94,894 | $94,894 | $81,456 | $88,933 | $94,158 | $292,559 |
| # of Families | 216 | NA | NA | NA | NA | NA | 465 |
| C. Other Family Support Payments | $85,000 | $169,528 | $195,000 | $335,944 | $377,587 | $635,007 | $1,400,316 |
| # of Families | 40 | 50 | 65 | 115 | 115 | 200 | 268 |

## Other Community Services Initiatives*

|  | 1986 | 1987 | 1988 | 1989 | 1990 | 1991 | 1992 |
|---|---|---|---|---|---|---|---|
| **AGING/DD SPENDING** | $0 | $0 | $0 | $0 | $0 | $0 | $783,720 |
| # of Persons Served | 0 | 0 | 0 | 0 | 0 | 0 | 178 |
| **ASSISTIVE TECHNOLOGY SPENDING** |  |  |  |  |  |  | $0 |
| # of Persons Served |  |  |  |  |  |  | 0 |
| **EARLY INTERVENTION SPENDING** | $4,364,980 | $4,350,050 | $4,350,050 | $4,142,569 | $4,451,636 | $4,533,375 | $3,325,583 |
| # of Persons Served | 1,336 | 1,330 | 1,316 | 1,520 | 1,642 | 1,676 | 1,581 |
| **PERSONAL ASSISTANCE SPENDING** |  |  |  |  |  |  | $0 |
| # of Persons Served |  |  |  |  |  |  | 0 |
| **SUPPORTED EMPLOYMENT SPENDING** | $935,969 | $3,026,170 | $3,487,107 | $4,241,533 | $6,316,045 | $7,705,340 | $8,904,026 |
| # of Persons Served | 219 | 708 | 809 | 1,009 | 1,426 | 1,673 | 1,880 |
| **SUPPORTED LIVING SPENDING** |  |  |  |  |  |  | $0 |
| # of Persons Served |  |  |  |  |  |  | 0 |

*Expenditures associated with Special Community Initiatives are a subset of funding within the community services component of the state's chart series and spreadsheet; Family Support Client figures may include duplicate client counts; HCBS Waiver counts include Waiver case management numbers.
0= Services not provided in the state; NA= Data not available from state; blank= Services not applicable (eg. CSLA prior to authorization, Special Community Initiatives prior to request for data by this study)

*Source:*
Institute on Disability and Human Development (UAP),
University of Illinois at Chicago, 1994

# COLORADO

## Large Congregate Care Facilities: FY 1992 Revenue Sources*

### Private 16+Bed Settings

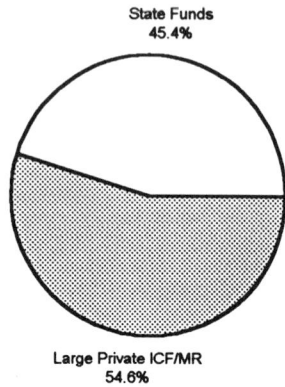

State Funds
45.4%

Large Private ICF/MR
54.6%

Total Funds: $7.9 Million

### Public Institutions

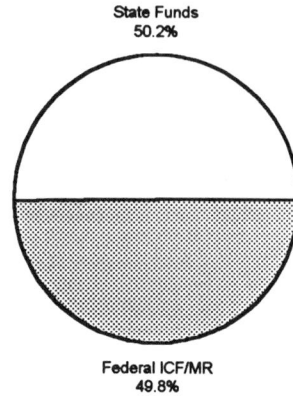

State Funds
50.2%

Federal ICF/MR
49.8%

Total Funds: $24.7 Million

*Excludes nursing homes

## Average Daily Residents in Institutions

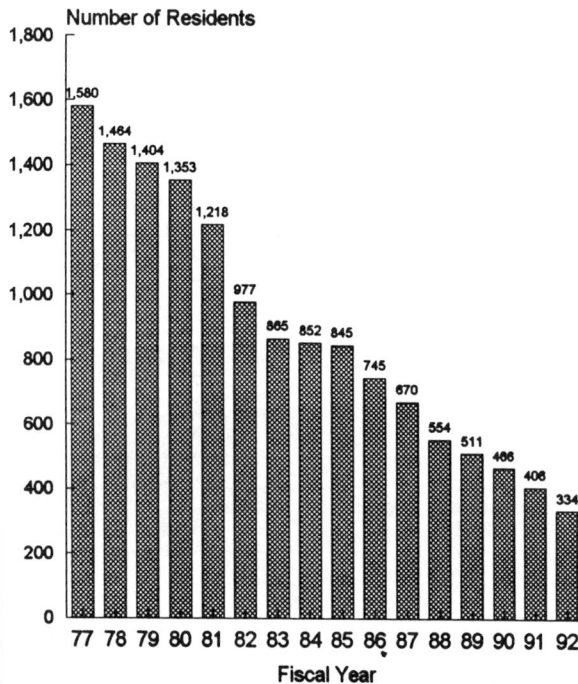

Number of Residents

| Fiscal Year | Number |
|---|---|
| 77 | 1,580 |
| 78 | 1,464 |
| 79 | 1,404 |
| 80 | 1,353 |
| 81 | 1,218 |
| 82 | 977 |
| 83 | 865 |
| 84 | 852 |
| 85 | 845 |
| 86 | 745 |
| 87 | 670 |
| 88 | 554 |
| 89 | 511 |
| 90 | 466 |
| 91 | 406 |
| 92 | 334 |

Fiscal Year

## Institutional Daily Costs Per Resident

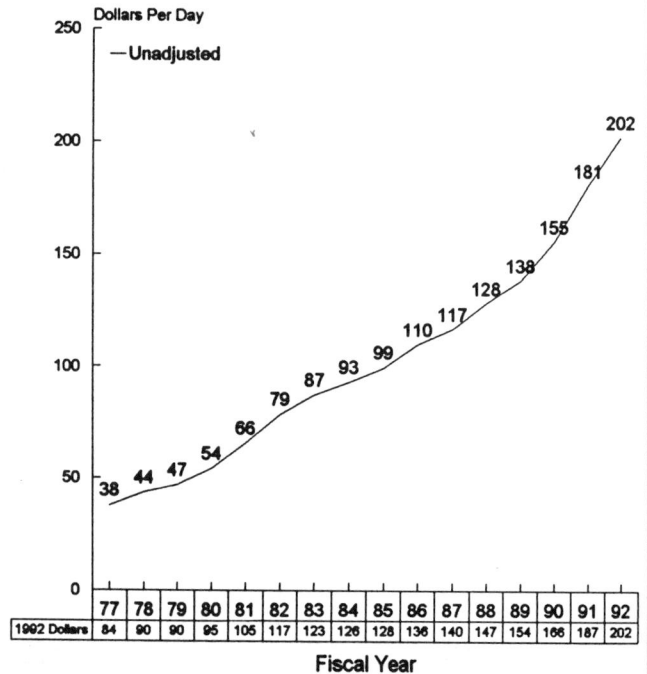

Dollars Per Day

—Unadjusted

| Fiscal Year | 77 | 78 | 79 | 80 | 81 | 82 | 83 | 84 | 85 | 86 | 87 | 88 | 89 | 90 | 91 | 92 |
|---|---|---|---|---|---|---|---|---|---|---|---|---|---|---|---|---|
| Unadjusted | 38 | 44 | 47 | 54 | 66 | 79 | 87 | 93 | 99 | 110 | 117 | 128 | 138 | 155 | 181 | 202 |
| 1992 Dollars | 84 | 90 | 90 | 95 | 105 | 117 | 123 | 126 | 128 | 136 | 140 | 147 | 154 | 166 | 187 | 202 |

Fiscal Year

*Source:*
Institute on Disability and Human Development (UAP),
University of Illinois at Chicago, 1994

# COLORADO FISCAL EFFORT

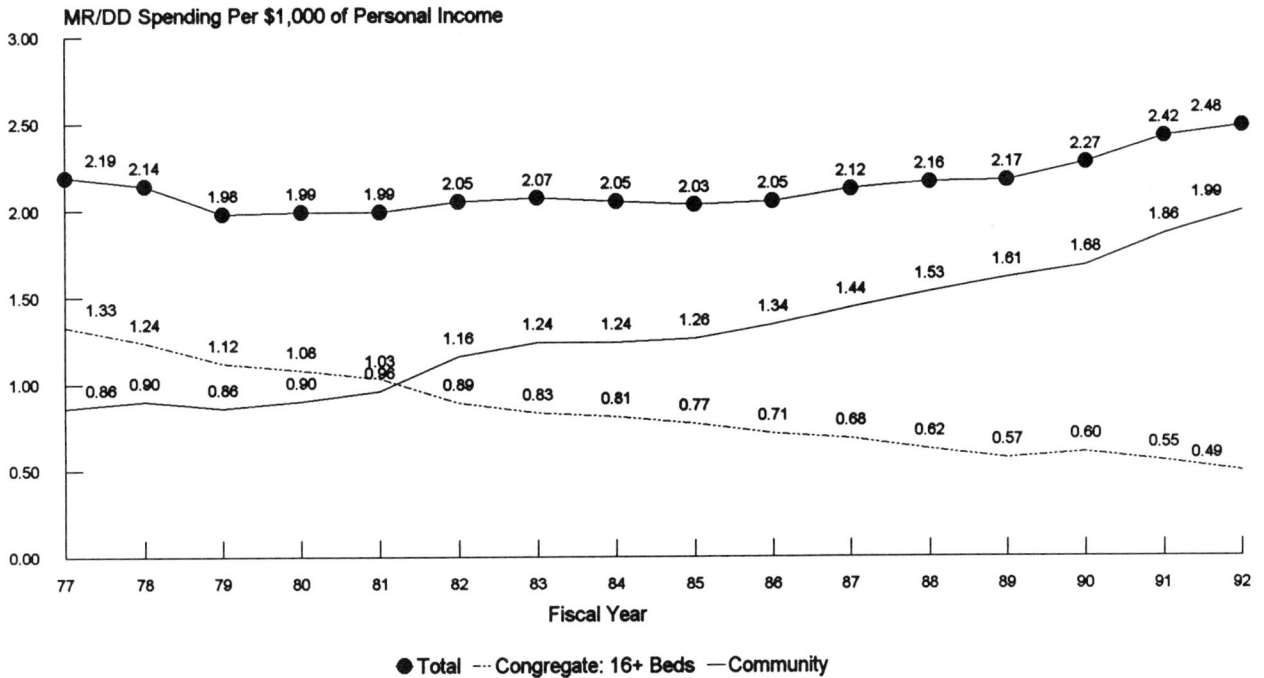

MR/DD Spending Per $1,000 of Personal Income

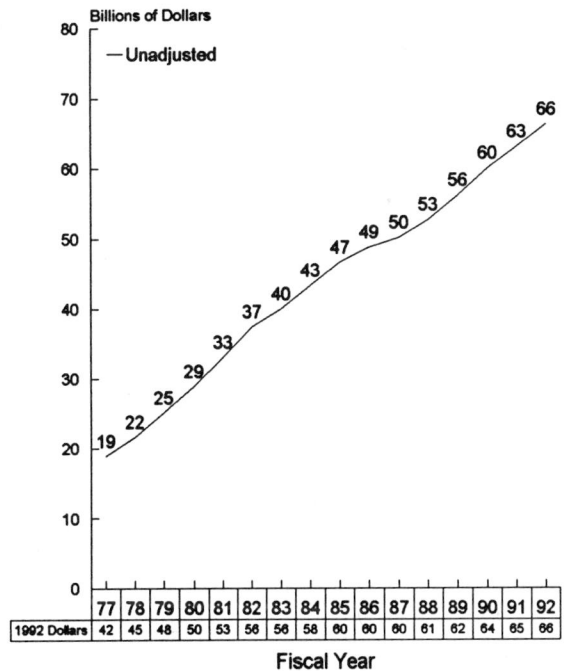

| | | |
|---|---|---|
| 3.00 | | |
| 2.50 | | 2.42  2.48 |
| 2.00 | 2.19  2.14  1.98  1.99  1.99  2.05  2.07  2.05  2.03  2.05  2.12  2.16  2.17  2.27 | 1.99 |
| 1.50 | 1.33  1.24 | 1.86 |
| 1.00 | 0.86  0.90  1.12  0.86  1.08  0.90  1.03  1.16  1.24  1.24  1.26  1.34  1.44  1.53  1.61  1.68 | |
| 0.50 | 0.96  0.89  0.83  0.81  0.77  0.71  0.68  0.62  0.57  0.60  0.55  0.49 | |
| 0.00 | | |

Fiscal Year: 77 78 79 80 81 82 83 84 85 86 87 88 89 90 91 92

● Total  --- Congregate: 16+ Beds  — Community

## Total MR/DD Spending

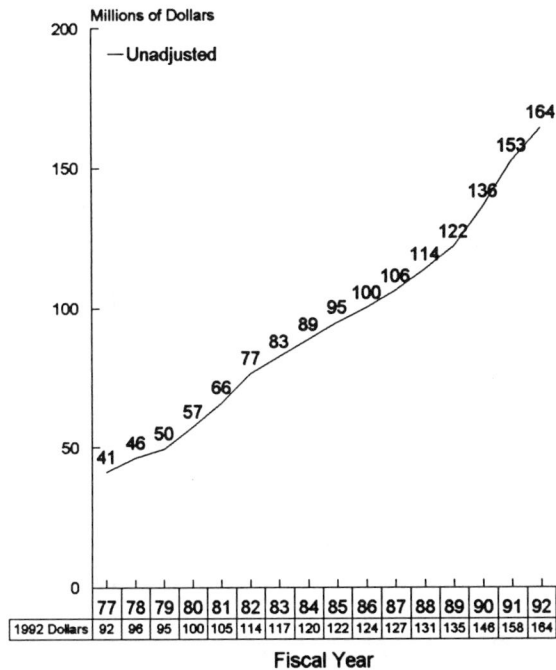

Millions of Dollars
—Unadjusted

| | |
|---|---|
| 200 | |
| 150 | 164  153 |
| 100 | 136  122  114  106  100  95  89  83 |
| 50 | 77  66  57  50  46  41 |
| 0 | |

| Fiscal Year | 77 | 78 | 79 | 80 | 81 | 82 | 83 | 84 | 85 | 86 | 87 | 88 | 89 | 90 | 91 | 92 |
|---|---|---|---|---|---|---|---|---|---|---|---|---|---|---|---|---|
| 1992 Dollars | 92 | 96 | 95 | 100 | 105 | 114 | 117 | 120 | 122 | 124 | 127 | 131 | 135 | 146 | 158 | 164 |

## Personal Income

Billions of Dollars
—Unadjusted

| | |
|---|---|
| 80 | |
| 70 | 66 |
| 60 | 63  60  56 |
| 50 | 53  50  49  47 |
| 40 | 43  40  37 |
| 30 | 33  29  25 |
| 20 | 22  19 |
| 10 | |
| 0 | |

| Fiscal Year | 77 | 78 | 79 | 80 | 81 | 82 | 83 | 84 | 85 | 86 | 87 | 88 | 89 | 90 | 91 | 92 |
|---|---|---|---|---|---|---|---|---|---|---|---|---|---|---|---|---|
| 1992 Dollars | 42 | 45 | 48 | 50 | 53 | 56 | 56 | 58 | 60 | 60 | 60 | 61 | 62 | 64 | 65 | 66 |

*Source:*
Institute on Disability and Human Development (UAP),
University of Illinois at Chicago, 1994

# COLORADO

## Financial Support for MR/DD Services: FY 1977-92

| | 1977 | 1978 | 1979 | 1980 | 1981 | 1982 | 1983 | 1984 |
|---|---|---|---|---|---|---|---|---|
| **TOTAL FUNDS** | $41,323,300 | $46,294,600 | $49,531,200 | $57,279,500 | $65,915,950 | $76,600,150 | $82,692,650 | $88,774,075 |
| **CONGREGATE 16+ BEDS** | 25,037,810 | 26,892,457 | 27,938,376 | 31,275,608 | 34,030,109 | 33,205,428 | 32,994,812 | 34,958,957 |
| INSTITUTIONAL SERVICES FUNDS | 21,765,000 | 23,325,000 | 24,027,000 | 26,903,000 | 29,274,654 | 28,055,523 | 27,559,655 | 29,035,287 |
| STATE FUNDS | 17,033,000 | 11,902,000 | 10,992,000 | 12,559,000 | 13,854,952 | 13,898,302 | 14,328,686 | 15,646,479 |
| General Funds | 16,970,000 | 11,843,000 | 10,986,000 | 12,549,000 | 13,845,952 | 13,146,802 | 12,480,120 | 13,690,972 |
| Local | 0 | 0 | 0 | 0 | 0 | 0 | 0 | 0 |
| Other State Funds | 63,000 | 59,000 | 6,000 | 10,000 | 9,000 | 751,500 | 1,848,566 | 1,955,507 |
| FEDERAL FUNDS | 4,732,000 | 11,423,000 | 13,035,000 | 14,344,000 | 15,419,702 | 14,157,221 | 13,230,969 | 13,388,808 |
| Federal ICF/MR | 3,802,000 | 10,114,000 | 11,974,000 | 13,429,000 | 14,548,702 | 13,598,721 | 12,842,669 | 13,138,708 |
| Title XX / SSBG Funds | 0 | 0 | 0 | 0 | 0 | 0 | 0 | 0 |
| Other Federal Funds | 930,000 | 1,309,000 | 1,061,000 | 915,000 | 871,000 | 558,500 | 388,300 | 250,100 |
| LARGE PRIVATE RESIDENTIAL | 3,272,810 | 3,567,457 | 3,911,376 | 4,372,608 | 4,755,455 | 5,149,905 | 5,435,157 | 5,923,670 |
| STATE FUNDS | 1,482,910 | 1,642,457 | 1,810,576 | 2,042,008 | 2,227,455 | 2,446,205 | 2,593,657 | 2,928,070 |
| General Funds | 0 | 0 | 0 | 0 | 0 | 0 | 0 | 0 |
| Other State Funds | 1,482,910 | 1,642,457 | 1,810,576 | 2,042,008 | 2,227,455 | 2,446,205 | 2,593,657 | 2,928,070 |
| Local/County Overmatch | 0 | 0 | 0 | 0 | 0 | 0 | 0 | 0 |
| FEDERAL FUNDS | 1,789,900 | 1,925,000 | 2,100,800 | 2,330,600 | 2,528,000 | 2,703,700 | 2,841,500 | 2,995,600 |
| Large Private ICF/MR | 1,789,900 | 1,925,000 | 2,100,800 | 2,330,600 | 2,528,000 | 2,703,700 | 2,841,500 | 2,995,600 |
| **COMMUNITY SERVICES FUNDS** | 16,285,490 | 19,402,143 | 21,592,824 | 26,003,892 | 31,885,841 | 43,394,722 | 49,697,838 | 53,815,118 |
| STATE FUNDS | 9,499,390 | 12,726,143 | 15,107,624 | 18,948,492 | 23,641,643 | 35,225,143 | 39,822,173 | 40,437,133 |
| General Funds | 7,394,090 | 10,541,543 | 12,930,424 | 16,795,992 | 21,224,593 | 32,447,993 | 36,683,223 | 37,130,158 |
| Other State Funds | 0 | 0 | 0 | 0 | 0 | 0 | 0 | 0 |
| Local/County Overmatch | 593,300 | 679,600 | 751,200 | 893,500 | 1,047,050 | 1,219,150 | 1,334,950 | 1,365,975 |
| SSI State Supplement | 1,512,000 | 1,505,000 | 1,426,000 | 1,259,000 | 1,370,000 | 1,558,000 | 1,804,000 | 1,941,000 |
| FEDERAL FUNDS | 6,786,100 | 6,676,000 | 6,485,200 | 7,055,400 | 8,244,198 | 8,169,579 | 9,875,665 | 13,377,985 |
| ICF/MR Funds | 1,265,100 | 1,938,000 | 2,359,200 | 3,173,400 | 4,477,198 | 8,169,579 | 9,875,665 | 5,817,885 |
| Small Public | 0 | 0 | 0 | 0 | 800,298 | 3,897,279 | 4,157,165 | 4,317,885 |
| Small Private | 1,265,100 | 1,938,000 | 2,359,200 | 3,173,400 | 3,676,900 | 4,272,300 | 5,718,500 | 1,500,000 |
| HCBS Waiver | | | | 0 | 0 | 0 | 0 | 5,508,100 |
| Model 50/200 Waiver | 0 | 0 | 0 | 0 | 0 | 0 | 0 | 0 |
| Other Title XIX Programs | 0 | 0 | 0 | 0 | 0 | 0 | 0 | 0 |
| Title XX / SSBG Funds | 4,612,000 | 4,091,000 | 3,543,000 | 3,758,000 | 3,767,000 | 0 | 0 | 0 |
| Other Federal Funds | 909,000 | 647,000 | 583,000 | 124,000 | 0 | 0 | 0 | 0 |
| Waiver Clients' SSI/ADC | 0 | 0 | 0 | 0 | 0 | 0 | 0 | 2,052,000 |

| | 1985 | 1986 | 1987 | 1988 | 1989 | 1990 | 1991 | 1992 |
|---|---|---|---|---|---|---|---|---|
| **TOTAL FUNDS** | $94,951,354 | $100,241,338 | $106,209,826 | $113,802,588 | $122,050,477 | $136,287,020 | $152,551,164 | $164,449,371 |
| **CONGREGATE 16+ BEDS** | 35,997,067 | 34,708,805 | 33,995,907 | 32,940,164 | 31,802,849 | 35,749,542 | 34,958,283 | 32,677,298 |
| INSTITUTIONAL SERVICES FUNDS | 30,651,267 | 29,870,467 | 28,527,389 | 25,986,820 | 25,801,991 | 26,440,895 | 26,750,811 | 24,697,000 |
| STATE FUNDS | 16,138,013 | 16,640,339 | 15,430,294 | 14,538,394 | 14,008,234 | 13,791,709 | 13,653,383 | 12,405,139 |
| General Funds | 14,156,706 | 14,157,971 | 13,121,503 | 12,211,915 | 11,825,480 | 11,873,056 | 12,002,196 | 10,632,704 |
| Local | 0 | 0 | 0 | 0 | 0 | 0 | 0 | 0 |
| Other State Funds | 1,981,307 | 2,482,368 | 2,308,791 | 2,326,479 | 2,182,754 | 1,918,653 | 1,651,187 | 1,772,435 |
| FEDERAL FUNDS | 14,513,254 | 13,230,128 | 13,097,095 | 11,448,426 | 11,793,757 | 12,649,186 | 13,097,428 | 12,291,861 |
| Federal ICF/MR | 14,320,754 | 13,005,925 | 12,913,820 | 11,273,420 | 11,793,757 | 12,649,186 | 13,097,428 | 12,291,861 |
| Title XX / SSBG Funds | 0 | 0 | 0 | 0 | 0 | 0 | 0 | 0 |
| Other Federal Funds | 192,500 | 224,203 | 183,275 | 175,006 | 0 | 0 | 0 | 0 |
| LARGE PRIVATE RESIDENTIAL | 5,345,800 | 4,838,338 | 5,468,518 | 6,953,344 | 6,000,858 | 9,308,647 | 8,207,472 | 7,980,298 |
| STATE FUNDS | 2,672,900 | 2,419,169 | 2,734,259 | 3,476,672 | 3,000,429 | 4,507,014 | 3,839,702 | 3,623,055 |
| General Funds | 0 | 0 | 0 | 0 | 0 | 0 | 0 | 0 |
| Other State Funds | 2,672,900 | 2,419,169 | 2,734,259 | 3,476,672 | 3,000,429 | 4,507,014 | 3,839,702 | 3,623,055 |
| Local/County Overmatch | 0 | 0 | 0 | 0 | 0 | 0 | 0 | 0 |
| FEDERAL FUNDS | 2,672,900 | 2,419,169 | 2,734,259 | 3,476,672 | 3,000,429 | 4,801,633 | 4,367,770 | 4,357,243 |
| Large Private ICF/MR | 2,672,900 | 2,419,169 | 2,734,259 | 3,476,672 | 3,000,429 | 4,801,633 | 4,367,770 | 4,357,243 |
| **COMMUNITY SERVICES FUNDS** | 58,954,287 | 65,532,533 | 72,213,919 | 80,862,424 | 90,247,628 | 100,537,478 | 117,592,881 | 131,772,073 |
| STATE FUNDS | 42,534,068 | 46,142,697 | 49,525,474 | 53,966,132 | 59,187,838 | 63,177,518 | 71,618,303 | 78,190,872 |
| General Funds | 38,741,694 | 42,257,992 | 44,720,085 | 48,837,799 | 52,333,365 | 55,134,162 | 63,023,232 | 69,364,482 |
| Other State Funds | 0 | 0 | 224,000 | 336,000 | 346,876 | 380,632 | 378,764 | 363,713 |
| Local/County Overmatch | 1,740,374 | 1,878,705 | 1,948,389 | 2,069,811 | 3,684,342 | 4,735,008 | 5,180,266 | 5,314,302 |
| SSI State Supplement | 2,052,000 | 2,006,000 | 2,633,000 | 2,722,522 | 2,823,255 | 2,927,716 | 3,036,041 | 3,148,375 |
| FEDERAL FUNDS | 16,420,219 | 19,389,836 | 22,688,445 | 26,896,292 | 31,059,790 | 37,359,960 | 45,974,578 | 53,581,201 |
| ICF/MR Funds | 4,745,339 | 4,888,133 | 5,396,821 | 5,697,758 | 7,326,341 | 8,228,810 | 10,599,993 | 11,173,856 |
| Small Public | 4,745,339 | 4,888,133 | 5,396,821 | 5,697,758 | 7,326,341 | 8,228,810 | 10,599,993 | 11,173,856 |
| Small Private | 0 | 0 | 0 | 0 | 0 | 0 | 0 | 0 |
| HCBS Waiver | 8,428,700 | 10,545,087 | 12,727,388 | 15,699,654 | 17,006,993 | 19,972,894 | 24,623,578 | 29,705,426 |
| Model 50/200 Waiver | 0 | 0 | 0 | 0 | 0 | 0 | 0 | 0 |
| Other Title XIX Programs | 0 | 0 | 0 | 0 | 0 | 1,371,266 | 1,589,036 | 1,556,601 |
| Title XX / SSBG Funds | 0 | 0 | 0 | 0 | 0 | 0 | 0 | 0 |
| Other Federal Funds | 0 | 0 | 0 | 0 | 0 | 125,230 | 452,371 | 717,978 |
| Waiver Clients' SSI/ADC | 3,246,180 | 3,956,616 | 4,564,236 | 5,498,880 | 6,726,456 | 7,661,760 | 8,709,600 | 10,427,340 |

*Source:*

Institute on Disability and Human Development (UAP),
University of Illinois at Chicago, 1994

# CONNECTICUT

## MR/DD Spending for Congregate Residential & Community Services

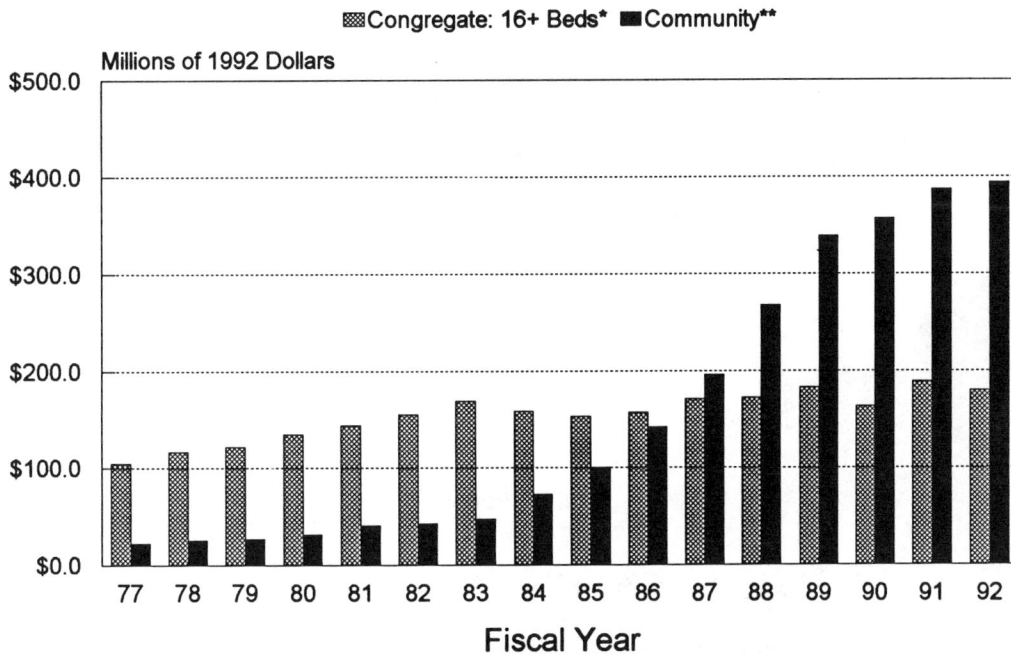

▨Congregate: 16+ Beds* ■Community**

Millions of 1992 Dollars

$500.0

$400.0

$300.0

$200.0

$100.0

$0.0

77 78 79 80 81 82 83 84 85 86 87 88 89 90 91 92

**Fiscal Year**

*Excludes nursing homes; ** Includes resources for
15 bed or less residential settings & non-residential community services

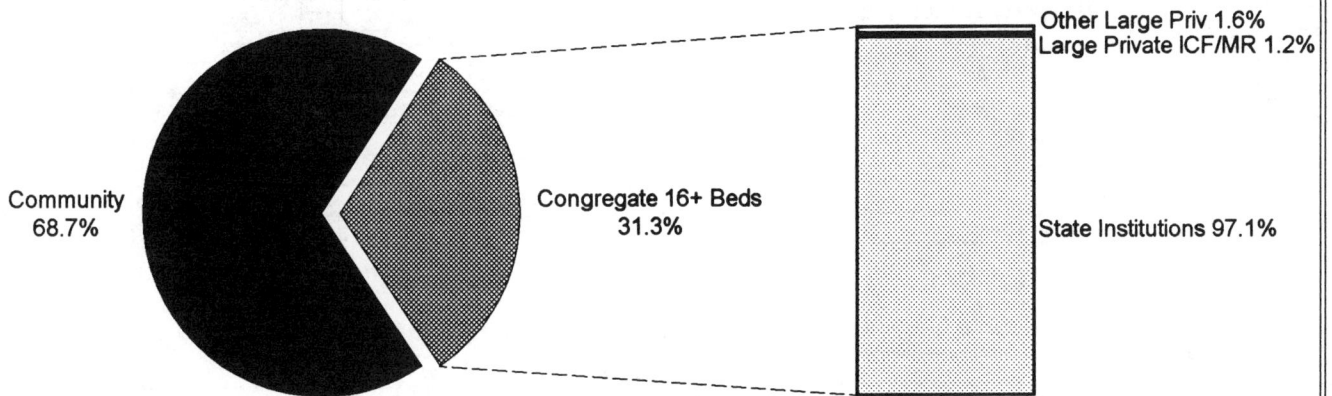

Community
68.7%

Congregate 16+ Beds
31.3%

Other Large Priv 1.6%
Large Private ICF/MR 1.2%

State Institutions 97.1%

FY 1992 Total Spending:
$573.4 Million

*Source:*
Institute on Disability and Human Development (UAP),
University of Illinois at Chicago, 1994

# CONNECTICUT

## Number of Persons Served by Residential Setting: FY 1992

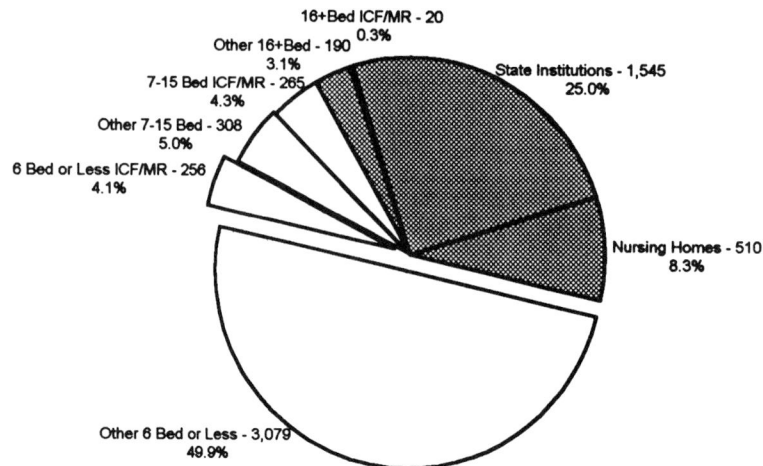

16+Bed ICF/MR - 20
0.3%

Other 16+Bed - 190
3.1%

7-15 Bed ICF/MR - 265
4.3%

Other 7-15 Bed - 308
5.0%

6 Bed or Less ICF/MR - 256
4.1%

State Institutions - 1,545
25.0%

Nursing Homes - 510
8.3%

Other 6 Bed or Less - 3,079
49.9%

Total Served: 6,173

## Persons Served by Residential Setting:1986-92

|  | 1986 | 1987 | 1988 | 1989 | 1990 | 1991 | 1992 |
|---|---|---|---|---|---|---|---|
| CONGREGATE 16 + BED SETTINGS | 3,818 | 3,728 | 3,465 | 2,933 | 2,560 | 2,400 | 2,265 |
| Nursing Homes | 1,097 | 1,095 | 1,016 | 702 | 571 | 540 | 510 |
| State Institutions | 2,430 | 2,342 | 2,157 | 1,943 | 1,727 | 1,626 | 1,545 |
| Private 16+Bed ICF/MR | 42 | 42 | 42 | 42 | 20 | 20 | 20 |
| Other 16+Bed Residential | 249 | 249 | 250 | 246 | 242 | 214 | 190 |
| 15 BED OR LESS RESIDENTIAL SETTINGS | 2,035 | 2,261 | 2,546 | 2,841 | 3,277 | 3,658 | 3,908 |
| Public 7-15 Bed ICF/MR | 279 | 284 | 321 | 308 | 266 | 274 | 211 |
| Private 7-15 Bed ICF/MR | 115 | 145 | 175 | 221 | 269 | 43 | 54 |
| Other 7-15 Bed Residential | 1,641 | 1,832 | 2,050 | 2,312 | 2,742 | 319 | 308 |
| Public 6 Bed or Less ICF/MR |  |  |  |  |  | 21 | 50 |
| Private 6 Bed or Less ICF/MR |  |  |  |  |  | 227 | 206 |
| Other 6 Bed or Less Residential |  |  |  |  |  | 2,774 | 3,079 |
| TOTAL PERSONS SERVED | 5,853 | 5,989 | 6,011 | 5,774 | 5,837 | 6,058 | 6,173 |

## Persons Served in Non-Residential Community Services:1986-92

|  | 1986 | 1987 | 1988 | 1989 | 1990 | 1991 | 1992 |
|---|---|---|---|---|---|---|---|
| DAY/WORK PROGRAMS | 3,735 | 4,369 | 4,754 | 6,437 | 6,940 | 6,339 | 6,850 |
| Sheltered Employment/Work Activity | 2,636 | 2,636 | 2,636 | 3,345 | 3,525 | 2,109 | 2,114 |
| Day Habilitation ("Day Training") | 431 | 741 | 958 | 1,710 | 1,839 | 2,170 | 2,416 |
| Supported/Competitive Employment | 668 | 992 | 1,160 | 1,382 | 1,576 | 2,060 | 2,320 |
| CASE MANAGEMENT | 8,592 | 8,789 | 9,120 | 9,835 | 10,211 | 11,033 | 11,444 |
| HCBS WAIVER | 0 | 0 | 644 | 1,127 | 1,517 | 1,655 | 1,920 |
| MODEL 50/200 WAIVER | 10 | 22 | 14 | 12 | 13 | 27 | 27 |

*Source:*
Institute on Disability and Human Development (UAP),
University of Illinois at Chicago, 1994

# CONNECTICUT

## Community Services: FY 1992 Revenue Sources

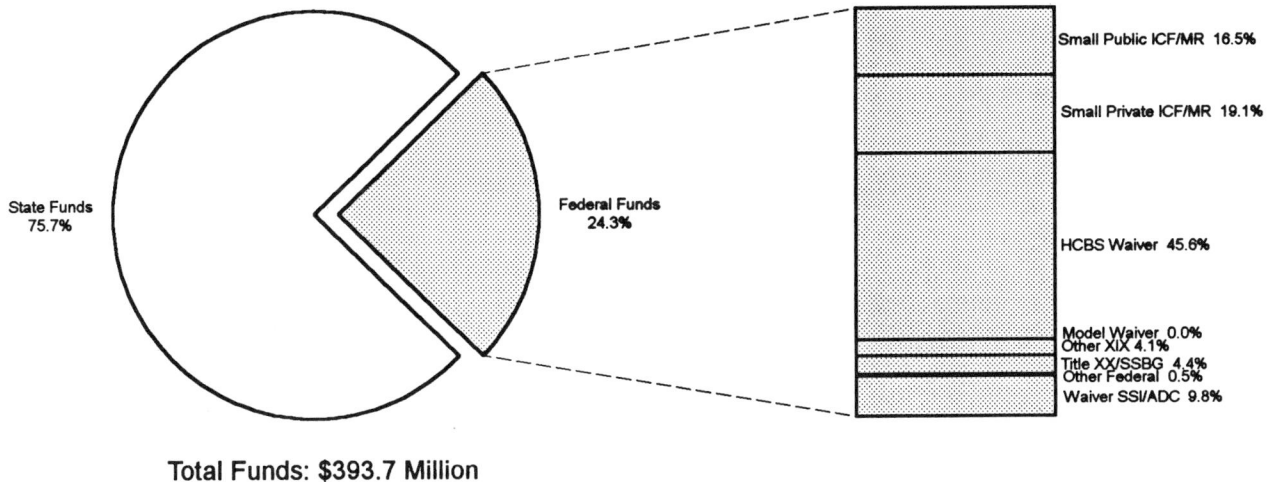

State Funds 75.7%

Federal Funds 24.3%

Small Public ICF/MR 16.5%

Small Private ICF/MR 19.1%

HCBS Waiver 45.6%

Model Waiver 0.0%
Other XIX 4.1%
Title XX/SSBG 4.4%
Other Federal 0.5%
Waiver SSI/ADC 9.8%

Total Funds: $393.7 Million

## Family Support Initiatives*

| | 1986 | 1987 | 1988 | 1989 | 1990 | 1991 | 1992 |
|---|---|---|---|---|---|---|---|
| FAMILY SUPPORT: TOTAL SPENDING | $271,158 | $1,061,265 | $1,903,409 | $2,175,396 | $2,039,888 | $2,543,455 | $4,219,866 |
| Total # of Families Supported | NA | NA | NA | NA | NA | NA | NA |
| A. Financial Subsidy/Payment | $0 | $0 | $0 | $38,232 | $50,976 | $280,840 | $589,820 |
| # of Families | 0 | 0 | 0 | 18 | 18 | 101 | 243 |
| B. Family Assistance Payments | NA | $331,472 | $836,228 | $630,260 | $793,280 | $1,316,462 | $1,273,244 |
| # of Families | NA | NA | NA | 640 | 968 | 1,110 | 1,483 |
| C. Other Family Support Payments | NA | $729,793 | $1,067,181 | $1,506,904 | $1,195,632 | $946,153 | $2,356,802 |
| # of Families | NA | NA | NA | NA | NA | NA | NA |

## Other Community Services Initiatives*

| | 1986 | 1987 | 1988 | 1989 | 1990 | 1991 | 1992 |
|---|---|---|---|---|---|---|---|
| AGING/DD SPENDING | $1,188,247 | $2,731,053 | $4,408,737 | $4,856,019 | $4,776,012 | $5,588,779 | $5,491,013 |
| # of Persons Served | NA | 286 | 424 | 516 | 613 | 629 | 679 |
| ASSISTIVE TECHNOLOGY SPENDING | | | | $0 | $0 | $0 | $0 |
| # of Persons Served | | | | 0 | 0 | 0 | 0 |
| EARLY INTERVENTION SPENDING | $2,272,263 | $2,355,064 | $2,540,668 | $4,680,489 | $4,543,136 | $6,704,066 | $6,645,468 |
| # of Persons Served | NA | 671 | 691 | 736 | 757 | 1,076 | 1,125 |
| PERSONAL ASSISTANCE SPENDING | | | | $0 | $0 | $0 | $0 |
| # of Persons Served | | | | 0 | 0 | 0 | 0 |
| SUPPORTED EMPLOYMENT SPENDING | $3,492,261 | $7,174,962 | $10,160,400 | $17,406,746 | $22,191,048 | $21,691,280 | $21,241,799 |
| # of Persons Served | 668 | 992 | 1,160 | 1,382 | 1,576 | 2,060 | 2,320 |
| SUPPORTED LIVING SPENDING | | | | $0 | $0 | $4,536,514 | $8,687,261 |
| # of Persons Served | | | | 0 | 0 | 125 | 638 |

*Expenditures associated with Special Community Initiatives are a subset of funding within the community services component of the state's chart series and spreadsheet; Family Support Client figures may include duplicate client counts; HCBS Waiver counts include Waiver case management numbers.
0= Services not provided in the state; NA= Data not available from state; blank= Services not applicable (eg. CSLA prior to authorization, Special Community Initiatives prior to request for data by this study)

*Source:*
Institute on Disability and Human Development (UAP),
University of Illinois at Chicago, 1994

# CONNECTICUT

## Large Congregate Care Facilities: FY 1992 Revenue Sources*

### Private 16+Bed Settings

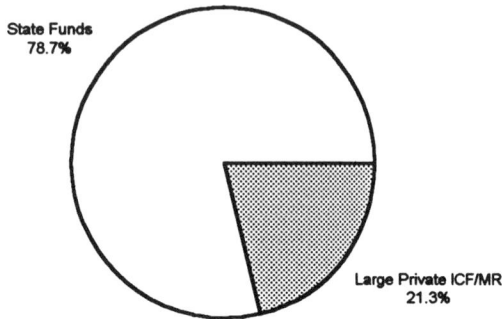

State Funds
78.7%

Large Private ICF/MR
21.3%

Total Funds: $5.1 Million

### Public Institutions

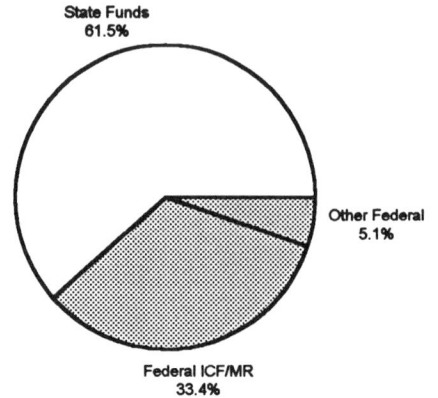

State Funds
61.5%

Other Federal
5.1%

Federal ICF/MR
33.4%

Total Funds: $174.6 Million

*Excludes nursing homes

## Average Daily Residents in Institutions

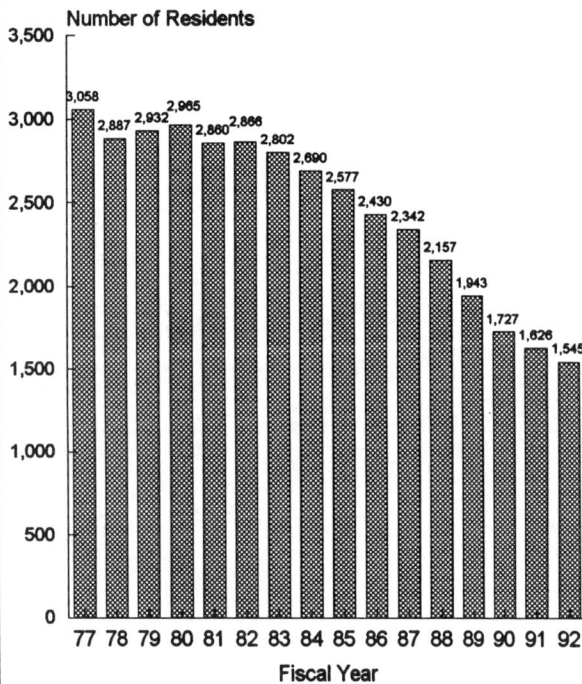

Number of Residents

| | |
|---|---|
| 3,058 | |

3,058  2,887  2,932  2,965  2,860  2,866  2,802  2,690  2,577  2,430  2,342  2,157  1,943  1,727  1,626  1,545

77 78 79 80 81 82 83 84 85 86 87 88 89 90 91 92

Fiscal Year

## Institutional Daily Costs Per Resident

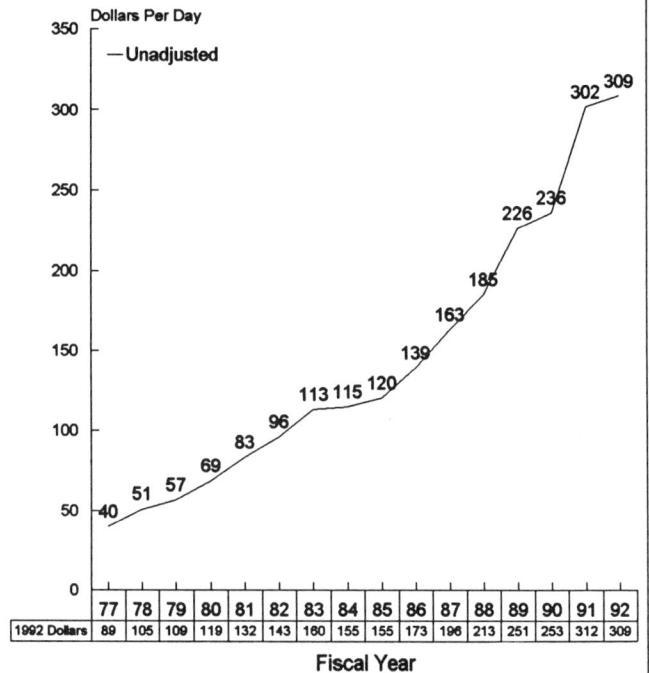

Dollars Per Day

—Unadjusted

40  51  57  69  83  96  113 115 120  139  163  185  226  236  302 309

| | 77 | 78 | 79 | 80 | 81 | 82 | 83 | 84 | 85 | 86 | 87 | 88 | 89 | 90 | 91 | 92 |
|---|---|---|---|---|---|---|---|---|---|---|---|---|---|---|---|---|
| 1992 Dollars | 89 | 105 | 109 | 119 | 132 | 143 | 160 | 155 | 155 | 173 | 196 | 213 | 251 | 253 | 312 | 309 |

Fiscal Year

*Source:*
Institute on Disability and Human Development (UAP),
University of Illinois at Chicago, 1994

# CONNECTICUT FISCAL EFFORT

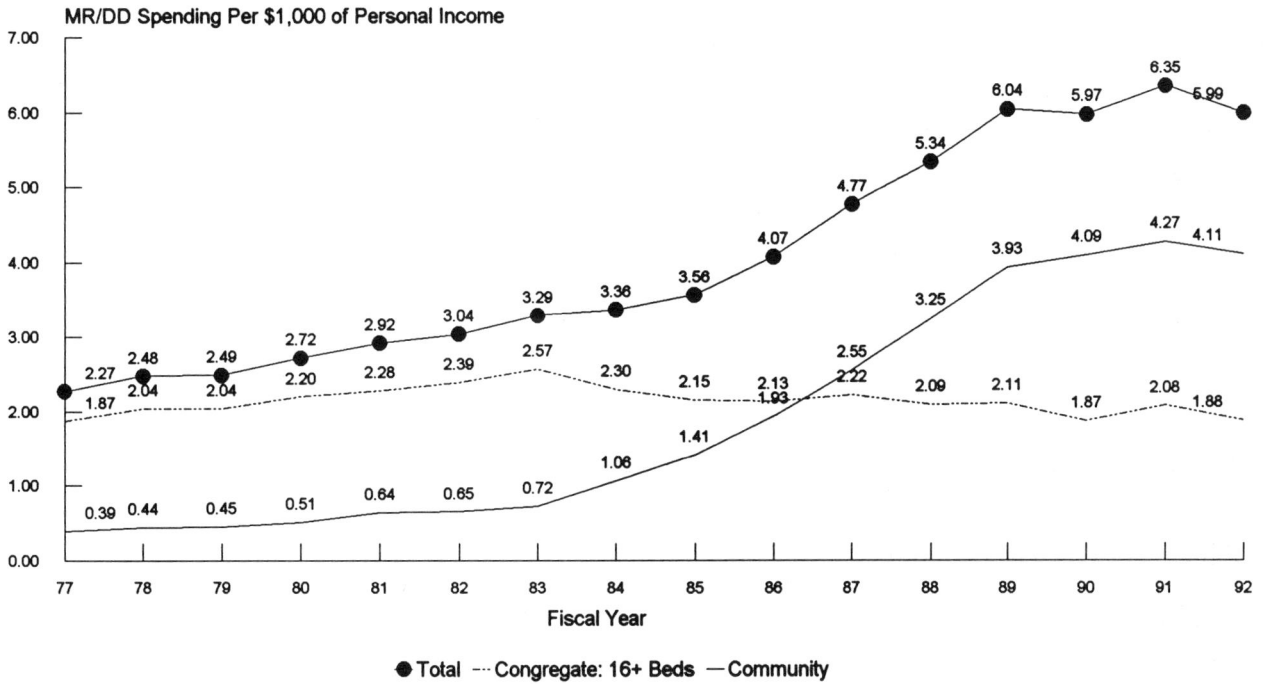

MR/DD Spending Per $1,000 of Personal Income

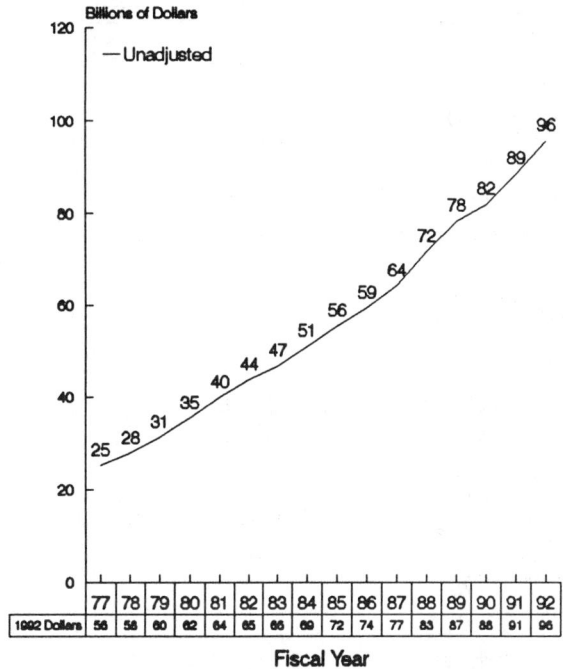

| | |
|---|---|
| 7.00 | |
| 6.00 | 6.35 5.99 |
| | 6.04 5.97 |
| 5.00 | 5.34 |
| | 4.77 |
| 4.00 | 4.07 4.27 4.11 |
| | 3.56 3.93 4.09 |
| 3.00 | 3.29 3.36 3.25 |

2.27 2.48 2.49 2.72 2.92 3.04
1.87 2.04 2.04 2.20 2.28 2.39 2.57 2.30 2.15 2.13 2.55 2.09 2.11 2.08 1.88
1.93 2.22 1.87
0.39 0.44 0.45 0.51 0.64 0.65 0.72 1.06 1.41

77 78 79 80 81 82 83 84 85 86 87 88 89 90 91 92

**Fiscal Year**

● Total  --- Congregate: 16+ Beds  — Community

## Total MR/DD Spending

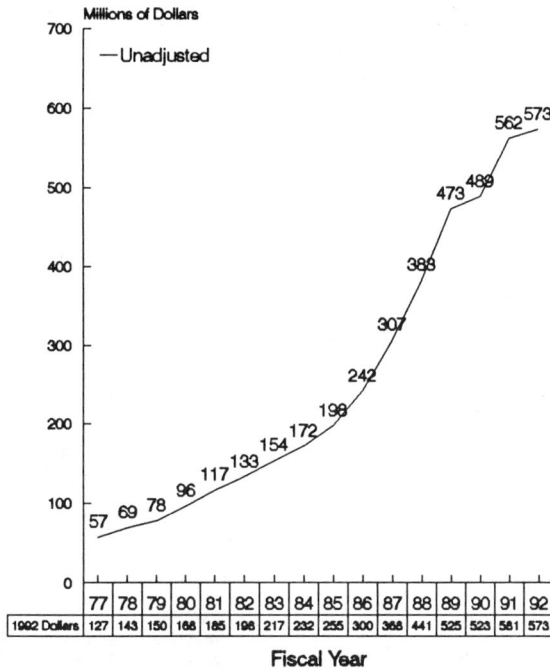

Millions of Dollars

— Unadjusted

| | |
|---|---|
| 700 | |
| 600 | 562 573 |
| 500 | 473 489 |
| 400 | 389 |
| 300 | 307 |
| 200 | 242 198 172 154 |
| 100 | 117 133 96 57 69 78 |
| 0 | |

| | 77 | 78 | 79 | 80 | 81 | 82 | 83 | 84 | 85 | 86 | 87 | 88 | 89 | 90 | 91 | 92 |
|---|---|---|---|---|---|---|---|---|---|---|---|---|---|---|---|
| 1992 Dollars | 127 | 143 | 150 | 168 | 185 | 198 | 217 | 232 | 255 | 300 | 368 | 441 | 525 | 523 | 581 | 573 |

**Fiscal Year**

## Personal Income

Billions of Dollars

— Unadjusted

| | |
|---|---|
| 120 | |
| 100 | 96 |
| | 89 |
| 80 | 82 78 |
| | 72 |
| 60 | 64 59 56 51 |
| | 47 44 |
| 40 | 40 35 31 |
| | 28 |
| 20 | 25 |
| 0 | |

| | 77 | 78 | 79 | 80 | 81 | 82 | 83 | 84 | 85 | 86 | 87 | 88 | 89 | 90 | 91 | 92 |
|---|---|---|---|---|---|---|---|---|---|---|---|---|---|---|---|
| 1992 Dollars | 56 | 58 | 60 | 62 | 64 | 65 | 66 | 69 | 72 | 74 | 77 | 83 | 87 | 88 | 91 | 96 |

**Fiscal Year**

*Source:*
Institute on Disability and Human Development (UAP),
University of Illinois at Chicago, 1994

# CONNECTICUT

## Financial Support for MR/DD Services: FY 1977-92

| | 1977 | 1978 | 1979 | 1980 | 1981 | 1982 | 1983 | 1984 |
|---|---|---|---|---|---|---|---|---|
| **TOTAL FUNDS** | $57,104,400 | $68,921,600 | $77,927,800 | $96,331,400 | $116,615,200 | $133,041,800 | $153,806,100 | $171,725,900 |
| **CONGREGATE 16+ BEDS** | 47,221,500 | 56,609,600 | 63,855,300 | 78,127,400 | 90,947,700 | 104,598,000 | 120,262,500 | 117,665,900 |
| INSTITUTIONAL SERVICES FUNDS | 44,385,000 | 53,562,000 | 60,504,000 | 74,438,000 | 86,896,000 | 100,314,000 | 115,740,000 | 112,920,600 |
| STATE FUNDS | 43,535,000 | 52,215,000 | 54,532,000 | 59,280,000 | 71,633,000 | 84,181,000 | 101,083,000 | 91,664,700 |
| General Funds | 43,533,000 | 52,198,000 | 54,524,000 | 59,259,000 | 71,563,000 | 84,142,000 | 101,048,000 | 86,017,900 |
| Local | 0 | 0 | 0 | 0 | 0 | 0 | 0 | 0 |
| Other State Funds | 2,000 | 17,000 | 8,000 | 21,000 | 70,000 | 39,000 | 35,000 | 5,646,800 |
| FEDERAL FUNDS | 850,000 | 1,347,000 | 5,972,000 | 15,158,000 | 15,263,000 | 16,133,000 | 14,657,000 | 21,255,900 |
| Federal ICF/MR | 0 | 12,000 | 4,971,000 | 14,268,000 | 14,494,000 | 15,585,000 | 14,082,000 | 17,508,700 |
| Title XX / SSBG Funds | 0 | 0 | 0 | 0 | 0 | 0 | 0 | 106,800 |
| Other Federal Funds | 850,000 | 1,335,000 | 1,001,000 | 890,000 | 769,000 | 548,000 | 575,000 | 3,640,400 |
| LARGE PRIVATE RESIDENTIAL | 2,836,500 | 3,047,600 | 3,351,300 | 3,689,400 | 4,051,700 | 4,284,000 | 4,522,500 | 4,745,300 |
| STATE FUNDS | 2,774,300 | 2,978,800 | 3,275,900 | 3,607,200 | 3,963,100 | 4,195,100 | 4,421,600 | 4,632,000 |
| General Funds | 2,774,300 | 2,978,800 | 3,275,900 | 3,607,200 | 3,963,100 | 4,195,100 | 4,421,600 | 4,632,000 |
| Other State Funds | 0 | 0 | 0 | 0 | 0 | 0 | 0 | 0 |
| Local/County Overmatch | 0 | 0 | 0 | 0 | 0 | 0 | 0 | 0 |
| FEDERAL FUNDS | 62,200 | 68,800 | 75,400 | 82,200 | 88,600 | 88,900 | 100,900 | 113,300 |
| Large Private ICF/MR | 62,200 | 68,800 | 75,400 | 82,200 | 88,600 | 88,900 | 100,900 | 113,300 |
| **COMMUNITY SERVICES FUNDS** | 9,882,900 | 12,312,000 | 14,072,500 | 18,204,000 | 25,667,500 | 28,443,800 | 33,543,600 | 54,060,000 |
| STATE FUNDS | 6,817,900 | 8,454,000 | 10,759,500 | 11,177,000 | 15,892,500 | 19,965,800 | 23,906,300 | 43,024,700 |
| General Funds | 4,820,900 | 6,080,000 | 7,829,500 | 7,628,000 | 12,162,500 | 16,236,800 | 19,393,300 | 37,383,700 |
| Other State Funds | 0 | 0 | 0 | 0 | 0 | 0 | 0 | 0 |
| Local/County Overmatch | 0 | 0 | 0 | 0 | 0 | 0 | 0 | 0 |
| SSI State Supplement | 1,997,000 | 2,374,000 | 2,930,000 | 3,549,000 | 3,730,000 | 3,729,000 | 4,513,000 | 5,641,000 |
| FEDERAL FUNDS | 3,065,000 | 3,858,000 | 3,313,000 | 7,027,000 | 9,775,000 | 8,478,000 | 9,637,300 | 11,035,300 |
| ICF/MR Funds | 0 | 0 | 0 | 4,747,000 | 5,515,000 | 5,751,000 | 6,288,300 | 6,712,300 |
| Small Public | 0 | 0 | 0 | 3,842,000 | 4,610,000 | 4,846,000 | 5,383,300 | 5,920,600 |
| Small Private | 0 | 0 | 0 | 905,000 | 905,000 | 905,000 | 905,000 | 791,700 |
| HCBS Waiver | 0 | 0 | 0 | 0 | 0 | 0 | 0 | 0 |
| Model 50/200 Waiver | 0 | 0 | 0 | 0 | 0 | 0 | 0 | 1,600 |
| Other Title XIX Programs | 0 | 0 | 0 | 0 | 0 | 0 | 0 | 0 |
| Title XX / SSBG Funds | 1,680,000 | 1,680,000 | 1,680,000 | 828,000 | 3,005,000 | 1,833,000 | 2,411,000 | 3,660,500 |
| Other Federal Funds | 1,385,000 | 2,178,000 | 1,633,000 | 1,452,000 | 1,255,000 | 894,000 | 938,000 | 660,900 |
| Waiver Clients' SSI/ADC | 0 | 0 | 0 | 0 | 0 | 0 | 0 | 0 |

| | 1985 | 1986 | 1987 | 1988 | 1989 | 1990 | 1991 | 1992 |
|---|---|---|---|---|---|---|---|---|
| **TOTAL FUNDS** | $197,565,200 | $241,853,400 | $306,632,700 | $383,227,840 | $473,075,557 | $488,639,583 | $562,251,404 | $573,413,062 |
| **CONGREGATE 16+ BEDS** | 119,540,400 | 126,927,200 | 142,920,100 | 150,130,500 | 165,570,776 | 153,507,666 | 184,458,677 | 179,716,076 |
| INSTITUTIONAL SERVICES FUNDS | 113,091,900 | 123,706,800 | 139,517,000 | 146,139,700 | 160,606,807 | 148,784,145 | 179,205,456 | 174,555,609 |
| STATE FUNDS | 89,702,700 | 92,049,100 | 104,653,700 | 102,328,600 | 111,911,765 | 91,039,626 | 106,242,582 | 107,334,450 |
| General Funds | 83,614,200 | 85,518,900 | 97,681,800 | 95,526,100 | 105,327,993 | 84,629,941 | 98,825,330 | 101,238,209 |
| Local | 0 | 0 | 0 | 0 | 0 | 0 | 0 | 0 |
| Other State Funds | 6,088,500 | 6,530,200 | 6,971,900 | 6,802,500 | 6,583,772 | 6,409,685 | 7,417,252 | 6,096,241 |
| FEDERAL FUNDS | 23,389,200 | 31,657,700 | 34,863,300 | 43,811,100 | 48,695,042 | 57,744,519 | 72,962,874 | 67,221,159 |
| Federal ICF/MR | 19,652,800 | 28,017,300 | 29,533,600 | 38,481,400 | 40,318,233 | 50,147,910 | 63,167,566 | 58,251,509 |
| Title XX / SSBG Funds | 96,000 | 0 | 0 | 0 | 0 | 0 | 0 | 0 |
| Other Federal Funds | 3,640,400 | 3,640,400 | 5,329,700 | 5,329,700 | 8,376,809 | 7,596,609 | 9,795,308 | 8,969,650 |
| LARGE PRIVATE RESIDENTIAL | 6,448,500 | 3,220,400 | 3,403,100 | 3,990,800 | 4,963,969 | 4,723,521 | 5,253,221 | 5,160,467 |
| STATE FUNDS | 6,323,500 | 3,083,300 | 3,254,000 | 3,828,700 | 4,567,029 | 4,091,741 | 4,386,601 | 4,059,006 |
| General Funds | 6,323,500 | 3,083,300 | 3,254,000 | 3,828,700 | 4,567,029 | 4,091,741 | 4,386,601 | 4,059,006 |
| Other State Funds | 0 | 0 | 0 | 0 | 0 | 0 | 0 | 0 |
| Local/County Overmatch | 0 | 0 | 0 | 0 | 0 | 0 | 0 | 0 |
| FEDERAL FUNDS | 125,000 | 137,100 | 149,100 | 162,100 | 396,940 | 631,780 | 866,620 | 1,101,461 |
| Large Private ICF/MR | 125,000 | 137,100 | 149,100 | 162,100 | 396,940 | 631,780 | 866,620 | 1,101,461 |
| **COMMUNITY SERVICES FUNDS** | 78,024,800 | 114,926,200 | 163,712,600 | 233,097,340 | 307,504,781 | 335,131,917 | 377,792,727 | 393,696,986 |
| STATE FUNDS | 65,224,400 | 101,647,600 | 143,059,700 | 202,977,684 | 262,456,377 | 265,313,556 | 291,693,689 | 297,919,742 |
| General Funds | 59,257,400 | 95,795,600 | 135,955,700 | 195,378,684 | 254,477,427 | 256,935,658 | 282,896,897 | 288,683,110 |
| Other State Funds | 0 | 0 | 0 | 0 | 0 | 0 | 0 | 0 |
| Local/County Overmatch | 0 | 0 | 0 | 0 | 0 | 0 | 0 | 0 |
| SSI State Supplement | 5,967,000 | 5,852,000 | 7,104,000 | 7,599,000 | 7,978,950 | 8,377,898 | 8,796,792 | 9,236,632 |
| FEDERAL FUNDS | 12,800,400 | 13,278,600 | 20,652,900 | 30,119,656 | 45,048,404 | 69,818,361 | 86,099,038 | 95,777,244 |
| ICF/MR Funds | 7,507,300 | 8,901,900 | 15,193,600 | 19,105,216 | 22,625,006 | 29,162,893 | 34,762,891 | 34,071,536 |
| Small Public | 6,457,900 | 6,995,200 | 11,228,500 | 12,726,084 | 12,857,423 | 15,167,960 | 18,060,924 | 15,777,745 |
| Small Private | 1,049,400 | 1,906,700 | 3,965,100 | 6,379,132 | 9,767,583 | 13,994,933 | 16,701,967 | 18,293,791 |
| HCBS Waiver | 0 | 0 | 0 | 3,864,600 | 13,088,843 | 29,589,896 | 36,408,372 | 43,696,015 |
| Model 50/200 Waiver | 1,600 | 1,600 | 3,500 | 4,136 | 406 | 754 | 1,375 | 1,375 |
| Other Title XIX Programs | 0 | 0 | 0 | 0 | 0 | 0 | 2,224,864 | 3,946,612 |
| Title XX / SSBG Funds | 4,626,700 | 3,618,200 | 4,739,300 | 4,544,600 | 4,311,272 | 4,019,532 | 4,285,380 | 4,236,150 |
| Other Federal Funds | 664,800 | 756,900 | 716,500 | 723,200 | 397,669 | 346,214 | 829,636 | 448,276 |
| Waiver Clients' SSI/ADC | 0 | 0 | 0 | 1,877,904 | 4,625,208 | 6,699,072 | 7,586,520 | 9,377,280 |

*Source:*

Institute on Disability and Human Development (UAP),
University of Illinois at Chicago, 1994

# DELAWARE

## MR/DD Spending for Congregate Residential & Community Services

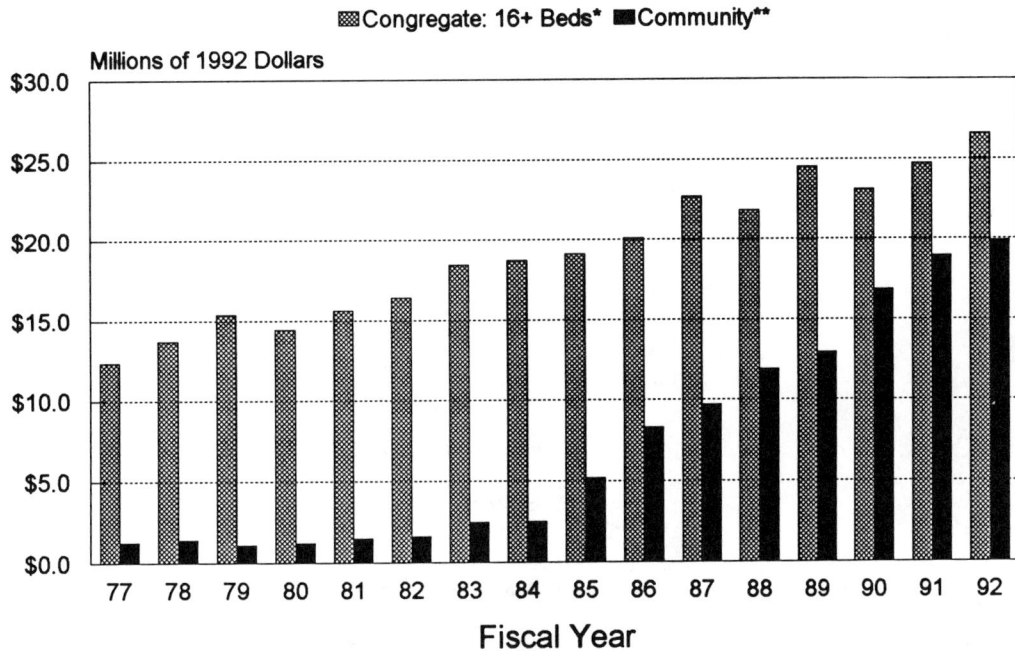

▓ Congregate: 16+ Beds*  ■ Community**

Millions of 1992 Dollars

Fiscal Year

*Excludes nursing homes; ** Includes resources for
15 bed or less residential settings & non-residential community services

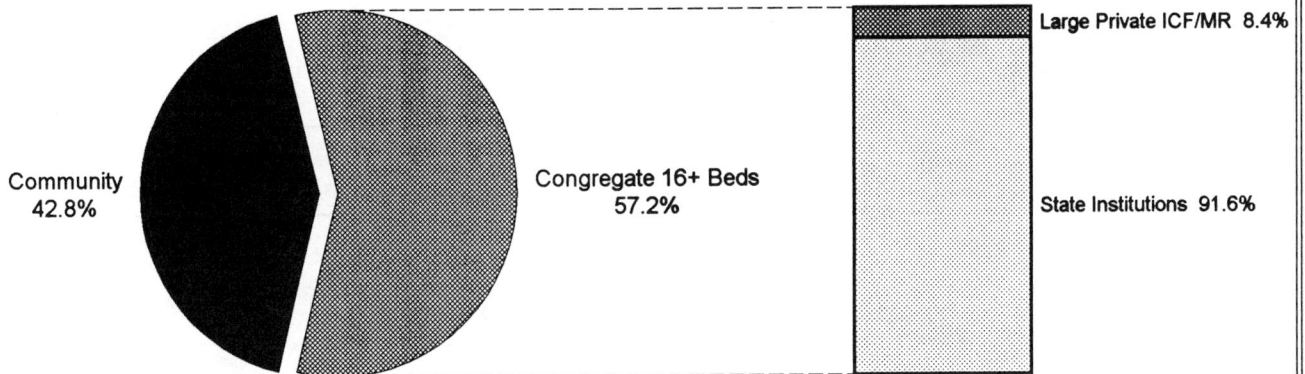

Community
42.8%

Congregate 16+ Beds
57.2%

Large Private ICF/MR  8.4%

State Institutions  91.6%

FY 1992 Total Spending:
$46.5 Million

*Source:*
Institute on Disability and Human Development (UAP),
University of Illinois at Chicago, 1994

# DELAWARE

## Number of Persons Served by Residential Setting: FY 1992

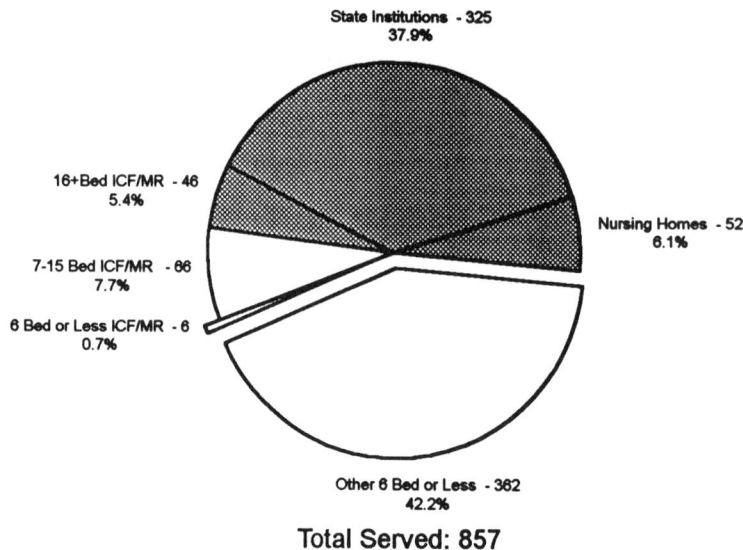

State Institutions - 325
37.9%

16+Bed ICF/MR - 46
5.4%

7-15 Bed ICF/MR - 66
7.7%

6 Bed or Less ICF/MR - 6
0.7%

Nursing Homes - 52
6.1%

Other 6 Bed or Less - 362
42.2%

Total Served: 857

## Persons Served by Residential Setting:1986-92

|  | 1986 | 1987 | 1988 | 1989 | 1990 | 1991 | 1992 |
|---|---|---|---|---|---|---|---|
| CONGREGATE 16 + BED SETTINGS | NA | NA | 683 | 435 | 452 | 427 | 423 |
| Nursing Homes | NA | NA | 305 | 75 | 64 | 44 | 52 |
| State Institutions | 404 | 392 | 378 | 360 | 342 | 337 | 325 |
| Private 16+Bed ICF/MR | 0 | 0 | 0 | 0 | 46 | 46 | 46 |
| Other 16+Bed Residential | 0 | 0 | 0 | 0 | 0 | 0 | 0 |
| 15 BED OR LESS RESIDENTIAL SETTINGS | 282 | 287 | 314 | 366 | 384 | 399 | 434 |
| Public 7-15 Bed ICF/MR | 0 | 0 | 0 | 0 | 0 | 0 | 0 |
| Private 7-15 Bed ICF/MR | 60 | 60 | 63 | 86 | 91 | 90 | 66 |
| Other 7-15 Bed Residential | 222 | 227 | 251 | 280 | 293 | 296 | 0 |
| Public 6 Bed or Less ICF/MR |  |  |  |  |  |  |  |
| Private 6 Bed or Less ICF/MR |  |  |  |  |  |  | 6 |
| Other 6 Bed or Less Residential |  |  |  |  |  | 13 | 362 |
| TOTAL PERSONS SERVED | NA | NA | 997 | 801 | 836 | 826 | 857 |

## Persons Served in Non-Residential Community Services:1986-92

|  | 1986 | 1987 | 1988 | 1989 | 1990 | 1991 | 1992 |
|---|---|---|---|---|---|---|---|
| DAY/WORK PROGRAMS | 446 | 633 | 630 | 655 | 676 | 652 | 719 |
| Sheltered Employment/Work Activity | NA | NA | NA | NA | NA | NA | NA |
| Day Habilitation ("Day Training") | NA | NA | NA | NA | NA | NA | NA |
| Supported/Competitive Employment | NA | NA | 70 | 87 | 113 | 106 | 144 |
| CASE MANAGEMENT | 506 | 552 | 579 | 678 | 711 | 963 | 1,230 |
| HCBS WAIVER | 60 | 81 | 130 | 185 | 196 | 245 | 272 |
| MODEL 50/200 WAIVER | 0 | 0 | 0 | 0 | 0 | 0 | 0 |

*Source:*
Institute on Disability and Human Development (UAP),
University of Illinois at Chicago, 1994

# DELAWARE

## Community Services: FY 1992 Revenue Sources

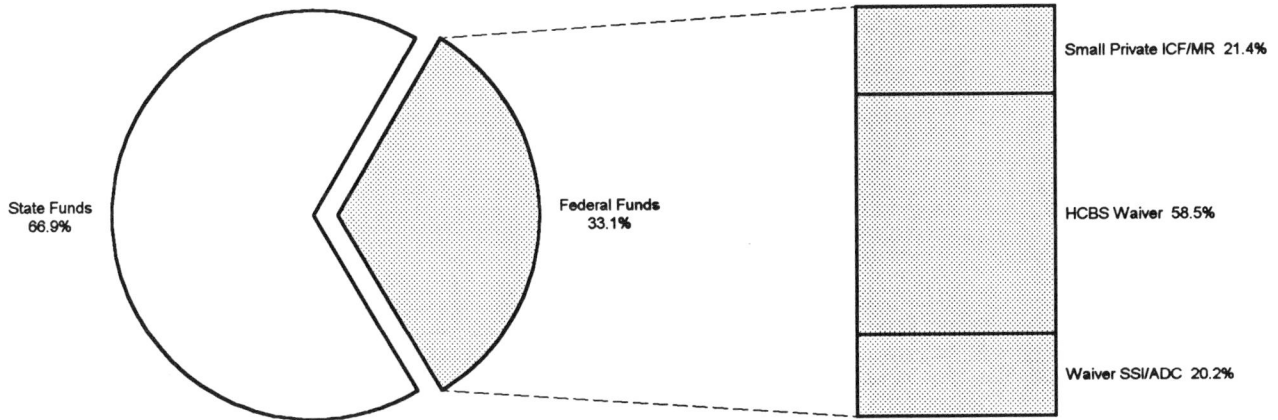

State Funds
66.9%

Federal Funds
33.1%

Small Private ICF/MR  21.4%

HCBS Waiver  58.5%

Waiver SSI/ADC  20.2%

Total Funds: $19.9 Million

## Family Support Initiatives*

|  | 1986 | 1987 | 1988 | 1989 | 1990 | 1991 | 1992 |
|---|---|---|---|---|---|---|---|
| **FAMILY SUPPORT: TOTAL SPENDING** | $39,515 | $58,128 | $80,352 | $74,048 | $86,344 | $67,192 | $63,444 |
| **Total # of Families Supported** | 74 | 85 | 266 | 0 | 318 | 559 | 824 |
| A. Financial Subsidy/Payment | $0 | $0 | $0 | $0 | $0 | $0 | $0 |
| # of Families | 0 | 0 | 0 | 0 | 0 | 0 | 0 |
| B. Family Assistance Payments | $39,515 | $58,128 | $71,818 | $74,048 | $86,344 | $67,192 | $63,444 |
| # of Families | 74 | 85 | 266 |  | 318 | 559 | 824 |
| C. Other Family Support Payments | $0 | $0 | $8,534 | $0 | $0 | $0 | $0 |
| # of Families | 0 | 0 | NA | 0 | 0 | 0 | 0 |

## Other Community Services Initiatives*

|  | 1986 | 1987 | 1988 | 1989 | 1990 | 1991 | 1992 |
|---|---|---|---|---|---|---|---|
| **AGING/DD SPENDING** | $0 | $0 | $0 | $0 | $0 | $0 | $0 |
| # of Persons Served | 0 | 0 | 0 | 0 | 0 | 0 | 0 |
| **ASSISTIVE TECHNOLOGY SPENDING** |  |  |  |  |  | $153,133 | $71,785 |
| # of Persons Served |  |  |  |  |  | NA | NA |
| **EARLY INTERVENTION SPENDING** | $86,982 | $154,270 | $181,753 | $223,776 | $181,440 | $229,176 | $150,384 |
| # of Persons Served | 338 | 356 | 417 | 433 | 418 | 440 | 461 |
| **PERSONAL ASSISTANCE SPENDING** |  |  |  |  |  |  | $0 |
| # of Persons Served |  |  |  |  |  |  | 0 |
| **SUPPORTED EMPLOYMENT SPENDING** | $40,615 | $65,840 | $251,732 | $221,466 | $1,086,679 | $744,176 | $810,402 |
| # of Persons Served | NA | 10 | 70 | 87 | 113 | 106 | 144 |
| **SUPPORTED LIVING SPENDING** |  |  |  |  |  | $128,179 | $161,332 |
| # of Persons Served |  |  |  |  |  | 13 | 28 |

*Expenditures associated with Special Community Initiatives are a subset of funding within the community services component of the state's chart series and spreadsheet; Family Support Client figures may include duplicate client counts; HCBS Waiver counts include Waiver case management numbers.
0= Services not provided in the state; NA= Data not available from state; blank= Services not applicable (eg. CSLA prior to authorization, Special Community Initiatives prior to request for data by this study)

*Source:*
Institute on Disability and Human Development (UAP),
University of Illinois at Chicago, 1994

# DELAWARE

## Large Congregate Care Facilities: FY 1992 Revenue Sources*

### Private 16+Bed Settings

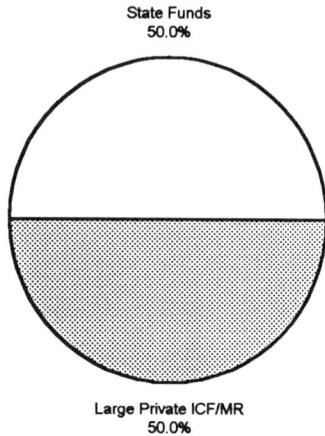

State Funds
50.0%

Large Private ICF/MR
50.0%

Total Funds: $2.2 Million

### Public Institutions

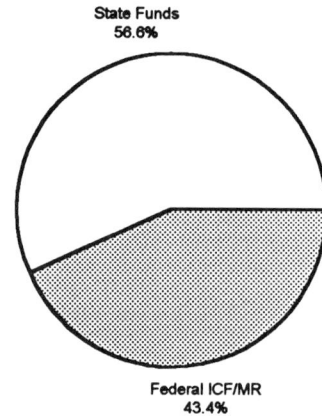

State Funds
56.6%

Federal ICF/MR
43.4%

Total Funds: $24.3 Million

*Excludes nursing homes

## Average Daily Residents in Institutions

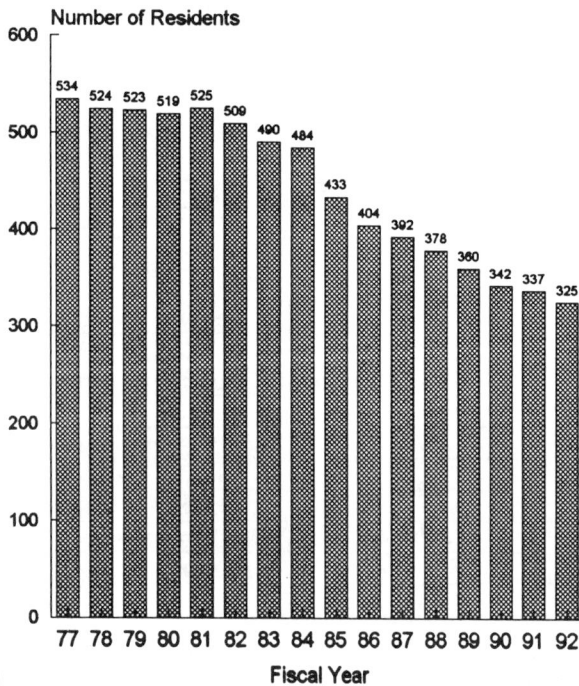

Number of Residents

| Fiscal Year | Residents |
|---|---|
| 77 | 534 |
| 78 | 524 |
| 79 | 523 |
| 80 | 519 |
| 81 | 525 |
| 82 | 509 |
| 83 | 490 |
| 84 | 484 |
| 85 | 433 |
| 86 | 404 |
| 87 | 392 |
| 88 | 378 |
| 89 | 360 |
| 90 | 342 |
| 91 | 337 |
| 92 | 325 |

## Institutional Daily Costs Per Resident

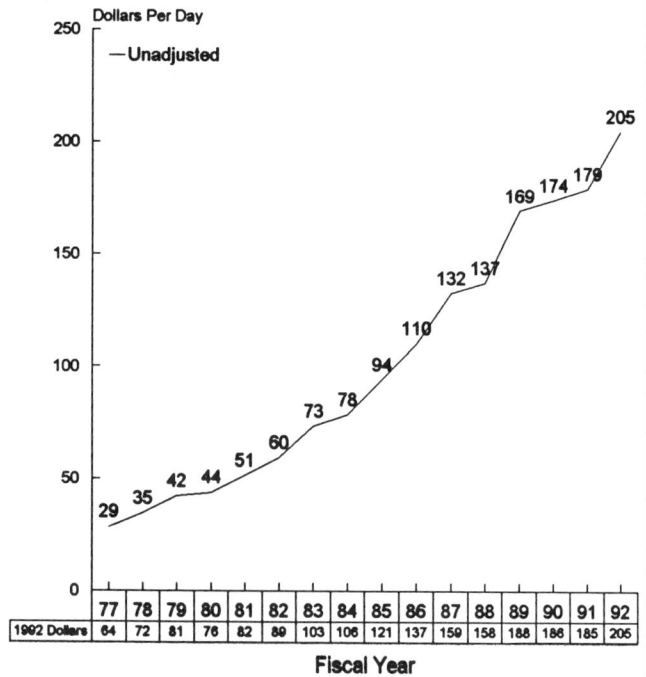

Dollars Per Day

—Unadjusted

| Fiscal Year | Unadjusted | 1992 Dollars |
|---|---|---|
| 77 | 29 | 64 |
| 78 | 35 | 72 |
| 79 | 42 | 81 |
| 80 | 44 | 76 |
| 81 | 51 | 82 |
| 82 | 60 | 89 |
| 83 | 73 | 103 |
| 84 | 78 | 106 |
| 85 | 94 | 121 |
| 86 | 110 | 137 |
| 87 | 132 | 159 |
| 88 | 137 | 158 |
| 89 | 169 | 188 |
| 90 | 174 | 186 |
| 91 | 179 | 185 |
| 92 | 205 | 205 |

Fiscal Year

*Source:*
Institute on Disability and Human Development (UAP),
University of Illinois at Chicago, 1994

# DELAWARE FISCAL EFFORT

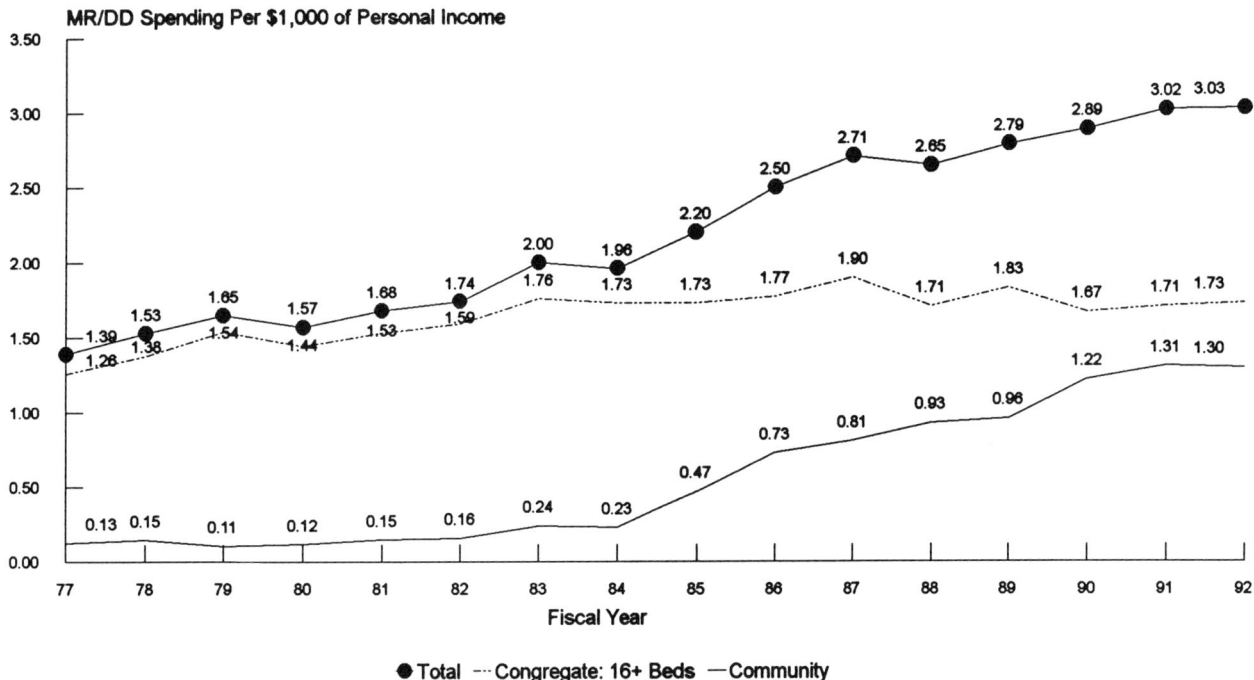

MR/DD Spending Per $1,000 of Personal Income

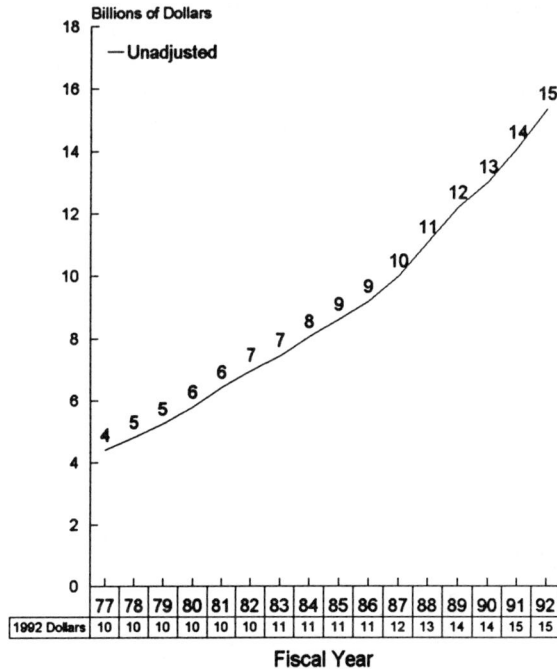

| | |
|---|---|
| Total | 1.39, 1.53, 1.65, 1.57, 1.68, 1.74, 1.76, 2.00, 1.96, 2.20, 2.50, 2.71, 2.65, 2.79, 2.89, 3.02, 3.03 |
| Congregate: 16+ Beds | 1.26, 1.38, 1.54, 1.44, 1.53, 1.59, 1.73, 1.73, 1.77, 1.90, 1.71, 1.83, 1.67, 1.71, 1.73 |
| Community | 0.13, 0.15, 0.11, 0.12, 0.15, 0.16, 0.24, 0.23, 0.47, 0.73, 0.81, 0.93, 0.96, 1.22, 1.31, 1.30 |

Fiscal Year

● Total  --- Congregate: 16+ Beds  — Community

## Total MR/DD Spending

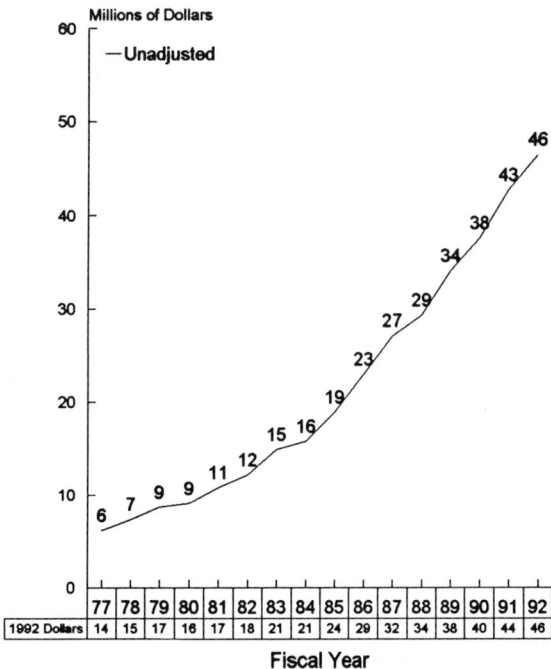

Millions of Dollars
— Unadjusted

6, 7, 9, 9, 11, 12, 15, 16, 19, 23, 27, 29, 34, 38, 43, 46

| | 77 | 78 | 79 | 80 | 81 | 82 | 83 | 84 | 85 | 86 | 87 | 88 | 89 | 90 | 91 | 92 |
|---|---|---|---|---|---|---|---|---|---|---|---|---|---|---|---|---|
| 1992 Dollars | 14 | 15 | 17 | 16 | 17 | 18 | 21 | 21 | 24 | 29 | 32 | 34 | 38 | 40 | 44 | 46 |

Fiscal Year

## Personal Income

Billions of Dollars
— Unadjusted

4, 5, 5, 6, 7, 7, 8, 9, 9, 10, 11, 12, 13, 14, 15

| | 77 | 78 | 79 | 80 | 81 | 82 | 83 | 84 | 85 | 86 | 87 | 88 | 89 | 90 | 91 | 92 |
|---|---|---|---|---|---|---|---|---|---|---|---|---|---|---|---|---|
| 1992 Dollars | 10 | 10 | 10 | 10 | 10 | 10 | 11 | 11 | 11 | 11 | 12 | 13 | 14 | 14 | 15 | 15 |

Fiscal Year

*Source:*
Institute on Disability and Human Development (UAP),
University of Illinois at Chicago, 1994

# DELAWARE
## Financial Support for MR/DD Services: FY 1977-92

| | 1977 | 1978 | 1979 | 1980 | 1981 | 1982 | 1983 | 1984 |
|---|---|---|---|---|---|---|---|---|
| **TOTAL FUNDS** | $6,144,644 | $7,348,159 | $8,663,400 | $9,072,700 | $10,814,800 | $12,169,200 | $14,889,600 | $15,776,100 |
| **CONGREGATE 16+ BEDS** | 5,578,244 | 6,643,959 | 8,076,700 | 8,349,600 | 9,865,000 | 11,072,000 | 13,117,100 | 13,900,400 |
| INSTITUTIONAL SERVICES FUNDS | 5,578,244 | 6,643,959 | 8,076,700 | 8,349,600 | 9,865,000 | 11,072,000 | 13,117,100 | 13,900,400 |
| STATE FUNDS | 5,578,244 | 5,552,959 | 6,051,700 | 5,137,600 | 5,982,000 | 7,618,000 | 8,231,100 | 8,794,100 |
| General Funds | 5,195,100 | 5,249,200 | 5,032,800 | 4,383,800 | 4,798,300 | 6,102,200 | 7,699,600 | 7,182,300 |
| Local | 0 | 0 | 0 | 0 | 0 | 0 | 0 | 0 |
| Other State Funds | 383,144 | 303,759 | 1,018,900 | 753,800 | 1,183,700 | 1,515,800 | 531,500 | 1,611,800 |
| FEDERAL FUNDS | 0 | 1,091,000 | 2,025,000 | 3,212,000 | 3,883,000 | 3,454,000 | 4,886,000 | 5,106,300 |
| Federal ICF/MR | 0 | 1,091,000 | 2,025,000 | 3,212,000 | 3,883,000 | 3,454,000 | 4,886,000 | 5,106,300 |
| Title XX / SSBG Funds | 0 | 0 | 0 | 0 | 0 | 0 | 0 | 0 |
| Other Federal Funds | 0 | 0 | 0 | 0 | 0 | 0 | 0 | 0 |
| LARGE PRIVATE RESIDENTIAL | 0 | 0 | 0 | 0 | 0 | 0 | 0 | 0 |
| STATE FUNDS | 0 | 0 | 0 | 0 | 0 | 0 | 0 | 0 |
| General Funds | 0 | 0 | 0 | 0 | 0 | 0 | 0 | 0 |
| Other State Funds | 0 | 0 | 0 | 0 | 0 | 0 | 0 | 0 |
| Local/County Overmatch | 0 | 0 | 0 | 0 | 0 | 0 | 0 | 0 |
| FEDERAL FUNDS | 0 | 0 | 0 | 0 | 0 | 0 | 0 | 0 |
| Large Private ICF/MR | 0 | 0 | 0 | 0 | 0 | 0 | 0 | 0 |
| **COMMUNITY SERVICES FUNDS** | 566,400 | 704,200 | 586,700 | 723,100 | 949,800 | 1,097,200 | 1,772,500 | 1,875,700 |
| STATE FUNDS | 471,400 | 704,200 | 524,700 | 673,100 | 925,800 | 908,100 | 1,280,100 | 1,327,900 |
| General Funds | 417,600 | 560,300 | 480,700 | 630,100 | 859,700 | 854,600 | 1,240,100 | 1,285,300 |
| Other State Funds | 2,800 | 95,900 | 0 | 0 | 25,100 | 11,500 | 0 | 600 |
| Local/County Overmatch | 0 | 0 | 0 | 0 | 0 | 0 | 0 | 0 |
| SSI State Supplement | 51,000 | 48,000 | 44,000 | 43,000 | 41,000 | 42,000 | 40,000 | 42,000 |
| FEDERAL FUNDS | 95,000 | 0 | 62,000 | 50,000 | 24,000 | 189,100 | 492,400 | 547,800 |
| ICF/MR Funds | 0 | 0 | 0 | 0 | 0 | 189,100 | 492,400 | 547,800 |
| Small Public | 0 | 0 | 0 | 0 | 0 | 0 | 0 | 0 |
| Small Private | 0 | 0 | 0 | 0 | 0 | 189,100 | 492,400 | 547,800 |
| HCBS Waiver | 0 | 0 | 0 | 0 | 0 | 0 | 0 | 0 |
| Model 50/200 Waiver | 0 | 0 | 0 | 0 | 0 | 0 | 0 | 0 |
| Other Title XIX Programs | 0 | 0 | 0 | 0 | 0 | 0 | 0 | 0 |
| Title XX / SSBG Funds | 95,000 | 0 | 62,000 | 50,000 | 24,000 | 0 | 0 | 0 |
| Other Federal Funds | 0 | 0 | 0 | 0 | 0 | 0 | 0 | 0 |
| Waiver Clients' SSI/ADC | 0 | 0 | 0 | 0 | 0 | 0 | 0 | 0 |

| | 1985 | 1986 | 1987 | 1988 | 1989 | 1990 | 1991 | 1992 |
|---|---|---|---|---|---|---|---|---|
| **TOTAL FUNDS** | $18,927,300 | $22,991,220 | $27,068,381 | $29,322,358 | $34,015,240 | $37,575,636 | $42,689,911 | $46,459,248 |
| **CONGREGATE 16+ BEDS** | 14,876,700 | 16,246,600 | 18,950,691 | 18,979,857 | 22,252,800 | 21,735,500 | 24,182,131 | 26,570,802 |
| INSTITUTIONAL SERVICES FUNDS | 14,876,700 | 16,246,600 | 18,950,691 | 18,979,857 | 22,252,800 | 21,735,500 | 22,019,999 | 24,339,946 |
| STATE FUNDS | 10,158,500 | 11,191,323 | 13,297,856 | 12,217,216 | 14,341,800 | 13,419,284 | 12,962,525 | 13,769,973 |
| General Funds | 8,579,600 | 9,556,123 | 11,406,556 | 11,523,916 | 12,049,100 | 11,392,484 | 11,717,325 | 12,569,973 |
| Local | 0 | 0 | 0 | 0 | 0 | 0 | 0 | 0 |
| Other State Funds | 1,578,900 | 1,635,200 | 1,891,300 | 693,300 | 2,292,700 | 2,026,800 | 1,245,200 | 1,200,000 |
| FEDERAL FUNDS | 4,718,200 | 5,055,277 | 5,652,835 | 6,762,641 | 7,911,000 | 8,316,216 | 9,057,474 | 10,569,973 |
| Federal ICF/MR | 4,718,200 | 5,055,277 | 5,652,835 | 6,762,641 | 7,911,000 | 8,316,216 | 9,057,474 | 10,569,973 |
| Title XX / SSBG Funds | 0 | 0 | 0 | 0 | 0 | 0 | 0 | 0 |
| Other Federal Funds | 0 | 0 | 0 | 0 | 0 | 0 | 0 | 0 |
| LARGE PRIVATE RESIDENTIAL | 0 | 0 | 0 | 0 | 0 | 0 | 2,162,132 | 2,230,856 |
| STATE FUNDS | 0 | 0 | 0 | 0 | 0 | 0 | 1,081,066 | 1,115,428 |
| General Funds | 0 | 0 | 0 | 0 | 0 | 0 | 1,081,066 | 1,115,428 |
| Other State Funds | 0 | 0 | 0 | 0 | 0 | 0 | 0 | 0 |
| Local/County Overmatch | 0 | 0 | 0 | 0 | 0 | 0 | 0 | 0 |
| FEDERAL FUNDS | 0 | 0 | 0 | 0 | 0 | 0 | 1,081,066 | 1,115,428 |
| Large Private ICF/MR | 0 | 0 | 0 | 0 | 0 | 0 | 1,081,066 | 1,115,428 |
| **COMMUNITY SERVICES FUNDS** | 4,050,600 | 6,744,620 | 8,117,690 | 10,342,501 | 11,762,440 | 15,840,136 | 18,507,780 | 19,888,446 |
| STATE FUNDS | 2,075,131 | 5,723,775 | 6,755,368 | 8,465,972 | 9,450,479 | 12,099,669 | 13,159,799 | 13,307,411 |
| General Funds | 2,018,231 | 5,648,875 | 6,484,068 | 8,200,972 | 9,248,979 | 11,899,669 | 12,959,799 | 13,107,411 |
| Other State Funds | 11,900 | 10,900 | 46,300 | 25,000 | 1,500 | 0 | 0 | 0 |
| Local/County Overmatch | 0 | 0 | 0 | 0 | 0 | 0 | 0 | 0 |
| SSI State Supplement | 45,000 | 64,000 | 225,000 | 240,000 | 200,000 | 200,000 | 200,000 | 200,000 |
| FEDERAL FUNDS | 1,975,469 | 1,020,845 | 1,362,322 | 1,876,529 | 2,311,961 | 3,740,467 | 5,347,981 | 6,581,035 |
| ICF/MR Funds | 1,676,500 | 548,400 | 633,405 | 719,785 | 707,365 | 1,043,171 | 1,244,122 | 1,405,809 |
| Small Public | 0 | 0 | 0 | 0 | 0 | 0 | 0 | 0 |
| Small Private | 1,676,500 | 548,400 | 633,405 | 719,785 | 707,365 | 1,043,171 | 1,244,122 | 1,405,809 |
| HCBS Waiver | 118,969 | 248,525 | 422,737 | 651,304 | 845,356 | 1,831,760 | 2,980,779 | 3,846,778 |
| Model 50/200 Waiver | 0 | 0 | 0 | 0 | 0 | 0 | 0 | 0 |
| Other Title XIX Programs | 0 | 0 | 0 | 0 | 0 | 0 | 0 | 0 |
| Title XX / SSBG Funds | 0 | 0 | 0 | 0 | 0 | 0 | 0 | 0 |
| Other Federal Funds | 0 | 0 | 0 | 0 | 0 | 0 | 0 | 0 |
| Waiver Clients' SSI/ADC | 180,000 | 223,920 | 306,180 | 505,440 | 759,240 | 865,536 | 1,123,080 | 1,328,448 |

Source:
Institute on Disability and Human Development (UAP),
University of Illinois at Chicago, 1994

# DISTRICT OF COLUMBIA

## MR/DD Spending for Congregate Residential & Community Services

▓ Congregate: 16+ Beds*   ■ Community**

Millions of 1992 Dollars

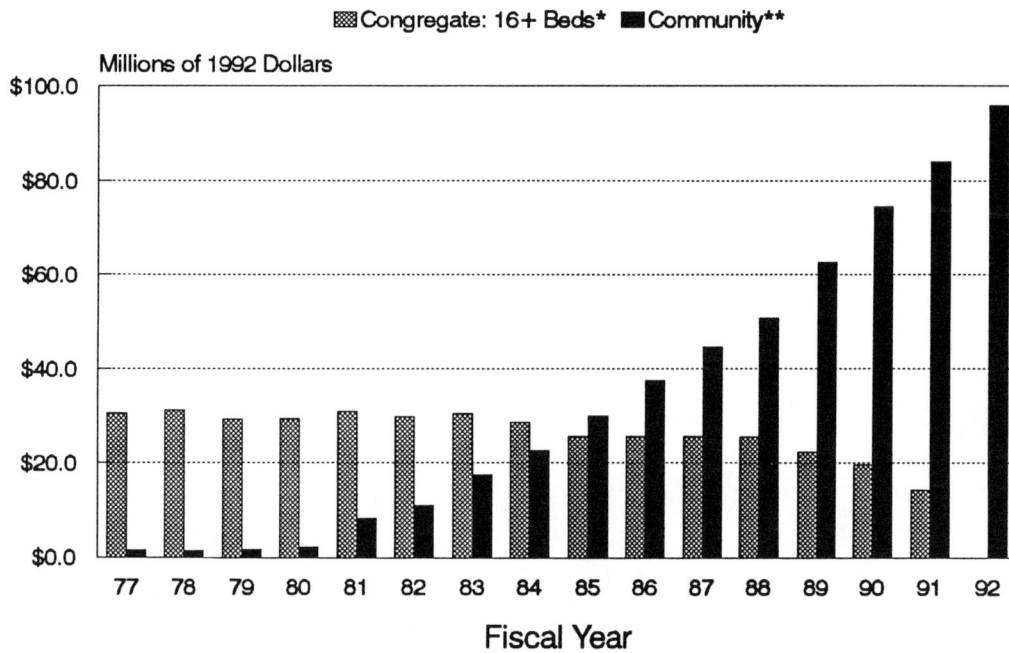

Fiscal Year

*Excludes nursing homes; ** Includes resources for
15 bed or less residential settings & non-residential community services

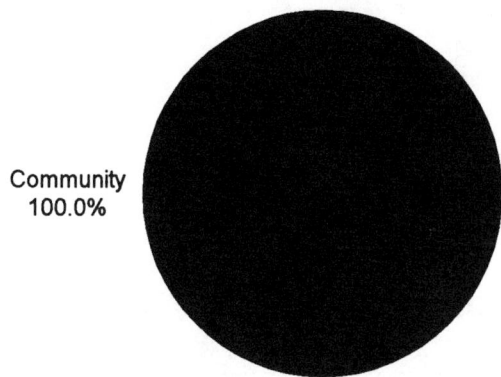

Community
100.0%

FY 1992 Total Spending:
$95.9 Million

*Source:*
Institute on Disability and Human Development (UAP),
University of Illinois at Chicago, 1994

# DISTRICT OF COLUMBIA

## Number of Persons Served by Residential Setting: FY 1992

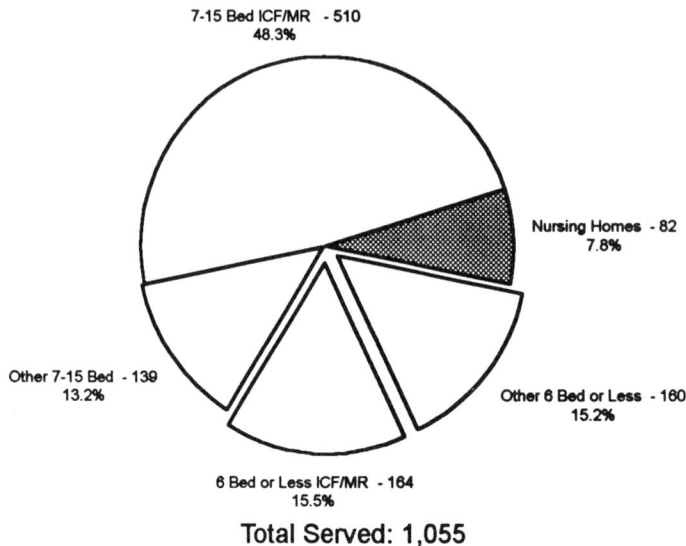

7-15 Bed ICF/MR - 510
48.3%

Nursing Homes - 82
7.8%

Other 7-15 Bed - 139
13.2%

Other 6 Bed or Less - 160
15.2%

6 Bed or Less ICF/MR - 164
15.5%

Total Served: 1,055

## Persons Served by Residential Setting:1986-92

|  | 1986 | 1987 | 1988 | 1989 | 1990 | 1991 | 1992 |
|---|---|---|---|---|---|---|---|
| **CONGREGATE 16 + BED SETTINGS** | NA | NA | 307 | 273 | 311 | 189 | 82 |
| Nursing Homes | NA | NA | 50 | 58 | 66 | 74 | 82 |
| State Institutions | 307 | 266 | 257 | 215 | 245 | 115 | 0 |
| Private 16+Bed ICF/MR | 0 | 0 | 0 | 0 | 0 | 0 | 0 |
| Other 16+Bed Residential | 0 | 0 | 0 | 0 | 0 | 0 | 0 |
| **15 BED OR LESS RESIDENTIAL SETTINGS** | 636 | 749 | 786 | 637 | 720 | 853 | 973 |
| Public 7-15 Bed ICF/MR | 0 | 0 | 0 | 0 | 0 | 0 | 0 |
| Private 7-15 Bed ICF/MR | 307 | 362 | 394 | 464 | 534 | 604 | 510 |
| Other 7-15 Bed Residential | 329 | 387 | 392 | 173 | 186 | 249 | 139 |
| Public 6 Bed or Less ICF/MR | 0 | 0 | 0 | 0 | 0 | 0 | 0 |
| Private 6 Bed or Less ICF/MR |  |  |  |  |  |  | 164 |
| Other 6 Bed or Less Residential |  |  |  |  |  |  | 160 |
| **TOTAL PERSONS SERVED** | NA | NA | 1,093 | 910 | 1,031 | 1,042 | 1,055 |

## Persons Served in Non-Residential Community Services:1986-92

|  | 1986 | 1987 | 1988 | 1989 | 1990 | 1991 | 1992 |
|---|---|---|---|---|---|---|---|
| **DAY/WORK PROGRAMS** | NA | 686 | 842 | 842 | 841 | 896 | 1,128 |
| Sheltered Employment/Work Activity | NA | 163 | 179 | 191 | 203 | 194 | 200 |
| Day Habilitation ("Day Training") | NA | 501 | 643 | 623 | 602 | 653 | 879 |
| Supported/Competitive Employment | NA | 22 | 20 | 28 | 36 | 49 | 49 |
| **CASE MANAGEMENT** | NA | NA | NA | 1,439 | 1,624 | 1,789 | 1,808 |
| **HCBS WAIVER** | 0 | 0 | 0 | 0 | 0 | 0 | 0 |
| **MODEL 50/200 WAIVER** | 0 | 0 | 0 | 0 | 0 | 0 | 0 |

*Source:*
Institute on Disability and Human Development (UAP),
University of Illinois at Chicago, 1994

# DISTRICT OF COLUMBIA

## Community Services: FY 1992 Revenue Sources

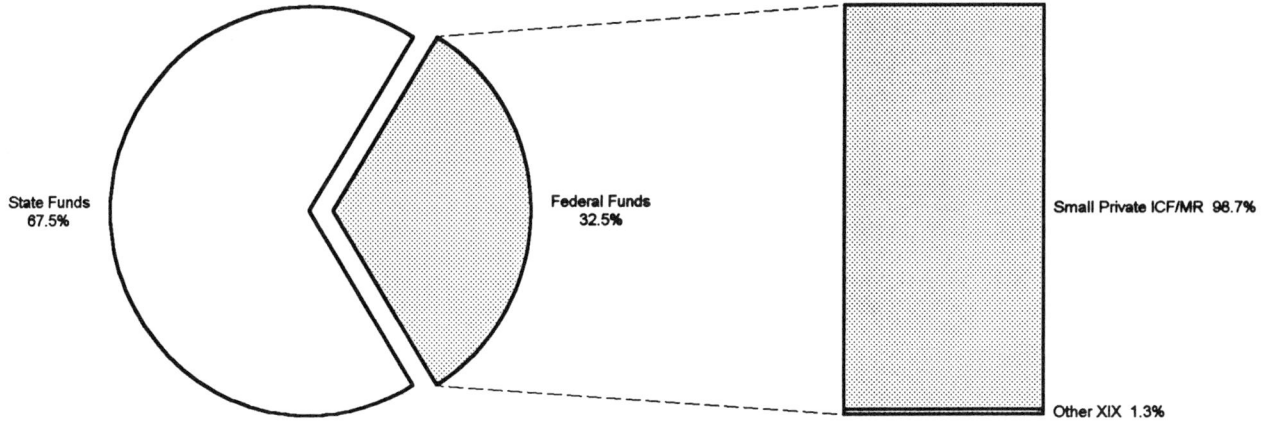

State Funds 67.5%

Federal Funds 32.5%

Small Private ICF/MR 98.7%

Other XIX 1.3%

Total Funds: $95.9 Million

## Family Support Initiatives*

|  | 1986 | 1987 | 1988 | 1989 | 1990 | 1991 | 1992 |
|---|---|---|---|---|---|---|---|
| **FAMILY SUPPORT: TOTAL SPENDING** | $0 | $406,000 | $493,082 | $780,760 | $987,987 | $1,110,771 | $1,399,012 |
| **Total # of Families Supported** | 0 | 408 | 860 | 976 | 1,110 | 1,268 | 1,492 |
| A. Financial Subsidy/Payment | $0 | $0 | NA | NA | NA | NA | NA |
| # of Families | 0 | 0 | 430 | 488 | 555 | 614 | 746 |
| B. Family Assistance Payments |  | $344,000 | $342,896 | $516,784 | $662,390 | $668,400 | $782,996 |
| # of Families |  | 343 | 400 | 450 | 494 | 570 | 655 |
| C. Other Family Support Payments |  | $62,000 | $150,186 | $263,976 | $325,597 | $442,371 | $616,016 |
| # of Families |  | 65 | 30 | 38 | 61 | 84 | 91 |

## Other Community Services Initiatives*

|  | 1986 | 1987 | 1988 | 1989 | 1990 | 1991 | 1992 |
|---|---|---|---|---|---|---|---|
| **AGING/DD SPENDING** | $0 | $0 | $0 | $0 | $0 | $0 | $0 |
| # of Persons Served | 0 | 0 | 0 | 0 | 0 | 0 | 0 |
| **ASSISTIVE TECHNOLOGY SPENDING** |  |  |  |  |  |  | $0 |
| # of Persons Served |  |  |  |  |  |  | 0 |
| **EARLY INTERVENTION SPENDING** | $0 | $0 | $0 | $0 | $0 | $0 | $0 |
| # of Persons Served | 0 | 0 | 0 | 0 | 0 | 0 | 0 |
| **PERSONAL ASSISTANCE SPENDING** |  |  |  |  |  |  | $0 |
| # of Persons Served |  |  |  |  |  |  | 0 |
| **SUPPORTED EMPLOYMENT SPENDING** | $0 | $55,000 | $58,000 | NA | NA | NA | NA |
| # of Persons Served | 0 | 22 | 20 | 28 | 36 | 49 | 49 |
| **SUPPORTED LIVING SPENDING** |  |  |  |  |  |  | $0 |
| # of Persons Served |  |  |  |  |  |  | 0 |

*Expenditures associated with Special Community Initiatives are a subset of funding within the community services component of the state's chart series and spreadsheet; Family Support Client figures may include duplicate client counts; HCBS Waiver counts include Waiver case management numbers.
0= Services not provided in the state; NA= Data not available from state; blank= Services not applicable (eg. CSLA prior to authorization, Special Community Initiatives prior to request for data by this study)

Source:
Institute on Disability and Human Development (UAP),
University of Illinois at Chicago, 1994

# DISTRICT OF COLUMBIA

## Large Congregate Care Facilities: FY 1992 Revenue Sources*

### Private 16+Bed Settings

**Public Institutions**

**Does Not Apply**

**Does Not Apply**

**\*Excludes nursing homes**

## Average Daily Residents in Institutions

Number of Residents

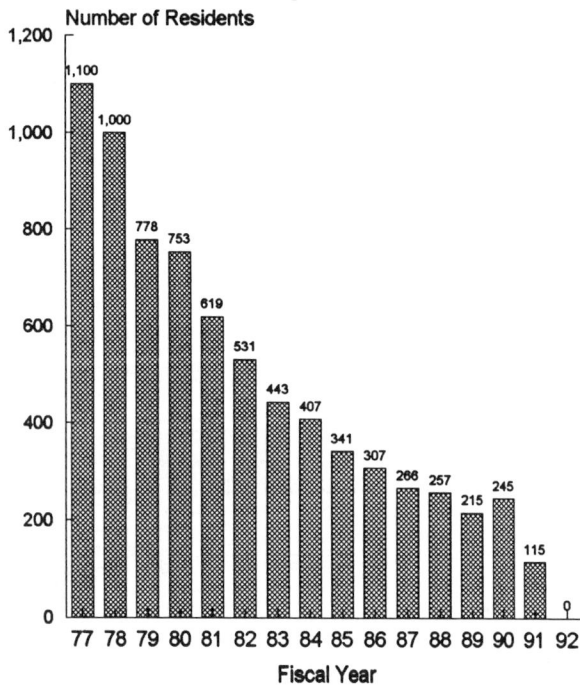

Fiscal Year

## Institutional Daily Costs Per Resident

Dollars Per Day

—Unadjusted

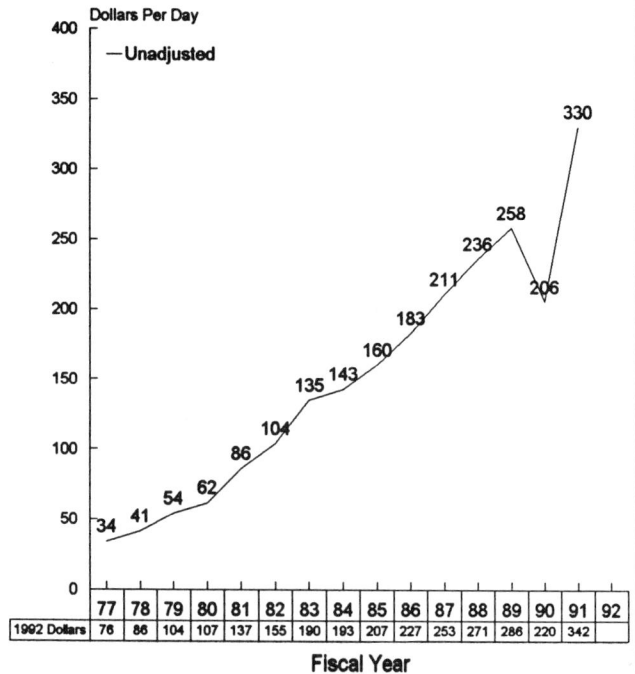

| | 77 | 78 | 79 | 80 | 81 | 82 | 83 | 84 | 85 | 86 | 87 | 88 | 89 | 90 | 91 | 92 |
|---|---|---|---|---|---|---|---|---|---|---|---|---|---|---|---|---|
| 1992 Dollars | 76 | 86 | 104 | 107 | 137 | 155 | 190 | 193 | 207 | 227 | 253 | 271 | 286 | 220 | 342 | |

Fiscal Year

*Source:*
Institute on Disability and Human Development (UAP),
University of Illinois at Chicago, 1994

# DISTRICT OF COLUMBIA FISCAL EFFORT

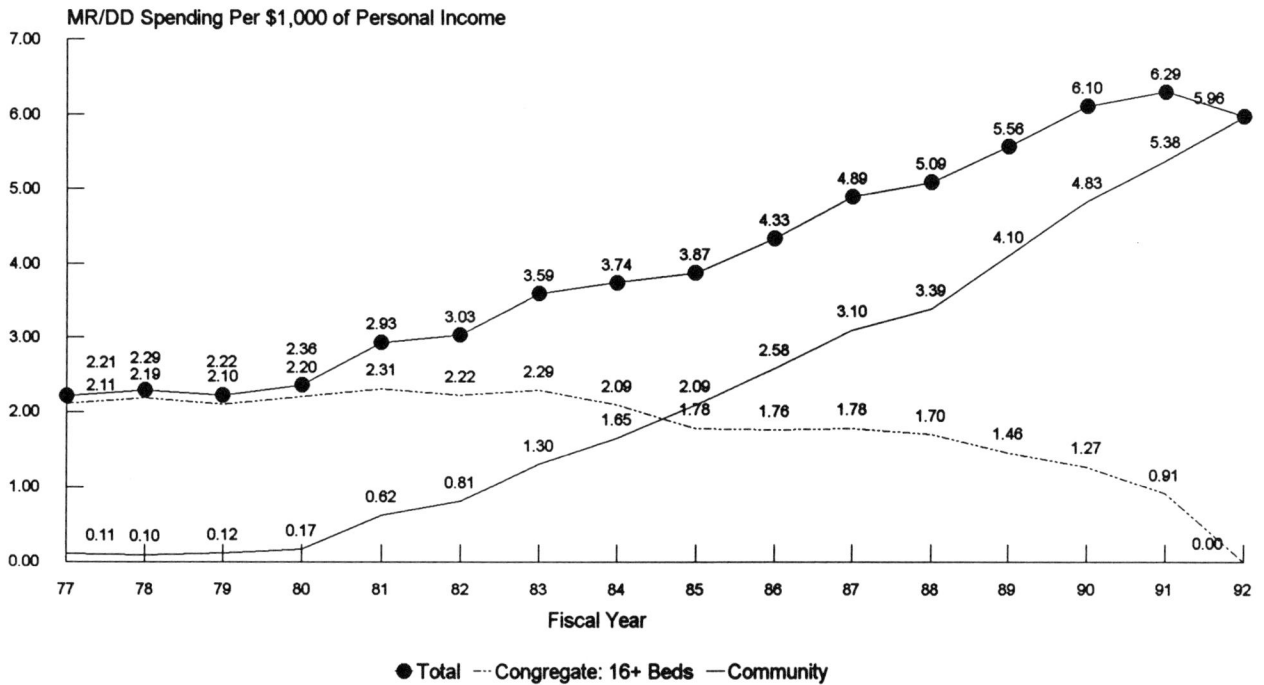

MR/DD Spending Per $1,000 of Personal Income

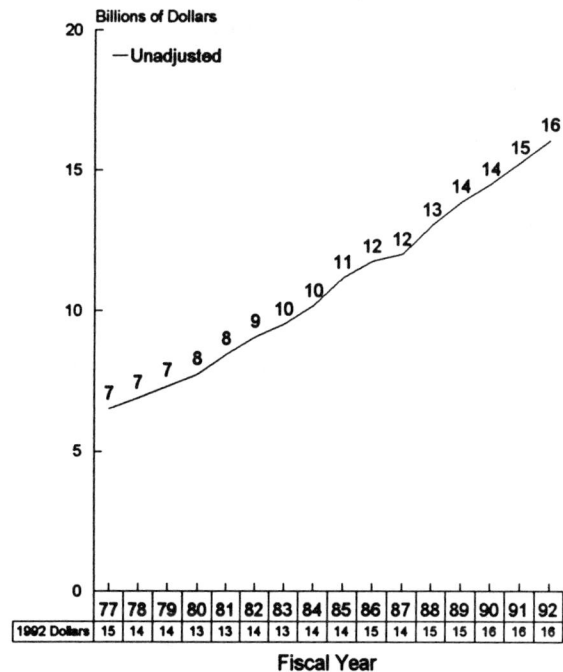

7.00

6.29
6.10
5.96
5.56
5.38
5.09
4.89
4.83
4.33
4.10
3.87
3.74
3.59
3.39
3.10
3.03
2.93
2.58
2.36
2.31
2.29  2.29
2.21  2.22  2.22
2.19  2.20  2.09  2.09
2.11  2.10  1.78  1.76  1.78  1.70
1.65  1.46
1.30  1.27
0.91
0.81
0.62
0.17  0.00
0.11  0.10  0.12

77  78  79  80  81  82  83  84  85  86  87  88  89  90  91  92

Fiscal Year

● Total  --- Congregate: 16+ Beds  — Community

## Total MR/DD Spending

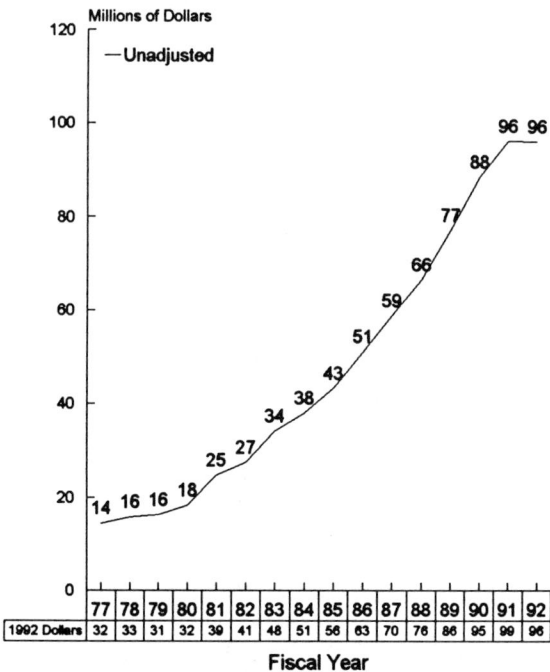

Millions of Dollars

—Unadjusted

120

100                                    96  96
                              88
80                         77
                      66
                  59
60            51
           43
        38
      34
60  25  27
      18
20  14  16  16

| | 77 | 78 | 79 | 80 | 81 | 82 | 83 | 84 | 85 | 86 | 87 | 88 | 89 | 90 | 91 | 92 |
|---|---|---|---|---|---|---|---|---|---|---|---|---|---|---|---|---|
| 1992 Dollars | 32 | 33 | 31 | 32 | 39 | 41 | 48 | 51 | 56 | 63 | 70 | 76 | 86 | 95 | 99 | 96 |

Fiscal Year

## Personal Income

Billions of Dollars

—Unadjusted

20

15                                    15  16
                              14  14
                        13
                  12  12
            11
20        10  10
        9
      8  8
7  7  7

| | 77 | 78 | 79 | 80 | 81 | 82 | 83 | 84 | 85 | 86 | 87 | 88 | 89 | 90 | 91 | 92 |
|---|---|---|---|---|---|---|---|---|---|---|---|---|---|---|---|---|
| 1992 Dollars | 15 | 14 | 14 | 13 | 13 | 14 | 13 | 14 | 14 | 15 | 14 | 15 | 15 | 16 | 16 | 16 |

Fiscal Year

*Source:*
Institute on Disability and Human Development (UAP),
University of Illinois at Chicago, 1994

# DISTRICT OF COLUMBIA

## Financial Support for MR/DD Services: FY 1977-92

| | 1977 | 1978 | 1979 | 1980 | 1981 | 1982 | 1983 | 1984 |
|---|---|---|---|---|---|---|---|---|
| **TOTAL FUNDS** | $14,418,000 | $15,772,000 | $16,256,000 | $18,293,000 | $24,754,000 | $27,486,000 | $34,159,300 | $38,010,000 |
| **CONGREGATE 16+ BEDS** | 13,733,000 | 15,084,000 | 15,354,000 | 17,015,000 | 19,496,000 | 20,102,000 | 21,761,000 | 21,257,000 |
| INSTITUTIONAL SERVICES FUNDS | 13,733,000 | 15,084,000 | 15,354,000 | 17,015,000 | 19,496,000 | 20,102,000 | 21,761,000 | 21,257,000 |
| STATE FUNDS | 9,895,000 | 10,638,000 | 8,666,000 | 12,192,000 | 16,589,000 | 17,867,000 | 15,771,000 | 14,537,600 |
| General Funds | 9,895,000 | 10,638,000 | 8,666,000 | 12,192,000 | 16,589,000 | 17,867,000 | 15,771,000 | 14,537,600 |
| Local | 0 | 0 | 0 | 0 | 0 | 0 | 0 | 0 |
| Other State Funds | 0 | 0 | 0 | 0 | 0 | 0 | 0 | 0 |
| FEDERAL FUNDS | 3,838,000 | 4,446,000 | 6,688,000 | 4,823,000 | 2,907,000 | 2,235,000 | 5,990,000 | 6,719,400 |
| Federal ICF/MR | 3,760,000 | 4,368,000 | 6,610,000 | 4,745,000 | 2,852,000 | 2,205,000 | 5,960,000 | 6,719,400 |
| Title XX / SSBG Funds | 0 | 0 | 0 | 0 | 0 | 0 | 0 | 0 |
| Other Federal Funds | 78,000 | 78,000 | 78,000 | 78,000 | 55,000 | 30,000 | 30,000 | |
| LARGE PRIVATE RESIDENTIAL | 0 | 0 | 0 | 0 | 0 | 0 | 0 | 0 |
| STATE FUNDS | 0 | 0 | 0 | 0 | 0 | 0 | 0 | 0 |
| General Funds | 0 | 0 | 0 | 0 | 0 | 0 | 0 | 0 |
| Other State Funds | 0 | 0 | 0 | 0 | 0 | 0 | 0 | 0 |
| Local/County Overmatch | 0 | 0 | 0 | 0 | 0 | 0 | 0 | 0 |
| FEDERAL FUNDS | 0 | 0 | 0 | 0 | 0 | 0 | 0 | 0 |
| Large Private ICF/MR | 0 | 0 | 0 | 0 | 0 | 0 | 0 | 0 |
| **COMMUNITY SERVICES FUNDS** | 685,000 | 688,000 | 902,000 | 1,278,000 | 5,258,000 | 7,384,000 | 12,398,300 | 16,753,000 |
| STATE FUNDS | 675,000 | 678,000 | 892,000 | 1,268,000 | 5,243,000 | 7,369,000 | 11,572,800 | 14,443,100 |
| General Funds | 635,000 | 617,000 | 712,000 | 912,000 | 4,890,000 | 7,015,000 | 11,195,800 | 14,057,100 |
| Other State Funds | 0 | 0 | 0 | 0 | 0 | 0 | 0 | 0 |
| Local/County Overmatch | 0 | 0 | 0 | 0 | 0 | 0 | 0 | 0 |
| SSI State Supplement | 40,000 | 61,000 | 180,000 | 356,000 | 353,000 | 354,000 | 377,000 | 386,000 |
| FEDERAL FUNDS | 10,000 | 10,000 | 10,000 | 10,000 | 15,000 | 15,000 | 825,500 | 2,309,900 |
| ICF/MR Funds | 0 | 0 | 0 | 0 | 0 | 0 | 810,500 | 2,294,900 |
| Small Public | 0 | 0 | 0 | 0 | 0 | 0 | 0 | 0 |
| Small Private | 0 | 0 | 0 | 0 | 0 | 0 | 810,500 | 2,294,900 |
| HCBS Waiver | 0 | 0 | 0 | 0 | 0 | 0 | 0 | 0 |
| Model 50/200 Waiver | 0 | 0 | 0 | 0 | 0 | 0 | 0 | 0 |
| Other Title XIX Programs | 0 | 0 | 0 | 0 | 0 | 0 | 0 | 0 |
| Title XX / SSBG Funds | 0 | 0 | 0 | 0 | 0 | 0 | 0 | 0 |
| Other Federal Funds | 10,000 | 10,000 | 10,000 | 10,000 | 15,000 | 15,000 | 15,000 | 15,000 |
| Waiver Clients' SSI/ADC | 0 | 0 | 0 | 0 | 0 | 0 | 0 | 0 |

| | 1985 | 1986 | 1987 | 1988 | 1989 | 1990 | 1991 | 1992 |
|---|---|---|---|---|---|---|---|---|
| **TOTAL FUNDS** | $43,310,160 | $51,002,820 | $58,695,480 | $66,388,140 | $77,095,498 | $88,350,082 | $95,981,509 | $95,878,193 |
| **CONGREGATE 16+ BEDS** | 19,949,460 | 20,691,920 | 21,434,380 | 22,176,840 | 20,249,732 | 18,378,460 | 13,871,093 | 0 |
| INSTITUTIONAL SERVICES FUNDS | 19,949,460 | 20,691,920 | 21,434,380 | 22,176,840 | 20,249,732 | 18,378,460 | 13,871,093 | 0 |
| STATE FUNDS | 13,660,210 | 13,280,420 | 12,900,630 | 12,520,840 | 10,124,866 | 9,189,230 | 6,935,547 | 0 |
| General Funds | 13,660,210 | 13,277,800 | 12,894,450 | 12,511,100 | 10,124,866 | 9,189,230 | 6,935,547 | 0 |
| Local | 0 | 0 | 0 | 0 | 0 | 0 | 0 | 0 |
| Other State Funds | 0 | 2,620 | 6,180 | 9,740 | 0 | 0 | 0 | 0 |
| FEDERAL FUNDS | 6,289,250 | 7,411,500 | 8,533,750 | 9,656,000 | 10,124,866 | 9,189,230 | 6,935,547 | 0 |
| Federal ICF/MR | 6,289,250 | 7,411,500 | 8,533,750 | 9,656,000 | 10,124,866 | 9,189,230 | 6,935,547 | 0 |
| Title XX / SSBG Funds | 0 | 0 | 0 | 0 | 0 | 0 | 0 | 0 |
| Other Federal Funds | 0 | 0 | 0 | 0 | 0 | 0 | 0 | 0 |
| LARGE PRIVATE RESIDENTIAL | 0 | 0 | 0 | 0 | 0 | 0 | 0 | 0 |
| STATE FUNDS | 0 | 0 | 0 | 0 | 0 | 0 | 0 | 0 |
| General Funds | 0 | 0 | 0 | 0 | 0 | 0 | 0 | 0 |
| Other State Funds | 0 | 0 | 0 | 0 | 0 | 0 | 0 | 0 |
| Local/County Overmatch | 0 | 0 | 0 | 0 | 0 | 0 | 0 | 0 |
| FEDERAL FUNDS | 0 | 0 | 0 | 0 | 0 | 0 | 0 | 0 |
| Large Private ICF/MR | 0 | 0 | 0 | 0 | 0 | 0 | 0 | 0 |
| **COMMUNITY SERVICES FUNDS** | 23,360,700 | 30,310,900 | 37,261,100 | 44,211,300 | 56,845,766 | 69,971,622 | 82,110,416 | 95,878,193 |
| STATE FUNDS | 17,871,400 | 22,810,300 | 27,749,200 | 32,688,100 | 40,478,703 | 48,676,497 | 55,887,229 | 64,726,943 |
| General Funds | 17,470,200 | 22,423,900 | 27,377,600 | 32,331,300 | 40,104,063 | 48,283,125 | 55,474,188 | 64,293,250 |
| Other State Funds | 0 | 0 | 0 | 0 | 0 | 0 | 0 | 0 |
| Local/County Overmatch | 0 | 0 | 0 | 0 | 0 | 0 | 0 | 0 |
| SSI State Supplement | 401,200 | 386,400 | 371,600 | 356,800 | 374,640 | 393,372 | 413,041 | 433,693 |
| FEDERAL FUNDS | 5,489,300 | 7,500,600 | 9,511,900 | 11,523,200 | 16,367,063 | 21,295,125 | 26,223,188 | 31,151,250 |
| ICF/MR Funds | 4,815,500 | 6,890,000 | 8,964,500 | 11,039,000 | 15,967,063 | 20,895,125 | 25,823,188 | 30,751,250 |
| Small Public | 0 | 0 | 0 | 0 | 0 | 0 | 0 | 0 |
| Small Private | 4,815,500 | 6,890,000 | 8,964,500 | 11,039,000 | 15,967,063 | 20,895,125 | 25,823,188 | 30,751,250 |
| HCBS Waiver | 0 | 0 | 0 | 0 | 0 | 0 | 0 | 0 |
| Model 50/200 Waiver | 0 | 0 | 0 | 0 | 0 | 0 | 0 | 0 |
| Other Title XIX Programs | 673,800 | 610,600 | 547,400 | 484,200 | 400,000 | 400,000 | 400,000 | 400,000 |
| Title XX / SSBG Funds | 0 | 0 | 0 | 0 | 0 | 0 | 0 | 0 |
| Other Federal Funds | 0 | 0 | 0 | 0 | 0 | 0 | 0 | 0 |
| Waiver Clients' SSI/ADC | 0 | 0 | 0 | 0 | 0 | 0 | 0 | 0 |

*Source:*

Institute on Disability and Human Development (UAP),
University of Illinois at Chicago, 1994

# FLORIDA

## MR/DD Spending for Congregate Residential & Community Services

▨ Congregate: 16+ Beds*  ■ Community**

Millions of 1992 Dollars

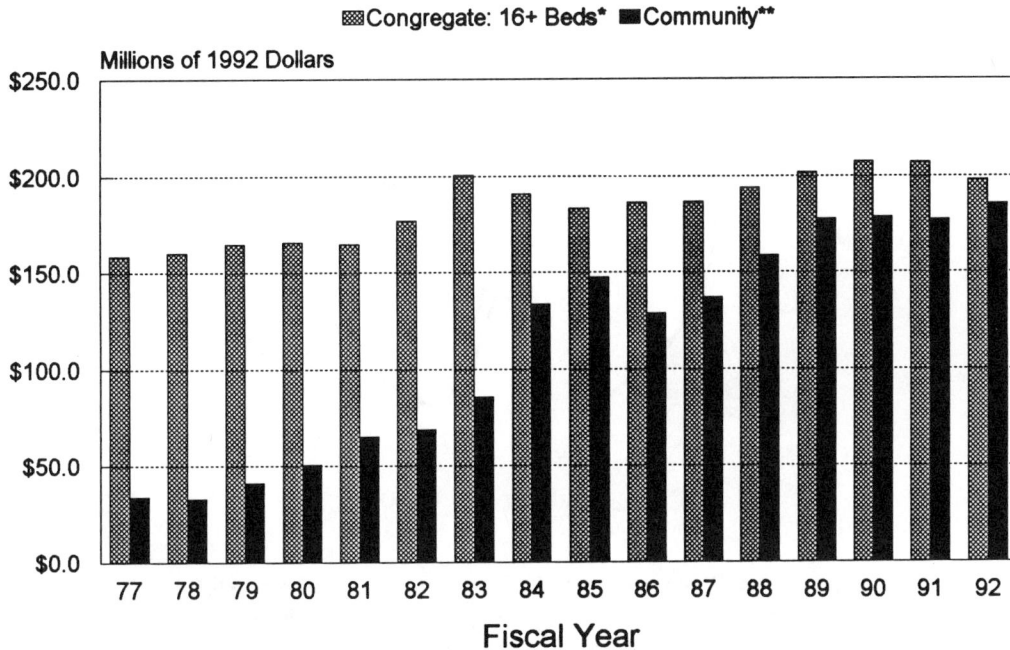

Fiscal Year

*Excludes nursing homes; ** Includes resources for
15 bed or less residential settings & non-residential community services

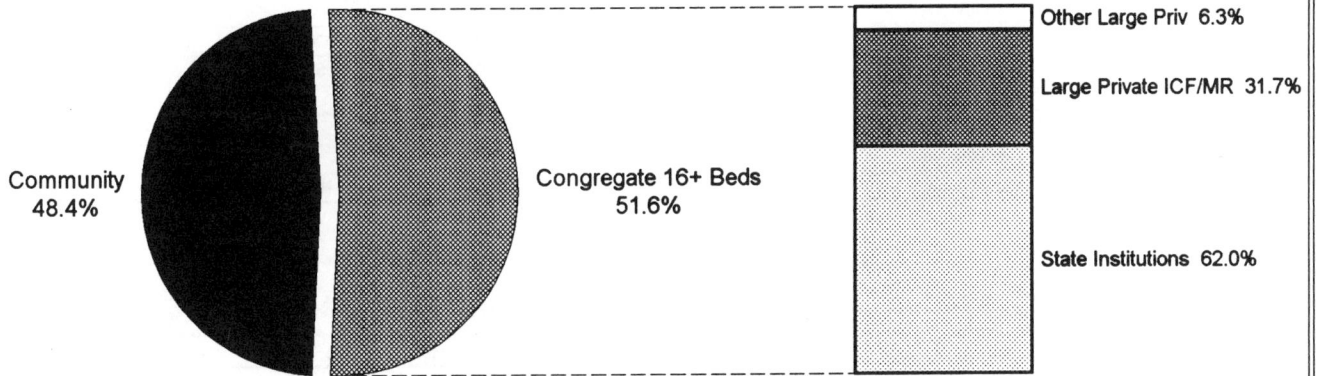

Community
48.4%

Congregate 16+ Beds
51.6%

Other Large Priv  6.3%

Large Private ICF/MR  31.7%

State Institutions  62.0%

FY 1992 Total Spending:
$383.3 Million

*Source:*
Institute on Disability and Human Development (UAP),
University of Illinois at Chicago, 1994

# FLORIDA

## Number of Persons Served by Residential Setting: FY 1992

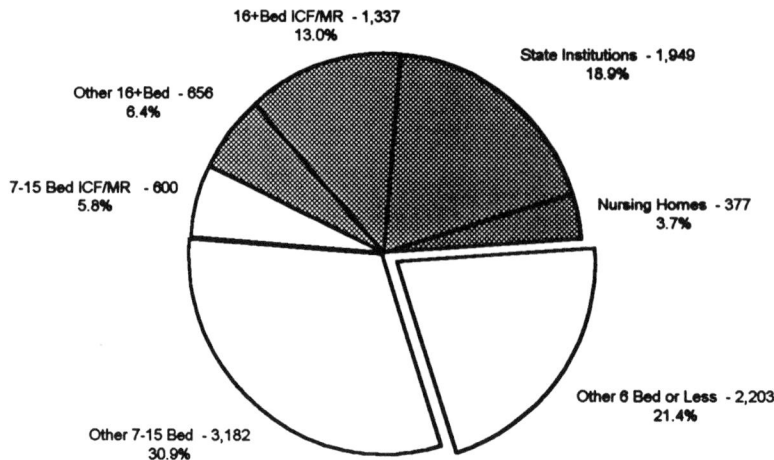

16+Bed ICF/MR - 1,337
13.0%

State Institutions - 1,949
18.9%

Other 16+Bed - 656
6.4%

7-15 Bed ICF/MR - 600
5.8%

Nursing Homes - 377
3.7%

Other 6 Bed or Less - 2,203
21.4%

Other 7-15 Bed - 3,182
30.9%

Total Served: 10,304

## Persons Served by Residential Setting:1986-92

|  | 1986 | 1987 | 1988 | 1989 | 1990 | 1991 | 1992 |
|---|---|---|---|---|---|---|---|
| CONGREGATE 16 + BED SETTINGS | NA | NA | 5,293 | NA | NA | NA | 4,319 |
| Nursing Homes* | NA | NA | 1,020 | NA | NA | NA | 377 |
| State Institutions | 2,125 | 2,039 | 1,993 | 1,990 | 1,992 | 1,982 | 1,949 |
| Private 16+Bed ICF/MR | 1,224 | 1,226 | 1,293 | 1,338 | 1,335 | 1,331 | 1,337 |
| Other 16+Bed Residential | 972 | 1,016 | 987 | 843 | 724 | 707 | 656 |
| 15 BED OR LESS RESIDENTIAL SETTINGS | 4,207 | 4,346 | 4,545 | 4,931 | 5,252 | 5,323 | 5,985 |
| Public 7-15 Bed ICF/MR | 0 | 0 | 0 | 0 | 0 | 0 | 0 |
| Private 7-15 Bed ICF/MR | 675 | 649 | 639 | 600 | 600 | 600 | 600 |
| Other 7-15 Bed Residential | 3,532 | 3,697 | 3,906 | 4,331 | 4,652 | 4,723 | 3,182 |
| Public 6 Bed or Less ICF/MR | 0 | 0 | 0 | 0 | 0 | 0 | 0 |
| Private 6 Bed or Less ICF/MR | 0 | 0 | 0 | 0 | 0 | 0 | 0 |
| Other 6 Bed or Less Residential | 0 | 0 | 0 | 0 | 0 | 0 | 2,203 |
| TOTAL PERSONS SERVED | NA | NA | 9,838 | NA | NA | NA | 10,304 |

## Persons Served in Non-Residential Community Services:1986-92

|  | 1986 | 1987 | 1988 | 1989 | 1990 | 1991 | 1992 |
|---|---|---|---|---|---|---|---|
| DAY/WORK PROGRAMS | 15,865 | 15,097 | 17,083 | 9,961 | 10,507 | 10,830 | 11,757 |
| Sheltered Employment/Work Activity | NA | NA | NA | NA | NA | NA | NA |
| Day Habilitation ("Day Training") | NA | NA | NA | 9,433 | 8,929 | 8,113 | 8,793 |
| Supported/Competitive Employment | NA | NA | 477 | 528 | 1,578 | 2,717 | 2,964 |
| CASE MANAGEMENT | 15,350 | 16,675 | 18,972 | 20,440 | 22,208 | 23,370 | 23,590 |
| HCBS WAIVER | 2,571 | 2,631 | 2,631 | 2,568 | 2,488 | 2,631 | 2,631 |
| MODEL 50/200 WAIVER | 0 | 0 | 0 | 0 | 0 | 0 | 0 |

*Source:*
Institute on Disability and Human Development (UAP),
University of Illinois at Chicago, 1994

# FLORIDA

## Community Services: FY 1992 Revenue Sources

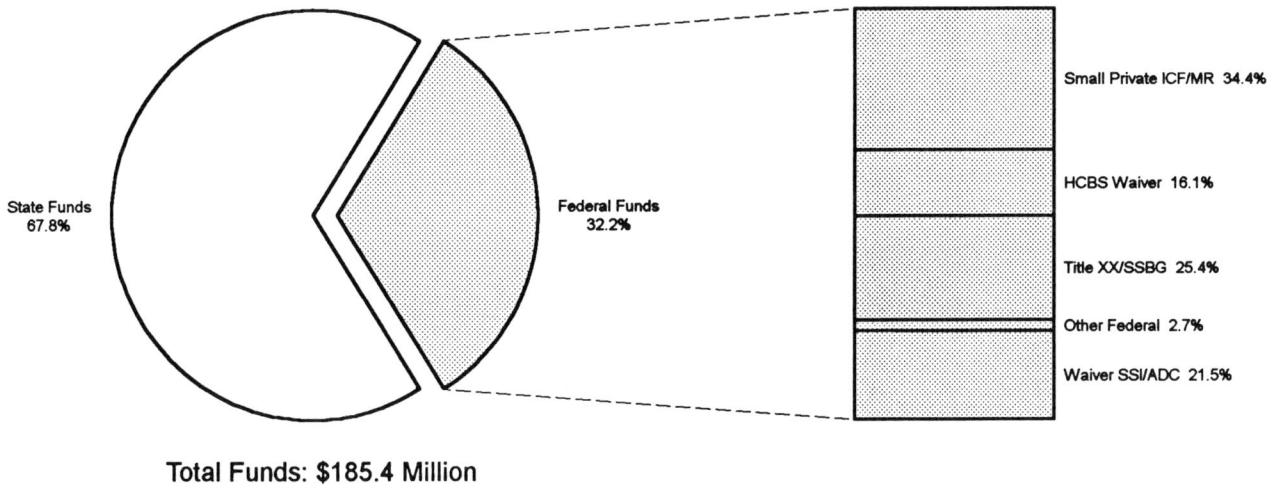

State Funds 67.8%

Federal Funds 32.2%

Small Private ICF/MR 34.4%

HCBS Waiver 16.1%

Title XX/SSBG 25.4%

Other Federal 2.7%

Waiver SSI/ADC 21.5%

Total Funds: $185.4 Million

## Family Support Initiatives*

|  | 1986 | 1987 | 1988 | 1989 | 1990 | 1991 | 1992 |
|---|---|---|---|---|---|---|---|
| FAMILY SUPPORT: TOTAL SPENDING | $1,233,902 | $1,740,212 | $1,979,991 | $1,915,734 | $1,750,935 | $1,147,659 | $699,840 |
| Total # of Families Supported | 4,935 | 5,150 | 4,385 | 2,497 | 2,421 | 1,493 | 1,255 |
| A. Financial Subsidy/Payment | $671,194 | $683,759 | $703,076 | $766,862 | $926,757 | $875,974 | $373,777 |
| # of Families | 262 | 278 | 276 | 258 | 293 | 302 | 232 |
| B. Family Assistance Payments | $419,593 | $487,908 | $586,118 | $968,913 | $1,245,409 | $1,147,659 | $699,840 |
| # of Families | 620 | 632 | 767 | 1,219 | 1,560 | 1,493 | 1,255 |
| C. Other Family Support Payments | $1,233,902 | $1,740,212 | $1,979,991 | $1,915,734 | $1,750,934 | $559,677 | $101,285 |
| # of Families | 4,935 | 5,150 | 4,385 | 2,497 | 2,421 | 893 | 385 |

## Other Community Services Initiatives*

|  | 1986 | 1987 | 1988 | 1989 | 1990 | 1991 | 1992 |
|---|---|---|---|---|---|---|---|
| AGING/DD SPENDING | $0 | $0 | $0 | $0 | $0 | $0 | $0 |
| # of Persons Served | 0 | 0 | 0 | 0 | 0 | 0 | 0 |
| ASSISTIVE TECHNOLOGY SPENDING |  |  |  | NA | $1,033,146 | $2,197,115 | $2,291,799 |
| # of Persons Served |  |  |  | NA | 1,440 | 2,333 | 2,848 |
| EARLY INTERVENTION SPENDING | NA | $1,859,568 | $2,364,251 | $2,973,931 | $4,830,181 | $3,551,175 | $3,183,952 |
| # of Persons Served | NA | 1,958 | 2,105 | 2,024 | 2,737 | 2,423 | 3,030 |
| PERSONAL ASSISTANCE SPENDING |  |  |  |  |  |  | $0 |
| # of Persons Served |  |  |  |  |  |  | 0 |
| SUPPORTED EMPLOYMENT SPENDING | NA | NA | $2,011,500 | $826,227 | $3,705,780 | $3,517,355 | $2,956,407 |
| # of Persons Served | NA | NA | 477 | 528 | 1,578 | 2,171 | 2,328 |
| SUPPORTED LIVING SPENDING |  |  |  |  |  | NA | $1,633,537 |
| # of Persons Served |  |  |  |  |  | 334 | 496 |

*Expenditures associated with Special Community Initiatives are a subset of funding within the community services component of the state's chart series and spreadsheet; Family Support Client figures may include duplicate client counts; HCBS Waiver counts include Waiver case management numbers.
0= Services not provided in the state; NA= Data not available from state; blank= Services not applicable (eg. CSLA prior to authorization, Special Community Initiatives prior to request for data by this study)

*Source:*
Institute on Disability and Human Development (UAP),
University of Illinois at Chicago, 1994

# FLORIDA

## Large Congregate Care Facilities: FY 1992 Revenue Sources*

### Private 16+Bed Settings

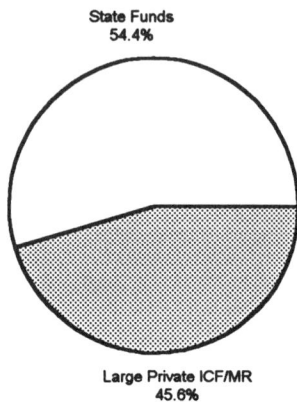

State Funds
54.4%

Large Private ICF/MR
45.6%

Total Funds: $75.1 Million

### Public Institutions

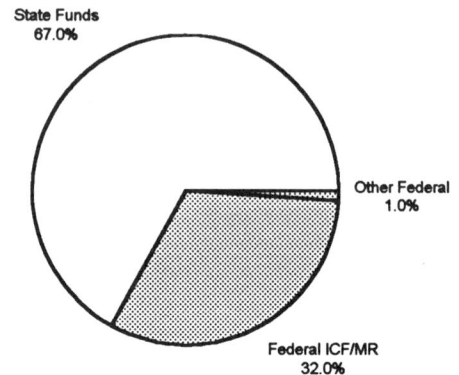

State Funds
67.0%

Other Federal
1.0%

Federal ICF/MR
32.0%

Total Funds: $122.7 Million

*Excludes nursing homes

## Average Daily Residents in Institutions

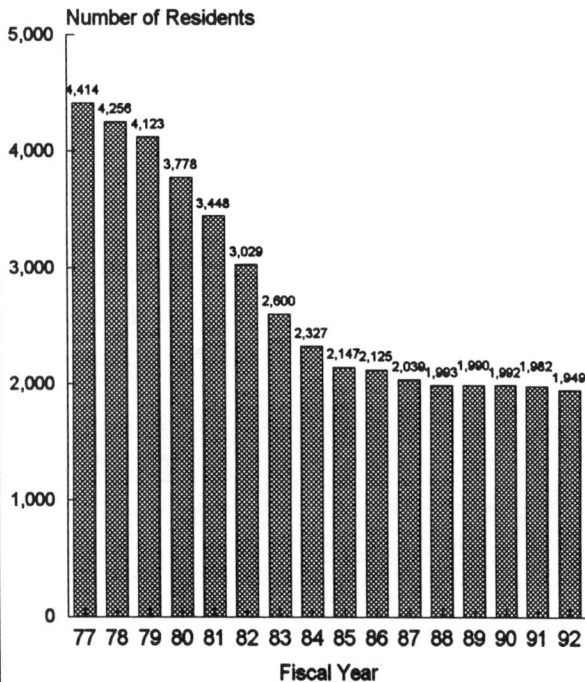

Number of Residents

| Fiscal Year | Residents |
|---|---|
| 77 | 4,414 |
| 78 | 4,256 |
| 79 | 4,123 |
| 80 | 3,778 |
| 81 | 3,448 |
| 82 | 3,029 |
| 83 | 2,600 |
| 84 | 2,327 |
| 85 | 2,147 |
| 86 | 2,125 |
| 87 | 2,039 |
| 88 | 1,993 |
| 89 | 1,990 |
| 90 | 1,992 |
| 91 | 1,982 |
| 92 | 1,949 |

## Institutional Daily Costs Per Resident

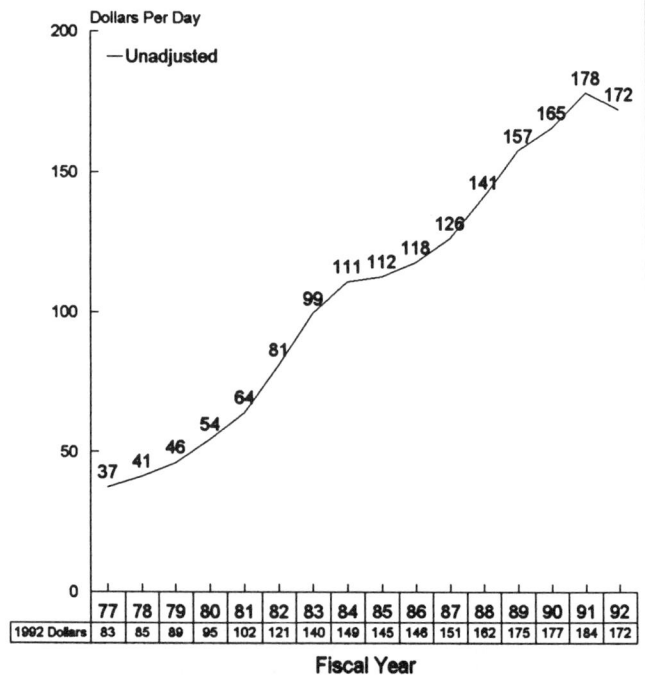

Dollars Per Day
—Unadjusted

| Fiscal Year | 77 | 78 | 79 | 80 | 81 | 82 | 83 | 84 | 85 | 86 | 87 | 88 | 89 | 90 | 91 | 92 |
|---|---|---|---|---|---|---|---|---|---|---|---|---|---|---|---|---|
| Unadjusted | 37 | 41 | 46 | 54 | 64 | 81 | 99 | 111 | 112 | 118 | 126 | 141 | 157 | 165 | 178 | 172 |
| 1992 Dollars | 83 | 85 | 89 | 95 | 102 | 121 | 140 | 149 | 145 | 146 | 151 | 162 | 175 | 177 | 184 | 172 |

*Source:*
Institute on Disability and Human Development (UAP),
University of Illinois at Chicago, 1994

# FLORIDA FISCAL EFFORT

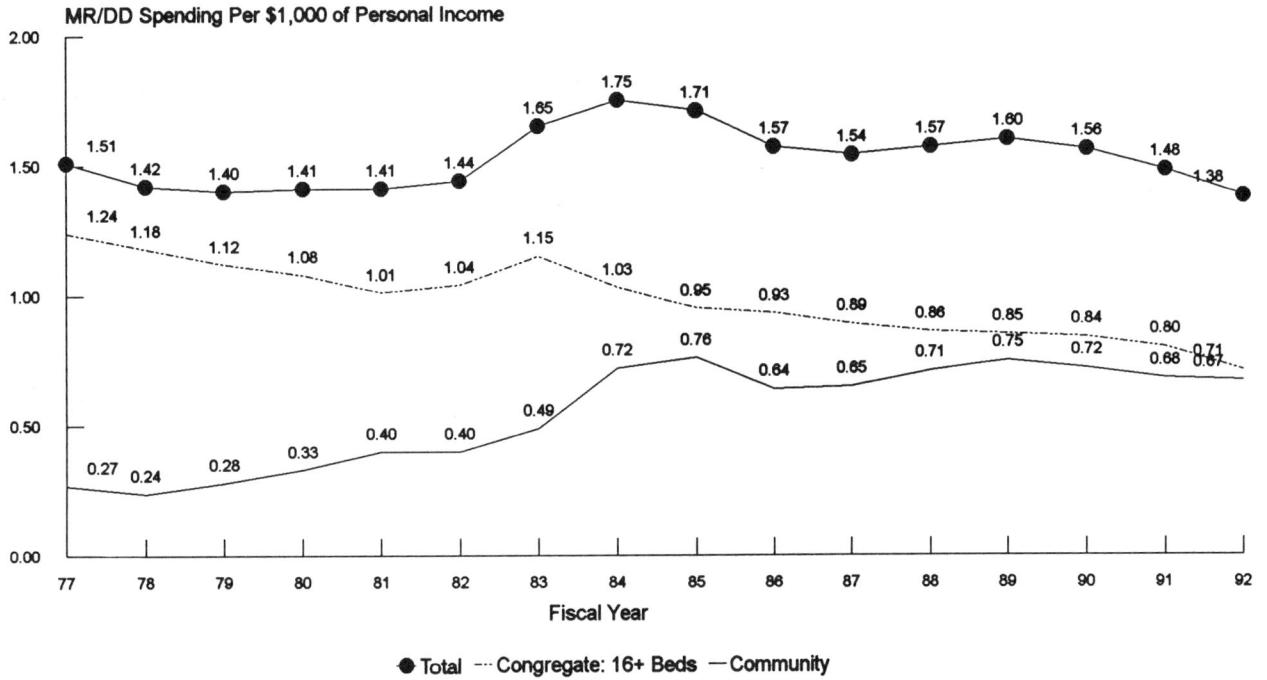

**MR/DD Spending Per $1,000 of Personal Income**

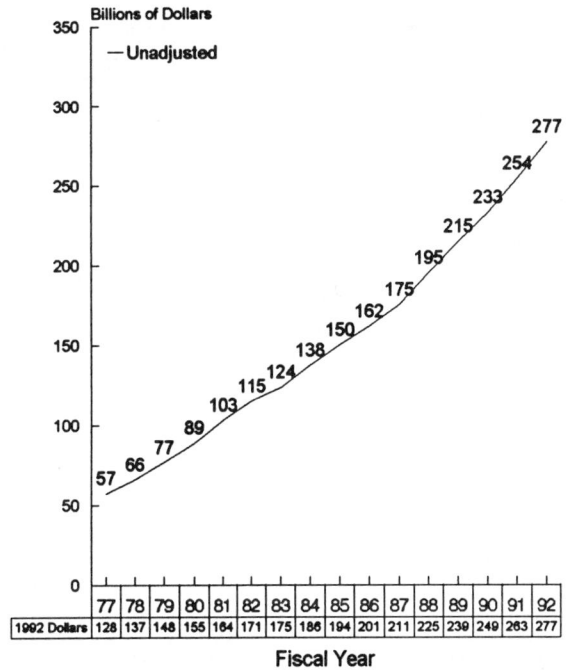

Total: 1.51, 1.42, 1.40, 1.41, 1.41, 1.44, 1.65, 1.75, 1.71, 1.57, 1.54, 1.57, 1.60, 1.56, 1.48, 1.38

Congregate: 16+ Beds: 1.24, 1.18, 1.12, 1.08, 1.01, 1.04, 1.15, 1.03, 0.95, 0.93, 0.89, 0.86, 0.85, 0.84, 0.80, 0.71, 0.67

Community: 0.27, 0.24, 0.28, 0.33, 0.40, 0.40, 0.49, 0.72, 0.76, 0.64, 0.65, 0.71, 0.75, 0.72, 0.68

**Fiscal Year**

● Total  --- Congregate: 16+ Beds  — Community

## Total MR/DD Spending

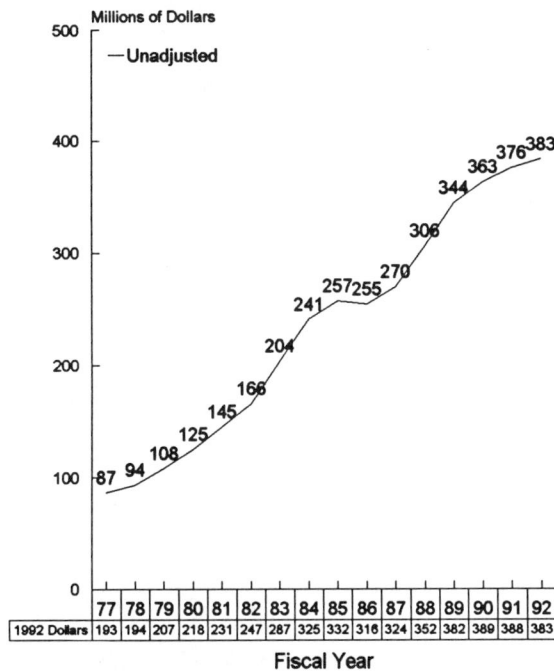

**Millions of Dollars**

—Unadjusted

87, 94, 108, 125, 145, 166, 204, 241, 257, 255, 270, 306, 344, 363, 376, 383

| | 77 | 78 | 79 | 80 | 81 | 82 | 83 | 84 | 85 | 86 | 87 | 88 | 89 | 90 | 91 | 92 |
|---|---|---|---|---|---|---|---|---|---|---|---|---|---|---|---|---|
| 1992 Dollars | 193 | 194 | 207 | 218 | 231 | 247 | 287 | 325 | 332 | 316 | 324 | 352 | 382 | 389 | 388 | 383 |

**Fiscal Year**

## Personal Income

**Billions of Dollars**

—Unadjusted

57, 66, 77, 89, 103, 115, 124, 138, 150, 162, 175, 195, 215, 233, 254, 277

| | 77 | 78 | 79 | 80 | 81 | 82 | 83 | 84 | 85 | 86 | 87 | 88 | 89 | 90 | 91 | 92 |
|---|---|---|---|---|---|---|---|---|---|---|---|---|---|---|---|---|
| 1992 Dollars | 128 | 137 | 148 | 155 | 164 | 171 | 175 | 186 | 194 | 201 | 211 | 225 | 239 | 249 | 263 | 277 |

**Fiscal Year**

*Source:*
Institute on Disability and Human Development (UAP),
University of Illinois at Chicago, 1994

# FLORIDA

## Financial Support for MR/DD Services: FY 1977-92

| | 1977 | 1978 | 1979 | 1980 | 1981 | 1982 | 1983 | 1984 |
|---|---|---|---|---|---|---|---|---|
| **TOTAL FUNDS** | $86,692,000 | $93,644,000 | $107,952,000 | $125,238,000 | $145,240,000 | $165,775,000 | $203,876,000 | $241,040,809 |
| **CONGREGATE 16+ BEDS** | 71,438,499 | 77,663,588 | 86,266,412 | 95,839,760 | 103,937,787 | 119,191,561 | 142,796,876 | 141,666,057 |
| INSTITUTIONAL SERVICES FUNDS | 60,201,000 | 64,084,000 | 69,370,000 | 75,294,000 | 80,464,000 | 89,606,000 | 94,287,000 | 94,238,065 |
| STATE FUNDS | 50,058,700 | 51,878,900 | 55,325,600 | 58,434,500 | 58,907,700 | 74,719,600 | 76,692,300 | 70,011,491 |
| General Funds | 49,751,000 | 51,533,000 | 54,803,000 | 57,774,000 | 57,494,000 | 73,184,000 | 74,819,000 | 66,671,200 |
| Local | 0 | 0 | 0 | 0 | 0 | 0 | 0 | 0 |
| Other State Funds | 307,700 | 345,900 | 522,600 | 660,500 | 1,413,700 | 1,535,600 | 1,873,300 | 3,340,291 |
| FEDERAL FUNDS | 10,142,300 | 12,205,100 | 14,044,400 | 16,859,500 | 21,556,300 | 14,886,400 | 17,594,700 | 24,226,574 |
| Federal ICF/MR | 2,723,145 | 3,061,215 | 4,625,010 | 5,845,425 | 12,511,245 | 13,590,060 | 16,578,705 | 22,316,428 |
| Title XX / SSBG Funds | 4,865,000 | 7,250,000 | 7,442,000 | 8,599,000 | 7,508,000 | 0 | 0 | 469,600 |
| Other Federal Funds | 2,554,155 | 1,893,885 | 1,977,390 | 2,415,075 | 1,537,055 | 1,296,340 | 1,015,995 | 1,440,546 |
| LARGE PRIVATE RESIDENTIAL | 11,237,499 | 13,579,588 | 16,896,412 | 20,545,760 | 23,473,787 | 29,585,561 | 48,509,876 | 47,427,992 |
| STATE FUNDS | 9,854,499 | 10,973,588 | 12,864,412 | 14,214,760 | 16,182,787 | 19,008,561 | 27,366,876 | 27,148,892 |
| General Funds | 9,854,499 | 10,973,588 | 12,864,412 | 14,214,760 | 16,182,787 | 19,008,561 | 27,366,876 | 27,148,892 |
| Other State Funds | 0 | 0 | 0 | 0 | 0 | 0 | 0 | 0 |
| Local/County Overmatch | 0 | 0 | 0 | 0 | 0 | 0 | 0 | 0 |
| FEDERAL FUNDS | 1,383,000 | 2,606,000 | 4,032,000 | 6,331,000 | 7,291,000 | 10,577,000 | 21,143,000 | 20,279,100 |
| Large Private ICF/MR | 1,383,000 | 2,606,000 | 4,032,000 | 6,331,000 | 7,291,000 | 10,577,000 | 21,143,000 | 20,279,100 |
| **COMMUNITY SERVICES FUNDS** | 15,253,501 | 15,980,412 | 21,685,588 | 29,398,240 | 41,302,213 | 46,583,439 | 61,079,124 | 99,374,752 |
| STATE FUNDS | 4,970,501 | 6,687,412 | 11,732,588 | 18,289,240 | 27,275,213 | 29,034,439 | 41,155,124 | 42,529,208 |
| General Funds | 4,802,501 | 6,488,412 | 11,527,588 | 17,977,240 | 26,837,213 | 28,593,439 | 40,566,124 | 40,393,508 |
| Other State Funds | 0 | 0 | 0 | 0 | 0 | 0 | 0 | 0 |
| Local/County Overmatch | 0 | 0 | 0 | 0 | 0 | 0 | 0 | 1,406,700 |
| SSI State Supplement | 168,000 | 199,000 | 205,000 | 312,000 | 438,000 | 441,000 | 589,000 | 729,000 |
| FEDERAL FUNDS | 10,283,000 | 9,293,000 | 9,953,000 | 11,109,000 | 14,027,000 | 17,549,000 | 19,924,000 | 56,845,544 |
| ICF/MR Funds | 0 | 0 | 0 | 0 | 2,000,000 | 2,500,000 | 3,500,000 | 6,571,600 |
| Small Public | 0 | 0 | 0 | 0 | 0 | 0 | 0 | 0 |
| Small Private | 0 | 0 | 0 | 0 | 2,000,000 | 2,500,000 | 3,500,000 | 6,571,600 |
| HCBS Waiver | 0 | 0 | 0 | 0 | 0 | 0 | 0 | 8,877,300 |
| Model 50/200 Waiver | 0 | 0 | 0 | 0 | 0 | 0 | 0 | 0 |
| Other Title XIX Programs | 0 | 0 | 0 | 0 | 0 | 0 | 0 | 0 |
| Title XX / SSBG Funds | 8,703,000 | 7,613,000 | 8,668,000 | 9,393,000 | 10,436,000 | 12,547,000 | 14,407,000 | 14,677,400 |
| Other Federal Funds | 1,580,000 | 1,680,000 | 1,285,000 | 1,716,000 | 1,591,000 | 2,502,000 | 2,017,000 | 2,432,840 |
| Waiver Clients' SSI/ADC | 0 | 0 | 0 | 0 | 0 | 0 | 0 | 24,286,404 |

| | 1985 | 1986 | 1987 | 1988 | 1989 | 1990 | 1991 | 1992 |
|---|---|---|---|---|---|---|---|---|
| **TOTAL FUNDS** | $257,450,665 | $254,515,948 | $270,010,273 | $306,444,116 | $344,241,584 | $363,006,523 | $375,787,606 | $383,250,469 |
| **CONGREGATE 16+ BEDS** | 142,650,669 | 150,447,761 | 155,687,781 | 168,405,226 | 183,133,573 | 195,098,150 | 202,569,484 | 197,862,780 |
| INSTITUTIONAL SERVICES FUNDS | 88,034,918 | 91,139,749 | 93,784,986 | 102,729,760 | 114,271,023 | 120,231,958 | 128,610,756 | 122,726,392 |
| STATE FUNDS | 56,144,928 | 65,039,474 | 65,583,935 | 75,193,674 | 85,002,008 | 86,111,318 | 90,032,243 | 82,283,056 |
| General Funds | 53,200,800 | 62,153,894 | 61,986,626 | 71,253,584 | 81,147,327 | 82,100,024 | 85,598,300 | 77,614,773 |
| Local | 0 | 0 | 0 | 0 | 0 | 0 | 0 | 0 |
| Other State Funds | 2,944,128 | 2,885,580 | 3,597,309 | 3,940,090 | 3,854,681 | 4,011,294 | 4,433,943 | 4,668,283 |
| FEDERAL FUNDS | 31,889,990 | 26,100,275 | 28,201,051 | 27,536,086 | 29,269,015 | 34,120,640 | 38,578,513 | 40,443,336 |
| Federal ICF/MR | 24,398,391 | 25,357,100 | 26,872,560 | 26,634,105 | 27,654,873 | 32,284,627 | 37,074,411 | 39,276,583 |
| Title XX / SSBG Funds | 6,679,700 | 0 | 0 | 0 | 0 | 0 | 0 | 0 |
| Other Federal Funds | 811,899 | 743,175 | 1,328,491 | 901,981 | 1,614,142 | 1,836,013 | 1,504,102 | 1,166,753 |
| LARGE PRIVATE RESIDENTIAL | 54,615,751 | 59,308,012 | 61,902,795 | 65,675,466 | 68,862,550 | 74,866,192 | 73,958,728 | 75,136,388 |
| STATE FUNDS | 30,485,051 | 33,627,555 | 35,808,918 | 38,555,351 | 38,067,982 | 41,044,347 | 40,562,407 | 40,891,553 |
| General Funds | 30,485,051 | 33,627,555 | 35,808,918 | 15,788,370 | 13,102,602 | 14,058,379 | 12,491,169 | 12,128,353 |
| Other State Funds | 0 | 0 | 0 | 22,766,981 | 24,965,380 | 26,985,968 | 28,071,238 | 28,763,200 |
| Local/County Overmatch | 0 | 0 | 0 | 0 | 0 | 0 | 0 | 0 |
| FEDERAL FUNDS | 24,130,700 | 25,680,457 | 26,093,877 | 27,120,115 | 30,794,568 | 33,821,845 | 33,396,321 | 34,244,835 |
| Large Private ICF/MR | 24,130,700 | 25,680,457 | 26,093,877 | 27,120,115 | 30,794,568 | 33,821,845 | 33,396,321 | 34,244,835 |
| **COMMUNITY SERVICES FUNDS** | 114,799,996 | 104,068,187 | 114,322,492 | 138,038,890 | 161,108,011 | 167,908,373 | 173,218,122 | 185,387,689 |
| STATE FUNDS | 49,598,234 | 50,906,273 | 62,815,182 | 87,759,502 | 105,350,912 | 114,955,467 | 118,644,414 | 125,625,800 |
| General Funds | 48,535,249 | 49,372,788 | 61,104,966 | 80,366,396 | 97,633,947 | 106,847,146 | 110,112,531 | 116,810,079 |
| Other State Funds | 291,985 | 288,485 | 403,216 | 290,054 | 290,285 | 291,713 | 290,727 | 290,785 |
| Local/County Overmatch | 0 | 0 | 0 | 0 | 0 | 0 | 0 | 0 |
| SSI State Supplement | 771,000 | 1,245,000 | 1,307,000 | 7,103,052 | 7,426,680 | 7,816,608 | 8,241,156 | 8,524,936 |
| FEDERAL FUNDS | 65,201,762 | 53,161,914 | 51,507,310 | 50,279,388 | 55,757,099 | 52,952,906 | 54,573,708 | 59,761,889 |
| ICF/MR Funds | 13,421,500 | 17,709,440 | 17,720,076 | 17,777,519 | 17,553,573 | 19,066,480 | 19,838,281 | 20,528,961 |
| Small Public | 0 | 0 | 0 | 0 | 0 | 0 | 0 | 0 |
| Small Private | 13,421,500 | 17,709,440 | 17,720,076 | 17,777,519 | 17,553,573 | 19,066,480 | 19,838,281 | 20,528,961 |
| HCBS Waiver | 9,617,100 | 8,776,271 | 7,216,445 | 7,739,185 | 10,603,708 | 9,496,782 | 9,575,025 | 9,594,343 |
| Model 50/200 Waiver | 0 | 0 | 0 | 0 | 0 | 0 | 0 | 0 |
| Other Title XIX Programs | 0 | 0 | 0 | 0 | 0 | 0 | 0 | 0 |
| Title XX / SSBG Funds | 14,416,700 | 14,416,780 | 13,201,107 | 13,647,076 | 14,667,377 | 11,840,770 | 11,197,137 | 15,163,353 |
| Other Federal Funds | 2,535,662 | 2,664,451 | 3,424,502 | 2,076,008 | 2,393,369 | 1,561,866 | 1,902,761 | 1,625,428 |
| Waiver Clients' SSI/ADC | 25,210,800 | 9,594,972 | 9,945,180 | 9,039,600 | 10,539,072 | 10,987,008 | 12,060,504 | 12,849,804 |

*Source:*
Institute on Disability and Human Development (UAP),
University of Illinois at Chicago, 1994

# GEORGIA

## MR/DD Spending for Congregate Residential & Community Services

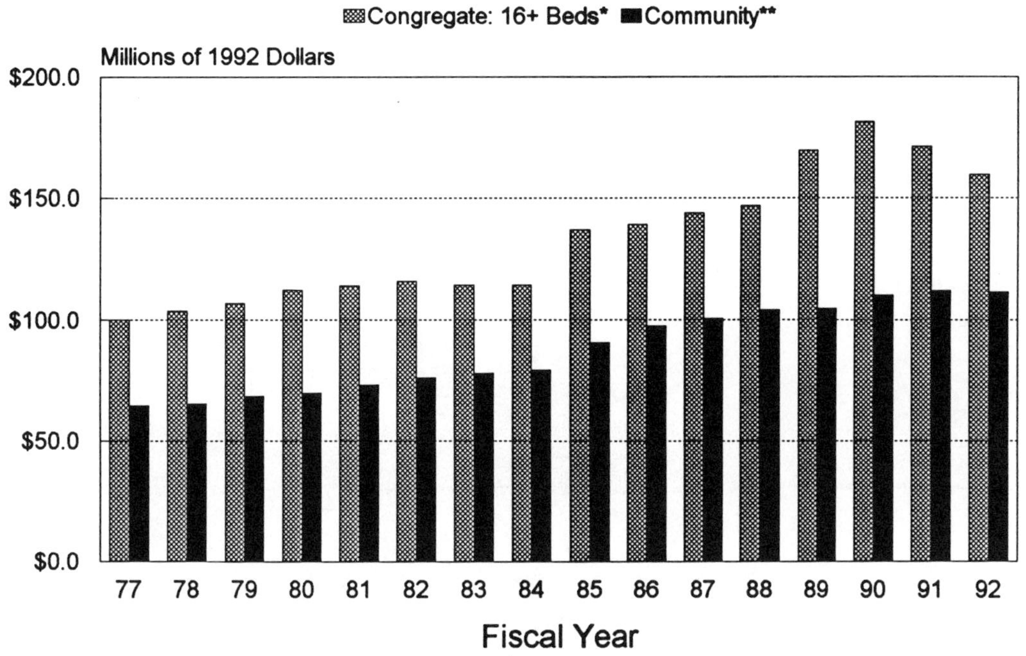
Congregate: 16+ Beds*
Community**
Millions of 1992 Dollars
$200.0
$150.0
$100.0
$50.0
$0.0
77
78
79
80
81
82
83
84
85
86
87
88
89
90
91
92
Fiscal Year

*Excludes nursing homes; ** Includes resources for 15 bed or less residential settings & non-residential community services

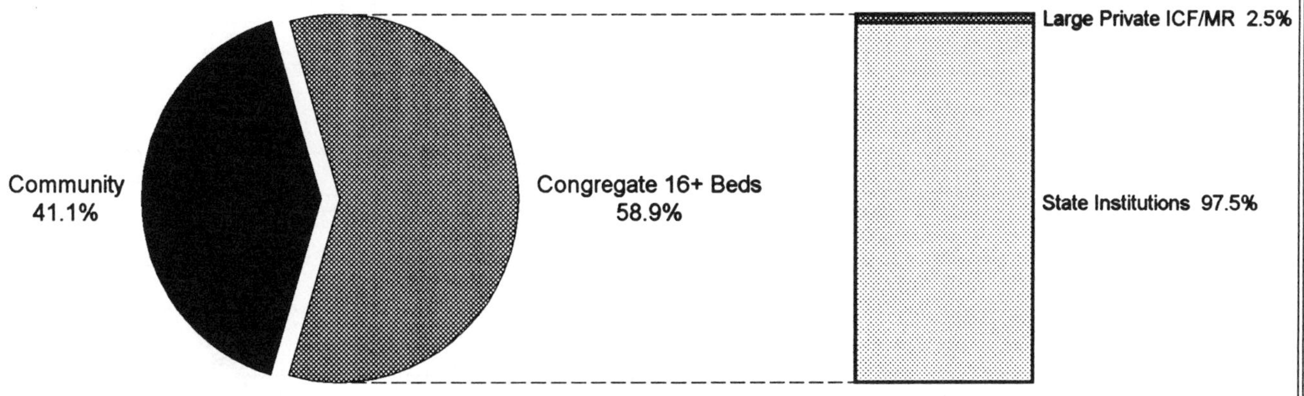
Community
41.1%
Congregate 16+ Beds
58.9%
Large Private ICF/MR 2.5%
State Institutions 97.5%

FY 1992 Total Spending:
$271.2 Million

*Source:*
Institute on Disability and Human Development (UAP), University of Illinois at Chicago, 1994

# GEORGIA

## Number of Persons Served by Residential Setting: FY 1992

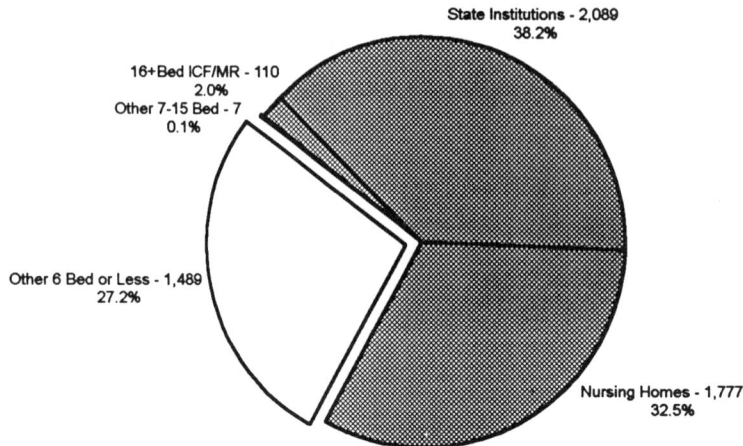

State Institutions - 2,089
38.2%

16+Bed ICF/MR - 110
2.0%

Other 7-15 Bed - 7
0.1%

Other 6 Bed or Less - 1,489
27.2%

Nursing Homes - 1,777
32.5%

Total Served: 5,472

## Persons Served by Residential Setting:1986-92

|  | 1986 | 1987 | 1988 | 1989 | 1990 | 1991 | 1992 |
|---|---|---|---|---|---|---|---|
| **CONGREGATE 16 + BED SETTINGS** | **4,075** | **4,160** | **4,240** | **4,110** | **3,998** | **3,894** | **3,976** |
| Nursing Homes | 1,845 | 1,948 | 2,050 | 1,928 | 1,807 | 1,685 | 1,777 |
| State Institutions | 2,121 | 2,103 | 2,080 | 2,072 | 2,081 | 2,099 | 2,089 |
| Private 16+Bed ICF/MR | 109 | 109 | 110 | 110 | 110 | 110 | 110 |
| Other 16+Bed Residential | 0 | 0 | 0 | 0 | 0 | 0 | 0 |
| **15 BED OR LESS RESIDENTIAL SETTINGS** | **NA** | **1,380** | **1,450** | **NA** | **NA** | **1,538** | **1,496** |
| Public 7-15 Bed ICF/MR | 0 | 0 | 0 | 0 | 0 | 0 | 0 |
| Private 7-15 Bed ICF/MR | 0 | 0 | 0 | 0 | 0 | 0 | 0 |
| Other 7-15 Bed Residential | 0 | 0 | 0 | 0 | 0 | 0 | 7 |
| Public 6 Bed or Less ICF/MR | 0 | 0 | 0 | 0 | 0 | 0 | 0 |
| Private 6 Bed or Less ICF/MR | 0 | 0 | 0 | 0 | 0 | 0 | 0 |
| Other 6 Bed or Less Residential | NA | 1,380 | 1,450 | NA | NA | 1,538 | 1,489 |
| **TOTAL PERSONS SERVED** | **NA** | **5,540** | **5,690** | **NA** | **NA** | **5,432** | **5,472** |

## Persons Served in Non-Residential Community Services:1986-92

|  | 1986 | 1987 | 1988 | 1989 | 1990 | 1991 | 1992 |
|---|---|---|---|---|---|---|---|
| **DAY/WORK PROGRAMS** | **9,247** | **9,199** | **9,199** | **8,095** | **8,415** | **8,686** | **8,514** |
| Sheltered Employment/Work Activity | NA | NA | NA | NA | NA | NA | NA |
| Day Habilitation ("Day Training") | NA | NA | NA | NA | NA | NA | NA |
| Supported/Competitive Employment | 10 | 248 | 462 | 596 | 810 | 891 | 986 |
| **CASE MANAGEMENT** | **NA** | **NA** | **NA** | **NA** | **NA** | **NA** | **NA** |
| **HCBS WAIVER** | **0** | **0** | **0** | **0** | **90** | **256** | **353** |
| **MODEL 50/200 WAIVER** | **0** | **0** | **0** | **0** | **0** | **0** | **0** |

*Source:*
Institute on Disability and Human Development (UAP),
University of Illinois at Chicago, 1994

# GEORGIA

## Community Services: FY 1992 Revenue Sources

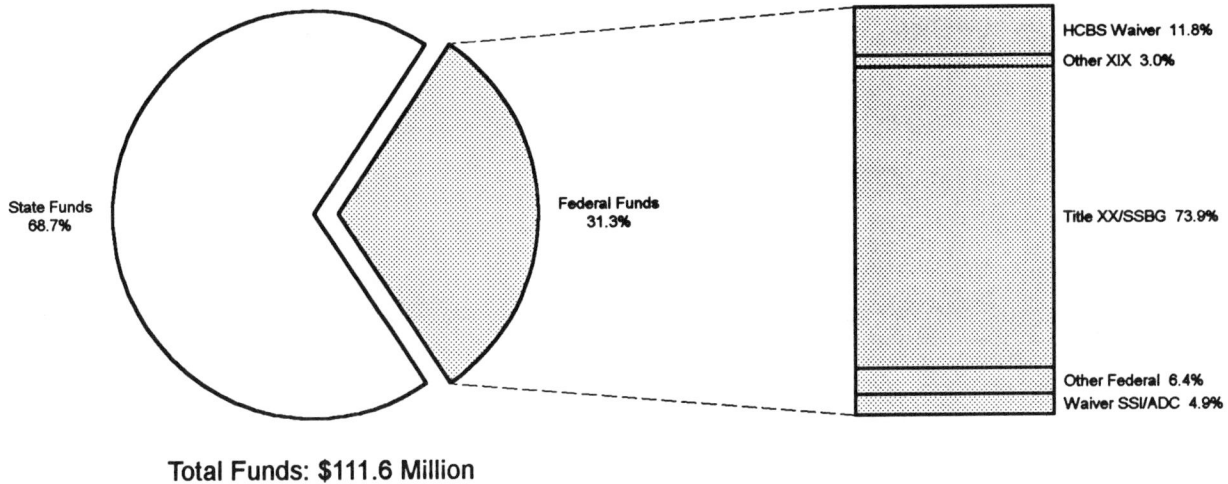

State Funds 68.7%

Federal Funds 31.3%

HCBS Waiver 11.8%
Other XIX 3.0%
Title XX/SSBG 73.9%
Other Federal 6.4%
Waiver SSI/ADC 4.9%

Total Funds: $111.6 Million

## Family Support Initiatives*

|  | 1986 | 1987 | 1988 | 1989 | 1990 | 1991 | 1992 |
|---|---|---|---|---|---|---|---|
| **FAMILY SUPPORT: TOTAL SPENDING** | $169,670 | $261,562 | $611,562 | $600,000 | $554,654 | $665,597 | $644,083 |
| **Total # of Families Supported** | 499 | 769 | 1,056 | 453 | 454 | 545 | 607 |
| A. Financial Subsidy/Payment | $0 | $0 | $0 | $0 | $0 | $0 | $0 |
| # of Families | 0 | 0 | 0 | 0 | 0 | 0 | 0 |
| B. Family Assistance Payments | $169,670 | $261,562 | $311,562 | $0 | $0 | $0 | $0 |
| # of Families | 499 | 769 | 856 | 0 | 0 | 0 | 0 |
| C. Other Family Support Payments | $0 | $0 | $300,000 | $600,000 | $554,654 | $665,597 | $644,083 |
| # of Families | 0 | 0 | 200 | 453 | 454 | 545 | 607 |

## Other Community Services Initiatives*

|  | 1986 | 1987 | 1988 | 1989 | 1990 | 1991 | 1992 |
|---|---|---|---|---|---|---|---|
| **AGING/DD SPENDING** | $0 | $0 | $0 | $0 | $0 | $0 | $0 |
| # of Persons Served | 0 | 0 | 0 | 0 | 0 | 0 | 0 |
| **ASSISTIVE TECHNOLOGY SPENDING** |  |  |  |  |  |  | $0 |
| # of Persons Served |  |  |  |  |  |  | 0 |
| **EARLY INTERVENTION SPENDING** | $0 | $0 | $0 | $0 | NA | $750,000 | $2,786,474 |
| # of Persons Served | 0 | 0 | 0 | 0 | 486 | 1,066 | 1,423 |
| **PERSONAL ASSISTANCE SPENDING** |  |  |  |  |  |  | $0 |
| # of Persons Served |  |  |  |  |  |  | 0 |
| **SUPPORTED EMPLOYMENT SPENDING** | $55,000 | $395,146 | $1,821,675 | $3,483,024 | $4,830,840 | $5,420,544 | $6,117,144 |
| # of Persons Served | 10 | 248 | 462 | 596 | 810 | 891 | 986 |
| **SUPPORTED LIVING SPENDING** |  |  |  |  |  |  | $0 |
| # of Persons Served |  |  |  |  |  |  | 0 |

*Expenditures associated with Special Community Initiatives are a subset of funding within the community services component of the state's chart series and spreadsheet; Family Support Client figures may include duplicate client counts; HCBS Waiver counts include Waiver case management numbers.
0= Services not provided in the state; NA= Data not available from state; blank= Services not applicable (eg. CSLA prior to authorization, Special Community Initiatives prior to request for data by this study)

*Source:*
Institute on Disability and Human Development (UAP),
University of Illinois at Chicago, 1994

# GEORGIA

## Large Congregate Care Facilities: FY 1992 Revenue Sources*

### Private 16+Bed Settings

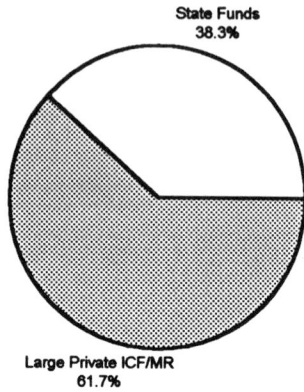

State Funds
38.3%

Large Private ICF/MR
61.7%

Total Funds: $4.0 Million

### Public Institutions

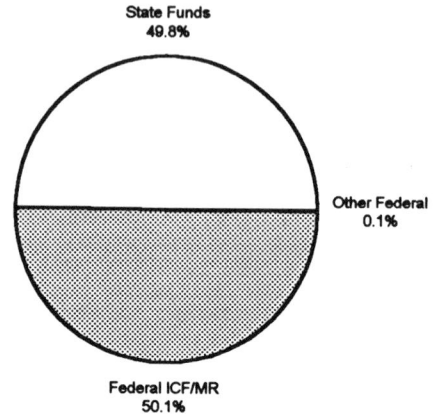

State Funds
49.8%

Other Federal
0.1%

Federal ICF/MR
50.1%

Total Funds: $155.6 Million

*Excludes nursing homes

## Average Daily Residents in Institutions

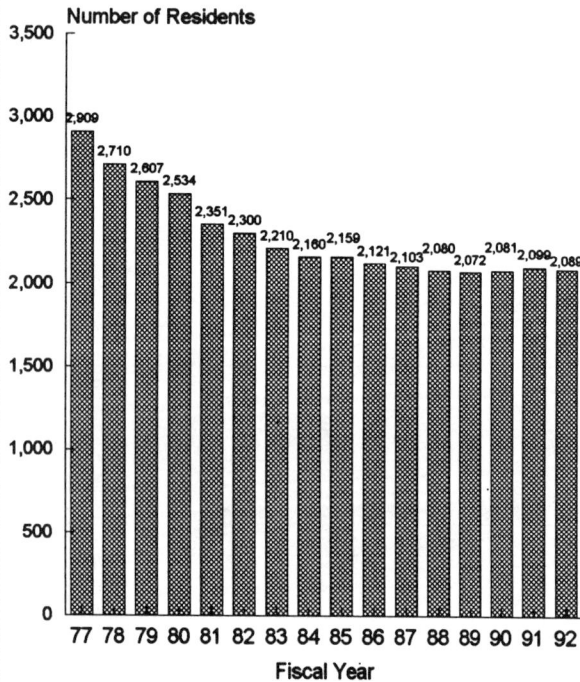

Number of Residents

| Fiscal Year | Number |
|---|---|
| 77 | 2,909 |
| 78 | 2,710 |
| 79 | 2,607 |
| 80 | 2,534 |
| 81 | 2,351 |
| 82 | 2,300 |
| 83 | 2,210 |
| 84 | 2,160 |
| 85 | 2,159 |
| 86 | 2,121 |
| 87 | 2,103 |
| 88 | 2,080 |
| 89 | 2,072 |
| 90 | 2,081 |
| 91 | 2,099 |
| 92 | 2,089 |

Fiscal Year

## Institutional Daily Costs Per Resident

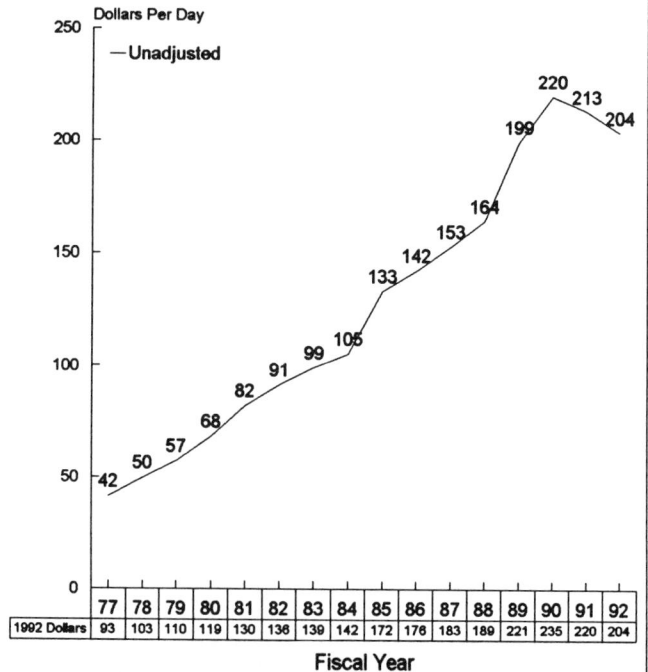

Dollars Per Day

—Unadjusted

Values: 42, 50, 57, 68, 82, 91, 99, 105, 133, 142, 153, 164, 199, 220, 213, 204

| Fiscal Year | 77 | 78 | 79 | 80 | 81 | 82 | 83 | 84 | 85 | 86 | 87 | 88 | 89 | 90 | 91 | 92 |
|---|---|---|---|---|---|---|---|---|---|---|---|---|---|---|---|---|
| 1992 Dollars | 93 | 103 | 110 | 119 | 130 | 136 | 139 | 142 | 172 | 176 | 183 | 189 | 221 | 235 | 220 | 204 |

Fiscal Year

*Source:*
Institute on Disability and Human Development (UAP),
University of Illinois at Chicago, 1994

# GEORGIA FISCAL EFFORT

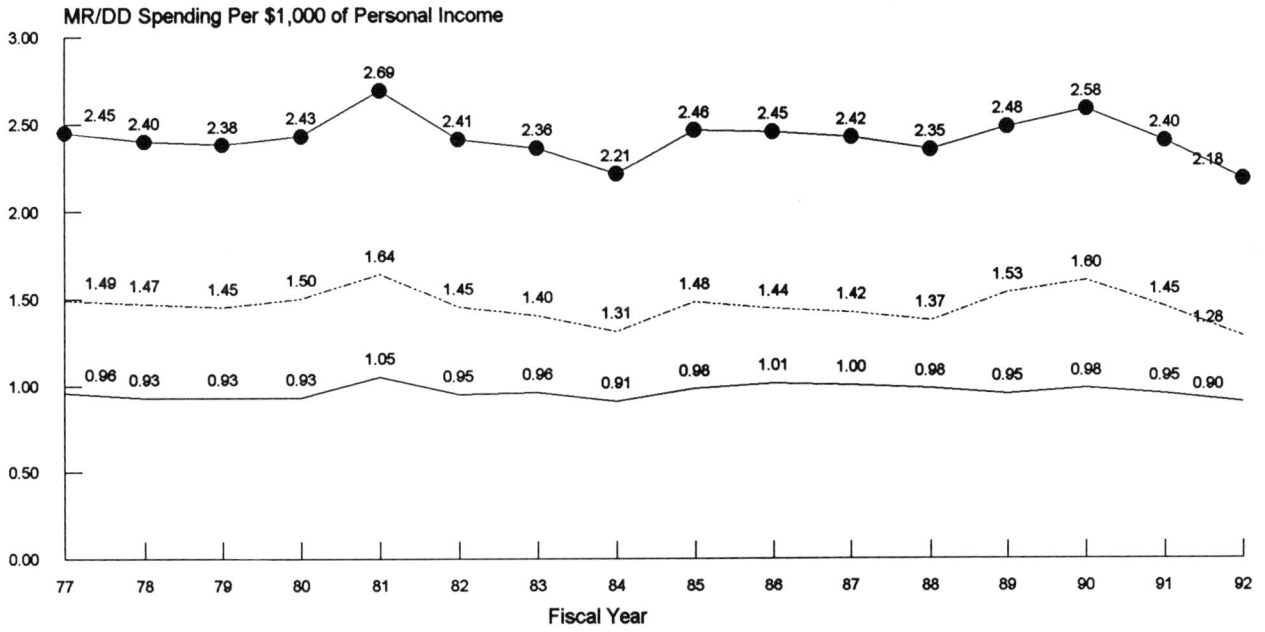

MR/DD Spending Per $1,000 of Personal Income

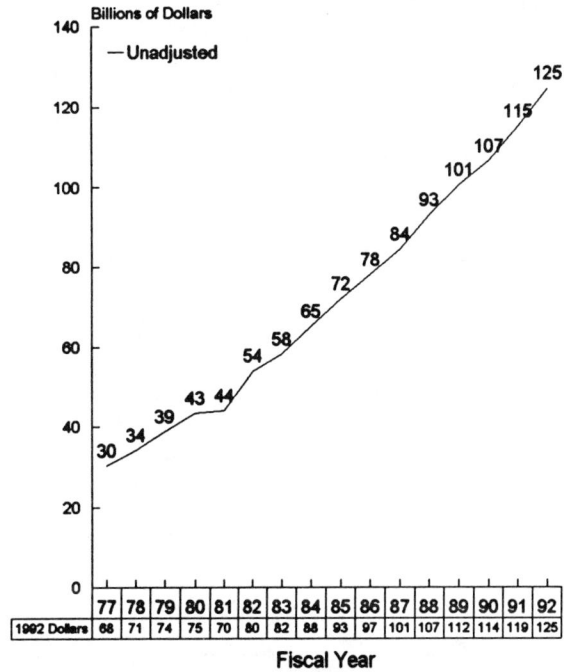

3.00

2.50   2.45  2.40        2.38        2.43              2.69              2.41                           2.46        2.45        2.42              2.35              2.48        2.58              2.40
                                                                                      2.36                                                                                                      2.18
                                                                                                  2.21

2.00

         1.49  1.47        1.45        1.50              1.64              1.45        1.40              1.48        1.44        1.42              1.37        1.53        1.60              1.45
1.50                                                                                                  1.31                                                                                      1.28

         0.96  0.93        0.93        0.93              1.05              0.95        0.96              0.98        1.01        1.00        0.98        0.95        0.98        0.95        0.90
1.00                                                                                      0.91

0.50

0.00
      77      78      79      80      81      82      83      84      85      86      87      88      89      90      91      92

Fiscal Year

● Total   --- Congregate: 16+ Beds   — Community

## Total MR/DD Spending

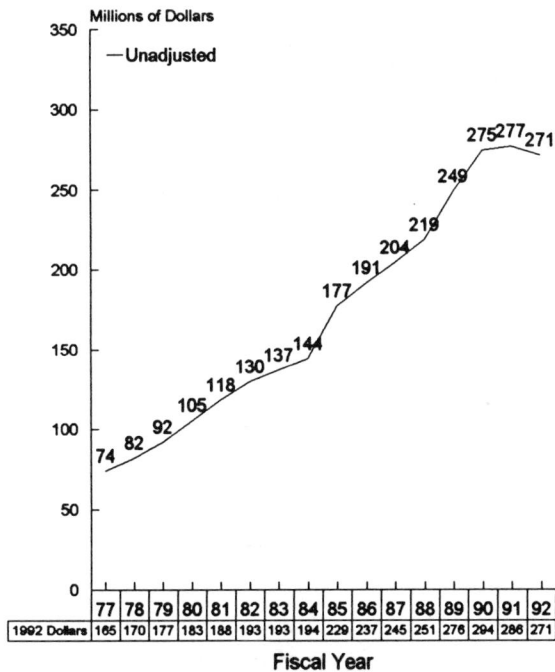

Millions of Dollars

350

—Unadjusted

300
                                                                            275 277 271
250                                                                   249

                                                            219
200                                                 204
                                              191
                                        177
150                         130 137 144
                      118
100             92  105
         82
      74
50

0
   | 77 | 78 | 79 | 80 | 81 | 82 | 83 | 84 | 85 | 86 | 87 | 88 | 89 | 90 | 91 | 92 |
   |----|----|----|----|----|----|----|----|----|----|----|----|----|----|----|----|
   1992 Dollars | 165 | 170 | 177 | 183 | 188 | 193 | 193 | 194 | 229 | 237 | 245 | 251 | 276 | 294 | 286 | 271 |

Fiscal Year

## Personal Income

Billions of Dollars

140

—Unadjusted

120                                                                                     115   125

                                                                            107
100                                                                   101
                                                                93
                                                          84
80                                              78
                                        72
                                  65
60                          58
                      54
               43  44
40       39
   30  34

20

0
   | 77 | 78 | 79 | 80 | 81 | 82 | 83 | 84 | 85 | 86 | 87 | 88 | 89 | 90 | 91 | 92 |
   |----|----|----|----|----|----|----|----|----|----|----|----|----|----|----|----|
   1992 Dollars | 68 | 71 | 74 | 75 | 70 | 80 | 82 | 88 | 93 | 97 | 101 | 107 | 112 | 114 | 119 | 125 |

Fiscal Year

*Source:*
**Institute on Disability and Human Development (UAP),
University of Illinois at Chicago, 1994**

# GEORGIA
## Financial Support for MR/DD Services: FY 1977-92

| | 1977 | 1978 | 1979 | 1980 | 1981 | 1982 | 1983 | 1984 |
|---|---|---|---|---|---|---|---|---|
| **TOTAL FUNDS** | $74,167,141 | $82,079,792 | $92,002,937 | $105,392,046 | $118,275,188 | $129,730,552 | $137,079,004 | $144,071,489 |
| **CONGREGATE 16+ BEDS** | 45,047,613 | 50,356,908 | 55,999,646 | 64,950,476 | 72,088,998 | 78,278,867 | 81,532,765 | 85,057,099 |
| INSTITUTIONAL SERVICES FUNDS | 44,152,000 | 49,197,400 | 54,547,200 | 63,255,000 | 70,302,000 | 76,562,000 | 79,763,000 | 83,240,000 |
| STATE FUNDS | 28,524,000 | 31,570,400 | 35,194,200 | 38,303,000 | 40,387,000 | 44,346,000 | 45,984,000 | 47,386,000 |
| General Funds | 23,764,000 | 26,201,400 | 30,491,200 | 36,622,000 | 37,678,000 | 39,554,000 | 44,523,000 | 45,380,000 |
| Local | 0 | 0 | 0 | 0 | 0 | 0 | 0 | 0 |
| Other State Funds | 4,760,000 | 5,369,000 | 4,703,000 | 1,681,000 | 2,709,000 | 4,792,000 | 1,461,000 | 2,006,000 |
| FEDERAL FUNDS | 15,628,000 | 17,627,000 | 19,353,000 | 24,952,000 | 29,915,000 | 32,216,000 | 33,779,000 | 35,854,000 |
| Federal ICF/MR | 15,328,000 | 17,288,000 | 18,985,000 | 24,550,000 | 29,915,000 | 32,216,000 | 33,779,000 | 35,854,000 |
| Title XX / SSBG Funds | 0 | 0 | 0 | 0 | 0 | 0 | 0 | 0 |
| Other Federal Funds | 300,000 | 339,000 | 368,000 | 402,000 | 0 | 0 | 0 | 0 |
| LARGE PRIVATE RESIDENTIAL | 895,613 | 1,159,508 | 1,452,446 | 1,695,476 | 1,786,998 | 1,716,867 | 1,769,765 | 1,817,099 |
| STATE FUNDS | 303,613 | 395,508 | 496,446 | 567,476 | 593,998 | 576,867 | 596,765 | 597,099 |
| General Funds | 303,613 | 395,508 | 496,446 | 567,476 | 593,998 | 576,867 | 596,765 | 597,099 |
| Other State Funds | 0 | 0 | 0 | 0 | 0 | 0 | 0 | 0 |
| Local/County Overmatch | 0 | 0 | 0 | 0 | 0 | 0 | 0 | 0 |
| FEDERAL FUNDS | 592,000 | 764,000 | 956,000 | 1,128,000 | 1,193,000 | 1,140,000 | 1,173,000 | 1,220,000 |
| Large Private ICF/MR | 592,000 | 764,000 | 956,000 | 1,128,000 | 1,193,000 | 1,140,000 | 1,173,000 | 1,220,000 |
| **COMMUNITY SERVICES FUNDS** | 29,119,528 | 31,722,884 | 36,003,291 | 40,441,570 | 46,186,190 | 51,451,685 | 55,546,239 | 59,014,390 |
| STATE FUNDS | 11,812,387 | 16,298,209 | 18,468,696 | 19,476,381 | 24,176,403 | 30,421,334 | 22,035,618 | 35,495,806 |
| General Funds | 11,812,387 | 16,298,209 | 18,468,696 | 19,476,381 | 24,176,403 | 30,421,334 | 22,035,618 | 35,495,806 |
| Other State Funds | 0 | 0 | 0 | 0 | 0 | 0 | 0 | 0 |
| Local/County Overmatch | 0 | 0 | 0 | 0 | 0 | 0 | 0 | 0 |
| SSI State Supplement | 0 | 0 | 0 | 0 | 0 | 0 | 0 | 0 |
| FEDERAL FUNDS | 17,307,141 | 15,424,675 | 17,534,595 | 20,965,189 | 22,009,787 | 21,030,351 | 33,510,621 | 23,518,584 |
| ICF/MR Funds | 0 | 0 | 0 | 0 | 0 | 0 | 0 | 0 |
| Small Public | 0 | 0 | 0 | 0 | 0 | 0 | 0 | 0 |
| Small Private | 0 | 0 | 0 | 0 | 0 | 0 | 0 | 0 |
| HCBS Waiver | 0 | 0 | 0 | 0 | 0 | 0 | 0 | 0 |
| Model 50/200 Waiver | 0 | 0 | 0 | 0 | 0 | 0 | 0 | 0 |
| Other Title XIX Programs | 0 | 0 | 0 | 0 | 0 | 0 | 0 | 0 |
| Title XX / SSBG Funds | 15,993,618 | 15,424,204 | 17,534,595 | 20,774,119 | 21,275,992 | 20,302,267 | 32,785,893 | 22,807,664 |
| Other Federal Funds | 1,313,523 | 471 | 0 | 191,070 | 733,795 | 728,084 | 724,728 | 710,920 |
| Waiver Clients' SSI/ADC | 0 | 0 | 0 | 0 | 0 | 0 | 0 | 0 |

| | 1985 | 1986 | 1987 | 1988 | 1989 | 1990 | 1991 | 1992 |
|---|---|---|---|---|---|---|---|---|
| **TOTAL FUNDS** | $177,342,000 | $191,473,955 | $204,317,924 | $218,652,454 | $248,961,568 | $274,541,826 | $277,020,991 | $271,203,382 |
| **CONGREGATE 16+ BEDS** | 106,805,427 | 112,541,502 | 120,231,512 | 127,862,549 | 153,962,071 | 170,651,122 | 167,300,674 | 159,636,294 |
| INSTITUTIONAL SERVICES FUNDS | 104,965,000 | 110,081,040 | 117,211,633 | 124,944,194 | 150,678,714 | 167,002,763 | 163,287,313 | 155,605,234 |
| STATE FUNDS | 63,680,000 | 74,735,469 | 77,912,106 | 81,534,311 | 86,248,612 | 97,244,263 | 93,440,769 | 77,491,046 |
| General Funds | 61,680,000 | 73,366,638 | 76,091,234 | 78,317,158 | 84,105,691 | 95,145,178 | 90,631,034 | 75,158,062 |
| Local | 0 | 0 | 0 | 0 | 0 | 0 | 0 | 0 |
| Other State Funds | 2,000,000 | 1,368,831 | 1,820,872 | 3,217,153 | 2,142,921 | 2,099,085 | 2,809,735 | 2,332,984 |
| FEDERAL FUNDS | 41,285,000 | 35,345,571 | 39,299,527 | 43,409,883 | 64,430,102 | 69,758,500 | 69,846,544 | 78,114,188 |
| Federal ICF/MR | 41,285,000 | 35,091,291 | 39,058,004 | 43,145,428 | 64,221,780 | 69,507,106 | 69,663,058 | 77,939,299 |
| Title XX / SSBG Funds | 0 | 0 | 0 | 0 | 0 | 0 | 0 | 0 |
| Other Federal Funds | 0 | 254,280 | 241,523 | 264,455 | 208,322 | 251,394 | 183,486 | 174,889 |
| LARGE PRIVATE RESIDENTIAL | 1,840,427 | 2,460,462 | 3,019,879 | 2,918,355 | 3,283,357 | 3,648,359 | 4,013,361 | 4,031,060 |
| STATE FUNDS | 599,427 | 826,715 | 1,025,249 | 1,039,226 | 1,207,464 | 1,375,702 | 1,543,940 | 1,545,105 |
| General Funds | 599,427 | 826,715 | 1,025,249 | 1,039,226 | 1,207,464 | 1,375,702 | 1,543,940 | 1,545,105 |
| Other State Funds | 0 | 0 | 0 | 0 | 0 | 0 | 0 | 0 |
| Local/County Overmatch | 0 | 0 | 0 | 0 | 0 | 0 | 0 | 0 |
| FEDERAL FUNDS | 1,241,000 | 1,633,747 | 1,994,630 | 1,879,129 | 2,075,893 | 2,272,657 | 2,469,421 | 2,485,955 |
| Large Private ICF/MR | 1,241,000 | 1,633,747 | 1,994,630 | 1,879,129 | 2,075,893 | 2,272,657 | 2,469,421 | 2,485,955 |
| **COMMUNITY SERVICES FUNDS** | 70,536,573 | 78,932,453 | 84,086,412 | 90,789,905 | 94,999,497 | 103,890,704 | 109,720,317 | 111,567,088 |
| STATE FUNDS | 43,016,573 | 53,009,266 | 55,568,470 | 62,018,274 | 68,148,731 | 74,353,337 | 76,202,568 | 76,645,698 |
| General Funds | 43,016,573 | 52,904,441 | 55,154,697 | 62,018,274 | 68,148,731 | 73,358,305 | 74,184,852 | 73,428,059 |
| Other State Funds | 0 | 104,825 | 413,773 | 0 | 0 | 995,032 | 2,017,716 | 3,217,639 |
| Local/County Overmatch | 0 | 0 | 0 | 0 | 0 | 0 | 0 | 0 |
| SSI State Supplement | 0 | 0 | 0 | 0 | 0 | 0 | 0 | 0 |
| FEDERAL FUNDS | 27,520,000 | 25,923,187 | 28,517,942 | 28,771,631 | 26,850,766 | 29,537,367 | 33,517,749 | 34,921,390 |
| ICF/MR Funds | 0 | 0 | 0 | 0 | 0 | 0 | 0 | 0 |
| Small Public | 0 | 0 | 0 | 0 | 0 | 0 | 0 | 0 |
| Small Private | 0 | 0 | 0 | 0 | 0 | 0 | 0 | 0 |
| HCBS Waiver | 0 | 0 | 0 | 0 | 0 | 1,037,770 | 2,208,314 | 4,137,720 |
| Model 50/200 Waiver | 0 | 0 | 0 | 0 | 0 | 0 | 0 | 0 |
| Other Title XIX Programs | 0 | 0 | 0 | 0 | 0 | 603,743 | 1,018,877 | 1,039,211 |
| Title XX / SSBG Funds | 27,000,000 | 24,712,858 | 27,687,479 | 27,721,000 | 25,801,945 | 25,155,824 | 26,596,050 | 25,800,455 |
| Other Federal Funds | 520,000 | 1,210,329 | 830,463 | 1,050,631 | 1,048,821 | 2,342,590 | 2,521,004 | 2,219,952 |
| Waiver Clients' SSI/ADC | 0 | 0 | 0 | 0 | 0 | 397,440 | 1,173,504 | 1,724,052 |

*Source:*
Institute on Disability and Human Development (UAP),
University of Illinois at Chicago, 1994

# HAWAII

## MR/DD Spending for Congregate Residential & Community Services

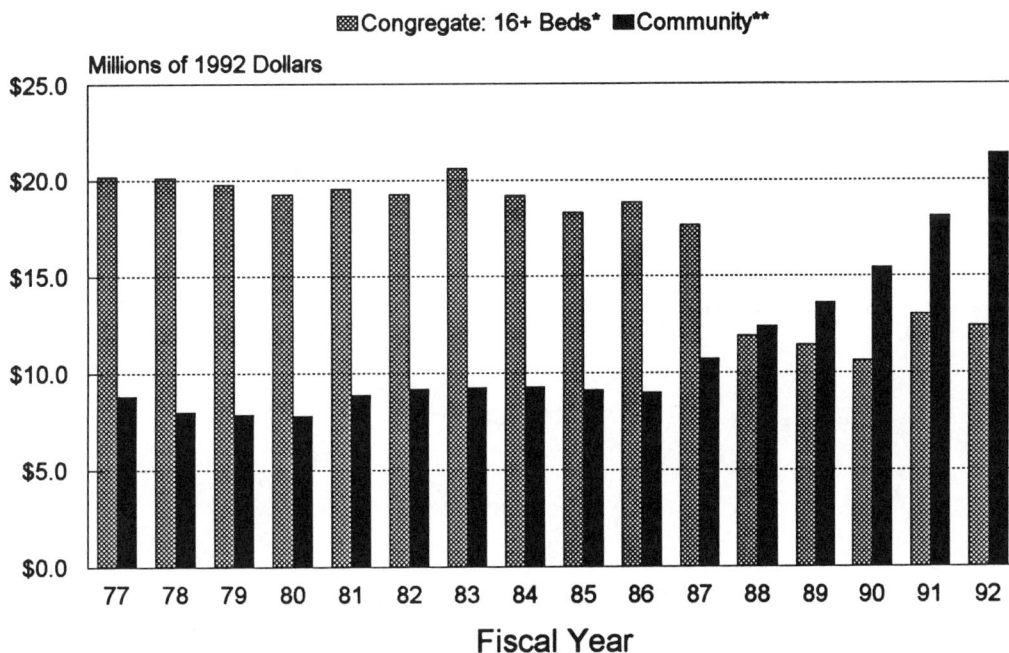

▨Congregate: 16+ Beds*  ■Community**

Millions of 1992 Dollars

Fiscal Year

*Excludes nursing homes; ** Includes resources for
15 bed or less residential settings & non-residential community services

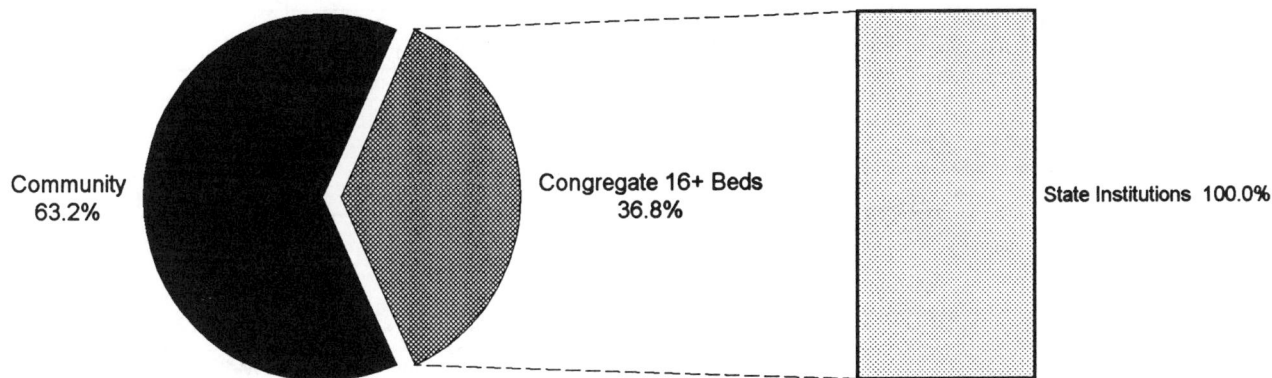

Community
63.2%

Congregate 16+ Beds
36.8%

State Institutions  100.0%

FY 1992 Total Spending:
$33.8 Million

*Source:*
Institute on Disability and Human Development (UAP),
University of Illinois at Chicago, 1994

# HAWAII

## Number of Persons Served by Residential Setting: FY 1992

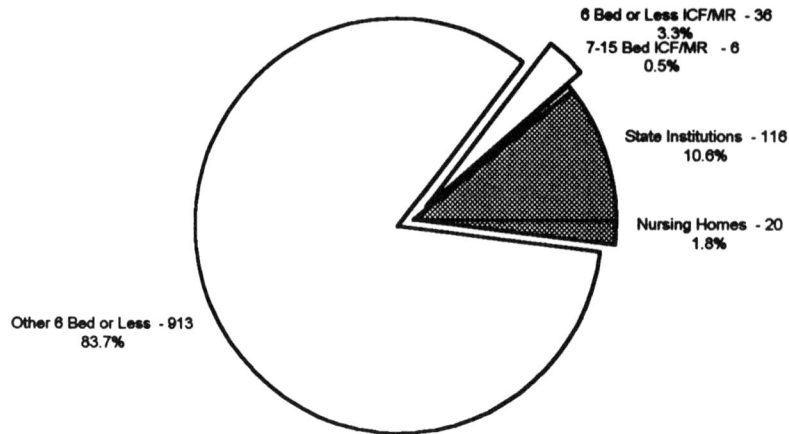

6 Bed or Less ICF/MR - 36
3.3%
7-15 Bed ICF/MR - 6
0.5%

State Institutions - 116
10.6%

Nursing Homes - 20
1.8%

Other 6 Bed or Less - 913
83.7%

Total Served: 1,091

## Persons Served by Residential Setting:1986-92

|  | 1986 | 1987 | 1988 | 1989 | 1990 | 1991 | 1992 |
|---|---|---|---|---|---|---|---|
| CONGREGATE 16 + BED SETTINGS | NA | NA | 288 | 249 | 217 | 181 | 136 |
| Nursing Homes | NA | NA | 61 | 62 | 59 | 35 | 20 |
| State Institutions | 279 | 266 | 227 | 187 | 158 | 146 | 116 |
| Private 16+Bed ICF/MR | 0 | 0 | 0 | 0 | 0 | 0 | 0 |
| Other 16+Bed Residential | 0 | 0 | 0 | 0 | 0 | 0 | 0 |
| 15 BED OR LESS RESIDENTIAL SETTINGS | 0 | 0 | 603 | 823 | 879 | 906 | 955 |
| Public 7-15 Bed ICF/MR | 0 | 0 | 0 | 0 | 0 | 0 | 0 |
| Private 7-15 Bed ICF/MR | NA | NA | 28 | 103 | 102 | 93 | 6 |
| Other 7-15 Bed Residential | NA | NA | 0 | 0 | 0 | 0 | 0 |
| Public 6 Bed or Less ICF/MR | 0 | 0 | 0 | 0 | 0 | 0 | 0 |
| Private 6 Bed or Less ICF/MR | NA | NA | NA | NA | NA | NA | 36 |
| Other 6 Bed or Less Residential | NA | NA | 575 | 720 | 777 | 813 | 913 |
| TOTAL PERSONS SERVED | NA | NA | 891 | 1,072 | 1,096 | 1,087 | 1,091 |

## Persons Served in Non-Residential Community Services:1986-92

|  | 1986 | 1987 | 1988 | 1989 | 1990 | 1991 | 1992 |
|---|---|---|---|---|---|---|---|
| DAY/WORK PROGRAMS | 800 | 800 | 780 | 795 | 795 | 800 | 825 |
| Sheltered Employment/Work Activity | NA | NA | NA | NA | NA | NA | NA |
| Day Habilitation ("Day Training") | NA | NA | NA | NA | NA | NA | NA |
| Supported/Competitive Employment | 0 | 0 | 112 | 115 | 115 | 125 | 126 |
| CASE MANAGEMENT | 1,034 | 1,034 | 1,034 | 1,200 | 1,209 | 1,307 | 1,374 |
| HCBS WAIVER | 32 | 52 | 56 | 108 | 125 | 274 | 401 |
| MODEL 50/200 WAIVER | 0 | 0 | 0 | 0 | 0 | 0 | 0 |

*Source:*
Institute on Disability and Human Development (UAP),
University of Illinois at Chicago, 1994

# HAWAII

## Community Services: FY 1992 Revenue Sources

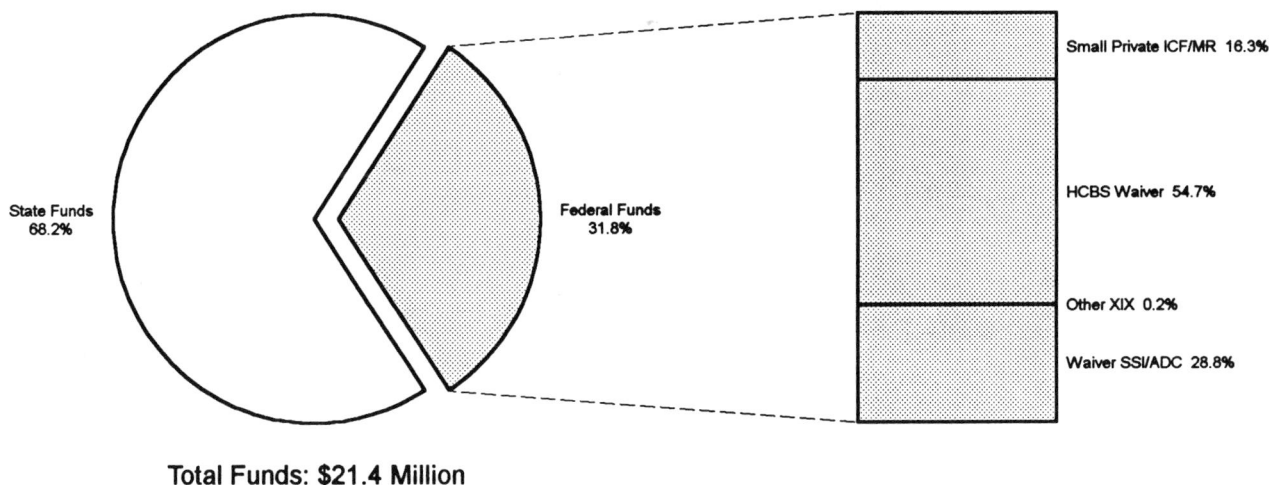

State Funds 68.2%

Federal Funds 31.8%

Small Private ICF/MR 16.3%

HCBS Waiver 54.7%

Other XIX 0.2%

Waiver SSI/ADC 28.8%

Total Funds: $21.4 Million

## Family Support Initiatives*

|  | 1986 | 1987 | 1988 | 1989 | 1990 | 1991 | 1992 |
|---|---|---|---|---|---|---|---|
| FAMILY SUPPORT: TOTAL SPENDING | $0 | $0 | $0 | $33,650 | $32,102 | $277,222 | $359,500 |
| Total # of Families Supported | 0 | 0 | 0 | 46 | 68 | 204 | 265 |
| A. Financial Subsidy/Payment | $0 | $0 | $0 | $0 | $0 | $0 | $0 |
| # of Families | 0 | 0 | 0 | 0 | 0 | 0 | 0 |
| B. Family Assistance Payments | $0 | $0 | $0 | $0 | $0 | $0 | $0 |
| # of Families | 0 | 0 | 0 | 0 | 0 | 0 | 0 |
| C. Other Family Support Payments | $0 | $0 | $0 | $33,650 | $32,102 | $277,222 | $359,500 |
| # of Families | 0 | 0 | 0 | 46 | 68 | 204 | 265 |

## Other Community Services Initiatives*

|  | 1986 | 1987 | 1988 | 1989 | 1990 | 1991 | 1992 |
|---|---|---|---|---|---|---|---|
| AGING/DD SPENDING | $0 | $0 | $0 | $0 | $0 | $0 | $0 |
| # of Persons Served | 0 | 0 | 0 | 0 | 0 | 0 | 0 |
| ASSISTIVE TECHNOLOGY SPENDING |  |  |  |  |  |  | $23,277 |
| # of Persons Served |  |  |  |  |  |  | 138 |
| EARLY INTERVENTION SPENDING | $1,391,200 | $1,302,600 | $0 | $0 | $0 | $0 | $0 |
| # of Persons Served | NA | NA | 0 | 0 | 0 | 0 | 0 |
| PERSONAL ASSISTANCE SPENDING |  |  |  |  |  |  | $0 |
| # of Persons Served |  |  |  |  |  |  | 0 |
| SUPPORTED EMPLOYMENT SPENDING | $0 | $0 | NA | NA | NA | NA | NA |
| # of Persons Served | 0 | 0 | 112 | 115 | 115 | 125 | 126 |
| SUPPORTED LIVING SPENDING |  |  |  |  |  |  | $0 |
| # of Persons Served |  |  |  |  |  |  | 0 |

*Expenditures associated with Special Community Initiatives are a subset of funding within the community services component of the state's chart series and spreadsheet; Family Support Client figures may include duplicate client counts; HCBS Waiver counts include Waiver case management numbers.
0= Services not provided in the state; NA= Data not available from state; blank= Services not applicable (eg. CSLA prior to authorization, Special Community Initiatives prior to request for data by this study)

Source:
Institute on Disability and Human Development (UAP),
University of Illinois at Chicago, 1994

# HAWAII

## Large Congregate Care Facilities: FY 1992 Revenue Sources*

### Private 16+Bed Settings

### Public Institutions

**Does Not Apply**

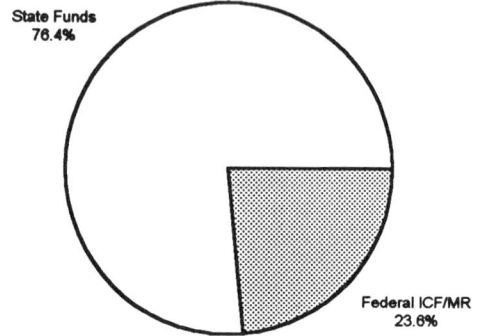

State Funds
76.4%

Federal ICF/MR
23.6%

Total Funds: $12.4 Million

*Excludes nursing homes

## Average Daily Residents in Institutions

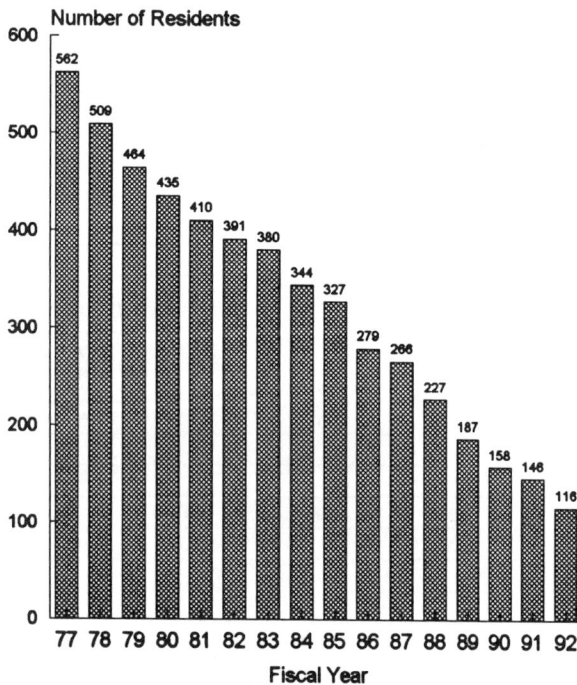

Number of Residents

| Fiscal Year | Residents |
|---|---|
| 77 | 562 |
| 78 | 509 |
| 79 | 464 |
| 80 | 435 |
| 81 | 410 |
| 82 | 391 |
| 83 | 380 |
| 84 | 344 |
| 85 | 327 |
| 86 | 279 |
| 87 | 266 |
| 88 | 227 |
| 89 | 187 |
| 90 | 158 |
| 91 | 146 |
| 92 | 116 |

## Institutional Daily Costs Per Resident

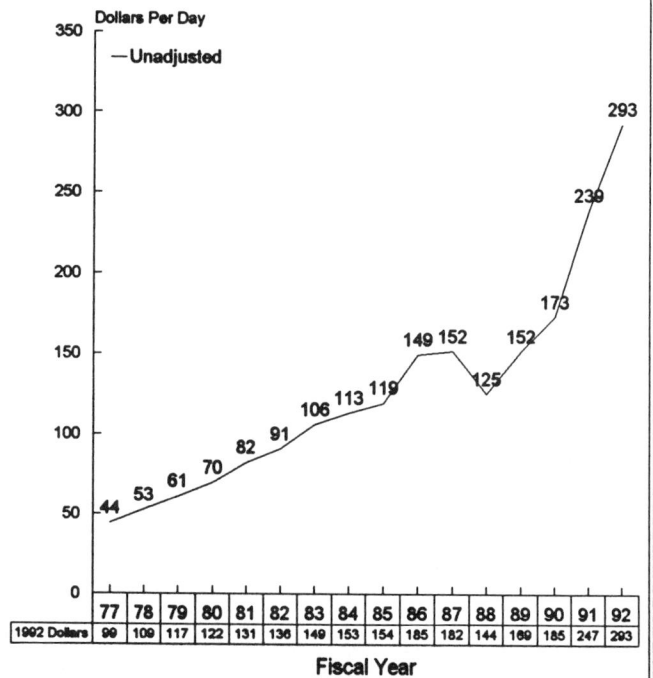

Dollars Per Day

— Unadjusted

| | 77 | 78 | 79 | 80 | 81 | 82 | 83 | 84 | 85 | 86 | 87 | 88 | 89 | 90 | 91 | 92 |
|---|---|---|---|---|---|---|---|---|---|---|---|---|---|---|---|---|
| Unadjusted | 44 | 53 | 61 | 70 | 82 | 91 | 106 | 113 | 119 | 149 | 152 | 125 | 152 | 173 | 239 | 293 |
| 1992 Dollars | 99 | 109 | 117 | 122 | 131 | 136 | 149 | 153 | 154 | 185 | 182 | 144 | 169 | 185 | 247 | 293 |

Fiscal Year

*Source:*
Institute on Disability and Human Development (UAP),
University of Illinois at Chicago, 1994

# HAWAII FISCAL EFFORT

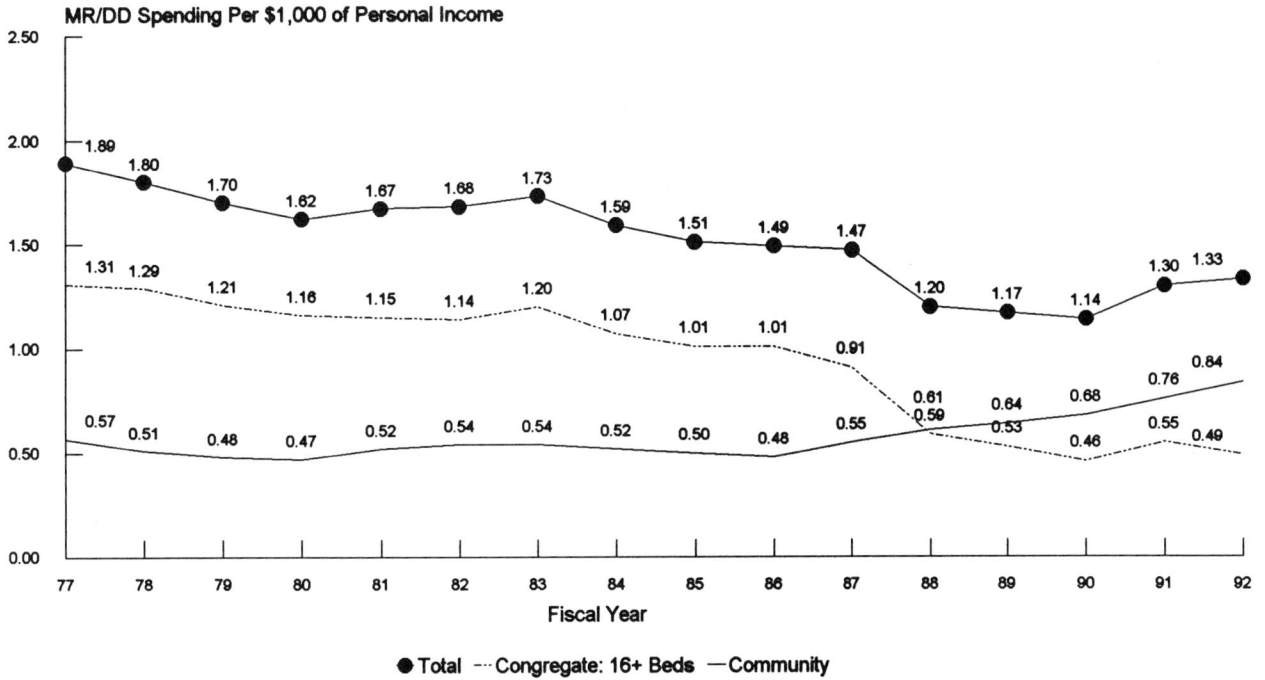

## MR/DD Spending Per $1,000 of Personal Income

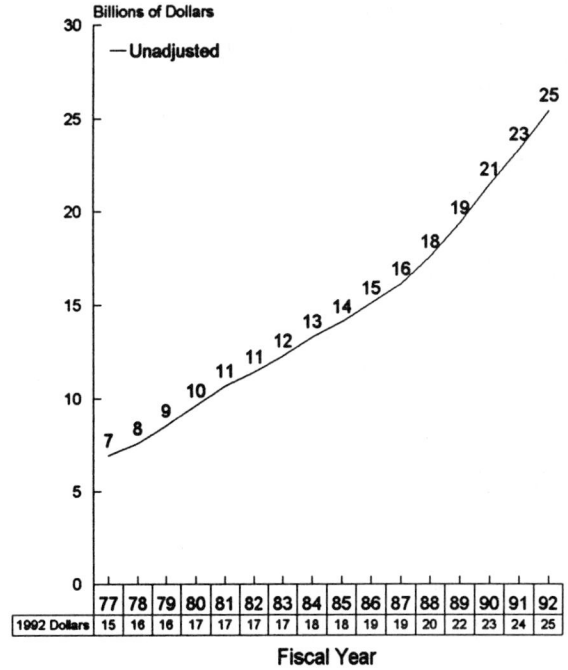

Total values: 1.89, 1.80, 1.70, 1.62, 1.67, 1.68, 1.73, 1.59, 1.51, 1.49, 1.47, 1.20, 1.17, 1.14, 1.30, 1.33

Congregate 16+ Beds: 1.31, 1.29, 1.21, 1.16, 1.15, 1.14, 1.20, 1.07, 1.01, 1.01, 0.91, 0.61, 0.64, 0.68, 0.76, 0.84

Community: 0.57, 0.51, 0.48, 0.47, 0.52, 0.54, 0.54, 0.52, 0.50, 0.48, 0.55, 0.59, 0.53, 0.46, 0.55, 0.49

Fiscal Year 77–92

● Total  --- Congregate: 16+ Beds  — Community

## Total MR/DD Spending

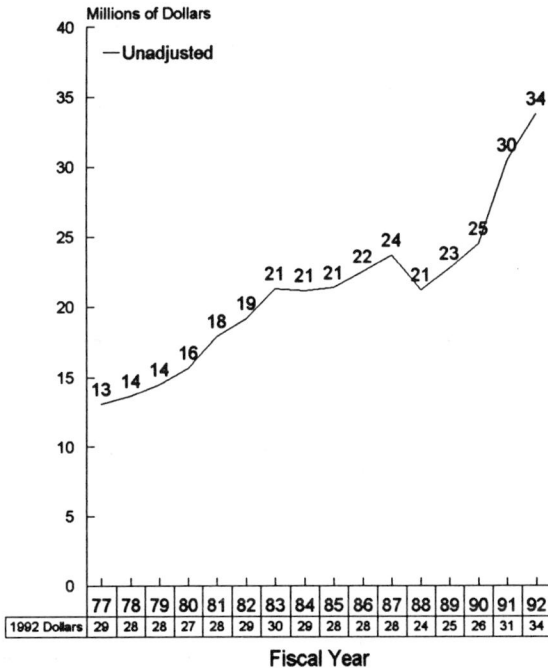

Millions of Dollars — Unadjusted

13, 14, 14, 16, 18, 19, 21, 21, 21, 22, 24, 21, 23, 25, 30, 34

| | 77 | 78 | 79 | 80 | 81 | 82 | 83 | 84 | 85 | 86 | 87 | 88 | 89 | 90 | 91 | 92 |
|---|---|---|---|---|---|---|---|---|---|---|---|---|---|---|---|---|
| 1992 Dollars | 29 | 28 | 28 | 27 | 28 | 29 | 30 | 29 | 28 | 28 | 28 | 24 | 25 | 26 | 31 | 34 |

Fiscal Year

## Personal Income

Billions of Dollars — Unadjusted

7, 8, 9, 10, 11, 11, 12, 13, 14, 15, 16, 18, 19, 21, 23, 25

| | 77 | 78 | 79 | 80 | 81 | 82 | 83 | 84 | 85 | 86 | 87 | 88 | 89 | 90 | 91 | 92 |
|---|---|---|---|---|---|---|---|---|---|---|---|---|---|---|---|---|
| 1992 Dollars | 15 | 16 | 16 | 17 | 17 | 17 | 17 | 18 | 18 | 19 | 19 | 20 | 22 | 23 | 24 | 25 |

Fiscal Year

*Source:*
Institute on Disability and Human Development (UAP),
University of Illinois at Chicago, 1994

# HAWAII
## Financial Support for MR/DD Services: FY 1977-92

| | 1977 | 1978 | 1979 | 1980 | 1981 | 1982 | 1983 | 1984 |
|---|---|---|---|---|---|---|---|---|
| **TOTAL FUNDS** | $13,063,300 | $13,639,900 | $14,479,300 | $15,644,500 | $17,903,500 | $19,161,200 | $21,264,300 | $21,113,264 |
| **CONGREGATE 16+ BEDS** | 9,093,400 | 9,763,400 | 10,361,400 | 11,129,800 | 12,315,800 | 12,982,700 | 14,684,100 | 14,235,700 |
| INSTITUTIONAL SERVICES FUNDS | 9,093,400 | 9,763,400 | 10,361,400 | 11,129,800 | 12,315,800 | 12,982,700 | 14,684,100 | 14,235,700 |
| STATE FUNDS | 7,521,900 | 5,626,200 | 5,472,700 | 6,139,200 | 6,809,300 | 7,311,800 | 8,286,500 | 8,063,500 |
| General Funds | 7,521,900 | 5,626,200 | 5,472,700 | 6,139,200 | 6,809,300 | 7,311,800 | 8,286,500 | 8,063,500 |
| Local | 0 | 0 | 0 | 0 | 0 | 0 | 0 | 0 |
| Other State Funds | 0 | 0 | 0 | 0 | 0 | 0 | 0 | 0 |
| FEDERAL FUNDS | 1,571,500 | 4,137,200 | 4,888,700 | 4,990,600 | 5,506,500 | 5,670,900 | 6,397,600 | 6,172,200 |
| Federal ICF/MR | 1,516,600 | 4,066,600 | 4,474,100 | 4,788,400 | 5,314,300 | 5,611,300 | 6,380,600 | 6,126,500 |
| Title XX / SSBG Funds | 0 | 0 | 0 | 0 | 0 | 0 | 0 | 0 |
| Other Federal Funds | 54,900 | 70,600 | 414,600 | 202,200 | 192,200 | 59,600 | 17,000 | 45,700 |
| LARGE PRIVATE RESIDENTIAL | 0 | 0 | 0 | 0 | 0 | 0 | 0 | 0 |
| STATE FUNDS | 0 | 0 | 0 | 0 | 0 | 0 | 0 | 0 |
| General Funds | 0 | 0 | 0 | 0 | 0 | 0 | 0 | 0 |
| Other State Funds | 0 | 0 | 0 | 0 | 0 | 0 | 0 | 0 |
| Local/County Overmatch | 0 | 0 | 0 | 0 | 0 | 0 | 0 | 0 |
| FEDERAL FUNDS | 0 | 0 | 0 | 0 | 0 | 0 | 0 | 0 |
| Large Private ICF/MR | 0 | 0 | 0 | 0 | 0 | 0 | 0 | 0 |
| **COMMUNITY SERVICES FUNDS** | 3,969,900 | 3,876,500 | 4,117,900 | 4,514,700 | 5,587,700 | 6,178,500 | 6,580,200 | 6,877,564 |
| STATE FUNDS | 2,709,900 | 2,065,500 | 2,341,900 | 2,760,100 | 3,787,200 | 5,448,700 | 6,362,200 | 6,432,700 |
| General Funds | 2,623,900 | 1,881,500 | 2,149,900 | 2,637,000 | 3,654,900 | 5,334,500 | 6,295,200 | 6,369,700 |
| Other State Funds | 28,000 | 123,000 | 129,000 | 57,100 | 62,300 | 42,200 | 0 | 0 |
| Local/County Overmatch | 0 | 0 | 0 | 0 | 0 | 0 | 0 | 0 |
| SSI State Supplement | 58,000 | 61,000 | 63,000 | 66,000 | 70,000 | 72,000 | 67,000 | 63,000 |
| FEDERAL FUNDS | 1,260,000 | 1,811,000 | 1,776,000 | 1,754,600 | 1,800,500 | 729,800 | 218,000 | 444,864 |
| ICF/MR Funds | 0 | 0 | 0 | 0 | 0 | 0 | 0 | 0 |
| Small Public | 0 | 0 | 0 | 0 | 0 | 0 | 0 | 0 |
| Small Private | 0 | 0 | 0 | 0 | 0 | 0 | 0 | 0 |
| HCBS Waiver | 0 | 0 | 0 | 0 | 0 | 0 | 0 | 63,400 |
| Model 50/200 Waiver | 0 | 0 | 0 | 0 | 0 | 0 | 0 | 0 |
| Other Title XIX Programs | 0 | 0 | 0 | 0 | 0 | 0 | 0 | 0 |
| Title XX / SSBG Funds | 85,000 | 369,000 | 386,000 | 228,200 | 249,200 | 168,900 | 0 | 0 |
| Other Federal Funds | 1,175,000 | 1,442,000 | 1,390,000 | 1,526,400 | 1,551,300 | 560,900 | 218,000 | 346,700 |
| Waiver Clients' SSI/ADC | 0 | 0 | 0 | 0 | 0 | 0 | 0 | 34,764 |

| | 1985 | 1986 | 1987 | 1988 | 1989 | 1990 | 1991 | 1992 |
|---|---|---|---|---|---|---|---|---|
| **TOTAL FUNDS** | $21,330,700 | $22,489,324 | $23,669,360 | $21,170,937 | $22,720,411 | $24,507,125 | $30,448,091 | $33,803,327 |
| **CONGREGATE 16+ BEDS** | 14,236,900 | 15,221,300 | 14,724,900 | 10,376,009 | 10,361,167 | 9,983,223 | 12,760,520 | 12,438,391 |
| INSTITUTIONAL SERVICES FUNDS | 14,236,900 | 15,221,300 | 14,724,900 | 10,376,009 | 10,361,167 | 9,983,223 | 12,760,520 | 12,438,391 |
| STATE FUNDS | 8,611,000 | 10,807,300 | 12,970,600 | 9,225,330 | 8,193,847 | 7,323,044 | 9,694,834 | 9,508,223 |
| General Funds | 8,611,000 | 10,807,300 | 12,970,600 | 9,147,231 | 8,038,435 | 7,111,838 | 9,409,540 | 9,259,453 |
| Local | 0 | 0 | 0 | 0 | 0 | 0 | 0 | 0 |
| Other State Funds | 0 | 0 | 0 | 78,099 | 155,412 | 211,206 | 285,294 | 248,770 |
| FEDERAL FUNDS | 5,625,900 | 4,414,000 | 1,754,300 | 1,150,679 | 2,167,320 | 2,660,179 | 3,065,686 | 2,930,168 |
| Federal ICF/MR | 5,602,500 | 4,398,400 | 1,754,300 | 1,150,679 | 2,167,320 | 2,660,179 | 3,065,686 | 2,930,168 |
| Title XX / SSBG Funds | 0 | 0 | 0 | 0 | 0 | 0 | 0 | 0 |
| Other Federal Funds | 23,400 | 15,600 | 0 | 0 | 0 | 0 | 0 | 0 |
| LARGE PRIVATE RESIDENTIAL | 0 | 0 | 0 | 0 | 0 | 0 | 0 | 0 |
| STATE FUNDS | 0 | 0 | 0 | 0 | 0 | 0 | 0 | 0 |
| General Funds | 0 | 0 | 0 | 0 | 0 | 0 | 0 | 0 |
| Other State Funds | 0 | 0 | 0 | 0 | 0 | 0 | 0 | 0 |
| Local/County Overmatch | 0 | 0 | 0 | 0 | 0 | 0 | 0 | 0 |
| FEDERAL FUNDS | 0 | 0 | 0 | 0 | 0 | 0 | 0 | 0 |
| Large Private ICF/MR | 0 | 0 | 0 | 0 | 0 | 0 | 0 | 0 |
| **COMMUNITY SERVICES FUNDS** | 7,093,800 | 7,268,024 | 8,944,460 | 10,794,928 | 12,359,244 | 14,523,902 | 17,687,571 | 21,364,936 |
| STATE FUNDS | 6,634,900 | 6,935,900 | 8,215,100 | 9,471,100 | 10,493,420 | 11,783,313 | 13,542,771 | 14,568,928 |
| General Funds | 6,568,900 | 6,869,900 | 8,144,300 | 9,399,500 | 10,418,240 | 11,704,374 | 13,459,885 | 14,481,898 |
| Other State Funds | 0 | 0 | 0 | 0 | 0 | 0 | 0 | 0 |
| Local/County Overmatch | 0 | 0 | 0 | 0 | 0 | 0 | 0 | 0 |
| SSI State Supplement | 66,000 | 66,000 | 70,800 | 71,600 | 75,180 | 78,939 | 82,886 | 87,030 |
| FEDERAL FUNDS | 458,900 | 332,124 | 729,360 | 1,323,828 | 1,865,824 | 2,740,589 | 4,144,800 | 6,796,008 |
| ICF/MR Funds | 0 | 4,100 | 243,600 | 763,400 | 789,401 | 1,208,677 | 1,238,023 | 1,105,914 |
| Small Public | 0 | 0 | 0 | 0 | 0 | 0 | 0 | 0 |
| Small Private | 0 | 4,100 | 243,600 | 763,400 | 789,401 | 1,208,677 | 1,238,023 | 1,105,914 |
| HCBS Waiver | 154,500 | 208,600 | 289,200 | 342,700 | 633,191 | 979,912 | 1,650,761 | 3,719,910 |
| Model 50/200 Waiver | 0 | 0 | 0 | 0 | 0 | 0 | 0 | 0 |
| Other Title XIX Programs | 0 | 0 | 0 | 0 | 0 | 0 | 0 | 11,700 |
| Title XX / SSBG Funds | 0 | 0 | 0 | 0 | 0 | 0 | 0 | 0 |
| Other Federal Funds | 218,000 | 0 | 0 | 0 | 0 | 0 | 0 | 0 |
| Waiver Clients' SSI/ADC | 86,400 | 119,424 | 196,560 | 217,728 | 443,232 | 552,000 | 1,256,016 | 1,958,484 |

*Source:*
Institute on Disability and Human Development (UAP),
University of Illinois at Chicago, 1994

# IDAHO

## MR/DD Spending for Congregate Residential & Community Services

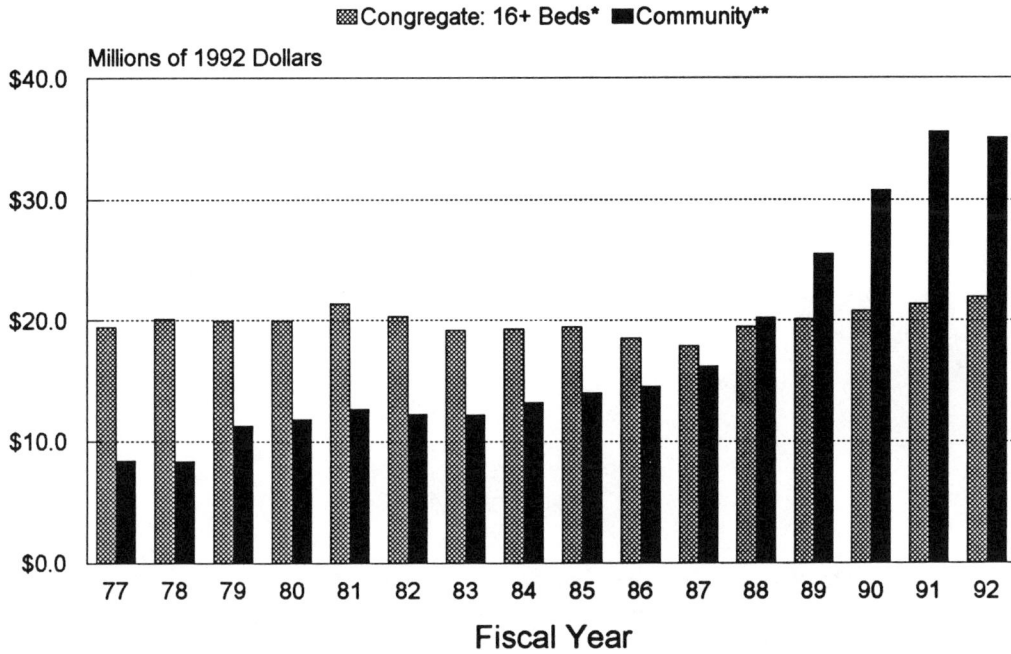

▨Congregate: 16+ Beds*  ■Community**

Millions of 1992 Dollars

### Fiscal Year

*Excludes nursing homes; ** Includes resources for
15 bed or less residential settings & non-residential community services

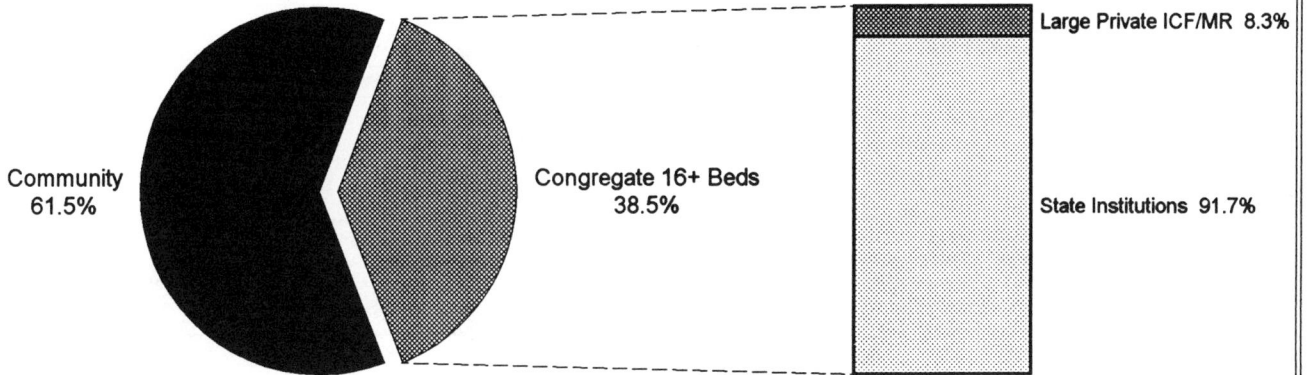

Community
61.5%

Congregate 16+ Beds
38.5%

Large Private ICF/MR 8.3%

State Institutions 91.7%

FY 1992 Total Spending:
$57.1 Million

*Source:*
Institute on Disability and Human Development (UAP),
University of Illinois at Chicago, 1994

# IDAHO

## Number of Persons Served by Residential Setting: FY 1992

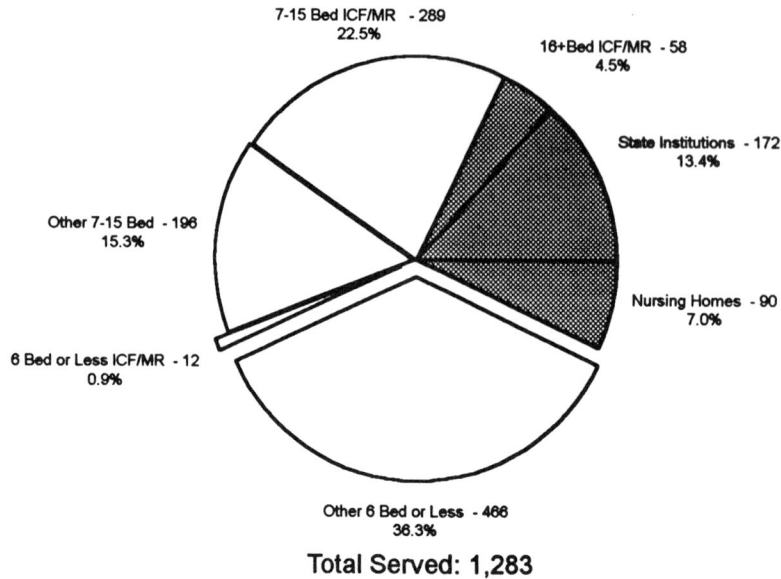

7-15 Bed ICF/MR - 289
22.5%

16+Bed ICF/MR - 58
4.5%

State Institutions - 172
13.4%

Other 7-15 Bed - 196
15.3%

Nursing Homes - 90
7.0%

6 Bed or Less ICF/MR - 12
0.9%

Other 6 Bed or Less - 466
36.3%

Total Served: 1,283

## Persons Served by Residential Setting:1986-92

|  | 1986 | 1987 | 1988 | 1989 | 1990 | 1991 | 1992 |
|---|---|---|---|---|---|---|---|
| CONGREGATE 16 + BED SETTINGS | NA | NA | 422 | NA | NA | 313 | 320 |
| Nursing Homes | NA | NA | 124 | NA | NA | 90 | 90 |
| State Institutions | 309 | 278 | 250 | 222 | 193 | 165 | 172 |
| Private 16+Bed ICF/MR | 72 | 72 | 48 | 51 | 55 | 58 | 58 |
| Other 16+Bed Residential | 0 | 0 | 0 | 0 | 0 | 0 | 0 |
| 15 BED OR LESS RESIDENTIAL SETTINGS | 100 | 115 | 744 | 784 | 823 | 863 | 963 |
| Public 7-15 Bed ICF/MR | 0 | 0 | 0 | 0 | 0 | 0 | 0 |
| Private 7-15 Bed ICF/MR | 100 | 115 | 183 | 216 | 248 | 281 | 289 |
| Other 7-15 Bed Residential | NA | NA | 561 | 568 | 575 | 582 | 196 |
| Public 6 Bed or Less ICF/MR |  |  |  |  |  |  | 0 |
| Private 6 Bed or Less ICF/MR |  |  |  |  |  |  | 12 |
| Other 6 Bed or Less Residential |  |  |  |  |  |  | 466 |
| TOTAL PERSONS SERVED | NA | NA | 1,166 | NA | NA | 1,176 | 1,283 |

## Persons Served in Non-Residential Community Services:1986-92

|  | 1986 | 1987 | 1988 | 1989 | 1990 | 1991 | 1992 |
|---|---|---|---|---|---|---|---|
| DAY/WORK PROGRAMS | 421 | 431 | 3,986 | NA | NA | 4,727 | 5,439 |
| Sheltered Employment/Work Activity | 421 | 431 | 525 | NA | NA | 463 | 388 |
| Day Habilitation ("Day Training") | NA | NA | 3,399 | NA | NA | 4,096 | 4,601 |
| Supported/Competitive Employment | 0 | 0 | 62 | NA | NA | 168 | 450 |
| CASE MANAGEMENT | NA | NA | NA | 0 | 0 | 24 | 0 |
| HCBS WAIVER | 115 | 168 | 204 | 270 | 346 | 380 | 385 |
| MODEL 50/200 WAIVER | 0 | 1 | 1 | 0 | 0 | 0 | 0 |

*Source:*
Institute on Disability and Human Development (UAP),
University of Illinois at Chicago, 1994

# IDAHO

## Community Services: FY 1992 Revenue Sources

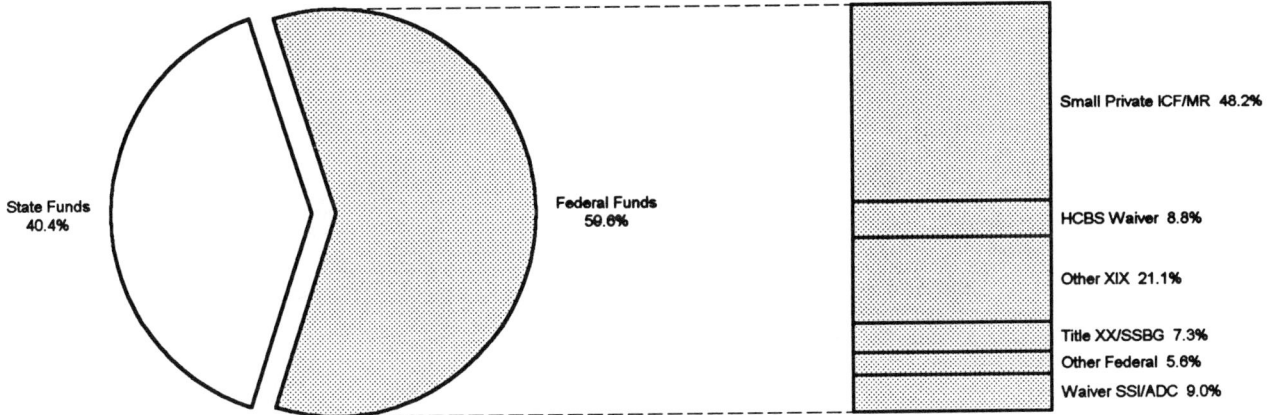

State Funds 40.4%

Federal Funds 59.6%

Small Private ICF/MR 48.2%

HCBS Waiver 8.8%

Other XIX 21.1%

Title XX/SSBG 7.3%

Other Federal 5.6%

Waiver SSI/ADC 9.0%

Total Funds: $35.1 Million

## Family Support Initiatives*

|  | 1986 | 1987 | 1988 | 1989 | 1990 | 1991 | 1992 |
|---|---|---|---|---|---|---|---|
| **FAMILY SUPPORT: TOTAL SPENDING** | **$86,600** | **$96,800** | **$113,500** | **NA** | **NA** | **$113,500** | **$147,000** |
| **Total # of Families Supported** | **295** | **311** | **372** | **NA** | **NA** | **471** | **468** |
| A. Financial Subsidy/Payment | $0 | $0 | $0 | $0 | $0 | $0 | $0 |
| # of Families | 0 | 0 | 0 | 0 | 0 | 0 | 0 |
| B. Family Assistance Payments | $48,300 | $57,000 | $71,500 | NA | NA | $71,500 | $77,000 |
| # of Families | 175 | 182 | 250 | NA | NA | 312 | 334 |
| C. Other Family Support Payments | $38,300 | $39,800 | $42,000 | NA | NA | $42,000 | $70,000 |
| # of Families | 120 | 129 | 122 | NA | NA | 159 | 134 |

## Other Community Services Initiatives*

|  | 1986 | 1987 | 1988 | 1989 | 1990 | 1991 | 1992 |
|---|---|---|---|---|---|---|---|
| **AGING/DD SPENDING** | **$0** | **$0** | **$0** | **$0** | **$0** | **$0** | **NA** |
| # of Persons Served | 0 | 0 | 0 | 0 | 0 | 0 | 217 |
| **ASSISTIVE TECHNOLOGY SPENDING** |  |  |  | **$0** | **$0** | **$0** | **$0** |
| # of Persons Served |  |  |  | 0 | 0 | 0 | 0 |
| **EARLY INTERVENTION SPENDING** | **$591,100** | **$695,800** | **$806,200** | **NA** | **NA** | **$1,200,000** | **NA** |
| # of Persons Served | 398 | 405 | 427 | NA | NA | 564 | 638 |
| **PERSONAL ASSISTANCE SPENDING** |  |  |  |  |  | **$2,500,000** | **NA** |
| # of Persons Served |  |  |  |  |  | 380 | 624 |
| **SUPPORTED EMPLOYMENT SPENDING** | **$0** | **$0** | **$252,000** | **NA** | **NA** | **$492,400** | **$502,000** |
| # of Persons Served | 0 | 0 | 62 | NA | NA | 168 | 450 |
| **SUPPORTED LIVING SPENDING** |  |  |  |  |  | **$50,000** | **NA** |
| # of Persons Served |  |  |  |  |  | 6 | 29 |

*Expenditures associated with Special Community Initiatives are a subset of funding within the community services component of the state's chart series and spreadsheet; Family Support Client figures may include duplicate client counts; HCBS Waiver counts include Waiver case management numbers.
0= Services not provided in the state; NA= Data not available from state; blank= Services not applicable (eg. CSLA prior to authorization, Special Community Initiatives prior to request for data by this study)

*Source:*
Institute on Disability and Human Development (UAP),
University of Illinois at Chicago, 1994

# IDAHO

## Large Congregate Care Facilities: FY 1992 Revenue Sources*

### Private 16+Bed Settings

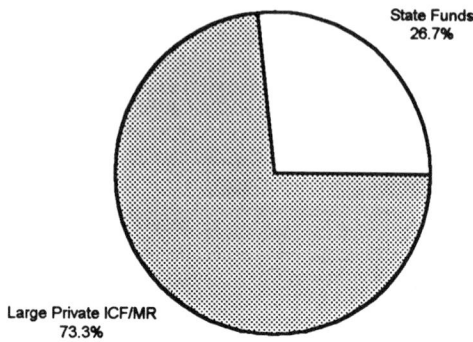

State Funds
26.7%

Large Private ICF/MR
73.3%

Total Funds: $1.8 Million

### Public Institutions

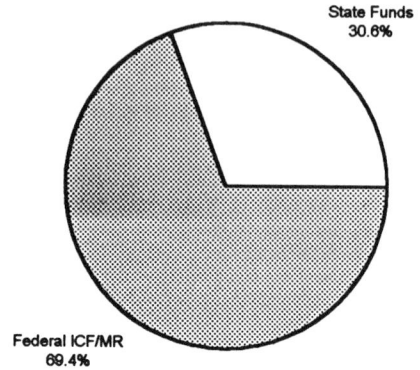

State Funds
30.6%

Federal ICF/MR
69.4%

Total Funds: $20.1 Million

*Excludes nursing homes

## Average Daily Residents in Institutions

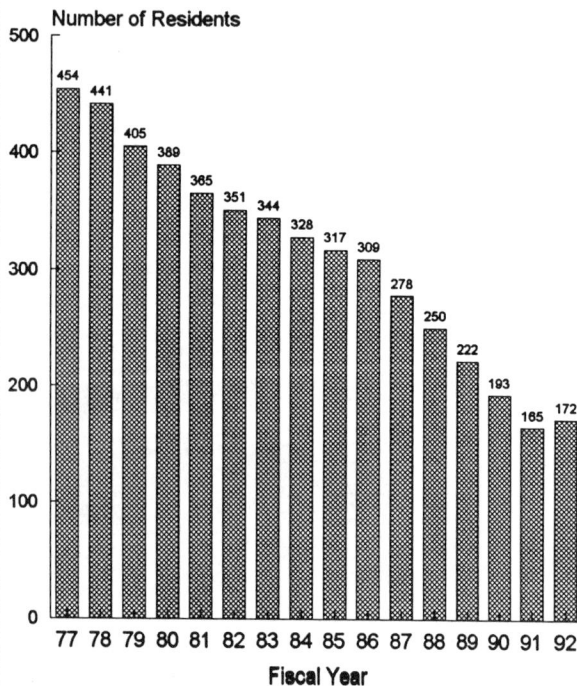

Number of Residents

| | |
|---|---|

454, 441, 405, 389, 365, 351, 344, 328, 317, 309, 278, 250, 222, 193, 165, 172

Fiscal Year: 77 78 79 80 81 82 83 84 85 86 87 88 89 90 91 92

## Institutional Daily Costs Per Resident

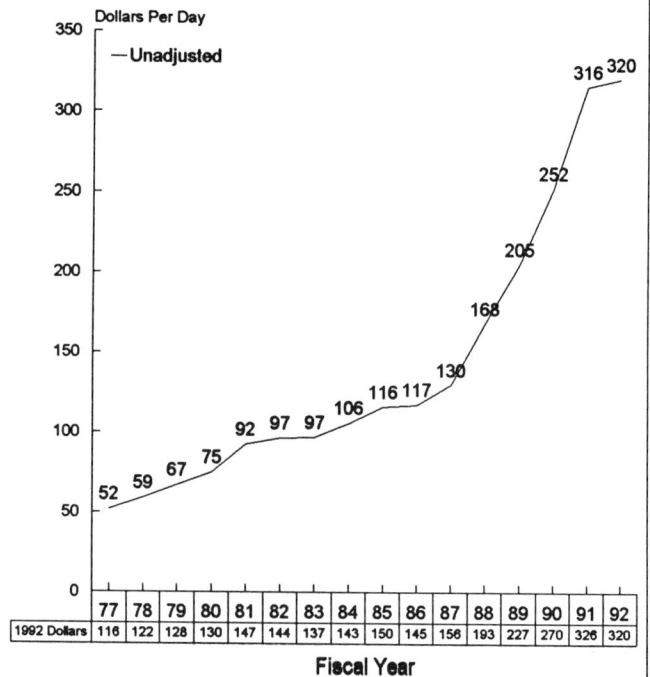

Dollars Per Day

—Unadjusted

52, 59, 67, 75, 92, 97, 97, 106, 116, 117, 130, 168, 205, 252, 316, 320

| Fiscal Year | 77 | 78 | 79 | 80 | 81 | 82 | 83 | 84 | 85 | 86 | 87 | 88 | 89 | 90 | 91 | 92 |
|---|---|---|---|---|---|---|---|---|---|---|---|---|---|---|---|---|
| 1992 Dollars | 116 | 122 | 128 | 130 | 147 | 144 | 137 | 143 | 150 | 145 | 156 | 193 | 227 | 270 | 326 | 320 |

*Source:*
Institute on Disability and Human Development (UAP),
University of Illinois at Chicago, 1994

# IDAHO FISCAL EFFORT

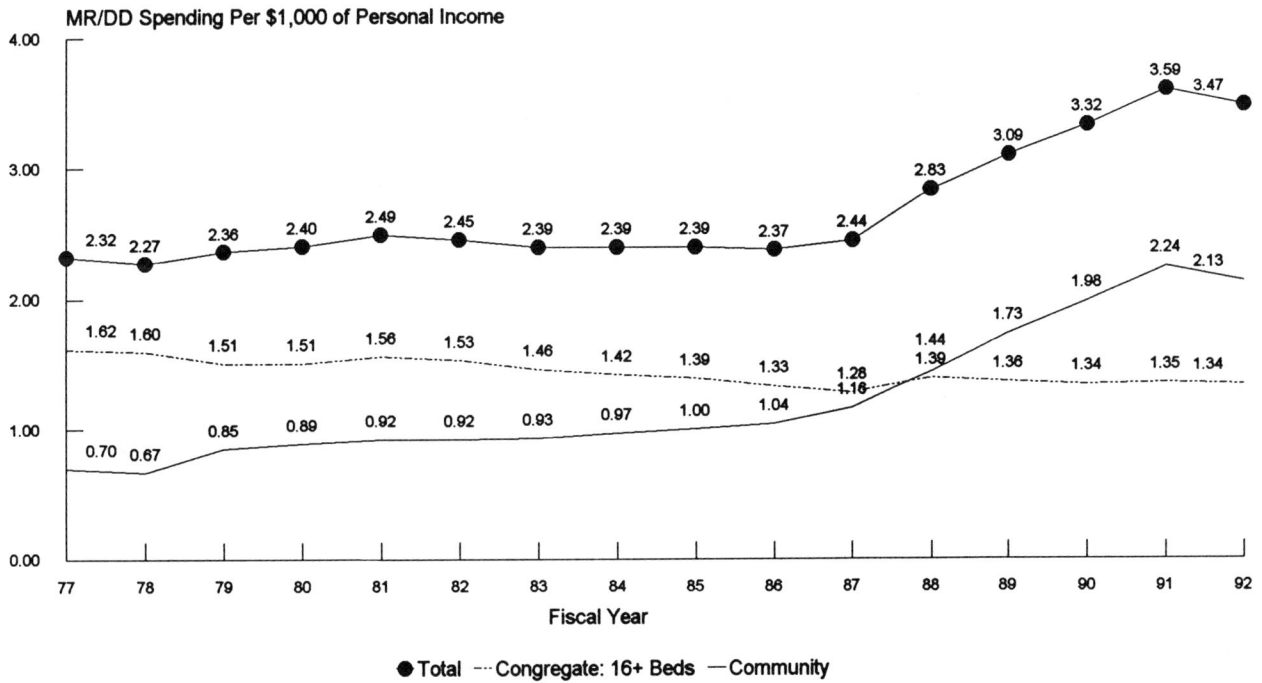

MR/DD Spending Per $1,000 of Personal Income

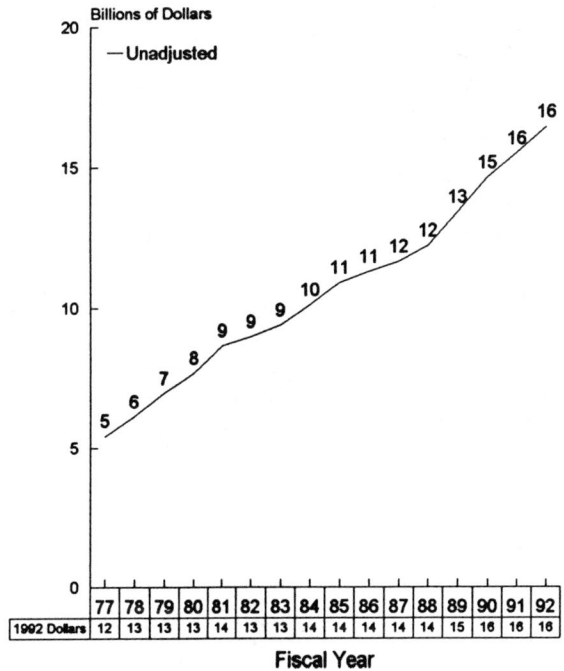

| Year | Total | Congregate: 16+ Beds | Community |
|------|-------|----------------------|-----------|
| 77 | 2.32 | 1.62 | 0.70 |
| 78 | 2.27 | 1.60 | 0.67 |
| 79 | 2.36 | 1.51 | 0.85 |
| 80 | 2.40 | 1.51 | 0.89 |
| 81 | 2.49 | 1.56 | 0.92 |
| 82 | 2.45 | 1.53 | 0.92 |
| 83 | 2.39 | 1.46 | 0.93 |
| 84 | 2.39 | 1.42 | 0.97 |
| 85 | 2.39 | 1.39 | 1.00 |
| 86 | 2.37 | 1.33 | 1.04 |
| 87 | 2.44 | 1.28 / 1.16 | |
| 88 | 2.83 | 1.44 / 1.39 | |
| 89 | 3.09 | 1.36 | 1.73 |
| 90 | 3.32 | 1.34 | 1.98 |
| 91 | 3.59 | 1.35 | 2.24 |
| 92 | 3.47 | 1.34 | 2.13 |

Fiscal Year

● Total   --- Congregate: 16+ Beds   — Community

## Total MR/DD Spending

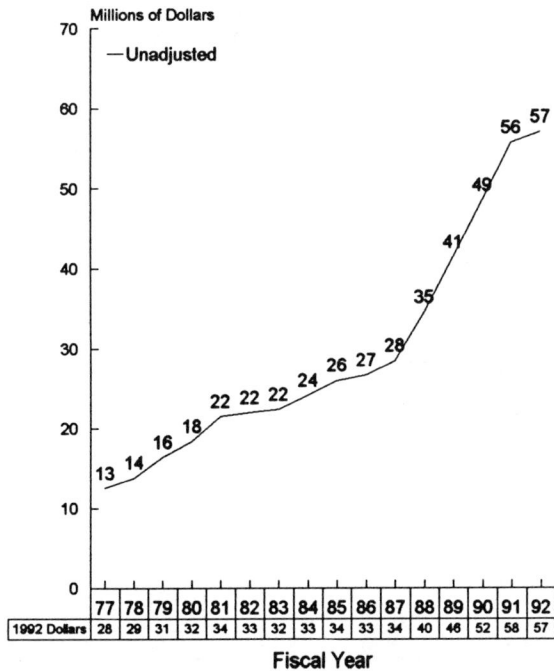

Millions of Dollars
— Unadjusted

| | 77 | 78 | 79 | 80 | 81 | 82 | 83 | 84 | 85 | 86 | 87 | 88 | 89 | 90 | 91 | 92 |
|--|----|----|----|----|----|----|----|----|----|----|----|----|----|----|----|----|
| Unadjusted | 13 | 14 | 16 | 18 | 22 | 22 | 22 | 24 | 26 | 27 | 28 | 35 | 41 | 49 | 56 | 57 |
| 1992 Dollars | 28 | 29 | 31 | 32 | 34 | 33 | 32 | 33 | 34 | 33 | 34 | 40 | 46 | 52 | 58 | 57 |

Fiscal Year

## Personal Income

Billions of Dollars
— Unadjusted

| | 77 | 78 | 79 | 80 | 81 | 82 | 83 | 84 | 85 | 86 | 87 | 88 | 89 | 90 | 91 | 92 |
|--|----|----|----|----|----|----|----|----|----|----|----|----|----|----|----|----|
| Unadjusted | 5 | 6 | 7 | 8 | 9 | 9 | 9 | 10 | 11 | 11 | 12 | 12 | 13 | 15 | 16 | 16 |
| 1992 Dollars | 12 | 13 | 13 | 13 | 14 | 13 | 13 | 14 | 14 | 14 | 14 | 14 | 15 | 16 | 16 | 16 |

Fiscal Year

*Source:*
Institute on Disability and Human Development (UAP),
University of Illinois at Chicago, 1994

# IDAHO
## Financial Support for MR/DD Services: FY 1977-92

| | 1977 | 1978 | 1979 | 1980 | 1981 | 1982 | 1983 | 1984 |
|---|---|---|---|---|---|---|---|---|
| **TOTAL FUNDS** | $12,542,000 | $13,831,000 | $16,405,000 | $18,417,000 | $21,514,000 | $21,984,000 | $22,370,000 | $24,119,482 |
| **CONGREGATE 16+ BEDS** | 8,759,058 | 9,764,907 | 10,468,416 | 11,562,849 | 13,515,350 | 13,728,221 | 13,660,002 | 14,318,417 |
| INSTITUTIONAL SERVICES FUNDS | 8,592,000 | 9,491,000 | 9,886,000 | 10,652,000 | 12,305,000 | 12,367,000 | 12,172,000 | 12,695,400 |
| STATE FUNDS | 3,611,000 | 4,690,000 | 4,645,000 | 4,688,000 | 3,664,000 | 5,045,000 | 4,832,000 | 4,922,500 |
| General Funds | 3,111,000 | 4,190,000 | 4,145,000 | 4,188,000 | 3,072,000 | 4,474,000 | 4,311,000 | 4,305,300 |
| Local | 0 | 0 | 0 | 0 | 0 | 0 | 0 | 0 |
| Other State Funds | 500,000 | 500,000 | 500,000 | 500,000 | 592,000 | 571,000 | 521,000 | 617,200 |
| FEDERAL FUNDS | 4,981,000 | 4,801,000 | 5,241,000 | 5,964,000 | 8,641,000 | 7,322,000 | 7,340,000 | 7,772,900 |
| Federal ICF/MR | 4,823,000 | 4,743,000 | 5,141,000 | 5,896,000 | 8,512,000 | 7,213,000 | 7,230,000 | 7,763,300 |
| Title XX / SSBG Funds | 0 | 0 | 0 | 0 | 0 | 0 | 0 | 0 |
| Other Federal Funds | 158,000 | 58,000 | 100,000 | 68,000 | 129,000 | 109,000 | 110,000 | 9,600 |
| LARGE PRIVATE RESIDENTIAL | 167,058 | 273,907 | 582,416 | 910,849 | 1,210,350 | 1,361,221 | 1,488,002 | 1,623,017 |
| STATE FUNDS | 53,158 | 96,607 | 212,116 | 317,249 | 415,150 | 469,621 | 514,402 | 538,517 |
| General Funds | 53,158 | 96,607 | 212,116 | 317,249 | 415,150 | 469,621 | 514,402 | 538,517 |
| Other State Funds | 0 | 0 | 0 | 0 | 0 | 0 | 0 | 0 |
| Local/County Overmatch | 0 | 0 | 0 | 0 | 0 | 0 | 0 | 0 |
| FEDERAL FUNDS | 113,900 | 177,300 | 370,300 | 593,600 | 795,200 | 891,600 | 973,600 | 1,084,500 |
| Large Private ICF/MR | 113,900 | 177,300 | 370,300 | 593,600 | 795,200 | 891,600 | 973,600 | 1,084,500 |
| **COMMUNITY SERVICES FUNDS** | 3,782,942 | 4,066,093 | 5,936,584 | 6,854,151 | 7,998,650 | 8,255,779 | 8,709,998 | 9,801,065 |
| STATE FUNDS | 2,799,842 | 3,005,393 | 3,882,884 | 4,371,751 | 4,844,850 | 4,941,379 | 5,098,598 | 5,639,444 |
| General Funds | 2,394,842 | 2,553,393 | 3,395,884 | 3,834,751 | 4,256,850 | 4,366,379 | 4,486,598 | 4,979,444 |
| Other State Funds | 0 | 0 | 0 | 0 | 0 | 0 | 0 | 0 |
| Local/County Overmatch | 0 | 0 | 0 | 0 | 0 | 0 | 0 | 0 |
| SSI State Supplement | 405,000 | 452,000 | 487,000 | 537,000 | 588,000 | 575,000 | 612,000 | 660,000 |
| FEDERAL FUNDS | 983,100 | 1,060,700 | 2,053,700 | 2,482,400 | 3,153,800 | 3,314,400 | 3,611,400 | 4,161,621 |
| ICF/MR Funds | 54,100 | 108,700 | 261,700 | 455,400 | 697,800 | 902,400 | 1,127,400 | 1,373,200 |
| Small Public | 0 | 0 | 0 | 0 | 0 | 0 | 0 | 0 |
| Small Private | 54,100 | 108,700 | 261,700 | 455,400 | 697,800 | 902,400 | 1,127,400 | 1,373,200 |
| HCBS Waiver | 0 | 0 | 0 | 0 | 0 | 0 | 0 | 13,997 |
| Model 50/200 Waiver | 0 | 0 | 0 | 0 | 0 | 0 | 0 | 0 |
| Other Title XIX Programs | 477,000 | 367,000 | 462,000 | 547,000 | 661,000 | 754,000 | 779,000 | 857,200 |
| Title XX / SSBG Funds | 202,000 | 335,000 | 1,080,000 | 1,230,000 | 1,545,000 | 1,408,000 | 1,455,000 | 1,478,700 |
| Other Federal Funds | 250,000 | 250,000 | 250,000 | 250,000 | 250,000 | 250,000 | 250,000 | 376,100 |
| Waiver Clients' SSI/ADC | 0 | 0 | 0 | 0 | 0 | 0 | 0 | 62,424 |

| | 1985 | 1986 | 1987 | 1988 | 1989 | 1990 | 1991 | 1992 |
|---|---|---|---|---|---|---|---|---|
| **TOTAL FUNDS** | $26,011,784 | $26,706,511 | $28,473,484 | $34,573,845 | $41,425,445 | $48,550,071 | $55,668,615 | $57,072,048 |
| **CONGREGATE 16+ BEDS** | 15,134,077 | 14,974,531 | 14,939,320 | 16,954,681 | 18,269,021 | 19,583,360 | 20,897,700 | 21,983,800 |
| INSTITUTIONAL SERVICES FUNDS | 13,425,100 | 13,227,000 | 13,162,700 | 15,357,900 | 16,577,833 | 17,797,767 | 19,017,700 | 20,164,000 |
| STATE FUNDS | 5,359,000 | 4,811,400 | 4,805,000 | 5,079,800 | 5,262,200 | 5,444,600 | 5,627,000 | 6,164,000 |
| General Funds | 4,734,000 | 4,362,000 | 4,206,800 | 4,358,400 | 4,561,100 | 4,763,800 | 4,966,500 | 5,503,500 |
| Local | 0 | 0 | 0 | 0 | 0 | 0 | 0 | 0 |
| Other State Funds | 625,000 | 449,400 | 598,200 | 721,400 | 701,100 | 680,800 | 660,500 | 660,500 |
| FEDERAL FUNDS | 8,066,100 | 8,415,600 | 8,357,700 | 10,278,100 | 11,315,633 | 12,353,167 | 13,390,700 | 14,000,000 |
| Federal ICF/MR | 8,056,500 | 8,406,000 | 8,357,700 | 10,278,100 | 11,315,633 | 12,353,167 | 13,390,700 | 14,000,000 |
| Title XX / SSBG Funds | 0 | 0 | 0 | 0 | 0 | 0 | 0 | 0 |
| Other Federal Funds | 9,600 | 9,600 | 0 | 0 | 0 | 0 | 0 | 0 |
| LARGE PRIVATE RESIDENTIAL | 1,708,977 | 1,747,531 | 1,776,620 | 1,596,781 | 1,691,187 | 1,785,594 | 1,880,000 | 1,819,800 |
| STATE FUNDS | 559,177 | 544,531 | 521,438 | 469,134 | 477,889 | 486,645 | 495,400 | 485,200 |
| General Funds | 559,177 | 544,531 | 521,438 | 469,134 | 477,889 | 486,645 | 495,400 | 485,200 |
| Other State Funds | 0 | 0 | 0 | 0 | 0 | 0 | 0 | 0 |
| Local/County Overmatch | 0 | 0 | 0 | 0 | 0 | 0 | 0 | 0 |
| FEDERAL FUNDS | 1,149,800 | 1,203,000 | 1,255,182 | 1,127,647 | 1,213,298 | 1,298,949 | 1,384,600 | 1,334,600 |
| Large Private ICF/MR | 1,149,800 | 1,203,000 | 1,255,182 | 1,127,647 | 1,213,298 | 1,298,949 | 1,384,600 | 1,334,600 |
| **COMMUNITY SERVICES FUNDS** | 10,877,707 | 11,731,980 | 13,534,164 | 17,619,164 | 23,156,424 | 28,966,711 | 34,770,915 | 35,088,248 |
| STATE FUNDS | 6,257,947 | 6,464,971 | 7,049,918 | 8,528,688 | 10,462,057 | 12,395,426 | 14,328,795 | 14,188,808 |
| General Funds | 5,559,947 | 5,712,971 | 6,040,918 | 7,532,688 | 9,413,725 | 11,294,763 | 13,175,800 | 12,978,163 |
| Other State Funds | 0 | 0 | 0 | 0 | 0 | 0 | 0 | 0 |
| Local/County Overmatch | 0 | 0 | 0 | 0 | 0 | 0 | 0 | 0 |
| SSI State Supplement | 698,000 | 752,000 | 1,009,000 | 996,000 | 1,048,332 | 1,100,663 | 1,152,995 | 1,210,645 |
| FEDERAL FUNDS | 4,619,760 | 5,267,009 | 6,484,246 | 9,090,476 | 12,694,367 | 16,571,285 | 20,442,120 | 20,899,440 |
| ICF/MR Funds | 1,630,500 | 1,705,800 | 2,481,182 | 4,622,282 | 6,437,721 | 8,253,161 | 10,068,600 | 10,068,600 |
| Small Public | 0 | 0 | 0 | 0 | 0 | 0 | 0 | 0 |
| Small Private | 1,630,500 | 1,705,800 | 2,481,182 | 4,622,282 | 6,437,721 | 8,253,161 | 10,068,600 | 10,068,600 |
| HCBS Waiver | 66,260 | 131,829 | 392,141 | 502,803 | 770,273 | 1,205,842 | 1,841,200 | 1,841,200 |
| Model 50/200 Waiver | 0 | 0 | 9,283 | 10,339 | 6,893 | 3,446 | 0 | 0 |
| Other Title XIX Programs | 852,500 | 1,082,500 | 1,013,700 | 1,189,400 | 2,263,567 | 3,337,733 | 4,411,900 | 4,411,900 |
| Title XX / SSBG Funds | 1,564,600 | 1,497,300 | 1,527,300 | 1,527,300 | 1,527,333 | 1,527,367 | 1,527,400 | 1,527,400 |
| Other Federal Funds | 322,300 | 420,400 | 425,600 | 445,200 | 580,500 | 715,800 | 851,100 | 1,170,000 |
| Waiver Clients' SSI/ADC | 183,600 | 429,180 | 635,040 | 793,152 | 1,108,080 | 1,527,936 | 1,741,920 | 1,880,340 |

*Source:*

Institute on Disability and Human Development (UAP),
University of Illinois at Chicago, 1994

# ILLINOIS

## MR/DD Spending for Congregate Residential & Community Services

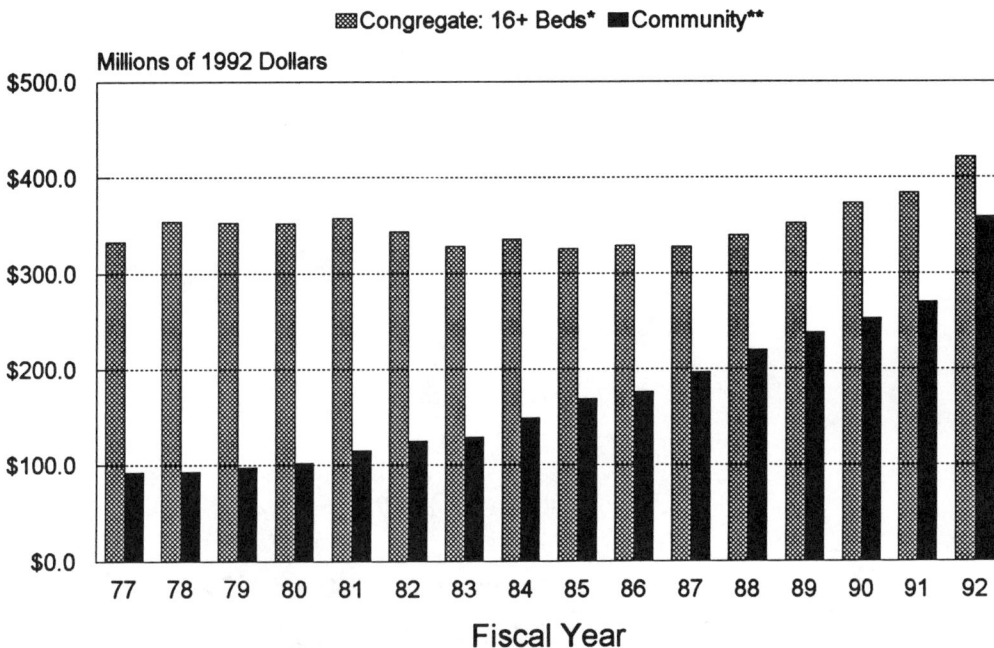

▨ Congregate: 16+ Beds*  ■ Community**

Millions of 1992 Dollars

**Fiscal Year**

*Excludes nursing homes; ** Includes resources for
15 bed or less residential settings & non-residential community services

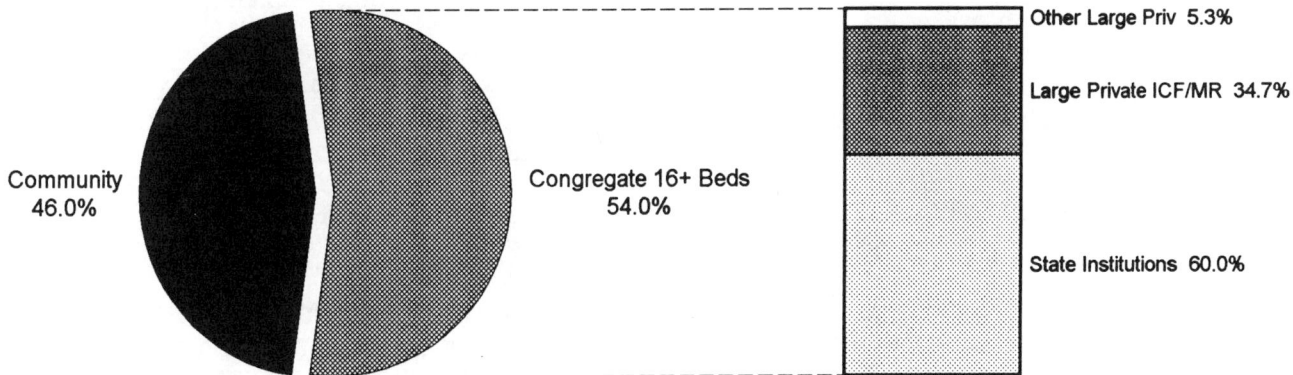

Community
46.0%

Congregate 16+ Beds
54.0%

Other Large Priv  5.3%

Large Private ICF/MR  34.7%

State Institutions  60.0%

FY 1992 Total Spending:
$780.1 Million

*Source:*
Institute on Disability and Human Development (UAP),
University of Illinois at Chicago, 1994

# ILLINOIS

## Number of Persons Served by Residential Setting: FY 1992

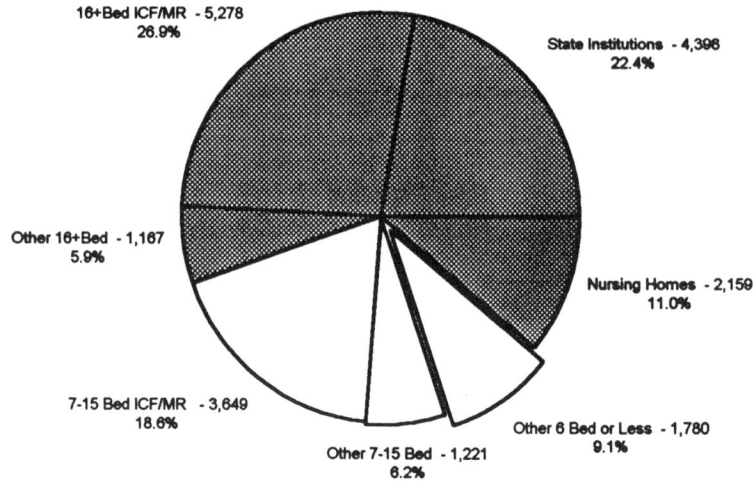

16+Bed ICF/MR - 5,278
26.9%

State Institutions - 4,398
22.4%

Other 16+Bed - 1,167
5.9%

Nursing Homes - 2,159
11.0%

7-15 Bed ICF/MR - 3,649
18.6%

Other 7-15 Bed - 1,221
6.2%

Other 6 Bed or Less - 1,780
9.1%

Total Served: 19,652

## Persons Served by Residential Setting:1986-92

|  | 1986 | 1987 | 1988 | 1989 | 1990 | 1991 | 1992 |
|---|---|---|---|---|---|---|---|
| CONGREGATE 16 + BED SETTINGS | 14,533 | 14,444 | 14,586 | 14,346 | 13,985 | 13,590 | 13,002 |
| Nursing Homes* | 4,432 | 4,432 | 4,490 | 4,191 | 3,906 | 3,629 | 2,159 |
| State Institutions | 4,601 | 4,521 | 4,518 | 4,507 | 4,473 | 4,348 | 4,398 |
| Private 16+Bed ICF/MR* | 4,093 | 4,093 | 4,223 | 4,298 | 4,188 | 4,212 | 5,278 |
| Other 16+Bed Residential | 1,407 | 1,398 | 1,355 | 1,350 | 1,418 | 1,401 | 1,167 |
| 15 BED OR LESS RESIDENTIAL SETTINGS | 2,073 | 2,284 | 2,888 | 3,697 | 4,318 | 5,093 | 6,650 |
| Public 7-15 Bed ICF/MR | 0 | 0 | 0 | 0 | 0 | 0 | 0 |
| Private 7-15 Bed ICF/MR | 375 | 510 | 1,095 | 1,600 | 1,670 | 2,279 | 3,649 |
| Other 7-15 Bed Residential | 1,698 | 1,774 | 1,793 | 2,097 | 2,648 | 2,814 | 1,221 |
| Public 6 Bed or Less ICF/MR |  |  |  |  |  |  | 0 |
| Private 6 Bed or Less ICF/MR |  |  |  |  |  |  | 0 |
| Other 6 Bed or Less Residential |  |  |  |  |  |  | 1,780 |
| TOTAL PERSONS SERVED | 16,606 | 16,728 | 17,474 | 18,043 | 18,303 | 18,683 | 19,652 |

*In 1992, 1,066 individuals in Nursing Homes were re-classified as Private 16+Bed ICF/MR. These former "skilled nursing facility/pediatrics" settings became certified as ICFs/MR.

## Persons Served in Non-Residential Community Services:1986-92

|  | 1986 | 1987 | 1988 | 1989 | 1990 | 1991 | 1992 |
|---|---|---|---|---|---|---|---|
| DAY/WORK PROGRAMS | 16,731 | 23,897 | 23,443 | 21,356 | 20,861 | 22,342 | 21,382 |
| Sheltered Employment/Work Activity | 4,172 | 8,524 | 8,377 | 6,666 | 6,750 | 7,264 | 6,657 |
| Day Habilitation ("Day Training") | 12,143 | 14,839 | 14,489 | 14,046 | 13,258 | 13,910 | 13,355 |
| Supported/Competitive Employment | 416 | 534 | 577 | 644 | 853 | 1,168 | 1,370 |
| CASE MANAGEMENT | 4,542 | 8,789 | 10,829 | 11,064 | 11,805 | 10,422 | 9,623 |
| HCBS WAIVER | 600 | 671 | 637 | 680 | 720 | 1,280 | 3,110 |
| MODEL 50/200 WAIVER | 0 | 0 | 0 | 0 | 0 | 0 | 0 |

*Source:*
Institute on Disability and Human Development (UAP),
University of Illinois at Chicago, 1994

# ILLINOIS

## Community Services: FY 1992 Revenue Sources

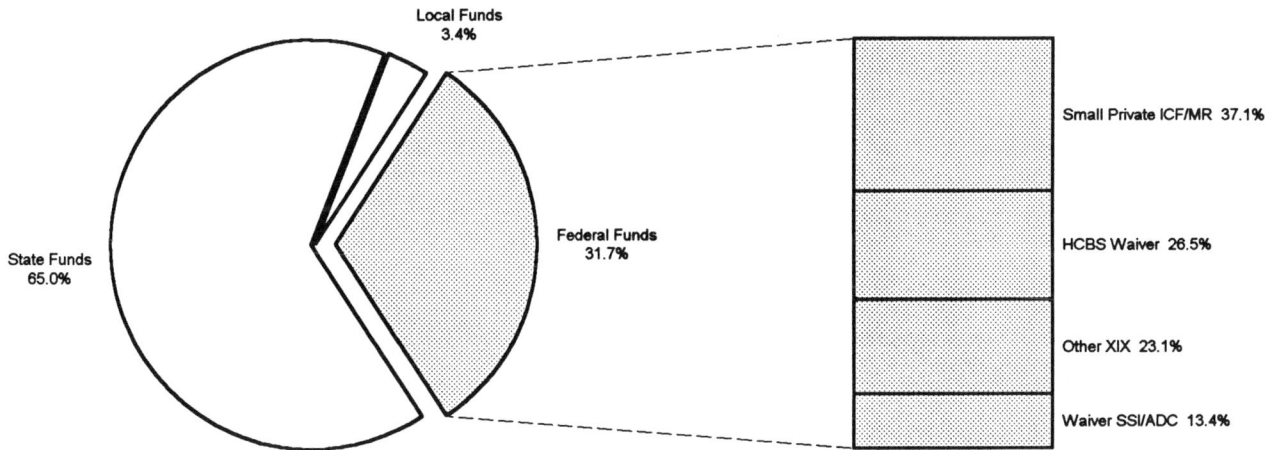

Local Funds
3.4%

State Funds
65.0%

Federal Funds
31.7%

Small Private ICF/MR 37.1%

HCBS Waiver 26.5%

Other XIX 23.1%

Waiver SSI/ADC 13.4%

Total Funds: $358.5 Million

## Family Support Initiatives*

|  | 1986 | 1987 | 1988 | 1989 | 1990 | 1991 | 1992 |
|---|---|---|---|---|---|---|---|
| FAMILY SUPPORT: TOTAL SPENDING | $8,862,900 | $10,300,000 | $12,315,500 | $15,647,400 | $17,581,300 | $19,206,300 | $20,966,900 |
| Total # of Families Supported | 6,033 | 9,923 | 12,060 | 13,273 | 15,709 | 17,354 | 21,252 |
| A. Financial Subsidy/Payment | $0 | $0 | $0 | $0 | $0 | $705,900 | $1,202,800 |
| # of Families | 0 | 0 | 0 | 0 | 0 | 204 | 250 |
| B. Family Assistance Payments | $3,597,600 | $4,355,000 | $4,409,600 | $4,882,900 | $5,874,000 | $6,106,400 | $6,072,500 |
| # of Families | 2,436 | 2,897 | 3,147 | 3,615 | 3,976 | 3,966 | 3,900 |
| C. Other Family Support Payments | $5,265,300 | $5,945,000 | $7,905,900 | $10,764,500 | $11,707,300 | $12,394,000 | $13,691,600 |
| # of Families | 3,597 | 7,026 | 8,913 | 9,658 | 11,733 | 13,184 | 17,102 |

## Other Community Services Initiatives*

|  | 1986 | 1987 | 1988 | 1989 | 1990 | 1991 | 1992 |
|---|---|---|---|---|---|---|---|
| AGING/DD SPENDING | $0 | $0 | $0 | $0 | $0 | $0 | $0 |
| # of Persons Served | 0 | 0 | 0 | 0 | 0 | 0 | 0 |
| ASSISTIVE TECHNOLOGY SPENDING |  |  |  |  |  | $171,600 | $172,500 |
| # of Persons Served |  |  |  |  |  | 112 | 170 |
| EARLY INTERVENTION SPENDING | $6,812,800 | $7,073,800 | $7,347,300 | $7,932,900 | $8,495,000 | $8,559,100 | $8,558,200 |
| # of Persons Served | $2,842 | $6,530 | 6,472 | 6,673 | 7,632 | 7,617 | 6,223 |
| PERSONAL ASSISTANCE SPENDING |  |  |  |  |  |  | $0 |
| # of Persons Served |  |  |  |  |  |  | 0 |
| SUPPORTED EMPLOYMENT SPENDING | $2,043,800 | $2,493,100 | $2,606,000 | $2,691,000 | $3,488,200 | $3,777,200 | $4,725,400 |
| # of Persons Served | 416 | 534 | 577 | 644 | 853 | 1,168 | 1,370 |
| SUPPORTED LIVING SPENDING |  |  |  |  |  |  | $99,000 |
| # of Persons Served |  |  |  |  |  |  | 200 |

*Expenditures associated with Special Community Initiatives are a subset of funding within the community services component of the state's chart series and spreadsheet; Family Support Client figures may include duplicate client counts; HCBS Waiver counts include Waiver case management numbers.
0= Services not provided in the state; NA= Data not available from state; blank= Services not applicable (eg. CSLA prior to authorization, Special Community Initiatives prior to request for data by this study)

Source:
Institute on Disability and Human Development (UAP),
University of Illinois at Chicago, 1994

# ILLINOIS

## Large Congregate Care Facilities: FY 1992 Revenue Sources*

### Private 16+Bed Settings

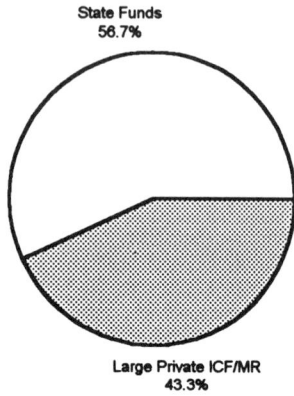

State Funds
56.7%

Large Private ICF/MR
43.3%

Total Funds: $168.8 Million

### Public Institutions

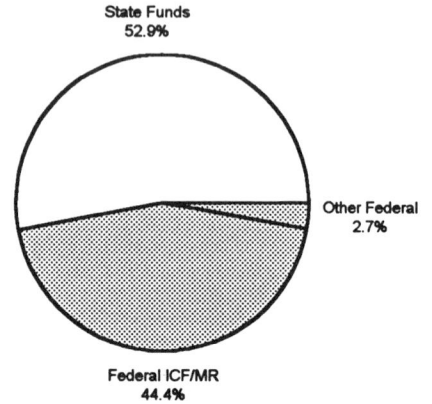

State Funds
52.9%

Other Federal
2.7%

Federal ICF/MR
44.4%

Total Funds: $252.8 Million

*Excludes nursing homes

## Average Daily Residents in Institutions

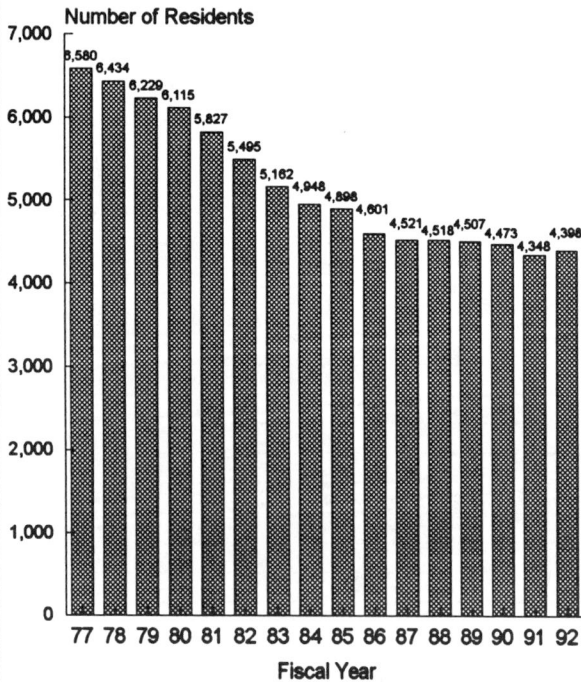

Number of Residents

6,580 · 6,434 · 6,229 · 6,115 · 5,827 · 5,495 · 5,162 · 4,948 · 4,898 · 4,601 · 4,521 · 4,518 · 4,507 · 4,473 · 4,348 · 4,398

Fiscal Year: 77 78 79 80 81 82 83 84 85 86 87 88 89 90 91 92

## Institutional Daily Costs Per Resident

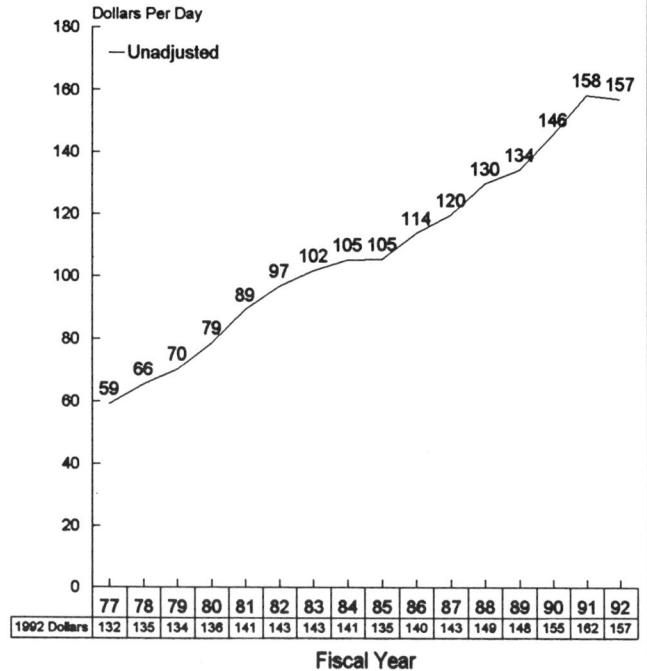

Dollars Per Day

— Unadjusted

59 · 66 · 70 · 79 · 89 · 97 · 102 · 105 · 105 · 114 · 120 · 130 · 134 · 146 · 158 · 157

| | 77 | 78 | 79 | 80 | 81 | 82 | 83 | 84 | 85 | 86 | 87 | 88 | 89 | 90 | 91 | 92 |
|---|----|----|----|----|----|----|----|----|----|----|----|----|----|----|----|----|
| 1992 Dollars | 132 | 135 | 134 | 136 | 141 | 143 | 143 | 141 | 135 | 140 | 143 | 149 | 148 | 155 | 162 | 157 |

Fiscal Year

*Source:*
Institute on Disability and Human Development (UAP),
University of Illinois at Chicago, 1994

# ILLINOIS FISCAL EFFORT

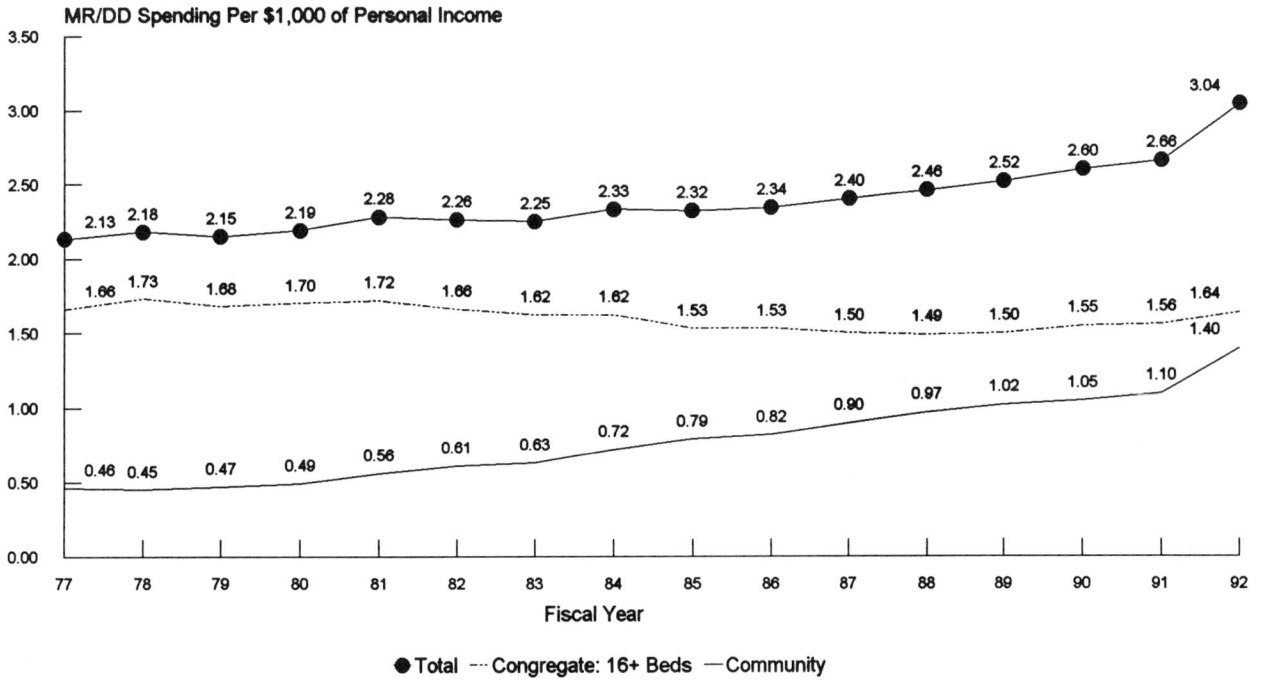

MR/DD Spending Per $1,000 of Personal Income

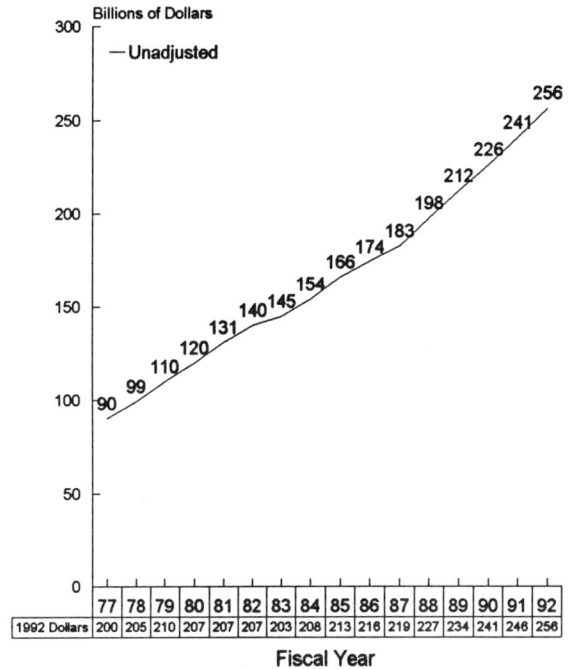

| | |
|---|---|
| 3.50 | |
| | 3.04 |
| 3.00 | |
| 2.50 | 2.13  2.18  2.15  2.19  2.28  2.26  2.25  2.33  2.32  2.34  2.40  2.46  2.52  2.60  2.66 |
| 2.00 | |
| 1.50 | 1.66  1.73  1.68  1.70  1.72  1.66  1.62  1.62  1.53  1.53  1.50  1.49  1.50  1.55  1.56  1.64 |
| | 1.40 |
| 1.00 | 0.90  0.97  1.02  1.05  1.10 |
| 0.50 | 0.46  0.45  0.47  0.49  0.56  0.61  0.63  0.72  0.79  0.82 |
| 0.00 | |

77   78   79   80   81   82   83   84   85   86   87   88   89   90   91   92

Fiscal Year

● Total  --- Congregate: 16+ Beds  — Community

## Total MR/DD Spending

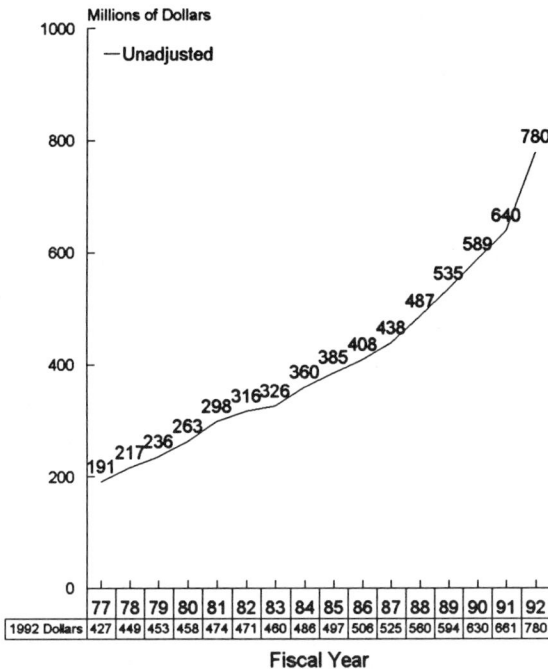

Millions of Dollars
— Unadjusted

| | |
|---|---|
| 1000 | |
| 800 | 780 |
| | 640 |
| 600 | 589 |
| | 535 |
| | 487 |
| 400 | 438 |
| | 385  408 |
| | 360 |
| | 298  316  326 |
| | 263 |
| 200 | 236 |
| | 191  217 |
| 0 | |

| | 77 | 78 | 79 | 80 | 81 | 82 | 83 | 84 | 85 | 86 | 87 | 88 | 89 | 90 | 91 | 92 |
|---|---|---|---|---|---|---|---|---|---|---|---|---|---|---|---|---|
| 1992 Dollars | 427 | 449 | 453 | 458 | 474 | 471 | 460 | 486 | 497 | 506 | 525 | 560 | 594 | 630 | 661 | 780 |

Fiscal Year

## Personal Income

Billions of Dollars
— Unadjusted

| | |
|---|---|
| 300 | |
| | 256 |
| 250 | 241 |
| | 226 |
| | 212 |
| 200 | 198 |
| | 183 |
| | 174 |
| | 166 |
| 150 | 154 |
| | 140  145 |
| | 131 |
| | 120 |
| 100 | 110 |
| | 99 |
| | 90 |
| 50 | |
| 0 | |

| | 77 | 78 | 79 | 80 | 81 | 82 | 83 | 84 | 85 | 86 | 87 | 88 | 89 | 90 | 91 | 92 |
|---|---|---|---|---|---|---|---|---|---|---|---|---|---|---|---|---|
| 1992 Dollars | 200 | 205 | 210 | 207 | 207 | 207 | 203 | 208 | 213 | 216 | 219 | 227 | 234 | 241 | 246 | 256 |

Fiscal Year

*Source:*
Institute on Disability and Human Development (UAP),
University of Illinois at Chicago, 1994

# ILLINOIS
## Financial Support for MR/DD Services: FY 1977-92

| | 1977 | 1978 | 1979 | 1980 | 1981 | 1982 | 1983 | 1984 |
|---|---|---|---|---|---|---|---|---|
| **TOTAL FUNDS** | $191,478,377 | $216,871,303 | $235,967,478 | $263,025,642 | $297,923,337 | $316,374,324 | $325,988,796 | $359,736,860 |
| **CONGREGATE 16+ BEDS** | 149,790,200 | 171,647,400 | 184,669,500 | 203,746,300 | 225,187,100 | 231,675,500 | 234,108,700 | 249,168,800 |
| INSTITUTIONAL SERVICES FUNDS | 142,290,200 | 153,867,400 | 159,909,500 | 176,106,300 | 189,716,100 | 193,786,500 | 191,537,100 | 190,091,400 |
| STATE FUNDS | 132,028,200 | 124,413,400 | 124,832,500 | 135,423,300 | 138,383,100 | 138,720,500 | 119,268,100 | 104,891,400 |
| General Funds | 132,028,200 | 124,413,400 | 124,832,500 | 135,423,300 | 138,383,100 | 138,720,500 | 119,268,100 | 104,891,400 |
| Local | 0 | 0 | 0 | 0 | 0 | 0 | 0 | 0 |
| Other State Funds | 0 | 0 | 0 | 0 | 0 | 0 | 0 | 0 |
| FEDERAL FUNDS | 10,262,000 | 29,454,000 | 35,077,000 | 40,683,000 | 51,333,000 | 55,066,000 | 72,269,000 | 85,200,000 |
| Federal ICF/MR | 8,383,000 | 26,136,000 | 32,925,000 | 36,618,000 | 49,168,000 | 52,852,000 | 70,010,000 | 78,100,000 |
| Title XX / SSBG Funds | 0 | 0 | 0 | 0 | 0 | 0 | 0 | 0 |
| Other Federal Funds | 1,879,000 | 3,318,000 | 2,152,000 | 4,065,000 | 2,165,000 | 2,214,000 | 2,259,000 | 7,100,000 |
| LARGE PRIVATE RESIDENTIAL | 7,500,000 | 17,780,000 | 24,760,000 | 27,640,000 | 35,471,000 | 37,889,000 | 42,571,600 | 59,077,400 |
| STATE FUNDS | 7,500,000 | 13,180,000 | 17,210,000 | 19,190,000 | 23,645,500 | 25,394,500 | 28,275,800 | 37,068,700 |
| General Funds | 0 | 4,600,000 | 7,550,000 | 8,450,000 | 11,825,500 | 12,494,500 | 14,295,800 | 22,008,700 |
| Other State Funds | 7,500,000 | 8,580,000 | 9,660,000 | 10,740,000 | 11,820,000 | 12,900,000 | 13,980,000 | 15,060,000 |
| Local/County Overmatch | 0 | 0 | 0 | 0 | 0 | 0 | 0 | 0 |
| FEDERAL FUNDS | 0 | 4,600,000 | 7,550,000 | 8,450,000 | 11,825,500 | 12,494,500 | 14,295,800 | 22,008,700 |
| Large Private ICF/MR | 0 | 4,600,000 | 7,550,000 | 8,450,000 | 11,825,500 | 12,494,500 | 14,295,800 | 22,008,700 |
| **COMMUNITY SERVICES FUNDS** | 41,688,177 | 45,223,903 | 51,297,978 | 59,279,342 | 72,736,237 | 84,698,824 | 91,880,096 | 110,568,060 |
| STATE FUNDS | 34,001,177 | 25,339,903 | 27,246,978 | 30,973,342 | 40,304,737 | 81,747,224 | 88,690,096 | 106,865,140 |
| General Funds | 10,445,000 | 4,950,000 | 5,495,000 | 9,560,000 | 17,719,500 | 53,714,400 | 61,866,400 | 81,902,600 |
| Other State Funds | 10,747,000 | 11,500,000 | 10,421,000 | 8,830,000 | 8,819,000 | 14,083,000 | 12,980,000 | 10,758,700 |
| Local/County Overmatch | 6,239,177 | 3,752,903 | 6,211,978 | 7,076,342 | 7,809,237 | 8,137,824 | 8,310,696 | 8,022,840 |
| SSI State Supplement | 6,570,000 | 5,137,000 | 5,119,000 | 5,507,000 | 5,957,000 | 5,812,000 | 5,533,000 | 6,181,000 |
| FEDERAL FUNDS | 7,687,000 | 19,884,000 | 24,051,000 | 28,306,000 | 32,431,500 | 2,951,600 | 3,190,000 | 3,702,920 |
| ICF/MR Funds | 0 | 0 | 0 | 0 | 74,500 | 159,500 | 254,200 | 495,400 |
| Small Public | 0 | 0 | 0 | 0 | 0 | 0 | 0 | 0 |
| Small Private | 0 | 0 | 0 | 0 | 74,500 | 159,500 | 254,200 | 495,400 |
| HCBS Waiver | 0 | 0 | 0 | 0 | 0 | 0 | 0 | 227,000 |
| Model 50/200 Waiver | 0 | 0 | 0 | 0 | 0 | 0 | 0 | 0 |
| Other Title XIX Programs | 0 | 0 | 0 | 0 | 0 | 0 | 0 | 0 |
| Title XX / SSBG Funds | 6,804,000 | 18,902,000 | 23,611,000 | 27,659,000 | 31,197,000 | 1,898,100 | 1,905,800 | 1,904,900 |
| Other Federal Funds | 883,000 | 982,000 | 440,000 | 647,000 | 1,160,000 | 894,000 | 1,030,000 | 936,900 |
| Waiver Clients' SSI/ADC | 0 | 0 | 0 | 0 | 0 | 0 | 0 | 138,720 |

| | 1985 | 1986 | 1987 | 1988 | 1989 | 1990 | 1991 | 1992 |
|---|---|---|---|---|---|---|---|---|
| **TOTAL FUNDS** | $385,200,762 | $408,237,915 | $437,865,825 | $486,614,940 | $534,997,659 | $588,888,641 | $639,683,072 | $780,128,968 |
| **CONGREGATE 16+ BEDS** | 253,604,200 | 265,879,900 | 273,534,500 | 295,459,300 | 319,239,436 | 350,729,402 | 375,471,562 | 421,600,500 |
| INSTITUTIONAL SERVICES FUNDS | 188,030,800 | 190,847,500 | 197,226,700 | 214,609,500 | 220,914,000 | 237,771,700 | 251,181,600 | 252,774,100 |
| STATE FUNDS | 107,030,800 | 102,584,600 | 137,314,200 | 130,796,700 | 102,593,700 | 125,462,000 | 136,133,000 | 133,698,000 |
| General Funds | 107,030,800 | 102,584,600 | 137,314,200 | 130,796,700 | 102,593,700 | 125,462,000 | 136,133,000 | 133,698,000 |
| Local | 0 | 0 | 0 | 0 | 0 | 0 | 0 | 0 |
| Other State Funds | 0 | 0 | 0 | 0 | 0 | 0 | 0 | 0 |
| FEDERAL FUNDS | 81,000,000 | 88,262,900 | 59,912,500 | 83,812,800 | 118,320,300 | 112,309,700 | 115,048,600 | 119,076,100 |
| Federal ICF/MR | 73,300,000 | 80,939,700 | 52,529,700 | 76,176,700 | 100,173,700 | 101,605,200 | 108,280,800 | 112,295,900 |
| Title XX / SSBG Funds | 0 | 0 | 0 | 0 | 0 | 0 | 0 | 0 |
| Other Federal Funds | 7,700,000 | 7,323,200 | 7,382,800 | 7,636,100 | 18,146,600 | 10,704,500 | 6,767,800 | 6,780,200 |
| LARGE PRIVATE RESIDENTIAL | 65,573,400 | 75,032,400 | 76,307,800 | 80,849,800 | 98,325,436 | 112,957,702 | 124,289,962 | 168,826,400 |
| STATE FUNDS | 40,856,700 | 46,154,700 | 47,302,900 | 49,348,200 | 58,868,418 | 68,055,051 | 74,676,431 | 95,672,150 |
| General Funds | 24,716,700 | 28,877,700 | 29,004,900 | 31,501,600 | 19,411,400 | 23,152,400 | 25,062,900 | 22,517,900 |
| Other State Funds | 16,140,000 | 17,277,000 | 18,298,000 | 17,846,600 | 39,457,018 | 44,902,651 | 49,613,531 | 73,154,250 |
| Local/County Overmatch | 0 | 0 | 0 | 0 | 0 | 0 | 0 | 0 |
| FEDERAL FUNDS | 24,716,700 | 28,877,700 | 29,004,900 | 31,501,600 | 39,457,018 | 44,902,651 | 49,613,531 | 73,154,250 |
| Large Private ICF/MR | 24,716,700 | 28,877,700 | 29,004,900 | 31,501,600 | 39,457,018 | 44,902,651 | 49,613,531 | 73,154,250 |
| **COMMUNITY SERVICES FUNDS** | 131,596,562 | 142,358,015 | 164,331,325 | 191,155,640 | 215,758,223 | 238,159,239 | 264,211,510 | 358,528,468 |
| STATE FUNDS | 120,818,762 | 119,640,415 | 137,430,845 | 152,696,384 | 170,147,403 | 186,544,301 | 201,964,734 | 245,032,207 |
| General Funds | 95,783,800 | 89,388,700 | 92,215,800 | 128,496,000 | 145,341,800 | 160,498,418 | 174,616,556 | 216,316,621 |
| Other State Funds | 10,036,400 | 9,920,100 | 22,319,000 | 576,000 | 0 | 0 | 0 | 0 |
| Local/County Overmatch | 8,460,562 | 8,866,615 | 9,541,045 | 9,978,384 | 10,477,303 | 11,001,168 | 11,551,227 | 12,128,788 |
| SSI State Supplement | 6,538,000 | 11,465,000 | 13,355,000 | 13,646,000 | 14,328,300 | 15,044,715 | 15,796,951 | 16,586,798 |
| FEDERAL FUNDS | 10,777,800 | 22,717,600 | 26,900,480 | 38,459,256 | 45,610,820 | 51,614,938 | 62,246,776 | 113,496,261 |
| ICF/MR Funds | 1,909,700 | 3,081,100 | 4,274,000 | 9,652,200 | 14,862,800 | 17,043,018 | 24,821,956 | 42,069,321 |
| Small Public | 0 | 0 | 0 | 0 | 0 | 0 | 0 | 0 |
| Small Private | 1,909,700 | 3,081,100 | 4,274,000 | 9,652,200 | 14,862,800 | 17,043,018 | 24,821,956 | 42,069,321 |
| HCBS Waiver | 3,088,600 | 5,545,900 | 6,419,800 | 6,678,300 | 7,242,800 | 7,867,400 | 8,700,000 | 30,038,700 |
| Model 50/200 Waiver | 0 | 0 | 0 | 0 | 0 | 0 | 0 | 0 |
| Other Title XIX Programs | 0 | 7,000,000 | 9,000,000 | 14,358,500 | 16,900,000 | 19,400,000 | 22,750,000 | 26,199,000 |
| Title XX / SSBG Funds | 2,026,300 | 1,540,300 | 1,728,100 | 1,728,100 | 0 | 0 | 0 | 0 |
| Other Federal Funds | 1,798,400 | 3,311,100 | 2,942,200 | 3,565,500 | 3,814,500 | 4,125,000 | 107,300 | 0 |
| Waiver Clients' SSI/ADC | 1,954,800 | 2,239,200 | 2,536,380 | 2,476,656 | 2,790,720 | 3,179,520 | 5,867,520 | 15,189,240 |

*Source:*

Institute on Disability and Human Development (UAP),
University of Illinois at Chicago, 1994

# INDIANA

## MR/DD Spending for Congregate Residential & Community Services

▨ Congregate: 16+ Beds*  ■ Community**

Millions of 1992 Dollars

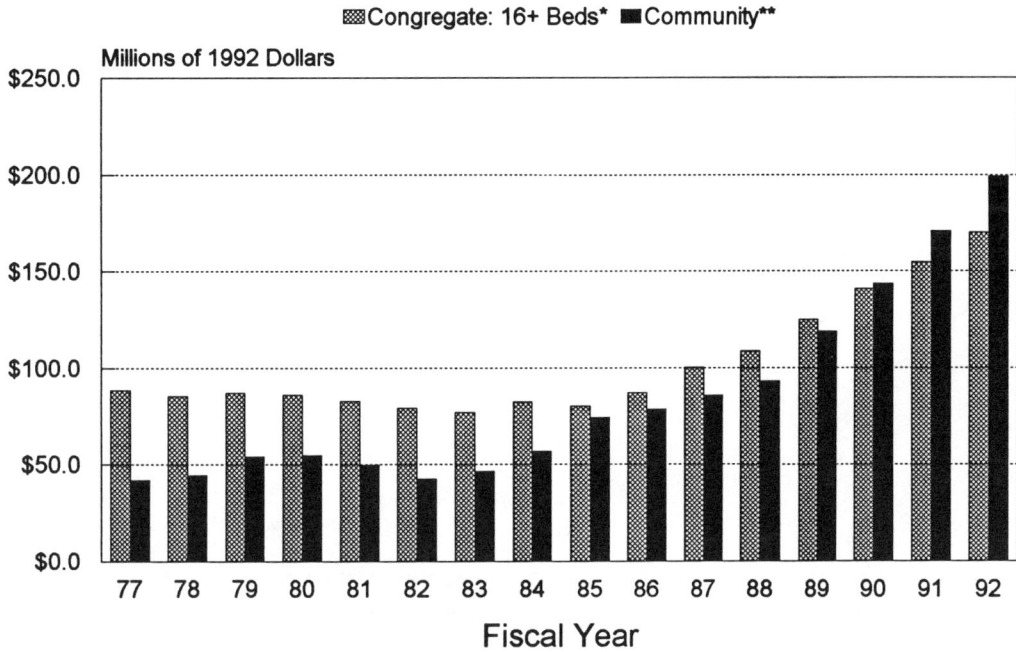

Fiscal Year

*Excludes nursing homes; ** Includes resources for
15 bed or less residential settings & non-residential community services

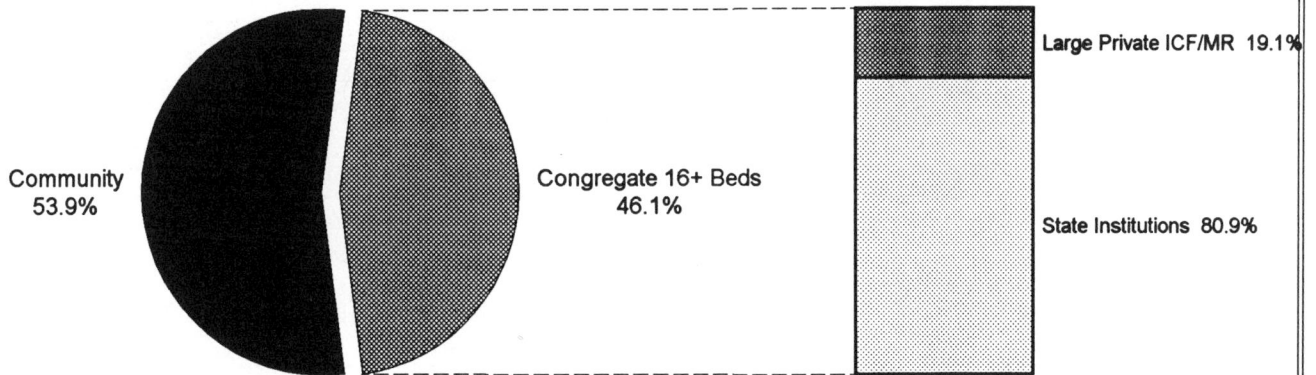

Community
53.9%

Congregate 16+ Beds
46.1%

Large Private ICF/MR 19.1%

State Institutions 80.9%

FY 1992 Total Spending:
$369.1 Million

*Source:*
Institute on Disability and Human Development (UAP),
University of Illinois at Chicago, 1994

# INDIANA

## Number of Persons Served by Residential Setting: FY 1992

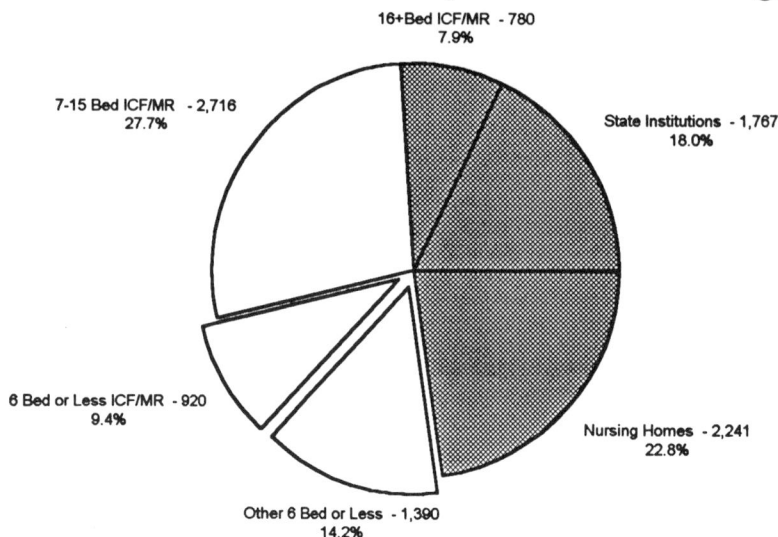

16+Bed ICF/MR - 780
7.9%

7-15 Bed ICF/MR - 2,716
27.7%

State Institutions - 1,767
18.0%

6 Bed or Less ICF/MR - 920
9.4%

Nursing Homes - 2,241
22.8%

Other 6 Bed or Less - 1,390
14.2%

Total Served: 9,814

## Persons Served by Residential Setting:1986-92

|  | 1986 | 1987 | 1988 | 1989 | 1990 | 1991 | 1992 |
|---|---|---|---|---|---|---|---|
| CONGREGATE 16 + BED SETTINGS | 6,422 | 5,970 | 5,053 | 5,192 | 5,133 | 4,998 | 4,788 |
| Nursing Homes | 3,702 | 3,355 | 2,500 | 2,435 | 2,371 | 2,306 | 2,241 |
| State Institutions | 2,114 | 2,009 | 1,945 | 2,038 | 1,983 | 1,912 | 1,767 |
| Private 16+Bed ICF/MR | 606 | 606 | 608 | 719 | 779 | 780 | 780 |
| Other 16+Bed Residential | 0 | 0 | 0 | 0 | 0 | 0 | 0 |
| 15 BED OR LESS RESIDENTIAL SETTINGS | 1,858 | 2,518 | 3,137 | NA | 4,527 | 4,829 | 5,026 |
| Public 7-15 Bed ICF/MR | 0 | 0 | 0 | 0 | 0 | 0 | 0 |
| Private 7-15 Bed ICF/MR | 1,858 | 2,036 | 2,418 | 2,873 | 3,327 | 3,474 | 2,716 |
| Other 7-15 Bed Residential |  | 482 | 719 | 960 | 0 | 0 | 0 |
| Public 6 Bed or Less ICF/MR |  | 0 | 0 | 0 | 0 | 0 | 0 |
| Private 6 Bed or Less ICF/MR |  | 0 | 0 | 0 | NA | NA | 920 |
| Other 6 Bed or Less Residential |  | 0 | 0 | 0 | 1,200 | 1,355 | 1,390 |
| TOTAL PERSONS SERVED | 8,280 | 8,488 | 8,190 | NA | 9,660 | 9,827 | 9,814 |

## Persons Served in Non-Residential Community Services:1986-92

|  | 1986 | 1987 | 1988 | 1989 | 1990 | 1991 | 1992 |
|---|---|---|---|---|---|---|---|
| DAY/WORK PROGRAMS | 9,366 | 9,181 | 10,263 | NA | 10,495 | NA | 10,642 |
| Sheltered Employment/Work Activity | 8,282 | 7,996 | 8,251 | NA | 8,234 | NA | 7,726 |
| Day Habilitation ("Day Training") | 1,084 | 1,185 | 1,415 | NA | 1,553 | NA | 2,035 |
| Supported/Competitive Employment | 0 | 0 | 597 | NA | 708 | NA | 881 |
| CASE MANAGEMENT | 14,872 | 15,910 | 16,896 | NA | 9,395 | NA | 10,011 |
| HCBS WAIVER | 0 | 0 | 0 | 0 | 3 | 11 | 28 |
| MODEL 50/200 WAIVER | 0 | 0 | 0 | 0 | 0 | 0 | 0 |

*Source:*
Institute on Disability and Human Development (UAP),
University of Illinois at Chicago, 1994

# INDIANA

## Community Services: FY 1992 Revenue Sources

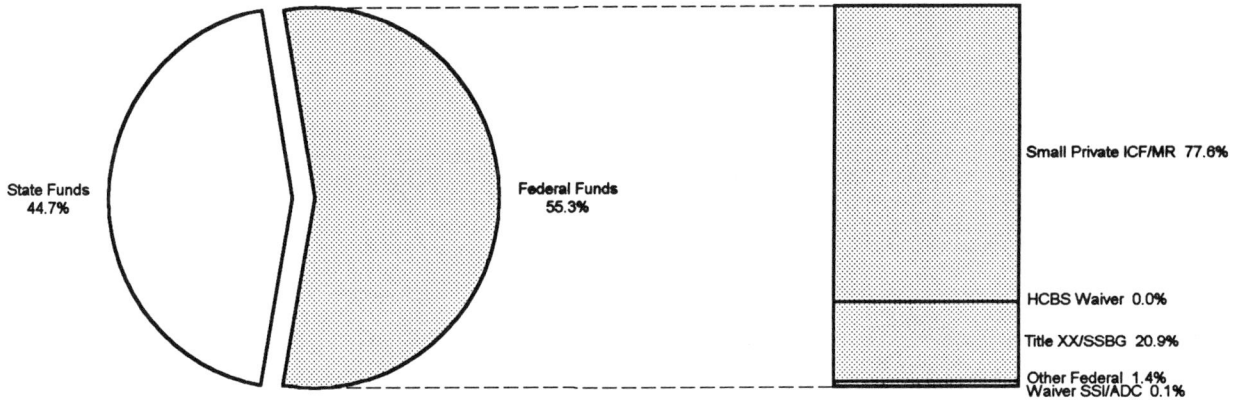

State Funds
44.7%

Federal Funds
55.3%

Small Private ICF/MR  77.6%

HCBS Waiver  0.0%

Title XX/SSBG  20.9%

Other Federal  1.4%
Waiver SSI/ADC  0.1%

### Total Funds: $199.1 Million

## Family Support Initiatives*

| | 1986 | 1987 | 1988 | 1989 | 1990 | 1991 | 1992 |
|---|---|---|---|---|---|---|---|
| **FAMILY SUPPORT: TOTAL SPENDING** | $240,501 | $326,234 | $370,542 | NA | NA | $502,350 | $502,350 |
| **Total # of Families Supported** | 585 | 800 | 1,000 | NA | NA | 1,500 | 1,500 |
| A. Financial Subsidy/Payment | $0 | $0 | $0 | $0 | $0 | $0 | $0 |
| # of Families | 0 | 0 | 0 | 0 | 0 | 0 | 0 |
| B. Family Assistance Payments | $216,451 | $293,611 | $333,488 | NA | NA | $502,350 | $502,350 |
| # of Families | | | | NA | NA | 1,500 | 1,500 |
| C. Other Family Support Payments | $24,050 | $32,623 | $37,054 | NA | NA | NA | NA |
| # of Families | NA | NA | NA | NA | NA | NA | NA |

## Other Community Services Initiatives*

| | 1986 | 1987 | 1988 | 1989 | 1990 | 1991 | 1992 |
|---|---|---|---|---|---|---|---|
| **AGING/DD SPENDING** | $0 | $0 | $140,877 | $0 | $0 | $0 | $0 |
| # of Persons Served | 0 | 0 | 22 | 0 | 0 | 0 | 0 |
| **ASSISTIVE TECHNOLOGY SPENDING** | | | | | | | $0 |
| # of Persons Served | | | | | | | 0 |
| **EARLY INTERVENTION SPENDING** | $0 | $0 | $1,372,351 | NA | $5,000,000 | NA | $6,000,000 |
| # of Persons Served | $0 | $0 | NA | NA | 1,573 | NA | 2,489 |
| **PERSONAL ASSISTANCE SPENDING** | | | | | | | $0 |
| # of Persons Served | | | | | | | 0 |
| **SUPPORTED EMPLOYMENT SPENDING** | $0 | $0 | $286,580 | NA | NA | NA | $2,100,000 |
| # of Persons Served | 0 | 0 | 597 | NA | 708 | NA | 881 |
| **SUPPORTED LIVING SPENDING** | | | | | | | $0 |
| # of Persons Served | | | | | | | 0 |

*Expenditures associated with Special Community Initiatives are a subset of funding within the community services component of the state's chart series and spreadsheet; Family Support Client figures may include duplicate client counts; HCBS Waiver counts include Waiver case management numbers.
0= Services not provided in the state; NA= Data not available from state; blank= Services not applicable (eg. CSLA prior to authorization, Special Community Initiatives prior to request for data by this study)

Source:
Institute on Disability and Human Development (UAP),
University of Illinois at Chicago, 1994

# INDIANA

## Large Congregate Care Facilities: FY 1992 Revenue Sources*

### Private 16+Bed Settings

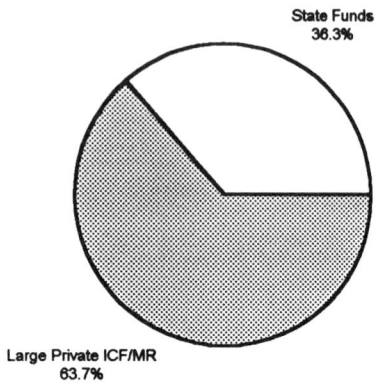

State Funds
36.3%

Large Private ICF/MR
63.7%

Total Funds: $32.5 Million

### Public Institutions

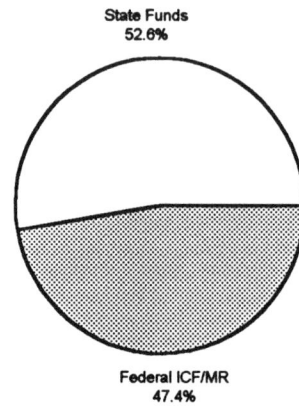

State Funds
52.6%

Federal ICF/MR
47.4%

Total Funds: $137.5 Million

*Excludes nursing homes

## Average Daily Residents in Institutions

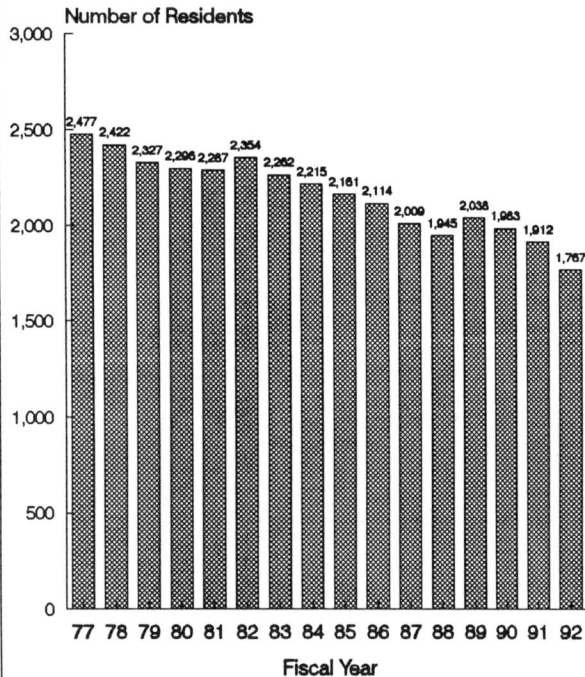

Number of Residents

| Fiscal Year | Residents |
|---|---|
| 77 | 2,477 |
| 78 | 2,422 |
| 79 | 2,327 |
| 80 | 2,296 |
| 81 | 2,287 |
| 82 | 2,354 |
| 83 | 2,262 |
| 84 | 2,215 |
| 85 | 2,161 |
| 86 | 2,114 |
| 87 | 2,009 |
| 88 | 1,945 |
| 89 | 2,038 |
| 90 | 1,983 |
| 91 | 1,912 |
| 92 | 1,767 |

Fiscal Year

## Institutional Daily Costs Per Resident

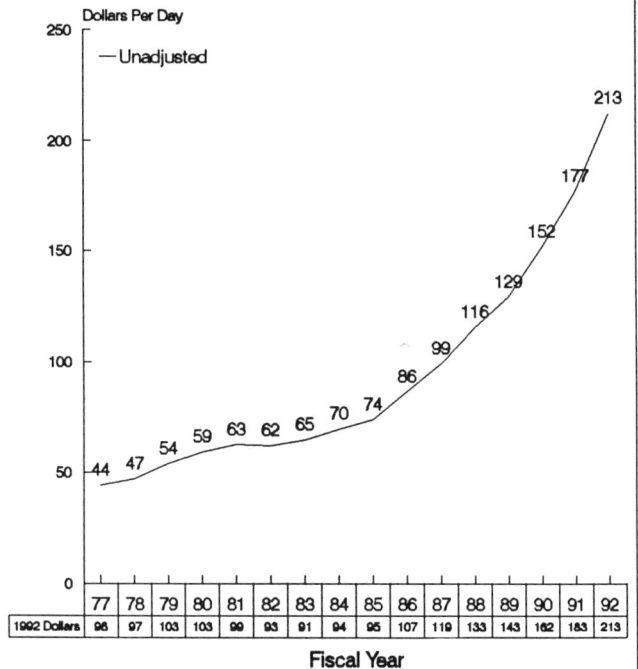

Dollars Per Day

— Unadjusted

| Fiscal Year | Unadjusted | 1992 Dollars |
|---|---|---|
| 77 | 44 | 98 |
| 78 | 47 | 97 |
| 79 | 54 | 103 |
| 80 | 59 | 103 |
| 81 | 63 | 99 |
| 82 | 62 | 93 |
| 83 | 65 | 91 |
| 84 | 70 | 94 |
| 85 | 74 | 95 |
| 86 | 86 | 107 |
| 87 | 99 | 119 |
| 88 | 116 | 133 |
| 89 | 129 | 143 |
| 90 | 152 | 162 |
| 91 | 177 | 183 |
| 92 | 213 | 213 |

Fiscal Year

*Source:*
Institute on Disability and Human Development (UAP),
University of Illinois at Chicago, 1994

# INDIANA FISCAL EFFORT

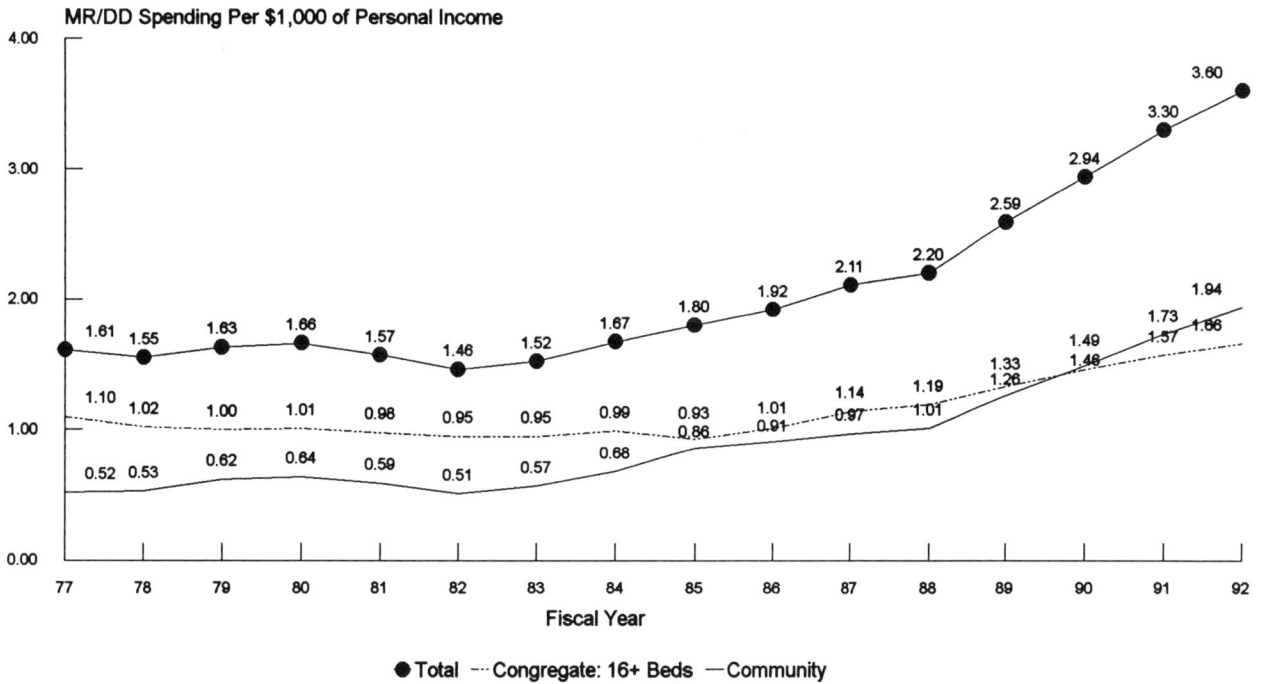

MR/DD Spending Per $1,000 of Personal Income

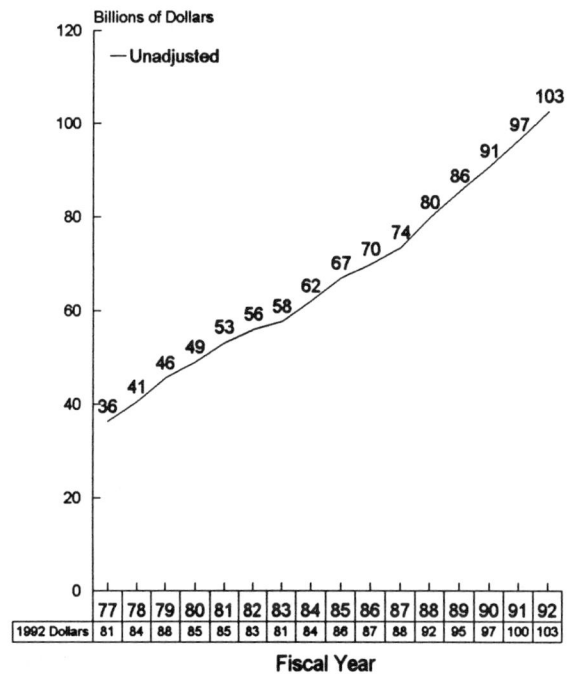

| | | | | | | | | | | | | | | | | |
|---|---|---|---|---|---|---|---|---|---|---|---|---|---|---|---|---|

Total values: 1.61, 1.55, 1.63, 1.66, 1.57, 1.46, 1.52, 1.67, 1.80, 1.92, 2.11, 2.20, 2.59, 2.94, 3.30, 3.60

Congregate: 16+ Beds values: 1.10, 1.02, 1.00, 1.01, 0.98, 0.95, 0.95, 0.99, 0.93, 0.86, 1.01, 0.91, 1.14, 0.97, 1.19, 1.01, 1.33, 1.26, 1.49, 1.46, 1.73, 1.57, 1.66, 1.94

Community values: 0.52, 0.53, 0.62, 0.64, 0.59, 0.51, 0.57, 0.68

Fiscal Year: 77 78 79 80 81 82 83 84 85 86 87 88 89 90 91 92

● Total  --- Congregate: 16+ Beds  — Community

## Total MR/DD Spending

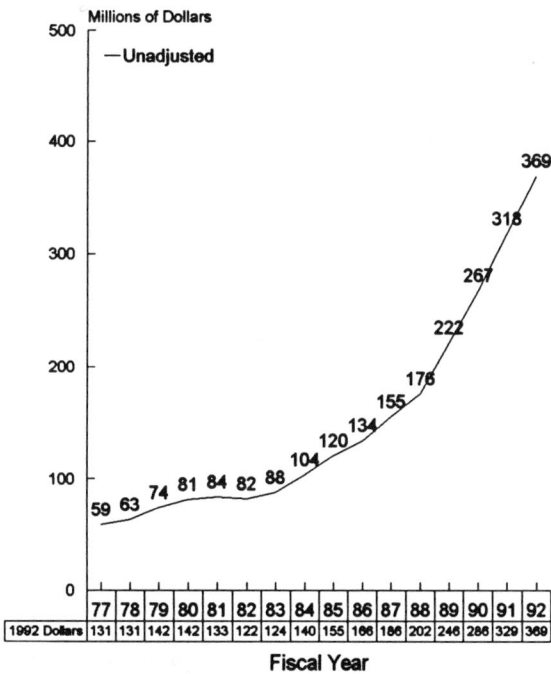

Millions of Dollars
— Unadjusted

Values: 369, 315, 267, 222, 176, 155, 134, 120, 104, 88, 82, 84, 81, 74, 63, 59

| Fiscal Year | 77 | 78 | 79 | 80 | 81 | 82 | 83 | 84 | 85 | 86 | 87 | 88 | 89 | 90 | 91 | 92 |
|---|---|---|---|---|---|---|---|---|---|---|---|---|---|---|---|---|
| 1992 Dollars | 131 | 131 | 142 | 142 | 133 | 122 | 124 | 140 | 155 | 166 | 186 | 202 | 246 | 286 | 329 | 369 |

Fiscal Year

## Personal Income

Billions of Dollars
— Unadjusted

Values: 103, 97, 91, 86, 80, 74, 70, 67, 62, 58, 56, 53, 49, 46, 41, 36

| Fiscal Year | 77 | 78 | 79 | 80 | 81 | 82 | 83 | 84 | 85 | 86 | 87 | 88 | 89 | 90 | 91 | 92 |
|---|---|---|---|---|---|---|---|---|---|---|---|---|---|---|---|---|
| 1992 Dollars | 81 | 84 | 88 | 85 | 85 | 83 | 81 | 84 | 86 | 87 | 88 | 92 | 95 | 97 | 100 | 103 |

Fiscal Year

*Source:*
Institute on Disability and Human Development (UAP),
University of Illinois at Chicago, 1994

# INDIANA

## Financial Support for MR/DD Services: FY 1977-92

| | 1977 | 1978 | 1979 | 1980 | 1981 | 1982 | 1983 | 1984 |
|---|---|---|---|---|---|---|---|---|
| **TOTAL FUNDS** | $58,666,185 | $63,107,635 | $74,002,400 | $81,341,532 | $83,661,426 | $81,971,361 | $87,924,305 | $103,655,049 |
| **CONGREGATE 16+ BEDS** | 39,875,100 | 41,508,673 | 45,718,400 | 49,757,532 | 52,223,276 | 53,355,481 | 54,879,805 | 61,323,577 |
| INSTITUTIONAL SERVICES FUND | 39,875,100 | 41,508,673 | 45,718,400 | 49,757,532 | 52,223,276 | 53,355,481 | 53,428,545 | 56,423,526 |
| STATE FUNDS | 38,833,000 | 36,108,025 | 34,548,000 | 35,553,647 | 35,434,324 | 31,356,105 | 33,207,912 | 33,088,878 |
| General Funds | 38,833,000 | 36,108,025 | 34,529,400 | 35,535,947 | 35,417,324 | 31,338,105 | 33,189,912 | 33,088,878 |
| Local | 0 | 0 | 0 | 0 | 0 | 0 | 0 | 0 |
| Other State Funds | 0 | 0 | 18,600 | 17,700 | 17,000 | 18,000 | 18,000 | 0 |
| FEDERAL FUNDS | 1,042,100 | 5,400,648 | 11,170,400 | 14,203,885 | 16,788,952 | 21,999,376 | 20,220,633 | 23,334,648 |
| Federal ICF/MR | 362,000 | 5,062,848 | 11,002,100 | 14,086,985 | 16,697,952 | 21,934,276 | 20,155,533 | 23,269,548 |
| Title XX / SSBG Funds | 0 | 0 | 0 | 0 | 0 | 0 | 0 | 0 |
| Other Federal Funds | 680,100 | 337,800 | 168,300 | 116,900 | 91,000 | 65,100 | 65,100 | 65,100 |
| LARGE PRIVATE RESIDENTIAL | 0 | 0 | 0 | 0 | 0 | 0 | 1,451,260 | 4,900,051 |
| STATE FUNDS | 0 | 0 | 0 | 0 | 0 | 0 | 627,960 | 2,002,651 |
| General Funds | 0 | 0 | 0 | 0 | 0 | 0 | 627,960 | 2,002,651 |
| Other State Funds | 0 | 0 | 0 | 0 | 0 | 0 | 0 | 0 |
| Local/County Overmatch | 0 | 0 | 0 | 0 | 0 | 0 | 0 | 0 |
| FEDERAL FUNDS | 0 | 0 | 0 | 0 | 0 | 0 | 823,300 | 2,897,400 |
| Large Private ICF/MR | 0 | 0 | 0 | 0 | 0 | 0 | 823,300 | 2,897,400 |
| **COMMUNITY SERVICES FUNDS** | 18,791,085 | 21,598,962 | 28,284,000 | 31,584,000 | 31,438,150 | 28,615,880 | 33,044,500 | 42,331,472 |
| STATE FUNDS | 9,024,000 | 9,600,000 | 12,397,000 | 13,655,000 | 13,791,043 | 10,535,849 | 14,601,800 | 21,148,000 |
| General Funds | 6,074,000 | 5,800,000 | 7,747,000 | 8,155,000 | 8,913,043 | 4,969,849 | 9,495,000 | 15,318,000 |
| Other State Funds | 2,950,000 | 3,800,000 | 4,650,000 | 5,500,000 | 4,878,000 | 5,566,000 | 5,106,800 | 5,830,000 |
| Local/County Overmatch | 0 | 0 | 0 | 0 | 0 | 0 | 0 | 0 |
| SSI State Supplement | 0 | 0 | 0 | 0 | 0 | 0 | 0 | 0 |
| FEDERAL FUNDS | 9,767,085 | 11,998,962 | 15,887,000 | 17,929,000 | 17,647,107 | 18,080,031 | 18,442,700 | 21,183,472 |
| ICF/MR Funds | 0 | 0 | 1,437,000 | 1,119,000 | 2,054,000 | 776,000 | 1,922,700 | 2,747,600 |
| Small Public | 0 | 0 | 0 | 0 | 0 | 0 | 0 | 0 |
| Small Private | 0 | 0 | 1,437,000 | 1,119,000 | 2,054,000 | 776,000 | 1,922,700 | 2,747,600 |
| HCBS Waiver | 0 | 0 | 0 | 0 | 0 | 0 | 0 | 0 |
| Model 50/200 Waiver | 0 | 0 | 0 | 0 | 0 | 0 | 0 | 0 |
| Other Title XIX Programs | 0 | 0 | 0 | 0 | 0 | 0 | 0 | 0 |
| Title XX / SSBG Funds | 8,850,000 | 11,400,000 | 13,950,000 | 16,500,000 | 14,633,000 | 16,697,000 | 15,320,000 | 17,491,000 |
| Other Federal Funds | 917,085 | 598,962 | 500,000 | 310,000 | 960,107 | 607,031 | 1,200,000 | 944,872 |
| Waiver Clients' SSI/ADC | 0 | 0 | 0 | 0 | 0 | 0 | 0 | 0 |

| | 1985 | 1986 | 1987 | 1988 | 1989 | 1990 | 1991 | 1992 |
|---|---|---|---|---|---|---|---|---|
| **TOTAL FUNDS** | $120,429,161 | $134,076,135 | $155,262,882 | $175,721,195 | $221,532,835 | $267,362,014 | $318,200,284 | $369,130,115 |
| **CONGREGATE 16+ BEDS** | 62,541,400 | 70,458,051 | 83,701,395 | 94,705,116 | 113,530,521 | 132,355,926 | 151,181,331 | 170,006,736 |
| INSTITUTIONAL SERVICES FUND | 58,123,245 | 66,596,215 | 72,754,753 | 82,272,357 | 96,069,772 | 109,867,187 | 123,664,601 | 137,462,016 |
| STATE FUNDS | 37,598,863 | 46,407,525 | 53,220,413 | 53,889,534 | 62,511,127 | 70,360,147 | 86,481,460 | 72,299,269 |
| General Funds | 37,593,098 | 46,388,155 | 53,201,043 | 53,886,534 | 62,511,127 | 70,360,147 | 86,478,260 | 72,296,069 |
| Local | 0 | 0 | 0 | 0 | 0 | 0 | 0 | 0 |
| Other State Funds | 5,765 | 19,370 | 19,370 | 3,000 | 0 | 0 | 3,200 | 3,200 |
| FEDERAL FUNDS | 20,524,382 | 20,188,690 | 19,534,340 | 28,382,823 | 33,558,645 | 39,507,040 | 37,183,141 | 65,162,747 |
| Federal ICF/MR | 20,506,604 | 20,175,302 | 19,521,340 | 28,377,323 | 33,558,645 | 39,507,040 | 36,985,142 | 65,112,748 |
| Title XX / SSBG Funds | 0 | 0 | 0 | 0 | 0 | 0 | 0 | 0 |
| Other Federal Funds | 17,778 | 13,388 | 13,000 | 5,500 | 0 | 0 | 197,999 | 49,999 |
| LARGE PRIVATE RESIDENTIAL | 4,418,155 | 3,861,836 | 10,946,642 | 12,432,759 | 17,460,749 | 22,488,739 | 27,516,730 | 32,544,720 |
| STATE FUNDS | 1,770,355 | 1,463,636 | 4,061,204 | 4,536,714 | 6,336,506 | 8,152,168 | 10,079,378 | 11,813,733 |
| General Funds | 1,770,355 | 1,463,636 | 4,061,204 | 4,536,714 | 6,336,506 | 8,152,168 | 10,079,378 | 11,813,733 |
| Other State Funds | 0 | 0 | 0 | 0 | 0 | 0 | 0 | 0 |
| Local/County Overmatch | 0 | 0 | 0 | 0 | 0 | 0 | 0 | 0 |
| FEDERAL FUNDS | 2,647,800 | 2,398,200 | 6,885,438 | 7,896,045 | 11,124,243 | 14,336,571 | 17,437,352 | 20,730,987 |
| Large Private ICF/MR | 2,647,800 | 2,398,200 | 6,885,438 | 7,896,045 | 11,124,243 | 14,336,571 | 17,437,352 | 20,730,987 |
| **COMMUNITY SERVICES FUNDS** | 57,887,761 | 63,618,084 | 71,561,487 | 81,016,079 | 108,002,314 | 135,006,088 | 167,018,953 | 199,123,379 |
| STATE FUNDS | 28,590,561 | 30,745,106 | 36,745,857 | 40,687,334 | 48,612,982 | 56,577,601 | 73,184,176 | 89,041,061 |
| General Funds | 22,865,561 | 25,095,106 | 31,268,064 | 35,179,857 | 34,121,013 | 33,101,141 | 47,843,679 | 61,836,527 |
| Other State Funds | 5,725,000 | 5,650,000 | 5,477,793 | 5,507,477 | 14,491,969 | 23,476,460 | 25,340,497 | 27,204,534 |
| Local/County Overmatch | 0 | 0 | 0 | 0 | 0 | 0 | 0 | 0 |
| SSI State Supplement | 0 | 0 | 0 | 0 | 0 | 0 | 0 | 0 |
| FEDERAL FUNDS | 29,297,200 | 32,872,978 | 34,815,630 | 40,328,745 | 59,389,332 | 78,428,487 | 93,834,777 | 110,082,318 |
| ICF/MR Funds | 10,394,000 | 14,564,400 | 17,210,287 | 22,663,114 | 38,406,516 | 54,112,503 | 69,378,346 | 85,409,209 |
| Small Public | 0 | 0 | 0 | 0 | 0 | 0 | 0 | 0 |
| Small Private | 10,394,000 | 14,564,400 | 17,210,287 | 22,663,114 | 38,406,516 | 54,112,503 | 69,378,346 | 85,409,209 |
| HCBS Waiver | 0 | 0 | 0 | 0 | 0 | 2,736 | 6,007 | 36,357 |
| Model 50/200 Waiver | 0 | 0 | 0 | 0 | 0 | 0 | 0 | 0 |
| Other Title XIX Programs | 0 | 0 | 0 | 0 | 0 | 0 | 0 | 0 |
| Title XX / SSBG Funds | 17,821,079 | 16,950,000 | 16,433,380 | 16,522,432 | 19,661,216 | 22,800,000 | 22,900,000 | 23,000,000 |
| Other Federal Funds | 1,082,121 | 1,358,578 | 1,171,963 | 1,143,199 | 1,321,600 | 1,500,000 | 1,500,000 | 1,500,000 |
| Waiver Clients' SSI/ADC | 0 | 0 | 0 | 0 | 0 | 13,248 | 50,424 | 136,752 |

*Source:*
Institute on Disability and Human Development (UAP),
University of Illinois at Chicago, 1994

# IOWA

## MR/DD Spending for Congregate Residential & Community Services

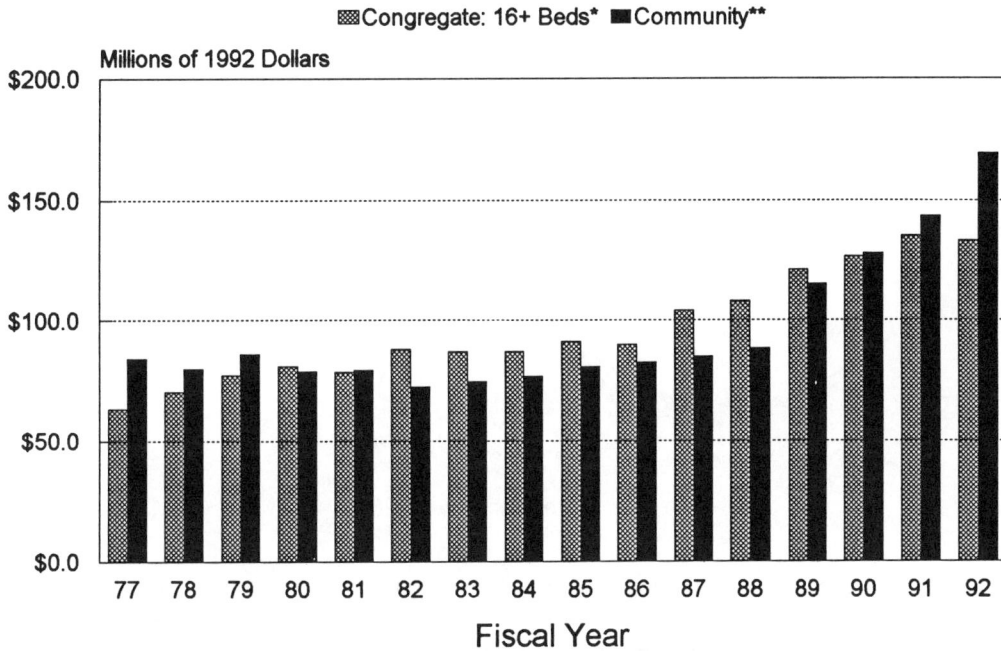

▨ Congregate: 16+ Beds*  ■ Community**

Millions of 1992 Dollars

Fiscal Year

*Excludes nursing homes; ** Includes resources for
15 bed or less residential settings & non-residential community services

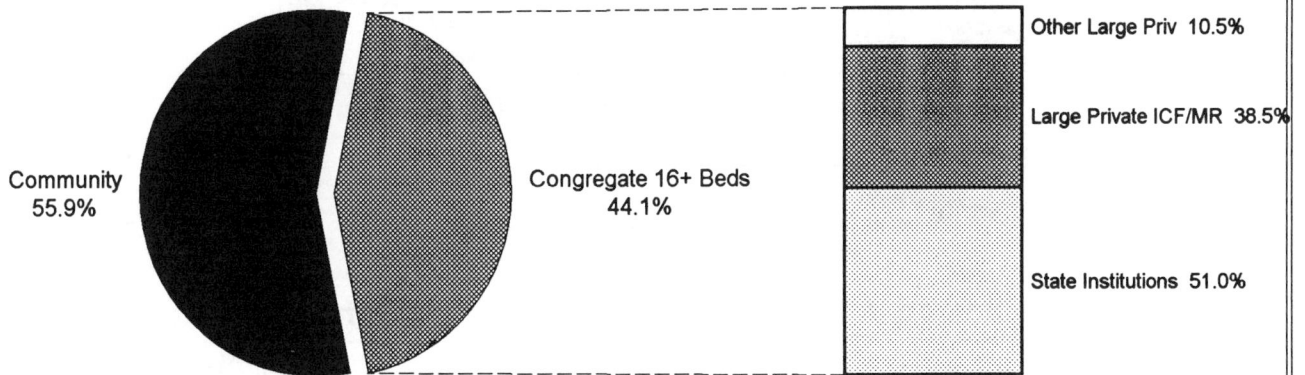

Community
55.9%

Congregate 16+ Beds
44.1%

Other Large Priv  10.5%

Large Private ICF/MR  38.5%

State Institutions  51.0%

FY 1992 Total Spending:
$302.5 Million

*Source:*
Institute on Disability and Human Development (UAP),
University of Illinois at Chicago, 1994

# IOWA

## Number of Persons Served by Residential Setting: FY 1992

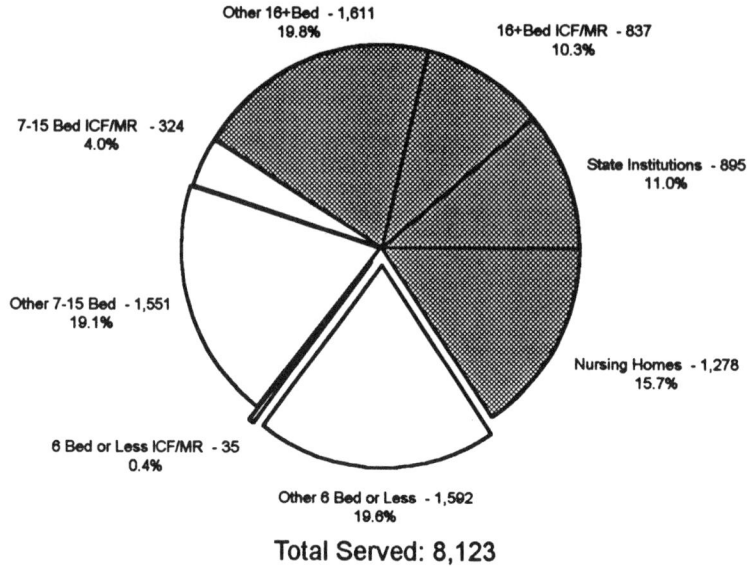

Other 16+Bed - 1,611
19.8%

16+Bed ICF/MR - 837
10.3%

7-15 Bed ICF/MR - 324
4.0%

State Institutions - 895
11.0%

Other 7-15 Bed - 1,551
19.1%

Nursing Homes - 1,278
15.7%

6 Bed or Less ICF/MR - 35
0.4%

Other 6 Bed or Less - 1,592
19.6%

Total Served: 8,123

## Persons Served by Residential Setting:1986-92

| | 1986 | 1987 | 1988 | 1989 | 1990 | 1991 | 1992 |
|---|---|---|---|---|---|---|---|
| CONGREGATE 16 + BED SETTINGS | NA | NA | 5,300 | 4,858 | 4,847 | 4,615 | 4,621 |
| Nursing Homes | NA | NA | 1,279 | 1,125 | 1,394 | 1,212 | 1,278 |
| State Institutions | 1,161 | 1,113 | 1,062 | 1,043 | 986 | 946 | 895 |
| Private 16+Bed ICF/MR | 565 | 692 | 819 | 800 | 821 | 837 | 837 |
| Other 16+Bed Residential | NA | 1,980 | 2,140 | 1,890 | 1,646 | 1,620 | 1,611 |
| 15 BED OR LESS RESIDENTIAL SETTINGS | 39 | 1,487 | 1,697 | 1,857 | 2,627 | 3,050 | 3,502 |
| Public 7-15 Bed ICF/MR | 0 | 0 | 0 | 0 | 0 | 0 | 0 |
| Private 7-15 Bed ICF/MR | 39 | 53 | 67 | 75 | 189 | 240 | 324 |
| Other 7-15 Bed Residential | NA | 1,434 | 1,630 | 1,782 | 1,409 | 1,469 | 1,551 |
| Public 6 Bed or Less ICF/MR | 0 | 0 | 0 | 0 | 0 | 0 | 0 |
| Private 6 Bed or Less ICF/MR | 0 | 0 | 0 | 0 | 0 | 0 | 35 |
| Other 6 Bed or Less Residential | | | | | 1,029 | 1,341 | 1,592 |
| TOTAL PERSONS SERVED | NA | NA | 6,997 | 6,715 | 7,474 | 7,665 | 8,123 |

## Persons Served in Non-Residential Community Services:1986-92

| | 1986 | 1987 | 1988 | 1989 | 1990 | 1991 | 1992 |
|---|---|---|---|---|---|---|---|
| DAY/WORK PROGRAMS | NA | 3,348 | 3,683 | NA | NA | NA | NA |
| Sheltered Employment/Work Activity | NA | 1,306 | 1,437 | 4,548 | 5,019 | 5,678 | 5,456 |
| Day Habilitation ("Day Training") | NA | 2,042 | 2,246 | NA | NA | NA | NA |
| Supported/Competitive Employment | 0 | 0 | 0 | 0 | 460 | 653 | 1,052 |
| CASE MANAGEMENT | 0 | 7,859 | 8,495 | 10,309 | 12,498 | 13,348 | 13,896 |
| HCBS WAIVER | 0 | 0 | 0 | 0 | 0 | 0 | 0 |
| MODEL 50/200 WAIVER | 2 | 3 | 8 | 85 | 161 | 183 | 179 |

*Source:*
Institute on Disability and Human Development (UAP),
University of Illinois at Chicago, 1994

# IOWA

## Community Services: FY 1992 Revenue Sources

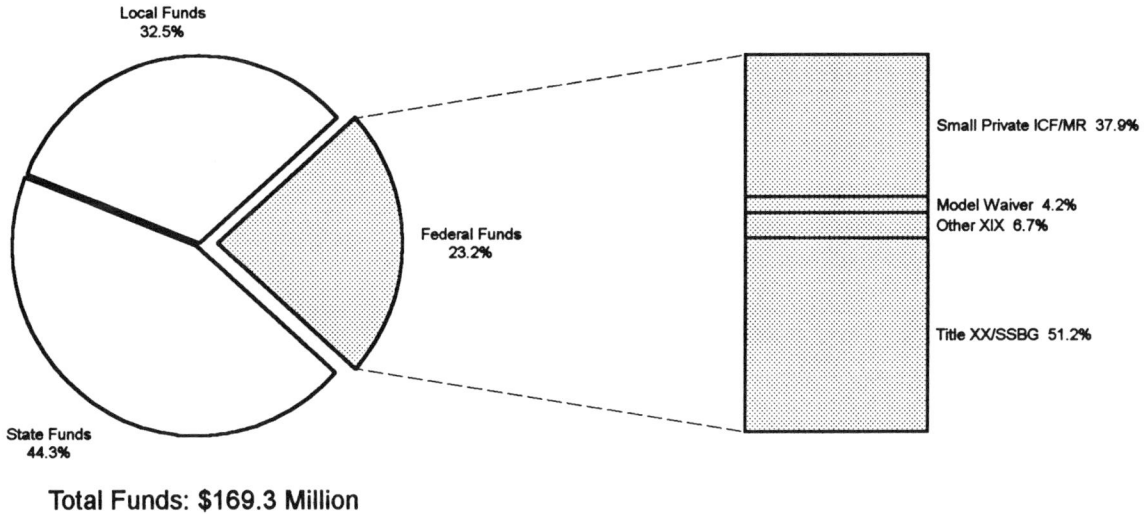

Local Funds
32.5%

State Funds
44.3%

Federal Funds
23.2%

Small Private ICF/MR 37.9%

Model Waiver 4.2%
Other XIX 6.7%

Title XX/SSBG 51.2%

Total Funds: $169.3 Million

## Family Support Initiatives*

|  | 1986 | 1987 | 1988 | 1989 | 1990 | 1991 | 1992 |
|---|---|---|---|---|---|---|---|
| FAMILY SUPPORT: TOTAL SPENDING | $0 | $0 | $0 | $95,000 | $430,000 | $497,000 | $708,000 |
| Total # of Families Supported | 0 | 0 | 0 | 60 | 166 | 182 | 235 |
| A. Financial Subsidy/Payment | $0 | $0 | $0 | $75,000 | $400,000 | $442,000 | $653,000 |
| # of Families | 0 | 0 | 0 | 40 | 136 | 137 | 193 |
| B. Family Assistance Payments | $0 | $0 | $0 | $0 | $0 | $0 | $0 |
| # of Families | 0 | 0 | 0 | 0 | 0 | 0 | 0 |
| C. Other Family Support Payments | $0 | $0 | $0 | $20,000 | $30,000 | $55,000 | $55,000 |
| # of Families | 0 | 0 | 0 | 20 | 30 | 45 | 42 |

## Other Community Services Initiatives*

|  | 1986 | 1987 | 1988 | 1989 | 1990 | 1991 | 1992 |
|---|---|---|---|---|---|---|---|
| AGING/DD SPENDING | $0 | $0 | $0 | $0 | $0 | $0 | $0 |
| # of Persons Served | 0 | 0 | 0 | 0 | 0 | 0 | 0 |
| ASSISTIVE TECHNOLOGY SPENDING |  |  |  |  |  |  | $0 |
| # of Persons Served |  |  |  |  |  |  | 0 |
| EARLY INTERVENTION SPENDING | $0 | $0 | $0 | $0 | $0 | $0 | $0 |
| # of Persons Served | 0 | 0 | 0 | 0 | 0 | 0 | 0 |
| PERSONAL ASSISTANCE SPENDING |  |  |  |  |  |  | $0 |
| # of Persons Served |  |  |  |  |  |  | 0 |
| SUPPORTED EMPLOYMENT SPENDING | $0 | $0 | $0 | $0 | $1,167,003 | $1,315,293 | $2,860,191 |
| # of Persons Served | 0 | 0 | 0 | 0 | 460 | 653 | 1,052 |
| SUPPORTED LIVING SPENDING |  |  |  |  |  |  | $1,171,284 |
| # of Persons Served |  |  |  |  |  |  | 1,380 |

*Expenditures associated with Special Community Initiatives are a subset of funding within the community services component of the state's chart series and spreadsheet; Family Support Client figures may include duplicate client counts; HCBS Waiver counts include Waiver case management numbers.
0= Services not provided in the state; NA= Data not available from state; blank= Services not applicable (eg. CSLA prior to authorization, Special Community Initiatives prior to request for data by this study)

Source:
Institute on Disability and Human Development (UAP),
University of Illinois at Chicago, 1994

# IOWA

## Large Congregate Care Facilities: FY 1992 Revenue Sources*

### Private 16+Bed Settings

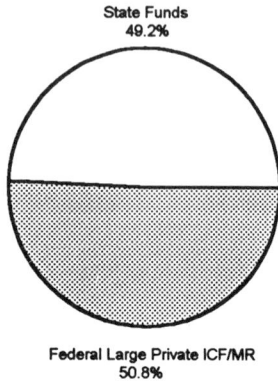

State Funds
49.2%

Federal Large Private ICF/MR
50.8%

Total Funds: $65.3 Million

### Public Institutions

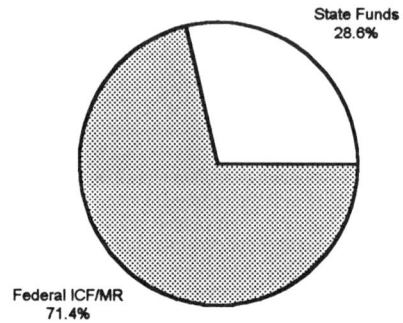

State Funds
28.6%

Federal ICF/MR
71.4%

Total Funds: $67.9 Million

*Excludes nursing homes

## Average Daily Residents in Institutions

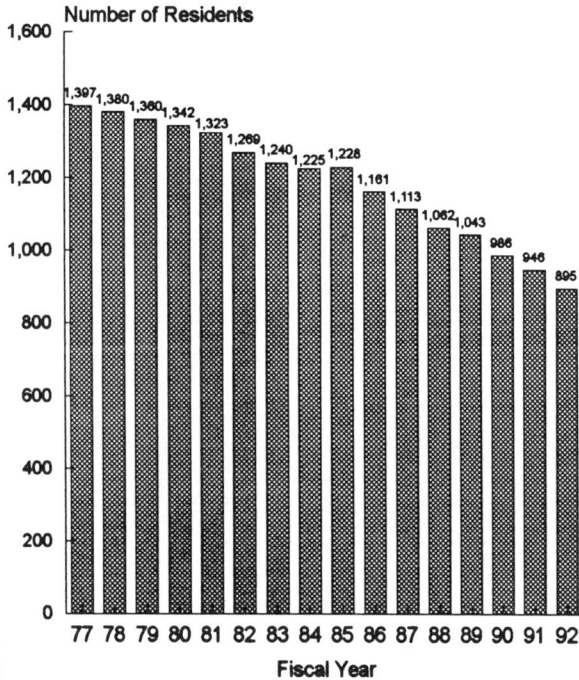

Number of Residents

| Fiscal Year | Number of Residents |
|---|---|
| 77 | 1,397 |
| 78 | 1,380 |
| 79 | 1,360 |
| 80 | 1,342 |
| 81 | 1,323 |
| 82 | 1,269 |
| 83 | 1,240 |
| 84 | 1,225 |
| 85 | 1,228 |
| 86 | 1,161 |
| 87 | 1,113 |
| 88 | 1,062 |
| 89 | 1,043 |
| 90 | 986 |
| 91 | 946 |
| 92 | 895 |

## Institutional Daily Costs Per Resident

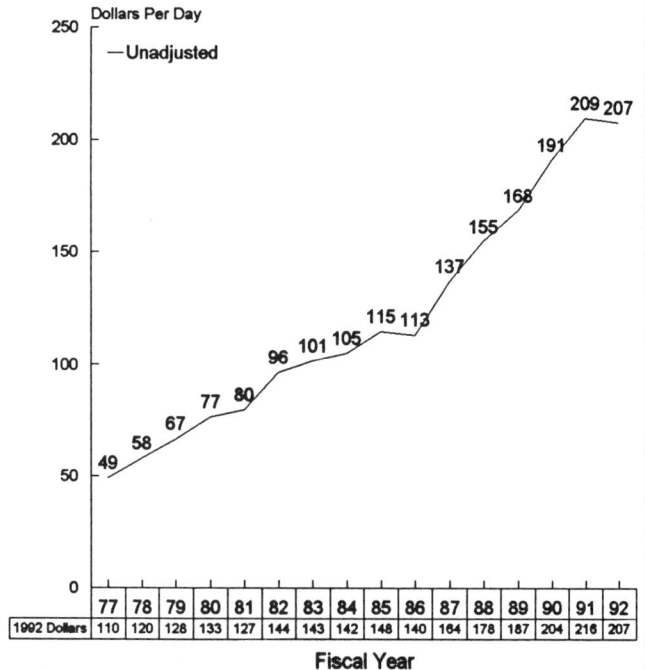

Dollars Per Day

—Unadjusted

| Fiscal Year | Unadjusted | 1992 Dollars |
|---|---|---|
| 77 | 49 | 110 |
| 78 | 58 | 120 |
| 79 | 67 | 128 |
| 80 | 80 | 133 |
| 81 | 77 | 127 |
| 82 | 96 | 144 |
| 83 | 101 | 143 |
| 84 | 105 | 142 |
| 85 | 115 | 148 |
| 86 | 113 | 140 |
| 87 | 137 | 164 |
| 88 | 155 | 178 |
| 89 | 168 | 187 |
| 90 | 191 | 204 |
| 91 | 209 | 216 |
| 92 | 207 | 207 |

*Source:*
Institute on Disability and Human Development (UAP),
University of Illinois at Chicago, 1994

# IOWA FISCAL EFFORT

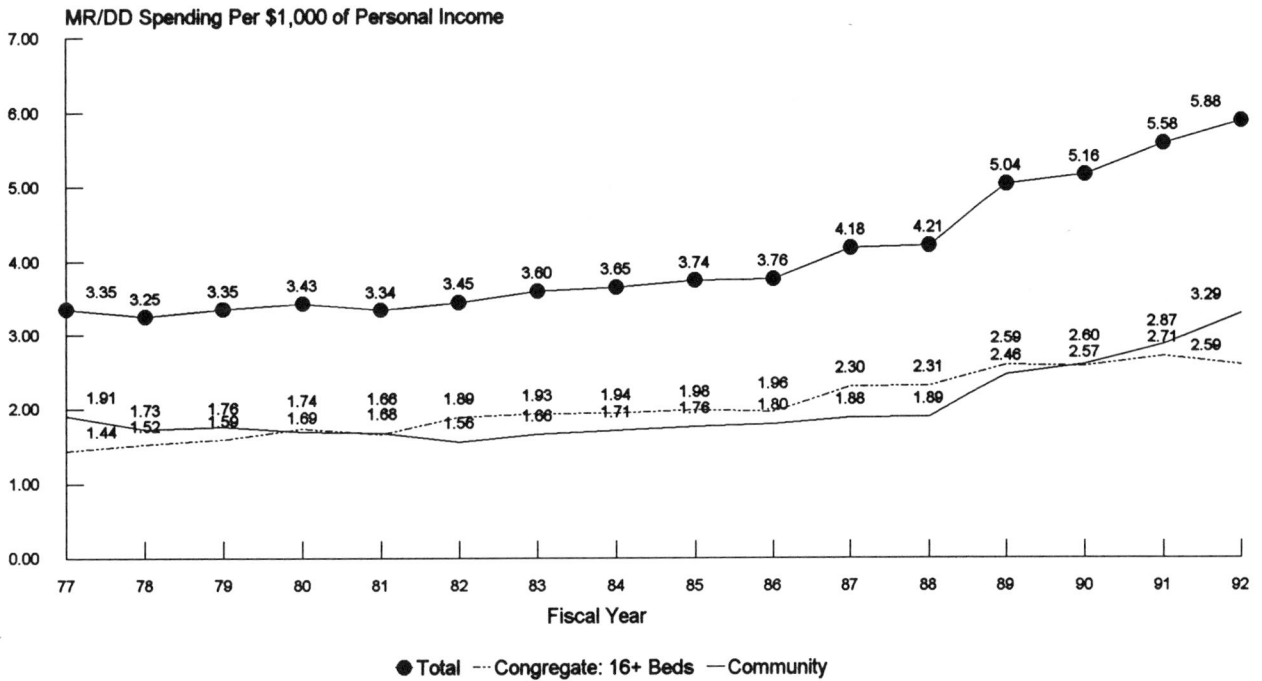

MR/DD Spending Per $1,000 of Personal Income

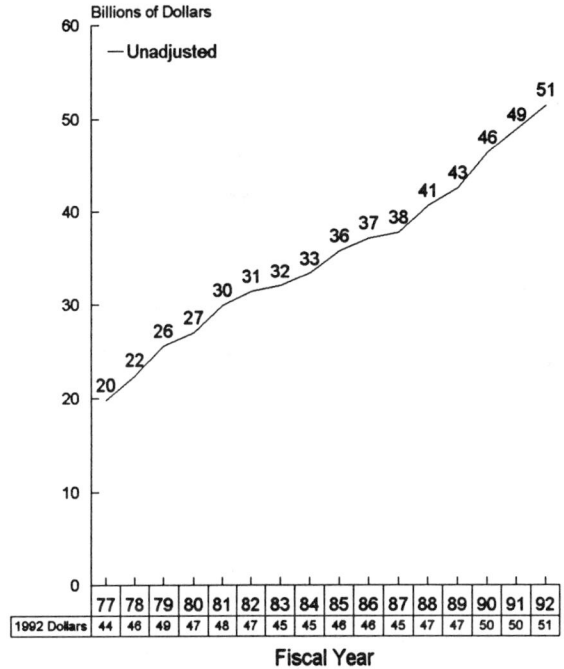

**Total** (●): 3.35, 3.25, 3.35, 3.43, 3.34, 3.45, 3.60, 3.65, 3.74, 3.76, 4.18, 4.21, 5.04, 5.16, 5.58, 5.88

**Congregate: 16+ Beds** (---): 1.44, 1.52, 1.59, 1.69, 1.68, 1.56, 1.66, 1.71, 1.76, 1.80, 1.88, 1.89, 2.46, 2.57, 2.71, 2.59

**Community** (—): 1.91, 1.73, 1.76, 1.74, 1.66, 1.89, 1.93, 1.94, 1.98, 1.96, 2.30, 2.31, 2.59, 2.60, 2.87, 3.29

Fiscal Year

● Total  --- Congregate: 16+ Beds  — Community

## Total MR/DD Spending

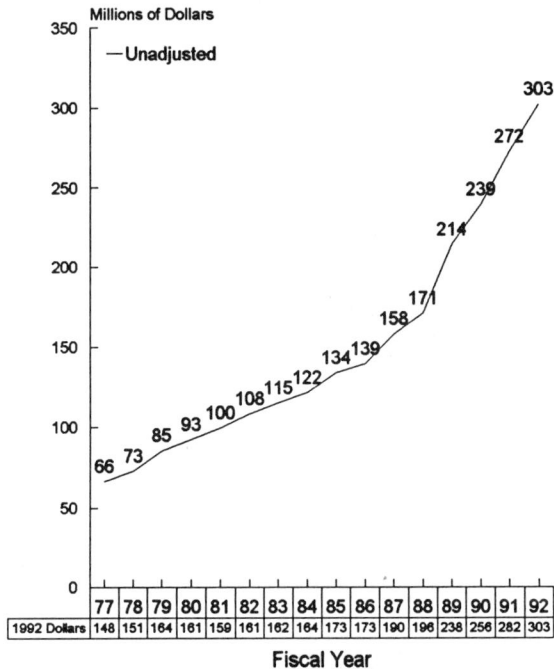

Millions of Dollars

— Unadjusted

66, 73, 85, 93, 100, 108, 115, 122, 134, 139, 158, 171, 214, 239, 272, 303

| | 77 | 78 | 79 | 80 | 81 | 82 | 83 | 84 | 85 | 86 | 87 | 88 | 89 | 90 | 91 | 92 |
|---|---|---|---|---|---|---|---|---|---|---|---|---|---|---|---|---|
| 1992 Dollars | 148 | 151 | 164 | 161 | 159 | 161 | 162 | 164 | 173 | 173 | 190 | 196 | 238 | 256 | 282 | 303 |

Fiscal Year

## Personal Income

Billions of Dollars

— Unadjusted

20, 22, 26, 27, 30, 31, 32, 33, 36, 37, 38, 41, 43, 46, 49, 51

| | 77 | 78 | 79 | 80 | 81 | 82 | 83 | 84 | 85 | 86 | 87 | 88 | 89 | 90 | 91 | 92 |
|---|---|---|---|---|---|---|---|---|---|---|---|---|---|---|---|---|
| 1992 Dollars | 44 | 46 | 49 | 47 | 48 | 47 | 45 | 45 | 46 | 46 | 45 | 47 | 47 | 50 | 50 | 51 |

Fiscal Year

*Source:*
Institute on Disability and Human Development (UAP),
University of Illinois at Chicago, 1994

# IOWA
## Financial Support for MR/DD Services: FY 1977-92

| | 1977 | 1978 | 1979 | 1980 | 1981 | 1982 | 1983 | 1984 |
|---|---|---|---|---|---|---|---|---|
| **TOTAL FUNDS** | $66,377,910 | $72,916,552 | $85,479,638 | $92,516,859 | $99,772,531 | $108,233,255 | $115,111,535 | $121,625,685 |
| **CONGREGATE 16+ BEDS** | 28,516,000 | 34,194,245 | 40,491,669 | 46,881,701 | 49,638,158 | 59,321,654 | 61,904,726 | 64,574,058 |
| INSTITUTIONAL SERVICES FUNDS | 25,075,000 | 29,276,700 | 33,117,000 | 37,599,000 | 38,455,800 | 44,655,900 | 45,908,400 | 47,007,300 |
| STATE FUNDS | 12,322,000 | 15,628,700 | 17,403,000 | 18,027,000 | 16,429,000 | 21,894,000 | 23,771,000 | 21,111,000 |
| General Funds | 0 | 0 | 0 | 0 | 0 | 0 | 0 | 0 |
| Local/County Overmatch | 0 | 0 | 0 | 0 | 0 | 0 | 0 | 0 |
| Other State Funds | 12,322,000 | 15,628,700 | 17,403,000 | 18,027,000 | 16,429,000 | 21,894,000 | 23,771,000 | 21,111,000 |
| FEDERAL FUNDS | 12,753,000 | 13,648,000 | 15,714,000 | 19,572,000 | 22,026,800 | 22,761,900 | 22,137,400 | 25,896,300 |
| Federal ICF/MR | 12,753,000 | 13,648,000 | 15,128,000 | 19,208,000 | 21,286,800 | 22,275,900 | 20,576,700 | 24,288,400 |
| Title XX / SSBG Funds | 0 | 0 | 0 | 0 | 0 | 0 | 0 | 0 |
| Other Federal Funds | 0 | 0 | 586,000 | 364,000 | 740,000 | 486,000 | 1,560,700 | 1,607,900 |
| LARGE PRIVATE RESIDENTIAL | 3,441,000 | 4,917,545 | 7,374,669 | 9,282,701 | 11,182,358 | 14,665,754 | 15,996,326 | 17,566,758 |
| STATE FUNDS | 3,441,000 | 4,348,545 | 5,779,669 | 6,806,701 | 7,903,358 | 9,855,754 | 10,861,326 | 12,022,758 |
| General Funds | 0 | 0 | 0 | 0 | 0 | 0 | 0 | 0 |
| Other State Funds | 0 | 499,545 | 1,474,669 | 1,991,701 | 2,517,358 | 3,831,754 | 4,124,326 | 4,486,758 |
| Local/County Overmatch | 3,441,000 | 3,849,000 | 4,305,000 | 4,815,000 | 5,386,000 | 6,024,000 | 6,737,000 | 7,536,000 |
| FEDERAL FUNDS | 0 | 569,000 | 1,595,000 | 2,476,000 | 3,279,000 | 4,810,000 | 5,135,000 | 5,544,000 |
| Large Private ICF/MR | 0 | 569,000 | 1,595,000 | 2,476,000 | 3,279,000 | 4,810,000 | 5,135,000 | 5,544,000 |
| **COMMUNITY SERVICES FUNDS** | 37,861,910 | 38,722,307 | 44,987,969 | 45,635,158 | 50,134,373 | 48,911,601 | 53,206,809 | 57,051,627 |
| STATE FUNDS | 24,473,455 | 25,423,628 | 29,484,122 | 30,410,508 | 33,643,574 | 33,604,694 | 37,351,838 | 40,911,993 |
| General Funds | 10,707,455 | 10,695,173 | 12,415,791 | 12,343,209 | 13,381,932 | 12,268,448 | 13,377,164 | 13,983,751 |
| Other State Funds | 5,361,000 | 5,152,455 | 6,153,331 | 5,621,299 | 6,067,642 | 5,152,246 | 5,512,674 | 5,873,242 |
| Local/County Overmatch | 8,364,000 | 9,538,000 | 10,878,000 | 12,406,000 | 14,148,000 | 16,135,000 | 18,401,000 | 20,985,000 |
| SSI State Supplement | 41,000 | 38,000 | 37,000 | 40,000 | 46,000 | 49,000 | 61,000 | 70,000 |
| FEDERAL FUNDS | 13,388,455 | 13,298,679 | 15,503,847 | 15,224,650 | 16,490,799 | 15,306,907 | 15,854,971 | 16,139,634 |
| ICF/MR Funds | 0 | 0 | 0 | 0 | 25,000 | 295,000 | 300,000 | 360,000 |
| Small Public | 0 | 0 | 0 | 0 | 0 | 0 | 0 | 0 |
| Small Private | 0 | 0 | 0 | 0 | 25,000 | 295,000 | 300,000 | 360,000 |
| HCBS Waiver | 0 | 0 | 0 | 0 | 0 | 0 | 0 | 0 |
| Model 50/200 Waiver | 0 | 0 | 0 | 0 | 0 | 0 | 0 | 0 |
| Other Title XIX Programs | 0 | 0 | 0 | 0 | 0 | 0 | 0 | 0 |
| Title XX / SSBG Funds | 13,388,455 | 13,298,679 | 15,503,847 | 15,224,650 | 16,465,799 | 14,667,907 | 15,190,971 | 15,415,634 |
| Other Federal Funds | 0 | 0 | 0 | 0 | 0 | 0 | 344,000 | 364,000 |
| Waiver Clients' SSI/ADC | 0 | 0 | 0 | 0 | 0 | 0 | 0 | 0 |

| | 1985 | 1986 | 1987 | 1988 | 1989 | 1990 | 1991 | 1992 |
|---|---|---|---|---|---|---|---|---|
| **TOTAL FUNDS** | $133,884,655 | $139,401,290 | $157,951,808 | $170,829,155 | $214,397,089 | $239,495,120 | $272,408,611 | $302,512,893 |
| **CONGREGATE 16+ BEDS** | 70,969,686 | 72,719,643 | 87,027,308 | 93,932,885 | 109,933,680 | 119,124,644 | 132,322,417 | 133,257,472 |
| INSTITUTIONAL SERVICES FUNDS | 51,382,700 | 47,904,300 | 55,538,384 | 60,082,000 | 64,044,842 | 68,725,016 | 72,321,713 | 67,962,492 |
| STATE FUNDS | 24,080,000 | 21,787,300 | 19,560,700 | 20,912,000 | 22,271,352 | 23,826,000 | 25,365,626 | 19,411,863 |
| General Funds | 0 | 0 | 0 | 0 | 0 | 0 | 0 | 0 |
| Local/County Overmatch | 0 | 0 | 0 | 0 | 0 | 0 | 0 | 0 |
| Other State Funds | 24,080,000 | 21,787,300 | 19,560,700 | 20,912,000 | 22,271,352 | 23,826,000 | 25,365,626 | 19,411,863 |
| FEDERAL FUNDS | 27,302,700 | 26,117,000 | 35,977,684 | 39,170,000 | 41,773,490 | 44,899,016 | 46,956,087 | 48,550,629 |
| Federal ICF/MR | 25,367,400 | 24,311,400 | 33,553,473 | 36,627,000 | 41,773,490 | 44,899,016 | 46,956,087 | 48,550,629 |
| Title XX / SSBG Funds | 0 | 0 | 0 | 0 | 0 | 0 | 0 | 0 |
| Other Federal Funds | 1,935,300 | 1,805,600 | 2,424,211 | 2,543,000 | 0 | 0 | 0 | 0 |
| LARGE PRIVATE RESIDENTIAL | 19,586,986 | 24,815,343 | 31,488,924 | 33,850,885 | 45,888,838 | 50,399,628 | 60,000,704 | 65,294,980 |
| STATE FUNDS | 13,422,986 | 15,891,643 | 18,747,924 | 19,580,885 | 29,383,165 | 26,223,428 | 29,673,281 | 32,155,612 |
| General Funds | 0 | 0 | 0 | 0 | 0 | 0 | 0 | 0 |
| Other State Funds | 4,994,986 | 6,464,643 | 8,486,924 | 8,686,885 | 9,735,461 | 14,425,429 | 17,666,600 | 18,136,151 |
| Local/County Overmatch | 8,428,000 | 9,427,000 | 10,261,000 | 10,894,000 | 19,647,704 | 11,797,999 | 12,006,681 | 14,019,461 |
| FEDERAL FUNDS | 6,164,000 | 8,923,700 | 12,741,000 | 14,270,000 | 16,505,673 | 24,176,200 | 30,327,423 | 33,139,368 |
| Large Private ICF/MR | 6,164,000 | 8,923,700 | 12,741,000 | 14,270,000 | 16,505,673 | 24,176,200 | 30,327,423 | 33,139,368 |
| **COMMUNITY SERVICES FUNDS** | 62,914,969 | 66,681,647 | 70,924,500 | 76,896,270 | 104,463,409 | 120,370,476 | 140,086,194 | 169,255,421 |
| STATE FUNDS | 45,174,053 | 48,659,887 | 50,362,818 | 55,198,995 | 78,552,378 | 91,347,320 | 108,071,300 | 129,983,271 |
| General Funds | 15,524,039 | 15,972,287 | 15,952,000 | 22,103,995 | 33,045,184 | 43,493,358 | 50,403,567 | 57,208,196 |
| Other State Funds | 5,644,014 | 5,308,600 | 4,444,818 | 759,000 | 2,764,235 | 4,713,035 | 5,622,625 | 8,984,190 |
| Local/County Overmatch | 23,932,000 | 27,293,000 | 29,751,000 | 32,075,000 | 35,226,959 | 34,875,927 | 43,235,108 | 55,019,885 |
| SSI State Supplement | 74,000 | 86,000 | 215,000 | 261,000 | 7,516,000 | 8,265,000 | 8,810,000 | 8,771,000 |
| FEDERAL FUNDS | 17,740,916 | 18,021,760 | 20,561,682 | 21,697,275 | 25,911,031 | 29,023,156 | 32,014,894 | 39,272,150 |
| ICF/MR Funds | 680,000 | 702,900 | 1,392,000 | 1,559,000 | 4,520,662 | 6,621,507 | 8,306,237 | 14,888,702 |
| Small Public | 0 | 0 | 0 | 0 | 0 | 0 | 0 | 0 |
| Small Private | 680,000 | 702,900 | 1,392,000 | 1,559,000 | 4,520,662 | 6,621,507 | 8,306,237 | 14,888,702 |
| HCBS Waiver | 0 | 0 | 0 | 0 | 0 | 0 | 0 | 0 |
| Model 50/200 Waiver | 0 | 0 | 3,682 | 26,275 | 357,106 | 795,834 | 1,229,602 | 1,647,360 |
| Other Title XIX Programs | 0 | 0 | 0 | 0 | 0 | 248,174 | 2,344,593 | 2,627,070 |
| Title XX / SSBG Funds | 16,450,916 | 16,708,860 | 19,166,000 | 20,112,000 | 20,785,089 | 19,261,222 | 20,109,018 | 20,109,018 |
| Other Federal Funds | 610,000 | 610,000 | 0 | 0 | 0 | 0 | 0 | 0 |
| Waiver Clients' SSI/ADC | 0 | 0 | 0 | 0 | 0 | 0 | 0 | 0 |

*Source:*
Institute on Disability and Human Development (UAP),
University of Illinois at Chicago, 1994

# KANSAS

## MR/DD Spending for Congregate Residential & Community Services

▨ Congregate: 16+ Beds*  ■ Community**

Millions of 1992 Dollars

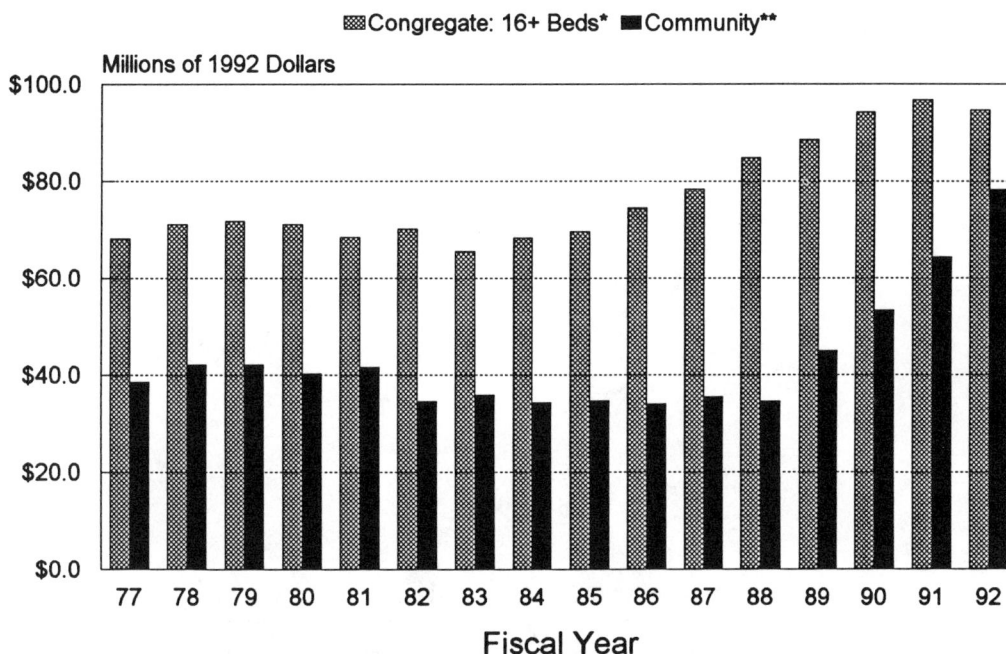

Fiscal Year

*Excludes nursing homes; ** Includes resources for
15 bed or less residential settings & non-residential community services

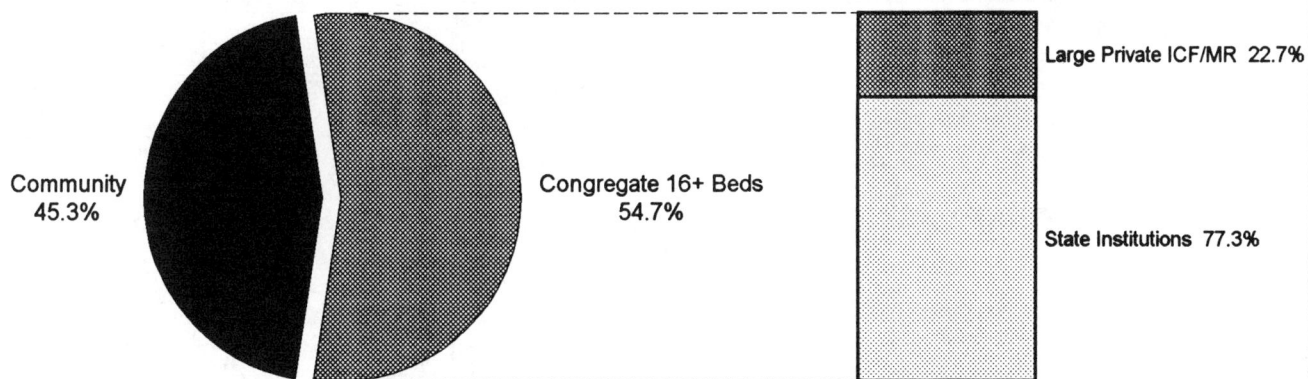

Community
45.3%

Congregate 16+ Beds
54.7%

Large Private ICF/MR  22.7%

State Institutions  77.3%

FY 1992 Total Spending:
$172.9 Million

*Source:*
Institute on Disability and Human Development (UAP),
University of Illinois at Chicago, 1994

# KANSAS

## Number of Persons Served by Residential Setting: FY 1992

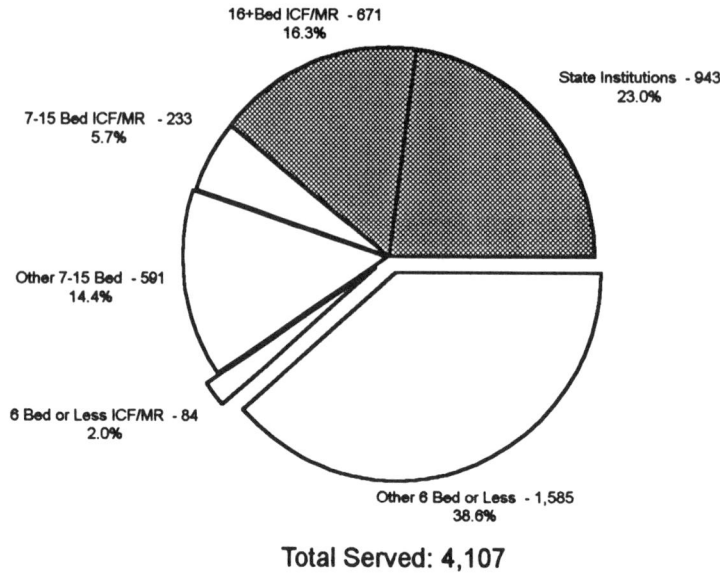

16+Bed ICF/MR - 671
16.3%

State Institutions - 943
23.0%

7-15 Bed ICF/MR - 233
5.7%

Other 7-15 Bed - 591
14.4%

6 Bed or Less ICF/MR - 84
2.0%

Other 6 Bed or Less - 1,585
38.6%

Total Served: 4,107

## Persons Served by Residential Setting:1986-92

|  | 1986 | 1987 | 1988 | 1989 | 1990 | 1991 | 1992 |
|---|---|---|---|---|---|---|---|
| CONGREGATE 16 + BED SETTINGS | 1,970 | 1,899 | 1,843 | 1,702 | 1,662 | 1,692 | 1,614 |
| Nursing Homes | NA | NA | 18 | NA | NA | 0 | 0 |
| State Institutions | 1,294 | 1,223 | 1,149 | 1,052 | 1,017 | 1,015 | 943 |
| Private 16+Bed ICF/MR | 676 | 676 | 676 | 650 | 645 | 677 | 671 |
| Other 16+Bed Residential | 0 | 0 | 0 | 0 | 0 | 0 | 0 |
| 15 BED OR LESS RESIDENTIAL SETTINGS | 1,343 | 1,485 | 1,605 | 238 | 2,039 | 2,352 | 2,493 |
| Public 7-15 Bed ICF/MR | 0 | 0 | 0 | 0 | 0 | 0 | 0 |
| Private 7-15 Bed ICF/MR | 187 | 187 | 203 | 238 | 278 | 241 | 233 |
| Other 7-15 Bed Residential | 1,156 | 1,298 | 1,402 | NA | 1,761 | 2,027 | 591 |
| Public 6 Bed or Less ICF/MR |  |  |  |  |  | 0 | 0 |
| Private 6 Bed or Less ICF/MR |  |  |  |  |  | 84 | 84 |
| Other 6 Bed or Less Residential |  |  |  |  |  | 0 | 1,585 |
| TOTAL PERSONS SERVED | 3,313 | 3,384 | 3,448 | 1,940 | 3,701 | 4,044 | 4,107 |

## Persons Served in Non-Residential Community Services:1986-92

|  | 1986 | 1987 | 1988 | 1989 | 1990 | 1991 | 1992 |
|---|---|---|---|---|---|---|---|
| DAY/WORK PROGRAMS | 2,336 | 2,378 | 2,570 | NA | 5,458 | 6,642 | 6,791 |
| Sheltered Employment/Work Activity | NA | NA | NA | NA | 2,042 | 2,543 | 2,508 |
| Day Habilitation ("Day Training") | NA | NA | NA | NA | 2,807 | 3,113 | 3,249 |
| Supported/Competitive Employment | 0 | 45 | 64 | NA | 609 | 986 | 1,034 |
| CASE MANAGEMENT | 2,555 | 2,570 | 2,812 | NA | 4,856 | 5,221 | 5,246 |
| HCBS WAIVER | 219 | 192 | 184 | 343 | 293 | 497 | 948 |
| MODEL 50/200 WAIVER | 0 | 0 | 0 | 0 | 0 | 0 | 0 |

*Source:*
Institute on Disability and Human Development (UAP),
University of Illinois at Chicago, 1994

# KANSAS

## Community Services: FY 1992 Revenue Sources

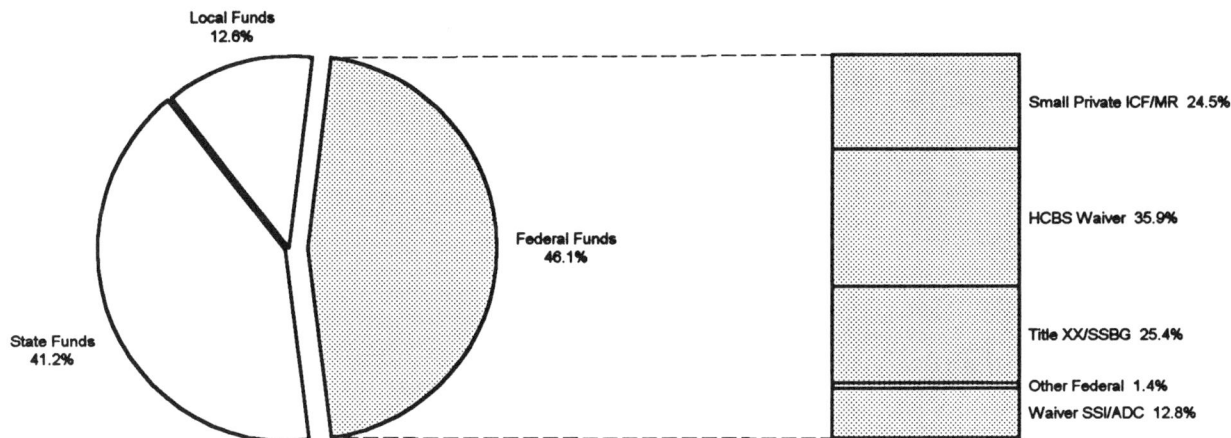

Local Funds
12.6%

State Funds
41.2%

Federal Funds
46.1%

Small Private ICF/MR  24.5%

HCBS Waiver  35.9%

Title XX/SSBG  25.4%

Other Federal  1.4%

Waiver SSI/ADC  12.8%

Total Funds: $78.3 Million

## Family Support Initiatives*

|  | 1986 | 1987 | 1988 | 1989 | 1990 | 1991 | 1992 |
|---|---|---|---|---|---|---|---|
| FAMILY SUPPORT: TOTAL SPENDING | $0 | $0 | $0 | $0 | $91,800 | $1,224,000 | $2,548,200 |
| Total # of Families Supported | 0 | 0 | 0 | 0 | 9 | 120 | 441 |
| A. Financial Subsidy/Payment | $0 | $0 | $0 | $0 | $0 | $0 | $600,000 |
| # of Families | 0 | 0 | 0 | 0 | 0 | 0 | 250 |
| B. Family Assistance Payments | $0 | $0 | $0 | $0 | $91,800 | $1,224,000 | $1,948,200 |
| # of Families | 0 | 0 | 0 | 0 | 9 | 120 | 191 |
| C. Other Family Support Payments | $0 | $0 | $0 | $0 | $0 | $0 | $0 |
| # of Families | 0 | 0 | 0 | 0 | 0 | 0 | 0 |

## Other Community Services Initiatives*

|  | 1986 | 1987 | 1988 | 1989 | 1990 | 1991 | 1992 |
|---|---|---|---|---|---|---|---|
| AGING/DD SPENDING | $0 | $0 | $0 | $0 | $0 | $0 | $0 |
| # of Persons Served | 0 | 0 | 0 | 0 | 0 | 0 | 0 |
| ASSISTIVE TECHNOLOGY SPENDING |  |  |  |  |  |  | $0 |
| # of Persons Served |  |  |  |  |  |  | 0 |
| EARLY INTERVENTION SPENDING | $0 | $0 | $0 | $0 | NA | NA | NA |
| # of Persons Served | 0 | 0 | 0 | 0 | 438 | 304 | 325 |
| PERSONAL ASSISTANCE SPENDING |  |  |  |  |  |  | $0 |
| # of Persons Served |  |  |  |  |  |  | 0 |
| SUPPORTED EMPLOYMENT SPENDING | $0 | $0 | $440,000 | $413,800 | $1,600,000 | $3,300,000 | $3,500,000 |
| # of Persons Served | 0 | 0 | 45 | 64 | 270 | 561 | 592 |
| SUPPORTED LIVING SPENDING |  |  |  |  |  |  | $0 |
| # of Persons Served |  |  |  |  |  |  | 0 |

*Expenditures associated with Special Community Initiatives are a subset of funding within the community services component of the state's chart series and spreadsheet; Family Support Client figures may include duplicate client counts; HCBS Waiver counts include Waiver case management numbers.
0= Services not provided in the state; NA= Data not available from state; blank= Services not applicable (eg. CSLA prior to authorization, Special Community Initiatives prior to request for data by this study)

*Source:*
Institute on Disability and Human Development (UAP),
University of Illinois at Chicago, 1994

# KANSAS

## Large Congregate Care Facilities: FY 1992 Revenue Sources*

### Private 16+Bed Settings

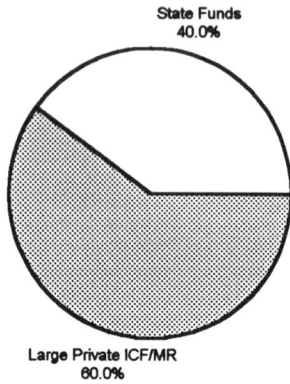

State Funds
40.0%

Large Private ICF/MR
60.0%

Total Funds: $21.1 Million

### Public Institutions

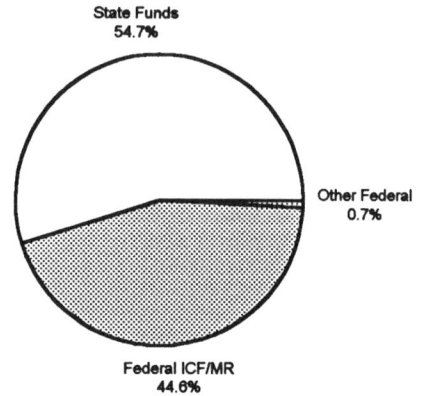

State Funds
54.7%

Other Federal
0.7%

Federal ICF/MR
44.6%

Total Funds: $73.5 Million

*Excludes nursing homes

## Average Daily Residents in Institutions

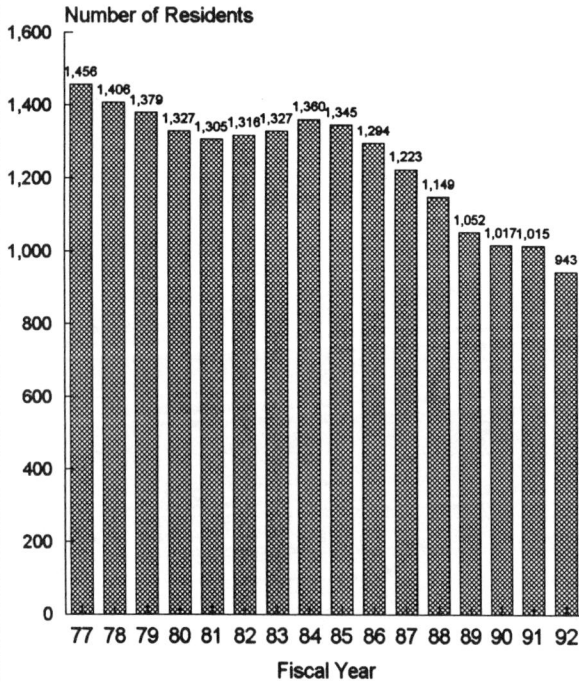

Number of Residents

| | |
|---|---|
| 1,456 | 77 |
| 1,406 | 78 |
| 1,379 | 79 |
| 1,327 | 80 |
| 1,305 | 81 |
| 1,316 | 82 |
| 1,327 | 83 |
| 1,360 | 84 |
| 1,345 | 85 |
| 1,294 | 86 |
| 1,223 | 87 |
| 1,149 | 88 |
| 1,052 | 89 |
| 1,017 | 90 |
| 1,015 | 91 |
| 943 | 92 |

Fiscal Year

## Institutional Daily Costs Per Resident

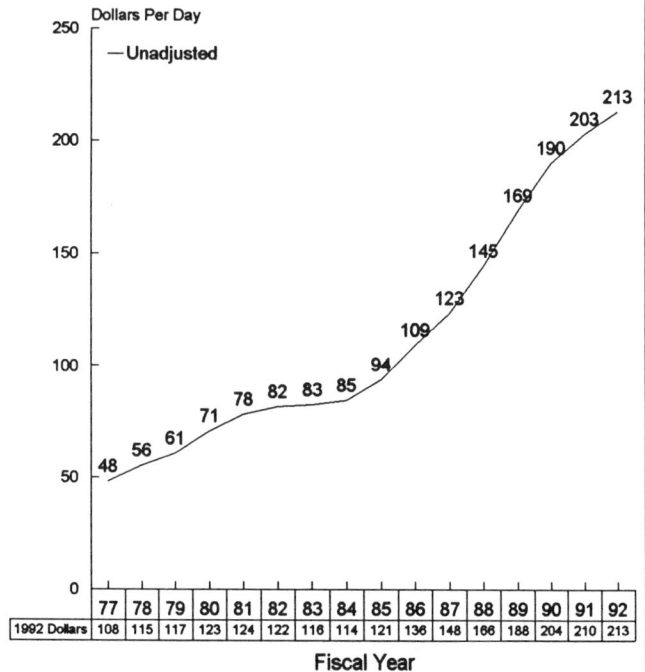

Dollars Per Day

—Unadjusted

48, 56, 61, 71, 78, 82, 83, 85, 94, 109, 123, 145, 169, 190, 203, 213

| | 77 | 78 | 79 | 80 | 81 | 82 | 83 | 84 | 85 | 86 | 87 | 88 | 89 | 90 | 91 | 92 |
|---|---|---|---|---|---|---|---|---|---|---|---|---|---|---|---|---|
| 1992 Dollars | 108 | 115 | 117 | 123 | 124 | 122 | 116 | 114 | 121 | 136 | 148 | 166 | 188 | 204 | 210 | 213 |

Fiscal Year

*Source:*
Institute on Disability and Human Development (UAP),
University of Illinois at Chicago, 1994

# KANSAS FISCAL EFFORT

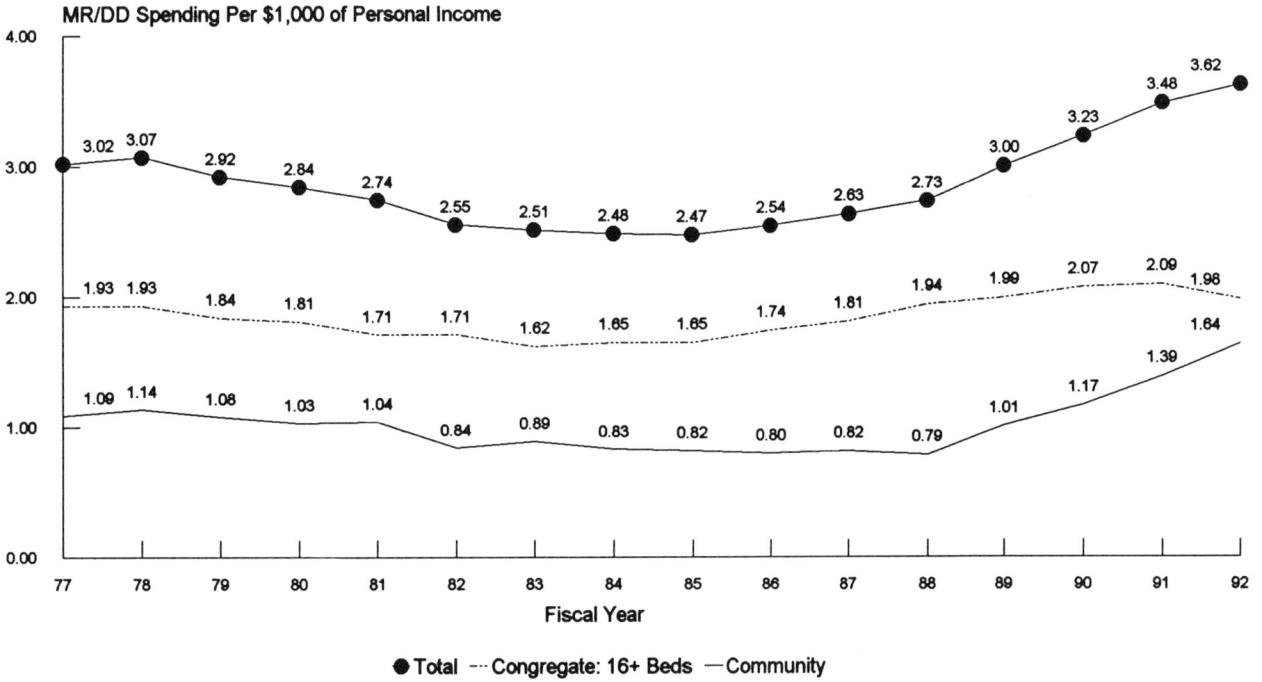

MR/DD Spending Per $1,000 of Personal Income

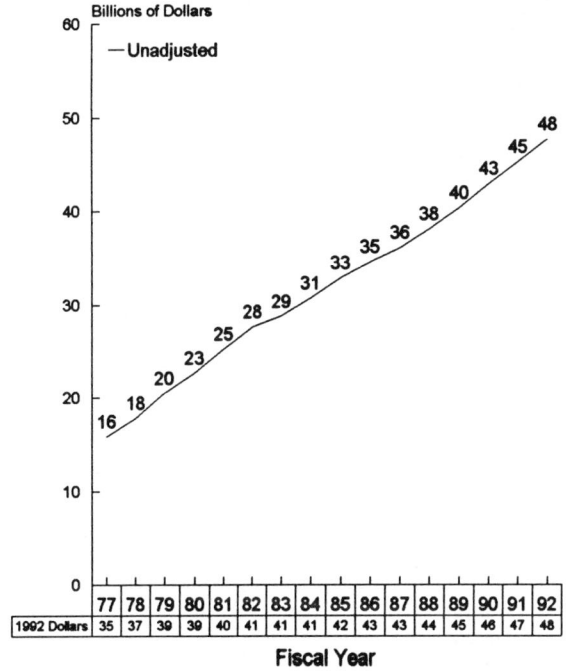

| | |
|---|---|
| 3.02 | 3.07 |
| 1.93 | 1.93 |
| 1.09 | 1.14 |

Total values: 3.02, 3.07, 2.92, 2.84, 2.74, 2.55, 2.51, 2.48, 2.47, 2.54, 2.63, 2.73, 3.00, 3.23, 3.48, 3.62

Congregate: 16+ Beds values: 1.93, 1.93, 1.84, 1.81, 1.71, 1.71, 1.62, 1.65, 1.65, 1.74, 1.81, 1.94, 1.99, 2.07, 2.09, 1.98

Community values: 1.09, 1.14, 1.08, 1.03, 1.04, 0.84, 0.89, 0.83, 0.82, 0.80, 0.82, 0.79, 1.01, 1.17, 1.39, 1.64

Fiscal Year: 77 78 79 80 81 82 83 84 85 86 87 88 89 90 91 92

● Total  ···Congregate: 16+ Beds  —Community

## Total MR/DD Spending

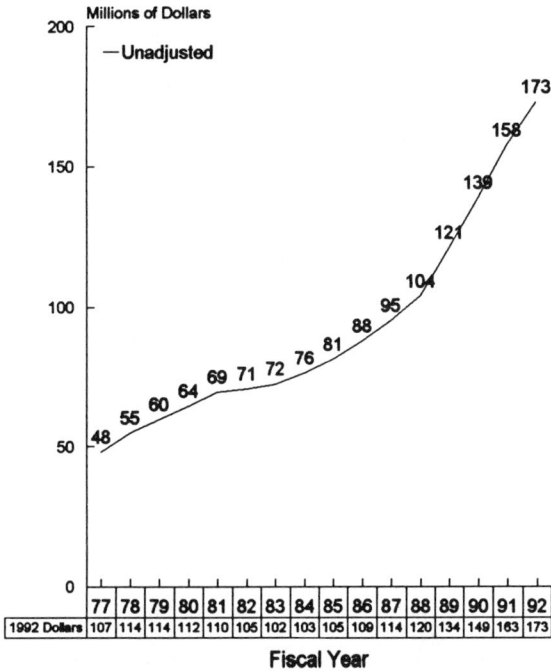

Millions of Dollars
—Unadjusted

Values: 48, 55, 60, 64, 69, 71, 72, 76, 81, 88, 95, 104, 121, 139, 158, 173

| Fiscal Year | 77 | 78 | 79 | 80 | 81 | 82 | 83 | 84 | 85 | 86 | 87 | 88 | 89 | 90 | 91 | 92 |
|---|---|---|---|---|---|---|---|---|---|---|---|---|---|---|---|---|
| 1992 Dollars | 107 | 114 | 114 | 112 | 110 | 105 | 102 | 103 | 105 | 109 | 114 | 120 | 134 | 149 | 163 | 173 |

Fiscal Year

## Personal Income

Billions of Dollars
—Unadjusted

Values: 16, 18, 20, 23, 25, 28, 29, 31, 33, 35, 36, 38, 40, 43, 45, 48

| Fiscal Year | 77 | 78 | 79 | 80 | 81 | 82 | 83 | 84 | 85 | 86 | 87 | 88 | 89 | 90 | 91 | 92 |
|---|---|---|---|---|---|---|---|---|---|---|---|---|---|---|---|---|
| 1992 Dollars | 35 | 37 | 39 | 39 | 40 | 41 | 41 | 41 | 42 | 43 | 43 | 44 | 45 | 46 | 47 | 48 |

Fiscal Year

*Source:*
Institute on Disability and Human Development (UAP),
University of Illinois at Chicago, 1994

# KANSAS
## Financial Support for MR/DD Services: FY 1977-92

| | 1977 | 1978 | 1979 | 1980 | 1981 | 1982 | 1983 | 1984 |
|---|---|---|---|---|---|---|---|---|
| **TOTAL FUNDS** | $48,014,541 | $54,861,977 | $59,632,157 | $64,356,989 | $69,351,050 | $70,605,135 | $72,291,455 | $76,201,715 |
| **CONGREGATE 16+ BEDS** | 30,690,660 | 34,460,776 | 37,590,791 | 41,105,317 | 43,123,045 | 47,256,287 | 46,718,905 | 50,757,622 |
| INSTITUTIONAL SERVICES FUNDS | 25,674,000 | 28,482,000 | 30,714,000 | 34,361,000 | 37,243,000 | 39,218,000 | 39,957,000 | 42,077,200 |
| STATE FUNDS | 12,217,000 | 17,006,000 | 14,631,000 | 19,553,000 | 18,706,000 | 20,619,000 | 21,151,000 | 24,386,900 |
| General Funds | 12,217,000 | 17,006,000 | 14,631,000 | 19,553,000 | 18,706,000 | 20,619,000 | 21,151,000 | 24,386,900 |
| Local | 0 | 0 | 0 | 0 | 0 | 0 | 0 | 0 |
| Other State Funds | 0 | 0 | 0 | 0 | 0 | 0 | 0 | 0 |
| FEDERAL FUNDS | 13,457,000 | 11,476,000 | 16,083,000 | 14,808,000 | 18,537,000 | 18,599,000 | 18,806,000 | 17,690,300 |
| Federal ICF/MR | 13,457,000 | 11,476,000 | 16,083,000 | 14,808,000 | 18,537,000 | 18,599,000 | 18,806,000 | 17,690,300 |
| Title XX / SSBG Funds | 0 | 0 | 0 | 0 | 0 | 0 | 0 | 0 |
| Other Federal Funds | 0 | 0 | 0 | 0 | 0 | 0 | 0 | 0 |
| LARGE PRIVATE RESIDENTIAL | 5,016,660 | 5,978,776 | 6,876,791 | 6,744,317 | 5,880,045 | 8,038,287 | 6,761,905 | 8,680,422 |
| STATE FUNDS | 2,306,660 | 2,823,776 | 3,276,791 | 3,154,317 | 2,733,045 | 3,797,287 | 3,211,905 | 4,242,122 |
| General Funds | 2,306,660 | 2,823,776 | 3,276,791 | 3,154,317 | 2,733,045 | 3,797,287 | 3,211,905 | 4,242,122 |
| Other State Funds | 0 | 0 | 0 | 0 | 0 | 0 | 0 | 0 |
| Local/County Overmatch | 0 | 0 | 0 | 0 | 0 | 0 | 0 | 0 |
| FEDERAL FUNDS | 2,710,000 | 3,155,000 | 3,600,000 | 3,590,000 | 3,147,000 | 4,241,000 | 3,550,000 | 4,438,300 |
| Large Private ICF/MR | 2,710,000 | 3,155,000 | 3,600,000 | 3,590,000 | 3,147,000 | 4,241,000 | 3,550,000 | 4,438,300 |
| **COMMUNITY SERVICES FUNDS** | 17,323,881 | 20,401,201 | 22,041,366 | 23,251,672 | 26,228,005 | 23,348,848 | 25,572,550 | 25,444,093 |
| STATE FUNDS | 7,426,181 | 9,028,101 | 10,167,666 | 11,159,472 | 13,566,605 | 13,324,548 | 15,103,050 | 14,086,929 |
| General Funds | 2,956,340 | 3,153,224 | 4,137,209 | 4,835,683 | 5,397,955 | 5,359,713 | 6,764,095 | 5,015,578 |
| Other State Funds | 2,927,600 | 3,396,400 | 3,497,900 | 3,535,100 | 3,788,800 | 2,525,600 | 2,707,900 | 2,842,700 |
| Local/County Overmatch | 1,542,241 | 2,478,477 | 2,532,557 | 2,788,689 | 4,379,850 | 5,439,235 | 5,631,055 | 6,228,651 |
| SSI State Supplement | 0 | 0 | 0 | 0 | 0 | 0 | 0 | 0 |
| FEDERAL FUNDS | 9,897,700 | 11,373,100 | 11,873,700 | 12,092,200 | 12,661,400 | 10,024,300 | 10,469,500 | 11,357,164 |
| ICF/MR Funds | 816,000 | 949,000 | 1,084,000 | 1,081,000 | 947,000 | 1,276,000 | 1,068,000 | 1,214,600 |
| Small Public | 0 | 0 | 0 | 0 | 0 | 0 | 0 | 0 |
| Small Private | 816,000 | 949,000 | 1,084,000 | 1,081,000 | 947,000 | 1,276,000 | 1,068,000 | 1,214,600 |
| HCBS Waiver | 0 | 0 | 0 | 0 | 0 | 0 | 0 | 36,300 |
| Model 50/200 Waiver | 0 | 0 | 0 | 0 | 0 | 0 | 0 | 0 |
| Other Title XIX Programs | 0 | 0 | 0 | 0 | 0 | 0 | 0 | 0 |
| Title XX / SSBG Funds | 8,782,700 | 10,189,100 | 10,493,700 | 10,605,200 | 11,366,400 | 8,455,300 | 9,065,500 | 9,516,900 |
| Other Federal Funds | 299,000 | 235,000 | 296,000 | 406,000 | 348,000 | 293,000 | 336,000 | 509,600 |
| Waiver Clients' SSI/ADC | 0 | 0 | 0 | 0 | 0 | 0 | 0 | 79,764 |

| | 1985 | 1986 | 1987 | 1988 | 1989 | 1990 | 1991 | 1992 |
|---|---|---|---|---|---|---|---|---|
| **TOTAL FUNDS** | $81,258,162 | $87,798,070 | $95,089,785 | $103,935,787 | $121,122,593 | $138,828,257 | $157,503,397 | $172,921,801 |
| **CONGREGATE 16+ BEDS** | 54,252,392 | 60,240,462 | 65,399,225 | 73,835,170 | 80,345,673 | 88,649,719 | 94,579,482 | 94,625,009 |
| INSTITUTIONAL SERVICES FUNDS | 46,087,600 | 51,616,384 | 55,086,725 | 60,782,744 | 64,923,261 | 70,659,191 | 75,261,553 | 73,478,632 |
| STATE FUNDS | 27,079,500 | 28,221,274 | 28,817,831 | 28,715,877 | 30,311,376 | 37,347,390 | 43,798,654 | 40,207,124 |
| General Funds | 27,079,500 | 28,221,274 | 28,817,831 | 26,332,017 | 28,235,692 | 35,166,946 | 38,543,072 | 37,218,660 |
| Local | 0 | 0 | 0 | 0 | 0 | 0 | 0 | 0 |
| Other State Funds | 0 | 0 | 0 | 2,383,860 | 2,075,684 | 2,180,444 | 5,255,582 | 2,988,464 |
| FEDERAL FUNDS | 19,008,100 | 23,395,110 | 26,268,894 | 32,066,867 | 34,611,885 | 33,311,801 | 31,462,899 | 33,271,508 |
| Federal ICF/MR | 19,008,100 | 23,395,110 | 26,268,894 | 31,486,613 | 34,093,806 | 32,819,827 | 30,956,093 | 32,754,395 |
| Title XX / SSBG Funds | 0 | 0 | 0 | 0 | 0 | 0 | 0 | 0 |
| Other Federal Funds | 0 | 0 | 0 | 580,254 | 518,079 | 491,974 | 506,806 | 517,113 |
| LARGE PRIVATE RESIDENTIAL | 8,164,792 | 8,624,078 | 10,312,500 | 13,052,426 | 15,422,412 | 17,990,528 | 19,317,929 | 21,146,377 |
| STATE FUNDS | 4,027,692 | 4,297,378 | 5,049,000 | 5,220,970 | 6,168,965 | 7,196,211 | 7,727,172 | 8,458,551 |
| General Funds | 4,027,692 | 4,297,378 | 5,049,000 | 5,220,970 | 6,168,965 | 7,196,211 | 7,727,172 | 8,458,551 |
| Other State Funds | 0 | 0 | 0 | 0 | 0 | 0 | 0 | 0 |
| Local/County Overmatch | 0 | 0 | 0 | 0 | 0 | 0 | 0 | 0 |
| FEDERAL FUNDS | 4,137,100 | 4,326,700 | 5,263,500 | 7,831,456 | 9,253,447 | 10,794,317 | 11,590,757 | 12,687,826 |
| Large Private ICF/MR | 4,137,100 | 4,326,700 | 5,263,500 | 7,831,456 | 9,253,447 | 10,794,317 | 11,590,757 | 12,687,826 |
| **COMMUNITY SERVICES FUNDS** | 27,005,770 | 27,557,608 | 29,690,560 | 30,100,617 | 40,776,920 | 50,178,538 | 62,923,915 | 78,296,792 |
| STATE FUNDS | 15,777,870 | 15,955,200 | 17,874,100 | 16,707,647 | 24,436,385 | 28,105,868 | 36,194,279 | 42,165,616 |
| General Funds | 6,416,808 | 1,777,700 | 2,239,600 | 1,663,472 | 2,777,689 | 5,083,114 | 7,978,432 | 11,562,793 |
| Other State Funds | 2,557,400 | 7,007,400 | 8,051,600 | 7,192,977 | 12,389,951 | 13,561,463 | 19,006,904 | 20,721,421 |
| Local/County Overmatch | 6,803,662 | 7,170,100 | 7,582,900 | 7,851,198 | 9,268,745 | 9,461,291 | 9,208,943 | 9,881,402 |
| SSI State Supplement | 0 | 0 | 0 | 0 | 0 | 0 | 0 | 0 |
| FEDERAL FUNDS | 11,227,900 | 11,602,408 | 11,816,460 | 13,392,970 | 16,340,535 | 22,072,670 | 26,729,636 | 36,131,176 |
| ICF/MR Funds | 1,296,100 | 1,389,900 | 1,941,700 | 1,528,360 | 2,041,414 | 4,504,697 | 7,452,365 | 8,858,551 |
| Small Public | 0 | 0 | 0 | 0 | 0 | 0 | 0 | 0 |
| Small Private | 1,296,100 | 1,389,900 | 1,941,700 | 1,528,360 | 2,041,414 | 4,504,697 | 7,452,365 | 8,858,551 |
| HCBS Waiver | 289,700 | 342,800 | 325,500 | 818,750 | 2,460,979 | 5,601,935 | 7,318,423 | 12,961,993 |
| Model 50/200 Waiver | 0 | 0 | 0 | 0 | 0 | 0 | 0 | 0 |
| Other Title XIX Programs | 0 | 0 | 0 | 0 | 0 | 0 | 0 | 0 |
| Title XX / SSBG Funds | 8,561,700 | 8,693,700 | 8,444,500 | 9,829,868 | 9,929,870 | 10,171,550 | 9,180,000 | 9,180,000 |
| Other Federal Funds | 410,800 | 358,700 | 379,000 | 500,600 | 500,600 | 500,600 | 500,600 | 500,600 |
| Waiver Clients' SSI/ADC | 669,600 | 817,308 | 725,760 | 715,392 | 1,407,672 | 1,293,888 | 2,278,248 | 4,630,032 |

*Source:*
Institute on Disability and Human Development (UAP),
University of Illinois at Chicago, 1994

# KENTUCKY

## MR/DD Spending for Congregate Residential & Community Services

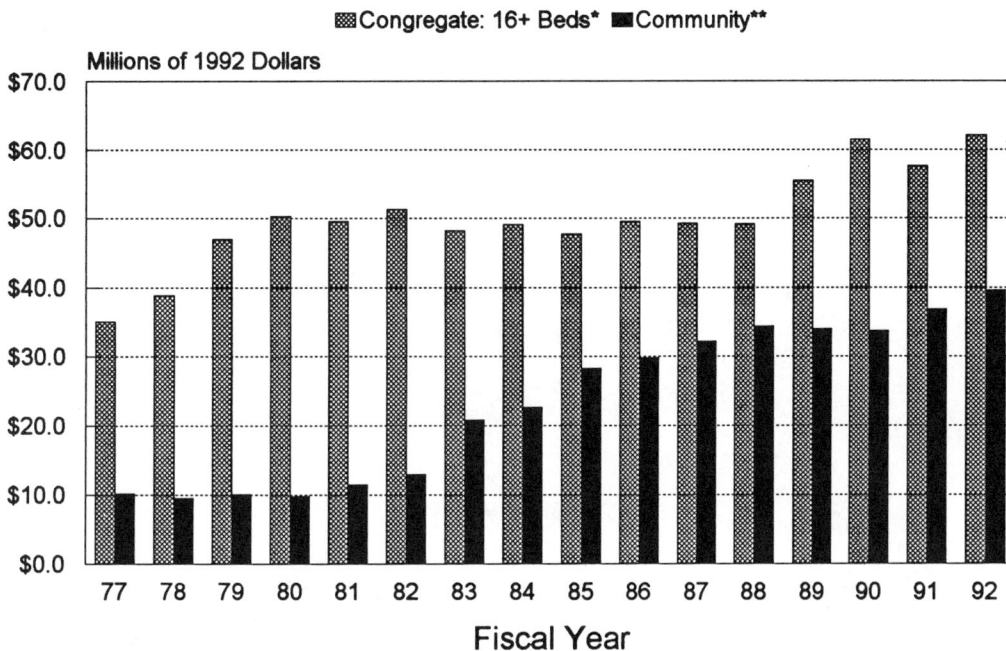

▨ Congregate: 16+ Beds* ■ Community**

Millions of 1992 Dollars

$70.0
$60.0
$50.0
$40.0
$30.0
$20.0
$10.0
$0.0

77 78 79 80 81 82 83 84 85 86 87 88 89 90 91 92

Fiscal Year

*Excludes nursing homes; ** Includes resources for
15 bed or less residential settings & non-residential community services

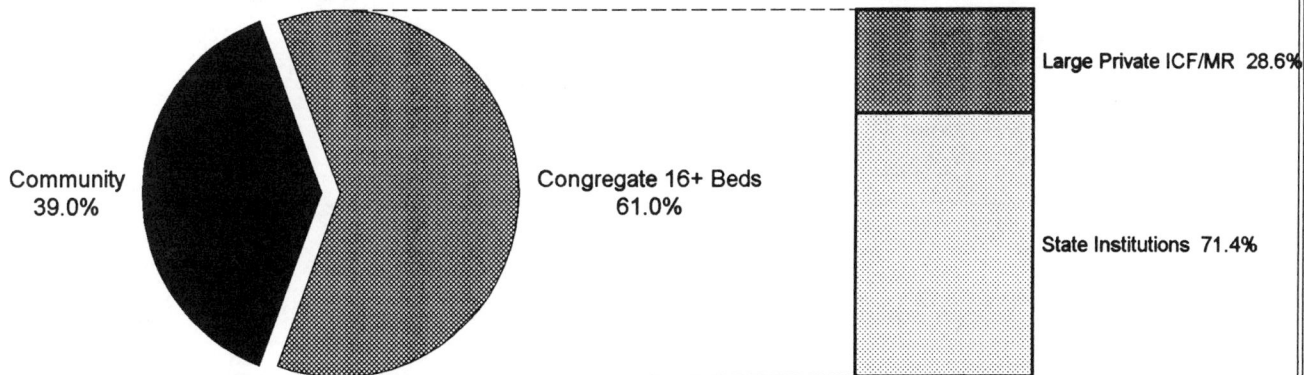

Community
39.0%

Congregate 16+ Beds
61.0%

Large Private ICF/MR 28.6%

State Institutions 71.4%

FY 1992 Total Spending:
$101.7 Million

Source:
Institute on Disability and Human Development (UAP),
University of Illinois at Chicago, 1994

# KENTUCKY

## Number of Persons Served by Residential Setting: FY 1992

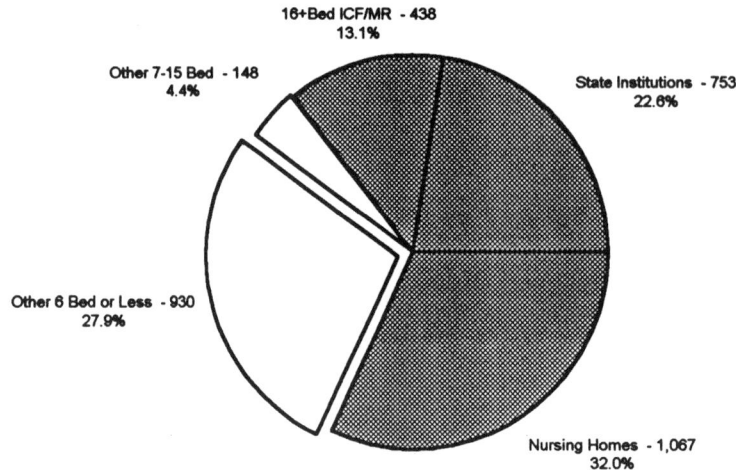

16+Bed ICF/MR - 438
13.1%

Other 7-15 Bed - 148
4.4%

State Institutions - 753
22.6%

Other 6 Bed or Less - 930
27.9%

Nursing Homes - 1,067
32.0%

Total Served: 3,336

## Persons Served by Residential Setting:1986-92

|  | 1986 | 1987 | 1988 | 1989 | 1990 | 1991 | 1992 |
|---|---|---|---|---|---|---|---|
| **CONGREGATE 16 + BED SETTINGS** | **NA** | **NA** | **1,914** | **NA** | **NA** | **NA** | **2,258** |
| Nursing Homes | NA | NA | 734 | NA | NA | NA | 1,067 |
| State Institutions | 748 | 745 | 742 | 741 | 744 | 750 | 753 |
| Private 16+Bed ICF/MR | 433 | 433 | 438 | 438 | 438 | 438 | 438 |
| Other 16+Bed Residential | 0 | 0 | 0 | 0 | 0 | 0 | 0 |
| **15 BED OR LESS RESIDENTIAL SETTINGS** | **452** | **546** | **705** | **725** | **757** | **786** | **1,078** |
| Public 7-15 Bed ICF/MR | 0 | 0 | 0 | 0 | 0 | 0 | 0 |
| Private 7-15 Bed ICF/MR | 0 | 0 | 0 | 0 | 0 | 0 | 0 |
| Other 7-15 Bed Residential | 452 | 546 | 705 | 725 | 757 | 786 | 148 |
| Public 6 Bed or Less ICF/MR | 0 | 0 | 0 | 0 | 0 | 0 | 0 |
| Private 6 Bed or Less ICF/MR | 0 | 0 | 0 | 0 | 0 | 0 | 0 |
| Other 6 Bed or Less Residential | NA | NA | NA | NA | NA | NA | 930 |
| **TOTAL PERSONS SERVED** | **NA** | **NA** | **2,619** | **NA** | **NA** | **NA** | **3,336** |

## Persons Served in Non-Residential Community Services:1986-92

|  | 1986 | 1987 | 1988 | 1989 | 1990 | 1991 | 1992 |
|---|---|---|---|---|---|---|---|
| **DAY/WORK PROGRAMS** | **2,891** | **2,945** | **3,171** | **3,629** | **2,520** | **2,327** | **2,582** |
| Sheltered Employment/Work Activity | NA | NA | NA | NA | NA | NA | NA |
| Day Habilitation ("Day Training") | NA | NA | NA | NA | NA | NA | NA |
| Supported/Competitive Employment | NA | NA | NA | NA | NA | NA | NA |
| **CASE MANAGEMENT** | **4,713** | **5,178** | **3,541** | **3,478** | **3,077** | **3,406** | **3,793** |
| **HCBS WAIVER** | **539** | **593** | **659** | **725** | **757** | **786** | **797** |
| **MODEL 50/200 WAIVER** | **0** | **0** | **1** | **0** | **0** | **0** | **0** |

*Source:*
Institute on Disability and Human Development (UAP),
University of Illinois at Chicago, 1994

# KENTUCKY

## Community Services: FY 1992 Revenue Sources

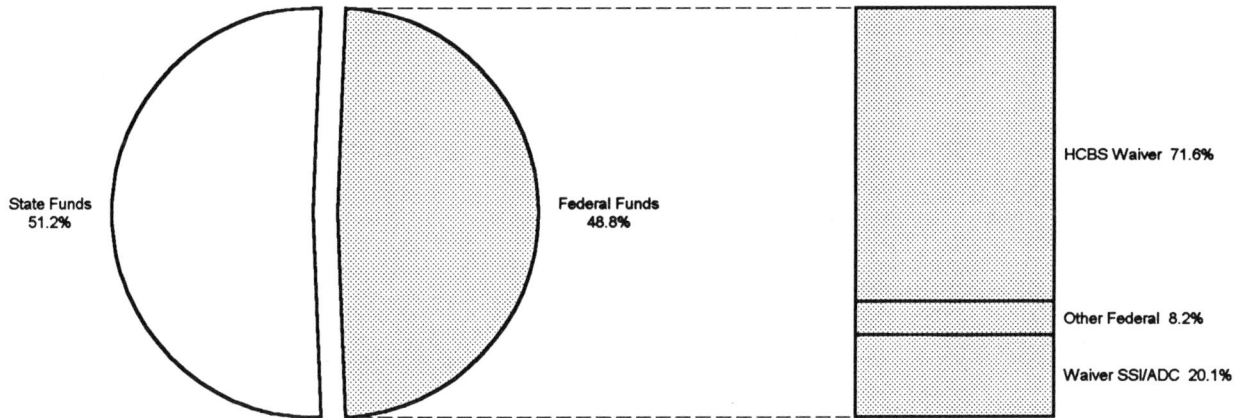

State Funds
51.2%

Federal Funds
48.8%

HCBS Waiver 71.6%

Other Federal 8.2%

Waiver SSI/ADC 20.1%

Total Funds: $39.6 Million

## Family Support Initiatives*

|  | 1986 | 1987 | 1988 | 1989 | 1990 | 1991 | 1992 |
|---|---|---|---|---|---|---|---|
| FAMILY SUPPORT: TOTAL SPENDING | $2,050,273 | $2,510,293 | $2,732,957 | $716,751 | $794,629 | $1,531,219 | $1,524,181 |
| Total # of Families Supported | NA | NA | NA | NA | NA | NA | NA |
| A. Financial Subsidy/Payment | $0 | $0 | $0 | $0 | $0 | $0 | $0 |
| # of Families | 0 | 0 | 0 | 0 | 0 | 0 | 0 |
| B. Family Assistance Payments | $604,814 | $895,401 | $991,312 | $348,966 | $460,514 | $1,221,203 | $1,175,832 |
| # of Families | NA | NA | NA | NA | NA | NA | NA |
| C. Other Family Support Payments | $1,445,459 | $1,614,892 | $1,741,645 | $367,785 | $334,115 | $310,016 | $348,349 |
| # of Families | NA | NA | NA | NA | NA | NA | NA |

## Other Community Services Initiatives*

|  | 1986 | 1987 | 1988 | 1989 | 1990 | 1991 | 1992 |
|---|---|---|---|---|---|---|---|
| AGING/DD SPENDING | $39,000 | $39,000 | $39,000 | $103,333 | $139,268 | $88,426 | $85,554 |
| # of Persons Served | NA | NA | NA | NA | NA | NA | NA |
| ASSISTIVE TECHNOLOGY SPENDING |  |  |  |  |  |  | $0 |
| # of Persons Served |  |  |  |  |  |  | 0 |
| EARLY INTERVENTION SPENDING | $605,357 | $586,840 | $678,459 | $2,452,170 | $2,594,810 | $3,016,230 | $2,185,749 |
| # of Persons Served | NA | NA | NA | NA | NA | NA | NA |
| PERSONAL ASSISTANCE SPENDING |  |  |  |  |  |  | $0 |
| # of Persons Served |  |  |  |  |  |  | 0 |
| SUPPORTED EMPLOYMENT SPENDING | $0 | $489,947 | $382,044 | $691,589 | $770,698 | $772,709 | $759,365 |
| # of Persons Served | 0 | NA | NA | NA | NA | NA | NA |
| SUPPORTED LIVING SPENDING |  |  |  |  |  |  | $0 |
| # of Persons Served |  |  |  |  |  |  | 0 |

*Expenditures associated with Special Community Initiatives are a subset of funding within the community services component of the state's chart series and spreadsheet; Family Support Client figures may include duplicate client counts; HCBS Waiver counts include Waiver case management numbers.
0= Services not provided in the state; NA= Data not available from state; blank= Services not applicable (eg. CSLA prior to authorization, Special Community Initiatives prior to request for data by this study)

Source:
Institute on Disability and Human Development (UAP),
University of Illinois at Chicago, 1994

# KENTUCKY

## Large Congregate Care Facilities: FY 1992 Revenue Sources*

### Private 16+Bed Settings

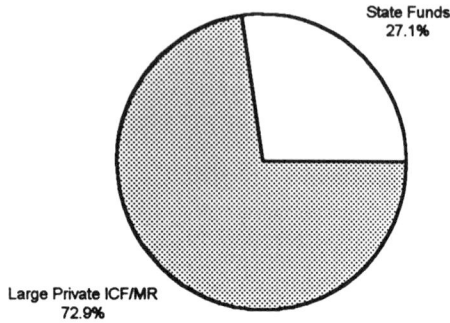

State Funds
27.1%

Large Private ICF/MR
72.9%

Total Funds: $17.7 Million

### Public Institutions

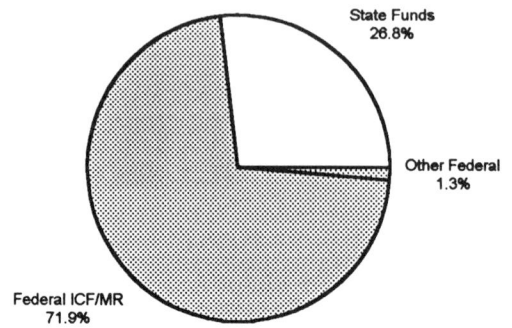

State Funds
26.8%

Other Federal
1.3%

Federal ICF/MR
71.9%

Total Funds: $44.4 Million

*Excludes nursing homes

## Average Daily Residents in Institutions

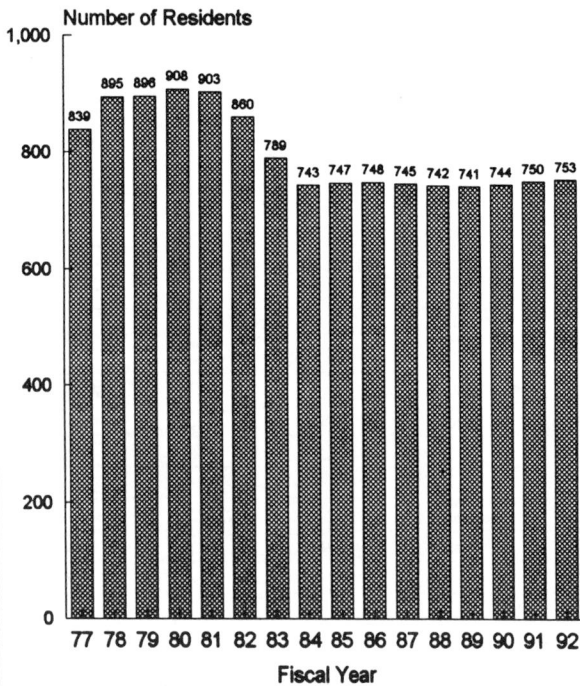

Number of Residents

| | |
|---|---|

1,000

800

600

400

200

0

839  895  896  908  903  860  789  743  747  748  745  742  741  744  750  753

77  78  79  80  81  82  83  84  85  86  87  88  89  90  91  92

Fiscal Year

## Institutional Daily Costs Per Resident

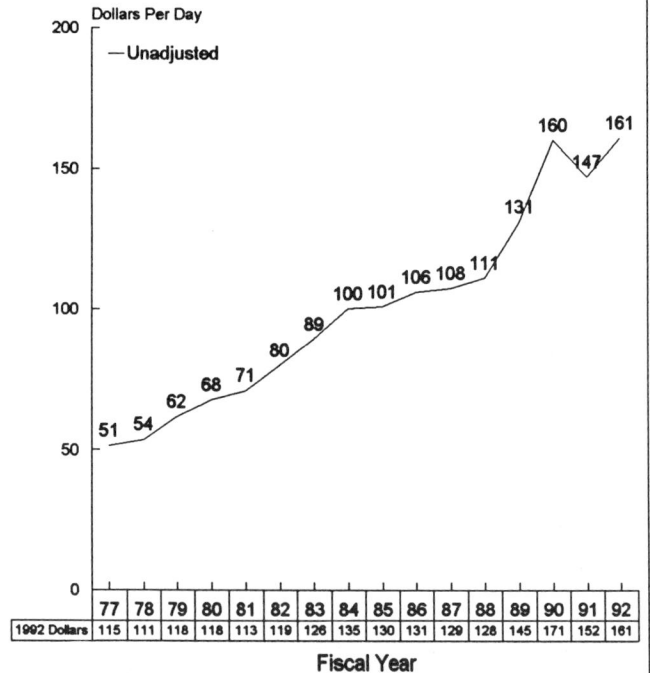

Dollars Per Day

—Unadjusted

200

150

100

50

0

51  54  62  68  71  80  89  100  101  106  108  111  131  160  147  161

| | 77 | 78 | 79 | 80 | 81 | 82 | 83 | 84 | 85 | 86 | 87 | 88 | 89 | 90 | 91 | 92 |
|---|---|---|---|---|---|---|---|---|---|---|---|---|---|---|---|---|
| 1992 Dollars | 115 | 111 | 118 | 118 | 113 | 119 | 126 | 135 | 130 | 131 | 129 | 128 | 145 | 171 | 152 | 161 |

Fiscal Year

*Source:*
Institute on Disability and Human Development (UAP),
University of Illinois at Chicago, 1994

# KENTUCKY FISCAL EFFORT

MR/DD Spending Per $1,000 of Personal Income

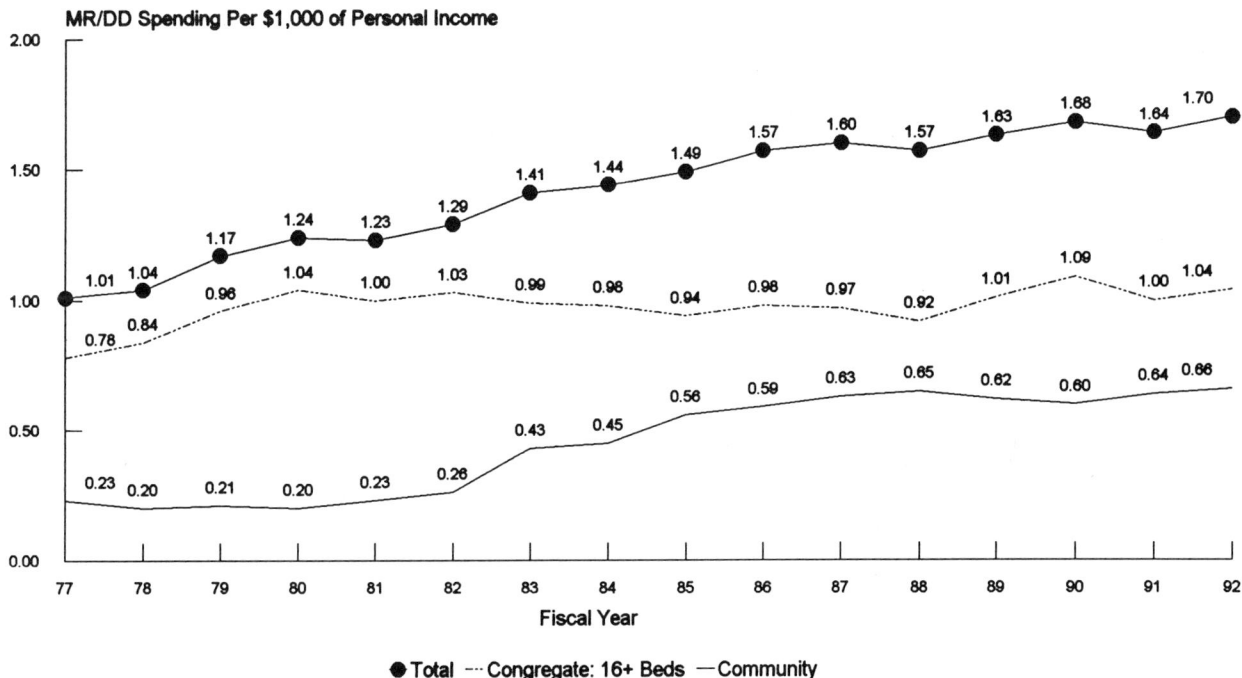

| | | | | | | | | | | | | | | | |
|---|---|---|---|---|---|---|---|---|---|---|---|---|---|---|---|

Total ● --- Congregate: 16+ Beds — Community

Fiscal Year

## Total MR/DD Spending

Millions of Dollars
— Unadjusted

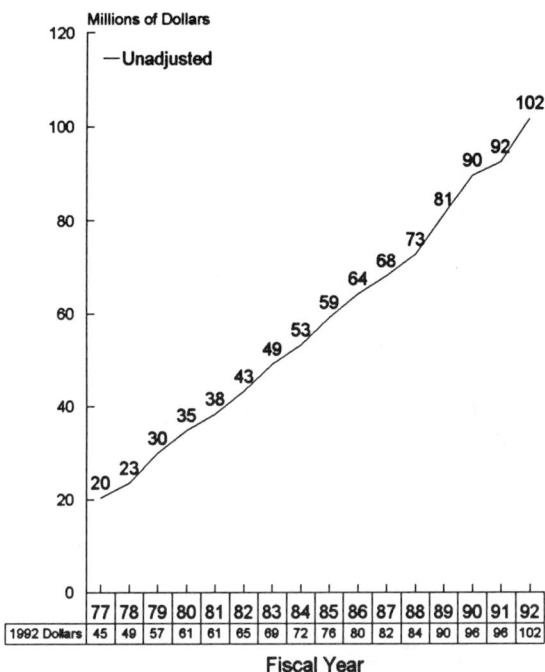

| | 77 | 78 | 79 | 80 | 81 | 82 | 83 | 84 | 85 | 86 | 87 | 88 | 89 | 90 | 91 | 92 |
|---|---|---|---|---|---|---|---|---|---|---|---|---|---|---|---|---|
| 1992 Dollars | 45 | 49 | 57 | 61 | 61 | 65 | 69 | 72 | 76 | 80 | 82 | 84 | 90 | 96 | 96 | 102 |

Fiscal Year

## Personal Income

Billions of Dollars
— Unadjusted

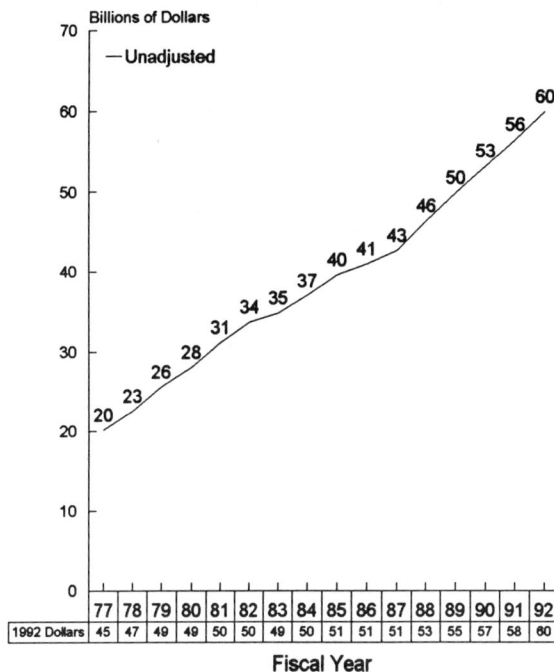

| | 77 | 78 | 79 | 80 | 81 | 82 | 83 | 84 | 85 | 86 | 87 | 88 | 89 | 90 | 91 | 92 |
|---|---|---|---|---|---|---|---|---|---|---|---|---|---|---|---|---|
| 1992 Dollars | 45 | 47 | 49 | 49 | 50 | 50 | 49 | 50 | 51 | 51 | 51 | 53 | 55 | 57 | 58 | 60 |

Fiscal Year

*Source:*
Institute on Disability and Human Development (UAP),
University of Illinois at Chicago, 1994

# KENTUCKY

## Financial Support for MR/DD Services: FY 1977-92

| | 1977 | 1978 | 1979 | 1980 | 1981 | 1982 | 1983 | 1984 |
|---|---|---|---|---|---|---|---|---|
| **TOTAL FUNDS** | $20,342,000 | $23,464,000 | $29,892,000 | $34,786,000 | $38,415,000 | $43,324,000 | $49,159,400 | $53,270,100 |
| **CONGREGATE 16+ BEDS** | 15,759,000 | 18,862,498 | 24,598,608 | 29,103,736 | 31,222,902 | 34,591,041 | 34,323,205 | 36,434,516 |
| INSTITUTIONAL SERVICES FUNDS | 15,759,000 | 17,515,000 | 20,176,000 | 22,458,000 | 23,356,000 | 25,050,000 | 25,668,900 | 27,238,600 |
| STATE FUNDS | 6,876,000 | 5,926,000 | 7,810,000 | 7,840,000 | 8,891,000 | 9,004,000 | 9,185,000 | 8,436,800 |
| General Funds | 6,876,000 | 5,926,000 | 7,810,000 | 7,840,000 | 8,891,000 | 9,004,000 | 9,185,000 | 8,436,800 |
| Local | 0 | 0 | 0 | 0 | 0 | 0 | 0 | 0 |
| Other State Funds | 0 | 0 | 0 | 0 | 0 | 0 | 0 | 0 |
| FEDERAL FUNDS | 8,883,000 | 11,589,000 | 12,366,000 | 14,618,000 | 14,465,000 | 16,046,000 | 16,483,900 | 18,801,800 |
| Federal ICF/MR | 8,732,000 | 11,254,000 | 11,787,000 | 13,876,000 | 13,729,000 | 15,275,000 | 15,600,300 | 18,086,100 |
| Title XX / SSBG Funds | 0 | 0 | 0 | 0 | 0 | 0 | 0 | 0 |
| Other Federal Funds | 151,000 | 335,000 | 579,000 | 742,000 | 736,000 | 771,000 | 883,600 | 715,700 |
| LARGE PRIVATE RESIDENTIAL | 0 | 1,347,498 | 4,422,608 | 6,645,736 | 7,866,902 | 9,541,041 | 8,654,305 | 9,195,916 |
| STATE FUNDS | 0 | 402,498 | 1,339,608 | 2,094,736 | 2,511,902 | 3,055,041 | 2,773,705 | 2,756,016 |
| General Funds | 0 | 402,498 | 1,339,608 | 2,094,736 | 2,511,902 | 3,055,041 | 2,773,705 | 2,756,016 |
| Other State Funds | 0 | 0 | 0 | 0 | 0 | 0 | 0 | 0 |
| Local/County Overmatch | 0 | 0 | 0 | 0 | 0 | 0 | 0 | 0 |
| FEDERAL FUNDS | 0 | 945,000 | 3,083,000 | 4,551,000 | 5,355,000 | 6,486,000 | 5,880,600 | 6,439,900 |
| Large Private ICF/MR | 0 | 945,000 | 3,083,000 | 4,551,000 | 5,355,000 | 6,486,000 | 5,880,600 | 6,439,900 |
| **COMMUNITY SERVICES FUNDS** | 4,583,000 | 4,601,502 | 5,293,392 | 5,682,264 | 7,192,098 | 8,732,959 | 14,836,195 | 16,835,584 |
| STATE FUNDS | 2,193,000 | 2,253,502 | 2,769,392 | 3,111,264 | 4,446,098 | 5,806,959 | 9,013,495 | 8,679,884 |
| General Funds | 979,000 | 921,502 | 1,296,392 | 1,617,264 | 2,966,098 | 4,336,959 | 7,568,495 | 7,266,884 |
| Other State Funds | 0 | 0 | 0 | 0 | 0 | 0 | 0 | 0 |
| Local/County Overmatch | 0 | 0 | 0 | 0 | 0 | 0 | 0 | 0 |
| SSI State Supplement | 1,214,000 | 1,332,000 | 1,473,000 | 1,494,000 | 1,480,000 | 1,470,000 | 1,445,000 | 1,413,000 |
| FEDERAL FUNDS | 2,390,000 | 2,348,000 | 2,524,000 | 2,571,000 | 2,746,000 | 2,926,000 | 5,822,700 | 8,155,700 |
| ICF/MR Funds | 0 | 0 | 0 | 0 | 0 | 0 | 0 | 0 |
| Small Public | 0 | 0 | 0 | 0 | 0 | 0 | 0 | 0 |
| Small Private | 0 | 0 | 0 | 0 | 0 | 0 | 0 | 0 |
| HCBS Waiver | 0 | 0 | 0 | 0 | 0 | 0 | 0 | 511,300 |
| Model 50/200 Waiver | 0 | 0 | 0 | 0 | 0 | 0 | 0 | 0 |
| Other Title XIX Programs | 0 | 0 | 0 | 0 | 0 | 0 | 0 | 0 |
| Title XX / SSBG Funds | 1,800,000 | 1,830,000 | 1,860,000 | 1,890,000 | 1,940,000 | 2,115,000 | 5,000,000 | 5,200,000 |
| Other Federal Funds | 590,000 | 518,000 | 664,000 | 681,000 | 806,000 | 811,000 | 822,700 | 797,100 |
| Waiver Clients' SSI/ADC | 0 | 0 | 0 | 0 | 0 | 0 | 0 | 1,647,300 |

| | 1985 | 1986 | 1987 | 1988 | 1989 | 1990 | 1991 | 1992 |
|---|---|---|---|---|---|---|---|---|
| **TOTAL FUNDS** | $59,140,200 | $64,217,848 | $68,079,340 | $72,694,949 | $81,231,277 | $89,611,109 | $92,466,002 | $101,745,062 |
| **CONGREGATE 16+ BEDS** | 37,151,184 | 40,111,500 | 41,192,376 | 42,790,334 | 50,379,745 | 57,858,663 | 56,379,375 | 62,104,805 |
| INSTITUTIONAL SERVICES FUNDS | 27,495,500 | 28,948,600 | 29,231,600 | 30,182,600 | 35,435,997 | 43,503,472 | 40,261,515 | 44,370,497 |
| STATE FUNDS | 8,514,600 | 9,209,500 | 9,597,800 | 9,148,900 | 9,446,666 | 11,630,313 | 10,738,016 | 11,889,247 |
| General Funds | 8,514,600 | 9,209,500 | 9,597,800 | 9,148,900 | 9,446,666 | 11,630,313 | 10,738,016 | 11,889,247 |
| Local | 0 | 0 | 0 | 0 | 0 | 0 | 0 | 0 |
| Other State Funds | 0 | 0 | 0 | 0 | 0 | 0 | 0 | 0 |
| FEDERAL FUNDS | 18,980,900 | 19,739,100 | 19,633,800 | 21,033,700 | 25,989,331 | 31,873,159 | 29,523,499 | 32,481,250 |
| Federal ICF/MR | 18,242,900 | 18,895,300 | 18,879,200 | 20,170,600 | 25,207,282 | 31,349,410 | 28,973,581 | 31,917,855 |
| Title XX / SSBG Funds | 0 | 0 | 0 | 0 | 0 | 0 | 0 | 0 |
| Other Federal Funds | 738,000 | 843,800 | 754,600 | 863,100 | 782,049 | 523,749 | 549,918 | 563,395 |
| LARGE PRIVATE RESIDENTIAL | 9,655,684 | 11,162,900 | 11,960,776 | 12,607,734 | 14,943,748 | 14,355,191 | 16,117,860 | 17,734,308 |
| STATE FUNDS | 2,827,184 | 3,309,800 | 3,514,076 | 3,544,034 | 4,073,666 | 3,884,515 | 4,358,269 | 4,813,091 |
| General Funds | 2,827,184 | 3,309,800 | 3,514,076 | 3,544,034 | 4,073,666 | 3,884,515 | 4,358,269 | 4,813,091 |
| Other State Funds | 0 | 0 | 0 | 0 | 0 | 0 | 0 | 0 |
| Local/County Overmatch | 0 | 0 | 0 | 0 | 0 | 0 | 0 | 0 |
| FEDERAL FUNDS | 6,828,500 | 7,853,100 | 8,446,700 | 9,063,700 | 10,870,082 | 10,470,676 | 11,759,591 | 12,921,217 |
| Large Private ICF/MR | 6,828,500 | 7,853,100 | 8,446,700 | 9,063,700 | 10,870,082 | 10,470,676 | 11,759,591 | 12,921,217 |
| **COMMUNITY SERVICES FUNDS** | 21,989,016 | 24,106,348 | 26,886,964 | 29,904,615 | 30,851,532 | 31,752,446 | 36,086,627 | 39,640,257 |
| STATE FUNDS | 13,701,316 | 13,705,600 | 15,422,524 | 16,139,666 | 16,739,898 | 17,197,410 | 19,095,140 | 20,309,352 |
| General Funds | 12,206,316 | 12,366,600 | 13,992,524 | 14,709,666 | 15,238,398 | 14,979,432 | 17,073,181 | 18,571,178 |
| Other State Funds | 0 | 0 | 0 | 0 | 0 | 641,403 | 366,555 | 0 |
| Local/County Overmatch | 0 | 0 | 0 | 0 | 0 | 0 | 0 | 0 |
| SSI State Supplement | 1,495,000 | 1,339,000 | 1,430,000 | 1,430,000 | 1,501,500 | 1,576,575 | 1,655,404 | 1,738,174 |
| FEDERAL FUNDS | 8,287,700 | 10,400,748 | 11,464,440 | 13,764,949 | 14,111,634 | 14,555,036 | 16,991,487 | 19,330,905 |
| ICF/MR Funds | 0 | 0 | 0 | 0 | 0 | 0 | 0 | 0 |
| Small Public | 0 | 0 | 0 | 0 | 0 | 0 | 0 | 0 |
| Small Private | 0 | 0 | 0 | 0 | 0 | 0 | 0 | 0 |
| HCBS Waiver | 5,611,400 | 6,899,500 | 7,749,900 | 9,395,400 | 9,582,173 | 9,687,514 | 11,861,223 | 13,848,568 |
| Model 50/200 Waiver | 0 | 0 | 0 | 95,057 | 0 | 0 | 0 | 0 |
| Other Title XIX Programs | 0 | 0 | 0 | 0 | 0 | 0 | 0 | 0 |
| Title XX / SSBG Funds | 0 | 0 | 0 | 0 | 0 | 0 | 0 | 0 |
| Other Federal Funds | 818,700 | 1,489,700 | 1,473,000 | 1,712,300 | 1,554,061 | 1,524,610 | 1,527,240 | 1,589,789 |
| Waiver Clients' SSI/ADC | 1,857,600 | 2,011,548 | 2,241,540 | 2,562,192 | 2,975,400 | 3,342,912 | 3,603,024 | 3,892,548 |

Source:
Institute on Disability and Human Development (UAP),
University of Illinois at Chicago, 1994

# LOUISIANA

## MR/DD Spending for Congregate Residential & Community Services

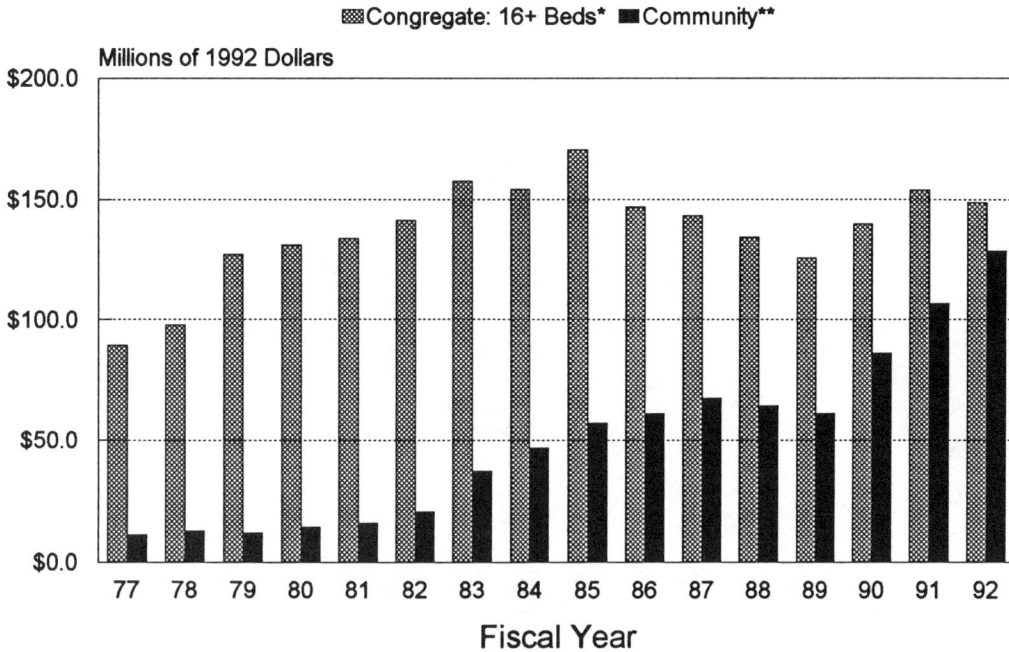

▨ Congregate: 16+ Beds*  ■ Community**

Millions of 1992 Dollars

$200.0

$150.0

$100.0

$50.0

$0.0

77  78  79  80  81  82  83  84  85  86  87  88  89  90  91  92

Fiscal Year

*Excludes nursing homes; ** Includes resources for
15 bed or less residential settings & non-residential community services

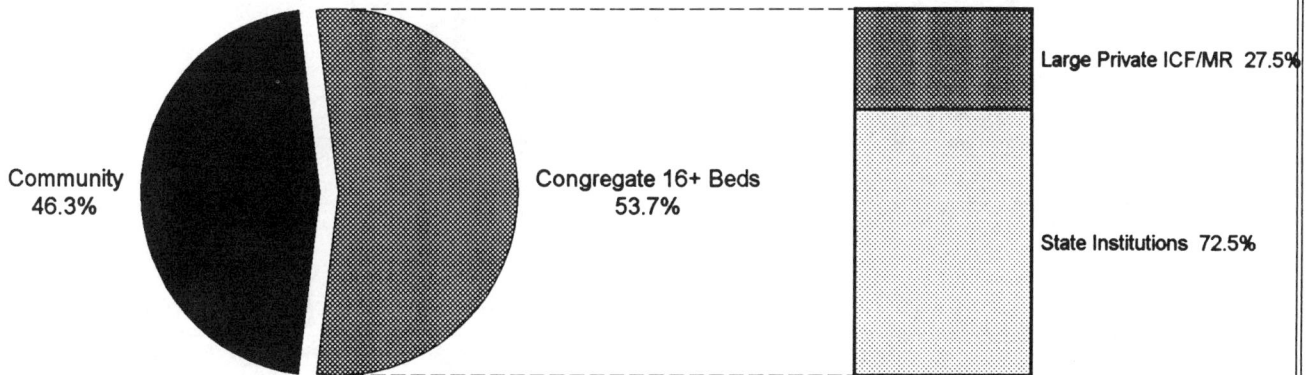

Community
46.3%

Congregate 16+ Beds
53.7%

Large Private ICF/MR  27.5%

State Institutions  72.5%

FY 1992 Total Spending:
$276.9 Million

Source:
Institute on Disability and Human Development (UAP),
University of Illinois at Chicago, 1994

# LOUISIANA

## Number of Persons Served by Residential Setting: FY 1992

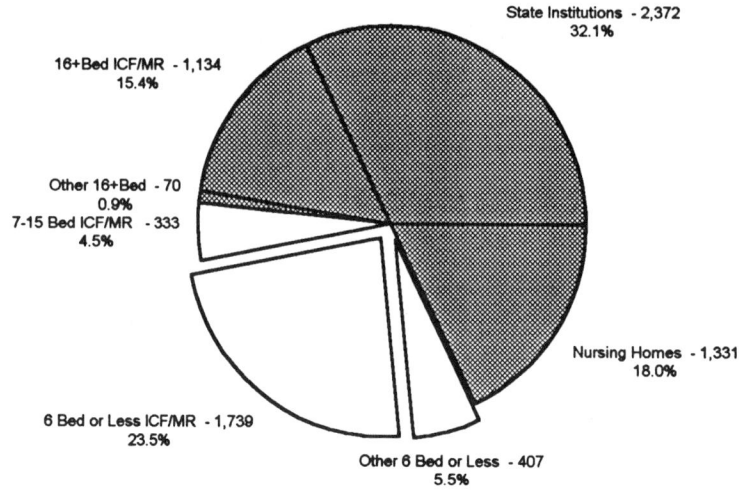

State Institutions - 2,372
32.1%

16+Bed ICF/MR - 1,134
15.4%

Other 16+Bed - 70
0.9%
7-15 Bed ICF/MR - 333
4.5%

Nursing Homes - 1,331
18.0%

6 Bed or Less ICF/MR - 1,739
23.5%

Other 6 Bed or Less - 407
5.5%

Total Served: 7,386

## Persons Served by Residential Setting:1986-92

|  | 1986 | 1987 | 1988 | 1989 | 1990 | 1991 | 1992 |
|---|---|---|---|---|---|---|---|
| CONGREGATE 16 + BED SETTINGS | NA | NA | 5,727 | 5,486 | 5,286 | 5,069 | 4,907 |
| Nursing Homes | NA | NA | 1,331 | 1,331 | 1,331 | 1,331 | 1,331 |
| State Institutions | 3,039 | 2,917 | 2,841 | 2,756 | 2,582 | 2,482 | 2,372 |
| Private 16+Bed ICF/MR | 1,527 | 1,541 | 1,555 | 1,329 | 1,303 | 1,186 | 1,134 |
| Other 16+Bed Residential | 0 | 0 | 0 | 70 | 70 | 70 | 70 |
| 15 BED OR LESS RESIDENTIAL SETTINGS | 949 | 1,292 | 1,657 | 1,870 | 2,181 | 2,496 | 2,479 |
| Public 7-15 Bed ICF/MR | 0 | 0 | 0 | 0 | 0 | 0 | 0 |
| Private 7-15 Bed ICF/MR | 272 | 272 | 272 | 272 | 272 | 272 | 333 |
| Other 7-15 Bed Residential | 0 | 0 | 0 | 0 | 0 | 0 | 0 |
| Public 6 Bed or Less ICF/MR | 35 | 33 | 30 | 30 | 36 | 36 | 58 |
| Private 6 Bed or Less ICF/MR | 401 | 676 | 951 | 1,163 | 1,460 | 1,776 | 1,681 |
| Other 6 Bed or Less Residential | 241 | 311 | 404 | 405 | 413 | 412 | 407 |
| TOTAL PERSONS SERVED | NA | NA | 7,384 | 7,356 | 7,467 | 7,565 | 7,386 |

## Persons Served in Non-Residential Community Services:1986-92

|  | 1986 | 1987 | 1988 | 1989 | 1990 | 1991 | 1992 |
|---|---|---|---|---|---|---|---|
| DAY/WORK PROGRAMS | 3,691 | 3,202 | 2,780 | 2,774 | 2,725 | 2,916 | 3,485 |
| Sheltered Employment/Work Activity | 3,691 | 3,202 | 1,979 | 1,932 | 1,964 | 1,771 | 1,620 |
| Day Habilitation ("Day Training") | NA | NA | 801 | 842 | 761 | 880 | 1,287 |
| Supported/Competitive Employment | 0 | 0 | 0 | NA | NA | 265 | 578 |
| CASE MANAGEMENT | NA | NA | NA | 1,071 | 1,071 | 3,900 | 2,800 |
| HCBS WAIVER | 0 | 0 | 0 | 0 | 59 | 190 | 494 |
| MODEL 50/200 WAIVER | 0 | 0 | 0 | 0 | 0 | 0 | 0 |

*Source:*
Institute on Disability and Human Development (UAP),
University of Illinois at Chicago, 1994

# LOUISIANA

## Community Services: FY 1992 Revenue Sources

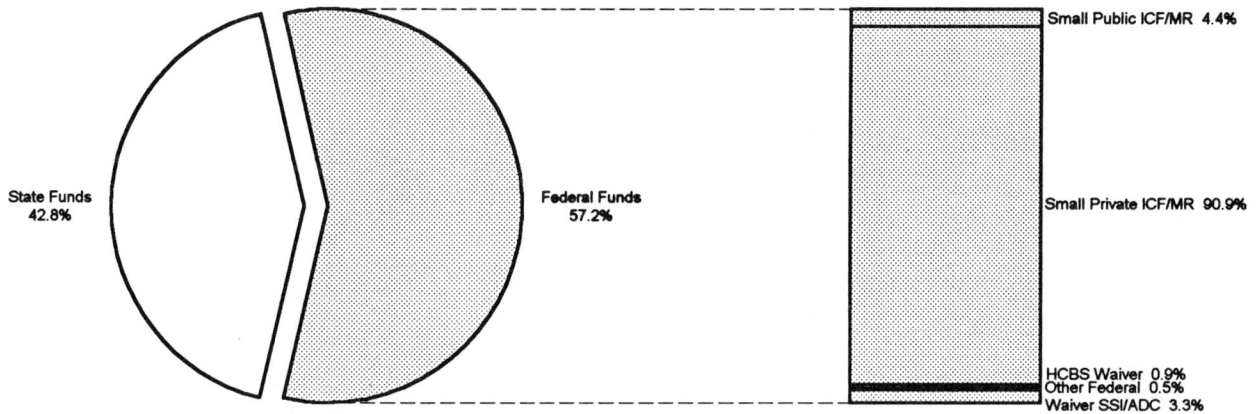

State Funds 42.8%

Federal Funds 57.2%

Small Public ICF/MR 4.4%

Small Private ICF/MR 90.9%

HCBS Waiver 0.9%
Other Federal 0.5%
Waiver SSI/ADC 3.3%

Total Funds: $128.3 Million

## Family Support Initiatives*

| | 1986 | 1987 | 1988 | 1989 | 1990 | 1991 | 1992 |
|---|---|---|---|---|---|---|---|
| FAMILY SUPPORT: TOTAL SPENDING | $38,260 | $40,919 | $561,648 | $1,810,075 | $1,847,291 | $2,610,913 | $3,735,924 |
| Total # of Families Supported | 0 | 0 | 150 | 846 | 895 | 980 | 1,480 |
| A. Financial Subsidy/Payment | $38,260 | $40,919 | $45,743 | $45,743 | $89,170 | $283,218 | $1,043,845 |
| # of Families | NA | NA | NA | 23 | 65 | 110 | 609 |
| B. Family Assistance Payments | $0 | $0 | $0 | $1,270,948 | $1,270,948 | $1,395,337 | $1,395,337 |
| # of Families | 0 | 0 | 0 | 672 | 672 | 715 | 715 |
| C. Other Family Support Payments | $0 | $0 | $515,905 | $493,384 | $487,173 | $932,358 | $1,296,742 |
| # of Families | 0 | 0 | 150 | 151 | 158 | 155 | 156 |

## Other Community Services Initiatives*

| | 1986 | 1987 | 1988 | 1989 | 1990 | 1991 | 1992 |
|---|---|---|---|---|---|---|---|
| AGING/DD SPENDING | $0 | $0 | $0 | $0 | $0 | $0 | $0 |
| # of Persons Served | 0 | 0 | 0 | 0 | 0 | 0 | 0 |
| ASSISTIVE TECHNOLOGY SPENDING | | | | | | | $0 |
| # of Persons Served | | | | | | | 0 |
| EARLY INTERVENTION SPENDING | $388,297 | $255,036 | $3,037,827 | $2,832,122 | $2,855,669 | $2,954,387 | $3,072,562 |
| # of Persons Served | NA | NA | 801 | 742 | 761 | 880 | 1,287 |
| PERSONAL ASSISTANCE SPENDING | | | | | | | $0 |
| # of Persons Served | | | | | | | 0 |
| SUPPORTED EMPLOYMENT SPENDING | $0 | $0 | $0 | NA | NA | $1,175,450 | $3,829,465 |
| # of Persons Served | 0 | 0 | 0 | NA | NA | 265 | 578 |
| SUPPORTED LIVING SPENDING | | | | | | | $30,824 |
| # of Persons Served | | | | | | | 23 |

*Expenditures associated with Special Community Initiatives are a subset of funding within the community services component of the state's chart series and spreadsheet; Family Support Client figures may include duplicate client counts; HCBS Waiver counts include Waiver case management numbers.
0= Services not provided in the state; NA= Data not available from state; blank= Services not applicable (eg. CSLA prior to authorization, Special Community Initiatives prior to request for data by this study)

Source:
Institute on Disability and Human Development (UAP),
University of Illinois at Chicago, 1994

# LOUISIANA

## Large Congregate Care Facilities: FY 1992 Revenue Sources*

### Private 16+Bed Settings

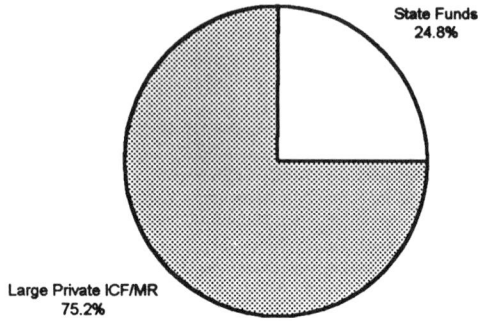

State Funds
24.8%

Large Private ICF/MR
75.2%

Total Funds: $40.8 Million

### Public Institutions

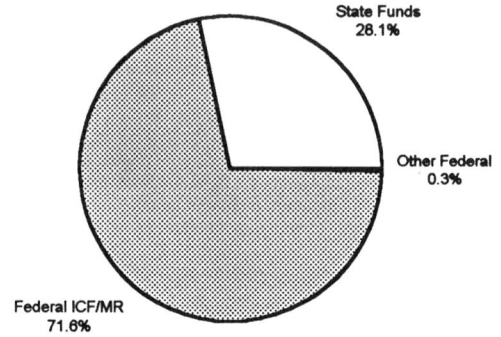

State Funds
28.1%

Other Federal
0.3%

Federal ICF/MR
71.6%

Total Funds: $107.7 Million

*Excludes nursing homes

## Average Daily Residents in Institutions

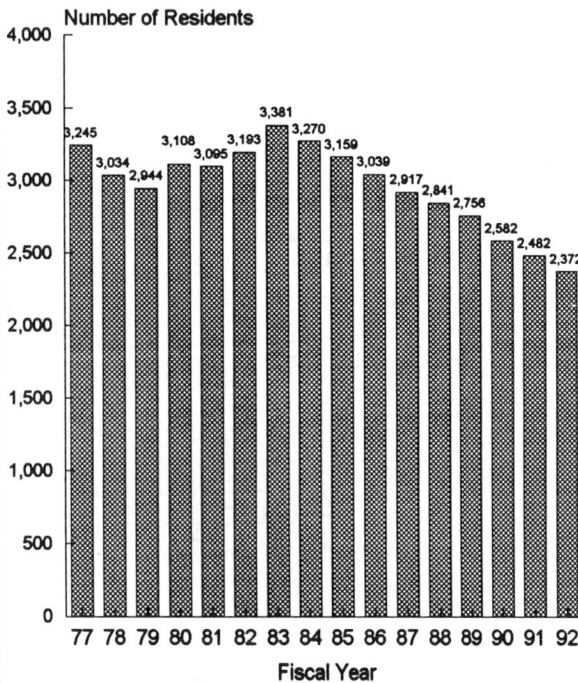

Number of Residents

| Fiscal Year | Residents |
|---|---|
| 77 | 3,245 |
| 78 | 3,034 |
| 79 | 2,944 |
| 80 | 3,108 |
| 81 | 3,095 |
| 82 | 3,193 |
| 83 | 3,381 |
| 84 | 3,270 |
| 85 | 3,159 |
| 86 | 3,039 |
| 87 | 2,917 |
| 88 | 2,841 |
| 89 | 2,756 |
| 90 | 2,582 |
| 91 | 2,482 |
| 92 | 2,372 |

Fiscal Year

## Institutional Daily Costs Per Resident

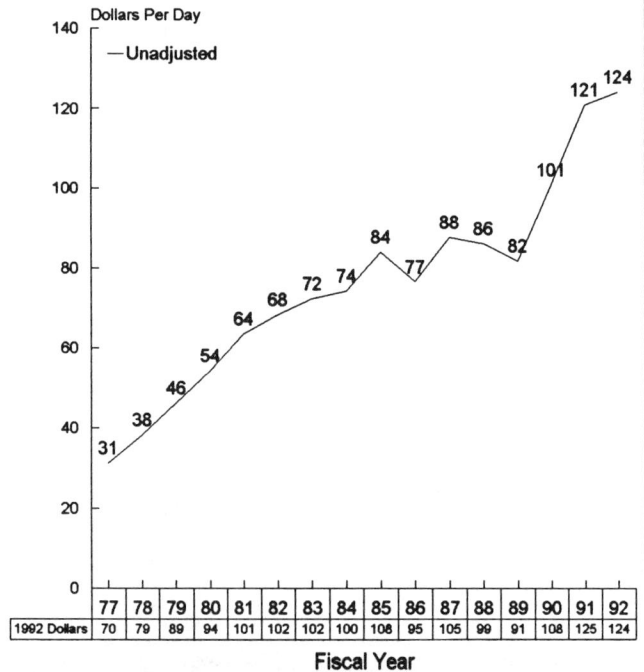

Dollars Per Day

— Unadjusted

| Fiscal Year | Unadjusted | 1992 Dollars |
|---|---|---|
| 77 | 31 | 70 |
| 78 | 38 | 79 |
| 79 | 46 | 89 |
| 80 | 54 | 94 |
| 81 | 64 | 101 |
| 82 | 68 | 102 |
| 83 | 72 | 102 |
| 84 | 74 | 100 |
| 85 | 84 | 108 |
| 86 | 77 | 95 |
| 87 | 88 | 105 |
| 88 | 86 | 99 |
| 89 | 82 | 91 |
| 90 | 101 | 108 |
| 91 | 121 | 125 |
| 92 | 124 | 124 |

Fiscal Year

Source:
Institute on Disability and Human Development (UAP),
University of Illinois at Chicago, 1994

# LOUISIANA FISCAL EFFORT

MR/DD Spending Per $1,000 of Personal Income

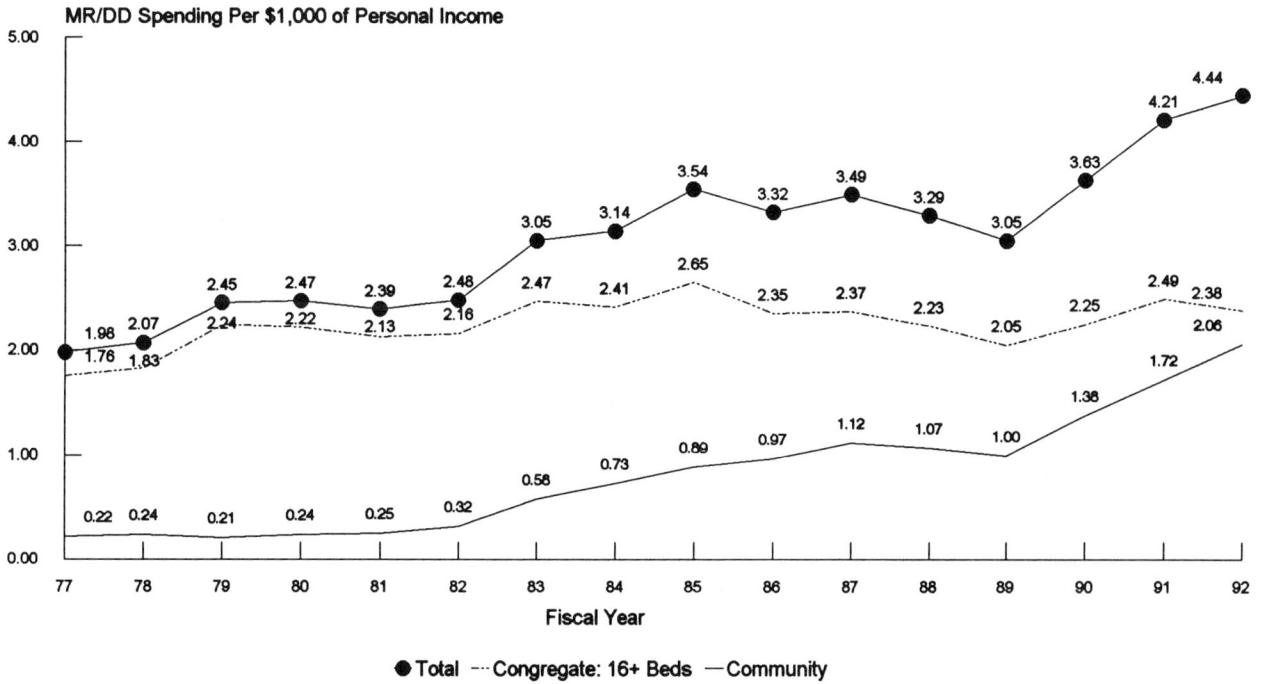

| | 77 | 78 | 79 | 80 | 81 | 82 | 83 | 84 | 85 | 86 | 87 | 88 | 89 | 90 | 91 | 92 |
|---|----|----|----|----|----|----|----|----|----|----|----|----|----|----|----|----|
| Total | 1.98 | 2.07 | 2.45 | 2.47 | 2.39 | 2.48 | 3.05 | 3.14 | 3.54 | 3.32 | 3.49 | 3.29 | 3.05 | 3.63 | 4.21 | 4.44 |
| Congregate: 16+ Beds | 1.76 | 1.83 | 2.24 | 2.22 | 2.13 | 2.16 | 2.47 | 2.41 | 2.65 | 2.35 | 2.37 | 2.23 | 2.05 | 2.25 | 2.49 | 2.38 |
| Community | 0.22 | 0.24 | 0.21 | 0.24 | 0.25 | 0.32 | 0.58 | 0.73 | 0.89 | 0.97 | 1.12 | 1.07 | 1.00 | 1.38 | 1.72 | 2.06 |

Fiscal Year

● Total    --- Congregate: 16+ Beds    — Community

## Total MR/DD Spending

Millions of Dollars
— Unadjusted

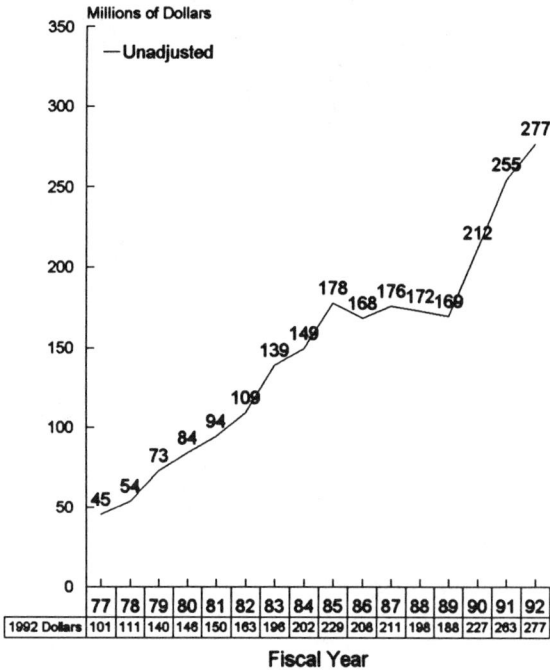

| | 77 | 78 | 79 | 80 | 81 | 82 | 83 | 84 | 85 | 86 | 87 | 88 | 89 | 90 | 91 | 92 |
|---|----|----|----|----|----|----|----|----|----|----|----|----|----|----|----|----|
| | 45 | 54 | 73 | 84 | 94 | 109 | 139 | 149 | 178 | 168 | 176 | 172 | 169 | 212 | 255 | 277 |
| 1992 Dollars | 101 | 111 | 140 | 146 | 150 | 163 | 196 | 202 | 229 | 208 | 211 | 198 | 188 | 227 | 263 | 277 |

Fiscal Year

## Personal Income

Billions of Dollars
— Unadjusted

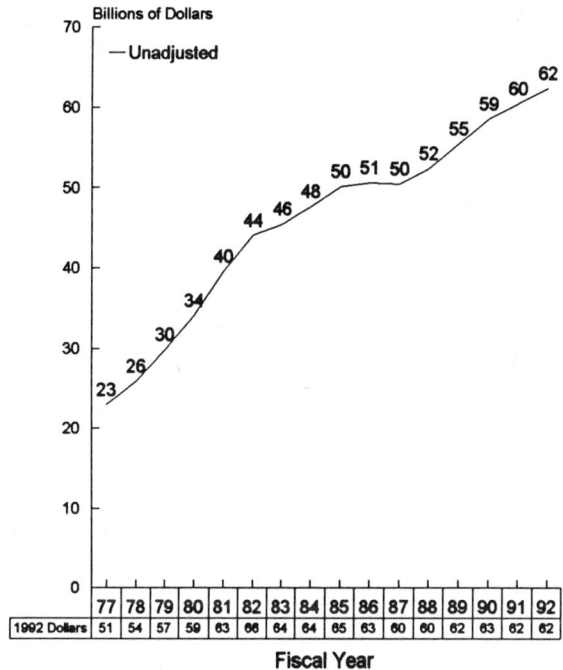

| | 77 | 78 | 79 | 80 | 81 | 82 | 83 | 84 | 85 | 86 | 87 | 88 | 89 | 90 | 91 | 92 |
|---|----|----|----|----|----|----|----|----|----|----|----|----|----|----|----|----|
| | 23 | 26 | 30 | 34 | 40 | 44 | 46 | 48 | 50 | 51 | 50 | 52 | 55 | 59 | 60 | 62 |
| 1992 Dollars | 51 | 54 | 57 | 59 | 63 | 66 | 64 | 64 | 65 | 63 | 60 | 60 | 62 | 63 | 62 | 62 |

Fiscal Year

*Source:*
Institute on Disability and Human Development (UAP),
University of Illinois at Chicago, 1994

# LOUISIANA
## Financial Support for MR/DD Services: FY 1977-92

| | 1977 | 1978 | 1979 | 1980 | 1981 | 1982 | 1983 | 1984 |
|---|---|---|---|---|---|---|---|---|
| **TOTAL FUNDS** | $45,348,000 | $53,651,000 | $72,899,000 | $84,014,000 | $94,426,000 | $109,235,800 | $138,883,598 | $149,366,928 |
| **CONGREGATE 16+ BEDS** | 40,244,313 | 47,432,699 | 66,588,057 | 75,727,711 | 84,338,898 | 95,229,190 | 112,303,985 | 114,536,820 |
| INSTITUTIONAL SERVICES FUNDS | 36,992,000 | 42,389,000 | 49,708,000 | 61,754,000 | 71,828,000 | 79,649,000 | 89,244,000 | 88,903,000 |
| STATE FUNDS | 15,641,000 | 18,657,000 | 23,501,000 | 26,059,000 | 28,160,000 | 29,889,000 | 35,814,000 | 34,119,000 |
| General Funds | 7,648,000 | 8,790,000 | 12,591,000 | 9,977,000 | 8,414,000 | 5,330,000 | 9,435,000 | 2,948,000 |
| Local | 0 | 0 | 0 | 0 | 0 | 0 | 0 | 0 |
| Other State Funds | 7,993,000 | 9,867,000 | 10,910,000 | 16,082,000 | 19,746,000 | 24,559,000 | 26,379,000 | 31,171,000 |
| FEDERAL FUNDS | 21,351,000 | 23,732,000 | 26,207,000 | 35,695,000 | 43,668,000 | 49,760,000 | 53,430,000 | 54,784,000 |
| Federal ICF/MR | 20,977,000 | 23,523,000 | 26,010,000 | 35,498,000 | 43,434,000 | 49,527,000 | 53,196,000 | 54,550,000 |
| Title XX / SSBG Funds | 0 | 0 | 0 | 0 | 0 | 0 | 0 | 0 |
| Other Federal Funds | 374,000 | 209,000 | 197,000 | 197,000 | 234,000 | 233,000 | 234,000 | 234,000 |
| LARGE PRIVATE RESIDENTIAL | 3,252,313 | 5,043,699 | 16,880,057 | 13,973,711 | 12,510,898 | 15,580,190 | 23,059,985 | 25,633,820 |
| STATE FUNDS | 897,313 | 1,465,699 | 4,988,057 | 4,299,711 | 3,900,898 | 5,088,490 | 7,644,385 | 8,959,020 |
| General Funds | 0 | 0 | 0 | 0 | 0 | 0 | 0 | 0 |
| Other State Funds | 897,313 | 1,465,699 | 4,988,057 | 4,299,711 | 3,900,898 | 5,088,490 | 7,644,385 | 8,959,020 |
| Local/County Overmatch | 0 | 0 | 0 | 0 | 0 | 0 | 0 | 0 |
| FEDERAL FUNDS | 2,355,000 | 3,578,000 | 11,892,000 | 9,674,000 | 8,610,000 | 10,491,700 | 15,415,600 | 16,674,800 |
| Large Private ICF/MR | 2,355,000 | 3,578,000 | 11,892,000 | 9,674,000 | 8,610,000 | 10,491,700 | 15,415,600 | 16,674,800 |
| **COMMUNITY SERVICES FUNDS** | 5,103,687 | 6,218,301 | 6,310,943 | 8,286,289 | 10,087,102 | 14,006,610 | 26,579,613 | 34,830,108 |
| STATE FUNDS | 2,680,687 | 2,281,301 | 2,118,943 | 3,001,289 | 3,574,102 | 8,535,610 | 16,398,115 | 17,020,080 |
| General Funds | 1,997,687 | 1,200,301 | 765,943 | 1,465,289 | 1,735,102 | 2,748,510 | 13,933,800 | 11,420,200 |
| Other State Funds | 683,000 | 1,081,000 | 1,353,000 | 1,536,000 | 1,839,000 | 5,787,100 | 2,464,315 | 5,599,880 |
| Local/County Overmatch | 0 | 0 | 0 | 0 | 0 | 0 | 0 | 0 |
| SSI State Supplement | 0 | 0 | 0 | 0 | 0 | 0 | 0 | 0 |
| FEDERAL FUNDS | 2,423,000 | 3,937,000 | 4,192,000 | 5,285,000 | 6,513,000 | 5,471,000 | 10,181,498 | 17,810,028 |
| ICF/MR Funds | 0 | 0 | 0 | 0 | 0 | 0 | 1,337,000 | 4,563,000 |
| Small Public | 0 | 0 | 0 | 0 | 0 | 0 | 0 | 0 |
| Small Private | 0 | 0 | 0 | 0 | 0 | 0 | 1,337,000 | 4,563,000 |
| HCBS Waiver | 0 | 0 | 0 | 0 | 0 | 0 | 1,574,000 | 5,156,500 |
| Model 50/200 Waiver | 0 | 0 | 0 | 0 | 0 | 0 | 0 | 0 |
| Other Title XIX Programs | 0 | 0 | 0 | 0 | 0 | 0 | 0 | 0 |
| Title XX / SSBG Funds | 2,049,000 | 3,245,000 | 3,498,000 | 4,610,000 | 5,518,000 | 4,611,000 | 0 | 0 |
| Other Federal Funds | 374,000 | 692,000 | 694,000 | 675,000 | 995,000 | 860,000 | 1,019,000 | 995,000 |
| Waiver Clients' SSI/ADC | 0 | 0 | 0 | 0 | 0 | 0 | 6,251,498 | 7,095,528 |

| | 1985 | 1986 | 1987 | 1988 | 1989 | 1990 | 1991 | 1992 |
|---|---|---|---|---|---|---|---|---|
| **TOTAL FUNDS** | $177,543,919 | $168,054,618 | $175,803,242 | $172,470,424 | $169,224,985 | $212,360,979 | $254,618,740 | $276,868,148 |
| **CONGREGATE 16+ BEDS** | 132,973,827 | 118,763,818 | 119,473,608 | 116,697,636 | 113,939,540 | 131,512,566 | 150,427,451 | 148,543,839 |
| INSTITUTIONAL SERVICES FUNDS | 96,849,700 | 84,887,470 | 93,237,723 | 89,416,350 | 82,227,539 | 94,951,850 | 109,537,890 | 107,694,278 |
| STATE FUNDS | 41,523,400 | 32,963,836 | 25,751,797 | 25,437,092 | 27,516,480 | 31,457,774 | 34,287,118 | 30,306,668 |
| General Funds | 11,052,600 | 4,394,273 | 114,828 | 323,700 | 1,192,979 | 3,639,193 | 4,172,423 | 0 |
| Local | 0 | 0 | 0 | 0 | 0 | 0 | 0 | 0 |
| Other State Funds | 30,470,800 | 28,569,563 | 25,636,969 | 25,113,392 | 26,323,501 | 27,818,581 | 30,114,695 | 30,306,668 |
| FEDERAL FUNDS | 55,326,300 | 51,923,634 | 67,485,926 | 63,979,258 | 54,711,059 | 63,494,076 | 75,250,772 | 77,387,610 |
| Federal ICF/MR | 55,055,300 | 51,406,834 | 66,969,126 | 63,462,458 | 54,422,247 | 63,201,244 | 74,961,195 | 77,099,610 |
| Title XX / SSBG Funds | 0 | 0 | 0 | 0 | 0 | 0 | 0 | 0 |
| Other Federal Funds | 271,000 | 516,800 | 516,800 | 516,800 | 288,812 | 292,832 | 289,577 | 288,000 |
| LARGE PRIVATE RESIDENTIAL | 36,124,127 | 33,876,348 | 26,235,885 | 27,281,286 | 31,712,001 | 36,560,716 | 40,889,561 | 40,849,561 |
| STATE FUNDS | 12,842,127 | 12,205,648 | 9,109,099 | 8,828,224 | 9,396,266 | 10,013,980 | 10,574,040 | 10,130,691 |
| General Funds | 0 | 0 | 0 | 0 | 0 | 0 | 0 | 0 |
| Other State Funds | 12,842,127 | 12,205,648 | 9,109,099 | 8,828,224 | 9,396,266 | 10,013,980 | 10,574,040 | 10,130,691 |
| Local/County Overmatch | 0 | 0 | 0 | 0 | 0 | 0 | 0 | 0 |
| FEDERAL FUNDS | 23,282,000 | 21,670,700 | 17,126,786 | 18,453,062 | 22,315,735 | 26,546,736 | 30,315,521 | 30,718,870 |
| Large Private ICF/MR | 23,282,000 | 21,670,700 | 17,126,786 | 18,453,062 | 22,315,735 | 26,546,736 | 30,315,521 | 30,718,870 |
| **COMMUNITY SERVICES FUNDS** | 44,570,092 | 49,290,800 | 56,329,634 | 55,772,788 | 55,285,445 | 80,848,413 | 104,191,289 | 128,324,309 |
| STATE FUNDS | 23,008,873 | 36,489,709 | 35,340,444 | 33,372,817 | 28,789,011 | 38,071,896 | 46,357,180 | 54,980,190 |
| General Funds | 15,812,600 | 30,010,909 | 24,810,194 | 23,162,599 | 18,057,768 | 21,937,562 | 25,735,475 | 31,046,912 |
| Other State Funds | 7,196,273 | 6,478,800 | 10,530,250 | 10,210,218 | 10,731,243 | 16,134,334 | 20,621,705 | 23,933,278 |
| Local/County Overmatch | 0 | 0 | 0 | 0 | 0 | 0 | 0 | 0 |
| SSI State Supplement | 0 | 0 | 0 | 0 | 0 | 0 | 0 | 0 |
| FEDERAL FUNDS | 21,561,219 | 12,801,091 | 20,989,190 | 22,399,971 | 26,496,434 | 42,776,517 | 57,834,109 | 73,344,119 |
| ICF/MR Funds | 8,313,600 | 11,502,900 | 19,798,809 | 20,788,749 | 24,775,361 | 42,017,876 | 56,620,095 | 69,906,666 |
| Small Public | 524,600 | 487,800 | 967,093 | 498,729 | 432,562 | 925,377 | 1,254,770 | 3,215,997 |
| Small Private | 7,789,000 | 11,015,100 | 18,831,716 | 20,290,020 | 24,342,799 | 41,092,499 | 55,365,325 | 66,690,669 |
| HCBS Waiver | 4,733,300 | 0 | 0 | 0 | 0 | 23,750 | 80,835 | 683,257 |
| Model 50/200 Waiver | 0 | 0 | 0 | 0 | 0 | 0 | 0 | 0 |
| Other Title XIX Programs | 0 | 0 | 0 | 0 | 0 | 0 | 0 | 0 |
| Title XX / SSBG Funds | 0 | 0 | 0 | 0 | 0 | 0 | 0 | 0 |
| Other Federal Funds | 1,001,119 | 1,298,191 | 1,190,381 | 1,611,222 | 1,721,073 | 474,347 | 262,219 | 341,500 |
| Waiver Clients' SSI/ADC | 7,513,200 | 0 | 0 | 0 | 0 | 260,544 | 870,960 | 2,412,696 |

*Source:*

Institute on Disability and Human Development (UAP),
University of Illinois at Chicago, 1994

# MAINE

## MR/DD Spending for Congregate Residential & Community Services

▨Congregate: 16+ Beds*  ■Community**

Millions of 1992 Dollars

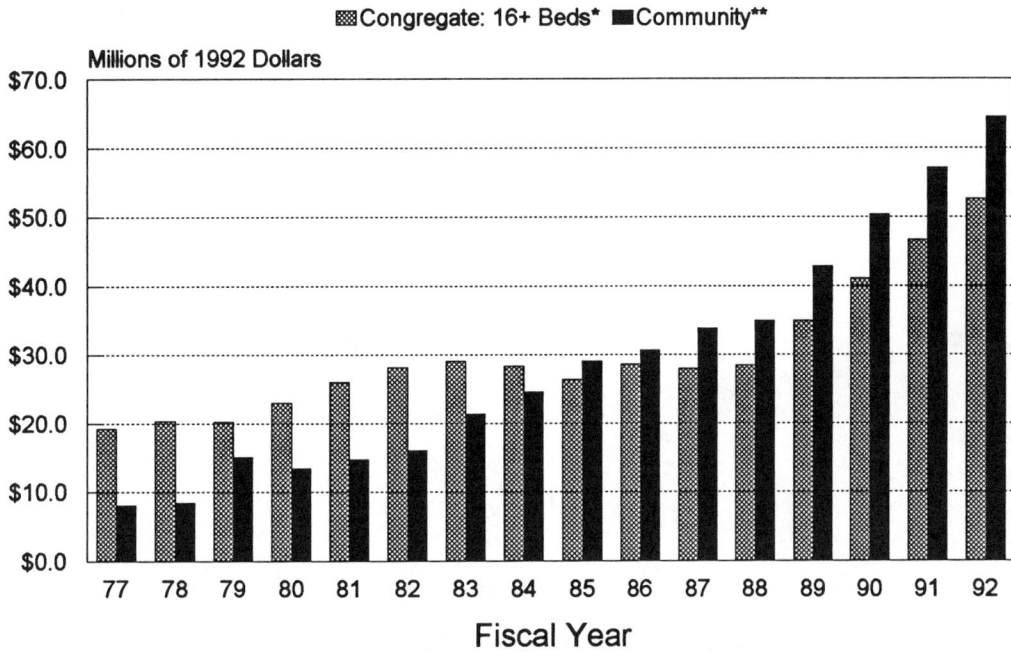

Fiscal Year

*Excludes nursing homes; ** Includes resources for
15 bed or less residential settings & non-residential community services

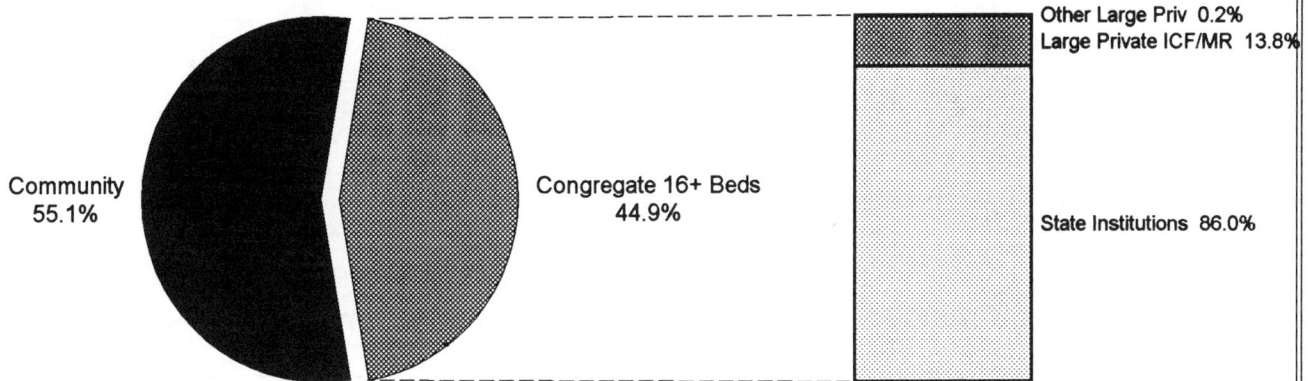

Community
55.1%

Congregate 16+ Beds
44.9%

Other Large Priv 0.2%
Large Private ICF/MR 13.8%

State Institutions 86.0%

FY 1992 Total Spending:
$117.1 Million

*Source:*
Institute on Disability and Human Development (UAP),
University of Illinois at Chicago, 1994

# MAINE

## Number of Persons Served by Residential Setting: FY 1992

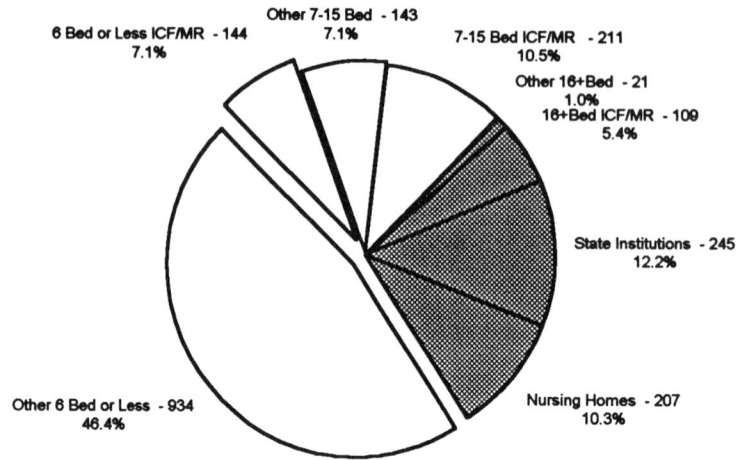

6 Bed or Less ICF/MR - 144
7.1%

Other 7-15 Bed - 143
7.1%

7-15 Bed ICF/MR - 211
10.5%

Other 16+Bed - 21
1.0%

16+Bed ICF/MR - 109
5.4%

State Institutions - 245
12.2%

Nursing Homes - 207
10.3%

Other 6 Bed or Less - 934
46.4%

Total Served: 2,014

## Persons Served by Residential Setting:1986-92

| | 1986 | 1987 | 1988 | 1989 | 1990 | 1991 | 1992 |
|---|---|---|---|---|---|---|---|
| CONGREGATE 16 + BED SETTINGS | 446 | 435 | 678 | 427 | 403 | 379 | 582 |
| Nursing Homes | NA | NA | 227 | NA | NA | NA | 207 |
| State Institutions | 302 | 291 | 307 | 292 | 276 | 261 | 245 |
| Private 16+Bed ICF/MR | 144 | 144 | 144 | 135 | 127 | 118 | 109 |
| Other 16+Bed Residential | 0 | 0 | 0 | 0 | 0 | 0 | 21 |
| 15 BED OR LESS RESIDENTIAL SETTINGS | NA | 617 | 689 | 771 | 852 | 934 | 1,432 |
| Public 7-15 Bed ICF/MR | 26 | 26 | 26 | 23 | 20 | 16 | 13 |
| Private 7-15 Bed ICF/MR | 205 | 232 | 241 | 256 | 272 | 287 | 198 |
| Other 7-15 Bed Residential | NA | 359 | 422 | 492 | 561 | 631 | 143 |
| Public 6 Bed or Less ICF/MR | | | | | | | 0 |
| Private 6 Bed or Less ICF/MR | | | | | | | 144 |
| Other 6 Bed or Less Residential | | | | | | | 934 |
| TOTAL PERSONS SERVED | NA | 1,052 | 1,367 | 1,198 | 1,255 | 1,312 | 2,014 |

## Persons Served in Non-Residential Community Services:1986-92

| | 1986 | 1987 | 1988 | 1989 | 1990 | 1991 | 1992 |
|---|---|---|---|---|---|---|---|
| DAY/WORK PROGRAMS | NA | 1,639 | 1,764 | NA | NA | NA | 2,689 |
| Sheltered Employment/Work Activity | NA | 844 | 855 | NA | NA | NA | NA |
| Day Habilitation ("Day Training") | NA | 696 | 743 | NA | NA | NA | 2,300 |
| Supported/Competitive Employment | NA | 99 | 166 | NA | NA | NA | 389 |
| CASE MANAGEMENT | NA | NA | 1,250 | NA | NA | NA | 4,626 |
| HCBS WAIVER | 350 | 390 | 430 | 453 | 454 | 453 | 584 |
| MODEL 50/200 WAIVER | 0 | 0 | 0 | 0 | 0 | 0 | 0 |

*Source:*
Institute on Disability and Human Development (UAP),
University of Illinois at Chicago, 1994

# MAINE

## Community Services: FY 1992 Revenue Sources

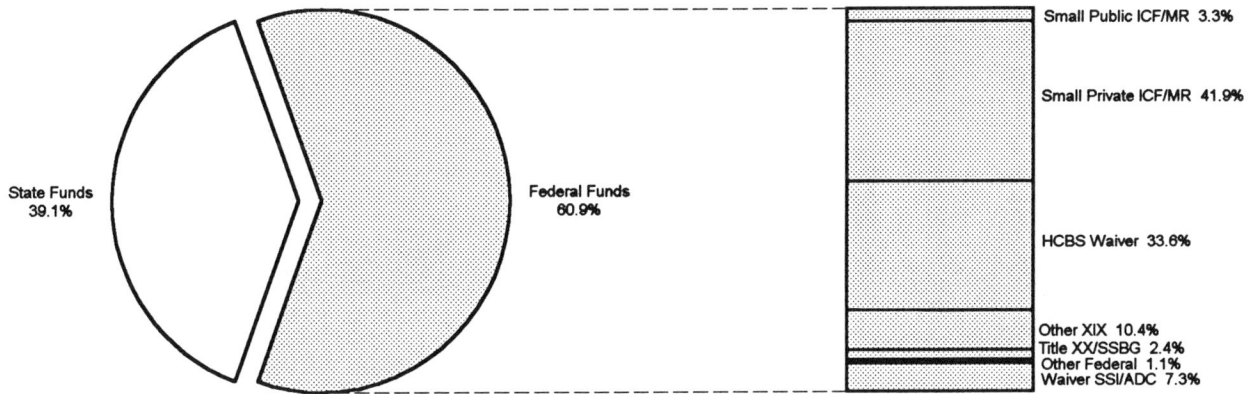

State Funds 39.1%

Federal Funds 60.9%

Small Public ICF/MR 3.3%

Small Private ICF/MR 41.9%

HCBS Waiver 33.6%

Other XIX 10.4%
Title XX/SSBG 2.4%
Other Federal 1.1%
Waiver SSI/ADC 7.3%

Total Funds: $64.5 Million

## Family Support Initiatives*

| | 1986 | 1987 | 1988 | 1989 | 1990 | 1991 | 1992 |
|---|---|---|---|---|---|---|---|
| **FAMILY SUPPORT: TOTAL SPENDING** | NA | NA | $197,306 | NA | NA | NA | $200,000 |
| **Total # of Families Supported** | NA | 300 | 500 | NA | NA | NA | 100 |
| A. Financial Subsidy/Payment | $0 | $0 | $0 | $0 | $0 | $0 | $0 |
| # of Families | 0 | 0 | 0 | 0 | 0 | 0 | 0 |
| B. Family Assistance Payments | NA | NA | $197,306 | NA | NA | NA | $200,000 |
| # of Families | NA | 300 | 500 | NA | NA | NA | 100 |
| C. Other Family Support Payments | $0 | $0 | $0 | $0 | $0 | $0 | $0 |
| # of Families | 0 | 0 | 0 | 0 | 0 | 0 | 0 |

## Other Community Services Initiatives*

| | 1986 | 1987 | 1988 | 1989 | 1990 | 1991 | 1992 |
|---|---|---|---|---|---|---|---|
| **AGING/DD SPENDING** | $0 | $0 | $0 | $0 | $0 | $0 | $0 |
| # of Persons Served | 0 | 0 | 0 | 0 | 0 | 0 | 0 |
| **ASSISTIVE TECHNOLOGY SPENDING** | | | | | | | NA |
| # of Persons Served | | | | | | | 436 |
| **EARLY INTERVENTION SPENDING** | $752,285 | $764,264 | $952,151 | NA | NA | NA | NA |
| # of Persons Served | NA | NA | NA | NA | NA | NA | NA |
| **PERSONAL ASSISTANCE SPENDING** | | | | | | | $0 |
| # of Persons Served | | | | | | | 0 |
| **SUPPORTED EMPLOYMENT SPENDING** | $200,000 | $250,000 | $300,000 | NA | NA | NA | $2,384,275 |
| # of Persons Served | 39 | 39 | 57 | NA | NA | NA | 389 |
| **SUPPORTED LIVING SPENDING** | | | | | | | $2,500,000 |
| # of Persons Served | | | | | | | 125 |

*Expenditures associated with Special Community Initiatives are a subset of funding within the community services component of the state's chart series and spreadsheet; Family Support Client figures may include duplicate client counts; HCBS Waiver counts include Waiver case management numbers.
0= Services not provided in the state; NA= Data not available from state; blank= Services not applicable (eg. CSLA prior to authorization, Special Community Initiatives prior to request for data by this study)

*Source:*
Institute on Disability and Human Development (UAP),
University of Illinois at Chicago, 1994

# MAINE

## Large Congregate Care Facilities: FY 1992 Revenue Sources*

### Private 16+Bed Settings

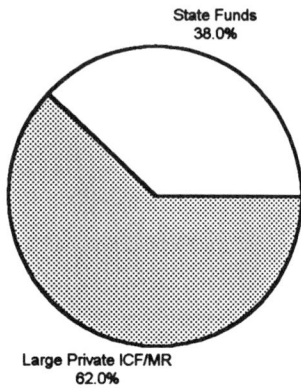

State Funds
38.0%

Large Private ICF/MR
62.0%

Total Funds: $7.4 Million

### Public Institutions

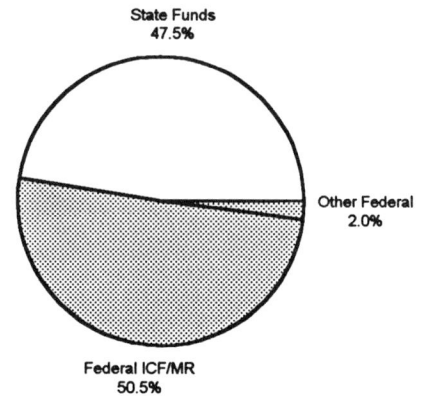

State Funds
47.5%

Other Federal
2.0%

Federal ICF/MR
50.5%

Total Funds: $45.3 Million

*Excludes nursing homes

## Average Daily Residents in Institutions

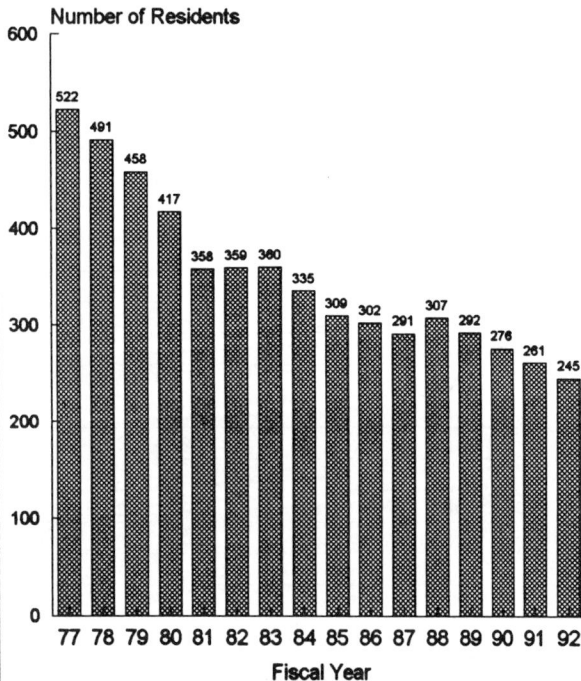

Number of Residents

| Fiscal Year | Residents |
|---|---|
| 77 | 522 |
| 78 | 491 |
| 79 | 458 |
| 80 | 417 |
| 81 | 358 |
| 82 | 359 |
| 83 | 360 |
| 84 | 335 |
| 85 | 309 |
| 86 | 302 |
| 87 | 291 |
| 88 | 307 |
| 89 | 292 |
| 90 | 276 |
| 91 | 261 |
| 92 | 245 |

Fiscal Year

## Institutional Daily Costs Per Resident

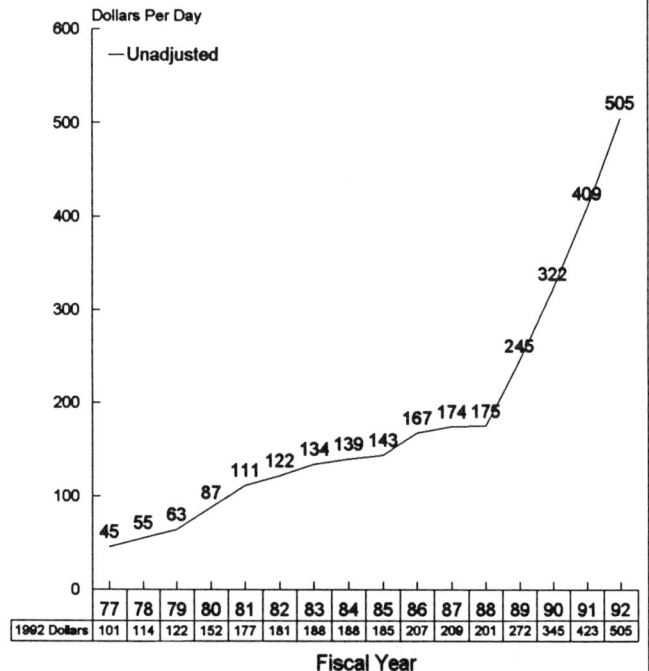

Dollars Per Day

— Unadjusted

| Fiscal Year | Unadjusted | 1992 Dollars |
|---|---|---|
| 77 | 45 | 101 |
| 78 | 55 | 114 |
| 79 | 63 | 122 |
| 80 | 87 | 152 |
| 81 | 111 | 177 |
| 82 | 122 | 181 |
| 83 | 134 | 188 |
| 84 | 139 | 188 |
| 85 | 143 | 185 |
| 86 | 167 | 207 |
| 87 | 174 | 209 |
| 88 | 175 | 201 |
| 89 | 245 | 272 |
| 90 | 322 | 345 |
| 91 | 409 | 423 |
| 92 | 505 | 505 |

Fiscal Year

*Source:*
Institute on Disability and Human Development (UAP),
University of Illinois at Chicago, 1994

# MAINE FISCAL EFFORT

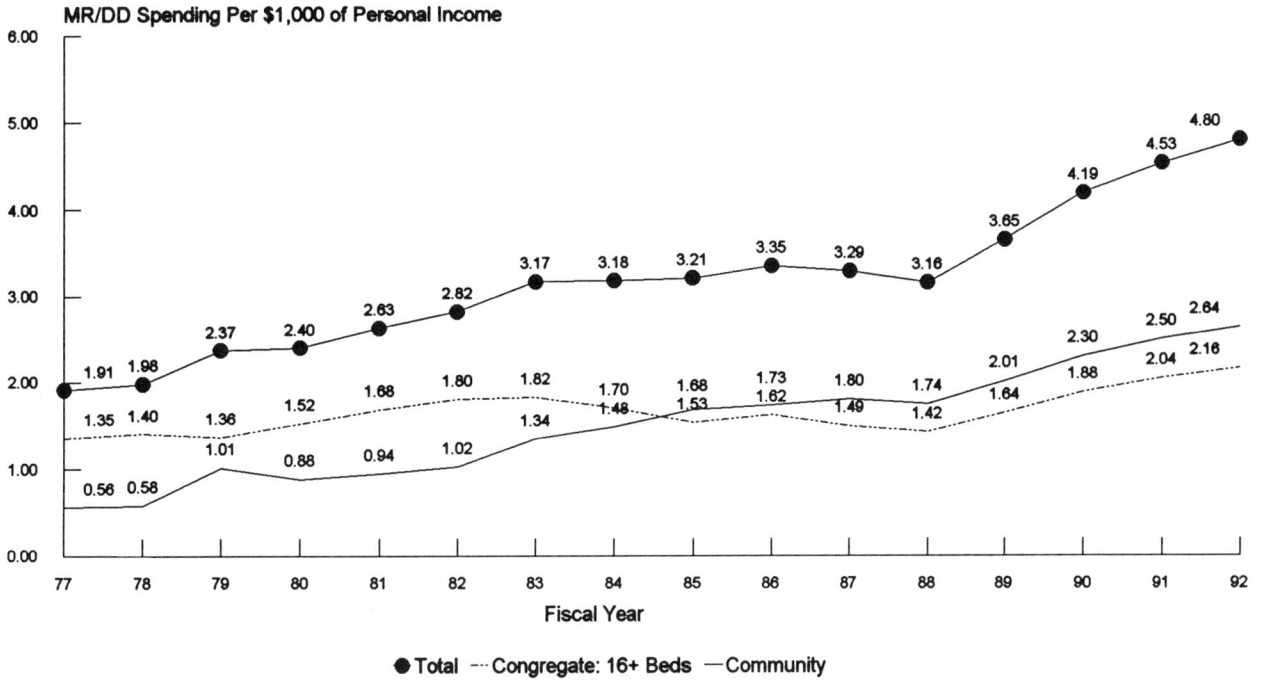

## MR/DD Spending Per $1,000 of Personal Income

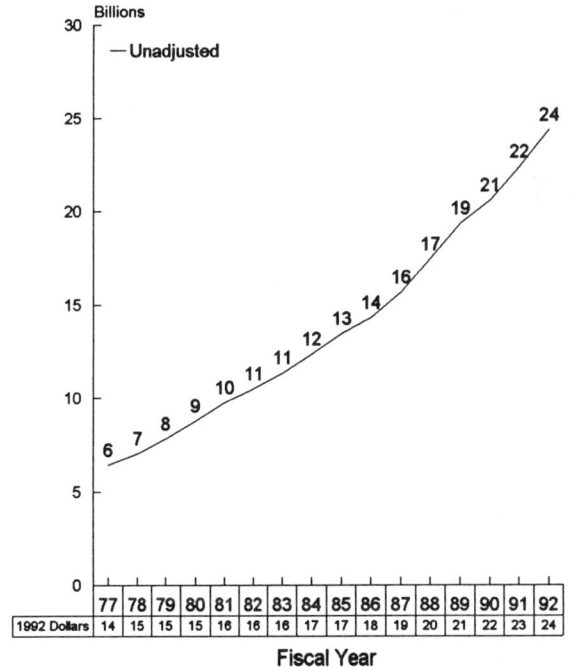

Total values (●): 1.91, 1.98, 2.37, 2.40, 2.63, 2.82, 3.17, 3.18, 3.21, 3.35, 3.29, 3.16, 3.65, 4.19, 4.53, 4.80

Congregate: 16+ Beds values: 1.35, 1.40, 1.36, 1.52, 1.68, 1.80, 1.82, 1.70, 1.68, 1.73, 1.80, 1.74, 2.01, 2.30, 2.50, 2.64
(with additional markings 1.48, 1.53, 1.62, 1.49, 1.42, 1.64, 1.88, 2.04, 2.16)

Community values: 0.56, 0.58, 1.01, 0.88, 0.94, 1.02, 1.34

Fiscal Year: 77 – 92

● Total   ···Congregate: 16+ Beds   —Community

## Total MR/DD Spending

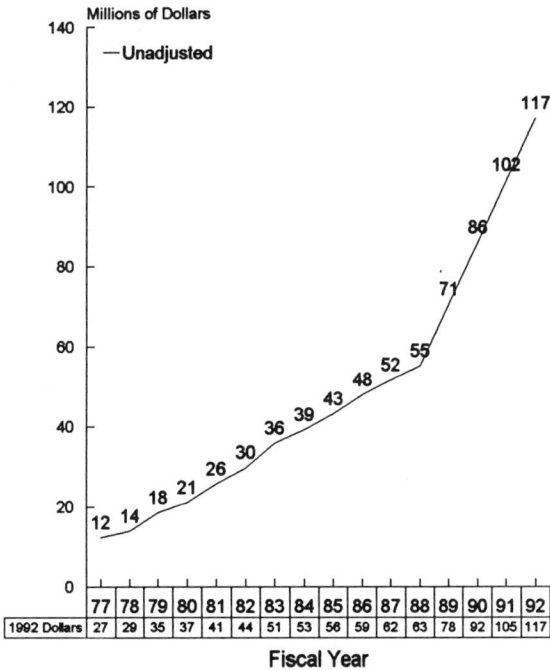

Millions of Dollars

—Unadjusted

117, 102, 86, 71, 55, 52, 48, 43, 39, 36, 30, 26, 21, 18, 14, 12

| | 77 | 78 | 79 | 80 | 81 | 82 | 83 | 84 | 85 | 86 | 87 | 88 | 89 | 90 | 91 | 92 |
|---|---|---|---|---|---|---|---|---|---|---|---|---|---|---|---|---|
| 1992 Dollars | 27 | 29 | 35 | 37 | 41 | 44 | 51 | 53 | 56 | 59 | 62 | 63 | 78 | 92 | 105 | 117 |

Fiscal Year

## Personal Income

Billions

—Unadjusted

24, 22, 21, 19, 17, 16, 14, 13, 12, 11, 11, 10, 9, 8, 7, 6

| | 77 | 78 | 79 | 80 | 81 | 82 | 83 | 84 | 85 | 86 | 87 | 88 | 89 | 90 | 91 | 92 |
|---|---|---|---|---|---|---|---|---|---|---|---|---|---|---|---|---|
| 1992 Dollars | 14 | 15 | 15 | 15 | 16 | 16 | 16 | 17 | 17 | 18 | 19 | 20 | 21 | 22 | 23 | 24 |

Fiscal Year

*Source:*
Institute on Disability and Human Development (UAP),
University of Illinois at Chicago, 1994

# MAINE

## Financial Support for MR/DD Services: FY 1977-92

| | 1977 | 1978 | 1979 | 1980 | 1981 | 1982 | 1983 | 1984 |
|---|---|---|---|---|---|---|---|---|
| **TOTAL FUNDS** | $12,255,338 | $13,923,948 | $18,469,418 | $21,067,366 | $25,654,719 | $29,738,076 | $35,928,583 | $39,273,940 |
| **CONGREGATE 16+ BEDS** | 8,652,504 | 9,858,827 | 10,589,950 | 13,315,311 | 16,435,338 | 18,960,514 | 20,698,961 | 21,031,692 |
| INSTITUTIONAL SERVICES FUNDS | 8,652,504 | 9,858,827 | 10,589,950 | 13,315,311 | 14,524,817 | 15,925,011 | 17,557,082 | 17,096,914 |
| STATE FUNDS | 7,769,155 | 8,426,447 | 9,039,605 | 10,789,351 | 10,527,348 | 9,697,448 | 11,422,973 | 9,361,950 |
| General Funds | 7,427,518 | 8,039,515 | 8,656,734 | 10,414,072 | 10,130,611 | 9,221,301 | 10,841,215 | 8,839,057 |
| Local | 0 | 0 | 0 | 0 | 0 | 0 | 0 | 0 |
| Other State Funds | 341,637 | 386,932 | 382,871 | 375,279 | 396,737 | 476,147 | 581,758 | 522,893 |
| FEDERAL FUNDS | 883,349 | 1,432,380 | 1,550,345 | 2,525,960 | 3,997,469 | 6,227,563 | 6,134,109 | 7,734,964 |
| Federal ICF/MR | 683,291 | 1,240,168 | 1,448,093 | 2,449,576 | 3,942,784 | 6,009,315 | 6,045,744 | 7,407,508 |
| Title XX / SSBG Funds | 0 | 0 | 0 | 0 | 0 | 0 | 0 | 0 |
| Other Federal Funds | 200,058 | 192,212 | 102,252 | 76,384 | 54,685 | 218,248 | 88,365 | 327,456 |
| LARGE PRIVATE RESIDENTIAL | 0 | 0 | 0 | 0 | 1,910,521 | 3,035,503 | 3,141,879 | 3,934,778 |
| STATE FUNDS | 0 | 0 | 0 | 0 | 582,136 | 899,723 | 922,770 | 1,155,644 |
| General Funds | 0 | 0 | 0 | 0 | 582,136 | 899,723 | 922,770 | 1,155,644 |
| Other State Funds | 0 | 0 | 0 | 0 | 0 | 0 | 0 | 0 |
| Local/County Overmatch | 0 | 0 | 0 | 0 | 0 | 0 | 0 | 0 |
| FEDERAL FUNDS | 0 | 0 | 0 | 0 | 1,328,385 | 2,135,780 | 2,219,109 | 2,779,134 |
| Large Private ICF/MR | 0 | 0 | 0 | 0 | 1,328,385 | 2,135,780 | 2,219,109 | 2,779,134 |
| **COMMUNITY SERVICES FUNDS** | 3,602,834 | 4,065,121 | 7,879,468 | 7,752,055 | 9,219,381 | 10,777,562 | 15,229,622 | 18,242,248 |
| STATE FUNDS | 1,973,834 | 2,408,121 | 6,074,468 | 6,022,055 | 6,719,794 | 7,305,134 | 10,443,034 | 10,832,834 |
| General Funds | 1,044,834 | 1,396,121 | 4,572,468 | 4,969,055 | 4,498,765 | 4,956,797 | 7,536,438 | 7,206,531 |
| Other State Funds | 475,000 | 493,000 | 931,000 | 491,000 | 1,658,029 | 1,745,337 | 2,301,596 | 3,019,303 |
| Local/County Overmatch | 0 | 0 | 0 | 0 | 0 | 0 | 0 | 0 |
| SSI State Supplement | 454,000 | 519,000 | 571,000 | 562,000 | 563,000 | 603,000 | 605,000 | 607,000 |
| FEDERAL FUNDS | 1,629,000 | 1,657,000 | 1,805,000 | 1,730,000 | 2,499,587 | 3,472,428 | 4,786,588 | 7,409,414 |
| ICF/MR Funds | 0 | 0 | 0 | 0 | 1,131,587 | 2,007,336 | 3,239,988 | 4,608,509 |
| Small Public | 0 | 0 | 0 | 0 | 0 | 190,916 | 266,420 | 493,511 |
| Small Private | 0 | 0 | 0 | 0 | 1,131,587 | 1,816,420 | 2,973,568 | 4,114,998 |
| HCBS Waiver | 0 | 0 | 0 | 0 | 0 | 0 | 0 | 223,172 |
| Model 50/200 Waiver | 0 | 0 | 0 | 0 | 0 | 0 | 0 | 0 |
| Other Title XIX Programs | 0 | 0 | 0 | 0 | 0 | 490,092 | 524,600 | 1,208,233 |
| Title XX / SSBG Funds | 1,450,000 | 1,479,000 | 1,553,000 | 1,475,000 | 1,118,000 | 716,000 | 770,000 | 859,400 |
| Other Federal Funds | 179,000 | 178,000 | 252,000 | 255,000 | 250,000 | 259,000 | 252,000 | 250,000 |
| Waiver Clients' SSI/ADC | 0 | 0 | 0 | 0 | 0 | 0 | 0 | 260,100 |

| | 1985 | 1986 | 1987 | 1988 | 1989 | 1990 | 1991 | 1992 |
|---|---|---|---|---|---|---|---|---|
| **TOTAL FUNDS** | $43,222,392 | $47,968,543 | $51,650,875 | $55,121,449 | $70,578,291 | $86,099,740 | $101,574,582 | $117,138,622 |
| **CONGREGATE 16+ BEDS** | 20,572,354 | 23,165,949 | 23,367,149 | 24,732,832 | 31,710,235 | 38,687,638 | 45,665,041 | 52,642,444 |
| INSTITUTIONAL SERVICES FUNDS | 16,164,619 | 18,442,956 | 18,466,324 | 19,674,812 | 26,075,728 | 32,476,643 | 38,877,559 | 45,278,474 |
| STATE FUNDS | 7,685,512 | 10,058,722 | 9,903,868 | 10,979,024 | 14,983,691 | 18,988,357 | 22,993,024 | 26,997,690 |
| General Funds | 7,196,085 | 9,404,709 | 9,239,935 | 10,267,396 | 14,428,720 | 18,590,043 | 22,751,367 | 26,912,690 |
| Local | 0 | 0 | 0 | 0 | 0 | 0 | 0 | 0 |
| Other State Funds | 489,427 | 654,013 | 663,933 | 711,628 | 554,971 | 398,314 | 241,657 | 85,000 |
| FEDERAL FUNDS | 8,479,107 | 8,384,234 | 8,562,456 | 8,695,788 | 11,092,037 | 13,488,286 | 15,884,535 | 18,280,784 |
| Federal ICF/MR | 8,155,806 | 8,301,736 | 8,479,645 | 8,608,756 | 11,026,763 | 13,444,770 | 15,862,777 | 18,280,784 |
| Title XX / SSBG Funds | 0 | 0 | 0 | 0 | 0 | 0 | 0 | 0 |
| Other Federal Funds | 323,301 | 82,498 | 82,811 | 87,032 | 65,274 | 43,516 | 21,758 | 0 |
| LARGE PRIVATE RESIDENTIAL | 4,407,735 | 4,722,993 | 4,900,825 | 5,058,020 | 5,634,508 | 6,210,995 | 6,787,483 | 7,363,970 |
| STATE FUNDS | 1,294,552 | 1,449,959 | 1,526,117 | 1,642,339 | 1,932,068 | 2,221,797 | 2,511,525 | 2,801,254 |
| General Funds | 1,294,552 | 1,449,959 | 1,526,117 | 1,642,339 | 1,932,068 | 2,221,797 | 2,511,525 | 2,801,254 |
| Other State Funds | 0 | 0 | 0 | 0 | 0 | 0 | 0 | 0 |
| Local/County Overmatch | 0 | 0 | 0 | 0 | 0 | 0 | 0 | 0 |
| FEDERAL FUNDS | 3,113,183 | 3,273,034 | 3,374,708 | 3,415,681 | 3,702,440 | 3,989,199 | 4,275,957 | 4,562,716 |
| Large Private ICF/MR | 3,113,183 | 3,273,034 | 3,374,708 | 3,415,681 | 3,702,440 | 3,989,199 | 4,275,957 | 4,562,716 |
| **COMMUNITY SERVICES FUNDS** | 22,650,038 | 24,802,594 | 28,283,726 | 30,388,617 | 38,868,056 | 47,412,102 | 55,909,541 | 64,496,178 |
| STATE FUNDS | 11,625,308 | 12,261,835 | 12,778,831 | 11,536,478 | 14,952,149 | 18,371,227 | 21,793,883 | 25,220,296 |
| General Funds | 7,381,605 | 7,557,964 | 6,906,374 | 4,953,669 | 4,215,252 | 3,476,835 | 2,738,417 | 2,000,000 |
| Other State Funds | 3,601,703 | 3,982,871 | 4,566,457 | 5,219,809 | 9,305,747 | 13,391,685 | 17,477,623 | 21,563,561 |
| Local/County Overmatch | 0 | 0 | 0 | 0 | 0 | 0 | 0 | 0 |
| SSI State Supplement | 642,000 | 721,000 | 1,306,000 | 1,363,000 | 1,431,150 | 1,502,708 | 1,577,843 | 1,656,735 |
| FEDERAL FUNDS | 11,024,730 | 12,540,759 | 15,504,895 | 18,852,139 | 23,915,907 | 29,040,875 | 34,115,658 | 39,275,882 |
| ICF/MR Funds | 5,676,147 | 5,830,876 | 6,825,688 | 7,546,423 | 10,105,917 | 12,665,410 | 15,224,904 | 17,784,397 |
| Small Public | 527,767 | 536,992 | 550,221 | 558,080 | 747,362 | 936,644 | 1,125,926 | 1,315,208 |
| Small Private | 5,148,380 | 5,293,884 | 6,275,467 | 6,988,343 | 9,358,555 | 11,728,766 | 14,098,978 | 16,469,189 |
| HCBS Waiver | 2,102,326 | 2,702,023 | 3,906,971 | 5,234,664 | 7,226,924 | 9,219,184 | 11,211,443 | 13,203,703 |
| Model 50/200 Waiver | 0 | 0 | 0 | 0 | 0 | 0 | 0 | 0 |
| Other Title XIX Programs | 1,365,357 | 1,510,688 | 1,880,238 | 3,081,107 | 3,333,556 | 3,586,005 | 3,838,453 | 4,090,902 |
| Title XX / SSBG Funds | 1,036,900 | 940,972 | 920,105 | 920,105 | 921,116 | 922,127 | 923,138 | 924,149 |
| Other Federal Funds | 250,000 | 250,000 | 497,693 | 398,000 | 403,619 | 409,238 | 414,856 | 420,475 |
| Waiver Clients' SSI/ADC | 594,000 | 1,306,200 | 1,474,200 | 1,671,840 | 1,924,776 | 2,238,912 | 2,502,864 | 2,852,256 |

*Source:*

Institute on Disability and Human Development (UAP),
University of Illinois at Chicago, 1994

# MARYLAND

## MR/DD Spending for Congregate Residential & Community Services

▨ Congregate: 16+ Beds*   ■ Community**

Millions of 1992 Dollars

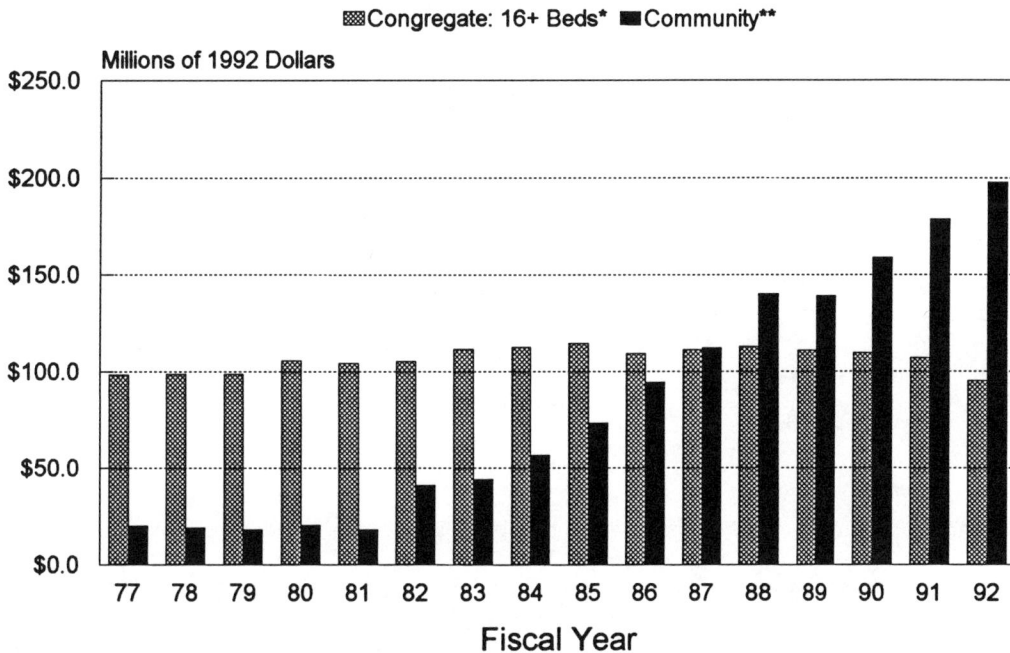

Fiscal Year

*Excludes nursing homes; ** Includes resources for
15 bed or less residential settings & non-residential community services

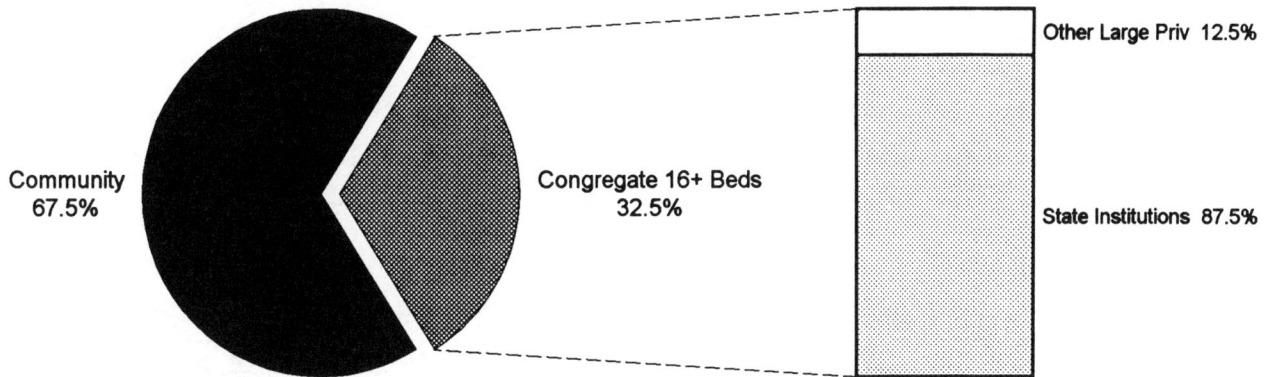

Community
67.5%

Congregate 16+ Beds
32.5%

Other Large Priv 12.5%

State Institutions 87.5%

FY 1992 Total Spending:
$292.4 Million

*Source:*
Institute on Disability and Human Development (UAP),
University of Illinois at Chicago, 1994

# MARYLAND

## Number of Persons Served by Residential Setting: FY 1992

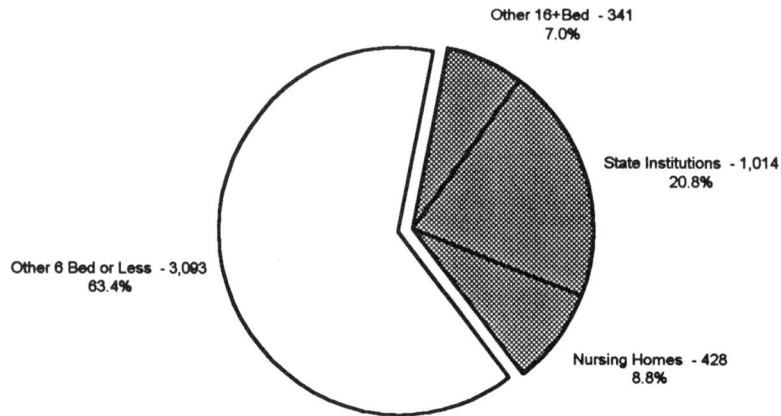

Other 16+Bed - 341
7.0%

State Institutions - 1,014
20.8%

Other 6 Bed or Less - 3,093
63.4%

Nursing Homes - 428
8.8%

Total Served: 4,876

## Persons Served by Residential Setting:1986-92

|  | 1986 | 1987 | 1988 | 1989 | 1990 | 1991 | 1992 |
|---|---|---|---|---|---|---|---|
| CONGREGATE 16 + BED SETTINGS | NA | NA | 2,218 | 2,183 | 2,086 | 1,951 | 1,783 |
| Nursing Homes | NA | NA | 506 | 487 | 467 | 448 | 428 |
| State Institutions | 1,753 | 1,528 | 1,441 | 1,395 | 1,291 | 1,168 | 1,014 |
| Private 16+Bed ICF/MR | 0 | 0 | 0 | 0 | 0 | 0 | 0 |
| Other 16+Bed Residential | 232 | 254 | 271 | 301 | 328 | 335 | 341 |
| 15 BED OR LESS RESIDENTIAL SETTINGS | 2,172 | 2,402 | 2,637 | 2,687 | 2,730 | 2,741 | 3,093 |
| Public 7-15 Bed ICF/MR | 0 | 0 | 0 | 0 | 0 | 0 | 0 |
| Private 7-15 Bed ICF/MR | 0 | 0 | 0 | 0 | 0 | 0 | 0 |
| Other 7-15 Bed Residential | 0 | 0 | 0 | 0 | 0 | 0 | 0 |
| Public 6 Bed or Less ICF/MR | 0 | 0 | 0 | 0 | 0 | 0 | 0 |
| Private 6 Bed or Less ICF/MR | 0 | 0 | 0 | 0 | 0 | 0 | 0 |
| Other 6 Bed or Less Residential | 2,172 | 2,402 | 2,637 | 2,687 | 2,730 | 2,741 | 3,093 |
| TOTAL PERSONS SERVED | NA | NA | 4,855 | 4,870 | 4,816 | 4,692 | 4,876 |

## Persons Served in Non-Residential Community Services:1986-92

|  | 1986 | 1987 | 1988 | 1989 | 1990 | 1991 | 1992 |
|---|---|---|---|---|---|---|---|
| DAY/WORK PROGRAMS | 6,242 | 7,086 | 6,313 | 5,495 | 5,653 | 5,295 | 5,927 |
| Sheltered Employment/Work Activity | NA | NA | NA | NA | NA | NA | NA |
| Day Habilitation ("Day Training") | 5,615 | 6,110 | 5,278 | 4,412 | 4,542 | 3,828 | 4,160 |
| Supported/Competitive Employment | 627 | 976 | 1,035 | 1,083 | 1,111 | 1,467 | 1,767 |
| CASE MANAGEMENT | 2,541 | 2,722 | 4,240 | 4,385 | 4,613 | 4,772 | 4,549 |
| HCBS WAIVER | 675 | 716 | 716 | 723 | 818 | 1,287 | 1,896 |
| MODEL 50/200 WAIVER | 0 | 0 | 0 | 0 | 0 | 0 | 0 |

*Source:*
Institute on Disability and Human Development (UAP),
University of Illinois at Chicago, 1994

# MARYLAND

## Community Services: FY 1992 Revenue Sources

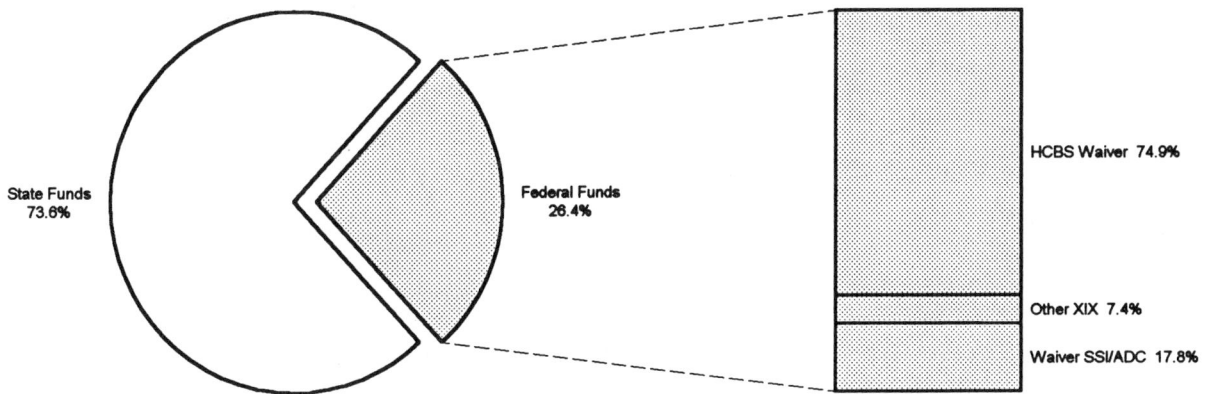

State Funds 73.6%

Federal Funds 26.4%

HCBS Waiver 74.9%

Other XIX 7.4%

Waiver SSI/ADC 17.8%

### Total Funds: $197.5 Million

## Family Support Initiatives*

|  | 1986 | 1987 | 1988 | 1989 | 1990 | 1991 | 1992 |
|---|---|---|---|---|---|---|---|
| FAMILY SUPPORT: TOTAL SPENDING | $405,888 | $961,043 | $4,050,136 | $6,327,349 | $8,055,573 | $9,633,301 | $11,116,817 |
| Total # of Families Supported | 112 | 359 | 2,008 | 2,342 | 2,877 | 3,879 | 3,880 |
| A. Financial Subsidy/Payment | $0 | $0 | $0 | $0 | $0 | $0 | $0 |
| # of Families | 0 | 0 | 0 | 0 | 0 | 0 | 0 |
| B. Family Assistance Payments | $0 | $0 | $0 | $0 | $0 | $0 | $0 |
| # of Families | 0 | 0 | 0 | 0 | 0 | 0 | 0 |
| C. Other Family Support Payments | $405,888 | $961,043 | $4,050,136 | $6,327,349 | $8,055,573 | $9,633,301 | $11,116,817 |
| # of Families | 112 | 359 | 2,008 | 2,342 | 2,877 | 3,879 | 3,880 |

## Other Community Services Initiatives*

|  | 1986 | 1987 | 1988 | 1989 | 1990 | 1991 | 1992 |
|---|---|---|---|---|---|---|---|
| AGING/DD SPENDING | $0 | $0 | $140,877 | $0 | $0 | $0 | $0 |
| # of Persons Served | 0 | 0 | 22 | 0 | 0 | 0 | 0 |
| ASSISTIVE TECHNOLOGY SPENDING |  |  |  |  |  |  | $0 |
| # of Persons Served |  |  |  |  |  |  | 0 |
| EARLY INTERVENTION SPENDING | $0 | $0 | $414,933 | $0 | $0 | $0 | $0 |
| # of Persons Served | 0 | 0 | 240 | 0 | 0 | 0 | 0 |
| PERSONAL ASSISTANCE SPENDING |  |  |  |  |  |  | $0 |
| # of Persons Served |  |  |  |  |  |  | 0 |
| SUPPORTED EMPLOYMENT SPENDING | $3,281,639 | $5,766,072 | $6,490,138 | $7,219,329 | $9,604,356 | $12,212,259 | $14,031,566 |
| # of Persons Served | 627 | 976 | 1,035 | 1,083 | 1,111 | 1,467 | 1,767 |
| SUPPORTED LIVING SPENDING |  |  |  |  |  |  | $0 |
| # of Persons Served |  |  |  |  |  |  | 0 |

*Expenditures associated with Special Community Initiatives are a subset of funding within the community services component of the state's chart series and spreadsheet; Family Support Client figures may include duplicate client counts; HCBS Waiver counts include Waiver case management numbers.
0= Services not provided in the state; NA= Data not available from state; blank= Services not applicable (eg. CSLA prior to authorization, Special Community Initiatives prior to request for data by this study)

*Source:*
Institute on Disability and Human Development (UAP),
University of Illinois at Chicago, 1994

# MARYLAND

## Large Congregate Care Facilities: FY 1992 Revenue Sources*

### Private 16+Bed Settings

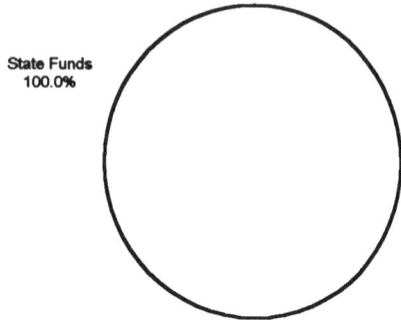

State Funds
100.0%

Total Funds: $11.8 Million

### Public Institutions

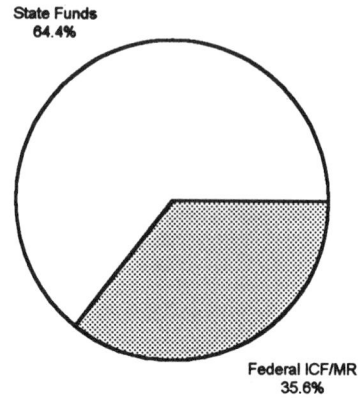

State Funds
64.4%

Federal ICF/MR
35.6%

Total Funds: $83.1 Million

*Excludes nursing homes

## Average Daily Residents in Institutions

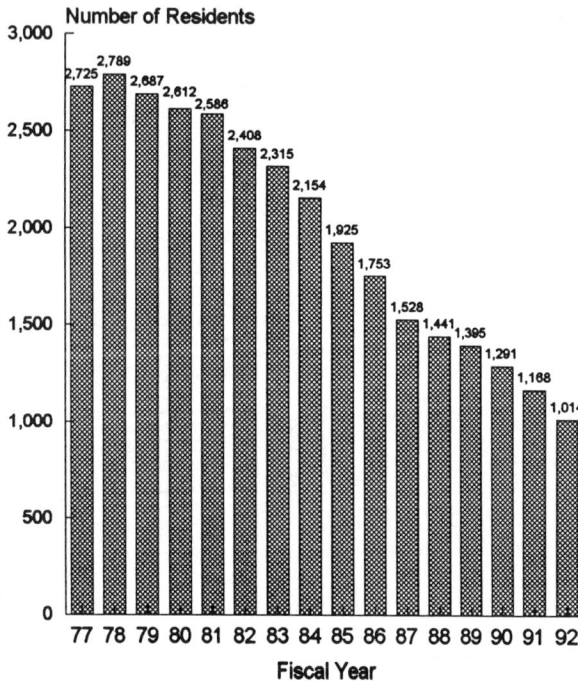

Number of Residents

| | |
|---|---|
| 2,725 | 77 |
| 2,789 | 78 |
| 2,687 | 79 |
| 2,612 | 80 |
| 2,586 | 81 |
| 2,408 | 82 |
| 2,315 | 83 |
| 2,154 | 84 |
| 1,925 | 85 |
| 1,753 | 86 |
| 1,528 | 87 |
| 1,441 | 88 |
| 1,395 | 89 |
| 1,291 | 90 |
| 1,168 | 91 |
| 1,014 | 92 |

Fiscal Year

## Institutional Daily Costs Per Resident

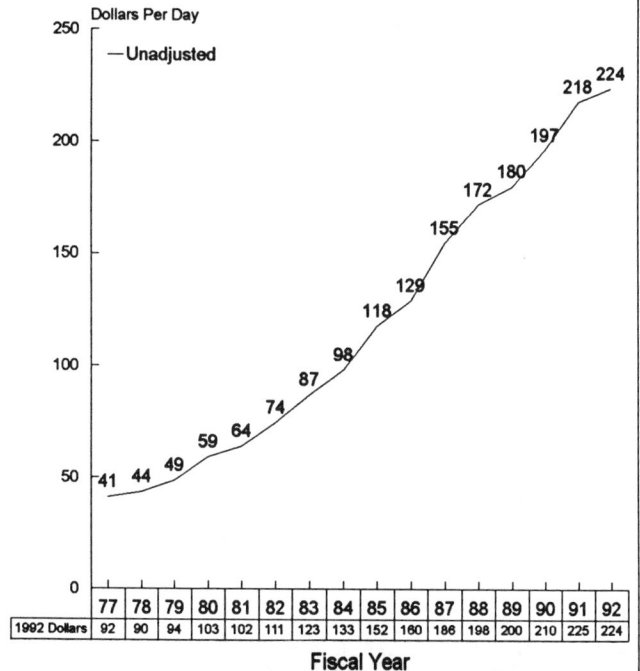

Dollars Per Day

— Unadjusted

| Data | 41 | 44 | 49 | 59 | 64 | 74 | 87 | 98 | 118 | 129 | 155 | 172 | 180 | 197 | 218 | 224 |
|---|---|---|---|---|---|---|---|---|---|---|---|---|---|---|---|---|
| Fiscal Year | 77 | 78 | 79 | 80 | 81 | 82 | 83 | 84 | 85 | 86 | 87 | 88 | 89 | 90 | 91 | 92 |
| 1992 Dollars | 92 | 90 | 94 | 103 | 102 | 111 | 123 | 133 | 152 | 160 | 186 | 198 | 200 | 210 | 225 | 224 |

Fiscal Year

*Source:*
Institute on Disability and Human Development (UAP),
University of Illinois at Chicago, 1994

# MARYLAND FISCAL EFFORT

## MR/DD Spending Per $1,000 of Personal Income

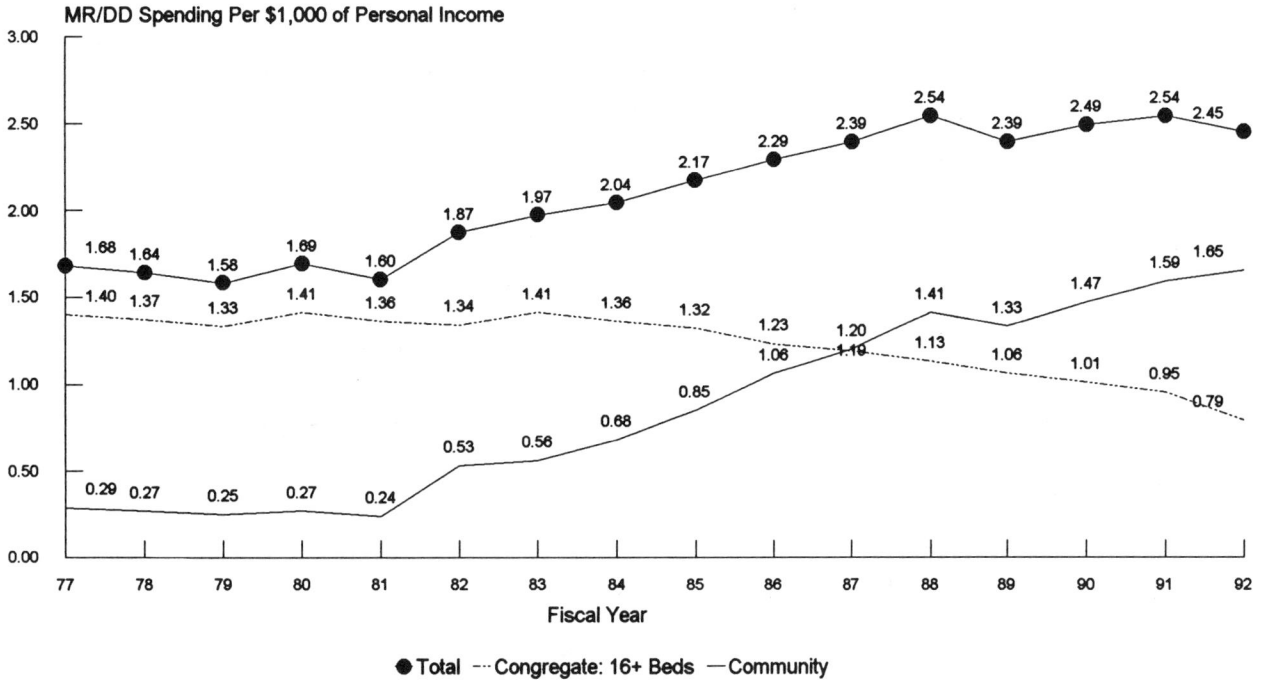

● Total  --- Congregate: 16+ Beds  — Community

Fiscal Year

## Total MR/DD Spending

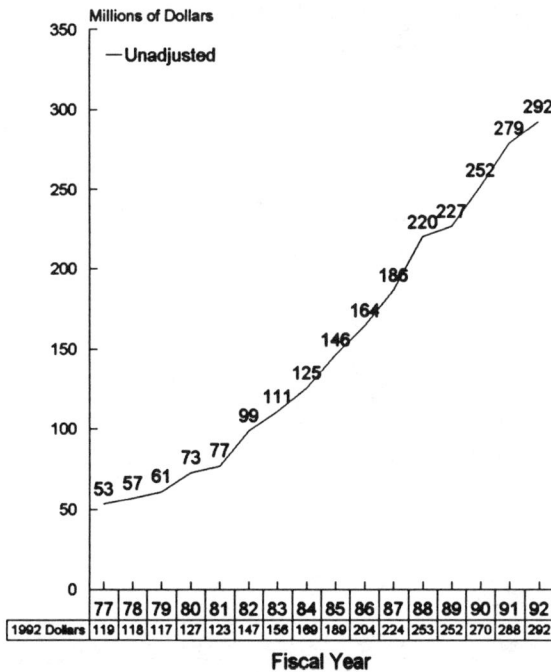

Millions of Dollars
— Unadjusted

| Fiscal Year | 77 | 78 | 79 | 80 | 81 | 82 | 83 | 84 | 85 | 86 | 87 | 88 | 89 | 90 | 91 | 92 |
|---|---|---|---|---|---|---|---|---|---|---|---|---|---|---|---|---|
| 1992 Dollars | 119 | 118 | 117 | 127 | 123 | 147 | 156 | 169 | 189 | 204 | 224 | 253 | 252 | 270 | 288 | 292 |

Fiscal Year

## Personal Income

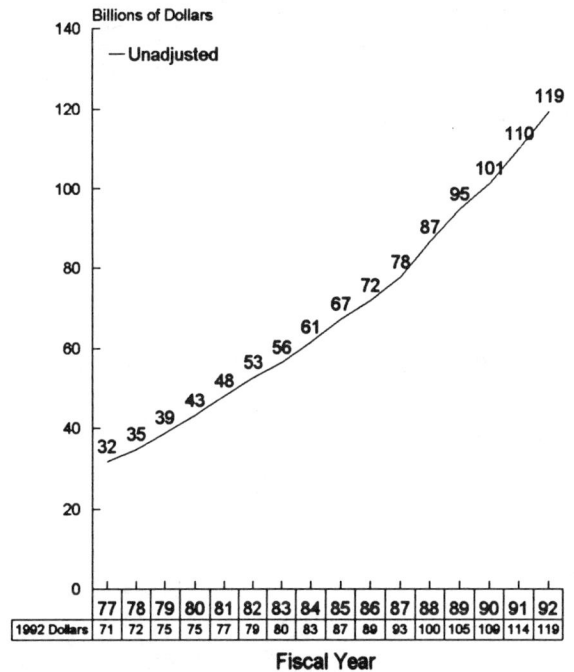

Billions of Dollars
— Unadjusted

| Fiscal Year | 77 | 78 | 79 | 80 | 81 | 82 | 83 | 84 | 85 | 86 | 87 | 88 | 89 | 90 | 91 | 92 |
|---|---|---|---|---|---|---|---|---|---|---|---|---|---|---|---|---|
| 1992 Dollars | 71 | 72 | 75 | 75 | 77 | 79 | 80 | 83 | 87 | 89 | 93 | 100 | 105 | 109 | 114 | 119 |

Fiscal Year

*Source:*
**Institute on Disability and Human Development (UAP),
University of Illinois at Chicago, 1994**

# MARYLAND

## Financial Support for MR/DD Services: FY 1977-92

| | 1977 | 1978 | 1979 | 1980 | 1981 | 1982 | 1983 | 1984 |
|---|---|---|---|---|---|---|---|---|
| **TOTAL FUNDS** | $53,389,000 | $57,075,000 | $61,182,000 | $72,872,000 | $77,106,000 | $98,730,000 | $110,919,000 | $125,373,204 |
| **CONGREGATE 16+ BEDS** | 44,298,734 | 47,726,186 | 51,618,290 | 61,012,569 | 65,591,620 | 70,975,285 | 79,378,028 | 83,406,508 |
| INSTITUTIONAL SERVICES FUNDS | 41,154,000 | 44,278,000 | 47,814,000 | 56,614,000 | 60,511,000 | 65,475,000 | 73,502,000 | 77,470,900 |
| STATE FUNDS | 34,085,000 | 32,327,000 | 29,585,000 | 32,237,700 | 32,210,380 | 36,261,900 | 37,205,500 | 43,045,700 |
| General Funds | 33,795,000 | 32,288,000 | 29,400,000 | 32,212,700 | 32,170,380 | 35,623,900 | 36,673,500 | 42,587,500 |
| Local | 0 | 0 | 0 | 0 | 0 | 0 | 0 | 0 |
| Other State Funds | 290,000 | 39,000 | 185,000 | 25,000 | 40,000 | 638,000 | 532,000 | 458,200 |
| FEDERAL FUNDS | 7,069,000 | 11,951,000 | 18,229,000 | 24,376,300 | 28,300,620 | 29,213,100 | 36,296,500 | 34,425,200 |
| Federal ICF/MR | 5,985,000 | 10,786,000 | 17,005,000 | 23,287,300 | 27,078,620 | 29,094,100 | 36,144,500 | 33,827,400 |
| Title XX / SSBG Funds | 0 | 0 | 0 | 0 | 0 | 0 | 0 | 0 |
| Other Federal Funds | 1,084,000 | 1,165,000 | 1,224,000 | 1,089,000 | 1,222,000 | 119,000 | 152,000 | 597,800 |
| LARGE PRIVATE RESIDENTIAL | 3,144,734 | 3,448,186 | 3,804,290 | 4,398,569 | 5,080,620 | 5,500,285 | 5,876,028 | 5,935,608 |
| STATE FUNDS | 3,144,734 | 3,448,186 | 3,804,290 | 4,398,569 | 5,080,620 | 5,500,285 | 5,876,028 | 5,935,608 |
| General Funds | 3,144,734 | 3,448,186 | 3,804,290 | 4,398,569 | 5,080,620 | 5,500,285 | 5,876,028 | 5,935,608 |
| Other State Funds | 0 | 0 | 0 | 0 | 0 | 0 | 0 | 0 |
| Local/County Overmatch | 0 | 0 | 0 | 0 | 0 | 0 | 0 | 0 |
| FEDERAL FUNDS | 0 | 0 | 0 | 0 | 0 | 0 | 0 | 0 |
| Large Private ICF/MR | 0 | 0 | 0 | 0 | 0 | 0 | 0 | 0 |
| **COMMUNITY SERVICES FUNDS** | 9,090,266 | 9,348,814 | 9,563,710 | 11,859,431 | 11,514,380 | 27,754,715 | 31,540,972 | 41,966,696 |
| STATE FUNDS | 4,590,266 | 4,374,814 | 4,577,710 | 6,794,431 | 6,540,380 | 21,486,715 | 26,474,972 | 35,358,792 |
| General Funds | 2,785,266 | 3,913,814 | 3,866,710 | 6,063,431 | 5,413,380 | 19,638,715 | 24,008,972 | 32,678,192 |
| Other State Funds | 1,805,000 | 461,000 | 711,000 | 731,000 | 1,127,000 | 1,848,000 | 2,466,000 | 2,680,600 |
| Local/County Overmatch | 0 | 0 | 0 | 0 | 0 | 0 | 0 | 0 |
| SSI State Supplement | 0 | 0 | 0 | 0 | 0 | 0 | 0 | 0 |
| FEDERAL FUNDS | 4,500,000 | 4,974,000 | 4,986,000 | 5,065,000 | 4,974,000 | 6,268,000 | 5,066,000 | 6,607,904 |
| ICF/MR Funds | 0 | 0 | 0 | 0 | 0 | 0 | 0 | 0 |
| Small Public | 0 | 0 | 0 | 0 | 0 | 0 | 0 | 0 |
| Small Private | 0 | 0 | 0 | 0 | 0 | 0 | 0 | 0 |
| HCBS Waiver | 0 | 0 | 0 | 0 | 0 | 0 | 0 | 256,000 |
| Model 50/200 Waiver | 0 | 0 | 0 | 0 | 0 | 0 | 0 | 0 |
| Other Title XIX Programs | 0 | 0 | 0 | 0 | 0 | 0 | 0 | 0 |
| Title XX / SSBG Funds | 4,243,000 | 4,874,000 | 4,867,000 | 4,863,000 | 4,874,000 | 3,842,000 | 3,899,000 | 3,883,600 |
| Other Federal Funds | 257,000 | 100,000 | 119,000 | 202,000 | 100,000 | 2,426,000 | 1,167,000 | 2,371,200 |
| Waiver Clients' SSI/ADC | 0 | 0 | 0 | 0 | 0 | 0 | 0 | 97,104 |

| | 1985 | 1986 | 1987 | 1988 | 1989 | 1990 | 1991 | 1992 |
|---|---|---|---|---|---|---|---|---|
| **TOTAL FUNDS** | $146,174,400 | $164,351,961 | $186,348,707 | $220,095,908 | $226,639,958 | $252,345,691 | $278,967,491 | $292,409,598 |
| **CONGREGATE 16+ BEDS** | 88,992,873 | 88,134,477 | 92,766,098 | 98,118,843 | 100,458,531 | 102,852,080 | 104,399,241 | 94,915,028 |
| INSTITUTIONAL SERVICES FUNDS | 82,644,200 | 82,638,013 | 86,406,880 | 90,740,910 | 91,670,367 | 92,614,852 | 92,890,620 | 83,083,461 |
| STATE FUNDS | 52,046,200 | 52,120,071 | 45,494,804 | 50,226,476 | 54,908,259 | 57,640,846 | 61,264,668 | 53,463,356 |
| General Funds | 51,870,900 | 51,958,773 | 45,338,452 | 50,116,958 | 54,785,089 | 57,527,511 | 61,174,164 | 53,376,244 |
| Local | 0 | 0 | 0 | 0 | 0 | 0 | 0 | 0 |
| Other State Funds | 175,300 | 161,298 | 156,352 | 109,518 | 123,170 | 113,335 | 90,504 | 87,112 |
| FEDERAL FUNDS | 30,598,000 | 30,517,942 | 40,912,076 | 40,514,434 | 36,762,108 | 34,974,006 | 31,625,952 | 29,620,105 |
| Federal ICF/MR | 30,230,200 | 30,307,254 | 40,749,465 | 40,403,053 | 36,652,122 | 34,911,590 | 31,573,946 | 29,584,594 |
| Title XX / SSBG Funds | 0 | 0 | 0 | 0 | 0 | 0 | 0 | 0 |
| Other Federal Funds | 367,800 | 210,688 | 162,611 | 111,381 | 109,986 | 62,416 | 52,006 | 35,511 |
| LARGE PRIVATE RESIDENTIAL | 6,348,673 | 5,496,464 | 6,359,218 | 7,377,933 | 8,788,164 | 10,237,228 | 11,508,621 | 11,831,567 |
| STATE FUNDS | 6,348,673 | 5,496,464 | 6,359,218 | 7,377,933 | 8,788,164 | 10,237,228 | 11,508,621 | 11,831,567 |
| General Funds | 6,348,673 | 5,496,464 | 6,359,218 | 7,377,933 | 8,788,164 | 10,237,228 | 11,508,621 | 11,831,567 |
| Other State Funds | 0 | 0 | 0 | 0 | 0 | 0 | 0 | 0 |
| Local/County Overmatch | 0 | 0 | 0 | 0 | 0 | 0 | 0 | 0 |
| FEDERAL FUNDS | 0 | 0 | 0 | 0 | 0 | 0 | 0 | 0 |
| Large Private ICF/MR | 0 | 0 | 0 | 0 | 0 | 0 | 0 | 0 |
| **COMMUNITY SERVICES FUNDS** | 57,181,527 | 76,217,484 | 93,582,609 | 121,977,065 | 126,181,427 | 149,493,611 | 174,568,250 | 197,494,570 |
| STATE FUNDS | 50,666,027 | 64,406,651 | 76,888,497 | 104,269,365 | 107,025,937 | 122,394,609 | 134,532,416 | 145,338,578 |
| General Funds | 47,928,827 | 61,685,898 | 74,067,184 | 101,553,460 | 104,394,161 | 119,762,833 | 131,900,640 | 142,706,802 |
| Other State Funds | 2,737,200 | 2,720,753 | 2,821,313 | 2,715,905 | 2,631,776 | 2,631,776 | 2,631,776 | 2,631,776 |
| Local/County Overmatch | 0 | 0 | 0 | 0 | 0 | 0 | 0 | 0 |
| SSI State Supplement | 0 | 0 | 0 | 0 | 0 | 0 | 0 | 0 |
| FEDERAL FUNDS | 6,515,500 | 11,810,833 | 16,694,112 | 17,707,700 | 19,155,490 | 27,099,002 | 40,035,834 | 52,155,992 |
| ICF/MR Funds | 0 | 0 | 0 | 0 | 0 | 0 | 0 | 0 |
| Small Public | 0 | 0 | 0 | 0 | 0 | 0 | 0 | 0 |
| Small Private | 0 | 0 | 0 | 0 | 0 | 0 | 0 | 0 |
| HCBS Waiver | 3,228,100 | 6,117,454 | 10,854,008 | 11,830,801 | 13,488,298 | 20,066,714 | 30,626,226 | 39,045,928 |
| Model 50/200 Waiver | 0 | 0 | 0 | 0 | 0 | 0 | 0 | 0 |
| Other Title XIX Programs | 0 | 1,350,000 | 2,700,000 | 2,700,000 | 2,700,000 | 3,420,000 | 3,510,000 | 3,850,000 |
| Title XX / SSBG Funds | 0 | 0 | 0 | 0 | 0 | 0 | 0 | 0 |
| Other Federal Funds | 2,005,800 | 1,824,279 | 433,624 | 393,091 | 0 | 0 | 0 | 0 |
| Waiver Clients' SSI/ADC | 1,281,600 | 2,519,100 | 2,706,480 | 2,783,808 | 2,967,192 | 3,612,288 | 5,899,608 | 9,260,064 |

*Source:*

Institute on Disability and Human Development (UAP), University of Illinois at Chicago, 1994

# MASSACHUSETTS

## MR/DD Spending for Congregate Residential & Community Services

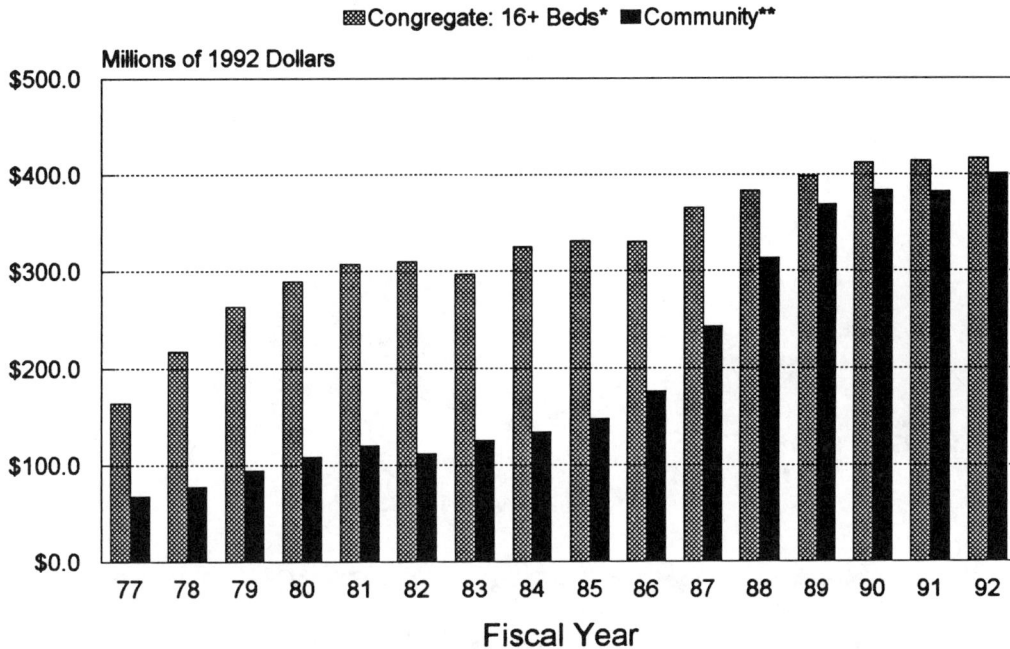

▨Congregate: 16+ Beds*  ■Community**

Millions of 1992 Dollars

$500.0

$400.0

$300.0

$200.0

$100.0

$0.0

77  78  79  80  81  82  83  84  85  86  87  88  89  90  91  92

### Fiscal Year

*Excludes nursing homes; ** Includes resources for
15 bed or less residential settings & non-residential community services

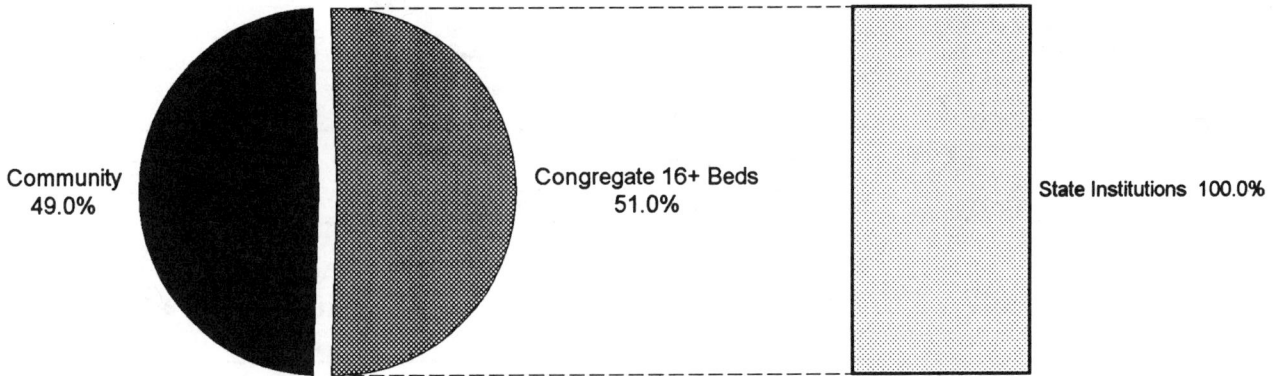

Community
49.0%

Congregate 16+ Beds
51.0%

State Institutions  100.0%

FY 1992 Total Spending:
$817.9 Million

*Source:*
Institute on Disability and Human Development (UAP),
University of Illinois at Chicago, 1994

# MASSACHUSETTS

## Number of Persons Served by Residential Setting: FY 1992

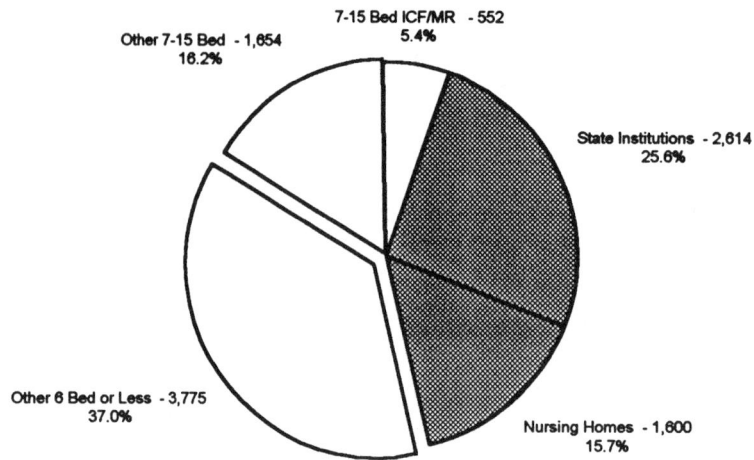

Other 7-15 Bed - 1,654
16.2%

7-15 Bed ICF/MR - 552
5.4%

State Institutions - 2,614
25.6%

Nursing Homes - 1,600
15.7%

Other 6 Bed or Less - 3,775
37.0%

Total Served: 10,195

## Persons Served by Residential Setting:1986-92

|  | 1986 | 1987 | 1988 | 1989 | 1990 | 1991 | 1992 |
|---|---|---|---|---|---|---|---|
| CONGREGATE 16 + BED SETTINGS | 4,930 | 4,785 | 4,680 | NA | NA | NA | 4,214 |
| Nursing Homes | 1,360 | 1,360 | 1,360 | NA | NA | NA | 1,600 |
| State Institutions | 3,570 | 3,425 | 3,320 | 3,100 | 2,905 | 2,778 | 2,614 |
| Private 16+Bed ICF/MR | 0 | 0 | 0 | 0 | 0 | 0 | 0 |
| Other 16+Bed Residential | 0 | 0 | 0 | 0 | 0 | 0 | 0 |
| 15 BED OR LESS RESIDENTIAL SETTINGS | 4,260 | 4,533 | 4,922 | 5,213 | 5,473 | 5,592 | 5,981 |
| Public 7-15 Bed ICF/MR | 0 | 32 | 168 | 184 | 232 | 232 | 232 |
| Private 7-15 Bed ICF/MR | 279 | 296 | 304 | 304 | 309 | 320 | 320 |
| Other 7-15 Bed Residential | 3,981 | 4,205 | 4,450 | 4,725 | 4,932 | 5,040 | 1,654 |
| Public 6 Bed or Less ICF/MR |  |  |  |  |  |  | 0 |
| Private 6 Bed or Less ICF/MR |  |  |  |  |  |  | 0 |
| Other 6 Bed or Less Residential |  |  |  |  |  |  | 3,775 |
| TOTAL PERSONS SERVED | 9,190 | 9,318 | 9,602 | NA | NA | NA | 10,195 |

## Persons Served in Non-Residential Community Services:1986-92

|  | 1986 | 1987 | 1988 | 1989 | 1990 | 1991 | 1992 |
|---|---|---|---|---|---|---|---|
| DAY/WORK PROGRAMS | 6,720 | 7,500 | NA | NA | 7,053 | 7,645 | 8,225 |
| Sheltered Employment/Work Activity | 5,670 | 6,300 | 5,000 | 5,300 | 4,651 | 4,920 | 5,400 |
| Day Habilitation ("Day Training") | 1,050 | 1,200 | 1,200 | 1,215 | 1,349 | 1,500 | 1,500 |
| Supported/Competitive Employment | 0 | 0 | NA | NA | 1,053 | 1,225 | 1,325 |
| CASE MANAGEMENT | 12,240 | 14,400 | 12,000 | 18,932 | 18,794 | 20,416 | 20,706 |
| HCBS WAIVER | 530 | 499 | 740 | 1,210 | 1,600 | 1,925 | 2,811 |
| MODEL 50/200 WAIVER | 0 | 0 | 0 | 0 | 0 | 0 | 0 |

Source:
Institute on Disability and Human Development (UAP),
University of Illinois at Chicago, 1994

# MASSACHUSETTS

## Community Services: FY 1992 Revenue Sources

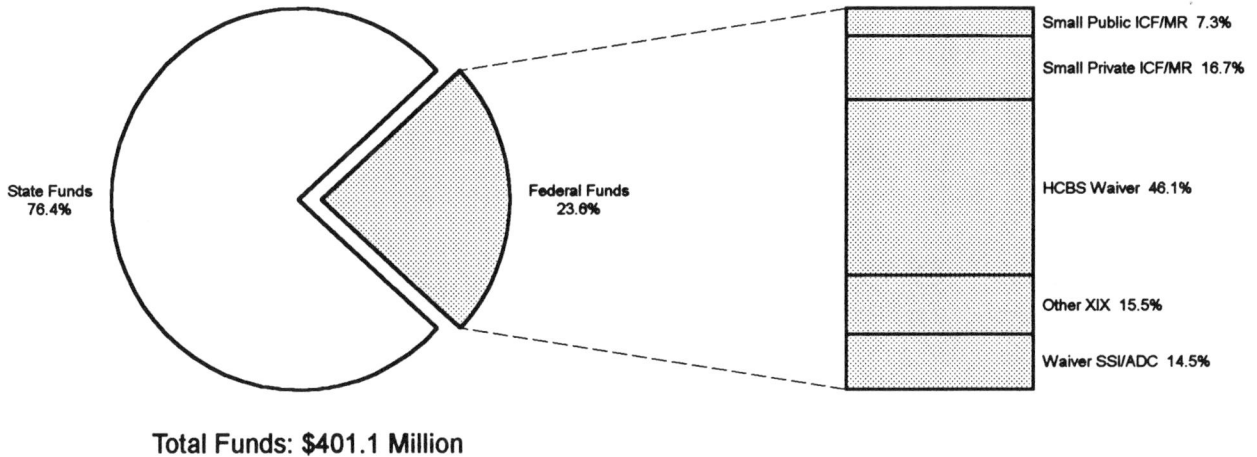

State Funds 76.4%

Federal Funds 23.6%

Small Public ICF/MR 7.3%

Small Private ICF/MR 16.7%

HCBS Waiver 46.1%

Other XIX 15.5%

Waiver SSI/ADC 14.5%

Total Funds: $401.1 Million

## Family Support Initiatives*

| | 1986 | 1987 | 1988 | 1989 | 1990 | 1991 | 1992 |
|---|---|---|---|---|---|---|---|
| FAMILY SUPPORT: TOTAL SPENDING | $0 | $0 | $17,000,000 | $18,000,000 | $20,300,000 | $19,200,000 | $18,000,000 |
| Total # of Families Supported | 0 | 0 | NA | NA | NA | NA | NA |
| A. Financial Subsidy/Payment | $0 | $0 | $0 | $0 | $0 | $0 | $0 |
| # of Families | 0 | 0 | 0 | 0 | 0 | 0 | 0 |
| B. Family Assistance Payments | $0 | $0 | $15,000,000 | $15,500,000 | $16,500,000 | $15,700,000 | $14,600,000 |
| # of Families | 0 | 0 | NA | NA | NA | NA | NA |
| C. Other Family Support Payments | $0 | $0 | $2,000,000 | $2,500,000 | $3,800,000 | $3,500,000 | $3,400,000 |
| # of Families | 0 | 0 | NA | NA | NA | NA | NA |

## Other Community Services Initiatives*

| | 1986 | 1987 | 1988 | 1989 | 1990 | 1991 | 1992 |
|---|---|---|---|---|---|---|---|
| AGING/DD SPENDING | $0 | $0 | $0 | $0 | $0 | $0 | $0 |
| # of Persons Served | 0 | 0 | 0 | 0 | 0 | 0 | 0 |
| ASSISTIVE TECHNOLOGY SPENDING | | | | | | | $0 |
| # of Persons Served | | | | | | | 0 |
| EARLY INTERVENTION SPENDING | $0 | $0 | $0 | $16,000,000 | $16,600,000 | $17,900,000 | $19,000,000 |
| # of Persons Served | 0 | 0 | 0 | 7,066 | 7,421 | 7,900 | 8,500 |
| PERSONAL ASSISTANCE SPENDING | | | | | | | $0 |
| # of Persons Served | | | | | | | 0 |
| SUPPORTED EMPLOYMENT SPENDING | $0 | $0 | $7,800,000 | $8,000,000 | $8,300,000 | $9,600,000 | $10,100,000 |
| # of Persons Served | 0 | 0 | NA | NA | 1,053 | 1,225 | 1,325 |
| SUPPORTED LIVING SPENDING | | | | | | | $0 |
| # of Persons Served | | | | | | | 0 |

*Expenditures associated with Special Community Initiatives are a subset of funding within the community services component of the state's chart series and spreadsheet; Family Support Client figures may include duplicate client counts; HCBS Waiver counts include Waiver case management numbers.
0= Services not provided in the state; NA= Data not available from state; blank= Services not applicable (eg. CSLA prior to authorization, Special Community Initiatives prior to request for data by this study)

Source:
Institute on Disability and Human Development (UAP),
University of Illinois at Chicago, 1994

# MASSACHUSETTS

## Large Congregate Care Facilities: FY 1992 Revenue Sources*

### Private 16+Bed Settings

**Does Not Apply**

### Public Institutions

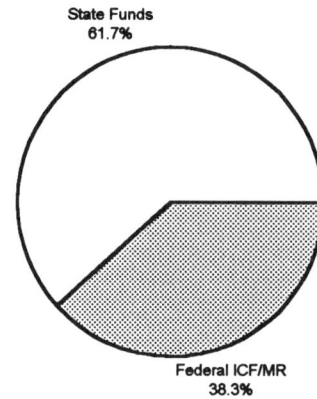

State Funds
61.7%

Federal ICF/MR
38.3%

Total Funds: $416.9 Million

*Excludes nursing homes

## Average Daily Residents in Institutions

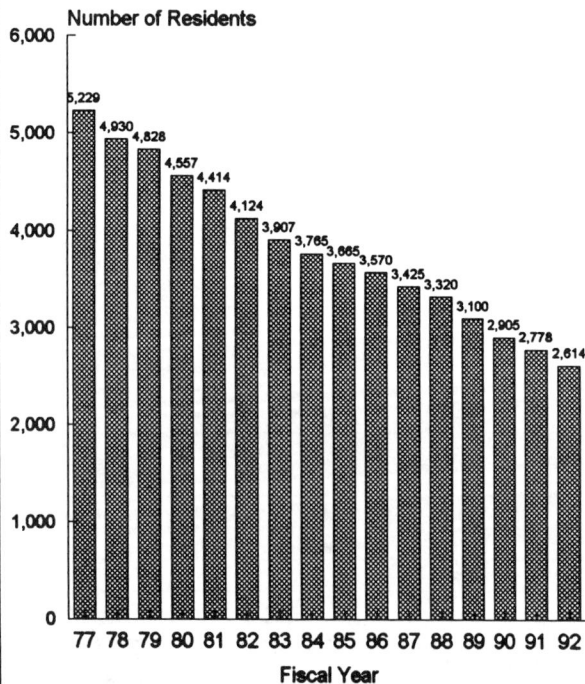

Number of Residents

| Fiscal Year | Residents |
|---|---|
| 77 | 5,229 |
| 78 | 4,930 |
| 79 | 4,828 |
| 80 | 4,557 |
| 81 | 4,414 |
| 82 | 4,124 |
| 83 | 3,907 |
| 84 | 3,765 |
| 85 | 3,665 |
| 86 | 3,570 |
| 87 | 3,425 |
| 88 | 3,320 |
| 89 | 3,100 |
| 90 | 2,905 |
| 91 | 2,778 |
| 92 | 2,614 |

## Institutional Daily Costs Per Resident

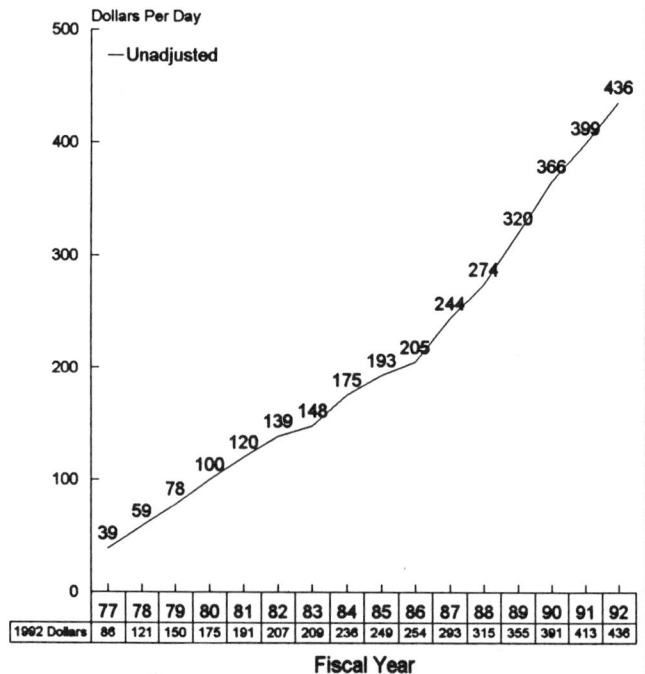

Dollars Per Day

—Unadjusted

39, 59, 78, 100, 120, 139, 148, 175, 193, 205, 244, 274, 320, 366, 399, 436

| Fiscal Year | 77 | 78 | 79 | 80 | 81 | 82 | 83 | 84 | 85 | 86 | 87 | 88 | 89 | 90 | 91 | 92 |
|---|---|---|---|---|---|---|---|---|---|---|---|---|---|---|---|---|
| 1992 Dollars | 86 | 121 | 150 | 175 | 191 | 207 | 209 | 236 | 249 | 254 | 293 | 315 | 355 | 391 | 413 | 436 |

*Source:*
Institute on Disability and Human Development (UAP),
University of Illinois at Chicago, 1994

# MASSACHUSETTS FISCAL EFFORT

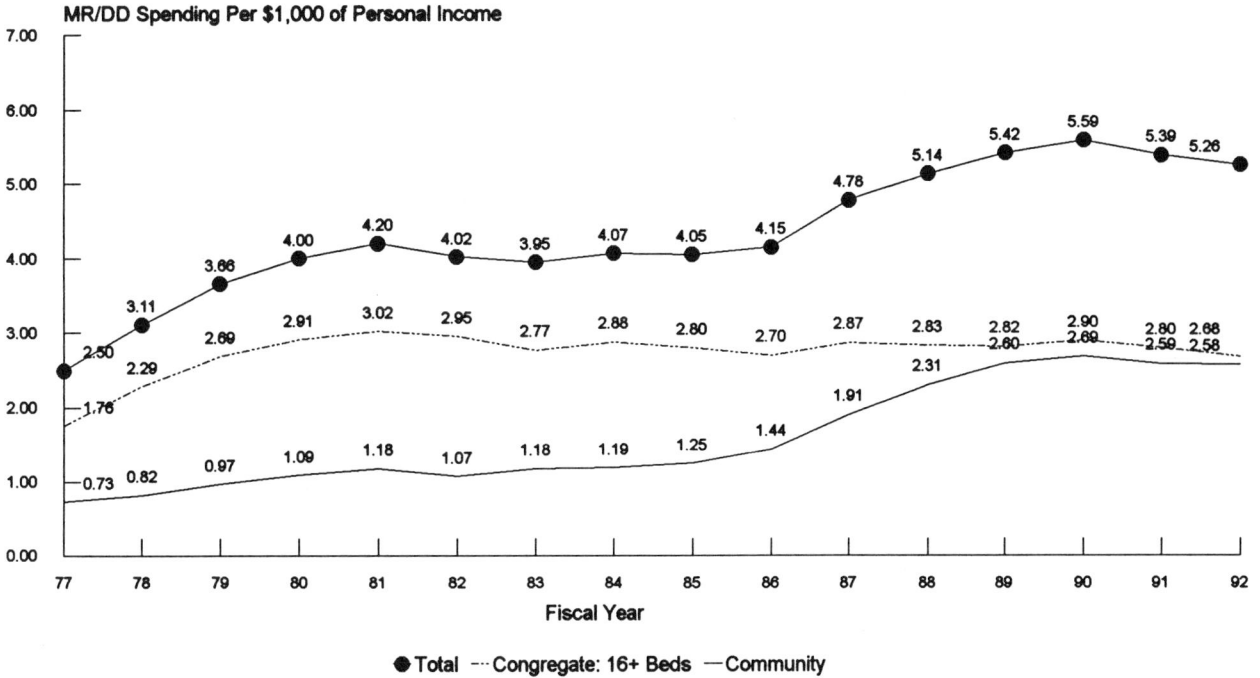

MR/DD Spending Per $1,000 of Personal Income

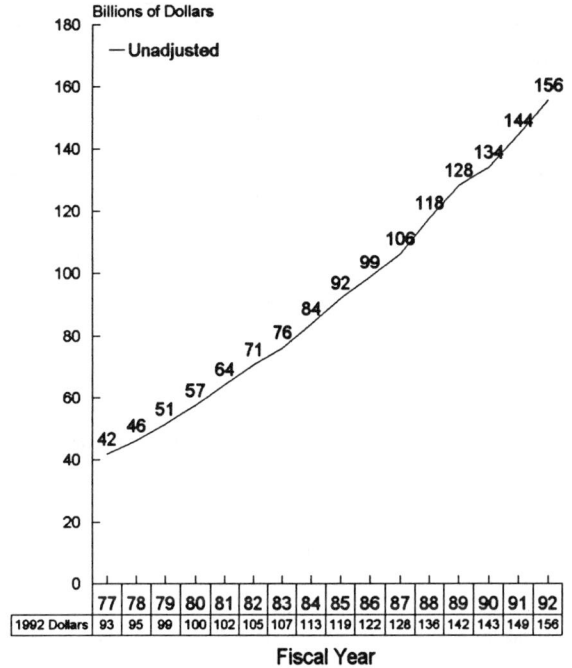

Total values (Fiscal Year 77–92): 2.50, 3.11, 3.66, 4.00, 4.20, 4.02, 3.95, 4.07, 4.05, 4.15, 4.78, 5.14, 5.42, 5.59, 5.39, 5.26

Congregate: 16+ Beds values: 1.76, 2.29, 2.69, 2.91, 3.02, 2.95, 2.77, 2.88, 2.80, 2.70, 2.87, 2.83, 2.82, 2.60, 2.90, 2.69, 2.80, 2.59, 2.68, 2.58

Community values: 0.73, 0.82, 0.97, 1.09, 1.18, 1.07, 1.18, 1.19, 1.25, 1.44, 1.91, 2.31

Fiscal Year

●Total  ---Congregate: 16+ Beds  —Community

## Total MR/DD Spending

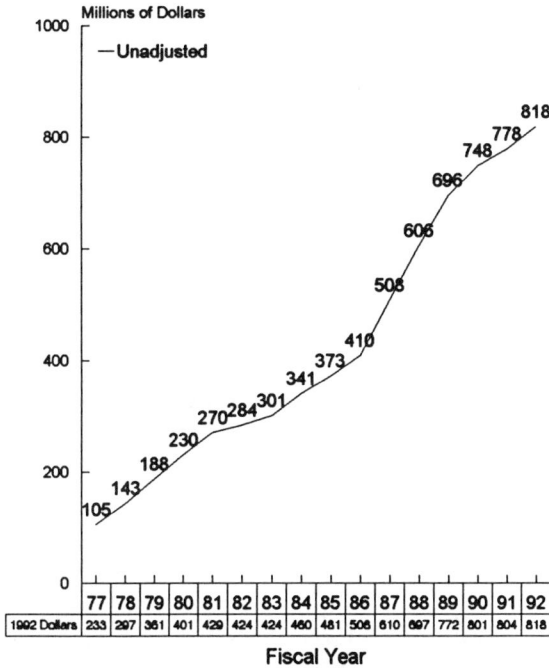

Millions of Dollars
—Unadjusted

Values: 105, 143, 188, 230, 270, 284, 301, 341, 373, 410, 505, 606, 696, 748, 778, 818

| | 77 | 78 | 79 | 80 | 81 | 82 | 83 | 84 | 85 | 86 | 87 | 88 | 89 | 90 | 91 | 92 |
|---|---|---|---|---|---|---|---|---|---|---|---|---|---|---|---|---|
| 1992 Dollars | 233 | 297 | 361 | 401 | 429 | 424 | 424 | 460 | 481 | 508 | 610 | 697 | 772 | 801 | 804 | 818 |

Fiscal Year

## Personal Income

Billions of Dollars
—Unadjusted

Values: 42, 46, 51, 57, 64, 71, 76, 84, 92, 99, 106, 118, 128, 134, 144, 156

| | 77 | 78 | 79 | 80 | 81 | 82 | 83 | 84 | 85 | 86 | 87 | 88 | 89 | 90 | 91 | 92 |
|---|---|---|---|---|---|---|---|---|---|---|---|---|---|---|---|---|
| 1992 Dollars | 93 | 95 | 99 | 100 | 102 | 105 | 107 | 113 | 119 | 122 | 128 | 136 | 142 | 143 | 149 | 156 |

Fiscal Year

*Source:*
Institute on Disability and Human Development (UAP),
University of Illinois at Chicago, 1994

# MASSACHUSETTS

## Financial Support for MR/DD Services: FY 1977-92

| | 1977 | 1978 | 1979 | 1980 | 1981 | 1982 | 1983 | 1984 |
|---|---|---|---|---|---|---|---|---|
| **TOTAL FUNDS** | **$104,685,600** | **$143,338,354** | **$187,788,740** | **$230,210,933** | **$269,976,685** | **$284,452,671** | **$300,785,640** | **$340,985,212** |
| **CONGREGATE 16+ BEDS** | 73,906,420 | 105,591,722 | 138,027,920 | 167,489,428 | 193,888,971 | 209,005,380 | 211,231,974 | 241,176,110 |
| INSTITUTIONAL SERVICES FUNDS | 73,906,420 | 105,591,722 | 138,027,920 | 167,489,428 | 193,888,971 | 209,005,380 | 211,231,974 | 241,176,110 |
| STATE FUNDS | 55,546,420 | 56,983,722 | 79,232,920 | 100,472,428 | 125,666,971 | 131,295,380 | 94,222,974 | 120,527,110 |
| General Funds | 55,546,420 | 56,983,722 | 79,232,920 | 100,472,428 | 125,666,971 | 131,295,380 | 94,222,974 | 120,527,110 |
| Local | 0 | 0 | 0 | 0 | 0 | 0 | 0 | 0 |
| Other State Funds | 0 | 0 | 0 | 0 | 0 | 0 | 0 | 0 |
| FEDERAL FUNDS | 18,360,000 | 48,608,000 | 58,795,000 | 67,017,000 | 68,222,000 | 77,710,000 | 117,009,000 | 120,649,000 |
| Federal ICF/MR | 18,360,000 | 48,608,000 | 58,795,000 | 67,017,000 | 68,222,000 | 77,710,000 | 117,009,000 | 120,649,000 |
| Title XX / SSBG Funds | 0 | 0 | 0 | 0 | 0 | 0 | 0 | 0 |
| Other Federal Funds | 0 | 0 | 0 | 0 | 0 | 0 | 0 | 0 |
| LARGE PRIVATE RESIDENTIAL | 0 | 0 | 0 | 0 | 0 | 0 | 0 | 0 |
| STATE FUNDS | 0 | 0 | 0 | 0 | 0 | 0 | 0 | 0 |
| General Funds | 0 | 0 | 0 | 0 | 0 | 0 | 0 | 0 |
| Other State Funds | 0 | 0 | 0 | 0 | 0 | 0 | 0 | 0 |
| Local/County Overmatch | 0 | 0 | 0 | 0 | 0 | 0 | 0 | 0 |
| FEDERAL FUNDS | 0 | 0 | 0 | 0 | 0 | 0 | 0 | 0 |
| Large Private ICF/MR | 0 | 0 | 0 | 0 | 0 | 0 | 0 | 0 |
| **COMMUNITY SERVICES FUNDS** | 30,779,180 | 37,746,632 | 49,760,820 | 62,721,505 | 76,087,714 | 75,447,291 | 89,553,666 | 99,809,102 |
| STATE FUNDS | 21,946,180 | 27,765,632 | 39,908,820 | 51,603,605 | 66,342,414 | 72,036,291 | 84,919,666 | 93,974,102 |
| General Funds | 17,133,480 | 22,819,932 | 34,787,520 | 46,393,305 | 61,794,714 | 69,979,291 | 82,859,666 | 92,020,102 |
| Other State Funds | 2,638,700 | 2,949,700 | 3,103,300 | 3,197,300 | 2,539,700 | 0 | 0 | 0 |
| Local/County Overmatch | 0 | 0 | 0 | 0 | 0 | 0 | 0 | 0 |
| SSI State Supplement | 2,174,000 | 1,996,000 | 2,018,000 | 2,013,000 | 2,008,000 | 2,057,000 | 2,060,000 | 1,954,000 |
| FEDERAL FUNDS | 8,833,000 | 9,981,000 | 9,852,000 | 11,117,900 | 9,745,300 | 3,411,000 | 4,634,000 | 5,835,000 |
| ICF/MR Funds | 0 | 0 | 0 | 154,900 | 569,300 | 1,168,000 | 1,786,000 | 2,557,000 |
| Small Public | 0 | 0 | 0 | 0 | 0 | 0 | 0 | 0 |
| Small Private | 0 | 0 | 0 | 154,900 | 569,300 | 1,168,000 | 1,786,000 | 2,557,000 |
| HCBS Waiver | 0 | 0 | 0 | 0 | 0 | 0 | 0 | 0 |
| Model 50/200 Waiver | 0 | 0 | 0 | 0 | 0 | 0 | 0 | 0 |
| Other Title XIX Programs | 0 | 0 | 0 | 450,000 | 600,000 | 1,100,000 | 1,650,000 | 1,900,000 |
| Title XX / SSBG Funds | 7,916,000 | 8,849,000 | 9,310,000 | 9,592,000 | 7,619,000 | 0 | 0 | 0 |
| Other Federal Funds | 917,000 | 1,132,000 | 542,000 | 921,000 | 957,000 | 1,143,000 | 1,198,000 | 1,378,000 |
| Waiver Clients' SSI/ADC | 0 | 0 | 0 | 0 | 0 | 0 | 0 | 0 |

| | 1985 | 1986 | 1987 | 1988 | 1989 | 1990 | 1991 | 1992 |
|---|---|---|---|---|---|---|---|---|
| **TOTAL FUNDS** | **$373,109,364** | **$409,557,236** | **$508,337,250** | **$605,835,795** | **$695,648,518** | **$748,263,397** | **$778,418,063** | **$817,945,560** |
| **CONGREGATE 16+ BEDS** | 258,028,696 | 267,051,260 | 305,202,920 | 333,213,900 | 361,637,252 | 387,568,509 | 404,750,349 | 416,892,859 |
| INSTITUTIONAL SERVICES FUNDS | 258,028,696 | 267,051,260 | 305,202,920 | 333,213,900 | 361,637,252 | 387,568,509 | 404,750,349 | 416,892,859 |
| STATE FUNDS | 149,057,696 | 140,842,260 | 183,414,920 | 190,555,900 | 214,175,912 | 240,907,764 | 241,613,307 | 257,181,006 |
| General Funds | 147,336,696 | 139,047,260 | 181,262,920 | 188,224,900 | 211,702,234 | 237,985,363 | 239,131,568 | 254,215,606 |
| Local | 0 | 0 | 0 | 0 | 0 | 0 | 0 | 0 |
| Other State Funds | 1,721,000 | 1,795,000 | 2,152,000 | 2,331,000 | 2,473,678 | 2,922,401 | 2,481,739 | 2,965,400 |
| FEDERAL FUNDS | 108,971,000 | 126,209,000 | 121,788,000 | 142,658,000 | 147,461,340 | 146,660,745 | 163,137,042 | 159,711,853 |
| Federal ICF/MR | 108,971,000 | 126,209,000 | 121,788,000 | 142,658,000 | 147,461,340 | 146,660,745 | 163,137,042 | 159,711,853 |
| Title XX / SSBG Funds | 0 | 0 | 0 | 0 | 0 | 0 | 0 | 0 |
| Other Federal Funds | 0 | 0 | 0 | 0 | 0 | 0 | 0 | 0 |
| LARGE PRIVATE RESIDENTIAL | 0 | 0 | 0 | 0 | 0 | 0 | 0 | 0 |
| STATE FUNDS | 0 | 0 | 0 | 0 | 0 | 0 | 0 | 0 |
| General Funds | 0 | 0 | 0 | 0 | 0 | 0 | 0 | 0 |
| Other State Funds | 0 | 0 | 0 | 0 | 0 | 0 | 0 | 0 |
| Local/County Overmatch | 0 | 0 | 0 | 0 | 0 | 0 | 0 | 0 |
| FEDERAL FUNDS | 0 | 0 | 0 | 0 | 0 | 0 | 0 | 0 |
| Large Private ICF/MR | 0 | 0 | 0 | 0 | 0 | 0 | 0 | 0 |
| **COMMUNITY SERVICES FUNDS** | 115,080,668 | 142,505,976 | 203,134,330 | 272,621,895 | 334,011,266 | 360,694,888 | 373,667,714 | 401,052,701 |
| STATE FUNDS | 104,224,668 | 126,212,016 | 182,713,575 | 245,286,567 | 291,445,165 | 299,856,062 | 304,210,085 | 306,211,087 |
| General Funds | 102,157,668 | 124,186,016 | 175,487,575 | 237,514,567 | 283,085,909 | 290,865,176 | 294,539,843 | 295,810,157 |
| Other State Funds | 0 | 0 | 0 | 0 | 0 | 0 | 0 | 0 |
| Local/County Overmatch | 0 | 0 | 0 | 0 | 0 | 0 | 0 | 0 |
| SSI State Supplement | 2,067,000 | 2,026,000 | 7,226,000 | 7,772,000 | 8,359,256 | 8,990,886 | 9,670,242 | 10,400,930 |
| FEDERAL FUNDS | 10,856,000 | 16,293,960 | 20,420,755 | 27,335,328 | 42,566,101 | 60,838,826 | 69,457,629 | 94,841,614 |
| ICF/MR Funds | 3,910,000 | 6,016,000 | 7,395,535 | 11,258,208 | 16,504,447 | 19,834,225 | 21,436,278 | 22,720,437 |
| Small Public | 0 | 0 | 745,535 | 4,058,208 | 5,464,742 | 5,484,622 | 6,369,195 | 6,900,000 |
| Small Private | 3,910,000 | 6,016,000 | 6,650,000 | 7,200,000 | 11,039,705 | 14,349,603 | 15,067,083 | 15,820,437 |
| HCBS Waiver | 2,900,000 | 4,500,000 | 6,639,000 | 7,900,000 | 13,064,424 | 21,064,925 | 24,774,474 | 43,706,099 |
| Model 50/200 Waiver | 0 | 0 | 0 | 0 | 0 | 0 | 0 | 0 |
| Other Title XIX Programs | 3,200,000 | 3,800,000 | 4,500,000 | 5,300,000 | 8,031,390 | 12,874,076 | 14,422,677 | 14,686,154 |
| Title XX / SSBG Funds | 0 | 0 | 0 | 0 | 0 | 0 | 0 | 0 |
| Other Federal Funds | 0 | 0 | 0 | 0 | 0 | 0 | 0 | 0 |
| Waiver Clients' SSI/ADC | 846,000 | 1,977,960 | 1,886,220 | 2,877,120 | 4,965,840 | 7,065,600 | 8,824,200 | 13,728,924 |

*Source:*
Institute on Disability and Human Development (UAP),
University of Illinois at Chicago, 1994

# MICHIGAN

## MR/DD Spending for Congregate Residential & Community Services

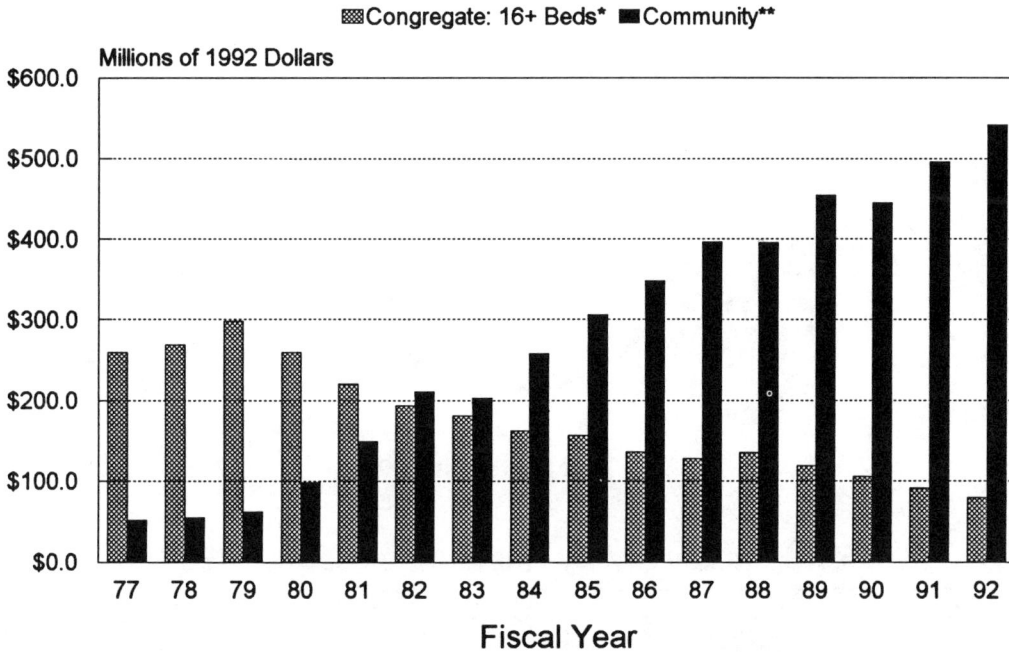

▨Congregate: 16+ Beds*  ■Community**

Millions of 1992 Dollars

$600.0

$500.0

$400.0

$300.0

$200.0

$100.0

$0.0

77 78 79 80 81 82 83 84 85 86 87 88 89 90 91 92

Fiscal Year

*Excludes nursing homes; ** Includes resources for
15 bed or less residential settings & non-residential community services

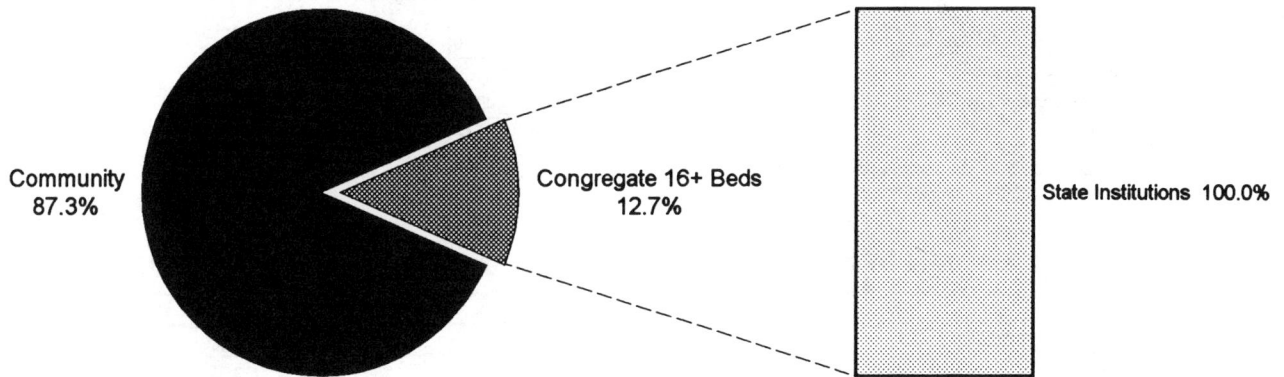

Community
87.3%

Congregate 16+ Beds
12.7%

State Institutions  100.0%

FY 1992 Total Spending:
$620.8 Million

*Source:*
Institute on Disability and Human Development (UAP),
University of Illinois at Chicago, 1994

# MICHIGAN

## Number of Persons Served by Residential Setting: FY 1992

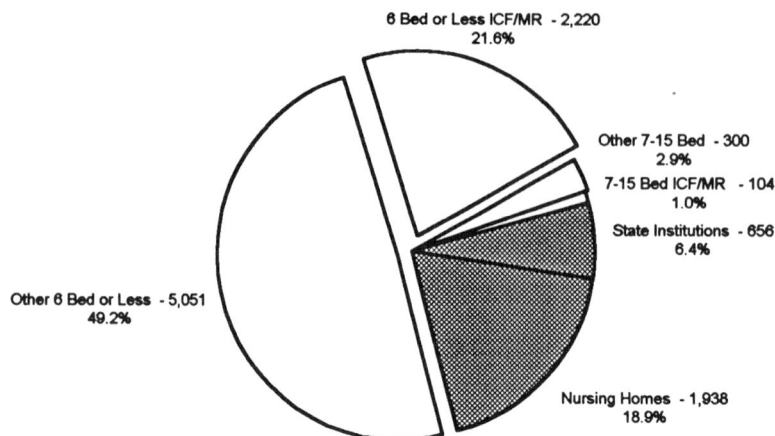

6 Bed or Less ICF/MR - 2,220
21.6%

Other 7-15 Bed - 300
2.9%

7-15 Bed ICF/MR - 104
1.0%

State Institutions - 656
6.4%

Other 6 Bed or Less - 5,051
49.2%

Nursing Homes - 1,938
18.9%

Total Served: 10,269

## Persons Served by Residential Setting:1986-92

| | 1986 | 1987 | 1988 | 1989 | 1990 | 1991 | 1992 |
|---|---|---|---|---|---|---|---|
| CONGREGATE 16 + BED SETTINGS | 1,867 | 1,724 | 4,294 | 3,901 | 3,537 | 3,136 | 2,594 |
| Nursing Homes* | NA | NA | 2,817 | 2,655 | 2,482 | 2,266 | 1,938 |
| State Institutions | 1,867 | 1,724 | 1,477 | 1,246 | 1,055 | 870 | 656 |
| Private 16+ Bed ICF/MR | 0 | 0 | 0 | 0 | 0 | 0 | 0 |
| Other 16+ Bed Residential | 0 | 0 | 0 | 0 | 0 | 0 | 0 |
| 15 BED OR LESS RESIDENTIAL SETTINGS | 5,189 | 5,348 | 5,562 | 6,014 | 6,804 | 7,379 | 7,675 |
| Public 7-15 Bed ICF/MR | 0 | 0 | 0 | 0 | 0 | 0 | 0 |
| Private 7-15 Bed ICF/MR | NA | NA | NA | NA | NA | 112 | 104 |
| Other 7-15 Bed Residential | 700 | 700 | 650 | 550 | 450 | 350 | 300 |
| Public 6 Bed or Less ICF/MR | 0 | 0 | 0 | 0 | 0 | 0 | 0 |
| Private 6 Bed or Less ICF/MR | 1,446 | 1,774 | 2,162 | 2,157 | 2,025 | 1,967 | 2,220 |
| Other 6 Bed or Less Residential | 3,043 | 2,874 | 2,750 | 3,307 | 4,329 | 4,950 | 5,051 |
| TOTAL PERSONS SERVED | 7,056 | 7,072 | 9,856 | 9,915 | 10,341 | 10,515 | 10,269 |

## Persons Served in Non-Residential Community Services:1986-92

| | 1986 | 1987 | 1988 | 1989 | 1990 | 1991 | 1992 |
|---|---|---|---|---|---|---|---|
| DAY/WORK PROGRAMS | 11,000 | 10,322 | NA | NA | 11,455 | 12,489 | 11,630 |
| Sheltered Employment/Work Activity | 6,000 | 5,000 | 5,000 | NA | 3,411 | 3,530 | 2,650 |
| Day Habilitation ("Day Training") | 5,000 | 5,000 | NA | 5,000 | 7,051 | 6,314 | 5,980 |
| Supported/Competitive Employment | NA | 322 | 603 | 752 | 993 | 2,645 | 3,000 |
| CASE MANAGEMENT | 11,500 | 14,500 | 11,000 | NA | 14,700 | 15,750 | 15,750 |
| HCBS WAIVER | 0 | 0 | 616 | 971 | 1,483 | 1,820 | 2,228 |
| MODEL 50/200 WAIVER | NA | 2 | 18 | 46 | 70 | 112 | 146 |

*Approximately 1,800 of the 1,938 individuals in Nursing Homes in 1992 are not supported by the Department of Mental Health (DMH), although DMH is working to arrange alternatives.
Expenditures for the total 1,938 individuals are not included in other graphics & tables.

*Source:*
Institute on Disability and Human Development (UAP),
University of Illinois at Chicago, 1994

# MICHIGAN

## Community Services: FY 1992 Revenue Sources

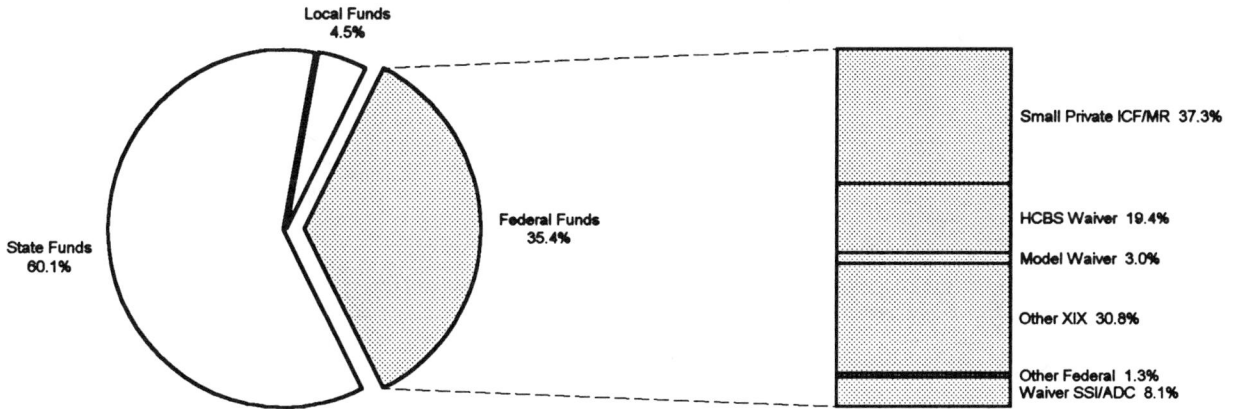

Local Funds
4.5%

State Funds
60.1%

Federal Funds
35.4%

Small Private ICF/MR 37.3%

HCBS Waiver 19.4%

Model Waiver 3.0%

Other XIX 30.8%

Other Federal 1.3%
Waiver SSI/ADC 8.1%

Total Funds: $541.7 Million

## Family Support Initiatives*

|  | 1986 | 1987 | 1988 | 1989 | 1990 | 1991 | 1992 |
|---|---|---|---|---|---|---|---|
| FAMILY SUPPORT: TOTAL SPENDING | $10,470,101 | $12,353,359 | $14,679,251 | $16,810,155 | $20,497,776 | $19,290,662 | $19,236,918 |
| Total # of Families Supported | NA | 3,067 | 3,288 | 10,131 | 12,549 | 13,604 | 13,684 |
| A. Financial Subsidy/Payment | $7,220,101 | $8,453,359 | $9,429,251 | $10,304,371 | $11,174,100 | $10,467,881 | $10,414,137 |
| # of Families | 2,771 | 3,067 | 3,288 | 3,499 | 3,687 | 3,842 | 3,922 |
| B. Family Assistance Payments | $0 | $0 | $0 | $0 | $0 | $0 | $0 |
| # of Families | 0 | 0 | 0 | 0 | 0 | 0 | 0 |
| C. Other Family Support Payments | $3,250,000 | $3,900,000 | $5,250,000 | $6,505,784 | $9,323,676 | $8,822,781 | $8,822,781 |
| # of Families | NA | NA | NA | 6,632 | 8,862 | 9,762 | 9,762 |

## Other Community Services Initiatives*

|  | 1986 | 1987 | 1988 | 1989 | 1990 | 1991 | 1992 |
|---|---|---|---|---|---|---|---|
| AGING/DD SPENDING | $456,700 | $456,700 | $483,700 | $483,700 | $483,700 | $483,700 | $558,700 |
| # of Persons Served | NA | NA | NA | NA | NA | NA | NA |
| ASSISTIVE TECHNOLOGY SPENDING |  |  |  |  |  |  | $0 |
| # of Persons Served |  |  |  |  |  |  | 0 |
| EARLY INTERVENTION SPENDING | $30,800 | $30,800 | $30,000 | NA | NA | $133,500 | $133,500 |
| # of Persons Served | NA | NA | NA | NA | NA | 64 | 64 |
| PERSONAL ASSISTANCE SPENDING |  |  |  |  |  |  | $0 |
| # of Persons Served |  |  |  |  |  |  | 0 |
| SUPPORTED EMPLOYMENT SPENDING | $800,000 | $1,450,000 | $1,955,500 | $1,113,000 | $1,113,000 | $1,113,000 | NA |
| # of Persons Served | NA | 322 | 603 | 752 | 993 | 2,645 | 3,000 |
| SUPPORTED LIVING SPENDING |  |  |  |  | NA | NA | NA |
| # of Persons Served |  |  |  |  | 442 | 528 | 301 |

*Expenditures associated with Special Community Initiatives are a subset of funding within the community services component of the state's chart series and spreadsheet; Family Support Client figures may include duplicate client counts; HCBS Waiver counts include Waiver case management numbers.
0= Services not provided in the state; NA= Data not available from state; blank= Services not applicable (eg. CSLA prior to authorization, Special Community Initiatives prior to request for data by this study)

*Source:*
Institute on Disability and Human Development (UAP),
University of Illinois at Chicago, 1994

# MICHIGAN

## Large Congregate Care Facilities: FY 1992 Revenue Sources*

### Private 16+Bed Settings

### Public Institutions

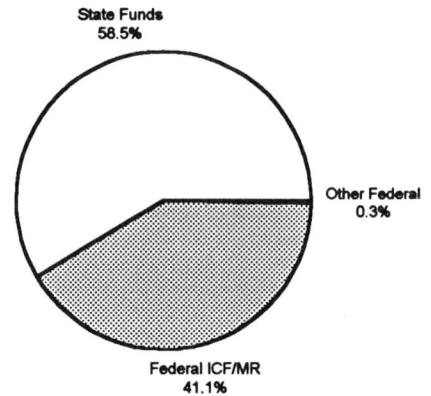

**Does Not Apply**

State Funds
58.5%

Other Federal
0.3%

Federal ICF/MR
41.1%

Total Funds: $79.1 Million

*Excludes nursing homes

## Average Daily Residents in Institutions

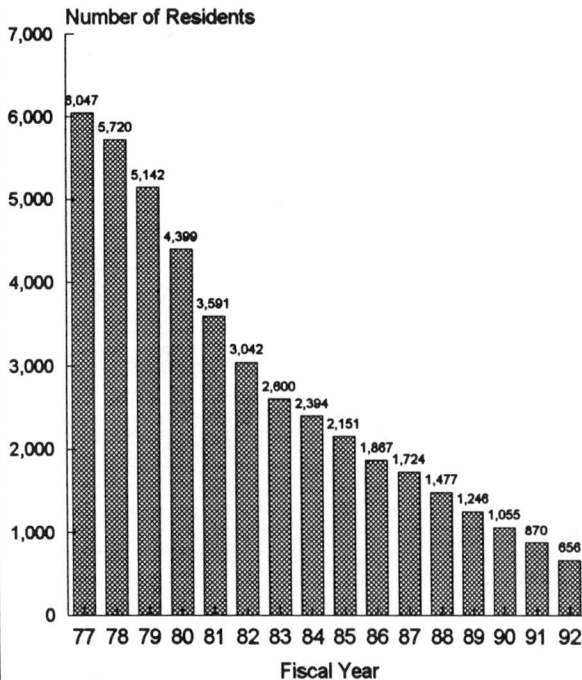

Number of Residents

| Fiscal Year | Number of Residents |
|---|---|
| 77 | 6,047 |
| 78 | 5,720 |
| 79 | 5,142 |
| 80 | 4,399 |
| 81 | 3,591 |
| 82 | 3,042 |
| 83 | 2,600 |
| 84 | 2,394 |
| 85 | 2,151 |
| 86 | 1,867 |
| 87 | 1,724 |
| 88 | 1,477 |
| 89 | 1,246 |
| 90 | 1,055 |
| 91 | 870 |
| 92 | 656 |

Fiscal Year

## Institutional Daily Costs Per Resident

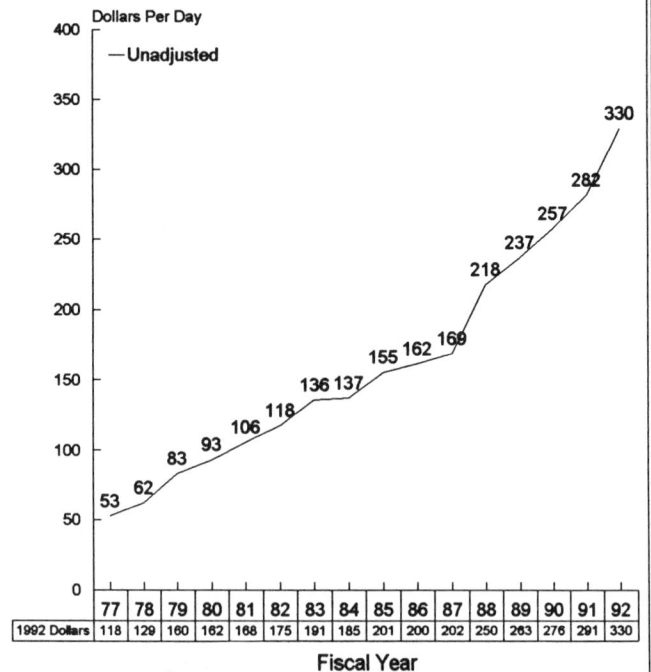

Dollars Per Day

— Unadjusted

| Fiscal Year | Unadjusted | 1992 Dollars |
|---|---|---|
| 77 | 53 | 118 |
| 78 | 62 | 129 |
| 79 | 83 | 160 |
| 80 | 93 | 162 |
| 81 | 106 | 168 |
| 82 | 118 | 175 |
| 83 | 136 | 191 |
| 84 | 137 | 185 |
| 85 | 155 | 201 |
| 86 | 162 | 200 |
| 87 | 169 | 202 |
| 88 | 218 | 250 |
| 89 | 237 | 263 |
| 90 | 257 | 276 |
| 91 | 282 | 291 |
| 92 | 330 | 330 |

Fiscal Year

*Source:*
Institute on Disability and Human Development (UAP),
University of Illinois at Chicago, 1994

# MICHIGAN FISCAL EFFORT

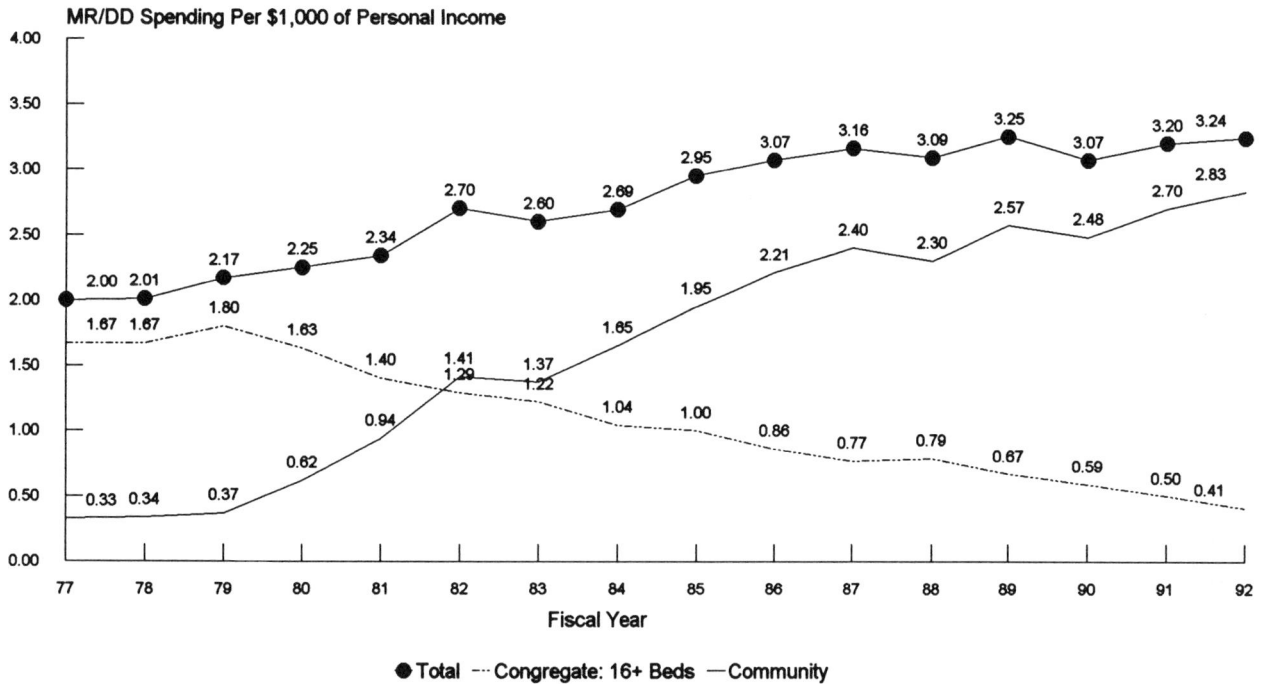

MR/DD Spending Per $1,000 of Personal Income

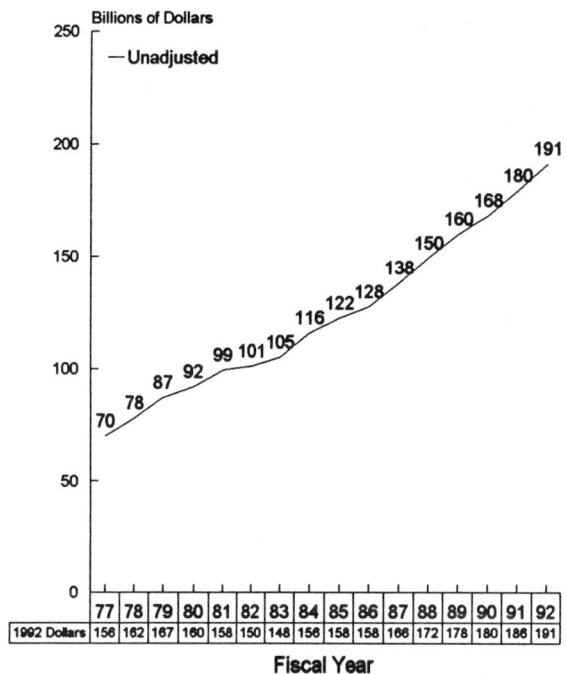

| | |
|---|---|
| 4.00 | |
| 3.50 | |
| 3.00 | |
| 2.50 | |
| 2.00 | |
| 1.50 | |
| 1.00 | |
| 0.50 | |
| 0.00 | |

Total values: 2.00  2.01  2.17  2.25  2.34  2.70  2.60  2.69  2.95  3.07  3.16  3.09  3.25  3.07  3.20  3.24

Congregate: 16+ Beds values: 1.67  1.67  1.80  1.63  1.40  1.41  1.37  1.04  1.00  0.86  0.77  0.79  0.67  0.59  0.50  0.41

Community values: 0.33  0.34  0.37  0.62  0.94  1.29  1.22  1.65  1.95  2.21  2.40  2.30  2.57  2.48  2.70  2.83

Fiscal Year: 77 78 79 80 81 82 83 84 85 86 87 88 89 90 91 92

● Total  --- Congregate: 16+ Beds  — Community

## Total MR/DD Spending

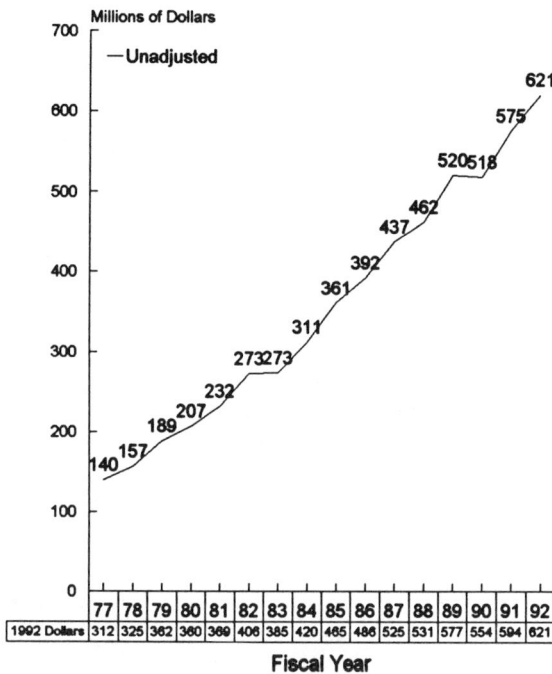

Millions of Dollars
— Unadjusted

| 700 | |
| 600 | |
| 500 | |
| 400 | |
| 300 | |
| 200 | |
| 100 | |
| 0 | |

Values: 140 157 189 207 232 273 273 311 361 392 437 462 520 518 575 621

| Fiscal Year | 77 | 78 | 79 | 80 | 81 | 82 | 83 | 84 | 85 | 86 | 87 | 88 | 89 | 90 | 91 | 92 |
|---|---|---|---|---|---|---|---|---|---|---|---|---|---|---|---|---|
| 1992 Dollars | 312 | 325 | 362 | 360 | 369 | 406 | 385 | 420 | 465 | 486 | 525 | 531 | 577 | 554 | 594 | 621 |

Fiscal Year

## Personal Income

Billions of Dollars
— Unadjusted

| 250 | |
| 200 | |
| 150 | |
| 100 | |
| 50 | |
| 0 | |

Values: 70 78 87 92 99 101 105 116 122 128 138 150 160 168 180 191

| Fiscal Year | 77 | 78 | 79 | 80 | 81 | 82 | 83 | 84 | 85 | 86 | 87 | 88 | 89 | 90 | 91 | 92 |
|---|---|---|---|---|---|---|---|---|---|---|---|---|---|---|---|---|
| 1992 Dollars | 156 | 162 | 167 | 160 | 158 | 150 | 148 | 156 | 158 | 158 | 166 | 172 | 178 | 180 | 186 | 191 |

Fiscal Year

*Source:*
Institute on Disability and Human Development (UAP),
University of Illinois at Chicago, 1994

# MICHIGAN

## Financial Support for MR/DD Services: FY 1977-92

| | 1977 | 1978 | 1979 | 1980 | 1981 | 1982 | 1983 | 1984 |
|---|---|---|---|---|---|---|---|---|
| **TOTAL FUNDS** | $140,109,617 | $156,963,778 | $188,758,727 | $206,849,554 | $232,091,222 | $272,665,386 | $272,983,878 | $311,444,285 |
| **CONGREGATE 16+ BEDS** | 116,950,000 | 130,214,000 | 156,222,000 | 149,946,000 | 138,632,000 | 130,605,000 | 128,659,618 | 119,951,195 |
| INSTITUTIONAL SERVICES FUNDS | 116,950,000 | 130,214,000 | 156,222,000 | 149,946,000 | 138,632,000 | 130,605,000 | 128,659,618 | 119,951,195 |
| STATE FUNDS | 94,253,000 | 80,708,000 | 101,102,000 | 97,224,000 | 72,457,000 | 64,052,000 | 65,057,795 | 70,474,755 |
| General Funds | 85,345,260 | 73,223,150 | 92,002,820 | 87,682,140 | 65,116,870 | 57,468,320 | 58,862,468 | 63,775,697 |
| Local | 8,440,740 | 7,241,850 | 9,099,180 | 8,671,860 | 6,440,130 | 5,683,680 | 5,821,563 | 6,307,487 |
| Other State Funds | 467,000 | 243,000 | 0 | 870,000 | 900,000 | 900,000 | 373,764 | 391,571 |
| FEDERAL FUNDS | 22,697,000 | 49,506,000 | 55,120,000 | 52,722,000 | 66,175,000 | 66,553,000 | 63,601,823 | 49,476,440 |
| Federal ICF/MR | 22,172,000 | 48,454,000 | 54,320,000 | 51,688,000 | 65,332,000 | 65,710,000 | 63,022,400 | 48,703,400 |
| Title XX / SSBG Funds | 0 | 0 | 0 | 0 | 0 | 0 | 0 | 0 |
| Other Federal Funds | 525,000 | 1,052,000 | 800,000 | 1,034,000 | 843,000 | 843,000 | 579,423 | 773,040 |
| LARGE PRIVATE RESIDENTIAL | 0 | 0 | 0 | 0 | 0 | 0 | 0 | 0 |
| STATE FUNDS | 0 | 0 | 0 | 0 | 0 | 0 | 0 | 0 |
| General Funds | 0 | 0 | 0 | 0 | 0 | 0 | 0 | 0 |
| Other State Funds | 0 | 0 | 0 | 0 | 0 | 0 | 0 | 0 |
| Local/County Overmatch | 0 | 0 | 0 | 0 | 0 | 0 | 0 | 0 |
| FEDERAL FUNDS | 0 | 0 | 0 | 0 | 0 | 0 | 0 | 0 |
| Large Private ICF/MR | 0 | 0 | 0 | 0 | 0 | 0 | 0 | 0 |
| **COMMUNITY SERVICES FUNDS** | 23,159,617 | 26,749,778 | 32,536,727 | 56,903,554 | 93,459,222 | 142,060,386 | 144,324,260 | 191,493,090 |
| STATE FUNDS | 23,159,617 | 26,749,778 | 31,101,527 | 53,458,754 | 86,069,497 | 127,268,361 | 117,803,660 | 162,734,490 |
| General Funds | 14,038,617 | 15,477,078 | 17,508,927 | 38,317,154 | 68,728,695 | 106,669,249 | 97,978,467 | 138,496,027 |
| Other State Funds | 0 | 0 | 0 | 0 | 0 | 0 | 0 | 0 |
| Local/County Overmatch | 1,478,000 | 1,614,700 | 1,803,600 | 3,978,600 | 7,334,802 | 10,897,112 | 10,051,193 | 14,190,463 |
| SSI State Supplement | 7,643,000 | 9,658,000 | 11,789,000 | 11,163,000 | 10,006,000 | 9,702,000 | 9,774,000 | 10,048,000 |
| FEDERAL FUNDS | 0 | 0 | 1,435,200 | 3,444,800 | 7,389,725 | 14,792,025 | 26,520,600 | 28,758,600 |
| ICF/MR Funds | 0 | 0 | 300,000 | 1,100,000 | 5,500,000 | 12,000,000 | 18,000,000 | 20,000,000 |
| Small Public | 0 | 0 | 0 | 0 | 0 | 0 | 0 | 0 |
| Small Private | 0 | 0 | 300,000 | 1,100,000 | 5,500,000 | 12,000,000 | 18,000,000 | 20,000,000 |
| HCBS Waiver | 0 | 0 | 0 | 0 | 0 | 0 | 0 | 0 |
| Model 50/200 Waiver | 0 | 0 | 0 | 0 | 0 | 0 | 0 | 0 |
| Other Title XIX Programs | 0 | 0 | 0 | 0 | 260,625 | 1,106,925 | 6,964,000 | 7,166,100 |
| Title XX / SSBG Funds | 0 | 0 | 0 | 0 | 0 | 0 | 0 | 0 |
| Other Federal Funds | 0 | 0 | 1,135,200 | 2,344,800 | 1,629,100 | 1,685,100 | 1,556,600 | 1,592,500 |
| Waiver Clients' SSI/ADC | 0 | 0 | 0 | 0 | 0 | 0 | 0 | 0 |

| | 1985 | 1986 | 1987 | 1988 | 1989 | 1990 | 1991 | 1992 |
|---|---|---|---|---|---|---|---|---|
| **TOTAL FUNDS** | $360,549,393 | $391,912,226 | $437,467,453 | $461,858,619 | $519,954,294 | $517,579,026 | $574,944,986 | $620,814,090 |
| **CONGREGATE 16+ BEDS** | 122,033,610 | 110,114,026 | 106,163,321 | 117,693,976 | 107,573,893 | 99,153,952 | 89,422,911 | 79,130,809 |
| INSTITUTIONAL SERVICES FUNDS | 122,033,610 | 110,114,026 | 106,163,321 | 117,693,976 | 107,573,893 | 99,153,952 | 89,422,911 | 79,130,809 |
| STATE FUNDS | 70,141,010 | 47,034,456 | 47,334,151 | 59,026,878 | 53,849,254 | 53,623,165 | 57,938,856 | 46,320,009 |
| General Funds | 63,475,239 | 42,548,102 | 42,816,730 | 51,858,459 | 47,146,821 | 46,945,580 | 50,877,359 | 40,087,396 |
| Local | 6,277,771 | 4,208,054 | 4,234,622 | 5,168,419 | 4,702,433 | 4,677,585 | 5,061,497 | 3,989,413 |
| Other State Funds | 388,000 | 278,300 | 282,799 | 2,000,000 | 2,000,000 | 2,000,000 | 2,000,000 | 2,243,200 |
| FEDERAL FUNDS | 51,892,600 | 63,079,570 | 58,829,170 | 58,667,098 | 53,724,639 | 45,530,787 | 31,484,055 | 32,810,800 |
| Federal ICF/MR | 51,565,600 | 62,492,000 | 58,227,000 | 58,267,098 | 53,324,639 | 45,180,787 | 31,184,055 | 32,560,800 |
| Title XX / SSBG Funds | 0 | 0 | 0 | 0 | 0 | 0 | 0 | 0 |
| Other Federal Funds | 327,000 | 587,570 | 602,170 | 400,000 | 400,000 | 350,000 | 300,000 | 250,000 |
| LARGE PRIVATE RESIDENTIAL | 0 | 0 | 0 | 0 | 0 | 0 | 0 | 0 |
| STATE FUNDS | 0 | 0 | 0 | 0 | 0 | 0 | 0 | 0 |
| General Funds | 0 | 0 | 0 | 0 | 0 | 0 | 0 | 0 |
| Other State Funds | 0 | 0 | 0 | 0 | 0 | 0 | 0 | 0 |
| Local/County Overmatch | 0 | 0 | 0 | 0 | 0 | 0 | 0 | 0 |
| FEDERAL FUNDS | 0 | 0 | 0 | 0 | 0 | 0 | 0 | 0 |
| Large Private ICF/MR | 0 | 0 | 0 | 0 | 0 | 0 | 0 | 0 |
| **COMMUNITY SERVICES FUNDS** | 238,515,783 | 281,798,200 | 331,304,132 | 344,164,643 | 412,380,401 | 418,425,074 | 485,522,075 | 541,683,281 |
| STATE FUNDS | 205,441,082 | 220,305,365 | 264,490,555 | 228,004,570 | 284,428,275 | 270,932,671 | 311,987,437 | 349,765,880 |
| General Funds | 176,508,222 | 189,646,177 | 225,059,121 | 190,594,412 | 241,195,549 | 228,414,826 | 266,566,101 | 301,564,440 |
| Other State Funds | 0 | 0 | 0 | 4,271,800 | 4,350,486 | 4,470,269 | 3,814,152 | 4,232,200 |
| Local/County Overmatch | 18,303,860 | 19,525,188 | 23,024,434 | 16,871,358 | 21,801,890 | 20,113,208 | 22,776,098 | 24,196,600 |
| SSI State Supplement | 10,629,000 | 11,134,000 | 16,407,000 | 16,267,000 | 17,080,350 | 17,934,368 | 18,831,086 | 19,772,640 |
| FEDERAL FUNDS | 33,074,701 | 61,492,835 | 66,813,577 | 116,160,073 | 127,952,126 | 147,492,403 | 173,534,638 | 191,917,401 |
| ICF/MR Funds | 21,000,000 | 48,419,200 | 49,600,000 | 67,823,602 | 60,448,861 | 64,984,593 | 74,609,675 | 71,672,173 |
| Small Public | 0 | 0 | 0 | 0 | 0 | 0 | 0 | 0 |
| Small Private | 21,000,000 | 48,419,200 | 49,600,000 | 67,823,602 | 60,448,861 | 64,984,593 | 74,609,675 | 71,672,173 |
| HCBS Waiver | 0 | 0 | 0 | 6,829,314 | 14,719,311 | 19,955,326 | 22,789,753 | 37,299,151 |
| Model 50/200 Waiver | 0 | 0 | 45,400 | 617,750 | 1,235,327 | 2,235,267 | 2,922,900 | 5,832,727 |
| Other Title XIX Programs | 10,439,201 | 11,198,135 | 15,293,477 | 36,226,336 | 43,318,205 | 48,945,819 | 59,048,615 | 59,148,310 |
| Title XX / SSBG Funds | 0 | 0 | 0 | 0 | 0 | 0 | 0 | 0 |
| Other Federal Funds | 1,635,500 | 1,875,500 | 1,874,700 | 2,268,063 | 2,657,190 | 4,129,158 | 4,482,287 | 2,409,500 |
| Waiver Clients' SSI/ADC | 0 | 0 | 0 | 2,395,008 | 5,573,232 | 7,242,240 | 9,681,408 | 15,555,540 |

*Source:*
Institute on Disability and Human Development (UAP),
University of Illinois at Chicago, 1994

# MINNESOTA

## MR/DD Spending for Congregate Residential & Community Services

▨Congregate: 16+ Beds*  ■Community**

Millions of 1992 Dollars

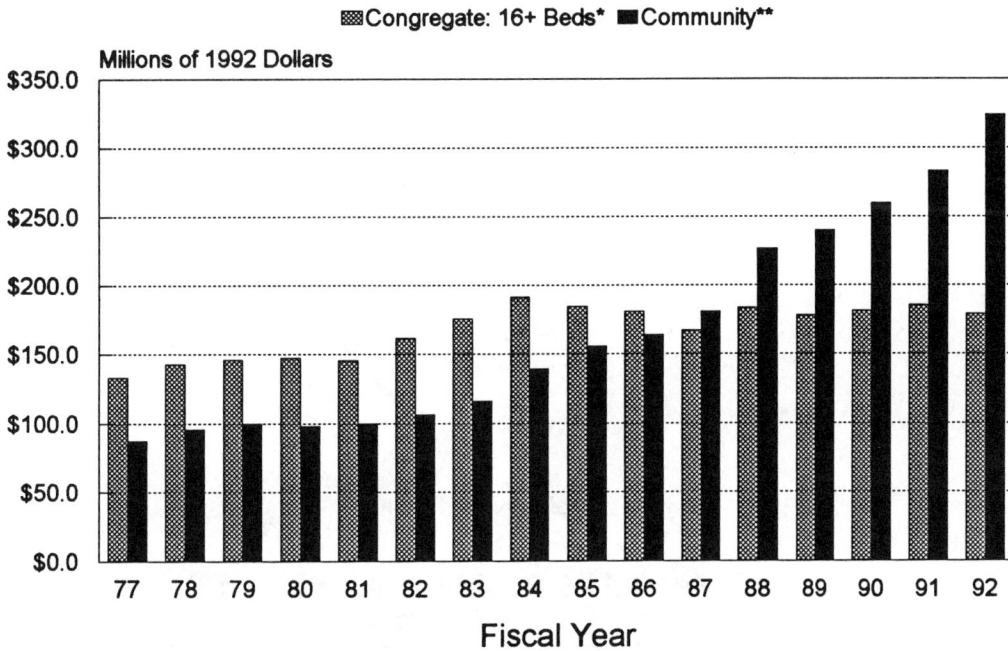

### Fiscal Year

*Excludes nursing homes; ** Includes resources for
15 bed or less residential settings & non-residential community services

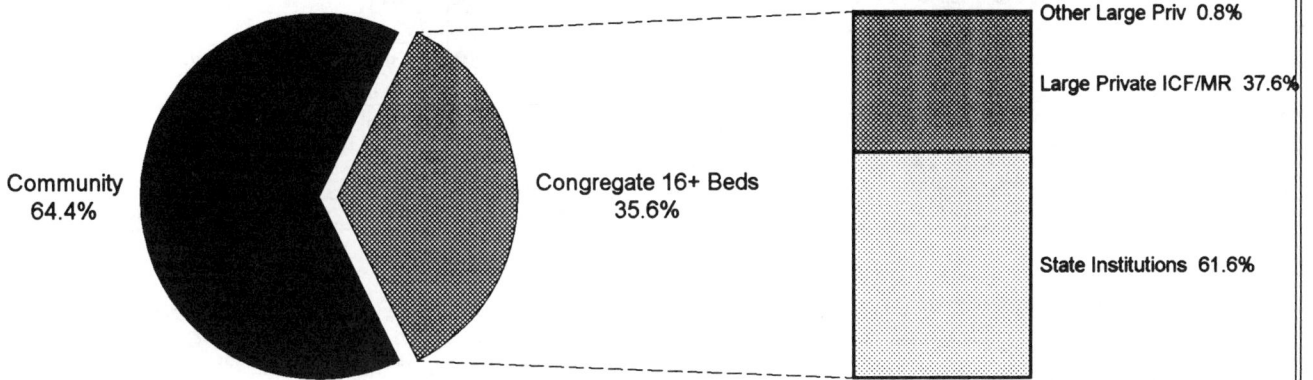

Community
64.4%

Congregate 16+ Beds
35.6%

Other Large Priv  0.8%

Large Private ICF/MR  37.6%

State Institutions  61.6%

FY 1992 Total Spending:
$502.8 Million

Source:
Institute on Disability and Human Development (UAP),
University of Illinois at Chicago, 1994

# MINNESOTA

## Number of Persons Served by Residential Setting: FY 1992

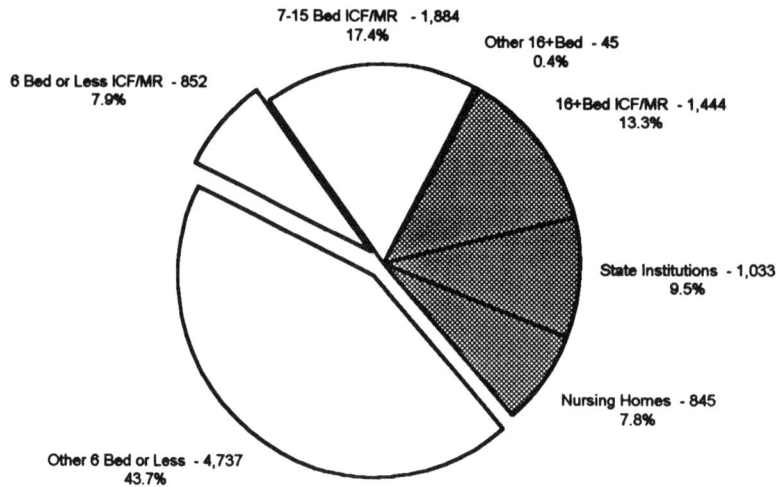

7-15 Bed ICF/MR - 1,884
17.4%

Other 16+Bed - 45
0.4%

6 Bed or Less ICF/MR - 852
7.9%

16+Bed ICF/MR - 1,444
13.3%

State Institutions - 1,033
9.5%

Nursing Homes - 845
7.8%

Other 6 Bed or Less - 4,737
43.7%

Total Served: 10,840

## Persons Served by Residential Setting:1986-92

| | 1986 | 1987 | 1988 | 1989 | 1990 | 1991 | 1992 |
|---|---|---|---|---|---|---|---|
| CONGREGATE 16 + BED SETTINGS | 5,169 | 4,901 | 4,487 | 4,165 | 3,971 | 3,652 | 3,367 |
| Nursing Homes | 1,200 | 1,080 | 900 | 850 | 802 | 827 | 845 |
| State Institutions | 1,880 | 1,703 | 1,556 | 1,442 | 1,352 | 1,177 | 1,033 |
| Private 16+Bed ICF/MR | 2,016 | 2,045 | 1,958 | 1,800 | 1,747 | 1,588 | 1,444 |
| Other 16+Bed Residential | 73 | 73 | 73 | 73 | 70 | 60 | 45 |
| 15 BED OR LESS RESIDENTIAL SETTINGS | 2,608 | 2,614 | 5,226 | 5,607 | 5,889 | 6,737 | 7,473 |
| Public 7-15 Bed ICF/MR | 0 | 0 | 0 | 0 | 0 | 0 | 0 |
| Private 7-15 Bed ICF/MR | 2,002 | 1,948 | 1,949 | 1,936 | 1,874 | 1,849 | 1,884 |
| Other 7-15 Bed Residential | 0 | 0 | 0 | 0 | 0 | 0 | 0 |
| Public 6 Bed or Less ICF/MR | 0 | 0 | 0 | 0 | 0 | 18 | 18 |
| Private 6 Bed or Less ICF/MR | 606 | 666 | 672 | 636 | 662 | 708 | 834 |
| Other 6 Bed or Less Residential | NA | NA | 2,605 | 3,035 | 3,353 | 4,162 | 4,737 |
| TOTAL PERSONS SERVED | 7,777 | 7,515 | 9,713 | 9,772 | 9,860 | 10,389 | 10,840 |

## Persons Served in Non-Residential Community Services:1986-92

| | 1986 | 1987 | 1988 | 1989 | 1990 | 1991 | 1992 |
|---|---|---|---|---|---|---|---|
| DAY/WORK PROGRAMS | 10,894 | 11,727 | 11,376 | 12,426 | 12,118 | 12,524 | 13,048 |
| Sheltered Employment/Work Activity | 2,967 | 3,315 | 4,457 | 4,301 | 3,989 | 3,874 | 3,904 |
| Day Habilitation ("Day Training") | 7,927 | 8,412 | 3,821 | 3,951 | 4,103 | 4,308 | 4,686 |
| Supported/Competitive Employment | NA | NA | 3,098 | 4,174 | 4,026 | 4,342 | 4,458 |
| CASE MANAGEMENT | 15,526 | 16,512 | 16,912 | 18,039 | 17,754 | 17,899 | 18,197 |
| HCBS WAIVER | 614 | 991 | 1,644 | 2,109 | 2,369 | 2,644 | 2,942 |
| MODEL 50/200 WAIVER | 0 | 0 | 0 | 0 | 0 | 0 | 0 |

*Source:*
Institute on Disability and Human Development (UAP),
University of Illinois at Chicago, 1994

# MINNESOTA

## Community Services: FY 1992 Revenue Sources

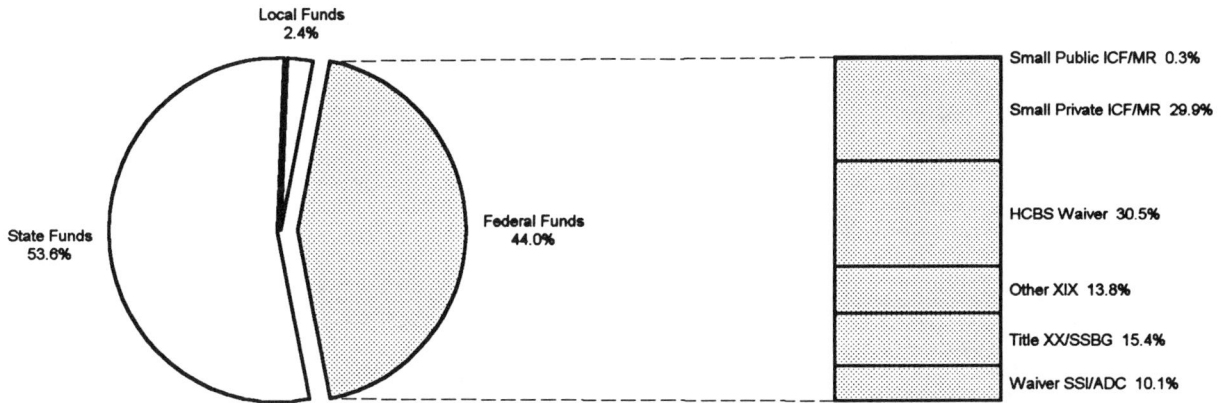

Local Funds
2.4%

State Funds
53.6%

Federal Funds
44.0%

Small Public ICF/MR  0.3%

Small Private ICF/MR  29.9%

HCBS Waiver  30.5%

Other XIX  13.8%

Title XX/SSBG  15.4%

Waiver SSI/ADC  10.1%

Total Funds: $323.8 Million

## Family Support Initiatives*

|  | 1986 | 1987 | 1988 | 1989 | 1990 | 1991 | 1992 |
|---|---|---|---|---|---|---|---|
| FAMILY SUPPORT: TOTAL SPENDING | NA | $1,560,000 | $4,717,955 | $5,233,198 | $5,888,826 | $8,696,343 | $9,396,280 |
| Total # of Families Supported | NA | NA | 2,297 | 2,411 | 2,331 | 2,795 | 2,981 |
| A. Financial Subsidy/Payment | $705,000 | $730,000 | $1,062,700 | $1,062,700 | $1,128,700 | $1,195,000 | $1,410,000 |
| # of Families | 240 | 245 | 410 | 418 | 435 | 455 | 641 |
| B. Family Assistance Payments | NA | NA | $1,305,255 | $1,470,498 | $1,485,126 | $2,148,629 | $2,400,000 |
| # of Families | NA | NA | 1,312 | 1,418 | 1,196 | 1,343 | 1,343 |
| C. Other Family Support Payments | NA | $830,000 | $2,350,000 | $2,700,000 | $3,275,000 | $5,352,714 | $5,586,280 |
| # of Families | NA | NA | 575 | 575 | 700 | 997 | 997 |

## Other Community Services Initiatives*

|  | 1986 | 1987 | 1988 | 1989 | 1990 | 1991 | 1992 |
|---|---|---|---|---|---|---|---|
| AGING/DD SPENDING | $0 | $0 | $0 | $0 | $0 | $0 | $0 |
| # of Persons Served | 0 | 0 | 0 | 0 | 0 | 0 | 0 |
| ASSISTIVE TECHNOLOGY SPENDING |  |  |  |  |  |  | $0 |
| # of Persons Served |  |  |  |  |  |  | 0 |
| EARLY INTERVENTION SPENDING | $8,215,514 | $5,770,216 | $5,500,000 | NA | NA | NA | NA |
| # of Persons Served | 1,522 | 1,053 | 1,000 | NA | NA | NA | NA |
| PERSONAL ASSISTANCE SPENDING |  |  |  |  |  |  | $0 |
| # of Persons Served |  |  |  |  |  |  | 0 |
| SUPPORTED EMPLOYMENT SPENDING | NA | NA | $8,182,951 | $11,153,788 | $11,038,415 | $12,113,633 | $13,584,625 |
| # of Persons Served | NA | NA | 3,098 | 4,174 | 4,026 | 4,342 | 4,453 |
| SUPPORTED LIVING SPENDING |  |  |  |  |  |  | $0 |
| # of Persons Served |  |  |  |  |  |  | 0 |

*Expenditures associated with Special Community Initiatives are a subset of funding within the community services component of the state's chart series and spreadsheet; Family Support Client figures may include duplicate client counts; HCBS Waiver counts include Waiver case management numbers.
0= Services not provided in the state; NA= Data not available from state; blank= Services not applicable (eg. CSLA prior to authorization, Special Community Initiatives prior to request for data by this study)

*Source:*
Institute on Disability and Human Development (UAP),
University of Illinois at Chicago, 1994

# MINNESOTA

## Large Congregate Care Facilities: FY 1992 Revenue Sources*

### Private 16+Bed Settings

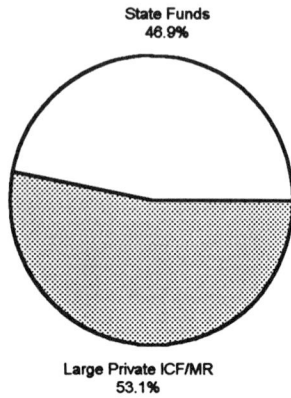

State Funds
46.9%

Large Private ICF/MR
53.1%

Total Funds: $68.7 Million

### Public Institutions

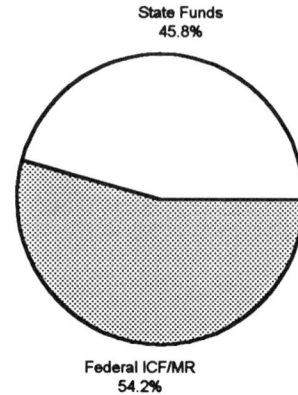

State Funds
45.8%

Federal ICF/MR
54.2%

Total Funds: $110.4 Million

**\*Excludes nursing homes**

## Average Daily Residents in Institutions

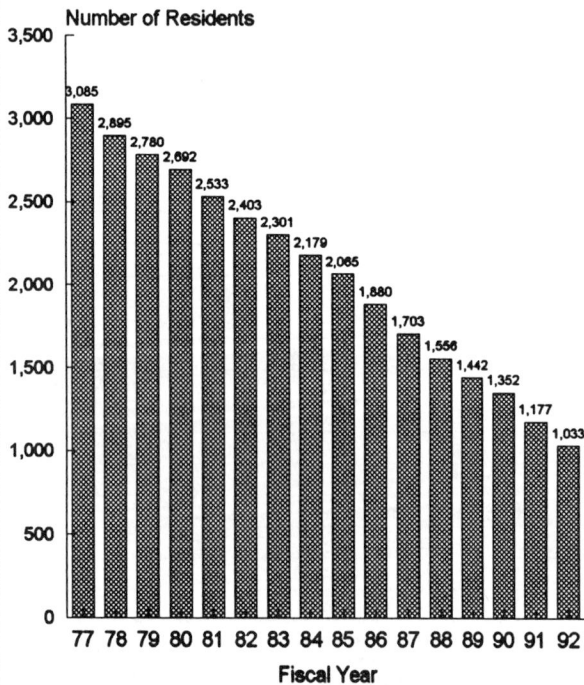

Number of Residents

| Fiscal Year | Residents |
|---|---|
| 77 | 3,085 |
| 78 | 2,895 |
| 79 | 2,780 |
| 80 | 2,692 |
| 81 | 2,533 |
| 82 | 2,403 |
| 83 | 2,301 |
| 84 | 2,179 |
| 85 | 2,065 |
| 86 | 1,880 |
| 87 | 1,703 |
| 88 | 1,556 |
| 89 | 1,442 |
| 90 | 1,352 |
| 91 | 1,177 |
| 92 | 1,033 |

## Institutional Daily Costs Per Resident

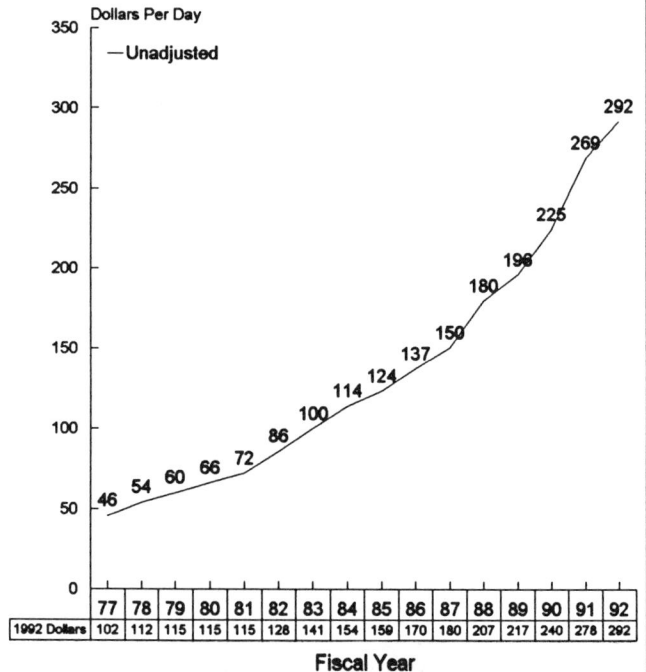

Dollars Per Day

—Unadjusted

| Fiscal Year | 77 | 78 | 79 | 80 | 81 | 82 | 83 | 84 | 85 | 86 | 87 | 88 | 89 | 90 | 91 | 92 |
|---|---|---|---|---|---|---|---|---|---|---|---|---|---|---|---|---|
| Unadjusted | 46 | 54 | 60 | 66 | 72 | 86 | 100 | 114 | 124 | 137 | 150 | 180 | 198 | 225 | 269 | 292 |
| 1992 Dollars | 102 | 112 | 115 | 115 | 115 | 128 | 141 | 154 | 159 | 170 | 180 | 207 | 217 | 240 | 278 | 292 |

Fiscal Year

*Source:*
Institute on Disability and Human Development (UAP),
University of Illinois at Chicago, 1994

# MINNESOTA FISCAL EFFORT

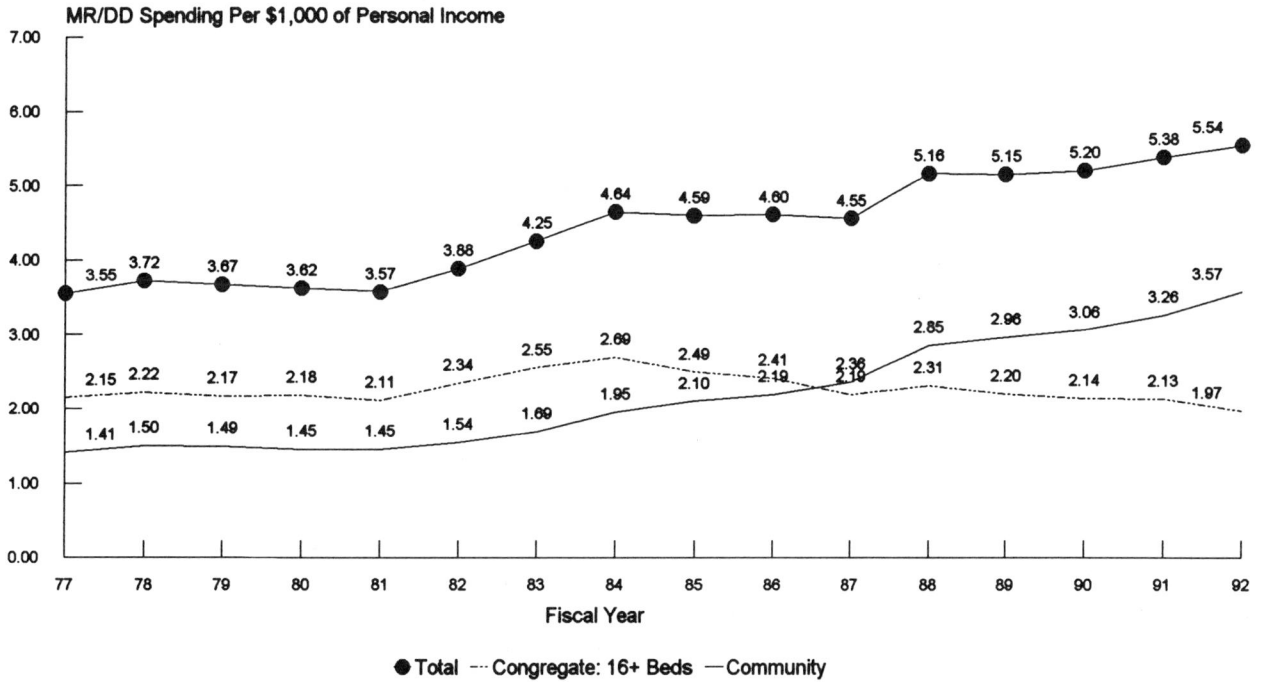

## MR/DD Spending Per $1,000 of Personal Income

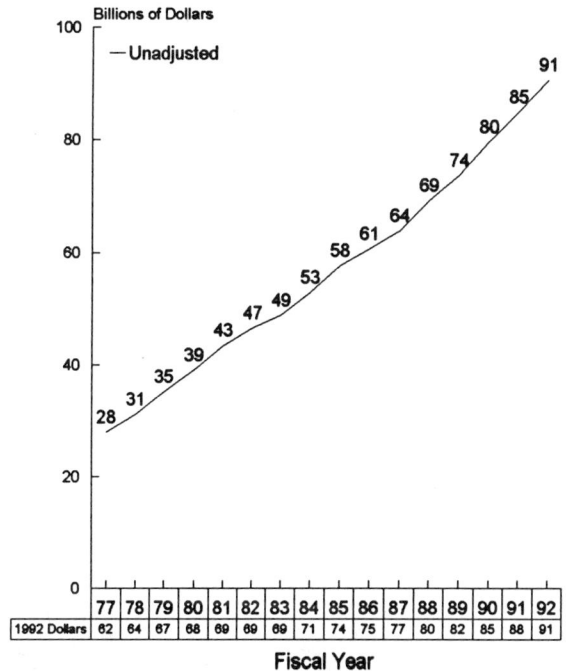

| Fiscal Year | Total | Congregate: 16+ Beds | Community |
|---|---|---|---|
| 77 | 3.55 | 2.15 | 1.41 |
| 78 | 3.72 | 2.22 | 1.50 |
| 79 | 3.67 | 2.17 | 1.49 |
| 80 | 3.62 | 2.18 | 1.45 |
| 81 | 3.57 | 2.11 | 1.45 |
| 82 | 3.88 | 2.34 | 1.54 |
| 83 | 4.25 | 2.55 | 1.69 |
| 84 | 4.64 | 2.69 | 1.95 |
| 85 | 4.59 | 2.49 | 2.10 |
| 86 | 4.60 | 2.41 | 2.19 |
| 87 | 4.55 | 2.36 / 2.19 | 2.19 |
| 88 | 5.16 | 2.31 | 2.85 |
| 89 | 5.15 | 2.20 | 2.96 |
| 90 | 5.20 | 2.14 | 3.06 |
| 91 | 5.38 | 2.13 | 3.26 |
| 92 | 5.54 | 1.97 | 3.57 |

● Total　---Congregate: 16+ Beds　—Community

## Total MR/DD Spending

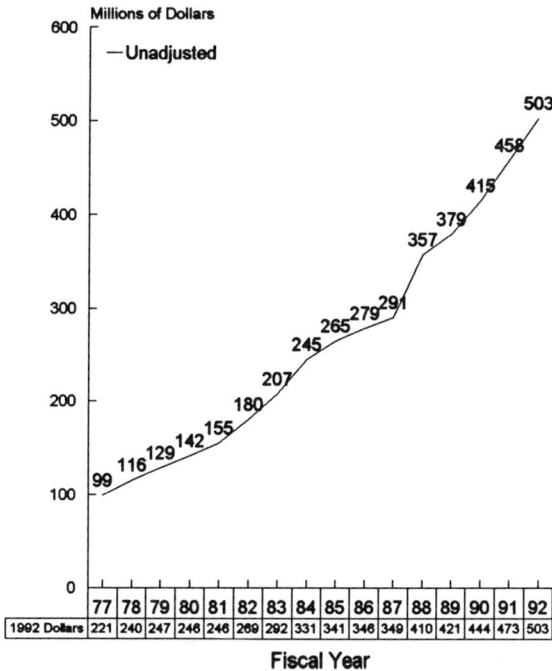

Millions of Dollars
—Unadjusted

| | 77 | 78 | 79 | 80 | 81 | 82 | 83 | 84 | 85 | 86 | 87 | 88 | 89 | 90 | 91 | 92 |
|---|---|---|---|---|---|---|---|---|---|---|---|---|---|---|---|---|
| Unadjusted | 99 | 116 | 129 | 142 | 155 | 180 | 207 | 245 | 265 | 279 | 291 | 357 | 379 | 415 | 458 | 503 |
| 1992 Dollars | 221 | 240 | 247 | 246 | 246 | 269 | 292 | 331 | 341 | 346 | 349 | 410 | 421 | 444 | 473 | 503 |

Fiscal Year

## Personal Income

Billions of Dollars
—Unadjusted

| | 77 | 78 | 79 | 80 | 81 | 82 | 83 | 84 | 85 | 86 | 87 | 88 | 89 | 90 | 91 | 92 |
|---|---|---|---|---|---|---|---|---|---|---|---|---|---|---|---|---|
| Unadjusted | 28 | 31 | 35 | 39 | 43 | 47 | 49 | 53 | 58 | 61 | 64 | 69 | 74 | 80 | 85 | 91 |
| 1992 Dollars | 62 | 64 | 67 | 68 | 69 | 69 | 69 | 71 | 74 | 75 | 77 | 80 | 82 | 85 | 88 | 91 |

Fiscal Year

*Source:*
Institute on Disability and Human Development (UAP),
University of Illinois at Chicago, 1994

# MINNESOTA

## Financial Support for MR/DD Services: FY 1977-92

| | 1977 | 1978 | 1979 | 1980 | 1981 | 1982 | 1983 | 1984 |
|---|---|---|---|---|---|---|---|---|
| **TOTAL FUNDS** | $99,050,474 | $115,758,895 | $128,560,432 | $141,607,554 | $154,950,292 | $180,490,334 | $207,387,610 | $245,198,404 |
| **CONGREGATE 16+ BEDS** | 59,836,812 | 69,222,362 | 76,291,509 | 85,001,176 | 91,794,787 | 108,817,802 | 124,646,802 | 142,057,734 |
| INSTITUTIONAL SERVICES FUNDS | 51,405,000 | 57,068,000 | 60,816,000 | 65,326,000 | 66,844,000 | 75,305,000 | 83,978,000 | 90,976,500 |
| STATE FUNDS | 24,247,000 | 29,962,000 | 35,093,000 | 24,910,500 | 29,562,700 | 31,466,800 | 33,528,100 | 43,498,300 |
| General Funds | 24,247,000 | 29,962,000 | 35,089,000 | 24,909,500 | 29,561,700 | 28,245,000 | 29,136,200 | 38,174,100 |
| Local | 0 | 0 | 0 | 0 | 0 | 0 | 0 | 0 |
| Other State Funds | 0 | 0 | 4,000 | 1,000 | 1,000 | 3,221,800 | 4,391,900 | 5,324,200 |
| FEDERAL FUNDS | 27,158,000 | 27,106,000 | 25,723,000 | 40,415,500 | 37,281,300 | 43,838,200 | 50,449,900 | 47,478,200 |
| Federal ICF/MR | 26,485,000 | 26,305,000 | 24,979,000 | 39,986,500 | 36,929,300 | 43,559,200 | 50,231,900 | 47,478,200 |
| Title XX / SSBG Funds | 0 | 0 | 0 | 0 | 0 | 0 | 0 | 0 |
| Other Federal Funds | 673,000 | 801,000 | 744,000 | 429,000 | 352,000 | 279,000 | 218,000 | 0 |
| LARGE PRIVATE RESIDENTIAL | 8,431,812 | 12,154,362 | 15,475,509 | 19,675,176 | 24,950,787 | 33,512,802 | 40,668,802 | 51,081,234 |
| STATE FUNDS | 4,026,222 | 5,795,929 | 7,367,881 | 9,237,178 | 11,609,272 | 15,745,178 | 19,138,879 | 24,558,861 |
| General Funds | 3,691,695 | 5,289,402 | 6,711,465 | 8,401,950 | 10,545,596 | 14,247,287 | 17,257,930 | 22,100,297 |
| Other State Funds | 334,527 | 506,527 | 656,416 | 835,228 | 1,063,676 | 1,497,891 | 1,880,949 | 2,458,564 |
| Local/County Overmatch | 0 | 0 | 0 | 0 | 0 | 0 | 0 | 0 |
| FEDERAL FUNDS | 4,405,590 | 6,358,433 | 8,107,628 | 10,437,998 | 13,341,515 | 17,767,624 | 21,529,923 | 26,522,373 |
| Large Private ICF/MR | 4,405,590 | 6,358,433 | 8,107,628 | 10,437,998 | 13,341,515 | 17,767,624 | 21,529,923 | 26,522,373 |
| **COMMUNITY SERVICES FUNDS** | 39,213,662 | 46,536,533 | 52,268,923 | 56,606,378 | 63,155,505 | 71,672,532 | 82,740,808 | 103,140,670 |
| STATE FUNDS | 21,670,852 | 26,742,165 | 30,870,550 | 30,101,375 | 32,219,009 | 39,059,719 | 50,531,556 | 61,007,468 |
| General Funds | 10,463,715 | 13,417,574 | 15,843,301 | 15,680,504 | 17,087,704 | 22,475,710 | 29,878,431 | 38,876,902 |
| Other State Funds | 7,035,330 | 8,399,731 | 9,486,336 | 8,415,905 | 8,560,286 | 9,647,937 | 13,189,999 | 14,328,387 |
| Local/County Overmatch | 3,122,807 | 3,355,860 | 3,588,913 | 3,821,966 | 4,055,019 | 4,288,072 | 4,521,126 | 4,754,179 |
| SSI State Supplement | 1,049,000 | 1,569,000 | 1,952,000 | 2,183,000 | 2,516,000 | 2,648,000 | 2,942,000 | 3,048,000 |
| FEDERAL FUNDS | 17,542,810 | 19,794,368 | 21,398,373 | 26,505,003 | 30,936,496 | 32,612,813 | 32,209,252 | 42,133,202 |
| ICF/MR Funds | 4,918,410 | 7,098,568 | 9,051,373 | 11,653,003 | 14,894,496 | 19,835,813 | 24,036,052 | 29,609,633 |
| Small Public | 0 | 0 | 0 | 0 | 0 | 0 | 0 | 0 |
| Small Private | 4,918,410 | 7,098,568 | 9,051,373 | 11,653,003 | 14,894,496 | 19,835,813 | 24,036,052 | 29,609,633 |
| HCBS Waiver | 0 | 0 | 0 | 0 | 0 | 0 | 0 | 0 |
| Model 50/200 Waiver | 0 | 0 | 0 | 0 | 0 | 0 | 0 | 0 |
| Other Title XIX Programs | | 0 | 0 | 0 | 0 | 0 | 0 | 3,303,699 |
| Title XX / SSBG Funds | 12,347,000 | 12,347,000 | 12,347,000 | 14,852,000 | 16,042,000 | 12,777,000 | 8,173,200 | 9,219,870 |
| Other Federal Funds | 277,400 | 348,800 | 0 | 0 | 0 | 0 | 0 | 0 |
| Waiver Clients' SSI/ADC | 0 | 0 | 0 | 0 | 0 | 0 | 0 | 0 |

| | 1985 | 1986 | 1987 | 1988 | 1989 | 1990 | 1991 | 1992 |
|---|---|---|---|---|---|---|---|---|
| **TOTAL FUNDS** | $264,696,464 | $278,853,612 | $290,552,681 | $356,923,472 | $379,038,673 | $414,515,348 | $457,753,857 | $502,825,952 |
| **CONGREGATE 16+ BEDS** | 143,631,720 | 146,224,426 | 139,621,452 | 159,664,252 | 161,616,030 | 170,350,461 | 180,968,385 | 179,025,696 |
| INSTITUTIONAL SERVICES FUNDS | 93,098,100 | 94,268,923 | 93,471,384 | 102,268,362 | 103,076,433 | 110,862,121 | 115,675,220 | 110,351,643 |
| STATE FUNDS | 43,072,600 | 42,880,566 | 42,797,725 | 47,212,582 | 48,136,694 | 52,304,749 | 54,066,624 | 50,563,123 |
| General Funds | 38,577,200 | 38,363,566 | 38,377,418 | 42,488,256 | 43,323,025 | 47,072,057 | 48,664,544 | 50,563,123 |
| Local | 0 | 0 | 0 | 0 | 0 | 0 | 0 | 0 |
| Other State Funds | 4,495,400 | 4,517,000 | 4,420,307 | 4,724,326 | 4,813,669 | 5,232,692 | 5,402,080 | 0 |
| FEDERAL FUNDS | 50,025,500 | 51,388,357 | 50,673,659 | 55,055,780 | 54,939,739 | 58,557,372 | 61,608,596 | 59,788,520 |
| Federal ICF/MR | 50,025,500 | 51,388,357 | 50,673,659 | 55,055,780 | 54,939,739 | 58,557,372 | 61,608,596 | 59,788,520 |
| Title XX / SSBG Funds | 0 | 0 | 0 | 0 | 0 | 0 | 0 | 0 |
| Other Federal Funds | 0 | 0 | 0 | 0 | 0 | 0 | 0 | 0 |
| LARGE PRIVATE RESIDENTIAL | 50,533,620 | 51,955,503 | 46,150,068 | 57,395,890 | 58,539,597 | 59,488,340 | 65,293,165 | 68,674,053 |
| STATE FUNDS | 24,544,296 | 24,960,222 | 22,188,047 | 27,255,560 | 28,368,271 | 28,893,250 | 31,236,578 | 32,238,003 |
| General Funds | 22,179,746 | 22,587,802 | 20,097,819 | 23,607,256 | 24,169,145 | 24,971,647 | 27,225,913 | 31,102,371 |
| Other State Funds | 2,364,550 | 2,372,420 | 2,090,228 | 3,648,304 | 4,199,126 | 3,921,603 | 4,010,665 | 1,135,632 |
| Local/County Overmatch | 0 | 0 | 0 | 0 | 0 | 0 | 0 | 0 |
| FEDERAL FUNDS | 25,989,324 | 26,995,281 | 23,962,021 | 30,140,330 | 30,171,326 | 30,595,090 | 34,056,587 | 36,436,050 |
| Large Private ICF/MR | 25,989,324 | 26,995,281 | 23,962,021 | 30,140,330 | 30,171,326 | 30,595,090 | 34,056,587 | 36,436,050 |
| **COMMUNITY SERVICES FUNDS** | 121,064,744 | 132,629,186 | 150,931,229 | 197,259,220 | 217,422,643 | 244,164,887 | 276,785,472 | 323,800,256 |
| STATE FUNDS | 73,091,963 | 77,829,882 | 86,075,439 | 106,453,385 | 121,575,059 | 137,832,534 | 156,749,959 | 181,174,429 |
| General Funds | 46,173,233 | 49,711,471 | 56,197,504 | 61,875,556 | 72,928,050 | 82,519,695 | 93,557,513 | 116,068,690 |
| Other State Funds | 17,865,530 | 18,318,217 | 19,634,748 | 34,047,062 | 37,490,294 | 41,398,013 | 47,307,713 | 46,748,366 |
| Local/County Overmatch | 5,829,200 | 5,499,194 | 5,169,187 | 4,839,181 | 5,258,170 | 5,718,953 | 6,478,822 | 7,630,633 |
| SSI State Supplement | 3,224,000 | 4,301,000 | 5,074,000 | 5,691,586 | 5,898,545 | 8,195,873 | 9,405,911 | 10,726,740 |
| FEDERAL FUNDS | 47,972,781 | 54,799,304 | 64,855,790 | 90,805,835 | 95,847,584 | 106,332,353 | 120,035,513 | 142,625,827 |
| ICF/MR Funds | 29,014,536 | 30,137,588 | 33,777,788 | 29,543,488 | 29,573,874 | 32,617,906 | 36,163,180 | 43,119,153 |
| Small Public | 0 | 0 | 0 | 0 | 0 | 0 | 0 | 484,709 |
| Small Private | 29,014,536 | 30,137,588 | 33,777,788 | 29,543,488 | 29,573,874 | 32,617,906 | 36,163,180 | 42,634,444 |
| HCBS Waiver | 469,217 | 3,224,141 | 7,034,097 | 29,543,488 | 29,573,874 | 32,617,906 | 36,217,606 | 43,562,408 |
| Model 50/200 Waiver | 0 | 0 | 0 | 0 | 0 | 0 | 0 | 0 |
| Other Title XIX Programs | 8,032,298 | 9,549,797 | 10,701,595 | 11,414,340 | 12,926,662 | 14,193,048 | 16,908,017 | 19,637,469 |
| Title XX / SSBG Funds | 9,596,330 | 9,596,330 | 9,596,330 | 13,912,647 | 15,117,238 | 16,441,989 | 18,626,614 | 21,938,069 |
| Other Federal Funds | 0 | 0 | 0 | 0 | 0 | 0 | 0 | 0 |
| Waiver Clients' SSI/ADC | 860,400 | 2,291,448 | 3,745,980 | 6,391,872 | 8,655,936 | 10,461,504 | 12,120,096 | 14,368,728 |

*Source:*

Institute on Disability and Human Development (UAP),
University of Illinois at Chicago, 1994

# MISSISSIPPI

## MR/DD Spending for Congregate Residential & Community Services

▨ Congregate: 16+ Beds*  ■ Community**

Millions of 1992 Dollars

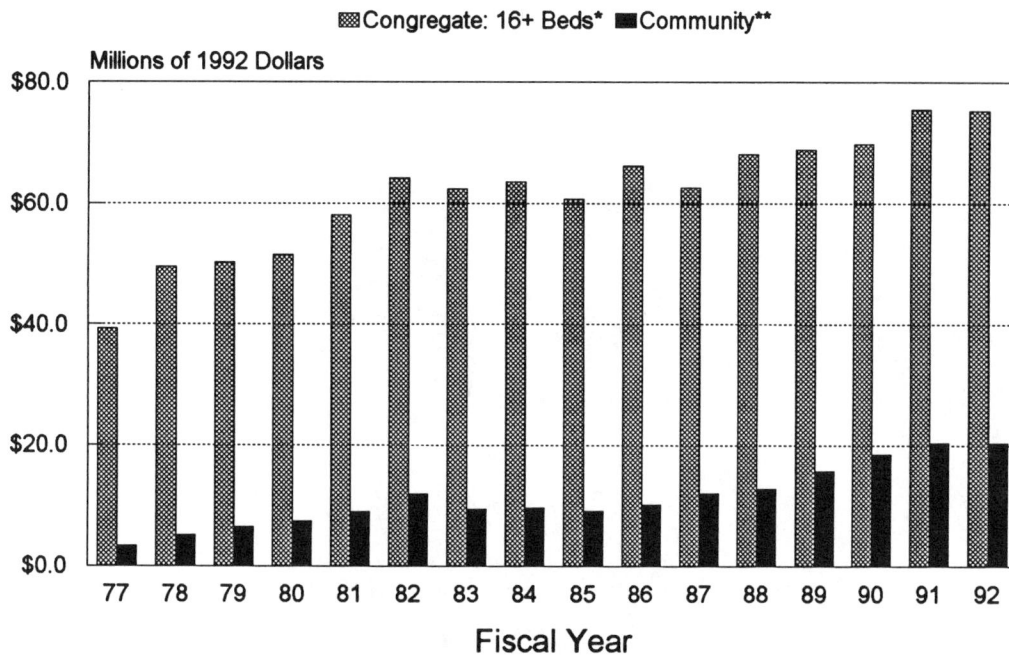

Fiscal Year

*Excludes nursing homes; ** Includes resources for
15 bed or less residential settings & non-residential community services

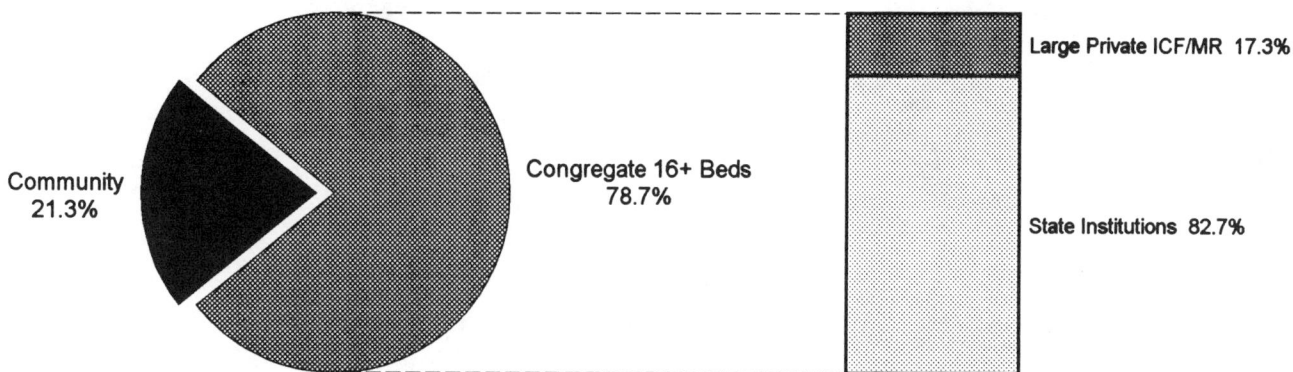

Community
21.3%

Congregate 16+ Beds
78.7%

Large Private ICF/MR 17.3%

State Institutions 82.7%

FY 1992 Total Spending:
$95.8 Million

*Source:*
Institute on Disability and Human Development (UAP),
University of Illinois at Chicago, 1994

# MISSISSIPPI

## Number of Persons Served by Residential Setting: FY 1992

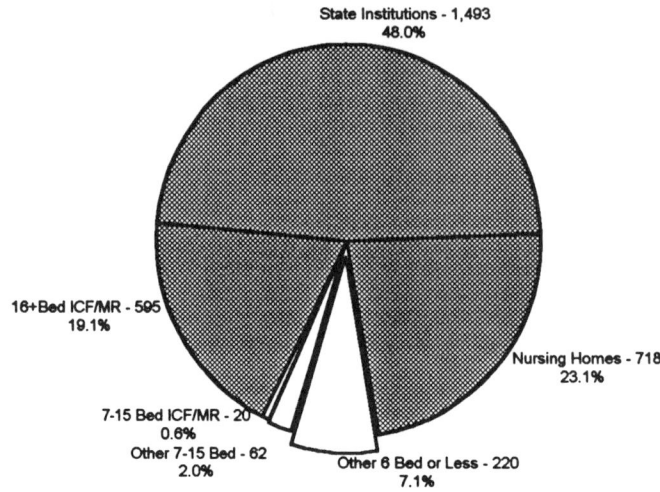

State Institutions - 1,493
48.0%

16+Bed ICF/MR - 595
19.1%

7-15 Bed ICF/MR - 20
0.6%

Other 7-15 Bed - 62
2.0%

Nursing Homes - 718
23.1%

Other 6 Bed or Less - 220
7.1%

Total Served: 3,108

## Persons Served by Residential Setting:1986-92

|  | 1986 | 1987 | 1988 | 1989 | 1990 | 1991 | 1992 |
|---|---|---|---|---|---|---|---|
| CONGREGATE 16 + BED SETTINGS | NA | NA | 2,382 | 2,335 | 2,286 | 2,583 | 2,806 |
| Nursing Homes | NA | NA | 329 | 265 | 200 | 480 | 718 |
| State Institutions | 1,553 | 1,506 | 1,458 | 1,475 | 1,491 | 1,508 | 1,493 |
| Private 16+Bed ICF/MR | 595 | 595 | 595 | 595 | 595 | 595 | 595 |
| Other 16+Bed Residential | 0 | 0 | 0 | 0 | 0 | 0 | 0 |
| 15 BED OR LESS RESIDENTIAL SETTINGS | 228 | 271 | 285 | 276 | 268 | 259 | 302 |
| Public 7-15 Bed ICF/MR | 0 | 0 | 0 | 0 | 0 | 0 | 20 |
| Private 7-15 Bed ICF/MR | 0 | 0 | 0 | 0 | 0 | 0 | 0 |
| Other 7-15 Bed Residential | 228 | 271 | 285 | 276 | 268 | 259 | 62 |
| Public 6 Bed or Less ICF/MR | 0 | 0 | 0 | 0 | 0 | 0 | 0 |
| Private 6 Bed or Less ICF/MR | 0 | 0 | 0 | 0 | 0 | 0 | 0 |
| Other 6 Bed or Less Residential | 0 | 0 | 0 | 0 | 0 | 0 | 220 |
| TOTAL PERSONS SERVED | NA | NA | 2,667 | 2,611 | 2,554 | 2,842 | 3,108 |

## Persons Served in Non-Residential Community Services:1986-92

|  | 1986 | 1987 | 1988 | 1989 | 1990 | 1991 | 1992 |
|---|---|---|---|---|---|---|---|
| DAY/WORK PROGRAMS | 1,140 | 1,250 | 1,380 | NA | NA | NA | NA |
| Sheltered Employment/Work Activity | 1,140 | 1,250 | 1,280 | 1,406 | 1,440 | 1,540 | 1,618 |
| Day Habilitation ("Day Training") | NA | NA | NA | NA | NA | NA | NA |
| Supported/Competitive Employment | 0 | 0 | 100 | 301 | 461 | 508 | 451 |
| CASE MANAGEMENT | 800 | 950 | 1,500 | 2,104 | 1,856 | 2,078 | 2,380 |
| HCBS WAIVER | 0 | 0 | 0 | 0 | 0 | 0 | 0 |
| MODEL 50/200 WAIVER | 0 | 0 | 0 | 0 | 0 | 0 | 0 |

*Source:*
Institute on Disability and Human Development (UAP),
University of Illinois at Chicago, 1994

# MISSISSIPPI

## Community Services: FY 1992 Revenue Sources

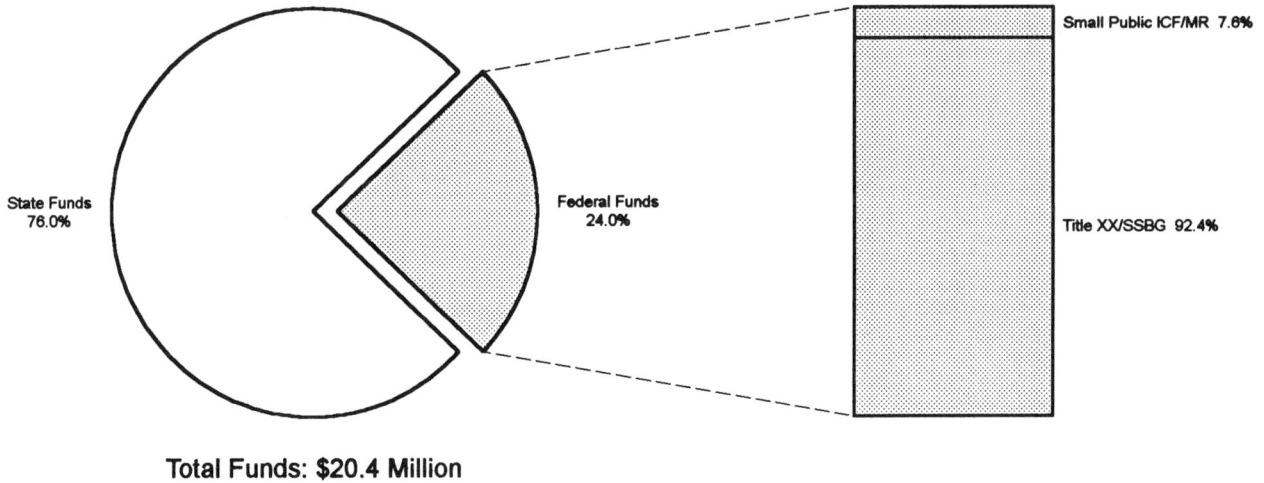

State Funds 76.0%

Federal Funds 24.0%

Small Public ICF/MR 7.6%

Title XX/SSBG 92.4%

Total Funds: $20.4 Million

## Family Support Initiatives*

|  | 1986 | 1987 | 1988 | 1989 | 1990 | 1991 | 1992 |
|---|---|---|---|---|---|---|---|
| **FAMILY SUPPORT: TOTAL SPENDING** | $0 | $0 | $0 | $0 | $0 | $0 | $0 |
| **Total # of Families Supported** | 0 | 0 | 0 | 0 | 0 | 0 | 0 |
| A. Financial Subsidy/Payment | $0 | $0 | $0 | $0 | $0 | $0 | $0 |
| # of Families | 0 | 0 | 0 | 0 | 0 | 0 | 0 |
| B. Family Assistance Payments | $0 | $0 | $0 | $0 | $0 | $0 | $0 |
| # of Families | 0 | 0 | 0 | 0 | 0 | 0 | 0 |
| C. Other Family Support Payments | $0 | $0 | $0 | $0 | $0 | $0 | $0 |
| # of Families | 0 | 0 | 0 | 0 | 0 | 0 | 0 |

## Other Community Services Initiatives*

|  | 1986 | 1987 | 1988 | 1989 | 1990 | 1991 | 1992 |
|---|---|---|---|---|---|---|---|
| **AGING/DD SPENDING** | $0 | $0 | $45,882 | $0 | $0 | $0 | $0 |
| # of Persons Served | 0 | 0 | NA | 0 | 0 | 0 | 0 |
| **ASSISTIVE TECHNOLOGY SPENDING** |  |  |  |  |  |  | $0 |
| # of Persons Served |  |  |  |  |  |  | 0 |
| **EARLY INTERVENTION SPENDING** | $353,533 | $500,000 | $600,000 | $758,380 | $800,006 | $758,380 | $800,006 |
| # of Persons Served | 150 | 175 | 184 | 391 | 397 | 395 | 430 |
| **PERSONAL ASSISTANCE SPENDING** |  |  |  |  |  |  | $0 |
| # of Persons Served |  |  |  |  |  |  | 0 |
| **SUPPORTED EMPLOYMENT SPENDING** | $0 | $0 | $298,542 | NA | NA | NA | NA |
| # of Persons Served | 0 | 0 | 100 | 301 | 461 | 508 | 451 |
| **SUPPORTED LIVING SPENDING** |  |  |  |  |  |  | $0 |
| # of Persons Served |  |  |  |  |  |  | 0 |

*Expenditures associated with Special Community Initiatives are a subset of funding within the community services component of the state's chart series and spreadsheet; Family Support Client figures may include duplicate client counts; HCBS Waiver counts include Waiver case management numbers.
0= Services not provided in the state; NA= Data not available from state; blank= Services not applicable (eg. CSLA prior to authorization, Special Community Initiatives prior to request for data by this study)

Source:
Institute on Disability and Human Development (UAP),
University of Illinois at Chicago, 1994

# MISSISSIPPI

## Large Congregate Care Facilities: FY 1992 Revenue Sources*

### Private 16+Bed Settings

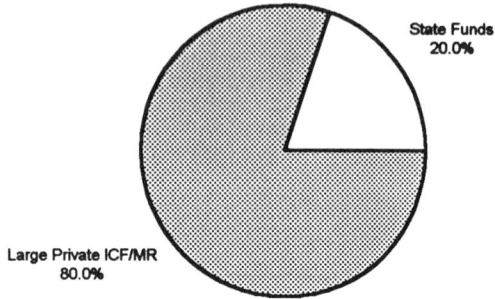

State Funds
20.0%

Large Private ICF/MR
80.0%

Total Funds: $13.0 Million

### Public Institutions

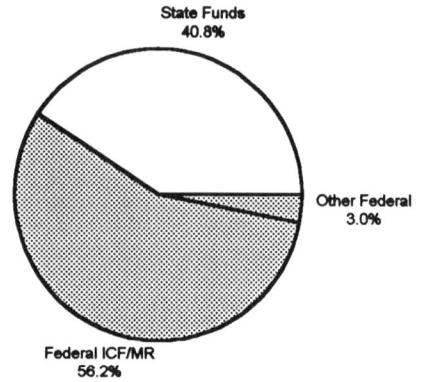

State Funds
40.8%

Other Federal
3.0%

Federal ICF/MR
56.2%

Total Funds: $62.3 Million

*Excludes nursing homes

## Average Daily Residents in Institutions

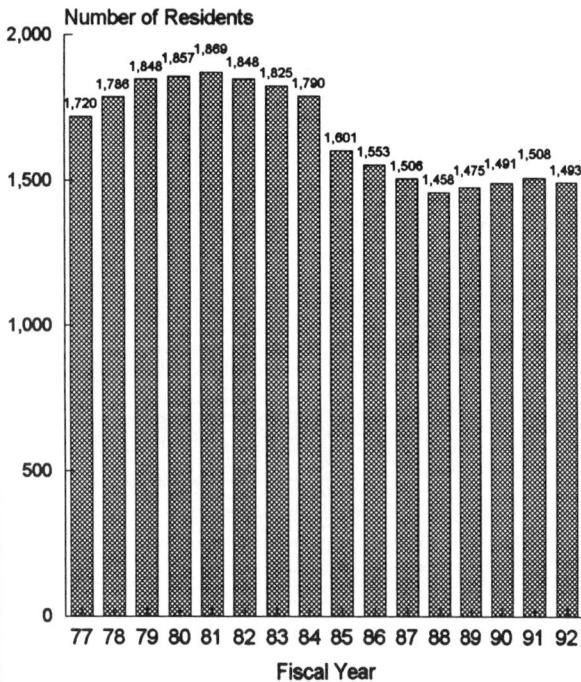

Number of Residents

2,000

1,500

1,000

500

0

1,720 1,786 1,848 1,857 1,869 1,848 1,825 1,790 1,601 1,553 1,506 1,458 1,475 1,491 1,508 1,493

77 78 79 80 81 82 83 84 85 86 87 88 89 90 91 92

Fiscal Year

## Institutional Daily Costs Per Resident

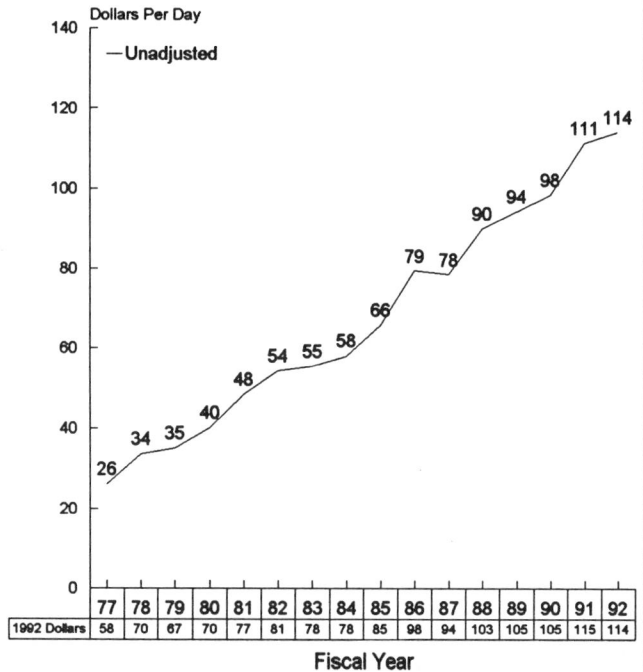

Dollars Per Day

140

120

100

80

60

40

20

0

—Unadjusted

26 34 35 40 48 54 55 58 66 79 78 90 94 98 111 114

| | 77 | 78 | 79 | 80 | 81 | 82 | 83 | 84 | 85 | 86 | 87 | 88 | 89 | 90 | 91 | 92 |
|---|---|---|---|---|---|---|---|---|---|---|---|---|---|---|---|---|
| 1992 Dollars | 58 | 70 | 67 | 70 | 77 | 81 | 78 | 78 | 85 | 98 | 94 | 103 | 105 | 105 | 115 | 114 |

Fiscal Year

*Source:*
Institute on Disability and Human Development (UAP),
University of Illinois at Chicago, 1994

# MISSISSIPPI FISCAL EFFORT

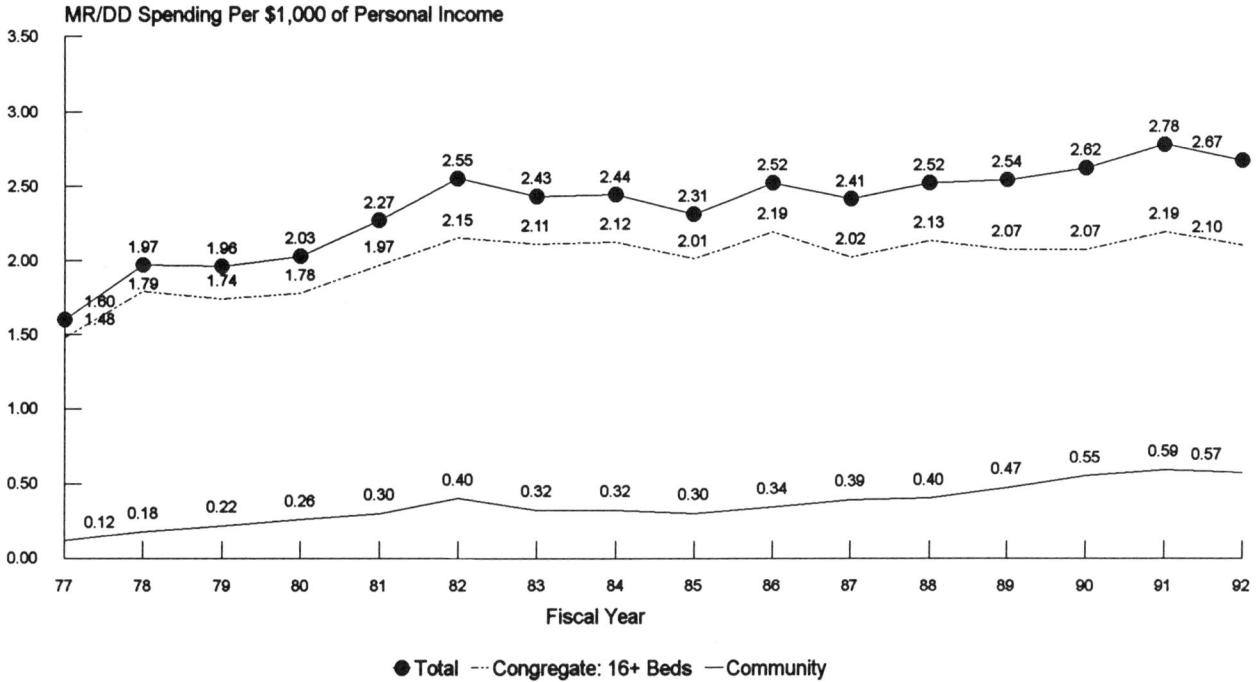

MR/DD Spending Per $1,000 of Personal Income

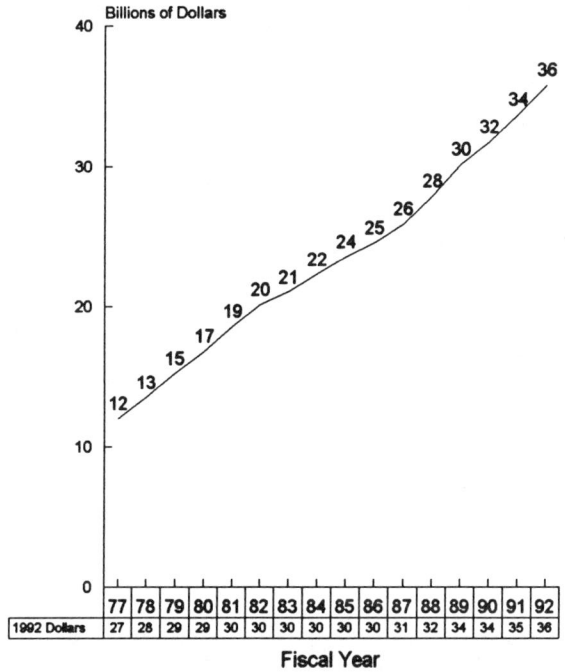

| | | | | | | | | | | | | | | | |
|---|---|---|---|---|---|---|---|---|---|---|---|---|---|---|---|

Total values: 1.60, 1.97, 1.96, 2.03, 2.27, 2.55, 2.43, 2.44, 2.31, 2.52, 2.41, 2.52, 2.54, 2.62, 2.78, 2.67

Congregate: 16+ Beds values: 1.48, 1.79, 1.74, 1.78, 1.97, 2.15, 2.11, 2.12, 2.01, 2.19, 2.02, 2.13, 2.07, 2.07, 2.19, 2.10

Community values: 0.12, 0.18, 0.22, 0.26, 0.30, 0.40, 0.32, 0.32, 0.30, 0.34, 0.39, 0.40, 0.47, 0.55, 0.59, 0.57

Fiscal Year

● Total   --- Congregate: 16+ Beds   — Community

## Total MR/DD Spending

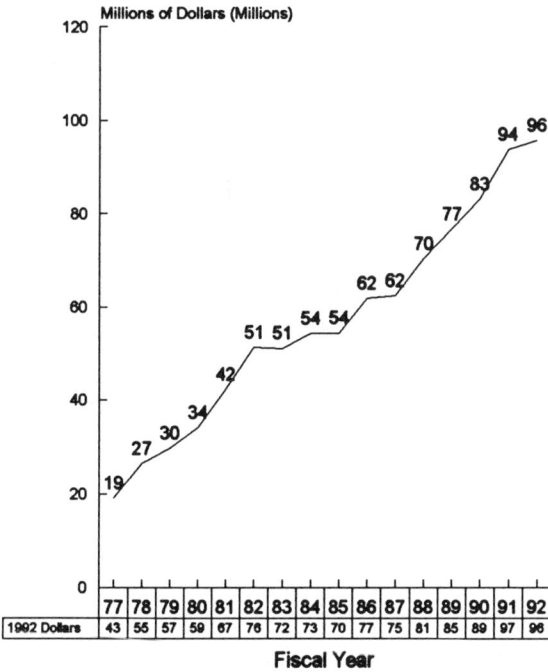

Millions of Dollars (Millions)

Values: 19, 27, 30, 34, 42, 51, 51, 54, 54, 62, 62, 70, 77, 83, 94, 96

| | 77 | 78 | 79 | 80 | 81 | 82 | 83 | 84 | 85 | 86 | 87 | 88 | 89 | 90 | 91 | 92 |
|---|---|---|---|---|---|---|---|---|---|---|---|---|---|---|---|---|
| 1992 Dollars | 43 | 55 | 57 | 59 | 67 | 76 | 72 | 73 | 70 | 77 | 75 | 81 | 85 | 89 | 97 | 96 |

Fiscal Year

## Personal Income

Billions of Dollars

Values: 12, 13, 15, 17, 19, 20, 21, 22, 24, 25, 26, 28, 30, 32, 34, 36

| | 77 | 78 | 79 | 80 | 81 | 82 | 83 | 84 | 85 | 86 | 87 | 88 | 89 | 90 | 91 | 92 |
|---|---|---|---|---|---|---|---|---|---|---|---|---|---|---|---|---|
| 1992 Dollars | 27 | 28 | 29 | 29 | 30 | 30 | 30 | 30 | 30 | 30 | 31 | 32 | 34 | 34 | 35 | 36 |

Fiscal Year

*Source:*
Institute on Disability and Human Development (UAP),
University of Illinois at Chicago, 1994

# MISSISSIPPI
## Financial Support for MR/DD Services: FY 1977-92

| | 1977 | 1978 | 1979 | 1980 | 1981 | 1982 | 1983 | 1984 |
|---|---|---|---|---|---|---|---|---|
| **TOTAL FUNDS** | $19,166,500 | $26,519,667 | $29,739,833 | $34,123,000 | $42,284,000 | $51,295,000 | $51,136,000 | $54,329,156 |
| **CONGREGATE 16+ BEDS** | 17,686,570 | 24,061,952 | 26,364,953 | 29,826,381 | 36,633,258 | 43,279,556 | 44,427,829 | 47,176,698 |
| INSTITUTIONAL SERVICES FUNDS | 16,381,000 | 21,935,000 | 23,613,000 | 27,337,000 | 33,033,000 | 36,606,000 | 36,933,000 | 38,024,300 |
| STATE FUNDS | 13,341,000 | 18,071,000 | 17,778,000 | 19,976,000 | 23,695,000 | 24,990,000 | 25,003,000 | 27,622,800 |
| General Funds | 11,369,000 | 15,939,000 | 17,494,000 | 18,236,000 | 21,062,000 | 20,828,000 | 19,748,000 | 17,392,700 |
| Local | 0 | 0 | 0 | 0 | 0 | 0 | 0 | 0 |
| Other State Funds | 1,972,000 | 2,132,000 | 284,000 | 1,740,000 | 2,633,000 | 4,162,000 | 5,255,000 | 10,230,100 |
| FEDERAL FUNDS | 3,040,000 | 3,864,000 | 5,835,000 | 7,361,000 | 9,338,000 | 11,616,000 | 11,930,000 | 10,401,500 |
| Federal ICF/MR | 1,409,000 | 2,290,000 | 4,121,000 | 5,073,000 | 7,201,000 | 9,633,000 | 10,351,000 | 10,125,100 |
| Title XX / SSBG Funds | 0 | 0 | 0 | 0 | 0 | 0 | 0 | 0 |
| Other Federal Funds | 1,631,000 | 1,574,000 | 1,714,000 | 2,288,000 | 2,137,000 | 1,983,000 | 1,579,000 | 276,400 |
| LARGE PRIVATE RESIDENTIAL | 1,305,570 | 2,126,952 | 2,751,953 | 2,489,381 | 3,600,258 | 6,673,556 | 7,494,829 | 9,152,398 |
| STATE FUNDS | 283,570 | 464,952 | 602,953 | 555,381 | 808,258 | 1,507,556 | 1,696,829 | 2,053,798 |
| General Funds | 283,570 | 464,952 | 602,953 | 555,381 | 808,258 | 1,507,556 | 1,696,829 | 2,053,798 |
| Other State Funds | 0 | 0 | 0 | 0 | 0 | 0 | 0 | 0 |
| Local/County Overmatch | 0 | 0 | 0 | 0 | 0 | 0 | 0 | 0 |
| FEDERAL FUNDS | 1,022,000 | 1,662,000 | 2,149,000 | 1,934,000 | 2,792,000 | 5,166,000 | 5,798,000 | 7,098,600 |
| Large Private ICF/MR | 1,022,000 | 1,662,000 | 2,149,000 | 1,934,000 | 2,792,000 | 5,166,000 | 5,798,000 | 7,098,600 |
| **COMMUNITY SERVICES FUNDS** | 1,479,930 | 2,457,715 | 3,374,880 | 4,296,619 | 5,650,742 | 8,015,444 | 6,708,171 | 7,152,458 |
| STATE FUNDS | 570,430 | 885,048 | 1,139,047 | 1,397,619 | 2,738,742 | 3,665,444 | 3,529,171 | 4,227,158 |
| General Funds | 267,430 | 361,048 | 394,047 | 431,619 | 1,768,742 | 2,215,444 | 2,470,171 | 3,252,058 |
| Other State Funds | 303,000 | 524,000 | 745,000 | 966,000 | 970,000 | 1,450,000 | 1,059,000 | 975,100 |
| Local/County Overmatch | 0 | 0 | 0 | 0 | 0 | 0 | 0 | 0 |
| SSI State Supplement | 0 | 0 | 0 | 0 | 0 | 0 | 0 | 0 |
| FEDERAL FUNDS | 909,500 | 1,572,667 | 2,235,833 | 2,899,000 | 2,912,000 | 4,350,000 | 3,179,000 | 2,925,300 |
| ICF/MR Funds | 0 | 0 | 0 | 0 | 0 | 0 | 0 | 0 |
| Small Public | 0 | 0 | 0 | 0 | 0 | 0 | 0 | 0 |
| Small Private | 0 | 0 | 0 | 0 | 0 | 0 | 0 | 0 |
| HCBS Waiver | 0 | 0 | 0 | 0 | 0 | 0 | 0 | 0 |
| Model 50/200 Waiver | 0 | 0 | 0 | 0 | 0 | 0 | 0 | 0 |
| Other Title XIX Programs | 0 | 0 | 0 | 0 | 0 | 0 | 0 | 0 |
| Title XX / SSBG Funds | 909,500 | 1,572,667 | 2,235,833 | 2,899,000 | 2,912,000 | 4,350,000 | 3,179,000 | 2,925,300 |
| Other Federal Funds | 0 | 0 | 0 | 0 | 0 | 0 | 0 | 0 |
| Waiver Clients' SSI/ADC | 0 | 0 | 0 | 0 | 0 | 0 | 0 | 0 |

| | 1985 | 1986 | 1987 | 1988 | 1989 | 1990 | 1991 | 1992 |
|---|---|---|---|---|---|---|---|---|
| **TOTAL FUNDS** | $54,427,149 | $61,840,687 | $62,382,643 | $70,359,690 | $76,734,160 | $83,108,629 | $93,776,739 | $95,782,629 |
| **CONGREGATE 16+ BEDS** | 47,316,971 | 53,605,257 | 52,317,043 | 59,301,249 | 62,511,982 | 65,722,715 | 73,857,593 | 75,337,549 |
| INSTITUTIONAL SERVICES FUNDS | 38,430,200 | 45,007,200 | 43,124,000 | 47,976,400 | 50,760,721 | 53,545,041 | 61,253,506 | 62,307,049 |
| STATE FUNDS | 25,668,600 | 34,041,800 | 31,303,700 | 33,558,900 | 30,009,519 | 26,460,138 | 26,664,062 | 25,442,727 |
| General Funds | 14,568,000 | 14,983,300 | 13,952,600 | 18,522,400 | 25,143,965 | 20,049,609 | 18,480,652 | 16,683,857 |
| Local | 0 | 0 | 0 | 0 | 0 | 0 | 0 | 0 |
| Other State Funds | 11,100,600 | 19,058,500 | 17,351,100 | 15,036,500 | 4,865,554 | 6,410,529 | 8,183,410 | 8,758,870 |
| FEDERAL FUNDS | 12,761,600 | 10,965,400 | 11,820,300 | 14,417,500 | 20,751,202 | 27,084,903 | 34,589,444 | 36,864,322 |
| Federal ICF/MR | 11,433,000 | 9,629,200 | 10,258,900 | 12,767,500 | 19,277,252 | 25,787,003 | 32,713,194 | 34,991,730 |
| Title XX / SSBG Funds | 0 | 0 | 0 | 0 | 0 | 0 | 0 | 0 |
| Other Federal Funds | 1,328,600 | 1,336,200 | 1,561,400 | 1,650,000 | 1,473,950 | 1,297,900 | 1,876,250 | 1,872,592 |
| LARGE PRIVATE RESIDENTIAL | 8,886,771 | 8,598,057 | 9,193,043 | 11,324,849 | 11,751,261 | 12,177,674 | 12,604,087 | 13,030,500 |
| STATE FUNDS | 1,987,971 | 1,872,657 | 1,978,343 | 2,337,449 | 2,405,263 | 2,473,077 | 2,540,892 | 2,608,706 |
| General Funds | 1,987,971 | 1,872,657 | 1,978,343 | 2,337,449 | 2,405,263 | 2,473,077 | 2,540,892 | 2,608,706 |
| Other State Funds | 0 | 0 | 0 | 0 | 0 | 0 | 0 | 0 |
| Local/County Overmatch | 0 | 0 | 0 | 0 | 0 | 0 | 0 | 0 |
| FEDERAL FUNDS | 6,898,800 | 6,725,400 | 7,214,700 | 8,987,400 | 9,345,998 | 9,704,597 | 10,063,195 | 10,421,794 |
| Large Private ICF/MR | 6,898,800 | 6,725,400 | 7,214,700 | 8,987,400 | 9,345,998 | 9,704,597 | 10,063,195 | 10,421,794 |
| **COMMUNITY SERVICES FUNDS** | 7,110,178 | 8,235,430 | 10,065,600 | 11,058,441 | 14,222,178 | 17,385,914 | 19,919,146 | 20,445,080 |
| STATE FUNDS | 4,359,078 | 5,242,430 | 5,626,100 | 6,532,541 | 9,696,278 | 12,860,014 | 15,393,246 | 15,545,880 |
| General Funds | 3,442,078 | 4,244,730 | 4,146,300 | 5,023,941 | 8,187,678 | 11,351,414 | 13,884,646 | 14,037,280 |
| Other State Funds | 917,000 | 997,700 | 1,479,800 | 1,508,600 | 1,508,600 | 1,508,600 | 1,508,600 | 1,508,600 |
| Local/County Overmatch | 0 | 0 | 0 | 0 | 0 | 0 | 0 | 0 |
| SSI State Supplement | 0 | 0 | 0 | 0 | 0 | 0 | 0 | 0 |
| FEDERAL FUNDS | 2,751,100 | 2,993,000 | 4,439,500 | 4,525,900 | 4,525,900 | 4,525,900 | 4,525,900 | 4,899,200 |
| ICF/MR Funds | 0 | 0 | 0 | 0 | 0 | 0 | 0 | 373,300 |
| Small Public | 0 | 0 | 0 | 0 | 0 | 0 | 0 | 373,300 |
| Small Private | 0 | 0 | 0 | 0 | 0 | 0 | 0 | 0 |
| HCBS Waiver | 0 | 0 | 0 | 0 | 0 | 0 | 0 | 0 |
| Model 50/200 Waiver | 0 | 0 | 0 | 0 | 0 | 0 | 0 | 0 |
| Other Title XIX Programs | 0 | 0 | 0 | 0 | 0 | 0 | 0 | 0 |
| Title XX / SSBG Funds | 2,751,100 | 2,993,000 | 4,439,500 | 4,525,900 | 4,525,900 | 4,525,900 | 4,525,900 | 4,525,900 |
| Other Federal Funds | 0 | 0 | 0 | 0 | 0 | 0 | 0 | 0 |
| Waiver Clients' SSI/ADC | 0 | 0 | 0 | 0 | 0 | 0 | 0 | 0 |

*Source:*
Institute on Disability and Human Development (UAP),
University of Illinois at Chicago, 1994

# MISSOURI

## MR/DD Spending for Congregate Residential & Community Services

▨ Congregate: 16+ Beds* ■ Community**

Millions of 1992 Dollars

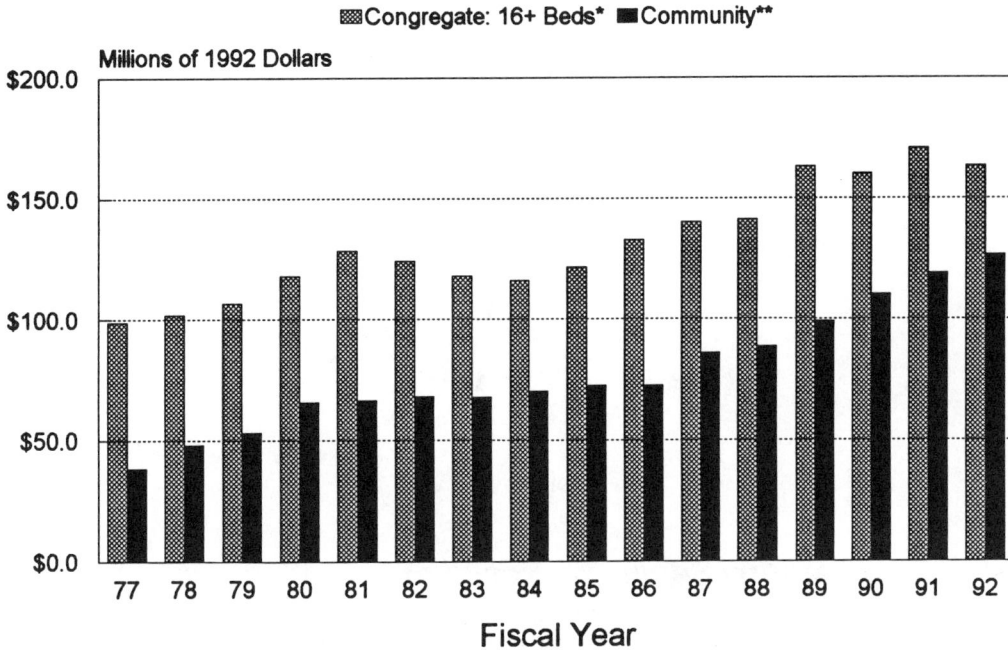

Fiscal Year

*Excludes nursing homes; ** Includes resources for
15 bed or less residential settings & non-residential community services

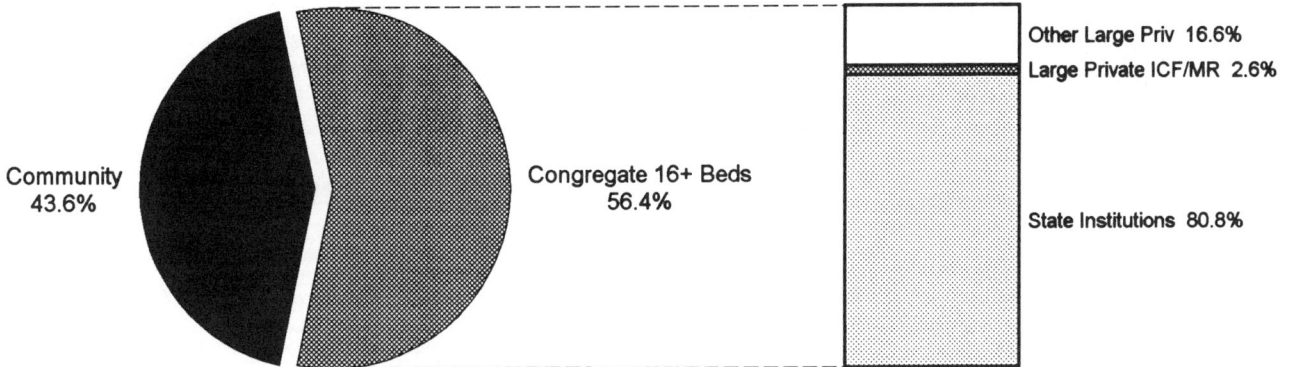

Community
43.6%

Congregate 16+ Beds
56.4%

Other Large Priv 16.6%
Large Private ICF/MR 2.6%

State Institutions 80.8%

FY 1992 Total Spending:
$290.3 Million

*Source:*
Institute on Disability and Human Development (UAP),
University of Illinois at Chicago, 1994

# MISSOURI

## Number of Persons Served by Residential Setting: FY 1992

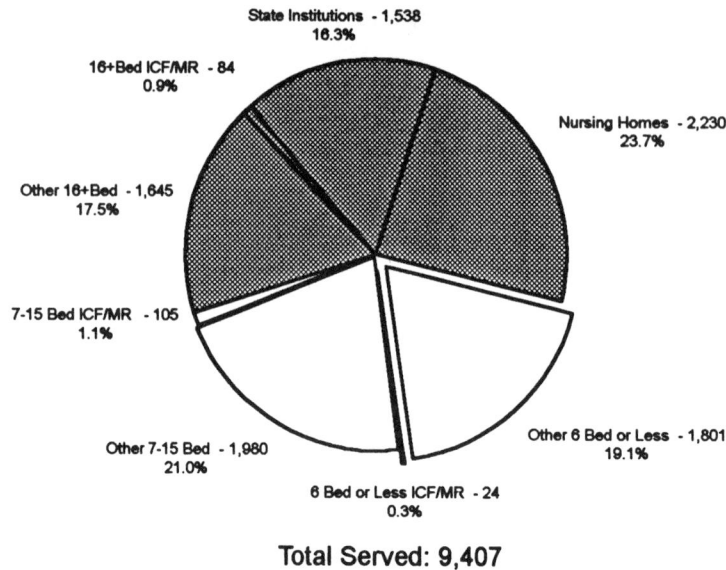

State Institutions - 1,538
16.3%

16+Bed ICF/MR - 84
0.9%

Nursing Homes - 2,230
23.7%

Other 16+Bed - 1,645
17.5%

7-15 Bed ICF/MR - 105
1.1%

Other 7-15 Bed - 1,980
21.0%

6 Bed or Less ICF/MR - 24
0.3%

Other 6 Bed or Less - 1,801
19.1%

Total Served: 9,407

## Persons Served by Residential Setting:1986-92

|  | 1986 | 1987 | 1988 | 1989 | 1990 | 1991 | 1992 |
|---|---|---|---|---|---|---|---|
| **CONGREGATE 16 + BED SETTINGS** | NA | NA | 6,910 | 6,509 | 6,444 | 5,873 | 5,497 |
| Nursing Homes | NA | NA | 3,000 | 2,600 | 2,600 | 2,244 | 2,230 |
| State Institutions | 1,838 | 1,888 | 1,888 | 1,899 | 1,868 | 1,687 | 1,538 |
| Private 16+Bed ICF/MR | 136 | 136 | 160 | 160 | 176 | 192 | 84 |
| Other 16+Bed Residential | 1,856 | 1,844 | 1,862 | 1,850 | 1,800 | 1,750 | 1,645 |
| **15 BED OR LESS RESIDENTIAL SETTINGS** | 2,058 | 2,084 | 1,963 | 2,484 | 2,240 | 2,661 | 3,910 |
| Public 7-15 Bed ICF/MR | 16 | 16 | 16 | 16 | 16 | 8 | 0 |
| Private 7-15 Bed ICF/MR | 76 | 84 | 102 | 131 | 157 | 120 | 105 |
| Other 7-15 Bed Residential | 1,966 | 1,984 | 1,845 | 1,338 | 1,178 | 1,448 | 1,980 |
| Public 6 Bed or Less ICF/MR | 0 | 0 | 0 | 0 | 0 | 0 | 0 |
| Private 6 Bed or Less ICF/MR |  |  |  | 30 | 36 | 36 | 24 |
| Other 6 Bed or Less Residential |  |  |  | 969 | 853 | 1,049 | 1,801 |
| **TOTAL PERSONS SERVED** | NA | NA | 8,873 | 8,993 | 8,684 | 8,534 | 9,407 |

## Persons Served in Non-Residential Community Services:1986-92

|  | 1986 | 1987 | 1988 | 1989 | 1990 | 1991 | 1992 |
|---|---|---|---|---|---|---|---|
| **DAY/WORK PROGRAMS** | NA | NA | 4,067 | 3,393 | 1,919 | 1,878 | 1,894 |
| Sheltered Employment/Work Activity | NA | NA | NA | NA | NA | NA | NA |
| Day Habilitation ("Day Training") | NA | NA | 3,977 | 3,313 | 1,866 | 1,773 | 1,763 |
| Supported/Competitive Employment | NA | NA | 90 | 80 | 105 | 105 | 131 |
| **CASE MANAGEMENT** | 11,790 | 11,940 | 11,682 | 11,865 | 12,266 | 12,409 | 13,863 |
| **HCBS WAIVER** | 0 | 0 | 0 | 348 | 1,089 | 1,452 | 2,280 |
| **MODEL 50/200 WAIVER** | 0 | 0 | 0 | 0 | 0 | 0 | 0 |

*Source:*
Institute on Disability and Human Development (UAP),
University of Illinois at Chicago, 1994

# MISSOURI

## Community Services: FY 1992 Revenue Sources

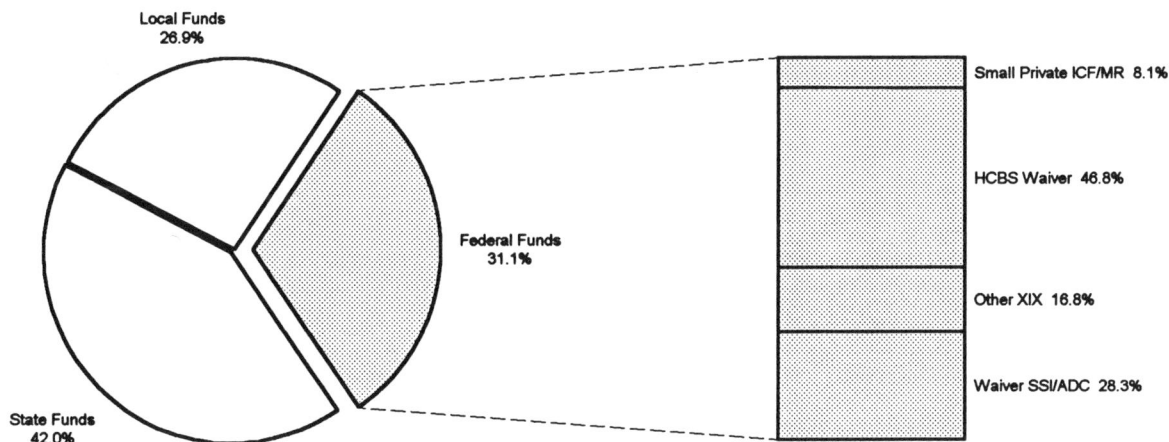

Local Funds
26.9%

State Funds
42.0%

Federal Funds
31.1%

Small Private ICF/MR  8.1%

HCBS Waiver  46.8%

Other XIX  16.8%

Waiver SSI/ADC  28.3%

Total Funds: $126.7 Million

## Family Support Initiatives*

|  | 1986 | 1987 | 1988 | 1989 | 1990 | 1991 | 1992 |
|---|---|---|---|---|---|---|---|
| **FAMILY SUPPORT: TOTAL SPENDING** | $0 | $0 | $536,655 | $2,107,711 | $3,837,885 | $3,777,396 | $3,442,130 |
| **Total # of Families Supported** | 0 | 0 | 500 | 1,808 | 2,538 | 2,329 | 2,429 |
| A. Financial Subsidy/Payment | $0 | $0 | $0 | $0 | $0 | $0 | $0 |
| # of Families | 0 | 0 | 0 | 0 | 0 | 0 | 0 |
| B. Family Assistance Payments | $0 | $0 | $362,500 | $785,575 | $1,186,984 | $845,399 | $1,007,407 |
| # of Families | 0 | 0 | 340 | 923 | 1,041 | 756 | 682 |
| C. Other Family Support Payments | $0 | $0 | $174,155 | $1,322,136 | $2,650,901 | $2,931,997 | $2,434,723 |
| # of Families | 0 | 0 | 160 | 885 | 1,497 | 1,573 | 1,747 |

## Other Community Services Initiatives*

|  | 1986 | 1987 | 1988 | 1989 | 1990 | 1991 | 1992 |
|---|---|---|---|---|---|---|---|
| **AGING/DD SPENDING** | $0 | $0 | $0 | $0 | $0 | $0 | $0 |
| # of Persons Served | 0 | 0 | 0 | 0 | 0 | 0 | 0 |
| **ASSISTIVE TECHNOLOGY SPENDING** |  |  |  |  |  |  | $0 |
| # of Persons Served |  |  |  |  |  |  | 0 |
| **EARLY INTERVENTION SPENDING** | $0 | $0 | $1,177,700 | $1,309,071 | $1,440,442 | $1,502,477 | $929,220 |
| # of Persons Served | 0 | 0 | 510 | 697 | 844 | 855 | 1,101 |
| **PERSONAL ASSISTANCE SPENDING** |  |  |  |  |  |  | $0 |
| # of Persons Served |  |  |  |  |  |  | 0 |
| **SUPPORTED EMPLOYMENT SPENDING** | $0 | $0 | $315,744 | $151,667 | $197,875 | $235,095 | $393,936 |
| # of Persons Served | 0 | 0 | 90 | 80 | 105 | 105 | 131 |
| **SUPPORTED LIVING SPENDING** |  |  |  |  |  | NA | NA |
| # of Persons Served |  |  |  |  |  | 118 | 661 |

*Expenditures associated with Special Community Initiatives are a subset of funding within the community services component of the state's chart series and spreadsheet; Family Support Client figures may include duplicate client counts; HCBS Waiver counts include Waiver case management numbers.
0= Services not provided in the state; NA= Data not available from state; blank= Services not applicable (eg. CSLA prior to authorization, Special Community Initiatives prior to request for data by this study)

*Source:*
Institute on Disability and Human Development (UAP),
University of Illinois at Chicago, 1994

# MISSOURI

## Large Congregate Care Facilities: FY 1992 Revenue Sources*

### Private 16+Bed Settings

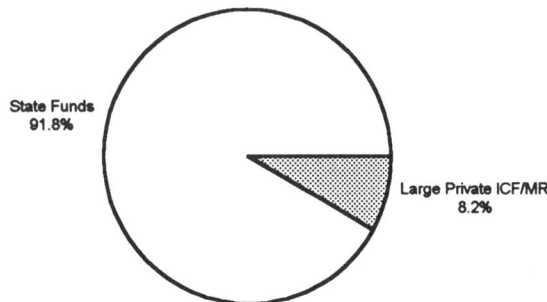

State Funds
91.8%

Large Private ICF/MR
8.2%

Total Funds: $31.4 Million

### Public Institutions

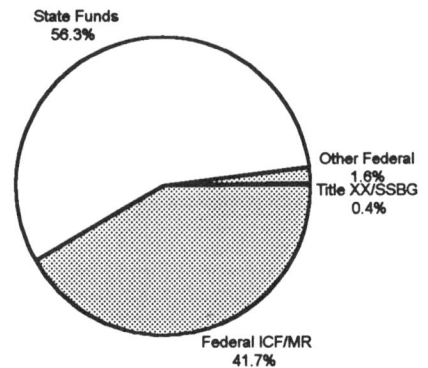

State Funds
56.3%

Other Federal
1.6%
Title XX/SSBG
0.4%

Federal ICF/MR
41.7%

Total Funds: $132.3 Million

*Excludes nursing homes

## Average Daily Residents in Institutions

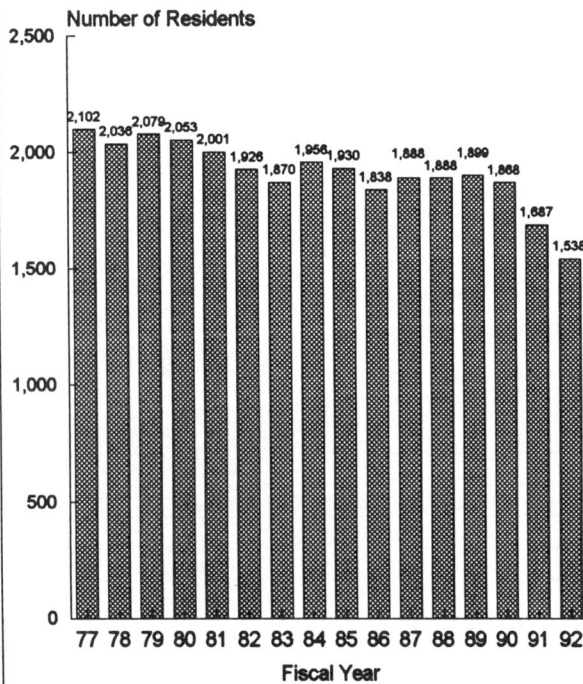

Number of Residents

| | | | | | | | | | | | | | | | |
|77|78|79|80|81|82|83|84|85|86|87|88|89|90|91|92|

2,102 2,036 2,079 2,053 2,001 1,926 1,870 1,958 1,930 1,838 1,888 1,888 1,899 1,868 1,687 1,538

Fiscal Year

## Institutional Daily Costs Per Resident

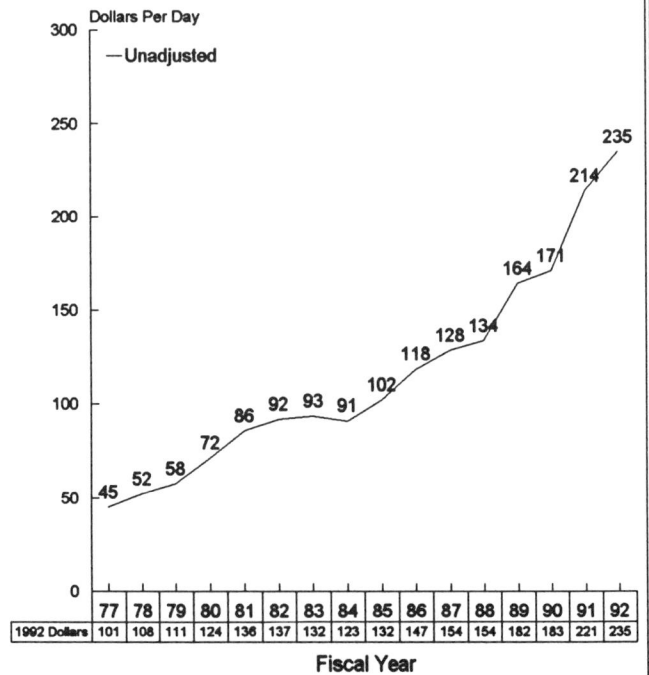

Dollars Per Day

—Unadjusted

45 52 58 72 86 92 93 91 102 118 128 134 164 171 214 235

| Fiscal Year | 77 | 78 | 79 | 80 | 81 | 82 | 83 | 84 | 85 | 86 | 87 | 88 | 89 | 90 | 91 | 92 |
|---|---|---|---|---|---|---|---|---|---|---|---|---|---|---|---|---|
| 1992 Dollars | 101 | 108 | 111 | 124 | 136 | 137 | 132 | 123 | 132 | 147 | 154 | 154 | 182 | 183 | 221 | 235 |

*Source:*
Institute on Disability and Human Development (UAP),
University of Illinois at Chicago, 1994

# MISSOURI FISCAL EFFORT

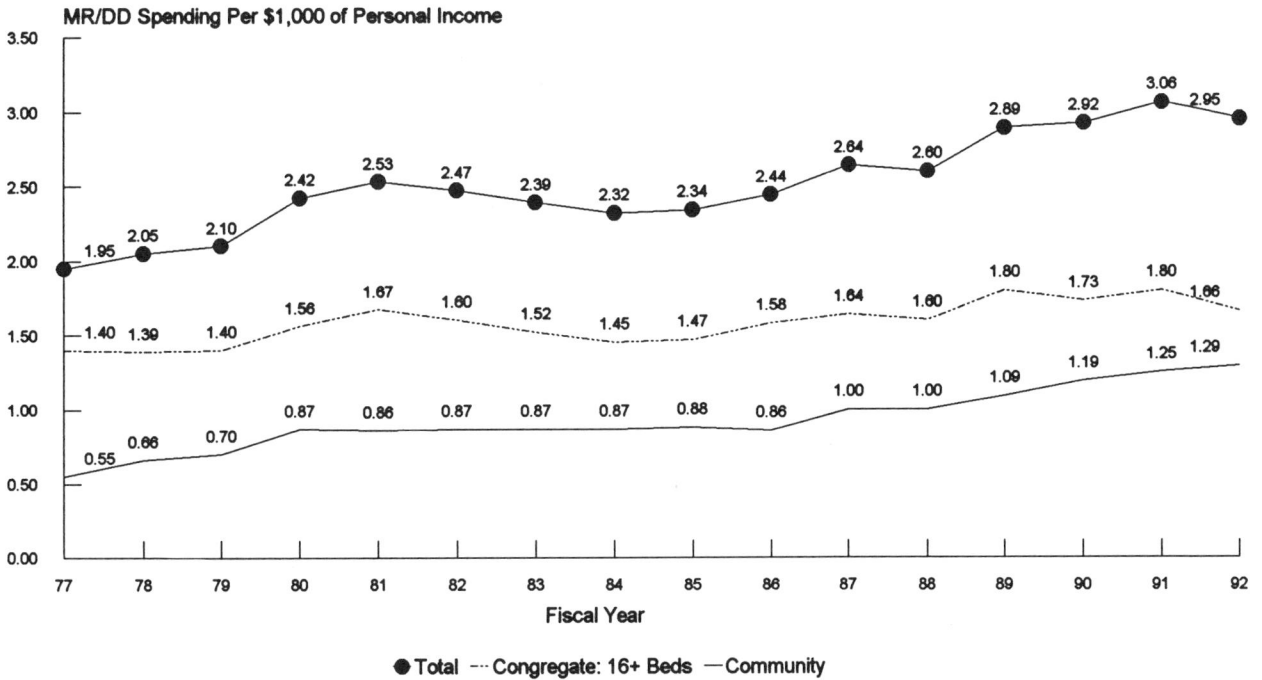

**MR/DD Spending Per $1,000 of Personal Income**

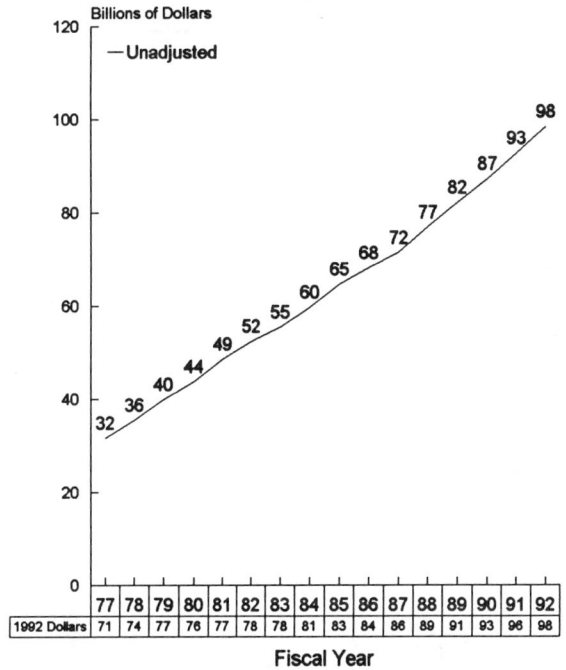

| Fiscal Year | Total | Congregate: 16+ Beds | Community |
|---|---|---|---|
| 77 | 1.95 | 1.40 | 0.55 |
| 78 | 2.05 | 1.39 | 0.66 |
| 79 | 2.10 | 1.40 | 0.70 |
| 80 | 2.42 | 1.56 | 0.87 |
| 81 | 2.53 | 1.67 | 0.86 |
| 82 | 2.47 | 1.60 | 0.87 |
| 83 | 2.39 | 1.52 | 0.87 |
| 84 | 2.32 | 1.45 | 0.87 |
| 85 | 2.34 | 1.47 | 0.88 |
| 86 | 2.44 | 1.58 | 0.86 |
| 87 | 2.64 | 1.64 | 1.00 |
| 88 | 2.60 | 1.60 | 1.00 |
| 89 | 2.89 | 1.80 | 1.09 |
| 90 | 2.92 | 1.73 | 1.19 |
| 91 | 3.06 | 1.80 | 1.25 |
| 92 | 2.95 | 1.66 | 1.29 |

● Total  --- Congregate: 16+ Beds  — Community

## Total MR/DD Spending

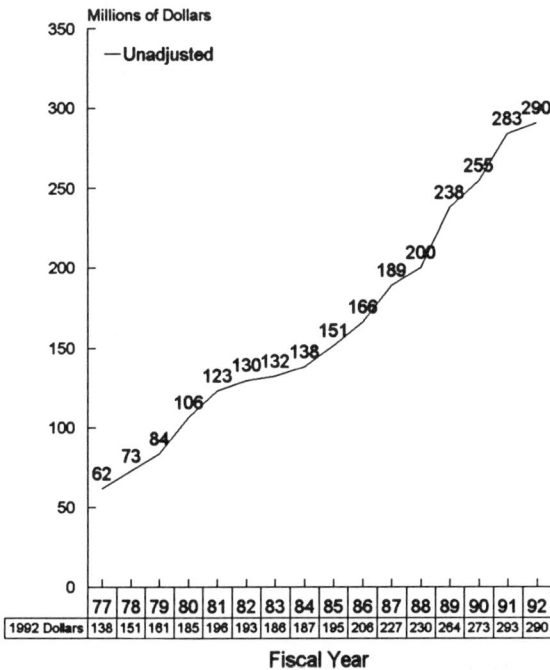

Millions of Dollars
—Unadjusted

| Fiscal Year | 77 | 78 | 79 | 80 | 81 | 82 | 83 | 84 | 85 | 86 | 87 | 88 | 89 | 90 | 91 | 92 |
|---|---|---|---|---|---|---|---|---|---|---|---|---|---|---|---|---|
| (Unadjusted) | 62 | 73 | 84 | 106 | 123 | 130 | 132 | 138 | 151 | 166 | 189 | 200 | 238 | 255 | 283 | 290 |
| 1992 Dollars | 138 | 151 | 161 | 185 | 196 | 193 | 186 | 187 | 195 | 206 | 227 | 230 | 264 | 273 | 293 | 290 |

## Personal Income

Billions of Dollars
—Unadjusted

| Fiscal Year | 77 | 78 | 79 | 80 | 81 | 82 | 83 | 84 | 85 | 86 | 87 | 88 | 89 | 90 | 91 | 92 |
|---|---|---|---|---|---|---|---|---|---|---|---|---|---|---|---|---|
| (Unadjusted) | 32 | 36 | 40 | 44 | 49 | 52 | 55 | 60 | 65 | 68 | 72 | 77 | 82 | 87 | 93 | 98 |
| 1992 Dollars | 71 | 74 | 77 | 76 | 77 | 78 | 78 | 81 | 83 | 84 | 86 | 89 | 91 | 93 | 96 | 98 |

*Source:*
Institute on Disability and Human Development (UAP),
University of Illinois at Chicago, 1994

# MISSOURI
## Financial Support for MR/DD Services: FY 1977-92

| | 1977 | 1978 | 1979 | 1980 | 1981 | 1982 | 1983 | 1984 |
|---|---|---|---|---|---|---|---|---|
| **TOTAL FUNDS** | $61,783,501 | $72,802,359 | $83,768,740 | $106,220,232 | $123,024,166 | $129,630,670 | $132,268,070 | $138,304,668 |
| **CONGREGATE 16+ BEDS** | 44,506,398 | 49,460,087 | 55,880,762 | 68,243,027 | 81,007,942 | 83,741,511 | 84,011,699 | 86,242,996 |
| INSTITUTIONAL SERVICES FUNDS | 34,601,750 | 38,876,750 | 43,722,250 | 53,747,300 | 62,693,500 | 64,567,750 | 63,774,750 | 65,133,400 |
| STATE FUNDS | 23,532,750 | 26,665,750 | 31,530,250 | 33,207,300 | 35,703,500 | 38,127,750 | 31,920,750 | 32,719,900 |
| General Funds | 20,171,000 | 22,699,000 | 26,764,000 | 27,837,000 | 27,320,000 | 30,414,000 | 22,952,000 | 19,309,100 |
| Local | 0 | 0 | 0 | 0 | 0 | 0 | 0 | 0 |
| Other State Funds | 3,361,750 | 3,966,750 | 4,766,250 | 5,370,300 | 8,383,500 | 7,713,750 | 8,968,750 | 13,410,800 |
| FEDERAL FUNDS | 11,069,000 | 12,211,000 | 12,192,000 | 20,540,000 | 26,990,000 | 26,440,000 | 31,854,000 | 32,413,500 |
| Federal ICF/MR | 10,446,000 | 11,671,000 | 11,658,000 | 19,907,000 | 26,383,000 | 25,918,000 | 31,347,000 | 31,700,300 |
| Title XX / SSBG Funds | 0 | 0 | 0 | 0 | 0 | 0 | 0 | 210,700 |
| Other Federal Funds | 623,000 | 540,000 | 534,000 | 633,000 | 607,000 | 522,000 | 507,000 | 502,500 |
| LARGE PRIVATE RESIDENTIAL | 9,904,648 | 10,583,337 | 12,158,512 | 14,495,727 | 18,314,442 | 19,173,761 | 20,236,949 | 21,109,596 |
| STATE FUNDS | 9,904,648 | 10,583,337 | 12,158,512 | 14,495,727 | 17,169,442 | 18,076,761 | 19,137,949 | 20,329,696 |
| General Funds | 9,904,648 | 10,583,337 | 12,158,512 | 14,495,727 | 17,169,442 | 18,076,761 | 19,137,949 | 20,329,696 |
| Other State Funds | 0 | 0 | 0 | 0 | 0 | 0 | 0 | 0 |
| Local/County Overmatch | 0 | 0 | 0 | 0 | 0 | 0 | 0 | 0 |
| FEDERAL FUNDS | 0 | 0 | 0 | 0 | 1,145,000 | 1,097,000 | 1,099,000 | 779,900 |
| Large Private ICF/MR | 0 | 0 | 0 | 0 | 1,145,000 | 1,097,000 | 1,099,000 | 779,900 |
| **COMMUNITY SERVICES FUNDS** | 17,277,103 | 23,342,272 | 27,887,978 | 37,977,205 | 42,016,224 | 45,889,159 | 48,256,371 | 52,061,672 |
| STATE FUNDS | 16,281,103 | 19,129,272 | 22,975,978 | 30,364,205 | 35,889,224 | 40,632,159 | 42,742,371 | 44,684,772 |
| General Funds | 11,623,853 | 11,994,772 | 15,034,108 | 20,342,955 | 23,701,224 | 24,811,665 | 26,567,911 | 27,829,258 |
| Other State Funds | 803,250 | 922,500 | 1,191,870 | 1,420,250 | 2,689,000 | 2,921,494 | 3,349,460 | 2,326,070 |
| Local/County Overmatch | 2,500,000 | 4,900,000 | 5,500,000 | 7,500,000 | 8,500,000 | 12,000,000 | 12,000,000 | 13,768,444 |
| SSI State Supplement | 1,354,000 | 1,312,000 | 1,250,000 | 1,101,000 | 999,000 | 899,000 | 825,000 | 761,000 |
| FEDERAL FUNDS | 996,000 | 4,213,000 | 4,912,000 | 7,613,000 | 6,127,000 | 5,257,000 | 5,514,000 | 7,376,900 |
| ICF/MR Funds | 0 | 0 | 0 | 0 | 0 | 0 | 0 | 545,500 |
| Small Public | 0 | 0 | 0 | 0 | 0 | 0 | 0 | 0 |
| Small Private | 0 | 0 | 0 | 0 | 0 | 0 | 0 | 545,500 |
| HCBS Waiver | 0 | 0 | 0 | 0 | 0 | 0 | 0 | 0 |
| Model 50/200 Waiver | 0 | 0 | 0 | 0 | 0 | 0 | 0 | 0 |
| Other Title XIX Programs | 0 | 0 | 0 | 0 | 0 | 0 | 0 | 952,000 |
| Title XX / SSBG Funds | 164,000 | 3,291,000 | 4,064,000 | 6,875,000 | 5,363,000 | 4,627,000 | 4,631,000 | 4,889,500 |
| Other Federal Funds | 832,000 | 922,000 | 848,000 | 738,000 | 764,000 | 630,000 | 883,000 | 989,900 |
| Waiver Clients' SSI/ADC | 0 | 0 | 0 | 0 | 0 | 0 | 0 | 0 |

| | 1985 | 1986 | 1987 | 1988 | 1989 | 1990 | 1991 | 1992 |
|---|---|---|---|---|---|---|---|---|
| **TOTAL FUNDS** | $151,299,572 | $166,291,763 | $188,861,128 | $200,104,458 | $237,881,075 | $254,596,725 | $283,457,878 | $290,277,309 |
| **CONGREGATE 16+ BEDS** | 94,670,702 | 107,480,119 | 117,102,632 | 123,044,743 | 148,046,142 | 150,767,027 | 167,150,641 | 163,605,611 |
| INSTITUTIONAL SERVICES FUNDS | 71,887,450 | 79,332,300 | 88,392,300 | 92,270,500 | 113,880,142 | 116,515,252 | 131,642,641 | 132,254,396 |
| STATE FUNDS | 45,123,650 | 55,148,400 | 60,746,300 | 57,559,600 | 74,149,669 | 77,774,449 | 76,187,990 | 74,445,176 |
| General Funds | 30,000,500 | 38,137,700 | 42,309,400 | 37,985,800 | 70,707,352 | 75,586,916 | 71,702,425 | 70,540,714 |
| Local | 0 | 0 | 0 | 0 | 0 | 0 | 0 | 0 |
| Other State Funds | 15,123,150 | 17,010,700 | 18,436,900 | 19,573,800 | 3,442,317 | 2,187,533 | 4,485,565 | 3,904,462 |
| FEDERAL FUNDS | 26,763,800 | 24,183,900 | 27,646,000 | 34,710,900 | 39,730,473 | 38,740,803 | 55,454,651 | 57,809,220 |
| Federal ICF/MR | 26,174,400 | 23,741,300 | 27,455,300 | 34,270,400 | 38,014,669 | 37,041,586 | 54,410,543 | 55,216,062 |
| Title XX / SSBG Funds | 166,400 | 117,000 | 56,700 | 98,900 | 1,332,324 | 1,334,628 | 483,412 | 483,412 |
| Other Federal Funds | 423,000 | 325,600 | 134,000 | 341,600 | 383,480 | 364,589 | 560,696 | 2,109,746 |
| LARGE PRIVATE RESIDENTIAL | 22,783,252 | 28,147,819 | 28,710,332 | 30,774,243 | 34,166,000 | 34,251,775 | 35,508,000 | 31,351,215 |
| STATE FUNDS | 21,892,352 | 25,629,619 | 26,005,632 | 27,350,743 | 29,087,647 | 29,524,557 | 30,429,647 | 28,766,673 |
| General Funds | 21,892,352 | 25,629,619 | 26,005,632 | 27,350,743 | 29,087,647 | 29,524,557 | 30,429,647 | 28,766,673 |
| Other State Funds | 0 | 0 | 0 | 0 | 0 | 0 | 0 | 0 |
| Local/County Overmatch | 0 | 0 | 0 | 0 | 0 | 0 | 0 | 0 |
| FEDERAL FUNDS | 890,900 | 2,518,200 | 2,704,700 | 3,423,500 | 5,078,353 | 4,727,218 | 5,078,353 | 2,584,542 |
| Large Private ICF/MR | 890,900 | 2,518,200 | 2,704,700 | 3,423,500 | 5,078,353 | 4,727,218 | 5,078,353 | 2,584,542 |
| **COMMUNITY SERVICES FUNDS** | 56,628,870 | 58,811,644 | 71,758,496 | 77,059,715 | 89,834,933 | 103,829,698 | 116,307,237 | 126,671,698 |
| STATE FUNDS | 46,380,870 | 48,144,744 | 58,972,696 | 64,044,015 | 79,123,454 | 87,191,043 | 91,284,514 | 87,281,590 |
| General Funds | 27,388,469 | 26,995,986 | 31,535,211 | 36,745,600 | 47,616,184 | 51,035,830 | 52,807,373 | 46,407,257 |
| Other State Funds | 2,650,513 | 3,221,425 | 4,050,295 | 4,514,225 | 4,631,424 | 5,187,195 | 5,809,658 | 6,506,817 |
| Local/County Overmatch | 15,536,888 | 17,305,333 | 23,113,190 | 22,578,190 | 26,659,546 | 30,740,903 | 32,429,012 | 34,117,122 |
| SSI State Supplement | 805,000 | 622,000 | 274,000 | 206,000 | 216,300 | 227,115 | 238,471 | 250,394 |
| FEDERAL FUNDS | 10,248,000 | 10,666,900 | 12,785,800 | 13,015,700 | 10,711,479 | 16,638,655 | 25,022,723 | 39,390,108 |
| ICF/MR Funds | 749,700 | 745,900 | 1,575,000 | 2,496,600 | 4,751,087 | 4,887,331 | 4,751,087 | 3,181,250 |
| Small Public | 0 | 27,100 | 72,300 | 218,300 | 206,403 | 391,099 | 206,403 | 0 |
| Small Private | 749,700 | 718,800 | 1,502,700 | 2,278,300 | 4,544,684 | 4,496,232 | 4,544,684 | 3,181,250 |
| HCBS Waiver | 0 | 0 | 0 | 0 | 4,532,200 | 6,942,300 | 13,615,668 | 18,438,892 |
| Model 50/200 Waiver | 0 | 0 | 0 | 0 | 0 | 0 | 0 | 0 |
| Other Title XIX Programs | 3,879,300 | 4,408,200 | 4,868,900 | 4,124,400 | 0 | 0 | 0 | 6,634,446 |
| Title XX / SSBG Funds | 4,818,100 | 4,756,300 | 4,758,500 | 4,808,800 | 0 | 0 | 0 | 0 |
| Other Federal Funds | 800,900 | 756,500 | 1,583,400 | 1,585,900 | 0 | 0 | 0 | 0 |
| Waiver Clients' SSI/ADC | 0 | 0 | 0 | 0 | 1,428,192 | 4,809,024 | 6,655,968 | 11,135,520 |

*Source:*
Institute on Disability and Human Development (UAP),
University of Illinois at Chicago, 1994

# MONTANA

## MR/DD Spending for Congregate Residential & Community Services

▨ Congregate: 16+ Beds*  ■ Community**

Millions of 1992 Dollars

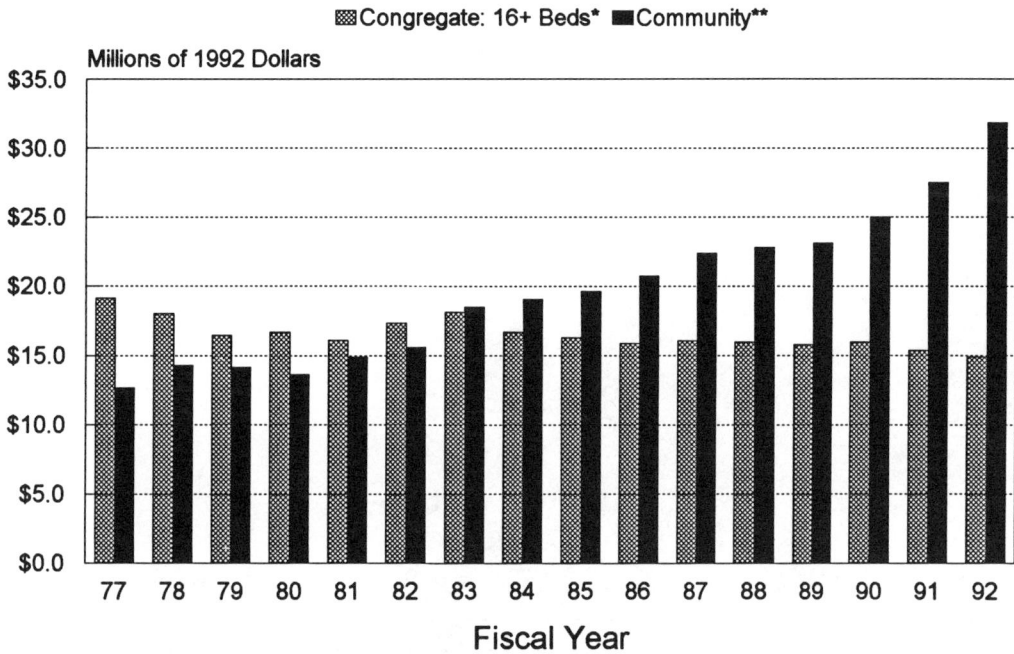

Fiscal Year

*Excludes nursing homes; ** Includes resources for
15 bed or less residential settings & non-residential community services

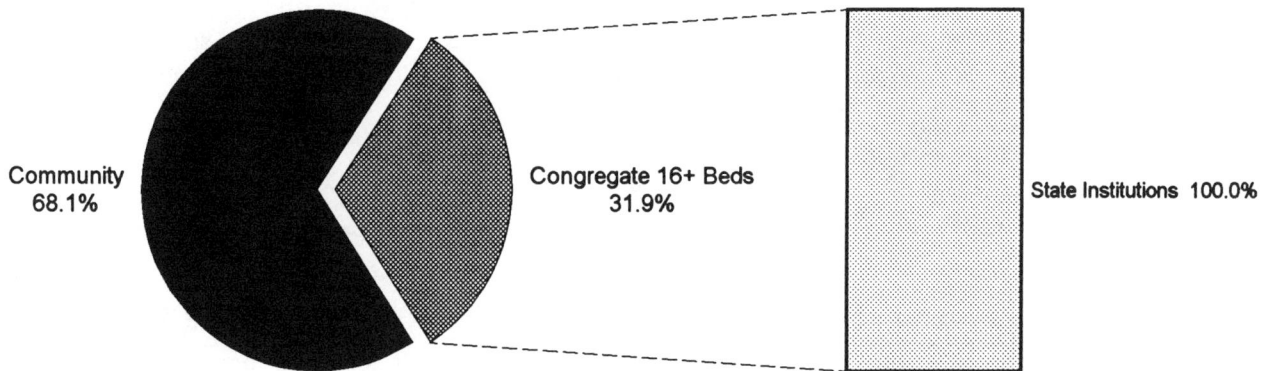

Community
68.1%

Congregate 16+ Beds
31.9%

State Institutions  100.0%

FY 1992 Total Spending:
$46.8 Million

*Source:*
Institute on Disability and Human Development (UAP),
University of Illinois at Chicago, 1994

# MONTANA

## Number of Persons Served by Residential Setting: FY 1992

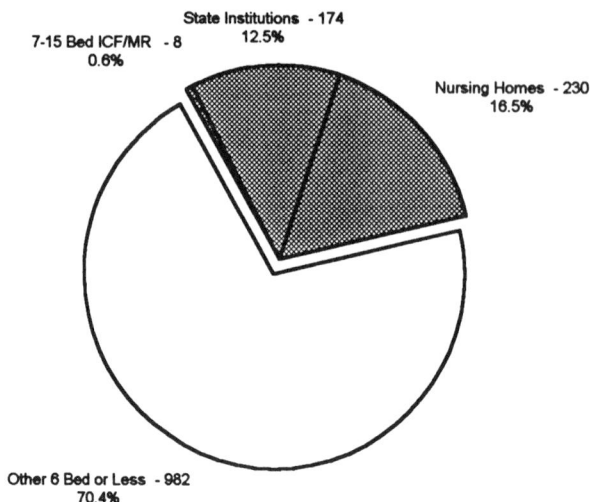

State Institutions - 174
12.5%

7-15 Bed ICF/MR - 8
0.6%

Nursing Homes - 230
16.5%

Other 6 Bed or Less - 982
70.4%

Total Served: 1,394

## Persons Served by Residential Setting:1986-92

|  | 1986 | 1987 | 1988 | 1989 | 1990 | 1991 | 1992 |
|---|---|---|---|---|---|---|---|
| CONGREGATE 16 + BED SETTINGS | NA | NA | 559 | 480 | 473 | 444 | 404 |
| Nursing Homes | NA | NA | 306 | 240 | 238 | 237 | 230 |
| State Institutions | 255 | 257 | 253 | 240 | 235 | 207 | 174 |
| Private 16+Bed ICF/MR | 0 | 0 | 0 | 0 | 0 | 0 | 0 |
| Other 16+Bed Residential | 0 | 0 | 0 | 0 | 0 | 0 | 0 |
| 15 BED OR LESS RESIDENTIAL SETTINGS | 819 | 912 | 909 | 908 | 912 | 929 | 990 |
| Public 7-15 Bed ICF/MR | 0 | 0 | 0 | 0 | 0 | 0 | 0 |
| Private 7-15 Bed ICF/MR | 10 | 10 | 10 | 10 | 10 | 10 | 8 |
| Other 7-15 Bed Residential | 0 | 0 | 0 | 0 | 0 | 0 | 0 |
| Public 6 Bed or Less ICF/MR | 0 | 0 | 0 | 0 | 0 | 0 | 0 |
| Private 6 Bed or Less ICF/MR | 0 | 0 | 0 | 0 | 0 | 0 | 0 |
| Other 6 Bed or Less Residential | 809 | 902 | 899 | 898 | 902 | 919 | 982 |
| TOTAL PERSONS SERVED | NA | NA | 1,468 | 1,388 | 1,385 | 1,373 | 1,394 |

## Persons Served in Non-Residential Community Services:1986-92

|  | 1986 | 1987 | 1988 | 1989 | 1990 | 1991 | 1992 |
|---|---|---|---|---|---|---|---|
| DAY/WORK PROGRAMS | 1,224 | 1,284 | 1,325 | 1,382 | 1,407 | 1,440 | 1,542 |
| Sheltered Employment/Work Activity | 981 | 1,000 | 1,043 | 1,047 | 1,031 | 1,021 | 1,022 |
| Day Habilitation ("Day Training") | 202 | 208 | 203 | 216 | 214 | 221 | 287 |
| Supported/Competitive Employment | 41 | 76 | 79 | 119 | 162 | 198 | 233 |
| CASE MANAGEMENT | 2,100 | 2,100 | 2,100 | 2,375 | 2,409 | 2,553 | 2,745 |
| HCBS WAIVER | 174 | 210 | 285 | 290 | 300 | 370 | 459 |
| MODEL 50/200 WAIVER | 0 | 0 | 0 | 0 | 0 | 0 | 0 |

Source:
Institute on Disability and Human Development (UAP),
University of Illinois at Chicago, 1994

# MONTANA

## Community Services: FY 1992 Revenue Sources

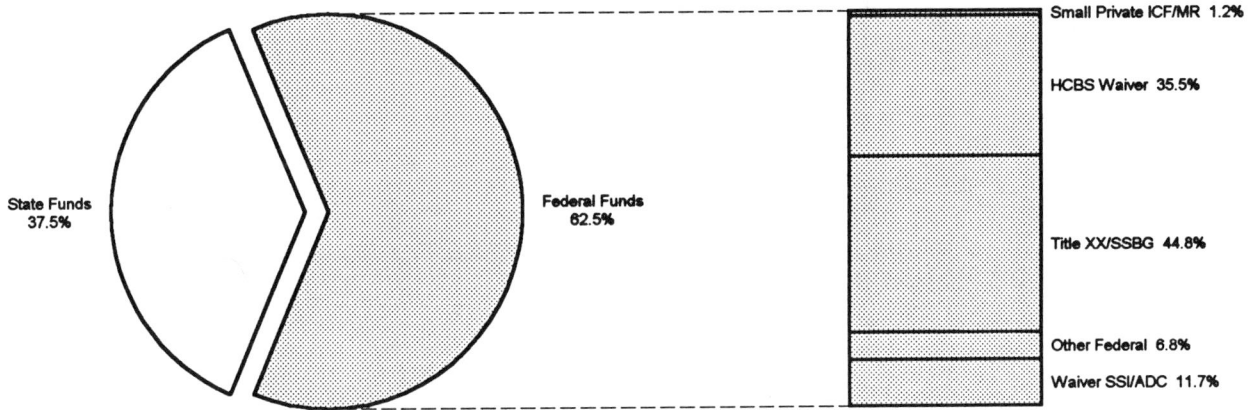

State Funds
37.5%

Federal Funds
62.5%

Small Private ICF/MR 1.2%

HCBS Waiver 35.5%

Title XX/SSBG 44.8%

Other Federal 6.8%

Waiver SSI/ADC 11.7%

Total Funds: $31.8 Million

## Family Support Initiatives*

|  | 1986 | 1987 | 1988 | 1989 | 1990 | 1991 | 1992 |
|---|---|---|---|---|---|---|---|
| FAMILY SUPPORT: TOTAL SPENDING | $2,249,634 | $2,558,542 | $2,844,400 | $3,424,652 | $3,848,117 | $4,087,895 | $5,115,442 |
| Total # of Families Supported | 1,595 | 1,678 | 1,755 | 1,428 | 1,509 | 1,831 | 2,352 |
| A. Financial Subsidy/Payment | $0 | $0 | $0 | $0 | $0 | $0 | $0 |
| # of Families | 0 | 0 | 0 | 0 | 0 | 0 | 0 |
| B. Family Assistance Payments | $241,900 | $260,900 | $269,400 | $280,021 | $335,783 | $348,355 | $352,775 |
| # of Families | 506 | 542 | 557 | 542 | 485 | 631 | 599 |
| C. Other Family Support Payments | $2,007,734 | $2,297,642 | $2,575,000 | $3,144,631 | $3,512,334 | $3,739,540 | $4,762,667 |
| # of Families | 1,089 | 1,136 | 1,198 | 886 | 1,024 | 1,200 | 1,753 |

## Other Community Services Initiatives*

|  | 1986 | 1987 | 1988 | 1989 | 1990 | 1991 | 1992 |
|---|---|---|---|---|---|---|---|
| AGING/DD SPENDING | $548,000 | $609,500 | $609,200 | $623,691 | $702,783 | $731,503 | $756,636 |
| # of Persons Served | 113 | 113 | 103 | 117 | 118 | 122 | 122 |
| ASSISTIVE TECHNOLOGY SPENDING |  |  |  |  |  |  | $0 |
| # of Persons Served |  |  |  |  |  |  | 0 |
| EARLY INTERVENTION SPENDING | $0 | $0 | $123,600 | $242,389 | $271,059 | $276,500 | $1,195,191 |
| # of Persons Served | 0 | 0 | 109 | 57 | 75 | 99 | 153 |
| PERSONAL ASSISTANCE SPENDING |  |  |  |  |  |  | $0 |
| # of Persons Served |  |  |  |  |  |  | 0 |
| SUPPORTED EMPLOYMENT SPENDING | $101,200 | $209,800 | $244,359 | $401,692 | $579,922 | $758,119 | $973,367 |
| # of Persons Served | 41 | 76 | 75 | 119 | 162 | 198 | 233 |
| SUPPORTED LIVING SPENDING |  |  |  |  |  |  | $0 |
| # of Persons Served |  |  |  |  |  |  | 0 |

*Expenditures associated with Special Community Initiatives are a subset of funding within the community services component of the state's chart series and spreadsheet; Family Support Client figures may include duplicate client counts; HCBS Waiver counts include Waiver case management numbers.
0= Services not provided in the state; NA= Data not available from state; blank= Services not applicable (eg. CSLA prior to authorization, Special Community Initiatives prior to request for data by this study)

Source:
Institute on Disability and Human Development (UAP),
University of Illinois at Chicago, 1994

# MONTANA

## Large Congregate Care Facilities: FY 1992 Revenue Sources*

### Private 16+Bed Settings

## Does Not Apply

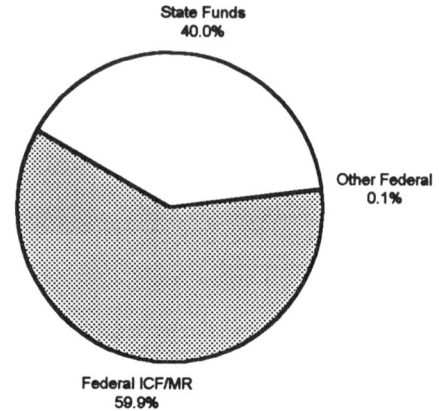

### Public Institutions

State Funds
40.0%

Other Federal
0.1%

Federal ICF/MR
59.9%

Total Funds: $14.9 Million

*Excludes nursing homes

## Average Daily Residents in Institutions

Number of Residents

299 305 314 309 303 272 275 256 256 255 257 253 240 235 207 174

77 78 79 80 81 82 83 84 85 86 87 88 89 90 91 92

Fiscal Year

## Institutional Daily Costs Per Resident

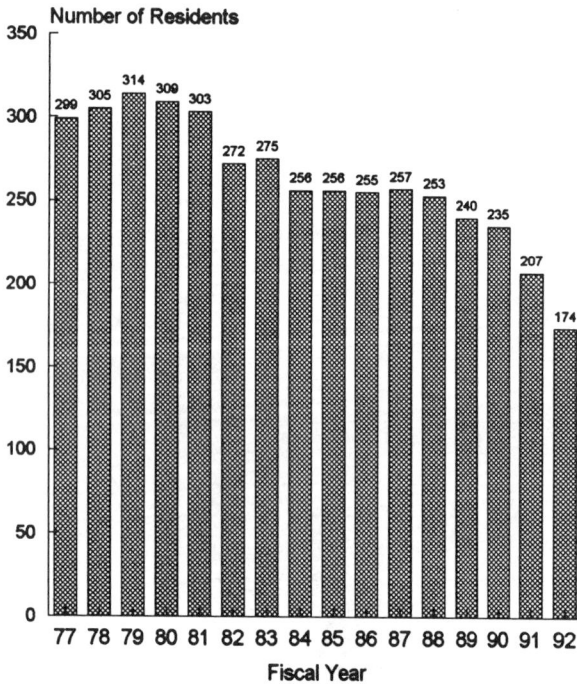

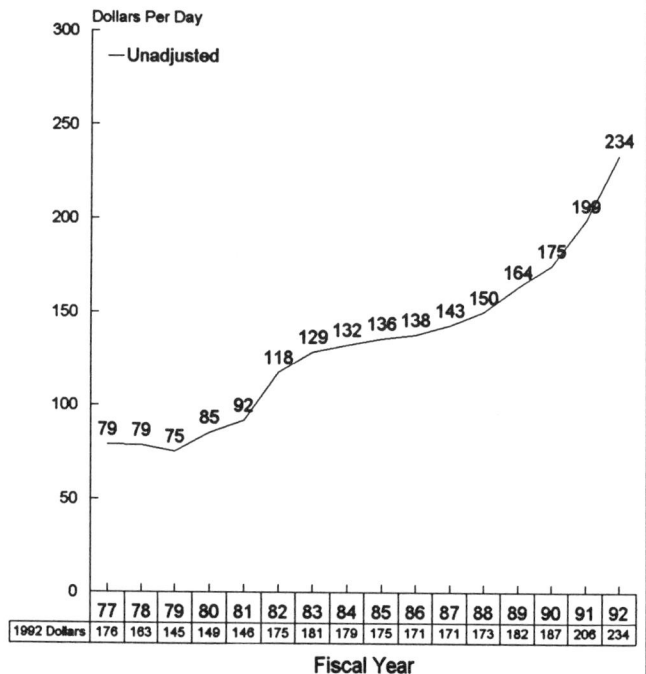

Dollars Per Day

— Unadjusted

234
199
175
164
150
143
138
136
132
129
118
92
85
79 79 75

| | 77 | 78 | 79 | 80 | 81 | 82 | 83 | 84 | 85 | 86 | 87 | 88 | 89 | 90 | 91 | 92 |
|---|---|---|---|---|---|---|---|---|---|---|---|---|---|---|---|---|
| 1992 Dollars | 176 | 163 | 145 | 149 | 146 | 175 | 181 | 179 | 175 | 171 | 171 | 173 | 182 | 187 | 206 | 234 |

Fiscal Year

*Source:*
Institute on Disability and Human Development (UAP),
University of Illinois at Chicago, 1994

# MONTANA FISCAL EFFORT

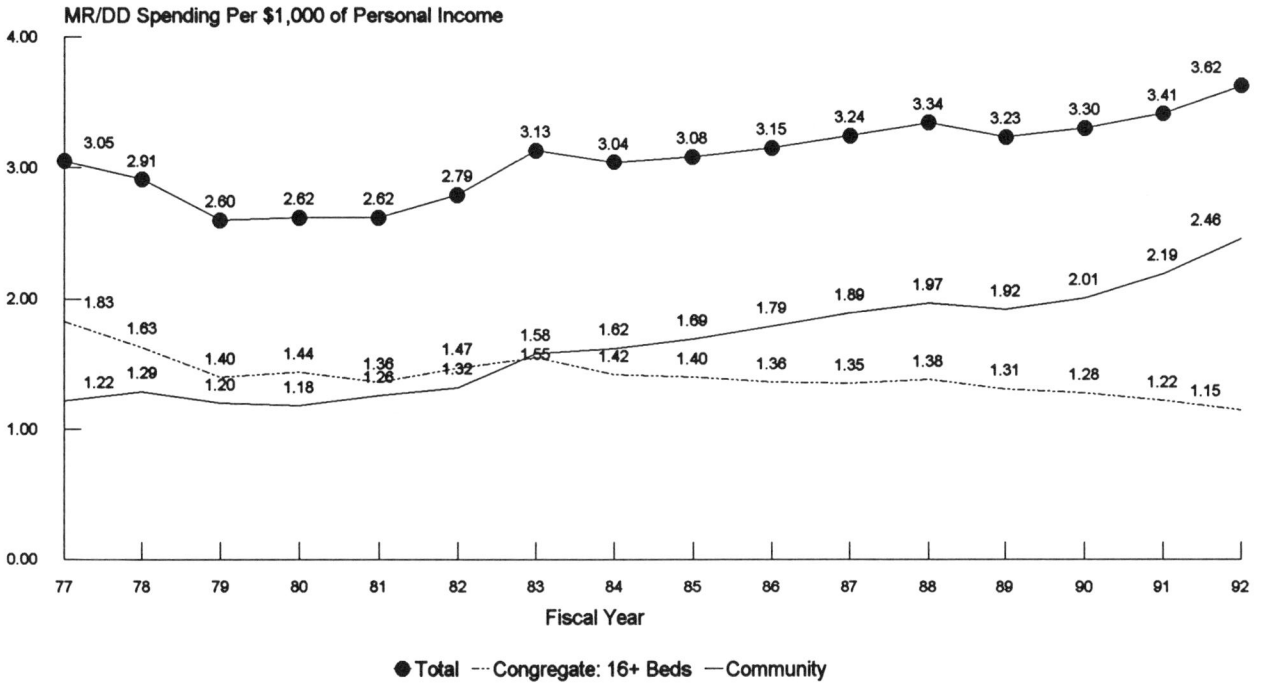

MR/DD Spending Per $1,000 of Personal Income

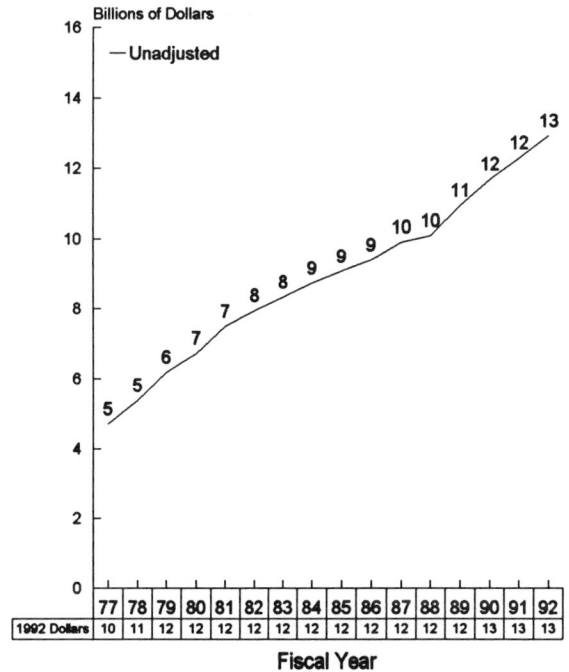

| | |
|---|---|
| 4.00 | |

Total values: 3.05, 2.91, 2.60, 2.62, 2.62, 2.79, 3.13, 3.04, 3.08, 3.15, 3.24, 3.34, 3.23, 3.30, 3.41, 3.62

Community values: 1.22, 1.29, 1.20, 1.18, 1.26, 1.32, 1.55, 1.62, 1.69, 1.79, 1.89, 1.97, 1.92, 2.01, 2.19, 2.46

Congregate values: 1.83, 1.63, 1.40, 1.44, 1.36, 1.47, 1.58, 1.42, 1.40, 1.36, 1.35, 1.38, 1.31, 1.28, 1.22, 1.15

Fiscal Year: 77 78 79 80 81 82 83 84 85 86 87 88 89 90 91 92

● Total ---Congregate: 16+ Beds —Community

## Total MR/DD Spending

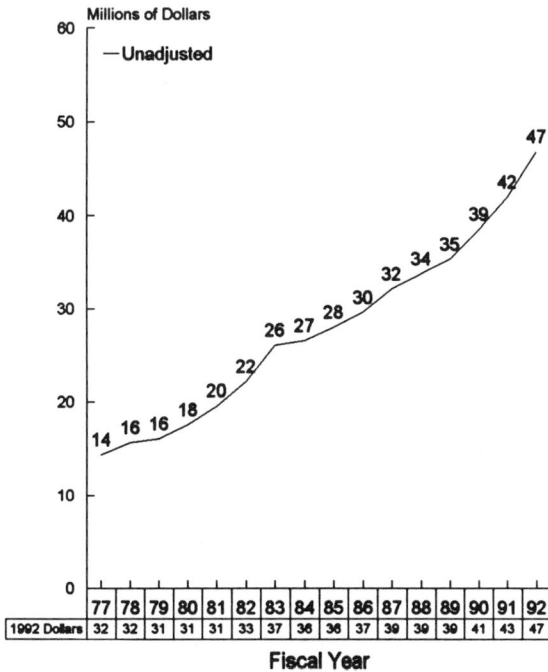

Millions of Dollars
—Unadjusted

Values: 14, 16, 16, 18, 20, 22, 26, 27, 28, 30, 32, 34, 35, 39, 42, 47

| | 77 | 78 | 79 | 80 | 81 | 82 | 83 | 84 | 85 | 86 | 87 | 88 | 89 | 90 | 91 | 92 |
|---|---|---|---|---|---|---|---|---|---|---|---|---|---|---|---|---|
| 1992 Dollars | 32 | 32 | 31 | 31 | 31 | 33 | 37 | 36 | 36 | 37 | 39 | 39 | 39 | 41 | 43 | 47 |

Fiscal Year

## Personal Income

Billions of Dollars
—Unadjusted

Values: 5, 5, 6, 7, 7, 8, 8, 9, 9, 9, 10, 10, 11, 12, 12, 13

| | 77 | 78 | 79 | 80 | 81 | 82 | 83 | 84 | 85 | 86 | 87 | 88 | 89 | 90 | 91 | 92 |
|---|---|---|---|---|---|---|---|---|---|---|---|---|---|---|---|---|
| 1992 Dollars | 10 | 11 | 12 | 12 | 12 | 12 | 12 | 12 | 12 | 12 | 12 | 12 | 12 | 13 | 13 | 13 |

Fiscal Year

*Source:*
Institute on Disability and Human Development (UAP),
University of Illinois at Chicago, 1994

# MONTANA
## Financial Support for MR/DD Services: FY 1977-92

| | 1977 | 1978 | 1979 | 1980 | 1981 | 1982 | 1983 | 1984 |
|---|---|---|---|---|---|---|---|---|
| **TOTAL FUNDS** | $14,331,000 | $15,671,000 | $16,063,000 | $17,553,000 | $19,563,000 | $22,197,652 | $26,067,772 | $26,548,916 |
| **CONGREGATE 16+ BEDS** | 8,606,000 | 8,740,000 | 8,628,000 | 9,652,000 | 10,165,000 | 11,680,000 | 12,911,000 | 12,395,400 |
| INSTITUTIONAL SERVICES FUNDS | 8,606,000 | 8,740,000 | 8,628,000 | 9,652,000 | 10,165,000 | 11,680,000 | 12,911,000 | 12,395,400 |
| STATE FUNDS | 6,534,000 | 5,716,000 | 5,772,000 | 6,255,000 | 6,036,000 | 8,160,000 | 7,988,000 | 6,151,500 |
| General Funds | 6,264,000 | 5,456,000 | 5,516,000 | 5,929,000 | 5,810,000 | 6,978,000 | 7,764,000 | 5,986,600 |
| Local | 0 | 0 | 0 | 0 | 0 | 0 | 0 | 0 |
| Other State Funds | 270,000 | 260,000 | 256,000 | 326,000 | 226,000 | 1,182,000 | 224,000 | 164,900 |
| FEDERAL FUNDS | 2,072,000 | 3,024,000 | 2,856,000 | 3,397,000 | 4,129,000 | 3,520,000 | 4,923,000 | 6,243,900 |
| Federal ICF/MR | 2,015,000 | 2,830,000 | 2,731,000 | 3,268,000 | 4,027,000 | 3,429,000 | 4,873,000 | 6,191,300 |
| Title XX / SSBG Funds | 0 | 0 | 0 | 0 | 0 | 0 | 0 | 0 |
| Other Federal Funds | 57,000 | 194,000 | 125,000 | 129,000 | 102,000 | 91,000 | 50,000 | 52,600 |
| LARGE PRIVATE RESIDENTIAL | 0 | 0 | 0 | 0 | 0 | 0 | 0 | 0 |
| STATE FUNDS | 0 | 0 | 0 | 0 | 0 | 0 | 0 | 0 |
| General Funds | 0 | 0 | 0 | 0 | 0 | 0 | 0 | 0 |
| Other State Funds | 0 | 0 | 0 | 0 | 0 | 0 | 0 | 0 |
| Local/County Overmatch | 0 | 0 | 0 | 0 | 0 | 0 | 0 | 0 |
| FEDERAL FUNDS | 0 | 0 | 0 | 0 | 0 | 0 | 0 | 0 |
| Large Private ICF/MR | 0 | 0 | 0 | 0 | 0 | 0 | 0 | 0 |
| **COMMUNITY SERVICES FUNDS** | 5,725,000 | 6,931,000 | 7,435,000 | 7,901,000 | 9,398,000 | 10,517,652 | 13,156,772 | 14,153,516 |
| STATE FUNDS | 2,473,000 | 4,342,000 | 4,260,000 | 3,771,000 | 4,962,000 | 9,241,000 | 9,689,000 | 10,289,600 |
| General Funds | 2,284,000 | 4,128,000 | 4,051,000 | 3,554,000 | 4,737,000 | 9,006,000 | 9,423,000 | 10,044,600 |
| Other State Funds | 0 | 0 | 0 | 0 | 0 | 0 | 0 | 0 |
| Local/County Overmatch | 0 | 0 | 0 | 0 | 0 | 0 | 0 | 0 |
| SSI State Supplement | 189,000 | 214,000 | 209,000 | 217,000 | 225,000 | 235,000 | 266,000 | 245,000 |
| FEDERAL FUNDS | 3,252,000 | 2,589,000 | 3,175,000 | 4,130,000 | 4,436,000 | 1,276,652 | 3,467,772 | 3,863,916 |
| ICF/MR Funds | 18,000 | 20,000 | 23,000 | 40,000 | 44,000 | 20,000 | 21,000 | 90,300 |
| Small Public | 0 | 0 | 0 | 0 | 0 | 0 | 0 | 0 |
| Small Private | 18,000 | 20,000 | 23,000 | 40,000 | 44,000 | 20,000 | 21,000 | 90,300 |
| HCBS Waiver | 0 | 0 | 0 | 0 | 0 | 244,000 | 534,000 | 808,000 |
| Model 50/200 Waiver | 0 | 0 | 0 | 0 | 0 | 0 | 0 | 0 |
| Other Title XIX Programs | 0 | 0 | 0 | 0 | 0 | 0 | 0 | 0 |
| Title XX / SSBG Funds | 3,234,000 | 2,381,000 | 3,083,000 | 4,019,000 | 4,234,000 | 902,000 | 2,698,000 | 1,351,800 |
| Other Federal Funds | 0 | 188,000 | 69,000 | 71,000 | 158,000 | 56,000 | 87,000 | 1,398,800 |
| Waiver Clients' SSI/ADC | 0 | 0 | 0 | 0 | 0 | 54,652 | 127,772 | 215,016 |

| | 1985 | 1986 | 1987 | 1988 | 1989 | 1990 | 1991 | 1992 |
|---|---|---|---|---|---|---|---|---|
| **TOTAL FUNDS** | $27,988,400 | $29,611,268 | $32,091,500 | $33,730,580 | $35,306,224 | $38,515,969 | $41,950,994 | $46,751,645 |
| **CONGREGATE 16+ BEDS** | 12,682,900 | 12,830,100 | 13,405,200 | 13,893,700 | 14,326,882 | 14,992,261 | 15,035,093 | 14,913,005 |
| INSTITUTIONAL SERVICES FUNDS | 12,682,900 | 12,830,100 | 13,405,200 | 13,893,700 | 14,326,882 | 14,992,261 | 15,035,093 | 14,913,005 |
| STATE FUNDS | 7,029,400 | 6,122,800 | 6,407,500 | 5,965,400 | 6,490,825 | 5,970,987 | 5,474,002 | 5,966,134 |
| General Funds | 6,888,600 | 6,109,300 | 6,404,300 | 5,960,400 | 6,485,073 | 5,921,162 | 5,375,833 | 5,887,060 |
| Local | 0 | 0 | 0 | 0 | 0 | 20,559 | 62,362 | 47,394 |
| Other State Funds | 140,800 | 13,500 | 3,200 | 5,000 | 5,752 | 29,266 | 35,807 | 31,680 |
| FEDERAL FUNDS | 5,653,500 | 6,707,300 | 6,997,700 | 7,928,300 | 7,836,057 | 9,021,274 | 9,561,091 | 8,946,871 |
| Federal ICF/MR | 5,607,700 | 6,668,900 | 6,930,900 | 7,901,800 | 7,808,385 | 8,999,002 | 9,550,892 | 8,929,864 |
| Title XX / SSBG Funds | 0 | 0 | 0 | 0 | 0 | 0 | 0 | 0 |
| Other Federal Funds | 45,800 | 38,400 | 66,800 | 26,500 | 27,672 | 22,272 | 10,199 | 17,007 |
| LARGE PRIVATE RESIDENTIAL | 0 | 0 | 0 | 0 | 0 | 0 | 0 | 0 |
| STATE FUNDS | 0 | 0 | 0 | 0 | 0 | 0 | 0 | 0 |
| General Funds | 0 | 0 | 0 | 0 | 0 | 0 | 0 | 0 |
| Other State Funds | 0 | 0 | 0 | 0 | 0 | 0 | 0 | 0 |
| Local/County Overmatch | 0 | 0 | 0 | 0 | 0 | 0 | 0 | 0 |
| FEDERAL FUNDS | 0 | 0 | 0 | 0 | 0 | 0 | 0 | 0 |
| Large Private ICF/MR | 0 | 0 | 0 | 0 | 0 | 0 | 0 | 0 |
| **COMMUNITY SERVICES FUNDS** | 15,305,500 | 16,781,168 | 18,686,300 | 19,836,880 | 20,979,342 | 23,523,708 | 26,915,901 | 31,838,640 |
| STATE FUNDS | 10,990,000 | 3,522,600 | 5,722,900 | 5,723,600 | 6,027,173 | 8,609,061 | 9,916,579 | 11,950,951 |
| General Funds | 10,731,000 | 3,249,800 | 5,174,000 | 5,226,600 | 5,237,873 | 7,754,061 | 9,001,625 | 11,040,451 |
| Other State Funds | 0 | 10,800 | 12,900 | 0 | 0 | 0 | 0 | 0 |
| Local/County Overmatch | 0 | 0 | 0 | 0 | 0 | 0 | 0 | 0 |
| SSI State Supplement | 259,000 | 262,000 | 536,000 | 497,000 | 789,300 | 855,000 | 914,954 | 910,500 |
| FEDERAL FUNDS | 4,315,500 | 13,258,568 | 12,963,400 | 14,113,280 | 14,952,169 | 14,914,647 | 16,999,322 | 19,887,689 |
| ICF/MR Funds | 86,500 | 93,200 | 103,700 | 108,500 | 151,590 | 170,786 | 217,801 | 233,582 |
| Small Public | 0 | 0 | 0 | 0 | 0 | 0 | 0 | 0 |
| Small Private | 86,500 | 93,200 | 103,700 | 108,500 | 151,590 | 170,786 | 217,801 | 233,582 |
| HCBS Waiver | 980,700 | 2,268,000 | 2,415,700 | 3,024,500 | 3,344,644 | 3,726,206 | 5,233,788 | 7,064,410 |
| Model 50/200 Waiver | 0 | 0 | 0 | 0 | 0 | 0 | 0 | 0 |
| Other Title XIX Programs | 0 | 0 | 0 | 0 | 0 | 0 | 0 | 0 |
| Title XX / SSBG Funds | 1,348,800 | 10,186,000 | 9,602,200 | 9,496,200 | 9,760,012 | 9,136,839 | 9,243,732 | 8,909,035 |
| Other Federal Funds | 1,629,500 | 62,000 | 48,000 | 376,000 | 415,283 | 491,216 | 496,921 | 1,356,286 |
| Waiver Clients' SSI/ADC | 270,000 | 649,368 | 793,800 | 1,108,080 | 1,280,640 | 1,389,600 | 1,807,080 | 2,324,376 |

*Source:*

Institute on Disability and Human Development (UAP),
University of Illinois at Chicago, 1994

# NEBRASKA

## MR/DD Spending for Congregate Residential & Community Services

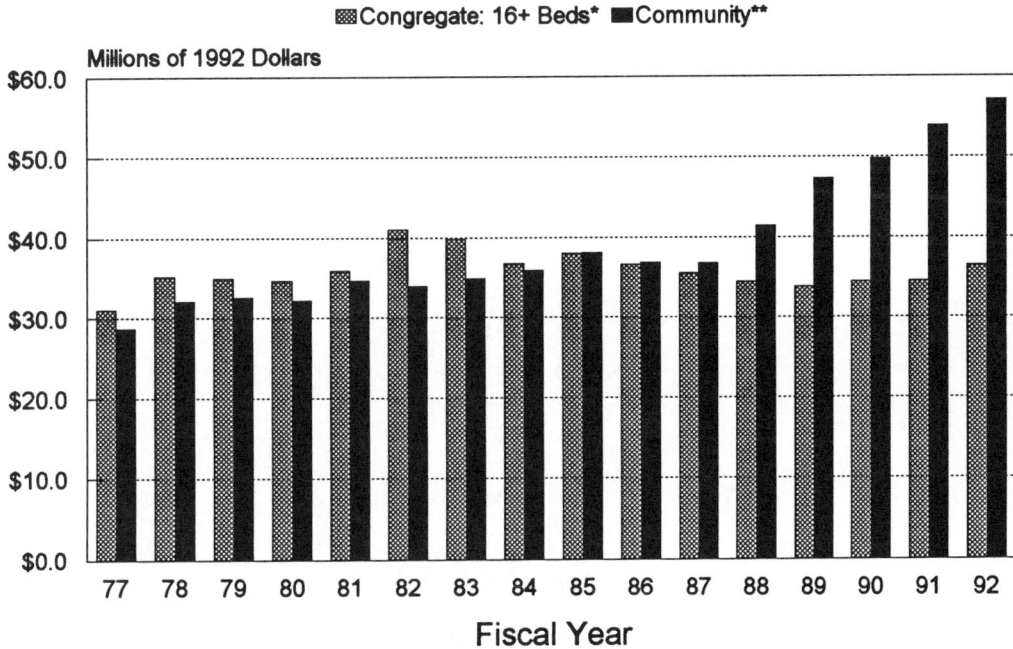

▨ Congregate: 16+ Beds*  ■ Community**

Millions of 1992 Dollars

### Fiscal Year

*Excludes nursing homes; ** Includes resources for
15 bed or less residential settings & non-residential community services

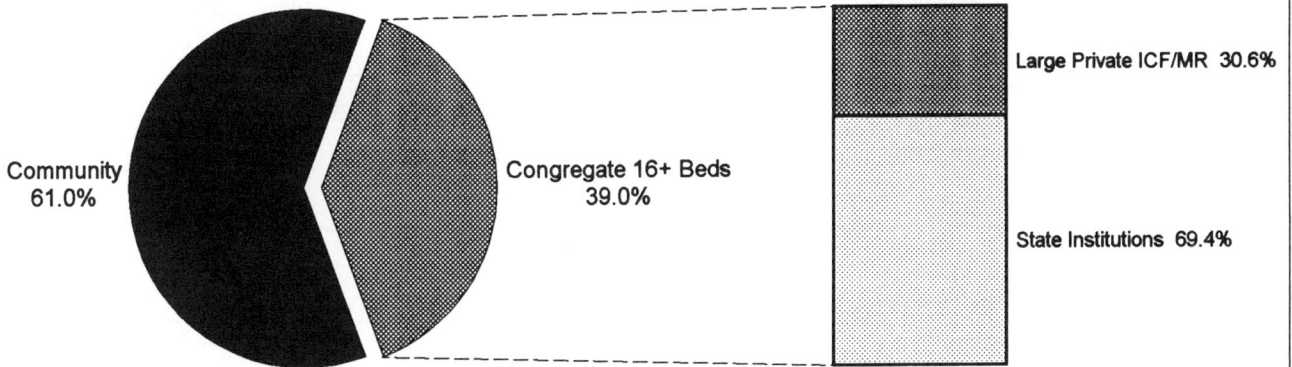

Community
61.0%

Congregate 16+ Beds
39.0%

Large Private ICF/MR 30.6%

State Institutions 69.4%

FY 1992 Total Spending:
$93.7 Million

*Source:*
Institute on Disability and Human Development (UAP),
University of Illinois at Chicago, 1994

# NEBRASKA

## Number of Persons Served by Residential Setting: FY 1992

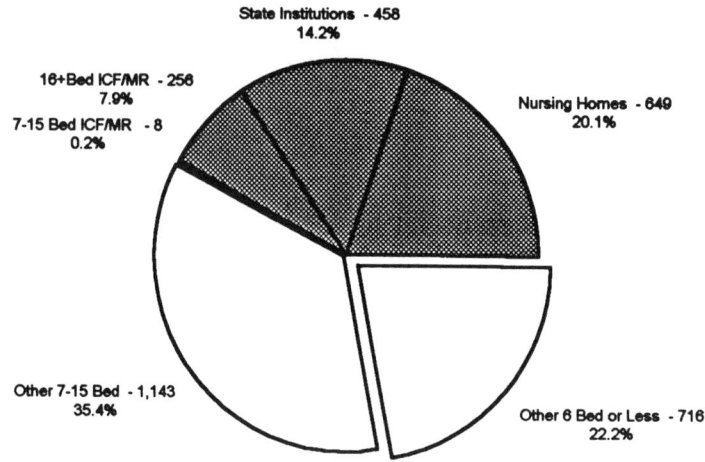

State Institutions - 458
14.2%

16+Bed ICF/MR - 256
7.9%

7-15 Bed ICF/MR - 8
0.2%

Nursing Homes - 649
20.1%

Other 7-15 Bed - 1,143
35.4%

Other 6 Bed or Less - 716
22.2%

Total Served: 3,230

## Persons Served by Residential Setting:1986-92

|  | 1986 | 1987 | 1988 | 1989 | 1990 | 1991 | 1992 |
|---|---|---|---|---|---|---|---|
| CONGREGATE 16 + BED SETTINGS | NA | NA | 1,159 | NA | NA | 1,185 | 1,363 |
| Nursing Homes | NA | NA | 387 | NA | NA | 461 | 649 |
| State Institutions | 459 | 468 | 470 | 467 | 466 | 466 | 458 |
| Private 16+Bed ICF/MR | 397 | 390 | 302 | 273 | 243 | 258 | 256 |
| Other 16+Bed Residential | 0 | 0 | 0 | 0 | 0 | 0 | 0 |
| 15 BED OR LESS RESIDENTIAL SETTINGS | 1,073 | 1,218 | 1,392 | 1,655 | 1,782 | 1,856 | 1,867 |
| Public 7-15 Bed ICF/MR | 0 | 0 | 0 | 0 | 0 | 0 | 0 |
| Private 7-15 Bed ICF/MR | 0 | 0 | 0 | 8 | 8 | 8 | 8 |
| Other 7-15 Bed Residential | 871 | 769 | 861 | 1,042 | 1,079 | 1,134 | 1,143 |
| Public 6 Bed or Less ICF/MR | 0 | 0 | 0 | 0 | 0 | 0 | 0 |
| Private 6 Bed or Less ICF/MR | 0 | 0 | 4 | 0 | 0 | 0 | 0 |
| Other 6 Bed or Less Residential | 202 | 449 | 527 | 605 | 695 | 714 | 716 |
| TOTAL PERSONS SERVED | NA | NA | 2,551 | NA | NA | 3,041 | 3,230 |

## Persons Served in Non-Residential Community Services:1986-92

|  | 1986 | 1987 | 1988 | 1989 | 1990 | 1991 | 1992 |
|---|---|---|---|---|---|---|---|
| DAY/WORK PROGRAMS | 1,648 | 1,897 | 2,144 | NA | NA | NA | 2,167 |
| Sheltered Employment/Work Activity | 1,389 | 1,601 | 1,737 | 1,756 | 1,774 | 1,831 | 1,720 |
| Day Habilitation ("Day Training") | 22 | 20 | 30 | NA | NA | NA | 50 |
| Supported/Competitive Employment | 237 | 276 | 377 | 362 | 382 | 367 | 397 |
| CASE MANAGEMENT | 2,141 | 2,108 | 2,671 | 2,608 | 2,586 | 2,711 | 2,731 |
| HCBS WAIVER | 0 | 0 | 553 | 557 | 675 | 707 | 931 |
| MODEL 50/200 WAIVER | 0 | 0 | 0 | 0 | 0 | 0 | 0 |

*Source:*
Institute on Disability and Human Development (UAP),
University of Illinois at Chicago, 1994

# NEBRASKA

## Community Services: FY 1992 Revenue Sources

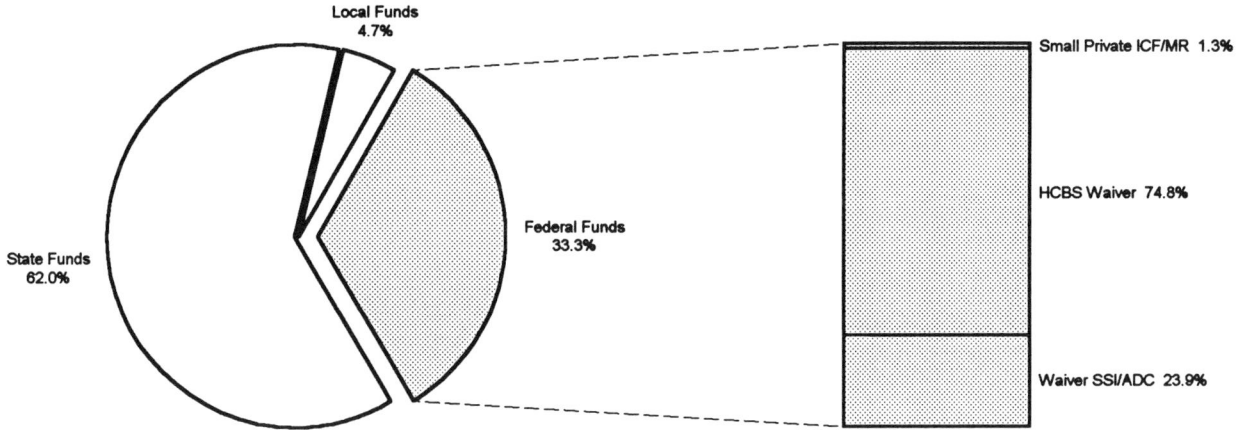

Local Funds
4.7%

Small Private ICF/MR 1.3%

HCBS Waiver 74.8%

State Funds
62.0%

Federal Funds
33.3%

Waiver SSI/ADC 23.9%

Total Funds: $57.1 Million

## Family Support Initiatives*

|  | 1986 | 1987 | 1988 | 1989 | 1990 | 1991 | 1992 |
|---|---|---|---|---|---|---|---|
| FAMILY SUPPORT: TOTAL SPENDING | $0 | $0 | $0 | $0 | $0 | $0 | $0 |
| Total # of Families Supported | 0 | 0 | 0 | 0 | 0 | 0 | 0 |
| A. Financial Subsidy/Payment |  |  |  |  |  |  |  |
| # of Families |  |  |  |  |  |  |  |
| B. Family Assistance Payments |  |  |  |  |  |  |  |
| # of Families |  |  |  |  |  |  |  |
| C. Other Family Support Payments |  |  |  |  |  |  |  |
| # of Families |  |  |  |  |  |  |  |

## Other Community Services Initiatives*

|  | 1986 | 1987 | 1988 | 1989 | 1990 | 1991 | 1992 |
|---|---|---|---|---|---|---|---|
| AGING/DD SPENDING |  |  |  | $0 | $0 | $0 | $0 |
| # of Persons Served |  |  |  | 0 | 0 | 0 | 0 |
| ASSISTIVE TECHNOLOGY SPENDING |  |  |  |  |  |  | $0 |
| # of Persons Served |  |  |  |  |  |  | 0 |
| EARLY INTERVENTION SPENDING |  |  |  | $0 | $0 | $0 | $0 |
| # of Persons Served |  |  |  | 0 | 0 | 0 | 0 |
| PERSONAL ASSISTANCE SPENDING |  |  |  |  |  |  | $0 |
| # of Persons Served |  |  |  |  |  |  | 0 |
| SUPPORTED EMPLOYMENT SPENDING | NA | NA | NA | NA | NA | NA | NA |
| # of Persons Served | 237 | 276 | 377 | 362 | 382 | 367 | 397 |
| SUPPORTED LIVING SPENDING | NA | NA | NA | NA | NA | $3,866,542 | $3,967,394 |
| # of Persons Served | 202 | 449 | 527 | 605 | 695 | 713 | 714 |

*Expenditures associated with Special Community Initiatives are a subset of funding within the community services component of the state's chart series and spreadsheet; Family Support Client figures may include duplicate client counts; HCBS Waiver counts include Waiver case management numbers.
0= Services not provided in the state; NA= Data not available from state; blank= Services not applicable (eg. CSLA prior to authorization, Special Community Initiatives prior to request for data by this study)

*Source:*
Institute on Disability and Human Development (UAP),
University of Illinois at Chicago, 1994

# NEBRASKA

## Large Congregate Care Facilities: FY 1992 Revenue Sources*

### Private 16+Bed Settings

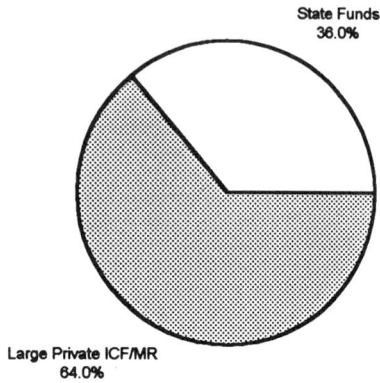

State Funds
36.0%

Large Private ICF/MR
64.0%

Total Funds: $11.2 Million

### Public Institutions

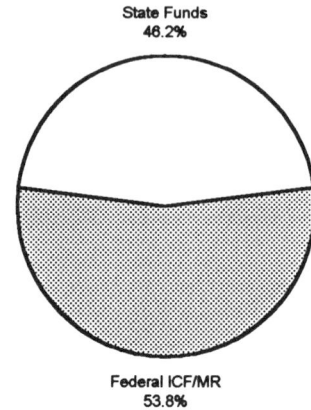

State Funds
46.2%

Federal ICF/MR
53.8%

Total Funds: $25.4 Million

*Excludes nursing homes

## Average Daily Residents in Institutions

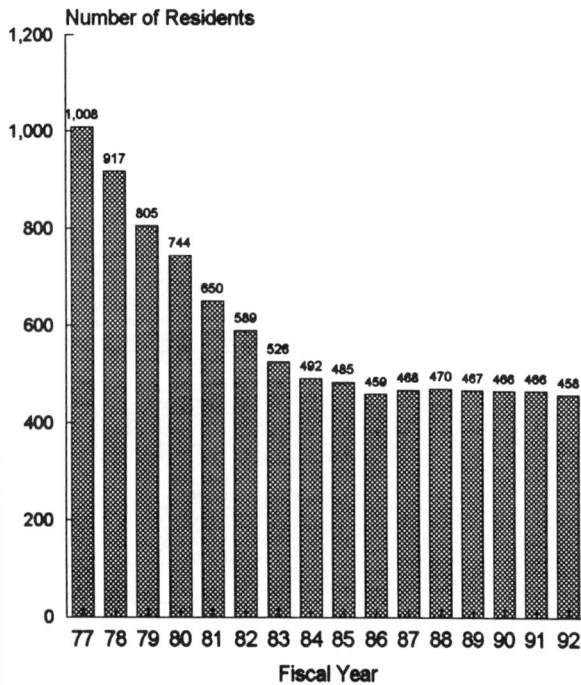

Number of Residents

| | |
|---|---|

77: 1,008
78: 917
79: 805
80: 744
81: 650
82: 589
83: 526
84: 492
85: 485
86: 459
87: 468
88: 470
89: 467
90: 466
91: 466
92: 458

Fiscal Year

## Institutional Daily Costs Per Resident

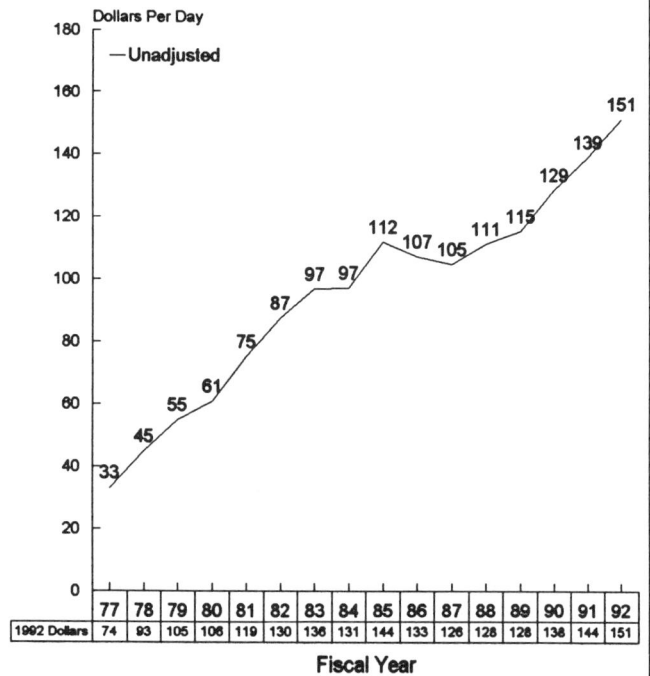

Dollars Per Day
—Unadjusted

33, 45, 55, 61, 75, 87, 97, 97, 112, 107, 105, 111, 115, 129, 139, 151

| | 77 | 78 | 79 | 80 | 81 | 82 | 83 | 84 | 85 | 86 | 87 | 88 | 89 | 90 | 91 | 92 |
|---|---|---|---|---|---|---|---|---|---|---|---|---|---|---|---|---|
| 1992 Dollars | 74 | 93 | 105 | 106 | 119 | 130 | 136 | 131 | 144 | 133 | 126 | 128 | 128 | 138 | 144 | 151 |

Fiscal Year

*Source:*
Institute on Disability and Human Development (UAP),
University of Illinois at Chicago, 1994

# NEBRASKA FISCAL EFFORT

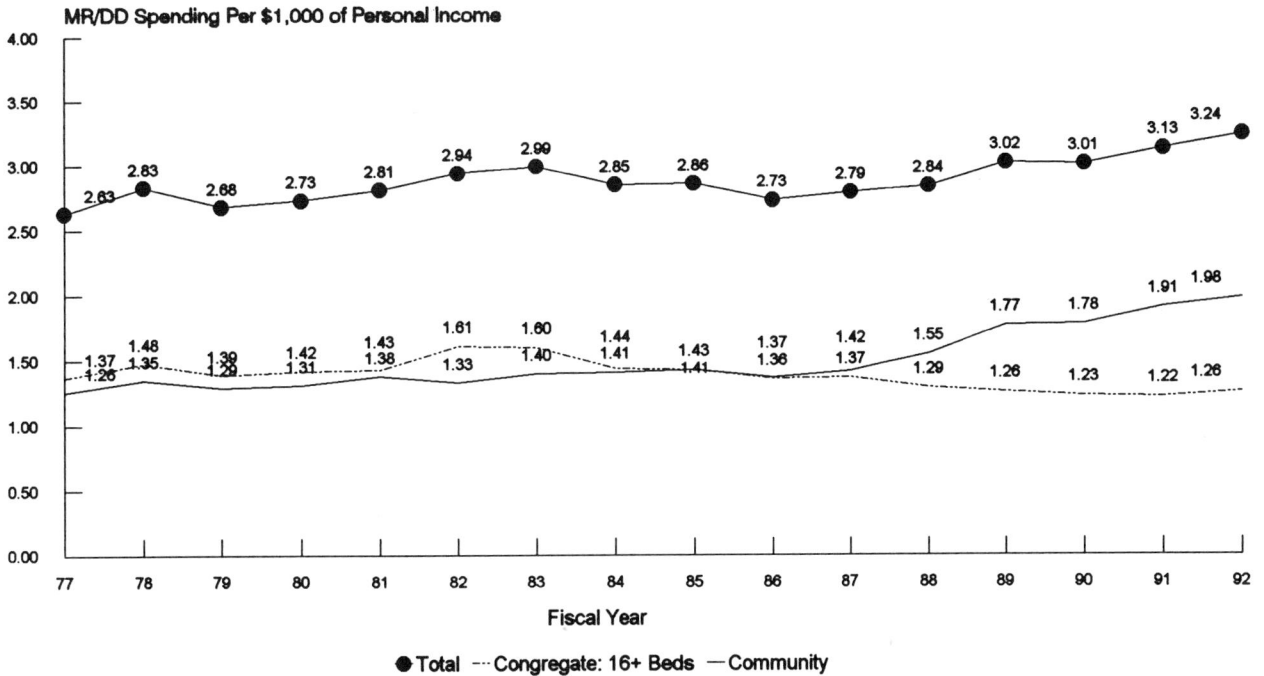

MR/DD Spending Per $1,000 of Personal Income

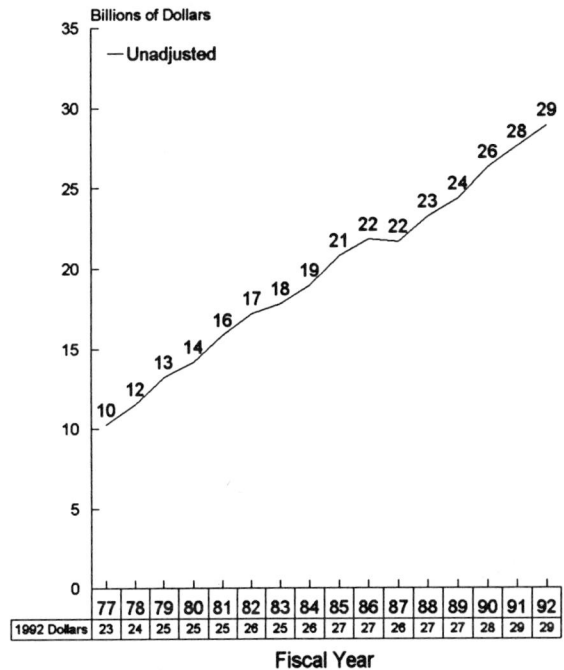

Values shown on the top chart:

Total: 2.63, 2.83, 2.68, 2.73, 2.81, 2.94, 2.99, 2.85, 2.86, 2.73, 2.79, 2.84, 3.02, 3.01, 3.13, 3.24

Congregate: 16+ Beds: 1.37, 1.35, 1.38, 1.31, 1.38, 1.33, 1.40, 1.41, 1.41, 1.36, 1.37, 1.29, 1.26, 1.23, 1.22, 1.26

Community: 1.26, 1.48, 1.29, 1.42, 1.43, 1.61, 1.60, 1.44, 1.43, 1.37, 1.42, 1.55, 1.77, 1.78, 1.91, 1.98

Fiscal Year

● Total   --- Congregate: 16+ Beds   — Community

## Total MR/DD Spending

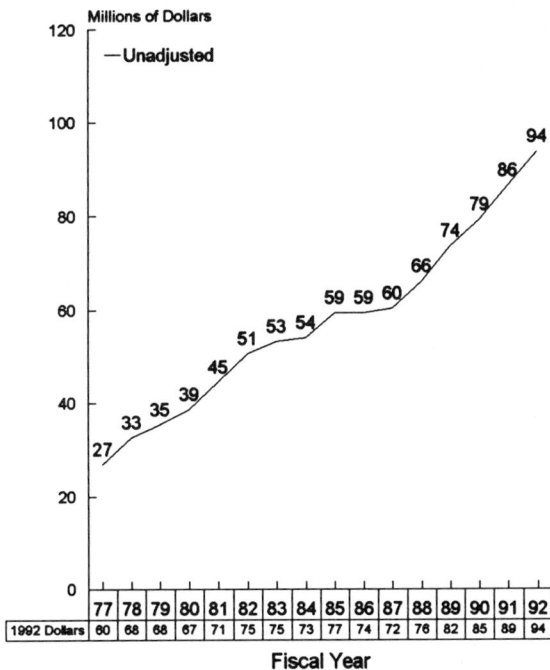

Millions of Dollars
— Unadjusted

Values: 27, 33, 35, 39, 45, 51, 53, 54, 59, 59, 60, 66, 74, 79, 86, 94

| | 77 | 78 | 79 | 80 | 81 | 82 | 83 | 84 | 85 | 86 | 87 | 88 | 89 | 90 | 91 | 92 |
|---|---|---|---|---|---|---|---|---|---|---|---|---|---|---|---|---|
| 1992 Dollars | 60 | 68 | 68 | 67 | 71 | 75 | 75 | 73 | 77 | 74 | 72 | 76 | 82 | 85 | 89 | 94 |

Fiscal Year

## Personal Income

Billions of Dollars
— Unadjusted

Values: 10, 12, 13, 14, 16, 17, 18, 19, 21, 22, 22, 23, 24, 26, 28, 29

| | 77 | 78 | 79 | 80 | 81 | 82 | 83 | 84 | 85 | 86 | 87 | 88 | 89 | 90 | 91 | 92 |
|---|---|---|---|---|---|---|---|---|---|---|---|---|---|---|---|---|
| 1992 Dollars | 23 | 24 | 25 | 25 | 25 | 26 | 25 | 26 | 27 | 27 | 26 | 27 | 27 | 28 | 29 | 29 |

Fiscal Year

*Source:*
Institute on Disability and Human Development (UAP),
University of Illinois at Chicago, 1994

# NEBRASKA

## Financial Support for MR/DD Services: FY 1977-92

| | 1977 | 1978 | 1979 | 1980 | 1981 | 1982 | 1983 | 1984 |
|---|---|---|---|---|---|---|---|---|
| **TOTAL FUNDS** | $26,894,116 | $32,609,061 | $35,371,607 | $38,643,097 | $44,519,139 | $50,611,327 | $53,251,347 | $54,049,846 |
| **CONGREGATE 16+ BEDS** | 13,986,771 | 17,072,755 | 18,323,259 | 20,054,558 | 22,658,200 | 27,708,786 | 28,403,210 | 27,331,773 |
| INSTITUTIONAL SERVICES FUNDS | 12,166,300 | 15,013,300 | 16,137,700 | 16,558,800 | 17,828,800 | 18,801,200 | 18,576,300 | 17,475,900 |
| STATE FUNDS | 7,948,300 | 10,379,300 | 11,267,700 | 8,314,800 | 9,157,800 | 8,378,200 | 8,639,300 | 9,719,500 |
| General Funds | 5,895,800 | 7,307,500 | 8,779,300 | 6,357,500 | 7,143,100 | 5,798,600 | 7,069,600 | 6,818,800 |
| Local | 0 | 0 | 0 | 0 | 0 | 0 | 0 | 0 |
| Other State Funds | 2,052,500 | 3,071,800 | 2,488,400 | 1,957,300 | 2,014,700 | 2,579,600 | 1,569,700 | 2,900,700 |
| FEDERAL FUNDS | 4,218,000 | 4,634,000 | 4,870,000 | 8,244,000 | 8,671,000 | 10,423,000 | 9,937,000 | 7,756,400 |
| Federal ICF/MR | 4,218,000 | 4,634,000 | 4,870,000 | 8,244,000 | 8,671,000 | 10,423,000 | 9,937,000 | 7,756,400 |
| Title XX / SSBG Funds | 0 | 0 | 0 | 0 | 0 | 0 | 0 | 0 |
| Other Federal Funds | 0 | 0 | 0 | 0 | 0 | 0 | 0 | 0 |
| LARGE PRIVATE RESIDENTIAL | 1,820,471 | 2,059,455 | 2,185,559 | 3,495,758 | 4,829,400 | 8,907,586 | 9,826,910 | 9,855,873 |
| STATE FUNDS | 808,471 | 947,555 | 1,017,159 | 1,517,858 | 2,046,700 | 3,741,186 | 4,115,510 | 4,200,573 |
| General Funds | 307,171 | 347,455 | 386,459 | 576,758 | 1,346,400 | 2,627,486 | 2,887,110 | 2,814,773 |
| Other State Funds | 501,300 | 600,100 | 630,700 | 941,100 | 700,300 | 1,113,700 | 1,228,400 | 1,385,800 |
| Local/County Overmatch | 0 | 0 | 0 | 0 | 0 | 0 | 0 | 0 |
| FEDERAL FUNDS | 1,012,000 | 1,111,900 | 1,168,400 | 1,977,900 | 2,782,700 | 5,166,400 | 5,711,400 | 5,655,300 |
| Large Private ICF/MR | 1,012,000 | 1,111,900 | 1,168,400 | 1,977,900 | 2,782,700 | 5,166,400 | 5,711,400 | 5,655,300 |
| **COMMUNITY SERVICES FUNDS** | 12,907,345 | 15,536,306 | 17,048,348 | 18,588,539 | 21,860,939 | 22,902,541 | 24,848,137 | 26,718,073 |
| STATE FUNDS | 7,032,345 | 9,611,306 | 11,123,348 | 12,663,539 | 15,935,939 | 17,769,541 | 19,904,137 | 21,774,073 |
| General Funds | 4,907,829 | 7,044,459 | 8,614,889 | 10,403,888 | 12,829,600 | 14,675,514 | 16,741,890 | 18,295,827 |
| Other State Funds | 0 | 0 | 0 | 0 | 0 | 0 | 0 | 0 |
| Local/County Overmatch | 1,315,516 | 1,487,847 | 1,364,459 | 1,170,651 | 1,930,339 | 1,791,027 | 1,948,247 | 2,024,246 |
| SSI State Supplement | 809,000 | 1,079,000 | 1,144,000 | 1,089,000 | 1,176,000 | 1,303,000 | 1,214,000 | 1,454,000 |
| FEDERAL FUNDS | 5,875,000 | 5,925,000 | 5,925,000 | 5,925,000 | 5,925,000 | 5,133,000 | 4,944,000 | 4,944,000 |
| ICF/MR Funds | 0 | 0 | 0 | 0 | 0 | 0 | 0 | 0 |
| Small Public | 0 | 0 | 0 | 0 | 0 | 0 | 0 | 0 |
| Small Private | 0 | 0 | 0 | 0 | 0 | 0 | 0 | 0 |
| HCBS Waiver | 0 | 0 | 0 | 0 | 0 | 0 | 0 | 0 |
| Model 50/200 Waiver | 0 | 0 | 0 | 0 | 0 | 0 | 0 | 0 |
| Other Title XIX Programs | 0 | 0 | 0 | 0 | 0 | 0 | 0 | 0 |
| Title XX / SSBG Funds | 5,875,000 | 5,925,000 | 5,925,000 | 5,925,000 | 5,925,000 | 5,133,000 | 4,944,000 | 4,944,000 |
| Other Federal Funds | 0 | 0 | 0 | 0 | 0 | 0 | 0 | 0 |
| Waiver Clients' SSI/ADC | 0 | 0 | 0 | 0 | 0 | 0 | 0 | 0 |

| | 1985 | 1986 | 1987 | 1988 | 1989 | 1990 | 1991 | 1992 |
|---|---|---|---|---|---|---|---|---|
| **TOTAL FUNDS** | $59,408,311 | $59,470,156 | $60,409,855 | $66,052,198 | $73,622,844 | $79,222,872 | $86,459,515 | $93,660,154 |
| **CONGREGATE 16+ BEDS** | 29,672,670 | 29,617,480 | 29,693,696 | 29,967,131 | 30,638,353 | 32,371,946 | 33,770,177 | 36,526,479 |
| INSTITUTIONAL SERVICES FUNDS | 19,807,100 | 17,946,400 | 17,889,300 | 19,129,400 | 19,644,939 | 21,883,779 | 23,642,510 | 25,355,411 |
| STATE FUNDS | 11,846,300 | 9,836,700 | 10,158,800 | 8,360,600 | 9,535,658 | 11,338,625 | 11,653,303 | 11,716,153 |
| General Funds | 8,373,600 | 7,722,500 | 8,135,800 | 6,333,500 | 6,680,755 | 6,761,845 | 7,252,017 | 7,655,446 |
| Local | 0 | 0 | 0 | 0 | 0 | 0 | 0 | 0 |
| Other State Funds | 3,472,700 | 2,114,200 | 2,023,000 | 2,027,100 | 2,854,903 | 4,576,780 | 4,401,286 | 4,060,707 |
| FEDERAL FUNDS | 7,960,800 | 8,109,700 | 7,730,500 | 10,768,800 | 10,109,281 | 10,545,154 | 11,989,207 | 13,639,258 |
| Federal ICF/MR | 7,960,800 | 8,109,700 | 7,730,500 | 10,768,800 | 10,109,281 | 10,545,154 | 11,989,207 | 13,639,258 |
| Title XX / SSBG Funds | 0 | 0 | 0 | 0 | 0 | 0 | 0 | 0 |
| Other Federal Funds | 0 | 0 | 0 | 0 | 0 | 0 | 0 | 0 |
| LARGE PRIVATE RESIDENTIAL | 9,865,570 | 11,671,080 | 11,804,396 | 10,837,731 | 10,993,414 | 10,488,167 | 10,127,667 | 11,171,068 |
| STATE FUNDS | 4,229,370 | 5,004,559 | 4,979,094 | 4,409,873 | 4,374,279 | 4,097,727 | 3,817,118 | 4,015,999 |
| General Funds | 3,308,870 | 4,574,659 | 4,979,094 | 4,409,873 | 4,374,279 | 4,097,727 | 3,817,118 | 4,015,999 |
| Other State Funds | 920,500 | 429,900 | 0 | 0 | 0 | 0 | 0 | 0 |
| Local/County Overmatch | 0 | 0 | 0 | 0 | 0 | 0 | 0 | 0 |
| FEDERAL FUNDS | 5,636,200 | 6,666,521 | 6,825,302 | 6,427,858 | 6,619,135 | 6,390,440 | 6,310,549 | 7,155,069 |
| Large Private ICF/MR | 5,636,200 | 6,666,521 | 6,825,302 | 6,427,858 | 6,619,135 | 6,390,440 | 6,310,549 | 7,155,069 |
| **COMMUNITY SERVICES FUNDS** | 29,735,641 | 29,852,676 | 30,716,159 | 36,085,067 | 42,984,491 | 46,850,926 | 52,689,338 | 57,133,675 |
| STATE FUNDS | 24,791,641 | 25,057,040 | 25,924,494 | 26,009,680 | 29,300,069 | 31,275,449 | 33,392,079 | 38,103,860 |
| General Funds | 21,028,930 | 21,240,469 | 22,096,626 | 22,178,515 | 25,616,168 | 27,181,624 | 28,801,034 | 33,717,447 |
| Other State Funds | 0 | 0 | 0 | 0 | 0 | 0 | 0 | 0 |
| Local/County Overmatch | 2,224,711 | 2,315,571 | 2,363,868 | 2,412,165 | 2,193,951 | 2,529,377 | 2,948,375 | 2,661,610 |
| SSI State Supplement | 1,538,000 | 1,501,000 | 1,464,000 | 1,419,000 | 1,489,950 | 1,564,448 | 1,642,670 | 1,724,803 |
| FEDERAL FUNDS | 4,944,000 | 4,795,636 | 4,791,665 | 10,075,387 | 13,684,422 | 15,575,477 | 19,297,259 | 19,029,815 |
| ICF/MR Funds | 0 | 0 | 4,007 | 32,007 | 185,131 | 220,384 | 225,794 | 250,345 |
| Small Public | 0 | 0 | 0 | 0 | 0 | 0 | 0 | 0 |
| Small Private | 0 | 0 | 4,007 | 32,007 | 185,131 | 220,384 | 225,794 | 250,345 |
| HCBS Waiver | 0 | 0 | 0 | 3,497,744 | 7,730,123 | 8,891,053 | 12,349,341 | 14,232,466 |
| Model 50/200 Waiver | 0 | 0 | 0 | 0 | 0 | 0 | 0 | 0 |
| Other Title XIX Programs | 0 | 0 | 0 | 0 | 0 | 0 | 0 | 0 |
| Title XX / SSBG Funds | 4,944,000 | 4,795,636 | 4,787,658 | 4,473,332 | 3,483,240 | 3,483,240 | 3,481,236 | 0 |
| Other Federal Funds | 0 | 0 | 0 | 0 | 0 | 0 | 0 | 0 |
| Waiver Clients' SSI/ADC | 0 | 0 | 0 | 2,072,304 | 2,285,928 | 2,980,800 | 3,240,888 | 4,547,004 |

*Source:*

Institute on Disability and Human Development (UAP),
University of Illinois at Chicago, 1994

# NEVADA

## MR/DD Spending for Congregate Residential & Community Services

▧ Congregate: 16+ Beds*  ■ Community**

Millions of 1992 Dollars

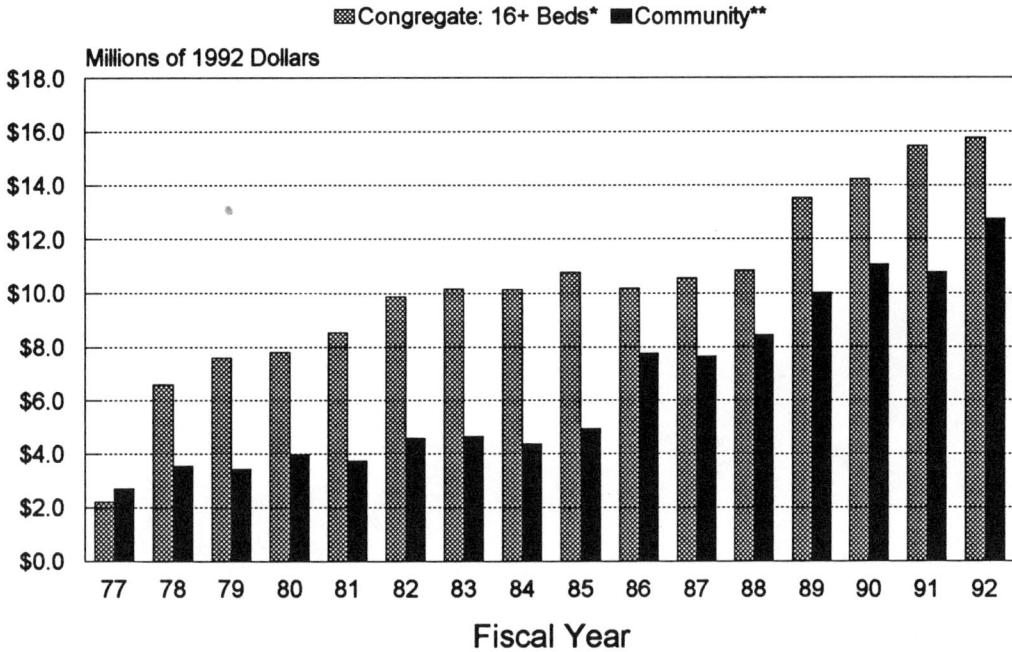

Fiscal Year

*Excludes nursing homes; ** Includes resources for
15 bed or less residential settings & non-residential community services

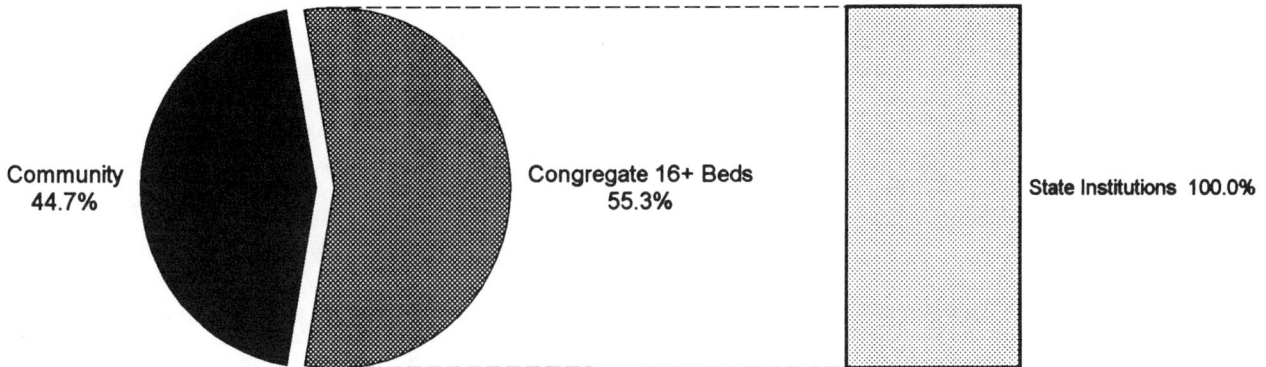

Community
44.7%

Congregate 16+ Beds
55.3%

State Institutions  100.0%

FY 1992 Total Spending:
$28.5 Million

*Source:*
Institute on Disability and Human Development (UAP),
University of Illinois at Chicago, 1994

# NEVADA

## Number of Persons Served by Residential Setting: FY 1992

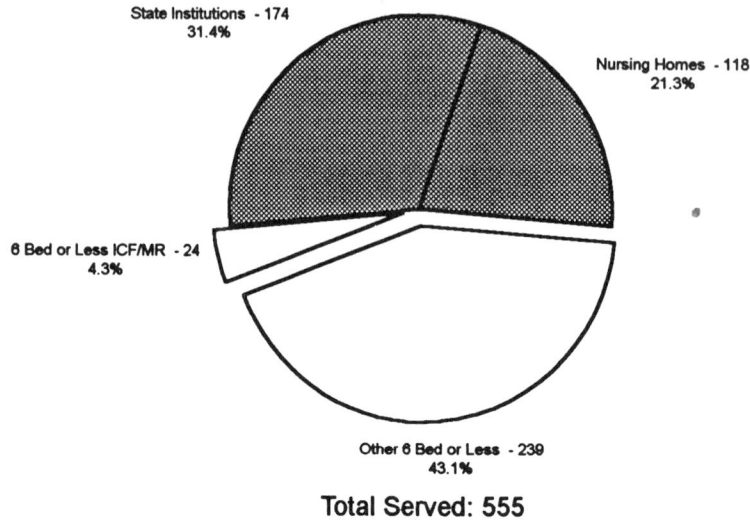

State Institutions  - 174
31.4%

Nursing Homes  - 118
21.3%

6 Bed or Less ICF/MR  - 24
4.3%

Other 6 Bed or Less  - 239
43.1%

Total Served: 555

## Persons Served by Residential Setting:1986-92

| | 1986 | 1987 | 1988 | 1989 | 1990 | 1991 | 1992 |
|---|---|---|---|---|---|---|---|
| CONGREGATE 16 + BED SETTINGS | NA | NA | 238 | 270 | 274 | 290 | 292 |
| Nursing Homes | NA | NA | 60 | 96 | 100 | 117 | 118 |
| State Institutions | 171 | 178 | 178 | 174 | 174 | 173 | 174 |
| Private 16+Bed ICF/MR | 0 | 0 | 0 | 0 | 0 | 0 | 0 |
| Other 16+Bed Residential | 0 | 0 | 0 | 0 | 0 | 0 | 0 |
| 15 BED OR LESS RESIDENTIAL SETTINGS | 15 | 244 | 265 | 254 | 283 | 274 | 263 |
| Public 7-15 Bed ICF/MR | 0 | 0 | 0 | 0 | 0 | 0 | 0 |
| Private 7-15 Bed ICF/MR | 15 | 15 | 15 | 0 | 0 | 0 | 0 |
| Other 7-15 Bed Residential | 0 | 0 | 0 | 0 | 0 | 0 | 0 |
| Public 6 Bed or Less ICF/MR | 0 | 0 | 0 | 0 | 0 | 0 | 0 |
| Private 6 Bed or Less ICF/MR | 0 | 0 | 0 | 0 | 0 | 13 | 24 |
| Other 6 Bed or Less Residential | NA | 229 | 250 | 254 | 283 | 261 | 239 |
| TOTAL PERSONS SERVED | NA | NA | 503 | 524 | 557 | 564 | 555 |

## Persons Served in Non-Residential Community Services:1986-92

| | 1986 | 1987 | 1988 | 1989 | 1990 | 1991 | 1992 |
|---|---|---|---|---|---|---|---|
| DAY/WORK PROGRAMS | 500 | 630 | 640 | 604 | 595 | 611 | 636 |
| Sheltered Employment/Work Activity | 483 | 593 | 618 | 548 | 521 | 520 | 545 |
| Day Habilitation ("Day Training") | 17 | 37 | 22 | 56 | 56 | 69 | 56 |
| Supported/Competitive Employment | 0 | 0 | 0 | 0 | 18 | 22 | 35 |
| CASE MANAGEMENT | 730 | 816 | 909 | 1,005 | 1,182 | 1,404 | 2,191 |
| HCBS WAIVER | 135 | 141 | 147 | 153 | 160 | 172 | 179 |
| MODEL 50/200 WAIVER | 0 | 0 | 0 | 0 | 0 | 0 | 0 |

*Source:*
Institute on Disability and Human Development (UAP),
University of Illinois at Chicago, 1994

# NEVADA

## Community Services: FY 1992 Revenue Sources

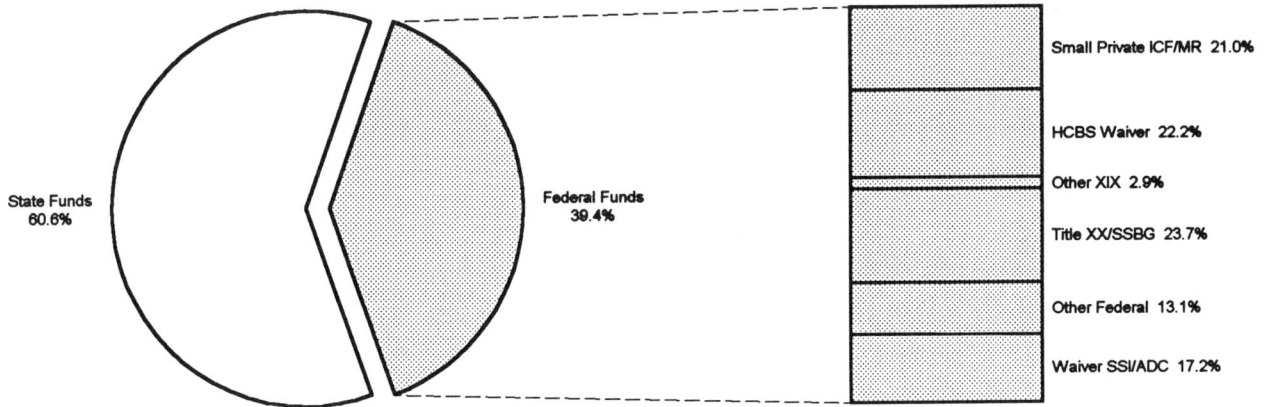

State Funds 60.6%
Federal Funds 39.4%

Small Private ICF/MR 21.0%
HCBS Waiver 22.2%
Other XIX 2.9%
Title XX/SSBG 23.7%
Other Federal 13.1%
Waiver SSI/ADC 17.2%

Total Funds: $12.8 Million

## Family Support Initiatives*

|  | 1986 | 1987 | 1988 | 1989 | 1990 | 1991 | 1992 |
|---|---|---|---|---|---|---|---|
| FAMILY SUPPORT: TOTAL SPENDING | $146,500 | $146,500 | $162,200 | $159,572 | $236,570 | $246,923 | $317,817 |
| Total # of Families Supported | 65 | 64 | 70 | 70 | 340 | 359 | 336 |
| A. Financial Subsidy/Payment | $146,500 | $146,500 | $162,200 | $159,572 | $178,478 | $188,688 | $266,740 |
| # of Families | 65 | 64 | 70 | 70 | 81 | 99 | 108 |
| B. Family Assistance Payments | $0 | $0 | $0 | $0 | $58,092 | $58,235 | $51,077 |
| # of Families | 0 | 0 | 0 | 0 | 259 | 260 | 228 |
| C. Other Family Support Payments | $0 | $0 | $0 | $0 | $0 | $0 | $0 |
| # of Families | 0 | 0 | 0 | 0 | 0 | 0 | 0 |

## Other Community Services Initiatives*

|  | 1986 | 1987 | 1988 | 1989 | 1990 | 1991 | 1992 |
|---|---|---|---|---|---|---|---|
| AGING/DD SPENDING | $0 | $0 | $0 | $0 | $0 | $0 | $0 |
| # of Persons Served | 0 | 0 | 0 | 0 | 0 | 0 | 0 |
| ASSISTIVE TECHNOLOGY SPENDING |  |  |  |  |  | $421,681 | $680,081 |
| # of Persons Served |  |  |  |  |  | 3,500 | 5,600 |
| EARLY INTERVENTION SPENDING | $788,000 | $1,199,900 | $1,258,600 | $907,035 | $1,083,227 | $877,993 | $978,531 |
| # of Persons Served | 131 | 238 | 222 | 329 | 290 | 239 | 253 |
| PERSONAL ASSISTANCE SPENDING |  |  |  |  |  |  | $0 |
| # of Persons Served |  |  |  |  |  |  | 0 |
| SUPPORTED EMPLOYMENT SPENDING | $0 | $0 | $0 | $0 | $35,230 | $63,635 | $76,292 |
| # of Persons Served | 0 | 0 | 0 | 0 | 18 | 22 | 35 |
| SUPPORTED LIVING SPENDING |  |  |  | $12,385 | $94,347 | $377,785 | $967,019 |
| # of Persons Served |  |  |  | 39 | 56 | 81 | 128 |

*Expenditures associated with Special Community Initiatives are a subset of funding within the community services component of the state's chart series and spreadsheet; Family Support Client figures may include duplicate client counts; HCBS Waiver counts include Waiver case management numbers.
0= Services not provided in the state; NA= Data not available from state; blank= Services not applicable (eg. CSLA prior to authorization, Special Community Initiatives prior to request for data by this study)

*Source:*
Institute on Disability and Human Development (UAP),
University of Illinois at Chicago, 1994

# NEVADA

## Large Congregate Care Facilities: FY 1992 Revenue Sources*

### Private 16+Bed Settings

### Public Institutions

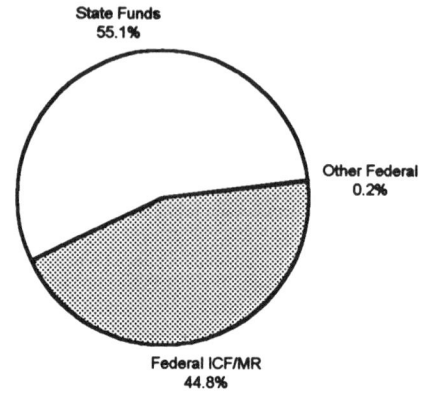

**Does Not Apply**

State Funds
55.1%

Other Federal
0.2%

Federal ICF/MR
44.8%

Total Funds: $15.8 Million

*Excludes nursing homes

## Average Daily Residents in Institutions

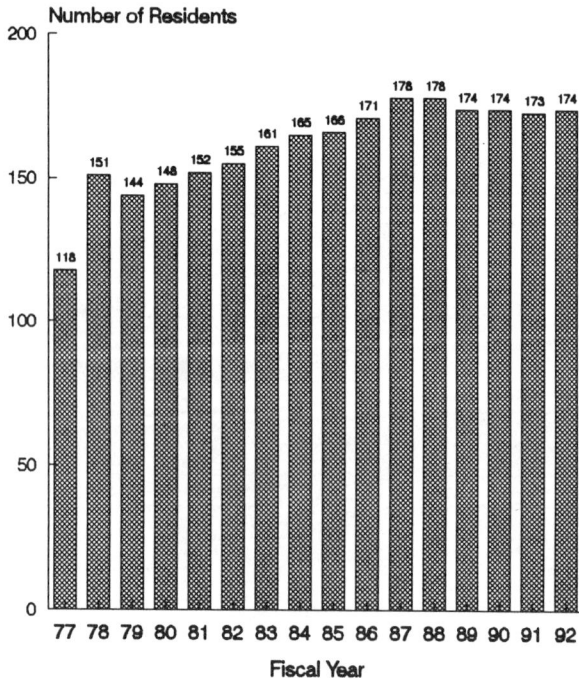

Number of Residents

| | |
|---|---|
| 77 | 118 |
| 78 | 151 |
| 79 | 144 |
| 80 | 148 |
| 81 | 152 |
| 82 | 155 |
| 83 | 161 |
| 84 | 165 |
| 85 | 166 |
| 86 | 171 |
| 87 | 178 |
| 88 | 178 |
| 89 | 174 |
| 90 | 174 |
| 91 | 173 |
| 92 | 174 |

Fiscal Year

## Institutional Daily Costs Per Resident

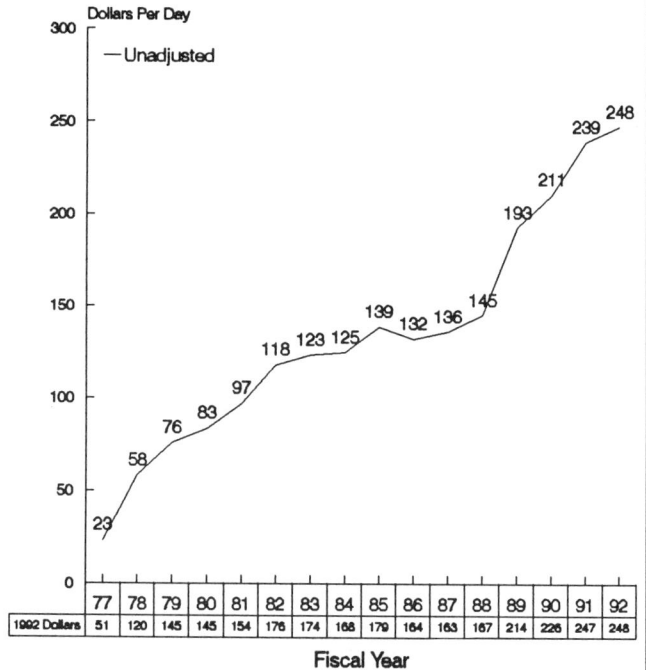

Dollars Per Day

— Unadjusted

23, 58, 76, 83, 97, 118, 123, 125, 139, 132, 136, 145, 193, 211, 239, 248

| | 77 | 78 | 79 | 80 | 81 | 82 | 83 | 84 | 85 | 86 | 87 | 88 | 89 | 90 | 91 | 92 |
|---|---|---|---|---|---|---|---|---|---|---|---|---|---|---|---|---|
| 1992 Dollars | 51 | 120 | 145 | 145 | 154 | 176 | 174 | 168 | 179 | 164 | 163 | 167 | 214 | 226 | 247 | 248 |

Fiscal Year

*Source:*
Institute on Disability and Human Development (UAP),
University of Illinois at Chicago, 1994

# NEVADA FISCAL EFFORT

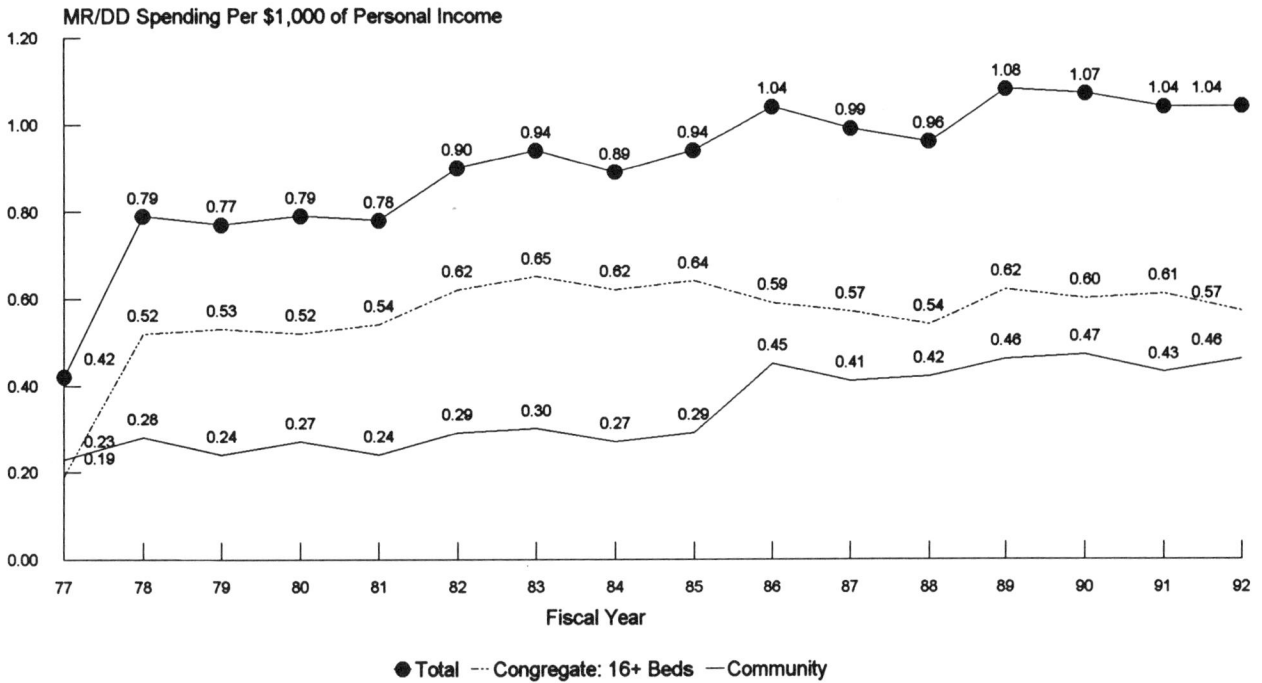

MR/DD Spending Per $1,000 of Personal Income

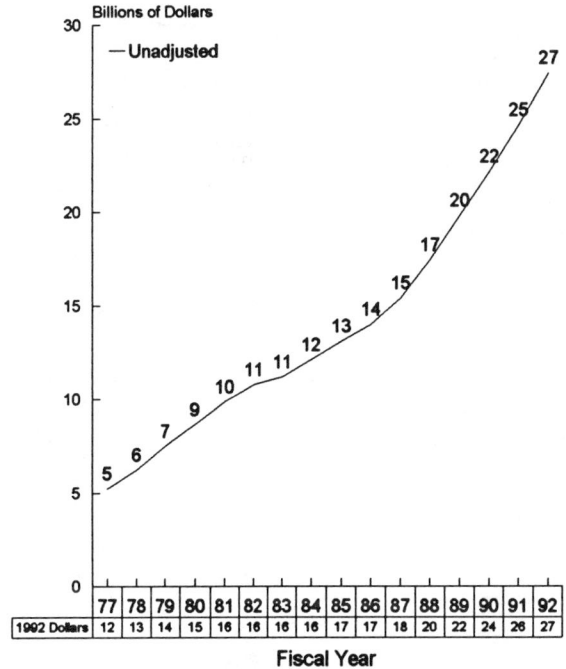

Total: 0.42, 0.79, 0.77, 0.79, 0.78, 0.90, 0.94, 0.89, 0.94, 1.04, 0.99, 0.96, 1.08, 1.07, 1.04, 1.04

Congregate: 16+ Beds: 0.23, 0.52, 0.53, 0.52, 0.54, 0.62, 0.65, 0.62, 0.64, 0.59, 0.57, 0.54, 0.62, 0.60, 0.61, 0.57

Community: 0.19, 0.28, 0.24, 0.27, 0.24, 0.29, 0.30, 0.27, 0.29, 0.45, 0.41, 0.42, 0.46, 0.47, 0.43, 0.46

Fiscal Year: 77, 78, 79, 80, 81, 82, 83, 84, 85, 86, 87, 88, 89, 90, 91, 92

● Total --- Congregate: 16+ Beds — Community

## Total MR/DD Spending

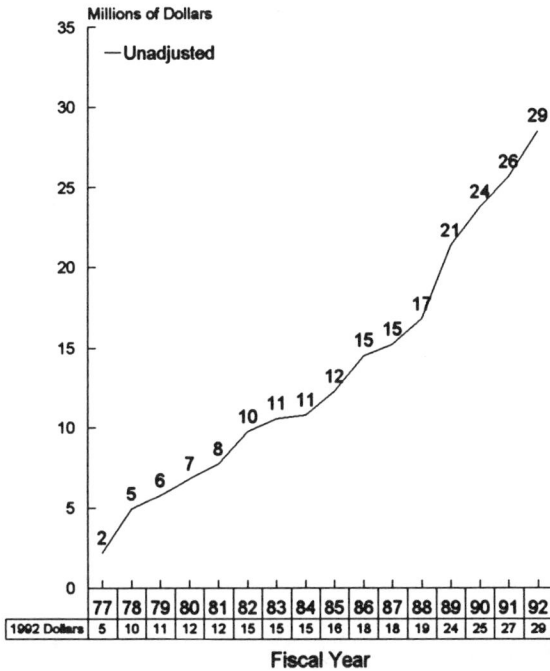

Millions of Dollars

— Unadjusted

Values: 2, 5, 6, 7, 8, 10, 11, 11, 12, 15, 15, 17, 21, 24, 26, 29

| | 77 | 78 | 79 | 80 | 81 | 82 | 83 | 84 | 85 | 86 | 87 | 88 | 89 | 90 | 91 | 92 |
|---|---|---|---|---|---|---|---|---|---|---|---|---|---|---|---|---|
| 1992 Dollars | 5 | 10 | 11 | 12 | 12 | 15 | 15 | 15 | 16 | 18 | 18 | 19 | 24 | 25 | 27 | 29 |

Fiscal Year

## Personal Income

Billions of Dollars

— Unadjusted

Values: 5, 6, 7, 9, 10, 11, 11, 12, 13, 14, 15, 17, 20, 22, 25, 27

| | 77 | 78 | 79 | 80 | 81 | 82 | 83 | 84 | 85 | 86 | 87 | 88 | 89 | 90 | 91 | 92 |
|---|---|---|---|---|---|---|---|---|---|---|---|---|---|---|---|---|
| 1992 Dollars | 12 | 13 | 14 | 15 | 16 | 16 | 16 | 16 | 17 | 17 | 18 | 20 | 22 | 24 | 26 | 27 |

Fiscal Year

*Source:*
Institute on Disability and Human Development (UAP),
University of Illinois at Chicago, 1994

# NEVADA
## Financial Support for MR/DD Services: FY 1977-92

| | 1977 | 1978 | 1979 | 1980 | 1981 | 1982 | 1983 | 1984 |
|---|---|---|---|---|---|---|---|---|
| **TOTAL FUNDS** | $2,206,000 | $4,930,000 | $5,773,000 | $6,826,000 | $7,745,000 | $9,763,000 | $10,576,000 | $10,787,700 |
| **CONGREGATE 16+ BEDS** | 990,000 | 3,205,000 | 3,978,000 | 4,519,000 | 5,381,000 | 6,672,000 | 7,248,000 | 7,526,100 |
| INSTITUTIONAL SERVICES FUNDS | 990,000 | 3,205,000 | 3,978,000 | 4,519,000 | 5,381,000 | 6,672,000 | 7,248,000 | 7,526,100 |
| STATE FUNDS | 925,000 | 2,659,000 | 2,846,000 | 2,708,000 | 3,129,000 | 3,330,000 | 3,915,000 | 3,873,500 |
| General Funds | 890,000 | 2,128,000 | 1,731,000 | 897,000 | 910,000 | 9,000 | 627,000 | 571,800 |
| Local | 0 | 0 | 0 | 0 | 0 | 0 | 0 | 0 |
| Other State Funds | 35,000 | 531,000 | 1,115,000 | 1,811,000 | 2,219,000 | 3,321,000 | 3,288,000 | 3,301,700 |
| FEDERAL FUNDS | 65,000 | 546,000 | 1,132,000 | 1,811,000 | 2,252,000 | 3,342,000 | 3,333,000 | 3,652,600 |
| Federal ICF/MR | 35,000 | 531,000 | 1,115,000 | 1,811,000 | 2,219,000 | 3,321,000 | 3,288,000 | 3,634,800 |
| Title XX / SSBG Funds | 0 | 0 | 0 | 0 | 0 | 0 | 0 | 0 |
| Other Federal Funds | 30,000 | 15,000 | 17,000 | 0 | 33,000 | 21,000 | 45,000 | 17,800 |
| LARGE PRIVATE RESIDENTIAL | 0 | 0 | 0 | 0 | 0 | 0 | 0 | 0 |
| STATE FUNDS | 0 | 0 | 0 | 0 | 0 | 0 | 0 | 0 |
| General Funds | 0 | 0 | 0 | 0 | 0 | 0 | 0 | 0 |
| Other State Funds | 0 | 0 | 0 | 0 | 0 | 0 | 0 | 0 |
| Local/County Overmatch | 0 | 0 | 0 | 0 | 0 | 0 | 0 | 0 |
| FEDERAL FUNDS | 0 | 0 | 0 | 0 | 0 | 0 | 0 | 0 |
| Large Private ICF/MR | 0 | 0 | 0 | 0 | 0 | 0 | 0 | 0 |
| **COMMUNITY SERVICES FUNDS** | 1,216,000 | 1,725,000 | 1,795,000 | 2,307,000 | 2,364,000 | 3,091,000 | 3,328,000 | 3,261,600 |
| STATE FUNDS | 781,000 | 947,000 | 969,000 | 1,168,000 | 1,569,000 | 1,720,000 | 2,107,000 | 2,106,400 |
| General Funds | 537,000 | 572,000 | 625,000 | 737,000 | 1,025,000 | 1,051,000 | 1,195,000 | 1,268,700 |
| Other State Funds | 244,000 | 375,000 | 344,000 | 431,000 | 544,000 | 669,000 | 912,000 | 837,700 |
| Local/County Overmatch | 0 | 0 | 0 | 0 | 0 | 0 | 0 | 0 |
| SSI State Supplement | 0 | 0 | 0 | 0 | 0 | 0 | 0 | 0 |
| FEDERAL FUNDS | 435,000 | 778,000 | 826,000 | 1,139,000 | 795,000 | 1,371,000 | 1,221,000 | 1,155,200 |
| ICF/MR Funds | 100,000 | 125,000 | 150,000 | 175,000 | 200,000 | 216,000 | 228,000 | 246,100 |
| Small Public | 0 | 0 | 0 | 0 | 0 | 0 | 0 | 0 |
| Small Private | 100,000 | 125,000 | 150,000 | 175,000 | 200,000 | 216,000 | 228,000 | 246,100 |
| HCBS Waiver | 0 | 0 | 0 | 0 | 0 | 0 | 181,000 | 431,700 |
| Model 50/200 Waiver | 0 | 0 | 0 | 0 | 0 | 0 | 0 | 0 |
| Other Title XIX Programs | 0 | 0 | 0 | 0 | 0 | 0 | 0 | 0 |
| Title XX / SSBG Funds | 69,000 | 455,000 | 410,000 | 614,000 | 460,000 | 999,000 | 654,000 | 327,700 |
| Other Federal Funds | 266,000 | 198,000 | 266,000 | 350,000 | 135,000 | 156,000 | 158,000 | 149,700 |
| Waiver Clients' SSI/ADC | 0 | 0 | 0 | 0 | 0 | 0 | 0 | 0 |

| | 1985 | 1986 | 1987 | 1988 | 1989 | 1990 | 1991 | 1992 |
|---|---|---|---|---|---|---|---|---|
| **TOTAL FUNDS** | $12,254,200 | $14,521,320 | $15,216,880 | $16,793,773 | $21,361,626 | $23,797,537 | $25,668,623 | $28,513,738 |
| **CONGREGATE 16+ BEDS** | 8,402,400 | 8,250,600 | 8,838,100 | 9,447,500 | 12,267,466 | 13,391,705 | 15,116,033 | 15,761,873 |
| INSTITUTIONAL SERVICES FUNDS | 8,402,400 | 8,250,600 | 8,838,100 | 9,447,500 | 12,267,466 | 13,391,705 | 15,116,033 | 15,761,873 |
| STATE FUNDS | 4,536,600 | 4,371,300 | 4,849,000 | 4,876,000 | 6,660,978 | 7,368,198 | 8,226,293 | 8,680,702 |
| General Funds | 529,200 | 430,900 | 852,600 | 332,100 | 862,550 | 973,642 | 1,030,146 | 1,218,774 |
| Local | 0 | 0 | 0 | 0 | 0 | 0 | 0 | 0 |
| Other State Funds | 4,007,400 | 3,940,400 | 3,996,400 | 4,543,900 | 5,798,428 | 6,394,556 | 7,196,147 | 7,461,928 |
| FEDERAL FUNDS | 3,865,800 | 3,879,300 | 3,989,100 | 4,571,500 | 5,606,488 | 6,023,507 | 6,889,740 | 7,081,171 |
| Federal ICF/MR | 3,841,800 | 3,842,000 | 3,960,300 | 4,543,900 | 5,580,007 | 5,998,404 | 6,864,870 | 7,054,680 |
| Title XX / SSBG Funds | 0 | 0 | 0 | 0 | 0 | 0 | 0 | 0 |
| Other Federal Funds | 24,000 | 37,300 | 28,800 | 27,600 | 26,481 | 25,103 | 24,870 | 26,491 |
| LARGE PRIVATE RESIDENTIAL | 0 | 0 | 0 | 0 | 0 | 0 | 0 | 0 |
| STATE FUNDS | 0 | 0 | 0 | 0 | 0 | 0 | 0 | 0 |
| General Funds | 0 | 0 | 0 | 0 | 0 | 0 | 0 | 0 |
| Other State Funds | 0 | 0 | 0 | 0 | 0 | 0 | 0 | 0 |
| Local/County Overmatch | 0 | 0 | 0 | 0 | 0 | 0 | 0 | 0 |
| FEDERAL FUNDS | 0 | 0 | 0 | 0 | 0 | 0 | 0 | 0 |
| Large Private ICF/MR | 0 | 0 | 0 | 0 | 0 | 0 | 0 | 0 |
| **COMMUNITY SERVICES FUNDS** | 3,851,800 | 6,270,720 | 6,378,780 | 7,346,273 | 9,094,160 | 10,405,832 | 10,552,590 | 12,751,865 |
| STATE FUNDS | 2,491,200 | 3,933,400 | 3,923,400 | 4,690,000 | 5,611,814 | 6,510,730 | 6,623,412 | 7,729,364 |
| General Funds | 1,459,700 | 2,845,600 | 3,103,600 | 3,967,700 | 4,002,787 | 4,877,425 | 4,896,536 | 5,936,654 |
| Other State Funds | 1,031,500 | 1,087,800 | 819,800 | 722,300 | 1,609,027 | 1,633,305 | 1,726,876 | 1,792,710 |
| Local/County Overmatch | 0 | 0 | 0 | 0 | 0 | 0 | 0 | 0 |
| SSI State Supplement | 0 | 0 | 0 | 0 | 0 | 0 | 0 | 0 |
| FEDERAL FUNDS | 1,360,600 | 2,337,320 | 2,455,380 | 2,656,273 | 3,482,346 | 3,895,102 | 3,929,178 | 5,022,501 |
| ICF/MR Funds | 367,000 | 396,900 | 396,900 | 399,537 | 396,234 | 467,171 | 503,091 | 1,054,703 |
| Small Public | 0 | 0 | 0 | 0 | 0 | 0 | 0 | 0 |
| Small Private | 367,000 | 396,900 | 396,900 | 399,537 | 396,234 | 467,171 | 503,091 | 1,054,703 |
| HCBS Waiver | 487,100 | 730,100 | 744,700 | 847,200 | 821,683 | 916,697 | 890,775 | 1,116,522 |
| Model 50/200 Waiver | 0 | 0 | 0 | 0 | 0 | 0 | 0 | 0 |
| Other Title XIX Programs | 0 | 0 | 0 | 0 | 0 | 0 | 13,295 | 144,660 |
| Title XX / SSBG Funds | 329,500 | 311,800 | 329,500 | 321,400 | 745,862 | 913,120 | 1,084,863 | 1,189,364 |
| Other Federal Funds | 177,000 | 394,700 | 451,300 | 516,600 | 855,771 | 874,274 | 619,810 | 655,712 |
| Waiver Clients' SSI/ADC | 0 | 503,820 | 532,980 | 571,536 | 662,796 | 723,840 | 817,344 | 861,540 |

*Source:*

Institute on Disability and Human Development (UAP),
University of Illinois at Chicago, 1994

# NEW HAMPSHIRE

## MR/DD Spending for Congregate Residential & Community Services

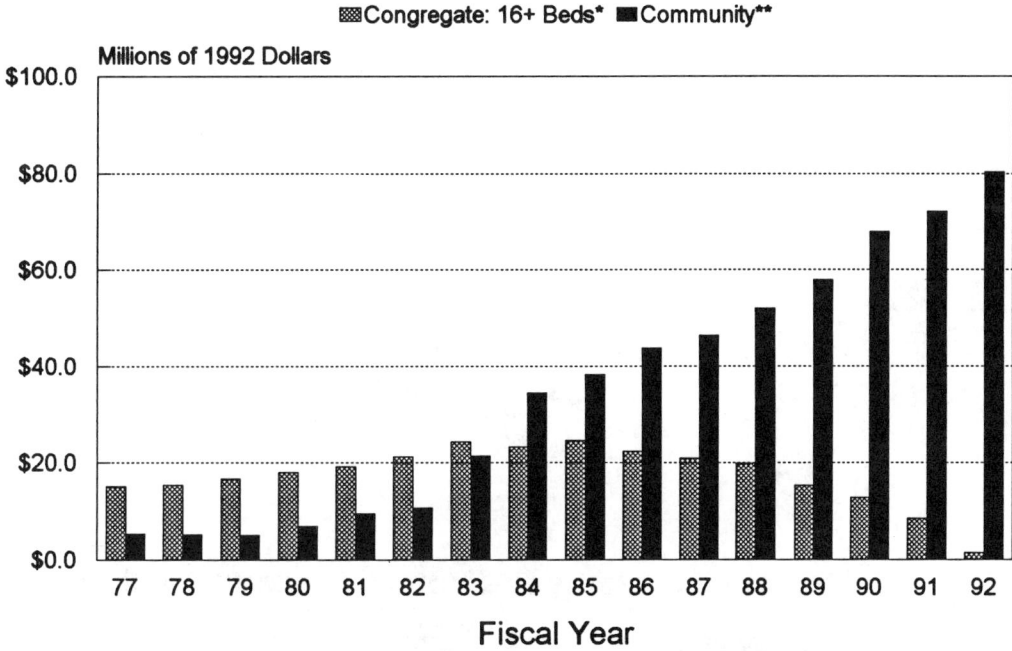

▨Congregate: 16+ Beds*  ■Community**

Millions of 1992 Dollars

### Fiscal Year
*Excludes nursing homes; ** Includes resources for
15 bed or less residential settings & non-residential community services

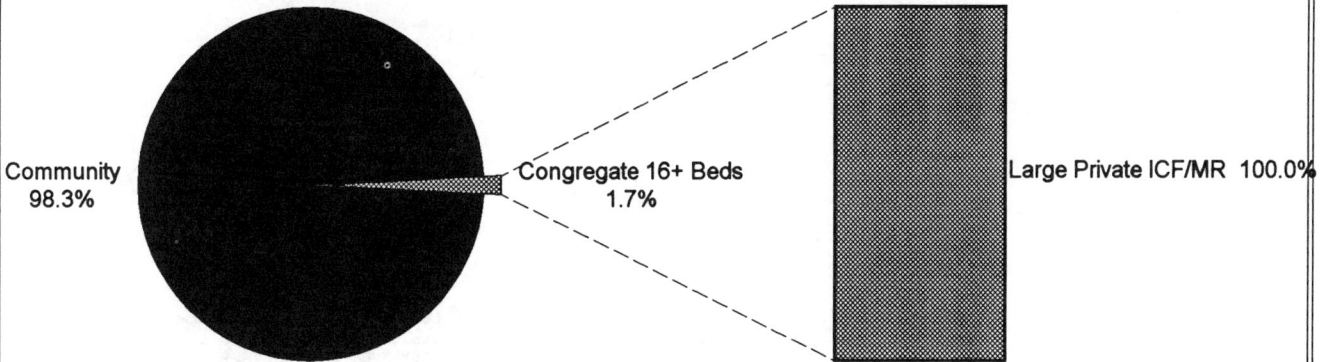

Community
98.3%

Congregate 16+ Beds
1.7%

Large Private ICF/MR  100.0%

FY 1992 Total Spending:
$81.7 Million

Source:
Institute on Disability and Human Development (UAP),
University of Illinois at Chicago, 1994

# NEW HAMPSHIRE

## Number of Persons Served by Residential Setting: FY 1992

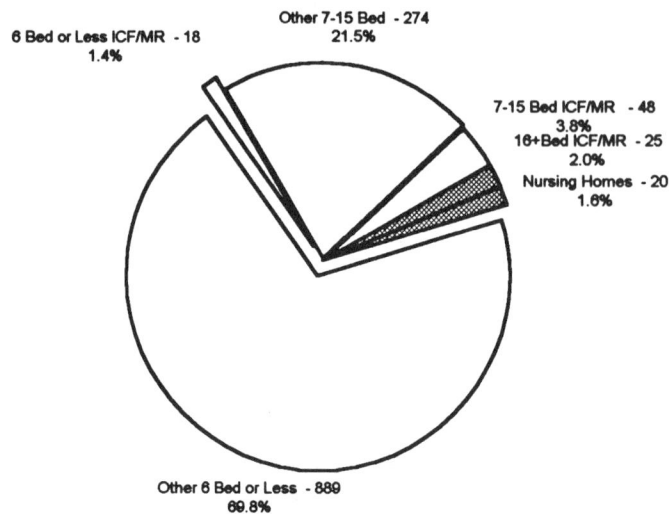

6 Bed or Less ICF/MR - 18
1.4%

Other 7-15 Bed - 274
21.5%

7-15 Bed ICF/MR - 48
3.8%
16+Bed ICF/MR - 25
2.0%
Nursing Homes - 20
1.6%

Other 6 Bed or Less - 889
69.8%

Total Served: 1,274

## Persons Served by Residential Setting:1986-92

|  | 1986 | 1987 | 1988 | 1989 | 1990 | 1991 | 1992 |
|---|---|---|---|---|---|---|---|
| CONGREGATE 16 + BED SETTINGS | NA | NA | 300 | 158 | 77 | 42 | 45 |
| Nursing Homes | NA | NA | 110 | 20 | 9 | 9 | 20 |
| State Institutions | 269 | 213 | 167 | 115 | 45 | 10 | 0 |
| Private 16+Bed ICF/MR | 24 | 24 | 23 | 23 | 23 | 23 | 25 |
| Other 16+Bed Residential | 0 | 0 | 0 | 0 | 0 | 0 | 0 |
| 15 BED OR LESS RESIDENTIAL SETTINGS | NA | NA | 866 | 934 | 991 | 1,152 | 1,229 |
| Public 7-15 Bed ICF/MR | 0 | 0 | 0 | 0 | 0 | 0 | 0 |
| Private 7-15 Bed ICF/MR | 36 | 45 | 54 | 54 | 54 | 66 | 48 |
| Other 7-15 Bed Residential | NA | NA | 812 | 880 | 937 | 1,086 | 274 |
| Public 6 Bed or Less ICF/MR | 0 | 0 | 0 | 0 | 0 | 0 | 0 |
| Private 6 Bed or Less ICF/MR |  |  |  |  |  |  | 18 |
| Other 6 Bed or Less Residential |  |  |  |  |  |  | 889 |
| TOTAL PERSONS SERVED | NA | NA | 1,166 | 1,092 | 1,068 | 1,194 | 1,274 |

## Persons Served in Non-Residential Community Services:1986-92

|  | 1986 | 1987 | 1988 | 1989 | 1990 | 1991 | 1992 |
|---|---|---|---|---|---|---|---|
| DAY/WORK PROGRAMS | NA | 1,041 | 1,049 | 1,205 | 1,336 | 1,456 | 1,569 |
| Sheltered Employment/Work Activity | NA | 509 | 243 | 417 | 276 | 451 | 598 |
| Day Habilitation ("Day Training") | 218 | 253 | 218 | 260 | 320 | 385 | 385 |
| Supported/Competitive Employment | NA | 279 | 588 | 528 | 740 | 620 | 586 |
| CASE MANAGEMENT | NA | NA | 1,590 | 1,634 | 1,974 | 2,056 | 1,890 |
| HCBS WAIVER | 482 | 541 | 635 | 756 | 822 | 925 | 1,055 |
| MODEL 50/200 WAIVER | 0 | 0 | 0 | 0 | 0 | 0 | 0 |

*Source:*
Institute on Disability and Human Development (UAP),
University of Illinois at Chicago, 1994

# NEW HAMPSHIRE

## Community Services: FY 1992 Revenue Sources

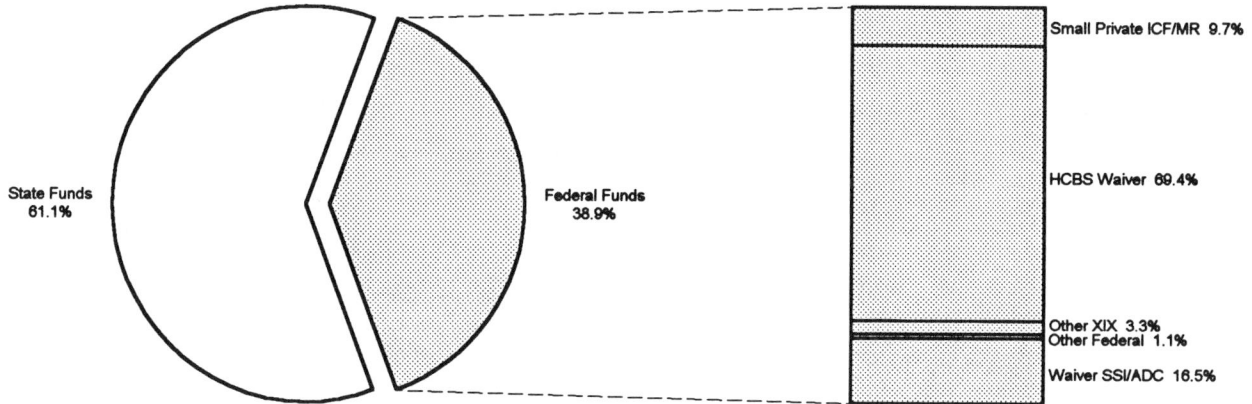

State Funds 61.1%

Federal Funds 38.9%

Small Private ICF/MR 9.7%

HCBS Waiver 69.4%

Other XIX 3.3%
Other Federal 1.1%

Waiver SSI/ADC 16.5%

Total Funds: $80.3 Million

## Family Support Initiatives*

|  | 1986 | 1987 | 1988 | 1989 | 1990 | 1991 | 1992 |
|---|---|---|---|---|---|---|---|
| FAMILY SUPPORT: TOTAL SPENDING | NA | NA | $936,174 | $1,098,337 | $1,911,162 | $2,116,460 | $2,693,049 |
| Total # of Families Supported | NA | NA | 1,285 | 1,404 | NA | NA | NA |
| A. Financial Subsidy/Payment | $0 | $0 | $0 | $0 | $0 | $0 | $0 |
| # of Families | 0 | 0 | 0 | 0 | 0 | 0 | 0 |
| B. Family Assistance Payments | NA | NA | $936,174 | $1,098,337 | $1,411,162 | $1,616,460 | $2,193,049 |
| # of Families | NA | NA | 1,285 | 1,404 | 1,718 | 2,415 | 2,609 |
| C. Other Family Support Payments | $0 | $0 | $0 | $0 | $500,000 | $500,000 | $500,000 |
| # of Families | 0 | 0 | 0 | 0 | NA | NA | NA |

## Other Community Services Initiatives*

|  | 1986 | 1987 | 1988 | 1989 | 1990 | 1991 | 1992 |
|---|---|---|---|---|---|---|---|
| AGING/DD SPENDING | $0 | $0 | $0 | $0 | $0 | $0 | $0 |
| # of Persons Served | 0 | 0 | 0 | 0 | 0 | 0 | 0 |
| ASSISTIVE TECHNOLOGY SPENDING |  |  | $125,000 | $650,000 | $675,000 | $698,000 | $703,000 |
| # of Persons Served |  |  | 45 | 180 | 185 | 288 | 220 |
| EARLY INTERVENTION SPENDING | $1,488,842 | $1,663,193 | $1,712,047 | $1,886,537 | $2,124,226 | $2,778,311 | $2,964,845 |
| # of Persons Served | 823 | 918 | 965 | 1,067 | 1,184 | 1,276 | 1,305 |
| PERSONAL ASSISTANCE SPENDING |  |  | $65,000 | $65,000 | $97,500 | $140,000 | $240,000 |
| # of Persons Served |  |  | 10 | 10 | 15 | 20 | 30 |
| SUPPORTED EMPLOYMENT SPENDING | $0 | NA | NA | $189,413 | $562,410 | $616,017 | $5,692,775 |
| # of Persons Served | 0 | 297 | 541 | 497 | 695 | 590 | 550 |
| SUPPORTED LIVING SPENDING |  |  |  |  |  |  | $0 |
| # of Persons Served |  |  |  |  |  |  | 0 |

*Expenditures associated with Special Community Initiatives are a subset of funding within the community services component of the state's chart series and spreadsheet; Family Support Client figures may include duplicate client counts; HCBS Waiver counts include Waiver case management numbers.
0= Services not provided in the state; NA= Data not available from state; blank= Services not applicable (eg. CSLA prior to authorization, Special Community Initiatives prior to request for data by this study)

Source:
Institute on Disability and Human Development (UAP),
University of Illinois at Chicago, 1994

# NEW HAMPSHIRE

## Large Congregate Care Facilities: FY 1992 Revenue Sources*

### Private 16+Bed Settings

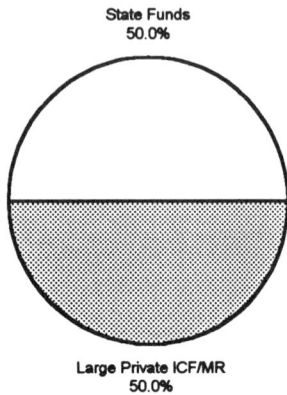

State Funds
50.0%

Large Private ICF/MR
50.0%

Total Funds: $1.4 Million

### Public Institutions

**Does Not Apply**

**\*Excludes nursing homes**

## Average Daily Residents in Institutions

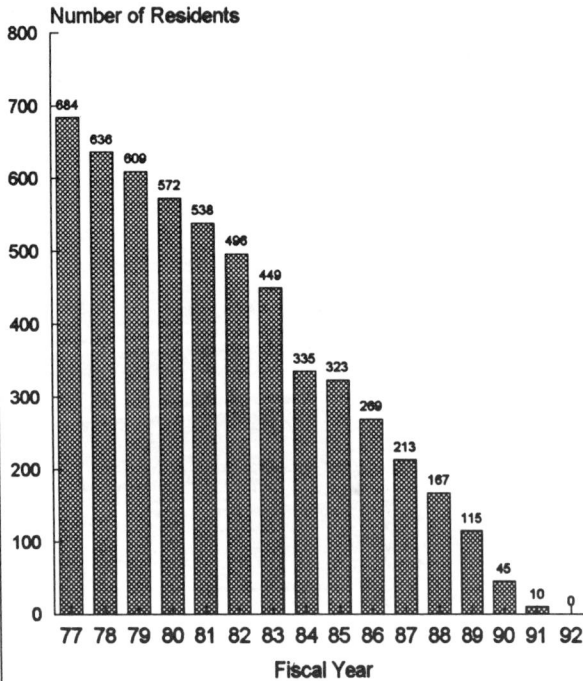

Number of Residents

| | |
|---|---|
| 684 | |

684, 636, 609, 572, 538, 496, 449, 335, 323, 269, 213, 167, 115, 45, 10, 0

77 78 79 80 81 82 83 84 85 86 87 88 89 90 91 92

Fiscal Year

## Institutional Daily Costs Per Resident

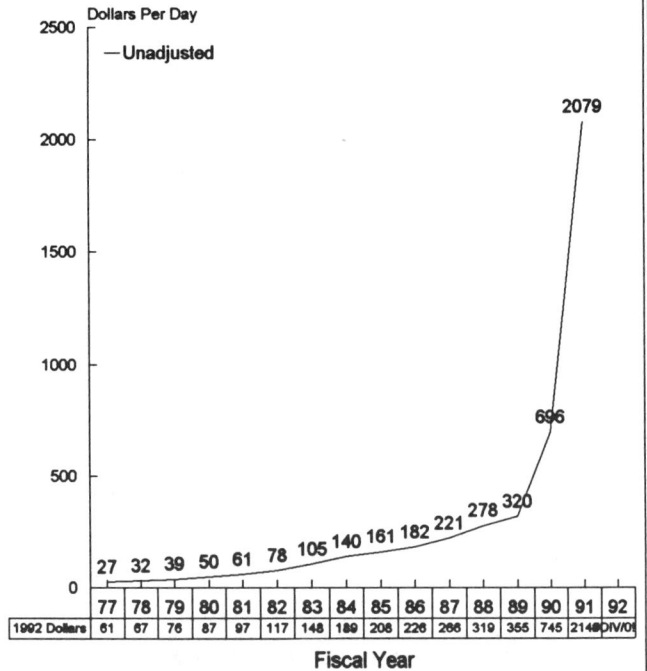

Dollars Per Day

—Unadjusted

2079

696

27  32  39  50  61  78  105  140  161  182  221  278  320

| | 77 | 78 | 79 | 80 | 81 | 82 | 83 | 84 | 85 | 86 | 87 | 88 | 89 | 90 | 91 | 92 |
|---|---|---|---|---|---|---|---|---|---|---|---|---|---|---|---|---|
| 1992 Dollars | 61 | 67 | 76 | 87 | 97 | 117 | 148 | 189 | 208 | 226 | 266 | 319 | 355 | 745 | 2148 | DIV/0! |

Fiscal Year

*Source:*
Institute on Disability and Human Development (UAP),
University of Illinois at Chicago, 1994

# NEW HAMPSHIRE FISCAL EFFORT

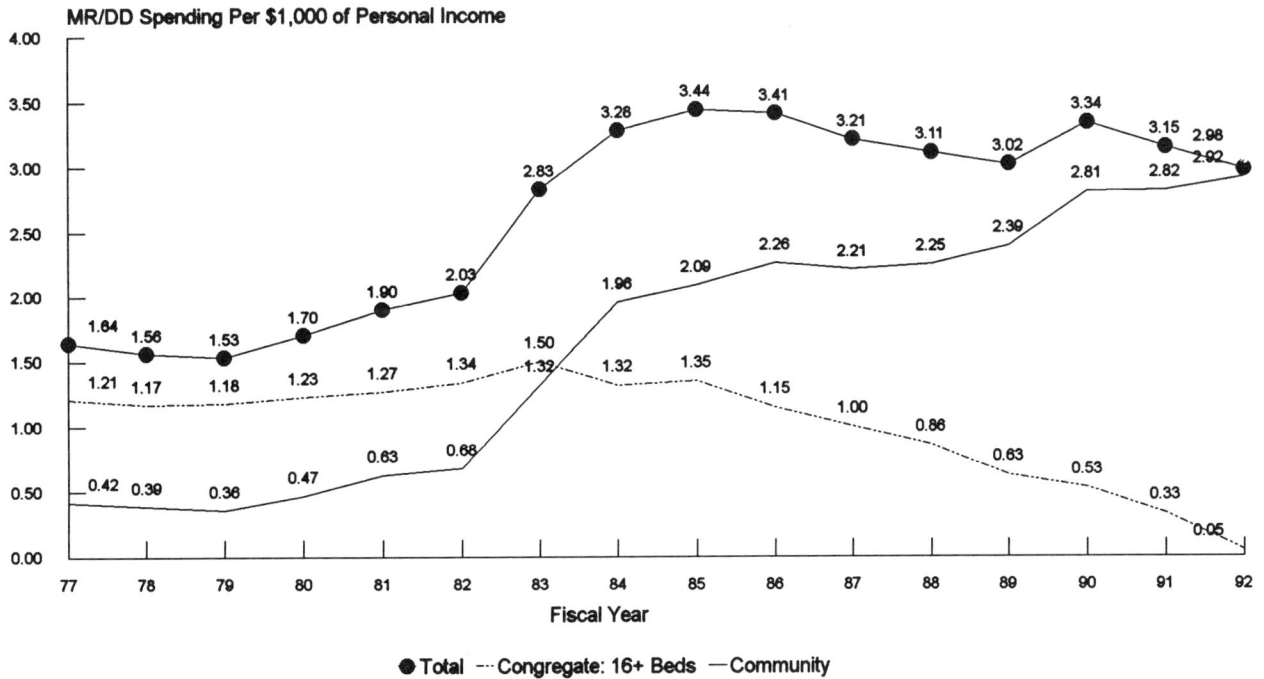

MR/DD Spending Per $1,000 of Personal Income

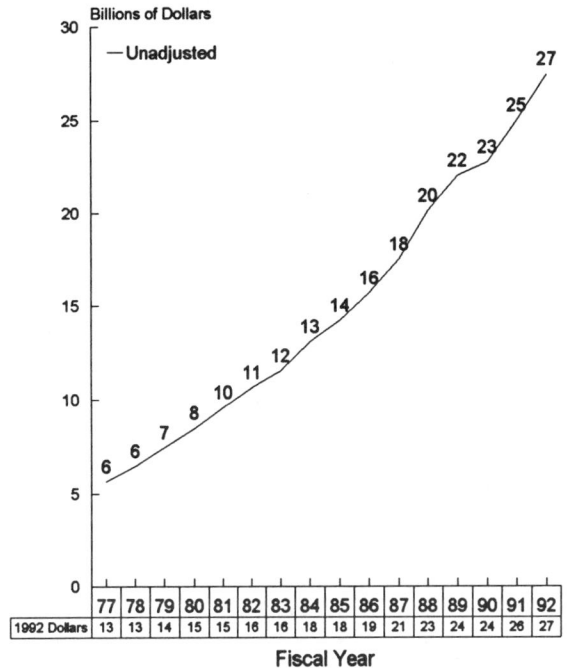

Values along Total line: 1.64, 1.56, 1.53, 1.70, 1.90, 2.03, 2.83, 3.28, 3.44, 3.41, 3.21, 3.11, 3.02, 3.34, 3.15, 2.98, 2.92

Values along Congregate line: 1.21, 1.17, 1.18, 1.23, 1.27, 1.34, 1.32, 1.32, 1.35, 1.15, 1.00, 0.86, 0.63, 0.53, 0.33, 0.05

Values along Community line: 0.42, 0.39, 0.36, 0.47, 0.63, 0.68, 1.50, 1.96, 2.09, 2.26, 2.21, 2.25, 2.39, 2.81, 2.82

Fiscal Year: 77 78 79 80 81 82 83 84 85 86 87 88 89 90 91 92

● Total  --- Congregate: 16+ Beds  — Community

## Total MR/DD Spending

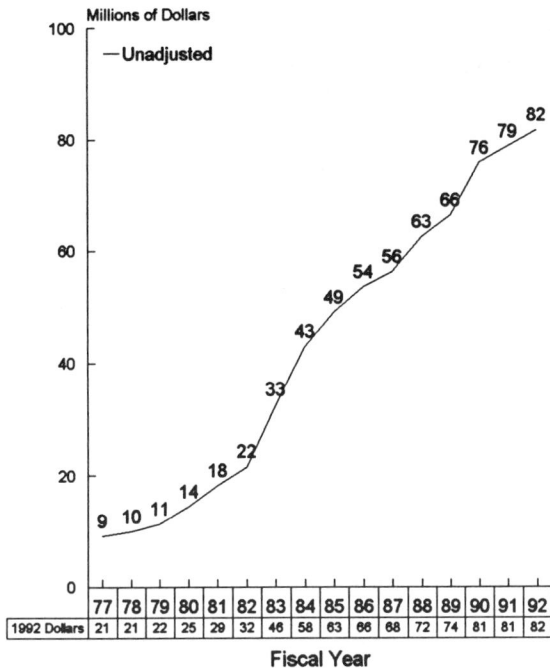

Millions of Dollars
— Unadjusted

Values: 9, 10, 11, 14, 18, 22, 33, 43, 49, 54, 56, 63, 66, 76, 79, 82

| Fiscal Year | 77 | 78 | 79 | 80 | 81 | 82 | 83 | 84 | 85 | 86 | 87 | 88 | 89 | 90 | 91 | 92 |
|---|---|---|---|---|---|---|---|---|---|---|---|---|---|---|---|---|
| 1992 Dollars | 21 | 21 | 22 | 25 | 29 | 32 | 46 | 58 | 63 | 66 | 68 | 72 | 74 | 81 | 81 | 82 |

Fiscal Year

## Personal Income

Billions of Dollars
— Unadjusted

Values: 6, 6, 7, 8, 10, 11, 12, 13, 14, 16, 18, 20, 22, 23, 25, 27

| Fiscal Year | 77 | 78 | 79 | 80 | 81 | 82 | 83 | 84 | 85 | 86 | 87 | 88 | 89 | 90 | 91 | 92 |
|---|---|---|---|---|---|---|---|---|---|---|---|---|---|---|---|---|
| 1992 Dollars | 13 | 13 | 14 | 15 | 15 | 16 | 16 | 18 | 18 | 19 | 21 | 23 | 24 | 24 | 26 | 27 |

Fiscal Year

*Source:*
Institute on Disability and Human Development (UAP),
University of Illinois at Chicago, 1994

# NEW HAMPSHIRE

## Financial Support for MR/DD Services: FY 1977-92

| | 1977 | 1978 | 1979 | 1980 | 1981 | 1982 | 1983 | 1984 |
|---|---|---|---|---|---|---|---|---|
| **TOTAL FUNDS** | $9,223,000 | $10,045,000 | $11,393,000 | $14,424,000 | $18,205,804 | $21,581,784 | $32,609,753 | $42,913,900 |
| **CONGREGATE 16+ BEDS** | 6,832,000 | 7,515,000 | 8,752,000 | 10,441,000 | 12,150,500 | 14,321,000 | 17,348,500 | 17,309,918 |
| INSTITUTIONAL SERVICES FUNDS | 6,832,000 | 7,515,000 | 8,752,000 | 10,441,000 | 12,024,000 | 14,186,000 | 17,205,000 | 17,158,000 |
| STATE FUNDS | 6,265,000 | 6,245,000 | 7,129,000 | 7,661,000 | 9,094,000 | 10,251,000 | 14,069,000 | 9,969,000 |
| General Funds | 5,576,000 | 5,555,000 | 6,486,000 | 7,014,000 | 8,268,000 | 9,370,000 | 13,324,000 | 9,044,000 |
| Local | 0 | 0 | 0 | 0 | 0 | 0 | 0 | 0 |
| Other State Funds | 689,000 | 690,000 | 643,000 | 647,000 | 826,000 | 881,000 | 745,000 | 925,000 |
| FEDERAL FUNDS | 567,000 | 1,270,000 | 1,623,000 | 2,780,000 | 2,930,000 | 3,935,000 | 3,136,000 | 7,189,000 |
| Federal ICF/MR | 567,000 | 1,270,000 | 1,623,000 | 2,720,000 | 2,890,000 | 3,902,000 | 3,111,000 | 6,963,000 |
| Title XX / SSBG Funds | 0 | 0 | 0 | 0 | 0 | 0 | 0 | 0 |
| Other Federal Funds | 0 | 0 | 0 | 60,000 | 40,000 | 33,000 | 25,000 | 226,000 |
| LARGE PRIVATE RESIDENTIAL | 0 | 0 | 0 | 0 | 126,500 | 135,000 | 143,500 | 151,918 |
| STATE FUNDS | 0 | 0 | 0 | 0 | 49,196 | 54,216 | 58,247 | 61,618 |
| General Funds | 0 | 0 | 0 | 0 | 0 | 0 | 0 | 0 |
| Other State Funds | 0 | 0 | 0 | 0 | 49,196 | 54,216 | 58,247 | 61,618 |
| Local/County Overmatch | 0 | 0 | 0 | 0 | 0 | 0 | 0 | 0 |
| FEDERAL FUNDS | 0 | 0 | 0 | 0 | 77,304 | 80,784 | 85,253 | 90,300 |
| Large Private ICF/MR | 0 | 0 | 0 | 0 | 77,304 | 80,784 | 85,253 | 90,300 |
| **COMMUNITY SERVICES FUNDS** | 2,391,000 | 2,530,000 | 2,641,000 | 3,983,000 | 6,055,304 | 7,260,784 | 15,261,253 | 25,603,982 |
| STATE FUNDS | 895,000 | 996,000 | 1,160,000 | 2,632,000 | 4,212,304 | 5,777,784 | 13,923,253 | 19,064,082 |
| General Funds | 399,000 | 432,000 | 436,000 | 1,700,000 | 3,078,304 | 4,448,784 | 12,243,253 | 17,311,082 |
| Other State Funds | 0 | 0 | 0 | 0 | 0 | 0 | 0 | 0 |
| Local/County Overmatch | 0 | 0 | 0 | 0 | 0 | 0 | 0 | 0 |
| SSI State Supplement | 496,000 | 564,000 | 724,000 | 932,000 | 1,134,000 | 1,329,000 | 1,680,000 | 1,753,000 |
| FEDERAL FUNDS | 1,496,000 | 1,534,000 | 1,481,000 | 1,351,000 | 1,843,000 | 1,483,000 | 1,338,000 | 6,539,900 |
| ICF/MR Funds | 0 | 0 | 0 | 0 | 0 | 0 | 0 | 0 |
| Small Public | 0 | 0 | 0 | 0 | 0 | 0 | 0 | 0 |
| Small Private | 0 | 0 | 0 | 0 | 0 | 0 | 0 | 0 |
| HCBS Waiver | 0 | 0 | 0 | 0 | 0 | 0 | 0 | 4,041,096 |
| Model 50/200 Waiver | 0 | 0 | 0 | 0 | 0 | 0 | 0 | 0 |
| Other Title XIX Programs | 0 | 0 | 0 | 0 | 209,000 | 270,000 | 1,178,000 | 1,304,000 |
| Title XX / SSBG Funds | 1,296,000 | 1,408,000 | 1,331,000 | 1,171,000 | 1,474,000 | 1,053,000 | 0 | 0 |
| Other Federal Funds | 200,000 | 126,000 | 150,000 | 180,000 | 160,000 | 160,000 | 160,000 | 144,000 |
| Waiver Clients' SSI/ADC | 0 | 0 | 0 | 0 | 0 | 0 | 0 | 1,050,804 |

| | 1985 | 1986 | 1987 | 1988 | 1989 | 1990 | 1991 | 1992 |
|---|---|---|---|---|---|---|---|---|
| **TOTAL FUNDS** | $48,960,235 | $53,513,274 | $56,263,759 | $62,592,894 | $66,425,326 | $75,862,815 | $78,787,685 | $81,706,546 |
| **CONGREGATE 16+ BEDS** | 19,206,946 | 18,112,802 | 17,466,397 | 17,284,036 | 13,922,377 | 12,022,289 | 8,305,815 | 1,397,812 |
| INSTITUTIONAL SERVICES FUNDS | 19,031,000 | 17,890,500 | 17,218,400 | 16,972,500 | 13,431,143 | 11,431,143 | 7,589,795 | 0 |
| STATE FUNDS | 8,729,000 | 7,810,800 | 9,591,300 | 9,476,300 | 7,760,094 | 7,440,101 | 5,939,143 | 0 |
| General Funds | 7,583,000 | 7,210,300 | 9,142,400 | 9,142,300 | 7,455,157 | 7,276,042 | 5,864,143 | 0 |
| Local | 0 | 0 | 0 | 0 | 0 | 0 | 0 | 0 |
| Other State Funds | 1,146,000 | 600,500 | 448,900 | 334,000 | 304,937 | 164,059 | 75,000 | 0 |
| FEDERAL FUNDS | 10,302,000 | 10,079,700 | 7,627,100 | 7,496,200 | 5,671,049 | 3,991,042 | 1,650,652 | 0 |
| Federal ICF/MR | 10,091,000 | 9,906,100 | 7,501,000 | 7,368,000 | 5,671,049 | 3,991,042 | 1,650,652 | 0 |
| Title XX / SSBG Funds | 0 | 0 | 0 | 0 | 0 | 0 | 0 | 0 |
| Other Federal Funds | 211,000 | 173,600 | 126,100 | 128,200 | 0 | 0 | 0 | 0 |
| LARGE PRIVATE RESIDENTIAL | 175,946 | 222,302 | 247,997 | 311,536 | 491,234 | 591,146 | 716,020 | 1,397,812 |
| STATE FUNDS | 71,346 | 97,702 | 111,797 | 151,936 | 245,617 | 295,573 | 358,010 | 698,906 |
| General Funds | 0 | 0 | 0 | 0 | 0 | 0 | 0 | 0 |
| Other State Funds | 71,346 | 97,702 | 111,797 | 151,936 | 245,617 | 295,573 | 358,010 | 698,906 |
| Local/County Overmatch | 0 | 0 | 0 | 0 | 0 | 0 | 0 | 0 |
| FEDERAL FUNDS | 104,600 | 124,600 | 136,200 | 159,600 | 245,617 | 295,573 | 358,010 | 698,906 |
| Large Private ICF/MR | 104,600 | 124,600 | 136,200 | 159,600 | 245,617 | 295,573 | 358,010 | 698,906 |
| **COMMUNITY SERVICES FUNDS** | 29,753,289 | 35,400,472 | 38,797,362 | 45,308,858 | 52,502,949 | 63,840,526 | 70,481,870 | 80,308,734 |
| STATE FUNDS | 22,145,054 | 25,969,799 | 28,022,403 | 30,880,291 | 34,976,025 | 41,591,942 | 42,603,343 | 49,055,720 |
| General Funds | 20,291,054 | 24,101,799 | 26,172,103 | 29,007,491 | 32,612,581 | 38,867,980 | 39,592,867 | 45,757,604 |
| Other State Funds | 0 | 0 | 0 | 0 | 0 | 0 | 0 | 0 |
| Local/County Overmatch | 0 | 0 | 0 | 0 | 0 | 0 | 0 | 0 |
| SSI State Supplement | 1,854,000 | 1,868,000 | 1,850,300 | 1,872,800 | 2,363,444 | 2,723,962 | 3,010,476 | 3,298,116 |
| FEDERAL FUNDS | 7,608,235 | 9,430,673 | 10,774,959 | 14,428,567 | 17,526,924 | 22,248,584 | 27,878,527 | 31,253,014 |
| ICF/MR Funds | 192,200 | 1,000,600 | 1,023,400 | 1,884,600 | 2,255,552 | 2,312,652 | 2,771,477 | 3,033,144 |
| Small Public | 0 | 0 | 0 | 0 | 0 | 0 | 0 | 0 |
| Small Private | 192,200 | 1,000,600 | 1,023,400 | 1,884,600 | 2,255,552 | 2,312,652 | 2,771,477 | 3,033,144 |
| HCBS Waiver | 5,669,535 | 6,272,349 | 7,424,279 | 9,799,787 | 11,837,000 | 15,782,000 | 19,800,000 | 21,700,000 |
| Model 50/200 Waiver | 0 | 0 | 0 | 0 | 0 | 0 | 0 | 0 |
| Other Title XIX Programs | 167,100 | 218,900 | 156,300 | 117,300 | 331,748 | 523,980 | 734,850 | 1,022,400 |
| Title XX / SSBG Funds | 0 | 0 | 0 | 0 | 0 | 0 | 0 | 0 |
| Other Federal Funds | 107,000 | 140,000 | 126,000 | 158,000 | 0 | 0 | 332,000 | 344,850 |
| Waiver Clients' SSI/ADC | 1,472,400 | 1,798,824 | 2,044,980 | 2,468,880 | 3,102,624 | 3,629,952 | 4,240,200 | 5,152,620 |

*Source:*
Institute on Disability and Human Development (UAP),
University of Illinois at Chicago, 1994

# NEW JERSEY

## MR/DD Spending for Congregate Residential & Community Services

▨ Congregate: 16+ Beds*  ■ Community**

Millions of 1992 Dollars

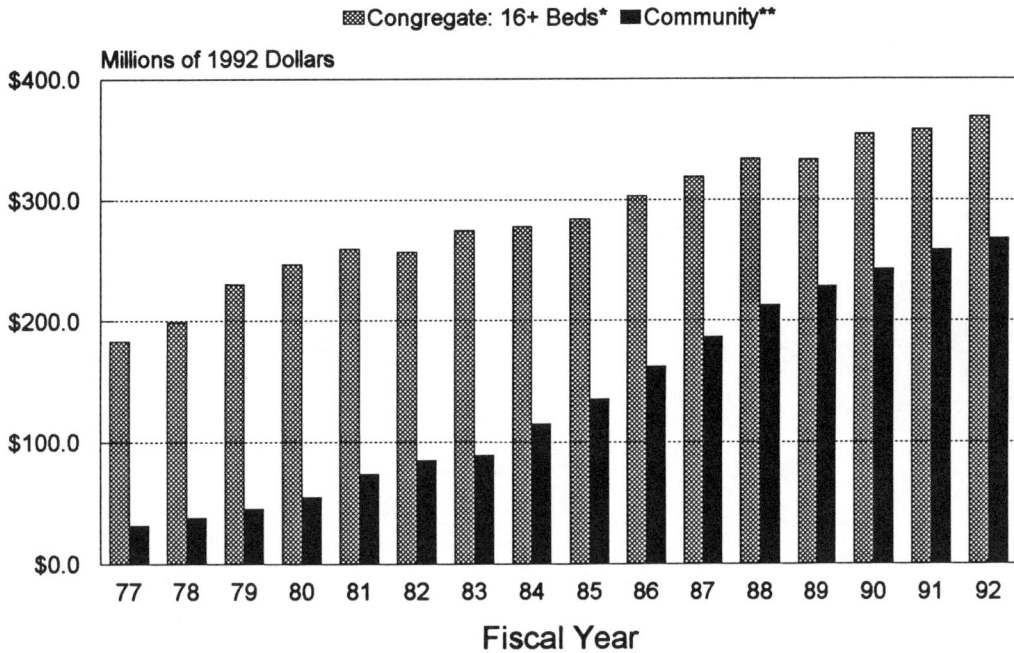

Fiscal Year

*Excludes nursing homes; ** Includes resources for
15 bed or less residential settings & non-residential community services

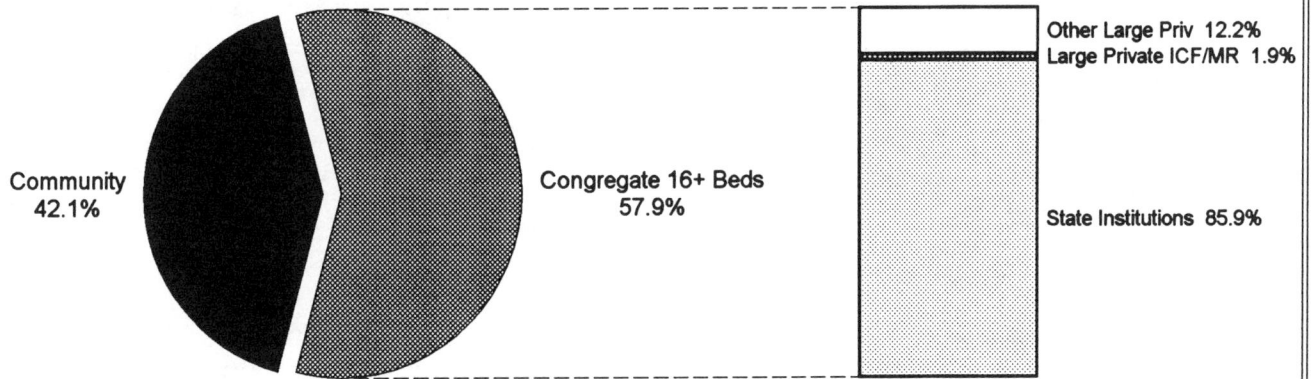

Community
42.1%

Congregate 16+ Beds
57.9%

Other Large Priv 12.2%
Large Private ICF/MR 1.9%

State Institutions 85.9%

FY 1992 Total Spending:
$636.4 Million

*Source:*
Institute on Disability and Human Development (UAP),
University of Illinois at Chicago, 1994

# NEW JERSEY

## Number of Persons Served by Residential Setting: FY 1992

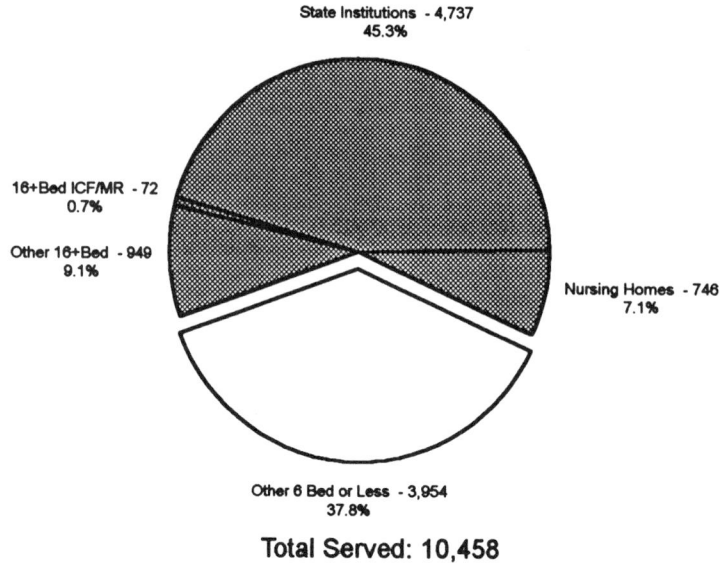

State Institutions - 4,737
45.3%

16+Bed ICF/MR - 72
0.7%

Other 16+Bed - 949
9.1%

Nursing Homes - 746
7.1%

Other 6 Bed or Less - 3,954
37.8%

Total Served: 10,458

## Persons Served by Residential Setting:1986-92

|  | 1986 | 1987 | 1988 | 1989 | 1990 | 1991 | 1992 |
|---|---|---|---|---|---|---|---|
| CONGREGATE 16 + BED SETTINGS | NA | NA | 8,770 | NA | NA | NA | 6,504 |
| Nursing Homes | NA | NA | 2,481 | NA | NA | NA | 746 |
| State Institutions | 5,507 | 5,381 | 5,236 | 5,143 | 5,110 | 4,988 | 4,737 |
| Private 16+Bed ICF/MR | 72 | 72 | 72 | 72 | 72 | 72 | 72 |
| Other 16+Bed Residential | 939 | 961 | 981 | 972 | 921 | 949 | 949 |
| 15 BED OR LESS RESIDENTIAL SETTINGS | 2,634 | 2,721 | 3,018 | 2,453 | 3,225 | 3,713 | 3,954 |
| Public 7-15 Bed ICF/MR | 0 | 0 | 0 | 0 | 0 | 0 | 0 |
| Private 7-15 Bed ICF/MR | 0 | 0 | 0 | 0 | 0 | 0 | 0 |
| Other 7-15 Bed Residential | 0 | 0 | 0 | 0 | 0 | 0 | 0 |
| Public 6 Bed or Less ICF/MR | 0 | 0 | 0 | 0 | 0 | 0 | 0 |
| Private 6 Bed or Less ICF/MR | 0 | 0 | 0 | 0 | 0 | 0 | 0 |
| Other 6 Bed or Less Residential | 2,634 | 2,721 | 3,018 | 2,453 | 3,225 | 3,713 | 3,954 |
| TOTAL PERSONS SERVED | NA | NA | 11,788 | NA | NA | NA | 10,458 |

## Persons Served in Non-Residential Community Services:1986-92

|  | 1986 | 1987 | 1988 | 1989 | 1990 | 1991 | 1992 |
|---|---|---|---|---|---|---|---|
| DAY/WORK PROGRAMS | 5,292 | 5,680 | 6,017 | 6,296 | 6,251 | 6,570 | 6,570 |
| Sheltered Employment/Work Activity | 4,121 | 4,277 | 4,409 | 4,632 | 4,615 | 4,645 | 4,645 |
| Day Habilitation ("Day Training") | 1,036 | 1,049 | 1,034 | 1,067 | 1,040 | 1,029 | 1,029 |
| Supported/Competitive Employment | 135 | 354 | 574 | 597 | 596 | 896 | 896 |
| CASE MANAGEMENT | 6,814 | 7,498 | 8,650 | 7,802 | 7,942 | 9,292 | 9,292 |
| HCBS WAIVER | 2,200 | 2,755 | 2,988 | 3,255 | 3,242 | 3,755 | 3,800 |
| MODEL 50/200 WAIVER | 0 | 0 | 0 | 0 | 0 | 0 | 0 |

*Source:*
Institute on Disability and Human Development (UAP),
University of Illinois at Chicago, 1994

# NEW JERSEY

## Community Services: FY 1992 Revenue Sources

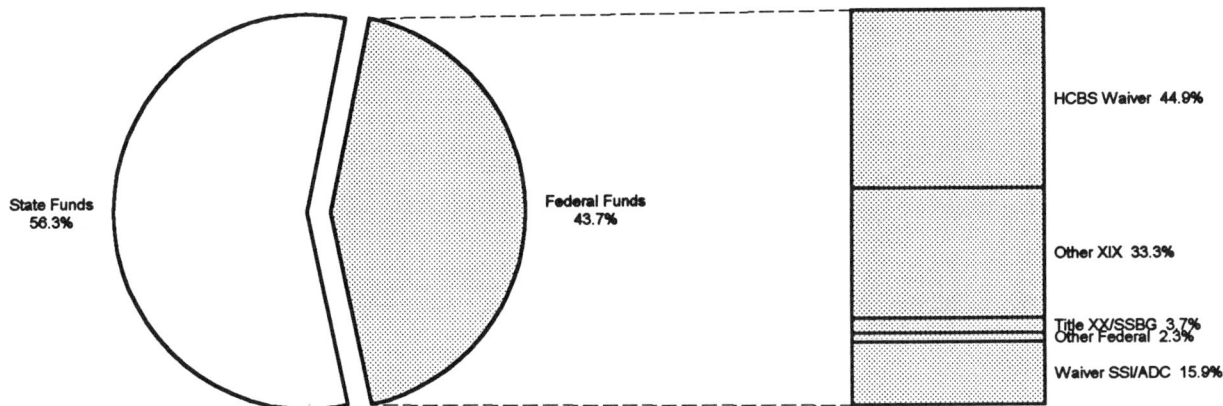

State Funds 56.3%

Federal Funds 43.7%

HCBS Waiver 44.9%

Other XIX 33.3%

Title XX/SSBG 3.7%
Other Federal 2.3%

Waiver SSI/ADC 15.9%

Total Funds: $267.6 Million

## Family Support Initiatives*

|  | 1986 | 1987 | 1988 | 1989 | 1990 | 1991 | 1992 |
|---|---|---|---|---|---|---|---|
| FAMILY SUPPORT: TOTAL SPENDING | $3,596,550 | $5,268,953 | $4,179,800 | $4,732,008 | $6,881,038 | $7,138,249 | $7,138,249 |
| Total # of Families Supported | NA | NA | NA | NA | NA | NA | NA |
| A. Financial Subsidy/Payment | $0 | $0 | $0 | $0 | $0 | $0 | $0 |
| # of Families | 0 | 0 | 0 | 0 | 0 | 0 | 0 |
| B. Family Assistance Payments | $1,608,535 | $2,571,874 | $4,171,000 | $4,731,903 | $6,710,038 | $7,041,249 | $6,973,249 |
| # of Families | NA | NA | NA | NA | NA | NA | NA |
| C. Other Family Support Payments | $1,988,015 | $2,697,079 | $8,800 | $105 | $171,000 | $97,000 | $165,000 |
| # of Families | NA | NA | NA | NA | NA | NA | NA |

## Other Community Services Initiatives*

|  | 1986 | 1987 | 1988 | 1989 | 1990 | 1991 | 1992 |
|---|---|---|---|---|---|---|---|
| AGING/DD SPENDING | $0 | $0 | $0 | $0 | $0 | $0 | $0 |
| # of Persons Served | 0 | 0 | 0 | 0 | 0 | 0 | 0 |
| ASSISTIVE TECHNOLOGY SPENDING |  |  |  |  |  |  | $200,000 |
| # of Persons Served |  |  |  |  |  |  | NA |
| EARLY INTERVENTION SPENDING | $0 | $0 | $0 | $0 | $0 | $0 | $0 |
| # of Persons Served | 0 | 0 | 0 | 0 | 0 | 0 | 0 |
| PERSONAL ASSISTANCE SPENDING |  |  |  |  |  |  | $0 |
| # of Persons Served |  |  |  |  |  |  | 0 |
| SUPPORTED EMPLOYMENT SPENDING | $600,000 | $1,519,000 | $1,824,000 | $2,235,000 | $2,235,000 | $3,400,000 | $6,300,000 |
| # of Persons Served | 135 | 354 | 574 | 454 | 566 | 632 | 823 |
| SUPPORTED LIVING SPENDING |  |  |  |  |  |  | $0 |
| # of Persons Served |  |  |  |  |  |  | 0 |

*Expenditures associated with Special Community Initiatives are a subset of funding within the community services component of the state's chart series and spreadsheet; Family Support Client figures may include duplicate client counts; HCBS Waiver counts include Waiver case management numbers.
0= Services not provided in the state; NA= Data not available from state; blank= Services not applicable (eg. CSLA prior to authorization, Special Community Initiatives prior to request for data by this study)

Source:
Institute on Disability and Human Development (UAP),
University of Illinois at Chicago, 1994

# NEW JERSEY

## Large Congregate Care Facilities: FY 1992 Revenue Sources*

### Private 16+Bed Settings

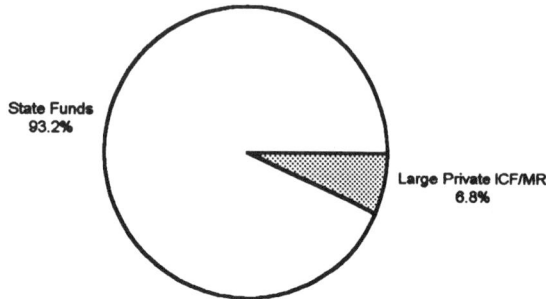

State Funds
93.2%

Large Private ICF/MR
6.8%

Total Funds: $52.0 Million

### Public Institutions

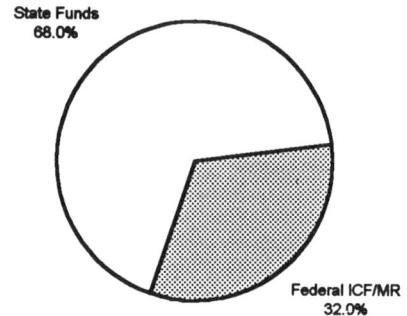

State Funds
68.0%

Federal ICF/MR
32.0%

Total Funds: $316.8 Million

**\*Excludes nursing homes**

## Average Daily Residents in Institutions

Number of Residents

| | |
|---|---|

7,603
7,810
7,589
7,262
6,942
6,551
6,046
5,886
5,699
5,507
5,381
5,236
5,143
5,110
4,988
4,737

10,000
8,000
6,000
4,000
2,000
0

77 78 79 80 81 82 83 84 85 86 87 88 89 90 91 92

Fiscal Year

## Institutional Daily Costs Per Resident

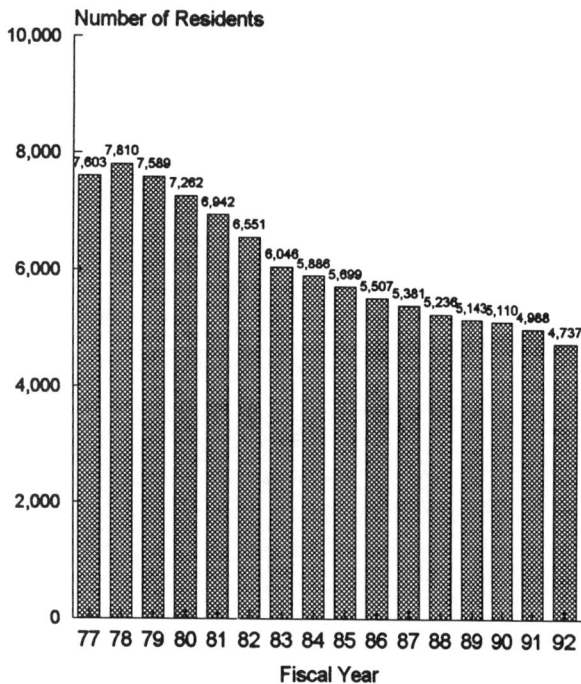

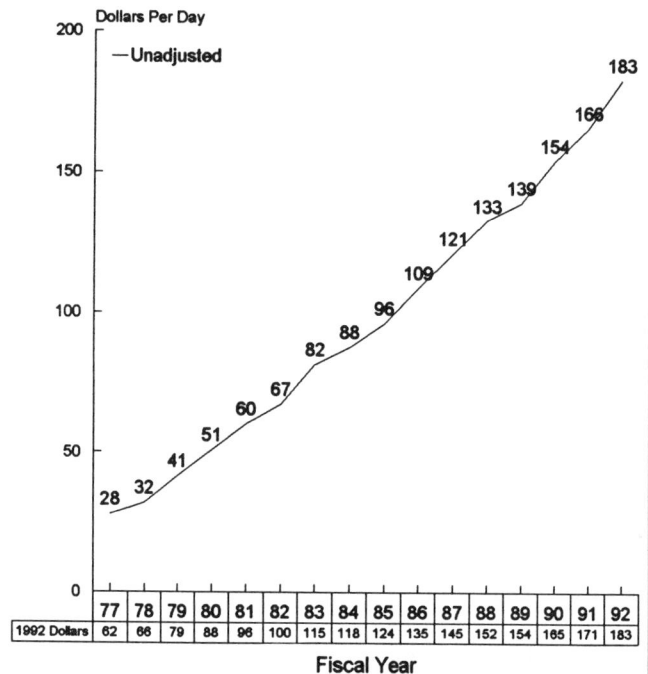

Dollars Per Day

—Unadjusted

200
150
100
50
0

28 32 41 51 60 67 82 88 96 109 121 133 139 154 166 183

| | 77 | 78 | 79 | 80 | 81 | 82 | 83 | 84 | 85 | 86 | 87 | 88 | 89 | 90 | 91 | 92 |
|---|---|---|---|---|---|---|---|---|---|---|---|---|---|---|---|---|
| 1992 Dollars | 62 | 66 | 79 | 88 | 96 | 100 | 115 | 118 | 124 | 135 | 145 | 152 | 154 | 165 | 171 | 183 |

Fiscal Year

*Source:*
Institute on Disability and Human Development (UAP),
University of Illinois at Chicago, 1994

# NEW JERSEY FISCAL EFFORT

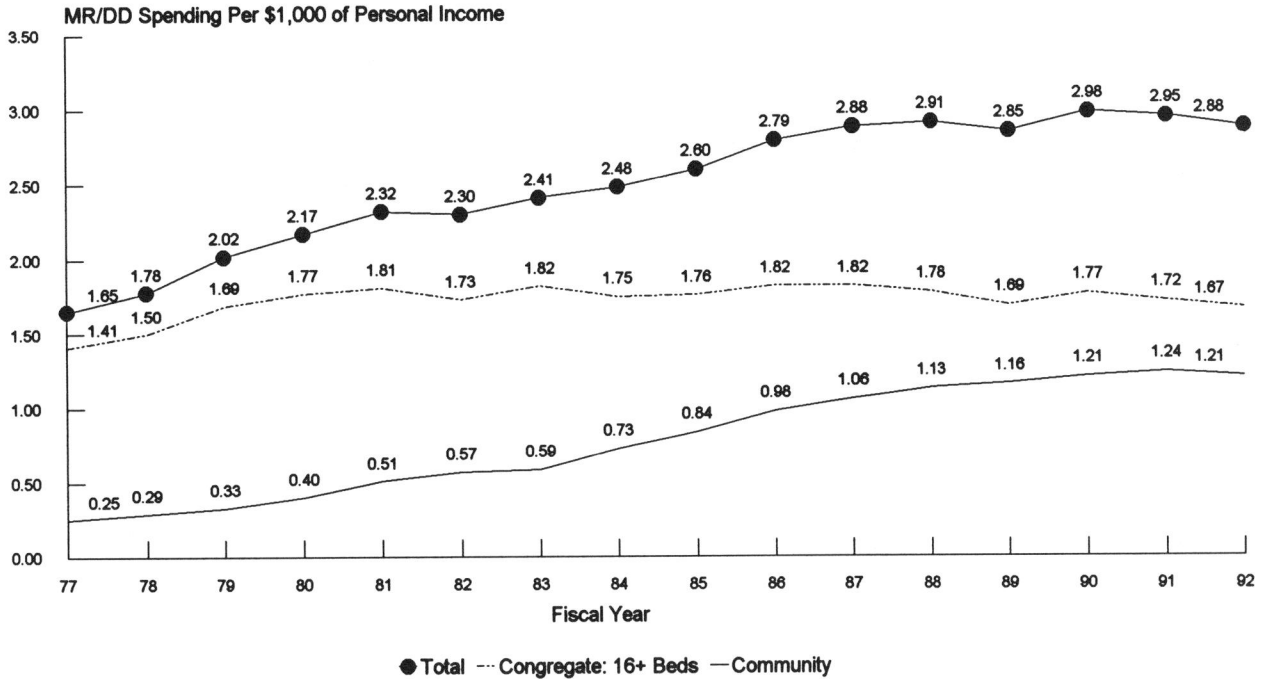

MR/DD Spending Per $1,000 of Personal Income

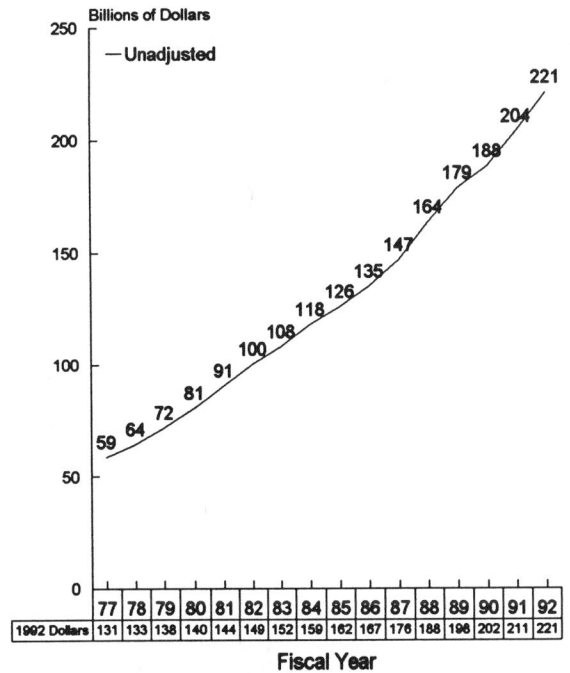

Total: 1.65, 1.78, 2.02, 2.17, 2.32, 2.30, 2.41, 2.48, 2.60, 2.79, 2.88, 2.91, 2.85, 2.98, 2.95, 2.88

Congregate: 16+ Beds: 1.41, 1.50, 1.69, 1.77, 1.81, 1.73, 1.82, 1.75, 1.76, 1.82, 1.82, 1.78, 1.69, 1.77, 1.72, 1.67

Community: 0.25, 0.29, 0.33, 0.40, 0.51, 0.57, 0.59, 0.73, 0.84, 0.98, 1.06, 1.13, 1.16, 1.21, 1.24, 1.21

Fiscal Year

● Total  --- Congregate: 16+ Beds  — Community

## Total MR/DD Spending

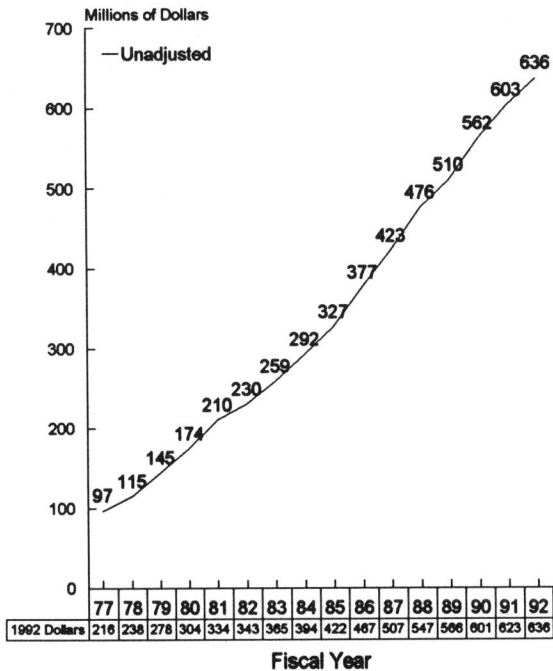

Millions of Dollars
— Unadjusted

97, 115, 145, 174, 210, 230, 259, 292, 327, 377, 423, 476, 510, 562, 603, 636

| | 77 | 78 | 79 | 80 | 81 | 82 | 83 | 84 | 85 | 86 | 87 | 88 | 89 | 90 | 91 | 92 |
|---|---|---|---|---|---|---|---|---|---|---|---|---|---|---|---|---|
| 1992 Dollars | 216 | 238 | 278 | 304 | 334 | 343 | 365 | 394 | 422 | 467 | 507 | 547 | 566 | 601 | 623 | 636 |

Fiscal Year

## Personal Income

Billions of Dollars
— Unadjusted

59, 64, 72, 81, 91, 100, 108, 118, 126, 135, 147, 164, 179, 188, 204, 221

| | 77 | 78 | 79 | 80 | 81 | 82 | 83 | 84 | 85 | 86 | 87 | 88 | 89 | 90 | 91 | 92 |
|---|---|---|---|---|---|---|---|---|---|---|---|---|---|---|---|---|
| 1992 Dollars | 131 | 133 | 138 | 140 | 144 | 149 | 152 | 159 | 162 | 167 | 176 | 188 | 196 | 202 | 211 | 221 |

Fiscal Year

*Source:*
Institute on Disability and Human Development (UAP),
University of Illinois at Chicago, 1994

# NEW JERSEY
## Financial Support for MR/DD Services: FY 1977-92

| | 1977 | 1978 | 1979 | 1980 | 1981 | 1982 | 1983 | 1984 |
|---|---|---|---|---|---|---|---|---|
| **TOTAL FUNDS** | $96,880,000 | $114,922,000 | $144,627,000 | $174,461,000 | $210,036,000 | $230,489,000 | $259,211,589 | $292,052,896 |
| **CONGREGATE 16+ BEDS** | 82,509,000 | 96,448,000 | 120,909,000 | 142,652,000 | 163,531,000 | 173,291,000 | 195,737,726 | 206,491,540 |
| INSTITUTIONAL SERVICES FUNDS | 77,344,000 | 90,877,000 | 114,552,000 | 134,947,000 | 152,449,000 | 160,429,000 | 179,895,000 | 188,537,000 |
| STATE FUNDS | 73,535,000 | 81,790,000 | 83,729,000 | 89,246,000 | 97,515,000 | 117,698,000 | 129,936,000 | 133,142,000 |
| General Funds | 73,501,000 | 81,357,000 | 83,701,000 | 89,183,000 | 93,291,000 | 113,066,000 | 124,632,000 | 128,114,000 |
| Local | 0 | 0 | 0 | 0 | 0 | 0 | 0 | 0 |
| Other State Funds | 34,000 | 433,000 | 28,000 | 63,000 | 4,224,000 | 4,632,000 | 5,304,000 | 5,028,000 |
| FEDERAL FUNDS | 3,809,000 | 9,087,000 | 30,823,000 | 45,701,000 | 54,934,000 | 42,731,000 | 49,959,000 | 55,395,000 |
| Federal ICF/MR | 0 | 1,877,000 | 28,453,000 | 43,545,000 | 52,845,000 | 41,183,000 | 48,171,000 | 53,994,000 |
| Title XX / SSBG Funds | 0 | 0 | 0 | 0 | 0 | 0 | 0 | 0 |
| Other Federal Funds | 3,809,000 | 7,210,000 | 2,370,000 | 2,156,000 | 2,089,000 | 1,548,000 | 1,788,000 | 1,401,000 |
| LARGE PRIVATE RESIDENTIAL | 5,165,000 | 5,571,000 | 6,357,000 | 7,705,000 | 11,082,000 | 12,862,000 | 15,842,726 | 17,954,540 |
| STATE FUNDS | 5,165,000 | 5,571,000 | 6,357,000 | 7,705,000 | 11,082,000 | 12,862,000 | 15,644,863 | 17,463,770 |
| General Funds | 5,165,000 | 5,571,000 | 6,357,000 | 7,705,000 | 11,082,000 | 12,862,000 | 15,447,000 | 16,973,000 |
| Other State Funds | 0 | 0 | 0 | 0 | 0 | 0 | 0 | 0 |
| Local/County Overmatch | 0 | 0 | 0 | 0 | 0 | 0 | 197,863 | 490,770 |
| FEDERAL FUNDS | 0 | 0 | 0 | 0 | 0 | 0 | 197,863 | 490,770 |
| Large Private ICF/MR | 0 | 0 | 0 | 0 | 0 | 0 | 197,863 | 490,770 |
| **COMMUNITY SERVICES FUNDS** | 14,371,000 | 18,474,000 | 23,718,000 | 31,809,000 | 46,505,000 | 57,198,000 | 63,473,863 | 85,561,356 |
| STATE FUNDS | 9,882,000 | 12,951,000 | 14,648,000 | 14,672,000 | 13,248,000 | 33,476,000 | 32,226,863 | 32,295,000 |
| General Funds | 7,290,000 | 9,931,000 | 11,279,000 | 10,545,000 | 3,693,000 | 20,756,000 | 19,389,000 | 15,753,000 |
| Other State Funds | 2,000 | 215,000 | 238,000 | 430,000 | 4,974,000 | 7,608,000 | 6,850,863 | 10,118,000 |
| Local/County Overmatch | 0 | 0 | 0 | 0 | 0 | 0 | 0 | 0 |
| SSI State Supplement | 2,590,000 | 2,805,000 | 3,131,000 | 3,697,000 | 4,581,000 | 5,112,000 | 5,987,000 | 6,424,000 |
| FEDERAL FUNDS | 4,489,000 | 5,523,000 | 9,070,000 | 17,137,000 | 33,257,000 | 23,722,000 | 31,247,000 | 53,266,356 |
| ICF/MR Funds | 0 | 0 | 0 | 0 | 0 | 0 | 0 | 0 |
| Small Public | 0 | 0 | 0 | 0 | 0 | 0 | 0 | 0 |
| Small Private | 0 | 0 | 0 | 0 | 0 | 0 | 0 | 0 |
| HCBS Waiver | 0 | 0 | 0 | 0 | 0 | 0 | 0 | 10,621,000 |
| Model 50/200 Waiver | 0 | 0 | 0 | 0 | 0 | 0 | 0 | 0 |
| Other Title XIX Programs | 0 | 63,000 | 3,112,000 | 11,143,000 | 22,735,000 | 17,212,000 | 24,430,000 | 30,128,000 |
| Title XX / SSBG Funds | 2,992,000 | 3,662,000 | 4,170,000 | 4,203,000 | 4,165,000 | 3,681,000 | 3,710,000 | 4,172,000 |
| Other Federal Funds | 1,497,000 | 1,798,000 | 1,788,000 | 1,791,000 | 6,357,000 | 2,829,000 | 3,107,000 | 3,778,000 |
| Waiver Clients' SSI/ADC | 0 | 0 | 0 | 0 | 0 | 0 | 0 | 4,567,356 |

| | 1985 | 1986 | 1987 | 1988 | 1989 | 1990 | 1991 | 1992 |
|---|---|---|---|---|---|---|---|---|
| **TOTAL FUNDS** | $326,785,748 | $376,531,140 | $422,657,080 | $475,721,298 | $509,838,242 | $561,677,097 | $602,837,772 | $636,420,435 |
| **CONGREGATE 16+ BEDS** | 221,222,748 | 245,057,740 | 266,936,180 | 290,588,954 | 302,307,472 | 333,491,562 | 350,210,946 | 368,802,734 |
| INSTITUTIONAL SERVICES FUNDS | 199,683,000 | 218,263,000 | 237,267,000 | 253,964,000 | 261,042,000 | 287,201,000 | 301,342,000 | 316,788,000 |
| STATE FUNDS | 143,718,000 | 155,533,000 | 168,497,000 | 180,416,000 | 182,308,000 | 202,497,000 | 208,166,000 | 215,468,000 |
| General Funds | 138,166,000 | 149,952,000 | 163,016,000 | 176,003,000 | 182,308,000 | 198,298,000 | 203,856,000 | 211,158,000 |
| Local | 0 | 0 | 0 | 0 | 0 | 0 | 0 | 0 |
| Other State Funds | 5,552,000 | 5,581,000 | 5,481,000 | 4,413,000 | 0 | 4,199,000 | 4,310,000 | 4,310,000 |
| FEDERAL FUNDS | 55,965,000 | 62,730,000 | 68,770,000 | 73,548,000 | 78,734,000 | 84,704,000 | 93,176,000 | 101,320,000 |
| Federal ICF/MR | 55,115,000 | 61,730,000 | 68,197,000 | 73,145,000 | 78,734,000 | 84,704,000 | 93,176,000 | 101,320,000 |
| Title XX / SSBG Funds | 0 | 0 | 0 | 0 | 0 | 0 | 0 | 0 |
| Other Federal Funds | 850,000 | 1,000,000 | 573,000 | 403,000 | 0 | 0 | 0 | 0 |
| LARGE PRIVATE RESIDENTIAL | 21,539,748 | 26,794,740 | 29,669,180 | 36,624,954 | 41,265,472 | 46,290,562 | 48,868,946 | 52,014,734 |
| STATE FUNDS | 20,205,874 | 25,195,870 | 28,093,090 | 34,410,477 | 37,155,736 | 42,141,781 | 45,212,973 | 48,497,000 |
| General Funds | 18,872,000 | 23,597,000 | 26,517,000 | 30,264,477 | 32,056,736 | 37,613,781 | 40,319,973 | 43,137,000 |
| Other State Funds | 1,333,874 | 1,598,870 | 1,576,090 | 4,146,000 | 5,099,000 | 4,528,000 | 4,893,000 | 5,360,000 |
| Local/County Overmatch | 0 | 0 | 0 | 0 | 0 | 0 | 0 | 0 |
| FEDERAL FUNDS | 1,333,874 | 1,598,870 | 1,576,090 | 2,214,477 | 4,109,736 | 4,148,781 | 3,655,973 | 3,517,734 |
| Large Private ICF/MR | 1,333,874 | 1,598,870 | 1,576,090 | 2,214,477 | 4,109,736 | 4,148,781 | 3,655,973 | 3,517,734 |
| **COMMUNITY SERVICES FUNDS** | 105,563,000 | 131,473,400 | 155,720,900 | 185,132,344 | 207,530,770 | 228,185,535 | 252,626,826 | 267,617,701 |
| STATE FUNDS | 58,107,000 | 82,190,000 | 92,428,000 | 114,894,000 | 123,833,250 | 140,008,863 | 149,483,906 | 150,730,501 |
| General Funds | 40,017,000 | 62,061,000 | 69,844,000 | 73,697,000 | 80,088,000 | 94,104,000 | 99,365,000 | 94,977,000 |
| Other State Funds | 11,294,000 | 12,764,000 | 14,181,000 | 32,652,000 | 34,773,000 | 36,484,000 | 40,227,000 | 45,367,000 |
| Local/County Overmatch | 0 | 0 | 0 | 0 | 0 | 0 | 0 | 0 |
| SSI State Supplement | 6,796,000 | 7,365,000 | 8,403,000 | 8,545,000 | 8,972,250 | 9,420,863 | 9,891,906 | 10,386,501 |
| FEDERAL FUNDS | 47,456,000 | 49,283,400 | 63,292,900 | 70,238,344 | 83,697,520 | 88,176,672 | 103,142,920 | 116,887,200 |
| ICF/MR Funds | 0 | 0 | 0 | 0 | 0 | 0 | 0 | 0 |
| Small Public | 0 | 0 | 0 | 0 | 0 | 0 | 0 | 0 |
| Small Private | 0 | 0 | 0 | 0 | 0 | 0 | 0 | 0 |
| HCBS Waiver | 10,571,000 | 10,774,000 | 17,944,000 | 18,046,000 | 26,932,000 | 30,868,000 | 39,379,000 | 52,462,000 |
| Model 50/200 Waiver | 0 | 0 | 0 | 0 | 0 | 0 | 0 | 0 |
| Other Title XIX Programs | 22,768,000 | 24,441,000 | 28,502,000 | 34,721,000 | 34,947,000 | 36,282,000 | 38,804,000 | 38,929,000 |
| Title XX / SSBG Funds | 3,815,000 | 3,907,000 | 3,906,000 | 3,906,000 | 4,490,000 | 4,337,000 | 4,370,000 | 4,296,000 |
| Other Federal Funds | 3,012,000 | 1,951,000 | 2,527,000 | 1,948,000 | 3,970,000 | 2,373,000 | 3,377,000 | 2,641,000 |
| Waiver Clients' SSI/ADC | 7,290,000 | 8,210,400 | 10,413,900 | 11,617,344 | 13,358,520 | 14,316,672 | 17,212,920 | 18,559,200 |

*Source:*
Institute on Disability and Human Development (UAP),
University of Illinois at Chicago, 1994

# NEW MEXICO

## MR/DD Spending for Congregate Residential & Community Services

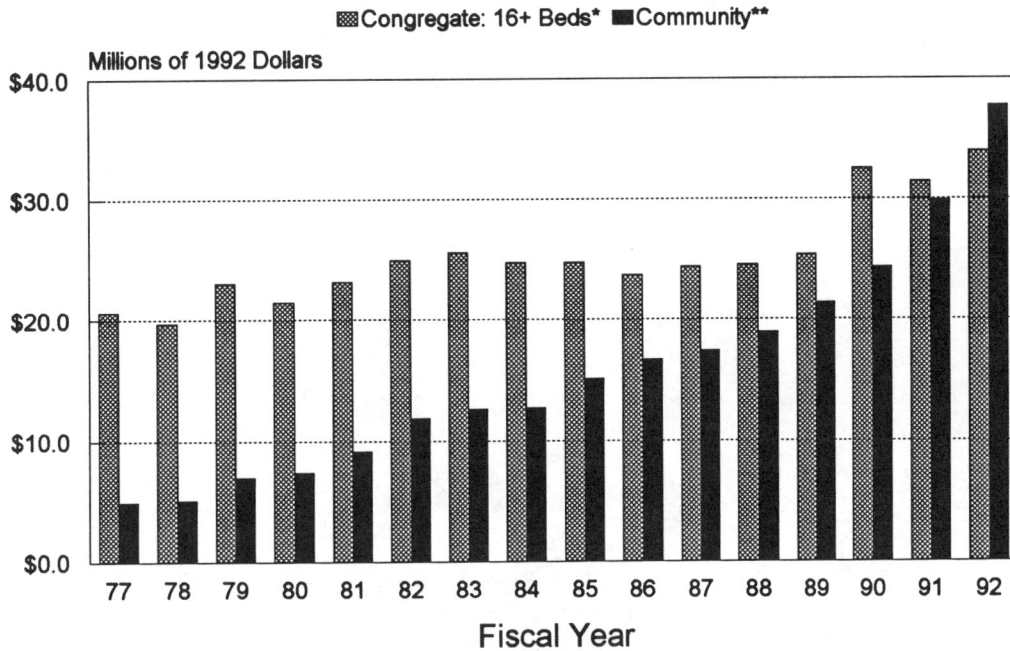

▧Congregate: 16+ Beds* ■Community**

Millions of 1992 Dollars

Fiscal Year

*Excludes nursing homes; ** Includes resources for
15 bed or less residential settings & non-residential community services

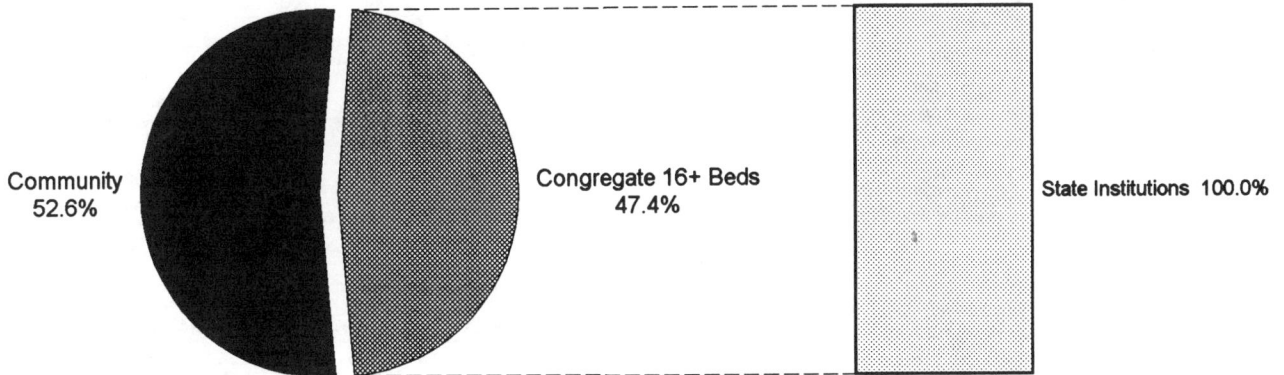

Community
52.6%

Congregate 16+ Beds
47.4%

State Institutions 100.0%

FY 1992 Total Spending:
$71.7 Million

*Source:*
Institute on Disability and Human Development (UAP),
University of Illinois at Chicago, 1994

# NEW MEXICO

## Number of Persons Served by Residential Setting: FY 1992

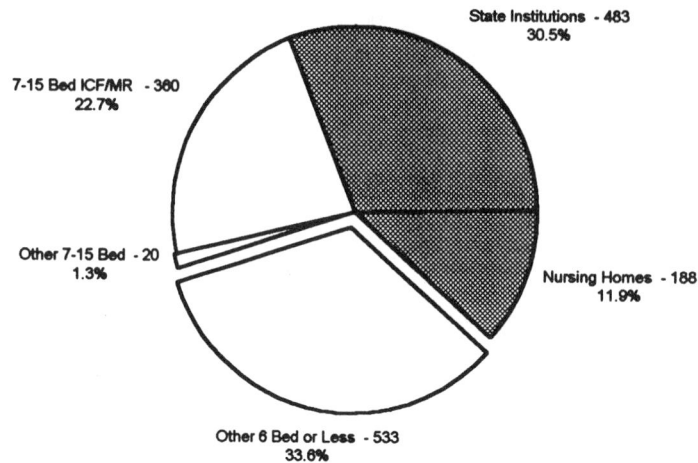

State Institutions - 483
30.5%

7-15 Bed ICF/MR - 360
22.7%

Other 7-15 Bed - 20
1.3%

Nursing Homes - 188
11.9%

Other 6 Bed or Less - 533
33.6%

Total Served: 1,584

## Persons Served by Residential Setting:1986-92

|  | 1986 | 1987 | 1988 | 1989 | 1990 | 1991 | 1992 |
|---|---|---|---|---|---|---|---|
| CONGREGATE 16 + BED SETTINGS | NA | NA | 559 | 625 | 618 | 617 | 671 |
| Nursing Homes | NA | NA | 66 | 125 | 125 | 128 | 188 |
| State Institutions | 470 | 484 | 493 | 500 | 493 | 489 | 483 |
| Private 16+Bed ICF/MR | 0 | 0 | 0 | 0 | 0 | 0 | 0 |
| Other 16+Bed Residential | 0 | 0 | 0 | 0 | 0 | 0 | 0 |
| 15 BED OR LESS RESIDENTIAL SETTINGS | 592 | 627 | 692 | 767 | 766 | 848 | 913 |
| Public 7-15 Bed ICF/MR | 0 | 0 | 0 | 0 | 0 | 0 | 0 |
| Private 7-15 Bed ICF/MR | 97 | 129 | 148 | 278 | 282 | 339 | 360 |
| Other 7-15 Bed Residential | 495 | 498 | 544 | 489 | 484 | 509 | 20 |
| Public 6 Bed or Less ICF/MR | 0 | 0 | 0 | 0 | 0 | 0 | 0 |
| Private 6 Bed or Less ICF/MR | 0 | 0 | 0 | 0 | 0 | 0 | 0 |
| Other 6 Bed or Less Residential | NA | NA | NA | NA | NA | NA | 533 |
| TOTAL PERSONS SERVED | NA | NA | 1,251 | 1,392 | 1,384 | 1,465 | 1,584 |

## Persons Served in Non-Residential Community Services:1986-92

|  | 1986 | 1987 | 1988 | 1989 | 1990 | 1991 | 1992 |
|---|---|---|---|---|---|---|---|
| DAY/WORK PROGRAMS | 782 | 770 | 832 | 652 | 634 | 816 | 916 |
| Sheltered Employment/Work Activity | 740 | 718 | 765 | 575 | 491 | 484 | 437 |
| Day Habilitation ("Day Training") | 30 | 33 | 33 | 41 | 12 | 12 | 11 |
| Supported/Competitive Employment | 12 | 19 | 34 | 36 | 131 | 320 | 468 |
| CASE MANAGEMENT | NA | NA | NA | NA | 151 | 788 | 1,070 |
| HCBS WAIVER | 85 | 128 | 120 | 156 | 151 | 170 | 282 |
| MODEL 50/200 WAIVER | 30 | 37 | 58 | 41 | 49 | 81 | 99 |

*Source:*
Institute on Disability and Human Development (UAP),
University of Illinois at Chicago, 1994

# NEW MEXICO

## Community Services: FY 1992 Revenue Sources

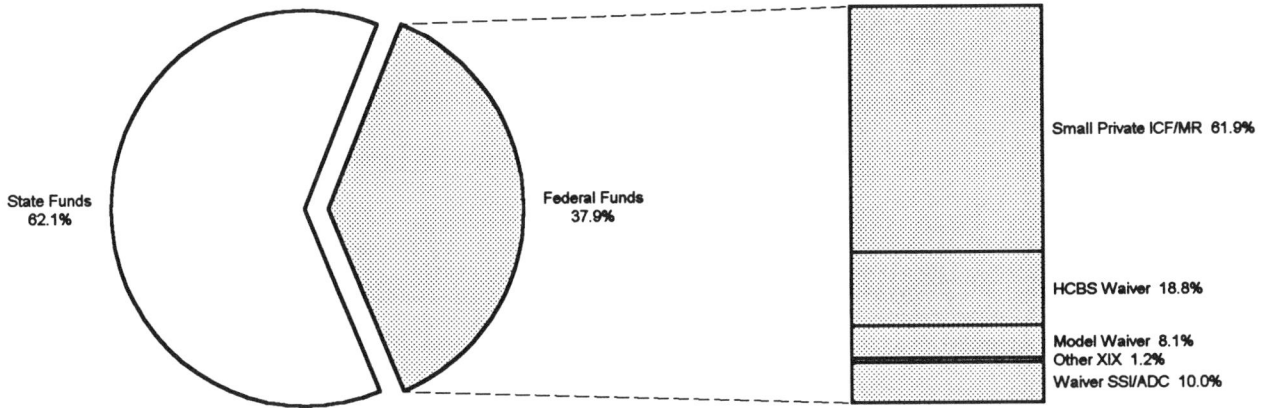

State Funds
62.1%

Federal Funds
37.9%

Small Private ICF/MR 61.9%

HCBS Waiver 18.8%

Model Waiver 8.1%
Other XIX 1.2%
Waiver SSI/ADC 10.0%

Total Funds: $37.7 Million

## Family Support Initiatives*

|  | 1986 | 1987 | 1988 | 1989 | 1990 | 1991 | 1992 |
|---|---|---|---|---|---|---|---|
| **FAMILY SUPPORT: TOTAL SPENDING** | NA | $145,935 | $187,770 | $191,618 | $332,598 | $514,338 | $617,175 |
| **Total # of Families Supported** | 222 | 211 | 224 | 265 | 321 | 508 | 522 |
| A. Financial Subsidy/Payment | $0 | $0 | $0 | $0 | $0 | $0 | $0 |
| # of Families | 0 | 0 | 0 | 0 | 0 | 0 | 0 |
| B. Family Assistance Payments | NA | $145,935 | $187,770 | $191,618 | $332,598 | $514,338 | $617,175 |
| # of Families | 222 | 211 | 224 | 265 | 321 | 508 | 522 |
| C. Other Family Support Payments | $0 | $0 | $0 | $0 | $0 | $0 | $0 |
| # of Families | 0 | 0 | 0 | 0 | 0 | 0 | 0 |

## Other Community Services Initiatives*

|  | 1986 | 1987 | 1988 | 1989 | 1990 | 1991 | 1992 |
|---|---|---|---|---|---|---|---|
| **AGING/DD SPENDING** | NA | NA | NA | $0 | $0 | $0 | $0 |
| # of Persons Served | 16 | 16 | 16 | 0 | 0 | 0 | 0 |
| **ASSISTIVE TECHNOLOGY SPENDING** |  |  |  |  |  |  | $0 |
| # of Persons Served |  |  |  |  |  |  | 0 |
| **EARLY INTERVENTION SPENDING** | NA | $1,826,156 | $1,971,171 | $2,328,517 | $2,408,706 | $2,926,701 | $2,674,636 |
| # of Persons Served | NA | 725 | 728 | 577 | 547 | 757 | 862 |
| **PERSONAL ASSISTANCE SPENDING** |  |  |  |  |  |  | $0 |
| # of Persons Served |  |  |  |  |  |  | 0 |
| **SUPPORTED EMPLOYMENT SPENDING** | NA | $37,874 | $134,824 | $129,424 | $557,334 | $1,546,096 | $2,413,636 |
| # of Persons Served | 12 | 19 | 34 | 36 | 131 | 320 | 436 |
| **SUPPORTED LIVING SPENDING** |  |  |  | $1,226,507 | $1,453,721 | $1,982,673 | $2,856,730 |
| # of Persons Served |  |  |  | 220 | 270 | 316 | 370 |

*Expenditures associated with Special Community Initiatives are a subset of funding within the community services component of the state's chart series and spreadsheet; Family Support Client figures may include duplicate client counts; HCBS Waiver counts include Waiver case management numbers.
0= Services not provided in the state; NA= Data not available from state; blank= Services not applicable (eg. CSLA prior to authorization, Special Community Initiatives prior to request for data by this study)

*Source:*
Institute on Disability and Human Development (UAP),
University of Illinois at Chicago, 1994

# NEW MEXICO

## Large Congregate Care Facilities: FY 1992 Revenue Sources*

### Private 16+Bed Settings

**Does Not Apply**

### Public Institutions

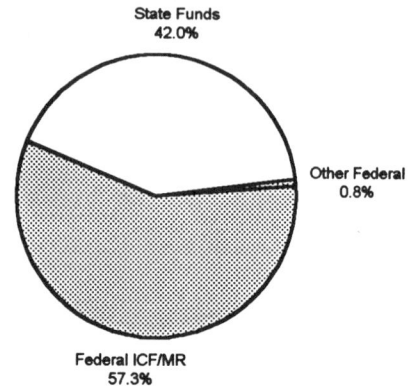

State Funds
42.0%

Other Federal
0.8%

Federal ICF/MR
57.3%

Total Funds: $34.0 Million

*Excludes nursing homes

## Average Daily Residents in Institutions

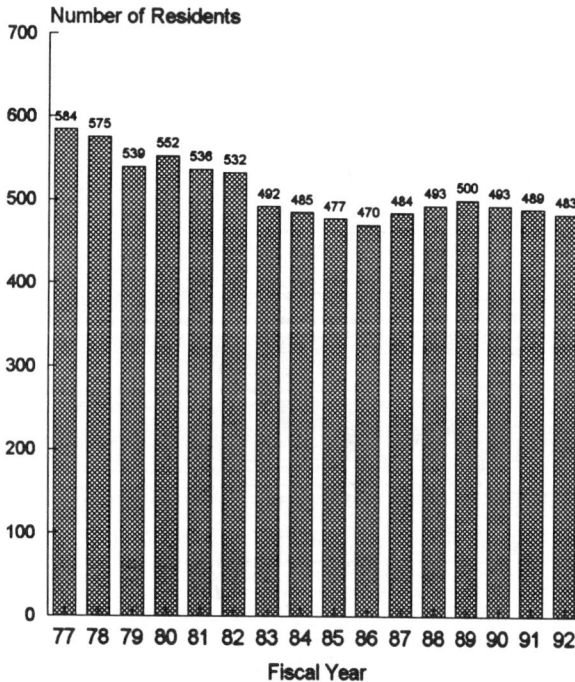

Number of Residents

| Fiscal Year | Residents |
|---|---|
| 77 | 584 |
| 78 | 575 |
| 79 | 539 |
| 80 | 552 |
| 81 | 536 |
| 82 | 532 |
| 83 | 492 |
| 84 | 485 |
| 85 | 477 |
| 86 | 470 |
| 87 | 484 |
| 88 | 493 |
| 89 | 500 |
| 90 | 493 |
| 91 | 489 |
| 92 | 483 |

Fiscal Year

## Institutional Daily Costs Per Resident

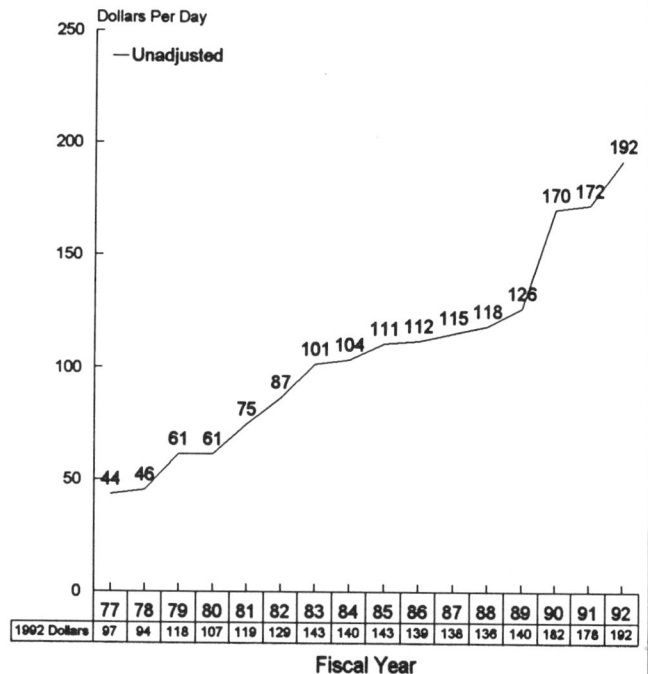

Dollars Per Day

—Unadjusted

Unadjusted values: 44, 46, 61, 61, 75, 87, 101, 104, 111, 112, 115, 118, 126, 170, 172, 192

| | 77 | 78 | 79 | 80 | 81 | 82 | 83 | 84 | 85 | 86 | 87 | 88 | 89 | 90 | 91 | 92 |
|---|---|---|---|---|---|---|---|---|---|---|---|---|---|---|---|---|
| 1992 Dollars | 97 | 94 | 118 | 107 | 119 | 129 | 143 | 140 | 143 | 139 | 138 | 136 | 140 | 182 | 178 | 192 |

Fiscal Year

*Source:*
Institute on Disability and Human Development (UAP),
University of Illinois at Chicago, 1994

# NEW MEXICO FISCAL EFFORT

**MR/DD Spending Per $1,000 of Personal Income**

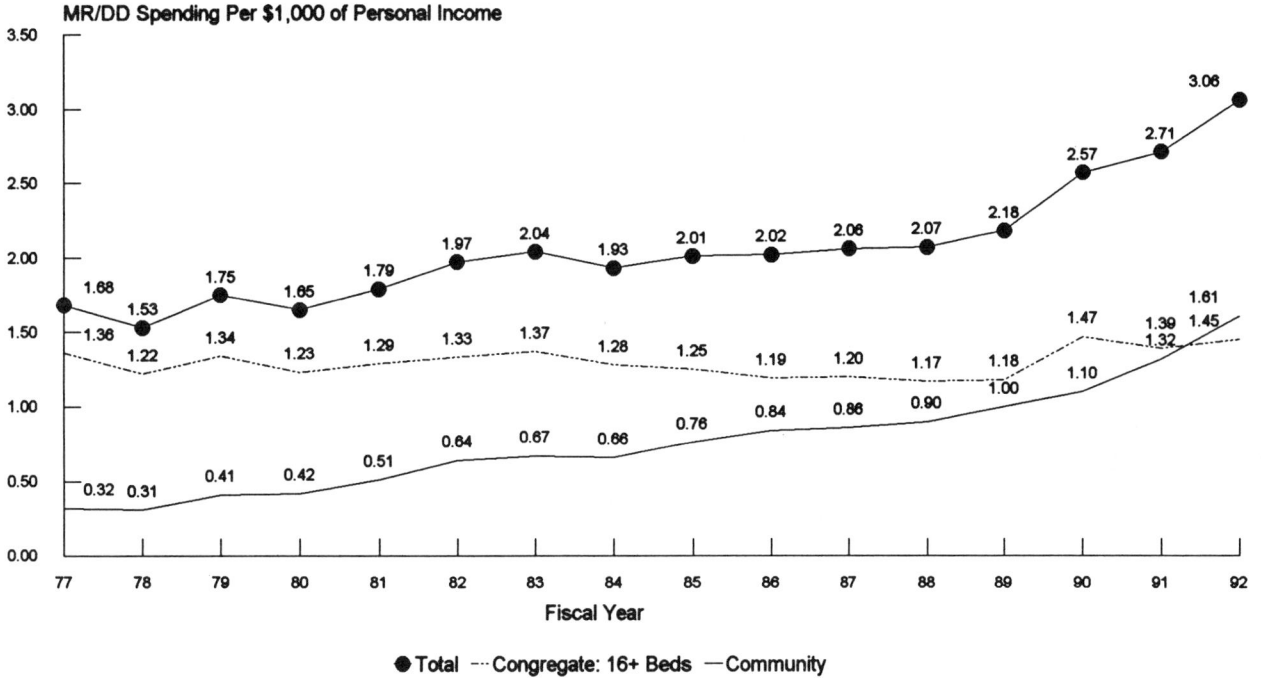

Total ●  ---Congregate: 16+ Beds  —Community

## Total MR/DD Spending

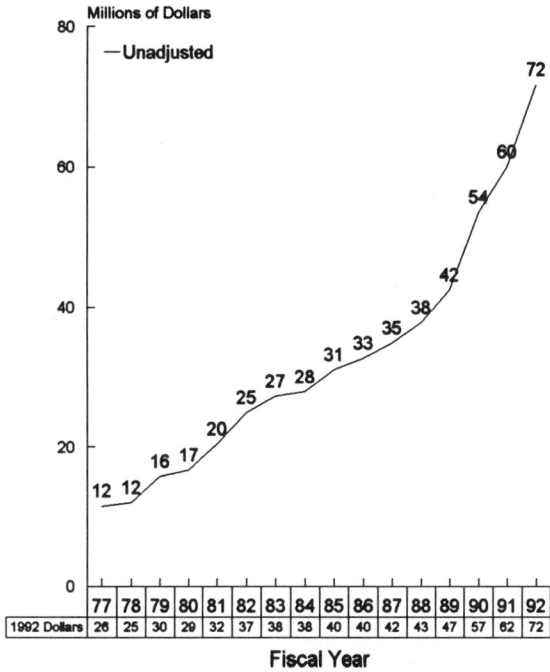

| | 77 | 78 | 79 | 80 | 81 | 82 | 83 | 84 | 85 | 86 | 87 | 88 | 89 | 90 | 91 | 92 |
|---|---|---|---|---|---|---|---|---|---|---|---|---|---|---|---|---|
| 1992 Dollars | 26 | 25 | 30 | 29 | 32 | 37 | 38 | 38 | 40 | 40 | 42 | 43 | 47 | 57 | 62 | 72 |

**Fiscal Year**

## Personal Income

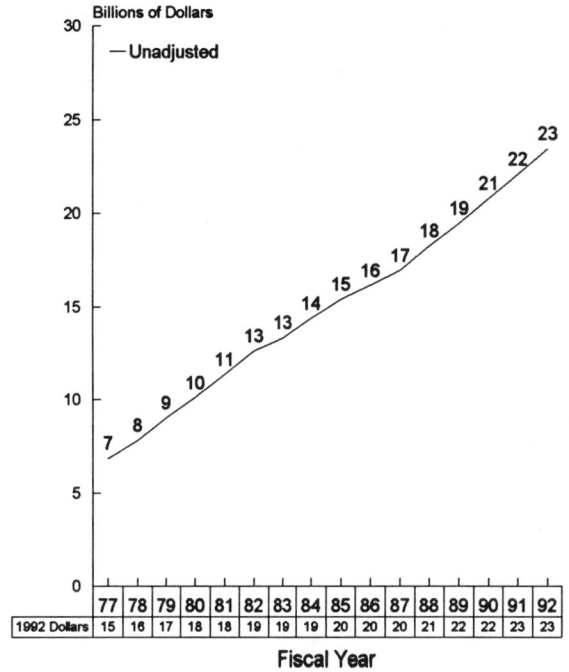

| | 77 | 78 | 79 | 80 | 81 | 82 | 83 | 84 | 85 | 86 | 87 | 88 | 89 | 90 | 91 | 92 |
|---|---|---|---|---|---|---|---|---|---|---|---|---|---|---|---|---|
| 1992 Dollars | 15 | 16 | 17 | 18 | 18 | 19 | 19 | 20 | 20 | 20 | 21 | 22 | 22 | 23 | 23 |

**Fiscal Year**

*Source:*
Institute on Disability and Human Development (UAP),
University of Illinois at Chicago, 1994

# NEW MEXICO

## Financial Support for MR/DD Services: FY 1977-92

| | 1977 | 1978 | 1979 | 1980 | 1981 | 1982 | 1983 | 1984 |
|---|---|---|---|---|---|---|---|---|
| **TOTAL FUNDS** | $11,517,000 | $12,009,400 | $15,731,400 | $16,684,476 | $20,391,972 | $24,848,789 | $27,197,400 | $27,825,256 |
| **CONGREGATE 16+ BEDS** | 9,300,000 | 9,563,400 | 12,075,400 | 12,423,600 | 14,622,400 | 16,820,000 | 18,213,400 | 18,372,200 |
| INSTITUTIONAL SERVICES FUNDS | 9,300,000 | 9,563,400 | 12,075,400 | 12,423,600 | 14,622,400 | 16,820,000 | 18,213,400 | 18,372,200 |
| STATE FUNDS | 6,735,600 | 7,123,800 | 7,714,600 | 6,674,100 | 8,620,200 | 8,367,800 | 9,942,700 | 6,726,744 |
| General Funds | 6,238,800 | 6,365,600 | 7,529,500 | 6,143,000 | 6,161,500 | 5,214,700 | 5,105,900 | 4,687,100 |
| Local | 0 | 0 | 0 | 0 | 0 | 0 | 0 | 0 |
| Other State Funds | 496,800 | 758,200 | 185,100 | 531,100 | 2,458,700 | 3,153,100 | 4,836,800 | 2,039,644 |
| FEDERAL FUNDS | 2,564,400 | 2,439,600 | 4,360,800 | 5,749,500 | 6,002,200 | 8,452,200 | 8,270,700 | 11,645,456 |
| Federal ICF/MR | 2,111,000 | 1,931,000 | 3,973,000 | 5,156,000 | 5,478,000 | 8,100,000 | 7,928,000 | 11,392,056 |
| Title XX / SSBG Funds | 0 | 0 | 0 | 0 | 0 | 0 | 0 | 0 |
| Other Federal Funds | 453,400 | 508,600 | 387,800 | 593,500 | 524,200 | 352,200 | 342,700 | 253,400 |
| LARGE PRIVATE RESIDENTIAL | 0 | 0 | 0 | 0 | 0 | 0 | 0 | 0 |
| STATE FUNDS | 0 | 0 | 0 | 0 | 0 | 0 | 0 | 0 |
| General Funds | 0 | 0 | 0 | 0 | 0 | 0 | 0 | 0 |
| Other State Funds | 0 | 0 | 0 | 0 | 0 | 0 | 0 | 0 |
| Local/County Overmatch | 0 | 0 | 0 | 0 | 0 | 0 | 0 | 0 |
| FEDERAL FUNDS | 0 | 0 | 0 | 0 | 0 | 0 | 0 | 0 |
| Large Private ICF/MR | 0 | 0 | 0 | 0 | 0 | 0 | 0 | 0 |
| **COMMUNITY SERVICES FUNDS** | 2,217,000 | 2,446,000 | 3,656,000 | 4,260,876 | 5,769,572 | 8,028,789 | 8,984,000 | 9,453,056 |
| STATE FUNDS | 591,000 | 820,000 | 2,014,000 | 2,549,876 | 3,884,572 | 5,379,789 | 6,866,878 | 7,084,651 |
| General Funds | 591,000 | 820,000 | 2,014,000 | 2,526,000 | 3,776,000 | 5,004,852 | 6,483,000 | 6,596,608 |
| Other State Funds | 0 | 0 | 0 | 23,876 | 108,572 | 374,937 | 383,878 | 488,043 |
| Local/County Overmatch | 0 | 0 | 0 | 0 | 0 | 0 | 0 | 0 |
| SSI State Supplement | 0 | 0 | 0 | 0 | 0 | 0 | 0 | 0 |
| FEDERAL FUNDS | 1,626,000 | 1,626,000 | 1,642,000 | 1,711,000 | 1,885,000 | 2,649,000 | 2,117,122 | 2,368,405 |
| ICF/MR Funds | 0 | 0 | 0 | 55,000 | 242,000 | 784,000 | 786,122 | 1,078,205 |
| Small Public | 0 | 0 | 0 | 0 | 0 | 0 | 0 | 0 |
| Small Private | 0 | 0 | 0 | 55,000 | 242,000 | 784,000 | 786,122 | 1,078,205 |
| HCBS Waiver | 0 | 0 | 0 | 0 | 0 | 0 | 0 | 0 |
| Model 50/200 Waiver | 0 | 0 | 0 | 0 | 0 | 0 | 0 | 0 |
| Other Title XIX Programs | 0 | 0 | 0 | 0 | 0 | 0 | 0 | 0 |
| Title XX / SSBG Funds | 1,626,000 | 1,626,000 | 1,642,000 | 1,656,000 | 1,643,000 | 1,865,000 | 1,331,000 | 1,290,200 |
| Other Federal Funds | 0 | 0 | 0 | 0 | 0 | 0 | 0 | 0 |
| Waiver Clients' SSI/ADC | 0 | 0 | 0 | 0 | 0 | 0 | 0 | 0 |

| | 1985 | 1986 | 1987 | 1988 | 1989 | 1990 | 1991 | 1992 |
|---|---|---|---|---|---|---|---|---|
| **TOTAL FUNDS** | $31,020,560 | $32,651,163 | $34,894,108 | $37,803,922 | $42,446,027 | $53,544,125 | $59,970,752 | $71,716,311 |
| **CONGREGATE 16+ BEDS** | 19,257,000 | 19,165,000 | 20,364,900 | 21,358,500 | 23,032,200 | 30,651,700 | 30,747,000 | 33,978,700 |
| INSTITUTIONAL SERVICES FUNDS | 19,257,000 | 19,165,000 | 20,364,900 | 21,358,500 | 23,032,200 | 30,651,700 | 30,747,000 | 33,978,700 |
| STATE FUNDS | 7,429,223 | 7,073,657 | 6,813,842 | 7,071,821 | 8,751,949 | 15,740,630 | 13,658,095 | 14,264,235 |
| General Funds | 572,300 | 679,300 | 993,100 | 1,366,300 | 2,255,600 | 8,841,100 | 6,352,000 | 6,474,300 |
| Local | 0 | 0 | 0 | 0 | 912,440 | 1,215,440 | 1,107,340 | 985,736 |
| Other State Funds | 6,856,923 | 6,394,357 | 5,820,742 | 5,705,521 | 5,583,909 | 5,684,090 | 6,198,755 | 6,804,199 |
| FEDERAL FUNDS | 11,827,777 | 12,091,343 | 13,551,058 | 14,286,679 | 14,280,251 | 14,911,070 | 17,088,905 | 19,714,465 |
| Federal ICF/MR | 11,578,277 | 11,824,743 | 13,263,658 | 14,009,479 | 14,036,291 | 14,667,110 | 16,844,945 | 19,456,701 |
| Title XX / SSBG Funds | 0 | 0 | 0 | 0 | 0 | 0 | 0 | 0 |
| Other Federal Funds | 249,500 | 266,600 | 287,400 | 277,200 | 243,960 | 243,960 | 243,960 | 257,764 |
| LARGE PRIVATE RESIDENTIAL | 0 | 0 | 0 | 0 | 0 | 0 | 0 | 0 |
| STATE FUNDS | 0 | 0 | 0 | 0 | 0 | 0 | 0 | 0 |
| General Funds | 0 | 0 | 0 | 0 | 0 | 0 | 0 | 0 |
| Other State Funds | 0 | 0 | 0 | 0 | 0 | 0 | 0 | 0 |
| Local/County Overmatch | 0 | 0 | 0 | 0 | 0 | 0 | 0 | 0 |
| FEDERAL FUNDS | 0 | 0 | 0 | 0 | 0 | 0 | 0 | 0 |
| Large Private ICF/MR | 0 | 0 | 0 | 0 | 0 | 0 | 0 | 0 |
| **COMMUNITY SERVICES FUNDS** | 11,763,560 | 13,486,163 | 14,529,208 | 16,445,422 | 19,413,827 | 22,892,425 | 29,223,752 | 37,737,611 |
| STATE FUNDS | 8,190,344 | 9,444,674 | 10,339,114 | 11,277,164 | 12,585,452 | 14,095,364 | 18,291,684 | 23,428,231 |
| General Funds | 7,407,341 | 8,650,587 | 8,894,300 | 9,505,700 | 10,139,300 | 10,950,000 | 14,560,400 | 18,918,500 |
| Other State Funds | 783,003 | 794,087 | 1,444,814 | 1,771,464 | 2,446,152 | 3,145,364 | 3,731,284 | 4,509,731 |
| Local/County Overmatch | 0 | 0 | 0 | 0 | 0 | 0 | 0 | 0 |
| SSI State Supplement | 0 | 0 | 0 | 0 | 0 | 0 | 0 | 0 |
| FEDERAL FUNDS | 3,573,216 | 4,041,489 | 4,190,094 | 5,168,258 | 6,828,375 | 8,797,061 | 10,932,068 | 14,309,380 |
| ICF/MR Funds | 1,774,995 | 1,771,623 | 2,308,304 | 2,856,991 | 4,547,915 | 6,194,547 | 7,419,669 | 8,858,390 |
| Small Public | 0 | 0 | 0 | 0 | 0 | 0 | 0 | 0 |
| Small Private | 1,774,995 | 1,771,623 | 2,308,304 | 2,856,991 | 4,547,915 | 6,194,547 | 7,419,669 | 8,858,390 |
| HCBS Waiver | 270,621 | 376,461 | 740,499 | 1,066,243 | 1,146,810 | 1,314,012 | 1,779,411 | 2,688,857 |
| Model 50/200 Waiver | 0 | 125,119 | 239,150 | 426,464 | 444,754 | 589,070 | 902,708 | 1,163,885 |
| Other Title XIX Programs | 0 | 0 | 0 | 0 | 0 | 0 | 0 | 170,200 |
| Title XX / SSBG Funds | 1,336,800 | 1,336,900 | 292,700 | 0 | 0 | 0 | 0 | 0 |
| Other Federal Funds | 0 | 114,166 | 125,601 | 352,000 | 0 | 0 | 0 | 0 |
| Waiver Clients' SSI/ADC | 190,800 | 317,220 | 483,840 | 466,560 | 688,896 | 699,432 | 830,280 | 1,428,048 |

*Source:*
Institute on Disability and Human Development (UAP),
University of Illinois at Chicago, 1994

# NEW YORK

## MR/DD Spending for Congregate Residential & Community Services

▨Congregate: 16+ Beds*  ■Community**

Millions of 1992 Dollars

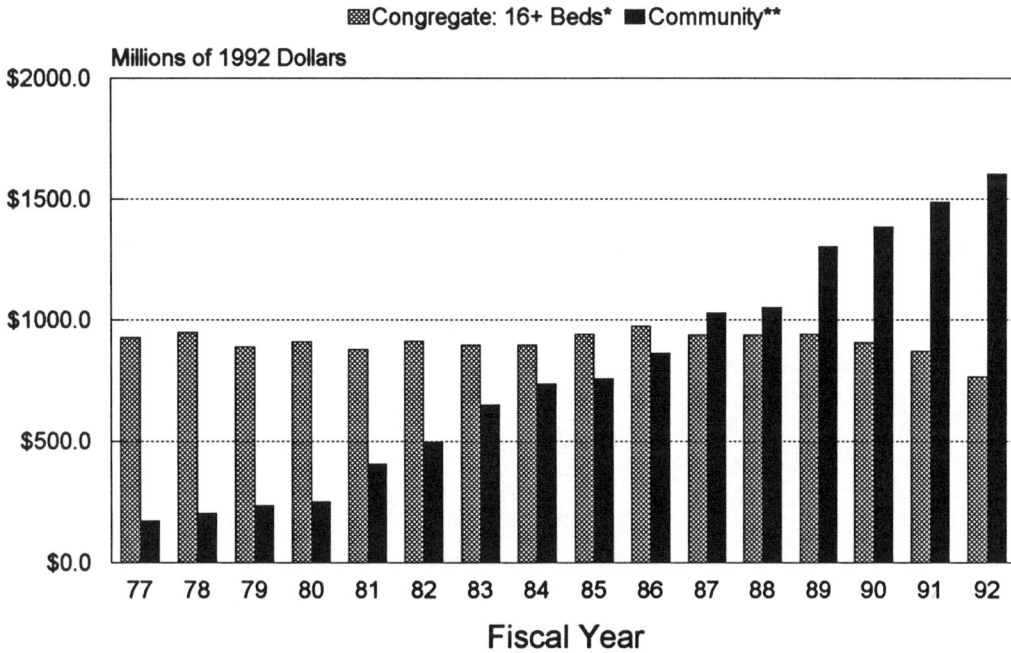

Fiscal Year

*Excludes nursing homes; ** Includes resources for
15 bed or less residential settings & non-residential community services

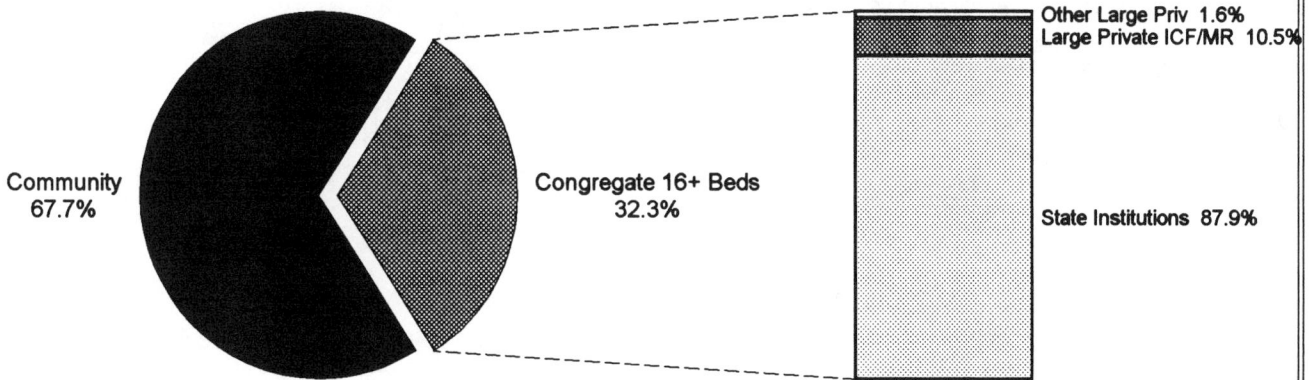

Community
67.7%

Congregate 16+ Beds
32.3%

Other Large Priv 1.6%
Large Private ICF/MR 10.5%

State Institutions 87.9%

FY 1992 Total Spending:
$2.37 Billion

*Source:*
Institute on Disability and Human Development (UAP),
University of Illinois at Chicago, 1994

# NEW YORK

## Number of Persons Served by Residential Setting: FY 1992

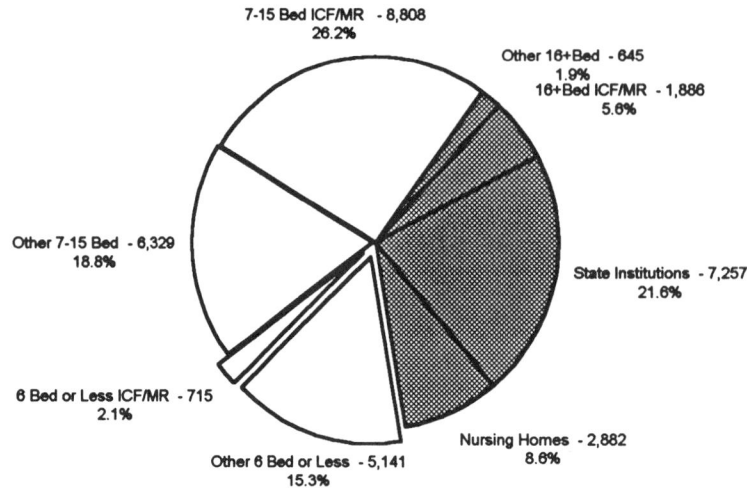

7-15 Bed ICF/MR - 8,808
26.2%

Other 16+Bed - 645
1.9%

16+Bed ICF/MR - 1,886
5.6%

Other 7-15 Bed - 6,329
18.8%

State Institutions - 7,257
21.6%

6 Bed or Less ICF/MR - 715
2.1%

Other 6 Bed or Less - 5,141
15.3%

Nursing Homes - 2,882
8.6%

Total Served: 33,663

## Persons Served by Residential Setting:1986-92

|  | 1986 | 1987 | 1988 | 1989 | 1990 | 1991 | 1992 |
|---|---|---|---|---|---|---|---|
| CONGREGATE 16 + BED SETTINGS | 15,776 | 15,408 | 14,827 | 14,199 | 13,718 | 13,250 | 12,670 |
| Nursing Homes | 2,645 | 2,645 | 2,645 | 2,704 | 2,763 | 2,823 | 2,882 |
| State Institutions | 10,828 | 10,203 | 9,534 | 8,853 | 8,519 | 7,964 | 7,257 |
| Private 16+Bed ICF/MR | 1,111 | 1,400 | 1,519 | 1,750 | 1,782 | 1,814 | 1,886 |
| Other 16+Bed Residential | 1,192 | 1,160 | 1,129 | 892 | 654 | 649 | 645 |
| 15 BED OR LESS RESIDENTIAL SETTINGS | 10,550 | 11,924 | 13,186 | 14,658 | 15,914 | 17,249 | 20,993 |
| Public 7-15 Bed ICF/MR | 1,582 | 1,800 | 1,973 | 2,302 | 2,630 | 2,838 | 3,011 |
| Private 7-15 Bed ICF/MR | 3,153 | 3,622 | 3,982 | 4,500 | 4,953 | 5,447 | 5,797 |
| Other 7-15 Bed Residential | 4,244 | 4,692 | 5,172 | 5,512 | 5,716 | 5,955 | 6,329 |
| Public 6 Bed or Less ICF/MR | 99 | 117 | 128 | 128 | 130 | 140 | 140 |
| Private 6 Bed or Less ICF/MR | 535 | 543 | 543 | 565 | 555 | 561 | 575 |
| Other 6 Bed or Less Residential | 937 | 1,150 | 1,388 | 1,651 | 1,930 | 2,308 | 5,141 |
| TOTAL PERSONS SERVED | 26,326 | 27,332 | 28,013 | 28,857 | 29,632 | 30,499 | 33,663 |

## Persons Served in Non-Residential Community Services:1986-92

|  | 1986 | 1987 | 1988 | 1989 | 1990 | 1991 | 1992 |
|---|---|---|---|---|---|---|---|
| DAY/WORK PROGRAMS | 2,569 | 2,656 | 35,580 | 63,987 | 64,841 | 65,426 | 41,966 |
| Sheltered Employment/Work Activity | NA | NA | 14,001 | 16,392 | 15,401 | 15,450 | 14,848 |
| Day Habilitation ("Day Training") | NA | NA | 19,512 | 44,764 | 44,921 | 46,224 | 22,201 |
| Supported/Competitive Employment | 600 | 800 | 2,067 | 2,831 | 4,519 | 3,752 | 4,917 |
| CASE MANAGEMENT | NA | NA | 45,929 | 51,809 | 53,053 | 58,123 | 69,566 |
| HCBS WAIVER | 0 | 0 | 0 | 0 | 0 | 0 | 168 |
| MODEL 50/200 WAIVER | 2 | 13 | 17 | 0 | 0 | 0 | 200 |

*Source:*
Institute on Disability and Human Development (UAP),
University of Illinois at Chicago, 1994

# NEW YORK

## Community Services: FY 1992 Revenue Sources

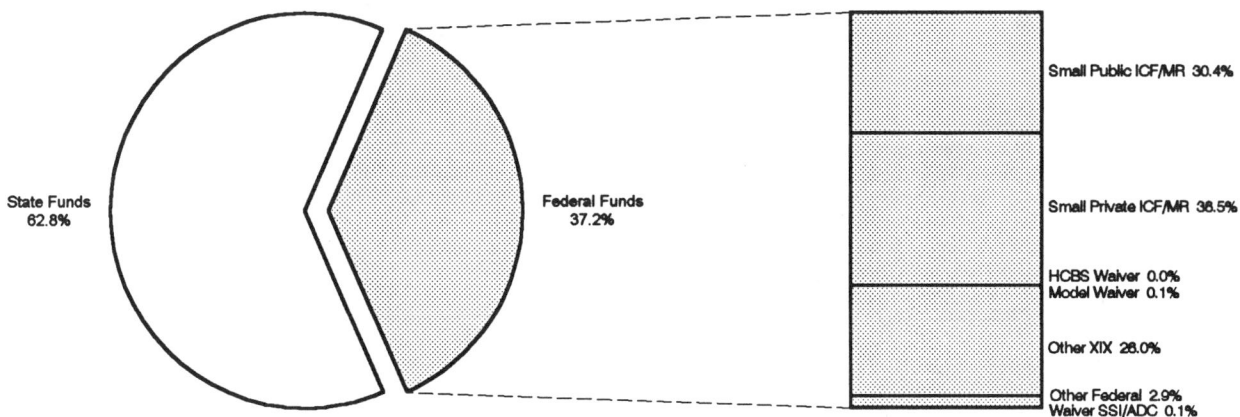

State Funds 62.8%

Federal Funds 37.2%

Small Public ICF/MR 30.4%

Small Private ICF/MR 38.5%

HCBS Waiver 0.0%
Model Waiver 0.1%

Other XIX 28.0%

Other Federal 2.9%
Waiver SSI/ADC 0.1%

Total Funds: $1.6 Billion

## Family Support Initiatives*

|  | 1986 | 1987 | 1988 | 1989 | 1990 | 1991 | 1992 |
|---|---|---|---|---|---|---|---|
| **FAMILY SUPPORT: TOTAL SPENDING** | $8,386,385 | $12,158,770 | $16,536,000 | $20,215,000 | $20,543,000 | $23,242,000 | $26,631,800 |
| **Total # of Families Supported** | 11,000 | 13,000 | 20,000 | 32,816 | 33,000 | 35,000 | 35,000 |
| A. Financial Subsidy/Payment | $0 | $0 | $0 | $0 | $0 | $317,200 | $700,000 |
| # of Families | 0 | 0 | 0 | 0 | 0 | 100 | 500 |
| B. Family Assistance Payments | $466,667 | $733,334 | $1,000,000 | $12,735,500 | $12,924,100 | $14,642,500 | $16,778,000 |
| # of Families | NA | NA | NA | 16,400 | 16,500 | 17,500 | 18,000 |
| C. Other Family Support Payments | $7,919,718 | $11,425,436 | $15,536,000 | $7,479,500 | $7,618,900 | $8,282,300 | $9,153,800 |
| # of Families | NA | NA | NA | 16,416 | 16,500 | 17,400 | 16,500 |

## Other Community Services Initiatives*

|  | 1986 | 1987 | 1988 | 1989 | 1990 | 1991 | 1992 |
|---|---|---|---|---|---|---|---|
| **AGING/DD SPENDING** | $0 | $0 | $0 | $494,000 | $985,000 | $1,195,000 | $2,562,000 |
| # of Persons Served | 0 | 0 | 0 | 179 | 179 | 221 | 538 |
| **ASSISTIVE TECHNOLOGY SPENDING** |  |  | $479,500 | $586,235 | $595,750 | $674,020 | $772,325 |
| # of Persons Served |  |  | 770 | 985 | 990 | 1,050 | 1,100 |
| **EARLY INTERVENTION SPENDING** | $0 | $1,072,216 | $1,091,203 | $505,375 | $513,575 | $581,050 | $665,800 |
| # of Persons Served | 0 | 660 | 700 | 5,100 | 5,115 | 5,425 | 5,500 |
| **PERSONAL ASSISTANCE SPENDING** |  |  | $2,291,000 | $2,443,000 | $1,721,000 | $1,782,000 | $1,639,000 |
| # of Persons Served |  |  | 1,492 | 1,703 | 1,746 | 1,826 | 1,922 |
| **SUPPORTED EMPLOYMENT SPENDING** | $800,000 | $2,425,000 | $4,757,000 | $6,512,000 | $9,088,000 | $7,852,000 | $9,725,000 |
| # of Persons Served | 600 | 800 | 2,067 | 2,831 | 4,519 | 3,752 | 4,917 |
| **SUPPORTED LIVING SPENDING** |  |  |  |  |  | $832,000 | $1,231,000 |
| # of Persons Served |  |  |  |  |  | 130 | 140 |

*Expenditures associated with Special Community Initiatives are a subset of funding within the community services component of the state's chart series and spreadsheet; Family Support Client figures may include duplicate client counts; HCBS Waiver counts include Waiver case management numbers.
0= Services not provided in the state; NA= Data not available from state; blank= Services not applicable (eg. CSLA prior to authorization, Special Community Initiatives prior to request for data by this study)

Source:
Institute on Disability and Human Development (UAP),
University of Illinois at Chicago, 1994

# NEW YORK

## Large Congregate Care Facilities: FY 1992 Revenue Sources*

### Private 16+Bed Settings

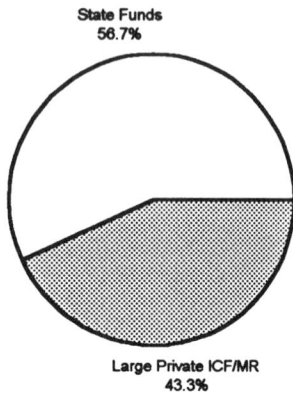

State Funds
56.7%

Large Private ICF/MR
43.3%

Total Funds: $92.8 Million

### Public Institutions

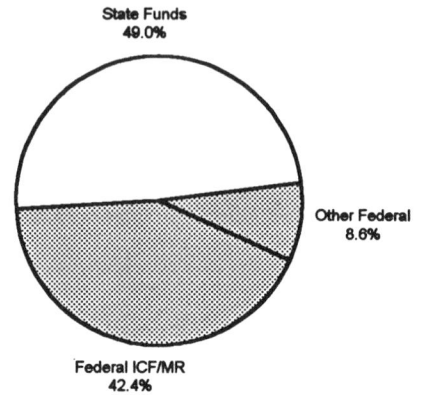

State Funds
49.0%

Other Federal
8.6%

Federal ICF/MR
42.4%

Total Funds: $672.3 Million

*Excludes nursing homes

## Average Daily Residents in Institutions

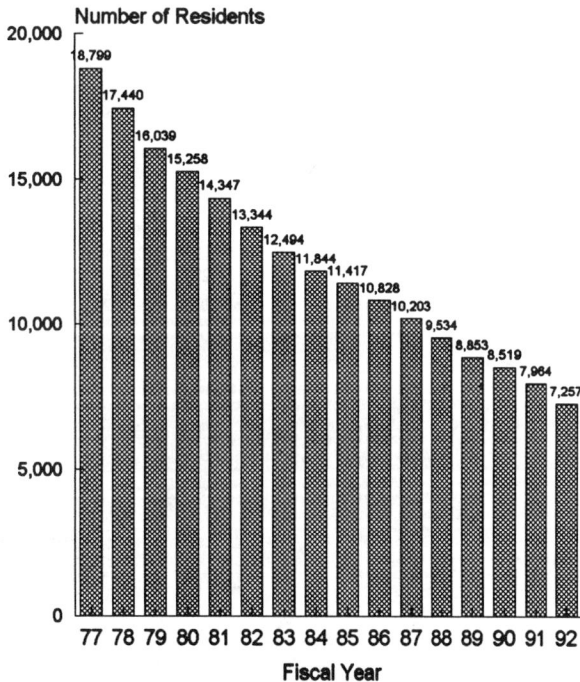

Number of Residents

- 77: 18,799
- 78: 17,440
- 79: 16,039
- 80: 15,258
- 81: 14,347
- 82: 13,344
- 83: 12,494
- 84: 11,844
- 85: 11,417
- 86: 10,828
- 87: 10,203
- 88: 9,534
- 89: 8,853
- 90: 8,519
- 91: 7,964
- 92: 7,257

Fiscal Year

## Institutional Daily Costs Per Resident

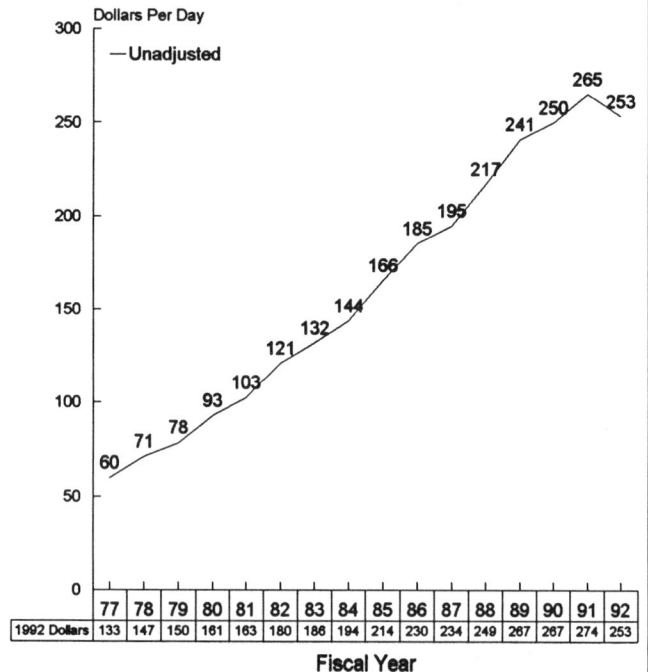

Dollars Per Day

—Unadjusted

- 77: 60
- 78: 71
- 79: 78
- 80: 93
- 81: 103
- 82: 121
- 83: 132
- 84: 144
- 85: 166
- 86: 185
- 87: 195
- 88: 217
- 89: 241
- 90: 250
- 91: 265
- 92: 253

| 1992 Dollars | 133 | 147 | 150 | 161 | 163 | 180 | 186 | 194 | 214 | 230 | 234 | 249 | 267 | 267 | 274 | 253 |
|---|---|---|---|---|---|---|---|---|---|---|---|---|---|---|---|---|

Fiscal Year

*Source:*
Institute on Disability and Human Development (UAP),
University of Illinois at Chicago, 1994

# NEW YORK FISCAL EFFORT

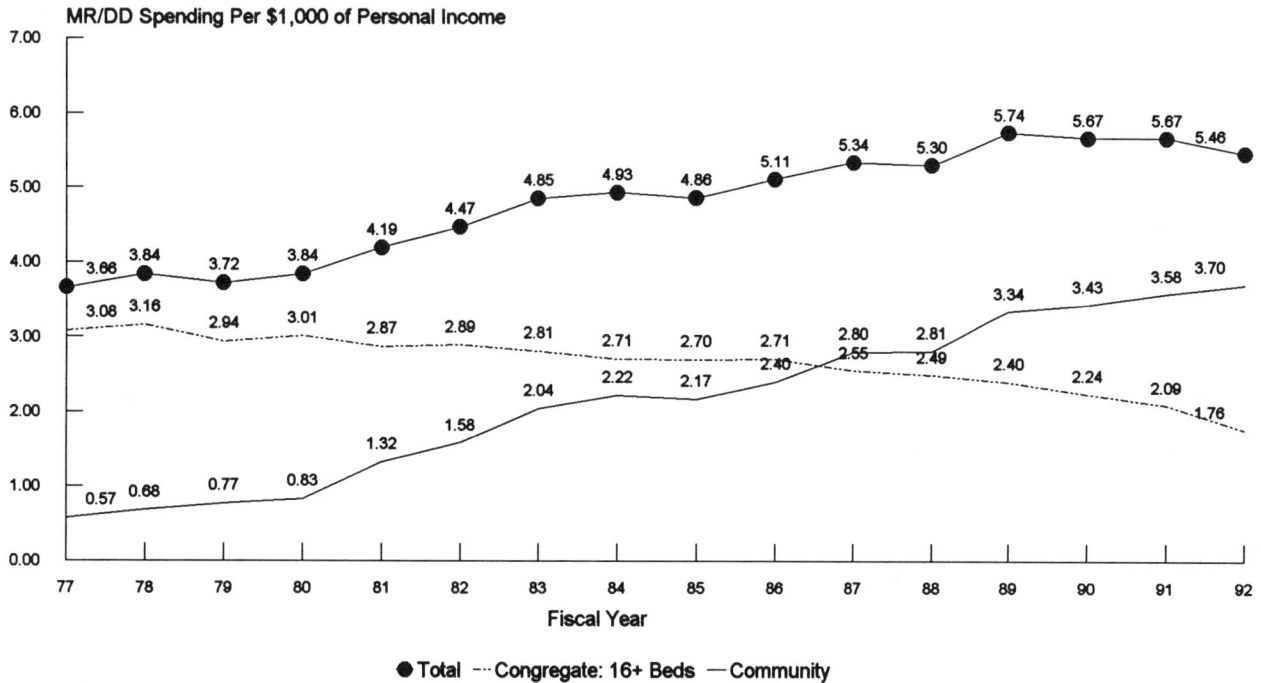

MR/DD Spending Per $1,000 of Personal Income

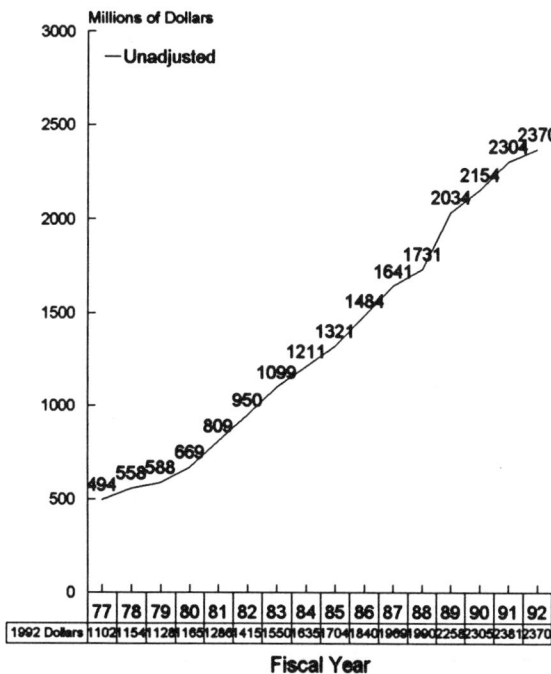

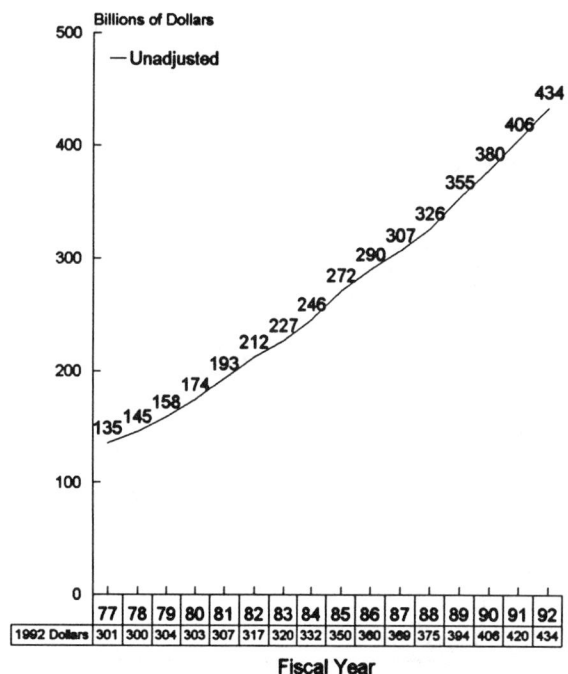

Total — Congregate: 16+ Beds — Community

| | Total | Congregate | Community |
|---|---|---|---|
| 77 | 3.66 | 3.08 | 0.57 |
| 78 | 3.84 | 3.16 | 0.68 |
| 79 | 3.72 | 2.94 | 0.77 |
| 80 | 3.84 | 3.01 | 0.83 |
| 81 | 4.19 | 2.87 | 1.32 |
| 82 | 4.47 | 2.89 | 1.58 |
| 83 | 4.85 | 2.81 | 2.04 |
| 84 | 4.93 | 2.71 | 2.22 |
| 85 | 4.86 | 2.70 | 2.17 |
| 86 | 5.11 | 2.71 | 2.40 |
| 87 | 5.34 | 2.80 | 2.55 |
| 88 | 5.30 | 2.81 | 2.49 |
| 89 | 5.74 | 2.40 | 3.34 |
| 90 | 5.67 | 2.24 | 3.43 |
| 91 | 5.67 | 2.09 | 3.58 |
| 92 | 5.46 | 1.76 | 3.70 |

Fiscal Year

## Total MR/DD Spending

Millions of Dollars
—Unadjusted

| | 77 | 78 | 79 | 80 | 81 | 82 | 83 | 84 | 85 | 86 | 87 | 88 | 89 | 90 | 91 | 92 |
|---|---|---|---|---|---|---|---|---|---|---|---|---|---|---|---|---|
| Unadjusted | 494 | 558 | 588 | 669 | 809 | 950 | 1099 | 1211 | 1321 | 1484 | 1641 | 1731 | 2034 | 2154 | 2304 | 2370 |
| 1992 Dollars | 1102 | 1154 | 1128 | 1165 | 1286 | 1415 | 1550 | 1635 | 1704 | 1840 | 1969 | 1990 | 2258 | 2305 | 2381 | 2370 |

Fiscal Year

## Personal Income

Billions of Dollars
—Unadjusted

| | 77 | 78 | 79 | 80 | 81 | 82 | 83 | 84 | 85 | 86 | 87 | 88 | 89 | 90 | 91 | 92 |
|---|---|---|---|---|---|---|---|---|---|---|---|---|---|---|---|---|
| Unadjusted | 135 | 145 | 158 | 174 | 193 | 212 | 227 | 246 | 272 | 290 | 307 | 326 | 355 | 380 | 406 | 434 |
| 1992 Dollars | 301 | 300 | 304 | 303 | 307 | 317 | 320 | 332 | 350 | 360 | 369 | 375 | 394 | 406 | 420 | 434 |

Fiscal Year

*Source:*
Institute on Disability and Human Development (UAP),
University of Illinois at Chicago, 1994

# NEW YORK
## Financial Support for MR/DD Services: FY 1977-92

| | 1977 | 1978 | 1979 | 1980 | 1981 | 1982 | 1983 | 1984 |
|---|---|---|---|---|---|---|---|---|
| **TOTAL FUNDS** | $493,970,486 | $557,703,486 | $587,657,486 | $669,274,422 | $808,987,768 | $949,981,814 | $1,099,260,090 | $1,211,257,779 |
| **CONGREGATE 16+ BEDS** | 416,415,929 | 459,126,929 | 465,256,929 | 524,643,109 | 553,386,045 | 614,487,979 | 636,940,915 | 665,315,099 |
| INSTITUTIONAL SERVICES FUNDS | 409,904,000 | 452,615,000 | 458,745,000 | 517,925,000 | 536,883,000 | 588,200,000 | 600,868,000 | 622,616,000 |
| STATE FUNDS | 299,607,000 | 325,424,000 | 319,603,000 | 266,924,000 | 244,343,000 | 175,553,000 | 242,949,000 | 256,821,000 |
| General Funds | 298,101,000 | 323,918,000 | 318,097,000 | 265,418,000 | 242,473,000 | 173,608,000 | 240,248,000 | 254,120,000 |
| Local | 0 | 0 | 0 | 0 | 0 | 0 | 0 | 0 |
| Other State Funds | 1,506,000 | 1,506,000 | 1,506,000 | 1,506,000 | 1,870,000 | 1,945,000 | 2,701,000 | 2,701,000 |
| FEDERAL FUNDS | 110,297,000 | 127,191,000 | 139,142,000 | 251,001,000 | 292,540,000 | 412,647,000 | 357,919,000 | 365,795,000 |
| Federal ICF/MR | 90,180,000 | 107,074,000 | 119,025,000 | 230,884,000 | 265,529,000 | 387,015,000 | 326,170,000 | 337,170,000 |
| Title XX / SSBG Funds | 0 | 0 | 0 | 0 | 0 | 0 | 0 | 0 |
| Other Federal Funds | 20,117,000 | 20,117,000 | 20,117,000 | 20,117,000 | 27,011,000 | 25,632,000 | 31,749,000 | 28,625,000 |
| LARGE PRIVATE RESIDENTIAL | 6,511,929 | 6,511,929 | 6,511,929 | 6,718,109 | 16,503,045 | 26,287,979 | 36,072,915 | 42,699,099 |
| STATE FUNDS | 6,511,929 | 6,511,929 | 6,511,929 | 6,615,019 | 11,507,487 | 16,399,954 | 21,292,422 | 24,605,514 |
| General Funds | 6,511,929 | 6,511,929 | 6,511,929 | 6,615,019 | 11,507,487 | 16,399,954 | 21,292,422 | 24,605,514 |
| Other State Funds | 0 | 0 | 0 | 0 | 0 | 0 | 0 | 0 |
| Local/County Overmatch | 0 | 0 | 0 | 0 | 0 | 0 | 0 | 0 |
| FEDERAL FUNDS | 0 | 0 | 0 | 103,090 | 4,995,558 | 9,888,025 | 14,780,493 | 18,093,585 |
| Large Private ICF/MR | 0 | 0 | 0 | 103,090 | 4,995,558 | 9,888,025 | 14,780,493 | 18,093,585 |
| **COMMUNITY SERVICES FUNDS** | 77,554,557 | 98,576,557 | 122,400,557 | 144,631,313 | 255,601,723 | 335,493,835 | 462,319,175 | 545,942,680 |
| STATE FUNDS | 74,718,557 | 95,640,557 | 119,164,557 | 139,912,042 | 199,736,694 | 258,598,097 | 355,185,499 | 415,254,961 |
| General Funds | 46,327,557 | 66,348,557 | 88,728,557 | 108,503,316 | 157,590,591 | 217,234,616 | 303,551,641 | 358,240,380 |
| Other State Funds | 14,027,000 | 14,720,000 | 15,449,000 | 16,278,726 | 26,600,103 | 25,738,481 | 35,899,858 | 41,466,581 |
| Local/County Overmatch | 0 | 0 | 0 | 0 | 0 | 0 | 0 | 0 |
| SSI State Supplement | 14,364,000 | 14,572,000 | 14,987,000 | 15,130,000 | 15,546,000 | 15,625,000 | 15,734,000 | 15,548,000 |
| FEDERAL FUNDS | 2,836,000 | 2,936,000 | 3,236,000 | 4,719,271 | 55,865,029 | 76,895,738 | 107,133,676 | 130,687,719 |
| ICF/MR Funds | 0 | 0 | 0 | 743,271 | 17,838,673 | 32,619,676 | 50,456,078 | 64,776,354 |
| Small Public | 0 | 0 | 0 | 434,000 | 2,852,000 | 2,955,600 | 6,114,600 | 10,495,600 |
| Small Private | 0 | 0 | 0 | 309,271 | 14,986,673 | 29,664,076 | 44,341,478 | 54,280,754 |
| HCBS Waiver | 0 | 0 | 0 | 0 | 0 | 0 | 0 | 0 |
| Model 50/200 Waiver | 0 | 0 | 0 | 0 | 0 | 0 | 0 | 0 |
| Other Title XIX Programs | 0 | 0 | 0 | 0 | 33,887,356 | 39,051,062 | 50,422,598 | 59,656,365 |
| Title XX / SSBG Funds | 836,000 | 836,000 | 836,000 | 620,000 | 391,000 | 391,000 | 261,000 | 261,000 |
| Other Federal Funds | 2,000,000 | 2,100,000 | 2,400,000 | 3,356,000 | 3,748,000 | 4,834,000 | 5,994,000 | 5,994,000 |
| Waiver Clients' SSI/ADC | 0 | 0 | 0 | 0 | 0 | 0 | 0 | 0 |

| | 1985 | 1986 | 1987 | 1988 | 1989 | 1990 | 1991 | 1992 |
|---|---|---|---|---|---|---|---|---|
| **TOTAL FUNDS** | $1,320,784,210 | $1,483,772,274 | $1,640,960,954 | $1,730,513,251 | $2,033,853,026 | $2,153,549,565 | $2,304,038,237 | $2,370,435,846 |
| **CONGREGATE 16+ BEDS** | 732,456,583 | 787,455,795 | 782,130,021 | 814,413,287 | 850,980,404 | 850,901,663 | 850,507,917 | 765,024,934 |
| INSTITUTIONAL SERVICES FUNDS | 689,959,000 | 732,874,000 | 725,332,000 | 756,786,000 | 778,282,025 | 776,822,931 | 770,212,651 | 672,270,019 |
| STATE FUNDS | 321,325,400 | 321,153,500 | 315,012,440 | 332,892,450 | 487,913,719 | 465,164,090 | 459,332,475 | 329,294,732 |
| General Funds | 319,355,400 | 318,876,500 | 313,448,500 | 331,261,520 | 486,334,029 | 463,584,400 | 457,757,594 | 327,842,878 |
| Local | 0 | 0 | 0 | 0 | 0 | 0 | 0 | 0 |
| Other State Funds | 1,970,000 | 2,277,000 | 1,563,940 | 1,630,930 | 1,579,690 | 1,579,690 | 1,574,881 | 1,451,854 |
| FEDERAL FUNDS | 368,633,600 | 411,720,500 | 410,319,560 | 423,893,550 | 290,368,306 | 311,658,841 | 310,880,176 | 342,975,287 |
| Federal ICF/MR | 343,133,000 | 382,829,800 | 369,296,000 | 388,038,480 | 241,722,500 | 255,966,529 | 255,966,529 | 285,158,848 |
| Title XX / SSBG Funds | 0 | 0 | 0 | 0 | 0 | 0 | 0 | 0 |
| Other Federal Funds | 25,500,600 | 28,890,700 | 41,023,560 | 35,855,070 | 48,645,806 | 55,692,312 | 54,913,647 | 57,816,439 |
| LARGE PRIVATE RESIDENTIAL | 42,497,583 | 54,581,795 | 56,798,021 | 57,627,287 | 72,698,379 | 74,078,732 | 80,295,266 | 92,754,915 |
| STATE FUNDS | 24,504,756 | 30,546,862 | 31,654,975 | 32,000,882 | 40,278,379 | 41,348,732 | 45,341,266 | 52,614,915 |
| General Funds | 24,504,756 | 30,546,862 | 31,654,975 | 6,374,476 | 7,858,379 | 8,618,732 | 10,387,266 | 12,474,915 |
| Other State Funds | 0 | 0 | 0 | 25,626,406 | 32,420,000 | 32,730,000 | 34,954,000 | 40,140,000 |
| Local/County Overmatch | 0 | 0 | 0 | 0 | 0 | 0 | 0 | 0 |
| FEDERAL FUNDS | 17,992,827 | 24,034,933 | 25,143,046 | 25,626,405 | 32,420,000 | 32,730,000 | 34,954,000 | 40,140,000 |
| Large Private ICF/MR | 17,992,827 | 24,034,933 | 25,143,046 | 25,626,405 | 32,420,000 | 32,730,000 | 34,954,000 | 40,140,000 |
| **COMMUNITY SERVICES FUNDS** | 588,327,627 | 696,316,479 | 858,830,933 | 916,099,964 | 1,182,872,622 | 1,302,647,902 | 1,453,530,320 | 1,605,410,912 |
| STATE FUNDS | 437,142,649 | 508,543,825 | 608,045,966 | 659,317,689 | 823,772,366 | 879,534,452 | 970,040,651 | 1,008,339,561 |
| General Funds | 376,786,297 | 440,645,447 | 519,452,725 | 416,779,415 | 505,606,512 | 517,538,751 | 566,534,083 | 574,915,901 |
| Other State Funds | 43,910,352 | 49,756,378 | 57,915,241 | 210,801,274 | 284,842,004 | 327,005,658 | 366,767,023 | 394,847,138 |
| Local/County Overmatch | 0 | 0 | 0 | 0 | 0 | 0 | 0 | 0 |
| SSI State Supplement | 16,446,000 | 18,142,000 | 30,678,000 | 31,737,000 | 33,323,850 | 34,990,043 | 36,739,545 | 38,576,522 |
| FEDERAL FUNDS | 151,184,978 | 187,772,654 | 250,784,967 | 256,782,275 | 359,100,256 | 423,113,450 | 483,489,669 | 597,071,351 |
| ICF/MR Funds | 77,455,381 | 105,730,298 | 127,997,745 | 165,052,365 | 249,137,970 | 298,499,636 | 335,985,712 | 411,537,866 |
| Small Public | 23,476,900 | 33,625,500 | 43,823,200 | 64,440,320 | 89,689,579 | 108,883,706 | 118,472,798 | 181,737,866 |
| Small Private | 53,978,481 | 72,104,798 | 84,174,545 | 100,612,045 | 159,448,391 | 189,615,930 | 217,512,914 | 229,800,000 |
| HCBS Waiver | 0 | 0 | 0 | 0 | 0 | 0 | 0 | 69,259 |
| Model 50/200 Waiver | 0 | 54,750 | 355,875 | 466,650 | 0 | 0 | 0 | 380,052 |
| Other Title XIX Programs | 67,380,797 | 75,415,606 | 115,505,307 | 82,280,000 | 99,685,138 | 113,257,086 | 133,895,666 | 167,029,622 |
| Title XX / SSBG Funds | 0 | 0 | 0 | 0 | 0 | 0 | 0 | 0 |
| Other Federal Funds | 6,348,800 | 6,572,000 | 6,926,040 | 8,983,260 | 10,277,148 | 11,356,728 | 13,608,291 | 17,234,040 |
| Waiver Clients' SSI/ADC | 0 | 0 | 0 | 0 | 0 | 0 | 0 | 820,512 |

*Source:*
Institute on Disability and Human Development (UAP),
University of Illinois at Chicago, 1994

# NORTH CAROLINA

## MR/DD Spending for Congregate Residential & Community Services

▨ Congregate: 16+ Beds*  ■ Community**

Millions of 1992 Dollars

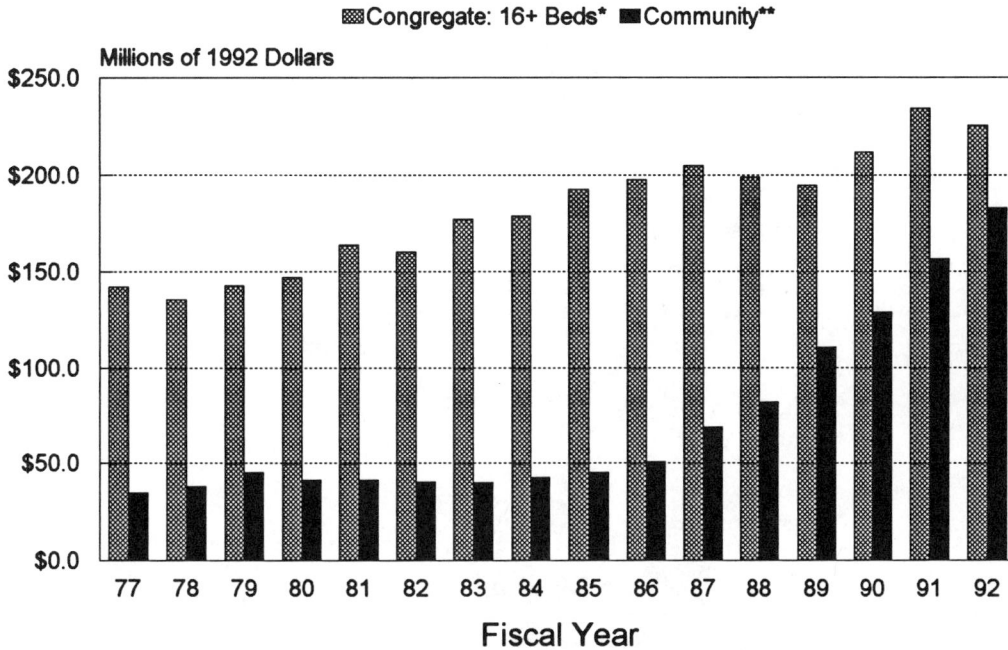

Fiscal Year

*Excludes nursing homes; ** Includes resources for
15 bed or less residential settings & non-residential community services

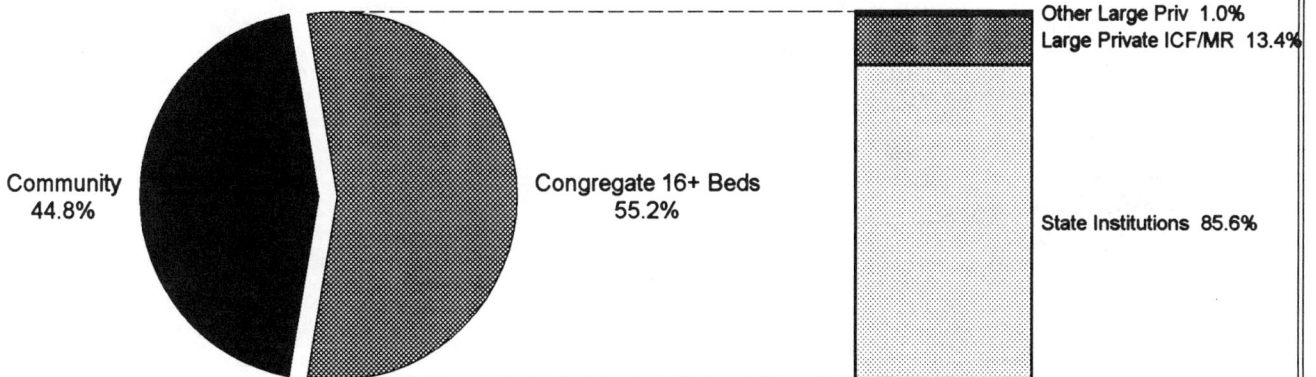

Community
44.8%

Congregate 16+ Beds
55.2%

Other Large Priv  1.0%
Large Private ICF/MR  13.4%

State Institutions  85.6%

FY 1992 Total Spending:
$408.3 Million

*Source:*
Institute on Disability and Human Development (UAP),
University of Illinois at Chicago, 1994

# NORTH CAROLINA

## Number of Persons Served by Residential Setting: FY 1992

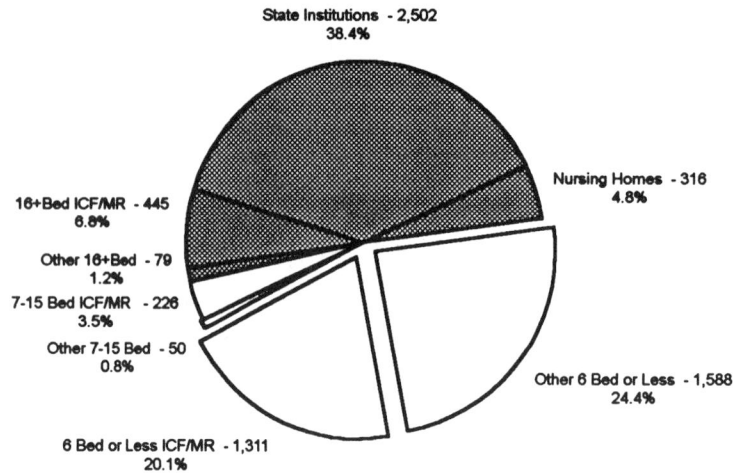

State Institutions - 2,502
38.4%

Nursing Homes - 316
4.8%

16+Bed ICF/MR - 445
6.8%

Other 16+Bed - 79
1.2%

7-15 Bed ICF/MR - 226
3.5%

Other 7-15 Bed - 50
0.8%

Other 6 Bed or Less - 1,588
24.4%

6 Bed or Less ICF/MR - 1,311
20.1%

Total Served: 6,517

## Persons Served by Residential Setting:1986-92

| | 1986 | 1987 | 1988 | 1989 | 1990 | 1991 | 1992 |
|---|---|---|---|---|---|---|---|
| CONGREGATE 16 + BED SETTINGS | NA | NA | 3,656 | 3,566 | 3,514 | 3,421 | 3,342 |
| Nursing Homes | NA | NA | 316 | 316 | 316 | 316 | 316 |
| State Institutions | 3,048 | 2,937 | 2,805 | 2,721 | 2,669 | 2,581 | 2,502 |
| Private 16+Bed ICF/MR | 395 | 395 | 395 | 445 | 445 | 445 | 445 |
| Other 16+Bed Residential | 140 | 140 | 140 | 84 | 84 | 79 | 79 |
| 15 BED OR LESS RESIDENTIAL SETTINGS | 1,263 | 1,456 | 1,847 | 2,086 | 2,448 | 2,999 | 3,175 |
| Public 7-15 Bed ICF/MR | 0 | 0 | 0 | 0 | 0 | 0 | 0 |
| Private 7-15 Bed ICF/MR | 77 | 122 | 187 | 202 | 217 | 217 | 226 |
| Other 7-15 Bed Residential | 50 | 50 | 50 | 50 | 50 | 50 | 50 |
| Public 6 Bed or Less ICF/MR | 30 | 53 | 64 | 86 | 98 | 125 | 137 |
| Private 6 Bed or Less ICF/MR | 143 | 217 | 409 | 527 | 729 | 1,055 | 1,174 |
| Other 6 Bed or Less Residential | 963 | 1,014 | 1,137 | 1,221 | 1,354 | 1,552 | 1,588 |
| TOTAL PERSONS SERVED | NA | NA | 5,503 | 5,652 | 5,962 | 6,420 | 6,517 |

## Persons Served in Non-Residential Community Services:1986-92

| | 1986 | 1987 | 1988 | 1989 | 1990 | 1991 | 1992 |
|---|---|---|---|---|---|---|---|
| DAY/WORK PROGRAMS | NA | NA | 5,413 | 5,657 | 5,672 | 5,594 | 5,594 |
| Sheltered Employment/Work Activity | NA | NA | 5,343 | 5,400 | 5,149 | 4,694 | 4,644 |
| Day Habilitation ("Day Training") | NA | NA | 0 | 0 | 0 | 0 | 0 |
| Supported/Competitive Employment | 0 | 0 | 70 | 257 | 523 | 900 | 950 |
| CASE MANAGEMENT | NA | NA | 369 | 1,252 | 2,095 | 2,505 | 2,864 |
| HCBS WAIVER | 296 | 306 | 369 | 504 | 642 | 821 | 1,075 |
| MODEL 50/200 WAIVER | 0 | 0 | 0 | 0 | 0 | 0 | 0 |

*Source:*
Institute on Disability and Human Development (UAP),
University of Illinois at Chicago, 1994

# NORTH CAROLINA

## Community Services: FY 1992 Revenue Sources

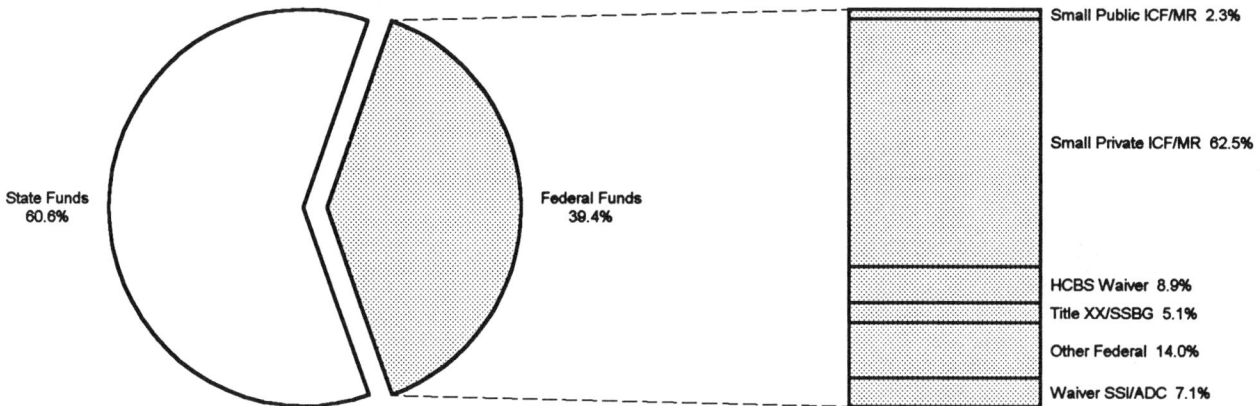

State Funds 60.6%

Federal Funds 39.4%

Small Public ICF/MR 2.3%

Small Private ICF/MR 62.5%

HCBS Waiver 8.9%

Title XX/SSBG 5.1%

Other Federal 14.0%

Waiver SSI/ADC 7.1%

Total Funds: $182.8 Million

## Family Support Initiatives*

|  | 1986 | 1987 | 1988 | 1989 | 1990 | 1991 | 1992 |
|---|---|---|---|---|---|---|---|
| FAMILY SUPPORT: TOTAL SPENDING | $908,100 | $986,100 | $1,072,900 | $826,627 | $871,880 | $465,466 | $479,326 |
| Total # of Families Supported | 1,387 | 1,385 | 1,395 | 1,653 | 1,799 | 1,933 | 2,039 |
| A. Financial Subsidy/Payment | $0 | $0 | $0 | $0 | $0 | $0 | $0 |
| # of Families | 0 | 0 | 0 | 0 | 0 | 0 | 0 |
| B. Family Assistance Payments | $903,400 | $983,700 | $1,070,200 | $768,884 | $812,154 | $404,581 | $416,936 |
| # of Families | 1,359 | 1,364 | 1,369 | 1,603 | 1,744 | 1,831 | 1,922 |
| C. Other Family Support Payments | $4,700 | $2,400 | $2,700 | $57,743 | $59,726 | $60,885 | $62,390 |
| # of Families | 28 | 21 | 26 | 50 | 55 | 102 | 117 |

## Other Community Services Initiatives*

|  | 1986 | 1987 | 1988 | 1989 | 1990 | 1991 | 1992 |
|---|---|---|---|---|---|---|---|
| AGING/DD SPENDING | NA | NA | NA | NA | NA | NA | NA |
| # of Persons Served | NA | NA | NA | NA | NA | NA | NA |
| ASSISTIVE TECHNOLOGY SPENDING |  |  |  | NA | NA | NA | NA |
| # of Persons Served |  |  |  | NA | NA | NA | NA |
| EARLY INTERVENTION SPENDING | $1,540,500 | $1,625,900 | $3,812,142 | $5,451,591 | $5,651,509 | $9,416,087 | $10,116,087 |
| # of Persons Served | 1,613 | 1,778 | 3,159 | 3,455 | 3,216 | 3,511 | 3,862 |
| PERSONAL ASSISTANCE SPENDING |  |  |  | $589,681 | $990,909 | $1,224,194 | $1,462,800 |
| # of Persons Served |  |  |  | 174 | 212 | 270 | 318 |
| SUPPORTED EMPLOYMENT SPENDING | $0 | $0 | $207,480 | $786,420 | $1,681,966 | $2,001,600 | $3,089,400 |
| # of Persons Served | 0 | 0 | 70 | 257 | 523 | 900 | 950 |
| SUPPORTED LIVING SPENDING |  |  |  | NA | NA | NA | NA |
| # of Persons Served |  |  |  | NA | NA | NA | NA |

*Expenditures associated with Special Community Initiatives are a subset of funding within the community services component of the state's chart series and spreadsheet; Family Support Client figures may include duplicate client counts; HCBS Waiver counts include Waiver case management numbers.
0= Services not provided in the state; NA= Data not available from state; blank= Services not applicable (eg. CSLA prior to authorization, Special Community Initiatives prior to request for data by this study)

*Source:*
Institute on Disability and Human Development (UAP),
University of Illinois at Chicago, 1994

# NORTH CAROLINA

## Large Congregate Care Facilities: FY 1992 Revenue Sources*

### Private 16+Bed Settings

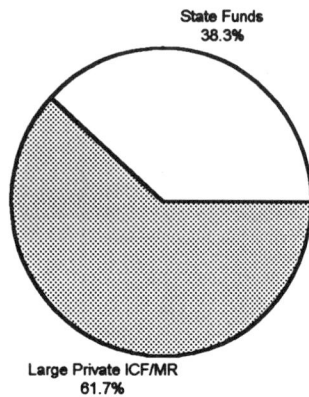

State Funds
38.3%

Large Private ICF/MR
61.7%

Total Funds: $32.5 Million

### Public Institutions

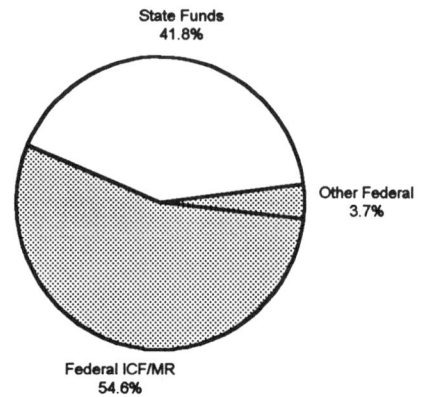

State Funds
41.8%

Other Federal
3.7%

Federal ICF/MR
54.6%

Total Funds: $193.0 Million

*Excludes nursing homes

## Average Daily Residents in Institutions

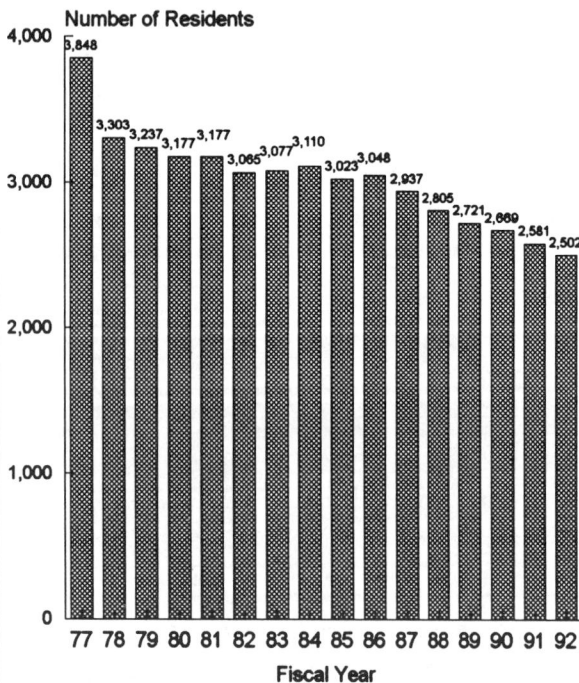

Number of Residents

3,848
3,303
3,237
3,177 3,177
3,065 3,077 3,110
3,023 3,048
2,937
2,805
2,721 2,669
2,581
2,502

77 78 79 80 81 82 83 84 85 86 87 88 89 90 91 92

Fiscal Year

## Institutional Daily Costs Per Resident

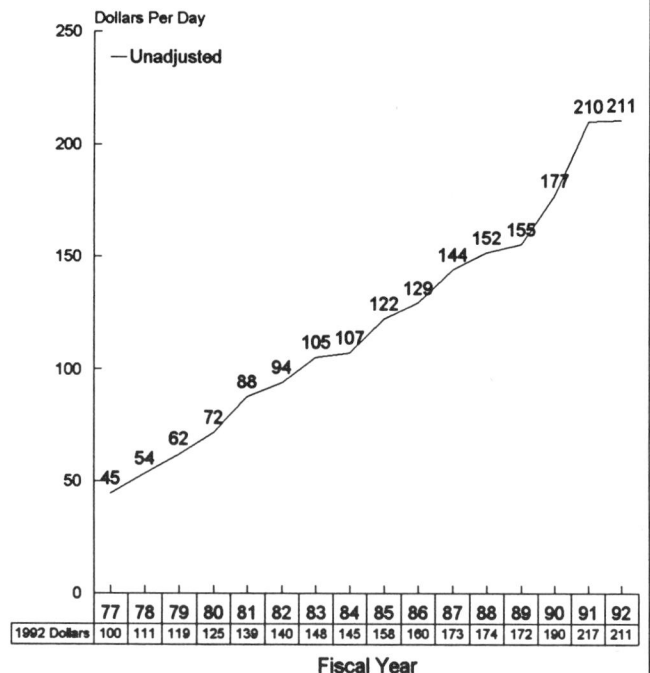

Dollars Per Day

— Unadjusted

210 211
177
152 155
144
129
122
105 107
94
88
72
62
54
45

| | 77 | 78 | 79 | 80 | 81 | 82 | 83 | 84 | 85 | 86 | 87 | 88 | 89 | 90 | 91 | 92 |
|---|---|---|---|---|---|---|---|---|---|---|---|---|---|---|---|---|
| 1992 Dollars | 100 | 111 | 119 | 125 | 139 | 140 | 148 | 145 | 158 | 160 | 173 | 174 | 172 | 190 | 217 | 211 |

Fiscal Year

*Source:*
Institute on Disability and Human Development (UAP),
University of Illinois at Chicago, 1994

# NORTH CAROLINA FISCAL EFFORT

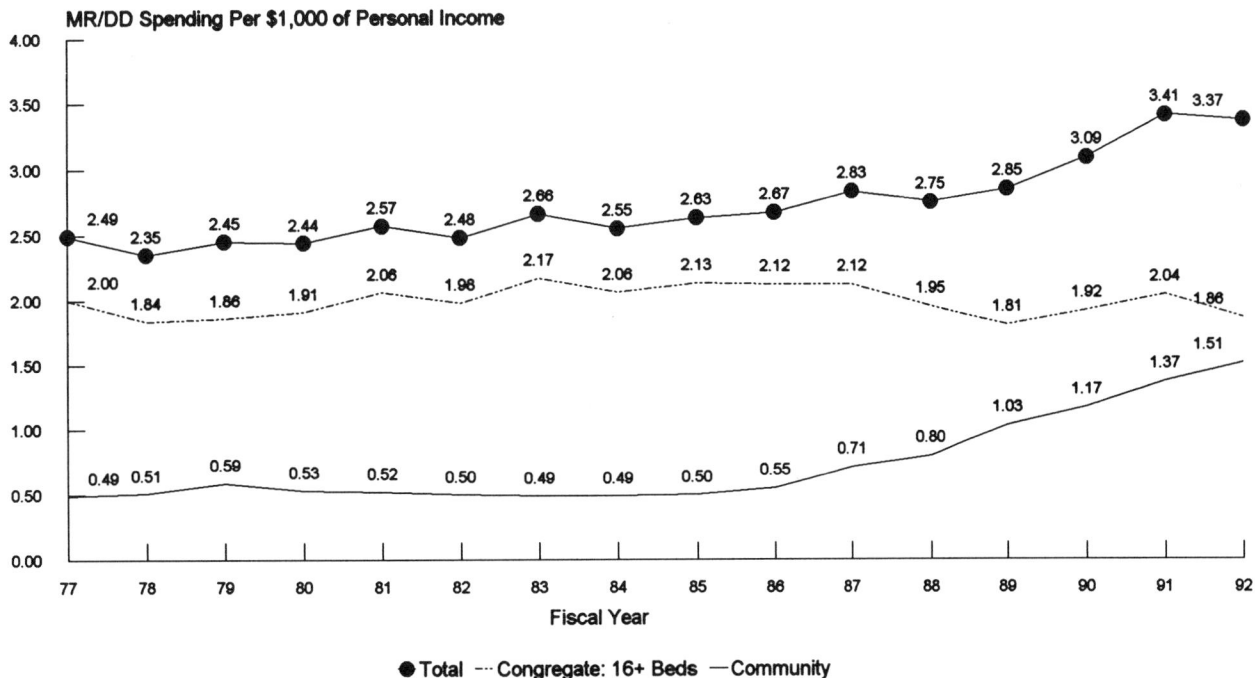

**MR/DD Spending Per $1,000 of Personal Income**

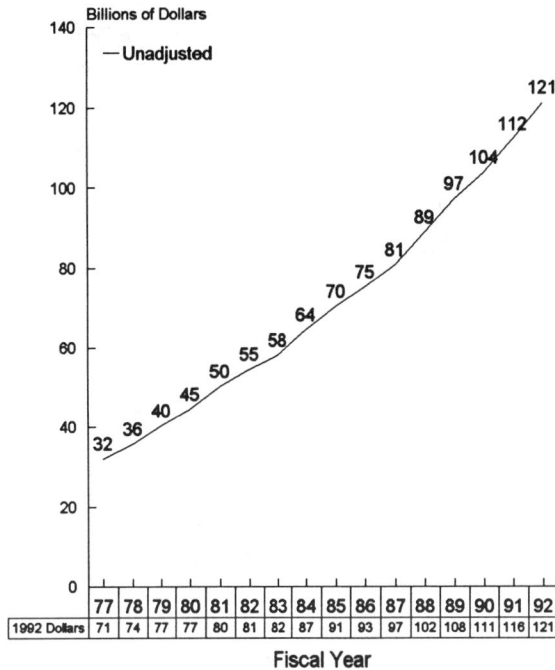

Total values: 2.49, 2.35, 2.45, 2.44, 2.57, 2.48, 2.66, 2.55, 2.63, 2.67, 2.83, 2.75, 2.85, 3.09, 3.41, 3.37

Congregate: 16+ Beds values: 2.00, 1.84, 1.86, 1.91, 2.06, 1.96, 2.17, 2.06, 2.13, 2.12, 2.12, 1.95, 1.81, 1.92, 2.04, 1.86

Community values: 0.49, 0.51, 0.59, 0.53, 0.52, 0.50, 0.49, 0.49, 0.50, 0.55, 0.71, 0.80, 1.03, 1.17, 1.37, 1.51

Fiscal Year: 77–92

● Total --- Congregate: 16+ Beds — Community

## Total MR/DD Spending

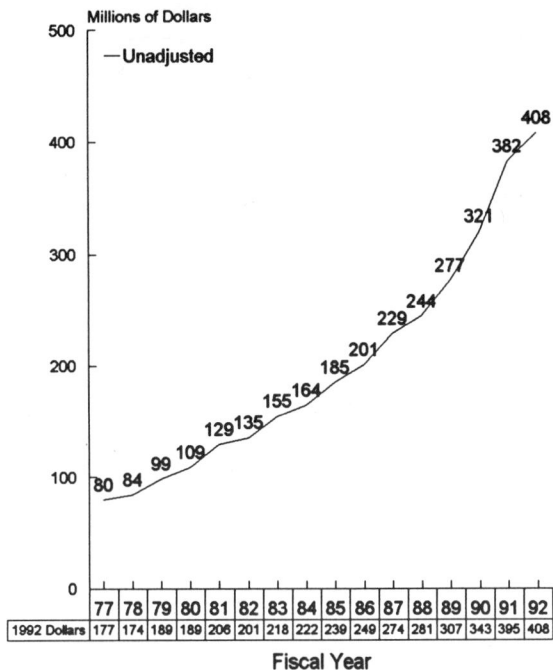

**Millions of Dollars**
— Unadjusted

Values: 80, 84, 99, 109, 129, 135, 155, 164, 185, 201, 229, 244, 277, 321, 382, 408

| | 77 | 78 | 79 | 80 | 81 | 82 | 83 | 84 | 85 | 86 | 87 | 88 | 89 | 90 | 91 | 92 |
|---|---|---|---|---|---|---|---|---|---|---|---|---|---|---|---|---|
| 1992 Dollars | 177 | 174 | 189 | 189 | 206 | 201 | 218 | 222 | 239 | 249 | 274 | 281 | 307 | 343 | 395 | 408 |

Fiscal Year

## Personal Income

**Billions of Dollars**
— Unadjusted

Values: 32, 36, 40, 45, 50, 55, 58, 64, 70, 75, 81, 89, 97, 104, 112, 121

| | 77 | 78 | 79 | 80 | 81 | 82 | 83 | 84 | 85 | 86 | 87 | 88 | 89 | 90 | 91 | 92 |
|---|---|---|---|---|---|---|---|---|---|---|---|---|---|---|---|---|
| 1992 Dollars | 71 | 74 | 77 | 77 | 80 | 81 | 82 | 87 | 91 | 93 | 97 | 102 | 108 | 111 | 116 | 121 |

Fiscal Year

*Source:*
Institute on Disability and Human Development (UAP),
University of Illinois at Chicago, 1994

# NORTH CAROLINA

## Financial Support for MR/DD Services: FY 1977-92

| | 1977 | 1978 | 1979 | 1980 | 1981 | 1982 | 1983 | 1984 |
|---|---|---|---|---|---|---|---|---|
| **TOTAL FUNDS** | $79,571,000 | $84,120,800 | $98,538,820 | $108,860,800 | $129,292,800 | $135,171,700 | $154,501,300 | $164,379,056 |
| **CONGREGATE 16+ BEDS** | 63,949,000 | 65,789,700 | 74,858,400 | 85,052,500 | 103,264,700 | 108,129,737 | 126,078,995 | 132,669,819 |
| INSTITUTIONAL SERVICES FUNDS | 62,758,000 | 64,511,800 | 73,452,700 | 83,504,800 | 101,563,800 | 105,150,700 | 118,205,300 | 121,976,100 |
| STATE FUNDS | 53,203,800 | 47,094,500 | 49,649,900 | 48,784,400 | 57,786,500 | 49,230,000 | 60,945,600 | 60,929,400 |
| General Funds | 40,127,000 | 38,756,000 | 38,551,600 | 33,340,200 | 37,732,300 | 23,289,500 | 33,829,400 | 26,639,800 |
| Local | 0 | 0 | 0 | 0 | 0 | 0 | 0 | 0 |
| Other State Funds | 13,076,800 | 8,338,500 | 11,098,300 | 15,444,200 | 20,054,200 | 25,940,500 | 27,116,200 | 34,289,600 |
| FEDERAL FUNDS | 9,554,200 | 17,417,300 | 23,802,800 | 34,720,400 | 43,777,300 | 55,920,700 | 57,259,700 | 61,046,700 |
| Federal ICF/MR | 7,909,200 | 14,963,300 | 21,516,800 | 30,848,400 | 40,719,300 | 52,048,700 | 54,168,700 | 57,341,500 |
| Title XX / SSBG Funds | 0 | 0 | 0 | 0 | 0 | 0 | 0 | 0 |
| Other Federal Funds | 1,645,000 | 2,454,000 | 2,286,000 | 3,872,000 | 3,058,000 | 3,872,000 | 3,091,000 | 3,705,200 |
| LARGE PRIVATE RESIDENTIAL | 1,191,000 | 1,277,900 | 1,405,700 | 1,547,700 | 1,700,900 | 2,979,037 | 7,873,695 | 10,693,719 |
| STATE FUNDS | 1,191,000 | 1,277,900 | 1,405,700 | 1,547,700 | 1,700,900 | 2,182,037 | 3,820,695 | 4,673,119 |
| General Funds | 1,191,000 | 1,277,900 | 1,405,700 | 1,547,700 | 1,700,900 | 2,182,037 | 3,820,695 | 4,673,119 |
| Other State Funds | 0 | 0 | 0 | 0 | 0 | 0 | 0 | 0 |
| Local/County Overmatch | 0 | 0 | 0 | 0 | 0 | 0 | 0 | 0 |
| FEDERAL FUNDS | 0 | 0 | 0 | 0 | 0 | 797,000 | 4,053,000 | 6,020,600 |
| Large Private ICF/MR | 0 | 0 | 0 | 0 | 0 | 797,000 | 4,053,000 | 6,020,600 |
| **COMMUNITY SERVICES FUNDS** | 15,622,000 | 18,331,100 | 23,680,420 | 23,808,300 | 26,028,100 | 27,041,963 | 28,422,305 | 31,709,237 |
| STATE FUNDS | 11,335,000 | 12,571,100 | 18,581,420 | 19,075,300 | 20,983,100 | 22,586,963 | 24,064,305 | 27,544,381 |
| General Funds | 8,497,000 | 9,329,100 | 15,372,300 | 15,600,300 | 17,318,100 | 18,457,963 | 19,872,305 | 22,952,881 |
| Other State Funds | 0 | 157,000 | 6,120 | 0 | 0 | 0 | 0 | 130,500 |
| Local/County Overmatch | 0 | 0 | 0 | 0 | 0 | 0 | 0 | 0 |
| SSI State Supplement | 2,838,000 | 3,085,000 | 3,203,000 | 3,475,000 | 3,665,000 | 4,129,000 | 4,192,000 | 4,461,000 |
| FEDERAL FUNDS | 4,287,000 | 5,760,000 | 5,099,000 | 4,733,000 | 5,045,000 | 4,455,000 | 4,358,000 | 4,164,856 |
| ICF/MR Funds | 0 | 0 | 0 | 0 | 0 | 33,000 | 169,000 | 251,000 |
| Small Public | 0 | 0 | 0 | 0 | 0 | 0 | 0 | 0 |
| Small Private | 0 | 0 | 0 | 0 | 0 | 33,000 | 169,000 | 251,000 |
| HCBS Waiver | 0 | 0 | 0 | 0 | 0 | 0 | 0 | 67,400 |
| Model 50/200 Waiver | 0 | 0 | 0 | 0 | 0 | 0 | 0 | 0 |
| Other Title XIX Programs | 0 | 0 | 0 | 0 | 0 | 0 | 0 | 0 |
| Title XX / SSBG Funds | 3,127,000 | 5,760,000 | 5,099,000 | 4,733,000 | 5,045,000 | 4,422,000 | 4,189,000 | 3,787,500 |
| Other Federal Funds | 1,160,000 | 0 | 0 | 0 | 0 | 0 | 0 | 0 |
| Waiver Clients' SSI/ADC | 0 | 0 | 0 | 0 | 0 | 0 | 0 | 58,956 |

| | 1985 | 1986 | 1987 | 1988 | 1989 | 1990 | 1991 | 1992 |
|---|---|---|---|---|---|---|---|---|
| **TOTAL FUNDS** | $184,957,300 | $200,853,696 | $228,726,278 | $244,488,899 | $276,760,433 | $320,683,868 | $382,356,744 | $408,313,123 |
| **CONGREGATE 16+ BEDS** | 149,722,249 | 159,730,607 | 171,216,936 | 173,140,942 | 176,437,801 | 199,212,490 | 229,156,806 | 225,465,812 |
| INSTITUTIONAL SERVICES FUNDS | 134,935,700 | 143,826,400 | 154,206,500 | 155,624,100 | 154,212,777 | 172,677,517 | 197,872,817 | 192,965,932 |
| STATE FUNDS | 59,983,000 | 66,487,400 | 70,977,200 | 71,811,900 | 63,275,858 | 70,091,615 | 82,118,281 | 80,598,313 |
| General Funds | 28,698,700 | 31,255,900 | 35,275,200 | 33,937,100 | 21,670,666 | 22,546,739 | 26,302,175 | 27,001,661 |
| Local | 0 | 0 | 0 | 0 | 0 | 0 | 0 | 0 |
| Other State Funds | 31,284,300 | 35,231,500 | 35,702,000 | 37,874,800 | 41,605,192 | 47,544,876 | 55,816,106 | 53,596,652 |
| FEDERAL FUNDS | 74,952,700 | 77,339,000 | 83,229,300 | 83,812,200 | 90,936,919 | 102,585,902 | 115,754,536 | 112,367,619 |
| Federal ICF/MR | 71,422,000 | 73,063,000 | 74,805,200 | 78,978,200 | 86,122,665 | 97,854,409 | 110,805,198 | 105,317,534 |
| Title XX / SSBG Funds | 0 | 0 | 0 | 0 | 0 | 0 | 0 | 0 |
| Other Federal Funds | 3,530,700 | 4,276,000 | 8,424,100 | 4,834,000 | 4,814,254 | 4,731,493 | 4,949,338 | 7,050,085 |
| LARGE PRIVATE RESIDENTIAL | 14,786,549 | 15,904,207 | 17,010,436 | 17,516,842 | 22,225,024 | 26,534,973 | 31,283,989 | 32,499,880 |
| STATE FUNDS | 5,951,249 | 6,391,007 | 6,798,336 | 7,063,542 | 8,298,956 | 9,855,722 | 11,870,544 | 12,433,165 |
| General Funds | 5,951,249 | 6,391,007 | 6,798,336 | 7,063,542 | 8,298,956 | 9,855,722 | 11,870,544 | 12,433,165 |
| Other State Funds | 0 | 0 | 0 | 0 | 0 | 0 | 0 | 0 |
| Local/County Overmatch | 0 | 0 | 0 | 0 | 0 | 0 | 0 | 0 |
| FEDERAL FUNDS | 8,835,300 | 9,513,200 | 10,212,100 | 10,453,300 | 13,926,068 | 16,679,251 | 19,413,445 | 20,066,715 |
| Large Private ICF/MR | 8,835,300 | 9,513,200 | 10,212,100 | 10,453,300 | 13,926,068 | 16,679,251 | 19,413,445 | 20,066,715 |
| **COMMUNITY SERVICES FUNDS** | 35,235,051 | 41,123,089 | 57,509,342 | 71,347,957 | 100,322,632 | 121,471,378 | 153,199,938 | 182,847,311 |
| STATE FUNDS | 30,612,951 | 32,414,587 | 40,863,328 | 49,252,015 | 67,099,324 | 77,778,863 | 92,758,593 | 110,785,762 |
| General Funds | 23,965,751 | 25,368,793 | 30,003,464 | 36,802,596 | 49,723,842 | 54,937,062 | 62,633,115 | 74,714,319 |
| Other State Funds | 1,928,200 | 1,123,794 | 4,608,864 | 6,034,419 | 10,325,397 | 15,093,758 | 21,610,378 | 26,713,348 |
| Local/County Overmatch | 0 | 0 | 0 | 0 | 0 | 0 | 0 | 0 |
| SSI State Supplement | 4,719,000 | 5,922,000 | 6,251,000 | 6,415,000 | 7,050,085 | 7,748,043 | 8,515,100 | 9,358,095 |
| FEDERAL FUNDS | 4,622,100 ' | 8,708,502 | 16,646,014 | 22,095,942 | 33,223,308 | 43,692,515 | 60,441,345 | 72,061,549 |
| ICF/MR Funds | 368,000 | 1,336,900 | 8,244,700 | 10,750,200 | 18,708,290 | 26,877,308 | 38,028,903 | 46,697,670 |
| Small Public | 0 | 0 | 0 | 0 | 890,930 | 1,268,482 | 1,625,917 | 1,680,630 |
| Small Private | 368,000 | 1,336,900 | 8,244,700 | 10,750,200 | 17,817,360 | 25,608,826 | 36,402,986 | 45,017,040 |
| HCBS Waiver | 301,100 | 1,196,100 | 2,100,500 | 2,562,600 | 3,415,706 | 4,614,607 | 5,491,458 | 6,425,645 |
| Model 50/200 Waiver | 0 | 25,830 | 15,634 | 0 | 0 | 0 | 0 | 0 |
| Other Title XIX Programs | 0 | 0 | 0 | 0 | 0 | 0 | 0 | 0 |
| Title XX / SSBG Funds | 3,683,000 | 3,504,500 | 3,502,600 | 3,513,000 | 3,579,305 | 3,714,019 | 3,741,433 | 3,693,947 |
| Other Federal Funds | 0 | 1,540,500 | 1,625,900 | 3,812,142 | 5,451,591 | 5,651,509 | 9,416,087 | 10,116,087 |
| Waiver Clients' SSI/ADC | 270,000 | 1,104,672 | 1,156,680 | 1,458,000 | 2,068,416 | 2,835,072 | 3,763,464 | 5,128,200 |

*Source:*

Institute on Disability and Human Development (UAP),
University of Illinois at Chicago, 1994

# NORTH DAKOTA

## MR/DD Spending for Congregate Residential & Community Services

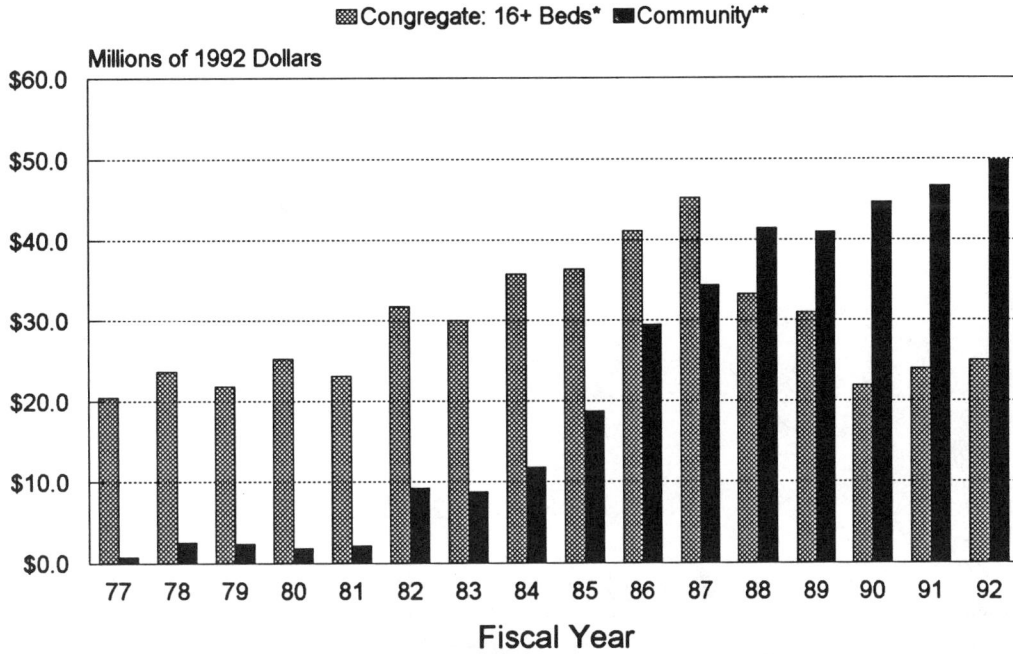

▨Congregate: 16+ Beds* ▉Community**

Millions of 1992 Dollars

$60.0

$50.0

$40.0

$30.0

$20.0

$10.0

$0.0

77  78  79  80  81  82  83  84  85  86  87  88  89  90  91  92

### Fiscal Year
*Excludes nursing homes; ** Includes resources for
15 bed or less residential settings & non-residential community services

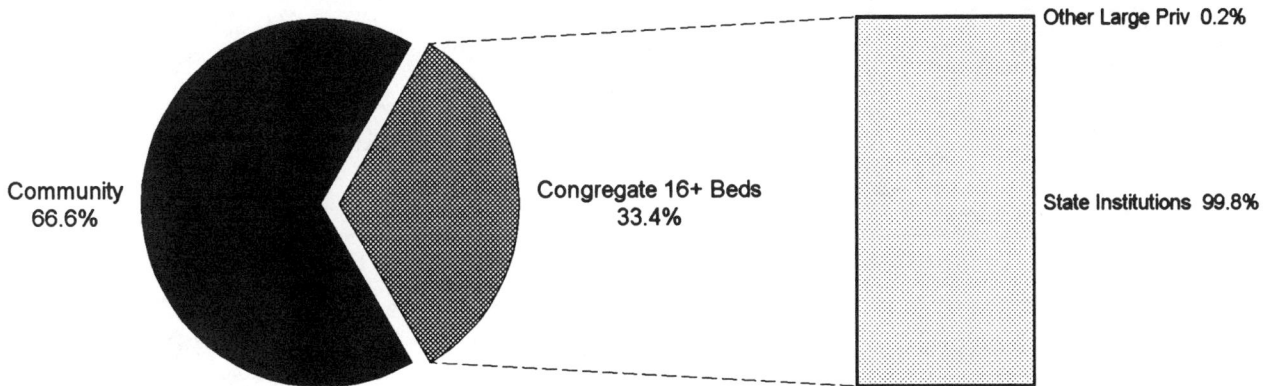

Community
66.6%

Congregate 16+ Beds
33.4%

Other Large Priv 0.2%

State Institutions 99.8%

FY 1992 Total Spending:
$74.8 Million

*Source:*
Institute on Disability and Human Development (UAP),
University of Illinois at Chicago, 1994

# NORTH DAKOTA

## Number of Persons Served by Residential Setting: FY 1992

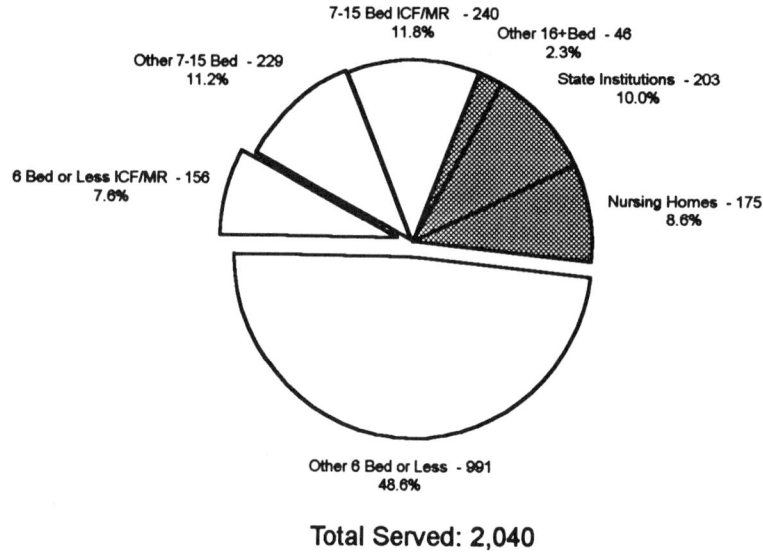

7-15 Bed ICF/MR - 240
11.8%

Other 16+Bed - 46
2.3%

Other 7-15 Bed - 229
11.2%

State Institutions - 203
10.0%

6 Bed or Less ICF/MR - 156
7.6%

Nursing Homes - 175
8.6%

Other 6 Bed or Less - 991
48.6%

Total Served: 2,040

## Persons Served by Residential Setting:1986-92

|  | 1986 | 1987 | 1988 | 1989 | 1990 | 1991 | 1992 |
|---|---|---|---|---|---|---|---|
| CONGREGATE 16 + BED SETTINGS | NA | NA | 614 | 564 | 489 | 458 | 424 |
| Nursing Homes | NA | NA | 221 | 202 | 192 | 186 | 175 |
| State Institutions | 497 | 392 | 347 | 316 | 251 | 226 | 203 |
| Private 16+Bed ICF/MR | 0 | 0 | 0 | 0 | 0 | 0 | 0 |
| Other 16+Bed Residential | 46 | 46 | 46 | 46 | 46 | 46 | 46 |
| 15 BED OR LESS RESIDENTIAL SETTINGS | 1,190 | 1,330 | 1,241 | 1,362 | 1,453 | 1,486 | 1,616 |
| Public 7-15 Bed ICF/MR | 0 | 0 | 0 | 0 | 0 | 0 | 0 |
| Private 7-15 Bed ICF/MR | 181 | 378 | 495 | 416 | 420 | 410 | 240 |
| Other 7-15 Bed Residential | 1,009 | 952 | 746 | 946 | 1,033 | 1,076 | 229 |
| Public 6 Bed or Less ICF/MR |  |  |  |  |  |  | 0 |
| Private 6 Bed or Less ICF/MR |  |  |  |  |  |  | 156 |
| Other 6 Bed or Less Residential |  |  |  |  |  |  | 991 |
| TOTAL PERSONS SERVED | NA | NA | 1,855 | 1,926 | 1,942 | 1,944 | 2,040 |

## Persons Served in Non-Residential Community Services:1986-92

|  | 1986 | 1987 | 1988 | 1989 | 1990 | 1991 | 1992 |
|---|---|---|---|---|---|---|---|
| DAY/WORK PROGRAMS | 495 | 445 | 436 | 943 | 1,040 | 1,083 | 1,547 |
| Sheltered Employment/Work Activity | 239 | 313 | 265 | 543 | 566 | 568 | 584 |
| Day Habilitation ("Day Training") | 99 | 84 | 171 | 400 | 474 | 515 | 514 |
| Supported/Competitive Employment | 157 | 48 | 0 | 0 | 0 | 0 | 449 |
| CASE MANAGEMENT | 2,432 | 2,555 | 2,634 | 2,710 | 1,793 | 2,853 | 2,893 |
| HCBS WAIVER | 618 | 741 | 741 | 1,112 | 1,234 | 1,238 | 1,339 |
| MODEL 50/200 WAIVER | 0 | 0 | 0 | 0 | 0 | 0 | 0 |

Source:
Institute on Disability and Human Development (UAP),
University of Illinois at Chicago, 1994

# NORTH DAKOTA

## Community Services: FY 1992 Revenue Sources

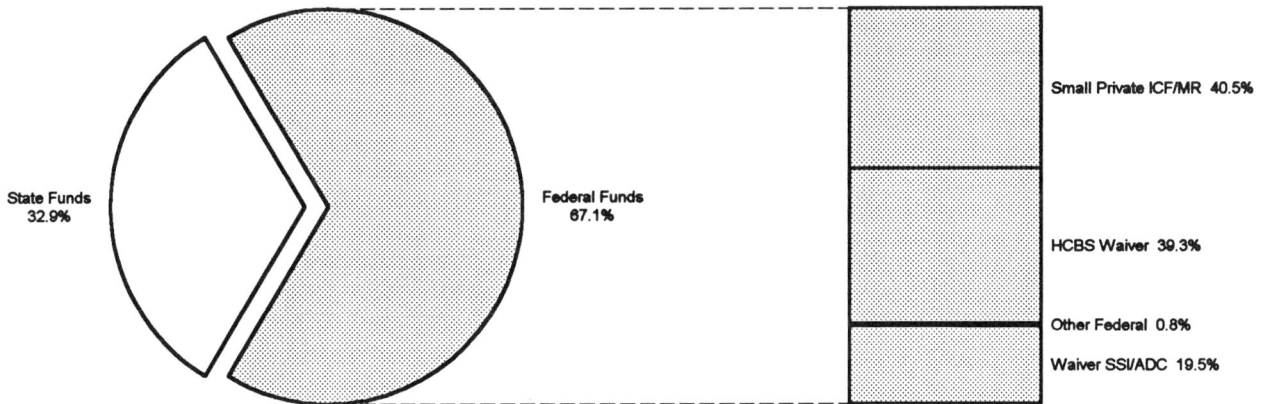

State Funds
32.9%

Federal Funds
67.1%

Small Private ICF/MR  40.5%

HCBS Waiver  39.3%

Other Federal  0.8%

Waiver SSI/ADC  19.5%

### Total Funds: $49.9 Million

## Family Support Initiatives*

|  | 1986 | 1987 | 1988 | 1989 | 1990 | 1991 | 1992 |
|---|---|---|---|---|---|---|---|
| **FAMILY SUPPORT: TOTAL SPENDING** | $680,700 | $446,600 | $489,841 | $670,511 | $546,109 | $677,701 | $1,388,954 |
| **Total # of Families Supported** | 272 | 207 | 330 | 337 | 360 | 475 | 564 |
| A. Financial Subsidy/Payment | $487,600 | $310,400 | $257,054 | $256,420 | $109,173 | $319,646 | $378,563 |
| # of Families | 272 | 207 | 216 | 195 | 106 | 197 | 226 |
| B. Family Assistance Payments | $193,100 | $136,200 | $186,569 | $268,544 | $273,036 | $325,781 | $108,161 |
| # of Families | NA | NA | 111 | 135 | 246 | 272 | 161 |
| C. Other Family Support Payments | $0 | $0 | $46,218 | $145,547 | $163,900 | $32,274 | $902,230 |
| # of Families | 0 | 0 | 3 | 7 | 8 | 6 | 345 |

## Other Community Services Initiatives*

|  | 1986 | 1987 | 1988 | 1989 | 1990 | 1991 | 1992 |
|---|---|---|---|---|---|---|---|
| **AGING/DD SPENDING** | $617,300 | $884,900 | $1,666,300 | $1,133,524 | $1,173,157 | $1,599,366 | $1,638,026 |
| # of Persons Served | 49 | 56 | 109 | 110 | 120 | 155 | 166 |
| **ASSISTIVE TECHNOLOGY SPENDING** |  |  |  |  |  |  | $0 |
| # of Persons Served |  |  |  |  |  |  | 0 |
| **EARLY INTERVENTION SPENDING** | $565,700 | $290,400 | $596,200 | $817,671 | $928,328 | $1,023,675 | $1,041,431 |
| # of Persons Served | 137 | 129 | 155 | NA | NA | NA | 455 |
| **PERSONAL ASSISTANCE SPENDING** |  |  |  |  |  |  | $0 |
| # of Persons Served |  |  |  |  |  |  | 0 |
| **SUPPORTED EMPLOYMENT SPENDING** | $343,000 | $590,100 | $0 | $0 | $0 | $0 | $908,963 |
| # of Persons Served | 157 | 48 | 0 | 0 | 0 | 0 | 449 |
| **SUPPORTED LIVING SPENDING** |  |  |  |  |  |  | $10,124,278 |
| # of Persons Served |  |  |  |  |  |  | 800 |

*Expenditures associated with Special Community Initiatives are a subset of funding within the community services component of the state's chart series and spreadsheet; Family Support Client figures may include duplicate client counts; HCBS Waiver counts include Waiver case management numbers.
0= Services not provided in the state; NA= Data not available from state; blank= Services not applicable (eg. CSLA prior to authorization, Special Community Initiatives prior to request for data by this study)

Source:
Institute on Disability and Human Development (UAP),
University of Illinois at Chicago, 1994

# NORTH DAKOTA

## Large Congregate Care Facilities: FY 1992 Revenue Sources*

### Private 16+Bed Settings

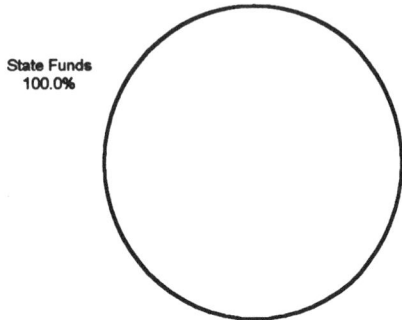

State Funds
100.0%

Total Funds: $53,728

### Public Institutions

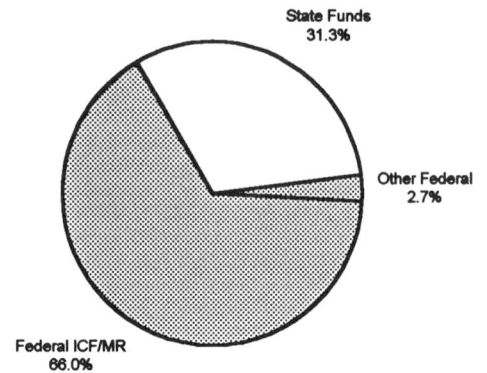

State Funds
31.3%

Other Federal
2.7%

Federal ICF/MR
66.0%

Total Funds: $24.9 Million

*Excludes nursing homes

## Average Daily Residents in Institutions

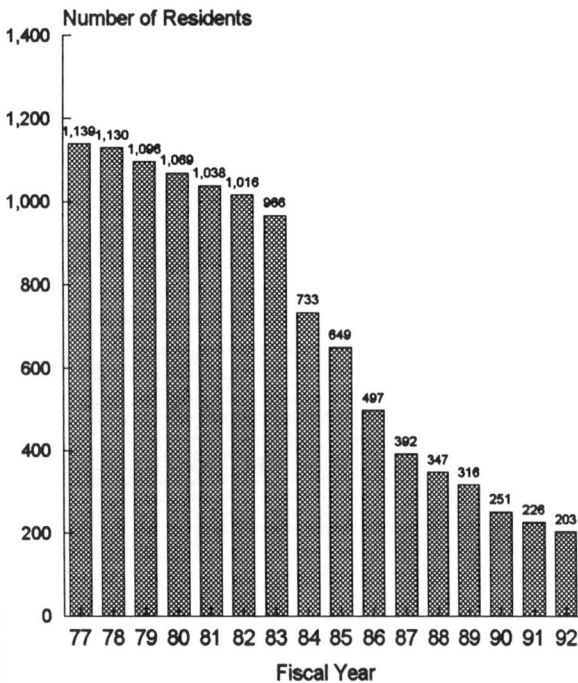

Number of Residents

| Fiscal Year | Residents |
|---|---|
| 77 | 1,139 |
| 78 | 1,130 |
| 79 | 1,096 |
| 80 | 1,069 |
| 81 | 1,038 |
| 82 | 1,016 |
| 83 | 966 |
| 84 | 733 |
| 85 | 649 |
| 86 | 497 |
| 87 | 392 |
| 88 | 347 |
| 89 | 316 |
| 90 | 251 |
| 91 | 226 |
| 92 | 203 |

Fiscal Year

## Institutional Daily Costs Per Resident

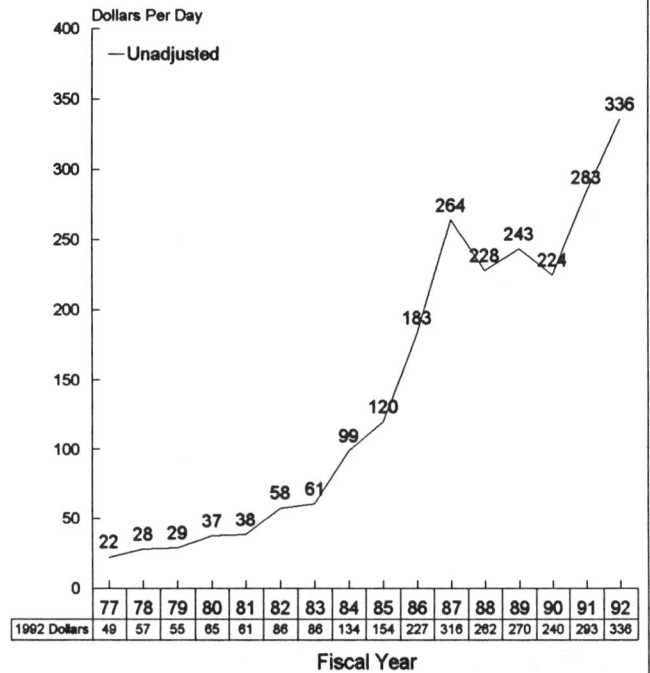

Dollars Per Day

—Unadjusted

| Fiscal Year | Unadjusted | 1992 Dollars |
|---|---|---|
| 77 | 22 | 49 |
| 78 | 28 | 57 |
| 79 | 29 | 55 |
| 80 | 37 | 65 |
| 81 | 38 | 61 |
| 82 | 58 | 86 |
| 83 | 61 | 86 |
| 84 | 99 | 134 |
| 85 | 120 | 154 |
| 86 | 183 | 227 |
| 87 | 264 | 316 |
| 88 | 228 | 262 |
| 89 | 243 | 270 |
| 90 | 224 | 240 |
| 91 | 283 | 293 |
| 92 | 336 | 336 |

Fiscal Year

*Source:*
Institute on Disability and Human Development (UAP),
University of Illinois at Chicago, 1994

# NORTH DAKOTA FISCAL EFFORT

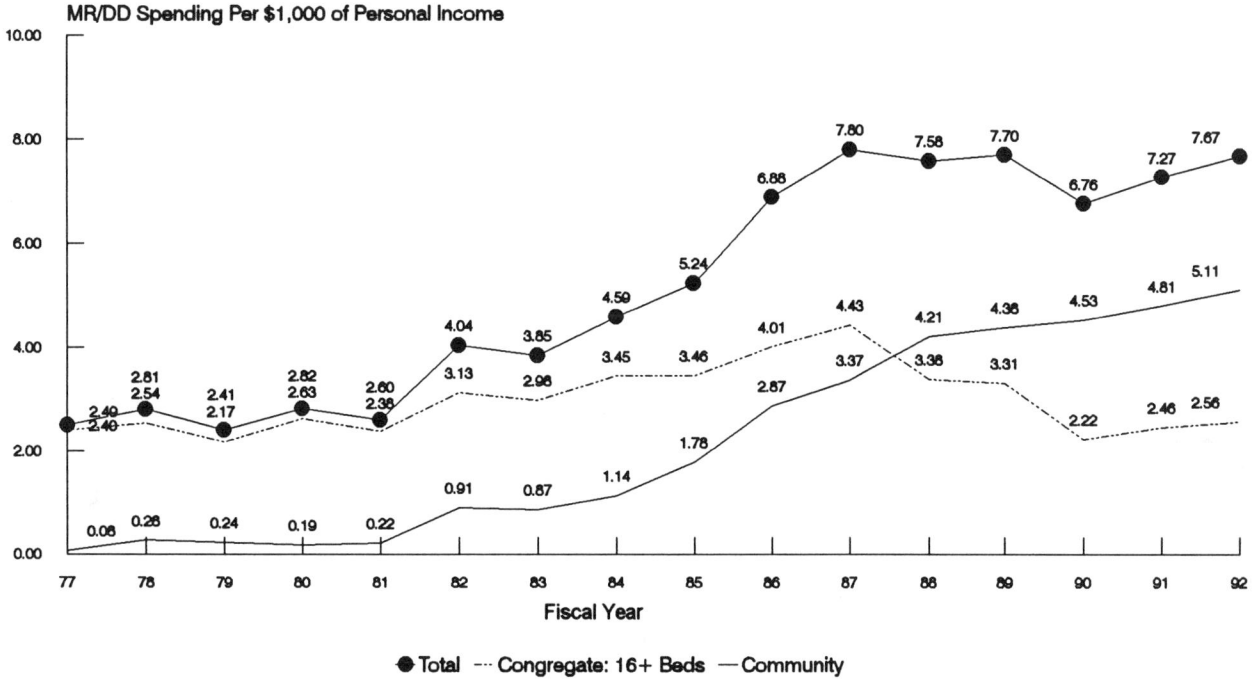

MR/DD Spending Per $1,000 of Personal Income

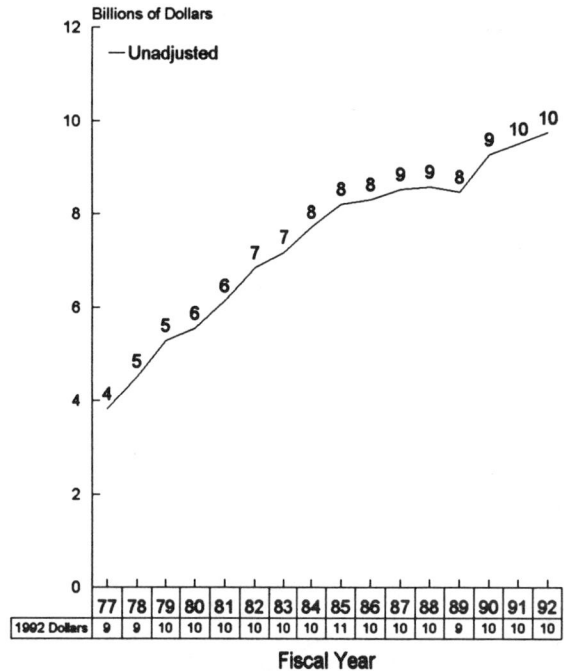

| | | | | | | | | | | | | | | | |
|---|---|---|---|---|---|---|---|---|---|---|---|---|---|---|---|

Total values: 2.40, 2.81, 2.54, 2.41, 2.17, 2.82, 2.63, 2.60, 2.38, 4.04, 3.85, 2.98, 4.59, 3.45, 5.24, 3.46, 6.88, 4.01, 7.80, 4.43, 3.37, 7.58, 4.21, 3.38, 7.70, 4.38, 3.31, 6.76, 4.53, 2.22, 7.27, 4.81, 2.46, 7.67, 5.11, 2.56

Community values: 0.06, 0.26, 0.24, 0.19, 0.22, 0.91, 0.87, 1.14, 1.78, 2.67

Fiscal Year

● Total   --- Congregate: 16+ Beds   — Community

## Total MR/DD Spending

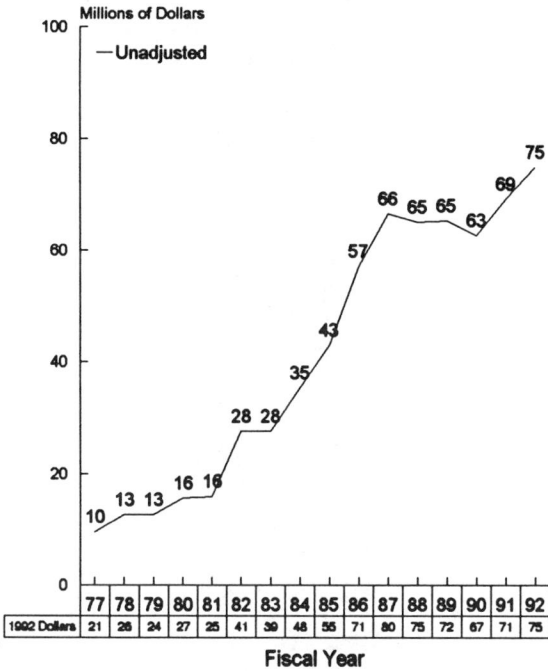

Millions of Dollars

— Unadjusted

Values: 10, 13, 13, 16, 16, 28, 28, 35, 43, 57, 66, 65, 65, 63, 69, 75

| | 77 | 78 | 79 | 80 | 81 | 82 | 83 | 84 | 85 | 86 | 87 | 88 | 89 | 90 | 91 | 92 |
|---|---|---|---|---|---|---|---|---|---|---|---|---|---|---|---|---|
| 1992 Dollars | 21 | 26 | 24 | 27 | 25 | 41 | 39 | 48 | 55 | 71 | 80 | 75 | 72 | 67 | 71 | 75 |

Fiscal Year

## Personal Income

Billions of Dollars

— Unadjusted

Values: 4, 5, 5, 6, 6, 7, 7, 8, 8, 8, 9, 9, 8, 9, 10, 10

| | 77 | 78 | 79 | 80 | 81 | 82 | 83 | 84 | 85 | 86 | 87 | 88 | 89 | 90 | 91 | 92 |
|---|---|---|---|---|---|---|---|---|---|---|---|---|---|---|---|---|
| 1992 Dollars | 9 | 9 | 10 | 10 | 10 | 10 | 10 | 10 | 11 | 10 | 10 | 10 | 9 | 10 | 10 | 10 |

Fiscal Year

*Source:*
Institute on Disability and Human Development (UAP),
University of Illinois at Chicago, 1994

# NORTH DAKOTA

## Financial Support for MR/DD Services: FY 1977-92

| | 1977 | 1978 | 1979 | 1980 | 1981 | 1982 | 1983 | 1984 |
|---|---|---|---|---|---|---|---|---|
| **TOTAL FUNDS** | $9,540,000 | $12,699,000 | $12,699,000 | $15,650,000 | $15,925,000 | $27,652,185 | $27,653,606 | $35,388,024 |
| **CONGREGATE 16+ BEDS** | 9,219,000 | 11,454,000 | 11,454,000 | 14,581,000 | 14,581,000 | 21,427,078 | 21,420,082 | 26,570,820 |
| INSTITUTIONAL SERVICES FUNDS | 9,219,000 | 11,454,000 | 11,454,000 | 14,581,000 | 14,581,000 | 21,382,000 | 21,382,000 | 26,531,100 |
| STATE FUNDS | 8,918,000 | 11,199,000 | 11,199,000 | 14,073,000 | 14,073,000 | 21,123,000 | 19,123,000 | 22,780,100 |
| General Funds | 8,204,000 | 10,055,000 | 10,055,000 | 12,983,000 | 12,983,000 | 19,511,000 | 17,511,000 | 14,529,000 |
| Local | 0 | 0 | 0 | 0 | 0 | 0 | 0 | 0 |
| Other State Funds | 714,000 | 1,144,000 | 1,144,000 | 1,090,000 | 1,090,000 | 1,612,000 | 1,612,000 | 8,251,100 |
| FEDERAL FUNDS | 301,000 | 255,000 | 255,000 | 508,000 | 508,000 | 259,000 | 2,259,000 | 3,751,000 |
| Federal ICF/MR | 0 | 0 | 0 | 0 | 0 | 0 | 2,000,000 | 3,500,000 |
| Title XX / SSBG Funds | 0 | 0 | 0 | 0 | 0 | 0 | 0 | 0 |
| Other Federal Funds | 301,000 | 255,000 | 255,000 | 508,000 | 508,000 | 259,000 | 259,000 | 251,000 |
| LARGE PRIVATE RESIDENTIAL | 0 | 0 | 0 | 0 | 0 | 45,078 | 38,082 | 39,720 |
| STATE FUNDS | 0 | 0 | 0 | 0 | 0 | 45,078 | 38,082 | 39,720 |
| General Funds | 0 | 0 | 0 | 0 | 0 | 45,078 | 38,082 | 39,720 |
| Other State Funds | 0 | 0 | 0 | 0 | 0 | 0 | 0 | 0 |
| Local/County Overmatch | 0 | 0 | 0 | 0 | 0 | 0 | 0 | 0 |
| FEDERAL FUNDS | 0 | 0 | 0 | 0 | 0 | 0 | 0 | 0 |
| Large Private ICF/MR | 0 | 0 | 0 | 0 | 0 | 0 | 0 | 0 |
| **COMMUNITY SERVICES FUNDS** | 321,000 | 1,245,000 | 1,245,000 | 1,069,000 | 1,344,000 | 6,225,107 | 6,233,524 | 8,817,204 |
| STATE FUNDS | 321,000 | 1,245,000 | 1,245,000 | 1,069,000 | 1,344,000 | 5,513,607 | 5,522,024 | 6,368,180 |
| General Funds | 321,000 | 1,245,000 | 1,245,000 | 1,069,000 | 1,344,000 | 5,215,607 | 5,224,024 | 6,368,180 |
| Other State Funds | 0 | 0 | 0 | 0 | 0 | 298,000 | 298,000 | 0 |
| Local/County Overmatch | 0 | 0 | 0 | 0 | 0 | 0 | 0 | 0 |
| SSI State Supplement | 0 | 0 | 0 | 0 | 0 | 0 | 0 | 0 |
| FEDERAL FUNDS | 0 | 0 | 0 | 0 | 0 | 711,500 | 711,500 | 2,449,024 |
| ICF/MR Funds | 0 | 0 | 0 | 0 | 0 | 400,500 | 400,500 | 1,385,600 |
| Small Public | 0 | 0 | 0 | 0 | 0 | 0 | 0 | 0 |
| Small Private | 0 | 0 | 0 | 0 | 0 | 400,500 | 400,500 | 1,385,600 |
| HCBS Waiver | 0 | 0 | 0 | 0 | 0 | 0 | 0 | 270,600 |
| Model 50/200 Waiver | 0 | 0 | 0 | 0 | 0 | 0 | 0 | 0 |
| Other Title XIX Programs | 0 | 0 | 0 | 0 | 0 | 0 | 0 | 0 |
| Title XX / SSBG Funds | 0 | 0 | 0 | 0 | 0 | 0 | 0 | 0 |
| Other Federal Funds | 0 | 0 | 0 | 0 | 0 | 311,000 | 311,000 | 557,000 |
| Waiver Clients' SSI/ADC | 0 | 0 | 0 | 0 | 0 | 0 | 0 | 235,824 |

| | 1985 | 1986 | 1987 | 1988 | 1989 | 1990 | 1991 | 1992 |
|---|---|---|---|---|---|---|---|---|
| **TOTAL FUNDS** | $43,021,200 | $57,113,576 | $66,470,780 | $65,034,408 | $65,216,694 | $62,639,046 | $69,122,783 | $74,833,601 |
| **CONGREGATE 16+ BEDS** | 28,391,867 | 33,271,150 | 37,771,077 | 28,950,953 | 28,073,535 | 20,610,793 | 23,428,833 | 24,983,322 |
| INSTITUTIONAL SERVICES FUNDS | 28,350,200 | 33,227,900 | 37,726,400 | 28,904,400 | 28,025,026 | 20,560,493 | 23,376,518 | 24,929,594 |
| STATE FUNDS | 20,268,300 | 21,506,400 | 21,291,300 | 13,955,300 | 10,502,152 | 7,673,222 | 8,291,830 | 7,806,330 |
| General Funds | 19,778,300 | 19,567,200 | 20,297,200 | 13,437,600 | 10,375,799 | 7,473,446 | 7,658,204 | 7,416,000 |
| Local | 0 | 0 | 0 | 0 | 126,353 | 199,776 | 633,626 | 390,330 |
| Other State Funds | 490,000 | 1,939,200 | 994,100 | 517,700 | 0 | 0 | 0 | 0 |
| FEDERAL FUNDS | 8,081,900 | 11,721,500 | 16,435,100 | 14,949,100 | 17,522,874 | 12,887,271 | 15,084,688 | 17,123,264 |
| Federal ICF/MR | 7,171,900 | 11,646,200 | 16,373,400 | 14,915,500 | 16,833,160 | 12,321,673 | 14,466,204 | 16,461,454 |
| Title XX / SSBG Funds | 0 | 0 | 0 | 0 | 0 | 0 | 0 | 0 |
| Other Federal Funds | 910,000 | 75,300 | 61,700 | 33,600 | 689,714 | 565,598 | 618,484 | 661,810 |
| LARGE PRIVATE RESIDENTIAL | 41,667 | 43,250 | 44,677 | 46,553 | 48,509 | 50,300 | 52,315 | 53,728 |
| STATE FUNDS | 41,667 | 43,250 | 44,677 | 46,553 | 48,509 | 50,300 | 52,315 | 53,728 |
| General Funds | 41,667 | 43,250 | 44,677 | 46,553 | 48,509 | 50,300 | 52,315 | 53,728 |
| Other State Funds | 0 | 0 | 0 | 0 | 0 | 0 | 0 | 0 |
| Local/County Overmatch | 0 | 0 | 0 | 0 | 0 | 0 | 0 | 0 |
| FEDERAL FUNDS | 0 | 0 | 0 | 0 | 0 | 0 | 0 | 0 |
| Large Private ICF/MR | 0 | 0 | 0 | 0 | 0 | 0 | 0 | 0 |
| **COMMUNITY SERVICES FUNDS** | 14,629,333 | 23,842,426 | 28,699,703 | 36,083,455 | 37,143,159 | 42,028,253 | 45,693,950 | 49,850,279 |
| STATE FUNDS | 8,620,033 | 16,293,850 | 16,184,223 | 19,654,847 | 13,205,225 | 15,571,773 | 15,610,077 | 16,398,011 |
| General Funds | 8,620,033 | 16,293,850 | 16,184,223 | 19,339,147 | 12,666,348 | 15,000,053 | 14,957,307 | 15,748,889 |
| Other State Funds | 0 | 0 | 0 | 315,700 | 538,877 | 571,720 | 652,770 | 649,122 |
| Local/County Overmatch | 0 | 0 | 0 | 0 | 0 | 0 | 0 | 0 |
| SSI State Supplement | 0 | 0 | 0 | 0 | 0 | 0 | 0 | 0 |
| FEDERAL FUNDS | 6,009,300 | 7,548,576 | 12,515,480 | 16,428,608 | 23,937,934 | 26,456,480 | 30,083,873 | 33,452,268 |
| ICF/MR Funds | 1,809,100 | 2,609,100 | 6,551,300 | 9,598,600 | 10,885,242 | 11,728,030 | 12,607,039 | 13,540,147 |
| Small Public | 0 | 0 | 0 | 0 | 0 | 0 | 0 | 0 |
| Small Private | 1,809,100 | 2,609,100 | 6,551,300 | 9,598,600 | 10,885,242 | 11,728,030 | 12,607,039 | 13,540,147 |
| HCBS Waiver | 1,757,200 | 2,501,800 | 3,050,300 | 3,835,200 | 8,231,271 | 8,946,181 | 11,380,717 | 13,145,248 |
| Model 50/200 Waiver | 0 | 0 | 0 | 0 | 0 | 0 | 0 | 0 |
| Other Title XIX Programs | 0 | 0 | 0 | 0 | 0 | 0 | 0 | 0 |
| Title XX / SSBG Funds | 0 | 0 | 0 | 0 | 0 | 0 | 0 | 0 |
| Other Federal Funds | 862,600 | 131,300 | 112,900 | 113,800 | 257,773 | 332,925 | 421,125 | 251,617 |
| Waiver Clients' SSI/ADC | 1,580,400 | 2,306,376 | 2,800,980 | 2,881,008 | 4,563,648 | 5,449,344 | 5,674,992 | 6,515,256 |

*Source:*
Institute on Disability and Human Development (UAP),
University of Illinois at Chicago, 1994

# OHIO

## MR/DD Spending for Congregate Residential & Community Services

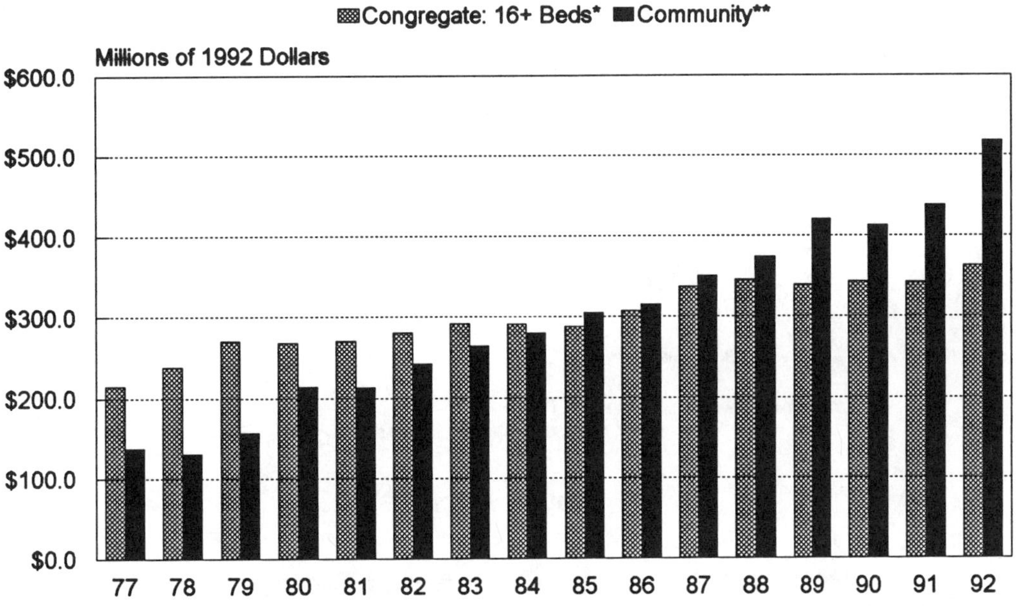
Congregate: 16+ Beds* Community**
Millions of 1992 Dollars
$600.0
$500.0
$400.0
$300.0
$200.0
$100.0
$0.0
77 78 79 80 81 82 83 84 85 86 87 88 89 90 91 92
Fiscal Year

*Excludes nursing homes; ** Includes resources for 15 bed or less residential settings & non-residential community services

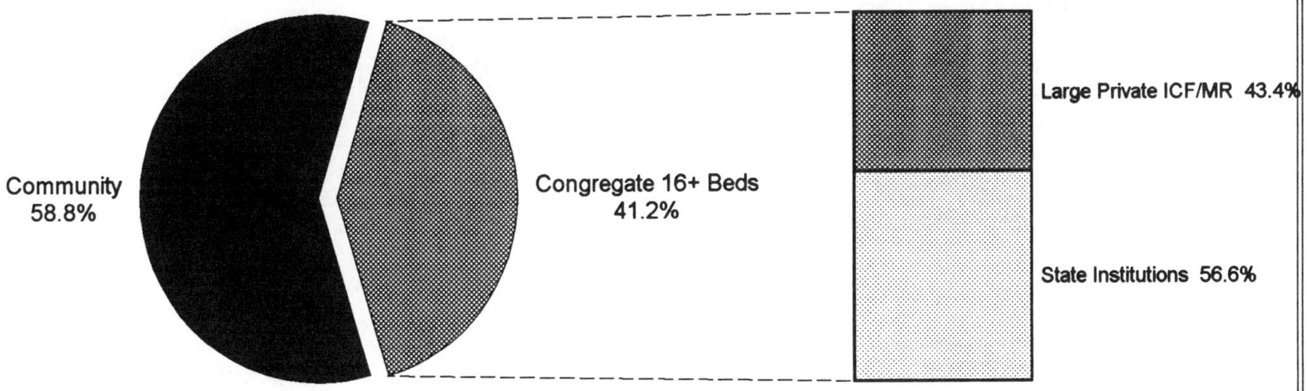
Community
58.8%
Congregate 16+ Beds
41.2%
Large Private ICF/MR 43.4%
State Institutions 56.6%

FY 1992 Total Spending:
$881.3 Million

*Source:*
Institute on Disability and Human Development (UAP), University of Illinois at Chicago, 1994

# OHIO

## Number of Persons Served by Residential Setting: FY 1992

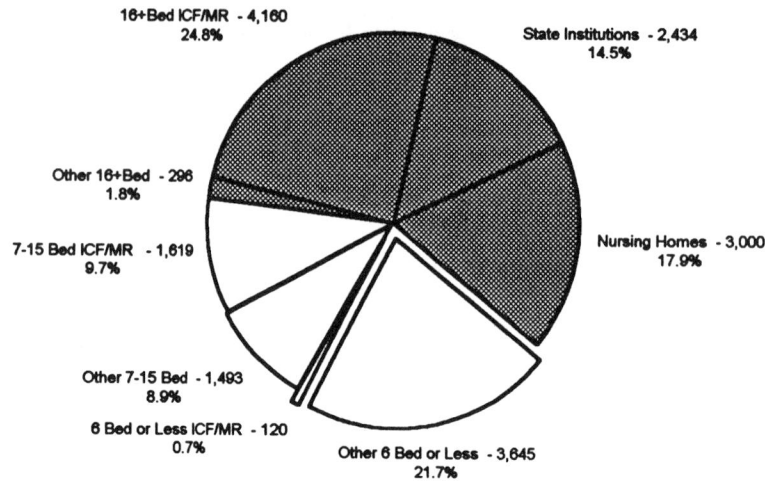

16+Bed ICF/MR - 4,160
24.8%

State Institutions - 2,434
14.5%

Other 16+Bed - 296
1.8%

7-15 Bed ICF/MR - 1,619
9.7%

Nursing Homes - 3,000
17.9%

Other 7-15 Bed - 1,493
8.9%

6 Bed or Less ICF/MR - 120
0.7%

Other 6 Bed or Less - 3,645
21.7%

Total Served: 16,767

## Persons Served by Residential Setting:1986-92

|  | 1986 | 1987 | 1988 | 1989 | 1990 | 1991 | 1992 |
|---|---|---|---|---|---|---|---|
| CONGREGATE 16 + BED SETTINGS | NA | NA | 11,938 | 10,471 | NA | NA | 9,890 |
| Nursing Homes | NA | NA | 4,756 | 3,184 | NA | NA | 3,000 |
| State Institutions | 2,993 | 3,051 | 2,990 | 2,753 | 2,656 | 2,540 | 2,434 |
| Private 16+Bed ICF/MR | 3,474 | 3,757 | 4,004 | 3,991 | 4,024 | 4,090 | 4,160 |
| Other 16+Bed Residential | 104 | 140 | 188 | 543 | 579 | 475 | 296 |
| 15 BED OR LESS RESIDENTIAL SETTINGS | 4,109 | 4,235 | 4,564 | 5,705 | 5,812 | 6,310 | 6,877 |
| Public 7-15 Bed ICF/MR | 0 | 0 | 0 | 0 | 0 | 0 | 0 |
| Private 7-15 Bed ICF/MR | 974 | 1,061 | 1,123 | 1,402 | 1,325 | 1,432 | 1,619 |
| Other 7-15 Bed Residential | 3,135 | 3,174 | 3,441 | 4,303 | 1,554 | 1,530 | 1,493 |
| Public 6 Bed or Less ICF/MR | 0 | 0 | 0 | 0 | 0 | 0 | 0 |
| Private 6 Bed or Less ICF/MR |  |  |  |  | 86 | 102 | 120 |
| Other 6 Bed or Less Residential |  |  |  |  | 2,847 | 3,246 | 3,645 |
| TOTAL PERSONS SERVED | NA | NA | 16,502 | 16,176 | NA | NA | 16,767 |

## Persons Served in Non-Residential Community Services:1986-92

|  | 1986 | 1987 | 1988 | 1989 | 1990 | 1991 | 1992 |
|---|---|---|---|---|---|---|---|
| DAY/WORK PROGRAMS | 19,715 | 20,981 | 22,458 | 23,836 | 25,794 | 28,560 | 27,736 |
| Sheltered Employment/Work Activity | 15,844 | 16,734 | 17,616 | 15,586 | 16,766 | 16,044 | 16,400 |
| Day Habilitation ("Day Training") | 3,522 | 3,843 | 4,271 | 5,556 | 5,963 | 5,804 | 5,976 |
| Supported/Competitive Employment | 349 | 404 | 571 | 2,694 | 3,486 | 5,617 | 6,228 |
| CASE MANAGEMENT | NA | 3,318 | 4,482 | 21,085 | 21,374 | 23,062 | 23,841 |
| HCBS WAIVER | 0 | 0 | 0 | 0 | 0 | 0 | 482 |
| MODEL 50/200 WAIVER | 59 | 106 | 90 | 192 | 242 | 243 | 242 |

*Source:*
Institute on Disability and Human Development (UAP),
University of Illinois at Chicago, 1994

# OHIO

## Community Services: FY 1992 Revenue Sources

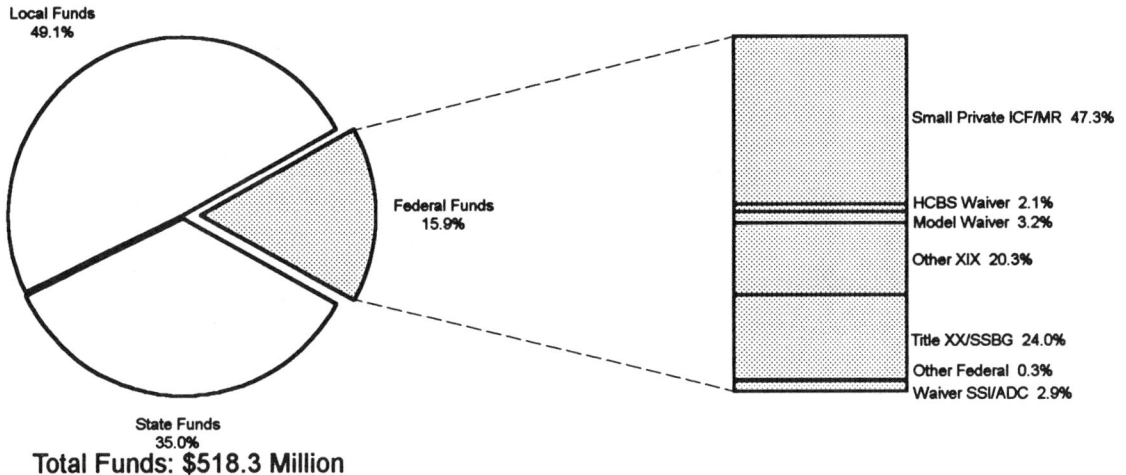

Local Funds 49.1%

Federal Funds 15.9%

State Funds 35.0%

Small Private ICF/MR 47.3%
HCBS Waiver 2.1%
Model Waiver 3.2%
Other XIX 20.3%
Title XX/SSBG 24.0%
Other Federal 0.3%
Waiver SSI/ADC 2.9%

Total Funds: $518.3 Million

## Family Support Initiatives*

|  | 1986 | 1987 | 1988 | 1989 | 1990 | 1991 | 1992 |
|---|---|---|---|---|---|---|---|
| FAMILY SUPPORT: TOTAL SPENDING | $2,056,223 | $2,142,462 | $3,562,462 | $4,638,160 | $4,638,160 | $4,777,305 | $4,777,305 |
| Total # of Families Supported | NA | NA | NA | 4,294 | 5,349 | 6,908 | 7,258 |
| A. Financial Subsidy/Payment | $0 | $0 | $0 | $0 | $0 | $0 | $0 |
| # of Families | 0 | 0 | 0 | 0 | 0 | 0 | 0 |
| B. Family Assistance Payments | $0 | $0 | $0 | $0 | $0 | $0 | $0 |
| # of Families | 0 | 0 | 0 | 0 | 0 | 0 | 0 |
| C. Other Family Support Payments | $2,056,223 | $2,142,462 | $3,562,462 | $4,638,160 | $4,638,160 | $4,777,305 | $4,777,305 |
| # of Families | NA | NA | NA | 4,294 | 5,349 | 6,908 | 7,258 |

## Other Community Services Initiatives*

|  | 1986 | 1987 | 1988 | 1989 | 1990 | 1991 | 1992 |
|---|---|---|---|---|---|---|---|
| AGING/DD SPENDING | $0 | $819,600 | $822,000 | NA | $505,200 | $966,000 | $1,041,600 |
| # of Persons Served | 0 | 683 | 685 | NA | 421 | 805 | 868 |
| ASSISTIVE TECHNOLOGY SPENDING |  |  |  |  |  |  | $0 |
| # of Persons Served |  |  |  |  |  |  | 0 |
| EARLY INTERVENTION SPENDING | $1,399,500 | $1,362,750 | $1,351,500 | $1,646,250 | $1,834,500 | $2,041,500 | $2,373,750 |
| # of Persons Served | 4,083 | 4,714 | 5,189 | 2,195 | 2,446 | 2,722 | 3,165 |
| PERSONAL ASSISTANCE SPENDING |  |  |  |  |  |  | $0 |
| # of Persons Served |  |  |  |  |  |  | 0 |
| SUPPORTED EMPLOYMENT SPENDING | $418,800 | $484,800 | $685,200 | $3,232,800 | $4,183,200 | $6,740,400 | $7,473,600 |
| # of Persons Served | 349 | 404 | 571 | 2,694 | 3,486 | 5,617 | 6,228 |
| SUPPORTED LIVING SPENDING |  |  |  |  | $2,865,315 | $10,228,954 | $12,712,360 |
| # of Persons Served |  |  |  |  | 260 | 698 | 1,099 |

*Expenditures associated with Special Community Initiatives are a subset of funding within the community services component of the state's chart series and spreadsheet; Family Support Client figures may include duplicate client counts; HCBS Waiver counts include Waiver case management numbers.
0= Services not provided in the state; NA= Data not available from state; blank= Services not applicable (eg. CSLA prior to authorization, Special Community Initiatives prior to request for data by this study)

*Source:*
Institute on Disability and Human Development (UAP),
University of Illinois at Chicago, 1994

# OHIO

## Large Congregate Care Facilities: FY 1992 Revenue Sources*

### Private 16+Bed Settings

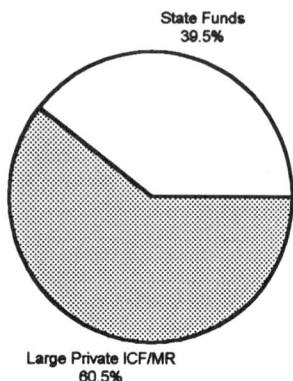

State Funds
39.5%

Large Private ICF/MR
60.5%

Total Funds: $157.4 Million

### Public Institutions

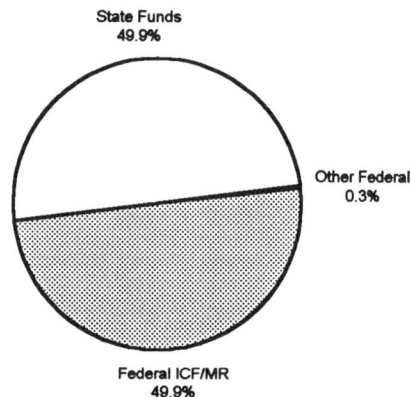

State Funds
49.9%

Other Federal
0.3%

Federal ICF/MR
49.9%

Total Funds: $205.5 Million

**\*Excludes nursing homes**

## Average Daily Residents in Institutions

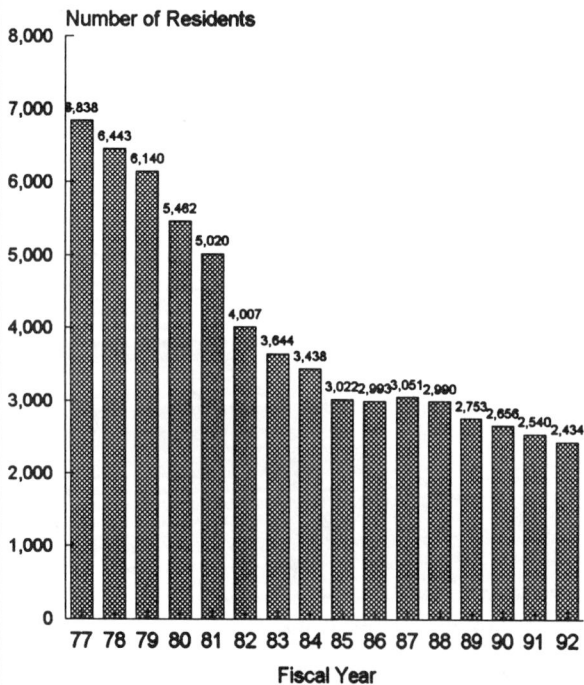

Number of Residents

| | |
|---|---|
| 77 | 6,838 |
| 78 | 6,443 |
| 79 | 6,140 |
| 80 | 5,462 |
| 81 | 5,020 |
| 82 | 4,007 |
| 83 | 3,644 |
| 84 | 3,438 |
| 85 | 3,022 |
| 86 | 2,993 |
| 87 | 3,051 |
| 88 | 2,990 |
| 89 | 2,753 |
| 90 | 2,656 |
| 91 | 2,540 |
| 92 | 2,434 |

Fiscal Year

## Institutional Daily Costs Per Resident

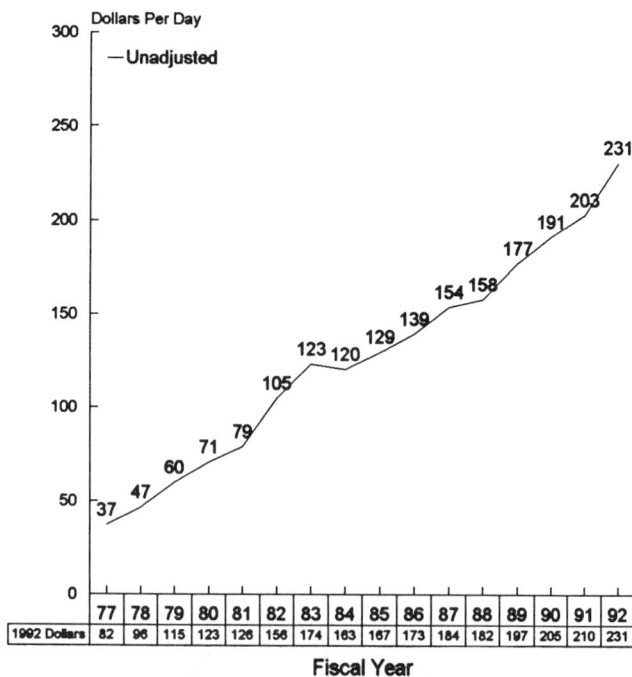

Dollars Per Day

—Unadjusted

| Fiscal Year | 77 | 78 | 79 | 80 | 81 | 82 | 83 | 84 | 85 | 86 | 87 | 88 | 89 | 90 | 91 | 92 |
|---|---|---|---|---|---|---|---|---|---|---|---|---|---|---|---|---|
| Unadjusted | 37 | 47 | 60 | 71 | 79 | 105 | 123 | 120 | 129 | 139 | 154 | 158 | 177 | 191 | 203 | 231 |
| 1992 Dollars | 82 | 96 | 115 | 123 | 126 | 156 | 174 | 163 | 167 | 173 | 184 | 182 | 197 | 205 | 210 | 231 |

Fiscal Year

*Source:*
Institute on Disability and Human Development (UAP),
University of Illinois at Chicago, 1994

# OHIO FISCAL EFFORT

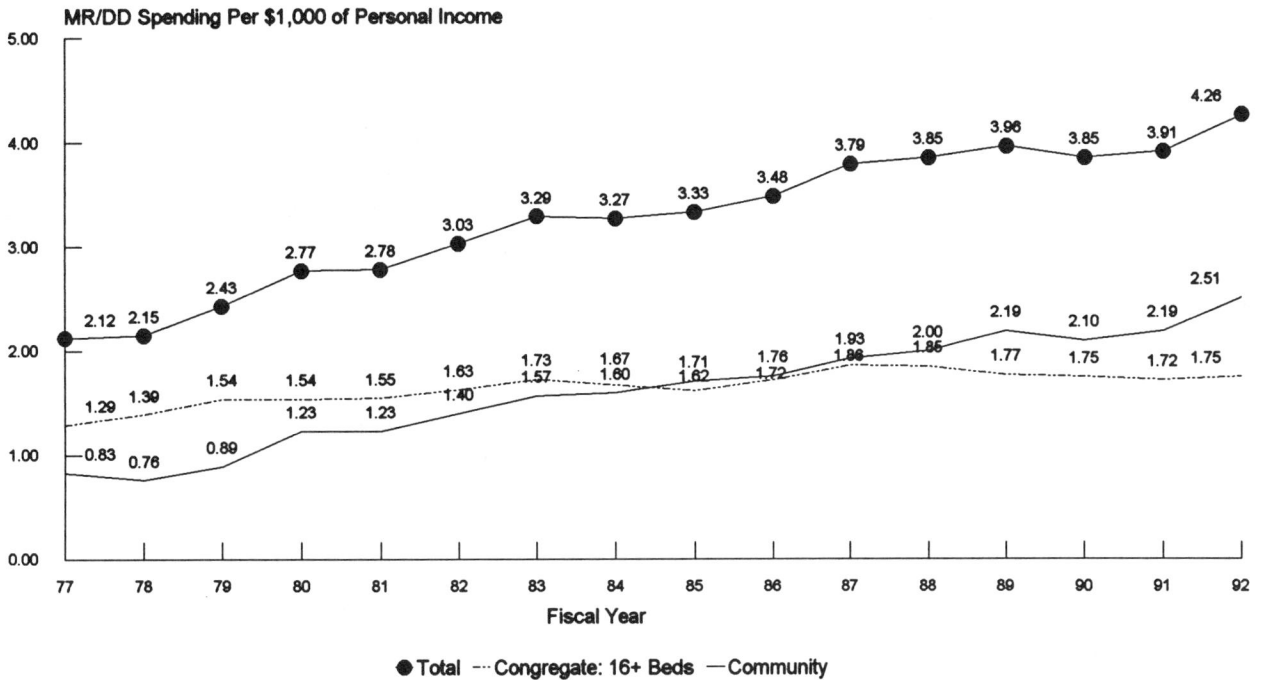

MR/DD Spending Per $1,000 of Personal Income

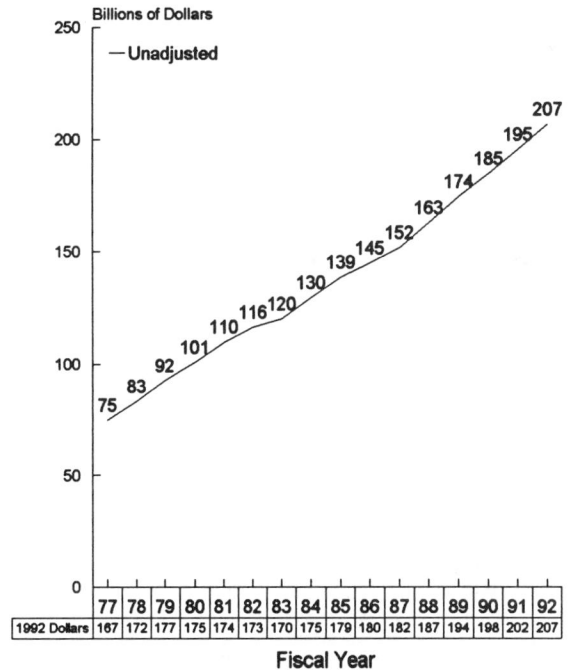

| | |
|---|---|
| 5.00 | |
| 4.00 | 4.26 |
| | 3.79  3.85  3.96  3.85  3.91 |
| 3.00 | 3.03  3.29  3.27  3.33  3.48 |
| | 2.77  2.78 |
| 2.00 | 2.12  2.15  2.43 |

(Total line) 2.12, 2.15, 2.43, 2.77, 2.78, 3.03, 3.29, 3.27, 3.33, 3.48, 3.79, 3.85, 3.96, 3.85, 3.91, 4.26

(Congregate: 16+ Beds) 1.29, 1.39, 1.54, 1.54, 1.55, 1.63, 1.73, 1.67, 1.71, 1.76, 1.93, 2.00, 1.86, 1.77, 1.75, 1.72, 1.75
1.57, 1.60, 1.62, 1.72, 1.86, 1.85

(Community) 0.83, 0.76, 0.89, 1.23, 1.23, 1.40, 1.57, 1.60, 1.62, 1.72, 1.86, 2.19, 2.10, 2.19, 2.51

Fiscal Year (77–92)

● Total  --- Congregate: 16+ Beds  — Community

## Total MR/DD Spending

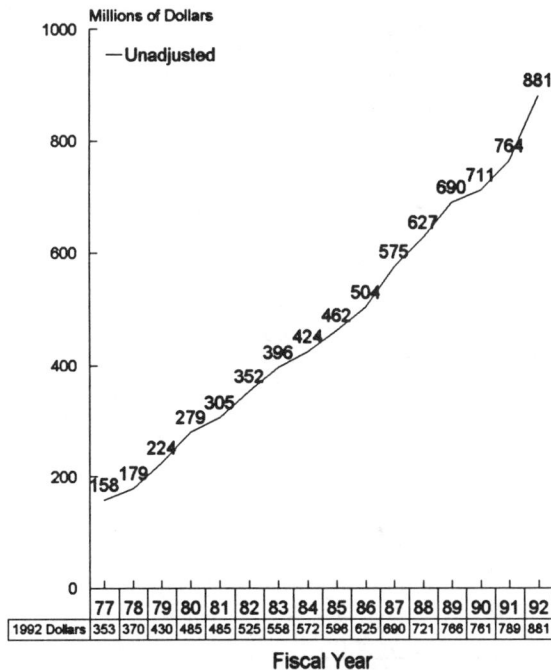

Millions of Dollars
— Unadjusted

| | |
|---|---|
| 1000 | |
| 800 | 881 |
| | 764 |
| | 690  711 |
| 600 | 627 |
| | 575 |
| | 504 |
| | 462 |
| 400 | 396  424 |
| | 352 |
| | 279  305 |
| 200 | 224 |
| | 158  179 |
| 0 | |

| | 77 | 78 | 79 | 80 | 81 | 82 | 83 | 84 | 85 | 86 | 87 | 88 | 89 | 90 | 91 | 92 |
|---|---|---|---|---|---|---|---|---|---|---|---|---|---|---|---|
| 1992 Dollars | 353 | 370 | 430 | 485 | 485 | 525 | 558 | 572 | 596 | 625 | 690 | 721 | 766 | 761 | 789 | 881 |

Fiscal Year

## Personal Income

Billions of Dollars
— Unadjusted

| | |
|---|---|
| 250 | |
| 200 | 207 |
| | 195 |
| | 185 |
| | 174 |
| | 163 |
| 150 | 152 |
| | 145 |
| | 139 |
| | 130 |
| | 110  116  120 |
| 100 | 101 |
| | 92 |
| | 83 |
| | 75 |
| 50 | |
| 0 | |

| | 77 | 78 | 79 | 80 | 81 | 82 | 83 | 84 | 85 | 86 | 87 | 88 | 89 | 90 | 91 | 92 |
|---|---|---|---|---|---|---|---|---|---|---|---|---|---|---|---|
| 1992 Dollars | 167 | 172 | 177 | 175 | 174 | 173 | 170 | 175 | 179 | 180 | 182 | 187 | 194 | 198 | 202 | 207 |

Fiscal Year

*Source:*
Institute on Disability and Human Development (UAP),
University of Illinois at Chicago, 1994

# OHIO
## Financial Support for MR/DD Services: FY 1977-92

| | 1977 | 1978 | 1979 | 1980 | 1981 | 1982 | 1983 | 1984 |
|---|---|---|---|---|---|---|---|---|
| **TOTAL FUNDS** | $158,360,259 | $178,809,421 | $224,050,177 | $278,963,526 | $304,908,468 | $352,432,703 | $396,079,832 | $424,063,448 |
| **CONGREGATE 16+ BEDS** | 96,554,401 | 115,540,973 | 141,887,022 | 155,187,508 | 170,372,880 | 189,163,589 | 207,868,074 | 216,196,196 |
| INSTITUTIONAL SERVICES FUNDS | 91,952,000 | 109,512,000 | 133,867,000 | 141,524,000 | 144,637,000 | 153,153,700 | 163,744,700 | 151,486,449 |
| STATE FUNDS | 78,287,000 | 93,237,000 | 96,944,000 | 108,632,000 | 107,839,000 | 106,677,300 | 97,817,600 | 87,901,242 |
| General Funds | 71,090,000 | 84,665,000 | 86,247,000 | 95,353,000 | 98,739,000 | 99,407,300 | 85,205,600 | 79,746,871 |
| Local | 0 | 0 | 0 | 0 | 0 | 0 | 0 | 0 |
| Other State Funds | 7,197,000 | 8,572,000 | 10,697,000 | 13,279,000 | 9,100,000 | 7,270,000 | 12,612,000 | 8,154,371 |
| FEDERAL FUNDS | 13,665,000 | 16,275,000 | 36,923,000 | 32,892,000 | 36,798,000 | 46,476,400 | 65,927,100 | 63,585,207 |
| Federal ICF/MR | 8,727,000 | 10,394,000 | 30,736,000 | 31,434,000 | 35,793,000 | 45,685,400 | 64,758,100 | 63,054,212 |
| Title XX / SSBG Funds | 0 | 0 | 0 | 0 | 0 | 0 | 0 | 0 |
| Other Federal Funds | 4,938,000 | 5,881,000 | 6,187,000 | 1,458,000 | 1,005,000 | 791,000 | 1,169,000 | 530,995 |
| LARGE PRIVATE RESIDENTIAL | 4,602,401 | 6,028,973 | 8,020,022 | 13,663,508 | 25,735,880 | 36,009,889 | 44,123,374 | 64,709,747 |
| STATE FUNDS | 2,605,401 | 3,203,973 | 4,079,022 | 6,642,508 | 12,089,880 | 16,718,889 | 20,378,374 | 29,473,247 |
| General Funds | 2,605,401 | 3,203,973 | 4,079,022 | 6,642,508 | 12,089,880 | 16,718,889 | 20,378,374 | 29,473,247 |
| Other State Funds | 0 | 0 | 0 | 0 | 0 | 0 | 0 | 0 |
| Local/County Overmatch | 0 | 0 | 0 | 0 | 0 | 0 | 0 | 0 |
| FEDERAL FUNDS | 1,997,000 | 2,825,000 | 3,941,000 | 7,021,000 | 13,646,000 | 19,291,000 | 23,745,000 | 35,236,500 |
| Large Private ICF/MR | 1,997,000 | 2,825,000 | 3,941,000 | 7,021,000 | 13,646,000 | 19,291,000 | 23,745,000 | 35,236,500 |
| **COMMUNITY SERVICES FUNDS** | 61,805,858 | 63,268,448 | 82,163,155 | 123,776,018 | 134,535,588 | 163,269,114 | 188,211,758 | 207,867,252 |
| STATE FUNDS | 55,002,858 | 56,273,448 | 75,785,155 | 90,868,018 | 108,078,588 | 130,065,114 | 159,502,758 | 175,870,705 |
| General Funds | 34,316,599 | 26,939,027 | 37,200,978 | 42,432,492 | 41,765,120 | 60,122,111 | 74,123,626 | 81,323,143 |
| Other State Funds | 0 | 0 | 0 | 0 | 7,425,000 | 0 | 3,780,000 | 690,708 |
| Local/County Overmatch | 20,686,259 | 29,334,421 | 38,584,177 | 48,435,526 | 58,888,468 | 69,943,003 | 81,599,132 | 93,856,854 |
| SSI State Supplement | 0 | 0 | 0 | 0 | 0 | 0 | 0 | 0 |
| FEDERAL FUNDS | 6,803,000 | 6,995,000 | 6,378,000 | 32,908,000 | 26,457,000 | 33,204,000 | 28,709,000 | 31,996,547 |
| ICF/MR Funds | 462,000 | 654,000 | 912,000 | 1,625,000 | 3,159,000 | 4,467,000 | 5,498,000 | 8,158,000 |
| Small Public | 0 | 0 | 0 | 0 | 0 | 0 | 0 | 0 |
| Small Private | 462,000 | 654,000 | 912,000 | 1,625,000 | 3,159,000 | 4,467,000 | 5,498,000 | 8,158,000 |
| HCBS Waiver | 0 | 0 | 0 | 0 | 0 | 0 | 0 | 0 |
| Model 50/200 Waiver | 0 | 0 | 0 | 0 | 0 | 0 | 0 | 53,768 |
| Other Title XIX Programs | 0 | 0 | 0 | 0 | 0 | 0 | 0 | 0 |
| Title XX / SSBG Funds | 0 | 0 | 0 | 25,379,000 | 16,957,000 | 22,029,000 | 16,835,000 | 18,622,480 |
| Other Federal Funds | 6,341,000 | 6,341,000 | 5,466,000 | 5,904,000 | 6,341,000 | 6,708,000 | 6,376,000 | 5,162,299 |
| Waiver Clients' SSI/ADC | 0 | 0 | 0 | 0 | 0 | 0 | 0 | 0 |

| | 1985 | 1986 | 1987 | 1988 | 1989 | 1990 | 1991 | 1992 |
|---|---|---|---|---|---|---|---|---|
| **TOTAL FUNDS** | $461,923,038 | $503,819,761 | $574,900,734 | $627,104,164 | $689,953,862 | $711,227,163 | $763,666,572 | $881,277,331 |
| **CONGREGATE 16+ BEDS** | 224,272,398 | 248,961,367 | 281,940,605 | 301,207,954 | 308,053,579 | 323,293,033 | 335,373,641 | 362,928,592 |
| INSTITUTIONAL SERVICES FUNDS | 142,824,124 | 152,058,911 | 171,125,317 | 172,722,013 | 177,928,219 | 185,531,652 | 188,351,709 | 205,483,304 |
| STATE FUNDS | 79,139,814 | 81,408,314 | 91,778,740 | 95,072,300 | 93,206,750 | 95,524,647 | 98,269,353 | 102,442,073 |
| General Funds | 71,515,488 | 73,275,572 | 81,043,620 | 88,054,600 | 86,182,900 | 88,515,456 | 91,053,270 | 94,199,073 |
| Local | 0 | 0 | 0 | 0 | 0 | 0 | 0 | 0 |
| Other State Funds | 7,624,326 | 8,132,742 | 10,735,120 | 7,017,700 | 7,023,850 | 7,009,191 | 7,216,083 | 8,243,000 |
| FEDERAL FUNDS | 63,684,310 | 70,650,597 | 79,346,577 | 77,649,713 | 84,721,469 | 90,007,005 | 90,082,356 | 103,041,231 |
| Federal ICF/MR | 62,756,562 | 69,513,689 | 77,546,963 | 76,827,713 | 83,899,469 | 89,377,005 | 89,452,356 | 102,453,296 |
| Title XX / SSBG Funds | 0 | 0 | 0 | 0 | 0 | 0 | 0 | 0 |
| Other Federal Funds | 927,748 | 1,136,908 | 1,799,614 | 822,000 | 822,000 | 630,000 | 630,000 | 587,935 |
| LARGE PRIVATE RESIDENTIAL | 81,448,274 | 96,902,456 | 110,815,288 | 128,485,941 | 130,125,360 | 137,761,381 | 147,021,932 | 157,445,288 |
| STATE FUNDS | 37,486,974 | 42,373,102 | 48,069,745 | 55,053,579 | 53,338,385 | 55,903,568 | 59,044,008 | 62,253,867 |
| General Funds | 37,486,974 | 42,373,102 | 48,069,745 | 55,053,579 | 53,338,385 | 55,903,568 | 59,044,008 | 62,253,867 |
| Other State Funds | 0 | 0 | 0 | 0 | 0 | 0 | 0 | 0 |
| Local/County Overmatch | 0 | 0 | 0 | 0 | 0 | 0 | 0 | 0 |
| FEDERAL FUNDS | 43,961,300 | 54,529,354 | 62,745,543 | 73,432,362 | 76,786,975 | 81,857,813 | 87,977,924 | 95,191,421 |
| Large Private ICF/MR | 43,961,300 | 54,529,354 | 62,745,543 | 73,432,362 | 76,786,975 | 81,857,813 | 87,977,924 | 95,191,421 |
| **COMMUNITY SERVICES FUNDS** | 237,650,640 | 254,858,394 | 292,960,129 | 325,896,210 | 381,900,283 | 387,934,130 | 428,292,931 | 518,348,739 |
| STATE FUNDS | 200,978,505 | 216,946,058 | 248,808,911 | 274,693,483 | 320,227,340 | 337,384,071 | 373,988,958 | 435,946,745 |
| General Funds | 94,262,336 | 96,768,981 | 118,404,746 | 127,970,889 | 148,438,884 | 138,069,748 | 145,969,244 | 181,631,166 |
| Other State Funds | 0 | 0 | 0 | 0 | 0 | 0 | 0 | 0 |
| Local/County Overmatch | 106,716,169 | 120,177,077 | 130,404,165 | 146,722,594 | 171,788,456 | 199,314,323 | 228,019,714 | 254,315,579 |
| SSI State Supplement | 0 | 0 | 0 | 0 | 0 | 0 | 0 | 0 |
| FEDERAL FUNDS | 36,672,135 | 37,912,336 | 44,151,218 | 51,202,727 | 61,672,943 | 50,550,059 | 54,303,973 | 82,401,994 |
| ICF/MR Funds | 10,178,000 | 12,625,089 | 16,367,557 | 20,159,738 | 26,403,693 | 28,095,710 | 32,298,815 | 38,950,666 |
| Small Public | 0 | 0 | 0 | 0 | 0 | 0 | 0 | 0 |
| Small Private | 10,178,000 | 12,625,089 | 16,367,557 | 20,159,738 | 26,403,693 | 28,095,710 | 32,298,815 | 38,950,666 |
| HCBS Waiver | 0 | 0 | 0 | 0 | 0 | 0 | 6,796 | 1,695,743 |
| Model 50/200 Waiver | 138,144 | 396,650 | 659,094 | 609,289 | 1,434,138 | 2,254,703 | 2,568,515 | 2,636,548 |
| Other Title XIX Programs | 0 | 0 | 0 | 10,500,000 | 14,000,000 | 419,646 | 1,764,847 | 16,734,949 |
| Title XX / SSBG Funds | 20,938,100 | 20,527,613 | 20,558,253 | 19,600,500 | 19,580,930 | 19,500,000 | 17,385,000 | 19,750,000 |
| Other Federal Funds | 5,417,891 | 4,362,984 | 6,566,314 | 333,200 | 254,182 | 280,000 | 280,000 | 280,000 |
| Waiver Clients' SSI/ADC | 0 | 0 | 0 | 0 | 0 | 0 | 0 | 2,354,088 |

*Source:*
Institute on Disability and Human Development (UAP),
University of Illinois at Chicago, 1994

# OKLAHOMA

## MR/DD Spending for Congregate Residential & Community Services

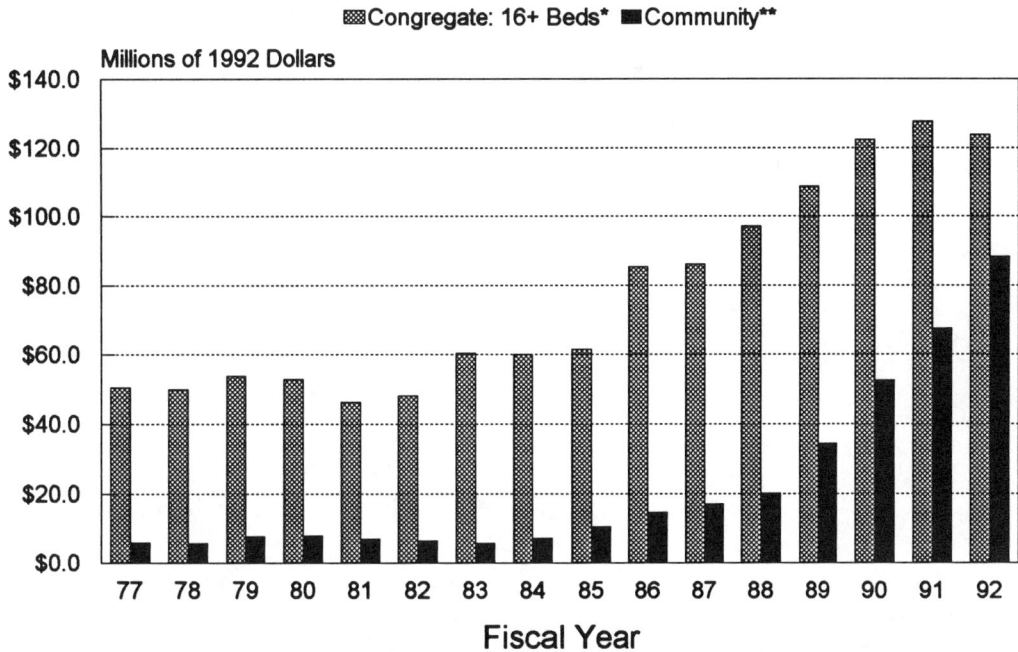

▨ Congregate: 16+ Beds* ■ Community**

Millions of 1992 Dollars

$140.0

$120.0

$100.0

$80.0

$60.0

$40.0

$20.0

$0.0

77 78 79 80 81 82 83 84 85 86 87 88 89 90 91 92

Fiscal Year

*Excludes nursing homes; ** Includes resources for
15 bed or less residential settings & non-residential community services

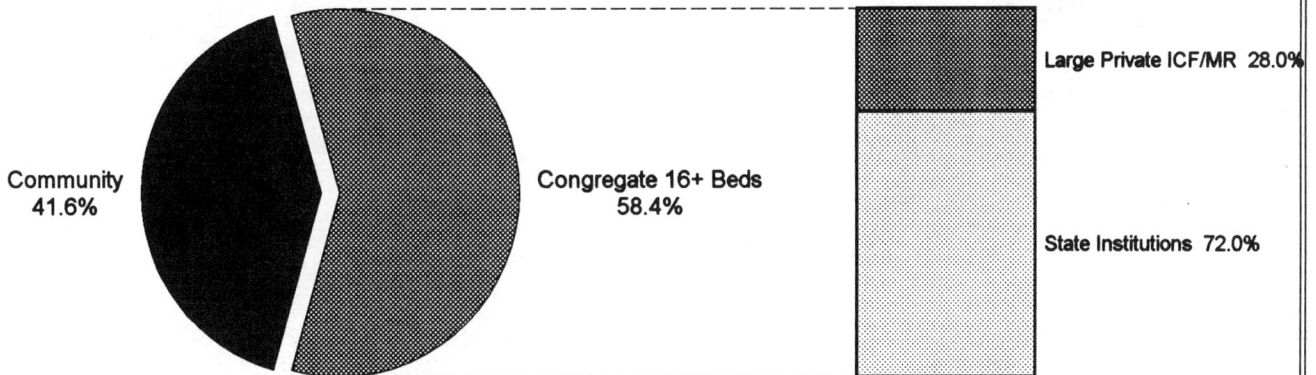

Community
41.6%

Congregate 16+ Beds
58.4%

Large Private ICF/MR 28.0%

State Institutions 72.0%

FY 1992 Total Spending:
$212.1 Million

*Source:*
Institute on Disability and Human Development (UAP),
University of Illinois at Chicago, 1994

# OKLAHOMA

## Number of Persons Served by Residential Setting: FY 1992

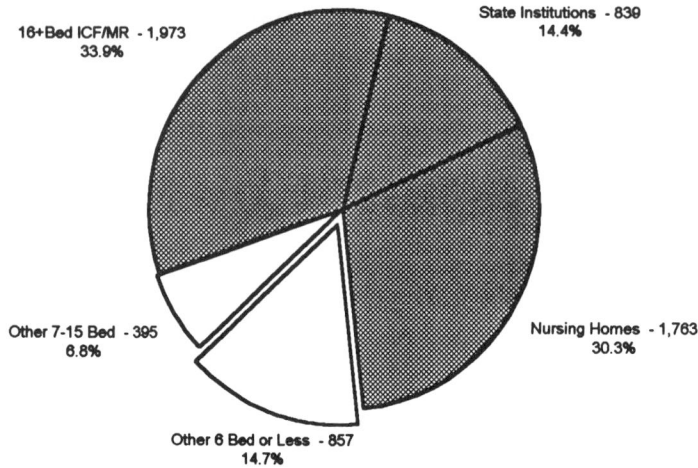

16+Bed ICF/MR - 1,973
33.9%

State Institutions - 839
14.4%

Other 7-15 Bed - 395
6.8%

Nursing Homes - 1,763
30.3%

Other 6 Bed or Less - 857
14.7%

Total Served: 5,827

## Persons Served by Residential Setting:1986-92

| | 1986 | 1987 | 1988 | 1989 | 1990 | 1991 | 1992 |
|---|---|---|---|---|---|---|---|
| CONGREGATE 16 + BED SETTINGS | 4,487 | 4,636 | 5,237 | 5,085 | 4,914 | 4,753 | 4,575 |
| Nursing Homes | 1,405 | 1,405 | 2,055 | 2,005 | 1,955 | 1,854 | 1,763 |
| State Institutions | 1,338 | 1,262 | 1,213 | 1,116 | 1,010 | 910 | 839 |
| Private 16+Bed ICF/MR | 1,744 | 1,969 | 1,969 | 1,964 | 1,949 | 1,989 | 1,973 |
| Other 16+Bed Residential | 0 | 0 | 0 | 0 | 0 | 0 | 0 |
| 15 BED OR LESS RESIDENTIAL SETTINGS | 512 | 619 | 689 | 777 | 890 | 1,133 | 1,252 |
| Public 7-15 Bed ICF/MR | 0 | 0 | 0 | 0 | 0 | 0 | 0 |
| Private 7-15 Bed ICF/MR | 0 | 0 | 0 | 0 | 0 | 0 | 0 |
| Other 7-15 Bed Residential | 512 | 619 | 689 | 777 | 890 | 1,133 | 395 |
| Public 6 Bed or Less ICF/MR | | | | | | | 0 |
| Private 6 Bed or Less ICF/MR | | | | | | | 0 |
| Other 6 Bed or Less Residential | | | | | | | 857 |
| TOTAL PERSONS SERVED | 4,999 | 5,255 | 5,926 | 5,862 | 5,804 | 5,886 | 5,827 |

## Persons Served in Non-Residential Community Services:1986-92

| | 1986 | 1987 | 1988 | 1989 | 1990 | 1991 | 1992 |
|---|---|---|---|---|---|---|---|
| DAY/WORK PROGRAMS | 1,143 | 1,143 | 1,588 | 1,709 | 1,903 | 2,037 | 2,171 |
| Sheltered Employment/Work Activity | 1,143 | 1,143 | 1,588 | 1,709 | 1,778 | 1,779 | 1,779 |
| Day Habilitation ("Day Training") | 0 | 0 | 0 | 0 | 0 | 0 | 0 |
| Supported/Competitive Employment | 0 | 0 | 0 | 0 | 125 | 258 | 392 |
| CASE MANAGEMENT | NA | NA | 134 | 305 | 621 | 844 | 1,050 |
| HCBS WAIVER | 56 | 85 | 134 | 305 | 621 | 844 | 1,050 |
| MODEL 50/200 WAIVER | 0 | 0 | 0 | 0 | 0 | 0 | 0 |

*Source:*
Institute on Disability and Human Development (UAP),
University of Illinois at Chicago, 1994

# OKLAHOMA

## Community Services: FY 1992 Revenue Sources

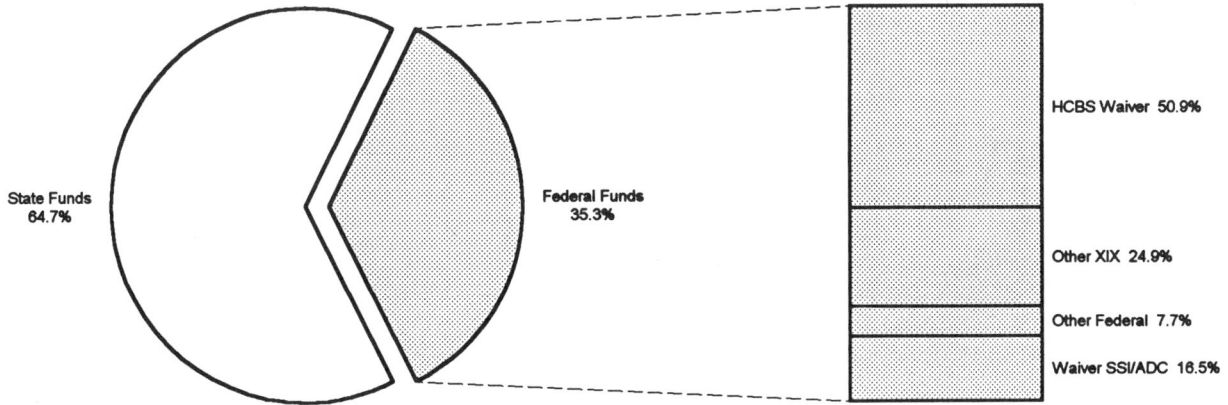

State Funds 64.7%

Federal Funds 35.3%

HCBS Waiver 50.9%

Other XIX 24.9%

Other Federal 7.7%

Waiver SSI/ADC 16.5%

Total Funds: $88.2 Million

## Family Support Initiatives*

|  | 1986 | 1987 | 1988 | 1989 | 1990 | 1991 | 1992 |
|---|---|---|---|---|---|---|---|
| FAMILY SUPPORT: TOTAL SPENDING | $0 | $0 | $0 | $8,010 | $50,984 | $79,120 | $504,007 |
| Total # of Families Supported | 0 | 0 | 0 | 33 | 124 | 155 | 385 |
| A. Financial Subsidy/Payment | $0 | $0 | $0 | $0 | $0 | $0 | $0 |
| # of Families | 0 | 0 | 0 | 0 | 0 | 0 | 0 |
| B. Family Assistance Spending | $0 | $0 | $0 | $8,010 | $50,984 | $79,120 | $408,580 |
| # of Families | 0 | 0 | 0 | 33 | 124 | 155 | 260 |
| C. Other Family Support Spending | $0 | $0 | $0 | $0 | $0 | $0 | $95,427 |
| # of Families | 0 | 0 | 0 | 0 | 0 | 0 | 125 |

## Other Community Services Initiatives*

|  | 1986 | 1987 | 1988 | 1989 | 1990 | 1991 | 1992 |
|---|---|---|---|---|---|---|---|
| AGING/DD SPENDING | $0 | $0 | $0 | $0 | $0 | $0 | $0 |
| # of Persons Served | 0 | 0 | 0 | 0 | 0 | 0 | 0 |
| ASSISTIVE TECHNOLOGY SPENDING |  |  |  |  |  |  | $0 |
| # of Persons Served |  |  |  |  |  |  | 0 |
| EARLY INTERVENTION SPENDING | $0 | $0 | $0 | $0 | $0 | $0 | $0 |
| # of Persons Served | 0 | 0 | 0 | 0 | 0 | 0 | 0 |
| PERSONAL ASSISTANCE SPENDING |  |  | $46,800 | $63,000 | $87,500 | $100,800 | $127,500 |
| # of Persons Served |  |  | 20 | 25 | 35 | 40 | 50 |
| SUPPORTED EMPLOYMENT SPENDING | $0 | $0 | $0 | $0 | $917,715 | $2,325,279 | $2,968,297 |
| # of Persons Served | 0 | 0 | 0 | 0 | 125 | 258 | 392 |
| SUPPORTED LIVING SPENDING |  |  |  |  | $4,535,788 | $13,493,894 | $24,573,133 |
| # of Persons Served |  |  |  |  | 87 | 220 | 349 |

*Expenditures associated with Special Community Initiatives are a subset of funding within the community services component of the state's chart series and spreadsheet; Family Support Client figures may include duplicate client counts; HCBS Waiver counts include Waiver case management numbers.
0= Services not provided in the state; NA= Data not available from state; blank= Services not applicable (eg. CSLA prior to authorization, Special Community Initiatives prior to request for data by this study)

Source:
Institute on Disability and Human Development (UAP),
University of Illinois at Chicago, 1994

# OKLAHOMA

## Large Congregate Care Facilities: FY 1992 Revenue Sources*

### Private 16+Bed Settings

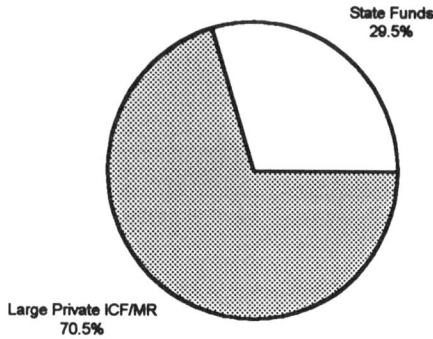

State Funds
29.5%

Large Private ICF/MR
70.5%

Total Funds: $34.6 Million

### Public Institutions

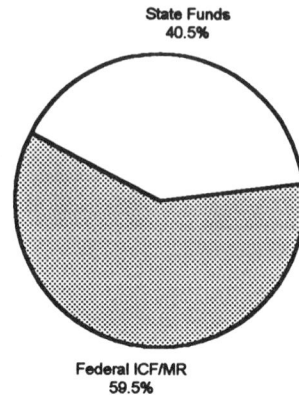

State Funds
40.5%

Federal ICF/MR
59.5%

Total Funds: $89.2 Million

*Excludes nursing homes

## Average Daily Residents in Institutions

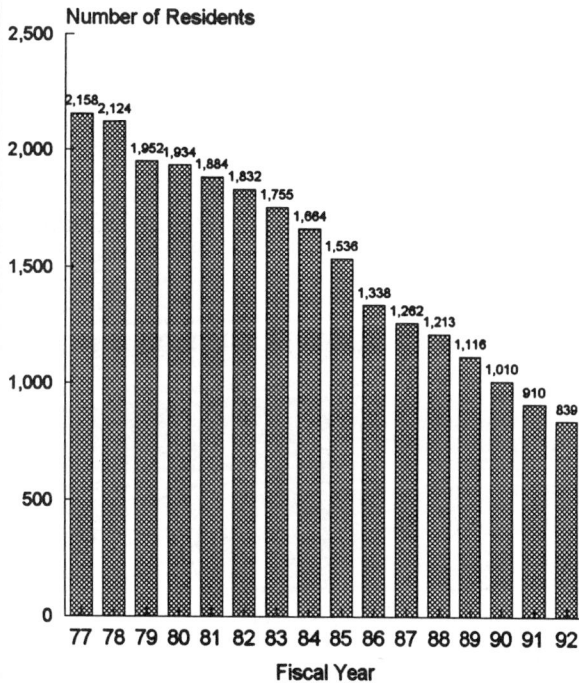

Number of Residents

| Fiscal Year | Number |
|---|---|
| 77 | 2,158 |
| 78 | 2,124 |
| 79 | 1,952 |
| 80 | 1,934 |
| 81 | 1,884 |
| 82 | 1,832 |
| 83 | 1,755 |
| 84 | 1,664 |
| 85 | 1,536 |
| 86 | 1,338 |
| 87 | 1,262 |
| 88 | 1,213 |
| 89 | 1,116 |
| 90 | 1,010 |
| 91 | 910 |
| 92 | 839 |

Fiscal Year

## Institutional Daily Costs Per Resident

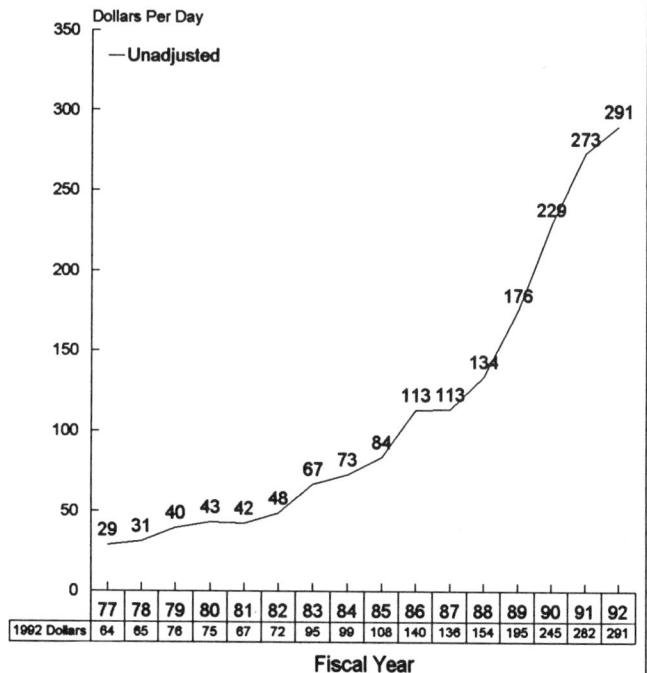

Dollars Per Day

— Unadjusted

29 31 40 43 42 48 67 73 84 113 113 134 176 229 273 291

| | 77 | 78 | 79 | 80 | 81 | 82 | 83 | 84 | 85 | 86 | 87 | 88 | 89 | 90 | 91 | 92 |
|---|---|---|---|---|---|---|---|---|---|---|---|---|---|---|---|---|
| 1992 Dollars | 64 | 65 | 76 | 75 | 67 | 72 | 95 | 99 | 108 | 140 | 136 | 154 | 195 | 245 | 282 | 291 |

Fiscal Year

Source:
Institute on Disability and Human Development (UAP),
University of Illinois at Chicago, 1994

# OKLAHOMA FISCAL EFFORT

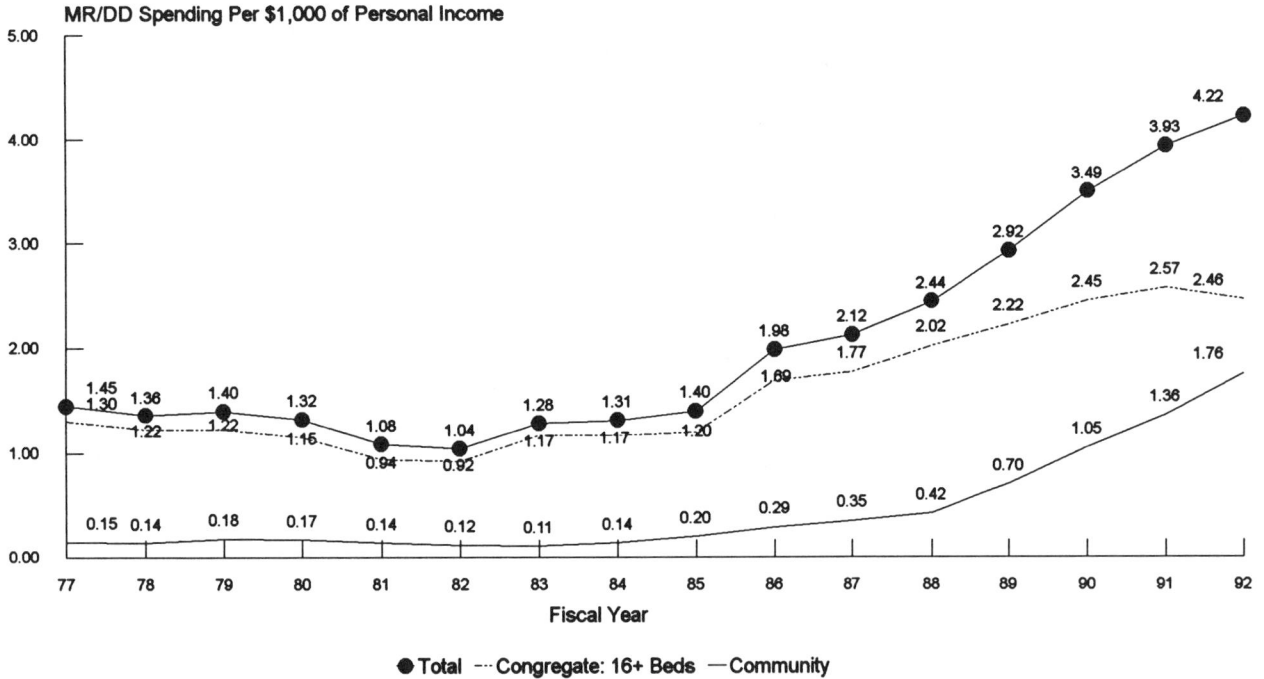

MR/DD Spending Per $1,000 of Personal Income

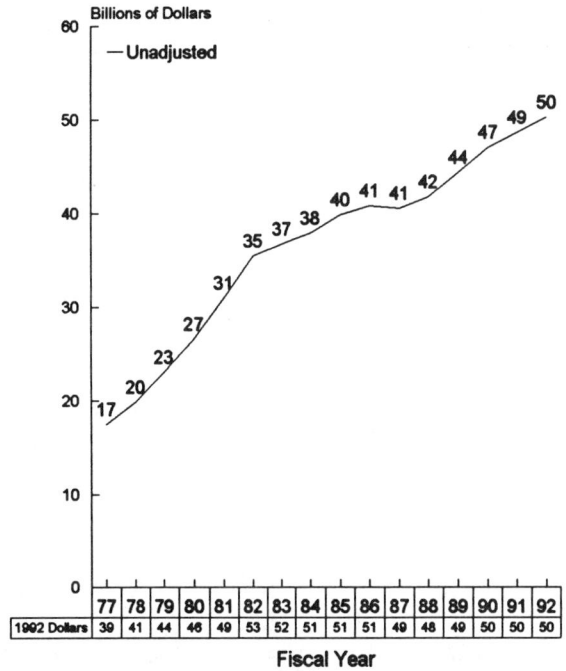

| | |
|---|---|
| 5.00 | |
| 4.00 | |
| 3.00 | |
| 2.00 | |
| 1.00 | |
| 0.00 | |

Total values: 1.45, 1.36, 1.40, 1.32, 1.08, 1.04, 1.28, 1.31, 1.40, 1.98, 2.12, 2.44, 2.92, 3.49, 3.93, 4.22

Congregate 16+ Beds values: 1.30, 1.22, 1.22, 1.16, 0.94, 0.92, 1.17, 1.17, 1.20, 1.69, 1.77, 2.02, 2.22, 2.45, 2.57, 2.46

Community values: 0.15, 0.14, 0.18, 0.17, 0.14, 0.12, 0.11, 0.14, 0.20, 0.29, 0.35, 0.42, 0.70, 1.05, 1.36, 1.76

Fiscal Year: 77 78 79 80 81 82 83 84 85 86 87 88 89 90 91 92

● Total  --- Congregate: 16+ Beds  — Community

## Total MR/DD Spending

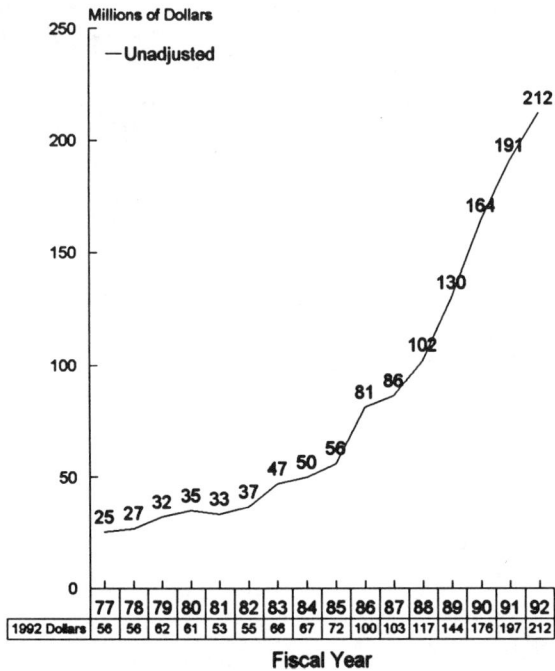

Millions of Dollars
— Unadjusted

| | |
|---|---|
| 250 | |
| 200 | 212 |
| 150 | 191 |
| 100 | 164 |
| 50 | 130 |
| 0 | |

Values: 25, 27, 32, 35, 33, 37, 47, 50, 56, 81, 86, 102, 130, 164, 191, 212

| Fiscal Year | 77 | 78 | 79 | 80 | 81 | 82 | 83 | 84 | 85 | 86 | 87 | 88 | 89 | 90 | 91 | 92 |
|---|---|---|---|---|---|---|---|---|---|---|---|---|---|---|---|---|
| 1992 Dollars | 56 | 56 | 62 | 61 | 53 | 55 | 66 | 67 | 72 | 100 | 103 | 117 | 144 | 176 | 197 | 212 |

## Personal Income

Billions of Dollars
— Unadjusted

| | |
|---|---|
| 60 | |
| 50 | 50 |
| 40 | |
| 30 | |
| 20 | |
| 10 | |
| 0 | |

Values: 17, 20, 23, 27, 31, 35, 37, 38, 40, 41, 41, 42, 44, 47, 49, 50

| Fiscal Year | 77 | 78 | 79 | 80 | 81 | 82 | 83 | 84 | 85 | 86 | 87 | 88 | 89 | 90 | 91 | 92 |
|---|---|---|---|---|---|---|---|---|---|---|---|---|---|---|---|---|
| 1992 Dollars | 39 | 41 | 44 | 46 | 49 | 53 | 52 | 51 | 51 | 51 | 49 | 48 | 49 | 50 | 50 | 50 |

*Source:*
Institute on Disability and Human Development (UAP),
University of Illinois at Chicago, 1994

# OKLAHOMA
## Financial Support for MR/DD Services: FY 1977-92

| | 1977 | 1978 | 1979 | 1980 | 1981 | 1982 | 1983 | 1984 |
|---|---|---|---|---|---|---|---|---|
| **TOTAL FUNDS** | $25,318,000 | $26,918,000 | $32,246,000 | $35,072,000 | $33,449,788 | $36,709,578 | $47,050,461 | $49,790,461 |
| **CONGREGATE 16+ BEDS** | 22,709,000 | 24,202,000 | 28,180,000 | 30,571,000 | 29,108,838 | 32,426,804 | 43,016,678 | 44,491,393 |
| INSTITUTIONAL SERVICES FUNDS | 22,709,000 | 24,202,000 | 28,180,000 | 30,571,000 | 29,108,838 | 32,426,804 | 43,016,678 | 44,491,393 |
| STATE FUNDS | 8,649,000 | 7,320,000 | 8,847,000 | 11,248,000 | 10,499,341 | 12,619,488 | 17,125,116 | 18,193,596 |
| General Funds | 0 | 0 | 0 | 0 | 0 | 0 | 0 | 0 |
| Local | 0 | 0 | 0 | 0 | 0 | 0 | 0 | 0 |
| Other State Funds | 8,649,000 | 7,320,000 | 8,847,000 | 11,248,000 | 10,499,341 | 12,619,488 | 17,125,116 | 18,193,596 |
| FEDERAL FUNDS | 14,060,000 | 16,882,000 | 19,333,000 | 19,323,000 | 18,609,497 | 19,807,316 | 25,891,562 | 26,297,797 |
| Federal ICF/MR | 13,657,000 | 16,544,000 | 19,182,000 | 19,182,000 | 18,416,497 | 19,618,316 | 25,591,562 | 25,997,797 |
| Title XX / SSBG Funds | 0 | 0 | 0 | 0 | 0 | 0 | 0 | 0 |
| Other Federal Funds | 403,000 | 338,000 | 151,000 | 141,000 | 193,000 | 189,000 | 300,000 | 300,000 |
| LARGE PRIVATE RESIDENTIAL | 0 | 0 | 0 | 0 | 0 | 0 | 0 | 0 |
| STATE FUNDS | 0 | 0 | 0 | 0 | 0 | 0 | 0 | 0 |
| General Funds | 0 | 0 | 0 | 0 | 0 | 0 | 0 | 0 |
| Other State Funds | 0 | 0 | 0 | 0 | 0 | 0 | 0 | 0 |
| Local/County Overmatch | 0 | 0 | 0 | 0 | 0 | 0 | 0 | 0 |
| FEDERAL FUNDS | 0 | 0 | 0 | 0 | 0 | 0 | 0 | 0 |
| Large Private ICF/MR | 0 | 0 | 0 | 0 | 0 | 0 | 0 | 0 |
| **COMMUNITY SERVICES FUNDS** | 2,609,000 | 2,716,000 | 4,066,000 | 4,501,000 | 4,340,950 | 4,282,774 | 4,033,783 | 5,299,068 |
| STATE FUNDS | 2,148,000 | 2,466,000 | 3,656,000 | 4,045,000 | 4,059,000 | 3,913,000 | 3,657,000 | 4,866,511 |
| General Funds | 0 | 0 | 0 | 0 | 0 | 0 | 0 | 0 |
| Other State Funds | 30,000 | 216,000 | 69,000 | 66,000 | 0 | 0 | 0 | 1,851,511 |
| Local/County Overmatch | 0 | 0 | 0 | 0 | 0 | 0 | 0 | 0 |
| SSI State Supplement | 2,118,000 | 2,250,000 | 3,587,000 | 3,979,000 | 4,059,000 | 3,913,000 | 3,657,000 | 3,015,000 |
| FEDERAL FUNDS | 461,000 | 250,000 | 410,000 | 456,000 | 281,950 | 369,774 | 376,783 | 432,557 |
| ICF/MR Funds | 0 | 0 | 0 | 0 | 0 | 0 | 0 | 0 |
| Small Public | 0 | 0 | 0 | 0 | 0 | 0 | 0 | 0 |
| Small Private | 0 | 0 | 0 | 0 | 0 | 0 | 0 | 0 |
| HCBS Waiver | 0 | 0 | 0 | 0 | 0 | 0 | 0 | 0 |
| Model 50/200 Waiver | 0 | 0 | 0 | 0 | 0 | 0 | 0 | 0 |
| Other Title XIX Programs | 0 | 0 | 0 | 0 | 0 | 0 | 0 | 0 |
| Title XX / SSBG Funds | 0 | 0 | 0 | 0 | 0 | 0 | 0 | 0 |
| Other Federal Funds | 461,000 | 250,000 | 410,000 | 456,000 | 281,950 | 369,774 | 376,783 | 432,557 |
| Waiver Clients' SSI/ADC | 0 | 0 | 0 | 0 | 0 | 0 | 0 | 0 |

| | 1985 | 1986 | 1987 | 1988 | 1989 | 1990 | 1991 | 1992 |
|---|---|---|---|---|---|---|---|---|
| **TOTAL FUNDS** | $55,919,810 | $80,994,931 | $86,115,697 | $101,988,275 | $129,782,311 | $164,322,714 | $190,887,837 | $212,128,795 |
| **CONGREGATE 16+ BEDS** | 47,812,990 | 69,082,689 | 71,854,384 | 84,493,389 | 98,491,793 | 115,050,932 | 124,957,378 | 123,890,830 |
| INSTITUTIONAL SERVICES FUNDS | 47,009,906 | 55,212,328 | 52,275,509 | 59,462,608 | 71,497,256 | 84,424,276 | 90,772,598 | 89,249,417 |
| STATE FUNDS | 19,295,630 | 23,159,681 | 21,174,582 | 22,228,101 | 24,754,130 | 35,485,738 | 38,124,433 | 36,183,239 |
| General Funds | 0 | 0 | 0 | 22,228,101 | 24,754,130 | 35,485,738 | 38,124,433 | 36,183,239 |
| Local | 0 | 0 | 0 | 0 | 0 | 0 | 0 | 0 |
| Other State Funds | 19,295,630 | 23,159,681 | 21,174,582 | 0 | 0 | 0 | 0 | 0 |
| FEDERAL FUNDS | 27,714,276 | 32,052,647 | 31,100,927 | 37,234,507 | 46,743,126 | 48,938,538 | 52,648,165 | 53,066,178 |
| Federal ICF/MR | 27,166,276 | 31,743,847 | 30,845,027 | 36,967,907 | 46,743,126 | 48,938,538 | 52,648,165 | 53,066,178 |
| Title XX / SSBG Funds | 0 | 0 | 0 | 0 | 0 | 0 | 0 | 0 |
| Other Federal Funds | 548,000 | 308,800 | 255,900 | 266,600 | 0 | 0 | 0 | 0 |
| LARGE PRIVATE RESIDENTIAL | 803,084 | 13,870,361 | 19,578,875 | 25,030,781 | 26,994,537 | 30,626,656 | 34,184,780 | 34,641,413 |
| STATE FUNDS | 333,521 | 5,850,518 | 7,968,602 | 9,396,555 | 9,346,184 | 9,350,189 | 10,485,171 | 10,230,471 |
| General Funds | 0 | 0 | 0 | 9,396,555 | 9,346,184 | 9,350,189 | 10,485,171 | 10,230,471 |
| Other State Funds | 333,521 | 5,850,518 | 7,968,602 | 0 | 0 | 0 | 0 | 0 |
| Local/County Overmatch | 0 | 0 | 0 | 0 | 0 | 0 | 0 | 0 |
| FEDERAL FUNDS | 469,563 | 8,019,843 | 11,610,273 | 15,634,226 | 17,648,353 | 21,276,467 | 23,699,609 | 24,410,942 |
| Large Private ICF/MR | 469,563 | 8,019,843 | 11,610,273 | 15,634,226 | 17,648,353 | 21,276,467 | 23,699,609 | 24,410,942 |
| **COMMUNITY SERVICES FUNDS** | 8,106,820 | 11,912,242 | 14,261,313 | 17,494,886 | 31,290,518 | 49,271,782 | 65,930,459 | 88,237,965 |
| STATE FUNDS | 7,546,192 | 10,631,021 | 12,688,970 | 14,622,291 | 23,726,704 | 36,240,917 | 47,429,802 | 57,118,058 |
| General Funds | 0 | 0 | 0 | 10,974,291 | 19,444,711 | 31,573,945 | 42,338,132 | 51,660,136 |
| Other State Funds | 4,357,192 | 7,431,021 | 9,271,970 | 0 | 174,099 | 282,206 | 299,618 | 424,801 |
| Local/County Overmatch | 0 | 0 | 0 | 0 | 0 | 0 | 0 | 0 |
| SSI State Supplement | 3,189,000 | 3,200,000 | 3,417,000 | 3,648,000 | 4,107,894 | 4,384,766 | 4,792,052 | 5,033,121 |
| FEDERAL FUNDS | 560,628 | 1,281,221 | 1,572,343 | 2,872,595 | 7,563,814 | 13,030,865 | 18,500,657 | 31,119,907 |
| ICF/MR Funds | 0 | 0 | 0 | 0 | 0 | 0 | 0 | 0 |
| Small Public | 0 | 0 | 0 | 0 | 0 | 0 | 0 | 0 |
| Small Private | 0 | 0 | 0 | 0 | 0 | 0 | 0 | 0 |
| HCBS Waiver | 0 | 34,711 | 232,483 | 976,358 | 1,611,471 | 3,251,346 | 6,599,648 | 15,847,994 |
| Model 50/200 Waiver | 0 | 0 | 0 | 0 | 0 | 0 | 0 | 0 |
| Other Title XIX Programs | 0 | 0 | 0 | 0 | 3,670,144 | 5,438,016 | 6,293,766 | 7,736,507 |
| Title XX / SSBG Funds | 0 | 0 | 0 | 0 | 0 | 0 | 0 | 0 |
| Other Federal Funds | 560,628 | 1,037,518 | 1,018,560 | 1,375,245 | 986,559 | 1,599,167 | 1,697,835 | 2,407,206 |
| Waiver Clients' SSI/ADC | 0 | 208,992 | 321,300 | 520,992 | 1,295,640 | 2,742,336 | 3,909,408 | 5,128,200 |

*Source:*
Institute on Disability and Human Development (UAP),
University of Illinois at Chicago, 1994

# OREGON

## MR/DD Spending for Congregate Residential & Community Services

▒Congregate: 16+ Beds*  ■Community**

Millions of 1992 Dollars

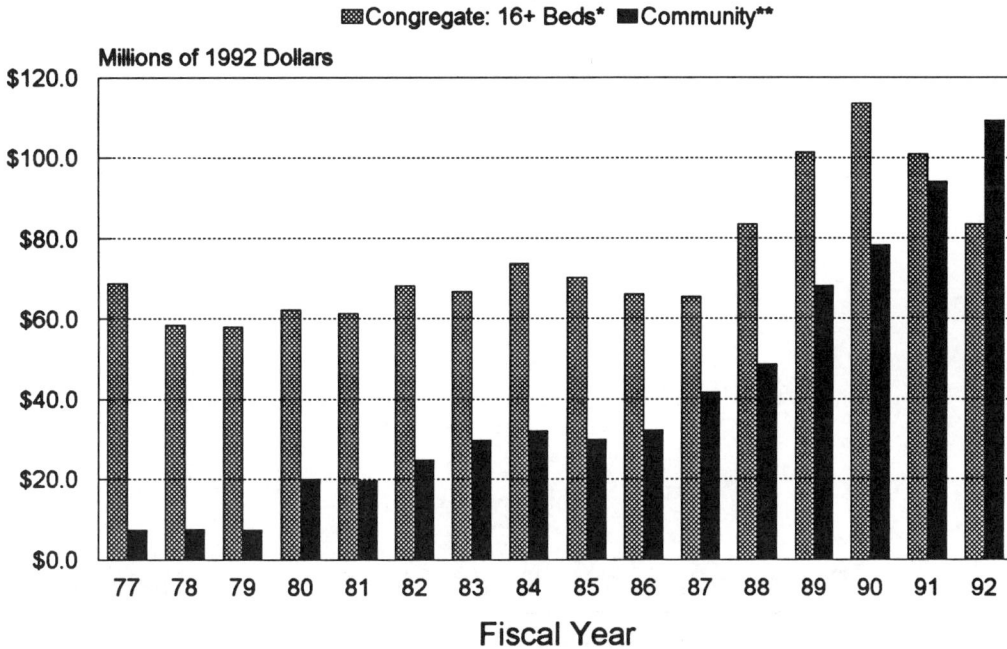

Fiscal Year

*Excludes nursing homes; ** Includes resources for
15 bed or less residential settings & non-residential community services

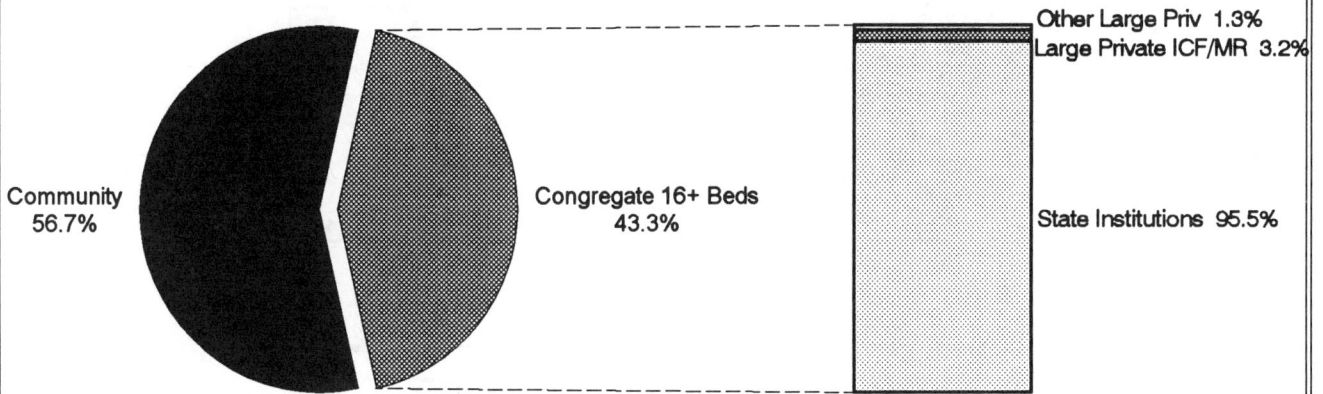

Community
56.7%

Congregate 16+ Beds
43.3%

Other Large Priv 1.3%
Large Private ICF/MR 3.2%

State Institutions 95.5%

FY 1992 Total Spending:
$192.9 Million

*Source:*
Institute on Disability and Human Development (UAP),
University of Illinois at Chicago, 1994

# OREGON

## Number of Persons Served by Residential Setting: FY 1992

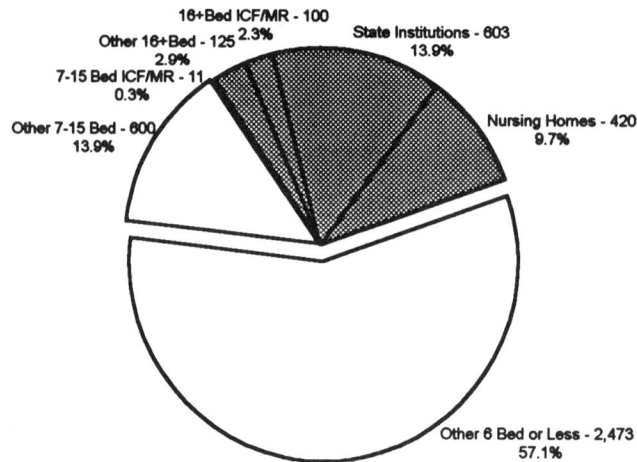

16+Bed ICF/MR - 100
2.3%

Other 16+Bed - 125
2.9%

7-15 Bed ICF/MR - 11
0.3%

Other 7-15 Bed - 600
13.9%

State Institutions - 603
13.9%

Nursing Homes - 420
9.7%

Other 6 Bed or Less - 2,473
57.1%

Total Served: 4,332

## Persons Served by Residential Setting:1986-92

| | 1986 | 1987 | 1988 | 1989 | 1990 | 1991 | 1992 |
|---|---|---|---|---|---|---|---|
| **CONGREGATE 16 + BED SETTINGS** | NA | NA | 1,734 | 1,769 | 1,556 | 1,422 | 1,248 |
| Nursing Homes | NA | NA | 238 | 450 | 443 | 435 | 420 |
| State Institutions | 1,356 | 1,214 | 1,130 | 1,026 | 840 | 754 | 603 |
| Private 16+Bed ICF/MR | 261 | 229 | 199 | 160 | 140 | 100 | 100 |
| Other 16+Bed Residential | 167 | 167 | 167 | 133 | 133 | 133 | 125 |
| **15 BED OR LESS RESIDENTIAL SETTINGS** | 22 | 1,805 | 2,055 | 2,390 | 2,612 | 2,811 | 3,084 |
| Public 7-15 Bed ICF/MR | 0 | 0 | 0 | 0 | 0 | 0 | 0 |
| Private 7-15 Bed ICF/MR | 22 | 22 | 22 | 22 | 22 | 22 | 11 |
| Other 7-15 Bed Residential | NA | 1,783 | 2,033 | 800 | 675 | 600 | 600 |
| Public 6 Bed or Less ICF/MR | | | | 0 | 0 | 0 | 0 |
| Private 6 Bed or Less ICF/MR | | | | 0 | 0 | 0 | 0 |
| Other 6 Bed or Less Residential | | | | 1,568 | 1,915 | 2,189 | 2,473 |
| **TOTAL PERSONS SERVED** | NA | NA | 3,789 | 4,159 | 4,168 | 4,233 | 4,332 |

## Persons Served in Non-Residential Community Services:1986-92

| | 1986 | 1987 | 1988 | 1989 | 1990 | 1991 | 1992 |
|---|---|---|---|---|---|---|---|
| **DAY/WORK PROGRAMS** | NA | 2,772 | 3,022 | 3,843 | 4,080 | 4,328 | 4,663 |
| Sheltered Employment/Work Activity | NA | 2,572 | 2,722 | 2,706 | 2,850 | 2,936 | 3,046 |
| Day Habilitation ("Day Training") | 0 | 0 | 0 | 0 | 0 | 0 | 0 |
| Supported/Competitive Employment | 39 | 200 | 300 | 1,137 | 1,230 | 1,392 | 1,617 |
| **CASE MANAGEMENT** | NA | NA | NA | NA | 3,531 | 3,783 | 3,988 |
| **HCBS WAIVER** | 693 | 903 | 1,157 | 1,156 | 1,306 | 1,429 | 1,471 |
| **MODEL 50/200 WAIVER** | 0 | 0 | 0 | 0 | 0 | 0 | 0 |

*Source:*
Institute on Disability and Human Development (UAP),
University of Illinois at Chicago, 1994

# OREGON

## Community Services: FY 1992 Revenue Sources

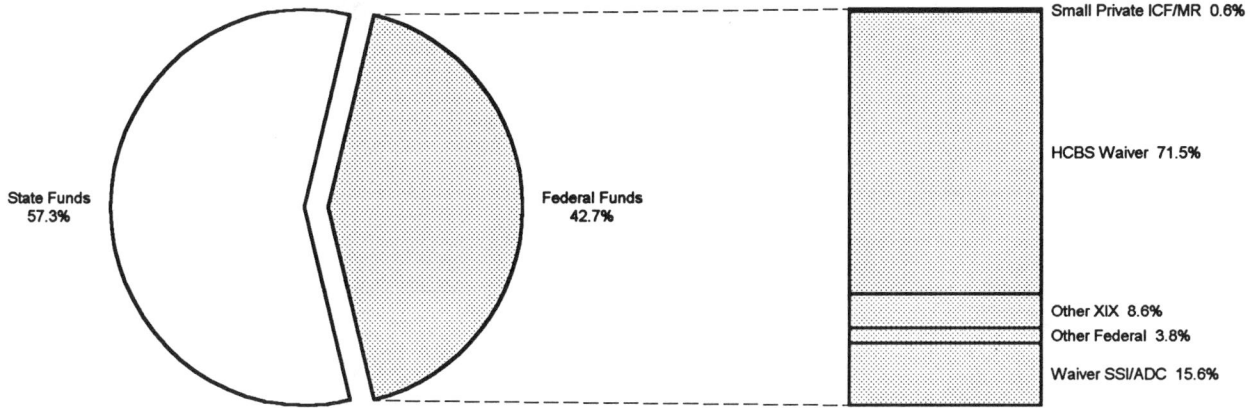

State Funds 57.3%

Federal Funds 42.7%

Small Private ICF/MR 0.6%

HCBS Waiver 71.5%

Other XIX 8.6%

Other Federal 3.8%

Waiver SSI/ADC 15.6%

Total Funds: $109.4 Million

## Family Support Initiatives*

|  | 1986 | 1987 | 1988 | 1989 | 1990 | 1991 | 1992 |
|---|---|---|---|---|---|---|---|
| FAMILY SUPPORT: TOTAL SPENDING | $0 | $0 | $0 | $867,202 | $824,356 | $1,041,602 | $941,106 |
| Total # of Families Supported | 0 | 0 | 0 | 334 | 334 | 435 | 435 |
| A. Financial Subsidy/Payment | $0 | $0 | $0 | $405,202 | $390,085 | $416,959 | $466,542 |
| # of Families | 0 | 0 | 0 | 183 | 183 | 183 | 183 |
| B. Family Assistance Payments | $0 | $0 | $0 | $0 | $0 | $0 | $0 |
| # of Families | 0 | 0 | 0 | 0 | 0 | 0 | 0 |
| C. Other Family Support Payments | $0 | $0 | $0 | $462,000 | $434,271 | $624,643 | $474,564 |
| # of Families | 0 | 0 | 0 | 151 | 151 | 252 | 252 |

## Other Community Services Initiatives*

|  | 1986 | 1987 | 1988 | 1989 | 1990 | 1991 | 1992 |
|---|---|---|---|---|---|---|---|
| AGING/DD SPENDING | $0 | $0 | $0 | $0 | $0 | $0 | $0 |
| # of Persons Served | 0 | 0 | 0 | 0 | 0 | 0 | 0 |
| ASSISTIVE TECHNOLOGY SPENDING |  |  |  |  |  |  | $0 |
| # of Persons Served |  |  |  |  |  |  | 0 |
| EARLY INTERVENTION SPENDING | $1,631,697 | $1,708,517 | $2,102,745 | $5,823,055 | $8,886,132 | $8,505,247 | $8,681,082 |
| # of Persons Served | 1,030 | 1,030 | 1,121 | 1,618 | 1,891 | 2,196 | 2,358 |
| PERSONAL ASSISTANCE SPENDING |  |  |  |  |  |  | $349,355 |
| # of Persons Served |  |  |  |  |  |  | 477 |
| SUPPORTED EMPLOYMENT SPENDING | $81,882 | $424,928 | $1,170,377 | $4,785,482 | $5,762,215 | $8,031,275 | $10,354,739 |
| # of Persons Served | 39 | 200 | 300 | 1,137 | 1,230 | 1,392 | 1,617 |
| SUPPORTED LIVING SPENDING |  |  |  |  |  |  | $0 |
| # of Persons Served |  |  |  |  |  |  | 0 |

*Expenditures associated with Special Community Initiatives are a subset of funding within the community services component of the state's chart series and spreadsheet; Family Support Client figures may include duplicate client counts; HCBS Waiver counts include Waiver case management numbers.
0= Services not provided in the state; NA= Data not available from state; blank= Services not applicable (eg. CSLA prior to authorization, Special Community Initiatives prior to request for data by this study)

*Source:*
Institute on Disability and Human Development (UAP),
University of Illinois at Chicago, 1994

# OREGON

## Large Congregate Care Facilities: FY 1992 Revenue Sources*

### Private 16+Bed Settings

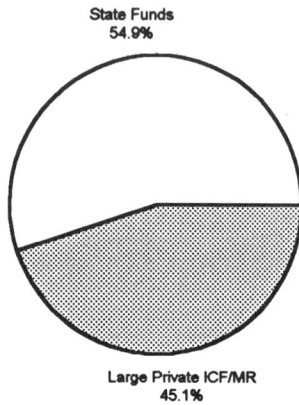

State Funds
54.9%

Large Private ICF/MR
45.1%

Total Funds: $3.7 Million

### Public Institutions

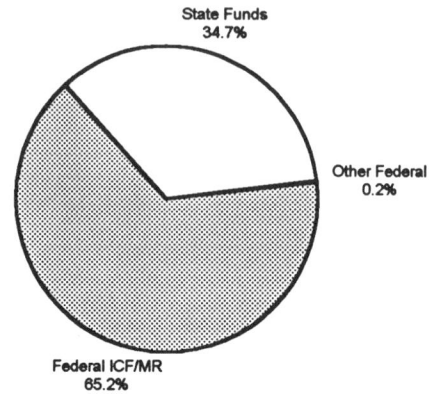

State Funds
34.7%

Other Federal
0.2%

Federal ICF/MR
65.2%

Total Funds: $79.8 Million

**\*Excludes nursing homes**

## Average Daily Residents in Institutions

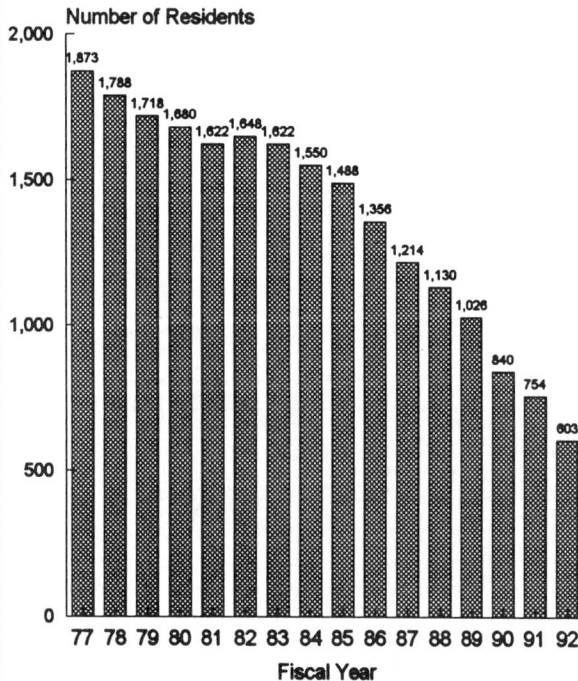

Number of Residents

| | | |
|---|---|---|

2,000

1,873
1,788
1,718
1,680
1,622 1,648 1,622
1,550
1,488
1,356
1,214
1,130
1,026
840
754
603

1,500

1,000

500

0

77 78 79 80 81 82 83 84 85 86 87 88 89 90 91 92
**Fiscal Year**

## Institutional Daily Costs Per Resident

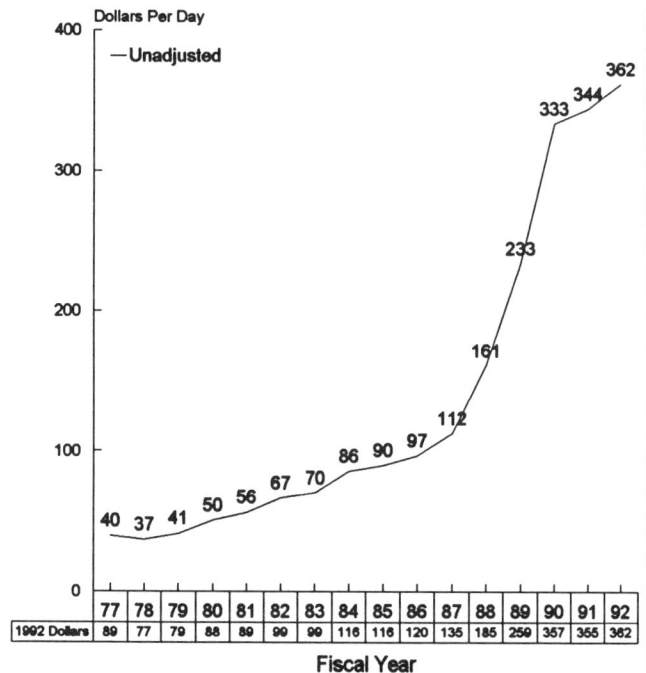

Dollars Per Day

400

—Unadjusted

362
344
333

233

161

112
97
86 90
70
67
50 56
40 37 41

300

200

100

0

| | 77 | 78 | 79 | 80 | 81 | 82 | 83 | 84 | 85 | 86 | 87 | 88 | 89 | 90 | 91 | 92 |
|---|----|----|----|----|----|----|----|----|----|----|----|----|----|----|----|----|
| 1992 Dollars | 89 | 77 | 79 | 88 | 89 | 99 | 99 | 116 | 116 | 120 | 135 | 185 | 259 | 357 | 355 | 362 |

**Fiscal Year**

*Source:*
Institute on Disability and Human Development (UAP),
University of Illinois at Chicago, 1994

# OREGON FISCAL EFFORT

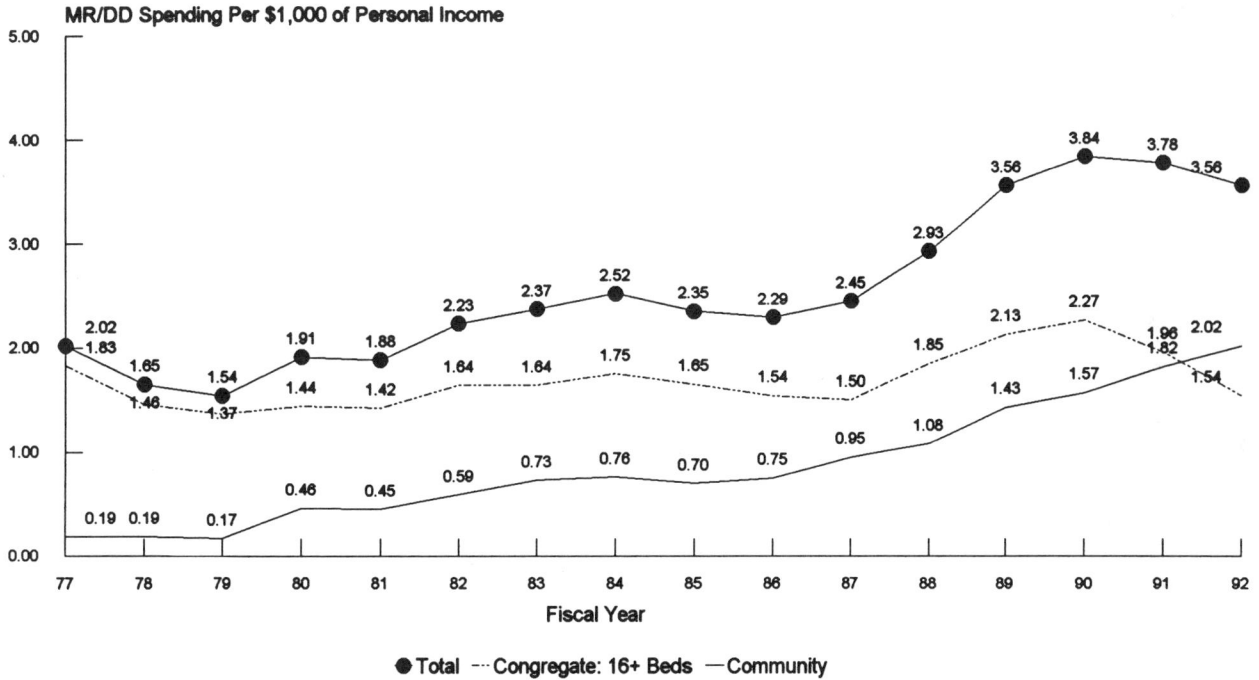

**MR/DD Spending Per $1,000 of Personal Income**

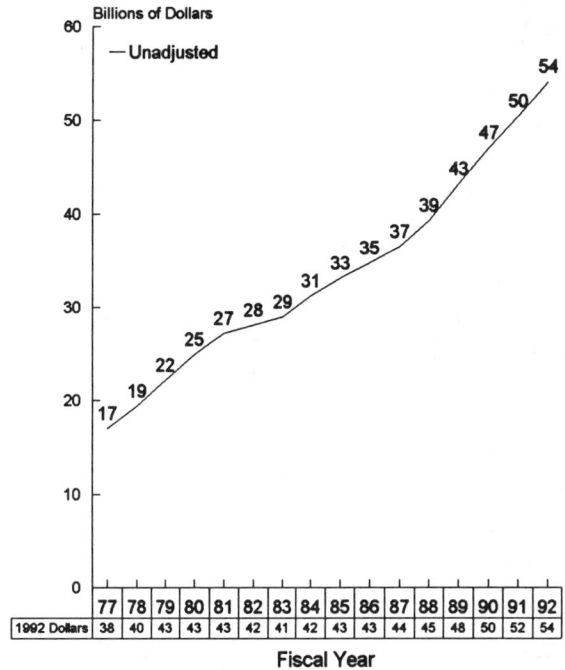

| | 77 | 78 | 79 | 80 | 81 | 82 | 83 | 84 | 85 | 86 | 87 | 88 | 89 | 90 | 91 | 92 |
|---|---|---|---|---|---|---|---|---|---|---|---|---|---|---|---|---|
| Total | 2.02 | 1.65 | 1.54 | 1.91 | 1.88 | 2.23 | 2.37 | 2.52 | 2.35 | 2.29 | 2.45 | 2.93 | 3.56 | 3.84 | 3.78 | 3.56 |
| Congregate: 16+ Beds | 1.83 | 1.46 | 1.37 | 1.44 | 1.42 | 1.64 | 1.64 | 1.75 | 1.65 | 1.54 | 1.50 | 1.85 | 2.13 | 2.27 | 1.96 | 1.54 |
| Community | 0.19 | 0.19 | 0.17 | 0.46 | 0.45 | 0.59 | 0.73 | 0.76 | 0.70 | 0.75 | 0.95 | 1.08 | 1.43 | 1.57 | 1.82 | 2.02 |

Fiscal Year

● Total  --- Congregate: 16+ Beds  — Community

## Total MR/DD Spending

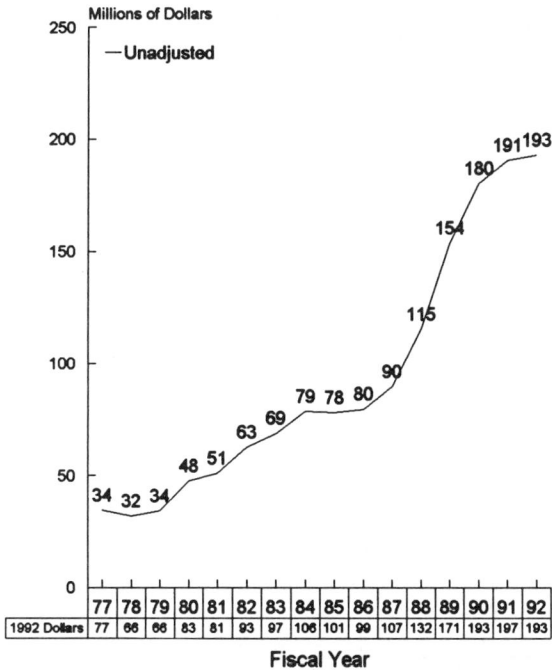

**Millions of Dollars**
—Unadjusted

| Fiscal Year | 77 | 78 | 79 | 80 | 81 | 82 | 83 | 84 | 85 | 86 | 87 | 88 | 89 | 90 | 91 | 92 |
|---|---|---|---|---|---|---|---|---|---|---|---|---|---|---|---|---|
| | 34 | 32 | 34 | 48 | 51 | 63 | 69 | 79 | 78 | 80 | 90 | 115 | 154 | 180 | 191 | 193 |
| 1992 Dollars | 77 | 66 | 66 | 83 | 81 | 93 | 97 | 106 | 101 | 99 | 107 | 132 | 171 | 193 | 197 | 193 |

## Personal Income

**Billions of Dollars**
—Unadjusted

| Fiscal Year | 77 | 78 | 79 | 80 | 81 | 82 | 83 | 84 | 85 | 86 | 87 | 88 | 89 | 90 | 91 | 92 |
|---|---|---|---|---|---|---|---|---|---|---|---|---|---|---|---|---|
| | 17 | 19 | 22 | 25 | 27 | 28 | 29 | 31 | 33 | 35 | 37 | 39 | 43 | 47 | 50 | 54 |
| 1992 Dollars | 38 | 40 | 43 | 43 | 43 | 42 | 41 | 42 | 43 | 43 | 44 | 45 | 48 | 50 | 52 | 54 |

*Source:*
Institute on Disability and Human Development (UAP),
University of Illinois at Chicago, 1994

# OREGON
## Financial Support for MR/DD Services: FY 1977-92

| | 1977 | 1978 | 1979 | 1980 | 1981 | 1982 | 1983 | 1984 |
|---|---|---|---|---|---|---|---|---|
| **TOTAL FUNDS** | $34,329,734 | $31,988,003 | $34,244,903 | $47,599,231 | $51,031,862 | $62,650,818 | $68,731,319 | $78,519,006 |
| **CONGREGATE 16+ BEDS** | 31,027,899 | 28,358,701 | 30,402,802 | 36,020,521 | 38,694,352 | 46,058,578 | 47,606,516 | 54,752,072 |
| INSTITUTIONAL SERVICES FUNDS | 27,166,000 | 24,142,000 | 25,845,000 | 31,032,000 | 33,304,000 | 40,094,000 | 41,520,000 | 48,684,200 |
| STATE FUNDS | 15,252,000 | 11,437,000 | 12,238,000 | 15,146,000 | 16,206,000 | 18,786,000 | 19,473,000 | 20,885,100 |
| General Funds | 15,252,000 | 11,437,000 | 12,238,000 | 15,146,000 | 16,206,000 | 18,786,000 | 19,473,000 | 20,885,100 |
| Local | 0 | 0 | 0 | 0 | 0 | 0 | 0 | 0 |
| Other State Funds | 0 | 0 | 0 | 0 | 0 | 0 | 0 | 0 |
| FEDERAL FUNDS | 11,914,000 | 12,705,000 | 13,607,000 | 15,886,000 | 17,098,000 | 21,308,000 | 22,047,000 | 27,799,100 |
| Federal ICF/MR | 11,398,000 | 12,390,000 | 13,258,000 | 15,436,000 | 16,616,000 | 21,024,000 | 21,792,000 | 27,521,700 |
| Title XX / SSBG Funds | 0 | 0 | 0 | 0 | 0 | 0 | 0 | 0 |
| Other Federal Funds | 516,000 | 315,000 | 349,000 | 450,000 | 482,000 | 284,000 | 255,000 | 277,400 |
| LARGE PRIVATE RESIDENTIAL | 3,861,899 | 4,216,701 | 4,557,802 | 4,988,521 | 5,390,352 | 5,964,578 | 6,086,516 | 6,067,872 |
| STATE FUNDS | 1,850,899 | 2,064,701 | 2,254,802 | 2,523,521 | 2,752,352 | 3,141,578 | 3,255,516 | 3,092,472 |
| General Funds | 1,850,899 | 2,064,701 | 2,254,802 | 2,523,521 | 2,752,352 | 3,141,578 | 3,255,516 | 3,092,472 |
| Other State Funds | 0 | 0 | 0 | 0 | 0 | 0 | 0 | 0 |
| Local/County Overmatch | 0 | 0 | 0 | 0 | 0 | 0 | 0 | 0 |
| FEDERAL FUNDS | 2,011,000 | 2,152,000 | 2,303,000 | 2,465,000 | 2,638,000 | 2,823,000 | 2,831,000 | 2,975,400 |
| Large Private ICF/MR | 2,011,000 | 2,152,000 | 2,303,000 | 2,465,000 | 2,638,000 | 2,823,000 | 2,831,000 | 2,975,400 |
| **COMMUNITY SERVICES FUNDS** | 3,301,835 | 3,629,302 | 3,842,101 | 11,578,710 | 12,337,510 | 16,592,240 | 21,124,803 | 23,766,934 |
| STATE FUNDS | 2,661,835 | 2,901,302 | 3,064,101 | 7,588,710 | 8,068,510 | 6,875,336 | 8,992,273 | 9,949,978 |
| General Funds | 1,896,835 | 2,137,302 | 2,256,101 | 6,740,710 | 7,178,510 | 5,717,336 | 7,324,273 | 8,215,978 |
| Other State Funds | 0 | 0 | 0 | 0 | 0 | 0 | 0 | 0 |
| Local/County Overmatch | 0 | 0 | 0 | 0 | 0 | 0 | 0 | 0 |
| SSI State Supplement | 765,000 | 764,000 | 808,000 | 848,000 | 890,000 | 1,158,000 | 1,668,000 | 1,734,000 |
| FEDERAL FUNDS | 640,000 | 728,000 | 778,000 | 3,990,000 | 4,269,000 | 9,716,904 | 12,132,530 | 13,816,956 |
| ICF/MR Funds | 0 | 0 | 0 | 0 | 0 | 0 | 0 | 0 |
| Small Public | 0 | 0 | 0 | 0 | 0 | 0 | 0 | 0 |
| Small Private | 0 | 0 | 0 | 0 | 0 | 0 | 0 | 0 |
| HCBS Waiver | 0 | 0 | 0 | 0 | 0 | 1,000,000 | 2,600,000 | 4,647,500 |
| Model 50/200 Waiver | 0 | 0 | 0 | 0 | 0 | 0 | 0 | 0 |
| Other Title XIX Programs | 0 | 0 | 0 | 0 | 0 | 0 | 0 | 356,600 |
| Title XX / SSBG Funds | 0 | 0 | 0 | 2,739,000 | 2,931,000 | 3,025,000 | 2,141,000 | 279,800 |
| Other Federal Funds | 640,000 | 728,000 | 778,000 | 1,251,000 | 1,338,000 | 1,780,000 | 1,514,000 | 1,624,800 |
| Waiver Clients' SSI/ADC | 0 | 0 | 0 | 0 | 0 | 3,911,904 | 5,877,530 | 6,908,256 |

| | 1985 | 1986 | 1987 | 1988 | 1989 | 1990 | 1991 | 1992 |
|---|---|---|---|---|---|---|---|---|
| **TOTAL FUNDS** | $77,944,372 | $79,529,764 | $89,557,198 | $115,149,531 | $153,985,837 | $180,384,920 | $190,606,232 | $192,933,150 |
| **CONGREGATE 16+ BEDS** | 54,724,506 | 53,500,107 | 54,759,894 | 72,724,086 | 92,029,723 | 106,760,862 | 98,690,920 | 83,567,022 |
| INSTITUTIONAL SERVICES FUNDS | 48,719,100 | 47,872,100 | 49,763,171 | 66,395,748 | 87,388,234 | 102,200,822 | 94,630,051 | 79,839,444 |
| STATE FUNDS | 20,797,700 | 18,881,000 | 28,656,481 | 24,754,599 | 34,381,701 | 44,416,850 | 26,060,613 | 27,668,981 |
| General Funds | 20,797,700 | 18,881,000 | 25,589,131 | 22,077,587 | 31,566,015 | 41,885,523 | 23,722,366 | 25,328,440 |
| Local | 0 | 0 | 0 | 0 | 0 | 0 | 0 | 0 |
| Other State Funds | 0 | 0 | 3,067,350 | 2,677,012 | 2,815,686 | 2,531,327 | 2,338,247 | 2,340,541 |
| FEDERAL FUNDS | 27,921,400 | 28,991,100 | 21,106,690 | 41,641,149 | 53,006,533 | 57,783,972 | 68,569,438 | 52,170,463 |
| Federal ICF/MR | 27,704,400 | 28,840,100 | 20,770,393 | 41,359,314 | 52,805,362 | 57,582,929 | 68,431,487 | 52,030,310 |
| Title XX / SSBG Funds | 0 | 0 | 0 | 0 | 0 | 0 | 0 | 0 |
| Other Federal Funds | 217,000 | 151,000 | 336,297 | 281,835 | 201,171 | 201,043 | 137,951 | 140,153 |
| LARGE PRIVATE RESIDENTIAL | 6,005,406 | 5,628,007 | 4,996,723 | 6,328,338 | 4,641,489 | 4,560,040 | 4,060,869 | 3,727,578 |
| STATE FUNDS | 3,030,006 | 2,707,866 | 2,420,065 | 2,942,670 | 2,344,997 | 2,321,156 | 2,144,864 | 2,048,080 |
| General Funds | 3,030,006 | 2,707,866 | 2,420,065 | 2,942,670 | 2,251,328 | 2,223,740 | 2,043,552 | 1,942,310 |
| Other State Funds | 0 | 0 | 0 | 0 | 93,669 | 97,416 | 101,312 | 105,770 |
| Local/County Overmatch | 0 | 0 | 0 | 0 | 0 | 0 | 0 | 0 |
| FEDERAL FUNDS | 2,975,400 | 2,920,141 | 2,576,658 | 3,385,668 | 2,296,492 | 2,238,884 | 1,916,005 | 1,679,498 |
| Large Private ICF/MR | 2,975,400 | 2,920,141 | 2,576,658 | 3,385,668 | 2,296,492 | 2,238,884 | 1,916,005 | 1,679,498 |
| **COMMUNITY SERVICES FUNDS** | 23,219,866 | 26,029,657 | 34,797,304 | 42,425,445 | 61,956,114 | 73,624,058 | 91,915,312 | 109,366,128 |
| STATE FUNDS | 11,228,966 | 13,531,770 | 20,133,939 | 22,508,800 | 37,433,857 | 40,648,197 | 54,057,224 | 62,631,374 |
| General Funds | 9,394,966 | 12,482,770 | 19,160,939 | 21,509,800 | 35,710,175 | 38,767,085 | 51,957,543 | 58,513,609 |
| Other State Funds | 0 | 0 | 0 | 0 | 674,732 | 779,714 | 943,214 | 2,903,474 |
| Local/County Overmatch | 0 | 0 | 0 | 0 | 0 | 0 | 0 | 0 |
| SSI State Supplement | 1,834,000 | 1,049,000 | 973,000 | 999,000 | 1,048,950 | 1,101,398 | 1,156,467 | 1,214,291 |
| FEDERAL FUNDS | 11,990,900 | 12,497,887 | 14,663,365 | 19,916,645 | 24,522,257 | 32,975,861 | 37,858,088 | 46,734,754 |
| ICF/MR Funds | 0 | 262,676 | 270,499 | 321,149 | 379,739 | 439,436 | 504,867 | 266,293 |
| Small Public | 0 | 0 | 0 | 0 | 0 | 0 | 0 | 0 |
| Small Private | 0 | 262,676 | 270,499 | 321,149 | 379,739 | 439,436 | 504,867 | 266,293 |
| HCBS Waiver | 3,775,700 | 2,628,123 | 5,169,534 | 8,092,798 | 13,955,082 | 20,679,446 | 27,119,537 | 33,408,612 |
| Model 50/200 Waiver | 0 | 0 | 0 | 0 | 0 | 0 | 0 | 0 |
| Other Title XIX Programs | 360,300 | 692,672 | 1,128,229 | 2,152,675 | 1,173,367 | 2,655,953 | 2,811,785 | 4,022,442 |
| Title XX / SSBG Funds | 2,688,300 | 5,499,209 | 3,689,204 | 3,782,103 | 2,475,844 | 1,812,250 | 0 | |
| Other Federal Funds | 1,663,800 | 828,931 | 992,559 | 1,069,504 | 1,530,433 | 1,511,776 | 663,587 | 1,764,783 |
| Waiver Clients' SSI/ADC | 3,502,800 | 2,586,276 | 3,413,340 | 4,498,416 | 5,007,792 | 5,877,000 | 6,758,312 | 7,272,624 |

*Source:*
Institute on Disability and Human Development (UAP),
University of Illinois at Chicago, 1994

# PENNSYLVANIA

## MR/DD Spending for Congregate Residential & Community Services

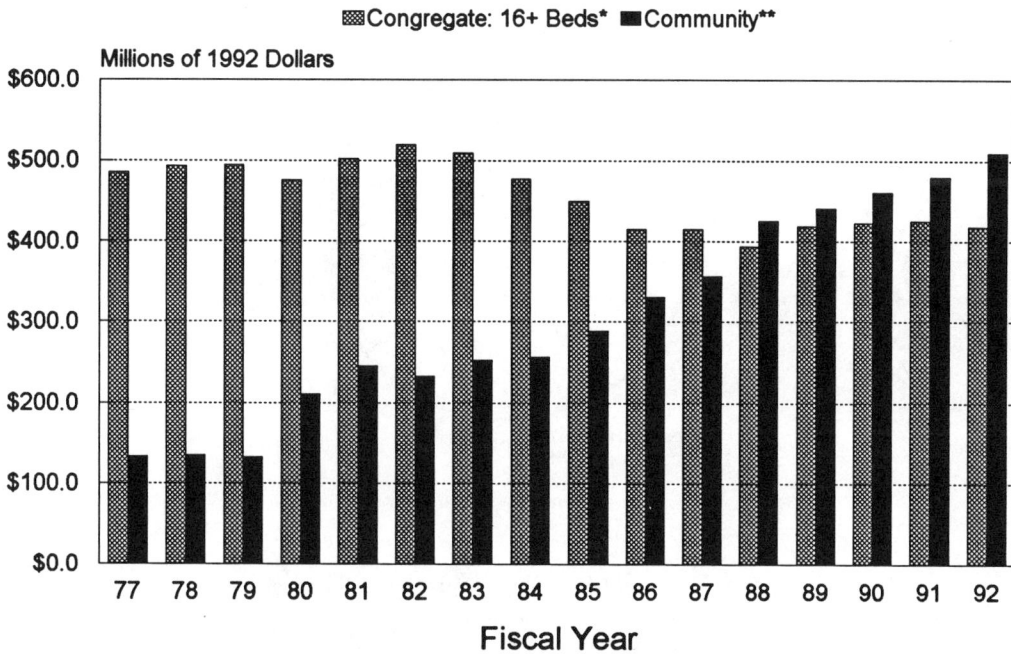

▦ Congregate: 16+ Beds*　■ Community**

Millions of 1992 Dollars

Fiscal Year

*Excludes nursing homes; ** Includes resources for
15 bed or less residential settings & non-residential community services

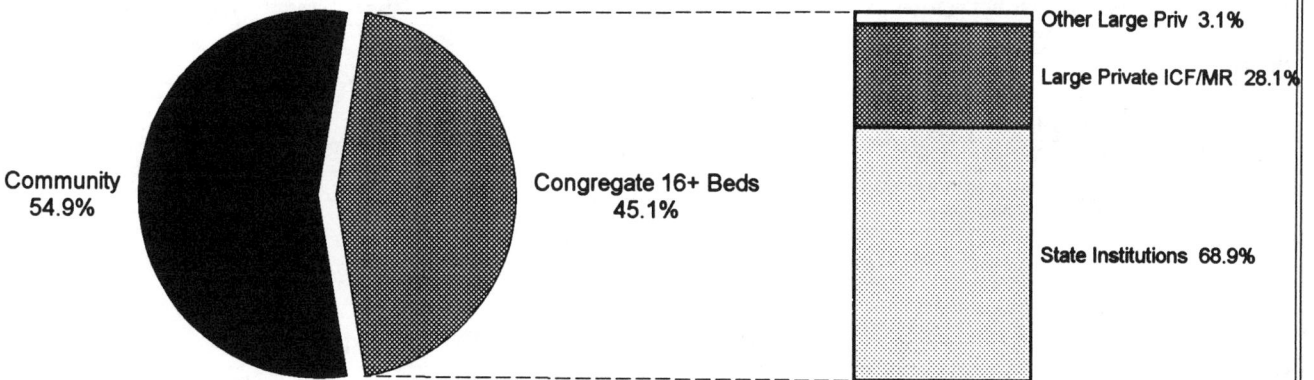

Community
54.9%

Congregate 16+ Beds
45.1%

Other Large Priv 3.1%

Large Private ICF/MR 28.1%

State Institutions 68.9%

FY 1992 Total Spending:
$928.0 Million

*Source:*
Institute on Disability and Human Development (UAP),
University of Illinois at Chicago, 1994

# PENNSYLVANIA

## Number of Persons Served by Residential Setting: FY 1992

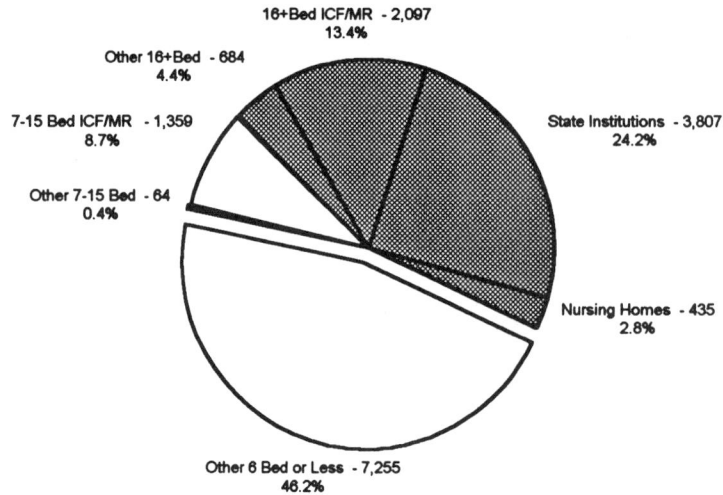

16+Bed ICF/MR - 2,097
13.4%

Other 16+Bed - 684
4.4%

7-15 Bed ICF/MR - 1,359
8.7%

Other 7-15 Bed - 64
0.4%

State Institutions - 3,807
24.2%

Nursing Homes - 435
2.8%

Other 6 Bed or Less - 7,255
46.2%

Total Served: 15,701

## Persons Served by Residential Setting:1986-92

|  | 1986 | 1987 | 1988 | 1989 | 1990 | 1991 | 1992 |
|---|---|---|---|---|---|---|---|
| CONGREGATE 16 + BED SETTINGS | NA | NA | 8,655 | NA | NA | 6,771 | 7,023 |
| Nursing Homes | NA | NA | 1,160 | NA | NA | 435 | 435 |
| State Institutions | 5,600 | 4,962 | 4,426 | 4,151 | 4,043 | 3,925 | 3,807 |
| Private 16+Bed ICF/MR | 1,573 | 1,924 | 1,945 | 2,037 | 2,041 | 2,079 | 2,097 |
| Other 16+Bed Residential | 1,195 | 1,159 | 1,124 | 895 | 483 | 332 | 684 |
| 15 BED OR LESS RESIDENTIAL SETTINGS | 5,941 | 6,898 | 7,348 | 7,888 | 8,440 | 8,622 | 8,678 |
| Public 7-15 Bed ICF/MR | 0 | 0 | 0 | 0 | 0 | 0 | 0 |
| Private 7-15 Bed ICF/MR | 517 | 762 | 815 | 966 | 1,135 | 1,143 | 1,359 |
| Other 7-15 Bed Residential | 5,424 | 6,136 | 6,533 | 873 | 294 | 537 | 64 |
| Public 6 Bed or Less ICF/MR | 0 | 0 | 0 | 0 | 0 | 0 | 0 |
| Private 6 Bed or Less ICF/MR | 0 | 0 | 0 | 0 | 0 | 0 | 0 |
| Other 6 Bed or Less Residential | NA | NA | NA | 6,049 | 7,011 | 6,942 | 7,255 |
| TOTAL PERSONS SERVED | NA | NA | 16,003 | NA | NA | 15,393 | 15,701 |

## Persons Served in Non-Residential Community Services:1986-92

|  | 1986 | 1987 | 1988 | 1989 | 1990 | 1991 | 1992 |
|---|---|---|---|---|---|---|---|
| DAY/WORK PROGRAMS | 12,544 | 14,084 | NA | 15,152 | 14,389 | 16,091 | 17,966 |
| Sheltered Employment/Work Activity | 3,386 | 4,024 | NA | 7,309 | 6,007 | 7,098 | 7,969 |
| Day Habilitation ("Day Training") | 9,158 | 10,060 | NA | 4,774 | 4,862 | 5,001 | 4,279 |
| Supported/Competitive Employment | NA | NA | NA | 3,069 | 3,520 | 3,992 | 5,718 |
| CASE MANAGEMENT | NA | NA | NA | NA | NA | NA | NA |
| HCBS WAIVER | 599 | 1,203 | 1,643 | 1,930 | 2,233 | 2,322 | 2,657 |
| MODEL 50/200 WAIVER | 0 | 0 | 0 | 0 | 0 | 0 | 0 |

*Source:*
Institute on Disability and Human Development (UAP),
University of Illinois at Chicago, 1994

# PENNSYLVANIA

## Community Services: FY 1992 Revenue Sources

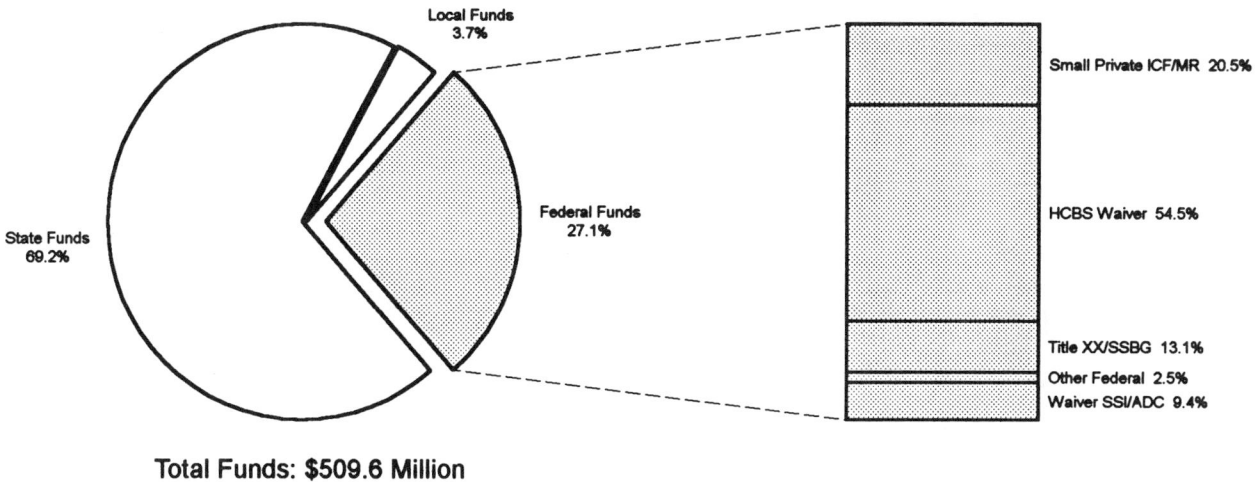

Total Funds: $509.6 Million

## Family Support Initiatives*

|  | 1986 | 1987 | 1988 | 1989 | 1990 | 1991 | 1992 |
|---|---|---|---|---|---|---|---|
| FAMILY SUPPORT: TOTAL SPENDING | $7,381,524 | $8,659,990 | $10,086,219 | $11,857,791 | $12,455,508 | $15,145,440 | $16,073,702 |
| Total # of Families Supported | 15,189 | 15,200 | 15,639 | 15,515 | 15,328 | 15,757 | 16,288 |
| A. Financial Subsidy/Payment | $0 | $0 | $0 | $0 | $0 | $0 | $0 |
| # of Families | 0 | 0 | 0 | 0 | 0 | 0 | 0 |
| B. Family Assistance Payments | $0 | $0 | $0 | $0 | $0 | $0 | $0 |
| # of Families | 0 | 0 | 0 | 0 | 0 | 0 | 0 |
| C. Other Family Support Payments | $7,381,524 | $8,659,990 | $10,086,219 | $11,857,791 | $12,455,508 | $15,145,440 | $16,073,702 |
| # of Families | 15,189 | 15,200 | 15,639 | 15,515 | 15,328 | 15,757 | 16,288 |

## Other Community Services Initiatives*

|  | 1986 | 1987 | 1988 | 1989 | 1990 | 1991 | 1992 |
|---|---|---|---|---|---|---|---|
| AGING/DD SPENDING | $2,200,000 | $2,200,000 | $2,200,000 | $0 | $0 | $0 | $0 |
| # of Persons Served | NA | NA | NA | 0 | 0 | 0 | 0 |
| ASSISTIVE TECHNOLOGY SPENDING |  |  |  |  |  |  | $0 |
| # of Persons Served |  |  |  |  |  |  | 0 |
| EARLY INTERVENTION SPENDING | $22,800,000 | $24,000,000 | $27,580,000 | $19,717,596 | $21,660,600 | $23,140,000 | $30,923,000 |
| # of Persons Served | 6,713 | 8,753 | 9,028 | 9,163 | 8,958 | 9,596 | 10,597 |
| PERSONAL ASSISTANCE SPENDING |  |  |  |  |  |  | $0 |
| # of Persons Served |  |  |  |  |  |  | 0 |
| SUPPORTED EMPLOYMENT SPENDING | $110,000 | $110,000 | $219,421 | $220,000 | $230,000 | $252,760 | $312,469 |
| # of Persons Served | NA | NA | NA | NA | NA | NA | NA |
| SUPPORTED LIVING SPENDING |  |  |  |  |  |  | $0 |
| # of Persons Served |  |  |  |  |  |  | 0 |

*Expenditures associated with Special Community Initiatives are a subset of funding within the community services component of the state's chart series and spreadsheet; Family Support Client figures may include duplicate client counts; HCBS Waiver counts include Waiver case management numbers.
0= Services not provided in the state; NA= Data not available from state; blank= Services not applicable (eg. CSLA prior to authorization, Special Community Initiatives prior to request for data by this study)

*Source:*
Institute on Disability and Human Development (UAP),
University of Illinois at Chicago, 1994

# PENNSYLVANIA

## Large Congregate Care Facilities: FY 1992 Revenue Sources*

### Private 16+Bed Settings

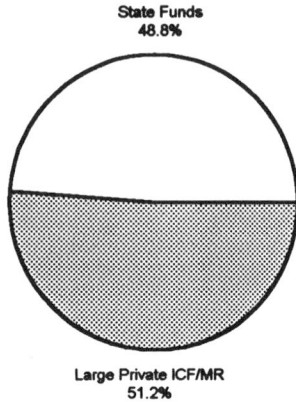

State Funds
48.8%

Large Private ICF/MR
51.2%

Total Funds: $130.3 Million

### Public Institutions

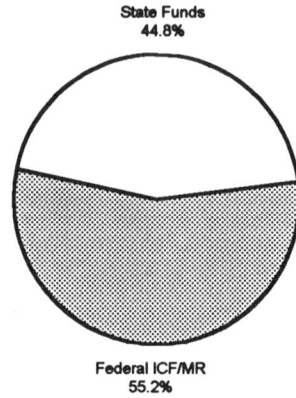

State Funds
44.8%

Federal ICF/MR
55.2%

Total Funds: $288.2 Million

*Excludes nursing homes

## Average Daily Residents in Institutions

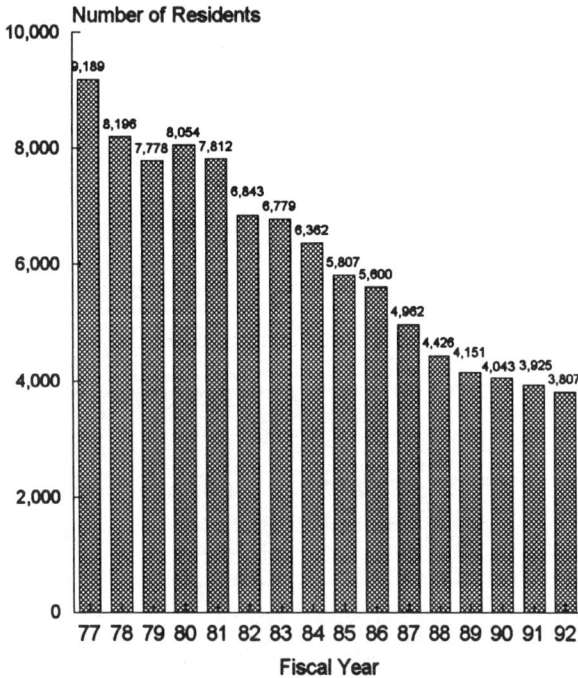

Number of Residents

| | |
|---|---|
| 10,000 | |
| | 9,189 |
| 8,000 | 8,196 7,778 8,054 7,812 |
| | 6,843 6,779 6,362 |
| 6,000 | 5,807 5,600 |
| | 4,962 4,426 4,151 |
| 4,000 | 4,043 3,925 3,807 |
| 2,000 | |
| 0 | |

77 78 79 80 81 82 83 84 85 86 87 88 89 90 91 92
Fiscal Year

## Institutional Daily Costs Per Resident

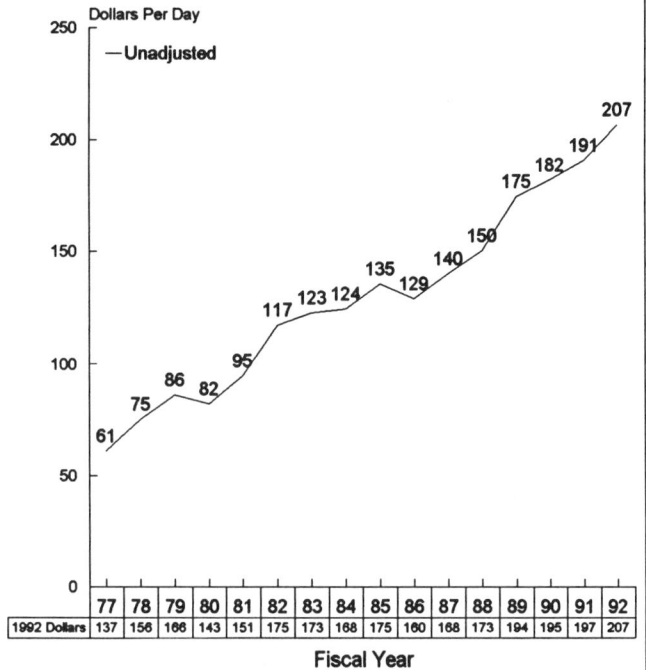

Dollars Per Day

—Unadjusted

250

200                                                                      207
                                                                  191
                                                              182
                                                         175
                                                   150
                                          135          140
                               123 124        129
                          117
200                    95
              86  82
         75
61

150

100

50

0

| | 77 | 78 | 79 | 80 | 81 | 82 | 83 | 84 | 85 | 86 | 87 | 88 | 89 | 90 | 91 | 92 |
|---|---|---|---|---|---|---|---|---|---|---|---|---|---|---|---|---|
| 1992 Dollars | 137 | 156 | 166 | 143 | 151 | 175 | 173 | 168 | 175 | 160 | 168 | 173 | 194 | 195 | 197 | 207 |

Fiscal Year

*Source:*
Institute on Disability and Human Development (UAP),
University of Illinois at Chicago, 1994

# PENNSYLVANIA FISCAL EFFORT

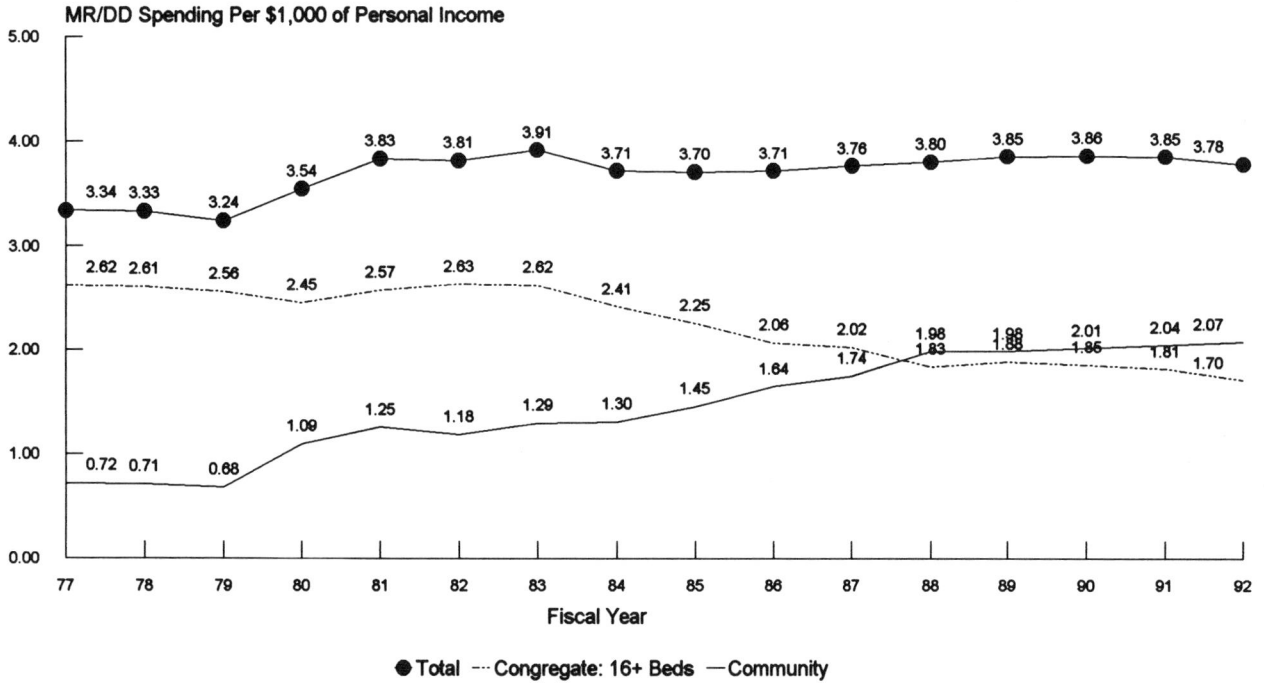

MR/DD Spending Per $1,000 of Personal Income

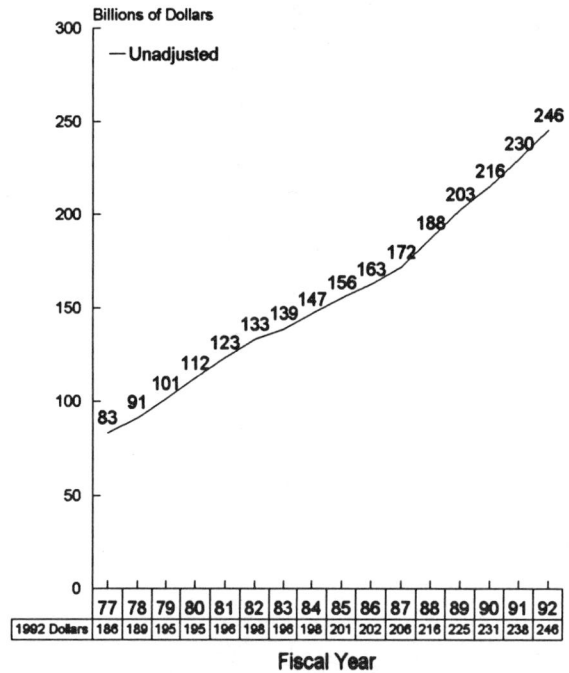

| Fiscal Year | 77 | 78 | 79 | 80 | 81 | 82 | 83 | 84 | 85 | 86 | 87 | 88 | 89 | 90 | 91 | 92 |
|---|---|---|---|---|---|---|---|---|---|---|---|---|---|---|---|---|
| Total | 3.34 | 3.33 | 3.24 | 3.54 | 3.83 | 3.81 | 3.91 | 3.71 | 3.70 | 3.71 | 3.76 | 3.80 | 3.85 | 3.86 | 3.85 | 3.78 |
| Congregate: 16+ Beds | 2.62 | 2.61 | 2.56 | 2.45 | 2.57 | 2.63 | 2.62 | 2.41 | 2.25 | 2.06 | 2.02 | 1.83 | 1.88 | 1.85 | 1.81 | 1.70 |
| Community | 0.72 | 0.71 | 0.68 | 1.09 | 1.25 | 1.18 | 1.29 | 1.30 | 1.45 | 1.64 | 1.74 | 1.98 | 1.98 | 2.01 | 2.04 | 2.07 |

● Total — Congregate: 16+ Beds — Community

## Total MR/DD Spending

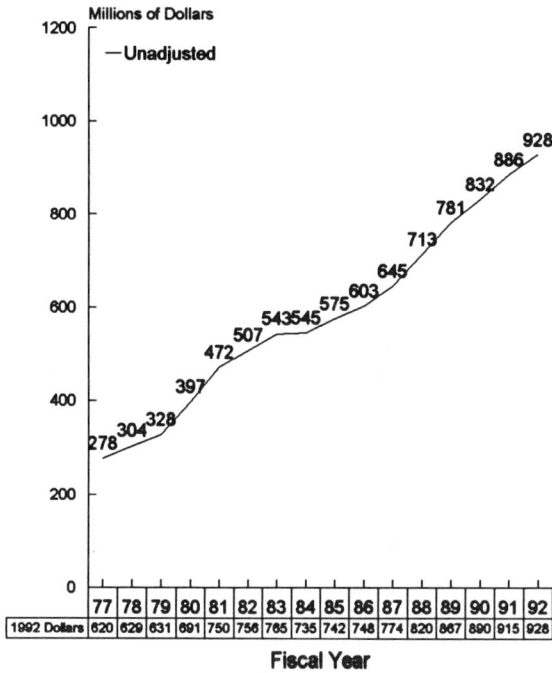

Millions of Dollars
—Unadjusted

| Fiscal Year | 77 | 78 | 79 | 80 | 81 | 82 | 83 | 84 | 85 | 86 | 87 | 88 | 89 | 90 | 91 | 92 |
|---|---|---|---|---|---|---|---|---|---|---|---|---|---|---|---|---|
| Unadjusted | 278 | 304 | 328 | 397 | 472 | 507 | 543 | 545 | 575 | 603 | 645 | 713 | 781 | 832 | 886 | 928 |
| 1992 Dollars | 620 | 629 | 631 | 691 | 750 | 756 | 785 | 735 | 742 | 748 | 774 | 820 | 867 | 890 | 915 | 928 |

Fiscal Year

## Personal Income

Billions of Dollars
—Unadjusted

| Fiscal Year | 77 | 78 | 79 | 80 | 81 | 82 | 83 | 84 | 85 | 86 | 87 | 88 | 89 | 90 | 91 | 92 |
|---|---|---|---|---|---|---|---|---|---|---|---|---|---|---|---|---|
| Unadjusted | 83 | 91 | 101 | 112 | 123 | 133 | 139 | 147 | 156 | 163 | 172 | 188 | 203 | 216 | 230 | 246 |
| 1992 Dollars | 186 | 189 | 195 | 195 | 196 | 198 | 196 | 198 | 201 | 202 | 206 | 216 | 225 | 231 | 238 | 246 |

Fiscal Year

*Source:*
Institute on Disability and Human Development (UAP),
University of Illinois at Chicago, 1994

# PENNSYLVANIA
## Financial Support for MR/DD Services: FY 1977-92

| | 1977 | 1978 | 1979 | 1980 | 1981 | 1982 | 1983 | 1984 |
|---|---|---|---|---|---|---|---|---|
| **TOTAL FUNDS** | $277,904,700 | $304,038,200 | $328,432,200 | $397,195,800 | $471,689,375 | $507,405,557 | $542,753,006 | $544,701,103 |
| **CONGREGATE 16+ BEDS** | 218,275,000 | 238,875,000 | 259,283,000 | 275,247,193 | 317,072,968 | 350,415,840 | 363,186,412 | 354,273,587 |
| INSTITUTIONAL SERVICES FUNDS | 205,423,000 | 225,558,000 | 244,988,000 | 242,334,000 | 270,322,000 | 292,628,000 | 303,604,000 | 289,586,742 |
| STATE FUNDS | 149,724,000 | 132,717,000 | 143,334,000 | 137,569,000 | 151,775,000 | 148,308,000 | 143,167,000 | 144,941,043 |
| General Funds | 145,996,000 | 127,909,000 | 134,464,000 | 123,089,000 | 144,945,000 | 138,743,000 | 132,000,000 | 130,189,643 |
| Local | 0 | 0 | 0 | 0 | 0 | 0 | 0 | 0 |
| Other State Funds | 3,728,000 | 4,808,000 | 8,870,000 | 14,480,000 | 6,830,000 | 9,565,000 | 11,167,000 | 14,751,400 |
| FEDERAL FUNDS | 55,699,000 | 92,841,000 | 101,654,000 | 104,765,000 | 118,547,000 | 144,320,000 | 160,437,000 | 144,645,699 |
| Federal ICF/MR | 51,699,000 | 87,856,000 | 98,406,000 | 102,688,000 | 113,897,000 | 143,635,000 | 159,649,000 | 144,366,000 |
| Title XX / SSBG Funds | 0 | 0 | 0 | 0 | 0 | 0 | 0 | 0 |
| Other Federal Funds | 4,000,000 | 4,985,000 | 3,248,000 | 2,077,000 | 4,650,000 | 685,000 | 788,000 | 279,699 |
| LARGE PRIVATE RESIDENTIAL | 12,852,000 | 13,317,000 | 14,295,000 | 32,913,193 | 46,750,968 | 57,787,840 | 59,582,412 | 64,686,845 |
| STATE FUNDS | 12,852,000 | 13,317,000 | 14,295,000 | 23,183,193 | 29,945,968 | 34,644,840 | 35,447,412 | 38,046,845 |
| General Funds | 12,852,000 | 13,317,000 | 14,295,000 | 23,183,193 | 29,945,968 | 34,644,840 | 35,447,412 | 38,046,845 |
| Other State Funds | 0 | 0 | 0 | 0 | 0 | 0 | 0 | 0 |
| Local/County Overmatch | 0 | 0 | 0 | 0 | 0 | 0 | 0 | 0 |
| FEDERAL FUNDS | 0 | 0 | 0 | 9,730,000 | 16,805,000 | 23,143,000 | 24,135,000 | 26,640,000 |
| Large Private ICF/MR | 0 | 0 | 0 | 9,730,000 | 16,805,000 | 23,143,000 | 24,135,000 | 26,640,000 |
| **COMMUNITY SERVICES FUNDS** | 59,629,700 | 65,163,200 | 69,149,200 | 121,948,607 | 154,616,407 | 156,989,717 | 179,566,594 | 190,427,516 |
| STATE FUNDS | 59,159,700 | 64,675,200 | 68,276,200 | 110,727,607 | 138,775,407 | 141,318,717 | 162,165,594 | 170,755,381 |
| General Funds | 46,013,000 | 50,796,000 | 53,980,000 | 96,783,807 | 124,385,032 | 126,449,767 | 145,570,069 | 153,761,281 |
| Other State Funds | 1,000 | 1,000 | 1,000 | 1,000 | 2,000 | 75,000 | 2,000 | 0 |
| Local/County Overmatch | 4,106,700 | 4,473,200 | 4,763,200 | 4,376,800 | 4,785,375 | 5,193,950 | 5,602,525 | 6,011,100 |
| SSI State Supplement | 9,039,000 | 9,405,000 | 9,532,000 | 9,566,000 | 9,603,000 | 9,600,000 | 10,991,000 | 10,983,000 |
| FEDERAL FUNDS | 470,000 | 488,000 | 873,000 | 11,221,000 | 15,841,000 | 15,671,000 | 17,401,000 | 19,672,135 |
| ICF/MR Funds | 0 | 0 | 0 | 0 | 0 | 3,107,000 | 5,522,000 | 6,332,000 |
| Small Public | 0 | 0 | 0 | 0 | 0 | 0 | 0 | 0 |
| Small Private | 0 | 0 | 0 | 0 | 3,107,000 | 5,522,000 | 5,927,000 | 6,332,000 |
| HCBS Waiver | 0 | 0 | 0 | 0 | 0 | 0 | 0 | 1,552,100 |
| Model 50/200 Waiver | 0 | 0 | 0 | 0 | 0 | 0 | 0 | 0 |
| Other Title XIX Programs | 0 | 0 | 0 | 0 | 0 | 0 | 0 | 0 |
| Title XX / SSBG Funds | 0 | 0 | 465,000 | 8,951,000 | 9,234,000 | 8,170,000 | 7,620,000 | 7,400,000 |
| Other Federal Funds | 470,000 | 488,000 | 408,000 | 2,270,000 | 3,500,000 | 1,979,000 | 3,854,000 | 3,899,047 |
| Waiver Clients' SSI/ADC | 0 | 0 | 0 | 0 | 0 | 0 | 0 | 488,988 |

| | 1985 | 1986 | 1987 | 1988 | 1989 | 1990 | 1991 | 1992 |
|---|---|---|---|---|---|---|---|---|
| **TOTAL FUNDS** | $575,323,492 | $603,039,111 | $645,319,848 | $713,174,421 | $780,967,968 | $831,779,185 | $885,543,745 | $928,016,136 |
| **CONGREGATE 16+ BEDS** | 350,472,630 | 335,550,523 | 346,767,606 | 342,765,817 | 380,433,421 | 398,034,780 | 416,280,485 | 418,432,590 |
| INSTITUTIONAL SERVICES FUNDS | 287,124,716 | 263,146,115 | 253,339,831 | 243,132,000 | 264,715,345 | 268,702,000 | 273,333,000 | 288,151,790 |
| STATE FUNDS | 135,455,716 | 113,479,115 | 112,625,831 | 105,406,000 | 105,816,001 | 112,918,000 | 121,462,000 | 129,053,790 |
| General Funds | 122,579,716 | 101,145,115 | 101,125,831 | 94,913,000 | 95,063,000 | 101,920,000 | 109,481,000 | 115,015,000 |
| Local | 0 | 0 | 0 | 0 | 0 | 0 | 0 | 0 |
| Other State Funds | 12,876,000 | 12,334,000 | 11,500,000 | 10,493,000 | 10,753,001 | 10,998,000 | 11,981,000 | 14,038,790 |
| FEDERAL FUNDS | 151,669,000 | 149,667,000 | 140,714,000 | 137,726,000 | 158,899,344 | 155,784,000 | 151,871,000 | 159,098,000 |
| Federal ICF/MR | 151,042,000 | 149,352,000 | 140,389,000 | 137,576,000 | 158,899,344 | 155,784,000 | 151,871,000 | 159,098,000 |
| Title XX / SSBG Funds | 0 | 0 | 0 | 0 | 0 | 0 | 0 | 0 |
| Other Federal Funds | 627,000 | 315,000 | 325,000 | 150,000 | 0 | 0 | 0 | 0 |
| LARGE PRIVATE RESIDENTIAL | 63,347,914 | 72,404,408 | 93,427,775 | 99,633,817 | 115,718,076 | 129,332,780 | 142,947,485 | 130,280,800 |
| STATE FUNDS | 37,725,914 | 41,545,408 | 50,283,775 | 52,818,817 | 59,489,409 | 65,126,114 | 70,762,818 | 63,577,030 |
| General Funds | 37,725,914 | 41,545,408 | 50,283,775 | 52,818,817 | 59,489,409 | 65,126,114 | 70,762,818 | 63,577,030 |
| Other State Funds | 0 | 0 | 0 | 0 | 0 | 0 | 0 | 0 |
| Local/County Overmatch | 0 | 0 | 0 | 0 | 0 | 0 | 0 | 0 |
| FEDERAL FUNDS | 25,622,000 | 30,859,000 | 43,144,000 | 46,815,000 | 56,228,667 | 64,206,667 | 72,184,667 | 66,703,770 |
| Large Private ICF/MR | 25,622,000 | 30,859,000 | 43,144,000 | 46,815,000 | 56,228,667 | 64,206,667 | 72,184,667 | 66,703,770 |
| **COMMUNITY SERVICES FUNDS** | 224,850,862 | 267,488,588 | 298,552,242 | 370,408,604 | 400,534,548 | 433,744,405 | 469,263,260 | 509,583,546 |
| STATE FUNDS | 188,010,462 | 222,473,120 | 239,979,902 | 281,548,620 | 303,200,605 | 326,117,531 | 349,107,295 | 371,707,414 |
| General Funds | 168,707,162 | 194,210,120 | 208,448,902 | 250,285,000 | 272,406,827 | 294,528,653 | 315,153,022 | 336,078,282 |
| Other State Funds | 576,000 | 2,724,000 | 2,200,000 | 0 | 0 | 0 | 0 | 0 |
| Local/County Overmatch | 7,109,300 | 13,322,000 | 15,861,000 | 17,660,620 | 16,510,628 | 16,591,570 | 18,207,100 | 19,094,600 |
| SSI State Supplement | 11,618,000 | 12,217,000 | 13,470,000 | 13,603,000 | 14,283,150 | 14,997,308 | 15,747,173 | 16,534,532 |
| FEDERAL FUNDS | 36,840,400 | 45,015,468 | 58,572,340 | 88,859,984 | 97,333,943 | 107,626,874 | 120,155,965 | 137,876,132 |
| ICF/MR Funds | 7,127,000 | 9,503,000 | 10,551,000 | 16,006,000 | 18,523,000 | 21,774,500 | 25,026,000 | 28,277,500 |
| Small Public | 0 | 0 | 0 | 0 | 0 | 0 | 0 | 0 |
| Small Private | 7,127,000 | 9,503,000 | 10,551,000 | 16,006,000 | 18,523,000 | 21,774,500 | 25,026,000 | 28,277,500 |
| HCBS Waiver | 4,542,000 | 10,371,000 | 20,556,000 | 40,501,000 | 47,908,223 | 55,315,446 | 63,454,917 | 75,113,844 |
| Model 50/200 Waiver | 0 | 0 | 0 | 0 | 0 | 0 | 0 | 0 |
| Other Title XIX Programs | 0 | 0 | 0 | 0 | 0 | 0 | 0 | 0 |
| Title XX / SSBG Funds | 20,362,000 | 20,362,000 | 19,157,000 | 19,723,000 | 18,522,000 | 17,998,000 | 17,998,000 | 17,998,000 |
| Other Federal Funds | 3,841,000 | 2,544,000 | 3,761,000 | 6,242,000 | 4,460,000 | 2,678,000 | 3,033,000 | 3,510,000 |
| Waiver Clients' SSI/ADC | 968,400 | 2,235,468 | 4,547,340 | 6,387,984 | 7,920,720 | 9,860,928 | 10,644,048 | 12,976,788 |

*Source:*
Institute on Disability and Human Development (UAP),
University of Illinois at Chicago, 1994

# RHODE ISLAND

## MR/DD Spending for Congregate Residential & Community Services

▨Congregate: 16+ Beds* ■Community**

Millions of 1992 Dollars

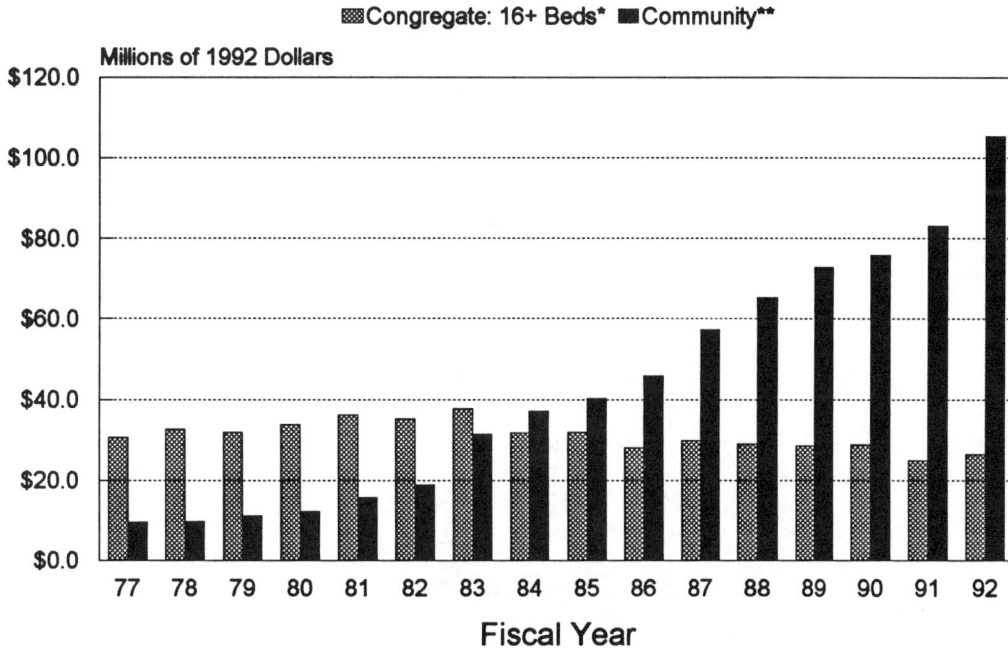

Fiscal Year

*Excludes nursing homes; ** Includes resources for
15 bed or less residential settings & non-residential community services

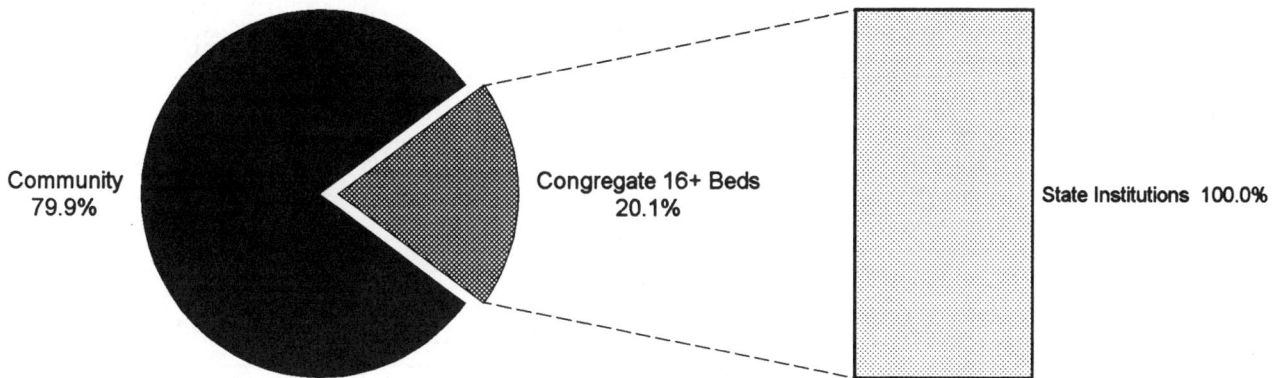

Community
79.9%

Congregate 16+ Beds
20.1%

State Institutions 100.0%

FY 1992 Total Spending:
$131.9 Million

*Source:*
Institute on Disability and Human Development (UAP),
University of Illinois at Chicago, 1994

# RHODE ISLAND

## Number of Persons Served by Residential Setting: FY 1992

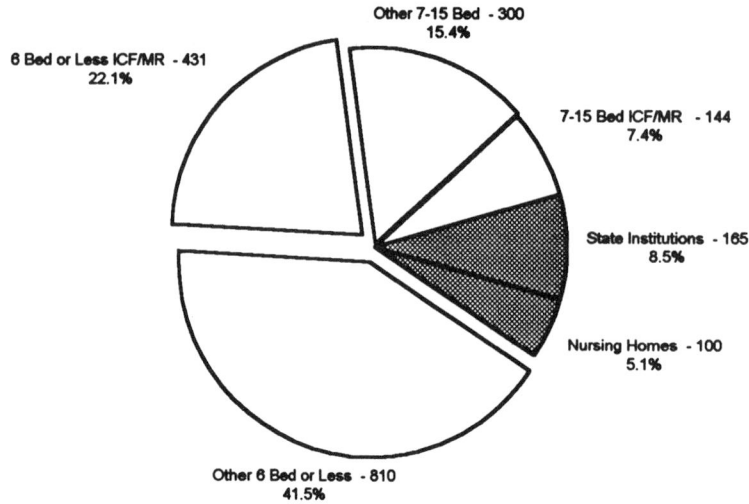

Other 7-15 Bed - 300
15.4%

6 Bed or Less ICF/MR - 431
22.1%

7-15 Bed ICF/MR - 144
7.4%

State Institutions - 165
8.5%

Nursing Homes - 100
5.1%

Other 6 Bed or Less - 810
41.5%

Total Served: 1,950

## Persons Served by Residential Setting:1986-92

|  | 1986 | 1987 | 1988 | 1989 | 1990 | 1991 | 1992 |
|---|---|---|---|---|---|---|---|
| CONGREGATE 16 + BED SETTINGS | NA | NA | 478 | NA | NA | NA | 265 |
| Nursing Homes | NA | NA | 195 | NA | NA | NA | 100 |
| State Institutions | 385 | 343 | 283 | 241 | 217 | 190 | 165 |
| Private 16+Bed ICF/MR | 0 | 0 | 0 | 0 | 0 | 0 | 0 |
| Other 16+Bed Residential | 0 | 0 | 0 | 0 | 0 | 0 | 0 |
| 15 BED OR LESS RESIDENTIAL SETTINGS | 1,326 | 1,480 | 1,632 | 1,665 | 1,710 | 1,749 | 1,685 |
| Public 7-15 Bed ICF/MR | 54 | 58 | 79 | 33 | 24 | 0 | 0 |
| Private 7-15 Bed ICF/MR | 532 | 594 | 612 | 603 | 594 | 584 | 144 |
| Other 7-15 Bed Residential | 740 | 828 | 941 | 1,029 | 1,092 | 1,165 | 300 |
| Public 6 Bed or Less ICF/MR | 0 | 0 | 0 | 0 | 0 | 0 | 0 |
| Private 6 Bed or Less ICF/MR |  |  |  |  |  |  | 431 |
| Other 6 Bed or Less Residential |  |  |  |  |  |  | 810 |
| TOTAL PERSONS SERVED | NA | NA | 2,110 | NA | NA | NA | 1,950 |

## Persons Served in Non-Residential Community Services:1986-92

|  | 1986 | 1987 | 1988 | 1989 | 1990 | 1991 | 1992 |
|---|---|---|---|---|---|---|---|
| DAY/WORK PROGRAMS | 1,108 | 1,224 | 1,021 | 1,228 | 1,276 | 1,490 | 1,799 |
| Sheltered Employment/Work Activity | NA | NA | NA | NA | NA | NA | NA |
| Day Habilitation ("Day Training") | 1,033 | 1,024 | 871 | 1,060 | 1,099 | 1,293 | 1,558 |
| Supported/Competitive Employment | 75 | 200 | 150 | 168 | 177 | 197 | 241 |
| CASE MANAGEMENT | 0 | 0 | 0 | 0 | 0 | NA | NA |
| HCBS WAIVER | 117 | 520 | 520 | 677 | 809 | 800 | 1,200 |
| MODEL 50/200 WAIVER | 0 | 0 | 0 | 0 | 0 | 0 | 0 |

Source:
Institute on Disability and Human Development (UAP),
University of Illinois at Chicago, 1994

# RHODE ISLAND

## Community Services: FY 1992 Revenue Sources

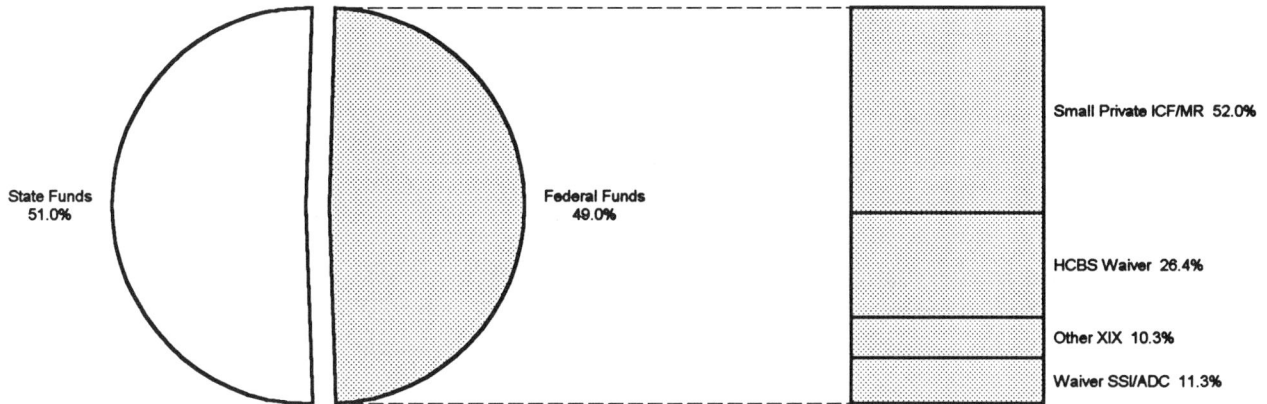

State Funds
51.0%

Federal Funds
49.0%

Small Private ICF/MR 52.0%

HCBS Waiver 26.4%

Other XIX 10.3%

Waiver SSI/ADC 11.3%

### Total Funds: $105.4 Million

## Family Support Initiatives*

|  | 1986 | 1987 | 1988 | 1989 | 1990 | 1991 | 1992 |
|---|---|---|---|---|---|---|---|
| **FAMILY SUPPORT: TOTAL SPENDING** | $0 | $0 | $1,700,000 | $1,761,612 | $1,772,185 | $2,403,423 | $2,735,176 |
| **Total # of Families Supported** | 0 | 0 | NA | NA | NA | NA | NA |
| A. Financial Subsidy/Payment |  |  | $320,000 | $336,612 | $336,185 | $305,094 | $273,244 |
| # of Families |  |  | 75 | NA | NA | NA | NA |
| B. Family Assistance Payments |  |  | $300,000 | $300,000 | $300,000 | $308,329 | $261,932 |
| # of Families |  |  | 100 | NA | NA | NA | NA |
| C. Other Family Support Payments |  |  | $1,080,000 | $1,125,000 | $1,136,000 | $1,790,000 | $2,200,000 |
| # of Families |  |  | NA | NA | NA | NA | NA |

## Other Community Services Initiatives*

|  | 1986 | 1987 | 1988 | 1989 | 1990 | 1991 | 1992 |
|---|---|---|---|---|---|---|---|
| **AGING/DD SPENDING** | $0 | $0 | $0 | $0 | $0 | $0 | $0 |
| # of Persons Served | 0 | 0 | 0 | 0 | 0 | 0 | 0 |
| **ASSISTIVE TECHNOLOGY SPENDING** |  |  |  |  |  |  | $0 |
| # of Persons Served |  |  |  |  |  |  | 0 |
| **EARLY INTERVENTION SPENDING** | $731,800 | $776,300 | $1,144,100 | $1,067,610 | $1,110,902 | $1,205,607 | ** |
| # of Persons Served | 268 | 261 | 261 | NA | NA | NA |  |
| **PERSONAL ASSISTANCE SPENDING** |  |  |  |  |  |  | $0 |
| # of Persons Served |  |  |  |  |  |  | 0 |
| **SUPPORTED EMPLOYMENT SPENDING** | $0 | $0 | $0 | $0 | $0 | $0 | $0 |
| # of Persons Served | 0 | 0 | 0 | 0 | 0 | 0 | 0 |
| **SUPPORTED LIVING SPENDING** |  |  |  |  |  |  | $0 |
| # of Persons Served |  |  |  |  |  |  | 0 |

*Expenditures associated with Special Community Initiatives are a subset of funding within the community services component of the state's chart series and spreadsheet; Family Support Client figures may include duplicate client counts; HCBS Waiver counts include Waiver case management numbers.
0= Services not provided in the state; NA= Data not available from state; blank= Services not applicable (eg. CSLA prior to authorization, Special Community Initiatives prior to request for data by this study)

** Early Intervention transferred to Department of Health

Source:
Institute on Disability and Human Development (UAP),
University of Illinois at Chicago, 1994

# RHODE ISLAND

## Large Congregate Care Facilities: FY 1992 Revenue Sources*

### Private 16+Bed Settings

### Public Institutions

#### Does Not Apply

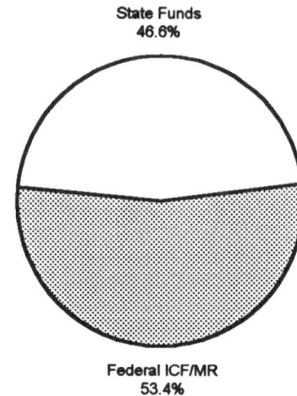

State Funds
46.6%

Federal ICF/MR
53.4%

Total Funds: $26.5 Million

*Excludes nursing homes

## Average Daily Residents in Institutions

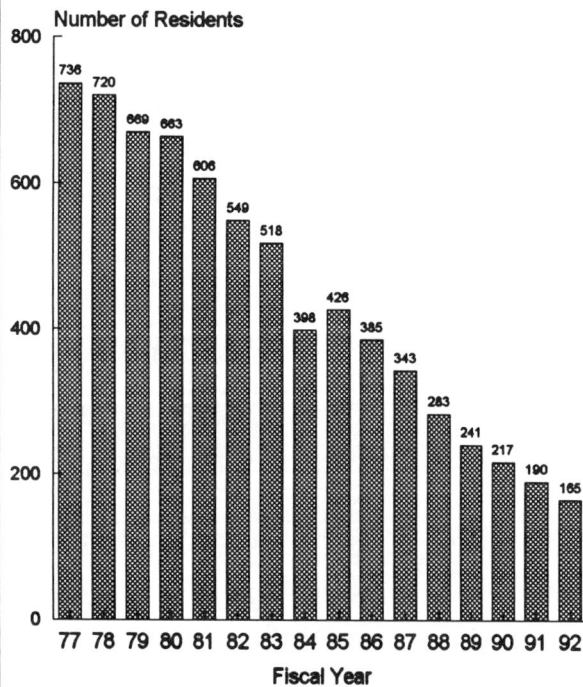

Number of Residents

| Fiscal Year | Residents |
|---|---|
| 77 | 736 |
| 78 | 720 |
| 79 | 669 |
| 80 | 663 |
| 81 | 606 |
| 82 | 549 |
| 83 | 518 |
| 84 | 398 |
| 85 | 426 |
| 86 | 385 |
| 87 | 343 |
| 88 | 283 |
| 89 | 241 |
| 90 | 217 |
| 91 | 190 |
| 92 | 165 |

## Institutional Daily Costs Per Resident

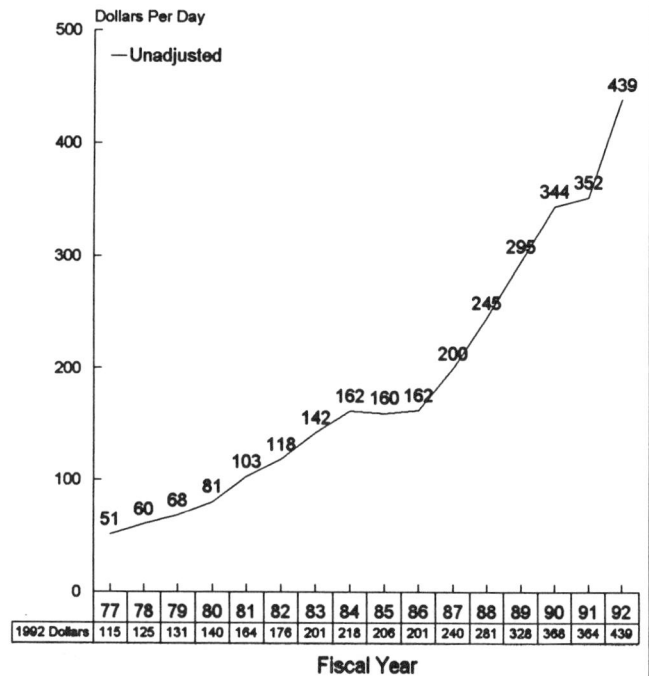

Dollars Per Day

—Unadjusted

| Fiscal Year | Unadjusted | 1992 Dollars |
|---|---|---|
| 77 | 51 | 115 |
| 78 | 60 | 125 |
| 79 | 68 | 131 |
| 80 | 81 | 140 |
| 81 | 103 | 164 |
| 82 | 118 | 176 |
| 83 | 142 | 201 |
| 84 | 162 | 218 |
| 85 | 160 | 206 |
| 86 | 162 | 201 |
| 87 | 200 | 240 |
| 88 | 245 | 281 |
| 89 | 295 | 328 |
| 90 | 344 | 368 |
| 91 | 352 | 364 |
| 92 | 439 | 439 |

Fiscal Year

*Source:*
Institute on Disability and Human Development (UAP),
University of Illinois at Chicago, 1994

# RHODE ISLAND FISCAL EFFORT

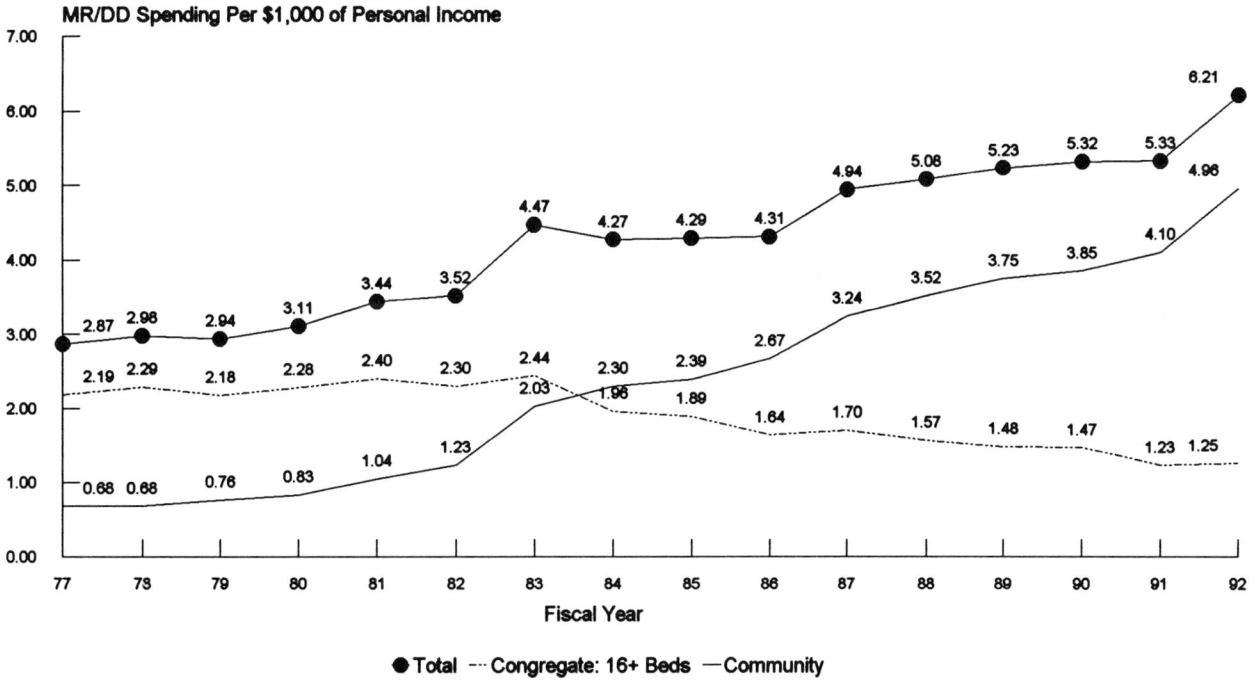

MR/DD Spending Per $1,000 of Personal Income

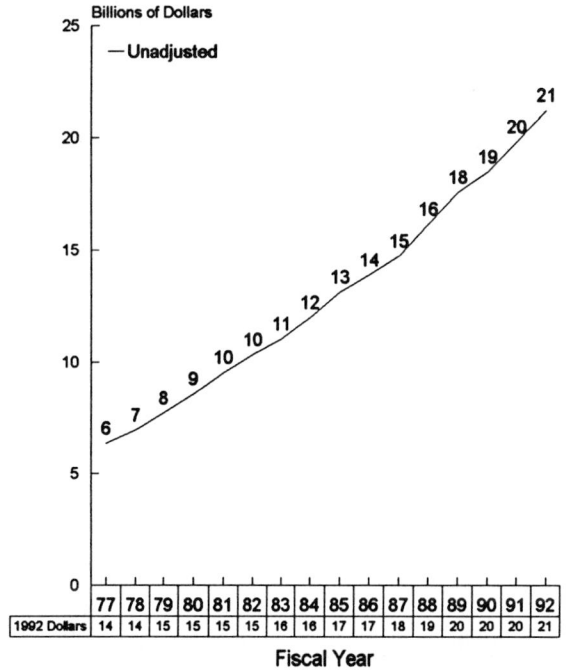

Total values: 2.87, 2.98, 2.94, 3.11, 3.44, 3.52, 4.47, 4.27, 4.29, 4.31, 4.94, 5.08, 5.23, 5.32, 5.33, 6.21

Congregate: 16+ Beds values: 2.19, 2.29, 2.18, 2.28, 2.40, 2.30, 2.44, 2.03, 1.98, 1.89, 1.64, 1.70, 1.57, 1.48, 1.47, 1.23, 1.25

Community values: 0.68, 0.68, 0.76, 0.83, 1.04, 1.23, 2.03, 2.30, 2.39, 2.67, 3.24, 3.52, 3.75, 3.85, 4.10, 4.96

Fiscal Year

● Total  --- Congregate: 16+ Beds  — Community

## Total MR/DD Spending

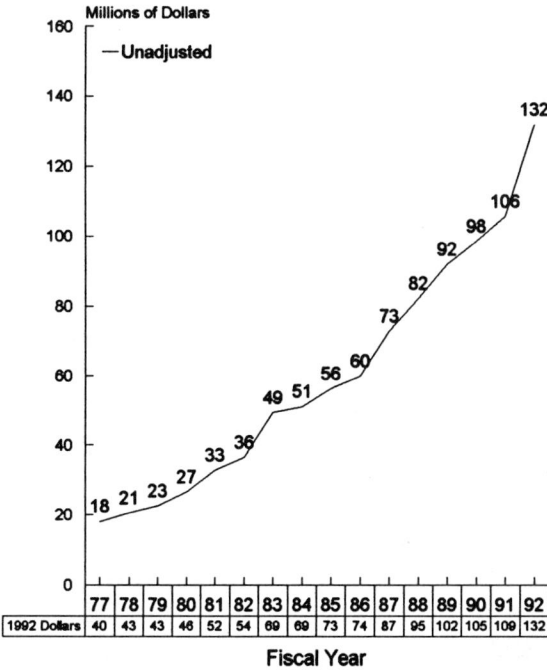

Millions of Dollars
— Unadjusted

18, 21, 23, 27, 33, 36, 49, 51, 56, 60, 73, 82, 92, 98, 106, 132

| | 77 | 78 | 79 | 80 | 81 | 82 | 83 | 84 | 85 | 86 | 87 | 88 | 89 | 90 | 91 | 92 |
|---|---|---|---|---|---|---|---|---|---|---|---|---|---|---|---|---|
| 1992 Dollars | 40 | 43 | 43 | 46 | 52 | 54 | 69 | 69 | 73 | 74 | 87 | 95 | 102 | 105 | 109 | 132 |

Fiscal Year

## Personal Income

Billions of Dollars
— Unadjusted

6, 7, 8, 9, 10, 10, 11, 12, 13, 14, 15, 16, 18, 19, 20, 21

| | 77 | 78 | 79 | 80 | 81 | 82 | 83 | 84 | 85 | 86 | 87 | 88 | 89 | 90 | 91 | 92 |
|---|---|---|---|---|---|---|---|---|---|---|---|---|---|---|---|---|
| 1992 Dollars | 14 | 14 | 15 | 15 | 15 | 15 | 16 | 16 | 17 | 17 | 18 | 19 | 20 | 20 | 20 | 21 |

Fiscal Year

*Source:*
Institute on Disability and Human Development (UAP),
University of Illinois at Chicago, 1994

# RHODE ISLAND

## Financial Support for MR/DD Services: FY 1977-92

| | 1977 | 1978 | 1979 | 1980 | 1981 | 1982 | 1983 | 1984 |
|---|---|---|---|---|---|---|---|---|
| **TOTAL FUNDS** | $18,118,000 | $20,567,000 | $22,519,000 | $26,613,000 | $32,737,000 | $36,401,000 | $49,277,000 | $51,078,748 |
| **CONGREGATE 16+ BEDS** | 13,828,000 | 15,839,000 | 16,685,000 | 19,536,000 | 22,825,000 | 23,730,000 | 26,911,000 | 23,529,300 |
| INSTITUTIONAL SERVICES FUNDS | 13,828,000 | 15,839,000 | 16,685,000 | 19,536,000 | 22,825,000 | 23,730,000 | 26,911,000 | 23,529,300 |
| STATE FUNDS | 5,990,000 | 6,789,000 | 7,145,000 | 8,232,000 | 9,630,000 | 10,299,000 | 11,680,000 | 10,110,300 |
| General Funds | 5,990,000 | 6,789,000 | 7,145,000 | 8,232,000 | 9,630,000 | 10,299,000 | 11,680,000 | 10,110,300 |
| Local | 0 | 0 | 0 | 0 | 0 | 0 | 0 | 0 |
| Other State Funds | 0 | 0 | 0 | 0 | 0 | 0 | 0 | 0 |
| FEDERAL FUNDS | 7,838,000 | 9,050,000 | 9,540,000 | 11,304,000 | 13,195,000 | 13,431,000 | 15,231,000 | 13,419,000 |
| Federal ICF/MR | 7,796,000 | 8,999,000 | 9,470,000 | 11,279,000 | 13,195,000 | 13,431,000 | 15,231,000 | 13,419,000 |
| Title XX / SSBG Funds | 0 | 0 | 0 | 0 | 0 | 0 | 0 | 0 |
| Other Federal Funds | 42,000 | 51,000 | 70,000 | 25,000 | 0 | 0 | 0 | 0 |
| LARGE PRIVATE RESIDENTIAL | 0 | 0 | 0 | 0 | 0 | 0 | 0 | 0 |
| STATE FUNDS | 0 | 0 | 0 | 0 | 0 | 0 | 0 | 0 |
| General Funds | 0 | 0 | 0 | 0 | 0 | 0 | 0 | 0 |
| Other State Funds | 0 | 0 | 0 | 0 | 0 | 0 | 0 | 0 |
| Local/County Overmatch | 0 | 0 | 0 | 0 | 0 | 0 | 0 | 0 |
| FEDERAL FUNDS | 0 | 0 | 0 | 0 | 0 | 0 | 0 | 0 |
| Large Private ICF/MR | 0 | 0 | 0 | 0 | 0 | 0 | 0 | 0 |
| **COMMUNITY SERVICES FUNDS** | 4,290,000 | 4,728,000 | 5,834,000 | 7,077,000 | 9,912,000 | 12,671,000 | 22,366,000 | 27,549,448 |
| STATE FUNDS | 4,088,000 | 4,576,000 | 5,406,000 | 5,932,000 | 7,667,000 | 9,000,000 | 15,293,000 | 17,753,200 |
| General Funds | 3,196,000 | 3,668,000 | 4,430,000 | 4,841,000 | 6,431,000 | 7,698,000 | 13,830,000 | 16,180,200 |
| Other State Funds | 0 | 0 | 0 | 0 | 0 | 0 | 0 | 0 |
| Local/County Overmatch | 0 | 0 | 0 | 0 | 0 | 0 | 0 | 0 |
| SSI State Supplement | 892,000 | 908,000 | 976,000 | 1,091,000 | 1,236,000 | 1,302,000 | 1,463,000 | 1,573,000 |
| FEDERAL FUNDS | 202,000 | 152,000 | 428,000 | 1,145,000 | 2,245,000 | 3,671,000 | 7,073,000 | 9,796,248 |
| ICF/MR Funds | 134,000 | 107,000 | 428,000 | 1,083,000 | 2,144,000 | 3,570,000 | 7,039,000 | 7,684,600 |
| Small Public | 0 | 0 | 0 | 0 | 196,000 | 744,000 | 2,438,000 | 1,339,600 |
| Small Private | 134,000 | 107,000 | 428,000 | 1,083,000 | 1,948,000 | 2,826,000 | 4,601,000 | 6,345,000 |
| HCBS Waiver | 0 | 0 | 0 | 0 | 0 | 0 | 0 | 241,400 |
| Model 50/200 Waiver | 0 | 0 | 0 | 0 | 0 | 0 | 0 | 0 |
| Other Title XIX Programs | 0 | 0 | 0 | 0 | 0 | 0 | 0 | 1,831,200 |
| Title XX / SSBG Funds | 0 | 0 | 0 | 0 | 0 | 0 | 0 | 0 |
| Other Federal Funds | 68,000 | 45,000 | 0 | 62,000 | 101,000 | 101,000 | 34,000 | 900 |
| Waiver Clients' SSI/ADC | 0 | 0 | 0 | 0 | 0 | 0 | 0 | 38,148 |

| | 1985 | 1986 | 1987 | 1988 | 1989 | 1990 | 1991 | 1992 |
|---|---|---|---|---|---|---|---|---|
| **TOTAL FUNDS** | $56,216,900 | $59,844,144 | $72,817,900 | $82,192,060 | $91,973,032 | $98,483,813 | $105,655,493 | $131,901,305 |
| **CONGREGATE 16+ BEDS** | 24,820,200 | 22,778,500 | 25,012,000 | 25,335,900 | 25,962,840 | 27,236,258 | 24,425,044 | 26,494,801 |
| INSTITUTIONAL SERVICES FUNDS | 24,820,200 | 22,778,500 | 25,012,000 | 25,335,900 | 25,962,840 | 27,236,258 | 24,425,044 | 26,494,801 |
| STATE FUNDS | 11,212,200 | 9,842,600 | 10,922,700 | 11,345,400 | 11,522,308 | 12,166,436 | 11,213,538 | 12,346,577 |
| General Funds | 11,212,200 | 9,842,600 | 10,922,700 | 11,345,400 | 11,522,308 | 12,166,436 | 11,213,538 | 12,346,577 |
| Local | 0 | 0 | 0 | 0 | 0 | 0 | 0 | 0 |
| Other State Funds | 0 | 0 | 0 | 0 | 0 | 0 | 0 | 0 |
| FEDERAL FUNDS | 13,608,000 | 12,935,900 | 14,089,300 | 13,990,500 | 14,440,532 | 15,069,822 | 13,211,506 | 14,148,224 |
| Federal ICF/MR | 13,608,000 | 12,935,900 | 14,089,300 | 13,990,500 | 14,440,532 | 15,069,822 | 13,211,506 | 14,148,224 |
| Title XX / SSBG Funds | 0 | 0 | 0 | 0 | 0 | 0 | 0 | 0 |
| Other Federal Funds | 0 | 0 | 0 | 0 | 0 | 0 | 0 | 0 |
| LARGE PRIVATE RESIDENTIAL | 0 | 0 | 0 | 0 | 0 | 0 | 0 | 0 |
| STATE FUNDS | 0 | 0 | 0 | 0 | 0 | 0 | 0 | 0 |
| General Funds | 0 | 0 | 0 | 0 | 0 | 0 | 0 | 0 |
| Other State Funds | 0 | 0 | 0 | 0 | 0 | 0 | 0 | 0 |
| Local/County Overmatch | 0 | 0 | 0 | 0 | 0 | 0 | 0 | 0 |
| FEDERAL FUNDS | 0 | 0 | 0 | 0 | 0 | 0 | 0 | 0 |
| Large Private ICF/MR | 0 | 0 | 0 | 0 | 0 | 0 | 0 | 0 |
| **COMMUNITY SERVICES FUNDS** | 31,396,700 | 37,065,644 | 47,805,900 | 56,856,160 | 66,010,192 | 71,247,555 | 81,230,449 | 105,406,504 |
| STATE FUNDS | 19,614,400 | 22,384,500 | 27,449,500 | 33,232,200 | 35,374,144 | 35,485,386 | 43,376,300 | 53,757,877 |
| General Funds | 17,950,400 | 20,625,500 | 25,763,500 | 31,620,200 | 33,681,544 | 33,708,156 | 41,510,208 | 51,798,481 |
| Other State Funds | 0 | 0 | 0 | 0 | 0 | 0 | 0 | 0 |
| Local/County Overmatch | 0 | 0 | 0 | 0 | 0 | 0 | 0 | 0 |
| SSI State Supplement | 1,664,000 | 1,759,000 | 1,686,000 | 1,612,000 | 1,692,600 | 1,777,230 | 1,866,092 | 1,959,396 |
| FEDERAL FUNDS | 11,782,300 | 14,681,144 | 20,356,400 | 23,623,960 | 30,636,048 | 35,762,169 | 37,854,149 | 51,648,627 |
| ICF/MR Funds | 9,251,300 | 10,458,000 | 13,782,900 | 16,598,400 | 19,895,124 | 23,127,995 | 23,559,357 | 26,834,767 |
| Small Public | 2,069,300 | 1,655,500 | 1,803,000 | 2,403,200 | 2,045,056 | 927,549 | 167,850 | 0 |
| Small Private | 7,182,000 | 8,802,500 | 11,979,900 | 14,195,200 | 17,850,068 | 22,200,446 | 23,391,507 | 26,834,767 |
| HCBS Waiver | 537,500 | 2,561,000 | 3,181,500 | 2,605,700 | 4,107,664 | 4,900,757 | 6,041,938 | 13,648,644 |
| Model 50/200 Waiver | 0 | 0 | 0 | 0 | 0 | 0 | 0 | 0 |
| Other Title XIX Programs | 1,903,500 | 1,115,900 | 1,426,400 | 2,398,100 | 3,854,852 | 4,160,873 | 4,585,654 | 5,304,416 |
| Title XX / SSBG Funds | 0 | 0 | 0 | 0 | 0 | 0 | 0 | 0 |
| Other Federal Funds | 0 | 109,600 | 0 | 0 | 0 | 0 | 0 | 0 |
| Waiver Clients' SSI/ADC | 90,000 | 436,644 | 1,965,600 | 2,021,760 | 2,778,408 | 3,572,544 | 3,667,200 | 5,860,800 |

*Source:*
Institute on Disability and Human Development (UAP),
University of Illinois at Chicago, 1994

# SOUTH CAROLINA

## MR/DD Spending for Congregate Residential & Community Services

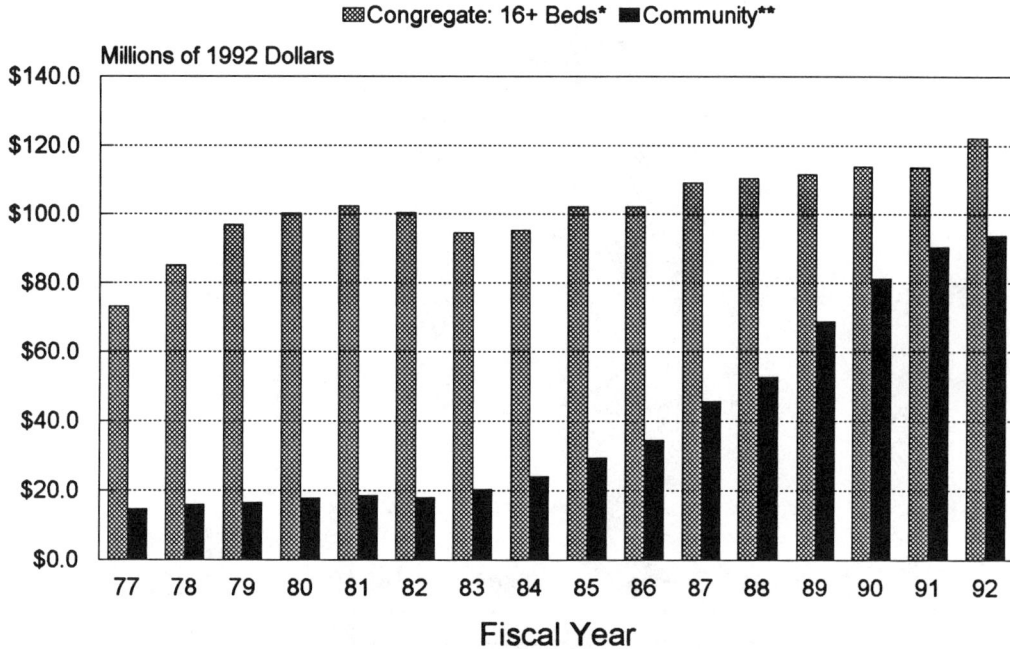

▨Congregate: 16+ Beds* ■Community**

Millions of 1992 Dollars

Fiscal Year
*Excludes nursing homes; ** Includes resources for
15 bed or less residential settings & non-residential community services

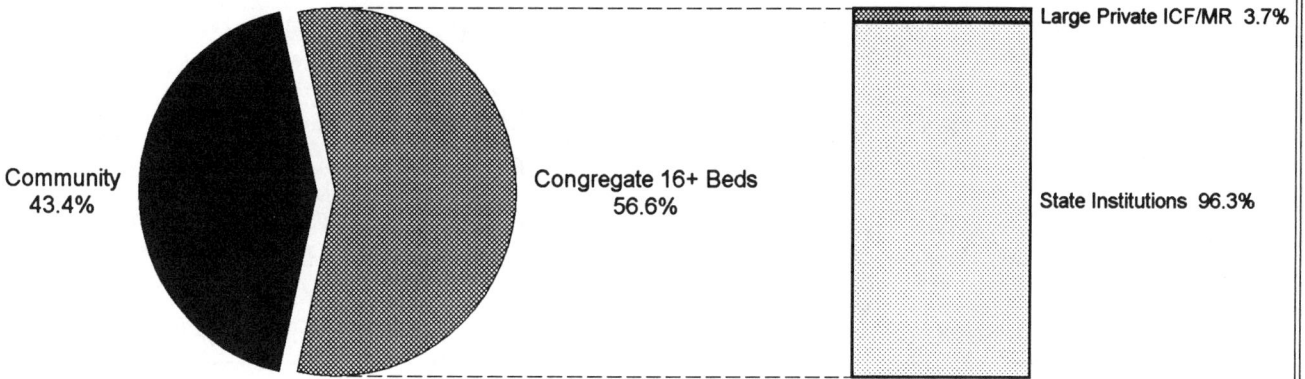

Community
43.4%

Congregate 16+ Beds
56.6%

Large Private ICF/MR 3.7%

State Institutions 96.3%

FY 1992 Total Spending:
$216.1 Million

*Source:*
Institute on Disability and Human Development (UAP),
University of Illinois at Chicago, 1994

# SOUTH CAROLINA

## Number of Persons Served by Residential Setting: FY 1992

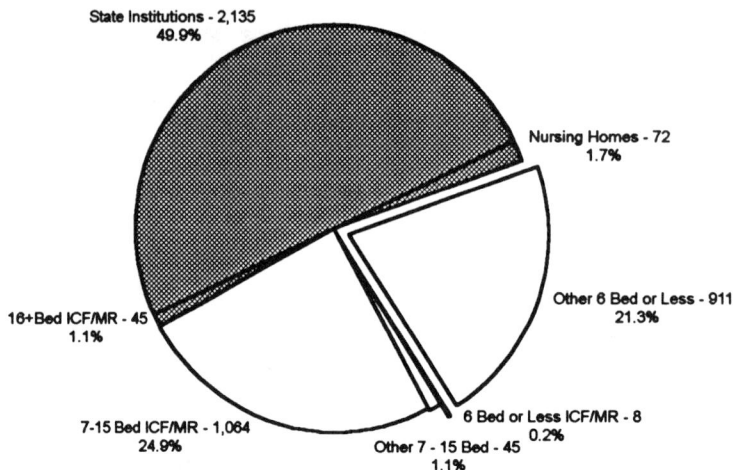

State Institutions - 2,135
49.9%

Nursing Homes - 72
1.7%

Other 6 Bed or Less - 911
21.3%

16+Bed ICF/MR - 45
1.1%

6 Bed or Less ICF/MR - 8
0.2%

7-15 Bed ICF/MR - 1,064
24.9%

Other 7 - 15 Bed - 45
1.1%

Total Served: 4,280

## Persons Served by Residential Setting:1986-92

|  | 1986 | 1987 | 1988 | 1989 | 1990 | 1991 | 1992 |
|---|---|---|---|---|---|---|---|
| CONGREGATE 16 + BED SETTINGS | NA | NA | 2,523 | 2,545 | 2,418 | 2,350 | 2,252 |
| Nursing Homes | NA | NA | 75 | 137 | 117 | 100 | 72 |
| State Institutions | 2,481 | 2,444 | 2,354 | 2,365 | 2,254 | 2,205 | 2,135 |
| Private 16+Bed ICF/MR | 94 | 94 | 94 | 43 | 47 | 45 | 45 |
| Other 16+Bed Residential | 0 | 0 | 0 | 0 | 0 | 0 | 0 |
| 15 BED OR LESS RESIDENTIAL SETTINGS | 656 | 1,212 | 1,354 | 1,316 | 1,572 | 1,849 | 2,028 |
| Public 7-15 Bed ICF/MR | 252 | 314 | 336 | 450 | 480 | 547 | 608 |
| Private 7-15 Bed ICF/MR | 68 | 157 | 266 | 335 | 414 | 452 | 456 |
| Other 7-15 Bed Residential | 336 | 741 | 752 | 531 | 678 | 850 | 45 |
| Public 6 Bed or Less ICF/MR |  |  |  |  |  |  | 8 |
| Private 6 Bed or Less ICF/MR |  |  |  |  |  |  | 0 |
| Other 6 Bed or Less Residential |  |  |  |  |  |  | 911 |
| TOTAL PERSONS SERVED | NA | NA | 3,877 | 3,861 | 3,990 | 4,199 | 4,280 |

## Persons Served in Non-Residential Community Services:1986-92

|  | 1986 | 1987 | 1988 | 1989 | 1990 | 1991 | 1992 |
|---|---|---|---|---|---|---|---|
| DAY/WORK PROGRAMS | NA | NA | NA | 5,178 | 5,832 | 6,431 | 6,585 |
| Sheltered Employment/Work Activity | NA | NA | NA | 3,099 | 3,376 | 3,699 | 3,970 |
| Day Habilitation ("Day Training") | 3,573 | 3,691 | 3,826 | 1,804 | 1,612 | 1,759 | 1,523 |
| Supported/Competitive Employment | 168 | 232 | 280 | 723 | 844 | 973 | 1,092 |
| CASE MANAGEMENT | 4,519 | 7,280 | 7,619 | 9,156 | 10,032 | 10,422 | 10,372 |
| HCBS WAIVER | 0 | 0 | 0 | 0 | 0 | 0 | 253 |
| MODEL 50/200 WAIVER | 0 | 0 | 0 | 0 | 0 | 0 | 0 |

*Source:*
Institute on Disability and Human Development (UAP),
University of Illinois at Chicago, 1994

# SOUTH CAROLINA

## Community Services: FY 1992 Revenue Sources

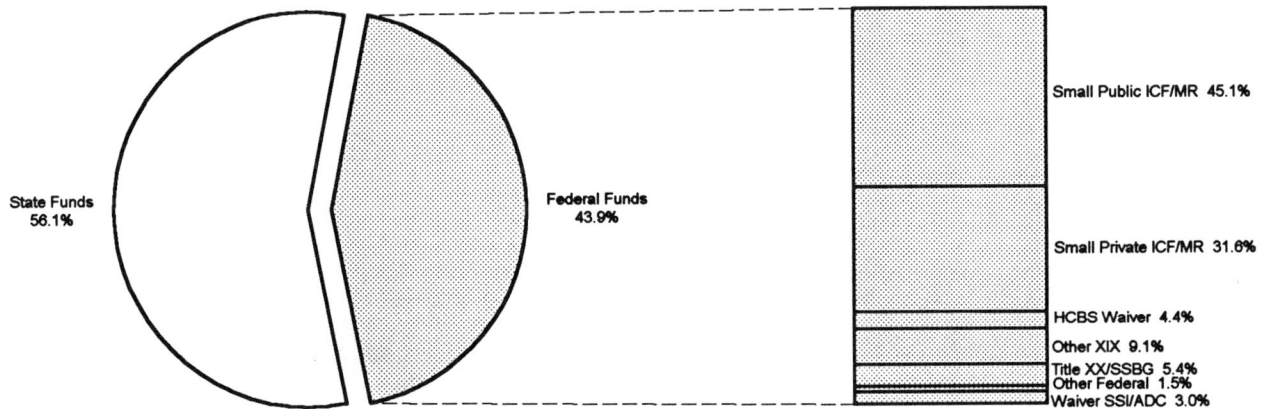

State Funds 56.1%

Federal Funds 43.9%

Small Public ICF/MR 45.1%

Small Private ICF/MR 31.6%

HCBS Waiver 4.4%
Other XIX 9.1%
Title XX/SSBG 5.4%
Other Federal 1.5%
Waiver SSI/ADC 3.0%

Total Funds: $93.8 Million

## Family Support Initiatives*

| | 1986 | 1987 | 1988 | 1989 | 1990 | 1991 | 1992 |
|---|---|---|---|---|---|---|---|
| FAMILY SUPPORT: TOTAL SPENDING | $484,100 | $1,114,700 | $1,422,100 | $4,276,453 | $5,757,212 | $6,743,686 | $7,304,259 |
| Total # of Families Supported | 138 | 215 | 241 | 981 | 1,155 | 1,326 | 1,496 |
| A. Financial Subsidy/Payment | $72,100 | $134,100 | $180,000 | $222,248 | $440,934 | $490,041 | $509,293 |
| # of Families | 75 | 150 | 175 | 251 | 413 | 476 | 512 |
| B. Family Assistance Payments | $412,000 | $980,600 | $1,242,100 | $4,054,205 | $5,316,278 | $6,253,645 | $6,794,966 |
| # of Families | 63 | 65 | 66 | 730 | 742 | 850 | 984 |
| C. Other Family Support Payments | $0 | $0 | $0 | $0 | $0 | $0 | $0 |
| # of Families | 0 | 0 | 0 | 0 | 0 | 0 | 0 |

## Other Community Services Initiatives*

| | 1986 | 1987 | 1988 | 1989 | 1990 | 1991 | 1992 |
|---|---|---|---|---|---|---|---|
| AGING/DD SPENDING | $0 | $0 | $0 | $0 | $0 | $0 | $0 |
| # of Persons Served | 0 | 0 | 0 | 0 | 0 | 0 | 0 |
| ASSISTIVE TECHNOLOGY SPENDING | | | | | | | $0 |
| # of Persons Served | | | | | | | 0 |
| EARLY INTERVENTION SPENDING | $3,177,900 | $3,582,600 | $3,819,700 | $4,090,930 | $4,221,163 | $4,699,624 | $4,040,500 |
| # of Persons Served | 927 | 943 | 1,081 | 1,000 | 1,000 | 1,156 | 1,144 |
| PERSONAL ASSISTANCE SPENDING | | | | | | | $0 |
| # of Persons Served | | | | | | | 0 |
| SUPPORTED EMPLOYMENT SPENDING | $208,000 | $439,000 | $713,000 | $990,779 | $927,078 | $1,875,126 | $1,867,761 |
| # of Persons Served | 168 | 232 | 280 | 723 | 844 | 973 | 1,092 |
| SUPPORTED LIVING SPENDING | | | | | | | $0 |
| # of Persons Served | | | | | | | 0 |

*Expenditures associated with Special Community Initiatives are a subset of funding within the community services component of the state's chart series and spreadsheet; Family Support Client figures may include duplicate client counts; HCBS Waiver counts include Waiver case management numbers.
0= Services not provided in the state; NA= Data not available from state; blank= Services not applicable (eg. CSLA prior to authorization, Special Community Initiatives prior to request for data by this study)

Source:
Institute on Disability and Human Development (UAP),
University of Illinois at Chicago, 1994

# SOUTH CAROLINA

## Large Congregate Care Facilities: FY 1992 Revenue Sources*

### Private 16+Bed Settings

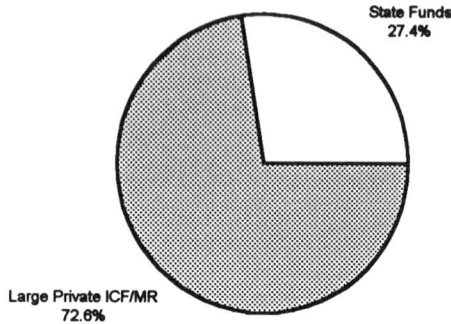

State Funds
27.4%

Large Private ICF/MR
72.6%

Total Funds: $4.5 Million

### Public Institutions

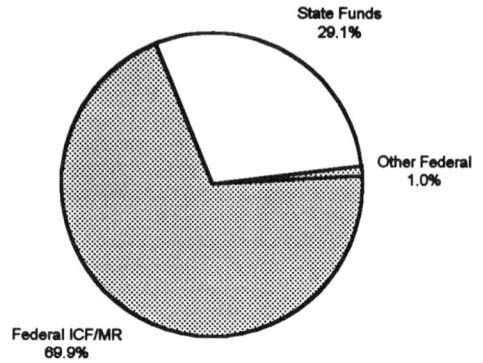

State Funds
29.1%

Other Federal
1.0%

Federal ICF/MR
69.9%

Total Funds: $117.7 Million

*Excludes nursing homes

## Average Daily Residents in Institutions

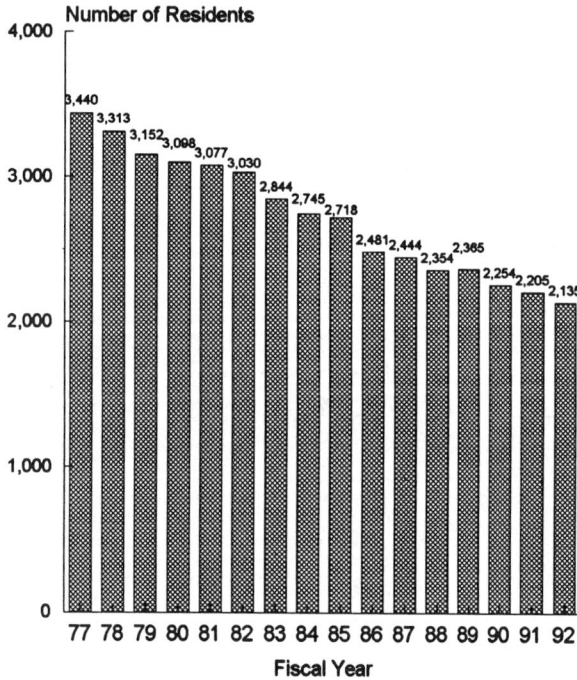

Number of Residents

3,440; 3,313; 3,152; 3,098; 3,077; 3,030; 2,844; 2,745; 2,718; 2,481; 2,444; 2,354; 2,365; 2,254; 2,205; 2,135

Fiscal Year 77-92

## Institutional Daily Costs Per Resident

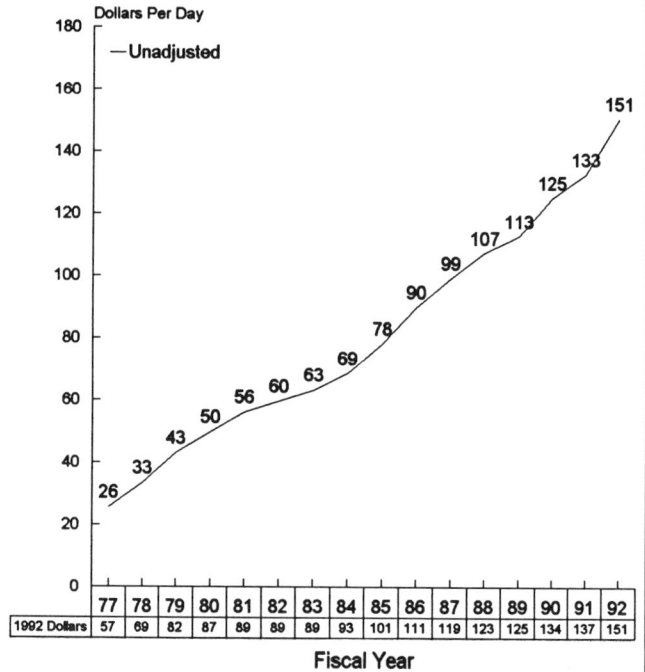

Dollars Per Day — Unadjusted

26, 33, 43, 50, 56, 60, 63, 69, 78, 90, 99, 107, 113, 125, 133, 151

| Fiscal Year | 77 | 78 | 79 | 80 | 81 | 82 | 83 | 84 | 85 | 86 | 87 | 88 | 89 | 90 | 91 | 92 |
|---|---|---|---|---|---|---|---|---|---|---|---|---|---|---|---|---|
| 1992 Dollars | 57 | 69 | 82 | 87 | 89 | 89 | 89 | 93 | 101 | 111 | 119 | 123 | 125 | 134 | 137 | 151 |

*Source:*
Institute on Disability and Human Development (UAP),
University of Illinois at Chicago, 1994

# SOUTH CAROLINA FISCAL EFFORT

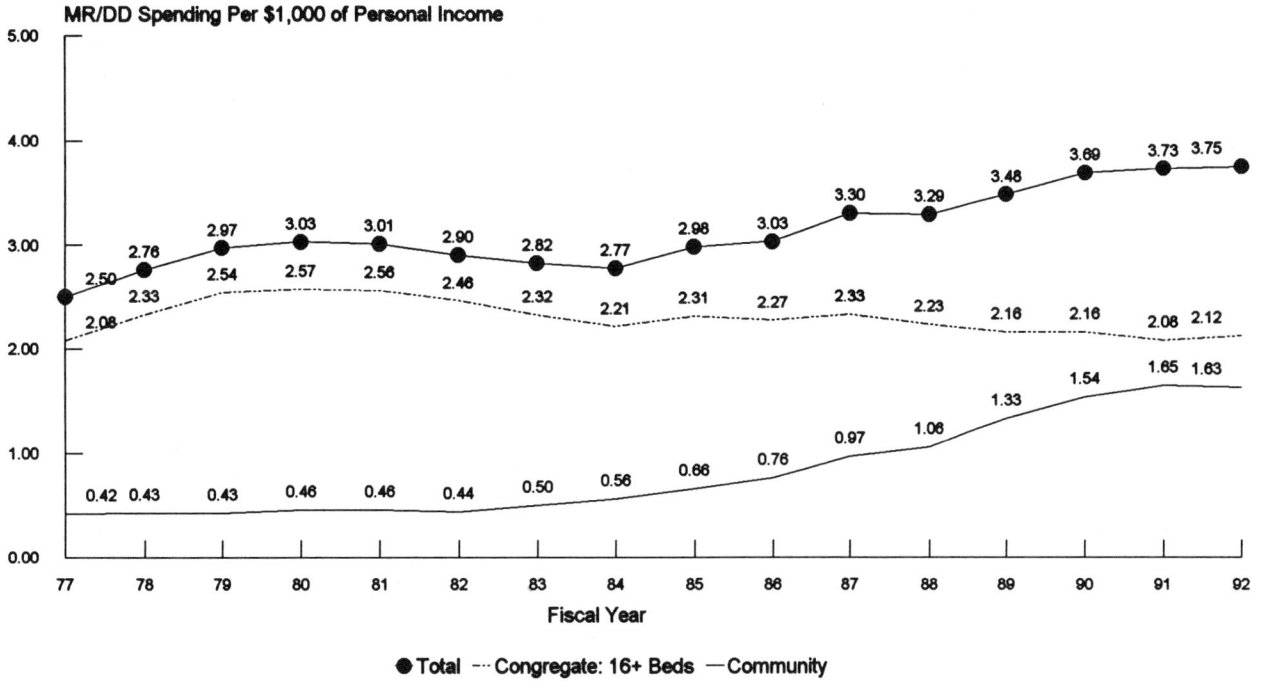

MR/DD Spending Per $1,000 of Personal Income

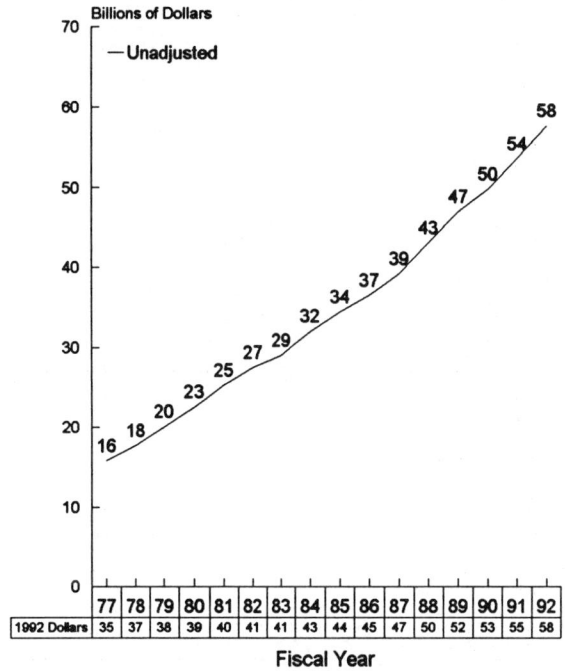

| | |
|---|---|
| 5.00 | |
| 4.00 | 3.69  3.73 3.75 |
| 3.00 | 2.50 2.76 2.97 3.03 3.01 2.90 2.82 2.77 2.98 3.03 3.30 3.29 3.48 |
| | 2.08 2.33 2.54 2.57 2.56 2.46 2.32 2.21 2.31 2.27 2.33 2.23 2.16 2.16 2.08 2.12 |
| | 1.54 1.65 1.63 |
| | 1.33 |
| 1.00 | 0.97 1.06 |
| | 0.42 0.43 0.43 0.46 0.46 0.44 0.50 0.56 0.66 0.76 |
| 0.00 | |

77  78  79  80  81  82  83  84  85  86  87  88  89  90  91  92

Fiscal Year

● Total  --- Congregate: 16+ Beds  — Community

## Total MR/DD Spending

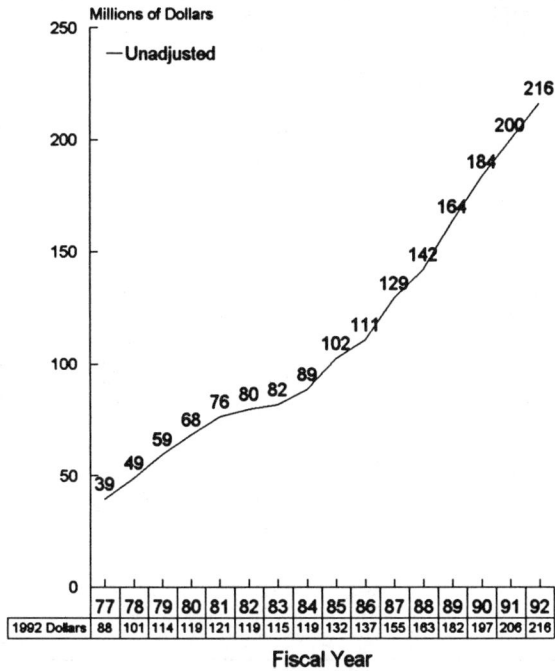

Millions of Dollars
— Unadjusted

| | |
|---|---|
| 250 | |
| | 216 |
| 200 | 200 |
| | 184 |
| 150 | 164 |
| | 142 |
| | 129 |
| | 102 111 |
| 100 | 89 |
| | 76 80 82 |
| | 68 |
| | 59 |
| 50 | 49 |
| | 39 |
| 0 | |

| | 77 | 78 | 79 | 80 | 81 | 82 | 83 | 84 | 85 | 86 | 87 | 88 | 89 | 90 | 91 | 92 |
|---|---|---|---|---|---|---|---|---|---|---|---|---|---|---|---|
| 1992 Dollars | 88 | 101 | 114 | 119 | 121 | 119 | 115 | 119 | 132 | 137 | 155 | 163 | 182 | 197 | 206 | 216 |

Fiscal Year

## Personal Income

Billions of Dollars
— Unadjusted

| | |
|---|---|
| 70 | |
| 60 | 58 |
| | 54 |
| | 50 |
| 50 | 47 |
| | 43 |
| 40 | 39 |
| | 37 |
| | 34 |
| | 32 |
| 30 | 29 |
| | 27 |
| | 25 |
| | 23 |
| 20 | 20 |
| | 18 |
| | 16 |
| 10 | |
| 0 | |

| | 77 | 78 | 79 | 80 | 81 | 82 | 83 | 84 | 85 | 86 | 87 | 88 | 89 | 90 | 91 | 92 |
|---|---|---|---|---|---|---|---|---|---|---|---|---|---|---|---|
| 1992 Dollars | 35 | 37 | 38 | 39 | 40 | 41 | 41 | 43 | 44 | 45 | 47 | 50 | 52 | 53 | 55 | 58 |

Fiscal Year

*Source:*
Institute on Disability and Human Development (UAP),
University of Illinois at Chicago, 1994

# SOUTH CAROLINA
## Financial Support for MR/DD Services: FY 1977-92

| | 1977 | 1978 | 1979 | 1980 | 1981 | 1982 | 1983 | 1984 |
|---|---|---|---|---|---|---|---|---|
| **TOTAL FUNDS** | $39,475,000 | $48,911,000 | $59,410,000 | $68,210,000 | $76,204,000 | $79,767,000 | $81,755,000 | $88,516,000 |
| **CONGREGATE 16+ BEDS** | 32,861,401 | 41,228,299 | 50,791,436 | 57,903,701 | 64,593,770 | 67,685,399 | 67,313,764 | 70,660,040 |
| INSTITUTIONAL SERVICES FUNDS | 32,224,000 | 40,327,000 | 49,429,000 | 56,498,000 | 63,072,000 | 65,878,000 | 65,604,000 | 68,909,800 |
| STATE FUNDS | 23,643,000 | 28,950,000 | 32,972,200 | 33,188,200 | 36,498,600 | 36,198,100 | 35,845,900 | 34,975,800 |
| General Funds | 23,546,000 | 28,609,000 | 32,260,200 | 32,853,200 | 36,420,600 | 35,396,100 | 35,057,900 | 34,438,400 |
| Local | 0 | 0 | 0 | 0 | 0 | 0 | 0 | 0 |
| Other State Funds | 97,000 | 341,000 | 712,000 | 335,000 | 78,000 | 802,000 | 788,000 | 537,400 |
| FEDERAL FUNDS | 8,581,000 | 11,377,000 | 16,456,800 | 23,309,800 | 26,573,400 | 29,679,900 | 29,758,100 | 33,934,000 |
| Federal ICF/MR | 6,039,000 | 9,398,000 | 14,598,800 | 21,677,800 | 25,024,400 | 27,877,900 | 28,042,100 | 32,464,300 |
| Title XX / SSBG Funds | 0 | 0 | 0 | 0 | 0 | 0 | 0 | 0 |
| Other Federal Funds | 2,542,000 | 1,979,000 | 1,858,000 | 1,632,000 | 1,549,000 | 1,802,000 | 1,716,000 | 1,469,700 |
| LARGE PRIVATE RESIDENTIAL | 637,401 | 901,299 | 1,362,436 | 1,405,701 | 1,521,770 | 1,807,399 | 1,709,764 | 1,750,240 |
| STATE FUNDS | 168,401 | 249,299 | 382,436 | 404,701 | 441,770 | 527,399 | 499,764 | 475,540 |
| General Funds | 168,401 | 249,299 | 382,436 | 404,701 | 441,770 | 527,399 | 499,764 | 475,540 |
| Other State Funds | 0 | 0 | 0 | 0 | 0 | 0 | 0 | 0 |
| Local/County Overmatch | 0 | 0 | 0 | 0 | 0 | 0 | 0 | 0 |
| FEDERAL FUNDS | 469,000 | 652,000 | 980,000 | 1,001,000 | 1,080,000 | 1,280,000 | 1,210,000 | 1,274,700 |
| Large Private ICF/MR | 469,000 | 652,000 | 980,000 | 1,001,000 | 1,080,000 | 1,280,000 | 1,210,000 | 1,274,700 |
| **COMMUNITY SERVICES FUNDS** | 6,613,599 | 7,682,701 | 8,618,564 | 10,306,299 | 11,610,230 | 12,081,601 | 14,441,236 | 17,855,960 |
| STATE FUNDS | 3,598,599 | 4,122,701 | 4,132,664 | 5,606,099 | 6,851,230 | 8,248,001 | 10,804,536 | 14,022,060 |
| General Funds | 3,436,599 | 3,910,701 | 3,883,664 | 5,231,099 | 6,474,230 | 7,834,001 | 10,312,536 | 13,483,060 |
| Other State Funds | 0 | 0 | 0 | 0 | 0 | 0 | 0 | 0 |
| Local/County Overmatch | 0 | 0 | 0 | 0 | 0 | 0 | 0 | 0 |
| SSI State Supplement | 162,000 | 212,000 | 249,000 | 375,000 | 377,000 | 414,000 | 492,000 | 539,000 |
| FEDERAL FUNDS | 3,015,000 | 3,560,000 | 4,485,900 | 4,700,200 | 4,759,000 | 3,833,600 | 3,636,700 | 3,833,900 |
| ICF/MR Funds | 0 | 0 | 898,900 | 1,337,200 | 1,797,000 | 2,145,600 | 2,013,700 | 1,942,700 |
| Small Public | 0 | 0 | 898,900 | 1,337,200 | 1,797,000 | 2,145,600 | 2,013,700 | 1,826,600 |
| Small Private | 0 | 0 | 0 | 0 | 0 | 0 | 0 | 116,100 |
| HCBS Waiver | 0 | 0 | 0 | 0 | 0 | 0 | 0 | 0 |
| Model 50/200 Waiver | 0 | 0 | 0 | 0 | 0 | 0 | 0 | 0 |
| Other Title XIX Programs | 0 | 0 | 0 | 0 | 0 | 0 | 0 | 0 |
| Title XX / SSBG Funds | 3,015,000 | 3,560,000 | 3,587,000 | 3,363,000 | 2,962,000 | 1,688,000 | 1,623,000 | 1,837,500 |
| Other Federal Funds | 0 | 0 | 0 | 0 | 0 | 0 | 0 | 53,700 |
| Waiver Clients' SSI/ADC | 0 | 0 | 0 | 0 | 0 | 0 | 0 | 0 |

| | 1985 | 1986 | 1987 | 1988 | 1989 | 1990 | 1991 | 1992 |
|---|---|---|---|---|---|---|---|---|
| **TOTAL FUNDS** | $102,413,700 | $110,610,400 | $129,260,469 | $141,891,804 | $163,639,087 | $183,646,682 | $199,802,222 | $216,121,691 |
| **CONGREGATE 16+ BEDS** | 79,614,646 | 82,738,161 | 91,162,269 | 96,088,604 | 101,313,811 | 107,244,929 | 111,272,328 | 122,275,732 |
| INSTITUTIONAL SERVICES FUNDS | 77,516,700 | 81,384,800 | 88,375,900 | 92,358,900 | 97,219,412 | 102,919,314 | 106,772,371 | 117,738,777 |
| STATE FUNDS | 33,960,500 | 38,999,900 | 37,652,800 | 36,264,300 | 39,936,994 | 36,237,061 | 33,175,706 | 34,289,047 |
| General Funds | 32,973,300 | 37,543,900 | 36,018,400 | 34,690,400 | 37,018,787 | 33,856,644 | 31,194,622 | 32,604,135 |
| Local | 0 | 0 | 0 | 0 | 0 | 0 | 0 | 0 |
| Other State Funds | 987,200 | 1,456,000 | 1,634,400 | 1,573,900 | 2,918,207 | 2,380,417 | 1,981,084 | 1,684,912 |
| FEDERAL FUNDS | 43,556,200 | 42,384,900 | 50,723,100 | 56,094,600 | 57,282,418 | 66,682,253 | 73,596,665 | 83,449,730 |
| Federal ICF/MR | 42,286,400 | 40,948,800 | 49,286,200 | 54,618,200 | 56,116,108 | 65,254,521 | 72,443,688 | 82,261,972 |
| Title XX / SSBG Funds | 0 | 0 | 0 | 0 | 0 | 0 | 0 | 0 |
| Other Federal Funds | 1,269,800 | 1,436,100 | 1,436,900 | 1,476,400 | 1,166,310 | 1,427,732 | 1,152,977 | 1,187,758 |
| LARGE PRIVATE RESIDENTIAL | 2,097,946 | 1,353,361 | 2,786,369 | 3,729,704 | 4,094,399 | 4,325,615 | 4,499,957 | 4,536,955 |
| STATE FUNDS | 555,746 | 366,761 | 760,679 | 996,204 | 1,098,118 | 1,164,888 | 1,228,488 | 1,241,311 |
| General Funds | 555,746 | 366,761 | 760,679 | 996,204 | 1,098,118 | 1,164,888 | 1,228,488 | 1,241,311 |
| Other State Funds | 0 | 0 | 0 | 0 | 0 | 0 | 0 | 0 |
| Local/County Overmatch | 0 | 0 | 0 | 0 | 0 | 0 | 0 | 0 |
| FEDERAL FUNDS | 1,542,200 | 986,600 | 2,025,690 | 2,733,500 | 2,996,281 | 3,160,727 | 3,271,469 | 3,295,644 |
| Large Private ICF/MR | 1,542,200 | 986,600 | 2,025,690 | 2,733,500 | 2,996,281 | 3,160,727 | 3,271,469 | 3,295,644 |
| **COMMUNITY SERVICES FUNDS** | 22,799,054 | 27,872,239 | 38,098,200 | 45,803,200 | 62,325,276 | 76,401,753 | 88,529,894 | 93,845,959 |
| STATE FUNDS | 18,198,554 | 19,608,339 | 24,622,300 | 27,562,800 | 37,973,682 | 47,586,742 | 54,574,666 | 52,602,725 |
| General Funds | 17,628,554 | 18,772,339 | 23,715,300 | 26,666,800 | 37,032,882 | 46,598,902 | 53,537,434 | 51,513,631 |
| Other State Funds | 0 | 0 | 0 | 0 | 0 | 0 | 0 | 0 |
| Local/County Overmatch | 0 | 0 | 0 | 0 | 0 | 0 | 0 | 0 |
| SSI State Supplement | 570,000 | 836,000 | 907,000 | 896,000 | 940,800 | 987,840 | 1,037,232 | 1,089,094 |
| FEDERAL FUNDS | 4,600,500 | 8,263,900 | 13,475,900 | 18,240,400 | 24,351,594 | 28,815,011 | 33,955,228 | 41,243,234 |
| ICF/MR Funds | 2,613,400 | 6,276,000 | 11,397,200 | 15,992,200 | 19,639,524 | 23,274,161 | 28,087,261 | 31,630,960 |
| Small Public | 2,501,700 | 4,936,600 | 7,589,100 | 8,952,400 | 11,771,652 | 14,323,045 | 17,460,320 | 18,602,734 |
| Small Private | 111,700 | 1,339,400 | 3,808,100 | 7,039,800 | 7,867,872 | 8,951,116 | 10,626,941 | 13,028,226 |
| HCBS Waiver | 0 | 0 | 0 | 0 | 0 | 0 | 0 | 1,798,354 |
| Model 50/200 Waiver | 0 | 0 | 0 | 0 | 0 | 0 | 0 | 0 |
| Other Title XIX Programs | 0 | 0 | 0 | 0 | 2,277,036 | 3,119,290 | 3,396,408 | 3,732,965 |
| Title XX / SSBG Funds | 1,947,900 | 1,850,400 | 1,944,200 | 1,947,700 | 1,929,153 | 1,998,779 | 2,026,267 | 2,217,314 |
| Other Federal Funds | 39,200 | 137,500 | 134,500 | 300,500 | 505,881 | 422,781 | 445,292 | 627,989 |
| Waiver Clients' SSI/ADC | 0 | 0 | 0 | 0 | 0 | 0 | 0 | 1,235,652 |

*Source:*
Institute on Disability and Human Development (UAP),
University of Illinois at Chicago, 1994

# SOUTH DAKOTA

## MR/DD Spending for Congregate Residential & Community Services

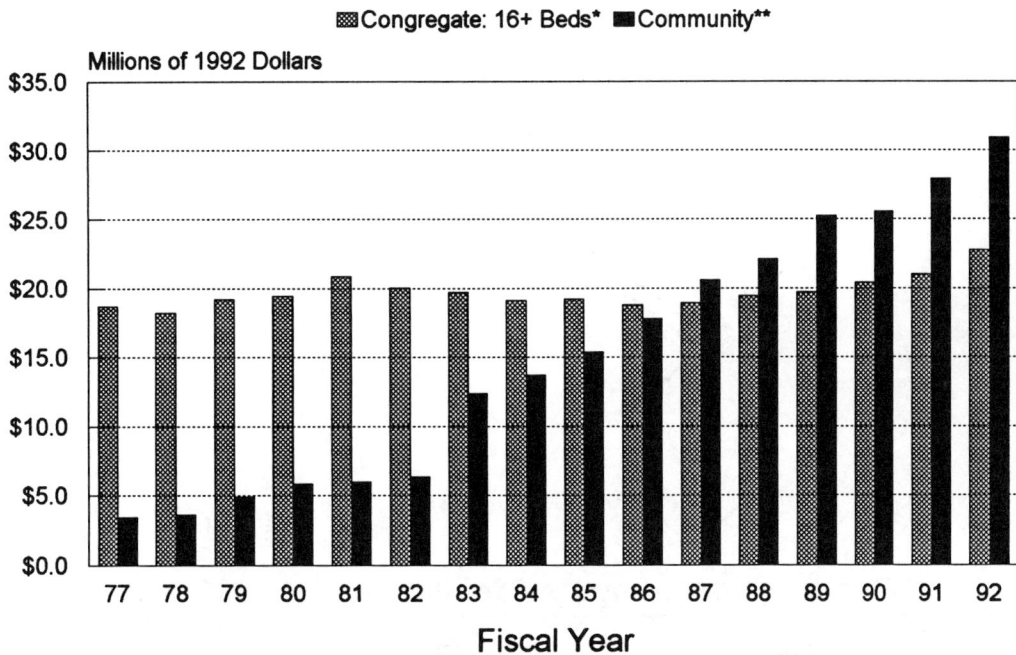

▨ Congregate: 16+ Beds*  ■ Community**

Millions of 1992 Dollars

Fiscal Year

*Excludes nursing homes; ** Includes resources for
15 bed or less residential settings & non-residential community services

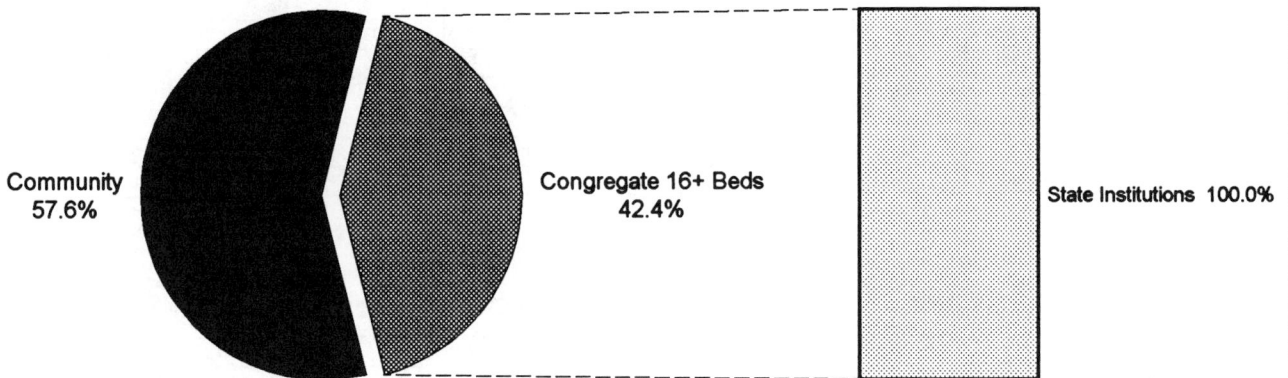

Community
57.6%

Congregate 16+ Beds
42.4%

State Institutions  100.0%

FY 1992 Total Spending:
$53.7 Million

Source:
Institute on Disability and Human Development (UAP),
University of Illinois at Chicago, 1994

# SOUTH DAKOTA

## Number of Persons Served by Residential Setting: FY 1992

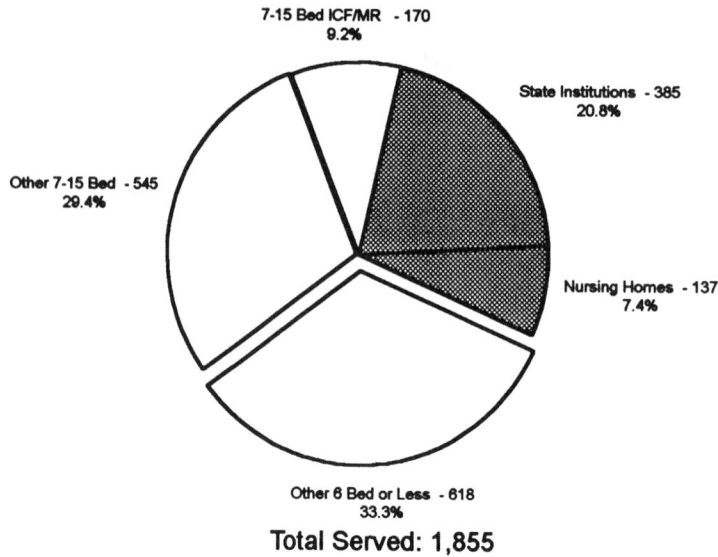

7-15 Bed ICF/MR  - 170
9.2%

State Institutions  - 385
20.8%

Other 7-15 Bed  - 545
29.4%

Nursing Homes  - 137
7.4%

Other 6 Bed or Less  - 618
33.3%

Total Served: 1,855

## Persons Served by Residential Setting:1986-92

|  | 1986 | 1987 | 1988 | 1989 | 1990 | 1991 | 1992 |
|---|---|---|---|---|---|---|---|
| CONGREGATE 16 + BED SETTINGS | NA | NA | 585 | 563 | 532 | 517 | 522 |
| Nursing Homes | NA | NA | 145 | 143 | 141 | 139 | 137 |
| State Institutions | 519 | 491 | 440 | 420 | 391 | 378 | 385 |
| Private 16+Bed ICF/MR | 0 | 0 | 0 | 0 | 0 | 0 | 0 |
| Other 16+Bed Residential | 0 | 0 | 0 | 0 | 0 | 0 | 0 |
| 15 BED OR LESS RESIDENTIAL SETTINGS | 843 | 886 | 932 | 990 | 1,014 | 1,026 | 1,333 |
| Public 7-15 Bed ICF/MR | 0 | 0 | 0 | 0 | 0 | 0 | 0 |
| Private 7-15 Bed ICF/MR | 166 | 177 | 213 | 203 | 184 | 178 | 170 |
| Other 7-15 Bed Residential | 677 | 709 | 555 | 530 | 531 | 529 | 545 |
| Public 6 Bed or Less ICF/MR | 0 | 0 | 0 | 0 | 0 | 0 | 0 |
| Private 6 Bed or Less ICF/MR | 0 | 0 | 0 | 0 | 0 | 0 | 0 |
| Other 6 Bed or Less Residential |  |  | 164 | 257 | 299 | 319 | 618 |
| TOTAL PERSONS SERVED | NA | NA | 1,517 | 1,553 | 1,546 | 1,543 | 1,855 |

## Persons Served in Non-Residential Community Services:1986-92

|  | 1986 | 1987 | 1988 | 1989 | 1990 | 1991 | 1992 |
|---|---|---|---|---|---|---|---|
| DAY/WORK PROGRAMS | 1,166 | 1,208 | 1,250 | 1,291 | 1,288 | 1,302 | 1,301 |
| Sheltered Employment/Work Activity | 722 | 770 | 818 | 866 | 853 | 838 | 835 |
| Day Habilitation ("Day Training") | 383 | 328 | 273 | 217 | 167 | 150 | 127 |
| Supported/Competitive Employment | 61 | 110 | 159 | 208 | 268 | 314 | 339 |
| CASE MANAGEMENT | 1,280 | 1,336 | 1,382 | 1,448 | 1,513 | 1,593 | 1,648 |
| HCBS WAIVER | 577 | 621 | 684 | 769 | 819 | 880 | 945 |
| MODEL 50/200 WAIVER | 0 | 0 | 0 | 0 | 0 | 0 | 0 |

Source:
Institute on Disability and Human Development (UAP),
University of Illinois at Chicago, 1994

# SOUTH DAKOTA

## Community Services: FY 1992 Revenue Sources

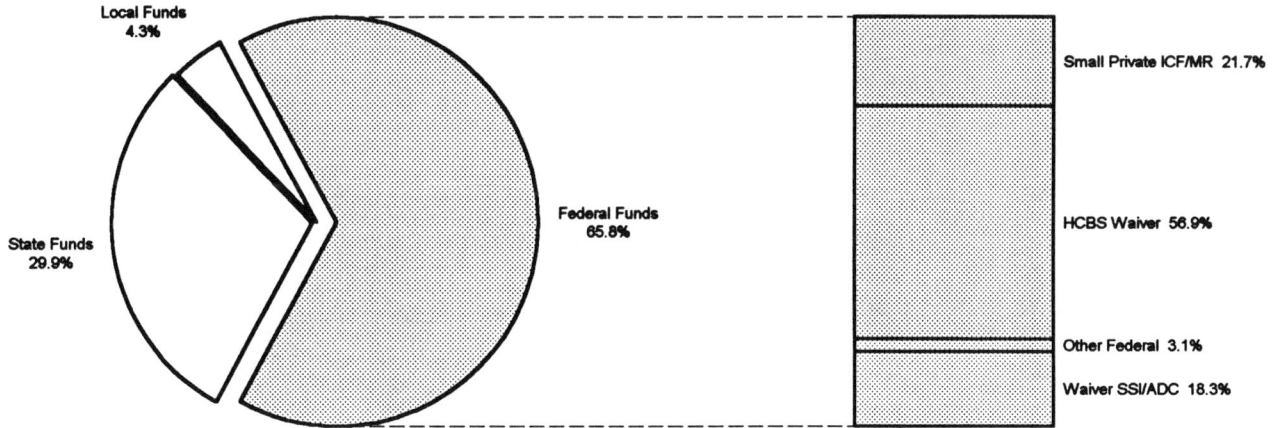

Local Funds 4.3%

State Funds 29.9%

Federal Funds 65.8%

Small Private ICF/MR 21.7%

HCBS Waiver 56.9%

Other Federal 3.1%

Waiver SSI/ADC 18.3%

Total Funds: $30.9 Million

## Family Support Initiatives*

|  | 1986 | 1987 | 1988 | 1989 | 1990 | 1991 | 1992 |
|---|---|---|---|---|---|---|---|
| **FAMILY SUPPORT: TOTAL SPENDING** | $0 | $0 | $0 | $0 | $52,034 | $51,648 | $33,686 |
| **Total # of Families Supported** | 0 | 0 | 0 | 0 | 6 | NA | NA |
| A. Financial Subsidy/Payment | $0 | $0 | $0 | $0 | $0 | $0 | $0 |
| # of Families | 0 | 0 | 0 | 0 | 0 | 0 | 0 |
| B. Family Assistance Payments | $0 | $0 | $0 | $0 | $0 | $0 | $33,686 |
| # of Families | 0 | 0 | 0 | 0 | 0 | 0 | NA |
| C. Other Family Support Payments | $0 | $0 | $0 | $0 | $52,034 | $51,648 | $0 |
| # of Families | 0 | 0 | 0 | 0 | 6 | NA | 0 |

## Other Community Services Initiatives*

|  | 1986 | 1987 | 1988 | 1989 | 1990 | 1991 | 1992 |
|---|---|---|---|---|---|---|---|
| **AGING/DD SPENDING** | $0 | $0 | $0 | $11,037 | $0 | $0 | $0 |
| # of Persons Served | 0 | 0 | 0 | 0 | 0 | 0 | 0 |
| **ASSISTIVE TECHNOLOGY SPENDING** |  |  |  |  |  |  | $0 |
| # of Persons Served |  |  |  |  |  |  | 0 |
| **EARLY INTERVENTION SPENDING** | $0 | $0 | $0 | $0 | $0 | $0 | $0 |
| # of Persons Served | 0 | 0 | 0 | 0 | 0 | 0 | 0 |
| **PERSONAL ASSISTANCE SPENDING** |  |  |  |  |  |  | $0 |
| # of Persons Served |  |  |  |  |  |  | 0 |
| **SUPPORTED EMPLOYMENT SPENDING** | NA | $76,414 | NA | NA | NA | NA | NA |
| # of Persons Served | 61 | 110 | 159 | 208 | 268 | 314 | 339 |
| **SUPPORTED LIVING SPENDING** |  |  |  | $35,508 | $138,928 | $29,786 | $0 |
| # of Persons Served |  |  |  | 5 | 14 | 4 | 0 |

*Expenditures associated with Special Community Initiatives are a subset of funding within the community services component of the state's chart series and spreadsheet; Family Support Client figures may include duplicate client counts; HCBS Waiver counts include Waiver case management numbers.
0= Services not provided in the state; NA= Data not available from state; blank= Services not applicable (eg. CSLA prior to authorization, Special Community Initiatives prior to request for data by this study)

*Source:*
Institute on Disability and Human Development (UAP),
University of Illinois at Chicago, 1994

# SOUTH DAKOTA

## Large Congregate Care Facilities: FY 1992 Revenue Sources*

### Private 16+Bed Settings

### Public Institutions

**Does Not Apply**

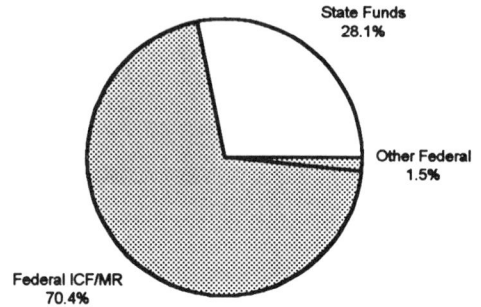

State Funds
28.1%

Other Federal
1.5%

Federal ICF/MR
70.4%

Total Funds: $22.7 Million

*Excludes nursing homes

## Average Daily Residents in Institutions

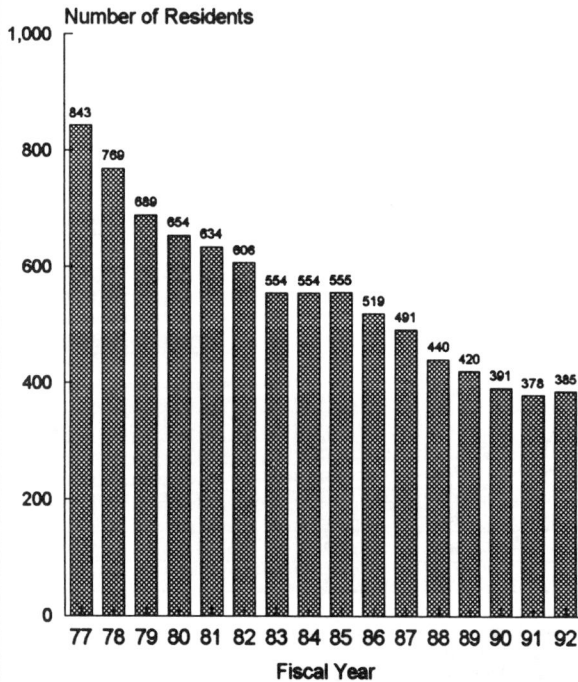

Number of Residents

| Fiscal Year | Residents |
|---|---|
| 77 | 843 |
| 78 | 769 |
| 79 | 689 |
| 80 | 654 |
| 81 | 634 |
| 82 | 606 |
| 83 | 554 |
| 84 | 554 |
| 85 | 555 |
| 86 | 519 |
| 87 | 491 |
| 88 | 440 |
| 89 | 420 |
| 90 | 391 |
| 91 | 378 |
| 92 | 385 |

## Institutional Daily Costs Per Resident

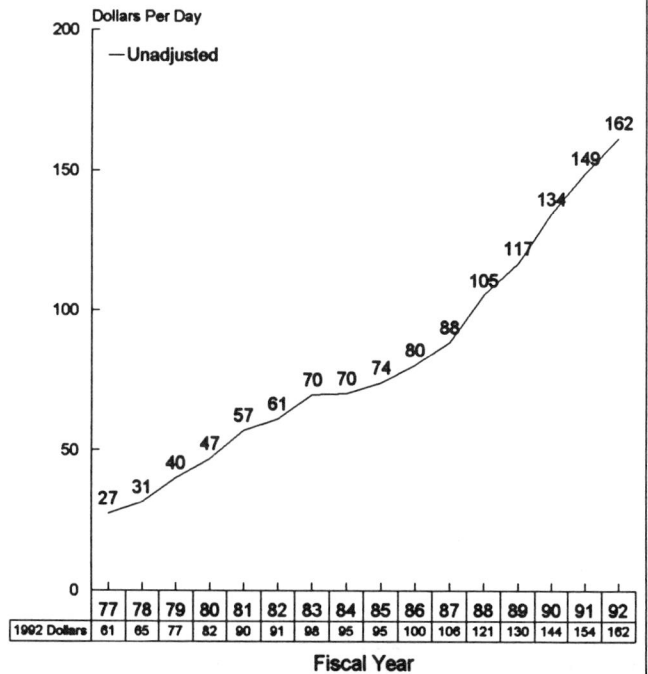

Dollars Per Day

—Unadjusted

| Fiscal Year | 77 | 78 | 79 | 80 | 81 | 82 | 83 | 84 | 85 | 86 | 87 | 88 | 89 | 90 | 91 | 92 |
|---|---|---|---|---|---|---|---|---|---|---|---|---|---|---|---|---|
| Unadjusted | 27 | 31 | 40 | 47 | 57 | 61 | 70 | 70 | 74 | 80 | 88 | 105 | 117 | 134 | 149 | 162 |
| 1992 Dollars | 61 | 65 | 77 | 82 | 90 | 91 | 98 | 95 | 95 | 100 | 106 | 121 | 130 | 144 | 154 | 162 |

Fiscal Year

*Source:*
Institute on Disability and Human Development (UAP),
University of Illinois at Chicago, 1994

# SOUTH DAKOTA FISCAL EFFORT

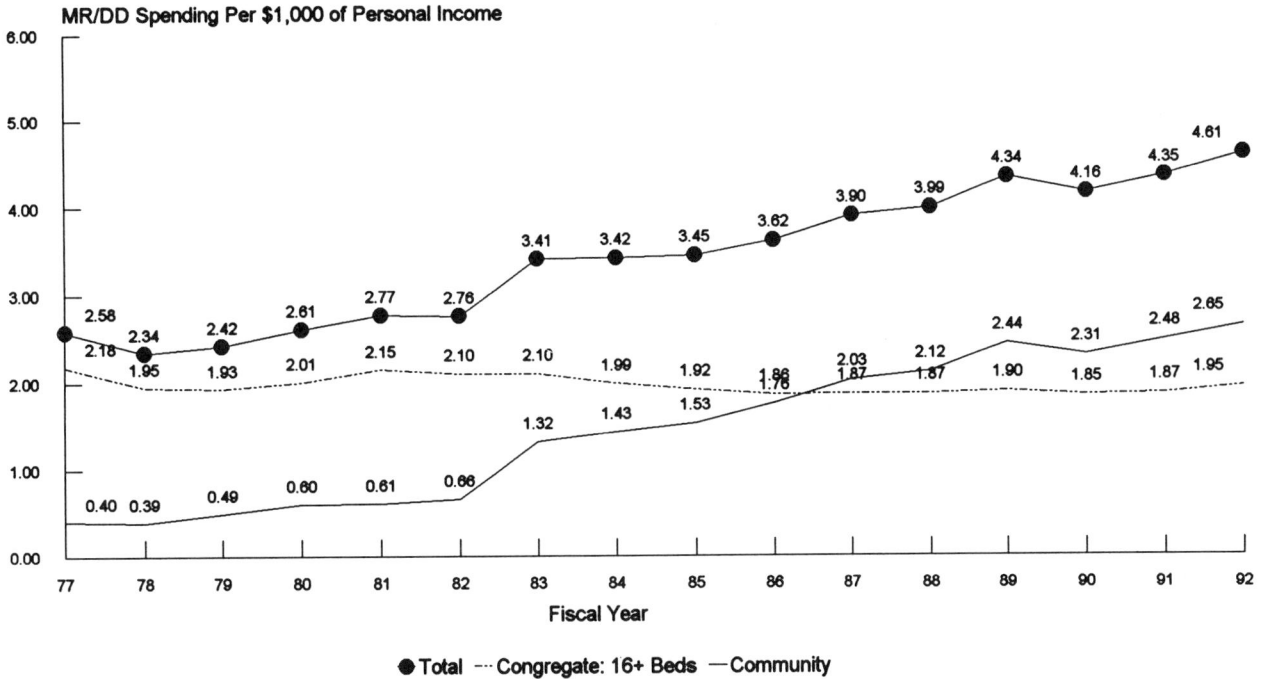

MR/DD Spending Per $1,000 of Personal Income

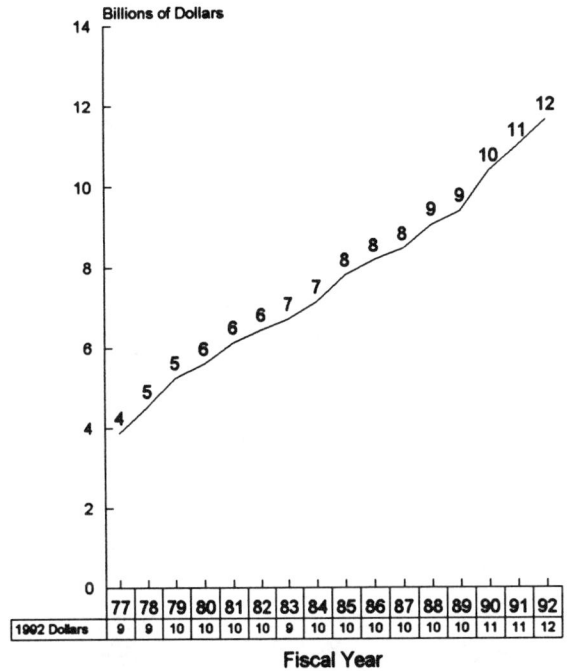

Total — Congregate: 16+ Beds — Community

Fiscal Year

Total line values: 2.58, 2.34, 2.42, 2.61, 2.77, 2.76, 3.41, 3.42, 3.45, 3.62, 3.90, 3.99, 4.34, 4.16, 4.35, 4.61

Congregate line values: 2.18, 1.95, 1.93, 2.01, 2.15, 2.10, 2.10, 1.99, 1.92, 1.86, 1.76, 2.03, 1.87, 2.12, 1.90, 1.85, 1.87, 1.95

Community line values: 0.40, 0.39, 0.49, 0.60, 0.61, 0.66, 1.32, 1.43, 1.53, 2.44, 2.31, 2.48, 2.65

## Total MR/DD Spending

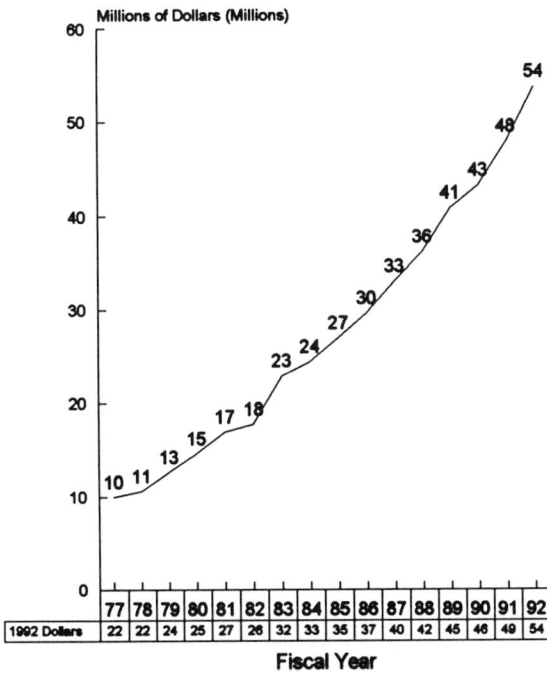

Millions of Dollars (Millions)

| 1992 Dollars | 77 | 78 | 79 | 80 | 81 | 82 | 83 | 84 | 85 | 86 | 87 | 88 | 89 | 90 | 91 | 92 |
|---|---|---|---|---|---|---|---|---|---|---|---|---|---|---|---|---|
| | 22 | 22 | 24 | 25 | 27 | 26 | 32 | 33 | 35 | 37 | 40 | 42 | 45 | 46 | 49 | 54 |

Values: 10, 11, 13, 15, 17, 18, 23, 24, 27, 30, 33, 36, 41, 43, 48, 54

Fiscal Year

## Personal Income

Billions of Dollars

| 1992 Dollars | 77 | 78 | 79 | 80 | 81 | 82 | 83 | 84 | 85 | 86 | 87 | 88 | 89 | 90 | 91 | 92 |
|---|---|---|---|---|---|---|---|---|---|---|---|---|---|---|---|---|
| | 9 | 9 | 10 | 10 | 10 | 10 | 9 | 10 | 10 | 10 | 10 | 10 | 10 | 11 | 11 | 12 |

Values: 4, 5, 5, 6, 6, 6, 7, 7, 8, 8, 8, 9, 9, 10, 11, 12

Fiscal Year

*Source:*
Institute on Disability and Human Development (UAP),
University of Illinois at Chicago, 1994

# SOUTH DAKOTA

## Financial Support for MR/DD Services: FY 1977-92

| | 1977 | 1978 | 1979 | 1980 | 1981 | 1982 | 1983 | 1984 |
|---|---|---|---|---|---|---|---|---|
| **TOTAL FUNDS** | $9,978,340 | $10,588,228 | $12,659,212 | $14,606,384 | $16,916,331 | $17,765,828 | $22,907,826 | $24,425,659 |
| **CONGREGATE 16+ BEDS** | 8,428,412 | 8,826,100 | 10,084,884 | 11,243,856 | 13,163,603 | 13,511,400 | 14,070,203 | 14,222,918 |
| INSTITUTIONAL SERVICES FUNDS | 8,428,412 | 8,826,100 | 10,084,884 | 11,243,856 | 13,163,603 | 13,511,400 | 14,070,203 | 14,222,918 |
| STATE FUNDS | 6,232,298 | 4,676,208 | 4,138,341 | 3,852,993 | 4,113,776 | 4,676,154 | 5,286,738 | 5,473,434 |
| General Funds | 6,047,794 | 4,575,708 | 3,985,901 | 3,770,955 | 3,959,194 | 4,519,647 | 5,133,258 | 5,321,988 |
| Local | 0 | 0 | 0 | 0 | 0 | 0 | 0 | 0 |
| Other State Funds | 184,504 | 100,500 | 152,440 | 82,038 | 154,582 | 156,507 | 153,480 | 151,446 |
| FEDERAL FUNDS | 2,196,114 | 4,149,892 | 5,946,543 | 7,390,863 | 9,049,827 | 8,835,246 | 8,783,465 | 8,749,484 |
| Federal ICF/MR | 2,054,114 | 4,007,892 | 5,804,543 | 7,248,863 | 8,907,827 | 8,693,246 | 8,591,465 | 8,361,484 |
| Title XX / SSBG Funds | 0 | 0 | 0 | 0 | 0 | 0 | 0 | 0 |
| Other Federal Funds | 142,000 | 142,000 | 142,000 | 142,000 | 142,000 | 142,000 | 192,000 | 388,000 |
| LARGE PRIVATE RESIDENTIAL | 0 | 0 | 0 | 0 | 0 | 0 | 0 | 0 |
| STATE FUNDS | 0 | 0 | 0 | 0 | 0 | 0 | 0 | 0 |
| General Funds | 0 | 0 | 0 | 0 | 0 | 0 | 0 | 0 |
| Other State Funds | 0 | 0 | 0 | 0 | 0 | 0 | 0 | 0 |
| Local/County Overmatch | 0 | 0 | 0 | 0 | 0 | 0 | 0 | 0 |
| FEDERAL FUNDS | 0 | 0 | 0 | 0 | 0 | 0 | 0 | 0 |
| Large Private ICF/MR | 0 | 0 | 0 | 0 | 0 | 0 | 0 | 0 |
| **COMMUNITY SERVICES FUNDS** | 1,549,928 | 1,762,128 | 2,574,328 | 3,362,528 | 3,752,728 | 4,254,428 | 8,837,623 | 10,202,741 |
| STATE FUNDS | 371,928 | 418,128 | 670,328 | 874,528 | 978,728 | 1,150,628 | 2,400,058 | 2,681,165 |
| General Funds | 321,000 | 368,000 | 616,000 | 815,000 | 919,000 | 1,090,700 | 1,214,400 | 1,425,900 |
| Other State Funds | 47,000 | 46,000 | 50,000 | 55,000 | 55,000 | 55,000 | 418,100 | 513,600 |
| Local/County Overmatch | 0 | 0 | 0 | 0 | 0 | 0 | 762,430 | 736,337 |
| SSI State Supplement | 3,928 | 4,128 | 4,328 | 4,528 | 4,728 | 4,928 | 5,128 | 5,328 |
| FEDERAL FUNDS | 1,178,000 | 1,344,000 | 1,904,000 | 2,488,000 | 2,774,000 | 3,103,800 | 6,437,565 | 7,521,576 |
| ICF/MR Funds | 0 | 0 | 203,000 | 653,000 | 911,000 | 1,095,100 | 1,393,000 | 1,425,600 |
| Small Public | 0 | 0 | 0 | 0 | 0 | 0 | 0 | 0 |
| Small Private | 0 | 0 | 203,000 | 653,000 | 911,000 | 1,095,100 | 1,393,000 | 1,425,600 |
| HCBS Waiver | 0 | 0 | 0 | 0 | 0 | 0 | 1,393,000 | 1,425,600 |
| Model 50/200 Waiver | 0 | 0 | 0 | 0 | 0 | 0 | 1,712,400 | 2,212,000 |
| Other Title XIX Programs | 0 | 0 | 0 | 0 | 0 | 0 | 0 | 0 |
| Title XX / SSBG Funds | 1,020,000 | 1,282,000 | 1,411,000 | 1,629,000 | 1,681,000 | 1,815,700 | 1,947,700 | 2,104,000 |
| Other Federal Funds | 158,000 | 62,000 | 290,000 | 206,000 | 182,000 | 193,000 | 194,000 | 195,100 |
| Waiver Clients' SSI/ADC | 0 | 0 | 0 | 0 | 0 | 0 | 1,190,465 | 1,584,876 |

| | 1985 | 1986 | 1987 | 1988 | 1989 | 1990 | 1991 | 1992 |
|---|---|---|---|---|---|---|---|---|
| **TOTAL FUNDS** | $26,947,271 | $29,618,122 | $33,053,048 | $36,189,326 | $40,809,137 | $43,236,377 | $47,888,241 | $53,713,689 |
| **CONGREGATE 16+ BEDS** | 14,977,747 | 15,220,980 | 15,846,081 | 16,948,473 | 17,888,222 | 19,193,585 | 20,567,825 | 22,772,901 |
| INSTITUTIONAL SERVICES FUNDS | 14,977,747 | 15,220,980 | 15,846,081 | 16,948,473 | 17,888,222 | 19,193,585 | 20,567,825 | 22,772,901 |
| STATE FUNDS | 5,734,623 | 5,230,732 | 5,846,020 | 5,722,037 | 5,741,349 | 5,737,387 | 6,241,582 | 6,394,285 |
| General Funds | 5,582,309 | 5,080,732 | 5,698,292 | 5,569,037 | 5,591,349 | 5,568,814 | 5,948,514 | 6,370,755 |
| Local | 0 | 0 | 0 | 0 | 0 | 0 | 0 | 0 |
| Other State Funds | 152,314 | 150,000 | 147,728 | 153,000 | 150,000 | 168,573 | 293,068 | 23,530 |
| FEDERAL FUNDS | 9,243,124 | 9,990,248 | 10,000,061 | 11,226,436 | 12,146,873 | 13,456,198 | 14,326,243 | 16,378,616 |
| Federal ICF/MR | 8,823,124 | 9,609,848 | 9,571,861 | 10,845,858 | 11,781,439 | 13,065,955 | 13,947,373 | 16,040,616 |
| Title XX / SSBG Funds | 0 | 0 | 0 | 0 | 0 | 0 | 0 | 0 |
| Other Federal Funds | 420,000 | 380,400 | 428,200 | 380,578 | 365,434 | 390,243 | 378,870 | 338,000 |
| LARGE PRIVATE RESIDENTIAL | 0 | 0 | 0 | 0 | 0 | 0 | 0 | 0 |
| STATE FUNDS | 0 | 0 | 0 | 0 | 0 | 0 | 0 | 0 |
| General Funds | 0 | 0 | 0 | 0 | 0 | 0 | 0 | 0 |
| Other State Funds | 0 | 0 | 0 | 0 | 0 | 0 | 0 | 0 |
| Local/County Overmatch | 0 | 0 | 0 | 0 | 0 | 0 | 0 | 0 |
| FEDERAL FUNDS | 0 | 0 | 0 | 0 | 0 | 0 | 0 | 0 |
| Large Private ICF/MR | 0 | 0 | 0 | 0 | 0 | 0 | 0 | 0 |
| **COMMUNITY SERVICES FUNDS** | 11,969,524 | 14,397,142 | 17,206,967 | 19,240,853 | 22,920,915 | 24,042,792 | 27,320,416 | 30,940,788 |
| STATE FUNDS | 2,949,324 | 3,563,178 | 4,564,787 | 5,610,848 | 6,409,336 | 8,567,047 | 9,509,381 | 10,587,495 |
| General Funds | 1,648,300 | 2,233,418 | 2,875,400 | 3,872,234 | 4,541,520 | 6,922,144 | 7,615,202 | 8,521,201 |
| Other State Funds | 523,100 | 494,300 | 584,900 | 582,998 | 429,328 | 596,655 | 672,018 | 733,250 |
| Local/County Overmatch | 772,396 | 829,732 | 1,098,559 | 1,149,488 | 1,432,014 | 1,041,425 | 1,215,172 | 1,325,880 |
| SSI State Supplement | 5,528 | 5,728 | 5,928 | 6,128 | 6,474 | 6,823 | 6,989 | 7,164 |
| FEDERAL FUNDS | 9,020,200 | 10,833,964 | 12,642,180 | 13,630,005 | 16,511,579 | 15,475,745 | 17,811,035 | 20,353,293 |
| ICF/MR Funds | 1,567,200 | 2,192,800 | 3,058,600 | 3,696,752 | 3,721,320 | 3,775,570 | 4,000,421 | 4,407,525 |
| Small Public | 0 | 0 | 0 | 0 | 0 | 0 | 0 | 0 |
| Small Private | 1,567,200 | 2,192,800 | 3,058,600 | 3,696,752 | 3,721,320 | 3,775,570 | 4,000,421 | 4,407,525 |
| HCBS Waiver | 2,891,500 | 3,448,300 | 4,173,200 | 4,843,010 | 6,541,130 | 7,713,309 | 9,530,354 | 11,584,315 |
| Model 50/200 Waiver | 0 | 0 | 0 | 0 | 0 | 0 | 0 | 0 |
| Other Title XIX Programs | 0 | 0 | 0 | 0 | 0 | 0 | 0 | 0 |
| Title XX / SSBG Funds | 2,322,500 | 2,647,000 | 2,572,800 | 1,904,723 | 2,672,674 | 0 | 0 | 0 |
| Other Federal Funds | 356,200 | 392,500 | 490,200 | 600,000 | 614,267 | 694,486 | 552,580 | 633,077 |
| Waiver Clients' SSI/ADC | 1,882,800 | 2,153,364 | 2,347,380 | 2,585,520 | 2,962,188 | 3,292,380 | 3,727,680 | 3,728,376 |

*Source:*
Institute on Disability and Human Development (UAP),
University of Illinois at Chicago, 1994

# TENNESSEE

## MR/DD Spending for Congregate Residential & Community Services

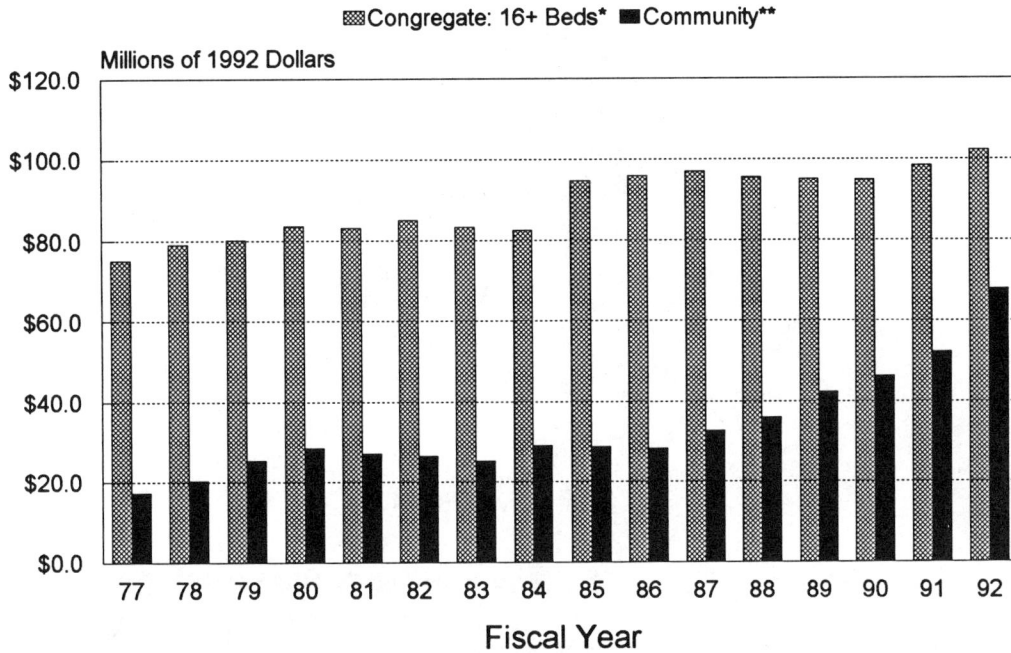

▨ Congregate: 16+ Beds*  ■ Community**

Millions of 1992 Dollars

Fiscal Year

*Excludes nursing homes; ** Includes resources for
15 bed or less residential settings & non-residential community services

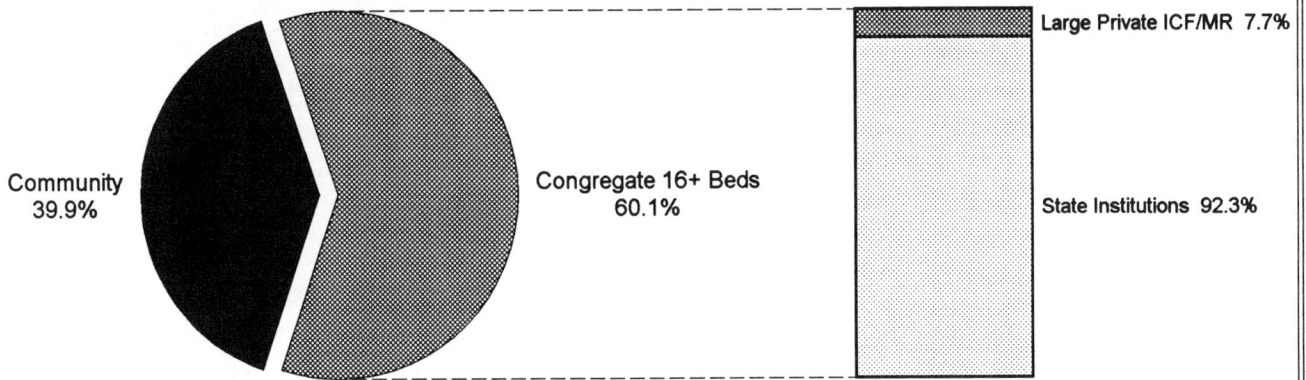

Community
39.9%

Congregate 16+ Beds
60.1%

Large Private ICF/MR  7.7%

State Institutions  92.3%

FY 1992 Total Spending:
$170.1 Million

*Source:*
Institute on Disability and Human Development (UAP),
University of Illinois at Chicago, 1994

# TENNESSEE

## Number of Persons Served by Residential Setting: FY 1992

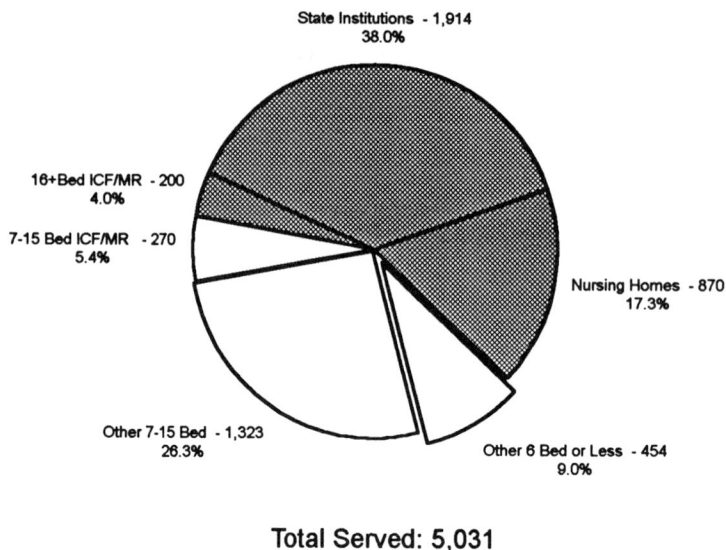

State Institutions - 1,914
38.0%

16+Bed ICF/MR - 200
4.0%

7-15 Bed ICF/MR - 270
5.4%

Nursing Homes - 870
17.3%

Other 7-15 Bed - 1,323
26.3%

Other 6 Bed or Less - 454
9.0%

Total Served: 5,031

## Persons Served by Residential Setting:1986-92

| | 1986 | 1987 | 1988 | 1989 | 1990 | 1991 | 1992 |
|---|---|---|---|---|---|---|---|
| CONGREGATE 16 + BED SETTINGS | NA | NA | 3,142 | NA | NA | 3,076 | 2,984 |
| Nursing Homes | NA | NA | 930 | NA | NA | 870 | 870 |
| State Institutions | 2,121 | 2,090 | 2,024 | 1,978 | 1,947 | 1,930 | 1,914 |
| Private 16+Bed ICF/MR | 188 | 188 | 188 | 264 | 284 | 276 | 200 |
| Other 16+Bed Residential | 0 | 0 | 0 | 0 | 0 | 0 | 0 |
| 15 BED OR LESS RESIDENTIAL SETTINGS | 1,155 | 1,176 | 1,492 | 1,707 | 1,792 | 1,969 | 2,047 |
| Public 7-15 Bed ICF/MR | 0 | 0 | 0 | 0 | 0 | 0 | 0 |
| Private 7-15 Bed ICF/MR | 94 | 12 | 12 | 14 | 30 | 182 | 270 |
| Other 7-15 Bed Residential | 1,061 | 1,164 | 1,184 | 1,291 | 1,301 | 1,307 | 1,323 |
| Public 6 Bed or Less ICF/MR | 0 | 0 | 0 | 0 | 0 | 0 | 0 |
| Private 6 Bed or Less ICF/MR | 0 | 0 | 0 | 0 | 0 | 0 | 0 |
| Other 6 Bed or Less Residential | NA | NA | 296 | 402 | 461 | 480 | 454 |
| TOTAL PERSONS SERVED | NA | NA | 4,634 | NA | NA | 5,045 | 5,031 |

## Persons Served in Non-Residential Community Services:1986-92

| | 1986 | 1987 | 1988 | 1989 | 1990 | 1991 | 1992 |
|---|---|---|---|---|---|---|---|
| DAY/WORK PROGRAMS | 2,827 | 3,161 | 3,252 | 3,390 | 3,458 | 3,462 | 3,644 |
| Sheltered Employment/Work Activity | NA | NA | NA | NA | NA | NA | NA |
| Day Habilitation ("Day Training") | NA | NA | 2,973 | 3,131 | 3,140 | 3,140 | 3,219 |
| Supported/Competitive Employment | 279 | 279 | 279 | 259 | 318 | 322 | 425 |
| CASE MANAGEMENT | NA | NA | 360 | 420 | 506 | 524 | 630 |
| HCBS WAIVER | 0 | 250 | 360 | 420 | 506 | 524 | 630 |
| MODEL 50/200 WAIVER | 0 | 50 | 50 | 52 | 42 | 56 | 96 |

Source:
Institute on Disability and Human Development (UAP),
University of Illinois at Chicago, 1994

# TENNESSEE

## Community Services: FY 1992 Revenue Sources

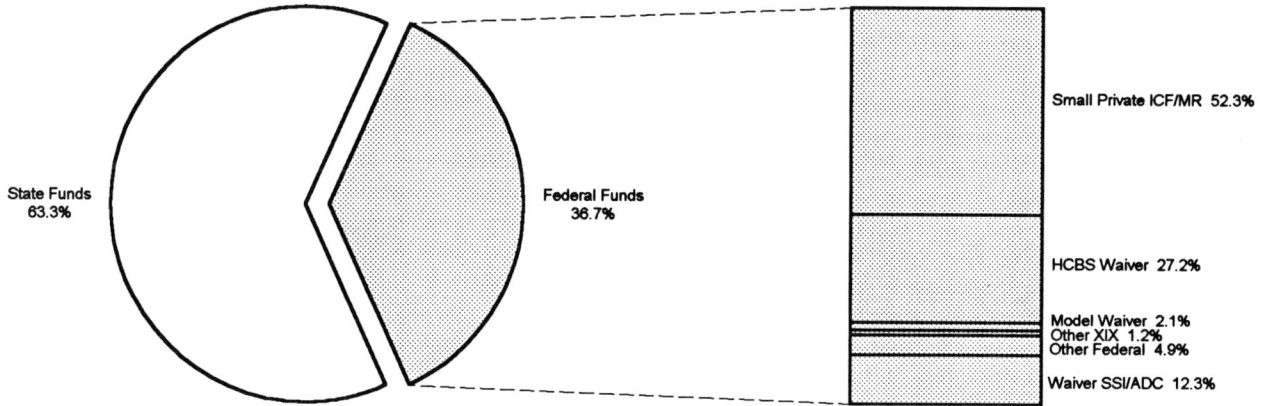

State Funds
63.3%

Federal Funds
36.7%

Small Private ICF/MR  52.3%

HCBS Waiver  27.2%

Model Waiver  2.1%
Other XIX  1.2%
Other Federal  4.9%

Waiver SSI/ADC  12.3%

Total Funds: $67.9 Million

## Family Support Initiatives*

|  | 1986 | 1987 | 1988 | 1989 | 1990 | 1991 | 1992 |
|---|---|---|---|---|---|---|---|
| **FAMILY SUPPORT: TOTAL SPENDING** | $90,976 | $110,108 | $104,860 | $221,200 | $330,352 | $559,620 | $643,470 |
| **Total # of Families Supported** | 85 | 232 | 357 | 569 | 642 | 905 | 875 |
| A. Financial Subsidy/Payment | $0 | $0 | $0 | $0 | $0 | $0 | $0 |
| # of Families | 0 | 0 | 0 | 0 | 0 | 0 | 0 |
| B. Family Assistance Payments | $90,976 | $110,108 | $104,860 | $112,200 | $157,852 | $153,720 | $165,810 |
| # of Families | 85 | 232 | 357 | 528 | 504 | 516 | 456 |
| C. Other Family Support Payments | $0 | $0 | $0 | $109,000 | $172,500 | $405,900 | $477,660 |
| # of Families | 0 | 0 | 0 | 41 | 138 | 389 | 419 |

## Other Community Services Initiatives*

|  | 1986 | 1987 | 1988 | 1989 | 1990 | 1991 | 1992 |
|---|---|---|---|---|---|---|---|
| **AGING/DD SPENDING** | $0 | $0 | $0 | $0 | $0 | $0 | $0 |
| # of Persons Served | 0 | 0 | 0 | 0 | 0 | 0 | 0 |
| **ASSISTIVE TECHNOLOGY SPENDING** |  |  |  | $0 | $0 | $305,400 | $608,300 |
| # of Persons Served |  |  |  | 0 | 0 | NA | 1,827 |
| **EARLY INTERVENTION SPENDING** | $3,219,370 | $3,771,762 | $3,273,903 | $3,698,329 | $4,202,617 | $4,524,561 | $4,511,658 |
| # of Persons Served | 1,334 | 1,376 | 1,218 | 1,225 | 1,234 | 1,219 | 1,117 |
| **PERSONAL ASSISTANCE SPENDING** |  |  |  | $0 | $0 | $0 | $0 |
| # of Persons Served |  |  |  | 0 | 0 | 0 | 0 |
| **SUPPORTED EMPLOYMENT SPENDING** | $1,186,842 | $1,216,021 | $1,243,229 | $1,089,527 | $1,061,751 | $1,084,800 | $1,283,800 |
| # of Persons Served | 279 | 279 | 279 | 259 | 318 | 322 | 425 |
| **SUPPORTED LIVING SPENDING** |  |  |  | $0 | $0 | $0 | $0 |
| # of Persons Served |  |  |  | 0 | 0 | 0 | 0 |

*Expenditures associated with Special Community Initiatives are a subset of funding within the community services component of the state's chart series and spreadsheet; Family Support Client figures may include duplicate client counts; HCBS Waiver counts include Waiver case management numbers.
0= Services not provided in the state; NA= Data not available from state; blank= Services not applicable (eg. CSLA prior to authorization, Special Community Initiatives prior to request for data by this study)

*Source:*
Institute on Disability and Human Development (UAP),
University of Illinois at Chicago, 1994

# TENNESSEE

## Large Congregate Care Facilities: FY 1992 Revenue Sources*

### Private 16+Bed Settings

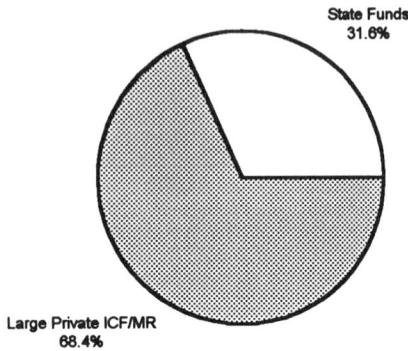

State Funds
31.6%

Large Private ICF/MR
68.4%

Total Funds: $7.8 Million

### Public Institutions

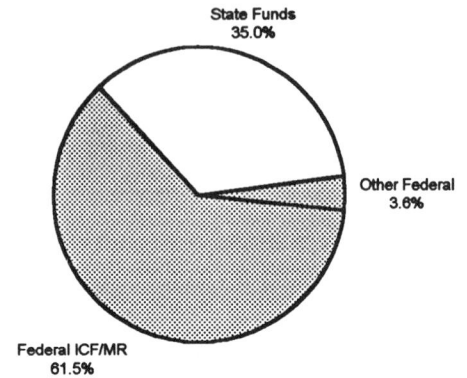

State Funds
35.0%

Other Federal
3.6%

Federal ICF/MR
61.5%

Total Funds: $94.4 Million

**\*Excludes nursing homes**

## Average Daily Residents in Institutions

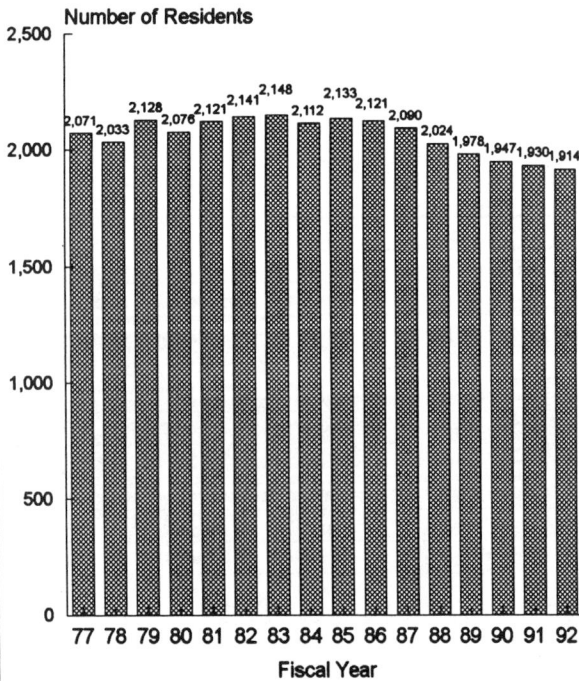

Number of Residents

| | |
|---|---|
| 77 | 2,071 |
| 78 | 2,033 |
| 79 | 2,128 |
| 80 | 2,076 |
| 81 | 2,121 |
| 82 | 2,141 |
| 83 | 2,148 |
| 84 | 2,112 |
| 85 | 2,133 |
| 86 | 2,121 |
| 87 | 2,090 |
| 88 | 2,024 |
| 89 | 1,978 |
| 90 | 1,947 |
| 91 | 1,930 |
| 92 | 1,914 |

Fiscal Year

## Institutional Daily Costs Per Resident

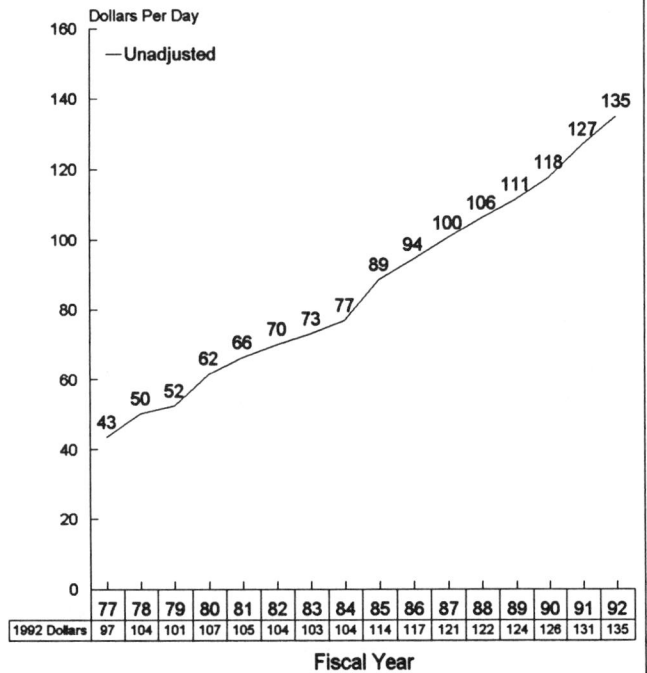

Dollars Per Day

—Unadjusted

43  50  52  62  66  70  73  77  89  94  100  106  111  118  127  135

| Fiscal Year | 77 | 78 | 79 | 80 | 81 | 82 | 83 | 84 | 85 | 86 | 87 | 88 | 89 | 90 | 91 | 92 |
|---|---|---|---|---|---|---|---|---|---|---|---|---|---|---|---|---|
| 1992 Dollars | 97 | 104 | 101 | 107 | 105 | 104 | 103 | 104 | 114 | 117 | 121 | 122 | 124 | 126 | 131 | 135 |

Fiscal Year

*Source:*
Institute on Disability and Human Development (UAP),
University of Illinois at Chicago, 1994

# TENNESSEE FISCAL EFFORT

**MR/DD Spending Per $1,000 of Personal Income**

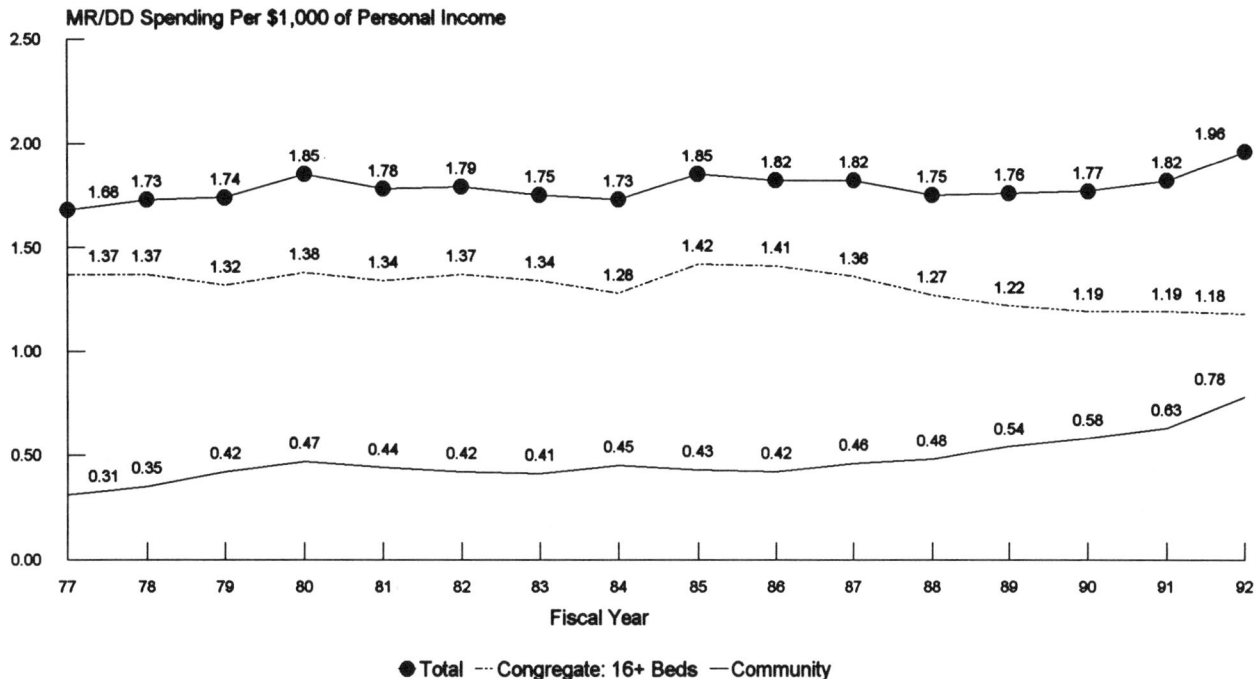

● Total  --- Congregate: 16+ Beds  — Community

## Total MR/DD Spending

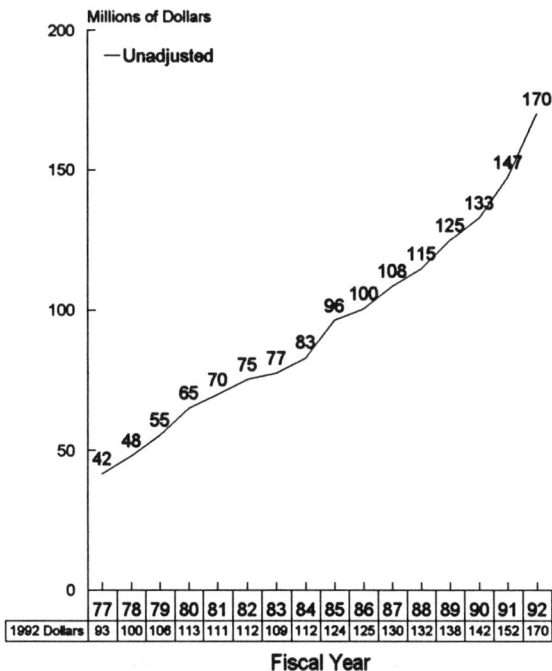

## Personal Income

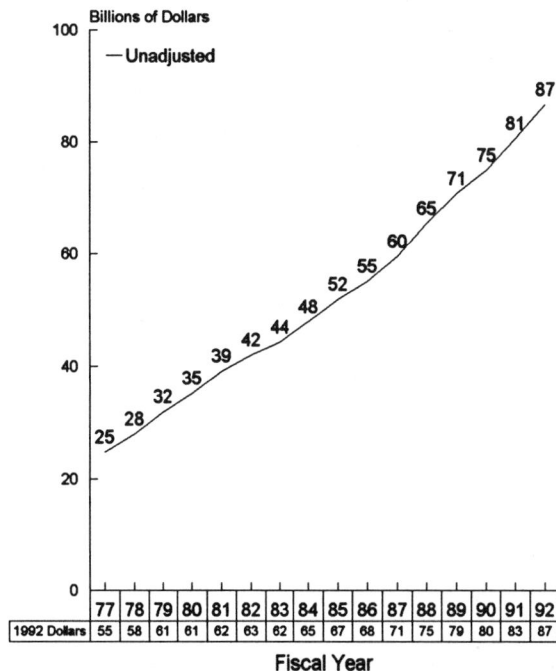

*Source:*
Institute on Disability and Human Development (UAP),
University of Illinois at Chicago, 1994

# TENNESSEE
## Financial Support for MR/DD Services: FY 1977-92

| | 1977 | 1978 | 1979 | 1980 | 1981 | 1982 | 1983 | 1984 |
|---|---|---|---|---|---|---|---|---|
| **TOTAL FUNDS** | $41,645,000 | $48,144,000 | $55,293,000 | $64,848,000 | $69,578,000 | $75,150,000 | $77,377,000 | $82,946,400 |
| **CONGREGATE 16+ BEDS** | 33,847,994 | 38,319,840 | 42,000,235 | 48,393,769 | 52,487,202 | 57,363,157 | 59,431,680 | 61,331,698 |
| INSTITUTIONAL SERVICES FUNDS | 32,847,000 | 37,253,000 | 40,682,000 | 46,825,000 | 51,322,000 | 54,693,000 | 57,202,000 | 59,369,200 |
| STATE FUNDS | 13,895,000 | 16,537,000 | 15,003,000 | 17,553,314 | 16,097,196 | 17,972,923 | 20,635,776 | 19,308,294 |
| General Funds | 6,199,000 | 7,413,000 | 3,516,000 | 5,006,000 | 1,080,000 | 1,501,000 | 2,076,000 | 1,267,600 |
| Local | 0 | 0 | 0 | 0 | 0 | 0 | 0 | 0 |
| Other State Funds | 7,696,000 | 9,124,000 | 11,487,000 | 12,547,314 | 15,017,196 | 16,471,923 | 18,559,776 | 18,040,694 |
| FEDERAL FUNDS | 18,952,000 | 20,716,000 | 25,679,000 | 29,271,686 | 35,224,804 | 36,720,077 | 36,566,224 | 40,060,906 |
| Federal ICF/MR | 18,329,000 | 20,192,000 | 25,423,000 | 28,934,000 | 34,883,000 | 36,452,000 | 36,291,000 | 39,798,300 |
| Title XX / SSBG Funds | 0 | 0 | 0 | 0 | 0 | 0 | 0 | 0 |
| Other Federal Funds | 623,000 | 524,000 | 256,000 | 337,686 | 341,804 | 268,077 | 275,224 | 262,606 |
| LARGE PRIVATE RESIDENTIAL | 1,000,994 | 1,066,840 | 1,318,235 | 1,568,769 | 1,165,202 | 2,670,157 | 2,229,680 | 1,962,498 |
| STATE FUNDS | 295,994 | 327,840 | 410,235 | 481,769 | 356,202 | 834,157 | 701,680 | 586,198 |
| General Funds | 0 | 0 | 0 | 0 | 0 | 0 | 0 | 0 |
| Other State Funds | 295,994 | 327,840 | 410,235 | 481,769 | 356,202 | 834,157 | 701,680 | 586,198 |
| Local/County Overmatch | 0 | 0 | 0 | 0 | 0 | 0 | 0 | 0 |
| FEDERAL FUNDS | 705,000 | 739,000 | 908,000 | 1,087,000 | 809,000 | 1,836,000 | 1,528,000 | 1,376,300 |
| Large Private ICF/MR | 705,000 | 739,000 | 908,000 | 1,087,000 | 809,000 | 1,836,000 | 1,528,000 | 1,376,300 |
| **COMMUNITY SERVICES FUNDS** | 7,797,006 | 9,824,160 | 13,292,765 | 16,454,231 | 17,090,798 | 17,786,843 | 17,945,320 | 21,614,702 |
| STATE FUNDS | 3,957,006 | 5,316,160 | 7,039,765 | 8,810,231 | 9,067,798 | 9,235,843 | 9,430,320 | 11,692,002 |
| General Funds | 3,454,006 | 4,981,160 | 6,628,765 | 8,330,231 | 8,710,798 | 8,243,843 | 8,625,320 | 10,930,102 |
| Other State Funds | 503,000 | 335,000 | 411,000 | 480,000 | 357,000 | 992,000 | 805,000 | 761,900 |
| Local/County Overmatch | 0 | 0 | 0 | 0 | 0 | 0 | 0 | 0 |
| SSI State Supplement | 0 | 0 | 0 | 0 | 0 | 0 | 0 | 0 |
| FEDERAL FUNDS | 3,840,000 | 4,508,000 | 6,253,000 | 7,644,000 | 8,023,000 | 8,551,000 | 8,515,000 | 9,922,700 |
| ICF/MR Funds | 0 | 0 | 0 | 0 | 383,000 | 1,046,000 | 1,303,000 | 1,501,100 |
| Small Public | 0 | 0 | 0 | 0 | 0 | 0 | 0 | 0 |
| Small Private | 0 | 0 | 0 | 0 | 383,000 | 1,046,000 | 1,303,000 | 1,501,100 |
| HCBS Waiver | 0 | 0 | 0 | 0 | 0 | 0 | 0 | 0 |
| Model 50/200 Waiver | 0 | 0 | 0 | 0 | 0 | 0 | 0 | 0 |
| Other Title XIX Programs | 0 | 0 | 0 | 0 | 0 | 0 | 0 | 0 |
| Title XX / SSBG Funds | 3,366,000 | 4,072,000 | 5,809,000 | 6,875,000 | 7,109,000 | 6,795,000 | 6,228,000 | 7,488,000 |
| Other Federal Funds | 474,000 | 436,000 | 444,000 | 769,000 | 531,000 | 710,000 | 984,000 | 933,600 |
| Waiver Clients' SSI/ADC | 0 | 0 | 0 | 0 | 0 | 0 | 0 | 0 |

| | 1985 | 1986 | 1987 | 1988 | 1989 | 1990 | 1991 | 1992 |
|---|---|---|---|---|---|---|---|---|
| **TOTAL FUNDS** | $96,206,700 | $100,487,657 | $108,441,174 | $114,610,034 | $124,694,005 | $132,774,295 | $147,227,124 | $170,149,693 |
| **CONGREGATE 16+ BEDS** | 73,797,594 | 77,554,677 | 81,097,141 | 83,274,785 | 86,290,714 | 89,365,877 | 96,229,205 | 102,266,641 |
| INSTITUTIONAL SERVICES FUNDS | 68,898,500 | 73,039,077 | 76,609,910 | 78,576,910 | 80,413,191 | 83,563,912 | 89,399,138 | 94,438,400 |
| STATE FUNDS | 28,781,695 | 24,171,231 | 23,762,033 | 25,377,023 | 25,117,362 | 26,964,407 | 28,837,989 | 33,012,266 |
| General Funds | 9,534,100 | 3,807,672 | 239,424 | 3,521,638 | 2,267,587 | 2,992,959 | 2,321,372 | 5,604,600 |
| Local | 0 | 0 | 0 | 654,101 | 572,246 | 676,287 | 607,377 | 559,100 |
| Other State Funds | 19,247,595 | 20,363,559 | 23,522,609 | 21,201,284 | 22,277,529 | 23,295,161 | 25,909,240 | 26,848,566 |
| FEDERAL FUNDS | 40,116,805 | 48,867,846 | 52,847,877 | 53,199,887 | 55,295,829 | 56,599,505 | 60,561,149 | 61,426,134 |
| Federal ICF/MR | 39,920,100 | 46,465,046 | 51,290,177 | 50,608,220 | 52,542,902 | 53,613,985 | 57,089,671 | 58,039,734 |
| Title XX / SSBG Funds | 0 | 0 | 0 | 0 | 0 | 0 | 0 | 0 |
| Other Federal Funds | 196,705 | 2,402,800 | 1,557,700 | 2,591,667 | 2,752,927 | 2,985,520 | 3,471,478 | 3,386,400 |
| LARGE PRIVATE RESIDENTIAL | 4,899,094 | 4,515,600 | 4,487,231 | 4,697,875 | 5,877,523 | 5,801,965 | 6,830,067 | 7,828,241 |
| STATE FUNDS | 1,437,394 | 1,340,230 | 1,334,951 | 1,383,524 | 1,746,213 | 1,753,935 | 2,128,249 | 2,469,811 |
| General Funds | 0 | 0 | 0 | 0 | 0 | 0 | 0 | 0 |
| Other State Funds | 1,437,394 | 1,340,230 | 1,334,951 | 1,383,524 | 1,746,213 | 1,753,935 | 2,128,249 | 2,469,811 |
| Local/County Overmatch | 0 | 0 | 0 | 0 | 0 | 0 | 0 | 0 |
| FEDERAL FUNDS | 3,461,700 | 3,175,370 | 3,152,280 | 3,314,351 | 4,131,310 | 4,048,030 | 4,701,818 | 5,358,430 |
| Large Private ICF/MR | 3,461,700 | 3,175,370 | 3,152,280 | 3,314,351 | 4,131,310 | 4,048,030 | 4,701,818 | 5,358,430 |
| **COMMUNITY SERVICES FUNDS** | 22,409,106 | 22,932,980 | 27,344,033 | 31,335,249 | 38,403,291 | 43,408,418 | 50,997,919 | 67,883,052 |
| STATE FUNDS | 12,366,706 | 20,714,542 | 23,683,569 | 24,992,108 | 30,611,064 | 33,884,512 | 36,771,359 | 42,958,190 |
| General Funds | 10,828,606 | 20,123,357 | 23,399,516 | 24,582,052 | 30,207,311 | 33,252,351 | 34,105,653 | 35,412,768 |
| Other State Funds | 1,538,100 | 591,185 | 284,053 | 410,056 | 403,753 | 632,161 | 2,665,706 | 7,545,422 |
| Local/County Overmatch | 0 | 0 | 0 | 0 | 0 | 0 | 0 | 0 |
| SSI State Supplement | 0 | 0 | 0 | 0 | 0 | 0 | 0 | 0 |
| FEDERAL FUNDS | 10,042,400 | 2,218,438 | 3,660,464 | 6,343,141 | 7,792,227 | 9,523,906 | 14,226,560 | 24,924,862 |
| ICF/MR Funds | 1,562,200 | 1,157,948 | 257,016 | 222,343 | 238,075 | 302,220 | 4,396,538 | 13,027,874 |
| Small Public | 0 | 0 | 0 | 0 | 0 | 0 | 0 | 0 |
| Small Private | 1,562,200 | 1,157,948 | 257,016 | 222,343 | 238,075 | 302,220 | 4,396,538 | 13,027,874 |
| HCBS Waiver | 0 | 0 | 1,127,720 | 3,010,733 | 4,123,216 | 5,156,489 | 5,830,723 | 6,776,723 |
| Model 50/200 Waiver | 0 | 0 | 174,112 | 451,931 | 467,066 | 374,773 | 325,122 | 515,154 |
| Other Title XIX Programs | 0 | 0 | 0 | 0 | 13,495 | 307,682 | 321,298 | 309,802 |
| Title XX / SSBG Funds | 7,488,000 | 0 | 0 | 0 | 0 | 0 | 0 | 0 |
| Other Federal Funds | 992,200 | 1,060,490 | 1,156,616 | 1,258,454 | 1,226,695 | 1,148,246 | 950,863 | 1,218,389 |
| Waiver Clients' SSI/ADC | 0 | 0 | 945,000 | 1,399,680 | 1,723,680 | 2,234,496 | 2,402,016 | 3,076,920 |

*Source:*
Institute on Disability and Human Development (UAP),
University of Illinois at Chicago, 1994

# TEXAS

## MR/DD Spending for Congregate Residential & Community Services

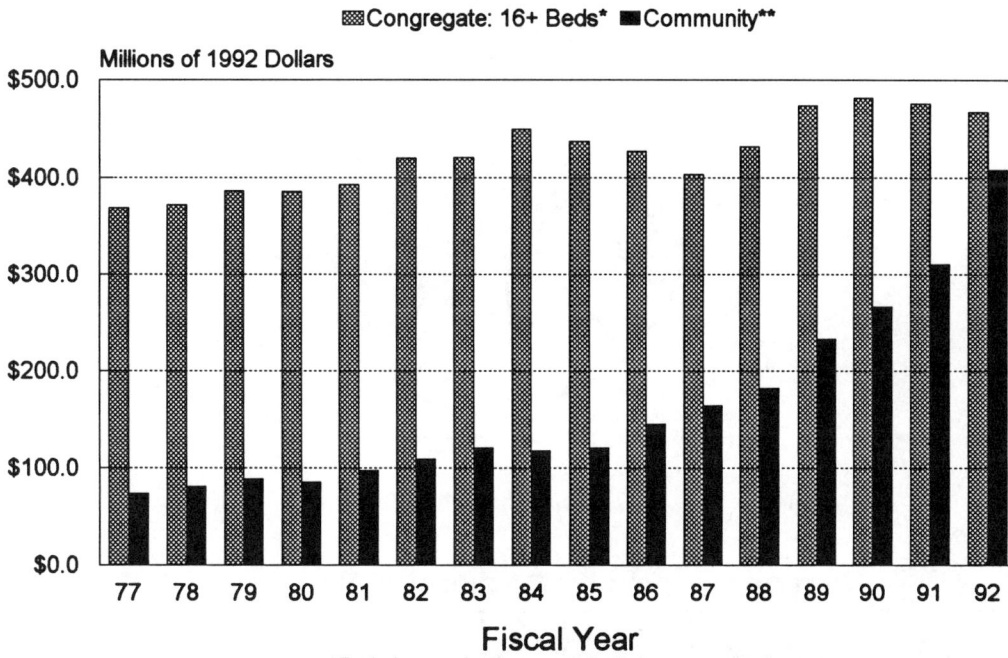

▨Congregate: 16+ Beds*  ■Community**

Millions of 1992 Dollars

Fiscal Year

*Excludes nursing homes; ** Includes resources for
15 bed or less residential settings & non-residential community services

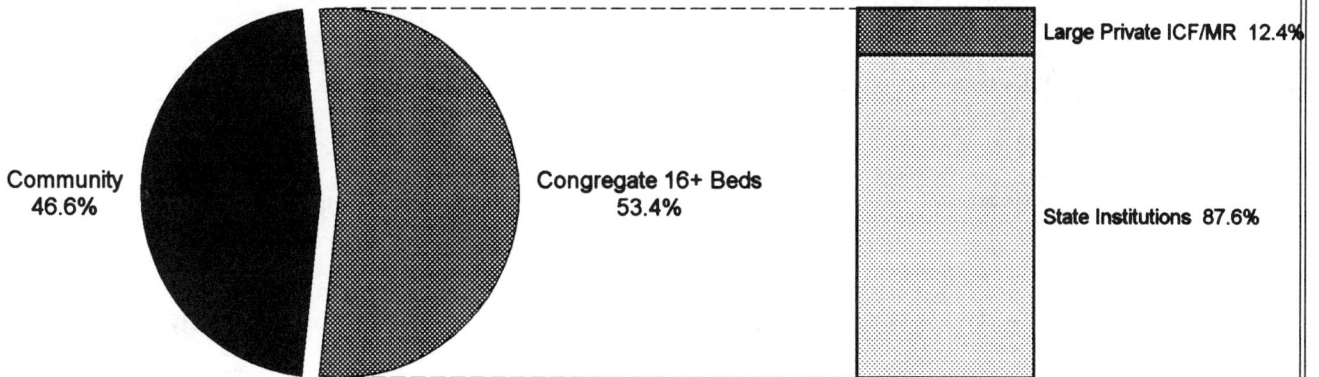

Community
46.6%

Congregate 16+ Beds
53.4%

Large Private ICF/MR  12.4%

State Institutions  87.6%

FY 1992 Total Spending:
$875.8 Million

*Source:*
Institute on Disability and Human Development (UAP),
University of Illinois at Chicago, 1994

# TEXAS

## Number of Persons Served by Residential Setting: FY 1992

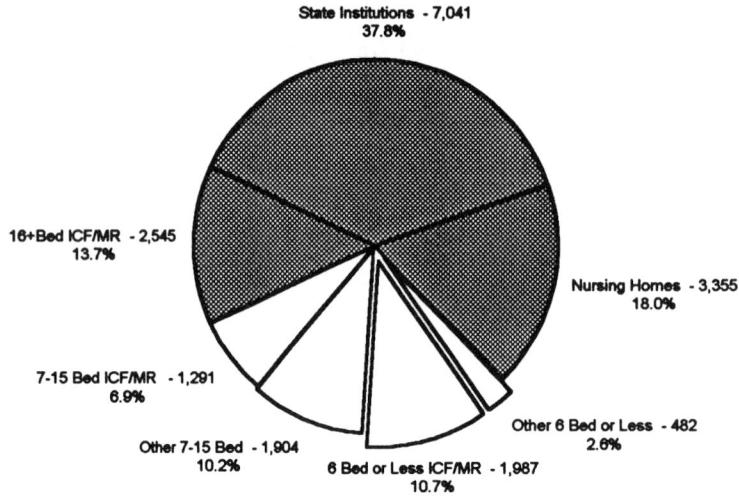

State Institutions - 7,041
37.8%

16+Bed ICF/MR - 2,545
13.7%

Nursing Homes - 3,355
18.0%

7-15 Bed ICF/MR - 1,291
6.9%

Other 6 Bed or Less - 482
2.6%

Other 7-15 Bed - 1,904
10.2%

6 Bed or Less ICF/MR - 1,987
10.7%

Total Served: 18,605

## Persons Served by Residential Setting:1986-92

|  | 1986 | 1987 | 1988 | 1989 | 1990 | 1991 | 1992 |
|---|---|---|---|---|---|---|---|
| **CONGREGATE 16 + BED SETTINGS** | **NA** | **NA** | **13,851** | **11,647** | **13,148** | **13,009** | **12,941** |
| Nursing Homes | NA | NA | 3,528 | 1,592 | 3,281 | 3,338 | 3,355 |
| State Institutions | 9,013 | 8,126 | 7,662 | 7,447 | 7,290 | 7,094 | 7,041 |
| Private 16+Bed ICF/MR | 2,477 | 2,765 | 2,661 | 2,608 | 2,577 | 2,577 | 2,545 |
| Other 16+Bed Residential | 0 | 0 | 0 | 0 | 0 | 0 | 0 |
| **15 BED OR LESS RESIDENTIAL SETTINGS** | **2,539** | **2,287** | **2,609** | **4,459** | **4,476** | **5,122** | **5,664** |
| Public 7-15 Bed ICF/MR | 24 | 24 | 24 | 24 | 24 | 24 | 24 |
| Private 7-15 Bed ICF/MR | 1,281 | 1,258 | 1,580 | 1,787 | 2,095 | 2,534 | 1,267 |
| Other 7-15 Bed Residential | 1,234 | 1,005 | 1,005 | 2,648 | 2,357 | 2,564 | 1,904 |
| Public 6 Bed or Less ICF/MR |  |  |  |  |  |  | 0 |
| Private 6 Bed or Less ICF/MR |  |  |  |  |  |  | 1,987 |
| Other 6 Bed or Less Residential |  |  |  |  |  |  | 482 |
| **TOTAL PERSONS SERVED** | **NA** | **NA** | **16,460** | **16,106** | **17,624** | **18,131** | **18,605** |

## Persons Served in Non-Residential Community Services:1986-92

|  | 1986 | 1987 | 1988 | 1989 | 1990 | 1991 | 1992 |
|---|---|---|---|---|---|---|---|
| **DAY/WORK PROGRAMS** | **NA** | **NA** | **12,846** | **12,111** | **12,443** | **12,888** | **17,235** |
| Sheltered Employment/Work Activity | NA | NA | 8,775 | 6,340 | 6,896 | 7,198 | 8,814 |
| Day Habilitation ("Day Training") | NA | NA | 4,071 | 5,521 | 5,197 | 5,240 | 7,771 |
| Supported/Competitive Employment | 0 | 0 | 0 | 250 | 350 | 450 | 650 |
| **CASE MANAGEMENT** | **NA** | **NA** | **3,556** | **4,562** | **4,904** | **5,823** | **9,000** |
| **HCBS WAIVER** | **68** | **199** | **288** | **373** | **420** | **650** | **1,335** |
| **MODEL 50/200 WAIVER** | **8** | **11** | **11** | **0** | **0** | **0** | **0** |

*Source:*
Institute on Disability and Human Development (UAP),
University of Illinois at Chicago, 1994

# TEXAS

## Community Services: FY 1992 Revenue Sources

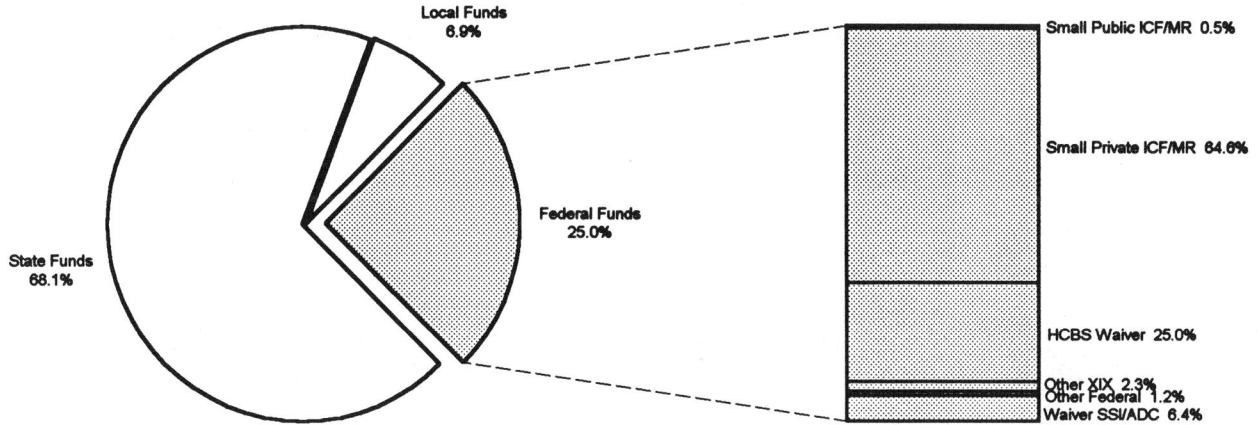

Local Funds 6.9%

State Funds 68.1%

Federal Funds 25.0%

Small Public ICF/MR 0.5%

Small Private ICF/MR 64.6%

HCBS Waiver 25.0%

Other XIX 2.3%
Other Federal 1.2%
Waiver SSI/ADC 6.4%

Total Funds: $408.2 Million

## Family Support Initiatives*

|  | 1986 | 1987 | 1988 | 1989 | 1990 | 1991 | 1992 |
|---|---|---|---|---|---|---|---|
| **FAMILY SUPPORT: TOTAL SPENDING** | $0 | $0 | $9,642,856 | $11,751,077 | $12,876,984 | $14,869,399 | $26,576,782 |
| **Total # of Families Supported** | 0 | 0 | 3,649 | 5,130 | 6,781 | 6,791 | 9,624 |
| A. Financial Subsidy/Payment | $0 | $0 | $1,000,000 | $2,000,000 | $3,500,000 | $4,500,000 | $7,600,000 |
| # of Families | 0 | 0 | 267 | 1,387 | 1,726 | 1,987 | 3,450 |
| B. Family Assistance Payments | NA | NA | $1,272,276 | $1,257,619 | $1,117,429 | $1,421,115 | $3,330,607 |
| # of Families | NA | NA | 498 | 955 | 976 | 1,011 | 1,513 |
| C. Other Family Support Payments | NA | NA | $7,370,580 | $8,493,458 | $8,259,555 | $8,948,284 | $15,646,175 |
| # of Families | NA | NA | 2,884 | 2,788 | 4,079 | 3,793 | 4,661 |

## Other Community Services Initiatives*

|  | 1986 | 1987 | 1988 | 1989 | 1990 | 1991 | 1992 |
|---|---|---|---|---|---|---|---|
| **AGING/DD SPENDING** | $0 | $0 | $0 | $0 | $0 | $0 | $0 |
| # of Persons Served | 0 | 0 | 0 | 0 | 0 | 0 | 0 |
| **ASSISTIVE TECHNOLOGY SPENDING** |  |  |  |  |  |  | $0 |
| # of Persons Served |  |  |  |  |  |  | 0 |
| **EARLY INTERVENTION SPENDING** | $9,248,600 | $9,103,000 | $11,574,000 | $4,000,000 | NA | NA | $5,500,000 |
| # of Persons Served | 8,695 | 9,165 | 10,220 | NA | NA | NA | NA |
| **PERSONAL ASSISTANCE SPENDING** |  |  |  |  |  |  | $0 |
| # of Persons Served |  |  |  |  |  |  | 0 |
| **SUPPORTED EMPLOYMENT SPENDING** | $0 | $0 | $0 | NA | NA | NA | NA |
| # of Persons Served | 0 | 0 | 0 | 250 | 350 | 450 | 650 |
| **SUPPORTED LIVING SPENDING** |  |  |  |  |  |  | $0 |
| # of Persons Served |  |  |  |  |  |  | 0 |

*Expenditures associated with Special Community Initiatives are a subset of funding within the community services component of the state's chart series and spreadsheet; Family Support Client figures may include duplicate client counts; HCBS Waiver counts include Waiver case management numbers.
0= Services not provided in the state; NA= Data not available from state; blank= Services not applicable (eg. CSLA prior to authorization, Special Community Initiatives prior to request for data by this study)

*Source:*
Institute on Disability and Human Development (UAP),
University of Illinois at Chicago, 1994

# TEXAS

## Large Congregate Care Facilities: FY 1992 Revenue Sources*

### Private 16+Bed Settings

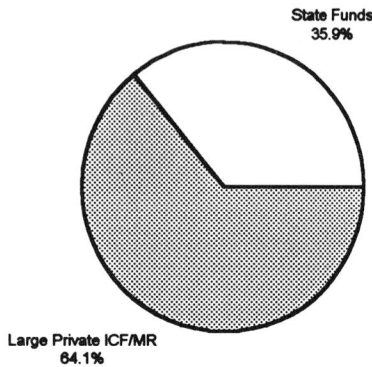

State Funds
35.9%

Large Private ICF/MR
64.1%

Total Funds: $58.1 Million

### Public Institutions

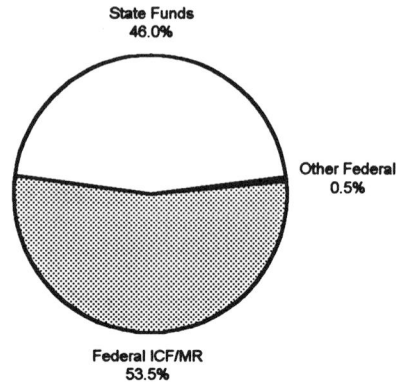

State Funds
46.0%

Other Federal
0.5%

Federal ICF/MR
53.5%

Total Funds: $409.4 Million

**\*Excludes nursing homes**

## Average Daily Residents in Institutions

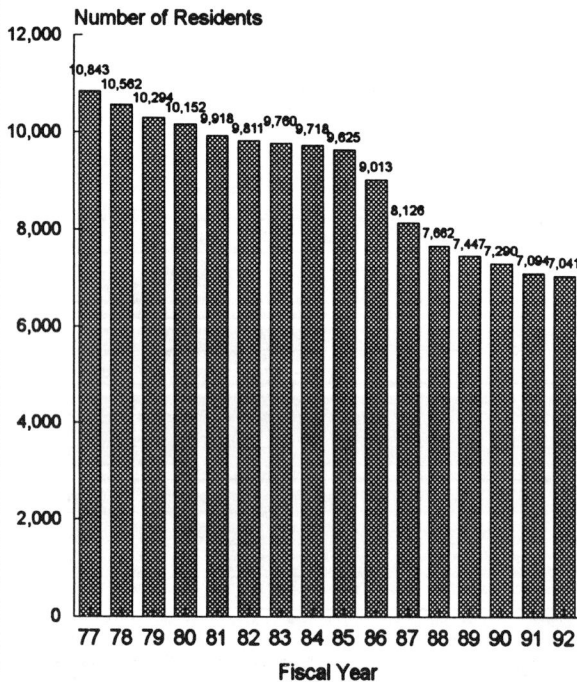

Number of Residents

10,843
10,562
10,294
10,152
9,918
9,811
9,760
9,718
9,625
9,013
8,126
7,662
7,447
7,290
7,094
7,041

Fiscal Year

## Institutional Daily Costs Per Resident

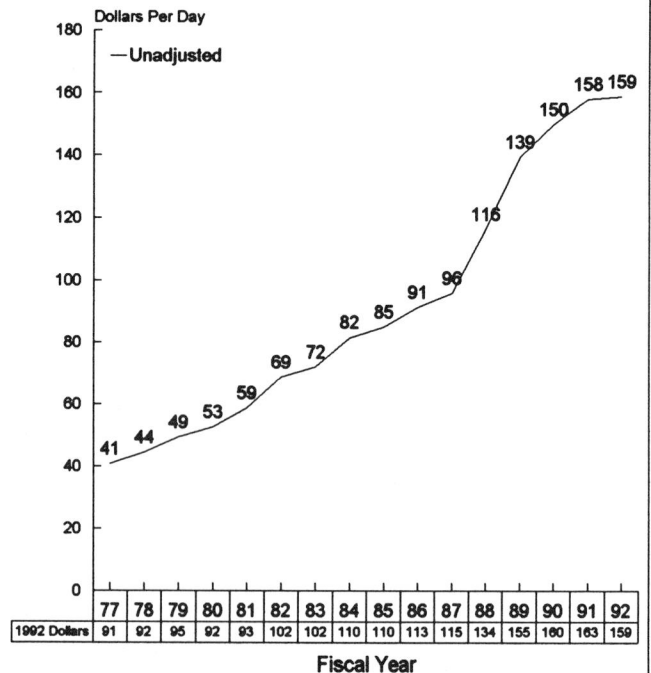

Dollars Per Day

—Unadjusted

41  44  49  53  59  69  72  82  85  91  96  116  139  150  158  159

| | 77 | 78 | 79 | 80 | 81 | 82 | 83 | 84 | 85 | 86 | 87 | 88 | 89 | 90 | 91 | 92 |
|---|---|---|---|---|---|---|---|---|---|---|---|---|---|---|---|---|
| 1992 Dollars | 91 | 92 | 95 | 92 | 93 | 102 | 102 | 110 | 110 | 113 | 115 | 134 | 155 | 160 | 163 | 159 |

Fiscal Year

*Source:*
Institute on Disability and Human Development (UAP),
University of Illinois at Chicago, 1994

# TEXAS FISCAL EFFORT

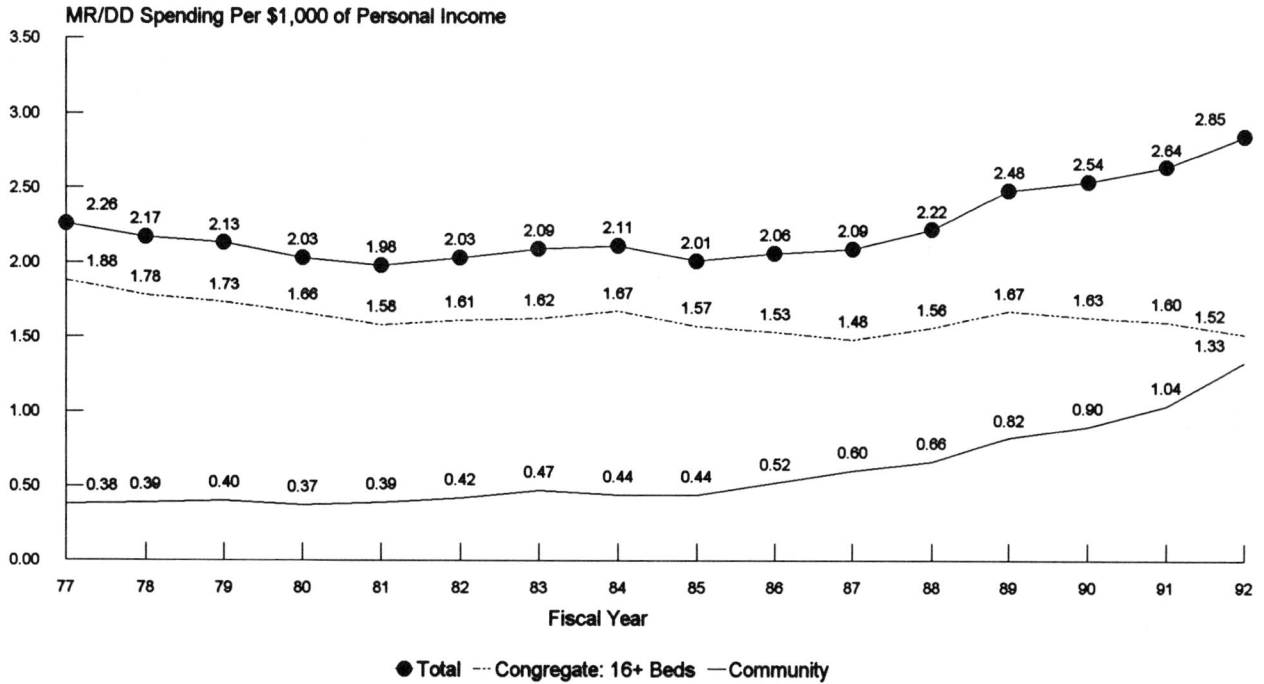

MR/DD Spending Per $1,000 of Personal Income

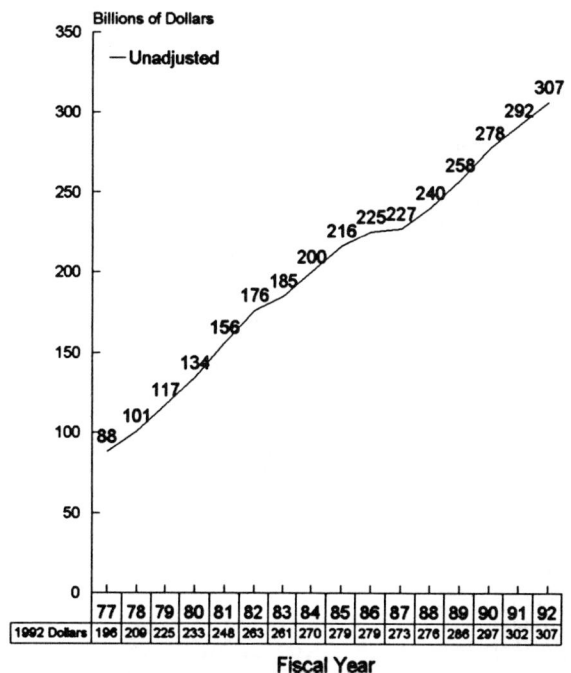

| Fiscal Year | Total | Congregate: 16+ Beds | Community |
|---|---|---|---|
| 77 | 2.26 | 1.88 | 0.38 |
| 78 | 2.17 | 1.78 | 0.39 |
| 79 | 2.13 | 1.73 | 0.40 |
| 80 | 2.03 | 1.66 | 0.37 |
| 81 | 1.98 | 1.58 | 0.39 |
| 82 | 2.03 | 1.61 | 0.42 |
| 83 | 2.09 | 1.62 | 0.47 |
| 84 | 2.11 | 1.67 | 0.44 |
| 85 | 2.01 | 1.57 | 0.44 |
| 86 | 2.06 | 1.53 | 0.52 |
| 87 | 2.09 | 1.48 | 0.60 |
| 88 | 2.22 | 1.56 | 0.66 |
| 89 | 2.48 | 1.67 | 0.82 |
| 90 | 2.54 | 1.63 | 0.90 |
| 91 | 2.64 | 1.60 | 1.04 |
| 92 | 2.85 | 1.52 | 1.33 |

● Total  --- Congregate: 16+ Beds  — Community

## Total MR/DD Spending

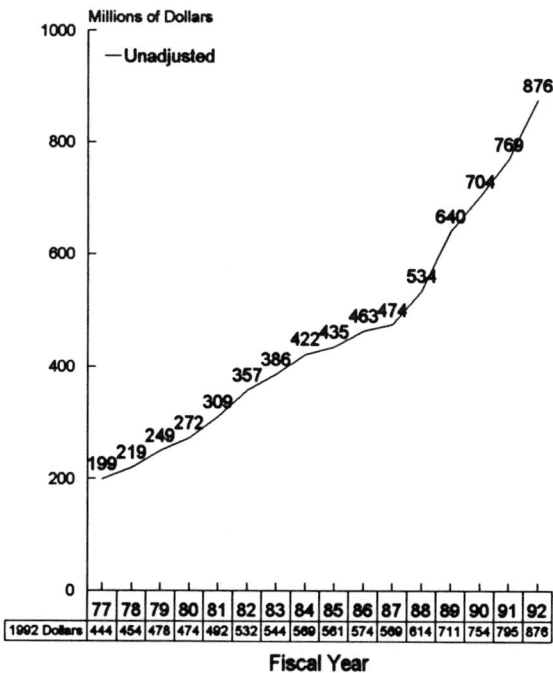

Millions of Dollars
—Unadjusted

| | 77 | 78 | 79 | 80 | 81 | 82 | 83 | 84 | 85 | 86 | 87 | 88 | 89 | 90 | 91 | 92 |
|---|---|---|---|---|---|---|---|---|---|---|---|---|---|---|---|---|
| Unadjusted | 199 | 219 | 249 | 272 | 309 | 357 | 386 | 422 | 435 | 463 | 474 | 534 | 640 | 704 | 769 | 876 |
| 1992 Dollars | 444 | 454 | 478 | 474 | 492 | 532 | 544 | 569 | 561 | 574 | 569 | 614 | 711 | 754 | 795 | 876 |

Fiscal Year

## Personal Income

Billions of Dollars
—Unadjusted

| | 77 | 78 | 79 | 80 | 81 | 82 | 83 | 84 | 85 | 86 | 87 | 88 | 89 | 90 | 91 | 92 |
|---|---|---|---|---|---|---|---|---|---|---|---|---|---|---|---|---|
| Unadjusted | 88 | 101 | 117 | 134 | 156 | 176 | 185 | 200 | 216 | 225 | 227 | 240 | 258 | 278 | 292 | 307 |
| 1992 Dollars | 196 | 209 | 225 | 233 | 248 | 263 | 261 | 270 | 279 | 279 | 273 | 276 | 286 | 297 | 302 | 307 |

Fiscal Year

*Source:*
Institute on Disability and Human Development (UAP),
University of Illinois at Chicago, 1994

# TEXAS
## Financial Support for MR/DD Services: FY 1977-92

| | 1977 | 1978 | 1979 | 1980 | 1981 | 1982 | 1983 | 1984 |
|---|---|---|---|---|---|---|---|---|
| **TOTAL FUNDS** | $199,152,805 | $219,395,654 | $248,920,515 | $272,367,870 | $309,254,844 | $357,021,350 | $385,725,978 | $421,500,968 |
| **CONGREGATE 16+ BEDS** | 165,782,390 | 180,019,322 | 202,129,963 | 222,641,612 | 247,568,903 | 283,271,579 | 299,582,084 | 334,115,910 |
| INSTITUTIONAL SERVICES FUNDS | 161,283,255 | 171,377,849 | 185,690,134 | 195,798,578 | 212,783,813 | 246,129,003 | 256,991,982 | 290,228,408 |
| STATE FUNDS | 112,556,720 | 127,293,674 | 123,104,564 | 113,501,424 | 124,200,376 | 140,202,258 | 139,523,594 | 173,002,226 |
| General Funds | 109,763,280 | 124,633,174 | 120,587,184 | 111,158,734 | 122,700,555 | 138,646,816 | 137,656,170 | 171,066,105 |
| Local | 0 | 0 | 0 | 0 | 0 | 0 | 0 | 0 |
| Other State Funds | 2,793,440 | 2,660,500 | 2,517,380 | 2,342,690 | 1,499,821 | 1,555,442 | 1,867,424 | 1,936,121 |
| FEDERAL FUNDS | 48,726,535 | 44,084,175 | 62,585,570 | 82,297,154 | 88,583,437 | 105,926,745 | 117,468,388 | 117,226,182 |
| Federal ICF/MR | 48,641,378 | 44,021,442 | 62,484,516 | 82,175,550 | 85,283,541 | 102,927,455 | 116,075,855 | 115,853,416 |
| Title XX / SSBG Funds | 0 | 0 | 0 | 0 | 0 | 0 | 0 | 0 |
| Other Federal Funds | 85,157 | 62,733 | 101,054 | 121,604 | 3,299,896 | 2,999,290 | 1,392,533 | 1,372,766 |
| LARGE PRIVATE RESIDENTIAL | 4,499,135 | 8,641,473 | 16,439,829 | 26,843,034 | 34,785,090 | 37,142,576 | 42,590,102 | 43,887,502 |
| STATE FUNDS | 1,638,135 | 3,336,473 | 6,467,429 | 11,024,434 | 14,487,990 | 16,353,876 | 18,837,602 | 19,973,202 |
| General Funds | 0 | 0 | 0 | 0 | 0 | 0 | 0 | 0 |
| Other State Funds | 1,638,135 | 3,336,473 | 6,467,429 | 11,024,434 | 14,487,990 | 16,353,876 | 18,837,602 | 19,973,202 |
| Local/County Overmatch | 0 | 0 | 0 | 0 | 0 | 0 | 0 | 0 |
| FEDERAL FUNDS | 2,861,000 | 5,305,000 | 9,972,400 | 15,818,600 | 20,297,100 | 20,788,700 | 23,752,500 | 23,914,300 |
| Large Private ICF/MR | 2,861,000 | 5,305,000 | 9,972,400 | 15,818,600 | 20,297,100 | 20,788,700 | 23,752,500 | 23,914,300 |
| **COMMUNITY SERVICES FUNDS** | 33,370,415 | 39,376,332 | 46,790,552 | 49,726,258 | 61,685,941 | 73,749,771 | 86,143,894 | 87,385,058 |
| STATE FUNDS | 29,893,535 | 34,368,908 | 39,571,260 | 42,843,154 | 50,430,510 | 60,587,031 | 71,376,391 | 72,047,997 |
| General Funds | 21,933,411 | 24,637,272 | 27,029,864 | 28,206,244 | 30,672,542 | 37,093,870 | 43,967,355 | 48,617,755 |
| Other State Funds | 342,607 | 356,485 | 1,408,612 | 1,746,492 | 5,109,917 | 7,087,476 | 7,877,980 | 8,510,546 |
| Local/County Overmatch | 7,617,517 | 9,375,151 | 11,132,784 | 12,890,418 | 14,648,051 | 16,405,685 | 19,531,056 | 14,919,696 |
| SSI State Supplement | 0 | 0 | 0 | 0 | 0 | 0 | 0 | 0 |
| FEDERAL FUNDS | 3,476,880 | 5,007,424 | 7,219,292 | 6,883,104 | 11,255,431 | 13,162,740 | 14,767,503 | 15,337,061 |
| ICF/MR Funds | 0 | 0 | 1,755,482 | 2,229,114 | 6,844,981 | 8,559,240 | 9,510,040 | 9,752,073 |
| Small Public | 0 | 0 | 131,882 | 225,714 | 241,081 | 173,940 | 192,540 | 158,173 |
| Small Private | 0 | 0 | 1,623,600 | 2,003,400 | 6,603,900 | 8,385,300 | 9,317,500 | 9,593,900 |
| HCBS Waiver | 0 | 0 | 0 | 0 | 0 | 0 | 0 | 0 |
| Model 50/200 Waiver | 0 | 0 | 0 | 0 | 0 | 0 | 0 | 0 |
| Other Title XIX Programs | 3,476,880 | 5,007,424 | 5,463,810 | 4,653,990 | 4,410,450 | 4,603,500 | 5,242,594 | 5,537,660 |
| Title XX / SSBG Funds | 0 | 0 | 0 | 0 | 0 | 0 | 0 | 0 |
| Other Federal Funds | 0 | 0 | 0 | 0 | 0 | 0 | 14,869 | 47,328 |
| Waiver Clients' SSI/ADC | 0 | 0 | 0 | 0 | 0 | 0 | 0 | 0 |

| | 1985 | 1986 | 1987 | 1988 | 1989 | 1990 | 1991 | 1992 |
|---|---|---|---|---|---|---|---|---|
| **TOTAL FUNDS** | $434,976,188 | $463,051,375 | $474,146,527 | $533,952,993 | $640,448,269 | $703,889,035 | $769,282,136 | $875,752,890 |
| **CONGREGATE 16+ BEDS** | 340,375,695 | 345,547,366 | 337,055,120 | 375,642,371 | 429,648,514 | 453,017,688 | 465,522,895 | 467,571,370 |
| INSTITUTIONAL SERVICES FUNDS | 298,395,187 | 300,304,955 | 284,027,252 | 326,002,807 | 378,996,255 | 398,800,694 | 409,230,038 | 409,424,190 |
| STATE FUNDS | 167,988,076 | 156,454,525 | 159,736,184 | 159,639,587 | 188,991,062 | 191,760,466 | 188,151,384 | 188,394,604 |
| General Funds | 165,793,042 | 154,263,807 | 157,361,930 | 157,560,730 | 186,451,420 | 189,269,190 | 186,027,886 | 186,271,106 |
| Local | 0 | 0 | 0 | 0 | 0 | 0 | 0 | 0 |
| Other State Funds | 2,195,034 | 2,190,718 | 2,374,254 | 2,078,857 | 2,539,642 | 2,491,276 | 2,123,498 | 2,123,498 |
| FEDERAL FUNDS | 130,407,111 | 143,850,430 | 124,291,068 | 166,363,220 | 190,005,193 | 207,040,228 | 221,078,654 | 221,029,586 |
| Federal ICF/MR | 125,090,591 | 138,494,218 | 119,610,299 | 163,045,697 | 187,527,801 | 204,644,619 | 219,049,138 | 219,017,605 |
| Title XX / SSBG Funds | 0 | 0 | 0 | 0 | 0 | 0 | 0 | 0 |
| Other Federal Funds | 5,316,520 | 5,356,212 | 4,680,769 | 3,317,523 | 2,477,392 | 2,395,609 | 2,029,516 | 2,011,981 |
| LARGE PRIVATE RESIDENTIAL | 41,980,508 | 45,242,411 | 53,027,868 | 49,639,564 | 50,652,259 | 54,216,994 | 56,292,857 | 58,147,180 |
| STATE FUNDS | 19,151,508 | 20,978,906 | 23,846,632 | 21,462,079 | 20,837,073 | 21,118,875 | 20,637,900 | 20,859,816 |
| General Funds | 0 | 0 | 0 | 0 | 0 | 0 | 0 | 0 |
| Other State Funds | 19,151,508 | 20,978,906 | 23,846,632 | 21,462,079 | 20,837,073 | 21,118,875 | 20,637,900 | 20,859,816 |
| Local/County Overmatch | 0 | 0 | 0 | 0 | 0 | 0 | 0 | 0 |
| FEDERAL FUNDS | 22,829,000 | 24,263,505 | 29,181,236 | 28,177,485 | 29,815,186 | 33,098,119 | 35,654,957 | 37,287,364 |
| Large Private ICF/MR | 22,829,000 | 24,263,505 | 29,181,236 | 28,177,485 | 29,815,186 | 33,098,119 | 35,654,957 | 37,287,364 |
| **COMMUNITY SERVICES FUNDS** | 94,600,493 | 117,504,009 | 137,091,407 | 158,310,622 | 210,799,755 | 250,871,347 | 303,759,241 | 408,181,520 |
| STATE FUNDS | 77,119,240 | 97,631,294 | 115,815,403 | 124,526,896 | 172,063,892 | 205,969,470 | 241,769,157 | 306,107,938 |
| General Funds | 49,865,371 | 64,632,465 | 76,697,775 | 80,857,842 | 117,447,324 | 145,004,127 | 170,703,095 | 216,666,946 |
| Other State Funds | 8,992,162 | 11,624,772 | 13,947,748 | 16,926,072 | 28,736,649 | 33,271,379 | 43,178,904 | 61,453,834 |
| Local/County Overmatch | 18,261,707 | 21,374,057 | 25,169,880 | 26,742,982 | 25,879,919 | 27,693,964 | 27,887,158 | 27,987,158 |
| SSI State Supplement | 0 | 0 | 0 | 0 | 0 | 0 | 0 | 0 |
| FEDERAL FUNDS | 17,481,253 | 19,872,715 | 21,276,004 | 33,783,726 | 38,735,863 | 44,901,877 | 61,990,084 | 102,073,582 |
| ICF/MR Funds | 10,294,125 | 11,517,880 | 11,302,061 | 17,233,941 | 23,454,591 | 32,282,426 | 44,747,028 | 66,532,562 |
| Small Public | 144,625 | 309,382 | 383,200 | 478,129 | 605,637 | 491,582 | 555,801 | 555,801 |
| Small Private | 10,149,500 | 11,208,498 | 10,918,861 | 16,755,812 | 22,848,954 | 31,790,844 | 44,191,227 | 65,976,761 |
| HCBS Waiver | 0 | 289,256 | 1,005,977 | 2,749,304 | 3,792,672 | 4,773,788 | 9,416,729 | 25,502,913 |
| Model 50/200 Waiver | 0 | 0 | 0 | 0 | 0 | 0 | 0 | 0 |
| Other Title XIX Programs | 5,934,588 | 6,270,726 | 6,898,130 | 7,317,090 | 9,613,072 | 3,496,518 | 2,107,002 | 2,310,000 |
| Title XX / SSBG Funds | 0 | 0 | 0 | 0 | 0 | 0 | 0 | 0 |
| Other Federal Funds | 1,252,540 | 1,541,077 | 1,317,616 | 4,978,735 | 0 | 1,730,457 | 1,708,325 | 1,207,967 |
| Waiver Clients' SSI/ADC | 0 | 253,776 | 752,220 | 1,504,656 | 1,875,528 | 2,618,688 | 4,011,000 | 6,520,140 |

*Source:*

Institute on Disability and Human Development (UAP),
University of Illinois at Chicago, 1994

# UTAH

## MR/DD Spending for Congregate Residential & Community Services

▨Congregate: 16+ Beds*  ■Community**

Millions of 1992 Dollars

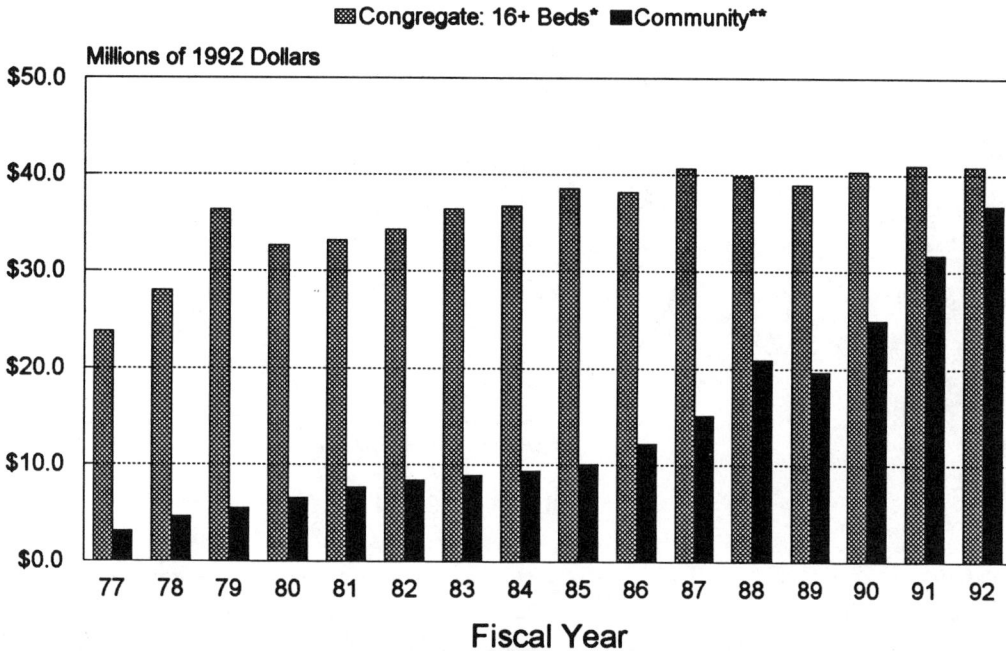

Fiscal Year

*Excludes nursing homes; ** Includes resources for
15 bed or less residential settings & non-residential community services

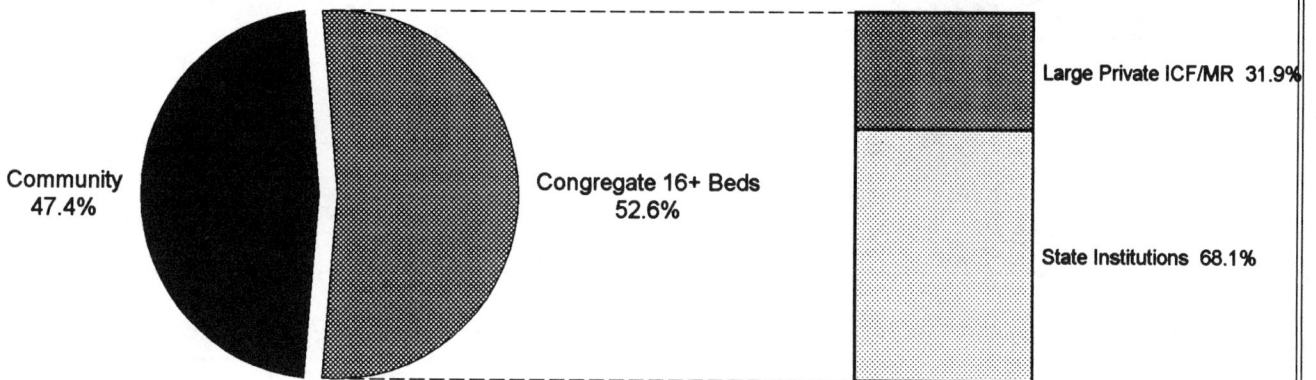

Community
47.4%

Congregate 16+ Beds
52.6%

Large Private ICF/MR  31.9%

State Institutions  68.1%

FY 1992 Total Spending:
$77.6 Million

*Source:*
Institute on Disability and Human Development (UAP),
University of Illinois at Chicago, 1994

# UTAH

## Number of Persons Served by Residential Setting: FY 1992

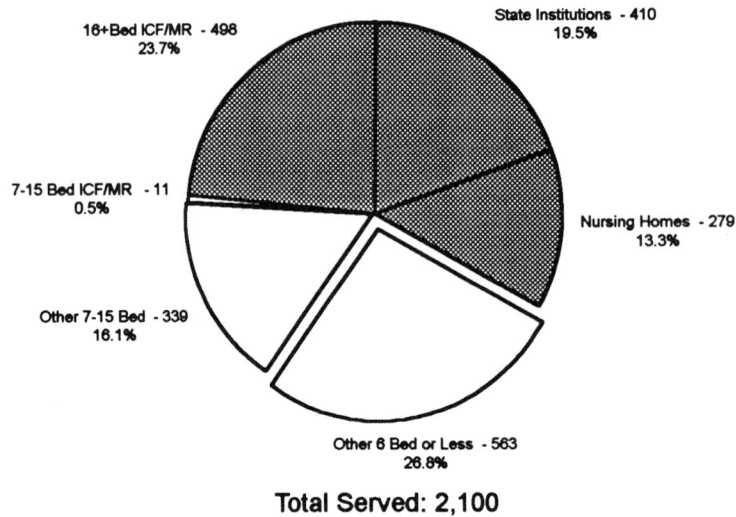

16+Bed ICF/MR - 498
23.7%

State Institutions - 410
19.5%

7-15 Bed ICF/MR - 11
0.5%

Nursing Homes - 279
13.3%

Other 7-15 Bed - 339
16.1%

Other 6 Bed or Less - 563
26.8%

Total Served: 2,100

## Persons Served by Residential Setting:1986-92

|  | 1986 | 1987 | 1988 | 1989 | 1990 | 1991 | 1992 |
|---|---|---|---|---|---|---|---|
| **CONGREGATE 16 + BED SETTINGS** | **NA** | **NA** | **1,487** | **NA** | **NA** | **1,195** | **1,187** |
| Nursing Homes | NA | NA | 360 | NA | NA | 279 | 279 |
| State Institutions | 701 | 594 | 527 | 481 | 464 | 434 | 410 |
| Private 16+Bed ICF/MR | 636 | 654 | 600 | 468 | 468 | 482 | 498 |
| Other 16+Bed Residential | 0 | 0 | 0 | 0 | 0 | 0 | 0 |
| **15 BED OR LESS RESIDENTIAL SETTINGS** | **476** | **644** | **837** | **801** | **772** | **849** | **913** |
| Public 7-15 Bed ICF/MR | 0 | 0 | 0 | 0 | 0 | 0 | 0 |
| Private 7-15 Bed ICF/MR | 30 | 45 | 57 | 10 | 12 | 11 | 11 |
| Other 7-15 Bed Residential | 446 | 599 | 780 | 459 | 366 | 359 | 339 |
| Public 6 Bed or Less ICF/MR | 0 | 0 | 0 | 0 | 0 | 0 | 0 |
| Private 6 Bed or Less ICF/MR | 0 | 0 | 0 | 0 | 0 | 0 | 0 |
| Other 6 Bed or Less Residential |  |  |  | 332 | 394 | 479 | 563 |
| **TOTAL PERSONS SERVED** | **NA** | **NA** | **2,324** | **NA** | **NA** | **2,044** | **2,100** |

## Persons Served in Non-Residential Community Services:1986-92

|  | 1986 | 1987 | 1988 | 1989 | 1990 | 1991 | 1992 |
|---|---|---|---|---|---|---|---|
| **DAY/WORK PROGRAMS** | **NA** | **NA** | **NA** | **934** | **1,041** | **1,220** | **1,267** |
| Sheltered Employment/Work Activity | 1,244 | 1,271 | 1,023 | 754 | 753 | 805 | 859 |
| Day Habilitation ("Day Training") | NA | NA | NA | NA | 48 | 43 | 32 |
| Supported/Competitive Employment | NA | 38 | 155 | 180 | 240 | 372 | 376 |
| **CASE MANAGEMENT** | **NA** | **NA** | **NA** | **999** | **1,166** | **1,324** | **1,500** |
| **HCBS WAIVER** | **0** | **0** | **898** | **999** | **1,166** | **1,324** | **1,500** |
| **MODEL 50/200 WAIVER** | **0** | **0** | **0** | **0** | **0** | **0** | **0** |

Source:
Institute on Disability and Human Development (UAP),
University of Illinois at Chicago, 1994

# UTAH

## Community Services: FY 1992 Revenue Sources

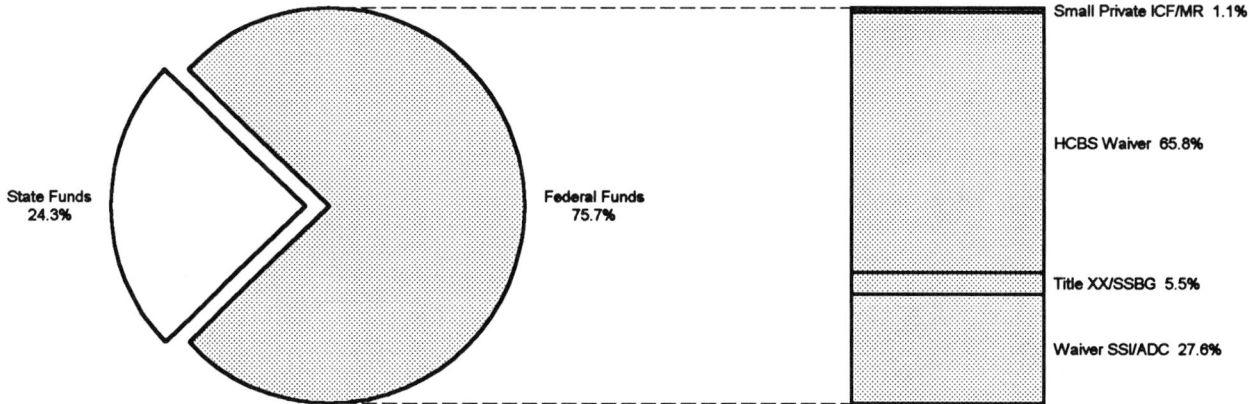

State Funds
24.3%

Federal Funds
75.7%

Small Private ICF/MR 1.1%

HCBS Waiver 65.8%

Title XX/SSBG 5.5%

Waiver SSI/ADC 27.6%

Total Funds: $36.8 Million

## Family Support Initiatives*

|  | 1986 | 1987 | 1988 | 1989 | 1990 | 1991 | 1992 |
|---|---|---|---|---|---|---|---|
| **FAMILY SUPPORT: TOTAL SPENDING** | **$76,600** | **$305,000** | **$447,100** | **$493,370** | **$677,726** | **$728,590** | **$1,241,832** |
| **Total # of Families Supported** | **NA** | **NA** | **NA** | **NA** | **NA** | **NA** | **NA** |
| A. Financial Subsidy/Payment | NA | $23,000 | $154,100 | $41,232 | $45,348 | $44,579 | $39,970 |
| # of Families | NA | NA | 21 | 127 | 140 | 137 | 123 |
| B. Family Assistance Payments | NA | $183,000 | $183,000 | $256,411 | $312,913 | $330,716 | $545,178 |
| # of Families | 354 | 345 | 354 | 380 | 464 | 527 | 808 |
| C. Other Family Support Payments | $76,600 | $99,000 | $110,000 | $195,727 | $319,465 | $353,295 | $656,684 |
| # of Families | NA | NA | NA | NA | NA | NA | NA |

## Other Community Services Initiatives*

|  | 1986 | 1987 | 1988 | 1989 | 1990 | 1991 | 1992 |
|---|---|---|---|---|---|---|---|
| **AGING/DD SPENDING** | $0 | $0 | $0 | $70,000 | $123,664 | $143,568 | $119,710 |
| # of Persons Served | 0 | 0 | 0 | 30 | 41 | 96 | 96 |
| **ASSISTIVE TECHNOLOGY SPENDING** |  |  |  |  |  |  | $0 |
| # of Persons Served |  |  |  |  |  |  | 0 |
| **EARLY INTERVENTION SPENDING** | $2,219,700 | $3,955,700 | $4,538,700 | NA | $1,672,300 | $2,261,468 | $2,627,310 |
| # of Persons Served | 1,554 | 1,811 | 1,201 | NA | 1,029 | 1,121 | 1,322 |
| **PERSONAL ASSISTANCE SPENDING** |  |  | $102,600 | $103,600 | $125,779 | $273,100 | $323,685 |
| # of Persons Served |  |  | 27 | 27 | NA | 50 | 50 |
| **SUPPORTED EMPLOYMENT SPENDING** | $261,000 | $460,600 | $193,200 | $1,063,465 | $1,549,658 | $2,265,832 | $2,357,185 |
| # of Persons Served | NA | 38 | 155 | 180 | 240 | 372 | 376 |
| **SUPPORTED LIVING SPENDING** |  |  |  | $62,600 | $151,980 | $361,280 | $336,150 |
| # of Persons Served |  |  |  | 20 | 105 | 149 | 156 |

*Expenditures associated with Special Community Initiatives are a subset of funding within the community services component of the state's chart series and spreadsheet; Family Support Client figures may include duplicate client counts; HCBS Waiver counts include Waiver case management numbers.
0= Services not provided in the state; NA= Data not available from state; blank= Services not applicable (eg. CSLA prior to authorization, Special Community Initiatives prior to request for data by this study)

*Source:*
Institute on Disability and Human Development (UAP),
University of Illinois at Chicago, 1994

# UTAH

## Large Congregate Care Facilities: FY 1992 Revenue Sources*

### Private 16+Bed Settings

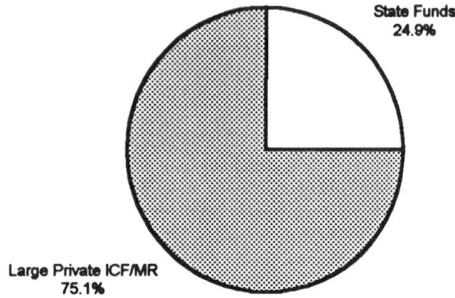

State Funds
24.9%

Large Private ICF/MR
75.1%

Total Funds: $13.0 Million

### Public Institutions

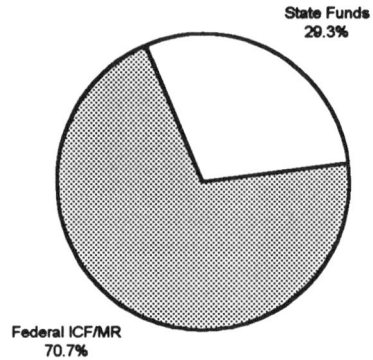

State Funds
29.3%

Federal ICF/MR
70.7%

Total Funds: $27.8 Million

*Excludes nursing homes

## Average Daily Residents in Institutions

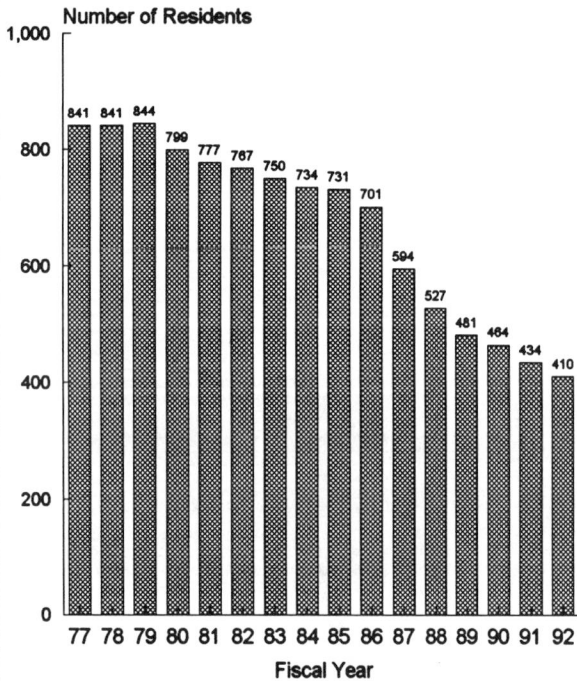

Number of Residents

| | |
|---|---|
| 841 | 77 |
| 841 | 78 |
| 844 | 79 |
| 799 | 80 |
| 777 | 81 |
| 767 | 82 |
| 750 | 83 |
| 734 | 84 |
| 731 | 85 |
| 701 | 86 |
| 594 | 87 |
| 527 | 88 |
| 481 | 89 |
| 464 | 90 |
| 434 | 91 |
| 410 | 92 |

Fiscal Year

## Institutional Daily Costs Per Resident

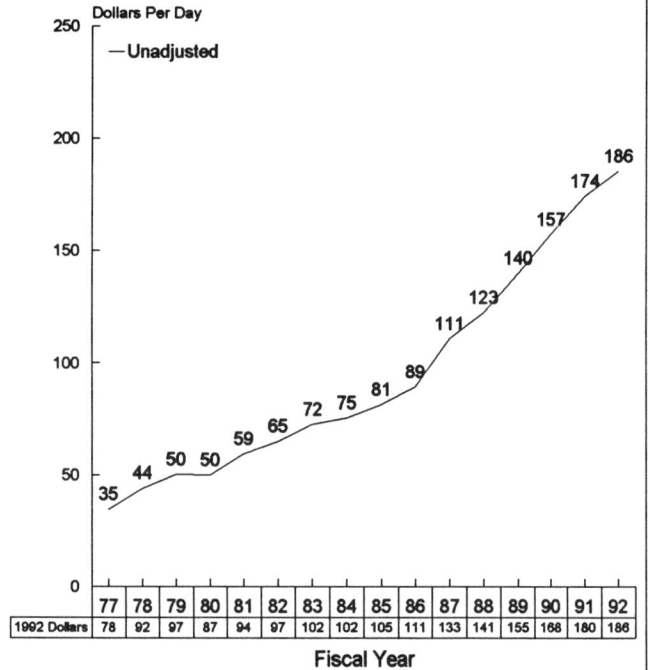

Dollars Per Day

—Unadjusted

35, 44, 50, 50, 59, 65, 72, 75, 81, 89, 111, 123, 140, 157, 174, 186

| | 77 | 78 | 79 | 80 | 81 | 82 | 83 | 84 | 85 | 86 | 87 | 88 | 89 | 90 | 91 | 92 |
|---|---|---|---|---|---|---|---|---|---|---|---|---|---|---|---|---|
| 1992 Dollars | 78 | 92 | 97 | 87 | 94 | 97 | 102 | 102 | 105 | 111 | 133 | 141 | 155 | 168 | 180 | 186 |

Fiscal Year

*Source:*
Institute on Disability and Human Development (UAP),
University of Illinois at Chicago, 1994

# UTAH FISCAL EFFORT

MR/DD Spending Per $1,000 of Personal Income

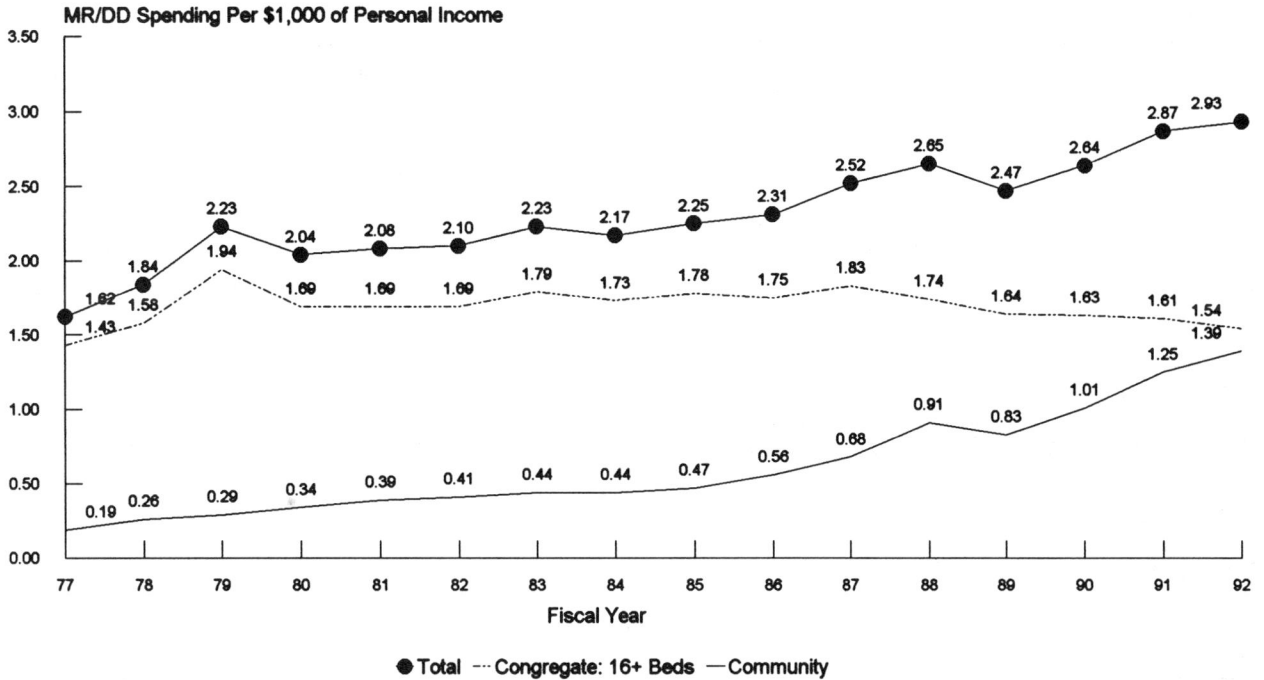

● Total  --- Congregate: 16+ Beds  — Community

## Total MR/DD Spending

Millions of Dollars

—Unadjusted

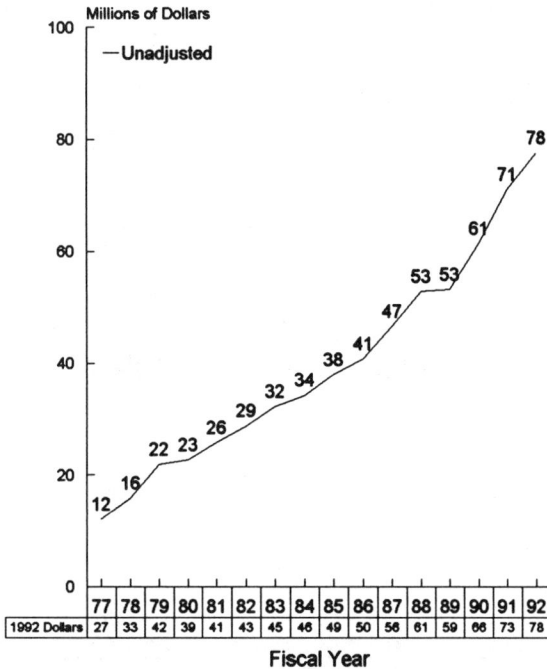

| | 77 | 78 | 79 | 80 | 81 | 82 | 83 | 84 | 85 | 86 | 87 | 88 | 89 | 90 | 91 | 92 |
|---|---|---|---|---|---|---|---|---|---|---|---|---|---|---|---|---|
| 1992 Dollars | 27 | 33 | 42 | 39 | 41 | 43 | 45 | 46 | 49 | 50 | 56 | 61 | 59 | 66 | 73 | 78 |

Fiscal Year

## Personal Income

Billions of Dollars

—Unadjusted

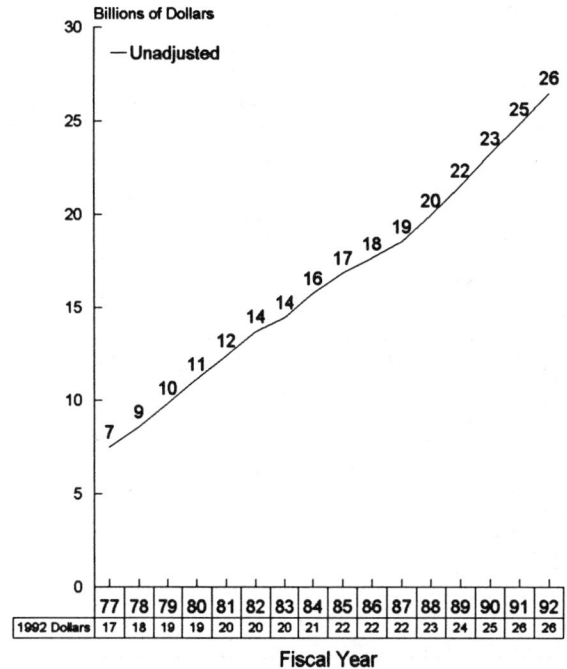

| | 77 | 78 | 79 | 80 | 81 | 82 | 83 | 84 | 85 | 86 | 87 | 88 | 89 | 90 | 91 | 92 |
|---|---|---|---|---|---|---|---|---|---|---|---|---|---|---|---|---|
| 1992 Dollars | 17 | 18 | 19 | 19 | 20 | 20 | 20 | 21 | 22 | 22 | 22 | 23 | 24 | 25 | 26 | 26 |

Fiscal Year

*Source:*
Institute on Disability and Human Development (UAP),
University of Illinois at Chicago, 1994

# UTAH
## Financial Support for MR/DD Services: FY 1977-92

| | 1977 | 1978 | 1979 | 1980 | 1981 | 1982 | 1983 | 1984 |
|---|---|---|---|---|---|---|---|---|
| **TOTAL FUNDS** | $12,112,000 | $15,820,000 | $21,911,000 | $22,648,000 | $25,731,000 | $28,748,000 | $32,228,000 | $34,205,500 |
| **CONGREGATE 16+ BEDS** | 10,717,000 | 13,580,000 | 19,035,417 | 18,858,725 | 20,896,588 | 23,124,168 | 25,905,632 | 27,277,636 |
| INSTITUTIONAL SERVICES FUNDS | 10,717,000 | 13,580,000 | 15,546,000 | 14,623,000 | 16,839,000 | 18,203,000 | 19,829,000 | 20,227,700 |
| STATE FUNDS | 3,938,000 | 5,028,000 | 4,891,000 | 5,040,000 | 5,460,000 | 5,578,000 | 6,107,000 | 5,845,000 |
| General Funds | 3,443,000 | 4,591,000 | 4,509,000 | 4,735,000 | 5,025,000 | 5,436,000 | 5,782,000 | 5,553,000 |
| Local | 0 | 0 | 0 | 0 | 0 | 0 | 0 | 0 |
| Other State Funds | 495,000 | 437,000 | 382,000 | 305,000 | 435,000 | 142,000 | 325,000 | 292,000 |
| FEDERAL FUNDS | 6,779,000 | 8,552,000 | 10,655,000 | 9,583,000 | 11,379,000 | 12,625,000 | 13,722,000 | 14,382,700 |
| Federal ICF/MR | 5,350,000 | 7,867,000 | 9,859,000 | 8,802,000 | 10,414,000 | 11,396,000 | 12,612,000 | 13,368,500 |
| Title XX / SSBG Funds | 0 | 0 | 0 | 0 | 57,000 | 77,000 | 84,000 | 77,200 |
| Other Federal Funds | 1,429,000 | 685,000 | 796,000 | 781,000 | 908,000 | 1,152,000 | 1,026,000 | 937,000 |
| LARGE PRIVATE RESIDENTIAL | 0 | 0 | 3,489,417 | 4,235,725 | 4,057,588 | 4,921,168 | 6,076,632 | 7,049,936 |
| STATE FUNDS | 0 | 0 | 1,082,417 | 1,342,725 | 1,295,588 | 1,550,168 | 1,905,632 | 2,094,536 |
| General Funds | 0 | 0 | 1,082,417 | 1,342,725 | 1,295,588 | 1,550,168 | 1,905,632 | 2,094,536 |
| Other State Funds | 0 | 0 | 0 | 0 | 0 | 0 | 0 | 0 |
| Local/County Overmatch | 0 | 0 | 0 | 0 | 0 | 0 | 0 | 0 |
| FEDERAL FUNDS | 0 | 0 | 2,407,000 | 2,893,000 | 2,762,000 | 3,371,000 | 4,171,000 | 4,955,400 |
| Large Private ICF/MR | 0 | 0 | 2,407,000 | 2,893,000 | 2,762,000 | 3,371,000 | 4,171,000 | 4,955,400 |
| **COMMUNITY SERVICES FUNDS** | 1,395,000 | 2,240,000 | 2,875,583 | 3,789,275 | 4,834,412 | 5,623,832 | 6,322,368 | 6,927,864 |
| STATE FUNDS | 854,000 | 1,371,000 | 1,760,583 | 1,928,275 | 2,577,412 | 2,795,832 | 2,734,868 | 3,138,464 |
| General Funds | 854,000 | 1,371,000 | 1,760,583 | 1,928,275 | 2,577,412 | 2,795,832 | 2,734,868 | 3,138,464 |
| Other State Funds | 0 | 0 | 0 | 0 | 0 | 0 | 0 | 0 |
| Local/County Overmatch | 0 | 0 | 0 | 0 | 0 | 0 | 0 | 0 |
| SSI State Supplement | 0 | 0 | 0 | 0 | 0 | 0 | 0 | 0 |
| FEDERAL FUNDS | 541,000 | 869,000 | 1,115,000 | 1,861,000 | 2,257,000 | 2,828,000 | 3,587,500 | 3,789,400 |
| ICF/MR Funds | 0 | 0 | 0 | 0 | 0 | 0 | 0 | 0 |
| Small Public | 0 | 0 | 0 | 0 | 0 | 0 | 0 | 0 |
| Small Private | 0 | 0 | 0 | 0 | 0 | 0 | 0 | 0 |
| HCBS Waiver | 0 | 0 | 0 | 0 | 0 | 0 | 0 | 0 |
| Model 50/200 Waiver | 0 | 0 | 0 | 0 | 0 | 0 | 0 | 0 |
| Other Title XIX Programs | 0 | 0 | 0 | 0 | 0 | 1,000,000 | 1,699,500 | 1,953,400 |
| Title XX / SSBG Funds | 541,000 | 869,000 | 1,114,000 | 1,841,000 | 2,226,000 | 1,828,000 | 1,888,000 | 1,836,000 |
| Other Federal Funds | 0 | 0 | 1,000 | 20,000 | 31,000 | 0 | 0 | 0 |
| Waiver Clients' SSI/ADC | 0 | 0 | 0 | 0 | 0 | 0 | 0 | 0 |

| | 1985 | 1986 | 1987 | 1988 | 1989 | 1990 | 1991 | 1992 |
|---|---|---|---|---|---|---|---|---|
| **TOTAL FUNDS** | $37,868,600 | $40,705,400 | $46,598,200 | $52,853,229 | $53,170,543 | $61,409,647 | $71,115,080 | $77,635,996 |
| **CONGREGATE 16+ BEDS** | 30,020,644 | 30,886,355 | 33,964,323 | 34,674,991 | 35,321,733 | 37,915,593 | 40,072,693 | 40,866,807 |
| INSTITUTIONAL SERVICES FUNDS | 21,733,800 | 22,857,400 | 24,048,500 | 23,645,100 | 24,565,000 | 26,621,869 | 27,597,756 | 27,838,901 |
| STATE FUNDS | 7,483,300 | 7,080,300 | 7,893,000 | 7,281,500 | 7,358,600 | 7,860,345 | 7,934,131 | 8,168,087 |
| General Funds | 6,479,700 | 5,949,800 | 6,763,900 | 6,278,900 | 6,001,300 | 6,594,700 | 6,774,660 | 7,055,456 |
| Local | 0 | 0 | 0 | 0 | 0 | 0 | 0 | 0 |
| Other State Funds | 1,003,600 | 1,130,500 | 1,129,100 | 1,002,600 | 1,357,300 | 1,265,645 | 1,159,471 | 1,112,631 |
| FEDERAL FUNDS | 14,250,500 | 15,777,100 | 16,155,500 | 16,363,600 | 17,206,400 | 18,761,524 | 19,663,625 | 19,670,814 |
| Federal ICF/MR | 14,140,100 | 15,439,800 | 15,972,400 | 16,363,600 | 17,206,400 | 18,761,524 | 19,663,625 | 19,670,814 |
| Title XX / SSBG Funds | 0 | 0 | 0 | 0 | 0 | 0 | 0 | 0 |
| Other Federal Funds | 110,400 | 337,300 | 183,100 | 0 | 0 | 0 | 0 | 0 |
| LARGE PRIVATE RESIDENTIAL | 8,286,844 | 8,028,955 | 9,915,823 | 11,029,891 | 10,756,733 | 11,293,724 | 12,474,937 | 13,027,906 |
| STATE FUNDS | 2,416,444 | 2,233,655 | 2,671,323 | 2,911,891 | 2,815,037 | 2,881,029 | 3,138,694 | 3,249,160 |
| General Funds | 2,416,444 | 2,233,655 | 2,671,323 | 2,911,891 | 2,815,037 | 2,881,029 | 3,138,694 | 3,249,160 |
| Other State Funds | 0 | 0 | 0 | 0 | 0 | 0 | 0 | 0 |
| Local/County Overmatch | 0 | 0 | 0 | 0 | 0 | 0 | 0 | 0 |
| FEDERAL FUNDS | 5,870,400 | 5,795,300 | 7,244,500 | 8,118,000 | 7,941,696 | 8,412,695 | 9,336,243 | 9,778,746 |
| Large Private ICF/MR | 5,870,400 | 5,795,300 | 7,244,500 | 8,118,000 | 7,941,696 | 8,412,695 | 9,336,243 | 9,778,746 |
| **COMMUNITY SERVICES FUNDS** | 7,847,956 | 9,819,045 | 12,633,877 | 18,178,238 | 17,848,810 | 23,494,054 | 31,042,387 | 36,769,189 |
| STATE FUNDS | 4,166,356 | 3,825,245 | 5,442,177 | 7,569,362 | 6,805,964 | 5,817,088 | 8,466,471 | 8,917,728 |
| General Funds | 3,913,956 | 3,545,945 | 5,126,577 | 7,369,362 | 6,524,264 | 5,712,556 | 8,456,574 | 8,912,530 |
| Other State Funds | 252,400 | 279,300 | 315,600 | 200,000 | 281,700 | 104,532 | 9,897 | 5,198 |
| Local/County Overmatch | 0 | 0 | 0 | 0 | 0 | 0 | 0 | 0 |
| SSI State Supplement | 0 | 0 | 0 | 0 | 0 | 0 | 0 | 0 |
| FEDERAL FUNDS | 3,681,600 | 5,993,800 | 7,191,700 | 10,608,876 | 11,042,846 | 17,676,966 | 22,575,916 | 27,851,461 |
| ICF/MR Funds | 0 | 273,100 | 495,300 | 773,600 | 175,094 | 268,414 | 270,922 | 305,286 |
| Small Public | 0 | 0 | 0 | 0 | 0 | 0 | 0 | 0 |
| Small Private | 0 | 273,100 | 495,300 | 773,600 | 175,094 | 268,414 | 270,922 | 305,286 |
| HCBS Waiver | 0 | 0 | 0 | 4,101,900 | 5,417,600 | 10,775,224 | 14,564,550 | 18,331,475 |
| Model 50/200 Waiver | 0 | 0 | 0 | 0 | 0 | 0 | 0 | 0 |
| Other Title XIX Programs | 1,989,300 | 3,718,600 | 4,291,400 | 0 | 0 | 0 | 0 | 0 |
| Title XX / SSBG Funds | 1,682,700 | 1,640,600 | 2,055,600 | 1,957,600 | 1,206,400 | 1,260,400 | 1,178,700 | 1,528,700 |
| Other Federal Funds | 9,600 | 361,500 | 349,400 | 560,400 | 0 | 0 | 0 | 0 |
| Waiver Clients' SSI/ADC | 0 | 0 | 0 | 3,215,376 | 4,243,752 | 5,372,928 | 6,561,744 | 7,686,000 |

*Source:*
Institute on Disability and Human Development (UAP),
University of Illinois at Chicago, 1994

# VERMONT

## MR/DD Spending for Congregate Residential & Community Services

▨ Congregate: 16+ Beds*  ■ Community**

Millions of 1992 Dollars

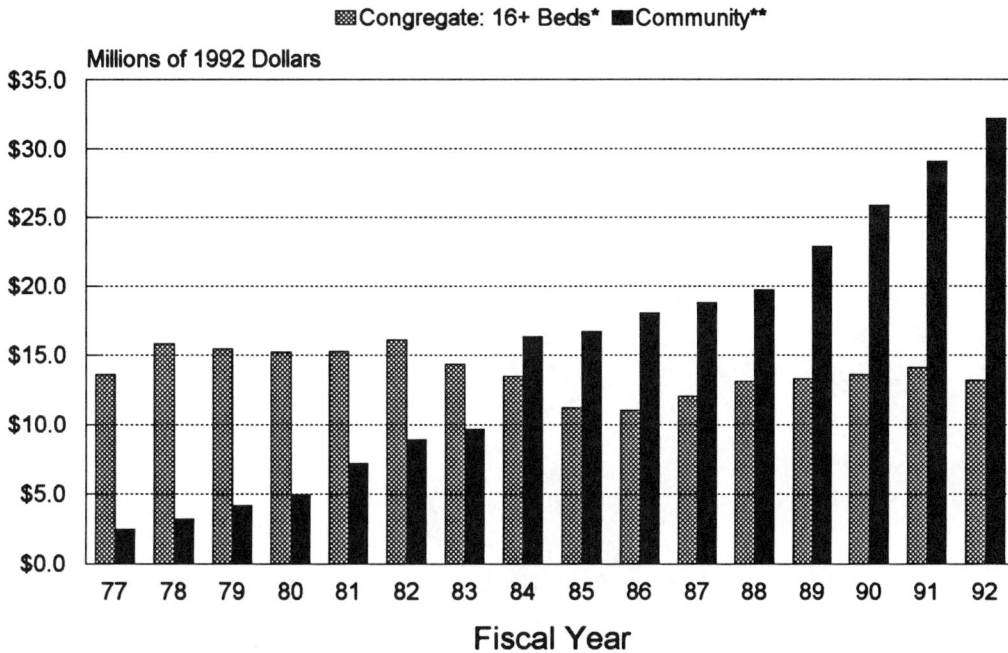

Fiscal Year

*Excludes nursing homes; ** Includes resources for
15 bed or less residential settings & non-residential community services

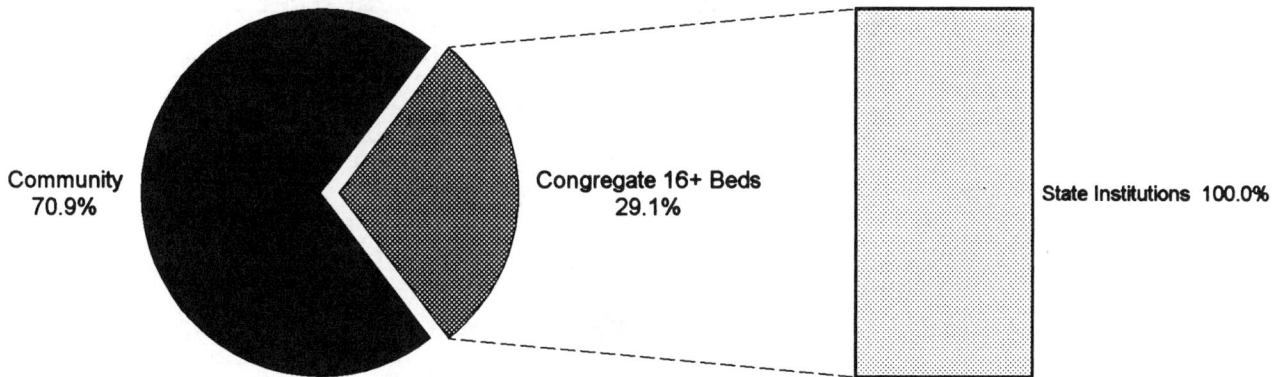

Community
70.9%

Congregate 16+ Beds
29.1%

State Institutions  100.0%

FY 1992 Total Spending:
$45.4 Million

*Source:*
Institute on Disability and Human Development (UAP),
University of Illinois at Chicago, 1994

# VERMONT

## Number of Persons Served by Residential Setting: FY 1992

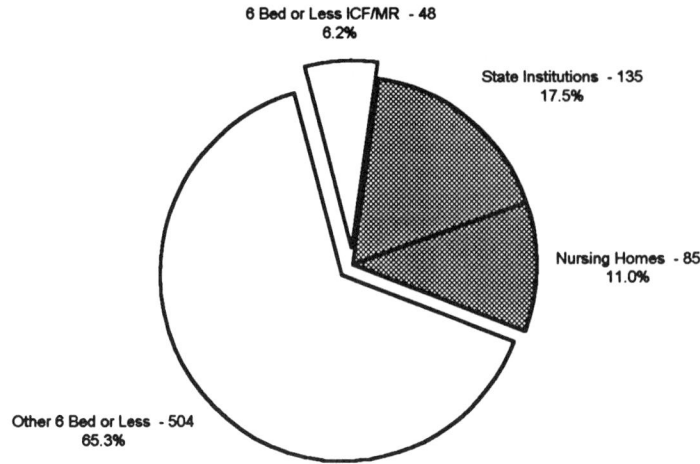

6 Bed or Less ICF/MR - 48
6.2%

State Institutions - 135
17.5%

Nursing Homes - 85
11.0%

Other 6 Bed or Less - 504
65.3%

Total Served: 772

## Persons Served by Residential Setting:1986-92

|  | 1986 | 1987 | 1988 | 1989 | 1990 | 1991 | 1992 |
|---|---|---|---|---|---|---|---|
| CONGREGATE 16 + BED SETTINGS | NA | NA | 316 | 278 | 268 | 262 | 220 |
| Nursing Homes | NA | NA | 125 | 95 | 89 | 92 | 85 |
| State Institutions | 196 | 194 | 191 | 183 | 179 | 170 | 135 |
| Private 16+Bed ICF/MR | 0 | 0 | 0 | 0 | 0 | 0 | 0 |
| Other 16+Bed Residential | 0 | 0 | 0 | 0 | 0 | 0 | 0 |
| 15 BED OR LESS RESIDENTIAL SETTINGS | 347 | 337 | 396 | 514 | 526 | 539 | 552 |
| Public 7-15 Bed ICF/MR | 0 | 0 | 0 | 0 | 0 | 0 | 0 |
| Private 7-15 Bed ICF/MR | 0 | 0 | 0 | 0 | 0 | 0 | 0 |
| Other 7-15 Bed Residential | 0 | 0 | 0 | 0 | 0 | 0 | 0 |
| Public 6 Bed or Less ICF/MR | 0 | 0 | 0 | 0 | 0 | 0 | 0 |
| Private 6 Bed or Less ICF/MR | 66 | 66 | 54 | 53 | 51 | 50 | 48 |
| Other 6 Bed or Less Residential | 281 | 271 | 342 | 461 | 475 | 490 | 504 |
| TOTAL PERSONS SERVED | NA | NA | 712 | 792 | 794 | 801 | 772 |

## Persons Served in Non-Residential Community Services:1986-92

|  | 1986 | 1987 | 1988 | 1989 | 1990 | 1991 | 1992 |
|---|---|---|---|---|---|---|---|
| DAY/WORK PROGRAMS | 780 | 752 | 670 | NA | NA | NA | 564 |
| Sheltered Employment/Work Activity | 50 | 50 | 50 | NA | NA | NA | 15 |
| Day Habilitation ("Day Training") | 579 | 517 | 400 | NA | NA | NA | 62 |
| Supported/Competitive Employment | 151 | 185 | 220 | NA | NA | NA | 487 |
| CASE MANAGEMENT | 0 | 0 | 0 | 0 | 0 | 0 | 910 |
| HCBS WAIVER | 93 | 205 | 243 | 296 | 353 | 405 | 545 |
| MODEL 50/200 WAIVER | 0 | 0 | 0 | 0 | 0 | 0 | 0 |

Source:
Institute on Disability and Human Development (UAP),
University of Illinois at Chicago, 1994

# VERMONT

## Community Services: FY 1992 Revenue Sources

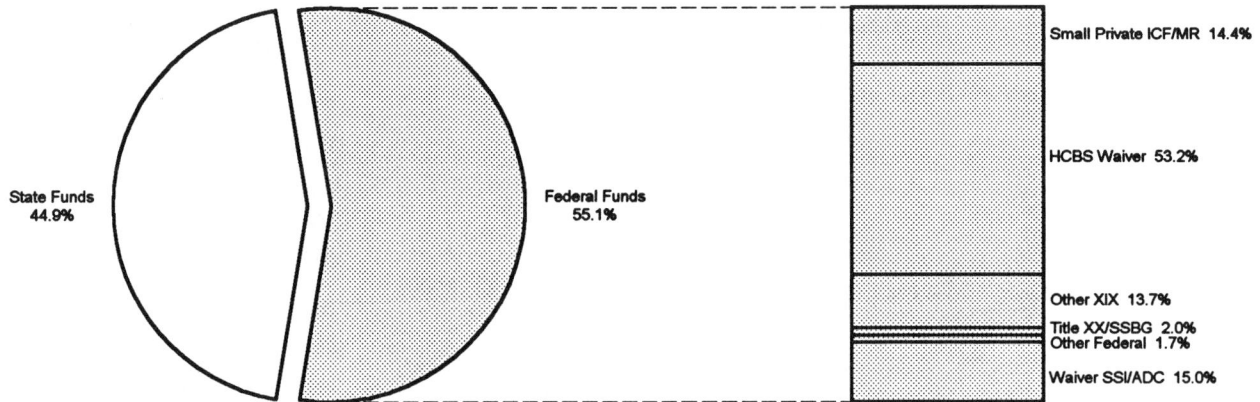

State Funds
44.9%

Federal Funds
55.1%

Small Private ICF/MR  14.4%

HCBS Waiver  53.2%

Other XIX  13.7%
Title XX/SSBG  2.0%
Other Federal  1.7%
Waiver SSI/ADC  15.0%

### Total Funds: $32.2 Million

## Family Support Initiatives*

|  | 1986 | 1987 | 1988 | 1989 | 1990 | 1991 | 1992 |
|---|---|---|---|---|---|---|---|
| **FAMILY SUPPORT: TOTAL SPENDING** | $478,300 | $501,900 | $588,500 | $469,276 | $548,255 | $560,977 | $568,591 |
| **Total # of Families Supported** | 311 | 282 | 420 | 445 | 481 | 490 | 510 |
| A. Financial Subsidy/Payment | $0 | $0 | $0 | $0 | $0 | $0 | $0 |
| # of Families | 0 | 0 | 0 | 0 | 0 | 0 | 0 |
| B. Family Assistance Payments | $465,300 | $488,300 | $572,500 | $454,276 | $533,255 | $541,977 | $548,591 |
| # of Families | 281 | 247 | 375 | 400 | 436 | 450 | 450 |
| C. Other Family Support Payments | $13,000 | $13,600 | $16,000 | $15,000 | $15,000 | $19,000 | $20,000 |
| # of Families | 30 | 35 | 45 | 45 | 45 | 40 | 60 |

## Other Community Services Initiatives*

|  | 1986 | 1987 | 1988 | 1989 | 1990 | 1991 | 1992 |
|---|---|---|---|---|---|---|---|
| **AGING/DD SPENDING** | $0 | $0 | $0 | $0 | $0 | $0 | $0 |
| # of Persons Served | 0 | 0 | 0 | 0 | 0 | 0 | 0 |
| **ASSISTIVE TECHNOLOGY SPENDING** |  |  |  | $0 | $0 | NA | $20,000 |
| # of Persons Served |  |  |  | 0 | 0 | 38 | 39 |
| **EARLY INTERVENTION SPENDING** | $0 | $0 | $0 | $0 | $0 | $0 | $0 |
| # of Persons Served | 0 | 0 | 0 | 0 | 0 | 0 | 0 |
| **PERSONAL ASSISTANCE SPENDING** |  |  |  |  |  |  | $0 |
| # of Persons Served |  |  |  |  |  |  | 0 |
| **SUPPORTED EMPLOYMENT SPENDING** | $0 | $0 | $29,500 | NA | NA | NA | $1,031,809 |
| # of Persons Served | 0 | 0 | 6 | NA | NA | NA | 487 |
| **SUPPORTED LIVING SPENDING** |  |  |  |  |  |  | $0 |
| # of Persons Served |  |  |  |  |  |  | 0 |

*Expenditures associated with Special Community Initiatives are a subset of funding within the community services component of the state's chart series and spreadsheet; Family Support Client figures may include duplicate client counts; HCBS Waiver counts include Waiver case management numbers.
0= Services not provided in the state; NA= Data not available from state; blank= Services not applicable (eg. CSLA prior to authorization, Special Community Initiatives prior to request for data by this study)

*Source:*
Institute on Disability and Human Development (UAP),
University of Illinois at Chicago, 1994

# VERMONT

## Large Congregate Care Facilities: FY 1992 Revenue Sources*

### Private 16+Bed Settings

### Public Institutions

### Does Not Apply

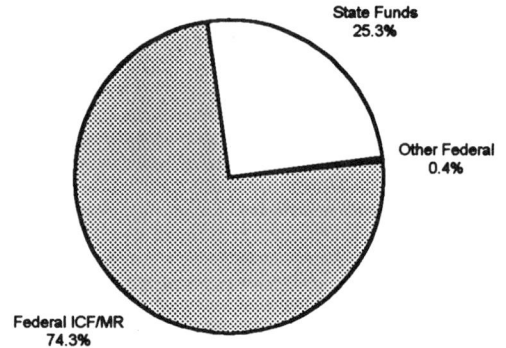

State Funds
25.3%

Other Federal
0.4%

Federal ICF/MR
74.3%

Total Funds: $13.2 Million

*Excludes nursing homes

## Average Daily Residents in Institutions

Number of Residents

| | | |
|---|---|---|

500 443 449
403
400 367 350
326
300
244
202 199 196 194 191 183 179 170
200
135
100

0
   77 78 79 80 81 82 83 84 85 86 87 88 89 90 91 92
Fiscal Year

## Institutional Daily Costs Per Resident

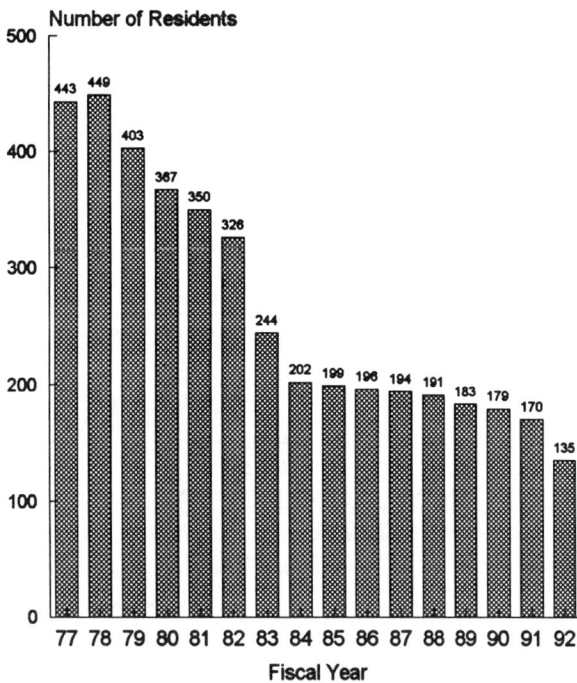

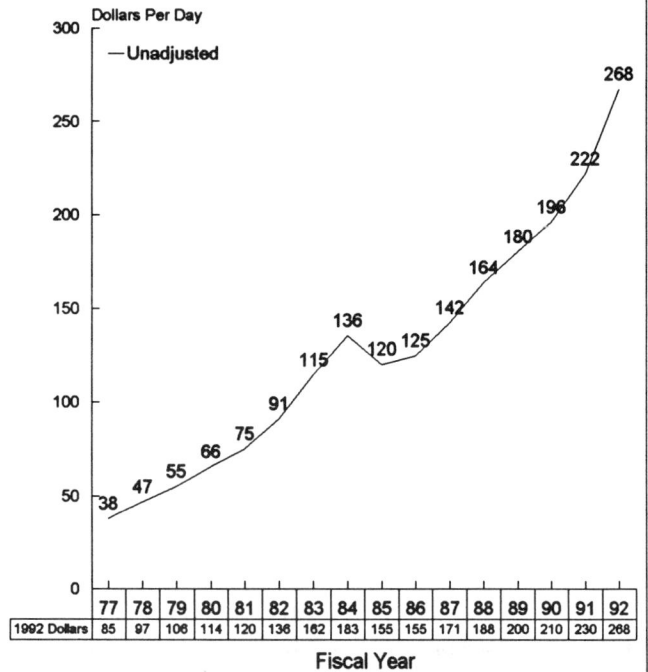

Dollars Per Day

300 —Unadjusted
268
250 222
196
200 180
164
142
150 136 125
120
115
100 91
75
55 66
50 47
38

0
   | 77 | 78 | 79 | 80 | 81 | 82 | 83 | 84 | 85 | 86 | 87 | 88 | 89 | 90 | 91 | 92 |
1992 Dollars | 85 | 97 | 106 | 114 | 120 | 136 | 162 | 183 | 155 | 155 | 171 | 188 | 200 | 210 | 230 | 268 |

Fiscal Year

*Source:*
Institute on Disability and Human Development (UAP),
University of Illinois at Chicago, 1994

# VERMONT FISCAL EFFORT

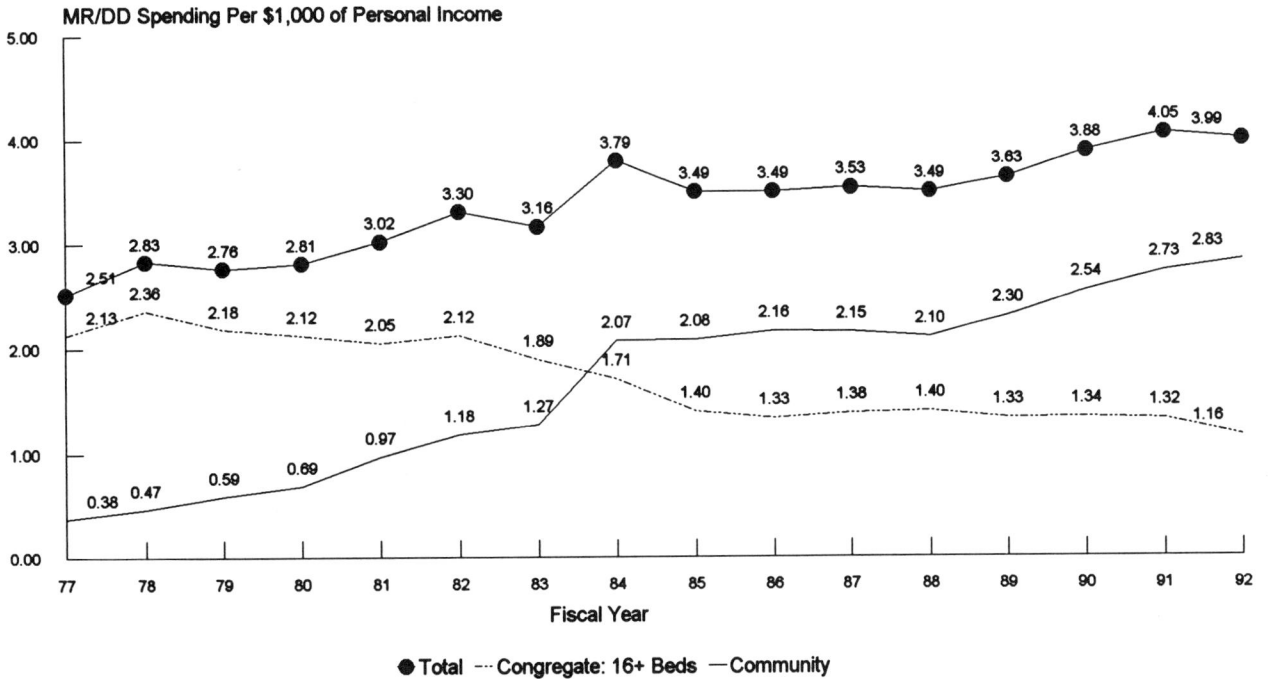

## MR/DD Spending Per $1,000 of Personal Income

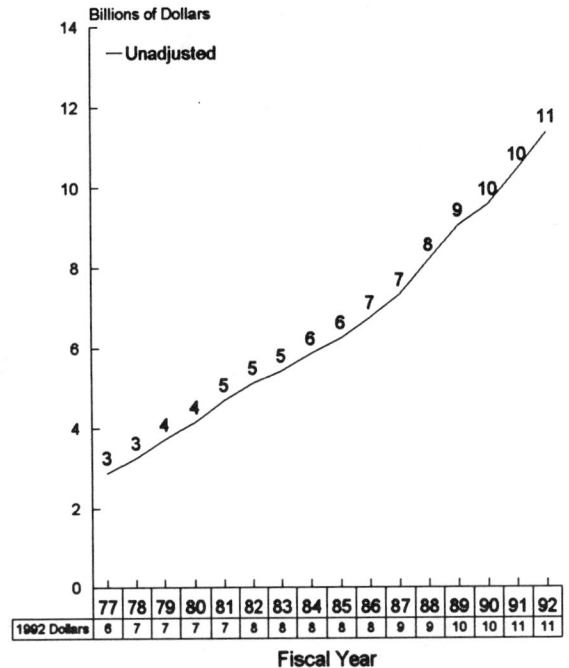

Total values (●): 2.51, 2.83, 2.76, 2.81, 3.02, 3.30, 3.16, 3.79, 3.49, 3.49, 3.53, 3.49, 3.63, 3.88, 4.05, 3.99

Congregate: 16+ Beds: 2.13, 2.36, 2.18, 2.12, 2.05, 2.12, 1.89, 1.71, 1.40, 1.33, 1.38, 1.40, 1.33, 1.34, 1.32, 1.16

Community: 0.38, 0.47, 0.59, 0.69, 0.97, 1.18, 1.27, 2.07, 2.08, 2.16, 2.15, 2.10, 2.30, 2.54, 2.73, 2.83

Fiscal Year: 77 78 79 80 81 82 83 84 85 86 87 88 89 90 91 92

● Total --- Congregate: 16+ Beds — Community

## Total MR/DD Spending

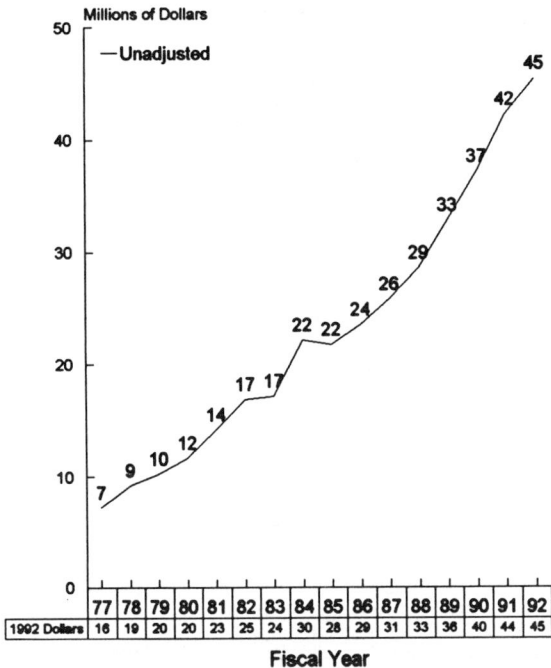

Millions of Dollars
— Unadjusted

Values: 7, 9, 10, 12, 14, 17, 17, 22, 22, 24, 26, 29, 33, 37, 42, 45

| Fiscal Year | 77 | 78 | 79 | 80 | 81 | 82 | 83 | 84 | 85 | 86 | 87 | 88 | 89 | 90 | 91 | 92 |
|---|---|---|---|---|---|---|---|---|---|---|---|---|---|---|---|---|
| 1992 Dollars | 16 | 19 | 20 | 20 | 23 | 25 | 24 | 30 | 28 | 29 | 31 | 33 | 36 | 40 | 44 | 45 |

## Personal Income

Billions of Dollars
— Unadjusted

Values: 3, 3, 4, 4, 5, 5, 5, 6, 6, 7, 7, 8, 9, 10, 10, 11

| Fiscal Year | 77 | 78 | 79 | 80 | 81 | 82 | 83 | 84 | 85 | 86 | 87 | 88 | 89 | 90 | 91 | 92 |
|---|---|---|---|---|---|---|---|---|---|---|---|---|---|---|---|---|
| 1992 Dollars | 6 | 7 | 7 | 7 | 7 | 8 | 8 | 8 | 8 | 8 | 9 | 9 | 10 | 10 | 11 | 11 |

*Source:*
Institute on Disability and Human Development (UAP),
University of Illinois at Chicago, 1994

# VERMONT
## Financial Support for MR/DD Services: FY 1977-92

| | 1977 | 1978 | 1979 | 1980 | 1981 | 1982 | 1983 | 1984 |
|---|---|---|---|---|---|---|---|---|
| **TOTAL FUNDS** | $7,227,000 | $9,200,400 | $10,268,600 | $11,661,900 | $14,159,800 | $16,846,000 | $17,111,280 | $22,152,132 |
| **CONGREGATE 16+ BEDS** | 6,127,000 | 7,660,500 | 8,090,100 | 8,802,700 | 9,615,900 | 10,841,100 | 10,215,200 | 10,023,900 |
| INSTITUTIONAL SERVICES FUNDS | 6,127,000 | 7,660,500 | 8,090,100 | 8,802,700 | 9,615,900 | 10,841,100 | 10,215,200 | 10,023,900 |
| STATE FUNDS | 3,803,000 | 2,753,900 | 2,992,500 | 2,085,700 | 2,097,300 | 2,729,100 | 2,713,600 | 3,409,100 |
| General Funds | 3,803,000 | 2,753,900 | 2,992,500 | 2,085,700 | 2,097,300 | 2,729,100 | 2,713,600 | 3,409,100 |
| Local | 0 | 0 | 0 | 0 | 0 | 0 | 0 | 0 |
| Other State Funds | 0 | 0 | 0 | 0 | 0 | 0 | 0 | 0 |
| FEDERAL FUNDS | 2,324,000 | 4,906,600 | 5,097,600 | 6,717,000 | 7,518,600 | 8,112,000 | 7,501,600 | 6,614,800 |
| Federal ICF/MR | 2,043,000 | 4,906,600 | 5,097,600 | 6,545,000 | 7,322,600 | 7,910,000 | 7,501,600 | 6,614,800 |
| Title XX / SSBG Funds | 0 | 0 | 0 | 0 | 0 | 0 | 0 | 0 |
| Other Federal Funds | 281,000 | 0 | 0 | 172,000 | 196,000 | 202,000 | 0 | 0 |
| LARGE PRIVATE RESIDENTIAL | 0 | 0 | 0 | 0 | 0 | 0 | 0 | 0 |
| STATE FUNDS | 0 | 0 | 0 | 0 | 0 | 0 | 0 | 0 |
| General Funds | 0 | 0 | 0 | 0 | 0 | 0 | 0 | 0 |
| Other State Funds | 0 | 0 | 0 | 0 | 0 | 0 | 0 | 0 |
| Local/County Overmatch | 0 | 0 | 0 | 0 | 0 | 0 | 0 | 0 |
| FEDERAL FUNDS | 0 | 0 | 0 | 0 | 0 | 0 | 0 | 0 |
| Large Private ICF/MR | 0 | 0 | 0 | 0 | 0 | 0 | 0 | 0 |
| **COMMUNITY SERVICES FUNDS** | 1,100,000 | 1,539,900 | 2,178,500 | 2,859,200 | 4,543,900 | 6,004,900 | 6,896,080 | 12,128,232 |
| STATE FUNDS | 600,000 | 1,156,000 | 1,593,500 | 1,964,400 | 2,903,100 | 3,919,800 | 4,286,700 | 7,288,800 |
| General Funds | 174,000 | 658,000 | 1,026,500 | 1,362,400 | 2,254,100 | 3,237,800 | 3,452,700 | 6,416,800 |
| Other State Funds | 0 | 0 | 0 | 0 | 0 | 0 | 0 | 0 |
| Local/County Overmatch | 0 | 0 | 0 | 0 | 0 | 0 | 0 | 0 |
| SSI State Supplement | 426,000 | 498,000 | 567,000 | 602,000 | 649,000 | 682,000 | 834,000 | 872,000 |
| FEDERAL FUNDS | 500,000 | 383,900 | 585,000 | 894,800 | 1,640,800 | 2,085,100 | 2,609,380 | 4,839,432 |
| ICF/MR Funds | 0 | 115,900 | 317,000 | 649,800 | 1,235,800 | 1,691,100 | 1,876,100 | 1,932,800 |
| Small Public | 0 | 0 | 0 | 0 | 0 | 0 | 0 | 0 |
| Small Private | 0 | 115,900 | 317,000 | 649,800 | 1,235,800 | 1,691,100 | 1,876,100 | 1,932,800 |
| HCBS Waiver | 0 | 0 | 0 | 0 | 0 | 0 | 334,000 | 2,300,000 |
| Model 50/200 Waiver | 0 | 0 | 0 | 0 | 0 | 0 | 0 | 0 |
| Other Title XIX Programs | 0 | 0 | 0 | 0 | 0 | 0 | 0 | 0 |
| Title XX / SSBG Funds | 500,000 | 268,000 | 268,000 | 245,000 | 405,000 | 394,000 | 365,000 | 350,000 |
| Other Federal Funds | 0 | 0 | 0 | 0 | 0 | 0 | 0 | 0 |
| Waiver Clients' SSI/ADC | 0 | 0 | 0 | 0 | 0 | 0 | 34,280 | 256,632 |

| | 1985 | 1986 | 1987 | 1988 | 1989 | 1990 | 1991 | 1992 |
|---|---|---|---|---|---|---|---|---|
| **TOTAL FUNDS** | $21,739,378 | $23,520,126 | $25,775,586 | $28,592,197 | $32,828,936 | $37,138,694 | $42,226,551 | $45,415,405 |
| **CONGREGATE 16+ BEDS** | 8,739,490 | 8,936,096 | 10,068,352 | 11,429,439 | 12,043,924 | 12,818,093 | 13,790,249 | 13,222,441 |
| INSTITUTIONAL SERVICES FUNDS | 8,739,490 | 8,936,096 | 10,068,352 | 11,429,439 | 12,043,924 | 12,818,093 | 13,790,249 | 13,222,441 |
| STATE FUNDS | 1,595,445 | 1,672,812 | 1,972,553 | 2,273,167 | 2,848,613 | 3,139,904 | 3,312,648 | 3,339,770 |
| General Funds | 1,595,445 | 1,672,812 | 1,972,553 | 2,273,167 | 2,848,613 | 3,139,904 | 3,312,648 | 3,339,770 |
| Local | 0 | 0 | 0 | 0 | 0 | 0 | 0 | 0 |
| Other State Funds | 0 | 0 | 0 | 0 | 0 | 0 | 0 | 0 |
| FEDERAL FUNDS | 7,144,045 | 7,263,284 | 8,095,799 | 9,156,272 | 9,195,311 | 9,678,189 | 10,477,601 | 9,882,671 |
| Federal ICF/MR | 7,031,149 | 7,168,877 | 8,014,022 | 9,074,936 | 9,127,572 | 9,613,624 | 10,379,430 | 9,828,371 |
| Title XX / SSBG Funds | 0 | 0 | 0 | 0 | 0 | 0 | 0 | 0 |
| Other Federal Funds | 112,896 | 94,407 | 81,777 | 81,336 | 67,739 | 64,565 | 98,171 | 54,300 |
| LARGE PRIVATE RESIDENTIAL | 0 | 0 | 0 | 0 | 0 | 0 | 0 | 0 |
| STATE FUNDS | 0 | 0 | 0 | 0 | 0 | 0 | 0 | 0 |
| General Funds | 0 | 0 | 0 | 0 | 0 | 0 | 0 | 0 |
| Other State Funds | 0 | 0 | 0 | 0 | 0 | 0 | 0 | 0 |
| Local/County Overmatch | 0 | 0 | 0 | 0 | 0 | 0 | 0 | 0 |
| FEDERAL FUNDS | 0 | 0 | 0 | 0 | 0 | 0 | 0 | 0 |
| Large Private ICF/MR | 0 | 0 | 0 | 0 | 0 | 0 | 0 | 0 |
| **COMMUNITY SERVICES FUNDS** | 12,999,888 | 14,584,030 | 15,707,234 | 17,162,758 | 20,785,012 | 24,320,601 | 28,436,302 | 32,192,964 |
| STATE FUNDS | 6,681,792 | 7,565,684 | 8,075,245 | 9,027,087 | 10,688,129 | 12,191,133 | 13,311,754 | 14,463,167 |
| General Funds | 5,730,086 | 6,497,684 | 6,808,196 | 7,686,994 | 9,262,897 | 10,706,662 | 11,755,556 | 12,828,197 |
| Other State Funds | 29,706 | 31,000 | 37,049 | 49,093 | 69,682 | 61,143 | 61,704 | 65,751 |
| Local/County Overmatch | 0 | 0 | 0 | 0 | 0 | 0 | 0 | 0 |
| SSI State Supplement | 922,000 | 1,037,000 | 1,230,000 | 1,291,000 | 1,355,550 | 1,423,328 | 1,494,494 | 1,569,219 |
| FEDERAL FUNDS | 6,318,096 | 7,018,346 | 7,631,989 | 8,135,671 | 10,096,883 | 12,129,468 | 15,124,548 | 17,729,797 |
| ICF/MR Funds | 1,755,600 | 1,631,300 | 1,526,500 | 1,758,500 | 1,872,555 | 1,986,610 | 2,100,665 | 2,555,389 |
| Small Public | 0 | 0 | 0 | 0 | 0 | 0 | 0 | 0 |
| Small Private | 1,755,600 | 1,631,300 | 1,526,500 | 1,758,500 | 1,872,555 | 1,986,610 | 2,100,665 | 2,555,389 |
| HCBS Waiver | 3,615,600 | 2,902,800 | 3,256,800 | 3,528,100 | 4,997,452 | 6,466,803 | 8,911,261 | 9,429,167 |
| Model 50/200 Waiver | 0 | 0 | 0 | 0 | 0 | 0 | 0 | 0 |
| Other Title XIX Programs | 0 | 1,601,400 | 1,531,300 | 1,356,300 | 1,465,595 | 1,574,890 | 1,684,185 | 2,427,863 |
| Title XX / SSBG Funds | 350,000 | 350,000 | 350,000 | 350,000 | 350,000 | 350,000 | 350,000 | 350,000 |
| Other Federal Funds | 179,296 | 185,770 | 192,489 | 197,987 | 188,289 | 192,317 | 203,581 | 305,598 |
| Waiver Clients' SSI/ADC | 417,600 | 347,076 | 774,900 | 944,784 | 1,222,992 | 1,558,848 | 1,874,856 | 2,661,780 |

*Source:*
Institute on Disability and Human Development (UAP),
University of Illinois at Chicago, 1994

# VIRGINIA

## MR/DD Spending for Congregate Residential & Community Services

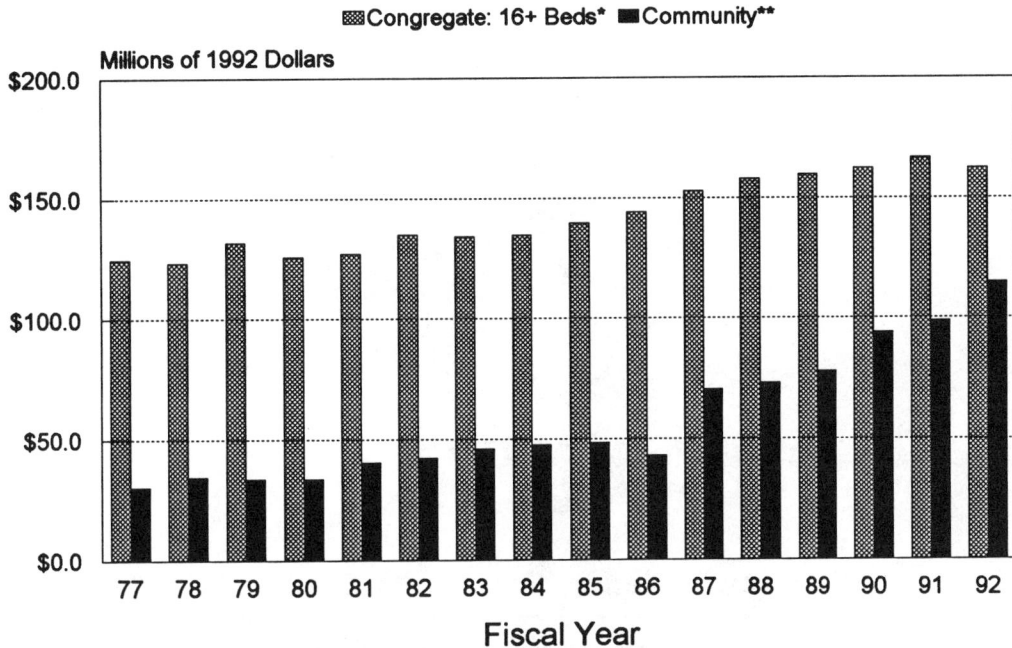

▨Congregate: 16+ Beds* ■Community**

Millions of 1992 Dollars

**Fiscal Year**

*Excludes nursing homes; ** Includes resources for
15 bed or less residential settings & non-residential community services

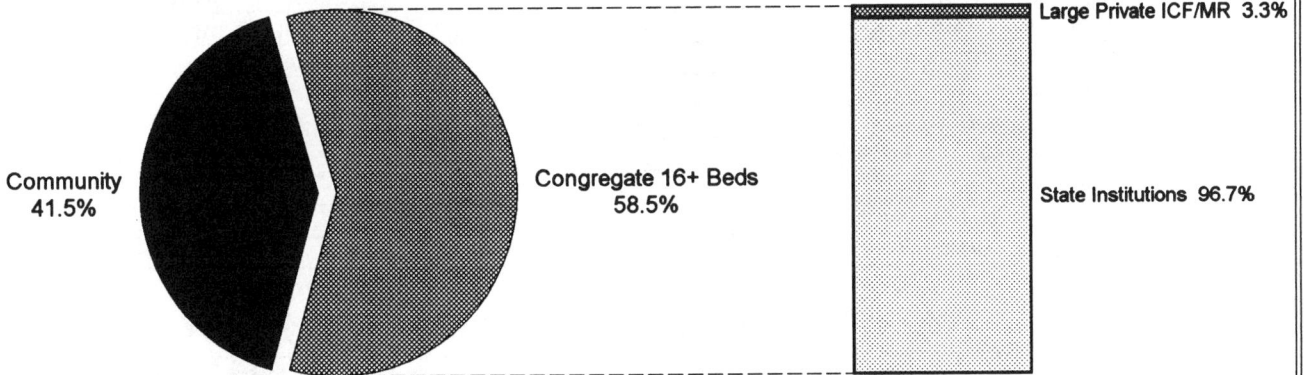

Community
41.5%

Congregate 16+ Beds
58.5%

Large Private ICF/MR  3.3%

State Institutions  96.7%

FY 1992 Total Spending:
$277.2 Million

*Source:*
Institute on Disability and Human Development (UAP),
University of Illinois at Chicago, 1994

# VIRGINIA

## Number of Persons Served by Residential Setting: FY 1992

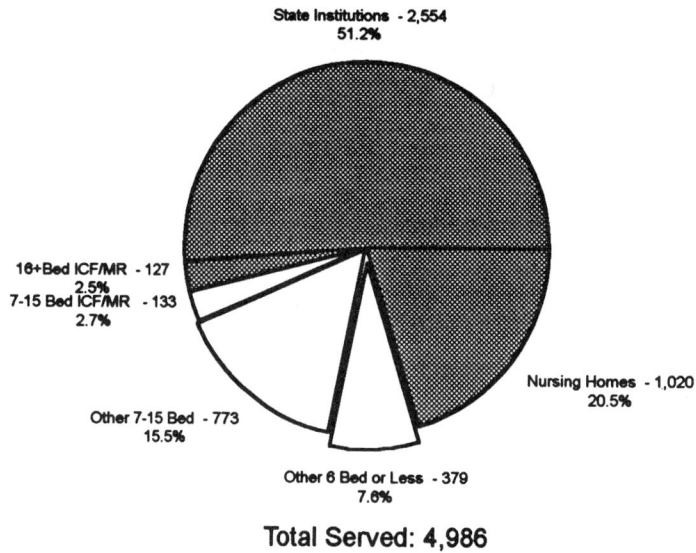

State Institutions - 2,554
51.2%

16+Bed ICF/MR - 127
2.5%
7-15 Bed ICF/MR - 133
2.7%

Nursing Homes - 1,020
20.5%

Other 7-15 Bed - 773
15.5%

Other 6 Bed or Less - 379
7.6%

Total Served: 4,986

## Persons Served by Residential Setting:1986-92

| | 1986 | 1987 | 1988 | 1989 | 1990 | 1991 | 1992 |
|---|---|---|---|---|---|---|---|
| **CONGREGATE 16 + BED SETTINGS** | **NA** | **NA** | **4,298** | **NA** | **NA** | **4,535** | **3,701** |
| Nursing Homes | NA | NA | 1,351 | NA | NA | 1,786 | 1,020 |
| State Institutions | 2,969 | 2,892 | 2,821 | 2,760 | 2,677 | 2,618 | 2,554 |
| Private 16+ Bed ICF/MR | 103 | 104 | 126 | 114 | 121 | 131 | 127 |
| Other 16+ Bed Residential | 0 | 0 | 0 | 0 | 0 | 0 | 0 |
| **15 BED OR LESS RESIDENTIAL SETTINGS** | **891** | **1,030** | **1,104** | **1,158** | **1,282** | **1,231** | **1,285** |
| Public 7-15 Bed ICF/MR | 0 | 0 | 0 | 0 | 0 | 0 | 0 |
| Private 7-15 Bed ICF/MR | 83 | 87 | 97 | 126 | 130 | 140 | 133 |
| Other 7-15 Bed Residential | 808 | 943 | 1,007 | 1,032 | 1,152 | 1,091 | 773 |
| Public 6 Bed or Less ICF/MR | 0 | 0 | 0 | 0 | 0 | 0 | 0 |
| Private 6 Bed or Less ICF/MR | | | | | | | 0 |
| Other 6 Bed or Less Residential | | | | | | | 379 |
| **TOTAL PERSONS SERVED** | **NA** | **NA** | **5,402** | **NA** | **NA** | **5,766** | **4,986** |

## Persons Served in Non-Residential Community Services:1986-92

| | 1986 | 1987 | 1988 | 1989 | 1990 | 1991 | 1992 |
|---|---|---|---|---|---|---|---|
| **DAY/WORK PROGRAMS** | **3,715** | **3,778** | **3,483** | **NA** | **NA** | **NA** | **NA** |
| Sheltered Employment/Work Activity | 2,666 | 2,681 | 2,584 | NA | NA | NA | NA |
| Day Habilitation ("Day Training") | 1,049 | 1,097 | 849 | NA | NA | NA | NA |
| Supported/Competitive Employment | 0 | 0 | 50 | NA | NA | NA | NA |
| **CASE MANAGEMENT** | **7,201** | **8,264** | **9,344** | **NA** | **NA** | **NA** | **NA** |
| **HCBS WAIVER** | **0** | **0** | **0** | **0** | **0** | **0** | **250** |
| **MODEL 50/200 WAIVER** | **0** | **0** | **0** | **0** | **0** | **0** | **0** |

*Source:*
Institute on Disability and Human Development (UAP),
University of Illinois at Chicago, 1994

# VIRGINIA

## Community Services: FY 1992 Revenue Sources

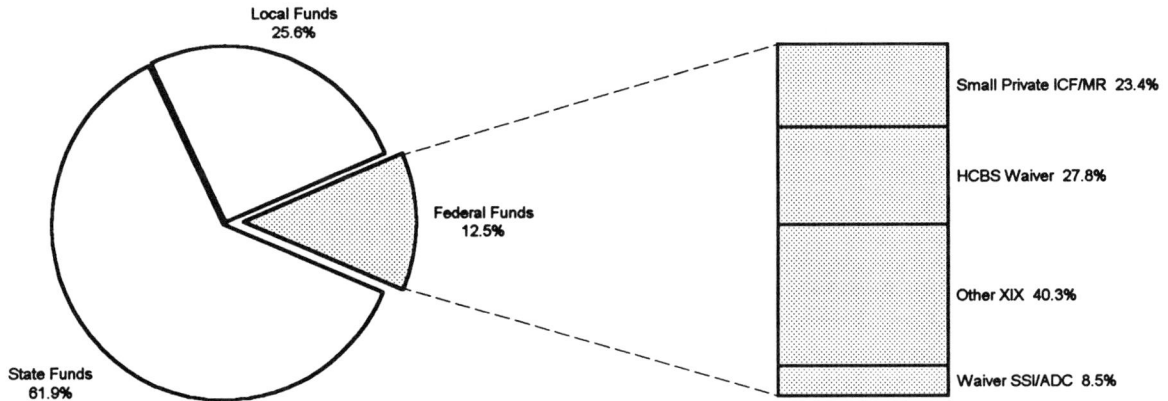

Local Funds 25.6%

Federal Funds 12.5%

State Funds 61.9%

Small Private ICF/MR 23.4%

HCBS Waiver 27.8%

Other XIX 40.3%

Waiver SSI/ADC 8.5%

Total Funds: $115.1 Million

## Family Support Initiatives*

|  | 1986 | 1987 | 1988 | 1989 | 1990 | 1991 | 1992 |
|---|---|---|---|---|---|---|---|
| **FAMILY SUPPORT: TOTAL SPENDING** | $0 | $0 | $0 | $0 | $0 | $550,000 | $600,000 |
| **Total # of Families Supported** | 0 | 0 | 0 | 0 | 0 | 565 | 600 |
| A. Financial Subsidy/Payment | $0 | $0 | $0 | $0 | $0 | $0 | $0 |
| # of Families | 0 | 0 | 0 | 0 | 0 | 0 | 0 |
| B. Family Assistance Payments | $0 | $0 | $0 | $0 | $0 | $0 | $0 |
| # of Families | 0 | 0 | 0 | 0 | 0 | 0 | 0 |
| C. Other Family Support Payments | $0 | $0 | $0 | $0 | $0 | $550,000 | $600,000 |
| # of Families | 0 | 0 | 0 | 0 | 0 | 565 | 600 |

## Other Community Services Initiatives*

|  | 1986 | 1987 | 1988 | 1989 | 1990 | 1991 | 1992 |
|---|---|---|---|---|---|---|---|
| **AGING/DD SPENDING** | $0 | $0 | $0 | $0 | $0 | $0 | $0 |
| # of Persons Served | 0 | 0 | 0 | 0 | 0 | 0 | 0 |
| **ASSISTIVE TECHNOLOGY SPENDING** |  |  |  |  |  |  | $0 |
| # of Persons Served |  |  |  |  |  |  | 0 |
| **EARLY INTERVENTION SPENDING** | $2,172,200 | $3,583,600 | $4,133,000 | $5,512,867 | $7,020,531 | $7,500,232 | $7,539,631 |
| # of Persons Served | 2,017 | 2,463 | 2,412 | NA | NA | NA | NA |
| **PERSONAL ASSISTANCE SPENDING** |  |  |  |  |  |  | $0 |
| # of Persons Served |  |  |  |  |  |  | 0 |
| **SUPPORTED EMPLOYMENT SPENDING** | $0 | $0 | $528,000 | $6,544,648 | $8,415,117 | $8,206,656 | $9,453,032 |
| # of Persons Served | 0 | 0 | 50 | NA | NA | NA | NA |
| **SUPPORTED LIVING SPENDING** |  |  |  | $2,513,891 | $3,104,437 | $3,312,720 | $3,173,563 |
| # of Persons Served |  |  |  | NA | NA | NA | NA |

*Expenditures associated with Special Community Initiatives are a subset of funding within the community services component of the state's chart series and spreadsheet; Family Support Client figures may include duplicate client counts; HCBS Waiver counts include Waiver case management numbers.
0= Services not provided in the state; NA= Data not available from state; blank= Services not applicable (eg. CSLA prior to authorization, Special Community Initiatives prior to request for data by this study)

*Source:*
Institute on Disability and Human Development (UAP),
University of Illinois at Chicago, 1994

# VIRGINIA

## Large Congregate Care Facilities: FY 1992 Revenue Sources*

### Private 16+Bed Settings

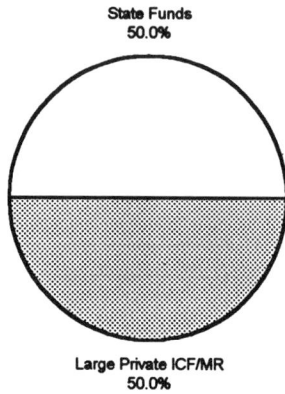

State Funds
50.0%

Large Private ICF/MR
50.0%

Total Funds: $5.4 Million

### Public Institutions

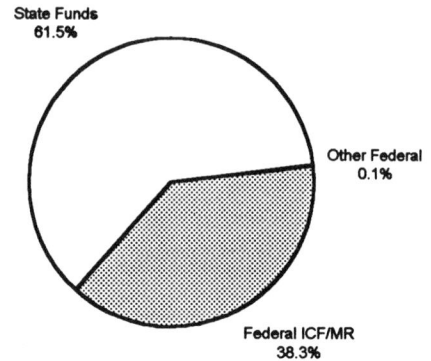

State Funds
61.5%

Other Federal
0.1%

Federal ICF/MR
38.3%

Total Funds: $156.7 Million

*Excludes nursing homes

## Average Daily Residents in Institutions

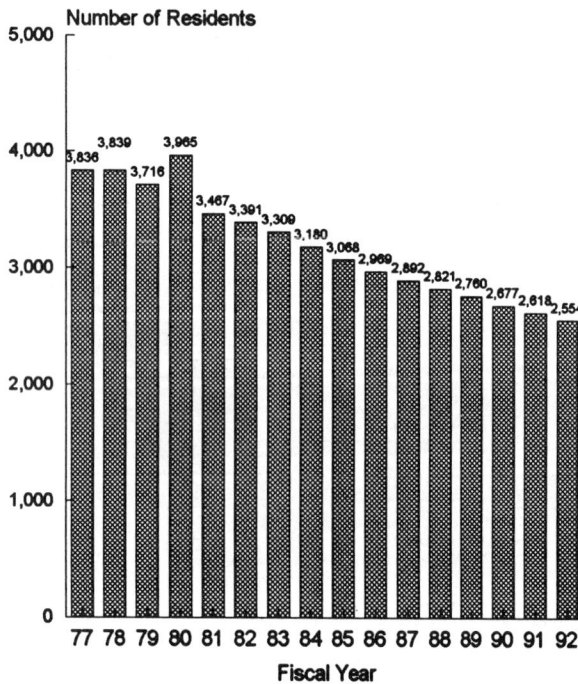

Number of Residents

| Fiscal Year | Residents |
|---|---|
| 77 | 3,836 |
| 78 | 3,839 |
| 79 | 3,716 |
| 80 | 3,965 |
| 81 | 3,467 |
| 82 | 3,391 |
| 83 | 3,309 |
| 84 | 3,180 |
| 85 | 3,068 |
| 86 | 2,969 |
| 87 | 2,892 |
| 88 | 2,821 |
| 89 | 2,760 |
| 90 | 2,677 |
| 91 | 2,618 |
| 92 | 2,554 |

Fiscal Year

## Institutional Daily Costs Per Resident

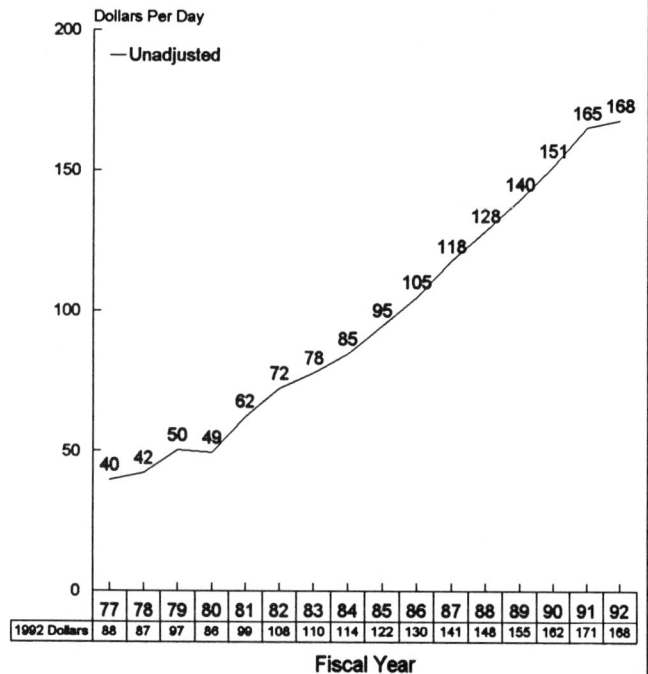

Dollars Per Day

—Unadjusted

40, 42, 50, 49, 62, 72, 78, 85, 95, 105, 118, 128, 140, 151, 165, 168

| Fiscal Year | 77 | 78 | 79 | 80 | 81 | 82 | 83 | 84 | 85 | 86 | 87 | 88 | 89 | 90 | 91 | 92 |
|---|---|---|---|---|---|---|---|---|---|---|---|---|---|---|---|---|
| 1992 Dollars | 88 | 87 | 97 | 86 | 99 | 108 | 110 | 114 | 122 | 130 | 141 | 148 | 155 | 162 | 171 | 168 |

Fiscal Year

*Source:*
Institute on Disability and Human Development (UAP),
University of Illinois at Chicago, 1994

# VIRGINIA FISCAL EFFORT

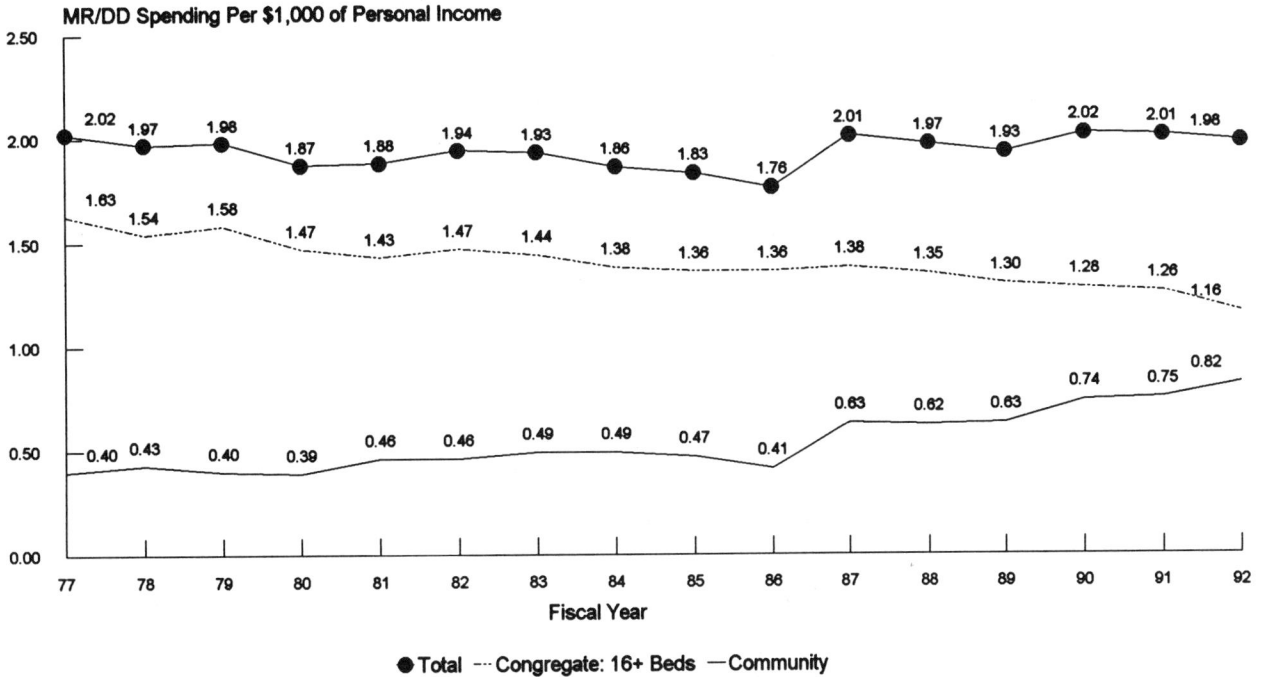

MR/DD Spending Per $1,000 of Personal Income

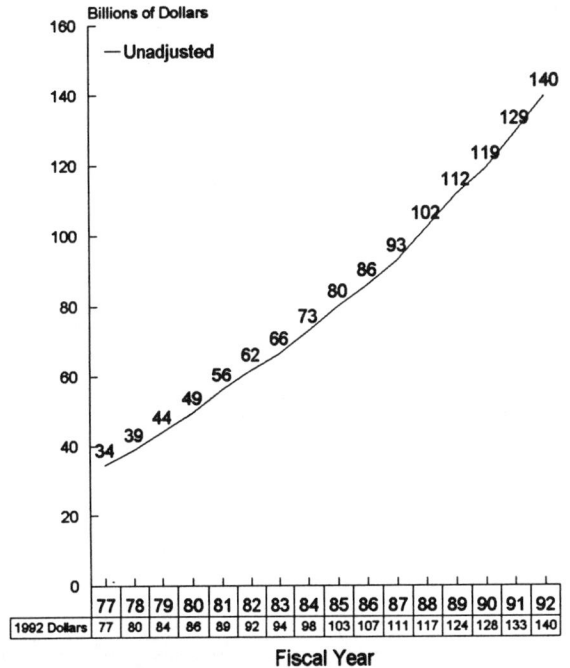

| | | | | | | | | | | | | | | | |
|---|---|---|---|---|---|---|---|---|---|---|---|---|---|---|---|

2.50

2.02  1.97  1.98  1.87  1.88  1.94  1.93  1.86  1.83  1.76  2.01  1.97  1.93  2.02  2.01  1.98

2.00

1.63  1.54  1.58  1.47  1.43  1.47  1.44  1.38  1.36  1.36  1.38  1.35  1.30  1.28  1.26  1.16

1.50

1.00

0.74  0.75  0.82

0.63  0.62  0.63

0.40  0.43  0.40  0.39  0.46  0.46  0.49  0.49  0.47  0.41

0.50

0.00

77   78   79   80   81   82   83   84   85   86   87   88   89   90   91   92

Fiscal Year

● Total   --- Congregate: 16+ Beds   — Community

## Total MR/DD Spending

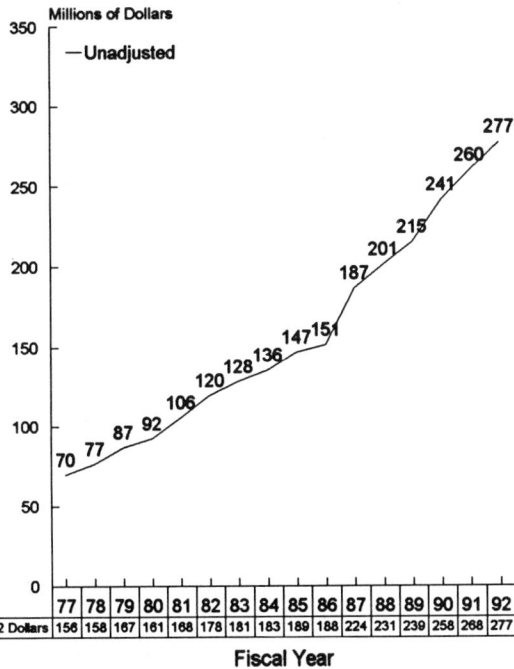

Millions of Dollars
—Unadjusted

350

300                                                          277
                                                        260
                                                   241
                                              215
                                         201
                                    187
                              147 151
                         136
                   120 128
              106
          87  92
      70  77

350
300
250
200
150
100
50
0

| | 77 | 78 | 79 | 80 | 81 | 82 | 83 | 84 | 85 | 86 | 87 | 88 | 89 | 90 | 91 | 92 |
|---|---|---|---|---|---|---|---|---|---|---|---|---|---|---|---|---|
| 1992 Dollars | 156 | 158 | 167 | 161 | 168 | 178 | 181 | 183 | 189 | 188 | 224 | 231 | 239 | 258 | 268 | 277 |

Fiscal Year

## Personal Income

Billions of Dollars
—Unadjusted

160                                                        140
                                                      129
                                                 119
                                            112
                                       102
                                  93
                             86
                        80
                   73
              62  66
         56
      49
   44
34  39

160
140
120
100
80
60
40
20
0

| | 77 | 78 | 79 | 80 | 81 | 82 | 83 | 84 | 85 | 86 | 87 | 88 | 89 | 90 | 91 | 92 |
|---|---|---|---|---|---|---|---|---|---|---|---|---|---|---|---|---|
| 1992 Dollars | 77 | 80 | 84 | 86 | 89 | 92 | 94 | 98 | 103 | 107 | 111 | 117 | 124 | 128 | 133 | 140 |

Fiscal Year

*Source:*
Institute on Disability and Human Development (UAP),
University of Illinois at Chicago, 1994

# VIRGINIA
## Financial Support for MR/DD Services: FY 1977-92

| | 1977 | 1978 | 1979 | 1980 | 1981 | 1982 | 1983 | 1984 |
|---|---|---|---|---|---|---|---|---|
| **TOTAL FUNDS** | $69,745,000 | $76,530,000 | $86,801,000 | $92,266,000 | $105,696,000 | $119,661,000 | $128,393,700 | $135,502,100 |
| **CONGREGATE 16+ BEDS** | 56,117,213 | 59,808,593 | 69,121,777 | 72,799,671 | 80,102,651 | 91,097,991 | 95,595,623 | 100,074,094 |
| INSTITUTIONAL SERVICES FUNDS | 55,483,000 | 59,111,000 | 68,250,000 | 71,596,000 | 78,785,000 | 89,648,000 | 94,081,700 | 98,501,100 |
| STATE FUNDS | 39,125,000 | 39,856,000 | 49,484,000 | 42,760,000 | 43,341,000 | 46,573,000 | 52,813,200 | 58,082,200 |
| General Funds | 24,965,000 | 22,716,000 | 32,029,000 | 17,147,000 | 12,012,000 | 9,077,000 | 16,299,700 | 24,679,700 |
| Local | 0 | 0 | 0 | 0 | 0 | 0 | 0 | 0 |
| Other State Funds | 14,160,000 | 17,140,000 | 17,455,000 | 25,613,000 | 31,329,000 | 37,496,000 | 36,513,500 | 33,402,500 |
| FEDERAL FUNDS | 16,358,000 | 19,255,000 | 18,766,000 | 28,836,000 | 35,444,000 | 43,075,000 | 41,268,500 | 40,418,900 |
| Federal ICF/MR | 15,890,000 | 18,756,000 | 18,137,000 | 28,177,000 | 34,642,000 | 42,162,000 | 40,297,400 | 37,821,500 |
| Title XX / SSBG Funds | 0 | 0 | 0 | 0 | 0 | 0 | 0 | 0 |
| Other Federal Funds | 468,000 | 499,000 | 629,000 | 659,000 | 802,000 | 913,000 | 971,100 | 2,597,400 |
| LARGE PRIVATE RESIDENTIAL | 634,213 | 697,593 | 871,777 | 1,203,671 | 1,317,651 | 1,449,991 | 1,513,923 | 1,572,994 |
| STATE FUNDS | 264,213 | 297,593 | 374,777 | 521,671 | 572,651 | 627,991 | 654,923 | 682,994 |
| General Funds | 264,213 | 297,593 | 374,777 | 521,671 | 572,651 | 627,991 | 654,923 | 682,994 |
| Other State Funds | 0 | 0 | 0 | 0 | 0 | 0 | 0 | 0 |
| Local/County Overmatch | 0 | 0 | 0 | 0 | 0 | 0 | 0 | 0 |
| FEDERAL FUNDS | 370,000 | 400,000 | 497,000 | 682,000 | 745,000 | 822,000 | 859,000 | 890,000 |
| Large Private ICF/MR | 370,000 | 400,000 | 497,000 | 682,000 | 745,000 | 822,000 | 859,000 | 890,000 |
| **COMMUNITY SERVICES FUNDS** | 13,627,787 | 16,721,407 | 17,679,223 | 19,466,329 | 25,593,349 | 28,563,009 | 32,798,077 | 35,428,006 |
| STATE FUNDS | 11,475,787 | 14,007,407 | 15,537,223 | 17,443,329 | 22,996,349 | 25,843,009 | 29,365,077 | 32,073,006 |
| General Funds | 4,095,787 | 5,316,407 | 5,938,223 | 7,073,329 | 9,369,349 | 11,294,009 | 13,278,077 | 15,391,006 |
| Other State Funds | 4,391,000 | 4,881,000 | 4,440,000 | 4,675,000 | 6,361,000 | 6,495,000 | 6,919,000 | 7,224,000 |
| Local/County Overmatch | 2,804,000 | 3,439,000 | 4,483,000 | 4,819,000 | 6,223,000 | 6,825,000 | 7,858,000 | 8,171,000 |
| SSI State Supplement | 185,000 | 371,000 | 676,000 | 876,000 | 1,043,000 | 1,229,000 | 1,310,000 | 1,287,000 |
| FEDERAL FUNDS | 2,152,000 | 2,714,000 | 2,142,000 | 2,023,000 | 2,597,000 | 2,720,000 | 3,433,000 | 3,355,000 |
| ICF/MR Funds | 0 | 0 | 0 | 0 | 0 | 541,000 | 1,062,000 | 1,104,000 |
| Small Public | 0 | 0 | 0 | 0 | 0 | 0 | 0 | 0 |
| Small Private | 0 | 0 | 0 | 0 | 0 | 541,000 | 1,062,000 | 1,104,000 |
| HCBS Waiver | 0 | 0 | 0 | 0 | 0 | 0 | 0 | 0 |
| Model 50/200 Waiver | 0 | 0 | 0 | 0 | 0 | 0 | 0 | 0 |
| Other Title XIX Programs | 0 | 0 | 0 | 0 | 0 | 0 | 0 | 0 |
| Title XX / SSBG Funds | 1,434,000 | 1,542,000 | 1,391,000 | 1,421,000 | 1,982,000 | 1,552,000 | 1,630,000 | 1,700,000 |
| Other Federal Funds | 718,000 | 1,172,000 | 751,000 | 602,000 | 615,000 | 627,000 | 741,000 | 551,000 |
| Waiver Clients' SSI/ADC | 0 | 0 | 0 | 0 | 0 | 0 | 0 | 0 |

| | 1985 | 1986 | 1987 | 1988 | 1989 | 1990 | 1991 | 1992 |
|---|---|---|---|---|---|---|---|---|
| **TOTAL FUNDS** | $146,564,176 | $151,473,768 | $186,511,995 | $201,063,838 | $215,264,730 | $241,243,008 | $259,621,550 | $277,232,471 |
| **CONGREGATE 16+ BEDS** | 108,836,198 | 116,525,181 | 127,730,377 | 137,358,307 | 144,695,903 | 152,675,969 | 163,039,107 | 162,133,796 |
| INSTITUTIONAL SERVICES FUNDS | 106,034,500 | 113,486,100 | 124,064,400 | 132,568,000 | 140,611,593 | 147,994,757 | 157,697,251 | 156,728,750 |
| STATE FUNDS | 67,766,200 | 65,571,400 | 72,469,600 | 78,274,800 | 88,149,163 | 90,965,130 | 96,178,625 | 96,444,324 |
| General Funds | 35,515,700 | 21,478,400 | 24,279,100 | 24,163,400 | 28,346,889 | 23,791,201 | 21,960,491 | 19,057,612 |
| Local | 0 | 0 | 0 | 0 | 0 | 0 | 0 | 0 |
| Other State Funds | 32,250,500 | 44,093,000 | 48,190,500 | 54,111,400 | 59,802,274 | 67,173,929 | 74,218,134 | 77,386,712 |
| FEDERAL FUNDS | 38,268,300 | 47,914,700 | 51,594,800 | 54,293,200 | 52,462,430 | 57,029,627 | 61,518,626 | 60,284,426 |
| Federal ICF/MR | 36,221,300 | 44,032,800 | 49,029,600 | 51,416,900 | 52,193,468 | 56,621,238 | 61,218,333 | 60,101,656 |
| Title XX / SSBG Funds | 0 | 0 | 0 | 0 | 0 | 0 | 0 | 0 |
| Other Federal Funds | 2,047,000 | 3,881,900 | 2,565,200 | 2,876,300 | 268,962 | 408,389 | 300,293 | 182,770 |
| LARGE PRIVATE RESIDENTIAL | 2,801,698 | 3,039,081 | 3,665,977 | 4,790,307 | 4,084,310 | 4,681,212 | 5,341,856 | 5,405,046 |
| STATE FUNDS | 1,217,898 | 1,398,281 | 1,717,877 | 2,309,407 | 1,991,510 | 2,326,562 | 2,670,928 | 2,702,523 |
| General Funds | 1,217,898 | 1,398,281 | 1,717,877 | 2,309,407 | 1,991,510 | 2,326,562 | 2,670,928 | 2,702,523 |
| Other State Funds | 0 | 0 | 0 | 0 | 0 | 0 | 0 | 0 |
| Local/County Overmatch | 0 | 0 | 0 | 0 | 0 | 0 | 0 | 0 |
| FEDERAL FUNDS | 1,583,800 | 1,640,800 | 1,948,100 | 2,480,900 | 2,092,800 | 2,354,650 | 2,670,928 | 2,702,523 |
| Large Private ICF/MR | 1,583,800 | 1,640,800 | 1,948,100 | 2,480,900 | 2,092,800 | 2,354,650 | 2,670,928 | 2,702,523 |
| **COMMUNITY SERVICES FUNDS** | 37,727,978 | 34,948,587 | 58,781,618 | 63,705,531 | 70,568,827 | 88,567,039 | 96,582,443 | 115,098,675 |
| STATE FUNDS | 35,970,378 | 31,940,287 | 53,674,718 | 57,944,131 | 67,891,403 | 85,569,963 | 90,370,635 | 100,693,659 |
| General Funds | 15,447,134 | 12,906,200 | 22,687,600 | 24,590,893 | 34,370,198 | 45,333,309 | 43,056,563 | 48,477,817 |
| Other State Funds | 10,696,500 | 8,592,600 | 15,887,600 | 14,775,500 | 11,797,527 | 13,777,597 | 16,990,619 | 20,512,061 |
| Local/County Overmatch | 8,465,744 | 8,760,487 | 13,294,518 | 16,766,738 | 19,822,128 | 24,462,429 | 28,226,994 | 29,502,499 |
| SSI State Supplement | 1,361,000 | 1,681,000 | 1,805,000 | 1,811,000 | 1,901,550 | 1,996,628 | 2,096,459 | 2,201,282 |
| FEDERAL FUNDS | 1,757,600 | 3,008,300 | 5,106,900 | 5,761,400 | 2,677,424 | 2,997,076 | 6,211,808 | 14,405,016 |
| ICF/MR Funds | 1,035,400 | 1,594,200 | 1,751,300 | 2,110,000 | 2,426,274 | 2,713,685 | 2,367,559 | 3,364,214 |
| Small Public | 0 | 0 | 0 | 0 | 0 | 0 | 0 | 0 |
| Small Private | 1,035,400 | 1,594,200 | 1,751,300 | 2,110,000 | 2,426,274 | 2,713,685 | 2,367,559 | 3,364,214 |
| HCBS Waiver | 0 | 0 | 0 | 0 | 0 | 0 | 0 | 4,010,000 |
| Model 50/200 Waiver | 0 | 0 | 0 | 0 | 0 | 0 | 0 | 0 |
| Other Title XIX Programs | 0 | 1,115,700 | 2,942,900 | 3,133,300 | 251,150 | 283,391 | 3,844,249 | 5,809,802 |
| Title XX / SSBG Funds | 484,100 | 241,100 | 338,600 | 412,800 | 0 | 0 | 0 | 0 |
| Other Federal Funds | 238,100 | 57,300 | 74,100 | 105,300 | 0 | 0 | 0 | 0 |
| Waiver Clients' SSI/ADC | 0 | 0 | 0 | 0 | 0 | 0 | 0 | 1,221,000 |

Source:
Institute on Disability and Human Development (UAP),
University of Illinois at Chicago, 1994

# WASHINGTON

## MR/DD Spending for Congregate Residential & Community Services

▓▓Congregate: 16+ Beds*  ■■Community**

Millions of 1992 Dollars

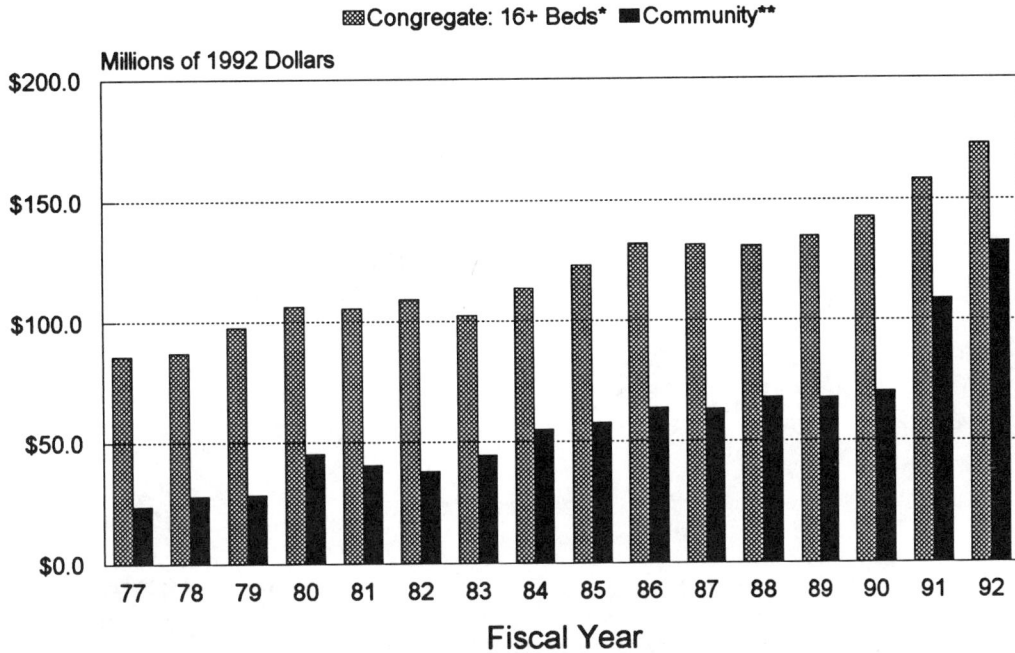

### Fiscal Year
*Excludes nursing homes; ** Includes resources for
15 bed or less residential settings & non-residential community services

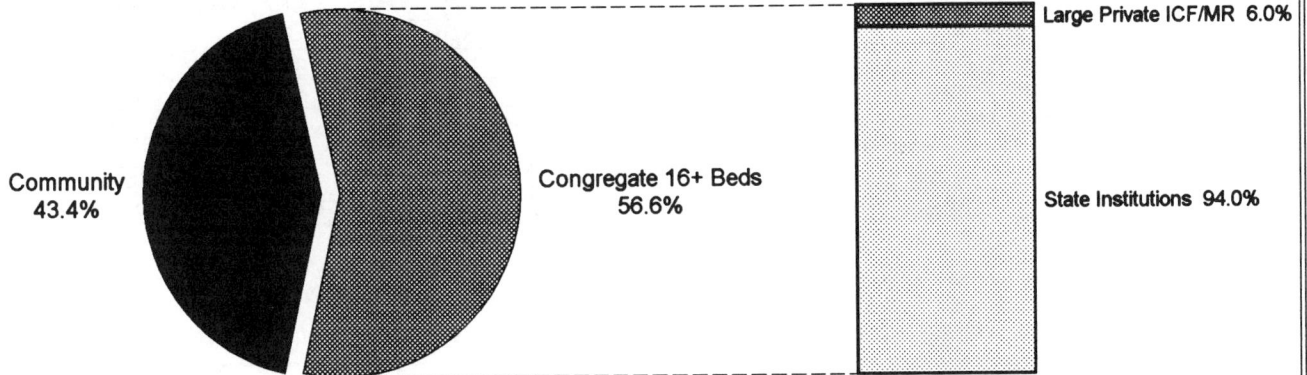

Community
43.4%

Congregate 16+ Beds
56.6%

Large Private ICF/MR  6.0%

State Institutions  94.0%

FY 1992 Total Spending:
$305.6 Million

*Source:*
Institute on Disability and Human Development (UAP),
University of Illinois at Chicago, 1994

# WASHINGTON

## Number of Persons Served by Residential Setting: FY 1992

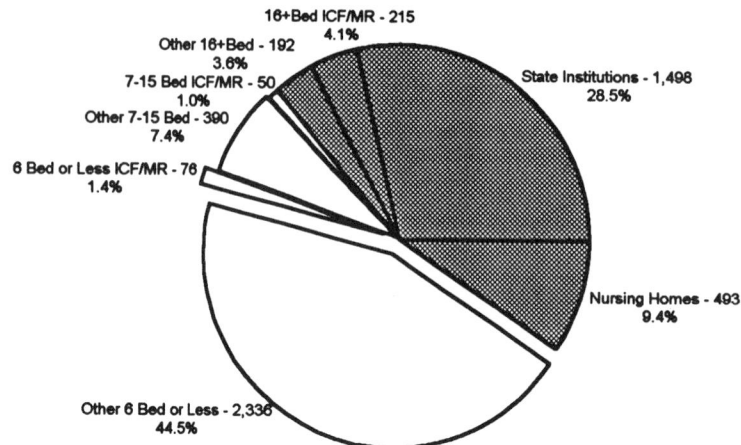

16+Bed ICF/MR - 215
4.1%

Other 16+Bed - 192
3.6%

7-15 Bed ICF/MR - 50
1.0%

Other 7-15 Bed - 390
7.4%

6 Bed or Less ICF/MR - 76
1.4%

State Institutions - 1,498
28.5%

Nursing Homes - 493
9.4%

Other 6 Bed or Less - 2,336
44.5%

Total Served: 5,250

## Persons Served by Residential Setting:1986-92

|  | 1986 | 1987 | 1988 | 1989 | 1990 | 1991 | 1992 |
|---|---|---|---|---|---|---|---|
| CONGREGATE 16 + BED SETTINGS | NA | NA | 3,176 | 3,069 | 2,743 | 2,497 | 2,398 |
| Nursing Homes | NA | NA | 595 | 562 | 523 | 491 | 493 |
| State Institutions | 1,847 | 1,829 | 1,794 | 1,776 | 1,605 | 1,535 | 1,498 |
| Private 16+Bed ICF/MR | 618 | 598 | 516 | 465 | 397 | 252 | 215 |
| Other 16+Bed Residential | NA | NA | 271 | 266 | 218 | 219 | 192 |
| 15 BED OR LESS RESIDENTIAL SETTINGS | 2,103 | 2,168 | 1,960 | 1,881 | 2,590 | 2,808 | 2,852 |
| Public 7-15 Bed ICF/MR | 0 | 0 | 0 | 0 | 0 | 0 | 0 |
| Private 7-15 Bed ICF/MR | 138 | 145 | 75 | 62 | 56 | 48 | 50 |
| Other 7-15 Bed Residential | 1,965 | 2,023 | 374 | 361 | 405 | 389 | 390 |
| Public 6 Bed or Less ICF/MR | 0 | 0 | 0 | 0 | 0 | 0 | 0 |
| Private 6 Bed or Less ICF/MR | NA | NA | 78 | 86 | 72 | 76 | 76 |
| Other 6 Bed or Less Residential | NA | NA | 1,433 | 1,372 | 2,057 | 2,295 | 2,336 |
| TOTAL PERSONS SERVED | NA | NA | 5,136 | 4,950 | 5,333 | 5,305 | 5,250 |

## Persons Served in Non-Residential Community Services:1986-92

|  | 1986 | 1987 | 1988 | 1989 | 1990 | 1991 | 1992 |
|---|---|---|---|---|---|---|---|
| DAY/WORK PROGRAMS | 3,260 | 3,436 | 3,755 | 3,894 | 4,224 | 4,252 | 4,869 |
| Sheltered Employment/Work Activity | 2,067 | 2,044 | 1,600 | 1,609 | 1,592 | 1,525 | 1,473 |
| Day Habilitation ("Day Training") | 297 | 327 | 570 | 531 | 644 | 713 | 890 |
| Supported/Competitive Employment | 896 | 1,065 | 1,585 | 1,754 | 1,988 | 2,014 | 2,506 |
| CASE MANAGEMENT | 13,549 | 13,954 | 14,462 | 14,848 | 15,716 | 16,828 | 17,823 |
| HCBS WAIVER | 980 | 905 | 1,049 | 1,047 | 1,271 | 1,725 | 2,078 |
| MODEL 50/200 WAIVER | 0 | 0 | 2 | 4 | 6 | 6 | 14 |

*Source:*
**Institute on Disability and Human Development (UAP),
University of Illinois at Chicago, 1994**

# WASHINGTON

## Community Services: FY 1992 Revenue Sources

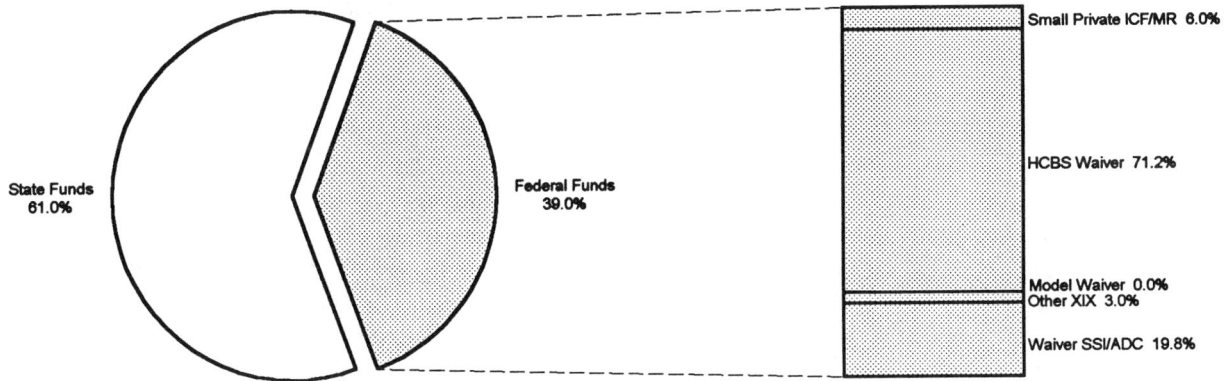

State Funds 61.0%

Federal Funds 39.0%

Small Private ICF/MR 6.0%

HCBS Waiver 71.2%

Model Waiver 0.0%
Other XIX 3.0%

Waiver SSI/ADC 19.8%

Total Funds: $132.5 Million

## Family Support Initiatives*

|  | 1986 | 1987 | 1988 | 1989 | 1990 | 1991 | 1992 |
|---|---|---|---|---|---|---|---|
| FAMILY SUPPORT: TOTAL SPENDING | NA | NA | $2,492,061 | $2,840,714 | $3,969,592 | $5,283,954 | $5,534,386 |
| Total # of Families Supported | NA | NA | 1,725 | 1,731 | 1,798 | 2,044 | 1,846 |
| A. Financial Subsidy/Payment | $0 | $0 | $0 | $0 | $0 | $0 | $0 |
| # of Families | 0 | 0 | 0 | 0 | 0 | 0 | 0 |
| B. Family Assistance Payments | NA | NA | $1,964,802 | $2,208,114 | $2,637,402 | $3,216,458 | $3,166,094 |
| # of Families | NA | NA | NA | NA | NA | NA | NA |
| C. Other Family Support Payments | NA | NA | $527,259 | $632,600 | $1,332,190 | $2,067,496 | $2,368,292 |
| # of Families | NA | NA | NA | NA | NA | NA | NA |

## Other Community Services Initiatives*

|  | 1986 | 1987 | 1988 | 1989 | 1990 | 1991 | 1992 |
|---|---|---|---|---|---|---|---|
| AGING/DD SPENDING | $239,946 | $260,453 | $1,506,294 | $1,470,457 | $1,599,355 | $2,244,693 | $2,762,497 |
| # of Persons Served | 183 | 175 | 212 | 202 | 219 | 232 | 259 |
| ASSISTIVE TECHNOLOGY SPENDING |  |  |  |  |  |  | $0 |
| # of Persons Served |  |  |  |  |  |  | 0 |
| EARLY INTERVENTION SPENDING | $1,727,429 | $2,085,588 | $2,049,941 | $2,127,548 | $2,388,562 | $959,290 | $2,492,516 |
| # of Persons Served | 1,353 | 1,413 | 1,222 | 1,292 | 1,299 | 1,310 | 1,583 |
| PERSONAL ASSISTANCE SPENDING |  |  |  |  |  |  | $0 |
| # of Persons Served |  |  |  |  |  |  | 0 |
| SUPPORTED EMPLOYMENT SPENDING | $3,180,431 | $3,585,067 | $5,161,697 | $5,919,494 | $6,950,054 | $7,566,180 | $8,822,954 |
| # of Persons Served | 896 | 1,065 | 1,585 | 1,754 | 1,988 | 2,014 | 2,506 |
| SUPPORTED LIVING SPENDING |  |  |  |  |  |  | $0 |
| # of Persons Served |  |  |  |  |  |  | 0 |

*Expenditures associated with Special Community Initiatives are a subset of funding within the community services component of the state's chart series and spreadsheet; Family Support Client figures may include duplicate client counts; HCBS Waiver counts include Waiver case management numbers.
0= Services not provided in the state; NA= Data not available from state; blank= Services not applicable (eg. CSLA prior to authorization, Special Community Initiatives prior to request for data by this study)

Source:
Institute on Disability and Human Development (UAP),
University of Illinois at Chicago, 1994

# WASHINGTON

## Large Congregate Care Facilities: FY 1992 Revenue Sources*

### Private 16+Bed Settings

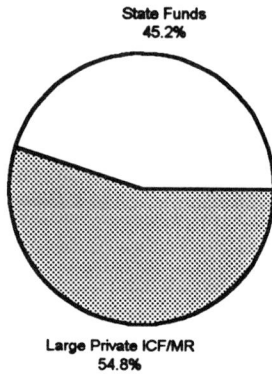

State Funds
45.2%

Large Private ICF/MR
54.8%

Total Funds: $10.3 Million

### Public Institutions

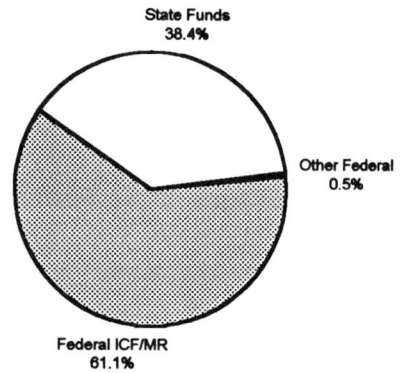

State Funds
38.4%

Other Federal
0.5%

Federal ICF/MR
61.1%

Total Funds: $162.7 Million

*Excludes nursing homes

## Average Daily Residents in Institutions

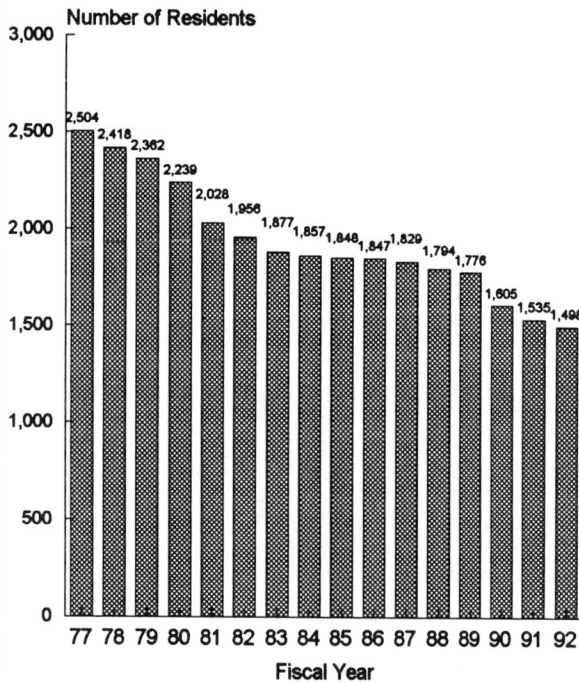

Number of Residents

| Fiscal Year | Residents |
|---|---|
| 77 | 2,504 |
| 78 | 2,418 |
| 79 | 2,362 |
| 80 | 2,239 |
| 81 | 2,028 |
| 82 | 1,956 |
| 83 | 1,877 |
| 84 | 1,857 |
| 85 | 1,848 |
| 86 | 1,847 |
| 87 | 1,829 |
| 88 | 1,794 |
| 89 | 1,776 |
| 90 | 1,605 |
| 91 | 1,535 |
| 92 | 1,498 |

Fiscal Year

## Institutional Daily Costs Per Resident

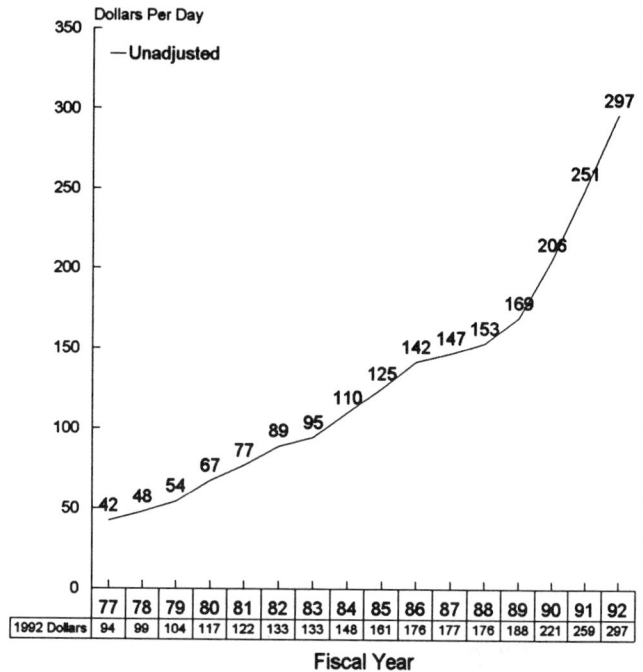

Dollars Per Day

—Unadjusted

| Fiscal Year | 77 | 78 | 79 | 80 | 81 | 82 | 83 | 84 | 85 | 86 | 87 | 88 | 89 | 90 | 91 | 92 |
|---|---|---|---|---|---|---|---|---|---|---|---|---|---|---|---|---|
| Unadjusted | 42 | 48 | 54 | 67 | 77 | 89 | 95 | 110 | 125 | 142 | 147 | 153 | 169 | 206 | 251 | 297 |
| 1992 Dollars | 94 | 99 | 104 | 117 | 122 | 133 | 133 | 148 | 161 | 176 | 177 | 176 | 188 | 221 | 259 | 297 |

Fiscal Year

*Source:*
Institute on Disability and Human Development (UAP),
University of Illinois at Chicago, 1994

# WASHINGTON FISCAL EFFORT

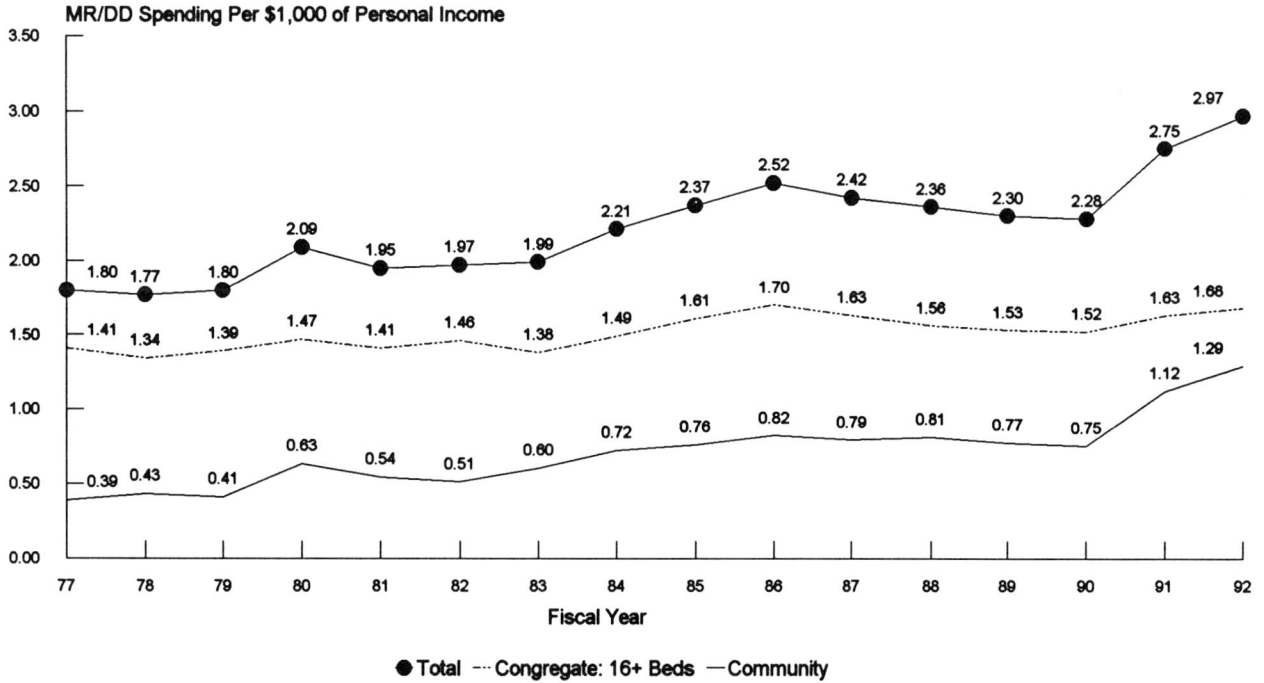

## MR/DD Spending Per $1,000 of Personal Income

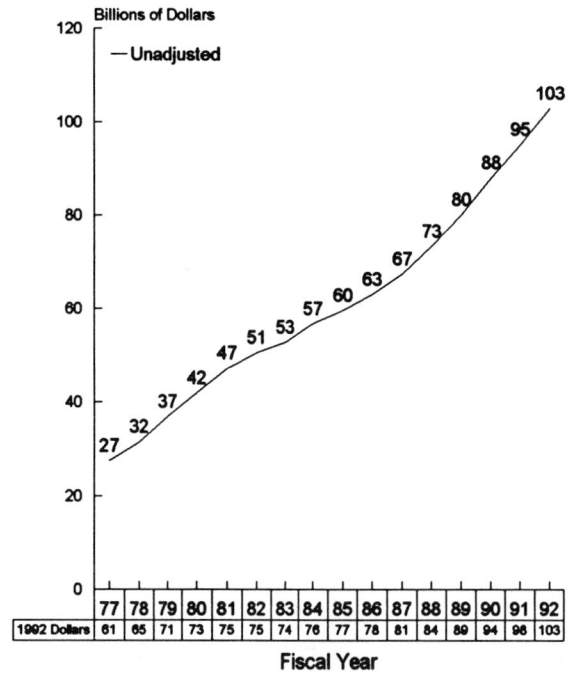

| | | | | | | | | | | | | | | | |
|---|---|---|---|---|---|---|---|---|---|---|---|---|---|---|---|
| 77 | 78 | 79 | 80 | 81 | 82 | 83 | 84 | 85 | 86 | 87 | 88 | 89 | 90 | 91 | 92 |

Total values: 1.80, 1.77, 1.80, 2.09, 1.95, 1.97, 1.99, 2.21, 2.37, 2.52, 2.42, 2.36, 2.30, 2.28, 2.75, 2.97

Congregate: 16+ Beds values: 1.41, 1.34, 1.39, 1.47, 1.41, 1.46, 1.38, 1.49, 1.61, 1.70, 1.63, 1.56, 1.53, 1.52, 1.63, 1.68

Community values: 0.39, 0.43, 0.41, 0.63, 0.54, 0.51, 0.60, 0.72, 0.76, 0.82, 0.79, 0.81, 0.77, 0.75, 1.12, 1.29

**Fiscal Year**

● Total  ⋯ Congregate: 16+ Beds  — Community

## Total MR/DD Spending

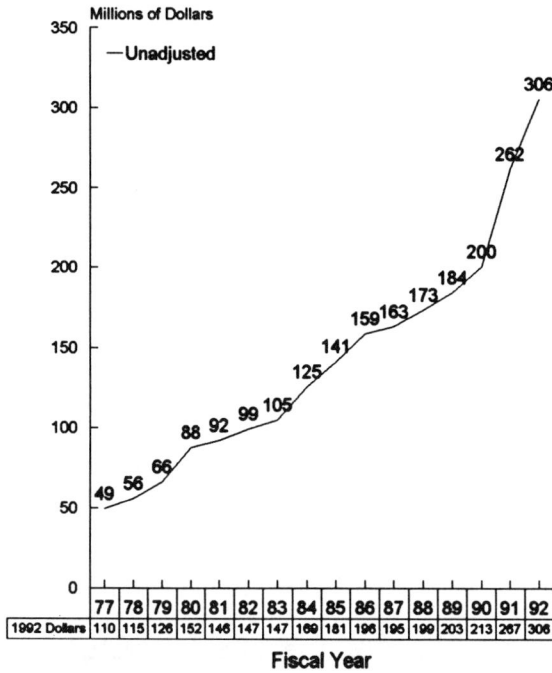

Millions of Dollars
— Unadjusted

Values: 49, 56, 66, 88, 92, 99, 105, 125, 141, 159, 163, 173, 184, 200, 262, 306

| | 77 | 78 | 79 | 80 | 81 | 82 | 83 | 84 | 85 | 86 | 87 | 88 | 89 | 90 | 91 | 92 |
|---|---|---|---|---|---|---|---|---|---|---|---|---|---|---|---|---|
| 1992 Dollars | 110 | 115 | 126 | 152 | 146 | 147 | 147 | 169 | 181 | 196 | 195 | 199 | 203 | 213 | 267 | 306 |

**Fiscal Year**

## Personal Income

Billions of Dollars
— Unadjusted

Values: 27, 32, 37, 42, 47, 51, 53, 57, 60, 63, 67, 73, 80, 88, 95, 103

| | 77 | 78 | 79 | 80 | 81 | 82 | 83 | 84 | 85 | 86 | 87 | 88 | 89 | 90 | 91 | 92 |
|---|---|---|---|---|---|---|---|---|---|---|---|---|---|---|---|---|
| 1992 Dollars | 61 | 65 | 71 | 73 | 75 | 75 | 74 | 76 | 77 | 78 | 81 | 84 | 89 | 94 | 98 | 103 |

**Fiscal Year**

*Source:*
Institute on Disability and Human Development (UAP),
University of Illinois at Chicago, 1994

# WASHINGTON
## Financial Support for MR/DD Services: FY 1977-92

| | 1977 | 1978 | 1979 | 1980 | 1981 | 1982 | 1983 | 1984 |
|---|---|---|---|---|---|---|---|---|
| **TOTAL FUNDS** | $49,387,000 | $55,828,000 | $66,184,000 | $87,790,000 | $92,181,000 | $99,383,000 | $104,616,000 | $125,341,992 |
| **CONGREGATE 16+ BEDS** | 38,668,000 | 42,261,000 | 51,220,405 | 61,525,085 | 66,580,000 | 73,766,000 | 72,954,000 | 84,480,000 |
| INSTITUTIONAL SERVICES FUNDS | 38,668,000 | 42,261,000 | 46,873,000 | 55,072,000 | 57,014,000 | 63,578,000 | 64,750,000 | 74,620,000 |
| STATE FUNDS | 38,151,000 | 35,920,000 | 25,845,000 | 27,687,000 | 32,732,000 | 29,988,000 | 41,357,000 | 42,956,000 |
| General Funds | 38,151,000 | 35,920,000 | 25,845,000 | 27,687,000 | 32,732,000 | 29,988,000 | 41,357,000 | 42,956,000 |
| Local | 0 | 0 | 0 | 0 | 0 | 0 | 0 | 0 |
| Other State Funds | 0 | 0 | 0 | 0 | 0 | 0 | 0 | 0 |
| FEDERAL FUNDS | 517,000 | 6,341,000 | 21,028,000 | 27,385,000 | 24,282,000 | 33,590,000 | 23,393,000 | 31,664,000 |
| Federal ICF/MR | 517,000 | 6,341,000 | 21,028,000 | 27,385,000 | 24,282,000 | 33,590,000 | 23,393,000 | 31,664,000 |
| Title XX / SSBG Funds | 0 | 0 | 0 | 0 | 0 | 0 | 0 | 0 |
| Other Federal Funds | 0 | 0 | 0 | 0 | 0 | 0 | 0 | 0 |
| LARGE PRIVATE RESIDENTIAL | 0 | 0 | 4,347,405 | 6,453,085 | 9,566,000 | 10,188,000 | 8,204,000 | 9,860,000 |
| STATE FUNDS | 0 | 0 | 2,102,405 | 3,200,085 | 4,783,000 | 5,094,000 | 4,102,000 | 4,930,000 |
| General Funds | 0 | 0 | 2,102,405 | 3,200,085 | 4,783,000 | 5,094,000 | 4,102,000 | 4,930,000 |
| Other State Funds | 0 | 0 | 0 | 0 | 0 | 0 | 0 | 0 |
| Local/County Overmatch | 0 | 0 | 0 | 0 | 0 | 0 | 0 | 0 |
| FEDERAL FUNDS | 0 | 0 | 2,245,000 | 3,253,000 | 4,783,000 | 5,094,000 | 4,102,000 | 4,930,000 |
| Large Private ICF/MR | 0 | 0 | 2,245,000 | 3,253,000 | 4,783,000 | 5,094,000 | 4,102,000 | 4,930,000 |
| **COMMUNITY SERVICES FUNDS** | 10,719,000 | 13,567,000 | 14,963,595 | 26,264,915 | 25,601,000 | 25,617,000 | 31,662,000 | 40,861,992 |
| STATE FUNDS | 4,591,000 | 9,551,000 | 10,042,595 | 19,043,915 | 11,200,000 | 21,685,000 | 20,309,000 | 21,311,000 |
| General Funds | 3,563,000 | 8,308,000 | 8,735,595 | 17,711,915 | 9,928,000 | 20,444,000 | 19,024,000 | 19,847,000 |
| Other State Funds | 0 | 0 | 0 | 0 | 0 | 0 | 0 | 0 |
| Local/County Overmatch | 0 | 0 | 0 | 0 | 0 | 0 | 0 | 0 |
| SSI State Supplement | 1,028,000 | 1,243,000 | 1,307,000 | 1,332,000 | 1,272,000 | 1,241,000 | 1,285,000 | 1,464,000 |
| FEDERAL FUNDS | 6,128,000 | 4,016,000 | 4,921,000 | 7,221,000 | 14,401,000 | 3,932,000 | 11,353,000 | 19,550,992 |
| ICF/MR Funds | 0 | 0 | 0 | 0 | 0 | 0 | 1,610,000 | 1,729,000 |
| Small Public | 0 | 0 | 0 | 0 | 0 | 0 | 0 | 0 |
| Small Private | 0 | 0 | | | | | 1,610,000 | 1,729,000 |
| HCBS Waiver | 0 | 0 | 0 | 0 | 0 | 0 | 0 | 1,689,000 |
| Model 50/200 Waiver | 0 | 0 | 0 | 0 | 0 | 0 | 0 | 0 |
| Other Title XIX Programs | 0 | 453,000 | 287,000 | 4,906,000 | 1,300,000 | 3,932,000 | 9,743,000 | 2,447,000 |
| Title XX / SSBG Funds | 6,128,000 | 3,563,000 | 4,634,000 | 2,315,000 | 13,101,000 | 0 | 0 | 10,759,000 |
| Other Federal Funds | 0 | 0 | 0 | 0 | 0 | 0 | 0 | 0 |
| Waiver Clients' SSI/ADC | 0 | 0 | 0 | 0 | 0 | 0 | 0 | 2,926,992 |

| | 1985 | 1986 | 1987 | 1988 | 1989 | 1990 | 1991 | 1992 |
|---|---|---|---|---|---|---|---|---|
| **TOTAL FUNDS** | $141,171,368 | $158,654,451 | $162,981,216 | $173,296,125 | $184,009,353 | $200,486,688 | $261,514,033 | $305,569,553 |
| **CONGREGATE 16+ BEDS** | 96,006,116 | 106,959,101 | 109,936,999 | 114,095,040 | 122,426,806 | 134,305,266 | 154,896,731 | 173,041,876 |
| INSTITUTIONAL SERVICES FUNDS | 84,441,878 | 95,535,681 | 98,188,646 | 100,572,264 | 109,809,367 | 120,687,924 | 140,544,259 | 162,710,127 |
| STATE FUNDS | 43,205,795 | 54,151,061 | 43,619,409 | 49,298,440 | 47,379,443 | 46,402,970 | 65,767,728 | 62,551,236 |
| General Funds | 43,205,795 | 54,151,061 | 43,619,409 | 49,298,440 | 47,379,443 | 46,402,970 | 65,767,728 | 62,551,236 |
| Local | 0 | 0 | 0 | 0 | 0 | 0 | 0 | 0 |
| Other State Funds | 0 | 0 | 0 | 0 | 0 | 0 | 0 | 0 |
| FEDERAL FUNDS | 41,236,083 | 41,384,620 | 54,569,237 | 51,273,824 | 62,429,924 | 74,284,954 | 74,776,531 | 100,158,891 |
| Federal ICF/MR | 40,154,309 | 40,402,745 | 53,741,534 | 50,465,597 | 61,621,692 | 73,522,065 | 74,313,795 | 99,404,823 |
| Title XX / SSBG Funds | 0 | 0 | 0 | 0 | 0 | 0 | 0 | 0 |
| Other Federal Funds | 1,081,774 | 981,875 | 827,703 | 808,227 | 808,232 | 762,889 | 462,736 | 754,068 |
| LARGE PRIVATE RESIDENTIAL | 11,564,238 | 11,423,420 | 11,748,353 | 13,522,776 | 12,617,439 | 13,617,342 | 14,352,472 | 10,331,749 |
| STATE FUNDS | 5,782,119 | 5,704,856 | 5,578,118 | 6,327,307 | 5,917,579 | 6,307,553 | 6,583,479 | 4,670,984 |
| General Funds | 5,782,119 | 5,704,856 | 5,578,118 | 6,327,307 | 5,917,579 | 6,307,553 | 6,583,479 | 4,670,984 |
| Other State Funds | 0 | 0 | 0 | 0 | 0 | 0 | 0 | 0 |
| Local/County Overmatch | 0 | 0 | 0 | 0 | 0 | 0 | 0 | 0 |
| FEDERAL FUNDS | 5,782,119 | 5,718,564 | 6,170,235 | 7,195,469 | 6,699,860 | 7,309,789 | 7,768,993 | 5,660,765 |
| Large Private ICF/MR | 5,782,119 | 5,718,564 | 6,170,235 | 7,195,469 | 6,699,860 | 7,309,789 | 7,768,993 | 5,660,765 |
| **COMMUNITY SERVICES FUNDS** | 45,165,252 | 51,695,350 | 53,044,217 | 59,201,085 | 61,582,547 | 66,181,422 | 106,617,302 | 132,527,677 |
| STATE FUNDS | 20,979,243 | 26,605,355 | 33,915,019 | 34,404,398 | 35,461,600 | 34,872,990 | 56,291,199 | 80,781,045 |
| General Funds | 19,430,243 | 24,862,355 | 32,014,019 | 32,688,533 | 33,732,079 | 33,116,908 | 54,519,908 | 79,006,724 |
| Other State Funds | 0 | 0 | 0 | 0 | 0 | 0 | 0 | 0 |
| Local/County Overmatch | 0 | 0 | 0 | 0 | 0 | 0 | 0 | 0 |
| SSI State Supplement | 1,549,000 | 1,743,000 | 1,901,000 | 1,715,865 | 1,729,521 | 1,756,082 | 1,771,291 | 1,774,321 |
| FEDERAL FUNDS | 24,186,009 | 25,089,995 | 19,129,198 | 24,796,687 | 26,120,947 | 31,308,432 | 50,326,103 | 51,746,632 |
| ICF/MR Funds | 1,093,086 | 1,753,072 | 2,153,234 | 2,398,490 | 2,392,343 | 2,630,977 | 3,428,918 | 3,105,635 |
| Small Public | 0 | 0 | 0 | 0 | 0 | 0 | 0 | 0 |
| Small Private | 1,093,086 | 1,753,072 | 2,153,234 | 2,398,490 | 2,392,343 | 2,630,977 | 3,428,918 | 3,105,635 |
| HCBS Waiver | 7,295,921 | 7,643,766 | 6,338,219 | 6,295,660 | 6,241,471 | 11,015,478 | 27,542,423 | 36,818,360 |
| Model 50/200 Waiver | 0 | 0 | 0 | 0 | 0 | 0 | 0 | 802 |
| Other Title XIX Programs | 1,977,122 | 1,865,522 | 1,488,480 | 1,264,975 | 1,357,805 | 1,449,254 | 664,339 | 1,573,139 |
| Title XX / SSBG Funds | 10,227,080 | 10,170,275 | 5,728,365 | 10,519,878 | 11,643,980 | 10,493,223 | 10,493,223 | 0 |
| Other Federal Funds | 0 | 0 | 0 | 0 | 0 | 0 | 0 | 0 |
| Waiver Clients' SSI/ADC | 3,592,800 | 3,657,360 | 3,420,900 | 4,317,684 | 4,485,348 | 5,719,500 | 8,197,200 | 10,248,696 |

*Source:*
Institute on Disability and Human Development (UAP),
University of Illinois at Chicago, 1994

# WEST VIRGINIA

## MR/DD Spending for Congregate Residential & Community Services

▨ Congregate: 16+ Beds*  ■ Community**

Millions of 1992 Dollars

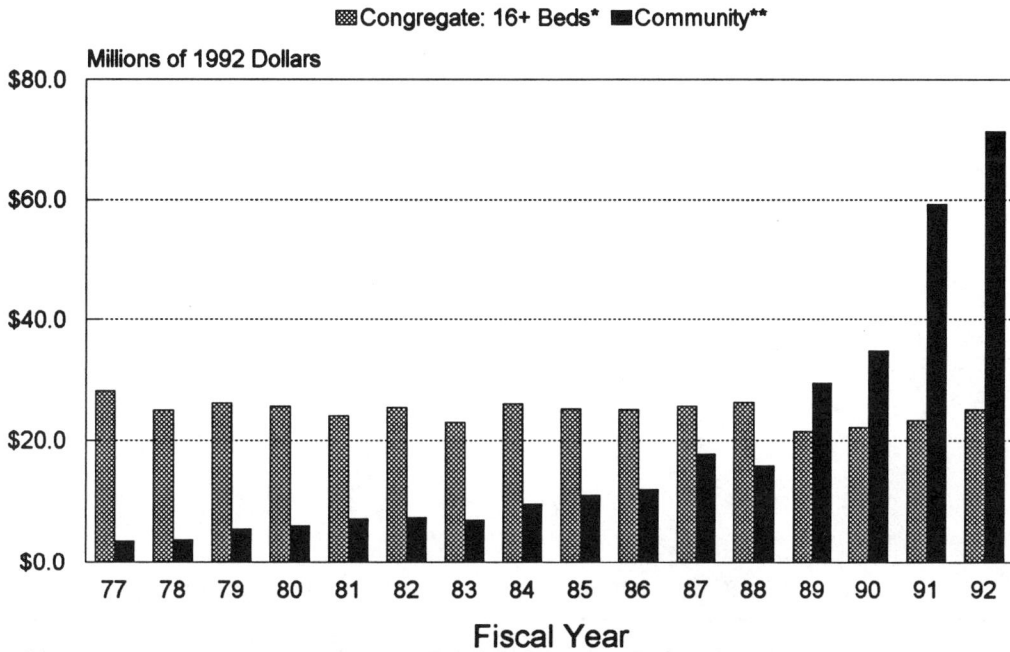

Fiscal Year

*Excludes nursing homes; ** Includes resources for
15 bed or less residential settings & non-residential community services

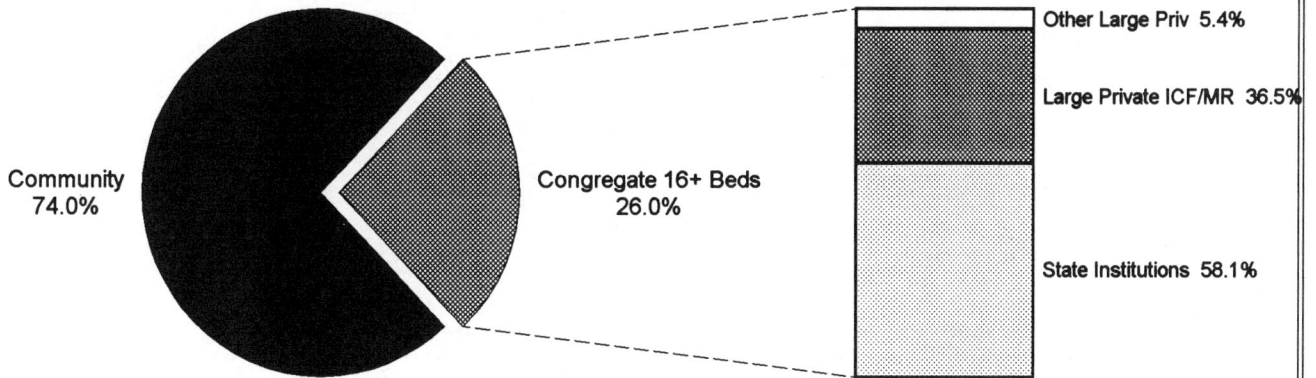

Community
74.0%

Congregate 16+ Beds
26.0%

Other Large Priv 5.4%

Large Private ICF/MR 36.5%

State Institutions 58.1%

FY 1992 Total Spending:
$96.6 Million

*Source:*
Institute on Disability and Human Development (UAP),
University of Illinois at Chicago, 1994

# WEST VIRGINIA

## Number of Persons Served by Residential Setting: FY 1992

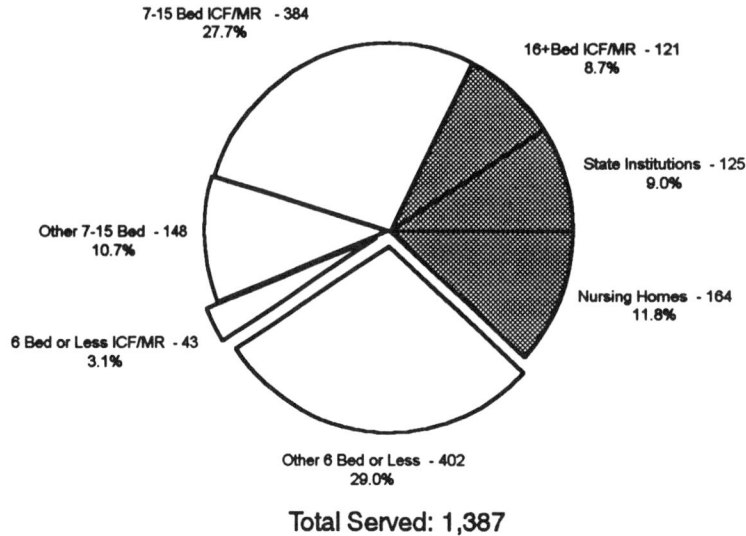

7-15 Bed ICF/MR - 384
27.7%

16+Bed ICF/MR - 121
8.7%

State Institutions - 125
9.0%

Other 7-15 Bed - 148
10.7%

Nursing Homes - 164
11.8%

6 Bed or Less ICF/MR - 43
3.1%

Other 6 Bed or Less - 402
29.0%

Total Served: 1,387

## Persons Served by Residential Setting:1986-92

|  | 1986 | 1987 | 1988 | 1989 | 1990 | 1991 | 1992 |
|---|---|---|---|---|---|---|---|
| CONGREGATE 16 + BED SETTINGS | 596 | 588 | 830 | 732 | 598 | 517 | 410 |
| Nursing Homes | NA | NA | 271 | 252 | 225 | 211 | 164 |
| State Institutions | 545 | 537 | 508 | 420 | 308 | 189 | 125 |
| Private 16+Bed ICF/MR | 51 | 51 | 51 | 60 | 65 | 117 | 121 |
| Other 16+Bed Residential | 0 | 0 | 0 | 0 | 0 | 0 | 0 |
| 15 BED OR LESS RESIDENTIAL SETTINGS | NA | NA | NA | 656 | 737 | 886 | 977 |
| Public 7-15 Bed ICF/MR | 0 | 0 | 0 | 0 | 0 | 0 | 0 |
| Private 7-15 Bed ICF/MR | 10 | 81 | 140 | 220 | 271 | 377 | 384 |
| Other 7-15 Bed Residential | NA | NA | NA | 111 | 118 | 126 | 148 |
| Public 6 Bed or Less ICF/MR | 0 | 0 | 0 | 0 | 0 | 0 | 0 |
| Private 6 Bed or Less ICF/MR | 0 | 9 | 16 | 25 | 30 | 42 | 43 |
| Other 6 Bed or Less Residential | NA | NA | NA | 300 | 318 | 341 | 402 |
| TOTAL PERSONS SERVED | NA | NA | NA | 1,388 | 1,335 | 1,403 | 1,387 |

## Persons Served in Non-Residential Community Services:1986-92

|  | 1986 | 1987 | 1988 | 1989 | 1990 | 1991 | 1992 |
|---|---|---|---|---|---|---|---|
| DAY/WORK PROGRAMS | 341 | 404 | 1,044 | 1,715 | 2,389 | 2,512 | 2,831 |
| Sheltered Employment/Work Activity | 300 | 320 | 464 | 914 | 1,363 | 1,111 | 1,318 |
| Day Habilitation ("Day Training") | 41 | 84 | 565 | 691 | 818 | 1,128 | 1,128 |
| Supported/Competitive Employment | 0 | 0 | 15 | 110 | 208 | 273 | 385 |
| CASE MANAGEMENT | NA | NA | NA | 2,058 | 2,429 | 3,463 | 4,805 |
| HCBS WAIVER | 55 | 105 | 126 | 224 | 308 | 413 | 513 |
| MODEL 50/200 WAIVER | 0 | 0 | 0 | 0 | 0 | 0 | 0 |

*Source:*
Institute on Disability and Human Development (UAP),
University of Illinois at Chicago, 1994

# WEST VIRGINIA

## Community Services: FY 1992 Revenue Sources

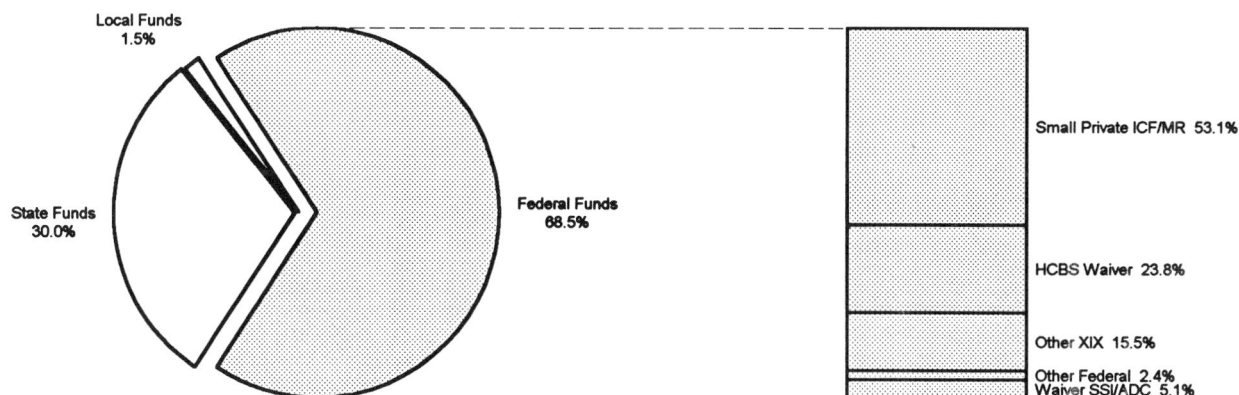

Local Funds 1.5%

State Funds 30.0%

Federal Funds 68.5%

Small Private ICF/MR 53.1%

HCBS Waiver 23.8%

Other XIX 15.5%

Other Federal 2.4%
Waiver SSI/ADC 5.1%

Total Funds: $71.5 Million

## Family Support Initiatives*

|  | 1986 | 1987 | 1988 | 1989 | 1990 | 1991 | 1992 |
|---|---|---|---|---|---|---|---|
| **FAMILY SUPPORT: TOTAL SPENDING** | $50,050 | $109,310 | $114,850 | $114,850 | $214,850 | $500,000 | $546,250 |
| **Total # of Families Supported** | 0 | 0 | 0 | NA | 145 | 450 | 600 |
| A. Financial Subsidy/Payment | $0 | $0 | $0 | $0 | $0 | $0 | $0 |
| # of Families | 0 | 0 | 0 | 0 | 0 | 0 | 0 |
| B. Family Assistance Payments | $50,050 | $109,310 | $114,850 | $114,850 | $114,850 | NA | NA |
| # of Families | NA | NA | NA | NA | $145 | NA | NA |
| C. Other Family Support Payments | $0 | $0 | $0 | $0 | $100,000 | $500,000 | $546,250 |
| # of Families | 0 | 0 | 0 | 0 | 0 | 0 | 600 |

## Other Community Services Initiatives*

|  | 1986 | 1987 | 1988 | 1989 | 1990 | 1991 | 1992 |
|---|---|---|---|---|---|---|---|
| **AGING/DD SPENDING** | $0 | $0 | $0 | $0 | $0 | $0 | $0 |
| # of Persons Served | 0 | 0 | 0 | 0 | 0 | 0 | 0 |
| **ASSISTIVE TECHNOLOGY SPENDING** | $0 | $0 | $0 | $0 | $0 | $0 | $0 |
| # of Persons Served | 0 | 0 | 0 | 0 | 0 | 0 | 0 |
| **EARLY INTERVENTION SPENDING** | $474,112 | $482,395 | $464,563 | $316,707 | $404,161 | $600,000 | $0 |
| # of Persons Served | NA | NA | NA | NA | NA | 1,400 | 0 |
| **PERSONAL ASSISTANCE SPENDING** |  |  |  | $14,600 | $20,984 | $186,495 | $2,090,243 |
| # of Persons Served |  |  |  | 144 | 211 | 1,391 | 1,872 |
| **SUPPORTED EMPLOYMENT SPENDING** | $0 | $0 | $22,500 | NA | NA | NA | NA |
| # of Persons Served | 0 | 0 | 15 | 110 | 208 | 273 | 385 |
| **SUPPORTED LIVING SPENDING** |  |  |  |  |  |  | $0 |
| # of Persons Served |  |  |  |  |  |  | 0 |

*Expenditures associated with Special Community Initiatives are a subset of funding within the community services component of the state's chart series and spreadsheet; Family Support Client figures may include duplicate client counts; HCBS Waiver counts include Waiver case management numbers.
0= Services not provided in the state; NA= Data not available from state; blank= Services not applicable (eg. CSLA prior to authorization, Special Community Initiatives prior to request for data by this study)

*Source:*
Institute on Disability and Human Development (UAP),
University of Illinois at Chicago, 1994

# WEST VIRGINIA

## Large Congregate Care Facilities: FY 1992 Revenue Sources*

### Private 16+Bed Settings

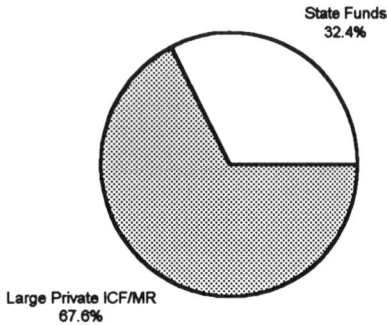

State Funds
32.4%

Large Private ICF/MR
67.6%

Total Funds: $10.5 Million

### Public Institutions

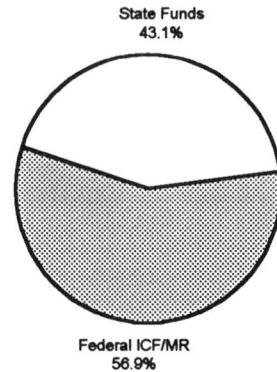

State Funds
43.1%

Federal ICF/MR
56.9%

Total Funds: $14.6 Million

*Excludes nursing homes

## Average Daily Residents in Institutions

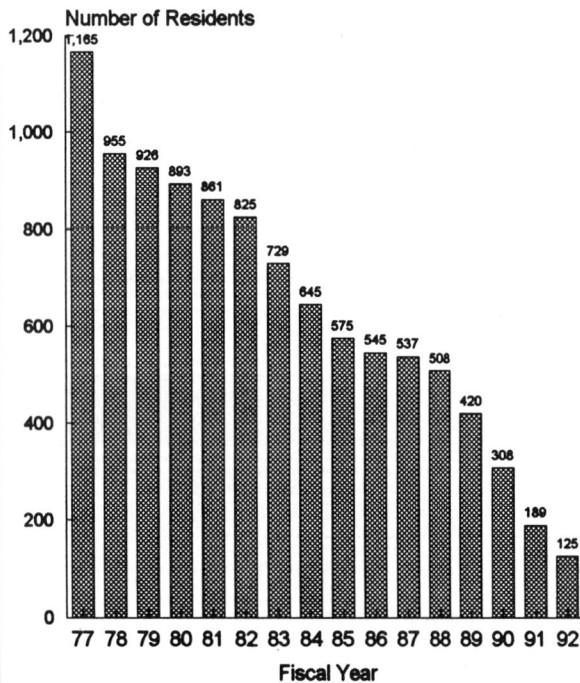

Number of Residents

| Fiscal Year | Number of Residents |
|---|---|
| 77 | 1,165 |
| 78 | 955 |
| 79 | 926 |
| 80 | 893 |
| 81 | 861 |
| 82 | 825 |
| 83 | 729 |
| 84 | 645 |
| 85 | 575 |
| 86 | 545 |
| 87 | 537 |
| 88 | 508 |
| 89 | 420 |
| 90 | 308 |
| 91 | 189 |
| 92 | 125 |

Fiscal Year

## Institutional Daily Costs Per Resident

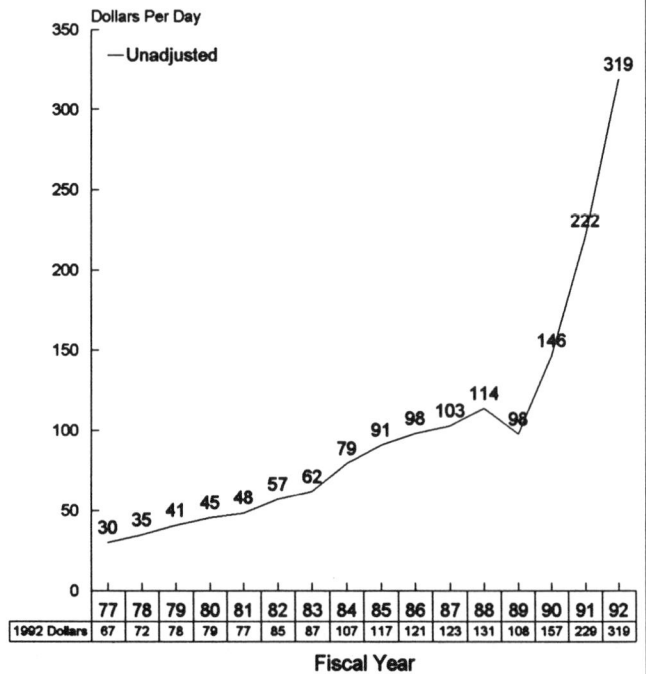

Dollars Per Day
— Unadjusted

| Fiscal Year | Unadjusted | 1992 Dollars |
|---|---|---|
| 77 | 30 | 67 |
| 78 | 35 | 72 |
| 79 | 41 | 78 |
| 80 | 45 | 79 |
| 81 | 48 | 77 |
| 82 | 57 | 85 |
| 83 | 62 | 87 |
| 84 | 79 | 107 |
| 85 | 91 | 117 |
| 86 | 98 | 121 |
| 87 | 103 | 123 |
| 88 | 114 | 131 |
| 89 | 98 | 108 |
| 90 | 146 | 157 |
| 91 | 222 | 229 |
| 92 | 319 | 319 |

Fiscal Year

*Source:*
Institute on Disability and Human Development (UAP),
University of Illinois at Chicago, 1994

# WEST VIRGINIA FISCAL EFFORT

MR/DD Spending Per $1,000 of Personal Income

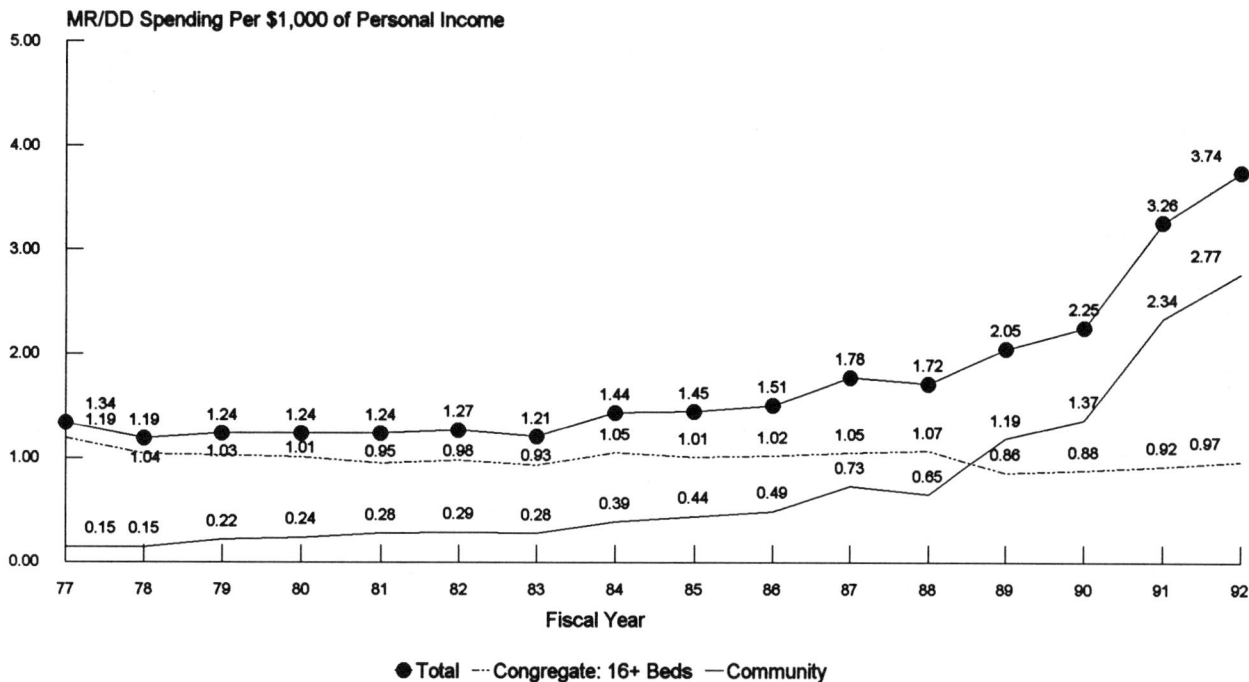

● Total  --- Congregate: 16+ Beds  — Community

## Total MR/DD Spending

Millions of Dollars
—Unadjusted

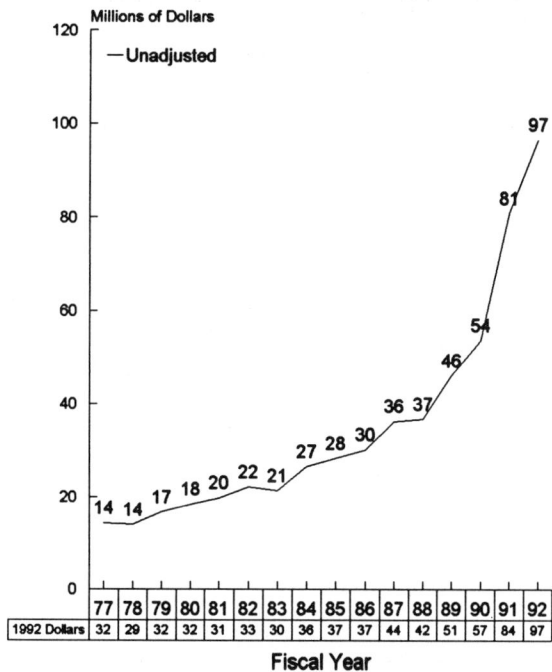

| Fiscal Year | 77 | 78 | 79 | 80 | 81 | 82 | 83 | 84 | 85 | 86 | 87 | 88 | 89 | 90 | 91 | 92 |
|---|---|---|---|---|---|---|---|---|---|---|---|---|---|---|---|---|
| 1992 Dollars | 32 | 29 | 32 | 32 | 31 | 33 | 30 | 36 | 37 | 37 | 44 | 42 | 51 | 57 | 84 | 97 |

Fiscal Year

## Personal Income

Billions of Dollars
—Unadjusted

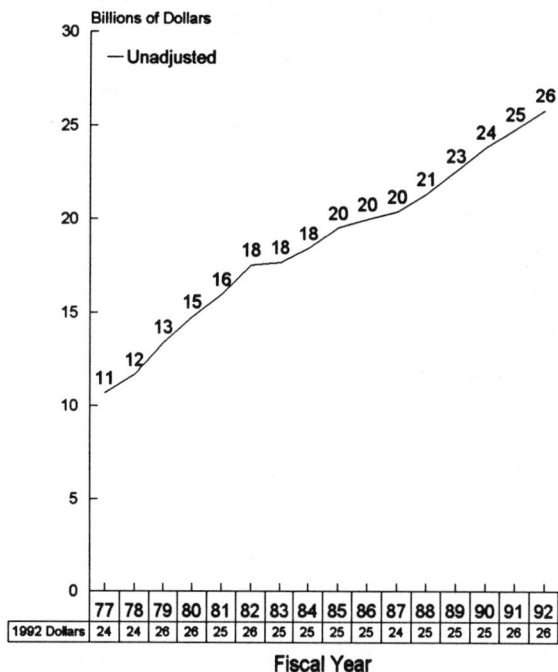

| Fiscal Year | 77 | 78 | 79 | 80 | 81 | 82 | 83 | 84 | 85 | 86 | 87 | 88 | 89 | 90 | 91 | 92 |
|---|---|---|---|---|---|---|---|---|---|---|---|---|---|---|---|---|
| 1992 Dollars | 24 | 24 | 26 | 26 | 25 | 26 | 25 | 25 | 25 | 25 | 25 | 24 | 25 | 25 | 25 | 26 | 26 |

Fiscal Year

*Source:*
Institute on Disability and Human Development (UAP),
University of Illinois at Chicago, 1994

# WEST VIRGINIA
## Financial Support for MR/DD Services: FY 1977-92

| | 1977 | 1978 | 1979 | 1980 | 1981 | 1982 | 1983 | 1984 |
|---|---|---|---|---|---|---|---|---|
| **TOTAL FUNDS** | $14,267,000 | $13,936,000 | $16,616,000 | $18,356,000 | $19,726,000 | $22,164,000 | $21,382,000 | $26,514,918 |
| **CONGREGATE 16+ BEDS** | 12,699,000 | 12,142,000 | 13,732,000 | 14,867,000 | 15,212,000 | 17,164,000 | 16,420,000 | 19,344,542 |
| INSTITUTIONAL SERVICES FUNDS | 12,699,000 | 12,142,000 | 13,732,000 | 14,867,000 | 15,212,000 | 17,164,000 | 16,420,000 | 18,705,812 |
| STATE FUNDS | 12,124,000 | 11,615,000 | 13,171,000 | 13,487,000 | 13,589,000 | 15,511,000 | 14,923,000 | 16,432,945 |
| General Funds | 11,994,000 | 11,477,000 | 12,974,000 | 13,223,000 | 13,222,000 | 15,054,000 | 14,377,000 | 15,951,664 |
| Local | 0 | 0 | 0 | 0 | 0 | 0 | 0 | 0 |
| Other State Funds | 130,000 | 138,000 | 197,000 | 264,000 | 367,000 | 457,000 | 546,000 | 481,281 |
| FEDERAL FUNDS | 575,000 | 527,000 | 561,000 | 1,380,000 | 1,623,000 | 1,653,000 | 1,497,000 | 2,272,867 |
| Federal ICF/MR | 0 | 0 | 0 | 763,000 | 1,036,000 | 1,082,000 | 980,000 | 1,767,583 |
| Title XX / SSBG Funds | 0 | 0 | 0 | 0 | 0 | 0 | 0 | 0 |
| Other Federal Funds | 575,000 | 527,000 | 561,000 | 617,000 | 587,000 | 571,000 | 517,000 | 505,284 |
| LARGE PRIVATE RESIDENTIAL | 0 | 0 | 0 | 0 | 0 | 0 | 0 | 638,730 |
| STATE FUNDS | 0 | 0 | 0 | 0 | 0 | 0 | 0 | 192,130 |
| General Funds | 0 | 0 | 0 | 0 | 0 | 0 | 0 | 0 |
| Other State Funds | 0 | 0 | 0 | 0 | 0 | 0 | 0 | 192,130 |
| Local/County Overmatch | 0 | 0 | 0 | 0 | 0 | 0 | 0 | 0 |
| FEDERAL FUNDS | 0 | 0 | 0 | 0 | 0 | 0 | 0 | 446,600 |
| Large Private ICF/MR | 0 | 0 | 0 | 0 | 0 | 0 | 0 | 446,600 |
| **COMMUNITY SERVICES FUNDS** | 1,568,000 | 1,794,000 | 2,884,000 | 3,489,000 | 4,514,000 | 5,000,000 | 4,962,000 | 7,170,376 |
| STATE FUNDS | 1,278,000 | 1,707,000 | 2,609,000 | 3,181,000 | 4,098,000 | 4,586,000 | 4,441,000 | 6,517,617 |
| General Funds | 1,278,000 | 1,707,000 | 2,609,000 | 3,181,000 | 4,098,000 | 4,586,000 | 4,441,000 | 6,517,617 |
| Other State Funds | 0 | 0 | 0 | 0 | 0 | 0 | 0 | 0 |
| Local/County Overmatch | 0 | 0 | 0 | 0 | 0 | 0 | 0 | 0 |
| SSI State Supplement | 0 | 0 | 0 | 0 | 0 | 0 | 0 | 0 |
| FEDERAL FUNDS | 290,000 | 87,000 | 275,000 | 308,000 | 416,000 | 414,000 | 521,000 | 652,759 |
| ICF/MR Funds | 0 | 0 | 0 | 0 | 0 | 0 | 0 | 91,000 |
| Small Public | 0 | 0 | 0 | 0 | 0 | 0 | 0 | 0 |
| Small Private | 0 | 0 | 0 | 0 | 0 | 0 | 0 | 91,000 |
| HCBS Waiver | 0 | 0 | 0 | 0 | 0 | 0 | 0 | 40,040 |
| Model 50/200 Waiver | 0 | 0 | 0 | 0 | 0 | 0 | 0 | 0 |
| Other Title XIX Programs | 0 | 0 | 0 | 0 | 0 | 0 | 0 | 0 |
| Title XX / SSBG Funds | 0 | 0 | 0 | 0 | 0 | 0 | 0 | 0 |
| Other Federal Funds | 290,000 | 87,000 | 275,000 | 308,000 | 416,000 | 414,000 | 521,000 | 445,423 |
| Waiver Clients' SSI/ADC | 0 | 0 | 0 | 0 | 0 | 0 | 0 | 76,296 |

| | 1985 | 1986 | 1987 | 1988 | 1989 | 1990 | 1991 | 1992 |
|---|---|---|---|---|---|---|---|---|
| **TOTAL FUNDS** | $28,325,544 | $30,121,290 | $36,259,231 | $36,691,522 | $46,179,097 | $53,641,825 | $80,845,372 | $96,594,311 |
| **CONGREGATE 16+ BEDS** | 19,668,954 | 20,370,220 | 21,423,564 | 22,886,563 | 19,429,271 | 20,919,487 | 22,884,444 | 25,123,172 |
| INSTITUTIONAL SERVICES FUNDS | 19,036,107 | 19,477,528 | 20,109,646 | 21,126,038 | 14,956,299 | 16,450,244 | 15,283,275 | 14,596,401 |
| STATE FUNDS | 17,328,146 | 17,349,024 | 15,570,558 | 14,259,033 | 9,431,313 | 7,728,294 | 8,997,093 | 6,291,233 |
| General Funds | 16,829,099 | 16,648,615 | 14,847,751 | 13,399,357 | 8,823,896 | 6,976,782 | 8,071,180 | 5,948,481 |
| Local | 0 | 0 | 0 | 0 | 0 | 0 | 0 | 0 |
| Other State Funds | 499,047 | 700,409 | 722,807 | 859,676 | 607,417 | 751,512 | 925,913 | 342,752 |
| FEDERAL FUNDS | 1,707,961 | 2,128,504 | 4,539,088 | 6,867,005 | 5,524,986 | 8,721,950 | 6,286,182 | 8,305,168 |
| Federal ICF/MR | 1,447,596 | 1,930,205 | 4,417,936 | 6,734,433 | 5,518,416 | 8,721,639 | 6,284,050 | 8,301,924 |
| Title XX / SSBG Funds | 0 | 0 | 0 | 0 | 0 | 0 | 0 | 0 |
| Other Federal Funds | 260,365 | 198,299 | 121,152 | 132,572 | 6,570 | 311 | 2,132 | 3,244 |
| LARGE PRIVATE RESIDENTIAL | 632,847 | 892,692 | 1,313,918 | 1,760,525 | 4,472,972 | 4,469,243 | 7,601,169 | 10,526,771 |
| STATE FUNDS | 186,247 | 256,292 | 363,561 | 452,807 | 2,221,786 | 2,172,639 | 2,269,656 | 3,413,389 |
| General Funds | 0 | 0 | 0 | 0 | 1,502,967 | 1,466,753 | 1,466,753 | 1,349,397 |
| Other State Funds | 186,247 | 256,292 | 363,561 | 452,807 | 718,819 | 705,886 | 802,903 | 2,063,992 |
| Local/County Overmatch | 0 | 0 | 0 | 0 | 0 | 0 | 0 | 0 |
| FEDERAL FUNDS | 446,600 | 636,400 | 950,357 | 1,307,718 | 2,251,186 | 2,296,604 | 5,331,513 | 7,113,382 |
| Large Private ICF/MR | 446,600 | 636,400 | 950,357 | 1,307,718 | 2,251,186 | 2,296,604 | 5,331,513 | 7,113,382 |
| **COMMUNITY SERVICES FUNDS** | 8,656,590 | 9,751,070 | 14,835,667 | 13,804,959 | 26,749,826 | 32,722,338 | 57,960,928 | 71,471,139 |
| STATE FUNDS | 7,620,484 | 8,460,559 | 11,400,087 | 7,139,455 | 13,802,867 | 15,183,985 | 20,960,384 | 22,544,196 |
| General Funds | 7,620,484 | 8,460,559 | 11,400,087 | 7,139,455 | 13,802,867 | 15,183,985 | 20,960,384 | 21,441,017 |
| Other State Funds | 0 | 0 | 0 | 0 | 0 | 0 | 0 | 0 |
| Local/County Overmatch | 0 | 0 | 0 | 0 | 0 | 0 | 0 | 1,103,179 |
| SSI State Supplement | 0 | 0 | 0 | 0 | 0 | 0 | 0 | 0 |
| FEDERAL FUNDS | 1,036,106 | 1,290,511 | 3,435,580 | 6,665,504 | 12,946,959 | 17,538,353 | 37,000,544 | 48,926,943 |
| ICF/MR Funds | 79,500 | 73,600 | 1,667,100 | 4,000,078 | 6,876,833 | 7,629,508 | 21,060,396 | 25,996,147 |
| Small Public | 0 | 0 | 0 | 0 | 0 | 0 | 0 | 0 |
| Small Private | 79,500 | 73,600 | 1,667,100 | 4,000,078 | 6,876,833 | 7,629,508 | 21,060,396 | 25,996,147 |
| HCBS Waiver | 196,103 | 252,157 | 562,163 | 1,345,420 | 2,850,033 | 5,297,763 | 8,896,066 | 11,628,000 |
| Model 50/200 Waiver | 0 | 0 | 0 | 0 | 0 | 0 | 0 | 0 |
| Other Title XIX Programs | 0 | 0 | 0 | 0 | 1,432,922 | 2,396,223 | 4,271,148 | 7,604,038 |
| Title XX / SSBG Funds | 0 | 0 | 0 | 0 | 0 | 0 | 0 | 0 |
| Other Federal Funds | 562,503 | 759,494 | 809,417 | 830,118 | 867,875 | 854,731 | 879,742 | 1,193,266 |
| Waiver Clients' SSI/ADC | 198,000 | 205,260 | 396,900 | 489,888 | 919,296 | 1,360,128 | 1,893,192 | 2,505,492 |

*Source:*
Institute on Disability and Human Development (UAP),
University of Illinois at Chicago, 1994

# WISCONSIN

## MR/DD Spending for Congregate Residential & Community Services

▨ Congregate: 16+ Beds*  ■ Community**

Millions of 1992 Dollars

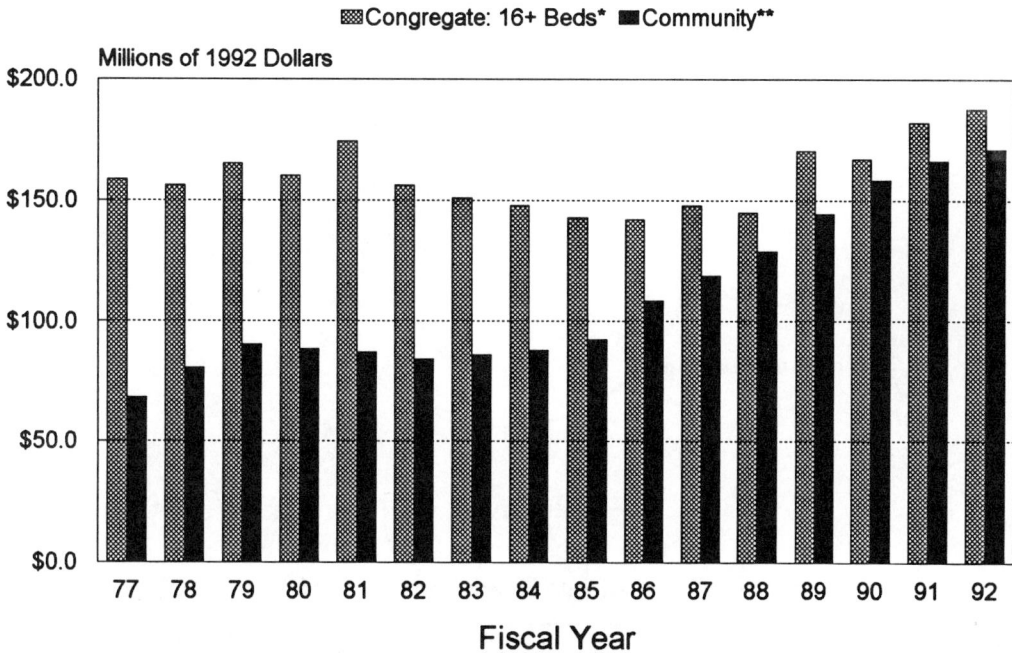

### Fiscal Year
*Excludes nursing homes; ** Includes resources for
15 bed or less residential settings & non-residential community services

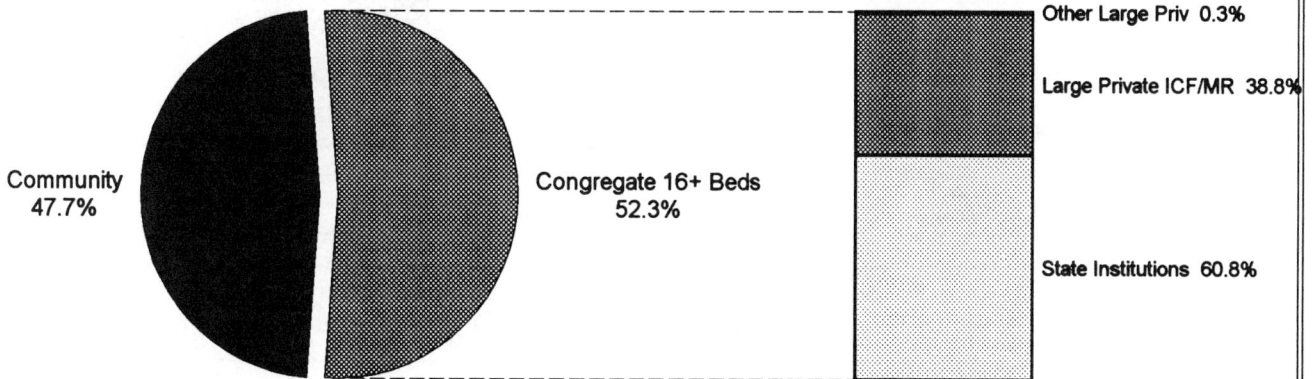

Community
47.7%

Congregate 16+ Beds
52.3%

Other Large Priv 0.3%

Large Private ICF/MR 38.8%

State Institutions 60.8%

FY 1992 Total Spending:
$358.6 Million

*Source:*
Institute on Disability and Human Development (UAP),
University of Illinois at Chicago, 1994

# WISCONSIN

## Number of Persons Served by Residential Setting: FY 1992

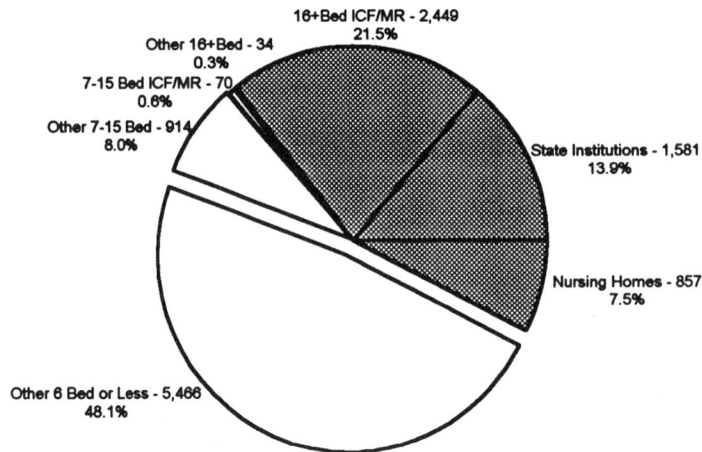

Other 16+Bed - 34
0.3%
7-15 Bed ICF/MR - 70
0.6%
Other 7-15 Bed - 914
8.0%

16+Bed ICF/MR - 2,449
21.5%

State Institutions - 1,581
13.9%

Nursing Homes - 857
7.5%

Other 6 Bed or Less - 5,466
48.1%

Total Served: 11,371

## Persons Served by Residential Setting:1986-92

|  | 1986 | 1987 | 1988 | 1989 | 1990 | 1991 | 1992 |
|---|---|---|---|---|---|---|---|
| **CONGREGATE 16 + BED SETTINGS** | **6,609** | **6,620** | **5,953** | **5,917** | **5,659** | **5,123** | **4,921** |
| Nursing Homes | 3,000 | 3,000 | 2,500 | 2,506 | 1,734 | 961 | 857 |
| State Institutions | 1,989 | 1,946 | 1,790 | 1,757 | 1,678 | 1,640 | 1,581 |
| Private 16+Bed ICF/MR* | 1,515 | 1,578 | 1,578 | 1,579 | 2,181 | 2,492 | 2,449 |
| Other 16+Bed Residential | 105 | 96 | 85 | 75 | 67 | 30 | 34 |
| **15 BED OR LESS RESIDENTIAL SETTINGS** | **5,528** | **5,004** | **6,042** | **6,524** | **7,150** | **7,244** | **6,450** |
| Public 7-15 Bed ICF/MR | 0 | 0 | 0 | 0 | 0 | 0 | 0 |
| Private 7-15 Bed ICF/MR | 136 | 70 | 70 | 70 | 70 | 70 | 70 |
| Other 7-15 Bed Residential | 5,392 | 4,934 | 5,972 | 6,454 | 7,080 | 7,174 | 914 |
| Public 6 Bed or Less ICF/MR |  |  |  |  |  |  | 0 |
| Private 6 Bed or Less ICF/MR |  |  |  |  |  |  | 0 |
| Other 6 Bed or Less Residential |  |  |  |  |  |  | 5,466 |
| **TOTAL PERSONS SERVED** | **12,137** | **11,624** | **11,995** | **12,441** | **12,809** | **12,367** | **11,371** |

*Includes approximately 1,000 individuals residing in county ICF/MRs.

## Persons Served in Non-Residential Community Services:1986-92

|  | 1986 | 1987 | 1988 | 1989 | 1990 | 1991 | 1992 |
|---|---|---|---|---|---|---|---|
| **DAY/WORK PROGRAMS** | **15,491** | **16,460** | **17,070** | **17,736** | **18,741** | **19,594** | **20,999** |
| Sheltered Employment/Work Activity | 6,932 | 6,951 | 6,631 | 6,748 | 6,859 | 6,786 | 6,832 |
| Day Habilitation ("Day Training") | 7,356 | 8,169 | 8,877 | 8,900 | 9,430 | 10,083 | 11,076 |
| Supported/Competitive Employment | 1,203 | 1,340 | 1,562 | 2,088 | 2,452 | 2,725 | 3,091 |
| **CASE MANAGEMENT** | **9,490** | **10,178** | **11,247** | **11,828** | **12,352** | **13,374** | **13,725** |
| **HCBS WAIVER** | **143** | **457** | **764** | **1,118** | **1,453** | **1,672** | **1,890** |
| **MODEL 50/200 WAIVER** | **0** | **0** | **0** | **0** | **0** | **0** | **0** |

*Source:*
Institute on Disability and Human Development (UAP),
University of Illinois at Chicago, 1994

# WISCONSIN

## Community Services: FY 1992 Revenue Sources

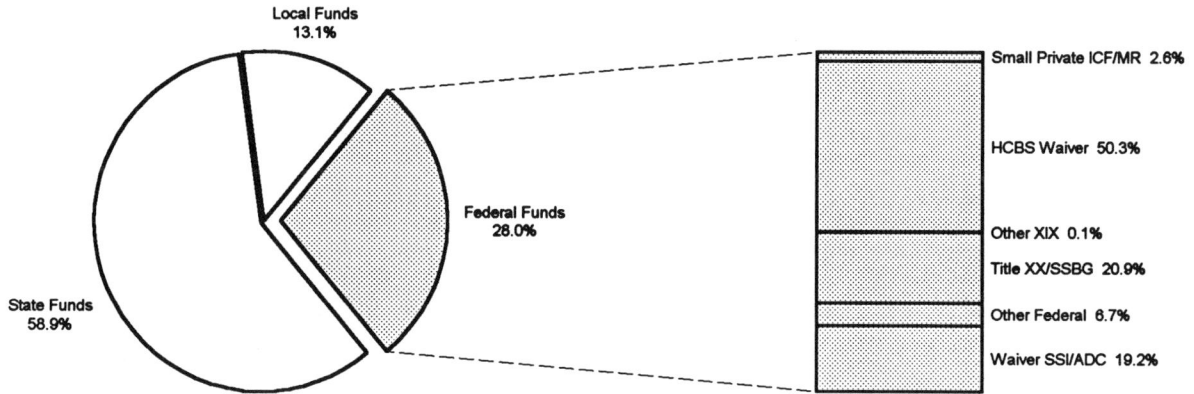

Local Funds 13.1%

State Funds 58.9%

Federal Funds 28.0%

Small Private ICF/MR 2.6%

HCBS Waiver 50.3%

Other XIX 0.1%

Title XX/SSBG 20.9%

Other Federal 6.7%

Waiver SSI/ADC 19.2%

Total Funds: $171.1 Million

## Family Support Initiatives*

| | 1986 | 1987 | 1988 | 1989 | 1990 | 1991 | 1992 |
|---|---|---|---|---|---|---|---|
| **FAMILY SUPPORT: TOTAL SPENDING** | $1,455,863 | $1,697,068 | $2,939,985 | $3,778,452 | $4,690,230 | $5,297,893 | $5,504,820 |
| **Total # of Families Supported** | 2,540 | 2,909 | 3,174 | 3,738 | 4,255 | 4,805 | 5,067 |
| A. Financial Subsidy/Payment | $0 | $0 | $0 | $0 | $0 | $0 | $0 |
| # of Families | 0 | 0 | 0 | 0 | 0 | 0 | 0 |
| B. Family Assistance Payments | $1,000,494 | $1,006,929 | $1,146,492 | $1,285,952 | $1,550,474 | $1,781,107 | $1,932,306 |
| # of Families | 2,001 | 2,250 | 2,031 | 2,249 | 2,435 | 2,566 | 2,716 |
| C. Other Family Support Payments | $455,369 | $690,139 | $1,793,493 | $2,492,500 | $3,139,756 | $3,516,786 | $3,572,514 |
| # of Families | 539 | 659 | 1,143 | 1,489 | 1,820 | 2,239 | 2,351 |

## Other Community Services Initiatives*

| | 1986 | 1987 | 1988 | 1989 | 1990 | 1991 | 1992 |
|---|---|---|---|---|---|---|---|
| **AGING/DD SPENDING** | $0 | $0 | $0 | $0 | $0 | $0 | $0 |
| # of Persons Served | 0 | 0 | 0 | 0 | 0 | 0 | 0 |
| **ASSISTIVE TECHNOLOGY SPENDING** | | | | | | | $0 |
| # of Persons Served | | | | | | | 0 |
| **EARLY INTERVENTION SPENDING** | $7,065,427 | $6,676,318 | $6,949,907 | $7,221,749 | $7,834,124 | $8,349,269 | $9,029,805 |
| # of Persons Served | 3,353 | 3,773 | 4,012 | 4,038 | 4,235 | 4,584 | 5,190 |
| **PERSONAL ASSISTANCE SPENDING** | | | | | | | $0 |
| # of Persons Served | | | | | | | 0 |
| **SUPPORTED EMPLOYMENT SPENDING** | $2,316,639 | $3,186,553 | $5,144,668 | $6,752,917 | $8,489,628 | $9,576,519 | $10,485,943 |
| # of Persons Served | 1,203 | 1,340 | 1,562 | 2,088 | 2,452 | 2,725 | 3,091 |
| **SUPPORTED LIVING SPENDING** | | | | | | | $1,637,818 |
| # of Persons Served | | | | | | | 159 |

*Expenditures associated with Special Community Initiatives are a subset of funding within the community services component of the state's chart series and spreadsheet; Family Support Client figures may include duplicate client counts; HCBS Waiver counts include Waiver case management numbers.
0= Services not provided in the state; NA= Data not available from state; blank= Services not applicable (eg. CSLA prior to authorization, Special Community Initiatives prior to request for data by this study)

*Source:*
Institute on Disability and Human Development (UAP),
University of Illinois at Chicago, 1994

# WISCONSIN

## Large Congregate Care Facilities: FY 1992 Revenue Sources*

### Private 16+Bed Settings

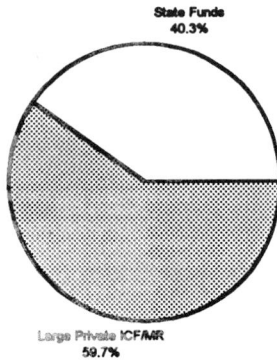

State Funds
40.3%

Large Private ICF/MR
59.7%

Total Funds: $73.4 Million

### Public Institutions

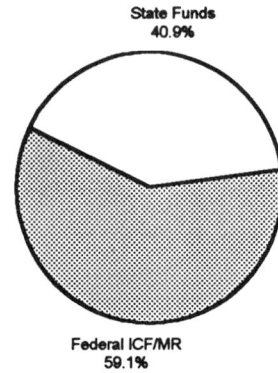

State Funds
40.9%

Federal ICF/MR
59.1%

Total Funds: $114.1 Million

*Excludes nursing homes

## Average Daily Residents in Institutions

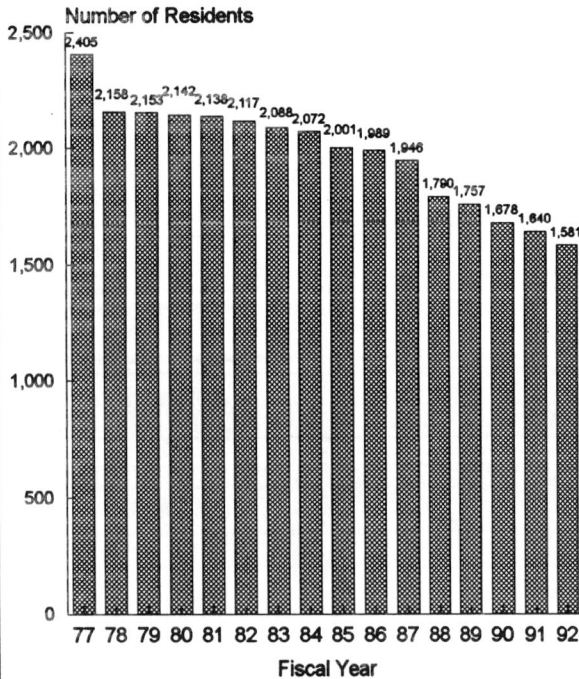

Number of Residents

2,500

2,405
2,158 2,153 2,142 2,138 2,117
2,088 2,072
2,001 1,989
1,946
1,790 1,757
1,678 1,640
1,581

2,000

1,500

1,000

500

0

77 78 79 80 81 82 83 84 85 86 87 88 89 90 91 92

Fiscal Year

## Institutional Daily Costs Per Resident

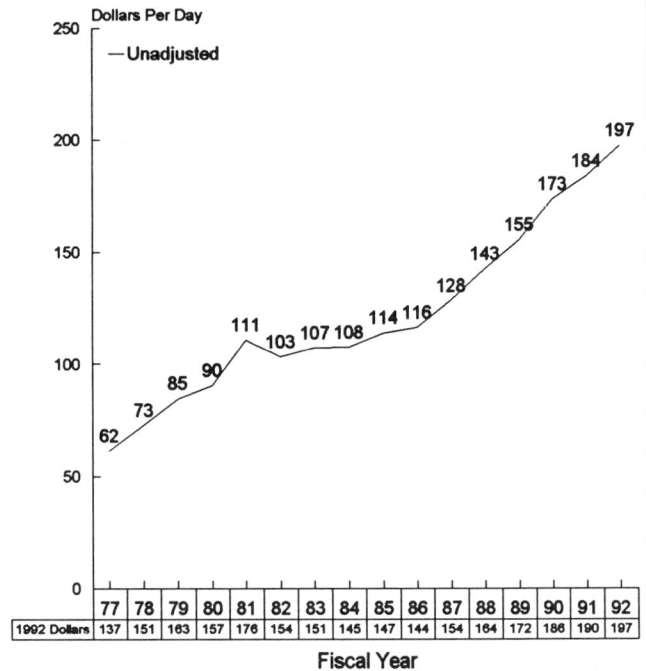

Dollars Per Day

250

—Unadjusted

200

197
184
173
155
143
128
114 116
111      107 108
103
90
85
73
62

150

100

50

0

| | 77 | 78 | 79 | 80 | 81 | 82 | 83 | 84 | 85 | 86 | 87 | 88 | 89 | 90 | 91 | 92 |
|---|---|---|---|---|---|---|---|---|---|---|---|---|---|---|---|---|
| 1992 Dollars | 137 | 151 | 163 | 157 | 176 | 154 | 151 | 145 | 147 | 144 | 154 | 164 | 172 | 186 | 190 | 197 |

Fiscal Year

*Source:*
Institute on Disability and Human Development (UAP),
University of Illinois at Chicago, 1994

# WISCONSIN FISCAL EFFORT

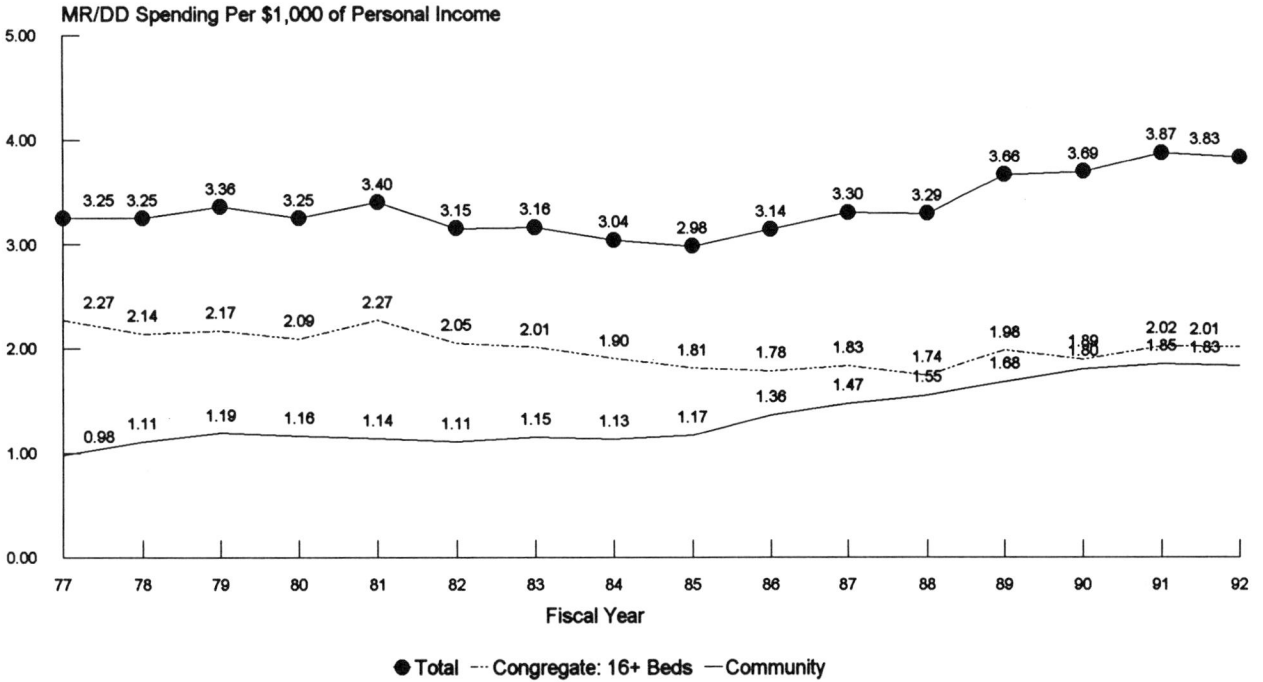

## MR/DD Spending Per $1,000 of Personal Income

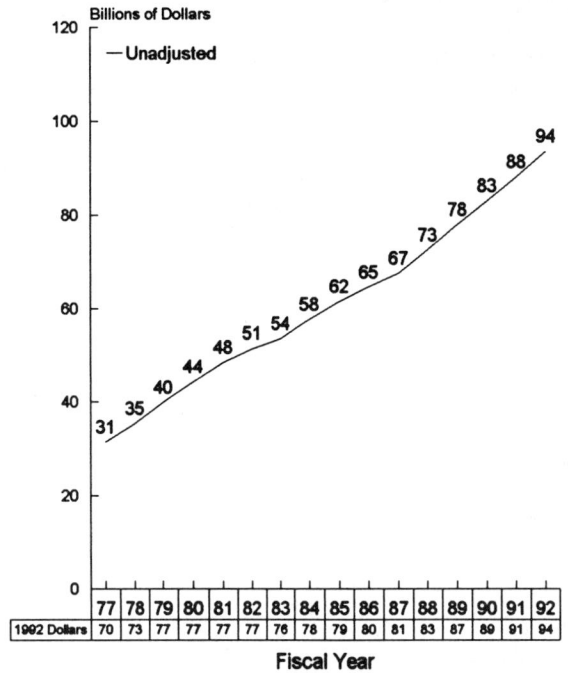

| Fiscal Year | Total | Congregate: 16+ Beds | Community |
|---|---|---|---|
| 77 | 3.25 | 2.27 | 0.98 |
| 78 | 3.25 | 2.14 | 1.11 |
| 79 | 3.36 | 2.17 | 1.19 |
| 80 | 3.25 | 2.09 | 1.16 |
| 81 | 3.40 | 2.27 | 1.14 |
| 82 | 3.15 | 2.05 | 1.11 |
| 83 | 3.16 | 2.01 | 1.15 |
| 84 | 3.04 | 1.90 | 1.13 |
| 85 | 2.98 | 1.81 | 1.17 |
| 86 | 3.14 | 1.78 | 1.36 |
| 87 | 3.30 | 1.83 | 1.47 |
| 88 | 3.29 | 1.74 | 1.55 |
| 89 | 3.66 | 1.98 | 1.68 |
| 90 | 3.69 | 1.89 | 1.80 |
| 91 | 3.87 | 2.02 | 1.85 |
| 92 | 3.83 | 2.01 | 1.83 |

● Total  --- Congregate: 16+ Beds  — Community

## Total MR/DD Spending

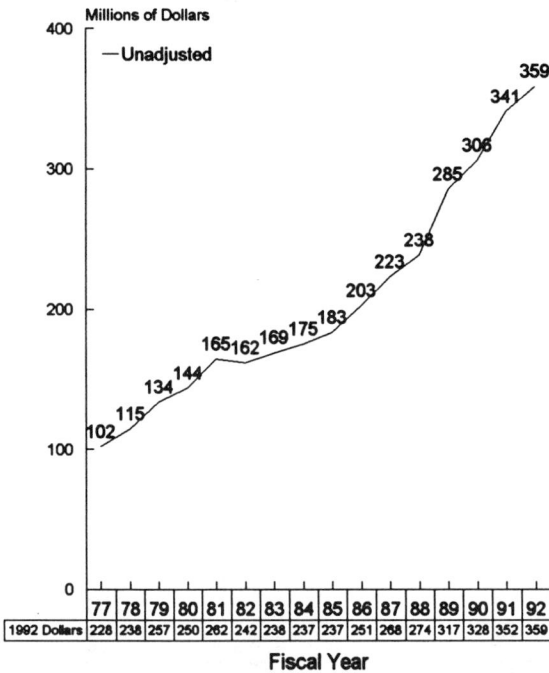

Millions of Dollars
— Unadjusted

| Fiscal Year | 77 | 78 | 79 | 80 | 81 | 82 | 83 | 84 | 85 | 86 | 87 | 88 | 89 | 90 | 91 | 92 |
|---|---|---|---|---|---|---|---|---|---|---|---|---|---|---|---|---|
| Unadjusted | 102 | 115 | 134 | 144 | 165 | 162 | 169 | 175 | 183 | 203 | 223 | 238 | 285 | 306 | 341 | 359 |
| 1992 Dollars | 228 | 238 | 257 | 250 | 262 | 242 | 238 | 237 | 237 | 251 | 268 | 274 | 317 | 328 | 352 | 359 |

## Personal Income

Billions of Dollars
— Unadjusted

| Fiscal Year | 77 | 78 | 79 | 80 | 81 | 82 | 83 | 84 | 85 | 86 | 87 | 88 | 89 | 90 | 91 | 92 |
|---|---|---|---|---|---|---|---|---|---|---|---|---|---|---|---|---|
| Unadjusted | 31 | 35 | 40 | 44 | 48 | 51 | 54 | 58 | 62 | 65 | 67 | 73 | 78 | 83 | 88 | 94 |
| 1992 Dollars | 70 | 73 | 77 | 77 | 77 | 77 | 76 | 78 | 79 | 80 | 81 | 83 | 87 | 89 | 91 | 94 |

*Source:*
Institute on Disability and Human Development (UAP),
University of Illinois at Chicago, 1994

# WISCONSIN

## Financial Support for MR/DD Services: FY 1977-92

| | 1977 | 1978 | 1979 | 1980 | 1981 | 1982 | 1983 | 1984 |
|---|---|---|---|---|---|---|---|---|
| **TOTAL FUNDS** | $102,175,434 | $114,895,393 | $133,988,490 | $143,911,706 | $164,962,205 | $162,174,347 | $169,098,564 | $175,211,471 |
| **CONGREGATE 16+ BEDS** | 71,377,195 | 75,703,557 | 86,592,688 | 92,661,528 | 109,882,207 | 105,281,724 | 107,606,862 | 109,816,661 |
| INSTITUTIONAL SERVICES FUNDS | 54,025,000 | 57,388,000 | 66,517,000 | 70,908,000 | 86,442,000 | 79,770,000 | 81,749,000 | 81,563,000 |
| STATE FUNDS | 22,913,000 | 27,860,000 | 33,849,000 | 35,674,000 | 42,608,000 | 40,630,000 | 40,786,000 | 41,725,000 |
| General Funds | 2,855,000 | 8,010,000 | 8,150,000 | 7,519,000 | 8,605,000 | 8,987,000 | 8,421,000 | 8,571,000 |
| Local | 0 | 0 | 0 | 0 | 0 | 0 | 0 | 0 |
| Other State Funds | 20,058,000 | 19,850,000 | 25,699,000 | 28,155,000 | 34,003,000 | 31,643,000 | 32,365,000 | 33,154,000 |
| FEDERAL FUNDS | 31,112,000 | 29,528,000 | 32,668,000 | 35,234,000 | 43,834,000 | 39,140,000 | 40,963,000 | 39,838,000 |
| Federal ICF/MR | 29,777,000 | 27,915,000 | 30,660,000 | 33,169,000 | 41,408,000 | 37,161,000 | 39,674,000 | 38,798,000 |
| Title XX / SSBG Funds | 0 | 0 | 0 | 0 | 0 | 0 | 0 | 0 |
| Other Federal Funds | 1,335,000 | 1,613,000 | 2,008,000 | 2,065,000 | 2,426,000 | 1,979,000 | 1,289,000 | 1,040,000 |
| LARGE PRIVATE RESIDENTIAL | 17,352,195 | 18,315,557 | 20,075,688 | 21,753,528 | 23,440,207 | 25,511,724 | 25,857,862 | 28,253,661 |
| STATE FUNDS | 8,753,795 | 9,297,757 | 10,081,288 | 10,857,728 | 11,595,107 | 12,454,924 | 12,277,562 | 13,910,361 |
| General Funds | 8,753,795 | 9,297,757 | 10,081,288 | 10,857,728 | 11,595,107 | 12,454,924 | 12,277,562 | 13,910,361 |
| Other State Funds | 0 | 0 | 0 | 0 | 0 | 0 | 0 | 0 |
| Local/County Overmatch | 0 | 0 | 0 | 0 | 0 | 0 | 0 | 0 |
| FEDERAL FUNDS | 8,598,400 | 9,017,800 | 9,994,400 | 10,895,800 | 11,845,100 | 13,056,800 | 13,580,300 | 14,343,300 |
| Large Private ICF/MR | 8,598,400 | 9,017,800 | 9,994,400 | 10,895,800 | 11,845,100 | 13,056,800 | 13,580,300 | 14,343,300 |
| **COMMUNITY SERVICES FUNDS** | 30,798,239 | 39,191,836 | 47,395,802 | 51,250,178 | 55,079,998 | 56,892,623 | 61,491,702 | 65,394,810 |
| STATE FUNDS | 25,525,639 | 34,131,636 | 42,175,202 | 45,861,978 | 49,932,098 | 51,560,823 | 56,106,802 | 59,798,468 |
| General Funds | 13,557,903 | 20,877,725 | 26,818,699 | 29,126,153 | 32,221,519 | 32,810,528 | 34,107,346 | 36,605,196 |
| Other State Funds | 1,752,000 | 1,741,000 | 1,833,000 | 2,125,000 | 1,958,767 | 2,378,500 | 4,931,353 | 4,071,478 |
| Local/County Overmatch | 3,317,736 | 3,705,911 | 4,139,503 | 4,623,825 | 5,164,812 | 5,696,795 | 5,582,103 | 7,014,794 |
| SSI State Supplement | 6,898,000 | 7,807,000 | 9,384,000 | 9,987,000 | 10,587,000 | 10,675,000 | 11,486,000 | 12,107,000 |
| FEDERAL FUNDS | 5,272,600 | 5,060,200 | 5,220,600 | 5,388,200 | 5,147,900 | 5,331,800 | 5,384,900 | 5,596,342 |
| ICF/MR Funds | 604,600 | 650,200 | 709,600 | 787,200 | 853,900 | 913,200 | 959,700 | 1,011,700 |
| Small Public | 0 | 0 | 0 | 0 | 0 | 0 | 0 | 0 |
| Small Private | 604,600 | 650,200 | 709,600 | 787,200 | 853,900 | 913,200 | 959,700 | 1,011,700 |
| HCBS Waiver | 0 | 0 | 0 | 0 | 0 | 0 | 0 | 68,016 |
| Model 50/200 Waiver | 0 | 0 | 0 | 0 | 0 | 0 | 0 | 0 |
| Other Title XIX Programs | 0 | 0 | 0 | 0 | 0 | 0 | 0 | 0 |
| Title XX / SSBG Funds | 3,998,000 | 3,740,000 | 3,789,000 | 3,851,000 | 3,544,000 | 3,728,000 | 3,728,000 | 3,728,000 |
| Other Federal Funds | 670,000 | 670,000 | 722,000 | 750,000 | 750,000 | 690,600 | 697,200 | 721,000 |
| Waiver Clients' SSI/ADC | 0 | 0 | 0 | 0 | 0 | 0 | 0 | 67,626 |

| | 1985 | 1986 | 1987 | 1988 | 1989 | 1990 | 1991 | 1992 |
|---|---|---|---|---|---|---|---|---|
| **TOTAL FUNDS** | $183,392,876 | $202,801,717 | $222,923,870 | $238,477,306 | $285,416,483 | $306,002,417 | $340,640,915 | $358,649,162 |
| **CONGREGATE 16+ BEDS** | 111,309,443 | 114,927,096 | 123,493,286 | 126,205,642 | 154,459,751 | 157,038,921 | 178,066,506 | 187,590,480 |
| INSTITUTIONAL SERVICES FUNDS | 83,192,700 | 84,390,967 | 91,218,833 | 93,365,112 | 99,553,998 | 106,207,030 | 110,014,960 | 114,142,861 |
| STATE FUNDS | 45,723,800 | 41,525,965 | 44,045,261 | 43,972,400 | 45,281,502 | 52,634,803 | 53,934,941 | 46,678,165 |
| General Funds | 6,657,500 | 6,028,900 | 5,628,203 | 5,316,365 | 3,659,619 | 11,355,842 | 11,002,147 | 0 |
| Local | 0 | 0 | 0 | 0 | 0 | 0 | 0 | 0 |
| Other State Funds | 39,066,300 | 35,497,065 | 38,417,058 | 38,656,035 | 41,621,883 | 41,278,961 | 42,932,794 | 46,678,165 |
| FEDERAL FUNDS | 37,468,900 | 42,865,002 | 47,173,572 | 49,392,712 | 54,272,496 | 53,572,227 | 56,080,019 | 67,464,696 |
| Federal ICF/MR | 36,820,100 | 42,580,092 | 46,819,198 | 49,078,224 | 54,272,496 | 53,572,227 | 56,080,019 | 67,464,696 |
| Title XX / SSBG Funds | 0 | 0 | 0 | 0 | 0 | 0 | 0 | 0 |
| Other Federal Funds | 648,800 | 284,910 | 354,374 | 314,488 | 0 | 0 | 0 | 0 |
| LARGE PRIVATE RESIDENTIAL | 28,116,743 | 30,536,129 | 32,274,453 | 32,840,530 | 54,905,753 | 50,831,891 | 68,051,546 | 73,447,619 |
| STATE FUNDS | 13,923,843 | 14,902,455 | 15,343,493 | 15,011,579 | 22,752,080 | 21,110,298 | 27,846,116 | 29,607,903 |
| General Funds | 13,923,843 | 14,902,455 | 15,343,493 | 15,011,579 | 22,752,080 | 21,110,298 | 27,846,116 | 29,607,903 |
| Other State Funds | 0 | 0 | 0 | 0 | 0 | 0 | 0 | 0 |
| Local/County Overmatch | 0 | 0 | 0 | 0 | 0 | 0 | 0 | 0 |
| FEDERAL FUNDS | 14,192,900 | 15,633,674 | 16,930,960 | 17,828,951 | 32,153,673 | 29,721,593 | 40,205,430 | 43,839,716 |
| Large Private ICF/MR | 14,192,900 | 15,633,674 | 16,930,960 | 17,828,951 | 32,153,673 | 29,721,593 | 40,205,430 | 43,839,716 |
| **COMMUNITY SERVICES FUNDS** | 72,083,433 | 87,874,621 | 99,430,584 | 112,271,664 | 130,956,732 | 148,963,496 | 162,574,409 | 171,058,682 |
| STATE FUNDS | 65,745,038 | 80,755,475 | 89,129,371 | 95,334,100 | 104,019,722 | 113,257,093 | 117,660,356 | 120,302,438 |
| General Funds | 40,584,608 | 52,366,273 | 59,283,313 | 64,308,858 | 69,661,141 | 74,809,726 | 75,180,263 | 74,239,895 |
| Other State Funds | 4,157,447 | 4,268,917 | 4,268,917 | 3,282,517 | 3,027,559 | 3,486,200 | 3,844,842 | 3,379,420 |
| Local/County Overmatch | 8,196,983 | 8,819,285 | 9,851,141 | 11,003,725 | 13,755,072 | 16,506,419 | 19,257,766 | 22,336,764 |
| SSI State Supplement | 12,806,000 | 15,301,000 | 15,726,000 | 16,739,000 | 17,575,950 | 18,454,748 | 19,377,485 | 20,346,359 |
| FEDERAL FUNDS | 6,338,395 | 7,119,146 | 10,301,213 | 16,937,564 | 26,937,010 | 35,706,403 | 44,914,053 | 50,756,244 |
| ICF/MR Funds | 1,070,300 | 1,070,197 | 575,166 | 607,331 | 1,425,402 | 953,907 | 1,129,374 | 1,253,084 |
| Small Public | 0 | 0 | 0 | 0 | 0 | 0 | 0 | 0 |
| Small Private | 1,070,300 | 1,070,197 | 575,166 | 607,331 | 1,425,402 | 953,907 | 1,129,374 | 1,253,084 |
| HCBS Waiver | 342,195 | 939,231 | 3,230,687 | 6,945,876 | 10,843,355 | 15,713,181 | 21,037,359 | 24,139,631 |
| Model 50/200 Waiver | 0 | 0 | 0 | 0 | 0 | 0 | 0 | 0 |
| Other Title XIX Programs | 0 | 0 | 0 | 986,400 | 1,900,000 | 2,100,000 | 2,400,000 | 2,871,004 |
| Title XX / SSBG Funds | 3,728,000 | 3,728,000 | 3,728,000 | 3,728,000 | 5,674,885 | 7,621,770 | 9,568,655 | 10,025,172 |
| Other Federal Funds | 996,300 | 848,042 | 1,039,900 | 1,699,525 | 2,505,096 | 2,901,097 | 3,116,509 | 3,236,593 |
| Waiver Clients' SSI/ADC | 201,600 | 533,676 | 1,727,460 | 2,970,432 | 4,588,272 | 6,416,448 | 7,662,156 | 9,230,760 |

*Source:*

Institute on Disability and Human Development (UAP),
University of Illinois at Chicago, 1994

# WYOMING

## MR/DD Spending for Congregate Residential & Community Services

▨Congregate: 16+ Beds* ■Community**

Millions of 1992 Dollars

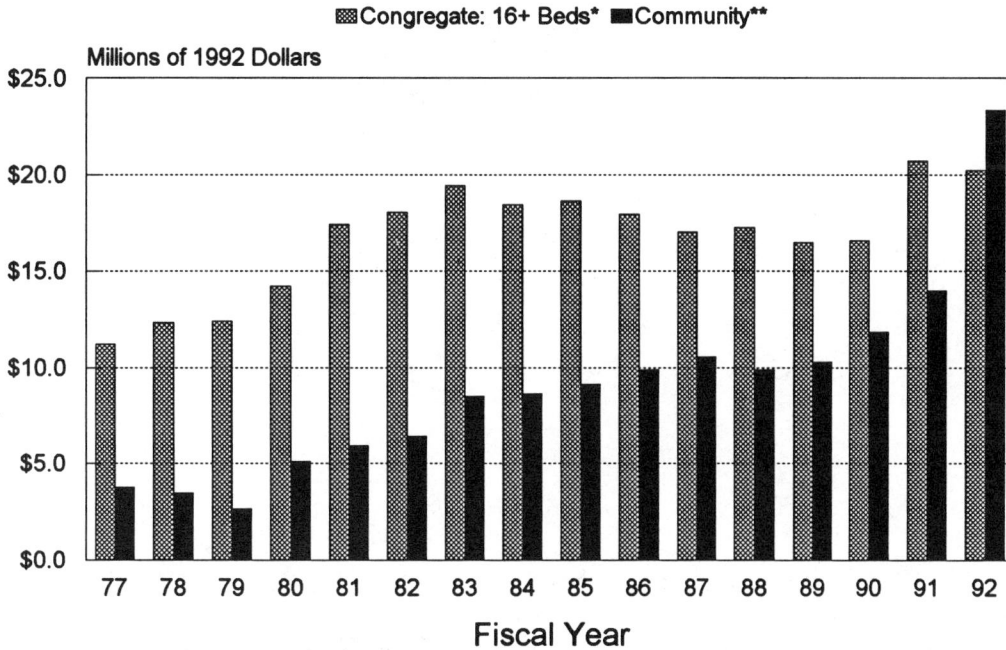

Fiscal Year

*Excludes nursing homes; ** Includes resources for
15 bed or less residential settings & non-residential community services

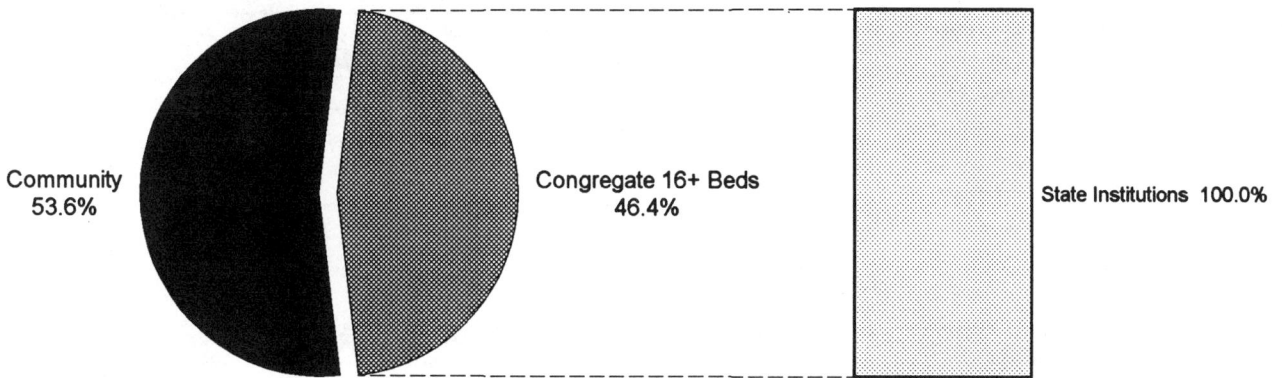

Community
53.6%

Congregate 16+ Beds
46.4%

State Institutions  100.0%

FY 1992 Total Spending:
$43.6 Million

*Source:*
Institute on Disability and Human Development (UAP),
University of Illinois at Chicago, 1994

# WYOMING

## Number of Persons Served by Residential Setting: FY 1992

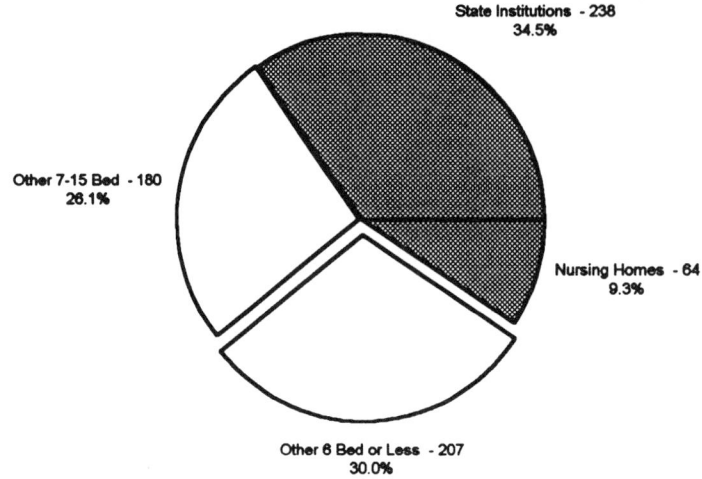

State Institutions - 238
34.5%

Other 7-15 Bed - 180
26.1%

Nursing Homes - 64
9.3%

Other 6 Bed or Less - 207
30.0%

Total Served: 689

## Persons Served by Residential Setting:1986-92

|  | 1986 | 1987 | 1988 | 1989 | 1990 | 1991 | 1992 |
|---|---|---|---|---|---|---|---|
| CONGREGATE 16 + BED SETTINGS | NA | NA | 453 | NA | NA | 290 | 302 |
| Nursing Homes | NA | NA | 79 | NA | NA | 21 | 64 |
| State Institutions | 438 | 432 | 374 | 342 | 311 | 269 | 238 |
| Private 16+Bed ICF/MR | 0 | 0 | 0 | 0 | 0 | 0 | 0 |
| Other 16+Bed Residential | 0 | 0 | 0 | 0 | 0 | 0 | 0 |
| 15 BED OR LESS RESIDENTIAL SETTINGS | 247 | 268 | 300 | 300 | 310 | 336 | 387 |
| Public 7-15 Bed ICF/MR | 0 | 0 | 0 | 0 | 0 | 0 | 0 |
| Private 7-15 Bed ICF/MR | 0 | 0 | 0 | 0 | 0 | 0 | 0 |
| Other 7-15 Bed Residential | 247 | 268 | 170 | 170 | 170 | 170 | 180 |
| Public 6 Bed or Less ICF/MR |  |  | 0 | 0 | 0 | 0 | 0 |
| Private 6 Bed or Less ICF/MR |  |  | 0 | 0 | 0 | 0 | 0 |
| Other 6 Bed or Less Residential |  |  | 130 | 130 | 140 | 166 | 207 |
| TOTAL PERSONS SERVED | NA | NA | 753 | NA | NA | 626 | 689 |

## Persons Served in Non-Residential Community Services:1986-92

|  | 1986 | 1987 | 1988 | 1989 | 1990 | 1991 | 1992 |
|---|---|---|---|---|---|---|---|
| DAY/WORK PROGRAMS | 400 | 408 | 400 | 400 | 620 | 644 | 640 |
| Sheltered Employment/Work Activity | NA | NA | NA | 400 | 450 | 404 | 308 |
| Day Habilitation ("Day Training") | NA | NA | NA | 0 | 50 | 150 | 96 |
| Supported/Competitive Employment | 0 | 0 | 0 | 0 | 120 | 90 | 236 |
| CASE MANAGEMENT | NA | NA | NA | NA | NA | 134 | 345 |
| HCBS WAIVER | 0 | 0 | 0 | 0 | 0 | 134 | 463 |
| MODEL 50/200 WAIVER | 0 | 0 | 0 | 0 | 0 | 0 | 0 |

*Source:*
Institute on Disability and Human Development (UAP),
University of Illinois at Chicago, 1994

# WYOMING

## Community Services: FY 1992 Revenue Sources

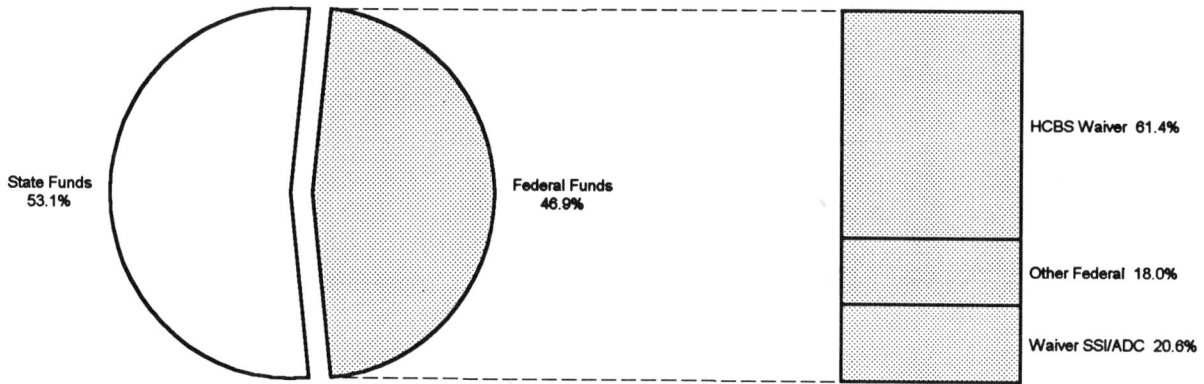

State Funds 53.1%

Federal Funds 46.9%

HCBS Waiver 61.4%

Other Federal 18.0%

Waiver SSI/ADC 20.6%

Total Funds: $23.3 Million

## Family Support Initiatives*

|  | 1986 | 1987 | 1988 | 1989 | 1990 | 1991 | 1992 |
|---|---|---|---|---|---|---|---|
| **FAMILY SUPPORT: TOTAL SPENDING** | $0 | $0 | $0 | $0 | $0 | $0 | $0 |
| **Total # of Families Supported** | 0 | 0 | 0 | 0 | 0 | 0 | 0 |
| A. Financial Subsidy/Payment | $0 | $0 | $0 | $0 | $0 | $0 | $0 |
| # of Families | 0 | 0 | 0 | 0 | 0 | 0 | 0 |
| B. Family Assistance Payments | $0 | $0 | $0 | $0 | $0 | $0 | $0 |
| # of Families | 0 | 0 | 0 | 0 | 0 | 0 | 0 |
| C. Other Family Support Payments | $0 | $0 | $0 | $0 | $0 | $0 | $0 |
| # of Families | 0 | 0 | 0 | 0 | 0 | 0 | 0 |

## Other Community Services Initiatives*

|  | 1986 | 1987 | 1988 | 1989 | 1990 | 1991 | 1992 |
|---|---|---|---|---|---|---|---|
| **AGING/DD SPENDING** | $0 | $0 | $0 | $0 | $0 | $0 | $0 |
| # of Persons Served | 0 | 0 | 0 | 0 | 0 | 0 | 0 |
| **ASSISTIVE TECHNOLOGY SPENDING** |  |  |  |  |  |  | $0 |
| # of Persons Served |  |  |  |  |  |  | 0 |
| **EARLY INTERVENTION SPENDING** | $4,784,900 | $4,629,400 | $4,587,000 | $5,080,000 | $5,830,000 | $5,800,000 | $6,650,000 |
| # of Persons Served | na | 1,089 | 1,122 | 1,190 | 1,321 | 1,286 | 1,422 |
| **PERSONAL ASSISTANCE SPENDING** |  |  |  |  |  |  | $0 |
| # of Persons Served |  |  |  |  |  |  | 0 |
| **SUPPORTED EMPLOYMENT SPENDING** | $0 | $0 | $0 | $0 | $1,080,000 | $810,000 | $1,995,616 |
| # of Persons Served | 0 | 0 | 0 | 0 | 120 | 90 | 236 |
| **SUPPORTED LIVING SPENDING** |  |  |  |  |  | $326,822 | $881,000 |
| # of Persons Served |  |  |  |  |  | 23 | 62 |

*Expenditures associated with Special Community Initiatives are a subset of funding within the community services component of the state's chart series and spreadsheet; Family Support Client figures may include duplicate client counts; HCBS Waiver counts include Waiver case management numbers.
0= Services not provided in the state; NA= Data not available from state; blank= Services not applicable (eg. CSLA prior to authorization, Special Community Initiatives prior to request for data by this study)

Source:
Institute on Disability and Human Development (UAP),
University of Illinois at Chicago, 1994

# WYOMING

## Large Congregate Care Facilities: FY 1992 Revenue Sources*

### Private 16+Bed Settings

### Public Institutions

### Does Not Apply

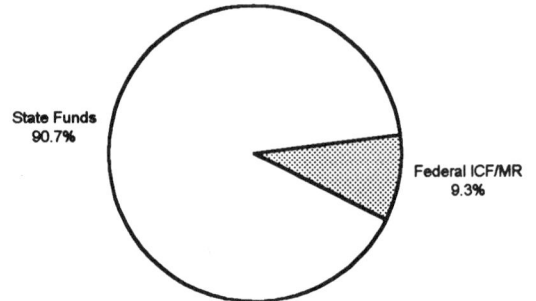

State Funds
90.7%

Federal ICF/MR
9.3%

Total Funds: $20.2 Million

*Excludes nursing homes

## Average Daily Residents in Institutions

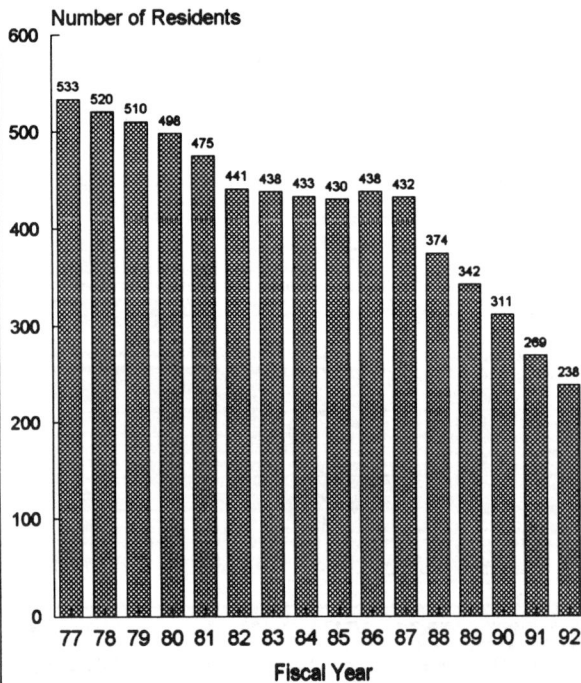

Number of Residents

| | |
|---|---|
| 77 | 533 |
| 78 | 520 |
| 79 | 510 |
| 80 | 498 |
| 81 | 475 |
| 82 | 441 |
| 83 | 438 |
| 84 | 433 |
| 85 | 430 |
| 86 | 438 |
| 87 | 432 |
| 88 | 374 |
| 89 | 342 |
| 90 | 311 |
| 91 | 269 |
| 92 | 238 |

Fiscal Year

## Institutional Daily Costs Per Resident

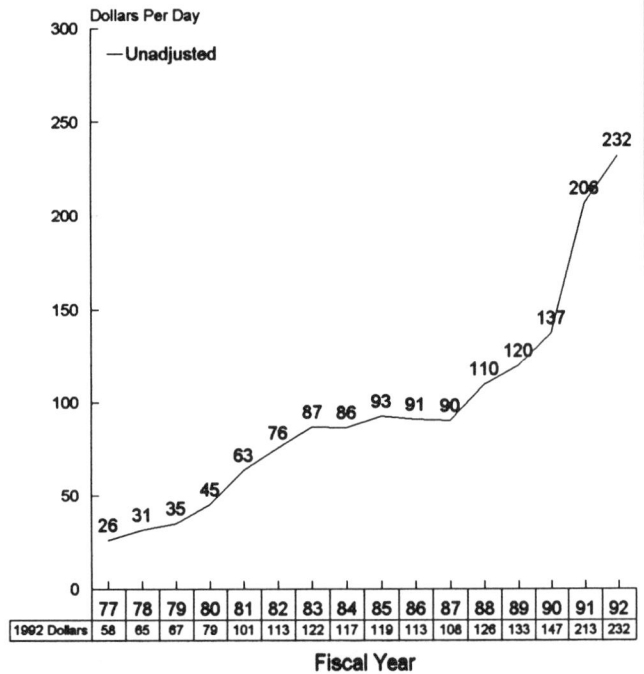

Dollars Per Day

— Unadjusted

26  31  35  45  63  76  87  86  93  91  90  110  120  137  206  232

| | 77 | 78 | 79 | 80 | 81 | 82 | 83 | 84 | 85 | 86 | 87 | 88 | 89 | 90 | 91 | 92 |
|---|---|---|---|---|---|---|---|---|---|---|---|---|---|---|---|---|
| 1992 Dollars | 58 | 65 | 67 | 79 | 101 | 113 | 122 | 117 | 119 | 113 | 108 | 126 | 133 | 147 | 213 | 232 |

Fiscal Year

*Source:*
Institute on Disability and Human Development (UAP),
University of Illinois at Chicago, 1994

# WYOMING FISCAL EFFORT

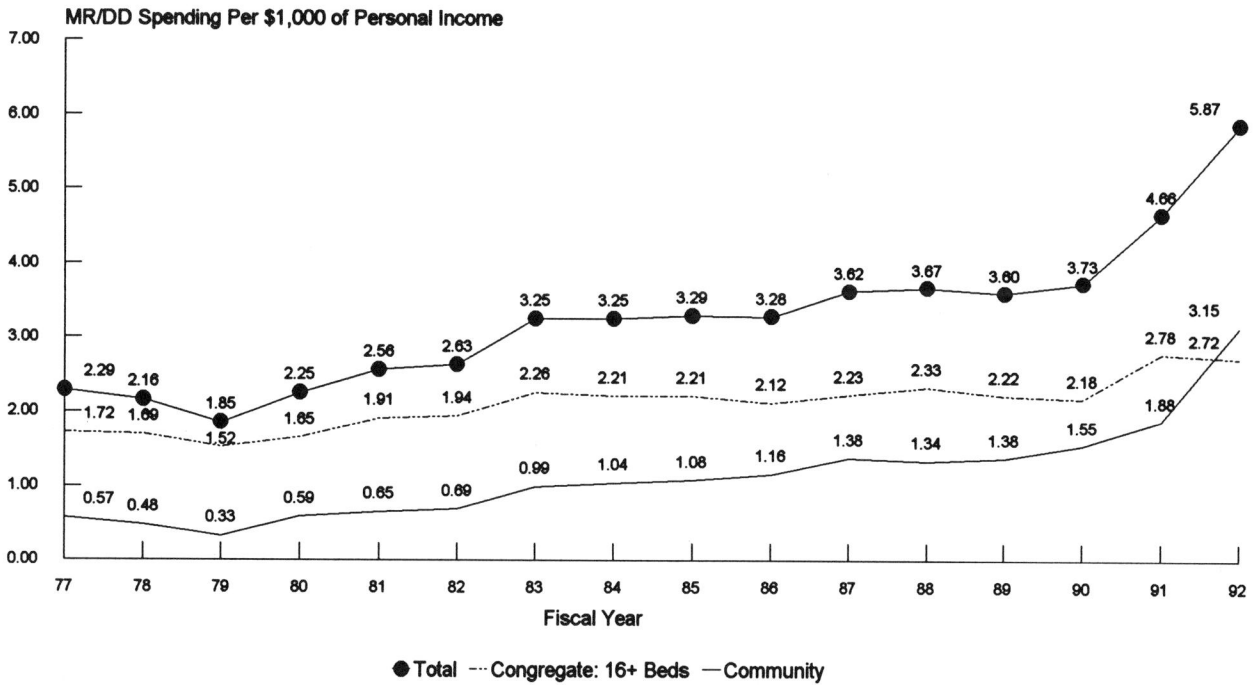

## MR/DD Spending Per $1,000 of Personal Income

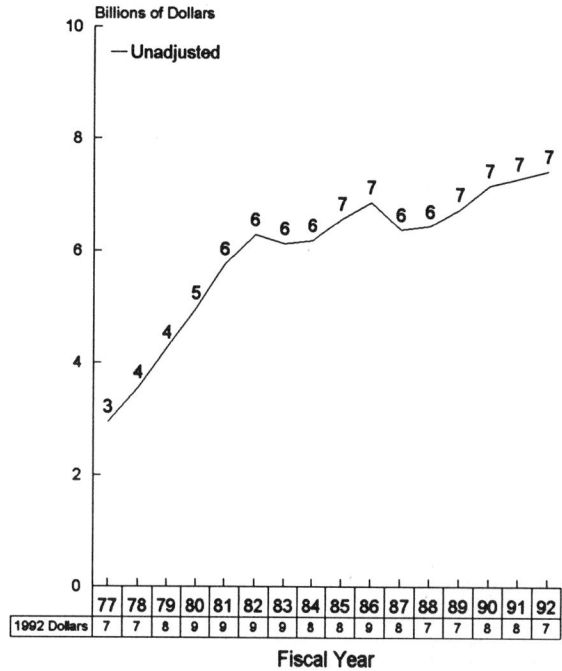

| Fiscal Year | Total | Congregate: 16+ Beds | Community |
|---|---|---|---|
| 77 | 2.29 | 1.72 | 0.57 |
| 78 | 2.16 | 1.69 | 0.48 |
| 79 | 1.85 | 1.52 | 0.33 |
| 80 | 2.25 | 1.65 | 0.59 |
| 81 | 2.56 | 1.91 | 0.65 |
| 82 | 2.63 | 1.94 | 0.69 |
| 83 | 3.25 | 2.26 | 0.99 |
| 84 | 3.25 | 2.21 | 1.04 |
| 85 | 3.29 | 2.21 | 1.08 |
| 86 | 3.28 | 2.12 | 1.16 |
| 87 | 3.62 | 2.23 | 1.38 |
| 88 | 3.67 | 2.33 | 1.34 |
| 89 | 3.60 | 2.22 | 1.38 |
| 90 | 3.73 | 2.18 | 1.55 |
| 91 | 4.66 | 2.78 | 1.88 |
| 92 | 5.87 | 2.72 | 3.15 |

● Total --- Congregate: 16+ Beds — Community

## Total MR/DD Spending

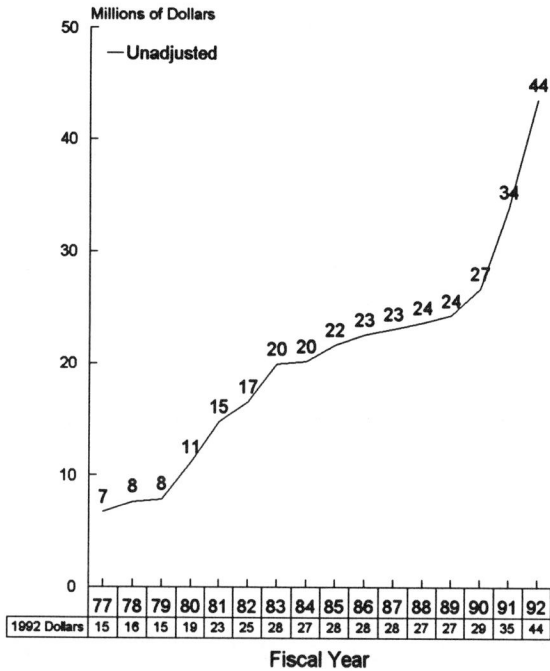

Millions of Dollars

— Unadjusted

Values plotted: 7, 8, 8, 11, 15, 17, 20, 20, 22, 23, 23, 24, 24, 27, 34, 44

| | 77 | 78 | 79 | 80 | 81 | 82 | 83 | 84 | 85 | 86 | 87 | 88 | 89 | 90 | 91 | 92 |
|---|---|---|---|---|---|---|---|---|---|---|---|---|---|---|---|---|
| 1992 Dollars | 15 | 16 | 15 | 19 | 23 | 25 | 28 | 27 | 28 | 28 | 28 | 27 | 27 | 29 | 35 | 44 |

Fiscal Year

## Personal Income

Billions of Dollars

— Unadjusted

Values plotted: 3, 4, 4, 5, 6, 6, 6, 6, 7, 7, 6, 6, 7, 7, 7, 7

| | 77 | 78 | 79 | 80 | 81 | 82 | 83 | 84 | 85 | 86 | 87 | 88 | 89 | 90 | 91 | 92 |
|---|---|---|---|---|---|---|---|---|---|---|---|---|---|---|---|---|
| 1992 Dollars | 7 | 7 | 8 | 9 | 9 | 9 | 9 | 9 | 8 | 8 | 9 | 8 | 7 | 7 | 8 | 7 |

Fiscal Year

*Source:*
Institute on Disability and Human Development (UAP),
University of Illinois at Chicago, 1994

# WYOMING
## Financial Support for MR/DD Services: FY 1977-92

| | 1977 | 1978 | 1979 | 1980 | 1981 | 1982 | 1983 | 1984 |
|---|---|---|---|---|---|---|---|---|
| **TOTAL FUNDS** | $6,728,000 | $7,660,000 | $7,879,000 | $11,175,000 | $14,726,000 | $16,500,000 | $19,916,000 | $20,121,900 |
| **CONGREGATE 16+ BEDS** | 5,043,000 | 5,975,000 | 6,489,000 | 8,225,000 | 10,998,000 | 12,168,000 | 13,843,000 | 13,691,600 |
| INSTITUTIONAL SERVICES FUNDS | 5,043,000 | 5,975,000 | 6,489,000 | 8,225,000 | 10,998,000 | 12,168,000 | 13,843,000 | 13,691,600 |
| STATE FUNDS | 4,894,000 | 5,861,000 | 6,365,000 | 8,071,000 | 10,837,000 | 12,020,000 | 13,751,000 | 13,622,600 |
| General Funds | 4,894,000 | 5,861,000 | 6,365,000 | 8,071,000 | 10,837,000 | 12,020,000 | 13,751,000 | 13,622,600 |
| Local | 0 | 0 | 0 | 0 | 0 | 0 | 0 | 0 |
| Other State Funds | 0 | 0 | 0 | 0 | 0 | 0 | 0 | 0 |
| FEDERAL FUNDS | 149,000 | 114,000 | 124,000 | 154,000 | 161,000 | 148,000 | 92,000 | 69,000 |
| Federal ICF/MR | 0 | 0 | 0 | 0 | 0 | 0 | 0 | 0 |
| Title XX / SSBG Funds | 0 | 0 | 0 | 0 | 0 | 0 | 0 | 0 |
| Other Federal Funds | 149,000 | 114,000 | 124,000 | 154,000 | 161,000 | 148,000 | 92,000 | 69,000 |
| LARGE PRIVATE RESIDENTIAL | 0 | 0 | 0 | 0 | 0 | 0 | 0 | 0 |
| STATE FUNDS | 0 | 0 | 0 | 0 | 0 | 0 | 0 | 0 |
| General Funds | 0 | 0 | 0 | 0 | 0 | 0 | 0 | 0 |
| Other State Funds | 0 | 0 | 0 | 0 | 0 | 0 | 0 | 0 |
| Local/County Overmatch | 0 | 0 | 0 | 0 | 0 | 0 | 0 | 0 |
| FEDERAL FUNDS | 0 | 0 | 0 | 0 | 0 | 0 | 0 | 0 |
| Large Private ICF/MR | 0 | 0 | 0 | 0 | 0 | 0 | 0 | 0 |
| **COMMUNITY SERVICES FUNDS** | 1,685,000 | 1,685,000 | 1,390,000 | 2,950,000 | 3,728,000 | 4,332,000 | 6,073,000 | 6,430,300 |
| STATE FUNDS | 335,000 | 335,000 | 338,000 | 1,998,000 | 2,878,000 | 3,482,000 | 5,623,000 | 5,558,400 |
| General Funds | 335,000 | 335,000 | 298,000 | 1,958,000 | 2,838,000 | 3,442,000 | 5,583,000 | 5,514,400 |
| Other State Funds | 0 | 0 | 0 | 0 | 0 | 0 | 0 | 0 |
| Local/County Overmatch | 0 | 0 | 0 | 0 | 0 | 0 | 0 | 0 |
| SSI State Supplement | 0 | 0 | 40,000 | 40,000 | 40,000 | 40,000 | 40,000 | 44,000 |
| FEDERAL FUNDS | 1,350,000 | 1,350,000 | 1,052,000 | 952,000 | 850,000 | 850,000 | 450,000 | 871,900 |
| ICF/MR Funds | 0 | 0 | 0 | 0 | 0 | 0 | 0 | 0 |
| Small Public | 0 | 0 | 0 | 0 | 0 | 0 | 0 | 0 |
| Small Private | 0 | 0 | 0 | 0 | 0 | 0 | 0 | 0 |
| HCBS Waiver | 0 | 0 | 0 | 0 | 0 | 0 | 0 | 0 |
| Model 50/200 Waiver | 0 | 0 | 0 | 0 | 0 | 0 | 0 | 0 |
| Other Title XIX Programs | 0 | 0 | 0 | 0 | 0 | 0 | 0 | 0 |
| Title XX / SSBG Funds | 1,000,000 | 1,000,000 | 600,000 | 600,000 | 400,000 | 400,000 | 0 | 0 |
| Other Federal Funds | 350,000 | 350,000 | 452,000 | 352,000 | 450,000 | 450,000 | 450,000 | 871,900 |
| Waiver Clients' SSI/ADC | 0 | 0 | 0 | 0 | 0 | 0 | 0 | 0 |

| | 1985 | 1986 | 1987 | 1988 | 1989 | 1990 | 1991 | 1992 |
|---|---|---|---|---|---|---|---|---|
| **TOTAL FUNDS** | $21,627,900 | $22,528,700 | $23,041,544 | $23,626,200 | $24,277,613 | $26,704,632 | $33,952,311 | $43,568,131 |
| **CONGREGATE 16+ BEDS** | 14,519,000 | 14,538,400 | 14,231,100 | 15,018,200 | 14,959,397 | 15,583,063 | 20,261,822 | 20,222,776 |
| INSTITUTIONAL SERVICES FUNDS | 14,519,000 | 14,538,400 | 14,231,100 | 15,018,200 | 14,959,397 | 15,583,063 | 20,261,822 | 20,222,776 |
| STATE FUNDS | 14,463,800 | 14,499,100 | 14,157,500 | 14,960,200 | 14,876,138 | 15,583,063 | 18,341,122 | 18,341,122 |
| General Funds | 14,463,800 | 14,408,200 | 13,902,600 | 14,960,200 | 14,876,138 | 15,583,063 | 18,341,122 | 18,341,122 |
| Local | 0 | 0 | 0 | 0 | 0 | 0 | 0 | 0 |
| Other State Funds | 0 | 90,900 | 254,900 | 0 | 0 | 0 | 0 | 0 |
| FEDERAL FUNDS | 55,200 | 39,300 | 73,600 | 58,000 | 83,259 | 0 | 1,920,700 | 1,881,654 |
| Federal ICF/MR | 0 | 0 | 0 | 0 | 0 | 0 | 1,829,245 | 1,881,654 |
| Title XX / SSBG Funds | 0 | 0 | 0 | 0 | 0 | 0 | 0 | 0 |
| Other Federal Funds | 55,200 | 39,300 | 73,600 | 58,000 | 83,259 | 0 | 91,455 | 0 |
| LARGE PRIVATE RESIDENTIAL | 0 | 0 | 0 | 0 | 0 | 0 | 0 | 0 |
| STATE FUNDS | 0 | 0 | 0 | 0 | 0 | 0 | 0 | 0 |
| General Funds | 0 | 0 | 0 | 0 | 0 | 0 | 0 | 0 |
| Other State Funds | 0 | 0 | 0 | 0 | 0 | 0 | 0 | 0 |
| Local/County Overmatch | 0 | 0 | 0 | 0 | 0 | 0 | 0 | 0 |
| FEDERAL FUNDS | 0 | 0 | 0 | 0 | 0 | 0 | 0 | 0 |
| Large Private ICF/MR | 0 | 0 | 0 | 0 | 0 | 0 | 0 | 0 |
| **COMMUNITY SERVICES FUNDS** | 7,108,900 | 7,990,300 | 8,810,444 | 8,608,000 | 9,318,216 | 11,121,569 | 13,690,489 | 23,345,355 |
| STATE FUNDS | 6,165,400 | 7,166,300 | 7,786,000 | 7,521,000 | 8,221,216 | 10,014,569 | 10,470,746 | 12,394,437 |
| General Funds | 6,118,400 | 7,110,300 | 7,727,000 | 7,465,000 | 8,160,000 | 9,940,000 | 10,394,646 | 12,299,912 |
| Other State Funds | 0 | 0 | 0 | 0 | 0 | 0 | 0 | 0 |
| Local/County Overmatch | 0 | 0 | 0 | 0 | 0 | 0 | 0 | 0 |
| SSI State Supplement | 47,000 | 56,000 | 59,000 | 56,000 | 61,216 | 74,569 | 76,100 | 94,525 |
| FEDERAL FUNDS | 943,500 | 824,000 | 1,024,444 | 1,087,000 | 1,097,000 | 1,107,000 | 3,219,743 | 10,950,918 |
| ICF/MR Funds | 0 | 0 | 0 | 0 | 0 | 0 | 0 | 0 |
| Small Public | 0 | 0 | 0 | 0 | 0 | 0 | 0 | 0 |
| Small Private | 0 | 0 | 0 | 0 | 0 | 0 | 0 | 0 |
| HCBS Waiver | 0 | 0 | 0 | 0 | 0 | 0 | 835,487 | 6,719,626 |
| Model 50/200 Waiver | 0 | 0 | 0 | 0 | 0 | 0 | 0 | 0 |
| Other Title XIX Programs | 0 | 0 | 0 | 0 | 0 | 0 | 0 | 0 |
| Title XX / SSBG Funds | 0 | 0 | 0 | 0 | 0 | 0 | 0 | 0 |
| Other Federal Funds | 943,500 | 824,000 | 1,024,444 | 1,087,000 | 1,097,000 | 1,107,000 | 1,770,000 | 1,970,000 |
| Waiver Clients' SSI/ADC | 0 | 0 | 0 | 0 | 0 | 0 | 614,256 | 2,261,292 |

*Source:*
Institute on Disability and Human Development (UAP),
University of Illinois at Chicago, 1994

# UNITED STATES

## MR/DD Spending for Congregate Residential & Community Services

▨Congregate: 16+ Beds*  ■Community**

Billions

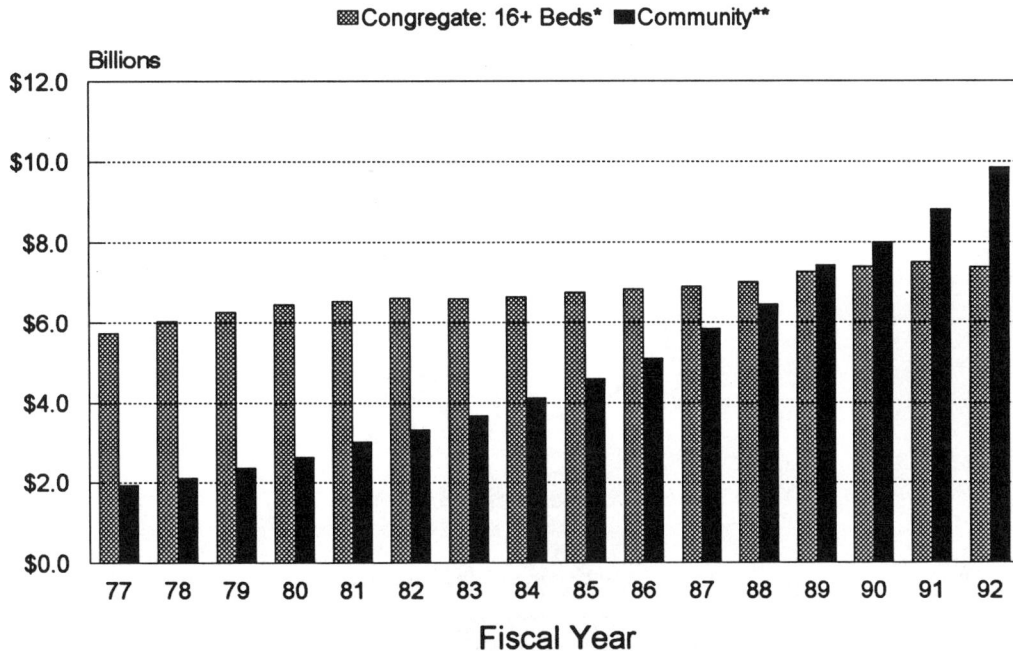

Fiscal Year

*Excludes nursing homes; ** Includes resources for
15 bed or less residential settings & non-residential community services

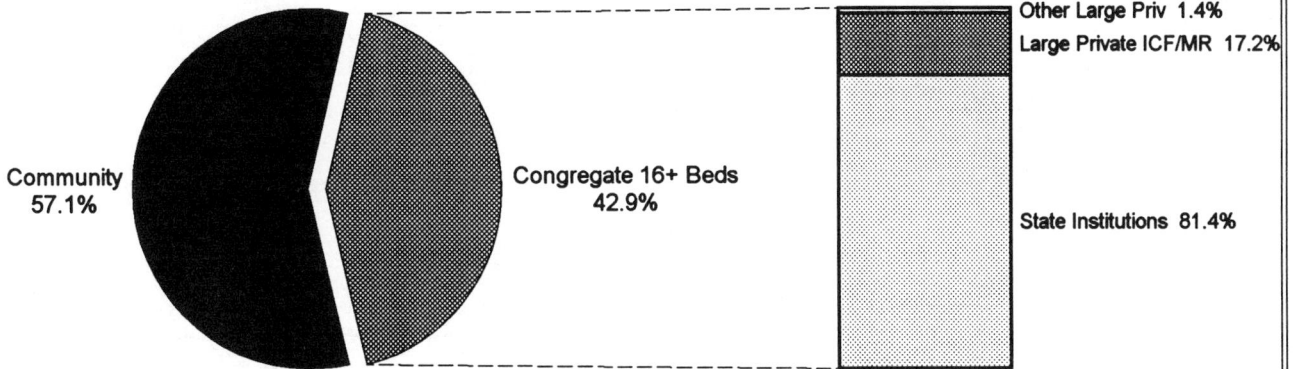

Community
57.1%

Congregate 16+ Beds
42.9%

Other Large Priv 1.4%
Large Private ICF/MR 17.2%

State Institutions 81.4%

FY 1992 Total Spending:
$17.228 Billion

*Source:*
Institute on Disability and Human Development (UAP),
University of Illinois at Chicago, 1994

# UNITED STATES

## Number of Persons Served by Residential Setting: FY 1992

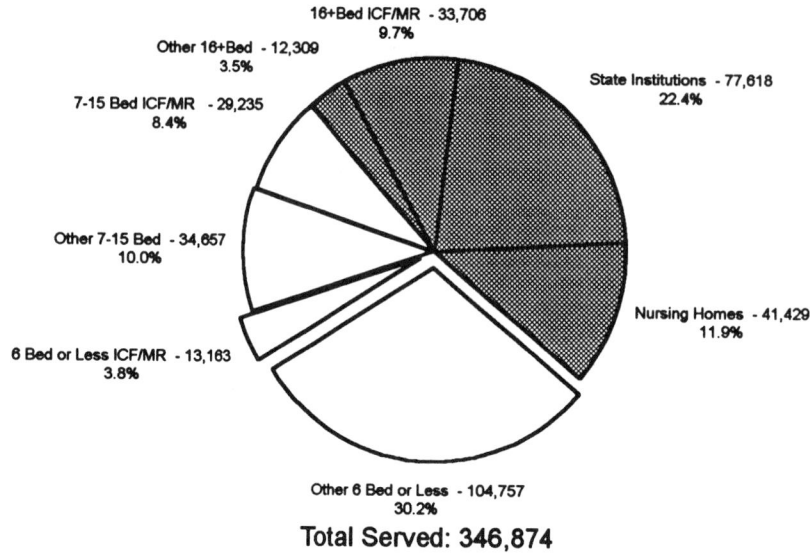

16+Bed ICF/MR - 33,706
9.7%

Other 16+Bed - 12,309
3.5%

7-15 Bed ICF/MR - 29,235
8.4%

State Institutions - 77,618
22.4%

Other 7-15 Bed - 34,657
10.0%

6 Bed or Less ICF/MR - 13,163
3.8%

Nursing Homes - 41,429
11.9%

Other 6 Bed or Less - 104,757
30.2%

Total Served: 346,874

## Persons Served by Residential Setting:1986-92

| | 1986 | 1987 | 1988 | 1989 | 1990 | 1991 | 1992 |
|---|---|---|---|---|---|---|---|
| CONGREGATE 16 + BED SETTINGS | 163,503 | 162,298 | 192,788 | 182,293 | 177,506 | 171,054 | 165,062 |
| Nursing Homes* | 20,686 | 20,320 | 54,202 | 47,105 | 46,452 | 43,992 | 41,429 |
| State Institutions | 100,522 | 95,766 | 91,432 | 87,998 | 84,739 | 81,180 | 77,618 |
| Private 16+Bed ICF/MR | 30,238 | 31,823 | 32,057 | 32,597 | 32,926 | 33,073 | 33,706 |
| Other 16+Bed Residential | 12,057 | 14,389 | 15,097 | 14,593 | 13,389 | 12,809 | 12,309 |
| 15 BED OR LESS RESIDENTIAL SETTINGS | 94,703 | 107,196 | 126,869 | 136,708 | 150,263 | 166,590 | 181,812 |
| Public 7-15 Bed ICF/MR | 2,513 | 2,834 | 3,223 | 3,614 | 3,969 | 4,214 | 4,369 |
| Private 7-15 Bed ICF/MR | 15,100 | 17,011 | 18,643 | 21,145 | 22,997 | 25,350 | 24,866 |
| Other 7-15 Bed Residential | 62,447 | 69,494 | 60,893 | 57,057 | 55,999 | 55,787 | 34,657 |
| Public 6 Bed or Less ICF/MR | 164 | 203 | 222 | 244 | 264 | 340 | 411 |
| Private 6 Bed or Less ICF/MR | 3,197 | 3,951 | 5,978 | 6,454 | 7,152 | 8,294 | 12,752 |
| Other 6 Bed or Less Residential | 11,282 | 13,703 | 37,910 | 48,195 | 59,882 | 72,606 | 104,757 |
| TOTAL PERSONS SERVED | 258,206 | 269,494 | 319,657 | 319,001 | 327,769 | 337,644 | 346,874 |

*Nursing home data for 1989-91 include imputed data for some states.

## Persons Served in Non-Residential Community Services:1986-92

| | 1986 | 1987 | 1988 | 1989 | 1990 | 1991 | 1992 |
|---|---|---|---|---|---|---|---|
| DAY/WORK PROGRAMS | 196,025 | 220,824 | 255,067 | 277,601 | 316,828 | 326,741 | 351,325 |
| Sheltered Employment/Work Activity | 79,508 | 90,564 | 114,115 | 108,437 | 121,951 | 115,077 | 137,236 |
| Day Habilitation ("Day Training") | 63,168 | 73,293 | 89,491 | 143,654 | 150,890 | 158,051 | 147,604 |
| Supported/Competitive Employment | 6,469 | 10,035 | 18,908 | 28,377 | 40,042 | 49,133 | 65,102 |
| CASE MANAGEMENT | 235,120 | 271,427 | 338,897 | 347,536 | 406,323 | 428,477 | 476,109 |
| HCBS WAIVER | 18,741 | 22,508 | 28,520 | 35,116 | 42,279 | 50,315 | 63,206 |
| MODEL 50/200 WAIVER | 111 | 245 | 270 | 432 | 583 | 708 | 1,003 |

*Source:*
Institute on Disability and Human Development (UAP),
University of Illinois at Chicago, 1994

# UNITED STATES

## Community Services: FY 1992 Revenue Sources

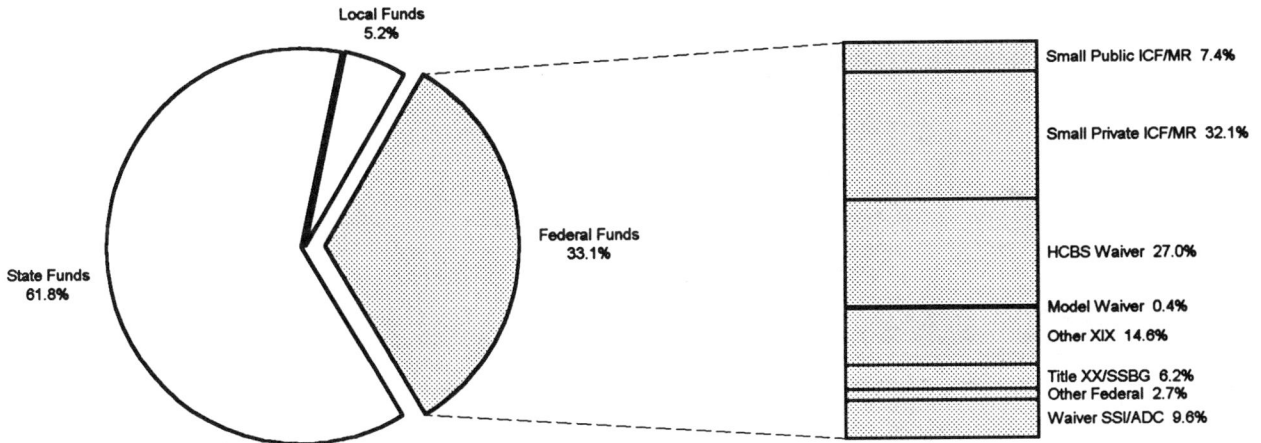

Local Funds
5.2%

State Funds
61.8%

Federal Funds
33.1%

Small Public ICF/MR  7.4%

Small Private ICF/MR  32.1%

HCBS Waiver  27.0%

Model Waiver  0.4%
Other XIX  14.6%

Title XX/SSBG  6.2%
Other Federal  2.7%
Waiver SSI/ADC  9.6%

Total Funds: $9.840 Billion

## Family Support Initiatives*

|  | 1986 | 1987 | 1988 | 1989 | 1990 | 1991 | 1992 |
|---|---|---|---|---|---|---|---|
| **FAMILY SUPPORT: TOTAL SPENDING** | $77,026,687 | $98,232,496 | $157,881,457 | $180,741,106 | $213,967,661 | $243,742,444 | $279,359,138 |
| **Total # of Families Supported** | 46,518 | 61,264 | 84,706 | 127,588 | 141,611 | 155,964 | 167,685 |
| A. Fincial Subsidy/Payment | $9,340,755 | $10,522,037 | $13,314,124 | $15,714,194 | $18,908,243 | $21,051,471 | $26,740,182 |
| # of Families | 3,685 | 4,011 | 5,228 | 6,957 | 7,903 | 9,020 | $12,304 |
| B. Family Assistance Payments | $18,218,928 | $24,288,278 | $51,830,516 | $71,238,916 | $85,678,205 | $100,074,091 | $107,029,562 |
| # of Families | 18,314 | 20,884 | 27,490 | 43,744 | 49,388 | 55,548 | $58,359 |
| C. Other Family Support Payments | $50,991,633 | $64,593,848 | $94,026,011 | $95,523,771 | $111,553,378 | $124,052,533 | $145,869,456 |
| # of Families | 45,180 | 52,960 | 63,769 | 80,951 | 91,230 | 98,504 | $105,503 |

## Other Community Services Initiatives*

|  | 1986 | 1987 | 1988 | 1989 | 1990 | 1991 | 1992 |
|---|---|---|---|---|---|---|---|
| **AGING/DD SPENDING** | $5,427,193 | $8,139,206 | $12,200,867 | $9,045,761 | $10,488,139 | $13,041,035 | $15,799,456 |
| # of Persons Served | 381 | 1,349 | 1,613 | 1,154 | 1,711 | 2,260 | 3,123 |
| **ASSISTIVE TECHNOLOGY SPENDING** | $0 | $0 | $1,342,310 | $2,066,142 | $3,508,525 | $6,153,563 | $6,782,564 |
| # of Persons Served | 0 | 0 | 1,720 | 2,243 | 4,004 | 9,060 | 13,702 |
| **EARLY INTERVENTION SPENDING** | $91,098,288 | $100,678,503 | $118,715,865 | $119,533,056 | $141,477,704 | $153,654,006 | $175,613,961 |
| # of Persons Served | 41,206 | 54,223 | 58,755 | 52,991 | 60,518 | 64,944 | 70,708 |
| **PERSONAL ASSISTANCE SPENDING** | $0 | $0 | $4,928,436 | $6,448,711 | $6,922,331 | $12,820,653 | $13,212,260 |
| # of Persons Served | 0 | 0 | 3,033 | 3,581 | 3,625 | 6,099 | 7,538 |
| **SUPPORTED EMPLOYMENT SPENDING** | $20,521,378 | $36,326,094 | $70,486,668 | $98,622,488 | $135,776,760 | $156,654,733 | $220,445,049 |
| # of Persons Served | 6,156 | 9,447 | 18,295 | 24,913 | 35,875 | 43,679 | 57,989 |
| **SUPPORTED LIVING SPENDING** | $0 | $0 | $10,250,427 | $15,623,111 | $27,231,546 | $62,387,908 | $102,373,852 |
| # of Persons Served | 202 | 449 | 4,602 | 5,006 | 6,617 | 10,294 | 14,779 |

*Expenditures associated with Special Community Initiatives are a subset of funding within the community services component of the state's chart series and spreadsheet; Family Support Client figures may include duplicate client counts; HCBS Waiver counts include Waiver case management numbers.
0= Services not provided in the state; NA= Data not available from state; blank= Services not applicable (eg. CSLA prior to authorization, Special Community Initiatives prior to request for data by this study)

*Source:*
Institute on Disability and Human Development (UAP),
University of Illinois at Chicago, 1994

# UNITED STATES

## Large Congregate Care Facilities: FY 1992 Revenue Sources*

### Private 16+Bed Settings

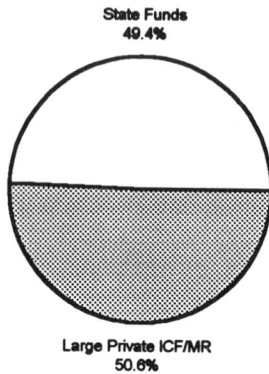

State Funds
49.4%

Large Private ICF/MR
50.6%

Total Funds: $1.372 Billion

### Public Institutions

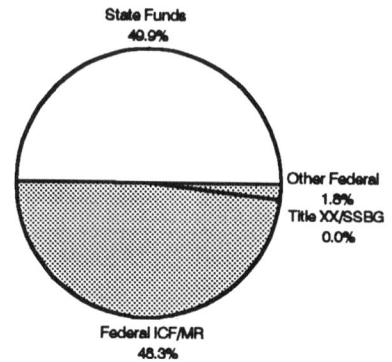

State Funds
49.9%

Other Federal
1.8%

Title XX/SSBG
0.0%

Federal ICF/MR
48.3%

Total Funds: $6.016 Billion

*Excludes nursing homes

## Average Daily Residents in Institutions

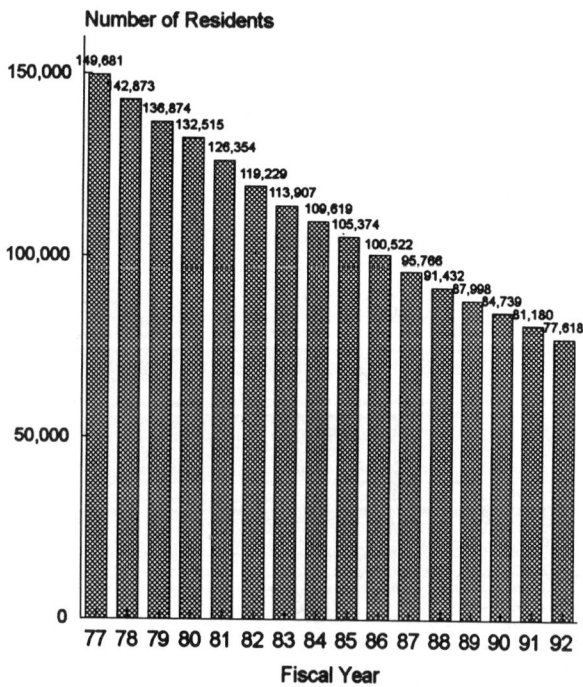

Number of Residents

| Fiscal Year | Number |
|---|---|
| 77 | 149,681 |
| 78 | 142,873 |
| 79 | 136,874 |
| 80 | 132,515 |
| 81 | 126,354 |
| 82 | 119,229 |
| 83 | 113,907 |
| 84 | 109,619 |
| 85 | 105,374 |
| 86 | 100,522 |
| 87 | 95,766 |
| 88 | 91,432 |
| 89 | 87,998 |
| 90 | 84,739 |
| 91 | 81,180 |
| 92 | 77,618 |

Fiscal Year

## Institutional Daily Costs Per Resident

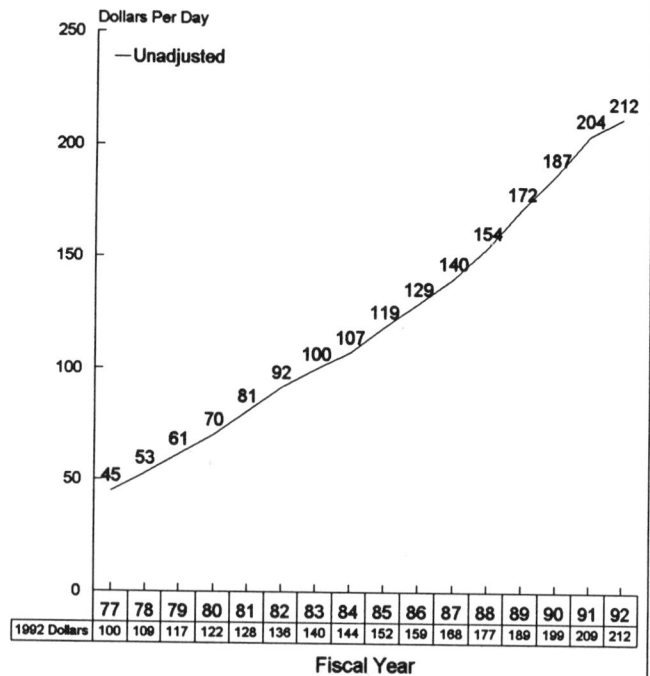

Dollars Per Day

— Unadjusted

| Fiscal Year | 77 | 78 | 79 | 80 | 81 | 82 | 83 | 84 | 85 | 86 | 87 | 88 | 89 | 90 | 91 | 92 |
|---|---|---|---|---|---|---|---|---|---|---|---|---|---|---|---|---|
| Unadjusted | 45 | 53 | 61 | 70 | 81 | 92 | 100 | 107 | 119 | 129 | 140 | 154 | 172 | 187 | 204 | 212 |
| 1992 Dollars | 100 | 109 | 117 | 122 | 128 | 136 | 140 | 144 | 152 | 159 | 168 | 177 | 189 | 199 | 209 | 212 |

Fiscal Year

*Source:*
Institute on Disability and Human Development (UAP),
University of Illinois at Chicago, 1994

# UNITED STATES FISCAL EFFORT

MR/DD Spending Per $1,000 of Personal Income

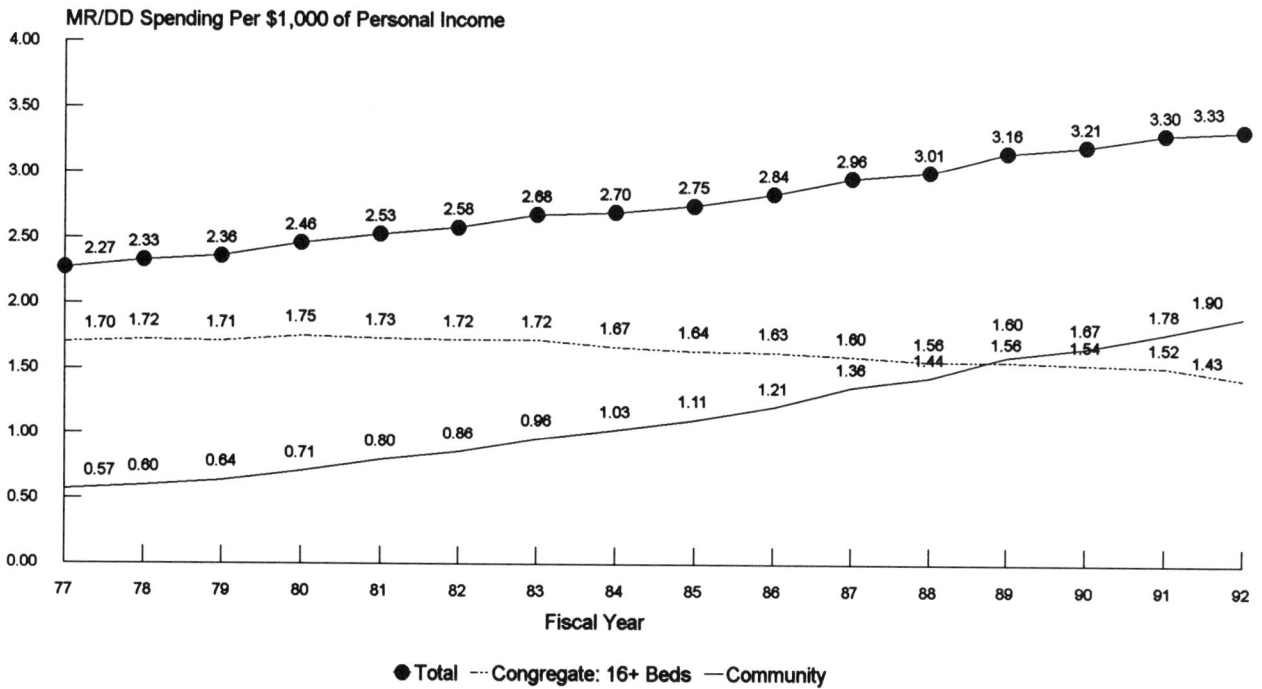

Total line values: 2.27, 2.33, 2.36, 2.46, 2.53, 2.58, 2.68, 2.70, 2.75, 2.84, 2.96, 3.01, 3.16, 3.21, 3.30, 3.33

Congregate: 16+ Beds values: 1.70, 1.72, 1.71, 1.75, 1.73, 1.72, 1.72, 1.67, 1.64, 1.63, 1.60, 1.56, 1.56, 1.54, 1.52, 1.43

Community values: 0.57, 0.60, 0.64, 0.71, 0.80, 0.86, 0.96, 1.03, 1.11, 1.21, 1.36, 1.44, 1.60, 1.67, 1.78, 1.90

Fiscal Year

● Total  --- Congregate: 16+ Beds  — Community

## Total MR/DD Spending

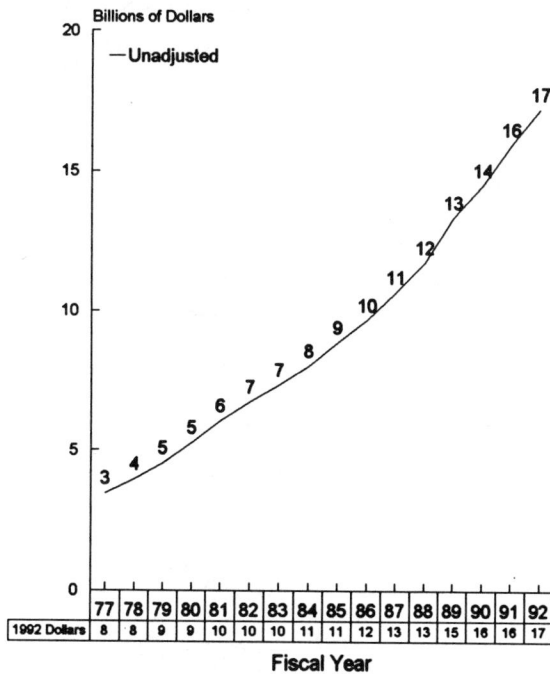

Billions of Dollars
—Unadjusted

Unadjusted line values: 3, 4, 5, 5, 6, 7, 7, 8, 9, 10, 11, 12, 13, 14, 16, 17

| | 77 | 78 | 79 | 80 | 81 | 82 | 83 | 84 | 85 | 86 | 87 | 88 | 89 | 90 | 91 | 92 |
|---|---|---|---|---|---|---|---|---|---|---|---|---|---|---|---|---|
| 1992 Dollars | 8 | 8 | 9 | 9 | 10 | 10 | 10 | 11 | 11 | 12 | 13 | 13 | 15 | 16 | 16 | 17 |

Fiscal Year

## Personal Income

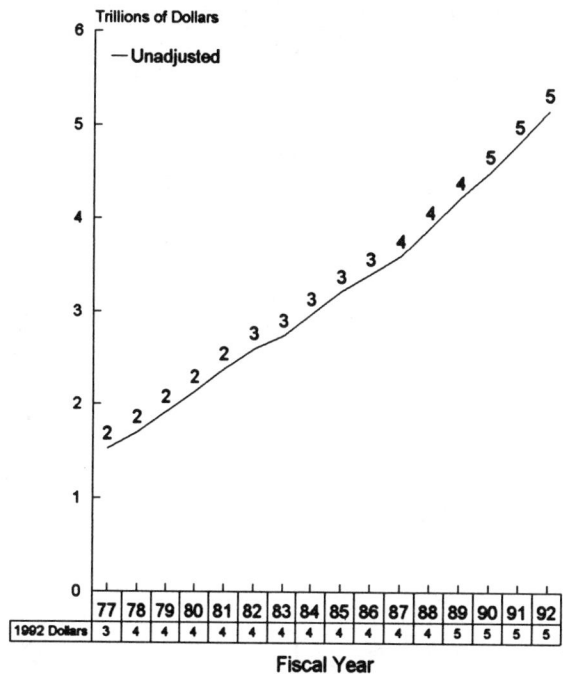

Trillions of Dollars
—Unadjusted

Unadjusted line values: 2, 2, 2, 2, 3, 3, 3, 3, 4, 4, 4, 4, 5, 5, 5, 5

| | 77 | 78 | 79 | 80 | 81 | 82 | 83 | 84 | 85 | 86 | 87 | 88 | 89 | 90 | 91 | 92 |
|---|---|---|---|---|---|---|---|---|---|---|---|---|---|---|---|---|
| 1992 Dollars | 3 | 4 | 4 | 4 | 4 | 4 | 4 | 4 | 4 | 4 | 4 | 4 | 5 | 5 | 5 | 5 |

Fiscal Year

*Source:*
Institute on Disability and Human Development (UAP),
University of Illinois at Chicago, 1994

# United States
## Financial Support for MR/DD Services: FY 1977-92

| | 1977 | 1978 | 1979 | 1980 | 1981 | 1982 | 1983 | 1984 |
|---|---|---|---|---|---|---|---|---|
| **TOTAL FUNDS** | $3,457,223,891 | $3,954,019,885 | $4,524,072,913 | $5,262,073,664 | $6,040,595,946 | $6,716,366,636 | $7,337,252,013 | $8,003,843,973 |
| **CONGREGATE 16+ BEDS** | 2,585,224,129 | 2,926,020,555 | 3,286,854,099 | 3,735,715,432 | 4,124,985,571 | 4,469,401,408 | 4,713,139,100 | 4,946,407,289 |
| INSTITUTIONAL SERVICES FUNDS | 2,461,323,585 | 2,766,422,780 | 3,066,870,238 | 3,413,147,471 | 3,725,023,874 | 3,986,903,173 | 4,154,365,465 | 4,298,058,101 |
| STATE FUNDS | 1,821,619,787 | 1,938,743,985 | 2,028,818,580 | 2,083,013,357 | 2,149,179,064 | 2,162,068,008 | 2,203,735,314 | 2,308,374,787 |
| General Funds | 1,672,938,772 | 1,773,311,594 | 1,839,761,559 | 1,860,326,276 | 1,910,749,757 | 1,886,708,171 | 1,918,814,617 | 1,976,676,885 |
| Local | 8,440,740 | 7,241,850 | 9,099,180 | 8,671,860 | 6,440,130 | 5,683,680 | 5,821,563 | 6,307,487 |
| Other State Funds | 140,240,275 | 158,190,541 | 179,957,841 | 214,015,221 | 231,989,177 | 269,676,157 | 279,099,134 | 325,390,415 |
| FEDERAL FUNDS | 639,703,798 | 827,678,795 | 1,038,051,658 | 1,330,134,114 | 1,575,844,810 | 1,824,835,165 | 1,950,630,151 | 1,989,683,314 |
| Federal ICF/MR | 573,486,028 | 752,071,965 | 969,461,262 | 1,262,765,899 | 1,499,616,168 | 1,765,579,789 | 1,886,295,233 | 1,919,419,140 |
| Title XX / SSBG Funds | 4,865,000 | 7,250,000 | 8,185,000 | 9,387,000 | 8,364,000 | 727,000 | 912,000 | 1,989,300 |
| Other Federal Funds | 61,352,770 | 68,356,830 | 60,405,396 | 57,981,215 | 67,864,642 | 58,528,376 | 63,422,918 | 68,274,874 |
| LARGE PRIVATE RESIDENTIAL | 123,900,544 | 159,597,775 | 219,983,861 | 322,567,961 | 399,961,697 | 482,498,235 | 558,773,635 | 648,349,188 |
| STATE FUNDS | 90,726,880 | 110,237,136 | 139,239,442 | 192,459,940 | 233,186,942 | 273,705,649 | 310,700,125 | 356,808,546 |
| General Funds | 74,635,701 | 89,429,495 | 108,836,360 | 155,288,989 | 190,677,867 | 223,561,360 | 252,716,016 | 292,690,416 |
| Other State Funds | 12,650,179 | 16,958,641 | 26,098,082 | 32,355,951 | 37,123,075 | 44,120,289 | 51,247,109 | 56,582,130 |
| Local/County Overmatch | 3,441,000 | 3,849,000 | 4,305,000 | 4,815,000 | 5,386,000 | 6,024,000 | 6,737,000 | 7,536,000 |
| FEDERAL FUNDS | 33,173,664 | 49,360,639 | 80,744,419 | 130,108,021 | 166,774,755 | 208,792,586 | 248,073,510 | 291,540,642 |
| Large Private ICF/MR | 33,173,664 | 49,360,639 | 80,744,419 | 130,108,021 | 166,774,755 | 208,792,586 | 248,073,510 | 291,540,64 |
| **COMMUNITY SERVICES FUNDS** | 871,999,762 | 1,027,999,330 | 1,237,218,814 | 1,526,358,232 | 1,915,610,374 | 2,246,965,227 | 2,624,112,914 | 3,057,436,68 |
| STATE FUNDS | 675,812,391 | 805,232,655 | 991,068,574 | 1,194,643,864 | 1,479,229,867 | 1,823,682,062 | 2,100,850,192 | 2,382,987,03 |
| General Funds | 406,112,423 | 505,311,786 | 628,538,006 | 805,967,271 | 1,029,969,220 | 1,336,452,773 | 1,577,511,075 | 1,820,196,38 |
| Other State Funds | 60,221,787 | 66,112,671 | 70,803,869 | 72,240,748 | 102,953,916 | 110,682,508 | 126,680,476 | 139,789,74 |
| Local/County Overmatch | 63,687,253 | 78,135,070 | 95,733,371 | 114,781,317 | 138,914,003 | 163,971,853 | 183,133,513 | 202,049,57 |
| SSI State Supplement | 145,790,928 | 155,673,128 | 195,993,328 | 201,654,528 | 207,392,728 | 212,574,928 | 213,525,128 | 220,951,32 |
| FEDERAL FUNDS | 196,187,371 | 222,766,675 | 246,150,240 | 331,714,368 | 436,380,507 | 423,283,165 | 523,262,722 | 674,449,64 |
| ICF/MR Funds | 8,878,210 | 12,361,368 | 20,573,255 | 33,697,288 | 77,517,235 | 119,676,144 | 166,486,445 | 205,055,65 |
| Small Public | 0 | 0 | 1,030,782 | 5,838,914 | 10,496,379 | 14,953,335 | 20,565,725 | 24,551,96 |
| Small Private | 8,878,210 | 12,361,368 | 19,542,473 | 27,858,374 | 67,020,856 | 104,722,809 | 145,920,720 | 180,503,69 |
| HCBS Waiver | 0 | 0 | 0 | 0 | 0 | 1,244,000 | 8,692,600 | 53,192,72 |
| Model 50/200 Waiver | 0 | 0 | 0 | 0 | 0 | 0 | 0 | 55,36 |
| Other Title XIX Programs | 3,953,880 | 5,890,424 | 9,324,810 | 21,699,990 | 64,063,431 | 69,519,579 | 102,633,292 | 120,432,25 |
| Title XX / SSBG Funds | 154,869,273 | 176,981,650 | 190,088,975 | 243,530,169 | 254,673,391 | 189,845,174 | 188,014,164 | 191,803,84 |
| Other Federal Funds | 28,486,008 | 27,533,233 | 26,163,200 | 32,786,921 | 40,126,450 | 39,031,712 | 41,436,625 | 44,255,96 |
| Waiver Clients' SSI/ADC | 0 | 0 | 0 | 0 | 0 | 3,966,556 | 15,999,596 | 59,653,83 |

| | 1985 | 1986 | 1987 | 1988 | 1989 | 1990 | 1991 | 1992 |
|---|---|---|---|---|---|---|---|---|
| **TOTAL FUNDS** | $8,848,495,007 | $9,665,036,853 | $10,658,554,079 | $11,733,029,599 | $13,355,248,433 | $14,491,668,782 | $15,949,796,635 | $17,227,897,59 |
| **CONGREGATE 16+ BEDS** | 5,272,532,074 | 5,533,509,005 | 5,772,785,398 | 6,107,253,332 | 6,598,512,744 | 6,959,983,842 | 7,340,392,718 | 7,388,126,85 |
| INSTITUTIONAL SERVICES FUNDS | 4,557,712,120 | 4,733,119,339 | 4,899,130,602 | 5,155,698,098 | 5,517,729,928 | 5,790,935,297 | 6,057,383,417 | 6,015,910,50 |
| STATE FUNDS | 2,480,799,945 | 2,497,870,435 | 2,625,386,996 | 2,683,057,026 | 2,957,773,314 | 3,070,309,992 | 3,176,461,517 | 2,999,472,78 |
| General Funds | 2,148,229,368 | 2,144,895,108 | 2,263,388,314 | 2,131,005,066 | 2,375,394,430 | 2,461,065,638 | 2,527,661,084 | 2,350,173,01 |
| Local | 6,277,771 | 4,208,054 | 4,234,622 | 5,822,520 | 6,313,472 | 6,789,647 | 7,472,202 | 5,971,97 |
| Other State Funds | 326,292,806 | 348,767,273 | 357,764,060 | 546,229,440 | 576,065,412 | 602,454,707 | 641,328,231 | 643,327,79 |
| FEDERAL FUNDS | 2,076,912,175 | 2,235,248,904 | 2,273,743,606 | 2,472,641,072 | 2,559,956,615 | 2,720,625,305 | 2,880,921,900 | 3,016,437,72 |
| Federal ICF/MR | 2,000,529,589 | 2,154,660,451 | 2,176,603,648 | 2,385,464,767 | 2,455,767,041 | 2,616,243,710 | 2,775,196,119 | 2,907,752,44 |
| Title XX / SSBG Funds | 8,067,500 | 1,198,200 | 1,182,100 | 1,223,200 | 1,332,324 | 1,334,628 | 483,412 | 483,4 |
| Other Federal Funds | 68,315,086 | 79,390,253 | 95,957,858 | 85,953,105 | 102,857,250 | 103,046,967 | 105,242,369 | 108,201,86 |
| LARGE PRIVATE RESIDENTIAL | 714,819,954 | 800,389,666 | 873,654,796 | 951,555,234 | 1,080,782,816 | 1,169,048,545 | 1,283,009,301 | 1,372,216,35 |
| STATE FUNDS | 391,865,705 | 433,057,434 | 465,253,334 | 497,975,950 | 555,827,658 | 590,947,506 | 640,059,821 | 677,920,57 |
| General Funds | 320,988,752 | 352,339,136 | 379,072,191 | 343,313,832 | 358,113,224 | 385,867,126 | 422,796,194 | 428,248,83 |
| Other State Funds | 62,448,953 | 71,291,298 | 75,920,143 | 143,768,118 | 178,066,730 | 193,282,381 | 205,256,946 | 235,652,27 |
| Local/County Overmatch | 8,428,000 | 9,427,000 | 10,261,000 | 10,894,000 | 19,647,704 | 11,797,999 | 12,006,681 | 14,019,46 |
| FEDERAL FUNDS | 322,954,249 | 367,332,232 | 408,401,462 | 453,579,284 | 524,955,157 | 578,101,039 | 642,949,480 | 694,295,77 |
| Large Private ICF/MR | 322,954,249 | 367,332,232 | 408,401,462 | 453,579,284 | 524,955,157 | 578,101,039 | 642,949,480 | 694,295,77 |
| **COMMUNITY SERVICES FUNDS** | 3,575,962,933 | 4,131,527,849 | 4,885,768,681 | 5,625,776,267 | 6,756,735,689 | 7,531,684,940 | 8,609,403,916 | 9,839,770,73 |
| STATE FUNDS | 2,750,871,165 | 3,176,097,492 | 3,725,314,020 | 4,200,602,127 | 4,967,028,602 | 5,398,607,215 | 6,021,740,879 | 6,586,414,30 |
| General Funds | 2,124,918,601 | 2,479,862,031 | 2,905,806,422 | 3,152,824,452 | 3,714,288,891 | 3,973,820,274 | 4,417,675,383 | 4,789,938,26 |
| Other State Funds | 159,890,280 | 173,490,989 | 220,341,694 | 410,107,188 | 586,182,276 | 695,303,425 | 806,039,656 | 922,241,88 |
| Local/County Overmatch | 232,353,556 | 263,136,344 | 298,173,276 | 318,721,534 | 364,982,533 | 406,103,377 | 458,030,379 | 508,922,59 |
| SSI State Supplement | 233,708,728 | 259,608,128 | 300,992,628 | 318,948,953 | 301,574,902 | 323,380,139 | 339,995,461 | 365,311,57 |
| FEDERAL FUNDS | 825,091,768 | 955,430,357 | 1,160,454,661 | 1,425,174,140 | 1,789,707,088 | 2,133,077,725 | 2,587,663,037 | 3,253,356,43 |
| ICF/MR Funds | 255,641,509 | 348,228,388 | 433,400,444 | 552,271,393 | 723,699,890 | 883,625,490 | 1,068,235,507 | 1,287,439,98 |
| Small Public | 40,448,131 | 53,462,207 | 72,558,970 | 100,031,208 | 132,037,687 | 157,028,876 | 175,899,897 | 241,817,84 |
| Small Private | 215,193,378 | 294,766,181 | 360,841,474 | 452,240,185 | 591,662,203 | 726,596,614 | 892,335,610 | 1,045,622,14 |
| HCBS Waiver | 101,900,647 | 123,128,098 | 166,910,983 | 254,387,328 | 375,572,822 | 484,643,389 | 629,093,719 | 876,812,08 |
| Model 50/200 Waiver | 139,744 | 603,949 | 1,505,730 | 2,707,891 | 3,945,690 | 6,253,847 | 7,950,222 | 12,177,90 |
| Other Title XIX Programs | 134,681,363 | 161,673,646 | 219,852,156 | 231,465,523 | 273,854,770 | 302,471,756 | 369,544,457 | 474,105,19 |
| Title XX / SSBG Funds | 203,427,705 | 204,162,233 | 200,913,381 | 211,391,864 | 208,899,144 | 204,825,922 | 206,840,531 | 202,002,18 |
| Other Federal Funds | 48,522,620 | 47,864,183 | 52,970,431 | 63,819,081 | 57,000,880 | 62,631,218 | 71,627,085 | 87,811,83 |
| Waiver Clients' SSI/ADC | 80,778,180 | 69,769,860 | 84,901,536 | 109,131,060 | 146,733,887 | 188,626,104 | 234,371,516 | 313,007,25 |

*Source:*
Institute on Disability and Human Development (UAP),
University of Illinois at Chicago, 1994

# PART III

## Technical Notes

Part III presents a summary of the data collection and technical notes to accompany each state's resource allocation profile in Part II. The fourth national study of public spending for mental retardation and developmental disabilities constituted an update and expansion of the twelve-year record of resource allocation constructed during three previous studies. The notes below focus on the 1989-92 period. Extensive narrative on the sources of FYs 1977-88 data are contained in Braddock et al. (1990).

**State-by-State Data Collection.** Project staff mailed detailed fiscal and programmatic worksheets to principal state MR/DD directors in 1991. The worksheets outlined the major revenue and expenditure categories employed in the study (see Table 1, Overview). The worksheets replicated each state's budget conventions corresponding to these study classification categories, listing the state-specific data lines identified for 1988 during the third national study. Four additional columns extended these data lines across fiscal years 1989-92.

There were four data collection worksheets. Worksheet 1A outlined revenues and expenditures for a) institutional services, b) large private (16+ bed) residential services, and c) community services. Worksheet 1B outlined data on institutional average daily residents, average daily expenditures per resident (per diems), full-time-equivalent (FTE) institutional staff, and numbers of individuals with mental retardation and related conditions in non-specialized adult nursing facilities and in specialized (i.e., pediatric) nursing facilities. Worksheet 1B also listed supplementary data including state population, statewide aggregate personal income, and federal income maintenance benefits/payments which were obtained by project staff from federal sources.

Worksheet 2 listed numbers of individuals served in the institutional, large private residential, and community (15 beds or less) categories of out-of-home residential services. Finally, Worksheet 3 summarized expenditures and numbers of individuals supported in the seven special community initiatives defined in the Overview (family support, aging/DD, assistive tech-

nology, early intervention, personal assistance, supported employment, and supported living).

**Outline of the Technical Notes.** The technical notes for each state include up to five categories of information about construction of the resource allocation profile.

1). The notes identify the principal state MR/DD agency, and describe the state's institutional, large private residential and community services housing options in 1992.

2). The notes describe, if applicable, any state budget publications, administrative records, or other documents used to construct the state's resource allocation profile.

3). The notes offer additional detail about certain program initiatives or budget lines. For example, in some states' notes there is clarification about *local/county overmatch* data sources or about the role of these local dollars in the state's service system.

4). The notes describe estimations used to impute missing data points or other calculations or estimates employed by project staff or by state officials. For example, the notes summarize the estimations used in some states to incorporate fringe benefit expenditures which were accounted for outside the principal state agency.

Project staff also made estimates based on a) states' different fiscal periods, b) Waiver participants' income maintenance benefits, and c) nursing home data. First, all but a few states (Alabama, District of Columbia, Michigan, New York, Texas) budgeted according to a July 1st through June 30th fiscal period. These four states' different fiscal periods are indicated in the notes below. Data on state general population, personal income, and federal medical assistance percentages (FMAP) were available on a federal fiscal year or on a calendar year basis and were adjusted to correspond to each state's fiscal period. For example, FMAP rates would be adjusted so that three quarters of federal fiscal year (FFY) 1992 and one quarter of FFY 1991 corresponded to fiscal year 1992 for those states with July through June fiscal periods.

Second, benefits available through Title II (Adults Disabled in Childhood) or Title XVI (Supplemental Security Income payments) were estimated by multiplying the non-duplicated number of Waiver participants by 12 months and then multiplying by the estimated monthly SSI/ADC amounts. These monthly amounts during 1988-92 (unless otherwise noted in the individual state's technical notes) were $324, $342, $368, $382, and $407.

Third, information about individuals with mental retardation and related disabilities residing in nursing facilities was generally available from states' "OBRA-87 coordinators" responsible for the implementation of PL 100-360, the federal 1987 Nursing Home Reform Act. Any exceptions or special details are noted.

5). Each state's technical notes conclude by identifying state budget or program officials who completed the project's worksheets or who otherwise provided access to the state's administrative records through telephone calls or correspondence.

## STATE TECHNICAL NOTES

**Alabama.** The principal state agency in Alabama was the Division of Mental Retardation in the Department of Mental Health/Mental Retardation (DMH/MR). *Congregate 16+ beds* services consisted of *institutional services* provided at a state school and four developmental centers. The facilities and their average daily populations in 1992 were Partlow State School, Tuscaloosa (340); L.B. Wallace Developmental Center, Decatur (304); Brewer DC, Mobile (230); Glenn Ireland DC, Tarrant City (200); and J.S. Tarwater DC, Wetumpka (188). *Large private residential services* in 1988 consisted of DMH/MR funding for 30 children with autism at the Glenwood Mental Health Center. The children subsequently received alternative placements in smaller settings.

*Community services* state funded community residences serving 7-15 individuals consisted primarily of group homes and special community living homes (SCLH). One hundred seventy-eight individuals were supported in semi-independent living and subsidized and independent living options of six beds or less.

*The State of Alabama Executive Budget: Fiscal Year 1991-1992* provided "actual" expenditure data for FY 1990 (October 1, 1989 through September 30, 1990); "budgeted" figures for FY 1991; and "estimated" data for FY 1992. The budget documents were organized by state department and by program, and contained line item data as well as a number of performance indicators. The primary source of data was administrative records which state officials reviewed to complete the project's worksheets. Ray Owens, Vince Campbell, and Jack Gifford, Division of Mental Retardation, DMH/MR, completed the worksheets developed by project staff.

**Alaska.** The principal state agency in Alaska was the Division of Mental Health and Developmental Disabilities Central Office, in the Department of Health and Social Services. *Congregate 16+ beds* services were provided in the Harborview Developmental Center in Valdez, serving 47 average daily residents in 1992. *Community services* were funded by state appropriations with the exception of federal ICF/MR reimbursements for the Hope Cottages, which consisted of four ten-bed private settings. Alaska's published state document

was *The Executive Operating Budget* containing line item detail and organized by state department and by program, and *The State of Alaska-Component Budget Summary*. All data necessary to construct the state's profile were transmitted on the project's worksheets by Diana Ray, Developmental Disabilities Project Assistant, and Stephanie Waldon, DD Central Office.

**Arizona.** Arizona's principal state agency was the Division of Developmental Disabilities, Arizona Department of Economic Security (DES). In May, 1987, the Governor signed Senate Bill 1418 establishing the Arizona Long Term Care System (ALTCS) under the Arizona Health Care Cost Containment System (AHCCCS). The ALTCS was a Section 1115 Waiver authorized under federal Medicaid regulations. This Waiver embodied competitively bid, risk-sharing, prepaid, and capitated contracts as outlined in the AHCCCS mission statement (*The Arizona Long Term Care System Section 1115 Demonstration Project*, no date, p. 1-25). The Arizona DD service system under ALTCS from 1989 through 1992 was fundamentally different from the system in place prior to 1989.

*Congregate 16+ beds* settings consisted of *institutional services* provided at Arizona Training Program (ATP) facilities in Coolidge and Tucson. In addition approximately forty individuals were served in institutional group homes at the site of the former ATP at Phoenix which closed in 1988. State officials were considering additional closures although no formal announcements have been made. Large private residential services consisted of a vendor-operated (private) ICF/MR, "Hacienda," which was formerly a skilled nursing facility and which served twenty-four individuals. Division appropriations also supported four individuals in larger vendor-operated settings not certified as ICFs/MR.

Substantial federal support for *community services* was available through the Section 1115 Waiver and associated federal income maintenance funding. Federal *other Title XIX program* funds represented ALTCS acute medical care revenues allocated to community services. Under ALTCS, 197 individuals resided in adult development homes in 1992, 297 in child development homes and 1,561 in group homes. All these settings were six beds or less. In addition, 4,894 individuals were covered under the demonstration waiver in home-based services, and 5,536 individuals received case management only. With the inclusion of 58 individuals residing in nursing facilities, the ALTCS served a total of 12,835 individuals with developmental disabilities.

All financial and programmatic data for 1990-92 were obtained from a series of computer-generated tables adapting the ALTCS data to the project's classification categories. The tables were developed by Mark Loudenslagel, in the DES budget section serving the Division office. Background information on AHCCCS and ALTCS were provided by Brian Lensch, Director, DD Division.

**Arkansas.** The Division of Developmental Disabilities, Arkansas Department of Human Services served as the principal state agency. *Congregate 16+ beds* services included *institutional services* which were provided at six Human Development Centers (HDCs). The facilities and their average daily populations in 1992 were Conway (613), Booneville (168), Arkadelphia (149), Alexander (136), Jonesboro (120), and the Southeast HDC in Warren (73). In addition, *large private residential services* consisted of four large (16+ beds) private ICFs/MR serving 183 individuals in 1992.

Small private ICFs/MR of 7-15 beds served 300 in 1992. Community residences of 7-15 beds also served 807 individuals in supervised homes and 389 individuals in supervised apartments. Six-or-less residential options consisted of five 5-bed supervised homes, 272 individuals receiving follow-along services, and 44 individuals in supported living.

*Other Title XIX program* funding consisted of Medicaid reimbursements for adult development and pre-school training, intervention and therapy services for children, and in 1992 $85.8 thousand for targeted case management serving 705 individuals. *Other state funds* consisted of local community programs' matches for small private ICFs/MR, for the HCBS Waiver, for targeted case management, and for the adult and child training and therapy services.

All financial and programmatic data for Arkansas were provided on the project's worksheets. Data were provided by Mike McCreight, Director, Donna Madden, Director's Office, Dennis Bonge, and Judy Routon, DD Division; and by Wilma Stuart, Arkansas Developmental Disabilities Council.

**California.** California's principal state agency was the Department of Developmental Services. *Congregate 16+ beds* services consisted of institutional services provided at developmental centers (DCs), sixteen bed or larger private Intermediate Care Facilities/Developmentally Disabled (ICFs/DD), and community care facilities (CCFs). The developmental centers and the average daily populations in 1992 were Sonoma, in Eldridge (1,366), Fairview, Costa Mesa (1,108), Lanterman, Pomona (1,090), Agnews, San Jose (1,038), Porterville (1,025), Camarillo State Hospital/Developmental Center (602), and Stockton (450). The Napa State Hospital/Developmental Center in Imola closed in 1988.

The *other state funds* category of revenues/expenditures for institutional services in 1992 included the federal Medi-Cal (ICF/MR) state match ($239.3 million), private payers ($17.5 million), California state lottery ($.6 million), special account for capital outlay ($.6 million), Department guardian ($.04 million) and other reimbursements ($6.3 million). *Other federal funds* for institutional services included Comprehensive Health and Medical Program for the Uniformed Services (CHAMPUS) ($.2 million), insurance/federal agencies ($1.8 million), Medicare ($7.0 million), and federal trust fund ($1.1 million). California's *large private residential services* consisted of ICFs/DD ranging in size from 50 to 150 beds and serving 1,964 individuals in 1992; distinct part skilled nursing facility ICF/DD units served 1,155 individuals; and state-funded CCFs served 3,509 individuals.

*Community services* options consisted of 7-15 bed and 4-6 bed private ICFs/DD and CCFs, and 6 bed or less state-funded supported living options for 6,815 individuals in 1992. The *other Title XIX program* component consisted of targeted case management ($32.7 million); federal CSLA ($.9 million), and nursing home reform ($.2 million). In 1995, 300 individuals were participating in CSLA options through 7 of the state's 21 regional centers (*Community Services Reporter*, 1994b). *Other federal funds* consisted of DD Program Development ($2.2 million), PL 99-457 early intervention ($10.5 million), and federal vocational rehabilitation funding for supported employment ($8.0 million) and for sheltered workshops ($2.9 million).

A revision to the FYs 1985-88 community services component of the data set reflects the inclusion of federal/state California Department of Rehabilitation funds. In 1982, funding for the "work activity program" serving individuals with developmental disabilities was transferred from the Department of Developmental Services to the state's Department of Rehabilitation. During FYs 1982-84, this state Department of Rehabilitation funding was included within the California financial profile ($35.1, $39.6 and $38.6 million, respectively). Project staff for the Third National Study (Braddock et al., 1986, p. 113) reported "...Department officials concluded that, at least for the first few years, the program would be conducted relatively intact, although with alternate funding...." In the present study, project staff consulted with California DDS officials who concurred that the Department of Rehabilitation's sheltered workshop and supported employment program for individuals with developmental disabilities has remained intact during 1985-92.

Department of Rehabilitation funding now included with the data set ranged from $44.9 million in 1985 to $88.7 million in 1992. The sheltered employment/work activity and supported employment expenditures for 1986-91 were estimated by interpolation, using annual increments of $6.26 million.

Dennis Amundson, Director, DDS, provided information about the DDS organizational structure and recent policy initiatives. The majority of revenue, expenditure and program data were provided on the project's worksheets by Dr. Roberta Marlowe, Chief, and Dr. Beverly Lozano, Information Systems, DDS. Additional information on FYs 1985-92 sheltered employment/work activity and supported employment clients, revenues, and expenditures was provided by Paul Carleton, Deputy Director, Administration Division, DDS.

**Colorado.** The principal state agency was the Division for Developmental Disabilities, Department of Institutions. *Congregate 16+ beds* services were provided in two state institutions and in large private ICFs/MR. The institutions and their average daily populations in 1992 were Grand Junction (199) and Wheat Ridge (135). The facility in Pueblo closed in 1989.

*Community services* residences included 7-15 bed public ICFs/MR, designated "Regional Center group homes," which served 250 individuals in 1992. Non-ICF/MR

group homes served 592 individuals. The majority of individuals, 2,163, resided in six bed or less settings. These included Personal Care Alternatives (PCAs); specialized and moderate supervision group homes and state-operated group homes; follow-along, intensive alternative residential services (ARS), host homes, and state-operated host homes. Federal HCBS Waiver funding of $29.7 million included $1.7 million available under the OBRA 87 Waiver for nursing home reform. *Other Title XIX program* reimbursements in Colorado consisted of targeted case management for 1,846 individuals in 1992. An additional 2,124 individuals were served through HCBS Waiver case management.

Colorado was one of the first CSLA states. Although no CSLA expenditures were reported in 1992, by 1995 13 of the state's 20 community centered boards were offering CSLA services to over 250 individuals (*Community Services Reporter*, 1994b).

All data were provided on the project's worksheets and in subsequent telephone conversations by Lynn Struxness, Data Management Section, Division for Developmental Disabilities.

**Connecticut.** The principal state agency was the Department of Mental Retardation (DMR). *Congregate 16+ beds* services in Connecticut consisted of 9 state centers, 2 training schools, services for 20 individuals in private ICFs/MR, and services for 190 individuals in homes for the aged, residential schools, and state-funded habilitative nurseries. The state-operated facilities and the numbers of average daily residents in 1992 were Southbury Training School (934), Mansfield Training School (135), Hartford Center, Newington (81), Ella T. Grasso Center, Stratford (71), Lower Fairfield Center, Norwalk (71), Seaside Center, Waterford (58), New Haven (51), Northwest Center, Torrington (46), Mystic Education Center (43) John Dempsey Center, Putnam (31), and Central State Center, Mariden (24). The Waterbury Center in Cheshire served 32 individuals in 1988 and closed in 1989. Mansfield closed in 1993, and New Haven closed in 1994.

*Community services* residential options underwent changes in classification between 1988 and 1992. Because many supervised apartments had 24-hour staffing, DMR began in 1992 to classify as "community living alternatives" (CLAs) all DMR-operated community residences with 24-hour staff. Those settings with less than 24-hour staffing were classified supported living. Six bed or less settings served 399 individuals in state-operated supported living, 239 individuals in private supported living, and 468 individuals in community training homes. There were also residential services for 298 individuals in public CLAs and 1,675 individuals in private CLAs. Beginning in 1991, targeted case management billings were separate from the HCBS Waiver. In 1992, 6,315 individuals were served in targeted case management, within the case management total of 11,444.

*The Governor's Budget* in Connecticut presented detailed performance data including budget initiative line items corresponding to the project's special community initiatives. However, because most fiscal data were presented in the *Budget* on a program basis, it was necessary for state officials and project staff to estimate the proportions of congregate residential and community services spending within several of the budget

campus settings beginning in 1989. Fringe benefits, which were accounted for in the state's Comptroller's Office, were estimated during 1988-92 on the basis of 41.65%, 46.42%, 40.08%, 45.56%, and 45.46%, respectively, of institutional and community services personnel. For example, fringe benefits in 1992 consisted of $45,359,412 for institutional staff and $43,621,565 for community staff.

Revenues classified as institutional services *other state funds* and *other federal funds* were obtained from *Bureau of Collection Services Annual Report 1991-92* and similar publications for preceding fiscal years. *Other state funds* consisted of "patient direct," "fiduciary," "substitute payee," "parent," "other insurer," "Blue Cross/Blue Shield," "trust-Bureau of Collection Services" and "court order." *Other federal funds* included Medicare, Medicare Part B, and "Medicaid 65 years and older." In 1992 the largest *other state fund* amount was "trust-

| Table III-1, Allocation of Connecticut DMR Budget Lines to Institutional Services | | | |
|---|---|---|---|
| | \% Allocated | | Estimated Expenditure |
| Budget Line | 1988 | 1989-92 | 1992 ($) |
| Specialized support and health | 70 | 65 | 9,810,046 |
| Recreational and social development | 70 | 60 | 3,271,595 |
| Case management | 23 | 23 | 1,755,117 |
| Unified school district | 74 | 100 | 1,424,923 |
| Staff development and training | 78 | 30 | 273,600 |

lines. The "campus unit" line in the *Budget* was classified as institutional services, and a number of other entire lines were classified as community services. These included "community work services," "early intervention," "supported employment," "non-vocational," "opportunities for older adults," "community training homes," "community living alternatives," "family support," and "field operations." DMR officials provided estimated percentages with which to allocate other budget amounts between institutional and community services. These budget lines are listed in Table III-1 with the percentages allocated to institutional services and the estimated institutional services expenditures in 1992.

In three lines (specialized support and health, recreational and social development, and staff development and training) the institutional percentages decreased, reflecting Connecticut's expanding community system. Unified School District funding was consolidated in the

BCS" totaling nearly $5 million and the largest *other federal fund* amount was Medicaid 65 years and older totaling $8.6 million. Community services *other Title XIX program* funding consisted of targeted case management. Another estimation employed in construction of the Connecticut financial profile was determination of developmental disabilities Model Waiver expenditures based on the proportion which these children represented of all children receiving Model Waiver case management.

Lawrence Johnson, Management Information Group, DMR, reviewed administrative records to provide data on the worksheets developed by project staff. Mr. Johnson also provided the percentages, per diem rates, and other data necessary to reclassify Connecticut's program-based line items according to the project's classification categories. Debbie Jo Garcia, Medicaid Policy Consultant, Department of Income Maintenance, provided Model 50/200 Waiver data.

**Delaware.** The principal state agency was the Division of Mental Retardation, Department of Health and Social Services. *Congregate 16+ beds* services in 1992 consisted of one state institution, the Stockley Center in Georgetown, serving 325 individuals, and a private ICF/MR setting serving 46 individuals. In Delaware, all individuals in *community services* out-of-home options resided in six bed or less settings, except 66 individuals in private 7-15 bed ICFs/MR. The other small residential category included foster care (81 individuals served in 1992), adult family living (79), neighborhood homes (88), apartments (86), and supported living (28).

All data for 1989-92 were provided by Dr. Henry Brown, Division of Mental Retardation, Department of Health and Social Services, in response to the project's worksheets. Dr. Brown noted that Delaware projected growth in community services, a decreased use of private ICFs/MR, and an increased use of neighborhood homes and support options under the HCBS Waiver.

**District of Columbia.** The principal state agency was the Bureau of Developmental Services, Department of Human Services. The District's single state institution, Forest Haven, was located in Laurel, Maryland. Forest Haven closed in 1991. *Community services* options in the 7-15 bed category included 27 individuals residing in out-of-District placements and 112 individuals residing in community residential facilities. Six bed or less options included 33 four-bed CRFs serving 132 individuals in 1992, specialized foster care serving 20 individuals, and supervised apartments serving 8 individuals.

The District's fiscal year corresponded to the federal fiscal year (October 1st through September 30th). Revenue, expenditure, and programmatic data for 1989-92 were provided by Charles Howard, Mental Retardation and Developmental Disabilities Administration, Department of Human Services. Additional Medicaid information was provided by Eric Bost, MR/DD Administration.

**Florida.** The principal state agency was Developmental Services, Department of Health and Rehabilitative Services. *Congregate 16+ beds* services in 1992 consisted of six institutional centers or units, large private ICFs/MR, and other large private residential habilitation centers (RHCs). The names and average daily populations of state centers in 1992 were Tacachale Center, in Gainesville (709), Marianna Center (409),

Gulf Coast Center, Fort Meyers (382), Landmark Center, Opa-Locka (357), Florida State Hospital, Chattahoochee (providing a secure program for persons with developmental disabilities in the criminal justice system and a program for persons with dual psychiatric and DD diagnoses) (77), and the Seguin Unit, Tacachale Center, Gainesville (15). The Seguin Unit, a secure defender transition program, was initiated in 1990. The Hillsborough Center in Seffner was transferred to the Florida Children, Youth and Families Program Office in 1992, and services became the responsibility of a private provider. Institutional services *other federal funds* included Medicaid hospital reimbursements and Medicare funds budgeted under the state's "operations and maintenance trust fund," and School Lunch, Library, and Foster Grandparents federal revenues budgeted under the "grants and donations trust fund."

The *community services* residential options of six beds or less included services for 1,329 individuals in long term residential center (LTRC) group homes and non-LTRC group facilities, 159 individuals in foster homes, 149 individuals in semi-independent living, 70 individuals in other small options, and 496 individuals in supported living. Community services *other state funds* consisted of Rish Park revenues ($2.5 thousand) and fees. *Other federal funds* consisted of Chapter 1 education funds and DD Act revenues budgeted under the "grants and donations trust fund," and federal revenues from Cuban/Haitian Assistance, Children's SOSC Council, and infants and toddlers education intervention.

Reimbursements in 1992 for small private ICFs/MR consisted of $20.7 million for "cluster Medicaid" facilities and the balance, $16.9 million, for group home settings. Total family support funding and numbers of families served did not equal the sum of *financial subsidy/payments*, *family assistance*, and *other family support*. Many families received more than one of the family support components. Florida officials recommended that the family support total be estimated during 1991-92 based on the *family assistance* subtotals, and that the 1986-90 estimate be based on the *other family support* subtotals of spending and numbers of families served.

Florida was one of the nation's eight CSLA states. Although funding had not been initiated in 1992, by June, 1994 the state had activated additional CSLA services including personal assistance and environmental modifications and was serving 686 individuals (*Community Services Reporter*, 1994b).

Revenue, expenditure, and program data for fiscal years 1987 through 1992 were provided by Susan Matus and John Obrzut, Developmental Disabilities Program Office (DDPO), Department of Health and Rehabilitative Services. Additional information on HCBS Waiver expenditures and numbers of individuals served was provided by Robbie Olmstead, Medicaid Office, and by Richard Lepore, Assistant Secretary for Developmental Services. Gail Harper, Program Manager, DDPO, provided data on nursing homes serving individuals with mental retardation and related conditions.

**Georgia.** The principal state agency was Mental Retardation Services, Division of Mental Health, Mental Retardation and Substance Abuse, Department of Human Resources. *Congregate 16+ beds* services in 1992 consisted of six institutional facilities and the Parkwood Developmental Center, a private ICF/MR. The facilities and their average daily populations were Gracewood School and Hospital (631), Central State Hospital, Milledgeville (579), Brook Run, formerly the Georgia Retardation Center, Atlanta (including River Crossing in Athens) (399), Southwest State Hospital, Thomasville (310), Northwest Georgia Regional Hospital, Rome (103), and Georgia Regional Hospital, Atlanta (67). The four facilities serving other populations and the percentage which individuals with mental retardation/developmental disabilities constituted of the total population were Central State Hospital (34.5%), Southwest State Hospital (61.1%), Northwest Georgia Regional Hospital (32.1%), and Georgia Regional Hospital (21.2%).

*Community services* reimbursements classified as *other Title XIX program* consisted of early intervention, case management, and outpatient clinic services. *Other federal funds* consisted of infant and toddler early intervention, foster grandparents, and Developmental Disabilities Act resources.

Revenue, expenditure, and programmatic data for FYs 1989-92 were provided by Jack Schmitt, Division of Mental Health, Mental Retardation and Substance Abuse, Department of Human Resources.

**Hawaii.** The principal state agency was the Developmental Disabilities Division, Department of Health.

*Congregate 16+ beds* services consisted of the Waimano Training School and Hospital in Pearl City, serving 116 individuals in 1992. *Community services* non-ICF/MR options were all six beds or less, consisting of care homes (630) and foster care (283). Six individuals funded by the Division resided in a cluster arrangement of three 5-bed facilities which were licensed as one 15-bed setting. This was classified *7-15 bed private ICF/MR*. *Other Title XIX program* funding consisted of targeted case management serving 150 individuals in 1992. HCBS Waiver case management served four individuals and the balance of case management recipients, 1,220 individuals, were supported with state funding.

Revenue, expenditure, and programmatic data for FYs 1989-92 were provided on the project's worksheets by Stanley Yee, Chief, and David Kanno, Developmental Disabilities Division, Department of Health.

**Idaho.** The principal state agency was the Bureau of Developmental Disabilities, Division of Community Rehabilitation, Department of Health and Welfare. *Congregate 16+ beds* services consisted of the Idaho State School and Hospital in Nampa, serving 172 individuals, and the Yellowstone and Green Acres private ICFs/MR. *Community services* six bed or less non-ICF/MR settings included sheltered homes, semi-independent living, child and adult foster care, and supported living. Funding in the community services category *other Title XIX services* consisted of support for adult and child development centers. *Other federal funds* consisted of Developmental Disabilities Act grant funds and early education incentive grants.

Data were provided in response to project worksheets by Dr. Paul Swatsenbarg, Director, Bureau of Developmental Disabilities, Department of Health and Welfare.

**Illinois.** The principal state agency was the Division of Developmental Disabilities, Department of Mental Health and Developmental Disabilities (DMH/DD). The *Illinois State Budget* was published in a consistent format during the 16 years encompassed by the 4 successive studies. The published executive budget each fiscal year consisted of three volumes: 1) a summary *Budget* with narrative and performance data on each department, agency, board, commission or constitutional/legislative office; 2) an *Appendix* providing line item detail; and 3) a *Personnel Detail* providing full time equivalent staffing data for each state-operated budget entity within the DMH/DD. This personnel detail was not available for state-supported services such as "grant-in-aid" or "purchase of care."

*Congregate 16+ beds* services consisted of nine developmental centers, five MH/DD centers, large private ICFs/DD, and other large residential settings. The state facilities and their average daily populations in 1992 were Shapiro Developmental Center, in Kankakee (820), Howe, Tinley Park (648), Ludeman, Park Forest (503), Lincoln (490), Kiley, Waukegan (471), Murray, Centralia (365), Jacksonville (320), Fox, Dwight (193), and Mabley, Dixon (107). The mental health and developmental disabilities centers were Choate, Anna (248), Alton (108), Singer, Rockford (75), Meyer, Decatur (40), and Chester (10). Developmental disabilities percentages of total population in these facilities were: Choate (51.4%), Alton (29.7%), Singer (25.1%), Meyer (31.4%), and Chester (3.0%). Fringe benefits for institutional employees were accounted for by Central Management Services and were estimated by DMH/DD officials on the basis of a percentage share of personnel costs. The fringe benefit total included in the Illinois profile for institutional services in 1992 was $12,516,700. *Other federal funds* included school lunch, Medicare Part A, Medicare Part B, Medicaid for skilled nursing facility units, and Division of Adult Vocational and Technical Education (DAVTE) funds.

Community "purchase of service" spending for day programs provided on developmental center grounds ($3.6 million in 1992 and comparable amounts in 1988-91) was classified as institutional services spending.

*Private 16+ bed ICF/MR* facilities of 50 beds or more, termed ICFs/DD, served 3,848 individuals in 1992. Specialized living centers (SLCs) consisted of ICFs/DD built by the state Capital Development Board and turned over to private providers. These facilities ranged from 50-100 beds in size and served 364 individuals. The *other 16+ bed residential* category included 595 individuals served in community living facilities (CLFs) and 572 individuals served in child care institutions. During 1992, former "skilled nursing facilities/pediatric (SNF/P)" serving 1,066 individuals were certified as ICFs/DD. The total 4,490 individuals served in nursing facilities in 1988 (displayed in the table on the second page of the Illinois profile) included 1,135 children who resided in the former SNF/P facilities. Excluding these former SNF/P children demonstrates that Illinois' adult

placements in non-specialized nursing facilities declined from 3,355 to 2,159 during 1988-92. Most of the 1,196 adults who left nursing homes during these five years received alternative placements in community options or in other specialized residential settings.

*Community services* residential options of 6 beds or less included community-integrated living arrangements (CILA), community residential alternatives (CRA), home/individual programs (H/IP), supported living arrangements (SLA), special home placements (SHP), one 6-bed community living facility (CLF), and child group homes. A number of private ICFs/DD initially licensed as 15-bed facilities had been re-certified with 16 beds during 1988-92. Project staff classified these homes as 7-15 bed ICFs/MR. Federal *HCBS Waiver* reimbursement in 1992 included $5.2 million for the OBRA 87 Waiver focusing on nursing home reform. *Other Title XIX program* funding consisted of $99.0 thousand for CSLA and the balance for Medicaid developmental training programs. The CSLA option was expected to expand to 750 participants in 1994.

*Local/county overmatch* funding was estimated on the basis of 5% annual increases during 1989-92. This local funding consisted of county and township millage tax funds and municipal (City of Chicago) funding authorized by three state statutes: House Bill 377, Senate Bill 553, and House Bill 708 (Braddock et al., 1990, p. 164).

Revenue, expenditure, and programmatic data during 1988-92 for the Division were provided by John Budny, Bureau of Planning and Program Development, by Marie Havens, and by Lynn Handy, Deputy Director, Division of Developmental Disabilities, DMH/DD. Additional data on individuals served in 6-bed or less settings were provided by Joe Rachunas, Division of Developmental Disabilities. Expenditure data and data on individuals served in ICFs/DD and in developmental training programs were provided by Dr. David Brooks, Chief, Office of Disability Services, Illinois Department of Public Aid, and data on individuals in nursing facilities was provided by Ray Carmody, Office of Disability Services.

**Indiana.** The principal state agency was Developmental Disabilities Services, Division of Mental Health, Department on Aging and Rehabilitation Services. *Congregate 16+ beds* services consisted of eight institutions and large private ICFs/MR. The four state developmental centers (DCs) and four mental health hospitals with DD units, and their average daily populations in 1992, were Fort Wayne (611), Muscatatuck, Butlerville (527), New Castle (265), Northern Indiana, South Bend (78), Central State Hospital DD Unit, Indianapolis (85), and mental health hospital DD units at Madison (72), Logansport (67) and Evansville (62). Central State Hospital closed in 1994.

Project staff determined total institutional services spending in 1992 on the basis of individual facility average daily population and per diem rates provided by state officials. Institutional spending during 1989-91 was estimated based on equal annual increments (interpolation) between 1988 and 1992. State officials provided 1989-92 federal/state ICF/MR reimbursement data, *other state funds* consisting of "farm revenue" from Muscatatuck and New Castle DCs, and *other federal funds* consisting of ESEA Title I grant funds for Northern Indiana State DC. The federal ICF/MR, Title I and state revenues were offset against total institutional spending. The remainder was designated institutional services *state general funds*.

State officials reported that 1992 federal/state ICF/MR revenues for individuals with MR/DD totaled $268.9 million. The institutional federal/state ICF/MR amount, $102.2 million, when subtracted from this total, left a balance of $166.7 million. This balance was allocated between large private (16+ beds) and small private ICFs/MR based upon the respective average daily residents and per diem rates in these two facility size groups. Federal/state ICF/MR revenues for the two ICF/MR groups during 1989-91 were then estimated based on equal annual increments between 1988 and 1992. Indiana's federal medical assistance percentage (FMAP) rate was employed to determine federal and state shares.

In addition to the annual federal/state revenues for small private ICFs/MR, Indiana officials provided other *community services* revenues and expenditures for 1990 and 1992 consisting of general funds, federal/state HCBS Waiver funds, and the associated federal income maintenance funds. They also provided federal Title XX/SSBG revenue data, the state match (classified as *other state funds*), and *other federal funds* consisting of DD Act funding. Project staff determined 1989 and 1991 amounts by interpolation. Individuals with mental retardation and related conditions residing in nursing

homes in 1992 included 1,888 individuals with developmental disabilities, 247 with dual psychiatric and DD diagnoses, and 106 children with severe disabilities served in Vernon Manor and the Camelot Care and Haven Centers.

The numbers of residents in private ICF/MR settings of 6 beds or less (920) and in 7-15 beds settings (2,716) were estimated on the basis of a listing by state officials of the numbers of ICF/MR homes by size. In 1992, there were 55 four-bed, 26 five-bed and 95 six-bed homes. In addition, there were 52 seven-bed and 294 eight-bed homes.

Revenue, expenditure, and programmatic data for FYs 1989-92 were provided by Ann January, Family and Social Services Administration, Division of Mental Health, and by Nancy Swaim, Division of Mental Health. John Viernes, Jr., Director, Developmental Disabilities Services, Division of Mental Health provided updated information on individuals served in community residences and Carol Warner, Division office, provided nursing home information.

**Iowa.** The principal state agency was Mental Retardation and Developmental Disabilities services, Division of Mental Health, Mental Retardation and Developmental Disabilities, Department of Human Services. *Congregate 16+ beds* services in 1992 included two Hospital/Schools, Glenwood and Woodward, serving 516 and 379 individuals, respectively. In addition there were large private ICFs/MR, and county funded facilities of 16 beds or more termed County Care Facilities (CCFs), Residential Care Facilities (RCFs) and RCFs/MR. Institutional *other state funds* consisted of county matching funds to the federal ICF/MR reimbursements. *Other state funds* for large private residential services consisted of the county ICF/MR match, and *local/county overmatch* represented the county funding for CCFs, RCFs, and RCFs/MR.

*Community* residences of six beds or less consisted of supervised apartments serving 800 individuals and RCFs and RCFs/MR serving 792. Iowa's community services were supported by substantial amounts of county funding. *Other state funds* included the county matches for small private ICFs/MR, for the Model 50/200 Waiver, and for targeted case management. *Local/county overmatch* consisted of funding for small RCFs, RCFs/MR and apartments ($26.6 million), for diagnosis and evaluation ($.05 million), and for vocational services ($28.4 million). Community services *general funds* consisted of Social Service Block Grant (SSBG) direct services state funds ($16.8 million), foster care ($32.2 million), MH/MR fund "general distributions" to counties ($2.5 million), MH/MR funds "special distribution" to counties ($.6 million), and county matches totaling $9 million for federal Medicaid programs. The Medicaid programs financed by these county matches were small private ICF/MR ($8.2 million), targeted case management ($.7 million), and Model 50/200 Waiver ($.1 million). *Other state funds* consisted of "SSBG local purchase" funds. Federal *other Title XIX program* funding consisted of targeted case management services.

Revenue, expenditure, and programmatic data for 1989-91 were provided by Charles M. Palmer, Director, Department of Human Services. Updated data for FY 1992 were provided by Larry Allen, Division of MR/DD.

**Kansas.** The principal state agency was Mental Retardation/Developmental Disabilities Services, Department of Social and Rehabilitation Services. *Congregate 16+ beds* services consisted of three state facilities and large private ICFs/MR. The state facilities and their average daily populations in 1992 were Kansas Neurological Institute, Topeka (333) and Training Centers at Winfield (340) and at Parsons (270). The DD Unit at Norton State Hospital closed in 1988.

*Community services* general funds consisted of the state match to federal reimbursements for small private ICFs/MR and the HCBS Waiver. *Other state funds* consisted of "special purpose" grants, "state aid" and a county match to federal Title XX/Social Services Block Grant revenues ($1.2 million in 1992). *Local/county overmatch* funding consisted of a mill levy for local property taxes supporting community day and residential programs.

Expenditures for MR/DD services were published in *The State of Kansas Budget Fiscal Year 1991* and *The State of Kansas Budget Fiscal Year 1992*. The institutional budgets in these documents provided funding sources and general program categories. The MR/DD community services expenditures were not broken out separately from expenditures for community mental health programs. These data for FYs 1989-92 were provided in response to the project's worksheets by Larry Sherraden, Administrator, Information Re-

sources, Mental Health and Retardation Services, Department of Social and Rehabilitation Services.

**Kentucky.** The principal state agency was the Division of Mental Retardation, Department for Mental Health and Mental Retardation Services, Cabinet for Human Resources. *Congregate 16+ beds* services consisted of four state-owned facilities and large private ICFs/MR. The state settings' names and average daily populations in 1992 were Oakwood, Somerset (413), Hazelwood, Louisville (214), Outwood, Dawson Springs (78), and Central State Hospital ICF/MR Unit, Louisville (48). The Outwood facility was privately operated. Six bed or less community residences consisted of group homes and apartments serving three or fewer individuals.

Judy Knowles, Division of Mental Retardation, provided revenue, expenditure, and programmatic data for FYs 1989-92 in response to the worksheets developed by project staff.

**Louisiana.** The principal state agency was the Office of Mental Retardation/Developmental Disabilities (OMR/DD), Department of Health and Hospitals. *Congregate 16+ beds* services consisted of 9 state institutions, 14 large private ICFs/MR, and a large private non-ICF/MR residence. The names and average daily populations of the state schools were Pinecrest, in Pineville (1,095), Hammond (448), Northwest, Bossier City (228), Ruston (122), Southwest, Iota (100), Thibodaux (44), Leesville (35), Columbia (23), and the Metropolitan Developmental Center, Belle Chasse (277). The total of 1,331 individuals served in nursing homes included 66 children served in specialized nursing facilities.

*Community services* expenditures in 1992 included federal/state small private ICF/MR spending for individuals with mental retardation and developmental disabilities in Jefferson Parish, a regional operation accounted for separately from other OMR/DD programs. Six bed or less residential options consisted of supervised apartments serving 251 individuals in 1992 and substitute family care serving 156 individuals.

Revenue, expenditure, and programmatic data for FYs 1989-92 were provided by William Payne, Jr., Director, Office of Human Services, Division of Fiscal Services, Department of Health and Hospitals, and by Alma Stewart, Director, Adult and Family Services. Data in the financial profile were reviewed by Susan Bowman, Assistant Secretary, Office for Citizens with Developmental Disabilities.

**Maine.** The principal state agency was the Division of Mental Retardation, Department of Mental Health and Mental Retardation. *Congregate 16+ beds* services consisted of two state centers, one private ICF/MR (Clearview) serving 29 individuals, four 20-bed private ICFs/MR, and a board and care facility serving 21 individuals. The state centers and their average daily populations in 1992 were Pineland Center, in Pownal (229), and Levinson Center, Bangor (16).

*Community services* settings of 7-15 beds included the 13-bed Aroostook Center, a public, non-institutional ICF/MR in Presque Isle; 14 "nursing" ICFs/MR; 6 other private ICFs/MR; and 15 board and care homes. Settings of six beds or less included 40 board and care homes, 1 six-bed "nursing" ICF/MR, 23 six-bed ICF/MR homes, and residential options for Waiver participants including foster homes, apartments, and board and care homes. Community *other Title XIX program* funding supported day habilitation programs.

Revenue, expenditure, and programmatic data for FYs 1992 were provided by Pete Thibodeaux, Resource Development Manager, Bureau of Mental Retardation, Department of Mental Health and Mental Retardation, by Mary Crichton, Division of MR, and by Kathryn McKimmy, Resource Development Manager, Division of MR. Project staff estimated 1989-91 data by interpolation (equal annual increments) between the 1988 data from the previous study and the 1992 data provided by DMH/MR staff.

**Maryland.** The principal state agency was the Developmental Disabilities Administration (DDA), Department of Health and Mental Hygiene (DHMH). *Congregate 16+ beds* services consisted of five state residential centers, DDA purchase of service funding for 166 individuals served in out-of-state residential programs, and four Department of Human Resources domiciliary care facilities (Belle Machre, Gallagher, Curtis Hall/Chimes and Anita Lynn) which met DDA licensure standards and served individuals with developmental disabilities. Two domiciliary care facilities for individuals with developmental disabilities (Kemp Horn and Angels Haven) closed in 1985, and the IBIS Rehabilitation program in Glendale was in operation only during 1989-91. The state residential centers and their average daily populations in 1992 were Rosewood, in Owings Mills (384), Great Oaks, Silver Spring

(242), Holly, Salisbury (194), Potomac, Hagerstown (133), and Brandenburg, Cumberland (61). There were four institutional closures: Victor Cullen, Sabillasville, in 1991; Walter P. Carter DD Unit, Baltimore, 1990; Highland Health, Baltimore, 1989; and Henryton, Sykesville, 1985.

*Community services* residential options in 1992 were all six beds or less in size. Nearly three-quarters of the options were alternative living units (ALUs) serving three or fewer individuals. In addition there were group homes averaging five individuals each and serving a total of 690 individuals, foster homes serving 175 individuals, and semi-independent living for 13 individuals. *Other Title XIX program* funding for community services in Maryland supported medical day care which served approximately 900 individuals.

*Other state funds* consisted of required county match funds paid to community services agencies. Maryland was one of the first eight states to be awarded federal Medicaid funding under the Community Supported Living Arrangement (CSLA) amendment to Medicaid (OBRA, 1990, P.L. 101-508). Maryland started receiving federal CSLA reimbursements in 1993 and there were 167 participants by 1995 (*Community Services Reporter*, 1994b). The Medicaid options, personal assistance services and targeted case management, were implemented in 1993.

Project staff utilized documents including *Review of service needs and costs in community and institutional programs* (Department of Fiscal Services, 1990) and *Maryland State Budget, Fiscal Year 1993, Vol. I*. The majority of data were provided in response to the project's worksheets. State officials, and the data they provided, were James Johnson, Chief, and Randy Greenwald, Budget Management Office, DHMH (state residential centers' expenditures, revenues, and individuals served); and Charles Spannare, Assistant Director for Administration and Management, DDA (community services expenditures, revenues, and individuals served).

Other data were provided by Kathleen Wolf, Deputy Director, DDA (program accomplishments, special federal funding initiatives, and system overview); Connie Holloway, PASARR Coordinator, DDA (individuals served in nursing facilities); Bill Wacker, Chief, Planning and Statistics Division, DDA (individuals served in community services, including HCBS Waiver participants); Hal Franklin, Assistant Director, DDA (family support); Diane Bolger, DDA (CSLA, family and individual support services); and Joseph Millstone, Director, Medical Care Policy Administration, DHMH (personal care assistance, targeted case management, and medical day programs).

**Massachusetts.** The principal state agency was the Department of Mental Retardation (DMR), established in 1988. The DMR was formerly a division within the Department of Mental Health. *Congregate 16+ beds* services consisted of seven developmental centers. The facilities and their average daily populations in 1992 were Fernald, in Waltham (including the Templeton Developmental Center in Templeton approximately 50 miles away) (809), Wrentham (550), Monson, Palmer (481), Hogan/Berry Retardation Facility, Hathorne (304), Dever, Taunton (280), Belchertown (130) and Glavin Regional Center, Shrewsbury (60). Belchertown closed in 1992, and Dever was scheduled to close in 1995. *Community services* residential options of six beds or less consisted of state-funded group homes, foster homes, and other small residences including apartments. Federal *other Title XIX program* funding consisted of targeted case management ($5.6 million in 1992) and day habilitation programs serving 1,500 individuals ($10.1 million).

Employee fringe benefits were accounted for in four separate agencies: Board of Retirement, Group Insurance Commission, Public Employee's Retirement Administration (accounting for worker's compensation), and Unemployment Insurance Trust Fund. DMR officials estimated these benefit amounts for institutional and small public ICF/MR employees, adding $66.2 million and $14.8 million to institutional services and community services, respectively, in 1992.

Expenditure data, data on numbers of individuals served, and expenditure and programmatic data for special community initiatives for fiscal years 1987 through 1992 were provided by Mary Fratto, Community Programs, DMR, and by Mary Cerreto, Assistant Commissioner. Data on individuals served in settings of six beds or less were provided by Ruth Saldinger, DMR. Information about fringe benefits and estimates for individuals served in individual developmental centers were provided by Michael Abrahams, DMR.

**Michigan.** The principal state agency was the Department of Mental Health (DMH). *Congregate 16+ beds* services in 1992 consisted of six state facilities. The facilities, and their 1992 average daily populations were Mt. Pleasant (204), Southgate (171), Caro (164), Muskegon (78), Newberry (26), and Coldwater (13). Coldwater, Muskegon, and Newberry closed during fiscal year 1992. Other closures in Michigan were Oakdale in Lapeer, 1991, Macomb-Oakland in Mt. Clemens, 1989, Plymouth, 1984, Northville, 1983, Alpine, 1981, and Fort Custer, 1972.

*Community services* residential options included alternative intermediate services/mentally retarded (AIS/MR) categorized by the project as ICFs/MR of 7-15 beds or 6-beds or less. Approximately 60% of the individuals served in AIS/MR settings were under the budgetary management of DMH, while the remaining 40% were managed by Community Mental Health (CMH) organizations. The non-ICF/MR residential settings consisted of "specialized residential" group homes which DMH designated by level, I through IV. Approximately 70% of specialized residential settings were managed by CMH organizations, and the balance by DMH.

*Other Title XIX program* federal funding in 1992 consisted of targeted case management ($18.9 million), CMH-managed personal care ($17.6 million), DMH clinic services ($14.9 million), and DMH-managed personal care ($7.7 million). Michigan was one of the first eight CSLA states, enrolling 125 participants at the end of 1992. There were over 400 participants by 1994 (*Community Services Reporter*, 1994b).

Data on numbers of individuals served and expenditure and programmatic data for special community initiatives for fiscal years 1987 through 1992 were provided by Marilyn Hill, Office of Federal Liaison/Entitlements, DMH. Expenditure data for institutional and community services was provided by Morris Hickman, Budget Section, DMH. Michigan officials provided data on individuals served at the end of the state's fiscal years. Project staff averaged these data to determine average daily population for the state fiscal year (e.g., average of September 30, 1991 and September 30, 1992 data for fiscal year 1992.)

**Minnesota.** The principal state agency was the Division for Persons with Developmental Disabilities, Department of Human Services. *Congregate 16+ beds* services consisted of seven regional treatment centers (RTCs), large private ICFs/MR, and one state-funded larger private setting, the Laura Baker School. The RTCs and their average daily populations in 1992 were Faribault (381), Cambridge (218), Brainerd (140), Fergus Falls (110), St. Peter (87), Willmar (50), and Moose Lake (47). Brainerd, Fergus Falls, St. Peter, Willmar, and Moose Lake served other populations (e.g., mental health, chemical dependency) in addition to persons with developmental disabilities.

Large private residential services *general funds* included Minnesota Supplemental Assistance (MSA) funds ($.3 million in 1992) for the Baker School. *Other state funds* consisted of the county matches for the Baker School.

Minnesota's small public ICF/MR funding, initiated in 1992, financed state-operated community services (SOCS), which were licensed as adult foster care and which served 18 individuals that year. An additional 28 SOCS residents resided in state-funded adult foster care settings. Other state-funded residences of six beds or less consisted of semi-independent living, foster care for adults and children, and non-ICF/MR group homes for six or fewer individuals.

*Other Title XIX program* funding consisted of developmental training and habilitation day programs for ICF/MR residents. The 1992 federal HCBS Waiver funding included $.4 million for OBRA 87 nursing home reform Waiver services. *Other state funds* in 1992 consisted of the semi-independent living services (SILS) county share ($2.9 million) and the Title XX/Social Services Block Grant county share. During 1988-92, *other state funds* also included county matches for small private ICFs/MR, the Waiver, and for other Title XIX services. The county match amounts in 1991 were small private ICF/MR ($3.2 million), HCBS Waiver ($3.0 million), and other Title XIX program ($1.5 million).

Revenue, expenditure, and programmatic data for FYs 1989-92 were provided by Jim Franczyk, Research, Evaluation and Planning Director, Department of Human Services, and Shirley Patterson, Director, Division for Persons with Developmental Disabilities.

**Mississippi.** The principal state agency was the Bureau of Mental Retardation, Department of Mental Health. *Congregate 16+ beds* services consisted of a state school, four retardation centers, and five large private ICFs/MR. The state facilities and their estimated average daily populations in 1992 were Ellisville State School (including Ellisville Farm) (584), Hudspeth Retardation Center, Whitfield (290), North Mississippi Retardation Center, Oxford (255), Boswell Retardation Center, Sanatorium (250), and South Mississippi Retardation Center, Long Beach (114).

The director of the Bureau of Mental Retardation, Roger McMurtry, could not provide some of the revenue and expenditure data for congregate residential and community services. It was therefore necessary to utilize state published budget documents, results from other studies, and estimations based on these sources to construct the Mississippi profile. First, data on state facility revenues, expenditures, average daily population, and staffing were obtained from the *State of Mississippi Proposed Budget for Fiscal Year July 1, 1991 to June 30, 1992 (Volume II)*. The budget presented "actual" data for 1990, "estimated" data for 1991, and "requested" data for 1992. The budget listed revenues and expenditures for each state residential center, along with "group home" and "community mental retardation treatment" lines at each facility except the Ellisville Farm.

Project staff determined institutional services revenues and expenditures as follows: 1) the budget document indicated "total funds" for each facility; 2) project staff classified "Social Security" and "VA/private/other federal" as *other federal funds*; 3) project staff determined that "Medicaid foods/drugs"(listed for Boswell) and "other funds" listed for the other facilities consisted of federal/state ICF/MR reimbursements (project staff utilized the state's fiscal year-adjusted federal medical assistance percentages, or FMAP, rate to calculate the federal and state match ICF/MR components); 4) "group home" and "community MR treatment" amounts were offset against total funds for each facility; and 5) project staff aggregated the individual facility revenue lines and total spending net of revenues and community spending.

In 1992 the "group home" and "community MR treatment" lines when aggregated across all facilities totaled $3.3 million and $3.4 million, respectively. Combining these amounts with the budget document listings for DMH-wide "MR service administration" and "MR administration service" ($2.2 million and $5.0 million, respectively) yielded the total $14.0 million for community services *general fund*. Institutional services revenues in 1992 consisted of *general funds,* which was the total aggregated spending for the facilities net of community spending and net of other revenues; *other state funds* consisting of the state share of the aggregated federal/state ICF/MR amounts; *federal ICF/MR;* and *other federal funds* consisting of the Social Security, VA, or other federal amounts aggregated across facilities. Fiscal year 1989 data were determined by interpolation between the 1988 data previously determined by project staff and Mississippi officials and the 1990 data available from the budget document.

It was necessary to determine four other Mississippi resource profile spending components: large private ICF/MR, community services Title XX/SSBG and the state match, federal small public ICF/MR spending, and a revision to FYs 1977-79 data.

First, project staff obtained the data for Mississippi's large private ICF/MR total spending in FY 1992 from Smith and Gettings (1993, p. 41). Mississippi's FMAP rate was used to determine federal and state shares, and the FYs 1989 to 1991 data were determined by interpolation (equal annual increments) between the 1988 data available from the previous study and the 1992 data available from the other national survey source (Smith & Gettings, 1992). Second, Director McMurtry estimated that federal Title XX/SSBG and the state match, classified by the project as community services *other state funds,* remained constant during 1988-92.

Third, McMurtry's correspondence (4/20/94) acknowledged receipt of the graphic profile for Mississippi, which incorporated the project staff estimations based on the state budget document and other sources outlined above. Although McMurtry could not "affirm or disavow" the data pertaining to privately operated programs, he did annotate a photocopy of the project's graphic profile. These additions/corrections to the state's profile included federal small public ICF/MR revenue in 1992; data on numbers of individuals served in 6-bed or less, in 7-15 bed, and in 16+ bed state residences in 1992, and 1989-92 information on sheltered employment/work activity, supported/competitive employment, case management, and early intervention services.

Fourth, project staff also consulted with McMurtry on revisions to the 1977-79 community services revenue and expenditure portion of the data set. Federal Title XX revenues were originally reported by Jane Lee, So-

cial Work Program Administrator, Mississippi Department of Public Welfare, 10/4/83 (Braddock et al., 1984, p. 469). These federal revenues (and the 25% state match) nearly doubled from 1977 to 1978 and again from 1978-79. However, between 1979 and 1980 federal/state Title XX funding for individuals with mental retardation dropped by $6 million.

Director McMurtry indicated that state directors of mental retardation centers began in 1974 to establish 18-20 "child development centers," mostly in southern Mississippi. The state facility directors initially used federal Titles IVA and VIB funding to develop these centers. During 1977-79, funding consisted of federal Title XX and the 25% state match. In 1980 the child development center funding was transferred from the MR state agency to the Mississippi Department of Public Welfare (DPW). Many of the development centers subsequently closed, and others were converted to child care centers serving primarily children without disabilities.

Mental Retardation Director McMurtry and project staff estimated that one-half ($1.2 million) of total federal and state Title XX spending in 1977, $3.9 million in 1978, and $6.9 million in 1979 was associated with these children's development centers subsequently transferred to DPW. These amounts were excluded from the data set.

The institutional average daily population for 1992 (1,493) was provided by Mr. McMurtry, and individual facility populations were estimated based on data from the state budget document. Data on individuals with mental retardation and related disabilities in nursing facilities were provided by Linda Giardina, Training Coordinator, Licensure and Certification, Division of Health Facilities, Mississippi State Department of Health. Through June, 1994, a total of 904 individuals with mental retardation and related conditions had undergone the OBRA-87 mandated screening process. The Health Department official anticipated that this number would not increase, since previous placements from state facilities had decreased. The state facilities developed special geriatric units.

**Missouri.** The principal state agency was the Division of Mental Retardation and Developmental Disabilities, Department of Mental Health. *Congregate 16+ beds* services in 1992 consisted of seven state centers, large private ICFs/MR, and other state-funded facilities of

16+ beds. The state centers and their 1992 average daily populations were Bellefontaine Habilitation Center, in St. Louis (387), Marshall (362), St. Louis Developmental Disabilities Treatment Center (320), Higginsville Habilitation Center (229), Nevada Center (150), Poplar Bluff Regional Center (50), and Sikeston Regional Center (40).

*Community services* residential options included 7-15 bed and 6-bed or less private ICFs/MR, and 7-15 bed and 6-bed or less residences not certified as ICFs/MR included group homes, supervised apartments and foster homes. *Local/county overmatch* funding consisted of Senate Bill 40 county property tax levies by three-fifths of Missouri's 114 counties (Braddock et al., 1990, p. 276). *Other Title XIX program* funding supported targeted case management.

Revenue, expenditure, and programmatic data for FYs 1989-92 were provided in response to the project's worksheets by Joann Leykam, Director, and John Bright, Division of MR/DD.

**Montana.** The principal state agency was the Developmental Disabilities Division, Department of Social Services. *Congregate 16+ beds* services consisted of two state centers, Montana Developmental Center in Boulder and Eastmont Center in Glendive. Their average daily populations in 1992 were 128 and 46, respectively. *Community services* small residential settings consisted of adult homes (637 individuals served in 1992), semi-independent living arrangements (298), and children's homes (47). *Other federal funds* consisted of Chapter 1 education funds and PL 99-457 early intervention funds.

Revenue, expenditure, and programmatic data for FYs 1989-92 were provided by Mike Hanshew, Administrator, Fritz Roos, and Janice Risch, Developmental Disabilities Division, in response to the project's worksheets.

**Nebraska.** The principal state agency was the Office of Mental Retardation, Department of Public Institutions. *Congregate 16+ beds* services consisted of the Beatrice State Developmental Center, serving 458 in 1992, and large private ICFs/MR. *Community services* residences consisted of one 8-bed private ICF/MR, 7-15 bed "training in independent living" settings, and 6-bed or less supported living services. Medicaid *targeted case management* was initiated in 1990 and served 822 in

1992. Expenditure estimates were not available. *Local/county overmatch* funding consisted of county tax funds supporting community services.

Revenue, expenditure, and programmatic data for FYs 1989-92 were provided in response to the project's worksheets by Jim Hanlon and Jackie Miller, Department of Public Institutions, and by Mary Steiner, Department of Social Services.

**Nevada.** The principal state agency was the Division of Mental Health and Mental Retardation, Department of Human Resources. *Congregate 16+ beds* services consisted of the Desert Developmental Center in Las Vegas and the Sierra Developmental Center in Sparks, with average daily populations in 1992 of 95 and 79, respectively. All *community services* residential options were 6 beds or less, including four private ICFs/MR, private group homes, and developmental homes. *Other Title XIX program* services funding supported targeted case management, which was initiated in 1991. There were no estimates for numbers of individuals served.

Revenue, expenditure, and programmatic data for FYs 1989-92 were provided in response to the project worksheets by David Luke, Administrator for Mental Retardation, Jean Wilcher, and Jean Laird, Division of MH and MR.

**New Hampshire.** The principal state agency was the Bureau of Developmental Services, Division of Mental Health and Developmental Services, Department of Health and Human Services. *Congregate 16+ beds* services in 1992 consisted of one private ICF/MR, Cedar Crest. New Hampshire closed the Laconia Developmental Center on January 31, 1991, and the Tobey Unit of New Hampshire State Hospital, located in Concord, closed in fiscal year 1991. New Hampshire thus became the first state without any state institutions or DD units within mental health facilities.

*Community services* residential options of six beds or less in New Hampshire consisted of single person residences (298 individuals served in 1992) and residences for two persons (190), three persons (165), four persons (136), five persons (70) and six persons (30). *Other Title XIX program* funding consisted of Medicaid reimbursement for targeted case management. The Medicaid day programs which constituted *other Title XIX program* funding during 1981-1988 were subsequently incorporated into the HCBS Waiver.

Revenue, expenditure, and programmatic data for FYs 1989-92 were provided by Dan Van Keuren, Program Analysis Unit, Division of Mental Health and Developmental Services.

**New Jersey.** The principal state agency was the Division of Developmental Disabilities, Department of Human Services. *Congregate 16+ beds* services consisted of 10 state developmental centers, 2 large private ICFs/MR, and approximately 40 large private facilities funded with "purchased care residential contracts." The state facilities and their estimated average daily populations in 1992 were Vineland (882), New Lisbon (696), Woodbine (668), Hunterdon, Clinton (625), Woodbridge (621), North Princeton (512), North Jersey, Totowa (446), Green Brook (115), Johnstone, Bordentown (114), and Ancora (58). The Johnstone facility closed at the end of 1992.

*Community services* residential options were all settings of six beds or less, supported by state funds or by the HCBS Waiver. The community residences consisted of small group homes, supervised apartments, supported living, and skill development homes. *Other state funds* consisted of revenues from the Casino Revenue Fund (CRF) and the State Facilities Education Act (SFEA). *Other Title XIX program* funding consisted of federal institutional ICF/MR revenues allocated by the Division to support community day and residential programs.

Expenditure and programmatic data for 1989-92 were provided by Angie Kamerdze, Planning and Operation Support, and by Lee Birkey and Tom Major, Division of Developmental Disabilities. Data on individuals with mental retardation and related conditions in nursing facilities were provided by Beth Gnozzio, Division of Developmental Disabilities. Data for Medicaid programs (including institutional ICF/MR, large private ICF/MR, community services *other Title XIX programs* and the HCBS Waiver) were provided by Ernest Rogers, Division of Medical Assistance and Health Services.

**New Mexico.** The principal state agency was the Developmental Disabilities Bureau, Behavioral Health Services Division, Health and the Environment Department. *Congregate 16+ beds* services consisted of two state institutions, Los Lunas, serving 339 individuals in 1992, and Fort Stanton, serving 144 individuals. Fort

Stanton was scheduled for closure in 1995. *Community services* residential options of six beds or less consisted of supported living (370), group homes (133), and surrogate family living (30). Twenty individuals were served in eight-bed group homes. *Other Title XIX program* funding in 1992 supported targeted case management serving 18 individuals; 282 individuals were served in the HCBS Waiver case management and the balance, 770 individuals, were in state-funded case management.

Revenue, expenditure, and programmatic data for FYs 1989-92 were provided in response to the project's worksheets by Steve Dossey, Management Services Bureau Chief, Behavioral Health Services Division.

**New York.** The principal state agency was the Office of Mental Retardation/Developmental Disabilities (OMR/DD). *Congregate 16+ beds* services in 1992 consisted of state developmental centers, special state-operated DD units, large private ICFs/MR, and state-operated and voluntary (private) facilities of 16 beds or more. Table III-2 summarizes, in order of average daily populations in 1992, the state Developmental Centers followed by the special state-operated DD units. Small residential units (SRUs) were facilities constructed or renovated adjacent to developmental centers. Other special units consisted of multiple disability units (MDUs), regional behavioral treatment units (RBTUs), secure units and autism units.

Staten Island Developmental Center closed in 1987. Craig in Sonyea and West Seneca closed in 1988. Rome closed in 1989; Bronx and Manhattan closed in 1992; J.N. Adams, Long Island, and Newark closed in 1993; and Wilton was projected to close in 1995. The Brooklyn, Broome, Fineson, Heck, Letchworth, Sunmount, Syracuse, Wassaic, and Westchester Developmental Centers were projected to close in 2000. The Letchworth Village MDU ceased operation in 1989, and state-operated intermediate care facilities at Staten Island were closed in 1989. The buildings were transferred to the City College of Staten Island.

The total 1,886 individuals in 1992 who were classified as large private ICF/MR residents included 344 individuals served in publicly operated settings. Other large private settings included residential schools serving 503 individuals and voluntary community residences of 16 beds or more serving 142 individuals. *Community services* residential options of 7-15 beds not

## TABLE III-2
*New York OMR/DD Developmental Centers and Special Units Ranked by Average Daily Population, 1992*

| Name | Location | Average Daily Population |
|---|---|---|
| **DEVELOPMENTAL CENTERS** | | |
| 1. Wassaic | Wassaic | 864.0 |
| 2. Westchester | Tarrytown | 612.0 |
| 3. Letchworth Village | Thiells | 603.0 |
| 4. Broome | Binghamtom | 450.0 |
| 5. Syracuse | Syracuse | 429.5 |
| 6. Bronx | Bronx | 413.5 |
| 7. Bernard M. Fineson | Corona | 413.5 |
| 8. Monroe | Rochester | 391.0 |
| 9. Brooklyn | Brooklyn | 382.0 |
| 10. Wilton | Wilton | 341.5 |
| 11. Sunmount | Tupper Lake | 297.5 |
| 12. Long Island | Melville | 259.0 |
| 13. Oswald D. Heck | Schenectady | 252.0 |
| 14. J.N. Adam | Perrysburg | 146.0 |
| 15. Manhattan | New York | 51.0 |
| 16. Newark | Newark | 18.0 |
| SUBTOTAL | | 5,923.5 |
| **SPECIAL UNITS** | | |
| 1. Long Island SRU | Melville | 211.0 |
| 2. Long Island MDU | Melville | 145.5 |
| 3. Rome SRU | Rome | 140.0 |
| 4. West Seneca MDU | West Seneca | 98.5 |
| 5. Rockland MDU | Rockland | 96.0 |
| 6. Newark SRU | Newark | 95.5 |
| 7. J.N. Adam MDU | Perrysburg | 91.5 |
| 8. Wassaic MDU | Wassaic | 87.5 |
| 9. South Beach MDU | Staten Island | 72.0 |
| 10. J.N. Adam SRU | Perrysburg | 71.0 |
| 11. Creedmoor Autism Unit | New York City | 47.5 |
| 12. O.D. Heck Autism Unit | Schenectady | 46.0 |
| 13. Sunmount MDU | Tupper Lake | 32.0 |
| 14. Sunmount SRU | Tupper Lake | 24.0 |
| 15. Wassaic RBTU | Wassaic | 23.5 |
| 16. Monroe Secure Unit | Rochester | 23.0 |
| 17. Metro RBTU | Brooklyn | 18.0 |
| 18. Metro Secure Unit | Brooklyn | 5.5 |
| 19. Sagamore Autism Unit | Melville | 5.0 |
| SUBTOTAL | | 1,333.0 |
| **TOTAL** | | **7,256.5** |

certified as ICFs/MR included publicly staffed community residences (1,364 individuals served in 1992), and voluntary community residences (4,965). Six bed or less non-ICF/MR settings included 4,795 voluntary beds and 346 public community residence (CR) beds.

Expenditures for state developmental centers and for the state-operated community residences and state-operated day programs included fringe benefits for these OMR/DD employees. Fringe benefit amounts, accounted for outside OMR/DD, were estimated by OMR/DD officials to constitute 25.2%, 26.2%, 29.0%, and 24.4% of personal service (salary) expenditures during 1989-92. Project staff classified fringe benefits as *general funds*. Also included with general funds for in-

stitutional and community services was "maintenance undistributed" consisting of a contingency account to cover repair and maintenance costs at state-operated developmental centers or community programs.

*Other state funds* and *other federal funds* for institutional and community services included "direct fees" consisting of private pay, federal income maintenance funds, and other contributions from service recipients. State officials estimated direct fees to be 93% federal funds and 7% state funds for institutional services; the allocation basis for community services was 99% and 1%. Institutional services *other federal funds*, in addition to the estimated 93% share of developmental center residents' fees, included Medicare Part B, school lunch/breakfast, foster grandparents, and salary sharing. Community services *other state funds* in 1992 consisted of state match funds for voluntary ICFs/DD ($183.8 million), "care at home III" Model 50/200 Waiver ($.4 million), Subchapter A voluntary Medicaid programs ($46.9 million), non-Subchapter A ($66.7 million), and the state Department of Social Services (DSS) match for voluntary ICFs/DD ($46.0 million). The balance of *other state funds* consisted of the estimated 1% of client fees for community programs ($.2 million), sheltered workshop demonstration funds ($9.7 million), and Chapter 978 and Unified Services local match funds ($41.2 million).

*Other Title XIX program* funds in 1992 consisted of voluntary non-Subchapter A day programs ($66.7 million), voluntary Subchapter A day programs ($46.9 million), state-operated day treatment ($27.3 million), voluntary clinics ($11.2 million), Medicaid transportation ($9.1 million), state-operated day treatment transportation ($5.5 million), voluntary vendor personal care ($.3 million), and state-operated clinics ($.04 million).

Revenue, expenditure, and programmatic data for FYs 1989-92 were provided by Paul Audino, Administration and Revenue Support, Budget and Fiscal Services, OMR/DD. Computer file data on individuals served in voluntary and state-operated community residences was provided by Tom Richards, OMR/DD. Bob Coyner, Chief Budgeting Analyst, Budget and Fiscal Services, provided additional information on individuals served in community residences. Special state institution unit population data were provided by Diane Sklaryk.

Correspondence from James F. Moran, Director, Administration Support, OMR/DD, noted that institutional per diem rates determined on the basis of federal Medicaid reimbursement methodology would be higher than those determined by the study's methodology. The Medicaid reimbursement per diem rates for 1989-92, including the allocation of Office-wide and other government expenses (but not including capital expenses), would be $280, $323, $364, and $408.

The OMR/DD supported/competitive employment data were provided by John Smith, Bureau of Budget Planning and Allocation, OMR/DD. Data for large private ICFs/MR and other large private residential facilities, sheltered employment/work activity, and day habilitation were provided by Mary Edmonds, OMR/DD Information Services Group. Data on nursing facilities were provided by Bob Welch, State Department of Health.

**North Carolina.** The principal state agency was Developmental Disabilities, Division of Mental Health, Mental Retardation, and Substance Abuse, Department of Human Resources. *Congregate 16+ beds* services consisted of five state centers, a mental retardation unit in a state mental health center, large private ICFs/MR, and other large private residences supported by state funding. The state facilities and their average daily populations in 1992 were Caswell, in Kinston (754), Murdock, Butner (693), O'Berry, Goldsboro (445), West Carolina, Morganton (436), Black Mountain (113), and Broughton MR Unit, Morganton (61). Institutional services *other state funds* included the 15% county match, totaling $8 million in 1992, for federal ICF/MR reimbursements.

*Community services* residential options of 7-15 beds which were not certified as ICFs/MR consisted of group homes. Six bed or less state funded residential options included group homes, family care homes, apartment living, foster care, subsidized family care, and specialized residential options. The case management total of 2,864 in 1992 included 983 individuals served under HCBS Waiver case management. *Other state funds* consisted of the state and local matches for small private and small public ICFs/MR and for the HCBS Waiver. State matches totaled $22.7 million in 1992, and local matches consisted of $2.4 million for small private ICFs/MR, $.1 million for small public ICFs/MR, and $.5 million for the Waiver.

Expenditure data and data on numbers of individuals served for fiscal years 1988 through 1992 were provided by Richard Parker and Janne E. Harris, Assistant Chief, Developmental Disabilities, Division of MH/MR/SAS. Additional data including HCBS waiver and ICF/MR expenditures were provided by Patsy Slaughter, Division of Medical Assistance. Lee Hoffman, Division of Facility Services, provided information on private ICFs/MR, and Jim Barnhill, Division of Medical Assistance, provided data for nursing homes serving individuals with mental retardation and related conditions.

**North Dakota.** The principal state agency was the Developmental Disabilities Division, Department of Human Services. *Congregate 16+ beds* services consisted of one state school in Grafton, and two private facilities. A transitional community living facility (TCLF) served 21 individuals, and a minimally supervised living arrangement (MSLA) served 25 individuals. Waiver federal funding (approximately $.4 million in 1992) supported services for 42 of the 46 individuals residing in these larger settings.

Community services *other state funds* consisted of the local match to federal HCBS Waiver services. Community residential options of six beds or less consisted of individualized supported living arrangements (ISLA), transitional community living, minimally supervised living, and foster care. In addition, specialized placements consisted of two 5-bed facilities serving individuals with dual psychiatric and developmental disabilities diagnoses. Data sources included the state's published budget, *The Executive Budget-- 1990-1992 Biennium,* and data provided in response to the project's worksheets by Sandi Noble, Director, and Robert Graham, Developmental Disabilities Division, Department of Human Services.

**Ohio.** The principal state agency was the Department of Mental Retardation and Developmental Disabilities (DMR/DD). *Congregate 16+ beds* services consisted of 13 developmental centers; 3 MR/DD units in state mental health or psychiatric centers; large private ICFs/MR; and other large residential settings including group homes and other homes. The table below summarizes, in order of average daily population in 1992, the state developmental centers and special state-operated MR/DD units.

**Table III-3**
*Ohio DMR/DD Developmental Centers and Special Units Ranked by Average Daily Population, 1992*

| Name | Location | Average Daily Population |
|---|---|---|
| **DEVELOPMENTAL CENTERS** | | |
| 1. Mount Vernon | Mt. Vernon | 329 |
| 2. Gallipolis | Gallipolis | 298 |
| 3. Apple Creek | Apple Creek | 276 |
| 4. Warrensville | Warrensville Twnshp. | 255 |
| 5. Tiffin | Tiffin | 220 |
| 6. Columbus | Columbus | 201 |
| 7. Northwest Ohio | Toledo | 170 |
| 8. Cambridge | Cambridge | 144 |
| 9. Youngstown | Mineral Ridge | 118 |
| 10. Southwest Ohio | Batavia | 112 |
| 11. Montgomery | Huber Heights | 104 |
| 12. Springview | Springfield | 90 |
| 13. Broadview | Broadview Heights | 84 |
| SUBTOTAL | | 2,401 |
| **SPECIAL UNITS** | | |
| 1. Central OH Psychiatric Hosp. | Columbus | 12 |
| 2. Pauline W. Lewis Center | Cincinnati | 12 |
| 3. Toledo Mental Health Center | Toledo | 9 |
| SUBTOTAL | | 33 |
| **TOTAL** | | **2,434** |

The Cleveland Developmental Center closed in 1988. Special MR/DD Units at Cambridge Mental Health Center and at Massillon Psychiatric Center closed in 1990, and units at Dayton Mental Health Center and Western Reserve Psychiatric Hospital in Cleveland closed in 1991.

*Community services* residential options of 7-15 beds included ICFs/MR serving 1,619 individuals and non-ICF/MR facilities which consisted of group homes (1,381 individuals served in 1992), family homes (66), and other homes (46). State funded residences of six beds or less included group homes serving 1,961 individuals, supported living (1,099), family homes (540), and other homes (45). Federal HCBS Waiver funding in 1992 consisted of the Individual Options Waiver ($1.5 million) and Ohio's OBRA 87 Waiver ($.2 million). *Other Title XIX program* federal funding consisted of targeted case management ($1.9 million) and day habilitation programs termed Community Alternative Funding Source (CAFS). The amount of CAFS federal Medicaid reimbursements, $10.5 and $14 million in 1988 and 1989, reflected retroactive funding due to a settlement between DMR/DD and the federal Health Care Financing Administration (HCFA). Federal CAFS funding was re-established January 1, 1992, with reimbursements totaling $14.9 million in fiscal year 1992.

*Local/county overmatch* funding consisting of "local effort" for "adult services," "infant services" "case management," "family resource services," and "residential services." These expenditures were listed by calendar year in the August 15, 1992, report of the Ohio Association of County Boards of MR/DD. Additional information on these data and other administrative records regarding the counties' local effort funding was provided by James Fabish and Charles Arndt of the Association.

Revenue, expenditure, and programmatic data for FYs 1989-92 were provided by Bob McDonald, Budget and Operations Office, DMR/DD. Data on the HCBS Waiver, the OBRA Waiver, Targeted Case Management, and Community Alternative Funding Source (CAFS) programs were provided by Mary Beth Wickerham, Administration, DMR/DD. Model 50/200 Waiver data were provided by Erin Higgins, Waiver Policy, Department of Human Services. Donna Wood, Office of Information Systems, DMR/DD, provided data on individuals served in large private and in community residential options. The data on average daily residents in private ICFs/MR of 16 beds or more and of 15 beds or less were the basis for estimating FYs 1989-92 expenditures for these settings. Per diem rates in 1989-92 were estimated to have increased at the rate of 5% per year since 1988. This method of estimation was confirmed by Lorin Ranbom and Harry Sax, Bureau of Facility Contracting and Audits, Office of Long Term Care, Department of Human Services. Dana Charlton and Linda Day, DMR/DD, provided information on supported living, and an explanation of trends in revenues and expenditures for Medicaid CAFS options. Revenues, expenditures, and average daily populations for the MR/DD units at mental health centers or hospitals were provided by Debra Miculka, Fiscal Planner, Fiscal Administration, Department of Mental Health.

**Oklahoma.** The principal state agency was the Developmental Disabilities Services Division, Department of Human Services. *Congregate 16+ beds* services consisted of 4 state centers and 24 large private ICFs/MR. The state centers and their average daily populations were Southern Oklahoma Resource Center (formerly Pauls Valley State School) (325), Northern Oklahoma Resource Center (formerly Enid State School) (251), Hissom Memorial Center, Sand Springs (227), and the Greer Center (36). Hissom closed in 1994. The Greer Center, a unit of the Northern Oklahoma Resource

Center, opened as an ICF/MR unit in 1990 for individuals with dual psychiatric and developmental disabilities diagnoses. An additional 16 beds were added in February, 1994.

*Community services* residences of six beds or less consisted of group homes (382 individuals served in 1992) and services for 475 individuals in foster homes and supported living. The supported living initiative primarily represented individualized options for former residents of the Hissom Memorial Center who were members of the *Homeward Bound* class action settlement. These 349 individual class members received substantial support to reside in their own apartments or homes. *Other Title XIX program* services consisted of day habilitation programs. All individuals receiving case management services were supported by the HCBS Waiver.

Revenue, expenditure, and programmatic data for 1989-92 were provided by David Goodell, Director of Administrative Services, and Priscilla Moore, DD Services Division. Four individuals served in nursing facilities in 1992, of the 1,763, were served in specialized (pediatric) settings.

**Oregon.** The principal state agency was Developmental Disability Services, Mental Health and Developmental Disability Services Division, Department of Human Resources. *Congregate 16+ beds* services consisted of two state facilities, large private ICFs/MR, and other large private residential services. State hospital and training centers and their average daily populations in 1992 were Fairview, in Salem (520), and Eastern Oregon, Pendelton (83).

*Community services* residential options included group homes of 7-15 beds serving 600 individuals in 1992 and group homes of 6 beds or less serving 1,249 individuals. Other 6-bed or less options in 1992 included semi-independent living (517 individuals served), non-relative foster care (477), and relative foster care (230). *General funds* (in 1992 only) included a local match for targeted case management services ($.34 thousand). *Other Title XIX program* funding consisted of targeted case management, serving 3,988 individuals in 1992.

Revenue, expenditure, and programmatic data for FYs 1989-92 were provided by Jack Morgan, Deputy, and Keith Baker, Office of Developmental Disability Services.

**Pennsylvania.** The principal state agency was the Office of Mental Retardation, Department of Public Welfare. *Congregate 16+ beds* services consisted of nine state developmental disabilities centers, three MR units in mental health facilities, large private ICFs/MR, and other large private settings called private living facilities (PLFs). The state centers and their average daily populations in 1992 were Polk Center (744), Selinsgrove Center (692), Ebensburg Center (473), White Haven Center (396), Western Center, in Canonsburg (360), Hamburg Center (348), Embreeville Center, Coatesville (235), Laurelton Center (210), Altoona Center (130), Mayview MR Unit, Bridgeville (78), Torrance MR Unit (71), and Somerset MR Unit (70). There have been 10 closures of state centers and MR units within mental health centers. Hollidaysburg Center and the Warren MR Unit closed in 1976; Cresson and Marcy Centers and the Harrisburg MR Unit closed in 1982; the Allentown and Wernersville MR Units and Pennhurst Center closed in 1988; the Philadelphia DD Unit closed in 1989; and Clarks Summit MR Unit closed in 1991.

*Community services* residential options consisted primarily of community living alternatives serving three or fewer individuals and 7-15 bed private ICFs/MR. Revenue, expenditure, and programmatic data for FYs 1989-92 were provided by Nancy Thaler, Deputy Secretary for Mental Retardation, and Mike Toth, OMR. Numbers of individuals with mental retardation and related conditions in nursing facilities were estimated by Phyllis Wellborn, OMR.

**Rhode Island.** The principal state agency was the Division of Retardation and Developmental Disabilities, Department of Mental Health, Retardation and Hospitals. *Congregate 16+ beds* services consisted of the Ladd Developmental Center, Exeter, serving 165 individuals in 1992. The Dix Building, Cranston, closed in 1990, and the Ladd Center closed in 1994.

Numbers of individuals served in *community services* residential options of 7-15 beds were estimated based on information from Division officials that there were 30 group homes averaging 10 beds each. Officials also estimated that there were 162 facilities and apartment options averaging 5 beds each. These small community residential options included "regular apartment" settings and 5-bed group homes funded by the Waiver; semi-independent apartments; semi-independent living; state-financed 5-bed community group homes; and adult family living. Funding categorized as *other Title*

*XIX program* funds included $122 thousand for targeted case management and $5.2 million in Medicaid reimbursements for day programs. Rhode Island ceased funding *small public ICFs/MR* in 1990. As one of the nation's first eight CSLA states, Rhode Island by 1995 had over 350 CSLA participants (*Community Services Reporter*, 1994b).

Revenue, expenditure, and programmatic data for 1989-92 were provided by Frank DiMaio, Administrator of Program Management, Division of Retardation and Developmental Disabilities.

**South Carolina.** The principal state agency was the Department of Disabilities and Special Needs. *Congregate 16+ beds* services consisted of four state regional centers and a large private ICF/MR. The state centers and their average daily populations in 1992 were: Whitten (formerly Piedmont Regional Center), in Clinton (877), Midlands, Columbia (501), Coastal, Ladson (298), Pee Dee, Florence (266), and (beginning in 1989) the Saleeby (125), Live Oak (48), and Clyde Street Units (20). The latter three centers' populations have been included prior to 1989 with the other four centers' populations. Live Oak, 10 miles from the Coastal Center, served older individuals with developmental disabilities. Clyde Street, also serving an older population, was adjacent to the Pee Dee Center in Florence. Saleeby served individuals with physical disabilities and medical needs, and was located in Hartsville, 20 miles from the Pee Dee Center. In 1989, one of two large private ICFs/MR operated by the Babcock Center was closed and individuals moved to six 8-bed ICFs/MR. The remaining large facility was the Pine Lake Center.

*Community services* residential options consisted of 76 eight-bed public ICFs/MR, 57 eight-bed private ICFs/MR, and services for 45 individuals in eight-bed group homes. Six bed or less options consisted of 2 four-bed public ICFs/MR, supervised apartments serving 651 individuals, community training homes (primarily single family homes) serving 254 individuals, and 1 six-bed group home. *Other Title XIX program* funding supported targeted case management, serving 9,782 individuals in 1992.

Revenue, expenditure, and programmatic data for FYs 1989-92 were provided by Bill Barfield, Budget Director, Department of Disabilities and Special Needs. Nancy Rumbaugh, Budget and Policy Analyst, provided data on individuals served in residential settings

of six beds or less. Jim Kirk, Deputy State Director, Fiscal Management, provided revised average daily population figures for 1977-79. The institutional average daily population data previously reported for those three years were 2,928, 2,704, and 3,015.

**South Dakota.** The principal state agency was the Division of Developmental Disabilities, Department of Human Services. *Congregate 16+ beds* services in 1992 consisted of two state developmental centers: Redfield serving 289 individuals and Custer serving 96 individuals. *Community services* residential options of six beds or less consisted of monitored apartments, supervised apartments, and individualized supported living. Options of 7-15 beds consisted of community residential facilities (CRFs).

Federal *Title XX/Social Services Block Grant* funding terminated in 1989. State *general funds* during 1990-92 supported these services previously financed by state/federal Title XX/SSBG funds, including prevocational, community living training, follow-along, and the Yankton Behavior Project. *Other state funds* in 1992 consisted of local school district matches for the children served in ICFs/MR ($.9 thousand), and the HCBS Waiver ($.6 million). The average monthly SSI/ADC amounts during 1988 to 1992 which were used to estimate Waiver participants' income maintenance payments/benefits were $315, $321, $335, $353, and $369. The number of HCBS participants used as the basis for calculating the income maintenance amount in 1992 was 842.

Revenue, expenditure, and programmatic data for 1989-92 were provided by Dr. Ed Campbell, Program Specialist Division of Developmental Disabilities.

**Tennessee.** The principal state agency was Mental Retardation Services, Department of Mental Health and Mental Retardation. *Congregate 16+ beds* services in 1992 consisted of five state developmental centers and large private ICFs/MR. The five state centers and their average daily populations were Greene Valley, in Greeneville (707), Clover Bottom, Donelson (557), Arlington (468), Nat T. Winston, Bolivar (145), and the Harold Jordan Habilitation Center, a secure MR unit at the Middle Tennessee Mental Health Institute, Nashville (37).

*Community services* residential options consisted of 7-15 bed private ICFs/MR, 8-bed group homes (including services to Waiver participants), and 6-bed or less options consisting of foster care serving 259 individuals in 1992 and semi-independent living supporting 195 individuals. *Other Title XIX program* funding consisted of Medicaid reimbursement for pre-admission screening and annual resident review (PASARR) activities mandated by federal nursing home reform legislation (P.L. 100-360, OBRA-87).

Revenue, expenditure, and programmatic data for FYs 1989-92 were provided by John Lewis, Director, MR Administrative Services.

**Texas.** The principal state agency was Mental Retardation Services, Texas Department of Mental Health/Mental Retardation (TDMH/MR). *Congregate 16+ beds* services consisted of thirteen state schools and two state centers. Table III-4 lists the state schools and centers in order of average daily population in 1992.

**TABLE III-4**
*Texas TDMH/MR State Schools and State Centers Ranked by Average Daily Population, 1992*

| Name | Location | Average Daily Population |
|------|----------|-------------------------|
| **DEVELOPMENTAL CENTERS** | | |
| 1. Mexia | Mexia | 740 |
| 2. Richmond | Richmond | 735 |
| 3. Abilene | Abilene | 721 |
| 4. Denton | Denton | 630 |
| 5. Travis | Austin | 582 |
| 6. Brenham | Brenham | 501 |
| 7. Lufkin | Lufkin | 494 |
| 8. Austin | Austin | 468 |
| 9. Lubbock | Lubbock | 429 |
| 10. San Angelo | Carlsbad | 425 |
| 11. Corpus Christi | Corpus Christi | 402 |
| 12. Fort Worth | Fort Worth | 342 |
| 13. San Antonio | San Antonio | 336 |
| SUBTOTAL | | 6,805 |
| | | |
| **STATE CENTERS** | | |
| 1. Rio Grande | Harlingen | 124 |
| 2. El Paso | El Paso | 112 |
| SUBTOTAL | | 236 |
| | | |
| **TOTAL** | | 7,041 |

Community services *other Title XIX program* funding during 1988-90 consisted of federal Medicaid funding for the "liaison worker program." Contractual Department of Human Services (DHS) personnel provided screening, evaluations, referrals, planning, follow-up, and other case coordination services. In 1990, $1.5 million classified as *other Title XIX program* funding con-

sisted of "liaison worker program" reimbursements, and the balance, $2.0 million, reimbursed targeted case management. All *Title XIX program* funds in 1991 and 1992 reimbursed targeted case management services. *Local/county overmatch* consisted of city, county, and other local tax funds supporting community mental retardation programs.

The biennium *Texas Legislative Budget* described funding for seven major components: (a) "program administration," (b) "state schools for the mentally retarded," (c) "state centers (mental retardation)," (d) "contracted community services (mental retardation)," (e) "home and community services," (f) "in-home and family support (mental retardation)," and (g) "state-wide client services." The *Texas Legislative Budget* (HB 1, 8/14/91) provided appropriations for FYs 1992-93. This state biennium period extended from September 1, 1991 to August 31, 1993.

Expenditure data, data on numbers of individuals served, and expenditure and programmatic data for special community initiatives during 1988-92 were provided by C.K. Roberts, Management Analysis, Don Henderson, Debbie Hankey, and Perry Young, TDMH/MR. Additional information on new developments in Texas was provided by Jaylon Fincannon, Deputy Commissioner for Mental Retardation, and Mark Johnston, *Lelsz* Coordinator, TDMH/MR.

**Utah.** The principal state agency was the Division of Services for People with Disabilities, Department of Human Services. *Congregate 16+ beds* services consisted of the Utah State Developmental Center in American Fork and large private ICFs/MR. *Community services* residences of 7-15 beds were group homes. Six bed or less options consisted of supervised apartments for 407 individuals in 1992 and supported living (also termed "apartment follow-along") for 156 individuals.

Adjusted community spending declined between 1988 and 1989 following a legislative mandate that small private ICFs/MR be closed and that residents transfer to state funding or to HCBS Waiver services. In addition, approximately $1.5 million in federal and state Title XX/SSBG funds were rebudgeted in 1988 to the state health department for federally mandated Part H early intervention services.

Revenue, expenditure, and programmatic data for FYs 1989-92 were provided by Dr. Ric Zaharia, Director, and Jodie Becker, Division of Services for People with Disabilities, Department of Human Services. Data on individuals with mental retardation and related conditions served in nursing facilities were provided by Deborah Wynkoop Green, Director, Bureau of Licensure, Department of Health.

**Vermont.** The principal state agency was the Division of Mental Retardation, Department of Mental Health and Mental Retardation, Agency of Human Services. *Congregate 16+ beds* services in 1992 consisted of Brandon Training School. Brandon closed on November 17, 1993. *Community services* residential options were all six beds or less. These included developmental homes serving 402 individuals in 1992, supervised apartments, staffed apartments, and small group homes. *Other Title XIX program* funding supported day programs, targeted case management, and social support. In 1992, 477 individuals received targeted case management, 267 received HCBS Waiver case management, and 166 received state-funded case management services.

Revenue, expenditure, and programmatic data for FYs 1989-92 were provided by Brenda Carey, Mark Davis, and June Bascom, Division of Mental Retardation. Joe Carlomagno provided data on supported employment. Clair McFadden, PASARR Coordinator, Division of Medicaid Services, provided information about individuals with mental retardation and related conditions in nursing homes.

**Virginia.** The principal state agency was the Office of Mental Retardation Services, Department of Mental Health, Mental Retardation, and Substance Abuse (DMH/MR/SA). *Congregate 16+ beds* services in 1992 consisted of five Virginia Training Centers (VTCs) and three large private ICFs/MR. The training centers and their average daily populations were Central, in Lynchburg (1,200), Southside, Petersburg (649), Northern, Fairfax (282), Southwestern, Hillsville (222), and Southeastern, Chesapeake (201).

*Community services* residential options of 7-15 beds consisted of group homes. Six bed or less options consisted of supervised apartments serving 208 individuals in 1992, sponsored placements serving 96 individuals, and domiciliary care serving 75 individuals. *Local/county overmatch* funds consisted of city and county dollars received by Community Services Boards. *Other Title XIX program* funding during 1986-90 supported case management, sheltered employment, work activ-

ity, early intervention, and intensive treatment and training. Targeted case management was supported with small amounts ($1.2 thousand and $31.4 thousand) of *Title XIX program* funds in 1989-90. By 1991 and 1992 all *Title XIX program* funding for individuals with mental retardation supported targeted case management.

Revenue, expenditure, and programmatic data for 1989-92 were provided by Paul Gilding, Central Office, by Boyd Newlin, Office of Finance and Administration, by Saundra Rollins, OBRA Coordinator, and by Shirley Ricks and Dorothy Ragsdale, Office of Mental Retardation, DMH/MR/SA. Linda Veldheer and Dr. Soosan Shahrokh, Senior Economist, Department of Medical Assistance Services, provided small and large private ICF/MR expenditure data and data on numbers of individuals served. Charlene Davidson, DMH/MR/SA, provided information about 759 individuals with mental retardation and 261 individuals with related conditions residing in nursing facilities in 1992.

**Washington.** The principal state agency was the Division of Developmental Disabilities, Department of Social and Health Services. *Congregate 16+ beds* services in 1992 consisted of six state schools, large private ICFs/MR and large private group homes of 16 beds or more. The state schools and their average daily populations in 1992 were Rainier, in Buckley (473), Fircrest, Seattle (403), Lakeland Village, Medical Lake (311), Yakima Valley, Selah (130), Interlake, Medical Lake (125), and Frances Haddon Morgan, Bremerton (56). The 192 individuals in 1992 who were served in the larger group homes were funded by the Division of Aging and Adult Services under their category of congregate care. Expenditures are not included within the financial profile.

*Community services* residential options of six beds or less consisted of group homes (164 individuals served in 1992), intensive tenant support (999), alternative living (558), tenant support (385), supportive living (159), and state operated living alternatives (SOLA) (71). HCBS Waiver reimbursements in 1992 included $1.6 million for the OBRA 87 Waiver. *Other Title XIX program* services consisted of day programs and medical/dental services.

Revenue, expenditure, and programmatic data for FYs 1989-92 were provided by Sue Elliot, Director, Division of Developmental Disabilities. Ron Sherman, Program

Financial Manager, and Jean Lewis, Division of DD, provided additional data on funding sources for specific program areas and data on individuals served in institutional services and in community residences.

**West Virginia.** The principal state agency was the Developmental Disabilities Division, Office of Behavioral Health Services, Bureau of Human Resources, Department of Health and Human Services. *Congregate 16+ beds* services consisted of one state-owned and staffed, but privately managed, facility: the Colin Anderson Center in St. Mary's. There also were three large private ICFs/MR (Greenbriar, Green Acres, and Potomac). The management of Greenbriar in Lewisburg was transferred from the state to a private agency, VOCA, on 8/1/90 and the facility closed on 12/31/93 as a result of an amendment to the 1983 court decree in *Hartley et al. v. Matin et al.* The Weston Hospital DD Unit closed in 1988, and Spencer Hospital DD Unit closed in 1989. The Green Acres and Potomac ICFs/MR began operation in 1984.

Community services *local/county overmatch* funding in 1992 consisted local funding raised by a "provider enhancement tax" constituting 23% of the state/federal reimbursement for Medicaid clinic, day, and other programs Federal *other Title XIX program* funding consisted of clinic services and day treatment ($5.1 million federal funding in 1992), personal assistance services ($1.6 million), and targeted case management ($.9 million). Medicaid targeted case management served 3,571 in 1992, three-quarters of the total served in case management in West Virginia.

Revenue, expenditure, and programmatic data for 1989-92 were provided by Steve Wiseman, Director, by Charles Harmon, and by Mark Hanna, Developmental Disabilities Division, Office of Behavioral Health Services.

**Wisconsin.** The principal state agency was the Bureau of Developmental Disability Services, Department of Health and Social Services (DHSS). *Congregate 16+ beds* services in 1992 consisted of three centers for the developmentally disabled, large private ICFs/MR, and child caring institutions. The three centers and their average daily populations were: Central Center, Madison (571), Southern Center, Union Grove (549), and Northern Center, Chippewa Falls (461). The large private ICFs/MR included county facilities serving approximately one thousand individuals.

*Community services* residential options were predominately six beds or less. These consisted of "supportive: other settings" (1,419 individuals served in 1992), "supportive: supervised apartments" (375), adult family homes (1,209), adult group homes (1,342), child group homes (39), child foster homes (130), CSLA and other supported living (631), and room and board home support (321). Community residences of 7-15 beds included group homes (736) and apartment options serving nine or more individuals. *Other Title XIX program* funding during 1988-91 consisted of targeted case management. In 1992, $2.8 million consisted of targeted case management reimbursement, and the balance, $71 thousand, constituted CSLA reimbursement. There were over 250 CSLA participants by June, 1994 (*Community Services Reporter*, 1994b). *Other federal funds* consisted of Title I education funds and federal vocational rehabilitation funding for supported employment.

Wisconsin had strong county participation in the delivery of services and supports for individuals with developmental disabilities. State statutes mandated county human services departments (HSD) and county departments of social services (DSS). To construct the financial profile, project staff used data provided by Steve Stanek, Wisconsin Council on Developmental Disabilities. Most of these data were provided on a spreadsheet entitled *Statewide 51/HSD DD Budget/Utilization Data 1986-92: Plan and Budget Data from the Annual County DD Data Form Reports to the Council.* The 23 "51/HSD DD Budget" line items on the Council's spreadsheet were the counties' "budgeted" data during 1986-92. It was therefore necessary for project staff to estimate expenditures by increasing each line item by a factor corresponding to the annual increases in the total 51/HSD/DSS expenditures. *Local/county overmatch* data were estimated by Steve Stanek for 1991 and 1992; data for 1989 and 1990 were determined by interpolation (equal annual increments between the 1991 figure and the 1988 figure determined in the previous study). *Other state funds,* consisting of the county match to 51/HSD "state aid" funding, was estimated in the same manner.

In addition to the data summarized above, Steve Stanek provided data on the individuals served in community residences of various sizes in 1992. Data on large and small private ICFs/MR were provided by Tom Swant and Eileen Mallow, Bureau of Health Care Planning,

Wisconsin Medical Assistance Program. Tim Mero, Division of Care and Treatment Facilities, DHSS, provided revenue, expenditure, average daily population and full-time equivalent staff data for the three state centers. Title I education fund data were provided by Donna Miller, Special Education Coordinator, Chapter 1 Programs, DHSS, and federal vocational rehabilitation funds data were provided by Sandy Hall, Division of Vocational Rehabilitation. Beverly Doherty, Family Support Coordinator, Division of Community Services, provided data on family support. Robin Cooper, Division of Community Services, provided data on CSLA, the HCBS Waiver, and background information on other community programs. Barbara Loftus, Bureau of Long Term Support, provided data on targeted case management.

**Wyoming.** The principal state agency was the Division of Developmental Disabilities, Wyoming Department of Health. *Congregate 16+ beds* services in 1992 consisted of the Wyoming State Training School in Lander. *Community services* residential options of six beds or less consisted of group homes and supported living for 207 individuals.

Revenue, expenditure, and programmatic data for FYs 1989-92 were provided by Dr. Jon Fortune, Adult Developmental Disabilities Consultant, Department of Health. Additional data on Wyoming State Training School were provided by Cliff Mikesell, Deputy Superintendent. Data on individuals with mental retardation and related conditions in nursing facilities were provided by George Crouch, Division of Health Care Financing, Department of Health.

**United States.** The data for the United States consist of the aggregated totals for the 50 states and the District of Columbia, with two exceptions. Numbers of individuals with mental retardation and related conditions served in nursing facilities during 1989-1991 were not available for many states. Project staff therefore imputed these data on a state-by-state basis by using equal annual increments between available data points. These interpolated values were then included in the aggregated United States totals.

Second, the single bar chart extending from the pie chart on the first page of the United States profile presents the proportion of total congregate (16+ beds) spending contributed by federal/state large private ICFs/MR. The aggregated U.S. amount for the states which funded these settings was determined by a) totaling each state's federal large private ICF/MR reimbursement; and b) totaling each state's state/local match as imputed according to the state's federal medical assistance percentage (FMAP). This produced a weighted average national FMAP rate for large private ICFs/MR of 59.04%.

The weighted national FMAP rates for the other Medicaid programs in fiscal year 1992 were state institutional ICFs/MR (57.81%), small public ICFs/MR (51.89%), small private ICFs/MR (57.21%), HCBS Waiver (56.76%), and other Title XIX programs (53.45%). The weighted FMAP nationally for all Medicaid programs serving individuals with mental retardation/developmental disabilities was 57.09%.

# REFERENCES

Bachelder, L., & Braddock, D. (1994, April). *Socialization practices and staff turnover in community homes for people with developmental disabilities.* Chicago: University of Illinois at Chicago, Institute on Disability and Human Development.

Bahl, R. (1982). Fiscal health of state and local governments: 1982 and beyond. *Public Budgeting and Finance, 2,* 5-21.

Bauer, L., & Smith, G. (1993). Community living for the developmentally disabled. *State Legislative Report (An information service of the National Conference of State Legislatures), 18*(12), 1-6.

Braddock, D. (1981). Deinstitutionalization of the retarded: Trends in public policy. *Hospital and Community Psychiatry, 32,* 607-615.

Braddock, D., & Bachelder, L. (1992). *An analysis of recent trends in West Virginia's service system for people with developmental disabilities.* Charleston, WV: West Virginia Developmental Disabilities Planning Council.

Braddock, D., & Fujiura, G.T. (1987a). State government financial effort in mental retardation. *American Journal of Mental Deficiency, 91,* 450-459.

Braddock, D., & Fujiura, G.T. (1987b). *Political and economic determinants of MR/DD spending in the states.* Paper presented at the annual meeting of the American Association on Mental Retardation, Los Angeles, California.

Braddock, D., & Fujiura, G.T. (1991). Politics, public policy, and the development of community mental retardation services in the United States. *American Journal on Mental Retardation, 95,* 369-387.

Braddock, D., & Heller, T. (1985). The closure of mental retardation institutions I: Trends in the United States. *Mental Retardation, 23,* 168-176.

Braddock D., & Hemp, R. (1993). *The allocation of resources for persons with developmental disabilities in Maryland: A report prepared for the Maryland State Planning Council on Developmental Disabilities.* Chicago: The University of Illinois at Chicago.

Braddock, D., Hemp, R., & Fujiura, G.T. (1986). *Public expenditures for mental retardation and developmental disabilities in the United States: State profiles* (Working Paper, 2nd Ed.). Chicago: University of Illinois at Chicago, Institute for the Study of Developmental Disabilities.

Braddock, D., Hemp, R., & Fujiura, G.T. (1987). National study of public spending for mental retardation and developmental disabilities. *American Journal of Mental Deficiency, 92,* 121-133.

Braddock, D., Hemp, R., Fujiura, G.T., Bachelder, L., & Mitchell, D. (1990). *The state of the states in developmental disabilities.* Baltimore: Paul H. Brookes Publishing Company.

Braddock, D., Hemp, R., & Howes, R. (1984). *Public expenditures for mental retardation and developmental disabilities in the United States: State profiles* (Working Paper, 1st Ed.). Chicago: University of Illinois at Chicago, Institute for the Study of Developmental Disabilities.

Bureau of Economic Analysis. (1987a). *Business statistics.* Washington, DC: U. S. Department of Commerce.

Bureau of Economic Analysis. (1987b). Table 1. *Survey of Current Business, 67*(7), 130-133.

Bureau of Economic Analysis. (1988a). Table 1. *Survey of Current Business, 68*(4), 72-73.

Bureau of Economic Analysis. (1988b). Table 7.4. *Survey of Current Business, 68*(7), 90.

Bureau of Economic Analysis. (1988c). Table 1. *Survey of Current Business, 68*(10), 25.

Bureau of Economic Analysis. (1989). Table 7.4. *Survey of Current Business, 69*(5), 15.

Bureau of Economic Analysis. (1993). Table 7.1. *Survey of Current Business, 73*(5), 19.

Caiden, N. (1978) *Collection of data on public expenditures for care of the mentally disabled.* (Memorandum prepared for Commission on the Mentally Disabled). Washington, DC: American Bar Association, Division of Public Service Activities.

*Community Services Reporter.* (1994a). Community Supported Living Arrangements: An update. *Reporter, 1*(1), 6. (Published by the National Association of State Directors of Developmental Disabilities Services, in collaboration with the University of Minnesota and University of Illinois at Chicago UAPs).

*Community Services Reporter.* (1994b). CSLA update... *Reporter, 1*(6), 8.

Consortium for Citizens with Disabilities -- CCD. (1991, October). *Recommended federal policy directions on personal assistance services for Americans with disabilities (draft position paper).* Washington: CCD Task Force on Personal Assistance Services.

Cyert, R.M., & March, J.G. (1963). *A behavioral theory of the firm.* Englewood Cliffs, NJ: Prentice Hall.

Department of Fiscal Services. (1990). *Review of service needs and costs in community and institutional programs.* Annapolis, MD: Maryland Developmental Disabilities Administration.

Dye, T. (1966). *Politics, economics, and the public.* Chicago: Rand McNally.

Dye, T., & Robey, J.S. (1980). Politics versus economics: Development of the literature on policy determination. In T.R. Dye & V. Gray (Eds.), *The determinants of public policy.* Lexington, MA: D.C. Heath and Company.

Epple, W.A., Jacobson, J.W., & Janicki, M.P. (1985). Staffing ratios in public institutions for persons with mental retardation in the United States. *Mental Retardation, 23,* 115-124.

Fabricant, S. (1952). *The trend of government activity in the United States since 1900.* New York: National Bureau of Economic Research.

Fujiura, G.T., Garza, J., & Braddock, D. (1990). *National survey of family support services in developmental disabilities.* Chicago: University of Illinois at Chicago, University Affiliated Program in Developmental Disabilities.

Gray, V. (1973). Innovation in the states: A diffusion study. *The American Political Science Review, 67,* 1174-1185.

Hemp, R. (1994). State agency and community provider perspectives on financing community services. In M.F. Hayden and B. Abery (Eds.), *Challenges for a service system in transition: Ensuring quality community experiences for persons with developmental disabilities,* 265-288. Baltimore: Paul H. Brookes Publishing Company.

Herr, S.S. (1983). *Rights and advocacy for retarded people.* Lexington, MA: D.C. Heath and Company.

Hofferbert, R.I. (1972). State and community policy studies: A review of comparative input-output analyses. In J.A.

Robinson (Ed.), *Political science annual: An international review (Vol. 3).* Indianapolis: Bobbs-Merrill Company.

Horowitz, A.R. (1968). A simultaneous equation approach to the problem of explaining interstate differences in state and local expenditures. *The Southern Economic Journal, 34,* 459-476.

Karan, O.C., Furey, E.M., & Granfield, J.M. (1991). *How University Affiliated Programs (UAPs) can contribute to supported living: The Connecticut experience.* East Hartford, CT: The A.J. Pappanikou Center on Special Education and Rehabilitation, A University Affiliated Program.

Karan, O.C., Granfield, J.M., & Furey, E.M. (1992). Supported living: Rethinking the rules of residential services. *AAMR News and Notes, 5*(1), 5.

Kennedy, M.J. (1990). What quality assurance means to me: Expectations of consumers. In V.J. Bradley and H.A. Bersani (Eds.), *Quality assurance for individuals with developmental disabilities: It's everybody's business.* Baltimore: Paul H. Brookes, 35-45.

Key, V.O., Jr. (1949) *Southern politics in state and nation.* New York: Knopf.

Lakin, K.C. (1979). *Demographic studies of residential facilities for mentally retarded people: A historical review of methodologies and findings.* Minneapolis: University of Minneosta, Center for Residential and Community Services.

Lakin, K.C., & Stehly, C. (1990). Supported community living: From community facilities to homes in the community. *DD Network News, 3* (3), 1-3.

Larson, S.A., Hewitt, A., & Lakin, K.C. (1994). Residential services personnel: recruitment, training, and retention. In M.F. Hayden and B. Abery (Eds.), *Community living for persons with mental retardation and related conditions,* 313-341. Baltimore: Paul H. Brookes Publishing Company.

Leavitt, H.J. (1975). Suppose we took groups seriously? In E.L. Cass and F.G. Zimmer (Eds.), *Man and work in society* (pp. 67-77). New York: Van Nostrand Reinhold.

Lepore, R. (1992). *Position paper regarding the expansion of supported living services (Memorandum to District Developmental Services Program Administrators Supported Living Technical Assistance Team).* Tallahassee: State of Florida Department of Health and Rehabilitative Services.

Longhurst, N. (1994). *The self-advocacy movement by persons with developmental disabilities: A demographic study and directory of groups in the United Sates.* Washington, DC, and Chicago: American Association on Mental Retardation, in cooperation with People First of Illinois and the Institute on Disability and Human Development (UAP).

Mitchell, D., & Braddock, D., (1993). Compensation and turnover of direct care staff in developmental disabilities residential facilities in the United States. I: Wages and Benefits. *Mental Retardation, 31*(6), 429-437.

Pittsley, R. (1990). North Dakota: Individualized supported living arrangement. *DD Network News, 3*(3), 7,8.

Racino, J.A., & Taylor, S.J. (1993). "People first": Approaches to housing and support. In J.A. Racino, P. Walker, S. O'Connor, & S.J. Taylor (Eds.), *Housing, support, and community: Choices and strategies for adults with disabilities,* 33-56. Baltimore: Paul H. Brookes.

Savage, R.L. (1978). Policy innovativeness as a trait of American states. *Journal of Politics, 40,* 212-224.

Smith, G.A. (1990). *Supported living: New directions in services to people with developmental disabilities.* Alexandria, VA: National Association of State Mental Retardation Program Directors.

Smith, G.A., & Gettings, R.M. (1992). *Medicaid in the community: The HCBS Waiver and CSLA programs.* Alexandria, VA: National Association of State Mental Retardation Program Directors.

Smith, G.A., & Gettings, R.M. (1993, May). *Medicaid's ICF/MR program: Present status and recent trends.* Alexandria, VA: National Association of State Directors of Developmental Disabilities Services.

Smith, M.F. (1993). Medicaid services for persons with developmental disabilities (Appendix D). In *Medicaid source book: Background data and analysis (A 1993 update),* 861-912. Washington, DC: Congressional Research Service, for the Subcommittee on Health and the Environment, Committee on Energy and Commerce, U.S. House of Representatives.

Smull, M. (1989). *Crisis in the community.* Baltimore: University of Maryland at Baltimore, Applied Research and Evaluation Unit, Department of Pediatrics, School of Medicine.

Smull, M. (1993). As we are learning about support... *AAMR News & Note, 6*(6), 6.

U.S. Bureau of the Census. (1993). *Statistical abstract of the United States: 1993 (113th Ed.).* Washington, DC: U.S. Government Printing Office.

Walker, J.L. (1969). The diffusion of innovation among the American states. *American Political Science Review, 63,* 880-899.

Wildavsky, A. (1974). *The politics of the budgetary process.* (2nd ed.) Boston: Little, Brown.

Winer, B.J. (1971). *Statistical principles in experimental design.* New York: McGraw-Hill.

# STATE OFFICIALS PROVIDING DATA FOR THE STUDY

| STATE | NAME, TITLE | DIVISION, OFFICE, BUREAU | DEPARTMENT |
|---|---|---|---|
| Alabama | Vince Campbell | Division of MR[1] | Department of MH[2]/MR |
| | Jack Gifford | Division of MR | Department of MH/MR |
| | Ray Owens | Division of MR | Department of MH/MR |
| Alaska | Diana Ray, DD[3] Project Assistant | DD Central Office, Division of MH | Department of Health and Social Services |
| | Stephanie Waldon | DD Central Office, Division of MH | Department of Health and Social Services |
| Arizona | Brian Lensch, Director | DD Division | Department of Economic Security |
| | Mark Loudenslagel | Budget Section | Department of Economic Security |
| Arkansas | Dennis Bonge | DD Division | Department of Human Services |
| | Donna Madden, Director's Office | DD Division | Department of Human Services |
| | Mike McCreight, Director | DD Division | Department of Human Services |
| | Judy Routon | DD Division | Department of Human Services |
| | Wilma Stuart | | Developmental Disabilities Council |
| California | Paul Carleton, Deputy Director | Administration Division | Department of Developmental Services |
| | Dr. Beverly Lozano | Information Systems | Department of Developmental Services |
| | Dr. Roberta Marlowe, Chief | Information Systems | Department of Developmental Services |
| Colorado | Lynn Struxness, Data Mgt. Section | Division for DD | Department of Institutions |
| Connecticut | Debbie Jo Garcia | Medicaid Policy | Department of Income Maintenance |
| | Lawrence Johnson | Management Information Group | Department of Mental Retardation |
| Delaware | Dr. Henry Brown | Division of MR | Department of Health and Social Services |
| DC | Eric Bost | MR/DD Administration | Department of Human Services |
| | Charles Howard | MR/DD Administration | Department of Human Services |
| Florida | Gail Harper, Program Manager | DD Program Office | Department of Health and Rehabilitative Services |
| | Richard Lepore, Assistant Secretary | Developmental Services | Department of Health and Rehabilitative Services |
| | Susan Matus | DD Program Office | Department of Health and Rehabilitative Services |
| | John Obrzut | DD Program Office | Department of Health and Rehabilitative Services |
| | Robbie Olmstead | Medicaid Office | Department of Health and Rehabilitative Services |
| Georgia | Jack Schmitt | Division of MH/MR and SA[4] | Department of Human Resources |
| Hawaii | David Kanno | DD Division | Department of Health |
| | Stanley Yee, Chief | DD Division | Department of Health |
| Idaho | Dr. Paul Swatsenbarg, Director | Bureau of DD | Department of Health and Welfare |
| Illinois | Dr. David Brooks, Chief | Office of Disability Services | Department of Public Aid |
| | John Budny, Planning and Program Dev. | Division of DD | Department of Mental Health/DD |
| | Ray Carmody | Office of Disability Services | Department of Public Aid |
| | Lynn Handy, Deputy Director | Division of DD | Department of Mental Health/DD |
| | Marie Havens | Division of DD | Department of Mental Health/DD |
| | Joe Rachunas | Division of DD | Department of Mental Health/DD |
| Indiana | Ann January, Family & Social Services | Division of MH | Department on Aging and Rehabilitation Services |
| | Nancy Swaim | Division of MH | Department on Aging and Rehabilitation Services |
| | John Viernes, Jr., Director | Division of MH | Department on Aging and Rehabilitation Services |
| | Carol Warner | Division of MH | Department on Aging and Rehabilitation Services |
| Iowa | Larry Allen, MR/DD Services | Division of MH/MR/DD | Department of Human Services |
| | Charles M. Palmer, Director | | Department of Human Services |
| Kansas | Larry Sherraden, Information Resources | MH and Retardation Services | Department of Social and Rehabilitation Services |
| Kentucky | Judy Knowles | Division of MR | Dept. for MH and MR, Cabinet for Human Resources |
| Louisiana | Susan Bowman, Assistant Secretary | Office for Citizens with DD | Department of Health and Hospitals |
| | William Payne, Jr., Fiscal Services | Office of Human Services | Department of Health and Hospitals |
| | Alma Stewart, Director, Adult & Family Serv. | Office for Citizens with DD | Department of Health and Hospitals |

*Abbreviations:* [1] *MR: Mental Retardation;* [2] *MH: Mental Health;* [3] *DD: Developmental Disability;* [4] *SA: Substance Abuse*

| STATE | NAME, TITLE | DIVISION, OFFICE, BUREAU | DEPARTMENT |
|---|---|---|---|
| Maine | Mary Crichton | Division of MR | Department of Mental Health and Mental Retardation |
| | Kathryn McKimmy, Resource Dev. Manager | Division of MR | Department of Mental Health and Mental Retardation |
| | Pete Thibodeaux, Resource Dev. Manager | Bureau of MR | Department of Mental Health and Mental Retardation |
| Maryland | Diane Bolger | DD Administration | Department of Health and Mental Hygiene |
| | Hal Franklin, Assistant Director | DD Administration | Department of Health and Mental Hygiene |
| | Randy Greenwald | Budget Management Office | Department of Health and Mental Hygiene |
| | Connie Holloway, PASARR Coordinator | DD Administration | Department of Health and Mental Hygiene |
| | James Johnson, Chief | Budget Management Office | Department of Health and Mental Hygiene |
| | Joseph Millstone, Director | Medical Care Policy Administration | Department of Health and Mental Hygiene |
| | Charles Spannare, Assistant Director | DD Administration | Department of Health and Mental Hygiene |
| | Bill Wacker, Chief, Planning & Statistics Div. | DD Administration | Department of Health and Mental Hygiene |
| | Kathleen Wolf, Deputy Director | DD Administration | Department of Health and Mental Hygiene |
| Massachusetts | Mary Cerreto, Assistant Commissioner | | Department of Mental Retardation |
| | Mary Fratto | Community Programs | Department of Mental Retardation |
| | Ruth Saldinger | | Department of Mental Retardation |
| Michigan | Morris Hickman | Budget Section | Department of Mental Health |
| | Marilyn Hill | Office of Federal Liaison/Entitlements | Department of Mental Health |
| Minnesota | Dr. Jim Franczyk, Director | Research, Evaluation & Planning | Department of Human Services |
| | Shirley Patterson, Director | Division for Persons with DD | Department of Human Services |
| Mississippi | Roger McMurtry, Director | Bureau of MR | Department of Mental Health |
| Missouri | John Bright | Division of MR/DD | Department of Mental Health |
| | Joann Leykam, Director | Division of MR/DD | Department of Mental Health |
| Montana | Mike Hanshew, Administrator | DD Division | Department of Social Services |
| | Janice Risch | DD Division | Department of Social Services |
| | Fritz Roos | DD Division | Department of Social Services |
| Nebraska | Jim Hanlon | Office of MR | Department of Public Institutions |
| | Jackie Miller | Office of MR | Department of Public Institutions |
| | Mary Steiner | | Department of Social Services |
| Nevada | Jean Laird | Division of MH/MR | Department of Human Resources |
| | David Luke, Administrator for MR | Division of MH/MR | Department of Human Resources |
| | Jean Wilcher | Division of MH/MR | Department of Human Resources |
| New Hampshire | Dan Van Keuren, Program Analysis Unit | Division of MH and Dev. Services | Department of MH and Developmental Services |
| New Jersey | Lee Birkey | Division of DD | Department of Human Services |
| | Angie Kamerdze, Planning & Operation Supp. | Division of DD | Department of Human Services |
| | Beth Gnozzio | Division of DD | Department of Human Services |
| | Tom Major | Division of DD | Department of Human Services |
| | Ernest Rogers | Division of Medical Assistance | Department of Human Services |
| New Mexico | Steve Dossey, Chief, Mgt. Services | Behavioral Health Services Division | Health and the Environment Department |
| New York | Paul Audino, Admin. & Revenue Supp. | Budget and Fiscal Services | Office of MR/DD |
| | Bob Coyner, Chief Budgeting Analyst | Budget and Fiscal Services | Office of MR/DD |
| | Mary Edmonds | Information Services Group | Office of MR/DD |
| | Diane Sklaryk | | Office of MR/DD |
| | Tom Richards | | Office of MR/DD |
| | John Smith | Bureau of Budget Planning & Alloc. | Office of MR/DD |
| | Bob Welch | | Department of Health |
| North Carolina | Jim Barnhill | Division of Medical Assistance | Department of Human Resources |
| | Janne E. Harris, Assistant Chief, DD | Division of MH/MR/SA | Department of Human Resources |
| | Lee Hoffman | Division of Facility Services | Department of Human Resources |
| | Richard Parker, Developmental Disabilities | Division of MH/MR/SA | Department of Human Resources |
| | Patsy Slaughter | Division of Medical Assistance | Department of Human Resources |

| STATE | NAME, TITLE | DIVISION, OFFICE, BUREAU | DEPARTMENT |
|---|---|---|---|
| **North Dakota** | Robert Graham | DD Division | Department of Human Services |
| | Sandi Noble, Director | DD Division | Department of Human Services |
| **Ohio** | Charles Arndt | | Ohio Assn. of County Boards of MR/DD |
| | Dana Charlton | | Department of MR/DD |
| | Linda Day | | Department of MR/DD |
| | James Fabish | | Ohio Assn. of County Boards of MR/DD |
| | Erin Higgins | Waiver Policy | Department of Human Services |
| | Bob McDonald | Budget & Operations Office | Department of MR/DD |
| | Debra Miculka, Fiscal Planner | Fiscal Administration | Department of Mental Health |
| | Lorin Ranbom, Fac. Contracting & Audits | Office of Long Term Care | Department of Human Services |
| | Harry Sax | Office of Long Term Care | Department of Human Services |
| | Mary Beth Wickerham | Administration | Department of MR/DD |
| | Donna Wood | Office of Information Systems | Department of MR/DD |
| **Oklahoma** | David Goodell, Dir. of Admin. Services | DD Services Division | Department of Human Services |
| | Priscilla Moore | DD Services Division | Department of Human Services |
| **Oregon** | Keith Baker, DD Services | MH/DD Services Division | Department of Human Resources |
| | Jack Morgan, Deputy, DD Services | MH/DD Services Division | Department of Human Resources |
| **Pennsylvania** | Nancy Thaler, Deputy Secretary | Office of Mental Retardation | Department of Public Welfare |
| | Mike Toth | Office of Mental Retardation | Department of Public Welfare |
| | Phyllis Wellborn | Office of Mental Retardation | Department of Public Welfare |
| **Rhode Island** | Frank DiMaio, Administrator of Pgm. Mgt. | Division of Retardation/DD | Department of MH, Retardation and Hospitals |
| **South Carolina** | Bill Barfield, Budget Director | | Department of Disabilities and Special Needs |
| | Jim Kirk, Deputy State Director | Fiscal Management | Department of Disabilities and Special Needs |
| | Nancy Rumbaugh, Budget & Policy Analyst | Fiscal Management | Department of Disabilities and Special Needs |
| **South Dakota** | Dr. Ed Campbell, Program Specialist | Division of DD | Department of Human Services |
| **Tennessee** | John Lewis, Director, Admin. Services | Mental Retardation Services | Department of Mental Health and Mental Retardation |
| **Texas** | Jaylon Fincannon, Deputy Commissioner | Mental Retardation Services | Department of Mental Health and Mental Retardation |
| | Debbie Hankey | | Department of Mental Health and Mental Retardation |
| | Don Henderson | | Department of Mental Health and Mental Retardation |
| | Mark Johnston, *Lelsz* Coordinator | | Department of Mental Health and Mental Retardation |
| | C.K. Roberts | Management Analysis | Department of Mental Health and Mental Retardation |
| | Perry Young | | Department of Mental Health and Mental Retardation |
| **Utah** | Jodie Becker | Serv. for People with Disabilities | Department of Human Services |
| | Deborah Wynkoop Green, Director | Bureau of Licensure | Department of Health |
| | Dr. Ric Zaharia, Director | Serv. for People with Disabilities | Department of Human Services |
| **Vermont** | June Bascom | Division of MR | Department of Mental Health and Mental Retardation |
| | Brenda Carey | Division of MR | Department of Mental Health and Mental Retardation |
| | Joe Carlomagno | Division of MR | Department of Mental Health and Mental Retardation |
| | Mark David | Division of MR | Department of Mental Health and Mental Retardation |
| | Clair McFadden, PASARR Coordinator | Division of Medicaid Services | Agency of Human Services |
| **Virginia** | Charlene Davidson | Office of Mental Retardation | Department of MH/MR and SA |
| | Paul Gilding | Central Office | Department of MH/MR and SA |
| | Boyd Newlin | Office of Finance & Administration | Department of MH/MR and SA |
| | Dorothy Ragsdale | Office of Mental Retardation | Department of MH/MR and SA |
| | Shirley Ricks | Office of Mental Retardation | Department of MH/MR and SA |
| | Saundra Rollins | Office of Mental Retardation | Department of MH/MR and SA |
| | Dr. Soosan Shahrokh, Senior Economist | | Department of Medical Assistance Services |
| | Linda Veldheer | | Department of Medical Assistance Services |
| **Washington** | Sue Elliot, Director | Division of DD | Department of Social and Health Services |
| | Jean Lewis | Division of DD | Department of Social and Health Services |
| | Ron Sherman, Program Financial Manager | Division of DD | Department of Social and Health Services |

| STATE | NAME, TITLE | DIVISION, OFFICE, BUREAU | DEPARTMENT |
|---|---|---|---|
| **West Virginia** | Mark Hanna, DD Division | Office of Behavioral Health Serv. | Bur. of Human Res., Dept. of Health & Human Serv. |
| | Charles Harmon, DD Division | Office of Behavioral Health Serv. | Bur. of Human Res., Dept. of Health & Human Serv. |
| | Steve Wiseman, Director, DD Division | Office of Behavioral Health Serv. | Bur. of Human Res., Dept. of Health & Human Serv. |
| **Wisconsin** | Robin Cooper, Division of Community Services | Bureau of DD Services | Department of Health and Social Services |
| | Beverly Doherty, Division of Community Serv. | Bureau of DD Services | Department of Health and Social Services |
| | Barbara Loftus | Bureau of Long Term Support | Department of Health and Social Services |
| | Eileen Mallow, Bureau of Health Care Planning | Medical Assistance Program | Department of Health and Social Services |
| | Tim Mero | Div. of Care & Treatment Facilities | Department of Health and Social Services |
| | Donna Miller, Special Education Coordinator | Title I Programs | Department of Health and Social Services |
| | Steven Stanek | | Wisconsin Council on Developmental Disabilities |
| | Tom Swant, Bureau of Health Care Planning | Medical Assistance Program | Department of Health and Social Services |
| **Wyoming** | George Crouch | Division of Health Care Financing | Department of Health |
| | Dr. Jon Fortune, Adult DD Consultant | Division of DD | Department of Health |
| | Cliff Mikesell, Deputy Superintendent | Wyoming State Training School | Department of Health |